Innovation and Entrepreneurship

This book presents a new model, the competency framework, for students, innovators, entrepreneurs, managers, and anyone who wants to better understand the dynamic world of innovation and entrepreneurship.

Focused on both the individual and strategic organizational level, this book is about people and the competencies each person needs to learn to be successful in creating a more dynamic future. The framework for innovation and entrepreneurship competencies empowers individuals to excel at innovation and new venture creation.

It provides a practical guide and clear and concise understanding of the knowledge, skills, attitudes, and experiences that are needed to increase imagination, creativity, innovation, and new venture creation capability. *Innovation and Entrepreneurship* will be attractive for students of entrepreneurship, innovation, management, and cross-disciplinary classes, such as design thinking.

Presented in a modular format, *Innovation and Entrepreneurship* informs the future direction of people and technology, as well as the educational systems producing the next generation of innovators and entrepreneurs.

Based on extensive academic research, this book is organized into two sections: 12 innovation elements and 12 competency categories. The **elements** are the foundation and the **competency categories** are the building blocks that inform our path toward a more precise understanding of how innovation and entrepreneurship play an important role in economic development and our daily lives.

Ralph F. Brueggemann is Adjunct Professor at the University of Cincinnati, USA. He has over 50 years of experience in all aspects of leadership, management, product management, quality improvement, and technology management in multiple business sectors. He has managed the development of commercial software products and applications, from mobile to high-end software systems.

Charles H. Matthews is Distinguished Teaching Professor of Entrepreneurship and Strategic Management, Founder and former Executive Director of the Center for Entrepreneurship Education & Research, and former Director of the Small Business Institute® at the University of Cincinnati, USA. He is an internationally recognized scholar and innovative teacher in the field of entrepreneurship.

Innovation and Entrepreneurship

A Competency Framework

Second Edition

**Ralph F. Brueggemann and
Charles H. Matthews**

Routledge
Taylor & Francis Group

NEW YORK AND LONDON

Designed cover image: BargotiPhotography / Getty Images

Second edition published 2025
by Routledge
605 Third Avenue, New York, NY 10158

and by Routledge
4 Park Square, Milton Park, Abingdon, Oxon, OX14 4RN

Routledge is an imprint of the Taylor & Francis Group, an informa business

© 2025 Taylor & Francis

First edition published by Routledge 2015

Library of Congress Cataloging-in-Publication Data
Names: Matthews, Charles H. (Economist), author. | Brueggemann, Ralph, author.
Title: Innovation and entrepreneurship : a competency framework / Charles
    H. Matthews and Ralph Brueggemann.
Description: Second edition. | New York, NY : Routledge, 2025. | Includes
    bibliographical references and index.
Identifiers: LCCN 2024027855 (print) | LCCN 2024027856 (ebook) |
    ISBN 9780367468569 (hardback) | ISBN 9780367898038 (paperback) |
    ISBN 9781003034308 (ebook)
Subjects: LCSH: Entrepreneurship. | Technological innovations. | Creative
    ability in business. | Knowledge management.
Classification: LCC HB615 .M3726 2025 (print) | LCC HB615 (ebook) |
    DDC 658.4—dc23/eng/20240715
LC record available at https://lccn.loc.gov/2024027855
LC ebook record available at https://lccn.loc.gov/2024027856

ISBN: 978-0-367-46856-9 (hbk)
ISBN: 978-0-367-89803-8 (pbk)
ISBN: 978-1-003-03430-8 (ebk)

DOI: 10.4324/9781003034308

Typeset in Times New Roman
by Apex CoVantage, LLC

This book is dedicated to our many students, past, present, and future, and all aspiring innovators and entrepreneurs.

Contents

About the Authors

Ralph F. Brueggemann, MBA, MEd, is Adjunct Professor at the College of Engineering and Applied Science, University of Cincinnati. At the University of Cincinnati, he has taught innovation, leadership, management, project management, software engineering, and database technology courses. His focus is on course development for Interdisciplinary Innovation for Engineers that uses the book *Innovation and Entrepreneurship: A Competency Framework*.

He has over 50 years of experience in all aspects of leadership, management, project management, product management, quality improvement, and technology management in multiple business sectors at regional, national, and international corporations. He has managed the development of commercial software products and applications, from mobile to high-end software systems. He has held positions at General Electric and Altafiber, as well as management positions at Macy's, Cincom Systems, and Dolbey Systems, and most recently he was the Director of Systems at the University of Cincinnati Medical Center and the Director of Data Systems at Cincinnati Children's Hospital Medical Center.

He is an advocate for community involvement as a volunteer educator for the Osher Lifelong Learning Institute, an outreach education program within the University of Cincinnati's College of Cooperative Education and Professional Studies. Additionally, he serves as a lead volunteer consultant, providing strategic planning services to local non-profit organizations. He is an Ohio Certified Volunteer Naturalist through the Ohio State University and is actively engaged in advancing nature-based sustainability, contributing to strategic planning initiatives for a national environmental organization. His commitment extends to serving on the board of a non-profit that provides service dogs for children with disabilities and another non-profit board dedicated to implementing a regional multi-purpose bike and running trail.

He has co-authored articles in *Academic Medicine* and the *Journal of the Medical Library Association*. He was a contributing author to the book *Information Technology for Managers*. He has received awards for his work in both teaching and the management of commercial software product development.

He is an inventor and a Life Senior Member of the Institute of Electrical and Electronics Engineers.

Charles H. Matthews, PhD, is Distinguished Teaching Professor of Entrepreneurship and Strategic Management, Founder and former Executive Director of the Center for Entrepreneurship Education & Research, and former Director of the Small Business Institute® (SBI), Lindner College of Business, University of Cincinnati. Dr. Matthews is an internationally recognized scholar and innovative teacher in the field of entrepreneurship. His teaching and research interests include curiosity, decision-making, entrepreneurship, innovation, leadership, and strategy. His research is published in *Small Business Economics*, the *Journal of Small Business Management*, the *Journal of Small Business Strategy*, *Entrepreneurship & Regional Development*, *Frontiers of Entrepreneurship Research*, *Family Business Review*, the *International Journal of Operations & Production Management*, the *Center for the Quality of Management Journal*, *Quality Management Journal*, *Industry & Higher Education*, and the *New England Journal of Entrepreneurship*. He has been quoted in numerous publications, including the *Wall Street Journal*, *Industry Week*, *Forbes*, *Business Week*, and *Inc*. He was a columnist on entrepreneurship and innovation for the *Cincinnati Post* from 1998 to 2001 and the *Cincinnati Enquirer* from 2011 to 2015. An award-winning teacher, Dr. Matthews has taught over 10,000 students worldwide, ranging from freshmen to doctoral students to executives, from individual instruction to classes of 540. He has facilitated over 750 faculty-guided, student-based field case studies and has served as a consultant to numerous organizations, including many family businesses.

In addition to his consulting practice, Dr. Matthews has entrepreneurship and family business experience in the automotive, photographic, and real estate industries. An educational entrepreneur, he is the founder of the UC Center for Entrepreneurship Education & Research in 1997, which was named one of the top 50 entrepreneurship programs in the United States in 2001 (*Success* magazine), a top tier and nationally recognized program in 2003, 2004, and 2005 (*Entrepreneur* magazine), and a top 25 undergraduate entrepreneurship program in 2008 (*Princeton Review*). He championed the creation of the undergraduate entrepreneurship/family business major, led the development of the Graduate Certificate in Entrepreneurship in the MBA program, including several new courses on entrepreneurship, e-business, and global entrepreneurship, and was part of the leadership team from the Colleges of Arts and Sciences; Business; Design, Art, Architecture, and Planning; Education; and Engineering that created the first cross-campus Certificate in Innovation Transformation and Entrepreneurship for all students across campus. He is a Fellow of the Small Business Institute® (SBI), Justin G. Longenecker Fellow of the US Association for Small Business and Entrepreneurship (USASBE), and a Wilford L. White Fellow of the International Council for Small Business (ICSB). He was a J. William Fulbright US Scholar in Lithuania in 2018. In 2024, he was honored to be named the Entrepreneurship Educator of the Year by the United States Association for Small Business and Entrepreneurship (USASBE).

Foreword

Welcome to the second edition of *Innovation and Entrepreneurship: A Competency Framework*. Echoing the sentiment of my good friend and colleague Dr. Mark Weaver, who wrote the foreword for the first edition, the authors bring over 100 years of combined experience in industry and education, both applied and theoretical.

Dr. Matthews is a leading scholar in the field of entrepreneurship, combining extensive business experience in the automotive, photographic, real estate, and fintech fields. He has successfully leveraged his business background to inform his work in academia and research over a 45-year career at the University of Cincinnati, having been named the 2024 Entrepreneurship Educator of the Year by the United States Association for Small Business and Entrepreneurship.

Mr. Brueggemann adds more than 50 years of direct experience building the competency model presented in this book both in practice and in the classroom. His experience in independent strategic consulting, non-profit boards, and positions at national and international corporations include General Electric, Altafiber, Macy's, Cincom Systems, Dolby Systems, University of Cincinnati Medical Center, and Cincinnati Children's Hospital Medical Center. He has received awards for his work in both teaching and the management of commercial software product development.

Together, they provide a tour-de-force of information, insights, and applications focused on the dynamic landscape of innovation and entrepreneurship. Without question, we find ourselves at the nexus of unprecedented change and opportunity. In a world marked by rapid technological advancements, shifting market dynamics, and evolving societal needs, the imperative for education in these fields has never been more pressing. Moreover, their innovation and entrepreneurship elements and competencies have stood the test of time and are timelier than ever.

This revised edition builds upon the foundation laid by its predecessor, delving deeper into the intricacies of the innovation and entrepreneurship competency framework. Developed as a comprehensive guide to navigate the complexities of innovation and entrepreneurship, it provides a roadmap for individuals and organizations seeking to thrive in an increasingly competitive and uncertain environment.

Even after a quick perusal of the chapters, the reader begins to develop an understanding of the fundamental elements of innovation and entrepreneurship. From identifying key elements and models to sharpening effective decision-making skills, each chapter offers invaluable insights and practical strategies to foster a culture of creativity, resilience, and growth. The first part of the book introduces readers to the core concepts of innovation and entrepreneurship. Through an exploration of their Competency Framework, readers gain a deeper understanding of the essential competencies, skills, and dynamics driving innovation and entrepreneurship forward. Subsequent chapters delve into myriad connected facets, exploring key topics such as problem-solving, creative thinking, knowledge building, and leadership. Through a combination of theoretical insights, practical examples, and actionable strategies, readers learn to navigate the complexities of the innovation and entrepreneurship landscape with confidence and agility.

One of the central themes that permeates this edition is the interconnectedness of innovation and entrepreneurship with broader societal and environmental challenges. As we confront pressing issues in business and society, the role of these concepts in driving positive change has never been more vital. By embracing sustainability principles and fostering a culture of responsible innovation, individuals and organizations can harness the transformative power of entrepreneurship to create a more sustainable future for all. Furthermore, this edition places a renewed emphasis on the importance of education and capacity-building in fostering a culture of innovation and entrepreneurship. From reimagining traditional educational paradigms to empowering individuals with the skills and mindset needed to thrive in the digital age, education plays a pivotal role in shaping the innovators and entrepreneurs of tomorrow.

Whether you plan to use this book as an undergraduate or graduate textbook or just to read for your own enlightenment, the second edition does not disappoint. Here are a few examples. In Chapters 1, 2, and 3, along with Chapter 11, readers gain a clear understanding of the competencies essential for success in innovation and entrepreneurship, including problem-solving, creative thinking, leadership, entrepreneurship, and strategic decision-making. Throughout the second edition, the authors masterfully show the power of the integration and overlap of the material.

More than just a theoretical review, as in the first edition, the second edition provides practical strategies and frameworks for fostering a culture of innovation and entrepreneurship individually and within organizations. For example, in Chapter 5, the authors provide a comprehensive overview of systems thinking and forming integrative thinking that fosters creativity, innovation, and entrepreneurship.

It is impressive to see the comprehensive coverage and integration of key topics including sustainability and responsibility, education and capacity building, and the interconnectedness of innovation and entrepreneurship within a broader ecosystem, revealing how to navigate complex environments and leverage ecosystem dynamics. As noted earlier, this is always combined with guidance on applying these principles in real-world contexts, with case studies and examples illustrating successful innovation strategies and practices.

As we navigate the complexities of the 21st century, it is clear that the ability to innovate and adapt will be the defining factor in determining future success. Whether you are a seasoned entrepreneur, a budding innovator, or one who is simply curious about the transformative power of innovation and entrepreneurship, this book serves as a guide, illuminating the path forward amidst uncertainty and change.

In closing, their authors' dedication to advancing the field of innovation and entrepreneurship is truly commendable, and their insights will undoubtedly inspire readers to embark on their own journey of discovery and transformation. I invite you to embark on this exhilarating journey through the pages of *Innovation and Entrepreneurship: A Competency Framework*. May it serve as a beacon of inspiration, guiding you toward new horizons of possibility and unlocking the boundless potential that lies within.

Here's to a future defined by innovation, entrepreneurship, and endless possibility.

Dr. George T. Solomon, Professor Emeritus,
The George Washington University, April 2024

Dr. George T. Solomon is a professor emeritus of management and the co-founder of the Center for Entrepreneurial Excellence (CFEE) at the George Washington University School of Business (GWSB). Dr. Solomon is the past president of the United States Association for Small Business and Entrepreneurship (USASBE) and the International Council for Small Business (ICSB). From 1976 until 2004, Dr. Solomon held various managerial positions at the SBA, including director of the Office of Special Initiatives and deputy associate administrator for Business Initiatives Education and Training, where he managed a staff of six to fifteen professionals. Dr. Solomon has published and edited over 130 articles, books of readings, book chapters, reference materials, and proceedings articles in both the areas of entrepreneurship/small business management and organizational behavior and dynamics.

Acknowledgments

Building on the first edition, the theme of this second edition is how to unlock human potential, both within ourselves and others. The theme of this book focuses on learning a framework for innovation and entrepreneurship competencies that empower individuals to excel at innovation and new venture creation. Ultimately, this book is about people and the competencies each person needs to learn to be successful in creating a more dynamic future. A significant obstacle to pursue the notion of what-might-be is imagination. With that in mind, our goal is for this book to help you develop all of your capabilities and aspirations.

On our writing journey, we were not alone. We would like to extend our deepest appreciation to all of those who have contributed to this effort. We especially acknowledge the unwavering support of our families, especially our spouses – Ralph Brueggemann's spouse, Diane, and Charles H. Matthews' spouse, Margie. We could not have successfully made this journey without their love and support.

We would also like to acknowledge the helpful comments made by several anonymous reviewers who provided valuable guidance at various stages of this effort. In particular, we would like to thank the editorial team at Routledge, whose support, guidance, and patience have made this book possible. A special thanks to Ms. Megan Moyer, UC Engineering student, for providing countless hours proofing many of the early draft chapters. We are also very grateful to Dr. George Solomon, Professor Emeritus, School of Business, The George Washington University, for reading the second edition manuscript and taking the time to critique our efforts and pen the foreword.

There were many of our colleagues and students whose insights contributed to this book directly and indirectly. Many of the concepts in this book came through *observation* and were tested in organizations and classes through practical *experimentation*. Ideas were initiated in many contexts; some worked and some did not. The accumulation of competencies – the attitudes, skills, and knowledge – described in this book came from our collective conclusion to *question* prevailing wisdom and *acknowledge* the value learned when progress was achieved. We gratefully acknowledge our *network* of colleagues whose role as valued guest speakers provided insights that reinforced the concepts. This shared body of knowledge created *associations* that combined the diverse thinking of many well-regarded proven professionals.

Finally, for our students, imagination, curiosity, creativity, and innovation require an additional mental model that is based on character, resilience, ideation, openness, trust, collaboration, and team building. Students have to develop the *confidence* to build this new mental model so that they are willing to take risks, manage their mistakes, and persist in pursuing their inspirations.

We are sincerely grateful for all the relationships experienced during the process of writing this book. Thank you!

Introduction to Innovation and Entrepreneurship

This introduction is currently organized into two parts.

Part I is the introductory content for the book.
Part II is an anthology of innovations that are organized into categories. *Part II is optional to read but would be useful for ideation browsing.*

PART I: ADVENTUROUS INNOVATORS AND ENTREPRENEURS

About This Book

This introduction presents an overview of key concepts discussed in this book. The focus of this book is how to unlock everyone's talents to build capability to be successful in the future by learning and applying innovation and entrepreneurship competencies. In general, competencies are the attitudes, skills, and knowledge that are needed to increase imagination, creativity, innovation, and entrepreneurship capability. Fundamental to this process is the concept of the Power of And, a unique model for combining all aspects of innovation and entrepreneurship into a unified framework.

This book is for anyone who wants to improve their ability to generate ideas, develop creative insights, and build innovation and entrepreneurial capabilities. Ultimately, this book is about people and the competencies each person needs to learn to be successful in his or her career while contributing to organizations of their choice. The thesis of this book is that by learning innovation and entrepreneurship through an organized framework, it facilitates learning, drives innovation, and enables successful new venture creation.

Innovators and entrepreneurs are focused on turning ideas that are often seen long before others into action. As discussed throughout this book, innovation and entrepreneurship are not random acts. Rather, they are the result of applying concepts based on evidence, systematic observation, experiences, theory, knowledge, application, experimentation, and more. Moreover, it includes concepts such as the Power of And – a holistic approach that prioritizes purpose as well as profits to act ethically and succeed financially.[1]

The Role of the Adventurer

To achieve meaningfully significant innovations and ultimately engage in transformative entrepreneurship, one needs to become an adventurer. For example, imagine you are a mountain climber. Do you have all the individual and team capability needed for the climb as well as to encounter the unexpected as you near the peak? While there is always a need for an eye on the future, it cannot

DOI: 10.4324/9781003034308-1

be accurately predicted. As a result, moving forward there is always less than full certainty. In order to address significant challenges and opportunities and devise solutions, innovation is critical. That is, doing the same things as they were done in the past and expecting different results does not work. Rather, there is a need to build the capability, individually and organizationally, to adapt or innovate to address a rapidly changing landscape.

For example, sporting events are zero-sum games resulting in a winner and loser. For-profit and non-profit organizations, on the other hand, do not participate as zero-sum games. Organizations are designed to provide value and produce many winners. However, if there are not effective organizations in place, as determined in part by their effective decision-making capability, failure or loss results. Among the most important elements for effective decision-making are to be *robust and nimble, take risks, and be willing to fail intentionally*. Intentional experimental failure is good failure because you learn how to be better. If failure is operational, it is not good failure.[2]

Innovation in Action

Innovation is a driving force behind progress and has shaped human history in remarkable ways – from pioneering inventors such as Thomas Edison, with over 1,000 US patents to his credit, to scientific and medical breakthroughs of the 21st century, to the so-called digital age driving change in modern times. In general, innovations throughout history can be viewed as distinct innovations, chains of causation, and associations.

Distinct Innovations

First there are innovations that are original, unique, impactful, and **distinct** from anything previously conceived. These innovations include the compass, glass, the transistor, antibiotics, and the steam engine. Some innovations are so unique, such as vaccines, that their development and acceptance are an ongoing process. Some innovations are initially rejected, such as xerography and the telephone, because the value is not immediately understood. Some original innovations are initially rejected because they had to shift or overturn prevailing thought. For instance, Mendel's theory of inheritance and heliocentrism, the astronomical model that describes the Earth and planets revolving around the Sun, had to displace the conventional wisdom at the time.

Chains of Causation

Second there are innovations that result from **chains of causation**, like dominos, or connecting the dots, where an innovation in one domain triggers unexpected breakthroughs in wholly different domains.[3] For example, the printing press, which was based on the winepress, enabled the mass printing of books available to everyone. Soon readers realized they could not see well closeup, triggering a development of magnifying lenses, and eventually microscopes, telescopes, and electron microscopes.

Associations

Third, innovation results from **associations**, or when two or more components are combined into an innovation. For example, steel is made from iron core and coke that is made from coal, gunpowder is made from sulfur, carbon, and potassium nitrate, and dynamite is made from nitroglycerine, sorbents, and stabilizers. Even more highly valued are those innovations that are combined to create new innovations. Electric vehicles, personal computers, and smartphones are examples of associated innovations.

To better understand the genesis of innovation, it is helpful to develop an innovation taxonomy. Essentially, a way of organizing or classifying innovation. One such approach would be a taxonomy of their functional value.

Innovation Taxonomy

The impactful innovations in history can be understood by organizing them into a taxonomy of their functional value.[4] While not exhaustive, these might include:

1. Innovations that **expand human intellect** include the alphabet, paper making, woodblock printing, the printing press, optical lens, microscopes, telescopes, the transistor, semiconductors, the microprocessor, the integrated circuit, the theory of relativity, quantum theory, artificial intelligence, and machine learning.
2. Innovations that **extend life** are agriculture, farming and animal domestication, pasteurization, fertilizers and nitrogen fixation, scientific plant breeding, germ theory, antibiotics like penicillin, radioactivity and x-rays, vaccinations, the structure of the DNA molecule, genomics, and gene editing (CRISPR).
3. Innovations that **improve work effectiveness and collaboration** encompass the Gregorian calendar and pendulum clock, paper currency, division of labor and scientific management, divisionalized organizational structure, economic and innovation theory, emotional intelligence and leadership theory, microfinance, activism for social change, and non-violent resistance to injustice.
4. Innovations that **inspire the creative arts** include cave painting, literature, painting, sound waves, music theory and composition, photography, and cinematography.
5. Innovations that form the **foundation for living effectively** include electricity generation and distribution systems, electromagnetic induction, diamagnetism and electrolysis, solar power, clean water and sanitation, refrigeration and air-conditioning, and lighting.
6. Innovations that **enable Industrial Revolutions** include the steam and internal combustion engine, steelmaking, the assembly line, sensors, and robotics.
7. Innovations that **accelerate digital communications** include the telegraph, the the telephone, the radio, the television, the Internet, satellites, and the global positioning system.
8. Innovations that **enable physical movement of people and goods** include the compass, the automobile, flight and the airplane, trains and railway systems, jet engines, and space travel.

The Framework

The innovation and entrepreneurship competency framework developed in this book provides an understanding of the attitudes, skills, and knowledge that are needed to increase imagination, creativity, innovation, and new venture creation capability. By learning and applying the innovation competencies, new venture start-ups and existing organizations are better able to innovate, create, develop competencies in current and future talent, and become more effective and efficient in both strategic directions and operations.

There are several compelling questions that have informed the development of the innovation and entrepreneurship competency framework: When it comes to organizational and economic development, has there been a general overemphasis on short-term market efficiency, incremental improvements, cost reduction, and outsourcing and a corresponding underemphasis on creativity, innovation, and entrepreneurship? Are future job opportunities, economic growth, improved education systems, sustainability and renewable energy sources, and enhanced health and wellness at risk as the future economic value of our collective imaginations, creativity, and innovation has been underestimated?

As noted previously, adventurers need to prepare for the future by learning competencies, taking risks, and developing resilience using interdisciplinary innovation, including the Power of And. The innovation and entrepreneurship competency framework facilitates the study, understanding, and application of the attitudes, skills, and knowledge that are needed to build capability.

The framework for the book is organized into two sections: innovation elements and competency categories.

1. The 12 elements are the foundation for understanding the discipline of innovation.
2. The competency categories are the building blocks that inform one's pathway toward a more precise understanding of how innovation drives all aspects of human development, behaviors, thinking, problem solving, knowledge building, creativity, culture, theory, entrepreneurship, strategy, leadership, ecosystems, and technology accelerators.

Innovation Elements

Before outlining the innovation and entrepreneurship competency framework, first the innovation elements that are the foundation for understanding innovation are described. The separating of innovation into discrete elements provides more clarity for learning how the pieces can be combined. Each element is described in Chapter 2 and depicted in Figure 0.1.

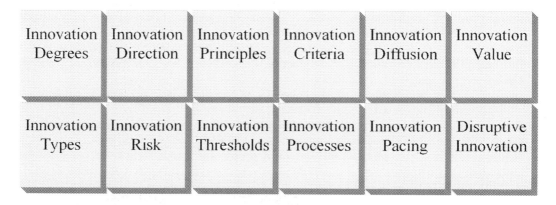

| Innovation Degrees | Innovation Direction | Innovation Principles | Innovation Criteria | Innovation Diffusion | Innovation Value |
| Innovation Types | Innovation Risk | Innovation Thresholds | Innovation Processes | Innovation Pacing | Disruptive Innovation |

Figure 0.1 Illustration of the Elements of Innovation

The concepts of innovation and entrepreneurship, while distinct and precise, are often hazily defined in a popular sense. Both terms are overused to the point that they are in danger of becoming meaningless. The field of strategic management encountered a similar crisis when the terms "strategy" and "strategic planning" became so ubiquitously used that management scholar Henry Mintzberg opined that if strategic planning is everything, then perhaps it is nothing.[5]

There is a natural tendency to skip past the foundational aspects of any practice and/or discipline, from science to sports. Consider the tendency in baseball to "swing for the fences." Although clearing the bases with a single swat of the bat is one exciting aspect of the game, hitting home runs is only made possible through a clear and precise understanding of the fundamentals of batting, from stance to swing. So, too, the elements of innovation require careful review because they serve as the prerequisites and foundation for innovation competencies. By clearly outlining the elements of innovation, we close the gap in our definitional understanding of innovation itself.

The Competency Framework

Building on the elements of innovation, the innovation and entrepreneurship competency framework is an integrated modular learning approach to innovation and entrepreneurship that is based on facts, evidence, and secondary research. The framework incorporates the scholarship of experts into a 12-category competency structure that is designed to improve innovation and entrepreneurship capability and success rates. Its genesis is driven by a deceptively simple question: why not *combine* the leading relevant philosophies together into a comprehensive set of competencies that can be practiced more readily?

American surgeon and journalist, Atul Gawande, writes,

> Élite performers, researchers say, must engage in "deliberate practice" – sustained, mindful efforts to develop the full range of abilities that success requires. You have to work at what you're not good at. In theory, people can do this themselves. But most people do not know where to start or how to proceed. Expertise, as the formula goes, requires going from unconscious incompetence to conscious incompetence to conscious competence and finally to unconscious competence.[6]

While not specifically addressing innovation and entrepreneurship, Gawande's words speak eloquently to the need for an innovation and entrepreneurship competency framework to help guide the innovation and entrepreneurship process from "unconscious incompetence to conscious incompetence to conscious competence and finally to unconscious competence."

Innovation and Entrepreneurship Competency Categories

The innovation and entrepreneurship competency categories are organized into a framework that enables the learner to develop the attitudes, skills, and knowledge that is necessary to improve everyone's innovation capability through practice. The innovation and entrepreneurship competency categories are depicted in Figure 0.2 as a set of circles illustrating the 12 competency categories described sequentially in this book.

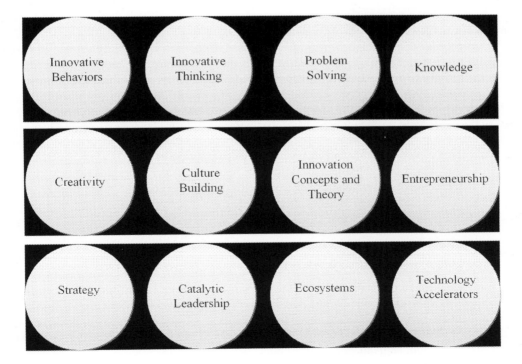

Figure 0.2 Illustration of the 12 Innovation and Entrepreneurship Competency Categories

Richard Feynman said, "Scientific knowledge is an enabling power to do either good or bad – but it does not carry instructions on how to use it."[7] The innovation competencies are the instructions on how we can improve our ability to expand our imaginations, our creativity and innovation potential, and our future. Innovative competencies are the behaviors, thinking, problem solving, and knowledge building. Next are creativity, culture building, and the realization of innovation through entrepreneurship and strategy. The final competencies are catalytic leadership, ecosystems, and technology accelerators. It is strengthening the innovation competencies individually and collectively that provides for renewal along the continuing quest for successful innovation and entrepreneurship.

What Is Entrepreneurship?

Entrepreneurship is the creation of new venture and value for multiple constituents, from customers to employees to communities and even countries. It includes both for-profit ventures as well as not-for-profit ventures. There are numerous success stories of entrepreneurs conceiving, formulating, founding, and leading new ventures to great success, including Apple, Google (now Alphabet), and Facebook (now Meta), to name just a few that have bloomed into iconic businesses. These entrepreneurs include small business, accelerated growth and serial venture founders, and corporate, social, and global entrepreneurs.

In its broadest terms, entrepreneurship is an economic phenomenon, a scholarly domain, and a teaching subject.[8] It is a multifaceted, complex, social, and economic phenomenon.[9] "Entrepreneurship is a mindset that can empower ordinary people to accomplish the extraordinary."[10]

Essentially, entrepreneurship at its core is the *discipline* of venture creation that transforms ideas into an enterprise that provides value. Entrepreneurship is the practice of new venture creation that addresses the vast opportunities and market inefficiencies that appear during the sometimes-troublesome nuances of creative destruction.

Entrepreneurs, acting alone or with others, take risks and actions to create the venture and value for multiple constituents. While entrepreneurship is ultimately about the creation of venture and value, as we shall see throughout the book, it is indeed a multidimensional subject that is intricately interwoven with innovation.

Entrepreneurs illustrate the 3D vision of drive, determination, and dedication needed to succeed in the ever-changing, technology-driven business and industry landscape. While Chapter 11, "Entrepreneurship," explores the intricacies of new venture creation, entrepreneurship is the foundational engine of any economy and creativity and innovation are its fuel.

Throughout this book, multiple exemplars of innovation and entrepreneurship illustrate the 3D vision of drive, determination, and dedication needed to succeed in the ever-changing, technology-driven business and industry landscape. There is much we can learn from these adventurous innovators and entrepreneurs.

Innovation and Entrepreneurship Competency Dynamics

The innovation and entrepreneurship competency framework is not linear. Rather, the competencies function as a holistic interactive and iterative set of dynamic back-and-forth flows. The bubble chart in Figure 0.3 more fully depicts the thinking processes of innovators and entrepreneurs. The central thrust of this dynamic interaction of competencies is the innovation pipeline, comprising imagination, creation, innovation, and the ultimate outcome.

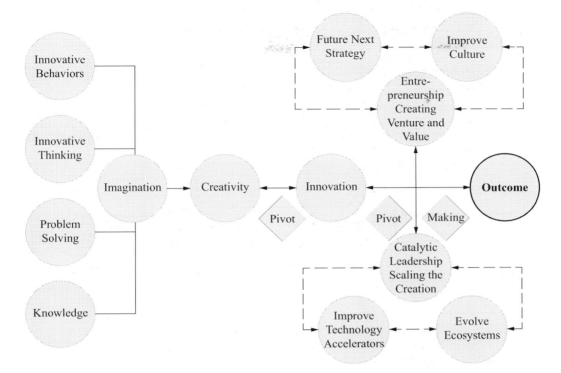

Figure 0.3 Illustration of the Dynamic Interaction of the Innovation and Entrepreneurship Competency Categories

Mind Map Innovation and Entrepreneurship Competencies

Looking at this complex interactive and iterative process another way, the innovation and entrepreneurship competencies can be depicted as a mind map illustrating the learnable concepts and behaviors. Figure 0.4 is a mind map that is a visual representation depicting the 12 innovation elements and the twelve competency categories.

Paradigm Shifts: Past, Current, and Future

We are living in an increasingly more complex world confronted with challenges that we have never experienced before. Today's challenges are unlikely to be solved with the thinking of the past. A paradigm shift, shown in Figure 0.5, is a way to describe the important changes that happen when conventional thinking is replaced by a new and better model, not simply a different one. It is important to understand paradigm shifts because they reveal opportunities and trends that require us to broaden our thinking and decision-making.

The eminent Danish philosopher, theologian, poet, and social critic Søren Kierkegaard is widely considered to be the first existentialist philosopher. His insight that life can only be understood backward, but it must be lived forward provides a window into a fundamental conundrum of innovation and entrepreneurship. Think of three curves: the past, *what was*; the present or current, *what is*; and the future, *what might be*. Innovation is often impeded by the fact that most people are part of organizations that are likely to be on the wrong "management of innovation curve" to be effective. Because of the dynamics of global change, including but not limited to advances in

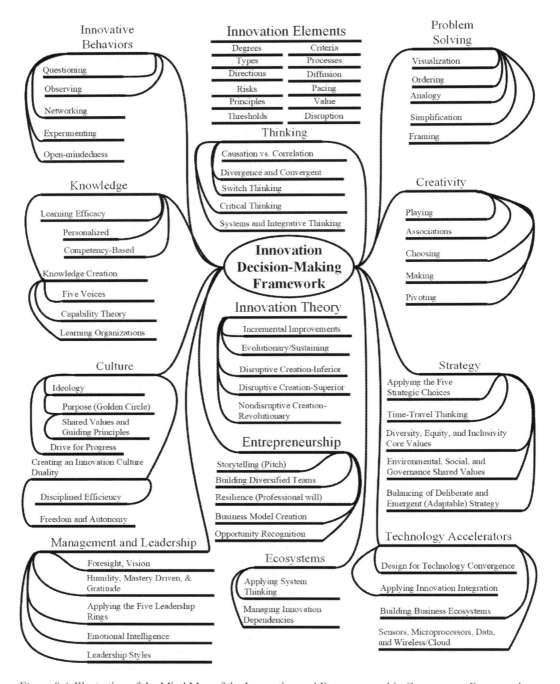

Figure 0.4 Illustration of the Mind Map of the Innovation and Entrepreneurship Competency Framework

communication, we are perpetually out of alignment with *what might be* because we are overly comfortable with the past, *what was*, and the present, *what is*.

The past provides a necessary foundation of understanding and proven concepts, which can be reused and rearranged in fresh ways to build something new by applying the Power of And. The present provides the dynamic environment required to execute thought and action with high

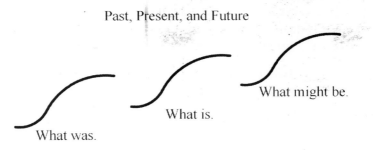

Past, Present, and Future

What might be.

What is.

What was.

Figure 0.5 Illustration of the Paradigm Shifts

Source: Thomas Kuhn, *The Structure of Scientific Revolutions.* 2d, enl ed. Vol. 2, no. 2. Chicago: University of Chicago Press, 1970. Wikipedia, s.v. "Paradigm shift," accessed December 11, 2020, https://en.wikipedia.org/ wiki/Paradigm_shift

precision to compete in current conditions and sustain (and exceed) the customer experience at the highest level, while being mindful of manageable costs. Yet as foundational and important as the past and present are, we are relentlessly moving toward an uncertain, but compelling, future. Moving organizations into the future demands a new catalytic leadership model that sparks, encourages, and supports the Power of And, as well as the imaginations of everyone, not just a few.

Research reveals that executives in innovative organizations have different behaviors than those leading less innovative organizations. Many organizations become stuck in the past and present rather than focused on *what might be,* even though they are following what they have been taught in the best business, engineering, and design schools. The sigmoid curves in Figure 0.5 illustrate the need to transition to a higher-level curve representing a new way of thinking about the future of innovation.

The turbulent times that we are experiencing are juxtaposed against organizations that have become fortresses resisting change. The average age of the companies in the S&P 500 has declined from more than 60 years in 1958, to less than 20 years today.[11] The ability to think strategically about the future relies on the premise that organizations should not only maximize return on capital (e.g., stockholders) but also actively contribute to the broader society (e.g., stakeholders).

Managerial thinking needs to be extended beyond the past and present into the future by studying, learning, and applying the innovation and entrepreneurship competency framework so that all individuals at all levels can improve their ability to innovate. It is not one competency, but all competencies working together synergistically that facilitate the development of people, our most critical resource for innovation.

Impenetrable Castles

For example, the Gordian knot, a legend of Phrygian Gordium, associated with Alexander the Great, is a metaphor for an intractable problem solved easily by finding a novel approach to the problem that renders the perceived constraints visible so the knot can be untied.[12]

When confronted with the gordian knot, people have a choice: leave the organization, move around the organization to fulfill a different role, or discover ways to create by benefiting from the resources but not get stymied by the culture.

In remarkable contrast, as the paradigm shifts occur, impenetrable castles, organizations that we rely on such as businesses, governments, and educational systems that are slow, unable, or unwilling to respond to the challenges surface. Established organizations are not particularly good at changing before they must or responding to nimble upstarts. Rosabeth Moss Kanter writes,[13]

The world is littered with literal and figurative castles. In Europe, they are museums to a medieval past. In America, castles take a more modern physical form as suburban corporate headquarter campuses, heavily guarded office towers, gated communities with hidden delivery entrances, or massive government buildings with intimidating security lines. These edifices are designed to protect executives and functionaries from unwelcome intrusion – or the need to change.

The fundamental question to be addressed is should organizations demonstrate respect and concern for the individual and contribute to the well-being of communities versus becoming impenetrable castles? For example, three key "impenetrable castles" can be identified each with compelling questions and issues for innovation and entrepreneurship:

1. Businesses. Is the purpose of a company just to create products and services? Should business only focus on the customer and seek out their wants, needs, and ideas? Should business only focus on superior profitability and maximizing shareholder value, or should they take responsibility for the broader goal of stakeholder needs? The rigidity that is prevalent in business castles is a source of opportunity for innovators.
2. Governments. What is the best way to achieve organizational bureaucracy and regulation on various levels to achieve the most effective balance? For example, how could governments build in mechanisms for continuous improvement? How can government best solicit input needs from their constituency in a meaningful way that is simple and convenient? What is the best way for governments to be held accountable for achieving transparent outcomes? How can governments encourage entrepreneurs and start-ups to experiment with new models?
3. Education systems. Education systems are powerful but often too slow-moving to adapt to paradigm shifts. Many education systems are designed to be job engines. Yet there are several purposes for education beyond economic.[14] Education is personal to enable all people to engage their unique talents. Education is social to enable all people to engage in active compassionate citizenship. Education is cultural to enable all people within their cultural groups to demonstrate their values and promote diversity, equity, and inclusion.[15] There are disparities in our society that can be ameliorated through our education system.[16]

The Power of And and Finding Your Voice

The Power of And is a concept for broadening an approach to transformational innovation.

It is applied by taking a multidimensional interdisciplinary perspective to combine multiple sources of intellectual capital to focus on increasingly more complex and changing circumstances within different domains to achieve what is next and what is after next. When combined with finding your voice, it provides a strong foundational process for innovation and entrepreneurship. The three voices illustrated in Figure 0.6. radiate outward and form a nexus for applying a multidimensional approach to innovation and entrepreneurship: find your voice, develop confidence to amplify your voice, and help others find their voice.[17]

The Three Voices

1. The first is finding your voice. Finding your voice requires all of us to unlock our talents, build on our strengths, and point to truth north. True north is a metaphor for character. As Gandhi said, "One person [man] cannot do right in one department of life whilst he is occupied in doing wrong in any other department. Life is one indivisible whole."
2. The second is to develop the confidence to amplify your voice. As Bullock and Sánchez note in their *Harvard Business Review* article, "Our voices matter as much as our words matter."[18] On developing confidence, Winston Churchill said, "Never give in. Never, never, never, never – in nothing, great or small, large or petty – never give in, except to convictions of honour and good sense."

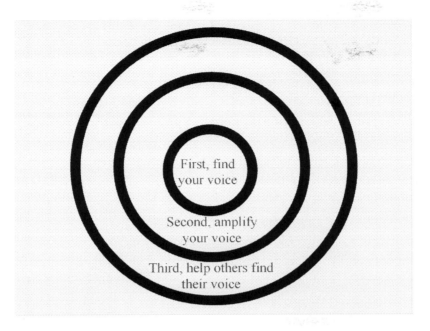

First, find
your voice

Second, amplify
your voice

Third, help others find
their voice

Figure 0.6 Illustration of the Three Voices

Source: Adapted from Stephen R. Covey, *The 8th Habit: From Effectiveness To Greatness*, (New York: Free Press, 2005).

3. The third is to help others find their voice by adding value to others. This is achieved by working together in teams to achieve meaningful results by building strength-on-strength through service. Just as John Kennedy said, "And so my fellow Americans, ask not what your country can do for you; ask what you can do for your country."

Stakeholder Capitalism

In the past, economic principles have focused primarily on the notion of maximation of shareholders' wealth. Because of the transformational changes, such as social and environmental challenges, the notion of only focusing on shareholder wealth is incomplete.

An argument can be raised that there is a compelling need to broaden the decision-making framework and choices dimensions to include stakeholder capitalism that goes beyond shareholder capitalism. For example, the Business Roundtable has adopted a modern standard for corporate responsibility and moving away from shareholder primacy and committing to an updated perspective that includes a commitment to all stakeholders.[19] The "Statement on the purpose of a corporation" was signed by 181 CEOs who committed to lead their companies for the benefit of all stakeholders – customers, employees, suppliers, communities, and shareholders.[20]

Abigail Disney, grandniece of Walt Disney, founder of The Walt Disney Company, speaks to a world where companies have a moral obligation to place their workers above shareholders, calling on all corporations to offer respect, dignity, and a living wage to everyone who works for them.[21] Abigail Disney describes the culture of Disney:[22]

Milton Friedman was the 1976 Nobel Memorial Prize in Economic Sciences who had a profound influence on business thought. "It was the essay heard round the world. Milton Friedman's 'The Social Responsibility of Business Is to Increase Its Profits' laid out arguably the most consequential economic idea of the latter half of the 20th century. The essay, published in The New York Times

Magazine on Sept. 13, 1970, was a call to arms for free market capitalism that influenced a generation of executives and political leaders, most notably Ronald Reagan and Margaret Thatcher."[23]

Milton Friedman's pivotal op-ed in the "New York Times" was followed by decades of concerted organizing and lobbying by business-focused activists along with a sustained assault on every law and regulation that had once held businesses' worst impulses in check. And soon enough, this new mindset had taken hold across every business school and across every sector. Profits were to be pursued by any means necessary, unions were kneecapped, taxes were slashed, and with the same machete, so was the safety net.

Figure 0.7 shows the stakeholder capitalism model that enlarges the purpose of organizations to include shareholder and stakeholder value.

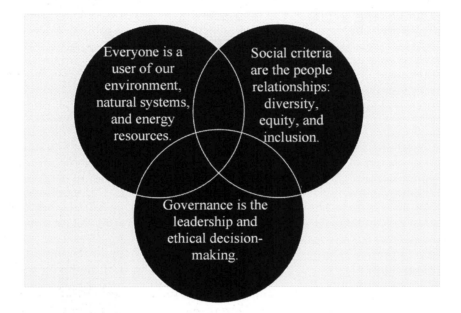

Figure 0.7 Illustration of Stakeholder Capitalism: Environmental, Social, and Governance

Source: Adapted from Witold Henisz, Tim Koller, and Robin Nuttall, "Five ways that ESG creates value," McKinsey & Company, November 2019, accessed January 5, 2020, https://www.mckinsey.com/business-functions/strategy-and-corporate-finance/our-insights/five-ways-that-esg-creates-value

Inclusive Excellence

Given that the Power of And encourages holistic thinking, recognizing that strength lies in combining diverse elements, ideas, and perspectives, another area for consideration in innovation and entrepreneurship is inclusive excellent. Combining the intellectual capability of people who have different backgrounds and perspectives can unleash more creative insights. Effective impactful solutions today need an interdisciplinary approach that is inclusive and able to fully use all resources across disciplines. Economies are more reliant on the intellectual capital of the workforce due to fast-paced types of technology achievement: biotechnology, automation, robotics, artificial intelligence, and more.

Organizations are needed that are fit for the future and fit for all human beings. Diversity, equity, and inclusion can enlarge organizational capability and expand networks of people and ideas to foster creativity and innovation.[24] Figure 0.8 describes DEI of the Power of And.

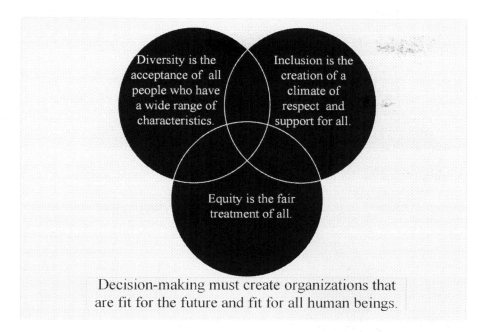

Figure 0.8 Illustration of Diversity, Equity, and Inclusion

Source: Acknowledgement: Gary Hamel and Michele Zanini, *Humanocracy*, (Boston (Massachusetts): Harvard Business Review Press, 2020).

The Interdisciplinary Power of And

Future organizations need to focus on decision-making that increasingly is based on the notion of interconnectedness of global systems. It is the interdisciplinary competencies of people that can integrate science, technology, engineering, art, design, and more.

The interdisciplinary model of the Power of And is the notion to describe the intersection of the competencies needed to transition into the future. The foundation of innovation is the intellectual capital that is the most significant contributor to address significant challenges and future opportunities. Figure 0.9 shows that different disciplines, science, technology, engineering, the arts, and design are effective ways to apply the Power of And.

Starting Questions

This book is about what we need to do to improve our innovation and entrepreneurship capabilities for the future. Gary Hamel's three-question survey gives us an insight to assess the innovation capability for front-line employees:[25]

1. **Innovators need training**. Have you been trained as business innovators? Imagine someone who has never swung a golf club. You can give a person a club and a beautiful fairway, but that does not mean they can play golf. You can give two people tennis rackets and a tennis court, but that does not mean they can play tennis together.
2. **Innovators need resources**. How easy is it for you to get the time and resources required to experiment? If you had an idea, how long would it take for you to clear your schedule and to procure experimental resources?

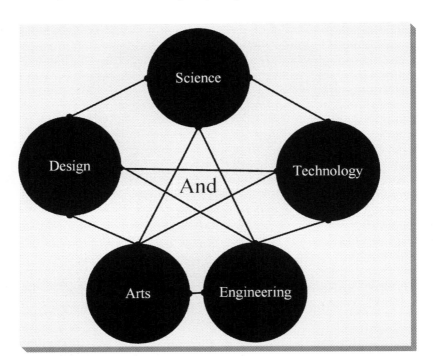

Figure 0.9 Illustration of The Power of And

Source: Adapted from Neri Oxman, *Abstract: The Art of Design*, Netflix, accessed July 24, 2020, https://www.netflix.com/title/80057883

3. **Innovators need to be held accountable**. Do you feel personally responsible for innovation? Are you and the people working above you held accountable? Is innovation measured in your organization in pace and in outcomes?

Hamel provides a three-point foundation for education in the art and science of innovation and entrepreneurship. Beginning with the elements of innovation, outlining the critical innovation and entrepreneurship competencies, our innovation and entrepreneurship quest will fully explore multiple dimensions of the 12 competency categories: behaviors, thinking, problem solving, knowledge building, creativity, culture, theory, entrepreneurship, strategy, leadership, ecosystems, and technology accelerators. Ultimately, we will see how all of these inform the way innovations come about.

Part I Summary

In this chapter the innovation and entrepreneurship competency framework is introduced. The framework is composed of 12 innovation elements and 12 competency categories that represent modular learning building blocks.

The focus of the framework includes the Power of And that describes how multiple aspects of intellectual capital can be combined to achieve meaningful significant innovations.

The first chapter describes the core innovation terminology. The second chapter describes the 12 innovation elements. The third chapter describes effective decision-making, a meta-competency, a process that is essential to building innovation capability.

The competency category chapters are organized into innovative behaviors, innovative thinking, problem solving, knowledge building, creativity, culture building, innovation concepts and theory, entrepreneurship, strategy, leadership, ecosystems, and technology accelerators.

The final chapters add supplemental topics that include intellectual capital, innovation processes, education architecture, sustainability, and innovation architecture.

It is in identifying, building, and strengthening these innovation competencies that new and existing ventures create competitive advantage and continuously seek renewal. You are invited to become an adventurer on this illuminating and exciting journey.

This is the end of Part I. Part II continues but is not required reading.

Part II: The Anthology Innovation and Entrepreneurship Competencies

Innovative thinking often spurs connections and actions that lead to new approaches, processes, products, and services, and sets the stage for problem solving. The discovery of new knowledge is one of the powerful instruments in the innovation tool chest. While innovative behaviors, thinking, problem solving, and new knowledge are individually and collectively powerful tools, creativity is often the catalyst that brings innovation to light and life. Creativity is represented in all forms through the arts: painting, photography, dance, drama, writing, movies, and music. The arts provide ways of learning creativity that can form the foundation for many of the building blocks of innovation. Entrepreneurship is the practice of new venture creation that addresses the vast opportunities and market inefficiencies that appear during the sometimes-troublesome nuances of creative destruction. Entrepreneurs take risks and actions to create the venture and value for multiple constituents. The intricate interrelationship between innovation and entrepreneurship is seen in the increasingly popular application of social entrepreneurship.

Building on the elements of innovation, in this anthology 12 innovation and entrepreneurship competencies are identified (the relationship of competencies, core competencies, and distinctive competencies is discussed in Chapter 1). The first seven innovation competencies are innovative behaviors, innovative thinking, problem solving, knowledge building, creativity, culture building, and innovation theory. In general, innovation becomes actionable through entrepreneurship and strategy. The entrepreneurship process, in brief, includes the entrepreneur (creativity, leadership, and communication), the engagement (opportunity, resource, team), the environment (uncertainty, ambiguity, outside forces), and the venture focus (product/service, customer, competition). Strategy becomes the overarching framework through which innovation is disseminated. The final three innovation competencies focus on the dynamic interaction of internal, catalytic leadership and external ecosystems (systems thinking and design thinking) and technology accelerators. It is in identifying, building, and strengthening these innovation competencies that new and existing ventures create competitive advantage and continuously seek renewal.

To set the stage for a better understanding of how and why each of these 12 innovation competencies is valuable and important, consider the following case vignettes and scenarios. Each underscores the integrative framework of the 12 innovation competencies.

Innovative Behaviors

Remove the Accounting

Intuit's Scott Cook said,

> My wife complained about doing the bills. It was a hassle. I had been trained at P&G to find a problem that everybody has and that you could solve with technology. And this struck me as a classic

entrepreneurial opportunity. Nobody likes to pay bills. There were about 20-plus personal-finance software products already on the market. I hired a computer-science student at Stanford, who later became Intuit's co-founder, and we tested the leading sellers. They were slow and a waste of time. So, we built our first product, Quicken, totally differently than every other competitor.[26]

Innovators are keen observers. Scott Cook, a former Procter & Gamble (P&G) employee, was trained to observe common problems and imagine a technology solution. That training paid off when he noticed how frustrated and irritated his wife became doing her home finances. Even though there were already personal financial software products available, he decided to build a new one. Scott hired a computer science student from Stanford and began studying the existing products on the market. Together they build an entirely new and unique personal finance product known as Quicken and formed the company Intuit.[27]

Innovators ask questions – lots of them. For example, Intuit did a study asking their customers about Quicken. They learned that half of their customers were using the Quicken product in small businesses. They contacted the customers to learn why this was. As Intuit co-founder Scott Cook describes, "Every small business has to keep books, but most don't understand debit and credit accounting. That's why they were buying and using Quicken. So then we built the first accounting software with no accounting in it and we called it QuickBooks."[28]

Innovators know how to network – both internally and externally. When we think of networking, we generally think of social, or external, networking. Yet, even within small firms, internal networking is just as important. For example, Intuit utilizes "'idea jams,' formal rotation programs for new employees, and four hours of 'unstructured time' per week for employees to experiment with projects of their own."[29] At the idea jams, gatherings of people are encouraged to generate ideas and be creative to stimulate innovation. Intuit's idea jams are an offshoot of their concept of unstructured time. They evolved after employees in product development wanted to gather passionate people in a room and focus their collective energy on innovation for a day. The "idea jam" concept began in their small business group and expanded beyond product development to all areas of the business. An idea jam has simple rules: You start by coming up with an idea either as a team or individually. You can either prepare your idea ahead of time or work on it at a one-day-sprint event. You present your concept at the idea jam, where a panel of executive judges selects the winners.[30]

Innovators are experimenters and learners. At Intuit, employees are given the freedom to spend 10% of their time on projects they're passionate about, like learning new skills or innovating to improve the work environment, learning, experimenting, and solving new customer problems. Intuit's Unstructured Time encourages creativity, innovation, and professional development.[31]

Taken collectively, these examples are a powerful testimony to how four behaviors individually and collectively spark innovation.

Innovative Thinking

Misdiagnosis

In his book *How Doctors Think,* Jerome Groopman tells the story of Anne Dodge, a woman who suffered through 15 years without an accurate diagnosis and therefore without treatment. Dodge was originally diagnosed with anorexia nervosa and bulimia, a disease that also carries a social stigma, and later with irritable bowel syndrome. Unfortunately, once a diagnosis becomes fixed in a doctor's mind, it often gains momentum and is strengthened as it gets passed from doctor to doctor, a form of parallel thinking.[32]

Despite eating a large amount of food, Dodge's weight was decreasing as though the food was just passing through her. Due to the nature of her diagnosis and its longevity, few physicians would welcome her. In her research on rapport between doctors and patients, Judy Hall discovered "that the sickest patients are the least liked by doctors, and that very sick people sense this disaffection."[33] Both patients and doctors are subject to emotions and egos that affect how we think about current conditions. This, in turn, can affect how we see things.

Eventually Dodge was seen by Dr. Myron Falchuk. Physicians like Dr. Falchuk are trained to evaluate patients in a linear way, gathering data through physical examination, ordering tests, and analyzing the results. After collecting the data, the physician formulates hypotheses (differential diagnoses) about what might be wrong. The likely diagnosis is inferred through probabilities, known as Bayesian analysis.

After 15 years of suffering, Anne Dodge had begun to lose hope. Then, realizing that Dodge was beaten down by her suffering, Dr. Falchuk examined her in a completely different way. While there was no direct reason to change the overarching frame, he took the extra step to create a second perspective to understand her suffering. In order to seek an alternative diagnosis, he challenged himself as to what he and others might be missing. Rather than using the existing medical records, he started afresh, seeking to hear her story in her own words.

Dr. Falchuk empathically listened; he asked open-ended questions. He made Dodge feel that he was really interested in hearing what she had to say. Eventually he determined that she had celiac disease, an autoimmune disorder caused by an allergy to gluten, a primary component of many grains. By changing Dodge's diet, he was able to greatly reduce her symptoms.

The first steps toward innovative thinking are seeking new information, gathering information in a new way, questioning past assumptions and thinking, and asking what might have been missed. While there is always a place for applying adages such as "If the wheel isn't broken, don't fix it," it is equally important to discern why *this* wheel, why here, why now, and "Is this even the wheel called for in this situation?" Innovative thinking often spurs connections and actions that lead to new approaches, processes, products, and services, and sets the stage for problem solving.

Problem Solving

Problem solving competencies, such as visualization, ordering, analogy, simplifications, and framing, facilitate your ability to create new solutions. For example, visualization is often a very effective tool because it uses the strengths of your visual senses (physical aspects such as core and peripheral vision) and mind (triggering neurochemical reactions in the brain).

Ordering is important because it enables innovations to be aligned for maximum effectiveness. If you have innovation partners that you are dependent on, you will need to sequence the co-dependencies. The order in which Apple rolls out its products and services, for example, is an important part of their success.[34]

The use of an analogy to compare similarities and/or contrasts between objects, events, or words is an effective approach to decision-making and problem solving as well. For example, in attacking the problem of creating a faster, more comfortable, lightweight, cost-effective swimsuit for competitive swimming, innovators use the analogy of "shark skin."[35]

Simplification is another competency that directly addresses the problem of complexity. Complex problems can be daunting at best and, at worst, overwhelming. The human mind can only handle so many simultaneous tasks; recent research suggests that the brain cannot effectively handle more than two complex, related activities at once.[36] Simplification often facilitates your brain's task management processes.

Similarly, framing opens the door to alternative ways of thinking about a particular problem. How a question is framed can be limiting (e.g., how much is two plus two?) or more expansive (e.g., the sum of what two numbers equals four?). Framing is contextual and allows you to choose the boundaries, allowing the mind to zoom in and zoom out to look at various perspectives of a problem.[37]

While problem solving can be valuable in new product development, it can also be used to facilitate the introduction of existing products in new markets. In the following, we illustrate the role of problem solving in new product development, using the examples of the vacuum cleaner and the inkjet printer, and on the new market introduction front, see the following discussion of P&G hair care in China.

The Vacuum Cleaner

One of the great challenges of housekeeping is finding the best way to clean the floor or carpet. The electric vacuum cleaner is a time- and labor-saving product comprising an air input port, an air output port, a fan, an electric motor, a porous filter bag, and housing. The machine operates by creating a partial vacuum that draws air into the input port along with dust and debris, and then sends the air out through the output port. Most (but not all) the dust and debris are caught in the porous filter bag.

As useful as it is, this vacuum cleaner design has a number of flaws. Some of the fine particles of dust and debris pass through the filter back into the room. The accumulation of dust and debris in the porous bag results in a reduction of suction. The material in the bag has a tendency to take on an odor that emanates into the room. Full bags require disposal, often resulting in additional messes while costing the consumer money for new bags.

While vacuuming his home, industrial designer James Dyson observed that the more he used the vacuum the worse its suction power became. Earlier in his career, he had invented a new type of wheelbarrow that used a ball instead of a wheel. When manufacturing the wheelbarrow, he noticed the filter to catch the overspray of an epoxy powder used to coat the wheelbarrow was clogged. "The spray-equipment maker said large industrial users collected airborne debris in a cyclone. The cyclone, it turned out, was a 30-ft-high cone that spun dust out of the air using centrifugal force – the kind of thing you might see on top of a saw mill."[38] Dyson went to a local sawmill to observe how wood dust was collected with a cyclone device that used centrifugal force and required no filter.[39] He thought to himself, why not use the same design for a vacuum cleaner?

Dyson's reasoning followed this analogy: the filter bag is to the sucking vacuum cleaner as centrifugal force is to the cyclone cleaner. Using Thomas Edison's trial-and-error method, "He set to work to solve this problem. Five years and 5,127 prototypes later, the world's first cyclonic bagless vacuum cleaner arrived."[40] Although Dyson approached major manufacturers with his invention, companies were more interested in pursuing the current marketing model, worth $500 million per year, than in pursuing new technology. "Later, Hoover's vice president for Europe, Mike Rutter, said on U.K. national TV, 'I do regret that Hoover as a company did not take the product technology off Dyson; it would have lain on the shelf and not been used.'"[41] Regrettable, indeed, as Dyson would go on to achieve over $10 billion in worldwide sales.[42]

The Inkjet Printer

Johannes Gutenberg's breakthrough innovation of mechanical moveable type, a substantial improvement over handwritten manuscripts and woodblock printing, is still considered to be one of the most important events in history. Moveable type and printing were instrumental in the efficient distribution of knowledge throughout the world.[43]

Similarly, the early mechanical typewriter was an innovation from the 1860s that was based on moveable type. The typewriter uses a keyboard wherein each key connects to a raised impression of an alphabetical character. The impact of the character is transferred onto a fabric carbon-embedded ribbon immediately on top of the paper. This design is workable but problematic due to jams caused by the typist going too fast for the design of the machine. Christopher Latham Sholes, in an effort to make his business ventures more efficient, along with Samuel Soule, James Densmore, and Carlos Glidden, developed an early typewriter. Sholes had to redesign the keyboard in response to the jamming problem and so he redesigned the arrangement to separate the most common sequences of letters like "th" or "he."[44]

While an excellent example that illustrates why things are developed in certain ways as well as how they need to change, as strange as it may seem, we still use this "flawed" QWERTY keyboard design even though most typing is now electronic. That is not to say new designs have not been proposed. Interestingly, a new variation on the QWERTY design for mobile devices by TrewGrip has gained some traction. Basically, it is a "rear-type" keyboard and air mouse for smartphones and mobile technology, where most typing is done with the user's thumbs.[45]

As is often the case, one innovation often creates the potential for more innovation. For example, with the advent of electricity, the potential of the electric vacuum was realized. Similarly, the development and refinement of computers enabled computer-driven impact printing, a carryover from the typewriter. The design was based on a group of pins mounted in a cluster on a print head that crossed back and forth over a fabric ribbon revealing the imprint on paper. The dot matrix cluster of pins was a better solution than using a character imprint like the typewriter because it was more flexible, allowing for more fonts and graphics.

American physicist and inventor Chester Carlson is largely credited with inventing electrophotography to replace the then-prevalent wet copy process (mimeograph) with a dry copy process. The copy-making solution was a "xerography" process that uses powdered ink that sticks to an electrostatic charge on a drum.[46] This xerographic printing process was instrumental in the later development of laser printers.

In the 1970s, companies began to realize that computer printing was so important that it required a new product design. At Hewlett-Packard, researchers were pursuing the idea of placing even more dots on the dot matrix printer. One day at HP Labs, engineer John Vaught was watching the small explosions of hot steamy water inside a percolator as the coffee brew trickled through the filter.[47] He realized that the metal pins are to the dot matrix printer as the percolator bursts are to the inkjet.[48] Perhaps you could spray heated ink onto the paper! In 1984, HP introduced the Think-jet, followed by the Deskjet in 1988.[49] At every turn, problem solving serves as the genesis for advancements in innovation, often driven by new technologies not previously available.

Introducing Shampoo in China

In 1988, the dominant hair care model in China involved using a bar of soap for cleansing both hair and body. There was neither a separate product category nor concept of using a separate product specially formulated for hair. This untapped market required innovative thinking and practice to solve the problem of introducing a new way to clean hair.

When it comes to innovating consumable product goods in the personal cleansing segment, Procter & Gamble has a long-standing record of bringing successful products to an increasingly global marketplace. In 1837, William Procter and James Gamble began innovating and creating what would become one of the leading consumer goods companies in the world. As we will see in Chapter 11, "Entrepreneurship," their entrepreneurial legacy includes continuous product and process innovation, introducing leading brands in laundry detergents, personal bathing, oral care products, and more around the world.

In 1989, P&G sought to change the dominant model of personal hair care in China with the introduction of Head & Shoulders. Doing so required product positioning as well as consumer education in order to gain an entry point in the marketplace. Introducing a product to a new market requires consumer education to change behaviors and create purchase patterns. Today, P&G is the leading provider of shampoos in the Chinese marketplace.[50] Moreover, they continue to lead product and brand innovation in a global marketplace, including Bounce Bursts, Febreze Allergen Reducer, Tide Pods Free and Gentle, Tide Simply Fresh, Tide Plus Collection, Tide Oxi Multi-Purpose Stain Remover, Gain Flings, Head & Shoulders Fresh Scent Technology, Secret Clinical Strength Collection, and more.

Knowledge Building

The discovery of new knowledge is essential to our economic, social, and individual well-being. In fact, new knowledge is one of the most powerful instruments in the innovation tool chest. For example, progress in medicine is dependent on understanding the mysteries in the biological sciences. Nowhere is this more evident than in the fascinating world of biology, genetics, and physiomics research and practice.

Genomics

The knowledge journey is often long and convoluted, with significant periods of misunderstanding, rejection, and persistence, followed by discovery. While physical traits in plants such as seed shape, seed color, and plant size are clearly visible, how such traits were transmitted from one generation to another was not always understood. In the period between 1856 and 1863, Gregor Mendel, an Augustinian friar, discovered the laws of inheritance by studying pea plants. Put simply, he discovered that round seeds dominated wrinkled seeds, tall plants dominated short plants, and yellow seed color dominated green seed color.[51] Although like many new discoveries Mendel's work was initially rejected, today he is considered the founder of the science of genetics.[52]

Another mystery on this new knowledge journey was solved in 1953, when James D. Watson and Francis Crick co-discovered the structure of deoxyribose nucleic acid, or DNA. DNA is a molecular structure that is present in nearly every cell in the body, representing the genetic code of each organism. The genetic code shows up in the new cells when they divide, carrying forward the characteristics of that person. Knowledge of DNA's structure enabled scientists to understand how genetic instructions are stored in the human body and how they are transferred from generation to generation.[53]

In 2000, Craig Ventor and Francis Collins jointly announced that they had created the initial draft of a map of the human genome.[54] This foundational breakthrough enabled scientists to develop in silico (using information technology and computers) simulation models that could be used to complement in vitro (in the glass, wet labs) and in vivo (in the living, organisms, animals, etc.) biological experiments. This three-part approach enables scientists to tackle big problems using a more economical and technology-based approach to conduct research and improve outcomes. In 2003, the Human Genome Project was declared complete when, after eight years, $1 billion, and thousands of researchers, a map of our human code was produced.[55] The human genome map is a blueprint of our human cells that is stored in a database for furthering science in areas such as molecular pharmacology, drug discovery, and cancer research.

In the late 1980s, the National Cancer Institute developed the NCI-60 protocol composed of human tumor samples from 60 different cell cultures (lines) used originally to test for anti-cancer agents by analyzing the anti-cancer properties of natural and synthetic compounds.[56] In 2013, the National Cancer Institute furthered this work by developing a more comprehensive list of the 60 human tumor cell lines (cultures) that include nine different types of cancer – breast, ovary, prostate, colon, lung, kidney, brain, leukemia, and melanoma – for use in identifying new cancer genes.[57] As exciting as this is, it only marks the continuing journey forward.

Pharmacogenomics and Personalized Medicine

Pharmacogenomics is the study of how genetic differences in patients affect an individual's response to a particular pharmaceutical.[58] In the field of pharmacogenomics, also known as personalized medicine, drugs can be used in more efficacious ways through an understanding of each person's unique set of genes.[59]

Because cancer drugs may work on one patient but not another, it has been difficult for physicians to predict how individual patients would benefit.

In 1985, scientists discovered that a specific receptor on the surface of cells, called human epidermal growth factor receptor 2 (HER2), was produced in excess in about 20–25% of breast tumors – suggesting to them that these tumors might be a different disease, defined by a unique molecular pathway through which those tumors propagated.[60]

This innovation of personalized medicine, which aims to match interventions with an individual's genetic instructions, was made possible by the ongoing search and discovery of new knowledge.

Herceptin was the first gene-targeted therapy for breast cancer. Herceptin was approved by the FDA in 1998 and was designed specifically to halt the growth of breast cancer cells. Herceptin works by attaching to the HER2 receptor on the surfaces of these cancer cells. A patient is first given a specific genetic test to determine whether they have the HER2 receptor gene pattern. If the patient has the matching gene pattern, Herceptin will likely result in successful treatment.

"Smart Bomb" Medicines

Another example of the power of new knowledge can be seen via chemotherapy, the traditional intervention for cancer. Chemotherapy uses cytotoxins, which kill both normal cells and cancer cells. This intervention can have side effects, including hair loss, nausea, infection, and even death. More effective interventions have since been developed to target the cancer more specifically. The first anti-cancer drug of this type was Gleevec, used to target the abnormal proteins in those who have chronic myeloid leukemia, a cancer of the white blood cells, and for the treatment of a rare form of stomach cancer called gastrointestinal stromal tumor.[61]

Based on the success of Herceptin and Gleevec, rather than using the traditional carpet-bombing blunderbuss approaches, new "smart bomb" medications are being developed. "The FDA approved Seattle Genetics' Adcetris in 2011, for the treatment of rare lymphomas, and this year the agency approved Genentech's Kadcyla for the treatment of metastatic breast cancer patients that are HER2 positive."[62]

New Knowledge and Creative Destruction

Noted economist Joseph Schumpeter emphasized the following positive consequences of economic downturns: the destruction of underperforming companies, the release of capital from dying sectors to new industries, and the movement of high-quality, skilled workers toward stronger employers. He is largely credited with popularizing the term "creative destruction." "For companies with cash and ideas, history shows that downturns can provide enormous strategic opportunities."[63]

As McKinsey's Tom Nicholas writes, "The experience of the 1930s also illustrates a broader point. Although deep downturns are destructive, they can also have an upside."

Synthetic rubber, a major innovation of the 20th century, is an excellent example of the power of new knowledge and effect of Schumpeter's concept of "creative destruction." Wallace Carothers, a DuPont research scientist, discovered neoprene (synthetic rubber) during the Great Depression. DuPont made a counterintuitive decision to invest in innovation during this major economic downturn. Synthetic rubber, made from petroleum, was a major innovation that is still used in many products, including cars and airplanes.[64]

DuPont developed an understanding of polymer chemistry through the development of their miracle fibers and, in so doing, created a technology enabler that got the job done better. Starting with trial-and-error processes, DuPont designed the world's first synthetic fiber, nylon, in 1945, then acrylic in 1944, and Dacron polyester in 1946. Next, DuPont developed an understanding of polymer chemistry which enabled scientists to design Nomex, a fire-retardant fiber, and then Kevlar, a fiber five times stronger than steel.

DuPont encapsulated the knowledge of polymer chemistry into software tools that enabled problem solving to be transitioned from a small group of expensive specialized experts to a larger group of less expensive experts. This effect allows specialized experts to perform new, innovative, high-order tasks as they delegate codified patterns of knowledge to software (or less experienced and less specialized individuals). They embedded knowledge into software that allowed them to more effectively share expertise on a larger scale. Today, DuPont's knowledge of polymer chemistry has been codified into software tools that allow the scientists and engineers to discover new synthetic fibers more quickly than before and spread this knowledge widely.[65]

Creativity

While innovative behaviors, thinking, problem solving, and new knowledge are individually and collectively powerful tools, creativity is often the catalyst that brings innovation to light and life. Creativity is represented in all forms through the arts: painting, photography, dance, drama, writing, movies, and music. The arts provide ways of learning creativity that can form the foundation for many of the building blocks of innovation.

The Orchestra

John Morris Russell, conductor of the Cincinnati Pops Orchestra, applies his creative, innovative, entrepreneurship, and leadership skills to develop new markets for audiences while multiplying the creativity of the Cincinnati Pops musicians. The orchestra and conductor are a metaphor for a creative model that shows the integration of the competencies.

For example, the planning of a performance requires that the conductor create a vision for the musical experience. Often this requires creating a unique new program that uses associative thinking and connects two or more ideas. Imagine that the conductor decides to use musical performances to facilitate the teaching of children, and teams up with teachers to combine music and education. For example, "From 1997 to 2009 Maestro Russell conducted the 'LinkUp!' educational series at Carnegie Hall, and the 'Sound Discoveries' series he developed with the Cincinnati Symphony Orchestra (CSO) that remains a model for educational concerts."[66] In 2012, Maestro Russell conducted a new program titled "Ballroom with a Twist" that combined orchestral music, dancing, and live vocals, encompassing *Dancing with the Stars*, *So You Think You Can Dance*, and *American Idol* all on the same stage.

One of the jobs of an orchestral conductor is to use social and venturing skills to grow the music business by building relationships with the community, increasing audience subscriptions, finding new markets, and encouraging patrons to provide resources so that the orchestra can grow, create, and thrive. A "Pops" conductor will learn the preferences of the audience, whether it is classical, jazz, bluegrass, or pop, and, at the same time, will provide new musical themes, pushing the audience in new directions they may have not experienced before.

Maestro Russell and his CSO team successfully engaged the African American community in CSO and Pops offerings. "He was recognized for his innovative programming and commitment to attracting new and diverse audiences to orchestral music, creating the Classical Roots: Spiritual Heights series, which brought the music of African-American composers and performers to thousands of listeners in area churches."[67] Beginning with smaller concerts in area churches in 2002, "Classical Roots" celebrates traditions that began in Africa, the spiritual and gospel, as well as blues, jazz, and concert music for orchestra and chorus.[68] Now performed in Cincinnati's Music Hall, the 2011 edition of "Classical Roots" was so successful that it sold out the 3,400-seat hall.

Musical performances are dynamic events crafted through the efforts of musicians, staff, and stage crew. During a rehearsal, a successful conductor establishes respect and trust with the musicians of his or her orchestra. The conductor provides a strong musical framework and empowers musicians to play their best by giving latitude within that framework. Although a conductor may have a solid concept for the sound and shape of any given work, musicians bring other creative ideas to a performance that complement and enhance it overall. The orchestral conductor is the leader that brings together the audience and musicians to create a fulfilling musical experience for both.

Culture Building

As an organization is conceived and develops, its founding culture adapts and grows. In general terms, culture represents the collective values and beliefs of key organizational members or, in the case of a new venture, often the founders. It is often the effect of an organization's history, products, markets, technologies, leaders, and employees. It becomes a set of learned group-specific behaviors that can take on both positive and negative conditions, as well as the development of subcultures within the organization. There are many types of venture cultures: results-oriented, bureaucratic, innovative, risk-taking, emergent and adaptable, people-oriented and team based, institutional, creative, and command and control. In general, a culture that is bureaucratic, risk-aversive, and control-oriented is likely to be less innovative than those that are entrepreneurial, emergent and adaptable, and people-oriented.

HP: The Company That Lost Their Way

Bill Hewlett and Dave Packard were classmates at Stanford and graduated with electrical engineering degrees in 1935.[69] After graduation, Packard was hired by General Electric and Hewlett went to MIT to work on a master's degree before going on to work for Jensen Speaker in Chicago.[70] They both had aspirations to become entrepreneurs, so in 1939, with a capital investment of $538, they established the Hewlett-Packard (HP) Company in Dave Packard's garage. "Hewlett and Packard tossed a coin to decide whether the company they founded would be called Hewlett-Packard or Packard-Hewlett. Packard won the coin toss but named their electronics manufacturing enterprise the 'Hewlett-Packard Company.' HP incorporated on August 18, 1947, and went public on November 6, 1957."[71]

Of the many projects they worked on, their very first financially successful product was a precision audio oscillator, the Model HP200A. Their innovation was the use of a small incandescent light bulb (known as a "pilot light") as a temperature dependent resistor in a critical portion of the circuit, the negative feedback loop which stabilized the amplitude of the output sinusoidal waveform. This allowed them to sell the Model HP200A for $54.40 when competitors were selling fewer stable oscillators for over $200.[72]

Walt Disney Studios purchased eight of the oscillators to develop and test an innovative sound system for the movie *Fantasia*.[73]

Hewlett and Packard worked to build and sustain the HP culture, known as the HP Way. The HP Way would come to be considered Silicon Valley's innovation model.[74] It is a lesson for the ages on how culture building and innovation are inextricably linked. Fortunately, shortly before his death, Packard wrote *The HP Way*, which describes HP history and how the culture was developed and sustained.

About David Packard, Jim Collins writes,

He never wanted to be part of the CEO club; he belonged to the Hewlett-Packard club. In an era when bosses dwelt in mahogany-panelled sanctums, Packard took an open-door workspace among his engineers. He practiced what would become famous as "management by walking around." Most radical of all for the time, he shared equity and profits with all employees.[75]

As Jim Collins writes,

The HP Way reflects the personal core values of Bill Hewlett and David Packard, and the translation of those values into a comprehensive set of operating practices, cultural norms, and business strategies. The point is not that every company should necessarily adopt the specifics of the HP Way, but that Hewlett and Packard exemplify the power of building a company based on a framework of principles that form the foundation of the HP Way or culture. The core essence of the HP Way consists of five fundamental precepts.1) The Hewlett-Packard company exists to make a technical contribution, and should only pursue opportunities consistent with this purpose; 2) The Hewlett-Packard company demands of itself and its people superior performance – profitable growth is both a means and a measure of enduring success; 3) The Hewlett-Packard company believes the best results come when you get the right people, trust them, give them freedom to find the best path to achieve objectives, and let them share in the rewards their work makes possible; 4) The Hewlett-Packard company has a responsibility to contribute directly to the well-being of the communities in which its operates; 5) Integrity, period.[76]

The question then becomes how to sustain the culture and/or recognize the best way to morph the culture for growth. After William Hewlett, John Young carried the HP ideology torch and served as president and CEO of Hewlett-Packard. Young was succeeded by Lewis E. Platt, who led HP's culture-building through 1999. Around 1999, HP felt it necessary to go outside for leadership, hiring people who departed from their core ideology.

Jim Collins writes,

If you are involved with an organization that feels it must go outside for a top manager, then look for candidates who are highly compatible with the core ideology. They can be different in managerial style, but they should share the core values at a gut level.[77]

During the period 1999 through 2010, HP experienced a set of leadership failures impacting the HP Way. All three of these leaders, Carly Fiorina, Patricia Dunn, and Mark Hurd, demonstrated questionable behaviors that impacted the core values and the culture established by HP's founders.

In a significant change of leadership, Hewlett-Packard appointed Carly Fiorina as chief executive officer in 1999, succeeding Lewis Platt. "Her strategy was to shift HP's culture away from organic growth through internal innovation and toward expansion through mergers with outside companies."[78] The culture that Dave and Bill established began to unravel as HP began transitioning from a model based on empowerment to one of control. Carly Fiorina was labeled "anti-Steve Jobs," and she was forced to resign in 2005.[79]

The managerial style of the leadership made another dramatic shift. After Carly Fiorina, Patricia Dunn, another outside director, was appointed as chairwoman of the board of HP from 2005 to 2006. In response to board-level leaks to the media, HP hired private investigators to identify the source. The investigators used inappropriate practices, such as the searching of board members' phone records.[80] Dunn said, "she was proud of her accomplishments at HP but regretted the use of 'inappropriate techniques' in the investigation and later resigned."[81]

After Patricia Dunn, Mark Hurd was appointed chairman, chief executive officer, and president of HP from 2006 to 2010. He focused on outsourcing and efficiency rather than building on HP's foundational core values. Hurd created distrust by implementing a program that fired the bottom 5% of staff each year, resulting in competition rather than collaboration among the employees.[82] He was replaced for violating proper standards of business conduct. "Many companies have fallen into HP's trap of managing for efficiency, not creativity. Whole industries, from steel to consumer electronics, have been gutted as a result of focusing on the short-term financial benefits resulting from efficiencies of scale at the expense of long-term investment in internal innovation."[83]

3M: The Company That Almost Lost Their Way

3M was founded in 1902 to mine corundum, a form of aluminum oxide. Corundum is a very hard mineral used as an abrasive for use in grinding wheels. Depending on the impurities, it can take on many different colors and is also used in jewelry. Unfortunately, 3M's mining business failed when they could not find any customers.[84]

3M shifted its expertise to manufacture sandpaper and, later, adhesives, including masking tape and a whole set of simple and flat products. How does 3M achieve continuous innovation? 3M is legendary for their ability to sustain an innovative culture that supports "intrapreneurial" activities from their founding in 1902 through today.[85]

The innovative culture at 3M is based on a set of management principles established by William L. McKnight and sustained using culture and innovator role models that included Richard Drew, Arthur Frey, Spence Silver, Patsy Sherman, and Sam Smith.

In *Built to Last*, Collins and Porras describe visionary companies like 3M as those which preserve a core ideology and simultaneously stimulate progress.[86] While visionary companies understand that profit is necessary, it is not the purpose of the firm or an end in itself. Rather, visionary companies focus on a clear purpose that continuously creates value for customers, employees, the business, communities, and others. In so doing, profit becomes possible, while failing to do so puts profits in jeopardy. 3M is an excellent example of the roles that core ideologies, drive for progress, and culture branching and pruning play in success.

Core Ideology

Core ideology has two parts: a purpose and a set of management guiding principles or core values. For 3M, the purpose was to solve unsolved problems innovatively.[87] Management's guiding principles or core values were respect for individual initiative, tolerance for honest mistakes, absolute integrity, and excellent products.

William L. McKnight created a set of management guiding principles that became the foundation of innovative culture.[88] These management guiding principles are based on empowering and trusting people. Considered to have been a business philosopher, McKnight was president of 3M from 1929 until 1949 and chairman of the board from 1949 through 1966.[89] His basic rules of management, outlined in 1948, are still listed on the company website:

> As our business grows, it becomes increasingly necessary to delegate responsibility and to encourage men and women to exercise their initiative. This requires considerable tolerance. Those men and women, to whom we delegate authority and responsibility, if they are good people, are going to want to do their jobs in their own way.
>   Mistakes will be made. But if a person is essentially right, the mistakes he or she makes are not as serious in the long run as the mistakes management will make if it undertakes to tell those in authority exactly how they must do their jobs.
>   Management that is destructively critical when mistakes are made kills initiative. And it's essential that we have many people with initiative if we are to continue to grow.

Drive for Progress

The drive for progress stimulates 3M to innovate, solve customer problems, and experiment. Based on McKnight's principles,[90] each division is expected to generate 30% of their annual sales from products and services offered in the last five years. 3M uses a program that allows technical people to spend 15% of their time on projects of their own choosing, doing experimental doodling.[91] 3M provides rewards such as the Golden Step award, given to those teams that earn $4 million or more in profitable revenues. 3M recognizes the accomplishments of its employees by peer nomination into the prestigious Carlton Society. Employees can receive a Genius grant, an internal venture capital fund, to develop prototypes and conduct market research. 3M has a split-career path, enabling opportunities for both technical and managerial talent development. 3Mers who champion new products may receive the opportunity to run a 3M division. The size of each division is kept small and encouraged to be autonomous.[92]

Culture: Branching and Pruning

3M recognized long before other companies that in order for a business to stay vibrant, it must continuously reinvent itself.

> Many say the company's success over the years is linked to its ability to change as 3M, its products and the world marketplace evolves. In fact, when the company greeted the new century in 2000, more than half the businesses that were 3M staples 20 years before had disappeared from the corporate portfolio.[93]

3M achieved innovation by anchoring their core ideology and simultaneously driving progress through an evolutionary process of branching and pruning that was an outgrowth of their culture. 3M's careful blending and balancing of deliberate and emergent strategy produced three excellent examples: Masking tape, Scotchgard™, and the now ubiquitous Post-it Notes™.

Masking Tape

3M employee Richard Drew was at a car paint shop when he noticed the painters having difficulty painting two-tone cars.[94] When the tape they were using to mark off sections was removed, some of the paint came off with it. Since 3M had expertise in the field of adhesives, Drew reasoned that 3M might be able to solve the car painting problem. Drew went back to 3M and discovered that they had no easily adaptable or relevant product in their labs. He began a self-initiated project to develop a solution by experimentally doodling with various materials and processes.

William L. McKnight, noticing that Drew was spending a lot of time on his car painting project, asked him to return to his assignment of incremental sandpaper improvement. Drew persisted, however, continuing work on the car painting problem. McKnight did not intervene, letting the maverick effort continue. The result was a new product that solved the problem at hand and could also be applied in numerous other situations: masking tape. Drew continued to improve on masking tape, later developing a transparent tape known as Scotch tape.

Scotch transparent tape was not deliberately conceived; it emerged as a by-product of the leadership and culture of 3M. Jim Collins writes,

> Scotch tape wasn't planned. No one at 3M had any idea in 1920, that 3M would enter the tape business and certainly no one expected that it would become the most important product line in the company by the mid-1930s. Scotch is a natural outgrowth of the organizational climate McKnight created, not the result of a brilliant strategic plan.[95]

Scotchgard™

In 1953, Patsy Sherman, 3M research chemist, was assigned to work on fluorochemicals. Her colleague, Sam Smith, was assigned to developing jet aircraft fuel lines.[96] The story goes like this:

> While Sherman and Smith were working in the lab one day, an assistant dropped a bottle of synthetic latex that Sherman had made, causing the compound to splash onto the assistant's white canvas tennis shoes. The two chemists were fascinated to find that while the substance did not change the look of the shoes, it could not be washed away by any solvents, and it repelled water, oil and other liquids.[97]

Sherman and Smith had inadvertently discovered a new, versatile fluorochemical polymer fabric-stain repellant. By 1956, their continued work on this accidental discovery led the 3M research team to offer the product known as Scotchgard™. By 1960, the research team had expanded the Scotchgard™ product line to include carpet treatment and automotive upholstery cleaner.[98]

Although the discovery of Scotchgard™ was a somewhat serendipitous event, the 3M culture is based on the combination of a tolerance for honest mistakes and empowerment and trust that encourages employees to take responsibility for the invention of new products that previously did not exist, thereby contributing to the realization of innovation.[99]

> Drawing from her own experiences, Sherman encourages aspiring inventors with advice that she herself learned decades ago: "Keep your eyes and mind open, and don't ignore something that doesn't come out the way you expect it to. Just keep looking at the world with inventor's eyes!"[100]

Post-it Note™

For a company in the adhesive business, Spence Silver's invention of "a new adhesive that would not dry or permanently bond to things," would be considered by many to be a failed product.[101] Meanwhile, Arthur Fry, another 3M employee, was in search of a better way to keep track of the hymns in his hymnal because the paper bookmarks kept falling out. Making the connection between his need for a sticky, yet moveable, bookmarker and Silver's weak glue, the idea for the Post-it Note™ was born.[102] As successful as the Post-it Note™ was to become, there was initial skepticism as to whether or not there would be a sufficient market for such a temporary bookmark. Once again, however, the culture at 3M allowed for the experimentation, connections, and persistence often needed to conceive, develop, and deliver a novel product that goes beyond its original conceptualization.

"Following the genesis of this idea, however, he spent much of his time suggesting variations of the invention, such as the Post-it Pop-up Note Dispenser and the Post-it Flag. Instead of generating novel ideas, he made incremental variations on his original idea."[103] Indeed, Fry would go on to develop a whole line of Post-it Note products and variations, sparking imitators and expansive markets.

Innovation Theory

Up to this point, the focus has been primarily on innovation in practice. It is equally important, though, to recognize the role that theory plays in both innovation and entrepreneurship. Quite simply, as psychologist Kurt Lewin is credited with saying, "there is nothing as practical as a good theory."

While there are many definitions of *theory*, for our purposes a *theory* describes a specific realm of knowledge and explains how it works.[104] In essence, a theory attempts to make sense from the observable world.[105] Innovation theory by its very nature is derived from multiple aspects of a broad spectrum of disciplines. For example, building on Clayton Christensen's theory of disruptive innovation, Michael Raynor conducted a number of experiments focusing on the role of disruption theory in informing innovation. Raynor suggests that disruption theory shapes innovation ideas and thus has implications for new venture success.[106] In addition, Jon-Arild Johannessen, Bjørn Olsen, and Johan Olaisen suggest that innovation theory is based in part on organizational vision and knowledge management which in turn informs innovation in practice.[107] Collectively, the work of Christensen, Raynor, Johannessen, et al., and others provides a window into the development of innovation theory that informs how we understand innovation and entrepreneurship.

IBM serves as an enduring case example of the importance of innovation theory in the world of innovation and entrepreneurship. IBM is one of the few companies with a history of entrepreneurial beginnings, and with both sustaining (incremental and evolutionary) and disruptive innovations along the way. A disruptive innovation is not necessarily a revolutionary innovation, such as the invention of electricity, electric motors, electric generators, and power plants, but all disruptive innovation is transformative. It can transform a historically expensive, complicated, and generally inaccessible product like a mainframe computer into the affordable, simple, and accessible personal computer.[108]

Interestingly, IBM's innovation started with the Jacquard loom that used punched cards to control the complex patterns in textile manufacturing.[109] This loom was an invention immediately ahead of the development of the punch-card concept patented by Herman Hollerith in 1889, and used in the 1890 US Census.[110] Based on the punch-card concept, unit record card handling equipment and the 80-column card were developed by IBM in 1928, for handling large volumes of data.

Since then, technology evolved from the mainframe computers of the 1960s, the minicomputers of the 1970s, and the microcomputers of the 1980s. In the 1960s and early 1970s, IBM was successful in outcompeting the "seven dwarfs" (Burroughs, Sperry Rand, Control Data, Honeywell, General Electric, RCA, and NCR) with the System/360 and System/370 mainframe computer. In the 1970s IBM started the Future System project, creating an autonomous minicomputer business unit in IBM's laboratory in Rochester, Minnesota to develop the System/38 minicomputer. This minicomputer included a relational database product based on technology that was invented by IBM to compete against DEC, Data General, Prime, HP, Nixdorf, and Stratus.

With the IBM mainframe computer, IBM gained market share and extended its value as a sustaining innovation. IBM mainframes were very complex, high-gross-margin products for medium to large organizations.

> Companies pursue these "sustaining innovations" at the higher tiers of their markets because this is what has historically helped them succeed: By charging the highest prices to their most demanding and sophisticated customers at the top of the market, companies will achieve the greatest profitability.[111]

Innovation theory suggests that incumbents like IBM are successful at sustaining innovations that incrementally evolve the existing products and services offered to their existing markets and customers. The incumbent will have a strong tendency to follow conventional business practices and stay very close to the current customers whom they depend on for immediate revenue. IBM did exactly what they should have based on the best managerial practices.

Innovation theory also suggests that, while incumbents are successful at incrementally evolving sustaining innovations, they are not always successful at disruptive innovations.

> An innovation that is disruptive allows a whole new population of consumers at the bottom of a market access to a product or service that was historically only accessible to consumers with a lot of money or a lot of skill. Characteristics of disruptive businesses, at least in their initial stages, can include lower gross margins, smaller target markets, and simpler products and services that may not appear as attractive as existing solutions.[112]

Entrepreneurs often see and seek market inefficiencies before incumbents do, creating new products, services, processes, and ventures. New entrepreneurial entrants often successfully pursue disruptive revolutionary innovation but struggle with sustaining innovations in the markets and products of incumbents. Four statements describe innovation theory in this regard:[113]

- An incumbent that offers a sustaining (incremental or evolutionary) innovation intended for its current customers can expect to succeed.
- An incumbent that attempts to offer a disruptive (revolutionary) innovation in its own markets can expect failure. The exception is for the incumbent to create a separate but linked organization that functions like a new entrepreneurial entrant with separate leadership, culture, and business models.
- The new entrepreneurial entrant that attempts to offer a sustaining innovation in the most valuable established markets of an incumbent can expect failure.
- The new entrepreneurial entrant that offers a disruptive innovation, one that is simple, affordable, and convenient in a new market for new consumers, can expect to succeed.

The incumbent cannot itself disrupt, unless it creates a separate organization that supports the new business model, products, and markets. IBM created the disruptive innovation, the IBM PC, through a separate organization. The IBM PC was simple instead of complex, affordable rather than expensive, and it was designed for ordinary, individual consumers, not for computer experts in large corporations.

IBM was able to create a new market disruption by providing non-consumers access to computing resources. IBM created a separate division known as the IBM Entry Systems Division in Boca

Raton, Florida to produce the IBM PC. This separate division allowed IBM to break away from the mainframe business model of offering a small number of expensive computing resources to a small number of organizations and replace that with the ability to offer a large number of inexpensive computing resources to a large number of people.

The IBM PC was released in 1981 and included components from Intel and Seagate with a Microsoft operating system.[114] Although customers were initially willing to pay premium prices for Apple products' performance and reliability over the IBM Personal Computers, "by the early 1990s Apple's computers had improved to levels beyond what customers in less-demanding tiers of the market needed – and the basis of competition changed."[115] Customers began switching from Apple computers to Dell Personal Computers because Dell offered customization and convenience. Instead of going to a retail store, you could configure and purchase your own computer on-line for direct shipment to you.

IBM has been successful at developing an entrepreneurial process and culture, and in adapting to change. They created subcultures that blended the best of efficiency with the most desirable aspects of innovative entrepreneurship. IBM achieved this by creating the Emerging Business Opportunities (EBO), a management process for identifying, staffing, funding, and tracking new business initiatives across IBM. They built a separate management process, one that fit with the existing process but counterbalanced the short-term orientation of IBM's management culture that enabled those who participated to take risks but fail early and fail small.[116] They added a new train track that intersected with the old track to ensure that the core IBM competencies were used by both tracks. They focused the new track on learning over profits to unleash rather than constrain emerging ideas.

On September 12, 2011, WellPoint, one of the nation's leading health benefits companies with 34.2 million members, announced in that it was planning to use the IBM supercomputer, Watson, for treating patients.[117] Watson, named after IBM's first president, Thomas J. Watson, is a massive parallel computer system that is designed for artificial intelligence and natural language processes. The more operations that can be done in parallel the faster the computer can provide results.

IBM's Watson received notoriety when it beat a set of highly qualified human *Jeopardy* contestants. The computer is innovative because of the manner in which it processes the algorithms to achieve the desired results.[118] WellPoint plans to use this powerhouse computer system and combine the patient's electronic healthcare records, the insurance company's history of medicines and treatments, and an electronic library of medical journals and textbooks. This combination of computing power and three sources of data is expected to rapidly reveal the best treatment interventions.[119]

Entrepreneurship

At its core, entrepreneurship is the creation of new venture and value for multiple constituents, from customers to employees to communities and even countries. It includes both for-profit ventures as well as not-for-profit ventures. There are numerous success stories of entrepreneurs ideating, conceiving, formulating, founding, and leading new ventures to great success, including Apple, Google (Alphabet), and Facebook (Meta), to name just a few, that have bloomed into iconic businesses. These entrepreneurs include small business owners, accelerated growth and serial venture founders, and corporate, social, and global entrepreneurs.

Essentially, entrepreneurship is the *discipline* of venture creation that transforms ideas into an enterprise that provides value. Entrepreneurship is the practice of new venture creation that addresses the vast opportunities and market inefficiencies that appear during the sometimes-troublesome nuances of creative destruction.

Entrepreneurs, acting alone or with others, take risks and actions to create the venture and value for multiple constituents. While entrepreneurship is ultimately about the creation of venture and value, as we shall see in the following examples, it is indeed a multidimensional subject that is intricately interwoven with innovation.

Entrepreneurs illustrate the 3D vision of drive, determination, and dedication needed to succeed in the ever-changing, technology-driven business and industry landscape.

There are several exemplars of innovation and entrepreneurship that illustrate the 3D vision of drive, determination, and dedication needed to succeed in the ever-changing, technology-driven business and industry landscape. What can we learn from these adventurous innovators and entrepreneurs?

Samuel Adams

Founded in 1983, by native Cincinnatian Mr. James Koch, the Boston Beer Company personifies the challenges of the entrepreneur. When Koch first conceived his new venture idea in 1983, entering the brewing industry was not very attractive. In fact, breweries were closing, not opening, growth was stagnant, and there was excess brewing capacity throughout the industry. Initial thoughts toward building a brewery were quickly abandoned, as potential investors were naturally reluctant to participate. Given this relative lack of overall industry attractiveness, what did Koch know that would set him apart? The short answer: focus on product/service, customers, and competitors.

Samuel Adams Lager would become the cornerstone of what would eventually become an entire product line of beer that would be targeted to just 2% of the beer drinking market. Pursuing a focused differentiation strategy demanded that the product attributes not only meet but exceed the customer's expectations. Since the premium product attributes (especially taste) were paramount, considerable time was spent perfecting the heart and soul of the company – the product. While the Boston Beer example focuses on product development, the same processes apply to service offerings. Service offerings can actually be thought of as "products" of service companies. For example, the product that a personal tax preparation service company offers is timely, accurate, quality tax analysis and preparation for individual taxpayers. In addition, product and service offerings frequently occur in combination. Starbucks is an excellent example of a product (a selection of premium coffee and tea beverages) and service (a premium coffee and tea beverage experience).

The customer segment was small but of sufficient size, quality, and durability to support a new entrant. By conceding 98% of the brew-drinking market to the dominant domestic breweries, Boston Beer was able to successfully focus on the 2% of beer drinkers that sought a premium or super premium product – an emerging segment addressed at that time only by the imported or specialty beer producers.

In the early years, Koch correctly assessed that the major domestic players would be unable and/ or unwilling to respond to a new entrant in the premium beer segment. They were committed to the larger, non-premium segment and had conceded the premium/specialty segment to the imported beers. While he knew the imported beer makers would respond, focusing on product attributes the customer sought, he would gain valuable time and space on his eventual emerging competitors. Through the early 1990s, microbrewing and craft brewing were still highly fragmented, giving Boston Beer first-mover advantage.

Tesla and Space X

Elon Musk is an adventurous innovator and entrepreneur. Musk has been compared to Apple Computer co-founder Steve Jobs for his big ideas and prolific innovations. Jobs pursued innovation in computers, movies, music, and entertainment,[120] while Musk has pursued innovation and entrepreneurship in computer software, electric cars, solar energy, and space travel. His first adventure was Zip2, a web software company that provided a "city guide" for the newspaper publishing industry. In 1999, Zip2 was sold to Compaq for $307 million in cash and $34 million in stock options. Musk's second adventure was the online payment processing system known as PayPal, which sold to eBay for $1.5 billion in common stock.[121]

Musk would go on to found and become CEO of Tesla Motors, an automotive company that designs and manufactures innovative electric sports cars. One of the constraints to the development of a production model electric car was the expense and weight of the battery. Musk's key breakthrough was to use a lithium-ion battery, like the ones in laptops, tablets, and phones, for improved price and performance characteristics. To reduce the prices of the batteries, Musk has announced plans to build the world's largest lithium-ion battery plant.[122]

Not content to innovate and create new ventures on the ground, in 2002, Musk founded Space Exploration Technologies, known as SpaceX. Instead of using a launch system once, SpaceX developed a launch system that could be reused, thereby reducing the cost of the spacecraft and its operation. SpaceX was the first private company to deliver cargo to the International Space Station. Musk's next big idea is to develop the means to make a round trip to Mars. The carbon dioxide in the atmosphere of Mars combined with water in the permafrost could be converted into oxygen and methane rocket fuel for the return trip. This way, a spaceship could go to Mars using fuel from Earth and then return to Earth using fuel from Mars.

As an eco-innovator, Musk proposed the concept for SolarCity, founded in 2006 – a residential installer of solar photovoltaic systems that promises to improve our future environment. Along with the anticipated decrease in the price of solar photovoltaic systems, the advancements in storage batteries allows renewable solar energy to be stored for later use during nights and cloudy days.[123] Finally, in 2012, Musk proposed a fifth form of transportation, known as the Hyperloop, as an alternative to boats, cars, planes, and trains. The Hyperloop is a design for an inter-city mass-transportation system where passengers would ride inside a capsule that is suspended on air-bearing skis and propelled inside a tube.[124]

Virgin Group

Elon Musk is not alone in his pursuit of innovation to advance science and humanity. Another noted entrepreneur and innovator, Sir Richard Branson, is also conceiving, innovating, and implementing private space travel. Beginning his first venture, Virgin Records, in 1972, by 2014, his many and varied innovative and entrepreneurial pursuits have grown to the Virgin Group which consists of over 400 companies. Branson has formed his latest venture, a US-based, UK-owned commercial spaceflight company called Virgin Galactic. Partnering with entrepreneur Paul Allen (co-founder of Microsoft) and visionary aerospace engineer Burt Rutan, Branson is focused on taking paying passengers into suborbital space.[125] Labeled a transformational leader, clearly never satisfied, his next proposed venture is Virgin Fuels, which hopes to address the need for alternative fuels in order to reduce the cost and environmental impact over traditional fossil-based fuels.[126]

GravityLight Energy

The intricate interrelationship between innovation and entrepreneurship can be clearly seen in the increasingly popular application of social entrepreneurship. For example, the use of fossil fuels, such as kerosene, for personal consumption is problematic, especially in developing countries, often creating health, safety, and environmental concerns. It is estimated that over 1.5 billion people worldwide have no reliable access to electricity, relying instead on fuels such as kerosene. Moreover, it is estimated that nearly 800 million women and children daily inhale an amount of smoke equivalent to smoking two packs of cigarettes. The results include high percentages of adult female lung cancer victims who are non-smokers, eye infections and cataracts, and severe burns from overturned kerosene lamps. Add to this the considerable cost burden, especially in impoverished areas, as well as the environmental impact from carbon emissions, and the problem is clear.[127]

As an alternative to kerosene lamps, Martin Riddiford, co-founder of the UK-based product design firm, Therefore, created a gravity-powered lamp that employs a 25-pound weight that falls about six feet per half-hour.[128] GravityLight is a revolutionary new approach to storing energy and creating illumination. It takes only three seconds to lift the weight, creating 30 minutes of light on its descent – for free.[129] In need of funds for scaling up the gravity-powered lamp, Riddiford turned to the crowd-funding site Indiegogo to acquire the resources to cover production costs and received $400,000 in one month – $345,000 more than the $55,000 the company sought.[130] "Once we have proved the design, we will be looking to link with NGOs and partners to distribute it as widely as possible. When mass produced the target cost for this light is less than $5."[131] It is an elegant solution to a vexing problem, with potential to address a critical social problem.

Strategy

Strategy is the continuous and dynamic process by which a firm analyzes both its internal (strengths and weaknesses) and external (opportunities and threats) environments, using this information to create a vision and set forth a direction or mission articulating specific goals, objectives, and tactics to achieve success. Management scholar Henry Mintzberg captured this concept of strategy nicely as a pattern in a stream of decisions.[132] In short, the powerful combination of strategy and innovation creates a set of choices that enables an organization to win.

These choices can be understood by following the growth of retailing starting with general stores. In the 19th-century United States, small-town general stores, staffed by behind-the-counter salesclerks, were the dominant retail model for local farmers to purchase merchandise. In 1888, the first Sears mail-order catalog was published, providing a more convenient way to access quality products at reasonable prices and introducing the concept of mass merchandising.[133] The Sears catalog was innovative because it provided a more convenient way to purchase what customers wanted and needed. While initially innovative in its strategy and implementation, Sears was not able to maintain its success in the 21st century, eventually downsizing before being purchased by Kmart. As we will see in Chapter 12, the continuous and dynamic aspects of strategy and innovation are critical over time.

In another example of strategy as a pattern of decisions, in the early days of the motorcar, gasoline was sold by pharmacists who would come from behind the counter to fill the vehicle. This gave rise to the proliferation of filling stations which offered full service by attendants pumping gasoline and oil, checking tire pressure, and cleaning the windshield, all while the customer sat in the comfort of his or her car.[134]

Eventually, the behind-the-counter approach to retailing was overtaken by the self-service model. Customers would select their own merchandise and wait in a checkout line as the price of each item was meticulously keyed into a cash register. The checkout process was streamlined with the introduction of electronic point-of-sale technology, used to scan uniform price codes printed on packages. In 1958, the general-purpose credit card and worldwide network was implemented.[135] The use of card readers enabled the more efficient use of credit cards and debit cards. Today, using self-service technology, customers are given the choice of "self-checkout," bypassing salesclerks entirely. In both of these examples, strategy is both deliberate and emergent. Initially, the deliberate, focus-differentiated strategy implemented via a catalog and attendant-friendly automobile service evolved and changed over time. Strategy and innovation alone are often insufficient to ensure success but, when combined, can become powerful allies in the quest for continued success.

Wal-Mart

Entrepreneur Sam Walton's core value for Wal-Mart is an unrelenting focus on providing value for the customer. Wal-Mart introduced radio frequency identification (RFID), enabling pallets of merchandise distributed to the stores to be tracked more effectively and efficiently, allowing Wal-Mart to pursue a low-cost strategy that could be translated into lower prices for consumers. Wal-Mart's innovations in automated supply and inventory control operations fundamentally changed retailing and the competitive landscape for both large and small operators.

Wal-Mart also introduced the use of large databases, known as data warehouses, to manage local inventory and identify merchandising opportunities that give them a competitive advantage. Their data warehouse is considered to be the largest commercial database in the world.[136] The information in retail data warehouses can be used to perform analytics such as affinity analysis to determine purchase patterns. For example, if two items are purchased together, reducing the price on the first affinity item may result in sales of the second affinity item, without having to reduce the price on that second item.[137] For example, people who purchase tuna are likely to purchase toothpaste so they can brush their teeth after they eat the tuna.[138]

Kroger

In the realm of grocery retail, the Great Atlantic and Pacific Team Company, A&P, stuck its head in the sand, arguing that you cannot change 100 years of success. By 1970, however, Kroger came to the inescapable conclusion that the old-model grocery store (which accounted for nearly 100% of Kroger's business) was soon to become extinct. Kroger completely changed its entire system in response to a more affluent economy, while A&P refused to change. Kroger pioneered the super combination stores, believing they were the way of the future and that you either had to be number one or number two in each market, or you had to exit. By the early 1990s, Kroger had rebuilt its entire system on the new model and was well on the way to becoming the number one grocery chain in America, a position it would attain in 1999.[139] A&P filed for bankruptcy in December 2010.[140]

Recognizing that future competitiveness would require increasing quality and quantity of customer data, both Tesco and Kroger acquired a 50% interest in dunnhumby. Dunnhumby has enabled Kroger to use its loyalty card to provide a competitive advantage by collecting information that helps them to retain customers. Innovations in the use of big data and analytics continue to improve their competitiveness.

Best Buy

While customers are generally the focus of retail sales, they can also be the source of competitive information. Jeff Severts, Best Buy VP of marketing, was concerned about the accuracy of the sales forecasts. Severts knew that any proposal for major change in forecasting sales would likely be met with staff resistance, as people had so much vested in the existing process. Severts encountered James Surowiecki's *The Wisdom of Crowds*, learning that the many are smarter than the few and that collective wisdom could shape business, economies, societies, and nations.[141] He decided to test the hypothesis that a crowd could forecast gift card sales for the following month. Severts provided employees with a single trend-line (gift card sales over the previous 12 months) and an incentive to win a $50 gift card. The crowd's estimate proved ten times more accurate than that of the experts.[142]

CVTE

Founded in 2003, CVTE has become the leading designer of interactive, flat panel displays in China. Located in Guangzhou Science Park, Guangzhou, Guangdong Province in the People's Republic of China, they now have research and development offices in Taipei, Shenzhen, and Ximaen, as well as a network of 26 sales and marketing offices in China. The only design house in China that develops Touch Module, PC Module, TV Board, Power Board, and ID with 100% IP ownership is CVTE. They introduced the first pluggable PC Module for education and conference market segments in 2011. They lead in the development of six-point touch and three-point writing technology and have developed a new interaction product line that integrates both the Windows and Android platforms to facilitate connectivity with smart devices and phones. Innovations include, but are not limited to, all-in-one designs for display, touch, PC, and AV; wireless screen sharing on multiple platforms including Android, Windows, and iOS, plus device screen sharing with IFP; smart interactive OSD with touch control; pluggable PC module; and smart energy saving technology.

CVTE's strategy in China centers on its SEEWO brand of interactive devices and flat panels. The Chinese education and conference market segments will benefit from EasiMeeting, EasiShow, Easi-Note, and SeewoLink, all providing innovative multi-user interactive touch and remote access solutions for sharing data, information, and knowledge. In addition, CVTE continues to innovate products for the Chinese market in smartphones, Quad Core high-speed CPUs, tablet PCs, digitizer tablets, Wi-Fi tablets, Android and Miracast dongles, GPS tracker, and wearable activity tracker devices.

Outside of China, CVTE's strategy centers around forming key strategic partnerships and serving as an OEM supplier to established name brands. Costs are contained through key supply partnerships to CVTE, and value is added via the application of CVTE's IP to products supplied to OEMs.

Amazon

Amazon's success is the result of the synergistic integration of the innovation competencies, especially emergent ecosystem strategy. At the beginning of the 21st century, Chris Anderson popularized the notion of the long tail.[143] The long tail strategy enables online retailers to sell small volumes of a broad selection of less popular and hard-to-find merchandise to customers, such as selling red-striped shoelaces. In contrast, conventional retailers sell large volumes of a narrow selection of more popular merchandise, such as Crest toothpaste, to customers.

Entrepreneur Jeff Bezos realized a physical retail store could only stock so many items, limited as it is by square footage.[144] Even when stores increased space, there was always a limitation on how many items the store could stock. Innovation and technology accelerate broad and narrow selection strategies in support of a profitable business model, facilitated by the use of the Internet and the network effect. Amazon's innovation solution provides a virtually limitless inventory by applying the long tail business model.

With effective technological web architecture via the Internet and large, highly efficient distribution centers, the number of products that could be offered grew substantially. Consumers were provided with more product choices, affordability, and convenience than ever before, leading to the success of Amazon.[145]

Amazon continues to enhance the consumer retail experience. For example, customers can purchase a service called Prime that provides them with free shipping. In addition, the Amazon multipurpose website provides access to tracking information about shipments. With digital books, there is no physical limit to the number of distinct books that can be offered. Furthermore, Amazon combined technology and creativity to produce the Kindle tablets. The Kindle provides affordability, simplicity (one-click shopping), and convenient access to Amazon's products and services. Customers can purchase a broad selection of merchandise and have access to e-books and videos. Customers can use Amazon's Whispernet to access the products and services without any monthly fee or wireless subscription.[146]

The Amazon Kindle Fire is a new way for customers to shop. "It's not just a low-end competitor to the iPad. There is scalable technology at its core that the present-generation iPad lacks – the extensive use of the Cloud. That is why Amazon can get away with shipping a device that has only 8GB of memory. What's more, the Fire has a business model advantage too – Amazon is using content to subsidize the hardware."[147] Comparing the Kindle Fire to the iPad demonstrates the difference between Amazon and Apple. Amazon competes on a low-cost strategy, translated into low prices for consumers, and sustainable margins, while Apple pursues a differentiation strategy with high prices and high margins.[148]

Catalytic Leadership

Remove the Barriers

While we will explore catalytic leadership and the role of the catalytic leader in innovation and entrepreneurship in more detail in Chapter 13, in short, a catalytic leader serves as a catalyst or agent for change. "Catalytic leadership is based on the leader engaging and motivating others to take on leadership roles, engaging everyone to work toward a common goal."[149] Innovation provides a challenging environment for leaders trying to connect key players in a changing world. A. G. Lafley, former chairman and CEO of Procter & Gamble, writes,

> Innovation is about connections, so we get everyone we can involve: P&Gers past and present, consumers and customers; suppliers; a wide range of "connect-and develop" partners; ideas, the more solutions. And because what gets measured gets managed, I establish a goal that half of new product and technology innovations come from outside P&G.[150]

Procter & Gamble provides a rare insight into how critical the role of leadership is in making innovation part of the corporate culture and not just the latest buzzword in management practice. It takes active, energetic leadership that not only raises awareness of potential change but creates leaders within the organization capable of sustaining collective action to achieve change.

> Consider the case of Procter & Gamble Company. Since A. G. Lafley became chief executive officer in 2000, the leaders of P&G have worked hard to make innovation part of the daily routine and to establish an innovation culture. Lafley and his team preserved the essential part of P&G's research and development capability – world-class technologists who are masters of the core technologies critical to the household and personal-care businesses – while also bringing more P&G employees outside R&D into the innovation game. They sought to create an enterprise-wide social system that would harness the skills and insights of people

throughout the company and give them one common focus: The consumer. Without that kind of culture of innovation, a strategy of sustainable organic growth is far more difficult to achieve.[151]

Culture can be either a barrier to or a facilitator of innovation.[152] Lafley writes,

> A culture is what people do day in and day out without being told. In an innovation-centered company, managers and employees have no fear of innovation since they have developed the know-how to manage its attendant risk; innovation builds their mental muscles, leading them to new core competencies.[153]

While P&G already fostered and facilitated innovation from within, Lafley also recognized the potential from outside the immediate corporate environment. He decided that 50% of P&G's new products should come from outside in what became known as "connect and develop." The P&G strategy focused on external collaboration to access innovation networks of entrepreneurs, inventors, and scientists.

Ecosystems

The environment or ecosystem in which innovation and new venture creation occur is of increasing importance. The role of technological and innovation interdependencies informs both theory and practice as it plays out in various contexts.[154] As we will see in more detail in Chapter 14, an ecosystem is a purposeful collaborating network of dynamic interacting subsystems that have an ever-changing set of dependencies within a given context. Most breakthrough innovations don't spring forth in isolation but rather rely on complementary innovation and/ or innovation activities to blossom and attract customers.[155] Nowhere can this be seen more clearly and abundantly than with the ideation, conceptualization, formulation, and continued implementation of Apple.

The Apple Secret

After an initial foray into the world of printed circuit boards, Apple began with limited and focused PC offerings using simple product designs like that of the Macintosh in 1984. Their success was achieved by providing excellent products that have a simple and natural design. It is most likely that their design was based on the Bauhaus movement, which advocated high simplicity and functionality over decoration and adornments.

With remarkable consistency, Apple has been ranked as a leading innovative company.[156] Apple was not the innovator behind the transistor (AT&T's Bell Labs), the microprocessor (Intel), the Ethernet (Xerox), or the Internet (ARPANET).[157] Apple was not the innovator behind the first large-scale commercial operating system (IBM's System 360), the mouse (Xerox), or Windows systems (Xerox). Apple was not the innovator of touchscreen technology, flash memory, or microdrives.

Apple's success was the result of their ability to apply a confluence of the innovation and entrepreneurship competencies with particular focus on ecosystem building and expansion by retaining and enlarging their customer base. The Apple ecosystem is more than devices. The Apple ecosystem comprises the iPod, the iPhone, the iMac, the iPad, operating systems, iTunes, retail stores, Apple TV, movies, the cloud, and the apps. The Apple ecosystem is growing integrated product and service all managed by one company.[158]

The iPod Ecosystem: Macintosh + iPod

In 2001, Apple released the first-generation iPod for the Macintosh. The release included "jukebox" software for creating and managing a personal music library on the Macintosh.[159] "The iPod drew on the company's well-known skills in software, user-friendly product design, and imaginative marketing – all underexploited capabilities."[160] There is very little that was new in the original iPod. The visual design of the original iPod is very similar to Dieter Rams' 1958 T3 Transistor Radio. Apple did not invent downloadable music, or the MP3 (digital compression) technology that is used to reduce the number of digital bits for speedy download and storage saving on the iPod. What Apple did was use existing technology and simple design concepts, connecting them together to create a unique product combination. In other words, Apple took full advantage of the external ecosystem and their internal innovation and entrepreneurship ecosystem to make connections that led to innovations that supported sustainable success.

Expanding the iPod Ecosystem: Macintosh + iPod + iTunes

The success of the iPod + iTunes can be attributed to understanding past advancements and combining them in unique ways to create the iPod ecosystem. In 2002, Apple released the second-generation iPod, and expanded the Macintosh + iPod product set by making it compatible with Windows products. In 2003, Apple released the third generation iPod and continued the expansion of the integrated set of products by offering the iTunes music store with 200,000 songs at 99 cents each, and music management software that worked with the Macintosh and Windows.[161] Apple's iTunes had a simple user interface that enabled customers to listen to music and manage music collections while on the move.[162]

Apple used the iPod ecosystem to retain and attract new customers through expansion of their products staged to secure a competitive advantage. The iPod + iTunes integrated product set was released at a time when Internet broadband was fast enough to support downloadable music and MP3 music was readily available. With iPod + iTunes, Apple became a world leader in online music, in part because the record companies were in denial about the potential of online music and failed to seize the market opportunity.[163] In 2004, the fourth-generation iPod product set evolved to include the iPod mini, available in five colors. Even the colorful launch of the iPod mini appears to be based on the 1929–1934 Kodak Petite, a version of the Kodak Vest Pocket Camera that came in five colors.[164] In 2005, Apple released the fifth-generation iPod, which plays music and displays photos and video. In 2007, Apple released the iPod Touch, a portable music and video player that uses wireless technology to connect directly to the Internet for purchasing and downloading content.[165]

The Apple Ecosystem: Macintosh + iPod + iTunes + iPhone

When the original iPhone was released in 2007, there were many rivals in the mobile phone market, such as Nokia and Motorola that had already established the smartphone ecosystem. The original iPhone combined a number of unique features, including the touch screen, the accelerator, and a web browser.[166] Apple partnered with only one wireless carrier in each country. In the United States, this was AT&T, a carrier that, at the time, had a relatively slow network. Instead of being a cellular device supplier to the wireless carriers, Apple developed exclusive partnerships with the carriers in a way that allowed them to generate revenue from the carrier and exert control over the carrier relationship.[167]

Apple's strength was in its combination of existing products, reshaping them, and developing ecosystems. At the time of the iPhone release, Apple did not have a mobile phone product. It was IBM, not Apple, who developed the first smartphone. The touch screen technology existed in the 1993 IBM Simon Personal Communicator, considered to be the first smartphone due to its combination of cellular phone with the personal digital assistant (PDA).[168] Apple's Newton and iPhone appear to be based in part on IBM's Simon in a similar way that Steve Jobs' visit to Xerox PARC in 1979 influenced the original Macintosh.

According to Jobs,

Creativity is just connecting things. When you ask creative people how they did something, they feel a little guilty because they didn't really *do* it, they just *saw* something. It seemed obvious to them after a while. That's because they were able to connect experiences they've had and synthesize new things. And the reason they were able to do that was that they've had more experiences, or they have thought more about their experiences than other people.[169]

The iPhone device was a subset of Apple's product line that included the iPod. The iPhone's integrated product set encompassed the music content of the iPod + iTunes and enabled Apple to continue to expand their ecosystem. By designing the iPod into the iPhone, Apple was able to build on the strengths of the iPod + iTunes momentum and expand the existing iPod customer base.[170] Apple's competitive advantage was in its ability to utilize its large customer base to expand the ecosystem.

In 2008, the Apple innovation and entrepreneurship ecosystem continued to expand with the launch of the App Store.[171] The App Store enabled customization of individual iPhones via a large number of downloadable, specialized applications. The unique value was that each customer could select the apps that they wanted, thereby expanding the functionality of the iPhone exponentially. Third-party application developers could use this platform to sell their apps after first being "certified" by Apple.

There has been considerable growth in the development and usage of mobile apps as evidenced by statistics on Google Play and the Apple Store. As of this writing, for both Google Play and the Apple Store, the number of published apps now exceeds 1,250,000. The Apple Store cumulative downloads is higher than Google Play with approximately 85 billion and approximately 50 billion, respectively. Games are the most popular apps for both.[172] The Apple Store generates more app revenue than Google Play, with approximately $10 billion and $1.3 billion, respectively. Each app provided Apple with 30% of the revenue for each chargeable app.[173]

The Apple Ecosystem: Macintosh + iPod + iTunes + iPhone + iPad

Both the iPod and the iPhone were introduced in existing markets that already had competing products. Apple continued to expand their ecosystem with the iPad, but this required a different strategy because the iPad was intended for new markets, not existing markets. Apple positioned the iPad as being better at many tasks than smartphones and laptops.[174] A new feature of the iPad included iBooks, placing Apple's iPad in direct competition with Amazon's Kindle.

Because the iPad was a new market opportunity, Apple was required to build partnerships with book publishers.

Apple was able to secure deals with the large publishing houses by giving them a viable alternative eBook platform, and offering them a lever with which to increase the asking price for eBooks: Apple deals used the same "agency" model adopted for the App store, in which the book sellers set their own price for the book (about $15 for new hardcovers) and Apple took a 30% cut. Amazon had been selling most hardcover books for $9.99 and taking a loss on each book in order to expand their dominance [in the] eBook market. In the weeks following the iPad release, Publishers one by one renegotiated their contracts with Amazon to use the agency model.[175]

The Apple Ecosystem: Premium and Value

In 2013, Apple made a fundamental shift in their ecosystem expansion from premium, forward-thinking products to a two-tier model. The two-tier approach introduced the Apple iPhone 5S for the affluent market and the more affordable Apple iPhone 5C for the value market.[176] This change allowed Apple to compete more effectively in the global smartphone market.

Technology Accelerators

Innovation and entrepreneurship occur at a fairly steady rate. Quickening the pace can be a considerable challenge, physically as well as strategically. In his book *Good to Great,* Jim Collins describes a technology accelerator as the utilization of a digital technology that transforms and facilitates the strategic intent. The strategic intent is composed of the future ideas of the visionaries, customers, and lead users. Although digital technology accelerators are important, they are strictly secondary in relation to strategic intent. Digital technology can accelerate innovation, but the real drivers are people and their teamwork, inspiration, competency, persistence, and talent.

High Tech vs. High Touch

Google's people-centric culture is considered to be unique, secretive, and innovation-oriented. The people-centric culture has a strong influence on enabling Google to provide a sustainable competitive advantage through its selective recruitment and retention of top talent. Google places high priority on engineering and expects its workers to devote 70% of their time to Google's core business, search and advertising, 20% on pursuits related to the core business, and 10% to experimenting with new ideas. The culture of Google motivates individuals to pursue high-order thinking, resulting in innovation. Google is an example of how to achieve "high tech/high touch" balance.[177] "High tech/high touch" is the concept that technological progress cannot occur effectively without an equivalent human response. Google's high technology is balanced with a high-touch people-centric culture.

The Network Is the Computer

John Gage of Sun Microsystems coined the phrase "the network is the computer" to describe distributed computing.[178] In a distributed computing model, processing functions and data can reside anywhere on a network or the commercial Internet. Google (Alphabet) overcame established competition to become one of the leading innovators in the global economy and applying the "the network is the computer" concept. Google is the now the main gateway to the world's largest digital network of publicly available information and knowledge. Google (Alphabet) is so dominant that its name is now a verb: *Google it.*

Google's vision is to provide the ability to search all information on the Web. To do that, Google has developed an enterprise architecture that combines software systems and technology infrastructure, enabling it to sustain its business and expand into new products. The Google business operating model uses a combination of its search engine and advertising that is changing how business is conducted. Google is the centerpiece for web searches, handling over one billion a day. It uses the accumulated information from the web searches to continually improve its search engine, enabling them to provide advancements that outpace their rivals, Yahoo and Microsoft.

Google has collected so much personally identifiable information that there are growing concerns over this accumulation of information. Most commercial advertising is inefficient because it is broadcast to anyone who happens to be listening, making it non-customer specific. Consider an advertisement on TV for a specific pharmaceutical such as Aricept®, used to treat Alzheimer's disease. That advertisement is broadcast to a much wider audience than is necessary. With Google, when a customer conducts a free search, advertisers pay Google to match consumers with their relevant products and services, resulting in more effective marketing.

Google uses an innovative, two-part strategic business model that combines a search engine and targeted advertising. The business operating model uses a page-ranking mechanism and targeted advertising. The targeted advertising is based on two functions: AdWords and AdSense.

AdWords is the posting of ads, based on what searches are performed, alongside of search results. AdWords uses the cost-per-click advertising business model where the advertiser pays Google if the user actually clicks on the advertisement link that is displayed. After a search, the Google AdWords™ program displays products and services advertisements that are identified by the title "Ads by Google." Companies pay for these links to have their products and services appear based on specific search terms. These listings are administered, sorted, and maintained by Google. If you search for a water faucet, for example, you may see a Lowes or Home Depot advertisement. If you click on that advertisement, it will take you to the Lowes or Home Depot website, and Lowes or Home Depot will pay Google.

AdSense is a service wherein you rent space on your website in which Google (Alphabet) can post advertisements. The advertisers bid to show their ads on your website. Context-relevant advertising is inserted into these third-party websites by Google. If the user actually clicks on the ad link, the advertiser will pay Google, and Google will then pay the website for the space. For example, Google might analyze the data collected from your Gmail account and discover that you have recently purchased clothing from Amazon. Later, you might see a Lands' End clothing advertisement on a third-party website that you are viewing.

Google's innovation-oriented culture enables it to thrive. They have achieved innovation not only through their own efforts but also by acquisition. Google's substantial financial resources allow growth through acquisition. For example, Google acquired YouTube, the popular video site used to share video clips between individuals. Google's YouTube has changed the way individuals are entertained and how they communicate.

Notes

1. R. E. Freeman, K. Martin, and B. Parmar, *The Power of And: Responsible Business Without Trafe-Offs* (New York: Columbia University Press, 2020).
2. Jeff Bezos, *Invent & Wander* (Boston: Harvard Business Review Press, 2021), 230–231.
3. Steven Johnson, *How We Got to Now: Six Innovations That Made the Modern World* (New York: Riverhead, 2014).
4. James Fallows, "The 50 Greatest Breakthroughs Since the Wheel," November 2013, accessed February 8, 2024, www.theatlantic.com/magazine/archive/2013/11/innovations-list/309536/.
5. Henry Mintzberg, "Rethinking Strategic Planning Part I: Pitfalls and Fallacies," *Long Range Planning* (1994), 12–21.
6. Atul Gawande, "Personal Best," *The New Yorker*, October 3, 2011, accessed February 18, 2024, www.newyorker.com/reporting/2011/10/03/111003fa_fact_gawande?currentPage=all.
7. Richard Feynman, accessed February 08, 2024, http://en.wikiquote.org/wiki/Richard_Feynman.

8. Scott Shane and Sankaran Venkataraman, "The Promise of Entrepreneurship as a Field of Research," *Academy of Management Review* 25, no. 1 (2000), 217–226.

9. David B. Audretsch, "The Dynamic Role of Small Firms: Evidence from the U.S.," *Small Business Economics* 18, no. 1 (2002), 13–40.

10. Clifton Taulbert and Gary Schoeniger, *Who Owns the Ice House?: Eight Lessons from an Unlikely Entrepreneur* (Mentor, OH: ELI Press, 2010).

11. B. Tom Hunsaker and Jonathan Knowles, "The Essence of Strategy Is Now How to Change When Environments Are Complex and Dynamic, Strategy Is about Adaptability," December 17, 2020, accessed February 8, 2024, https://sloanreview.mit.edu/article/the-essence-of-strategy-is-now-how-to-change/.

12. *Wikipedia*, s.v. "Gordian Knot," accessed December 23, 2020, Gordian Knot – Wikipedia.

13. Rosabeth Moss Kanter, *Think Outside the Building: How Advanced Leaders Can Change the World One Smart Innovation at a Time* (New York: Public Affairs, 2020), 1.

14. Ken Robinson and Lou Aronica, *Creative Schools: The Grassroots Revolution That's Transforming Education* (New York: Viking, 2015), 45–53.

15. National Center for Education Statistics, "Status and Trends in the Education of Racial and Ethnic Groups 2018," February 2019, accessed February 18, 2024, https://nces.ed.gov/pubs2019/2019038.pdf.

16. A Report by the American Psychological Association Presidential Task Force on Educational Disparities, "Ethnic and Racial Disparities in Education: Psychology's Contributions to Understanding and Reducing Disparities," *American Psychological Association*, August 3, 2012, accessed February 18, 2024, www.apa.org/ed/resources/racial-disparities.

17. Stephen R. Covey, *The 8th Habit: From Effectiveness to Greatness* (New York: The Free Press, 2004).

18. D. Bullock and R. Sanchez, "Don't Underestimate the Power of Your Voice," *Harvard Business Review*, April 13, 2022, accessed February 8, 2024, https://hbr.org/2022/04/dont-underestimate-the-power-of-your-voice.

19. Mike Borruso, Torea Frey, Gwyn Herbein, Philip Mathew, Janet Michaud, Nathan Wilson, and Paul Lasewicz, "From There to Here: 50 Years of Thinking on the Social Responsibility of Business," September 11, 2020, accessed February 18, 2024, www.mckinsey.com/featured-insights/corporate-purpose/from-there-to-here-50-years-of-thinking-on-the-social-responsibility-of-business.

20. Business Roundtable, "Business Roundtable Redefines the Purpose of a Corporation to Promote 'An Economy That Serves All Americans'," August 19, 2019, accessed February 18, 2024, www.business-roundtable.org/business-roundtable-redefines-the-purpose-of-a-corporation-to-promote-an-economy-that-serves-all-americans.

21. Abigail Disney, "Dignity Isn't a Privilege. It's a Worker's Right," May 2020, accessed February 18, 2024, www.ted.com/talks/abigail_disney_dignity_isn_t_a_privilege_it_s_a_worker_s_right/transcript.

22. Abigail Disney, "Dignity Isn't a Privilege. It's a Worker's Right," May 2020, accessed February 11, 2024, www.ted.com/talks/abigail_disney_dignity_isn_t_a_privilege_it_s_a_worker_s_right/transcript.

23. Andrew Ross Sorkin and Jason Karaian, "Greed Is Good. Except When It's Bad," accessed August 11, 2024, https://www.nytimes.com/2020/09/13/business/dealbook/milton-friedman-essay-anniversary.html

24. Gary Hamel and Michele Zanini, *Humanocracy* (Boston: Harvard Business Review Press, 2020).

25. Gary Hamel, "Who's Really Innovative?" *The Wall Street Journal* (November 22, 2010), accessed February 18, 2024, http://blogs.wsj.com/management/2010/11/22/whos-really-innovative/.

26. Sarah E. Needleman, "For Intuit Co-Founder, the Numbers Add Up," *The Wall Street Journal*, August 18, 2011, accessed February 18, 2024, www.wsj.com/articles/SB1000142405311190359690457651436414 42860224.

27. Sarah E. Needleman, "For Intuit Co-Founder, the Numbers Add Up," *The Wall Street Journal*, August 18, 2011, accessed February 18, 2024, www.wsj.com/articles/SB1000142405311190359690457651436414 42860224.

28. Sarah E. Needleman, "For Intuit Co-Founder, the Numbers Add Up," *The Wall Street Journal*, August 18, 2011, accessed February 18, 2024, www.wsj.com/articles/SB1000142405311190359690457651436414 42860224.

29. "100 Best Companies to Work For," *CNN*, accessed February 18, 2024, http://money.cnn.com/magazines/fortune/best-companies/2012/full_list/.

30. Nathan Donato-Weinstein, "Intuit Employees Get a Chance to Play in 'Idea Jams'," *San Francisco Business Times*, April 22, 2011, accessed February 18, 2024, www.bizjournals.com/sanfrancisco/print-edition/2011/04/22/intuit-employees-get-a-chance-to-play.html?page=all.

31. Intuit Blog Team, "Intuit's Newest Awards from Fast Company, Fortune, & More," *Life at Intuit*, September 12, 2019, accessed February 18, 2024, www.intuit.com/blog/life-at-intuit/intuits-newest-

awards-from-fast-company-fortune-more/#:~:text=All%20Intuit%20employees%20are%20 encouraged,the%20future%20of%20our%20company.

32. Jerome Groopman, "Anne Dodge Case," *How Doctors Think* (New York: Houghton Mifflin, 2007).
33. Jerome Groopman, "Anne Dodge Case," *How Doctors Think* (New York: Houghton Mifflin, 2007), 19.
34. Ron Adner, *The Wide Lens* (New York: Portfolio/Penguin, 2012), 217.
35. *Wikipedia*, s.v. "High-Technology Swimwear Fabric," accessed January 7, 2014, http://en.wikipedia. org/wiki/High-technology_swimwear_fabric.
36. Jim Taylor, "Technology: Myth of Multitasking," *Psychology Today*, March 30, 2011, accessed February 18, 2024, www.psychologytoday.com/blog/the-power-prime/201103/technology-myth-multitasking.
37. Noam Shpancer, "Framing: Your Most Important and Least Recognized Daily Mental Activity," *Psychology Today*, December 22, 2010, accessed February 18, 2024, www.psychologytoday.com/us/blog/ insight-therapy/201012/framing-your-most-important-and-least-recognized-daily-ment.
38. Patrick Mahoney, "Industrial Design: Design the Dyson Way," August 7, 2008, accessed February 18, 2024, http://machinedesign.com/news/industrial-design-design-dyson-way.
39. Charlie Burton, "The Seventh Disruption: How James Dyson Reinvented the Personal Heater," *Wired*, October 22, 2011, accessed February 18, 2024, www.wired.co.uk/magazine/archive/2011/11/features/ the-seventh-disruption-james-dyson?page=all.
40. James Dyson, "The Story of Dyson Vacuum Cleaners," *Dyson Company History*, accessed February 18, 2024, www.achooallergy.com/blog/learning/dyson-company-history/.
41. James Dyson, "The Story of Dyson Vacuum Cleaners," *Dyson Company History*, accessed February 18, 2024, www.achooallergy.com/blog/learning/dyson-company-history/.
42. James Dyson, "The Story of Dyson Vacuum Cleaners," *Dyson Company History*, accessed February 18, 2024, www.achooallergy.com/blog/learning/dyson-company-history/.
43. *Wikipedia*, s.v. "Johannes Gutenberg," accessed July 10, 2013, http://en.wikipedia.org/wiki/ Johannes_Gutenberg.
44. Jimmy Stamp, "Fact of Fiction? The Legend of the QWERTY Keyboard," *Smithsonian*, May 3, 2013, accessed February 18, 2024, www.smithsonianmag.com/arts-culture/fact-of-fiction-the-legend-of-the- qwerty-keyboard-49863249/?no-ist.
45. "TrewGrip," *TrewGrip*, accessed December 26, 2013, www.trewgrip.com/.
46. *Wikipedia*, s.v. "Chester Carlson," accessed July 10, 2013, http://en.wikipedia.org/wiki/Chester_Carlson.
47. "Spitting Image," *The Economist*, September 19, 2002, accessed February 18, 2024, www.economist. com/node/1324685.
48. Bruce Nussbaum, *Creative Intelligence* (New York: Harper Business, 2013), 190–197.
49. *Wikipedia*, s.v. "HP Deskjet," accessed July 10, 2013, https://en.wikipedia.org/wiki/HP_Deskjet.
50. "Market Segmentation of China's Shampoo Market: Main Players & Products," *daxueconsulting*, accessed February 18, 2024, https://daxueconsulting.com/shampoo-market-in-china/.
51. Tara Rodden Robinson, *Genetics for Dummies* (Hoboken, NJ: Wiley Publishing, 2005), 43.
52. *Wikipedia*, s.v. "Gregor Mendel," accessed July 24, 2013, http://en.wikipedia.org/wiki/Gregor_Mendel.
53. *Wikipedia*, s.v. "Molecular Structure of Nucleic Acids," accessed August 18, 2012, http://en.wikipedia. org/wiki/Molecular_Structure_of_Nucleic_Acids:_A_Structure_for_Deoxyribose_Nucleic_Acid.
54. *Wikipedia*, s.v. "Craig Ventor," accessed August 18, 2012, http://en.wikipedia.org/wiki/Craig_Venter.
55. Gina Kolata, "Human Genome, Then and Now," *The New York Times*, April 16, 2013, accessed February 18, 2024, www.nytimes.com/2013/04/16/science/the-human-genome-project-then-and-now.html.
56. Robert H. Shoemaker, "The NCI60 Human Tumour Cell Line Anticancer Drug Screen," *Nature Reviews Cancer* 6, no. 10 (2006), 813–823.
57. "Comprehensive List of Gene Variants Developed for Cancer Cells from Nine Tissue Types," July 15, 2013, accessed National Cancer Institute, February 18, 2024, www.sciencedaily.com/releases/2013/07/130715151103.htm.
58. "Pharmacogenomics," *Genetics Home Reference*, accessed February 18, 2024, http://ghr.nlm.nih.gov/ glossary=pharmacogenomics.
59. *Wikipedia*, s.v. "Pharmacogenomics," accessed August 18, 2012, http://en.wikipedia.org/wiki/Pharmacogenomics.
60. Clayton Christensen, Jerome Grossman, and Jason Hwang, *The Innovator's Prescription* (New York: McGraw Hill, 2009), 50.
61. "Gleevac," *National Cancer Institute*, accessed February 18, 2024, www.cancer.gov/research/progress/ discovery/gleevec.

62. Trevor Hallam, "Antibody-Drug Conjugates and Cancer Treatment: Making 'Smart Bombs' Smarter," *Scientific American* (blog), July 4, 2013, accessed February 18, 2024, http://blogs.scientificamerican.com/guest-blog/2013/07/04/antibody-drug-conjugates-and-cancer-treatment-making-smart-bombs-smarter/.

63. Tom Nicholas, "Innovation Lessons from the 1930s," *McKinsey Quarterly*, December 2008, accessed February 18, 2024, www.hbs.edu/ris/Publication%20Files/Tom_McKinsey_Quarterly_8421a1a0-0104-4cf1-843d-fc32fa51dd0a.pdf.

64. Tom Nicholas, "Innovation Lessons from the 1930s," *McKinsey Quarterly*, December 2008, accessed February 18, 2024, www.hbs.edu/ris/Publication%20Files/Tom_McKinsey_Quarterly_8421a1a0-0104-4cf1-843d-fc32fa51dd0a.pdf.

65. Clayton Christensen, Jerome Grossman, and Jason Hwang, *The Innovator's Prescription* (New York: McGraw Hill, 2009), 37.

66. *Cincinnati Symphony Orchestra Program 2012–2013* (Cincinnati, OH: Cincinnati Symphony Orchestra, 2012), 18.

67. *Cincinnati Symphony Orchestra Program 2012–2013* (Cincinnati, OH: Cincinnati Symphony Orchestra, 2012), 17.

68. "Classical Roots," *Cincinnati Symphony Orchestra*, accessed February 18, 2024, www.cincinnatisymphony.org/education-and-community/community-programs/classical-roots/.

69. "Hewlett-Packard History," *Hewlett-Packard*, accessed February 18, 2024, www.hp.com/us-en/shop/tech-takes/history-of-hp.

70. David Packard, *The HP Way: How Bill Hewlett and I Built Our Company* (New York: Harper Business, 2006).

71. *Wikipedia*, s.v. "Hewlett-Packard," accessed February 11, 2024, http://en.wikipedia.org/wiki/Hewlett-Packard.

72. *Wikipedia*, s.v. "Hewlett-Packard," accessed February 11, 2024, http://en.wikipedia.org/wiki/Hewlett-Packard.

73. "Hewlett-Packard History," *Hewlett-Packard*, accessed February 18, 2024, www.hp.com/us-en/shop/tech-takes/history-of-hp.

74. Reena Jana, "HP Cultural Revolution," *Business Week*, November 15, 2007, accessed February 11, 2024, www.bloomberg.com/news/articles/2007-11-15/hps-cultural-revolutionbusinessweek-business-news-stock-market-and-financial-advice?embedded-checkout=true.

75. Jim Collins, "The 10 Greatest CEOs of All Time," accessed February 11, 2024, www.jimcollins.com/article_topics/articles/10-greatest.html.

76. Jim Collins, "Forward to David Packard's *The HP Way*," May 2005, accessed February 11, 2024, www.jimcollins.com/article_topics/articles/the-hp-way.html.

77. Jim Collins and Jerry I. Porras, *Built to Last* (New York: HarperCollins, 2002), 182.

78. Bruce Nussbaum, *Creative Intelligence* (New York: Harper Business, 2013), 224.

79. *Wikipedia*, s.v. "Carly Fiorina," accessed February 11, 2024, http://en.wikipedia.org/wiki/Carly_Fiorina.

80. Scott Ard, "Leak Scandal Costs HP's Dunn Her Chairman's Job," *CNET*, September 22, 2006, accessed February 11, 2024, www.cnet.com/tech/tech-industry/leak-scandal-costs-hps-dunn-her-chairmans-job/.

81. "Patricia Dunn Dies at 58; Hewlett-Packard Chairwoman," *LA Times*, December 6, 2011, accessed February 11, 2024, http://articles.latimes.com/2011/dec/06/local/la-me-patricia-dunn-20111206.

82. Bruce Nussbaum, *Creative Intelligence* (New York: Harper Business, 2013), 225.

83. Bruce Nussbaum, *Creative Intelligence* (New York: Harper Business, 2013), 226–227.

84. Jim Collins and Jerry I. Porras, *Built to Last* (New York: HarperCollins, 2002), 256.

85. *Wikipedia*, s.v. "3M," accessed July 11, 2013, http://en.wikipedia.org/wiki/3M.

86. Jim Collins and Jerry I. Porras, *Built to Last* (New York: HarperCollins, 2002), 3, 14, 16, 94, 215, 246.

87. Jim Collins and Jerry I. Porras, *Built to Last* (New York: HarperCollins, 2002), 225.

88. "3M Principles," *3M*, accessed February 18, 2024, http://solutions.3m.com/wps/portal/3M/en_WW/History/3M/Company/McKnight-principles/.

89. *Wikipedia*, s.v. "William L. McKnight," accessed July 11, 2013, http://en.wikipedia.org/wiki/William_L._McKnight.

90. *Managing Creativity and Innovation* (Boston: Harvard Business Press, 2003), 108–109.

91. "A Century of Innovation, The 3M Story," *3M*, accessed February 18, 2024, https://multimedia.3m.com/mws/media/171240O/3m-century-of-innovation-book.pdf.

92. Jim Collins and Jerry I. Porras, *Built to Last* (New York: HarperCollins, 2002), 156–158.

93. "A Century of Innovation, the 3M Story," *3M*, accessed February 18, 2024, https://multimedia.3m.com/mws/media/171240O/3m-century-of-innovation-book.pdf.

94. *Wikipedia*, s.v. "Richard Drew," accessed July 2013, http://en.wikipedia.org/wiki/Richard_Gurley_Drew.
95. Jim Collins and Jerry I. Porras, *Built to Last* (New York: HarperCollins, 2002), 153.
96. Patsy Sherman, "Invention of Scotchgard™ Stain Repellent," accessed February 18, 2024, www.women-inventors.com/Patsy-Sherman.asp.
97. Patsy Sherman, "Invention of Scotchgard™ Stain Repellent," accessed February 18, 2024, www.women-inventors.com/Patsy-Sherman.asp.
98. Patsy Sherman, "Invention of Scotchgard™ Stain Repellent," accessed February 18, 2024, www.women-inventors.com/Patsy-Sherman.asp.
99. V. Govindarajan and S. Srinivas, "The Innovation Mindset in Action: 3M Corporation," *Harvard Business Review*, August 6, 2013, accessed February 18, 2024, https://hbr.org/2013/08/the-innovation-mindset-in-acti-3.
100. Patsy Sherman, "Invention of Scotchgard™ Stain Repellent," accessed February 18, 2024, www.women-inventors.com/Patsy-Sherman.asp.
101. Jeffry A. Timmons and Stephen Spinelli, *New Venture Creation* (New York: McGraw-Hill, 2003), 17, 61, 101, 310, 313.
102. *Wikipedia*, s.v. "Arthur Fry," accessed September 11, 2011, http://en.wikipedia.org/wiki/Arthur_Fry.
103. Pino G. Audia and Jack Goncalo, "Does Success Spoil Inventors?" *IEEE Spectrum*, May 2007, accessed February 18, 2024, https://spectrum.ieee.org/does-success-spoil-inventors.
104. Richard A. Swanson and Thomas J. Chermack, *Theory Building in Applied Disciplines* (San Francisco: Berrett-Koehler, 2013).
105. Robert Dubin, *Theory Building*, Rev. ed. (New York: Free Press, 1978).
106. Michael E. Raynor, "Disruption Theory as a Predictor of Innovation Success/Failure," *Strategy & Leadership* 39, no. 4 (2011), 27–30.
107. Jon-Arild Johannessen, Bjørn Olsen, and Johan Olaisen, "Aspects of Innovation Theory Based on Knowledge-management," *International Journal of Information Management* 19, no. 2 (1999), 121–139.
108. Clayton Christensen, "Disruptive Innovation Explained," *Harvard Business Review*, March 6, 2012, accessed February 18, 2024, http://blogs.hbr.org/2012/03/disruptive-innovation-explaine/.
109. *Wikipedia*, s.v. "Jacquard Loom," accessed September 3, 2011, http://en.wikipedia.org/wiki/Jacquard_loom.
110. *Wikipedia*, s.v. "Punched Card," September 3, 2011, http://en.wikipedia.org/wiki/Punched_card.
111. Clayton Christensen, "Disruptive Innovation," accessed February 18, 2024, www.claytonchristensen.com/key-concepts/.
112. Clayton Christensen, "Disruptive Innovation," accessed February 18, 2024, www.claytonchristensen.com/key-concepts/.
113. Michael E. Raynor, "Disruption Theory as a Predictor of Innovation Success/Failure," *Strategy & Leadership* 39, no. 4 (2011), 27–30.
114. Clayton Christensen, Jerome Grossman, and Jason Hwang, *The Innovator's Prescription* (New York: McGraw Hill, 2009), 197.
115. Clayton Christensen, Jerome Grossman, and Jason Hwang, *The Innovator's Prescription* (New York: McGraw Hill, 2009), 116.
116. Gary Hamel, "The Future of Management," *Harvard Business Review*, October 9, 2007, 216–219.
117. "WellPoint's New Hire: IBM Watson Technology Plays 'Doctor'," *IBM Times*, accessed February 18, 2024, www.ibtimes.com/articles/212340/20110912/wellpoint-ibm-watson-jeopardy.htm.
118. *Wikipedia*, s.v. "Watson," accessed September 12, 2011, http://en.wikipedia.org/wiki/Watson_(computer).
119. Stephanie Overby, "Can Watson, IBM's Supercomputer, Cure Cancer?" April 30, 2012, accessed February 18, 2024, www.cio.com/article/284234/healthcare-can-watson-ibm-s-supercomputer-cure-cancer.html.
120. Chris Anderson, "The Shared Genius of Elon Musk and Steve Jobs," *Fortune*, November 27, 2013, accessed February 18, 2024, https://fortune.com/2013/11/21/the-shared-genius-of-elon-musk-and-steve-jobs/.
121. *Wikipedia*, s.v. "Elon Musk," accessed December 22, 2013, http://en.wikipedia.org/wiki/Elon_Musk.
122. Anne Vandermey, "The World's Top 25 Eco-Innovators," *Fortune*, May 1, 2014, accessed February 18, 2024, https://fortune.com/2014/05/01/the-worlds-top-25-eco-innovators/.
123. Brian Dumaine, "Storing Solar Energy for a Rainy Day," *Fortune*, November 6, 2013, accessed February 18, 2024, https://fortune.com/2013/11/06/storing-solar-energy-for-a-rainy-day/.
124. Aaron Sankin, "Hyperloop: Billionaire Tech Mogul's New Idea Could Revolutionize Travel Forever," *Huffington Post*, September 25, 2012, accessed February 18, 2024, www.huffingtonpost.com/2012/09/25/hyperloop_n_1913683.html.

125. *Wikipedia*, s.v. "Sir Richard Branson," accessed February 05, 2014, http://en.wikipedia.org/wiki/Richard_Branson.
126. "Richard Branson," *Entrepreneur*, accessed February 18, 2024, www.entrepreneur.com/author/richard-branson.
127. "GravityLight: Lighting for Developing Countries," accessed February 18, 2024, www.indiegogo.com/projects/gravitylight-lighting-for-developing-countries.
128. Caroline Winter, "Innovator: Martin Riddiford's Gravity-Powered Lamp," *Bloomberg Businessweek*, March 2013, accessed February 18, 2024, www.bloomberg.com/news/articles/2013-03-14/innovator-martin-riddifords-gravity-powered-lampcom/news/articles/2013-03-14/innovator-martin-riddifords-gravity-powered-lamp.
129. "GravityLight: Lighting for Developing Countries," accessed February 18, 2024, www.indiegogo.com/projects/gravitylight-lighting-for-developing-countries.
130. Caroline Winter, "Innovator: Martin Riddiford's Gravity-Powered Lamp," *Bloomberg Businessweek*, March 2013, accessed February 18, 2024, www.bloomberg.com/news/articles/2013-03-14/innovator-martin-riddifords-gravity-powered-lamp.
131. "GravityLight: Lighting for Developing Countries," accessed February 18, 2024, www.indiegogo.com/projects/gravitylight-lighting-for-developing-countries.
132. Henry Mintzberg, "Patterns in Strategy Formation," *Management Science* 24, no. 9 (1978), 934–948.
133. *Wikipedia*, s.v. "Sears," accessed September 3, 2011, http://en.wikipedia.org/wiki/Sears; *Wikipedia*, s.v. "Sears Catalog," accessed October 17, 2012, http://en.wikipedia.org/wiki/Sears_Catalog_Home.
134. *Wikipedia*, s.v. "Filling Stations," accessed August 21, 2011, http://en.wikipedia.org/wiki/Filling_stations.
135. *Wikipedia*, s.v. "Credit Card," accessed September 3, 2011, http://en.wikipedia.org/wiki/Credit_card.
136. Charles Babcock, "Data, Data, Everywhere," *Information Week*, January 9, 2006, accessed February 18, 2024, www.informationweek.com/it-leadership/data-data-everywhere.
137. *Wikipedia*, s.v. "Affinity Analysis," accessed February 18, 2024, http://en.wikipedia.org/wiki/Affinity_analysis.
138. "Market Basket Analysis," accessed September 4, 2011, http://loyaltysquare.com/mba.php.
139. Jim Collins, *Good to Great: Why Some Companies Make the Leap . . . and Others Don't* (New York: HarperCollins, 2011).
140. *Wikipedia*, s.v. "The Great Atlantic & Pacific Tea Company," accessed February 18, 2024, http://en.wikipedia.org/wiki/The_Great_Atlantic_%26_Pacific_Tea_Company.
141. Phred Dvorak, "Best Buy 'Taps Prediction Market'," *The Wall Street Journal*, September 16, 2008, accessed February 18, 2024, http://online.wsj.com/article/SB122152452811139909.html.
142. Gary Hamel and Bill Breen, *The Future of Management* (Boston: Harvard Business Press, 2013), 229–232.
143. *Wikipedia*, s.v. "Long Tail," accessed February 18, 2024, http://en.wikipedia.org/wiki/Long_tail.
144. *Wikipedia*, s.v. "Jeff Bezos," accessed February 18, 2024, http://en.wikipedia.org/wiki/Jeff_Bezos.
145. *Wikipedia*, s.v. "Amazon.com," accessed February 18, 2024, http://en.wikipedia.org/wiki/Amazon.com.
146. *Wikipedia*, s.v. "Amazon Kindle," accessed February 18, 2024, http://en.wikipedia.org/wiki/Amazon_Kindle.
147. Rob Wheeler, "Amazon's Kindle Fire Is a Disruptive Innovation," *HBR Blog Network*, September 29, 2011, accessed February 18, 2024, http://blogs.hbr.org/cs/2011/09/amazon_kindle_fire_scare_apple.html.
148. Brad Stone, "Amazon, the Company That Ate the World," *Bloomberg Business Week*, October 3, 2011, accessed February 18, 2024, www.nbcnews.com/business/markets/amazon-com-company-ate-world-flna1c7101080.
149. "Catalytic Leadership: Strategies for an Interconnected World," *The Luke Center for Catalytic Leadership*, accessed February 18, 2024, www.thelukecenter.org/#!catalyticleadership/cl2k.
150. Alan G. Lafley and Ram Charan, *The Game Changer* (New York: Crown Business, 2008).
151. Alan G. Lafley and Ram Charan, "P&G's Innovation Culture," *Strategy and Business Magazine*, August 26, 2008, accessed February 18, 2024, www.strategy-business.com/article/08304?gko=b5105.
152. "Innosight," accessed February 18, 2024, www.innosight.com/services/develop-innovation-capabilities/#:~:text=Creating%20a%20Culture%20of%20Innovation&text=We%20can%20help%20build%20a,members%20of%20key%20governance%20functions.
153. Alan G. Lafley and Ram Charan, *The Game Changer* (New York: Crown Business, 2008), 15.
154. Ron Adner and Rahul Kapoor, "Value Creation in Innovation Ecosystems: How the Structure of Technological Interdependence Affects Firm Performance in New Technology Generations," *Strategic Management Journal* 31, no. 3 (2010), 306–333.

155. Ron Adner, "Match Your Innovation Strategy to Your Innovation Ecosystem," *Harvard Business Review* 84, no. 4 (2006), 98.
156. "The World's 50 Most Innovative Companies," *Fast Company*, accessed February 18, 2024, www.fastcompany.com/most-innovative-companies/2012/full-list.
157. Colin Wood, "Who Really, Really Invented the Internet?" July 27, 2012, February 11, 2024, www.govtech.com/e-government/Who-Invented-the-Internet.html; *Wikipedia*, s.v. "ARPANET," accessed February 11, 2024, http://en.wikipedia.org/wiki/ARPANET.
158. Michael deAgonia, Preston Gralla, and J. R. Raphael, "Battle of the Media Ecosystems: Amazon, Apple, Google and Microsoft," *Computer World*, September 3, 2013, accessed February 11, 2024, www.computer-world.com/s/article/9240650/Battle_of_the_media_ecosystems_Amazon_Apple_Google_and_Microsoft?taxonomyId=229&pageNumber=2.
159. *Wikipedia*, s.v. "iPod," accessed February 11, 2024, https://en.wikipedia.org/wiki/IPod.
160. Chris Zook, "Googling Growth," *The Wall Street Journal*, April 9, 2007, accessed February 11, 2024, http://online.wsj.com/news/articles/SB117607363963063539.
161. *Wikipedia*, s.v. "iPod," accessed February 11, 2024, https://en.wikipedia.org/wiki/IPod.
162. Dan Saffer, "The Cult of Innovation," *Business Week*, March 5, 2007, accessed February 11, 2024, www.bloomberg.com/news/articles/2007-03-04/the-cult-of-innovation?embedded-checkout=true.
163. Gary Hamel and Bill Breen, *The Future of Management* (Boston: Harvard Business Press, 2013), 44–45.
164. *Wikipedia*, s.v. "Kodak Petite," accessed February 11, 2024, http://camera-wiki.org/wiki/Kodak_Petite.
165. *Wikipedia*, s.v. "iPod Touch," accessed February 11, 2024, http://en.wikipedia.org/wiki/IPod_Touch.
166. "iPhone History," *Apple*, accessed February 11, 2024, http://apple-history.com/iphone.
167. Ron Adner, *The Wide Lens* (New York: Portfolio/Penguin, 2012), 214–216.
168. *Wikipedia*, s.v. "IBM Simon," accessed February 11, 2024, http://en.wikipedia.org/wiki/IBM_Simon.
169. Thomas Claburn, "Steve Jobs: 11 Acts of Vision," *Information Week*, October 7, 2011, accessed February 11, 2024, www.informationweek.com/it-infrastructure/steve-jobs-11-acts-of-vision.
170. Ron Adner, *The Wide Lens* (New York: Portfolio/Penguin, 2012), 213–216.
171. *Wikipedia*, s.v. "App Store," accessed February 11, 2024, http://en.wikipedia.org/wiki/App_Store_(iOS).
172. "Statista Inc.," accessed December 20, 2014, www.statista.com/.
173. *Wikipedia*, s.v. "Application Store," accessed February 11, 2024, http://en.wikipedia.org/wiki/Application_store.
174. "iPad History," *Apple*, accessed February 11, 2024, http://apple-history.com/ipad.
175. "iPad History," *Apple*, accessed February 11, 2024, http://apple-history.com/ipad.
176. Dominic Basulto, "Apple's New Strategy: Trickle-down Innovation," *The Washington Post*, September 11, 2013, accessed February 11, 2024, www.washingtonpost.com/blogs/innovations/wp/2013/09/11/apples-new-strategy-trickle-down-innovation/.
177. John Naisbitt and Patricia Aburdeen, *Megatrends* (New York: Warner Books, 1982).
178. *Wikipedia*, s.v. "John Gage," accessed February 11, 2024, http://en.wikipedia.org/wiki/John_Gage.

1 Innovation and Entrepreneurship Importance

Early innovations in drawing, writing, and printing were at the forefront of our ability to learn and share knowledge. These early innovations include cave writings, the papyrus, the Dead Sea Scrolls, the Gutenberg printing press, and moveable type. In the 21st century, major innovations have occurred in the areas of science and genomics, artificial intelligence, sustainable resources, renewable energy, biomimetics, transportation, digitalization, manufacturing, computerization, networking, and much more. Interestingly, with exceptions of communication and medical diagnostic, pharmacologic, surgical, and medical instrument development, many important social systems (e.g., management, education, government, and healthcare) have escaped major innovative breakthroughs.

Consistently a leader in innovation and entrepreneurship, recent data on global competitiveness and innovation suggests that the United States is not alone when it comes to recognizing the importance of innovation and entrepreneurship. While notable progress has occurred on several fronts, including medicine and engineering, the United States struggles with an education system showing evidence of decline, a healthcare system that is costly and cumbersome, and a natural environment that often suffers from neglect. Moreover, troublesome issues continue surrounding a government system that has all too often succumbed to partisan politics, and both public and private sector economic systems carrying far too much debt.

Many of the recent innovations worldwide are not initiated by established organizations with deep talent and research and development labs, but rather from dedicated, determined, and driven entrepreneurs who ideate and innovate big ideas to create new ventures that tap underserved and/or unserved existing and new markets.[1] Ventures such as Amazon, Apple, Facebook (now Meta), Grameen Bank, Google (now Alphabet), Kickstarter, Whole Foods, Wikipedia, and Uber in North America; Virgin Enterprises, Hamilton Bradshaw, Digital Champion, and Specsavers in the United Kingdom; and Alibaba, ByteDance, Tencent, Baidu, Xiaomi, and Yipin Fresh in China, as well as other innovative start-ups in the Asia Pacific region, are just a few among many leaders in this innovation and entrepreneurship revolution.

Building on the foundation that innovation and entrepreneurship is the right developmental growth model for the future, several challenging questions emerge. How can a viable pathway be identified to ensure the next generation of innovators, entrepreneurs, and leaders can successfully pursue their dreams and aspirations? What are the most effective competencies the future workforce needs to learn to enable solving the big problems facing society? Are present talents being underutilized jeopardizing future development? Are creative skills sufficiently encouraged and developed for those pursuing what's next?

In this chapter, we begin our journey to address these questions and more. The importance of competencies, as well as a review and outline of the role of core and distinctive competencies is examined. Learning competencies are outlined and the overarching meta-competency,

DOI: 10.4324/9781003034308-2

effective decision-making, is introduced. The terminology and importance of imagination, creativity, innovation, and entrepreneurship are described to build an innovation and entrepreneurship framework.

Three sources of innovation: people, trends, and advancements are explored. Improving competitiveness and the critical aspects of creativity, innovation, and entrepreneurship are explored and discussed. Education is considered in terms of both how it informs, as well as is a key driver of, innovation and entrepreneurship.

The Importance of Competencies

For any organization, and for new start-ups, from for-profit ventures to not-for-profit ventures, it is important to achieve a level of competence (what needs to be done well) to survive and thrive. An organization or business venture, at a minimum, needs to achieve one competence or internal action that is done better than other activities in the internal value chain. This minimal level of competence allows a venture to be effective and efficient in the delivery of goods and/or services.

C. K. Prahalad and Gary Hamel took this concept one step further by identifying what they termed the need for a "core competence" of the corporation. That is, a firm must not only have competence, but a core competence that is central to the venture's strategy, competitiveness, and its profitability. In addition to core competencies, which are internal to the venture, a distinctive competence is something that a venture does in its value chain better than any of its competitors.[2] In order to drive innovation and entrepreneurship, a better understanding is needed of the roles competence and competency play in building a viable innovation and entrepreneurship competency framework.

Competency

What is the difference between competency and competence? While often used interchangeably, there are subtle yet important differences. In general, competency is the necessary criteria for competence. There are individual and collective competencies:

1. **Individual competencies** are the combination of learnable behaviors that encompass attitudes (wanting to do), skills (how to do), knowledge (what to do), practical experiences (proven learning), and natural talents of a person to effectively accomplish an explicit goal within a specific context.
2. **Collective competencies** are the synergistic combination of the individual competencies of team members within organizations.[3] There is a continuum that exists from low-functioning teams to high-functioning teams. High-functioning teams, although very rare, are those that apply collective competencies the most effectively.

Competence

You learn or gain competencies to meet or exceed a level of competence. A competence is the ability to accomplish a work task up to a recognized standard for a particular profession. For example, professions such as engineering, law, accounting, and medicine require evidence that individuals can perform up to a level of competence: the professional engineer exam, the bar exam, the certified public accountant exam, and the medical licensing exam, respectively. As seen in Figure 1.1, attitudes, skills, and knowledge are overlapping types of competencies.

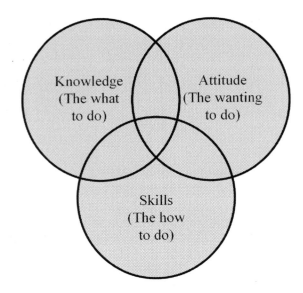

Figure 1.1 Illustration of Competency Types

Core Competencies

A core competency is a collective competency that includes the learnable behaviors the entire organization must practice achieving competence in relation to the organization's purpose and its competitive environment. A core competency encompasses the attitudes, skills, and knowledge that create unique customer value.

Manufacturing firms like Tesla, 3M, Intel, Huawei, and Boeing, for example, have three core competencies: detailed customer knowledge and focus, large-scale systems integration, and lean and efficient design and production systems.[4] These firms also have distinctive competencies that are better or unique as compared to the competition. Distinctive competencies are especially valuable drivers of competitiveness since they are hard to duplicate. A firm's intellectual property, such as patents, provides a unique competitive advantage that can often protect their distinctive competencies. As we will see in Chapter 16, "The Importance of Intellectual Property," there are multiple ways to go about providing that protection.

Competing for the Future

A breakthrough in strategic thinking occurred in 1996, with the publication of the book *Competing for the Future*, by business thinking experts C. K. Prahalad and Gary Hamel. They used the phrase "core competencies" to describe how businesses should define themselves through their key abilities rather than as a line of products or services. In the book, which *The Economist* magazine praised as "perhaps the best business book of the 1990s," the authors urged executives to ask themselves, "What are we really good at, and how can we build upon it?"[5] Prahalad and Hamel write, "Core competencies are the collective learning in the organization, especially how to coordinate diverse production skills and integrate multiple streams of technologies."[6]

Organizations need to identify what core competencies they need to cultivate in their precious human resources to meet a competence level that rises above the competition. The three tests to identify a core competence include:

1. First, does it provide potential access to a wide variety of markets?
2. Second, it does it make a significant contribution to the perceived benefit of the desired outcome?
3. Finally, is the core competence difficult for competitors to imitate?[7]

The core innovation and entrepreneurship competencies outlined in this book provide a framework for teaching and learning about innovation, to improve innovation competence to meet the threshold required for a business. Managers and entrepreneurs need to ask themselves the following questions:

1. What value will we deliver to our customers currently? In five or ten years from now?
2. What new "competencies" (a combination of skills and technologies) will we need to develop or obtain to offer that value?
3. What are the implications about how we interact with our customers?[8]

The Importance of Learning Competencies

Before diving into the overall innovation and entrepreneurship competency framework, it is suggested here that identifying and building a learning competency is critical. In general, overall effective decision-making relies on decision-making capability. This requires the building of human intellectual capability by developing competence (e.g., attitudes, skills, and knowledge), evidenced by learning, resulting in the application of behaviors/actions. Collectively, this process comprises what is called here a learning competency. See Figure 1.2. Building a strong learning competence creates a foundation for individuals and organizations to optimize the multifaceted role of innovation in the complex and multiple aspects of business, commerce, education, engineering, global trade, government, healthcare, and more.

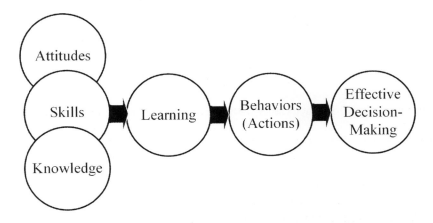

Figure 1.2 Illustration of the Value of Learning Competencies

The Innovation and Entrepreneurship Competency Framework

As important as building a strong learning competence is, it is only a prelude to the process of innovation and entrepreneurship. While the discipline of innovation suffers at times from a definitional crisis (for a review of various definitions of innovation, please see Table 2.1 in Chapter 2), in general, innovation is regarded as people applying a purposeful process to transform innovative ideas and opportunities that have value into results. The innovation and entrepreneurship competency framework is a holistic, integrated approach to facilitate effective evidence-based decision-making.

The purpose of the innovation and entrepreneurship competency framework is to enable the development of attitudes, skills, and knowledge to increase imagination, creativity, and innovation, which become actionable through entrepreneurship and strategy. By learning and applying the innovation and entrepreneurship competency framework, individuals and organizations are better able to develop future talent, make effective decisions, and compete for the future.

The 12 innovation and entrepreneurship competency framework categories are:

1. To learn how to apply the innovation *behaviors* (associating, questioning, observing, networking, and experimenting)
2. To learn how to think by applying *causation*, *critical thinking*, *divergence*, and *convergence*
3. To learn *problem solving* techniques in their appropriate contexts
4. To understand the importance of *knowledge* for innovation
5. To understand the development your *creative capabilities*
6. To understand the impact of *culture* on innovation and entrepreneurship
7. To understand *innovation* in-depth by examining and understanding the pathways to foster innovation
8. To understand and apply *entrepreneurship* in new ventures and large organizations
9. To understand how to use innovation *strategy* to create a competitive advantage
10. To understand modern evidence-based *leadership* concepts[9]
11. To understand *ecosystems*, systems thinking that encompasses people (relationships & connectedness), processes, and philosophies (whole, rather than just its parts and patterns) of systems[10]
12. To understand the application of *technology* accelerators

With a general framework outlined, the importance of decision-making, imagination, and creativity are explored in the following.

The Importance of Decision-Making

As discussed in more depth in Chapter 3, the effectiveness of our decision-making has a significant impact on our lives and on the lives of others. Decisions that matter the most in our individual lives and collectively in our organizations can dramatically achieve meaningful progress. Effective decision-making has several remarkable contrasts.

1. Decision-making is the *least* understood and *most* valuable high-order competency that we use in all aspects of our lives.
2. Decision-making is one of the most *frequent* cognitive tasks that we perform, yet we do not make the effort to learn how to do it effectively.
3. Decision-making has inherent invisible obstacles, such as implicit cognitive biases, which interfere with the clarity, completeness, and accuracy of our thoughts.

Why is decision-making so important? Decision-making is an overarching meta-competency (see Chapter 3) that is essential for individuals and organizations to leverage innovation and facilitate adaptation and flexibility. The five-step decision-making process depicted in Figure 1.3 provides a pathway to sharpen our ability to reflect on how we can improve our decisions.

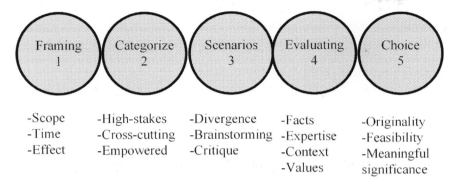

Framing 1	Categorize 2	Scenarios 3	Evaluating 4	Choice 5
-Scope	-High-stakes	-Divergence	-Facts	-Originality
-Time	-Cross-cutting	-Brainstorming	-Expertise	-Feasibility
-Effect	-Empowered	-Critique	-Context	-Meaningful significance
			-Values	

Figure 1.3 Illustration of the Decision-Making Process

Source: Acknowledgement: Johnson, Steven. 2018. Farsighted. New York: Riverhead.

Effective decision-making requires deliberate learning and the self-awareness of the templates that encompass our values and beliefs. Our values and belief templates play a key role in the formation of our perception of myths, cognitive biases, perceptions, and more.

Imagination, Creativity, Innovation, and Entrepreneurship

As illustrated in Figure 1.4, decision-making is the overarching competency that guides the iterative transformation from imagination, creativity, innovation, to entrepreneurship each informing the other.

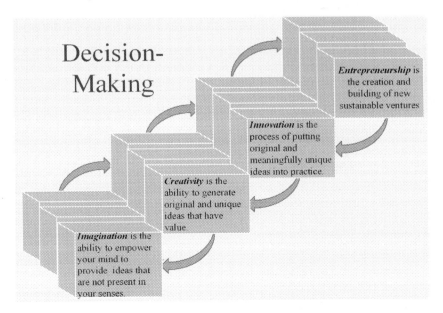

Figure 1.4 Illustration of Imagination, Creativity, Innovation, and Entrepreneurship

Source: Adapted from Robinson, K. (2011). *Out of our minds: Learning to be creative.* Oxford: Capstone, p. 220. Adapted from Robinson, K., & Aronica, L. (2011). *Finding your element.* New York: Viking, pp. 23–24.

The Importance of Imagination

Imagination is the power to see beyond what known or observable. It is the power to generate ideas that are not present in our senses.[11] Imagination is important because it provides open-mindedness to enlarge thinking beyond the here and now to search for what might be possible. Imagination is inherently something for which responsibility must be taken in order to achieve it.[12]

Whoever said "Imagination didn't matter" had none.

Today, someone just played some imaginary notes.
Today, someone just painted some imaginary colors.
Today, someone just blew some imaginary kisses to their partner.
Today, someone imagined a future generation that will change the world.
Today, someone just wrote down some imaginary words.
Today, someone just completed an imaginary exercise.
Today, someone just baked an imaginary recipe they thought up.
Today, someone just shared some imaginary ideas.
Today, someone saw a sky nobody else could.
Today someone just built a business with some imaginary notions.
Today, someone just helped another with some imaginary concepts.
Today, someone designed the next great brand no one thought of before.

Never forget:
Imagination isn't something you have.
It's something you are.

What will you imagine today?[13]

Imagination is the prerequisite of creativity in the process of identifying ideas that have value.

Imagination is the starting domino that kicks off meaningful innovation. Living in a global idea economy fuels the ability to turn an idea into a new product, service, or experience, which is now easier than ever. The tools that enable disruption – e.g., cloud computing, mobile technology, big data analytics – are increasingly accessible and affordable, giving rise to a new generation of entrepreneurs. In the global community, no organization is immune to disruption if it cannot imagine, identify, and adopt innovative ideas.

Taking Responsibility for Your Imagination

To awaken imagination, one needs to take responsibility for it. Imagination is the inception for the creativity, innovation, and entrepreneurship that follows. It can be enhanced by encouragement, exercise, and openness to new ideas, as well as diminished by stress, a lack of focus, and dysfunctional decision-making. Figure 1.5 summarizes the key aspects of awakening imagination.

Imagination Constraints

Idea Generation Declines with Formal Schooling

Interestingly, idea generation capability tends to decline with age and education. Ideation research suggests that student divergent thinking, the ability to generate ideas, decreases with

1. Block out time for reflection.	Take time to rest, exercise, reflect, and listen to or play music.
2. Ask active open questions.	Imagination involves reaching beyond our established habits and alternatives to ask questions that prompt the exploration of fresh ideas and approaches.
3. Allow yourself to be playful	Playing allows us to practice imagining, improvising, and being open to inspiration — all important skills when pursuing the unknown.
4. Set up a system for sharing ideas.	Build a network to share ideas while they are still in development: creating forums for people to communicate in a casual way, without hierarchy, reports, permissions, or financial justifications.
5. Seek out the anomalous and unexpected.	Adapt your mental models to consider new and different strategies and courses of action.
6. Encourage experimentation	Experiment with your ideas in the real world, often generating unexpected outcomes and stimulating further thinking and new ideas.
7. Stay hopeful and positive.	Set high expectations for your aspirational goals to activate a self-fulfilling prophesy.

Figure 1.5 Illustration of Awakening Your Imagination

Source: Adapted from Martin Reeves and Jack Fuller, *We Need Imagination Now More Than Ever*, April 10, 2020, accessed April 23, 2020, https://hbr.org/2020/04/we-need-imagination-now-more-than-ever

increased levels of formal schooling. In a landmark study conducted by Land and Jarman, they found that at the age of five, 98% of students scored in the highly creative range (for divergent thinking), with that number dropping to 32% by the age ten, 10% by the age fifteen, and down to 2% for adults.[14]

Idea Generation Is Impacted by the Leadership Culture

Idea generation is influenced by leadership styles, by country and company cultures, and the managerial orientation that is practiced in organizations. Everyone has a choice, to be silent or to speak up. Silence occurs when a person decides to withhold information. Silence can be detrimental if someone fails to share potentially important ideas and organizational information with someone who can act on the information. In contrast, speaking up refers to the escalation of discretionary communications about a person's actionable insights, thoughts, and ideas about work-related issues to those who have the authority and will take responsibility to make necessary changes.[15]

It is essential for leadership to understand that they can create a climate where people are willing to share task-relevant information. There are many everyday people who work for organizations that discover opportunities for improvement and uncover problems that need solutions. These everyday people on the frontlines are in direct contact with customers and are the first to imagine new possibilities. Unfortunately, it is not unusual for leaders to ignore the ideas of the frontline people.

In a study completed by Sheri, Tanqlrala, and Venkataramanib, they suggest that leaders and managers often fail to create bi-directional speak-up cultures because the leaders and managers are placed in impossible positions and not empowered to make changes.[16] "We found that managers face two distinct hurdles: They are not *empowered* to act on input from below, and they feel compelled to adopt a *short-term outlook* to work."[17] These two factors restrict a speak-up climate in organizations. They can lead even the best-intentioned leaders to avoid seeking employee ideas and potentially even stifle them.[18]

1. Leaders are not empowered with enough autonomy to change things because the authority to make decisions is upward, micromanaged by upper management, in their organization structure.
2. Leaders who are empowered to act may be expected to demonstrate short-term results over longer-term sustainability. In a study in which John Graham, Campbell Harvey, and Shiva Rajgopal interviewed 400 CFOs of large US public companies, 78% of executives reported that they would that they would sacrifice long-term economic value for their firm in order to improve their short-term (quarterly) earnings expectations.[19]

Idea Generation Contradictions

The brain is a complex network of billions of neurons that communicate with each other using electrical signals. These electrical signals regulate our thoughts, memories, sensory perception, vision, and movement.[20] Dyer, Gregersen, and Christensen write, "The more diverse knowledge the brain possesses, the more connections it can make when given fresh inputs of knowledge, and fresh inputs trigger the associations that lead to novel ideas."[21]

Imagine the possibilities if the mind can be freed for innovation. Freeing the mind involves understanding better how the brain works. The mind can be viewed as the software that runs on the brain, the hardware. The connections of the software of the mind (neurons) are strengthened as we learn and experience new things. Although genetics influence one's natural creative abilities, practicing the discovery skills can magnify those creative abilities.[22]

John Medina describes how the brain works in *Brain Rules*. He writes, "We are also terrific pattern matchers, constantly assessing our environment for similarities, and we tend to remember things if we think we have seen them before."[23] An individual can become so accustomed to the way they perform various tasks that they cannot imagine that there are different, and perhaps better, ways of thinking. The mind can be open or closed, and it is up to each person to know the difference. We are hardwired to think using well-established patterns. The strengthening of the patterns can result in a narrowing of our thinking processes, leading to our being uncreative. This can be overcome if we learn how to break out of patterned thinking. As we shall see, this has implications for creativity.

The Importance of Creativity

Creativity is the application of your imagination to *transform* ideas into all types of value and then combining those ideas into new associations. According to Jorgen Vig Knudstorp, chairperson of the LEGO Brand Group, "Creativity is the rearrangement of existing knowledge into new, useful combinations." It is like a key in a lock that can be turned in two directions. Turn it one way, and you unlock and facilitate creative talents; turn it the other way, and you lock and diminish creative talent inside each person.[24] It is a myth that creativity is the rare talent of a few select individuals. Creative thinking is available to everyone.

Creativity studies, however, have revealed that US creativity scores have been declining since 1990.[25] For example, according to Geoff Colvin, "A World Values Survey that asked people how important it is 'to think up new ideas and be creative' placed the U.S. 10th, while other major economies – Germany, France, the U.K. – ranked higher."[26]

Keith Sawyer writes, "The creative life is filled with new ideas. Your mind tirelessly generates possibilities. You don't clamp down, because you realize most of these ideas won't pan out – at least not for the current project. But successful creativity is a numbers game: When you have tons of ideas, some of them are sure to be great."[27] Let's explore how this might work in music.

Creativity in Music

Music is the creative expression of sounds organized in time that is a combination of unique songs, performances, production, film, and business. Music is created when a composer organizes melody, harmony, simultaneous pitches, and rhythm, which completes musical thoughts. It includes changes in the duration of the frequency of the sound or pitch, with varying degrees of loudness and tone qualities. The music is "described" on a score with the composer's symbols of notation, which performers can transform into musical sounds.

The Music Effect

This music effect is the positive impact that music can have on brain function and associated creativity and thinking skills. Creativity, the generation of ideas that have value, is the driving force behind all types of innovations. What is the effect of music on cognition and creativity?

Anita Collins performed a meta-analysis that provides evidence of the value of music education. The meta-analysis showed that music education could positively and permanently improve memory, cognitive skills, physical development, and emotional well-being."[28] In another study of the music effect, it is suggested that "[s]ix months of music-based multitask training improved executive function and benefited global cognitive function in older adults."[29] These findings illustrate not only the benefits of music education, but also the overall importance of creativity and its role in innovation.

The Importance of Innovation

Innovation is the process of *transforming* a creative concept into an innovation type (products, customer experience, solutions, systems, processes, business models, managerial, platforms, brands, and science and technology) that provides value to people while simultaneously generating revenue and profits.

An innovation differs from an invention in that innovation refers to the *use* of a novel idea or method, whereas an invention refers more directly to the creation of the *idea* or method itself.[30] The more impactful higher-degree innovations can change the way people live. The characteristics of an innovation are novel, useful, and implemented. Figure 1.6 illustrates this relationship.

"The most prominent development of this accelerating war for innovations is the severe decline of the average lifespan of S&P 500 companies, which has been going down from 90 years in 1935 to currently only 18 years – with 75 percent of current S&P 500 companies expected to disappear until 2027, according to research by McKinsey."[31]

McKinsey suggests that 51% of the activities of the US economy are potentially susceptible to automation, including robotics, artificial intelligence, and machine learning driven by ideation. McKinsey estimates that automation could raise productivity growth globally by 0.8 to 1.4% annually in the US.[32] While it brings substantial benefits, it also portends concerns for how people and technology interface.

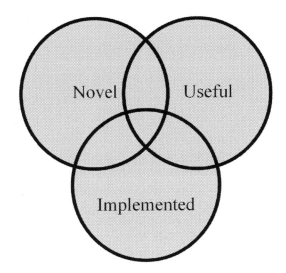

Figure 1.6 Illustration of Innovation Characteristics

Source: Adapted from Dyer, Jeff, Paul Godfrey, Robert Jensen, and David Bryce. 2018. *Strategic Management: Concepts and Cases.* Second ed. New York: John Wiley & Sons, Inc., 178–179.

Innovation is widely regarded as a driver for generating new knowledge, economic growth, and jobs. Just like keeping score in sports helps teams to strategize, it is important to know where countries stand in relation to one another so as to assess if the actions taken are increasing or decreasing their innovation capability.[33]

Business author and speaker Tom Peters famously notes, "Innovate or die."[34] The nature of innovation, however, invites debate. Are we witnessing an abundance of small innovations (incrementalism), akin to the ever-growing list of additives in toothpastes? Or are we experiencing fewer, impactful disruptions, like gunpowder and dynamite, flight, electricity, papermaking, printing, integrated circuits, and artificial intelligence? The answers remain unclear. The resulting ambiguity raises further questions. If innovation truly underpins the future of economic value, why is there no universally accepted innovation index, similar to the consumer price index? Should organizations be expected or mandated to quantify or measure their innovation capabilities?

The Importance of Entrepreneurship

Creativity, the generation of ideas that have value, is the root of innovation and entrepreneurship. At its very core, entrepreneurship is about the creation of venture and value for multiple constituents, including but not limited to customers, employees, cities, regions, and even countries. The potential for economic growth and employment is different depending on the business sector, and the size and age of the entrepreneurship ecosystem that currently exists. For economic growth and employment, small business firms are better positioned than large business firms; young small firms are better than small existing firms, and young high-tech firms are better overall, especially in the accelerated scalable growth segment.

According to Michael Porter and Jan Rivkin, "Research shows that innovation accounts for a large fraction of growth in national productivity, and the knowledge gained by one firm frequently spills over to others. Entrepreneurship is also key to job creation: Startups account for 3% of U.S. employment, but 20% of gross job creation."[35] According to the Bureau of Labor Statistics, start-up firms under one year old only had 1% of total employment but contributed 90% of the employment growth.[36]

Job Creation and Destruction

Entrepreneurs are a significant force in job creation, but some entrepreneurs have much more of an impact than others. "By now it is well understood," writes economist Tim Kane, "that firms large and small are continuously and simultaneously destroying and creating jobs."[37] Small businesses' job creation has significantly outpaced that of large businesses. According to the United States Small Business Administration, small businesses create the majority of employment growth. Small businesses have accounted for two out of every three jobs added in the past 25 years. "[L]arge businesses generated 6.7 million net new jobs over the past 25 years. During the same period, small businesses generated 12.9 million net new jobs, meaning small businesses have accounted for 66 percent of employment growth over the last 25 years."[38] According to the Automatic Data Processing Research Institute (ADP), which uses payroll data to provide monthly statistics on US non-farm private sector employment, small and medium-sized businesses historically create the most jobs.[39]

> High-tech startups are a key driver of job creation throughout the United States, according to research by technology policy coalition Engine and the Ewing Marion Kauffman Foundation. Though they start lean, new high-tech companies grow rapidly in the early years, adding thousands of jobs along the way.[40]

The innovative high technology sector is defined as those businesses with a large proportion of employees in the fields of science, technology, engineering, and math (STEM). The start-ups in this high-tech sector were 69% higher in 2011 than in 1980. More specifically, in the information and communications technology sector, new firm start-ups grew by 210% in contrast to private-sector business creation that decreased by 9% in the same period.[41]

Young Technology Firms

It is most effective to be both a young firm and a technology firm. Young technology firms contribute to net job creation rather than small businesses in general.

A report titled "Business Dynamics Statistics Briefing: Job Creation, Worker Churning, and Wages at Young Businesses" finds the following:

> Young firms, defined as employers in the first two years of their lives, have higher job creation and job destruction rates than older firms. A substantial fraction of the job creation for young firms is due to the job creation that occurs in the quarter of starting up. However, there is substantial subsequent job creation as well as job destruction in the succeeding quarters in the first two years. The overall net job creation (the difference between job creation and destruction) is much higher for young firms than for older firms.[42]

This research suggests that it is not so much small versus large ventures, but rather young firms that contribute most significantly to job creation. The Ewing Marion Kauffman Foundation reports in "The Importance of Startups in Job Creation and Job Destruction" that, in the last three decades (between 1977 and 2005), firms that were less than five years old added an average of three million jobs annually, while existing firms lost one million in net jobs annually.[43]

Additionally, a National Bureau of Economic Research[44] report concludes that the real drivers of disproportionate job growth are young companies. Start-up firms generate the surge of jobs that propel economic growth. According to Anthony Breitzman and Diana Hicks, "Small firms are a significant source of innovation and patent activity. Small businesses develop more patents per employee than larger businesses, with the smallest firms, those with fewer than 25 employees, producing the greatest number of patents per employee."[45]

The Drivers of Innovation

There are three drivers of innovation: people driving meaningful innovations, trends or megatrends that drive change, and advancements, especially in science and technology.

People, or more specifically, their intellectual capital, are the first driver of innovation. Innovation is a process that starts with the unique ideas that originate with people. Impactful innovations are based on meaningfully significant ideas that fulfill a job that customers need to have done. For maximum value, the ideas of people are aligned with the megatrends and with scientific and technological progress. These relationships are seen in Figure 1.7.

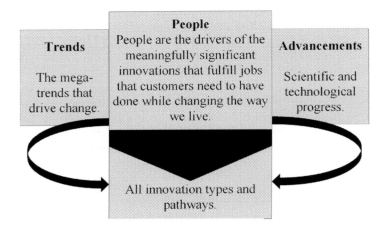

Figure 1.7 Illustration of the Drivers of Innovation

Because an innovation is the realization of an idea, it needs to be validated in practice. Often, this will require building and testing using a minimum viable prototype (MVP) to gather feedback that the idea can be implemented. While ideation, creativity, and innovation can have value in the process, business ideas need to be implementable to be commercialized.

Meaningfully Significant Progress Starts with People

Resilience

Keep in mind that the competencies discussed here all require resilience to become proficient. Resilience encompasses a person's willingness to face reality, to find a meaningful life purpose, and to continuously strive for improvement.[46]

In a study that was conducted at the Music Academy of West Berlin (Hochschule der Kuenste), violists were divided into three groups: the elite violinists, who had the potential to become world-class soloists; the good violinists; and the ordinary violists, who were unlikely to play professionally. The subjects were interviewed and were asked to estimate how many hours per week they had practiced alone with the violin for each year since they had started to practice.

The results indicated that the thing that distinguishes one performer from another was how hard they worked.[47] This was one of the studies that was used by Malcolm Gladwell to formulate the 10,000-hour rule of success using examples such as The Beatles who performed 1,200 sets before their first burst of success and Bill Gates who programmed for seven consecutive years before dropping out of Harvard to start Microsoft.[48]

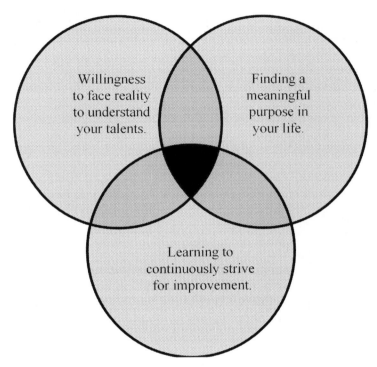

Figure 1.8 Illustration of Resilience

Source: Adapted from Coutu, D. L. (2002). How resilience works. *Harvard Business Review*, 80(5), 46–55.

Why is it that some organizations and individuals thrive when confronted with challenges while others fold? The answer in a word is *resilience*. Diane L. Coutu described the three essential components of resilience: facing down reality (confront the brutal facts), searching for meaning (core ideology), and continually improvising (drive for progress).[49] Figure 1.8 illustrates the interrelated aspects of resilience, as can be seen in numerous examples as in the following.

1. Australian Nicolas Vujicic was born in 1982, with no limbs and struggled both physically and mentally growing up. He has since become an evangelist and popular motivational speaker. Vujicic is an example of why it is often less important the challenge that individuals experience and more important how those individuals respond to the challenge.[50]
2. American Brandon Burlsworth was a walk-on underdog football player who through resilience became a starter for the University of Arizona's Razorback football team. He was selected for the 1998 College Football All-America Team. In the 1999 NFL draft Burlsworth was selected in the

third round (63rd overall) by the Indianapolis Colts. He was expected to be the right offensive guard starter in minicamp but was killed in an automobile accident 11 days after he was drafted.[51]

3. Englishman Robin Cavendish was stricken by polio and was required to stay on a respirator in the hospital. He refused to give up and became the longest surviving *responaut* in British history. While he was on the respirator, he experimented with wheelchair designs that included a battery-operated respirator that transformed the lives of thousands of disabled patients. He was a British advocate for disabled people and one of the longest-living polio survivors in Great Britain.[52]

4. When it came to winning the space race in the 1960s, engineers Christine Darden and Mary Jackson, mathematician Katherine Johnson, and computer programmer Dorothy Vaughan epitomized the concept of resilience on multiple fronts. Overcoming segregation and racial discrimination, these pioneers pursued their careers making critical contribution to the then-nascent US Space Program. In 2019, they were honored with the highest civilian recognition, the US Congressional Gold Medal, and in 2020, NASA announced that the agency's headquarters building in Washington, DC, will be named after Mary W. Jackson, the first African American female engineer at NASA.[53]

5. Olympian Al Oerter won consecutive gold medals from 1956 to 1968. Never the favorite, discounted at every turn, he overcame obstacle after obstacle. At the Tokyo Olympics in 1964, overcoming a cervical disc injury and torn cartilage in his ribcage, he was told not to compete. "Doctors told him not to compete, but Oerter wrapped his side with ice packs, injected Novocain and set another Olympic record. Asked why he went ahead and competed, Oerter said, these are the Olympics and you die before you don't compete in the Olympics."[54]

Growth Mindsets

The concept of a "fixed mindset" is based on the notion that your overall capabilities are fixed and do not change (refer to Figure 1.9). In contrast, the concept of a "growth mindset" is based on the notion that you can take responsibility for developing your overall capability to achieve your goals and the outcomes that you pursue. If you think you can improve, you will. McKinsey & Company reports the importance of determination, recognition, and grit in developing mindset for growth.

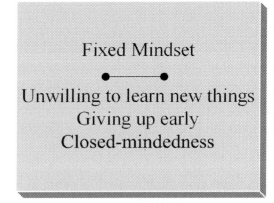
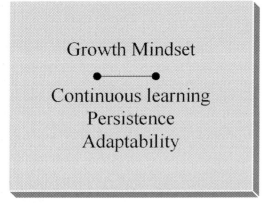

Figure 1.9 Illustration of Fixed and Growth Mindset

Source: Adapted from Carol Dweck, *Mindset: The New Psychology of Success.* 1st ed. New York: Random House, 2007.

[R]esearch by Stanford's Carol Dweck finds that students are more successful when they are praised and recognized for their contributions, hard work, practice, and effort – in short, for a mindset of growth. Such a mindset is valuable in corporate environments too, for it suggests that women can shape (and reshape) their own advancement and success. The good news is that these capabilities are coachable and that educational innovation (online, video, and experiential learning, for example) ought to help. Leaders should encourage experimentation to accelerate progress.[55]

People: Human Factors

It is the human factors that are essential for imagination, creativity, innovation, and entrepreneurship. Figure 1.10 outlines a few human factors that contribute to successful innovation.

Innovation Essentials
Inspire, train, and mentor everyone to facilitate creativity and innovation.
Think of innovation as a process of creating unique associations and combinations.
Innovation isn't necessarily about new things; it's about new value.
Discover meaningfully significant ideas that can change the world.
Focus on identifying and resolving uncertainties through experimentation.
Remember that being first to market is no guarantee of success.
Let your customers develop your next product.
Search for synergistic partnerships that combine talent.
Create a culture of systems and structures that support ongoing innovation.
Build a network of thought leaders and commercialization resources.
Facilite all the innovation types and pathways.
Create a network of customer advocates and communities

Figure 1.10 Illustration of the Innovation Essentials

Source: Adapted from Bruce Posner and Martha E. Mangelsdorf, "12 Essential Innovation Insights," September 12, 2017, accessed April 7, 2020, https://sloanreview.mit.edu/article/12-essential-innovation-i

Functional Fixedness: Enhancing Open-Mindedness

Functional fixedness occurs when a decision-maker's experience with a particular function of an object impedes using the object in a novel way when searching for a solution to a problem.[56] For instance, not realizing you can use a brick for a doorstop.

Functional fixedness, closed-mindedness, causes thinking errors that reduce your likelihood of generating valuable insights. Open-mindedness is the essential perspective for innovators. Open-mindedness can reduce the likelihood of thinking errors and ineffective decision-making by freeing yourself to extend the depth and breadth of your imagination.

The Door

It has been suggested that a traditional education model is incomplete and bound to conformity with its roots in the first industrial revolution of the steam engine. This mentality can lead to doing things more efficiently, but that has less and less value. In the traditional education model, teachers lecture; students listen, read textbooks, and may conduct research and author essays. This model fails to acknowledge that individuals have unique needs and learn in different ways. As Sir Ken Robinson notes, "First, all students have great natural abilities. Second, the key to developing them is to move beyond the narrow confines of academicism and conformity to systems that are personalized to the real abilities of everyday students."[57] Figure 1.11 illustrates opening the door to close-mindedness.

Figure 1.11 Illustration of Opening Door

The Window

On May 25, 2001, Erik Weihenmayer, an adventurer, athlete, and author reached the summit of Mount Everest. He is the only blind person to have climbed to the summit. He also has completed the 277 miles of the whitewater of the Colorado River that cuts through the Grand Canyon in a *kayak*. He became blind in the ninth grade from a disease known as juvenile retinoschisis.[58] Overcoming blindness is not just physical, as it can take different forms.

Prevention of Thinking Errors

Many thinking errors are caused by misperceptions. Improved thinking can reduce the likelihood of thinking errors and ineffective decision-making. For example, in a study using blindfolded violinists, six violins were compared: three high-quality modern violins with a Guarneri and two Stradivari instruments. There is a widespread belief that the Stradivari and Guarneri violins are tonally superior. Yet the blindfolded violinists in the test could not reliably distinguish the violins of the old experts from the modern violins. The Guarneri and Stradivari violins do not, according to this blindfolded play-off, sound better than high-quality modern violin instruments.[59]

MISPERCEPTIONS: THE FROSTY WINDOWS

Imagine a four-room house. In room number one, you and others see the same thing through a clear window. In room number two, however, you cannot see because the window is frosty, yet others still can see through a clear window. In room number three, neither you nor the others can see through the frosty window. In room number four, you can see though a clear window, but the others cannot see through the frosty window.[60] The four rooms are a metaphor for describing the visibility and mindset of organizations. We are perpetually seeing through an assortment of clear and frosty windows. At times we all have blind spots that block our effectiveness. How do we overcome these blind spots?

Johari Window

Individuals and organizations need to take responsibility for developing their self-awareness to overcome their functional blindness. The innovation and entrepreneurship mindsets require openness to ideas. We must reduce the gravitational pull that draws our thinking in the wrong direction by enlarging our ability to see through the frosty windows. By developing competencies, we are better able to overcome functional blindness.

The Johari window, depicted in Figure 1.12, is a way of viewing blind spots. Many leaders in many organizations become preoccupied with the status quo and with short-termism and fail to consider their own blind spots and their need for the inclusion and the involvement of others.

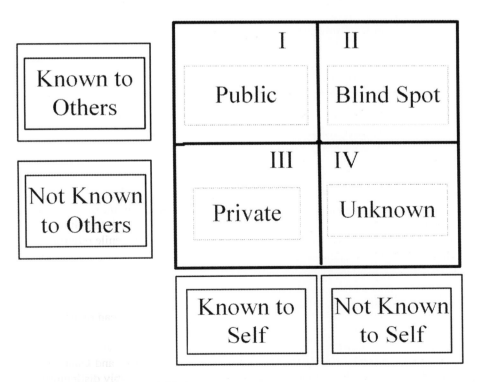

Figure 1.12 Illustration of the Johari Window

Source: Adapted from Johari Window, https://en.wikipedia.org/wiki/Johari_window

The innovators' blind spot is failing to see how their success also depends on partners who themselves would need to innovate and agree to adapt for their efforts to succeed. The more partners, the lower the probability of success. This innovation risk paradigm suggests that innovators consider the entire ecosystem by broadening their view to develop a clearer understanding of the full set of interdependences.

Innovation Obstacles

In addition to functional fixedness, Figure 1.13 illustrates several other obstacles to innovation. Respondents were asked in a survey to identify the most common obstacles to innovation in large companies. Awareness of the obstacles facilitates ways to remove these obstacles and thereby advance innovation.[61]

Obstacles to Innovation in Large Companies	
Politics, turf wars, and a lack of alignment.	55%
Inflexible cultures.	45%
Inability to act on signals.	42%
Lack of budget.	41%
Lack of the right strategy or vision.	36%

Figure 1.13 Illustration of Innovation Obstacles in Large Companies

Source: Adapted from Scott Kirsner, "The Biggest Obstacles to Innovation in Large Companies," July 30, 2018, accessed February 25, 2020, https://hbr.org/2018/07/the-biggest-obstacles-to-innovation-in-large-companies

Gordian Knot

The Gordian knot, illustrated in Figure 1.14, is used to describe a complex or unsolvable problem that can be traced back to the life of Alexander the Great.[62] It is used as a metaphor for the invisible curse of closed-minded organizations.

The term Gordian knot describes the notion that organizations create their own obstacles by implicitly tying knots that form cultures of conformity and rigidity. This results in their unwillingness to correct their culture or to adapt to the dynamics of change. There are many examples of companies that were unable to unravel the knot that they created. Big Tobacco, Theranos, Volkswagen, Wells Fargo, and Enron, to name a few, led their own employees down the path of wrongful behavior.

Behavior Change in Dysfunctional Organizations

The Gordian knot is caused by a collection of cognitive biases, closed-mindedness, and micro-cultures of rigid silos. Firms that are fixated with a mix of dysfunctional behaviors, such as overconfidence, confirmation bias, sunk cost fallacies, loss aversion, and the status quo biases, can be bypassed by start-ups even with inferior solutions.[63] The Gordian knot phenomenon is based on prospect theory that

Figure 1.14 Illustration of the Gordian Knot

was conceived by Amos Tversky and Nobel Prize winner Daniel Kahneman. Prospect theory describes why people hold onto what they know and own because they are more sensitive to losses compared to gains of similar magnitude.[64]

Closed-minded and Open-minded: The Gordian Knot

The Gordian knot mentality of rigidity is prevalent in incumbent organization. Those who work in Gordian knot cultures have choices.

1. People can get sent away because they cannot or will not adapt.
2. People go away voluntarily because of their frustrations with the leadership knot.
3. People can adapt to the knot by learning how to discover ways to benefit from corporate resources but not get stymied by the bureaucracy.

The Gordian knot is an invisible curse for the incumbents but a source of opportunities for entrepreneurs inside and outside the organization. Entrepreneurs (start-ups) with innovations can disrupt organizations that are unwilling to adapt, fail to see trends, or are unaware of science and technology advancements.[65]

Gordian-knot-oriented firms need to apply herculean effort to change their collective behaviors to survive using a two-step process and countervailing the hidden forces.

1. The first way to countervail the Gordian knot effect is to create diverse cross-functional teams that are trained in critical thinking and emotional intelligence. Critical thinking is a force that can be used to overcome closed-mindedness by ensuring that the claims that are made are based on validated evidence. Emotional intelligence is a package of competencies that include

self-awareness, self-management, social awareness, and relationship management. These can improve your ability to prevent cognitive biases that underlie decision-making.[66]

2. The second way to countervail the Gordian knot effect is to create organizations that are flat and dyadic. An organization should be flat with no more than five layers. A flat organization structure simplifies organization structures and simultaneously improves the pace of decision-making. Fewer layers mean faster decision, especially if each layer is composed of cross-functional teams.[67] A dyadic organization is one where there is a bi-directional flow of relevant information to promote meaningful communication.

Trends and Paradigm Shifts

The second driver of innovation is trends. A trend is movement in a distinct direction that can be used to detect early signs of new evolving behavior patterns. Trends are a source of innovation that reflect changing conditions and value shifts in our global society.

The most innovative impact can be achieved by aligning a meaningfully significant new concept with a megatrend or paradigm shift. A paradigm shift is a fundamental change in practices, ideology, and underlying assumptions. A change in thinking, or paradigm shift, occurred when our understanding that the sun revolved around the earth was wrong and that the earth revolved around the sun was right. Trends can be categorized in three groups: megatrends, macrotrends, and microtrends.[68] Refer to Figure 1.15.

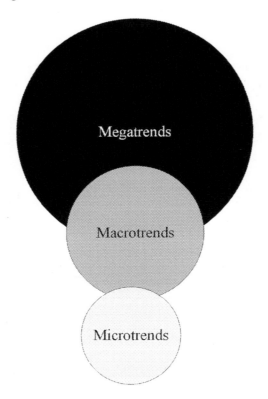

Figure 1.15 Illustration of Microtrends, Macrotrends, and Megatrends

Source: Adapted from Statista Trend Compass 2020 Report, accessed April 5, 2020, https://www.statista.com/study/69166/statista-trendcompass

1. The megatrends are the long-term paradigm shifts and wide-ranging transformation processes that shape society and future markets that can be projected at least 25 years into the future.
2. The macrotrends are the medium-term processes that range from 10 to 15 years that are consumer-related wants and needs of people and focus on lifestyles and the attitudes, expectations, and behaviors of people.
3. The microtrends are the short-term market-related trends that have lifecycles of 3 to 5 years that shape products, services, and experiences.

Four Super Forces Shaping the Trends

As depicted in Figure 1.16, the four drivers of change are the super forces that move our world and shape trends. These four super forces – technology, society, culture, and economy – help interpret and understand where trends emerge and what drives them.

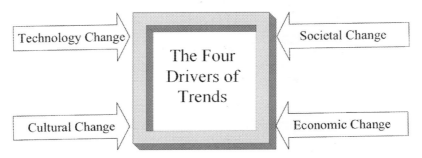

Figure 1.16 Illustration of the Four Drivers of Trends

Source: Adapted from Statista TrendCompass 2020 Report, accessed April 5, 2020, https://www.statista.com/study/69166/statista-trendcompass/

Figure 1.17 outlines key questions for each of the four super forces. Addressing these questions enables a more accurate future perspective detecting emerging trends.

Questions for the Four Drivers of Trends	
Technological Change	"Technology plays a vital role in consumer decision-making and the ability of a business to thrive in the future."
Key question:	"What opportunities do new technologies open up?"
Social Change	"Ongoing population shifts are reshaping consumer lifestyles and purchasing decisions."
Key question:	"How does the way people live together in a society change?"
Economic Change	"Global economic growth has seen a huge upheaval with advanced economies facing pushback."
Key question:	"How do trade and business ecosystems evolve?"
Cultural Change	"Consumers all over the world are taking action, changing the world with new values."
Key question:	"How do our values adapt to the changing conditions?"

Figure 1.17 Illustration of the Questions for the Four Trend Drivers

Source: Adapted from Statista TrendCompass 2020, Statista, accessed June 3, 2020, https://www.statista.com/study/69166/statista-trendcompass/

Twelve Megatrends

Speculative-fiction author William Gibson writes, "The future is already here – it's just not very evenly distributed."[69] During periods of dramatic and disruptive change, the leadership must take responsibility to transition to the new frontier, which focuses on the power to improve our global societies. Trends do not move independently but rather interact. Figure 1.18 suggests 12 global future megatrends that could affect innovation and entrepreneurship. What trends do you foresee?

Twelve Global Future Trends	
Connectivity:	"Digital and real are no longer separate entities but have become a collective environment. We are always on and permanently connected to everyone and everything."
Gender Shift:	"Time is up. Gender roles will no longer be accepted as being predetermined, but will increasingly be defined by individuals themselves."
Globalization:	"The internet has accelerated globalization all over the planet. New decentral partnerships open up and shake up global politics and economy."
Healthstyle:	"Health is becoming a lifestyle. Taking care of our bodies as well as our minds has become a necessity."
Individualization:	"The divergence between people's individual lifestyles has become a global phenomena and will increase in future."
Mobility:	"Our 21st century is not only marked by an increased need for mobility but also by its huge variety."
New Ecology:	"The environment is deeply suffering from the subsequent costs of the human lifestyle. The time to act has begun."
Silver Society:	"The increasing life expectancy in most regions throughout the world is turning the demographic pyramid on its head."
Singleization:	"The number of single households is growing constantly. Single cultures and individual lifestyles are increasingly being recognized."
Social Imbalance:	"The world is becoming less fair. Whilst inequalities between states are diminishing on the global level, they are increasing within specific regions and countries."
Urbanization:	"The majority of the world's population is living in cities – an amount that is only going to increase in the future."
Volatile Economy:	"Throughout the world, businesses are increasingly being confronted with dynamically changing commercial environments."

Figure 1.18 Twelve Global Future Trends

Source: Adapted from Statista TrendCompass 2020, Statista, accessed June 3, 2020, https://www.statista.com/study/69166/statista-trendcompass/

Black Swan Sentinel Events

Black swan sentinel events are dynamic, unpredictable, or unforeseen crises that can have extreme consequences. Black swan sentinel events can stimulate transformational change, propel organizations to adopt essential innovations, and disrupt slow adopters who will find themselves on "burning platforms." "Good leaders seize crises to remake organizational habits."[70] Throughout history, transformational events occur in real time creating a ripple effect moving forward.

In 1957, the Soviet Union successfully launched the world's first artificial satellite and woke up a sleeping United States and changed history. Sputnik was small, about the size of a beach ball (58 cm or 22.8 in in diameter) and only weighed only 83.6 kg or 183.9 lb, yet it introduced the start of the space age, a new era of political, military, technological, and scientific developments.[71]

NASA was unsuccessful in changing safety habits until the Challenger explosion in 1986. Airplane cockpit redesign was influenced by the runway error on the Spanish island of Tenerife in 1977, that killed 583 people. In England, a fire at King's Cross station facilitated changes made to improve fire prevention. In 2002, surgical mistakes at the Rhode Island Hospital stimulated changes to the corrosive culture and dysfunctional institutional habits.[72]

Thomas Edison's research laboratory created the Kinetograph (a motion picture camera) and the Kinetoscope (a peep-hole motion picture viewer) in the late 1890s.[73] Edison partnered with anti-tuberculosis health activists to produce short films to increase the awareness of how to prevent the transmission of the disease. The tuberculosis educational movies were the first films that many viewers had ever seen. Later educational films were used in public health campaigns in efforts to combat polio and to promote vaccinations.[74]

In a 2020 survey by Fortune 500 CEOs, during the COVID-19 pandemic, respondents were asked whether the pandemic would accelerate their technological transformation, slow their technological transformation, or have no significant effect. The result was 63% said "accelerate," while only 6% said "slow."[75] The restrictions imposed by the pandemic have stimulated a search for alternative solutions and simultaneously focused management on the importance of digital transformations and gathering of data to address the global implications of the crisis.

Advancements in Science and Technology

Advancements in science and technology are the third driver of innovation. Education plays a key role in societies, organizations, and countries competing for the future. If the United States is "serious about building an economy that lasts" and strengthening the middle class, "we had better be serious about education," former President Obama said. "We have to pick up our game and raise our standards."[76] The critical importance of the nexus of innovation, entrepreneurship, and education can be seen in the need for future knowledge creation, employment readiness, building a vibrant domestic economic base, and fostering competition for a rapidly changing global economy.

"Building the skills that lead to readiness for employment, career progress, and the ability to innovate is critical to America's economic future. The United States must build a more cohesive and effective system of education and talent development to cultivate a productive workforce that can meet the challenges of a technology-driven global economy."[77] Figure 1.19 identifies 12

The Future of Science and Technology		
Applied artificial intelligence	Industrializing machine learning	Generative artificial intelligence
Next-generation software development	Trust architectures and digital identity	Web3
Advanced connectivity	Immersive-reality technologies	Cloud and edge computing
Quantum technologies	Mobility	Bioengineering
Future of space technologies	Electrification and renewables	Climate techology

Figure 1.19 The Future of Science and Technology

Source: Adapted from Michael Chui, Mena Issler, Roger Roberts, and Lareina Yee, "Technology Trends Outlook 2023," July 20, 2023, accessed November 20, 2023, https://www.mckinsey.com/capabilities/mckinsey-digital/our-insights/the-top-trends-in-tech#new-and-notable

selected science and technology categories that are likely to be associated with future innovation and entrepreneurship.

Improvements in innovation capability and economic growth are dependent on worldwide education systems. We live in a world that demands creativity and innovation across multiple social, legal, technical, political, and educational sectors. Educators at all levels, and in specific sectors (e.g., science, technology, engineering, and math) in particular, are responsible for ensuring that the future workforce has the competencies required to ideate, conceptualize, develop, and implement the intellectual capital that drives progress.

The Importance of Global Comparisons

Measuring Global Competitiveness

The Global Competitiveness Index Rankings

The Global Competitiveness Index (GCI) is a composite indicator that uses over one hundred indicators that are organized into a 12-pillar framework. The 12 pillars are institutions, appropriate infrastructure, stable macroeconomic framework, good health and primary education, higher education and training, efficient goods markets, efficient labor markets, developed financial markets, ability to harness existing technology, market size (both domestic and international), effective production of new and different goods, and innovation.[78]

The GCI score is derived from international organizations, academic institutions, and nongovernmental organizations that include the World Economic Forum's Executive Opinion Survey and a global study that surveys every year approximately 15,000 business executives with the help of 150 partner institutes. The recent rankings on global competitiveness provided by the World Economic Forum are Singapore, the United States, Hong Kong, the Netherlands, Switzerland, Japan, Germany, Sweden, the United Kingdom, and Denmark.[79]

The GCI score focuses on productivity factors that will grow in significance as the Fourth Industrial Revolution (4IR) gathers pace: human capital, agility, resilience, and innovation. The GCI's most compelling insight is the overall critical role that innovation, in the form of new, value-added products and services, plays in the continuing global economic transformation.

The World Competitiveness Ranking

The International Institute for Management Development (IMD) World Competitiveness Ranking of 64 economies assesses the extent to which a country promotes the prosperity of its people by measuring economic well-being through data and survey responses from executives. "The World Competitiveness Ranking is based on 334 competitiveness criteria selected as a result of comprehensive research using economic literature, international, national and regional sources and feedback from the business community, government agencies and academics."[80] The criteria categories are economic performance, government efficiency, business efficiency, and infrastructure.[81]

The recent rankings expose the economic impact of the pandemic across the globe. The findings describe qualities such as investment in innovation, digitalization, welfare benefits, and leadership resulting in social cohesion that have helped economies better weather the crisis, allowing them to rank higher in competitiveness. Figure 1.20 shows the top rankings over a ten-year period.[82]

Nation/Territory	1997	2002	2007	2012	2017	2019	2020	2021	2022	2023
Denmark	13	6	5	13	7	8	2	3	1	1
Ireland	10	9	14	20	6	7	12	13	11	2
Switzerland	12	5	6	3	2	4	3	1	2	3
Singapore	2	8	2	4	3	1	1	5	3	4
Netherlands	4	4	8	11	5	6	4	4	6	5
Taiwan	18	20	18	7	14	16	11	8	7	6
Hong Kong	3	13	3	1	1	2	5	7	5	7
Sweden	19	12	9	5	9	9	6	2	4	8
United States	1	1	1	2	4	3	10	10	10	9
United Arab Emirates	-	-	-	16	10	5	9	9	12	10

Figure 1.20 Illustration of the World Competitiveness Ranking

Source: Adapted from International Institute for Management Development, "World Competitiveness Ranking," accessed November 20, 2023, https://www.imd.org/centers/wcc/world-competitiveness-center/rankings/world-competitiveness-ranking/2023/ and https://en.wikipedia.org/wiki/World_Competitiveness_Yearbook

Improving Global Competitiveness

The ability of any nation to improve its overall competitiveness can be facilitated by innovation and entrepreneurship. Innovation is important because it is a primary source of competitive advantage. "In a world where advanced knowledge is widespread and low-cost labor is readily available, U.S. advantages in the marketplace and in science and technology have begun to erode. A comprehensive and coordinated federal effort is urgently needed to bolster U.S. competitiveness and pre-eminence in these areas."[83]

Of course, improving competitiveness through innovation and entrepreneurship is not just a US goal, but a global one as well. For example, with over 60 national and provincial scientific institutions, 45.6 patents per 10,000 persons, and ever-increasing numbers of technology-based companies and R&D centers attracted to the region, the Laoshan district of Eastern Qingdao, China is ground zero for innovation and entrepreneurship in China. Successful ventures, such as the now-global appliance-maker Haier, maintain head offices and global R&D centers in the Laoshan district.[84]

On the ever-expanding Internet front, two formidable Chinese start-ups, Alibaba and Tencent, have redefined the concepts of innovation and entrepreneurship in practice. Alibaba, the brainchild of Chinese entrepreneur Jack Ma, is set to reap the benefits of one of the largest IPOs in recent history. Alibaba, akin to Amazon in the United States, has become the dominant web-portal player in China since its initial entry into the online market in 1999. Continual innovation and successive start-ups have fueled the company's growth. Alibaba has also spurred into action other players, now vying for a portion of the expanding online Chinese market. For example, Tencent, founded by Chinese entrepreneurs Ma Huateng and Zhang Zhidong in 1998, has become a chief rival of Alibaba through its continuous innovations in multiple industries and sectors on the web portal front.[85]

The list of innovations and start-ups by Tencent and Alibaba addresses consumers' near-limitless quest for goods and services via the Internet. For example, Tencent offers WeChat (messaging), Tencent Weibo (microblogging), Paipai (consumer-to-consumer ecommerce), Jingdong (business-to-business ecommerce), Tenpay (third-party pay), Licatong (savings investment), and Ten-Pay Credit Card (virtual credit cards), to name a few. Comparable rivals from Alibaba include Laiwang, Sina Weibo, Taobao, Tmall, Alipay, Yu'ebao, and Alipay Credit Card, respectively. Other services offered by both Alibaba and Tencent include travel booking, taxi hailing, ecommerce logistics, search engines, cloud storage, and navigation. As if this were not enough, both rivals pursue continual developments in Android ROM space, app stores, gaming, music, smart TV, and education.[86]

Measuring Global Innovation

The discipline of innovation provides a way for improving the livelihood of all of us. What is the state of global innovation? A way to measure innovation at the aggregate level is through comparative indices. As can be seen in Figure 1.21, the Global Innovation Index (GII) prepared by INSEAD, Cornell, and the World Intellectual Property Organization provides detailed metrics about the innovation performance of 126 countries which represent 90.8% of the world's population and 96.3% of the global gross domestic product. The GII uses 80 indicators to focus on innovation, including political environment, education, infrastructure, and business expertise.

Global Innovation Index			
2023		2022	
1	Switzerland	1	Switzerland
2	Sweden	2	United States
3	United States	3	Sweden
4	United Kingdom	4	United Kingdom
5	Singapore	5	Netherlands
6	Finland	6	Republic of Korea
7	Netherlands	7	Singapore
8	Germany	8	Germany
9	Denmark	9	Finland
10	Republic of Korea	10	Denmark
11	France	11	China
12	China	12	France
13	Japan	13	Japan
14	Israel	14	Hong Kong, China
15	Canada	15	Canada
16	Estonia	16	Israel
17	Hong Kong, China	17	Austria
18	Austria	18	Estonia
19	Norway	19	Luxembourg
20	Iceland	20	Iceland

Figure 1.21 Illustration of Global Innovation Index

Source: Adapted from World Intellectual Property Organization, Global Innovation Index 2023, accessed September 30, 2023, https://www.wipo.int/edocs/pubdocs/en/wipo-pub-2000-2023-sectionl-en-gii-2023-results-global-innovation-index-2023.pdf. Adapted from World Intellectual Property Organization, Global Innovation Index 2022, accessed November 3, 2022, https://www.globalinnovationindex.org/Home

Most government measurements focus on economic measures such as the gross domestic product rather than measurements of our innovation capability. Focusing on innovation measurements would provide a better understanding of the impact of policies on economic growth and prevent "innovation shortfalls."[87]

The Role of Education

The purpose of the education system is to transform lives, to unlock creative talents, and to enable each of us to build on our strengths by developing our talents, culturally and behaviorally: culturally, by deepening our understanding of the world, and behaviorally, by enhancing our knowledge, attitudes, skills, and practical experiences.[88]

Education plays a critical role in the development of both innovation and entrepreneurship, and the innovation and entrepreneurship competency framework we develop in this text causally relates to the importance of the role of education. Educators must adapt to the present and future needs of students and society by integrating relevant technology into scalable and adaptable learning architectures.

Ideally, the education system ought to encourage the development of the fundamentals of problem solving, thinking, and creativity skills within a team-oriented environment. Recognizing a knowledge-based global economy that is reliant on creativity and innovation should accelerate the rate at which educators work to address this need.

Education systems worldwide are struggling to provide opportunities for students to learn these vital innovation and entrepreneurship skills. Simply put, education systems now and in the future need to teach the competencies that enable diverse peoples to create, connect, and leverage different domains of knowledge that result in ongoing innovation and entrepreneurship. To be competitive in a global economy in times of change, we need to focus on high rates of learning. As the dynamic white water of change surges throughout the world, new knowledge is discovered, while existing knowledge becomes obsolete and needs to be updated or replaced.

Given that new learning is necessary to replenish the intellectual capital that becomes rusty, worn, and outdated, starting early in the education process becomes even more of a priority. Individually and collectively, educators are expected to provide environment, content, and curriculum that allows for students to develop creativity, innovation, and entrepreneurship skills to ensure our future competitiveness.[89]

Many colleges do not require courses on creativity or innovation, many colleges do not require that educators adopt instructional strategies to learn creativity, and many teacher education programs do not require creativity in their curriculums.[90] The evidence suggests, however, that education systems have at least four challenges: (1) a lack of emphasis placed on creativity skills, (2) weak foundational skills in reading and mathematics that are also not internationally competitive, (3) insufficient standards necessary for modern learning architectures, and (4) existing teaching and learning models which are not adequately systematized and developed for adaptability for the future.

Despite living in an era when we need more creativity to drive innovation, there is evidence that our creativity skills may be in decline.[91] Imagination, creativity, innovation, and entrepreneurship are vital to sustaining and improving an advanced standard of living. The innovation and entrepreneurship competency framework is designed to facilitate the needed learning experience to improve creativity, innovation, and entrepreneurship capability. The following are reasons that innovation and entrepreneurship competencies are essential.

The Innovation Discipline

Despite its importance, understanding innovation is much like traveling through a labyrinth. At the center of any new discipline, there is a need for an organizing system to provide a framework for learning and understanding. It is essential that innovation develops as a discipline like engineering, physics, chemistry, economics, psychology, sociology, mathematics, accounting, and others. Figure 1.22 summarizes some of the key aspects of the continued maturation of innovation as a discipline.

The Innovation Discipline
Innovation needs to become a discipline like engineering, physics, chemistry or accounting. We are in an early transition toward viewing innovation as a discipline with competencies that can be learned. Thus far, there have been no clearly defined competency areas that encompass innovation.
The innovation competencies propel intellectual capital, the knowledge of the workforce, and the underlying basis for competitiveness. Innovation requires a leadership style that supports a culture that can tolerate risk and an organization that has the resources to support all competency areas. Without resources and a climate supportive of risk takers, an innovative culture can be starved into non-existence.
The education system should be a priority on the development of the intellectual capital necessary for innovating in the new economy. The United States education system is dominated by knowledge transfer rather than ideation, but it is widely recognized that, in the new global economy, more ideation is required in order to remain competitive. Innovation, which requires higher levels of individual intellectual capital, is an important way for organizations to compete in the new global economy. Yet high schools, colleges, and universities do not place a high priority on offering academic courses or programs in creativity and innovation. Colleges and universities that provide innovation programs will be better positioned strategically for attracting students, prestige, and resources.
Innovation is much broader than simply product innovation. Innovation should encompass all facets of business. Innovation is polymorphic and has many different types. It is not just products and services; it is improved processes, new organizational forms, new platforms, and new branding. Innovation is without boundaries.

Figure 1.22 Illustration of Innovation Discipline

Source: Adapted from Peter Gray, "As Children's Freedom Has Declined, So Has Their Creativity," Psychology Today, September 17, 2012, accessed April 17, 2020, http://www.psychologytoday.com/blog/freedom-learn/201209/chilclren-s-freedom-has-declined-so-has-their-creativity.

Adapted from Fang qi Xu, Ginny McDonnell, and William R. Nash, "A Survey of Creativity Courses at Universities in Principal Countries," The Journal of Creative Behavior, 2005, accessed April 17. 2020, https://www.semanticscholar.org/paper/A-Survey-of-Creativity-Courses-at-Universities-in-Xu-Mcdonnell/26l6a0db4a50a68d0ec44c4dc0balab67acld716

Summary

In this chapter, the importance of competencies are outlined, and the role of core, distinctive, and collective competencies are reviewed. Imagination, creativity, innovation, entrepreneurship, and decision-making are defined to establish the foundation for the innovation discipline.

Organizations should mange innovation as a discipline to improve their long-term viability. Innovation is defined as people applying a purposeful process to transform innovative ideas and opportunities that have value into meaningful results. Yet leaders often fail to understand the causal mechanisms to stimulate innovation and improve the likelihood of transformational outcomes to achieve competitive separation.

Innovation is important for economic growth, suggesting the importance of advancing the foundation of innovation and entrepreneurship and how to best measure it. Without standard metrics for measuring innovation and entrepreneurship, it is not possible to know if improvements have occurred. In a subsequent chapter, we discuss the notion of measuring innovation in more detail.

The three key drivers of innovation: human intellectual capital, trends, and advancements in science and technology are discussed. A global comparison of competitiveness and innovation that are leading indicators for the standard of living of future economies is presented. Education, as a key driver that propels imagination, creativity, innovation, and entrepreneurship, is outlined. In the next chapter, we provide the elements of innovation as a springboard for the full innovation and entrepreneurship competency framework.

Notes

1. Bruce Nussbaum, *Creative Intelligence* (New York: Harper Business, 2013), 37.
2. Coimbatore K. Prahalad and Gary Hamel, "The Core Competence of the Corporation," *Harvard Business Review* 68, no. 3 (1990), 79–91.
3. Arup Barman and Jothika Konwar, "Competency Based Curriculum in Higher Education: A Necessity Grounded by Globalization," *Romanian Journal for Multidimensional Education*, accessed February 17, 2024, www.ceeol.com/search/article-detail?id=196610.
4. "MBE Core Competencies," *Boeing*, Model Based Engineering (MBE) Supplier Integration, accessed February 17, 2024, www.boeingsuppliers.com/MBE_SFA_Core_Competencies.html.
5. Matt Schudel, "C. K. Prahalad, Expert on Corporate Strategy, Dies at 68," *The Washington Post*, April 21, 2010, accessed February 17, 2024, www.washingtonpost.com/wp-dyn/content/article/2010/04/20/AR2010042005075.html.
6. Coimbatore K. Prahalad and Gary Hamel, "The Core Competence of the Corporation," *Harvard Business Review* 68, no. 3 (1990), 79–91.
7. Coimbatore K. Prahalad and Gary Hamel, "The Core Competence of the Corporation," *Harvard Business Review* 68, no. 3 (1990), 79–91.
8. Steven ten Have, Wouter ten Have, Frans Stevens, and Marcel van der Elst, *Key Management Models*, with Fiona Pol-Coyne (London: Prentice Hall | Financial Times, 2003), 69.
9. Clayton M. Christensen, James Allworth, and Karen Dillon, *How Will You Measure Your Life* (New York: Harper, 2012).
10. Russell L. Ackoff, *Systems Thinking for Curious Managers: With 40 New Management f-Laws* (Anixter: Triarchy Press Limited, 2010), 6.
11. Ken Robinson, *Out of Our Minds: Learning to Be Creative* (West Sussex: Capstone, 2011), 17.
12. David Brier, "Working from Home and the Importance of Imagination," April 8, 2020, accessed February 10, 2024, www.youtube.com/watch?v=EQTFBLHHVlM&feature=youtu.be.
13. David Brier, "Working from Home and the Importance of Imagination," April 8, 2020, accessed February 10, 2024, www.youtube.com/watch?v=EQTFBLHHVlM&feature=youtu.be.
14. George T. Land and Beth B. Jarman, *Breakpoint and Beyond* (New York: Harper Business, 1992).
15. Elizabeth W. Morrison, "Employee Voice and Silence," *Annual Review of Organizational Psychology and Organizational Behavior* 1, no. 1 (2014), 173–197.
16. Elad N. Sheri, Subrahmaniam Tanqlrala, and Vijaya Venkataramanib, "Why Managers Do Not Seek Voice from Employees: The Importance of Managers' Personal Control and Long-Term Orientation," *Organization Science* 30, no. 3 (2019), 447–466, accessed February 17, 2024, https://doi.org/10.1287/orsc.2018.1273.
17. Elad N. Sherf, Subra Tangirala, and Vijaya Venkataramani, "Research: Why Managers Ignore Employees' Ideas," April 8, 2019, accessed February 17, 2024, https://hbr.org/2019/04/research-why-managers-ignore-employees-ideas.
18. Elad N. Sherf, Subra Tangirala, and Vijaya Venkataramani, "Research: Why Managers Ignore Employees' Ideas," *Harvard Business Review*, April 8, 2019, accessed February 17, 2024, https://hbr.org/2019/04/research-why-managers-ignore-employees-ideas.
19. Roger L. Martin, "Yes, Short-Termism Really Is a Problem," October 9, 2015, accessed February 17, 2024, https://hbr.org/2015/10/yes-short-termism-really-is-a-problem.
20. Alice Park, "Alzheimer's Unlocked," *Time Magazine*, October 21, 2010, 58.
21. Jeff Dyer, Hal Gregersen, and Clayton M. Christensen, *The Innovator's DNA* (Boston: Harvard Business Review Press, 2011).
22. Jeff Dyer, Hal Gregersen, and Clayton M. Christensen, *The Innovator's DNA* (Boston: Harvard Business Review Press, 2011), 37.
23. John Medina, *Brain Rules* (Seattle, WA: Pear Press, 2008), 82.
24. Sir Ken Robinson, *Out of Our Minds: Learning to Be Creative* (West Sussex: Capstone, 2011).
25. Geoff Colvin, "A Mighty Culture of Innovation Cannot Be Taken for Granted," *Fortune*, September 16, 2013, accessed February 17, 2024, http://fortune.com/2013/08/29/a-mighty-culture-of-innovation-cannot-be-taken-for-granted/.
26. Geoff Colvin, "A Mighty Culture of Innovation Cannot Be Taken for Granted," *Fortune*, September 16, 2013, accessed February 17, 2024, http://fortune.com/2013/08/29/a-mighty-culture-of-innovation-cannot-be-taken-for-granted/.
27. Keith Sawyer, *Zig Zag* (San Francisco: Jossey-Bass, 2013), 6.

28. Anita Collins, "Music Education and the Brain: What Does It Take to Make a Change?" *Update – Applications of Research in Music Education* 32, no. 2 (2014), 1, https://doi.org/10.1177/8755123313502346.
29. Mélany Hars, Francois R. Herrmann, Gabriel Gold, René Rizzoli, and Andrea Trombetti, "Effect of Music-Based Multitask Training on Cognition and Mood in Older Adults," *Age and Ageing* 43, no. 2 (March 2014), 196–200, accessed February 17, 2024, https://doi.org/10.1093/ageing/aft163.
30. Jeff Dyer, Paul Godfrey, Robert Jensen, and David Bryce, *Strategic Management: Concepts and Cases*, 2nd ed. (New York: John Wiley & Sons, Inc., 2018), 178–179.
31. Statista Trend Compass 2020, *Statista*, accessed February 17, 2024, www.statista.com/study/69166/statista-trendcompass/.
32. James Manyika, Michael Chui, Mehdi Miremadi, Jacques Bughin, Katy George, Paul Willmott, and Martin Dewhurst, "Harnessing Automation for a Future That Works," *McKinsey Global Institute*, January 12, 2017, accessed February 10, 2024, www.mckinsey.com/global-themes/digital-disruption/harnessing-automation-for-a-future-that-works.
33. Jeff Dyer, Paul Godfrey, Robert Jensen, and David Bryce, *Strategic Management: Concepts and Cases*, 2nd ed. (New York: John Wiley & Sons, Inc., 2018), 178–179.
34. Tom Peters, "Innovate or Die: The Innovation121 A Menu of [Essential] Innovation Tactics," *Tom Peters* (blog), accessed February 17, 2024, http://tompeters.com/blogs/freestuff/uploads/Innov_tactics121_Appends011309.pdf.
35. Michael Porter and Jan Rivkin, "What Business Should Do to Restore Competitiveness," *Fortune*, October 15, 2012. Also, "Who Creates Jobs?" *The Digest*, National Bureau of Economic Research (NBER), 2011, accessed February 10, 2024.
36. U.S. Bureau of Labor Statistics, "Older Firms Have 86 Percent of Total Employment, But Startup Firms Have 90 Percent of Job Growth," 2019, accessed February 10, 2024, www.bls.gov/spotlight/2022/business-employment-dynamics-by-age-and-size/home.htm#:~:text=%E2%80%8B%20Source%3A%20U.S.%20Bureau%20of%20Labor%20Statistics.,-View%20Chart%20Data&text=In%20the%20year%20ended%20in%20March%202019%2C%20employment%20in%20firms,percent%20of%20the%20employment%20growth.
37. Tim Kane, "The Importance of Startups in Job Creation and Job Destruction," *Kauffman Foundation*, July, 2010, accessed February 10, 2024, www.kauffman.org/uploadedFiles/firm_formation_importance_of_startups.pdf.
38. "Small Business Facts," *U.S. Small Business Administration, Office of Advocacy*, April, 2022, accessed February 10, 2024, since 1990, small businesses added 8 million jobs to the economy.
39. Steven Hansen, "July 2013 ADP Jobs 200,000, A Second Good Jobs Report in a Row," *Global Economic Intersection*, July 31, 2013, accessed February 10, 2024, www.esrcheck.com/2013/07/31/july-2013-adp-national-employment-report-shows-200000-private-sector-jobs-added-during-month/.
40. Ian Hathaway, "Tech Starts: High-Technology Business Formation and Job Creation in the United States," *Kauffman Foundation*, August 20, 2013, accessed February 11, 2024, www.kauffman.org/what-we-do/research/firm-formation-and-growth-series/tech-starts-hightechnology-business-formation-and-job-creation-in-the-united-states.
41. Rose Levy and Joscelin Cooper, "Young High-Tech Firms Outpace Private Sector Job Creation," *Kauffman Foundation*, August 14, 2013, accessed February 11, 2024, www.kauffman.org/newsroom/2013/08/young-hightech-firms-outpace-private-sector-job-creation.
42. John Haltiwanger, "Business Dynamics Statistics Briefing: Job Creation, Worker Churning, and Wages at Young Businesses," *Kauffman Foundation*, November 2012, accessed February 11, 2024, www.kauffman.org/wp-content/uploads/2019/12/bds_report_7.pdf.
43. Tim Kane, "The Importance of Startups in Job Creation and Job Destruction," *Kauffman Foundation*, July 2010, accessed February 11, 2024, www.kauffman.org/uploadedFiles/firm_formation_importance_of_startups.pdf.
44. John C. Haltiwanger, Ron S. Jarmin, and Javier Miranda, "Who Creates Jobs? Small vs. Large vs. Young," *National Bureau of Economic Research*, August 2010, accessed February 11, 2024, www.nber.org/papers/w16300.
45. Anthony Breitzman and Diana Hicks, "An Analysis of Small Business Patents by Industry and Firm Size," *Small Business Association*, November 2008, accessed February 11, 2024, www.govinfo.gov/content/pkg/GOVPUB-SBA-PURL-LPS105711/pdf/GOVPUB-SBA-PURL-LPS105711.pdf.
46. Diane L. Coutu, "How Resilience Works," *Harvard Business Review*, May 2002, accessed February 11, 2024, http://hbr.org/2002/05/how-resilience-works/ar/1.
47. Karl Anders Ericsson, Ralf Th. Krampe, and Clemens Tesch-Romer, "The Role of Deliberate Practice in the Acquisition of Expert Performance," *Psychological Review* 100, no. 3 (1993), 363–406.

48. Malcolm Gladwell, *Outliers: The Story of Success* (New York: Little, Brown and Co., 2008), 38–39.
49. Diane L. Coutu, "How Resilience Works," *Harvard Business Review*, May 2002, accessed February 11, 2024, http://hbr.org/2002/05/how-resilience-works/ar/1.
50. *Wikipedia*, s.v. "Nicholas Vujicic," accessed February 11, 2024, http://en.wikipedia.org/wiki/Nick_Vujicic.
51. *Wikipedia*, s.v. "Brandon Burlsworth," accessed February 11, 2024, https://en.wikipedia.org/wiki/Brandon_Burlsworth.
52. *Wikipedia*, s.v. "Robin Cavendish," accessed February 17, 2024, https://en.wikipedia.org/wiki/Robin_Cavendish.
53. "NASA Names Headquarters after 'Hidden Figure' Mary W. Jackson," June 24, 2020, accessed February 11, 2024, www.nasa.gov/press-release/nasa-names-headquarters-after-hidden-figure-mary-w-jackson.
54. Tom Goldman, "Golden Olympic Great Oerter Dies," *NPR*, October 1, 2007, accessed January 4, 2024, www.npr.org/templates/story/story.php?storyId=14869678#:~:text=Transcript-,Al%20Oerter%2C%20the%20discus%20thrower%20who%20won%20consecutive%20gold%20medals,career%20as%20an%20abstract%20painter.
55. Lareina Yee, "Fostering Women Leaders: A Fitness Test for Your Top Team," *McKinsey & Company*, January 2015, accessed February 11, 2024, www.mckinsey.com/~/media/McKinsey/Business%20Functions/Organization/Our%20Insights/Fostering%20women%20leaders%20A%20fitness%20test%20for%20your%20top%20team/Fostering_women_leaders_A_fitness_test_for_your_top_team.pdf.
56. E. G. Chrysikou, K. Motyka, C. Nigro, S. Yang, and S. Thompson-Schill, "Functional Fixedness in Creative Thinking Tasks Depends on Stimulus Modality," *Psychology of Aesthetics, Creativity, and the Arts* 10, no. 4 (2016), 425–435, https://doi.org/10.1037/aca0000050.
57. Ken Robinson and Lou Aronica, *Creative Schools: The Grassroots Revolution That's Transforming Education* (New York: Viking, 2015), 82.
58. *Wikipedia*, s.v. "Erik Weihenmayer," accessed February 17, 2024, https://en.wikipedia.org/wiki/Erik_Weihenmayer.
59. Nicholas Wade, "In Classic vs. Modern Violins, Beauty Is in Ear of the Beholder," *The New York Times*, January 2, 2012, accessed February 11, 2024, www.nytimes.com/search?query=In+Classic+vs.+Modern+Violins%2C+Beauty+Is+in+Ear+of+the+Beholder.
60. *Wikipedia*, s.v. "Johari Window," accessed February 11, 2024, http://en.wikipedia.org/wiki/Johari_window.
61. Scott Kirsner, "The Biggest Obstacles to Innovation in Large Companies," July 30, 2018, accessed February 11, 2024, https://hbr.org/2018/07/the-biggest-obstacles-to-innovation-in-large-companies.
62. Evan Andrews, "What Was the Gordian Knot?" February 3, 2016, accessed February 17, 2024, www.history.com/news/what-was-the-gordian-knot.
63. Clayton Christensen, *The Innovator's Dilemma* (New York: HarperCollins, 2003).
64. Daniel Kahneman and Amos Tversky, "Prospect Theory: An Analysis of Decision Under Risk," *Econometrica* 47, no. 2 (March 1979), 263, accessed February 17, 2024, https://doi.org/10.2307/1914185.
65. Michael E. Raynor and Clayton M. Christensen, *The Innovator's Solution: Creating and Sustaining Successful Growth* (Boston, MA: Harvard Business School Press, 2003).
66. Daniel Goleman and Richard E. Boyatzis, "Emotional Intelligence Has 12 Elements. Which Do You Need to Work On?," February 11, 2024, https://hbr.org/2017/02/emotional-intelligence-has-12-elements-which-do-you-need-to-work-on.
67. Greg Lalicker and Peter Lambert, "Digging Deep for Organizational Innovation," *McKinsey Quarterly*, April 2018, accessed February 11, 2024, www.mckinsey.com/business-functions/organization/our-insights/digging-deep-for-organizational-innovation?cid=other-eml-alt-mkq-mck-oth-1804&hlkid=ed56243672324879ba5389819bf0fa9a&hctky=2468311&hdpid=7a46958e-e879-4514-8bd6-56926f9394f1.
68. Statista TrendCompass 2020, *Statista*, accessed February 17, 2024, www.statista.com/study/69166/statista-trendcompass/.
69. *Wikipedia*, s.v. "William Gibson," accessed February 17, 2024, http://en.wikiquote.org/wiki/William_Gibson.
70. Charles Duhigg, *The Power of Habit* (New York: Random House, 2014), 159–160.
71. "Sputnik and the Dawn of the Space Age," accessed February 11, 2024, https://history.nasa.gov/sputnik/.
72. Charles Duhigg, *The Power of Habit* (New York: Random House, 2014), 159–160.
73. "History of Edison Motion Pictures," accessed February 17, 2024, www.loc.gov/collections/edison-company-motion-pictures-and-sound-recordings/articles-and-essays/history-of-edison-motion-pictures/.

74. Katherine A. Foss, "How Epidemics of the Past Changed the Way Americans Lived," *Smithsonian*, April 1, 2020, accessed February 17, 2024, www.zocalopublicsquare.org/2020/04/01/what-we-can-learn-from-epidemics-covid-19-tuberculosis/ideas/essay/?xid=PS_smithsonian or www.smithsonianmag.com/history/how-epidemics-past-forced-americans-promote-health-ended-up-improving-life-this-country-180974555.

75. Alan Murray and David Meyer, "The Pandemic Has Been an Impetus for Innovation," *Fortune*, May 6, 2020, accessed November 27, 2023, https://fortune.com/2020/05/06/pandemic-innovation-impetus-ceo-daily/.

76. Margaret Talev, "Obama Says Better Public School System Key to Economic Recovery," *BusinessWeek*, September 2011, accessed November 27, 2023, www.bloomberg.com/news/articles/2011-09-24/obama-says-better-public-school-system-key-to-economic-recovery.

77. Susan Lund, James Manyika, Scott Nyquist, Lenny Mendonca, and Sreenivas Ramaswamy, "Game Changers: Five Opportunities for U.S. Growth and Renewal," *McKinsey*, July 2013, accessed November 27, 2023, www.mckinsey.com/featured-insights/americas/us-game-changers (McKinsey login may be required).

78. Klaus Schwab, "The Global Competitiveness Report 2020," *World Economic Forum*, accessed November 27, 2023, www.weforum.org/publications/the-global-competitiveness-report-2020/.

79. Klaus Schwab, "The Global Competitiveness Report 2020," *World Economic Forum*, accessed November 27, 2023, www.weforum.org/publications/the-global-competitiveness-report-2020/.

80. International Institute for Management Development, "World Competitiveness Ranking," accessed November 27, 2023, www.imd.org/centers/world-competitiveness-center/rankings/world-competitiveness/.

81. International Institute for Management Development, "World Competitiveness Ranking," accessed November 27, 2023, www.imd.org/centers/world-competitiveness-center/rankings/world-competitiveness/.

82. International Institute for Management Development, "World Competitiveness Ranking," accessed November 27, 2023, www.imd.org/centers/world-competitiveness-center/rankings/world-competitiveness/.

83. Institute of Medicine, National Academy of Sciences, and National Academy of Engineering, *Rising Above the Gathering Storm: Energizing and Employing America for a Brighter Economic Future* (Washington, DC: The National Academies Press, 2007), February 17, 2024, www.nap.edu/catalog.php?record_id=11463.

84. Hu Qing, "Laoshan District Nurtures Technology Innovation," *China Daily*, May 18, 2014, accessed February 17, 2024, www.chinadaily.com.cn/m/qingdao/2014-05/18/content_17548004.htm.

85. "Alibaba's IPO: From Bazar to Bonanza," *The Economist*, May 10, 2014, accessed February 17, 2024, www.economist.com/node/21601869/print.

86. "Tencent Versus Alibaba: A Complete Guide to an Increasingly Fierce Rivalry (INFOGRAPHIC)," *Techinasia*, accessed February 17, 2024, www.techinasia.com/tencent-alibaba-complete-guide-increasingly-fierce-rivalry-infographic/.

87. Michael Mandel, "The Failed Promise of Innovation in the U.S.," *BusinessWeek*, June 3, 2009, accessed February 17, 2024, www.bloomberg.com/news/articles/2009-06-03/the-failed-promise-of-innovation-in-the-u-dot-s.

88. Sir Ken Robinson, *Out of Our Minds* (Mankato, MN: Capstone, 2011), 67.

89. Tom Peters, "Educate for a Creative Society," *YouTube Video*, posted by "BetterLifeCoaches," March 8, 2007, accessed February 17, 2024, www.youtube.com/watch?v=h_w4AfflmeM.

90. Shanna R. Daly, Erika A. Mosyjowski, and Colleen M. Seifert. "Teaching Creativity in Engineering Courses," *Journal of Engineering Education* 103, no. 3 (July 2014), 417–449, https://onlinelibrary.wiley.com/doi/abs/10.1002/jee.20048.

91. Peter Gray, "As Children's Freedom Has Declined, So Has Their Creativity," *Psychology Today*, September 17, 2012, accessed February 17, 2024, www.psychologytoday.com/blog/freedom-learn/201209/children-s-freedom-has-declined-so-has-their-creativity.

2   The Elements of Innovation

It is important to clarify the meaning of the term innovation. In general, innovation is the application of a purposeful process to transform new ideas and opportunities that generate new or added value into results. Innovation involves a progression of ideation, creation, invention, innovation, and initiation of a new venture. Ideation is the generation of ideas, the more the better, by inspired people. Creativity is the selection, association, and combination of ideas that have value.

In this chapter, a common ground for what we mean by innovation, a term often overused to the point of meaninglessness, is addressed. We also provide working definitions of imagination, creativity, and innovation and briefly present and discuss 12 elements of innovation (degrees, direction, principles and tenets, criteria, diffusion, value, types, risk, thresholds, pacing, and finally, disruptive innovation), which in turn inform the full innovation and entrepreneurship competency framework presented throughout the book.

Defining Innovation

Creativity experts Teresa Amabile, Regina Conti, Heather Coon, Jeffrey Lazenby, and Michael Herron argue,

> All innovation begins with creative ideas. . . . We define innovation as the successful implementation of creative ideas within an organization. In this view, creativity by individuals and teams is a starting point for innovation; the first is necessary but not a sufficient condition for the second.[1]

Innovation requires first ideating and then acting on creative ideas to make a tangible difference in the goods and/or services around which the innovation occurs.

Keith Sawyer writes, "Creativity is largely domain-specific – that the ability to be creative in any given domain, whether physics, painting, or musical performance, is based on long years of study and mastery of a domain-specific set of cognitive structures."[2] When you have domain-specific knowledge, such as being knowledgeable in the field of medicine, engineering, or computer science, you are empowered to be creative and invent something entirely new.

An invention is the identification and documentation of an idea that has the potential for becoming an innovation and commercialization. It is possible to temporarily protect intellectual property with a patent. A patent is a form of exclusive rights to anything that can be made by an individual that is granted for a specified period. A patented invention may or may not result in an innovation. If your invention meets the criteria – technical feasibility, business viability, and consumer desirability – there is the possibility of an innovation. If the innovation meets the criteria, it is then feasible to further prototype, iterate, pivot, and commercialize the innovation into a new business

DOI: 10.4324/9781003034308-3

venture through the creation of a business model that anticipates costs and revenue to provide a framework for financial viability.

Table 2.1 provides some existing definitions of innovation considered in defining the discipline of innovation using new competency categories and elements.

Table 2.1 Illustration of Innovation Definitions

The ***Oxford Dictionary*** defines *innovation* as "the action process of innovating."[3] Innovating is defined as "make changes in something established, especially by introducing new methods, ideas, or products."[4] It traces its origins to the mid-16th century: from the Latin *innovat- "renewed,* altered," from the verb *innovare,* from *in-* "into" + *novare* "make new" (from *novus* "new"). The many synonyms include *change, alteration, revolution, upheaval, transformation, metamorphosis, reorganization, restructuring, rearrangement, recasting, remodeling, renovation, restyling, variation; new measures, new methods, new devices, novelty, newness, unconventionality, modernization, modernism*; a break with tradition, a shift of emphasis, a departure, a change of direction; *informally,* a shake up or a shakedown.[5]

Merriam-Webster defines *innovation* as "a new idea, device, or method: The act or process of introducing new ideas, devices, or methods."[6] Synonyms include *brainchild, coinage, concoction, contrivance, creation, invention,* and *wrinkle.*[7]

Joe Tidd and John Bessant, authors of ***Managing Innovation***, define *innovation* as "the process of turning ideas into reality and capturing value from them."[8] Their process is organized into four phases: searching for innovative opportunities, selecting the opportunity, implementing the opportunity, and capturing the value.

Jeffrey Dance, after reviewing 30+ definitions, synthesizes them down to define two key ingredients of innovation: (1) something fresh (new, original, or improved) and (2) something that creates value.[9]

Rod Coombs, Paolo Saviotti, and Vivien Walsh, from a more economic/academic perspective, and building on **Stephen Davies's *The Diffusion of Process Innovations,*** [10] identify two types of innovation: (1) innovation that consists of technologically simple and inexpensive processes (e.g., televisions, washing machines, etc.) and (2) innovation that consists of technologically complex expensive innovations (e.g., process innovation producing chemicals or steel).[11]

While the pursuit of a definition of innovation coalesces around the constructs of newness and value, the concept of innovation (and, as we will see, the concept of entrepreneurship) is often understood differently by multiple constituents across numerous disciplines. Researchers, practitioners, and politicians often overuse and under define the term to suit a too broad or narrow perspective. Because what constitutes innovation is frequently subject to each individual's perspective, it is difficult to objectively measure. The inability to precisely measure innovation makes it difficult to compare innovation effectiveness across companies and countries.

A review of electronic and non-electronic sources produces over 40 definitions of innovation. These range from problem solving to creating value and everything in between, including politicians positioning innovation as "the creation of something that improves the way we live our lives."[12]

Because innovation is essential to the viability of organizations and global economics, the purposeful outlining of the elements of innovation is necessary to inform the practice of innovation and facilitate the learning and practicing of the innovation competencies. Harnessing the collective learning of an organization through the innovation competencies also provides a better foundation for developing human capital (talent) for the future. While human capital is not explicitly outlined as one of the 12 elements, it is a key factor in the overall innovation process and is implicit in our understanding of innovation and creativity. Innovation and entrepreneurship cannot occur without individuals, working independently or with others, to ideate, innovate, and create value.

Definitions: Imagination, Creativity, and Innovation

People are the center of imagination, creativity, innovation, and entrepreneurship and collectively they provide the potential for human development and economic growth. All too often we use imagination as a synonym for creativity, creativity as a synonym for innovation, and creativity and innovation as synonyms for entrepreneurship. Given the highly interactive nature of imagination, creativity, innovation, and entrepreneurship, this is an easy mistake to make. Yet each of these contributes to the flow of our thinking in unique and powerful ways and therefore needs to be understood independently and without confusion. Mihaly Csikszentmihalyi writes, "This optimal experience is what I have called flow, because many of the respondents described the feeling when things are going well as an almost automatic, effortless, yet highly focused state of consciousness."[13]

Imagination is an extraordinary power. Creativity expert Sir Ken Robinson defines imagination as "the ability to bring to mind things that are not present in our senses."[14] Our imaginations provide us the opportunity to travel through time, looking back to *what was*, to the present at *what is*, and into the future at *what might be*. According to Karen Weintraub for *USA Today*,

> imagination depends on memory. Imagining what a new piece of music might sound like requires you to play with bits of music that you carry in your head, to have an understanding of and memory for music so that you can manipulate notes to create something new.[15]

But where do good ideas come from? They cannot be born of memory alone. While chance favors the connected mind, ideation also relies on time and what author Steve Johnson calls the "slow hunch."[16] The more building blocks of knowledge you have accumulated, the more likely you are to combine ideas in ways they have never been combined before. Imagination and creativity can be additionally amplified through catalytic leadership and by building organizational cultures that enable people to collaborate with others.

At their core, innovators and entrepreneurs are problem solvers. When faced with obstacles, innovators rethink essential features and produce better products. For example, a number of years ago the kitchen tool for peeling apples, carrots, and potatoes had a boxy, narrow handle that was difficult to grip. In the 1980s, Sam Farber, an industrial designer, observed his wife, Betsey, who had mild arthritis, struggling to peel an apple using this functional but uncomfortable peeler. This inspired Farber to redesign the tool with a soft, round handle to match the natural curvature of a hand. As we will see throughout this book, often the role of innovation in entrepreneurship is identifying the need for innovation in a specific market – in Farber's case, people with hands that suffered from arthritis.

Imagination is the cultivation of ideas that are not present in our senses. Creativity is the ability to generate ideas that have value – aesthetic, cultural, economic, legal, political, societal, environmental, educational, and technological. Creativity is achieved through expertise, questioning, observation, networking, experimentation, and association resulting in actionable insights: creations.[17] Imagination and creativity are predecessors to innovation, the transformation of ideas into results. Sam Farber used his creative insight to develop a better kitchen tool design, and then pivoted that design into a set of innovative kitchen utensils that were both functional and comfortable, called Oxo Good Grips. Oxo Good Grips utensils have a soft plastic handle that matches the natural curvature of the hand.[18]

Innovation can be more precisely defined as follows: people applying a purposeful process to transform ideas and opportunities that create new or added value into results that provide for economic growth. Innovation is more than adding incremental features to products. It is more than generating many ideas through brainstorming. It is more than producing many prototypes and it is more than following a trial-and-error process.

The Elements of Innovation

Because the word *innovation* is often imprecisely defined, it is overused and applied in situations where it is not entirely relevant. For example, *innovation* has been offered as an overarching solution for addressing economic problems and for implying that one product is more original than another. This leads to cascading misunderstandings about what innovation is. It is suggested here that this misunderstanding often stems from a lack of awareness of the many elements of innovation.

In essence, "[a]n academic discipline or field of study is a branch of knowledge, taught and researched as part of higher education."[19] Well-established disciplines have a set of elements that provide the foundation for ensuring understanding. Consider some examples of elements in science, writing and poetry, music, art, and film, as illustrated in Figure 2.1. As can be seen, discipline is linked by multiple elements that provide clarity of thought regarding what constitutes that discipline. For example, music as a discipline is connected by dynamics, rhythm, melody, harmony, and tempo.

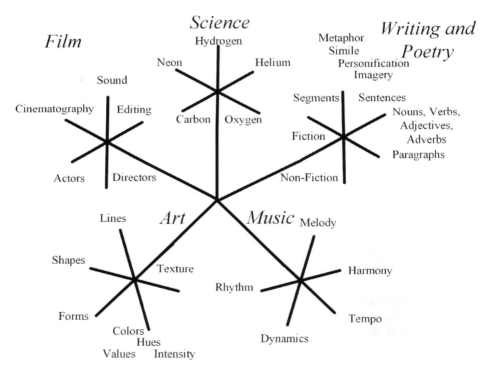

Figure 2.1 Illustration of the Elements in Disciplines

Similarly, innovation can be better understood by identifying and outlining its elements. Innovation can be separated into 12 discrete elements. Thinking about the innovation elements from a holistic perspective provides a richer understanding of what innovation is and suggests insights into how innovation can be viewed, learned, and practiced via 12 innovation and entrepreneurship competencies. The elements in Figure 2.2 provide a foundation for more precise and clearer understanding of innovation.

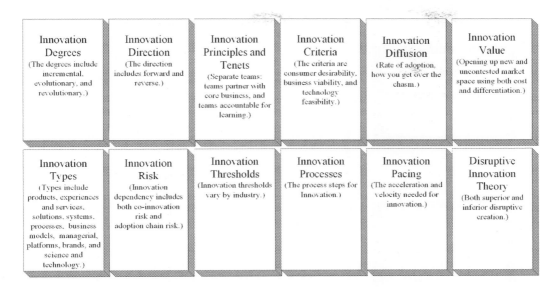

Figure 2.2 Illustration of the Elements of Innovation

The elements of innovation provide a more complete and accurate understanding of innovation and entrepreneurship, help to identify and build future talent, and increase our ability to innovate. Because research studies on competitiveness, innovation, and education reveal that we are at risk of underutilizing our overall potential, it is increasingly important to revisit these foundational elements so that we can innovate more effectively.

Innovation Degrees

Setting disruptive innovation aside for the moment (more on this in Chapter 10, "Innovation Theory"), there are three innovation degrees: incremental, evolutionary, and revolutionary.[20] Incremental innovations are small improvements, evolutionary innovations are medium improvements, and revolutionary innovations are large improvements. They differ in how they are positioned with respect to offerings, businesses, customers, and markets.

The chart in Figure 2.3 illustrates differences based on an innovation's offerings, businesses, customers, and markets and their impact on economic activity and employment. Incremental and evolutionary innovations are, at times, referred to as *continuous innovations*; revolutionary innovations are also called *discontinuous innovations*.

Incremental

Incremental innovations focus on existing offerings, businesses, customers, and markets. For example, incremental innovations might focus on improving efficiency-oriented processes by removing waste from operational systems to reduce cost and time constraints or on product and service improvements like providing less expensive computer memory in tablets or adding more features to toothpaste and detergents.

Incremental improvements include specific optimization interventions that organizations use to remove waste and inefficiencies. Both Six Sigma and Lean are well-regarded managerial quality

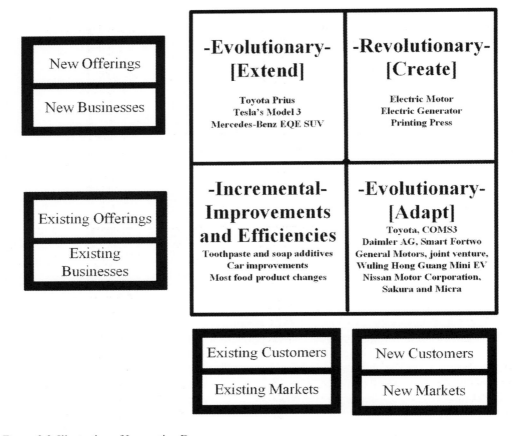

New Offerings

New Businesses

-Evolutionary-
[Extend]

Toyota Prius
Tesla's Model 3
Mercedes-Benz EQE SUV

-Revolutionary-
[Create]

Electric Motor
Electric Generator
Printing Press

Existing Offerings

Existing
Businesses

-Incremental-
Improvements
and Efficiencies

Toothpaste and soap additives
Car improvements
Most food product changes

-Evolutionary-
[Adapt]

Toyota, COMS3
Daimler AG, Smart Fortwo
General Motors, joint venture,
Wuling Hong Guang Mini EV
Nissan Motor Corporation,
Sakura and Micra

Existing Customers

Existing Markets

New Customers

New Markets

Figure 2.3 Illustration of Innovation Degrees

Source: Adapted from: Tim Brown, *Change by Design*, (New York: Harper, 2009), 161.

improvement programs that explicitly target the removal of many types of organizational waste and variability. These efficiency-oriented innovations are incremental and can result in decreased economic growth and reduction in employment opportunities.[21] Because the goal of the quality improvement programs is to remove inefficiencies and waste, the consequences can be a reduction of the workforce.

An incremental innovation can be used to differentiate products for marketing purposes. Kellogg CEO John Bryant claimed that the Peanut Butter Pop-Tart was an innovation and one of the cereal company's most important products of 2013. By reviewing the definition of innovation outlined here, though, we can see that while the peanut butter flavor is a creative addition to the Pop-Tart line of products, it does not create added value significant enough to stimulate economic growth and is therefore a merely incremental innovation.[22]

Evolutionary

Extended

Evolutionary extended innovations are created when new offerings and new business models are provided to existing customers in existing markets. Evolutionary extended innovations for transportation include cars, trucks, trains, planes, and e-bikes. Electronic vehicles of all types provide value because of their long-term savings on maintenance and repairs, lower operational costs, and less environmental impact.[23]

Adapted

Evolutionary adapted innovations are created when existing offerings and existing business models are provided to new customers and new markets. Examples of evolutionary adaptation are Lululemon Athletica's new apparel market category, athleisure, yoga pants, the microcar markets, and the retrofitting of residences and commercial buildings, a new market, to use less energy through insulation, heating, ventilation, and air-conditioning upgrades.

Revolutionary

Revolutionary innovations are those that have a higher impact and value. These innovations focus on new offerings, new businesses, and new customers and markets. Because of their discontinuity, the impact can be both substantial and scalable. Unlike both incremental and evolutionary innovations, revolutionary innovations are expected to have a positive impact on economic growth and employment. The personal computer, electric motors and generators, solar panels, the printing press, antibiotics, and vaccines are just a few examples of revolutionary innovations.

Before Johannes Gutenberg invented the moveable type printing press, books were produced entirely by hand. Gutenberg's movable metal type made mass production easy, quickly supplanting the handwritten manuscripts that came before and revolutionizing book production methods across the world.[24] Gutenberg's breakthrough would lead to thousands of innovations in printing, reading, and communication.

During the US Civil War from 1861 to 1865, more soldiers died of infections than all other causes.[25] Science had neither discerned nor discovered the concepts of germ theory and inoculation. The discovery of microorganisms and the development of vaccines resulted in a paradigm shift, leading to innovations in healthcare that dramatically improved our understanding of medicine and our collective well-being. Scientists such as Louis Pasteur and Joseph Lister pioneered work in microorganisms and antiseptic medicine leading to numerous innovations in science and healthcare. The Listerine antiseptic mouthwash, for example, was named after Joseph Lister, who advocated sterilizing instruments for surgery.[26]

Combinatorial

Combinatorial innovations combine two or more existing innovation concepts into a new unique concept for new markets and new customers. Combinatorial innovations include innovation degrees evolutionary and revolutionary, but not incremental. For instance, oceanic wind turbines that are integrated with electrolyzers can generate hydrogen from desalinated seawater. An electrolyzer is a device that uses electricity to split water into hydrogen and oxygen gas through electrolysis. Nearby chemical plants on dedicated platforms then process the hydrogen, combining it with nitrogen to make ammonia. No need to connect to underwater power cables.[27]

Innovation Types

Because there are many types, innovations have characteristics that are polymorphic. Organizing innovation into ten categories makes it is easier to understand how you can use multiple types of innovation simultaneously. The ten fundamental innovation types depicted in Figure 2.4 include products, customer experiences, solutions, systems, processes, business models, managerial, platforms, brands, and science. While each individually has the potential for value added impact, it is often the combination of the types that can have the most value for both non-profit and for-profit ventures.

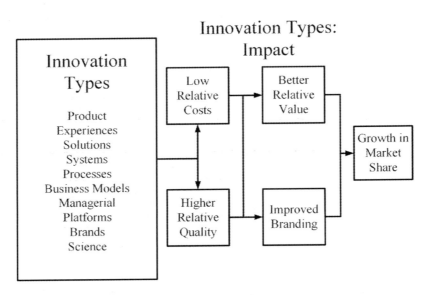

Figure 2.4 Illustration of Innovation Types

Source: Adapted from Tidd, J., & Bessant, J. R. (2013). *Managing innovation: Integrating technological, market and organizational change* (5th ed.) New York: John Wiley, p. 427.

Of course, innovation is about much more than new products. A discussion among experts in the field for *BusinessWeek* argues that it is also about reinventing business processes.

> Today, innovation is about much more than new products. It is about reinventing business processes and building entirely new markets that meet untapped customer needs. Most important, as the Internet and globalization widen the pool of new ideas, it's about selecting and executing the right ideas and bringing them to market in record time.[28]

Disney, Southwest Airlines, IKEA, and Starbucks, for example, have effectively used the concept of "customer experience innovation" by providing unique value-added solutions that have been difficult for competitors to duplicate. For example, Disney combines three related masteries: the mastery of the re-creation of famous settings, the mastery of interpersonal skills training for the cast, and the mastery of action where the cast are trained to manage combustion points. Combustion points are negative events that occur when the fine-tuned customer experience breaks down. The cast are trained to identify a combustion point and take action to rectify it prior to the explosion.[29]

Organizations and businesses continuously strive to provide new value for customers. Sales growth, high costs, commoditization, and increased competition are but a few of the drivers for this customer-centric approach. Innovation types, however, include many options other than products and customer experiences. Managerial innovation, for example, has the potential for sizable economic impact. Too often, however, traditional managerial thinking dominates most organizations, minimizing innovation opportunities.[30] Yet, over time, managerial innovation has a notable record of accomplishment upon which to build.

For example, in the late 1800s, American engineer Frederick Winslow Taylor developed "scientific management," a process that promotes efficiency by measuring and adjusting human movement to prevent waste.[31] For instance, Taylor determined the optimum quantity of coal to move per shovel-load for workers to stoke a furnace most efficiently. Similarly, revolutionary managerial innovations include Eli Whitney's development of standardized parts and Henry Ford's assembly line.[32] Together with the concept of standardized parts, Ford's assembly line enabled him to efficiently manufacture inexpensive products in high volumes. Ford's Model T made personal transportation affordable, changing the US economy and the world economy.

Peter Drucker was an exceptional managerial innovator. In 1993, Peter Drucker's *Concept of the Corporation* described the inner workings of General Motors and suggested that Alfred Sloan should decentralize the company. This suggestion met with the resistance characteristic of revolutionary innovations.[33] Drucker contributed to innovative managerial thinking by his focus on the conception of the knowledge worker. Drucker was a leader in thinking that organizations should contribute to their customers beyond profits and highlighted the importance of public, private, and non-profit organizations.[34]

It can be argued, however, that managerial innovation has not progressed very much since Taylor, Whitney, Ford, and Drucker. According to management expert Gary Hamel, management innovation is caught in a time warp. "Few companies have a well-honed process for continuous management innovation," writes Hamel.

> Most businesses have a formal methodology for product innovation, and many have R&D groups that explore the frontiers of science. Virtually every organization on the planet has in recent years worked systematically to reinvent its business processes for the sake of speed and efficiency. How odd, then, that so few companies apply a similar degree of diligence to the kind of innovation that matters most: Management innovation.[35]

At times it seems that the willingness to develop and apply managerial innovation to keep up with the increasing speed of change is comparable to driving a Ford Model T on the autobahn.

Hamel believes that this lack of managerial innovation is restricting organizations' ability to provide a competitive advantage.[36] "Most companies," he argues, "are built for continuous improvement, rather than for discontinuous innovation. They know how to get better, but they do not know how to get different."[37] Hamel notes that "we are prisoners of our own mental models about management."[38] Managerial innovations should receive more emphasis since they can have such high impact. Hamel's innovation stack ranks types of innovation, placing management innovation at the top because it provides a difficult-to-duplicate competitive advantage.[39] Lower in the stack are strategic innovation, ecosystem innovation, product innovation, and finally operational (process efficiency) innovation.

Innovation Matrix

To address this "managerial innovation roadblock," we suggest that innovation types and degrees can best be understood via an innovation matrix. Again, setting aside disruptive innovation for the moment, which is discussed in Chapter 10, the innovation matrix outlined in Figure 2.5 describes a more precise way of identifying an innovation through the intersection of types and degrees.

Innovation Direction

Innovation direction is a concept that encompasses forward and reverse innovation. Innovation direction is a notion that is based on the source and target of the innovation. A forward

The Innovation Matrix			
	Innovation Degrees		
	Incremental	Evolutionary	Revolutionary
Products	Product additives	Smartphones	Xerox, heart-lung machine
Services	Automated checkout	IKEA, Whole Foods	Disney, Sesame Street
Solutions	Airplane Wi-Fi	Heliocopter	Airplane
Systems	Windows and Apple OS	Artificial intelligence	The Internet
Processes	Design thinking	Lean and Six Sigma	Ford assembly line
Business Models	Subscription model	One-stop shopping	Microfinance
Managerial	Participative leadership styles	Statistical process control	Decentralization
Platforms	Jet engine efficiency	Airbnb and Uber	Intel x86 Microprocesors
Brands	Branded ecosystems	Coca-Cola	Trademarks
Science and Technology	Antibacterial paint	Refrigeration	Vaccines

(Left side vertical label: Innovation Types)

Figure 2.5 Illustration of Innovation Matrix

innovation would have its source in country X and the target in country X. A reverse innovation would have its source in country Y and later targeted to a different country such as country X. Country X or Y could be a developed or developing country. This overall concept of forward and reverse innovations is depicted in Figure 2.6, with country specific problem, solution, and value direction shown in Figure 2.7.

A forward innovation source would be from a developed country targeted to a developing country. A reverse innovation source, on the other hand, would be a developing country in which an innovation developed there spreads to a developing country. Reverse innovation is not meant to be pejorative. It is an innovation element that is addressing the realities of different economies and how the offering is matched with the consumer. These two concepts are based on the fact that a differential exists between developed and developing countries and that a solution that is designed to work in one country may or may not work in another.

Developing countries can potentially have a sizable advantage over developed countries. Economic growth rates outside the United States are higher than that of the US economy. Ninety-five percent of the world's consumers live outside of the United States.[40] Furthermore, of the world's eight billion people, the majority cannot purchase products from the United States.[41] This under-served market provides interesting possibilities and opportunities for innovation.

For example, it is estimated that in developing economies, there are 1.1 billion households that are underserved and not connected to the Internet.[42] By providing more efficient networks,

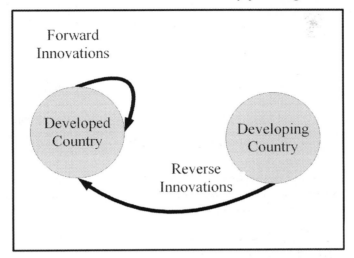

Figure 2.6 Illustration of Forward and Reverse Innovation

Source: Adapted from General Electric's Jeffrey Immelt; Vijay Govindarajan and Chris Trimble, *Reverse Innovation: Create Far From Home, Win Everywhere*; C. K. Prahalad, *The Fortune at the Bottom of the Pyramid.*

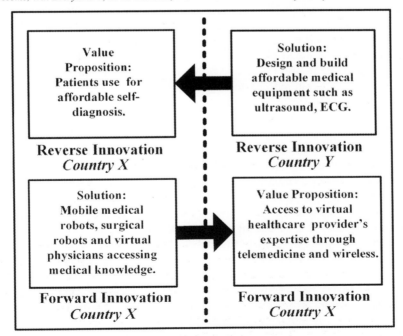

Figure 2.7 Illustration of Forward and Reverse Innovation Examples

Source: Adapted from General Electric's Jeffrey Immelt; Vijay Govindarajan and Chris Trimble, *Reverse Innovation: Create Far From Home, Win Everywhere*; C. K. Prahalad, *The Fortune at the Bottom of the Pyramid.*

affordable smartphones, and apps that use minimal amounts of data, billions of people worldwide could have mobile access. Internet.org is a consortium comprising Facebook, Samsung, Nokia, Qualcomm, and Ericsson, which have agreed to partner to pursue both humanitarian goals and potentially profitable new markets.[43] The Internet is the primary means of virtually connecting friends and families as well as the foundation of the knowledge-based worldwide economy.[44]

Forward Innovation

Forward innovations are those where the source and target of the innovation are the same country. The fundamental design of the innovation would be dependent on the characteristics of the country.

Cloud-based networks, artificial intelligence, knowledge databases, super computers (IBM's Watson), big data, and knowledge databases can be combined to provide a global virtual healthcare system to enable physicians to diagnose diseases more effectively. Google Glasses can potentially provide physicians with access to medical providers for consultations, medical records (IBM's Watson), expert systems, and knowledge bases.

In healthcare, new technology is available to extend the reach and improve the effectiveness and accessibility of physicians. InTouch Health's RP-VITA (Remote Presence Virtual + Independent Telemedicine Assistant) is a hospital robot that can assist a physician and help reduce time and effort by a physician and therefore a physician's costs. The RP-7i® allows a remote clinician to see and interact with patients. The da Vinci Surgical System is a robot that surgeons can use to perform less invasive procedures thereby improving recovery time.

Cholesterol and triglycerides are fatty materials that stick to the inside of arterial blood vessels causing them to thicken and limit blood flow. A stent is a medical device the size of a ballpoint pen spring for holding a cardiac artery open after mechanically widening an artery. There are many different types of stents such as bare-metal stents and drug-eluting stents dissolve and help prevent scarring. The dissolving heart stent, made of biodegradable plastic, can be used to keep a patient's artery open after surgery and eventually dissolve allowing the artery to more naturally heal while reducing the likelihood of blood clots.[45] Absorb™, Abbott's drug-eluting and dissolvable heart stent, is designed to assist in restoring blood flow to the heart by keeping a blocked heart vessel open to enable the artery to return to its healthy state.[46]

Reverse Innovation

Dartmouth professor Vijay Govindarajan, who helped to popularize the term, describes reverse innovation as innovation that occurs in developing countries and is later marketed as a low-cost innovation in more developed countries.[47] The goal of innovation in developing countries, as described by Govindarajan, is "to change our innovation paradigm from value for money to value for many. And value for many implies frugal innovation; frugal thinking."[48] The fundamental design of the innovation would be less dependent of the characteristics of the country.

If the direction is from the developing to a developed country the opportunities are viable because the innovation can be designed to be convenient, affordable, or customizable. If the direction is from a developed to a developing country the opportunities are not as viable because the innovation may be difficult to design for convenience, affordability, or customizability. This is because of the differential in per capita incomes and that the innovation may require infrastructure resources that are not in place, such as water, energy, or network capability.

Reverse innovations whose origins are in the developing countries are ideal for innovating in health and wellness because of the extent of the needs of the people and the size of the consumer market. There is a large need for medical devices in the developing countries that are portable, affordable, and convenient. Ultrasound and electrocardiogram medical devices are examples of reverse innovations designed for developing countries. These reverse innovations provide a more affordable value proposition because they can be specifically designed and marketed in the developing countries and then marketed back to the developed countries with minimal rework.

In developing countries, the design thinking process must take into consideration the limited quantities of aggregate resources and the population base. For example, there are dramatic differences in per capita income, resources, infrastructure, and the availability of healthcare professionals in developing versus developed countries. As a result, the process of innovation in developing countries, such as China and India, focuses on the need for affordable products. Once created, these products can be sold in industrialized countries creating new markets, adoption, and uses for these innovations.

Reverse innovations are potentially high payoff because focus on affordability in developing countries can create products that have the prospect of spreading to developed markets as well. In *The Fortune at the Bottom of the Pyramid: Eradicating Poverty Through Profits,* C. K. Prahalad describes the sales potential of the billions of underserved consumers in the world and how entrepreneurial ventures could unleash their economic power in developing markets.[49]

Low standards of living, shortage of food, and lack of access to necessities, such as clean water and healthcare, in developing countries mean potential for the growth of future markets. Value propositions created by entrepreneurs can address these poverties in developing countries, such as African countries, China, and India, and can increase the likelihood of their economic expansion. Nestle has marketed the Maggi noodle, low in fat and containing whole wheat for nutrition, in India and Pakistan as these emerging economies transition from non-consumers to consumers. This product created a growing market in developing countries and is now also sold in developed countries.

There are opportunities in both developing and developed countries for improving healthcare. A desirable healthcare system would provide early diagnosis, affordable care, improved outcomes, prevention of unnecessary infections, the elimination or reduction of physician and patient travel, reduced hospital visits and readmissions, reduced emergency department visits, and convenient access to the latest medical knowledge and expert medical professionals. Large numbers of people in developing countries do not have access to hospitals or medical centers. The number of physicians per capita is lower in developing countries compared to in developed ones. In 2010, for example, Africa had around two physicians per 10,000 people, while in Europe there were 33 physicians per 10,000 – 15 times as many.[50] Between 2012 and 2017, in each of the EU member states, the number of physicians per 100,000 inhabitants increased,[51] while the ratio in Africa remained largely unchanged over the same time span.[52]

Technology and medical knowledge can be integrated in a way that has the potential to improve the overall patient experience. For example, affordable smartphone medical devices for use in developing countries can diagnose diseases for early interventions; a head-worn sonar medical device can diagnose strokes, the third leading cause of death, for prompt treatment;[53] Healthspot's Telemedicine Kiosk (Doc-In-A-Box), now offered in retail pharmacies and rural areas, extends the reach of physicians by combining retail clinics with physicians and can be powered by solar panels for use in developing countries; Max Little developed a voice diagnostic tool that uses mathematical algorithms to detect Parkinson's disease *over the phone.*[54]

Reverse innovations, designed to provide affordable medical equipment to developing countries, can be remarketed to rural areas in developed countries, bringing the "hospital" to the patients. The low-cost GE portable ultrasound machine was developed for the China market and is now sold for use in ambulances and other emergency vehicles in the United States. GE's portable electrocardiograph (ECG) machine was originally built by GE Healthcare for doctors in India and China. The ECG is now offered in the United States at an 80% markdown compared to similar products. Affordable medical devices for self-diagnosis, such as those that collect biological data for blood pressure, glucose, and heart rates, can also help to improve health and to extend the reach of physicians.

In the realm of contemporary healthcare, the real world meets the world of science fiction. Gene Roddenberry's *Star Trek*, an American science-fiction series, is set in the Milky Way galaxy in the 23rd century. In the show, Dr. Leonard McCoy uses "the tricorder" to instantaneously diagnose patients aboard the USS *Enterprise*.[55] In the real world of the 21st century, five-year-old Nelson De Brouwer received a brain injury after falling from a 36-foot-high window. Nelson's father, Walter De Brouwer, carried him, unconscious and with the left side of his head caved in, to an emergency room in Brussels, Belgium. While his son was in the intensive care unit, Walter got the idea to build a handheld medical device that gathers and interprets vital signs.[56] The non-invasive Scanadu Scout uses a small sensing device to capture more than five vital signs: pulse transit time, heart rate (pulse), electrical heart activity, temperature, heart rate variability, and blood oxygenation (pulse oximetry). The Scanadu Scout is held up to your head, and the biological data is transferred via Bluetooth to a smartphone app in real time. While failure to obtain FDA approval in 2016[57] put Scanadu on hold, it reveals a path to innovation that continues in healthcare.[58,59]

Innovation Risk

Companies are expanding their customer promises, value propositions, by building ecosystems that integrate an expanding list of services and products. The innovation ecosystem encompasses internal ecosystems – what a company does that is independent of other companies – and external ecosystems – what a company does that is dependent on other companies.

In a world of co-dependent ecosystems, for everyone to win, all partners need to coordinate their efforts so that each executes their roles effectively and innovation risks are managed rather than ignored. If a company focuses on their own innovations without considering the broader ecosystems that they are dependent upon, their innovations can fail. These interdependencies are outlined in Figure 2.8.

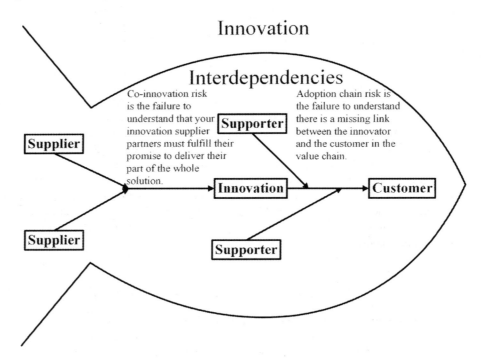

Figure 2.8 Illustration of Innovation Interdependencies

Source: Adapted from Ron Adner and Rahul Kapoor, "Value Creation in Innovation Ecosystems," *Strategic Management Journal*, 31:3, (2010): 309.

Apple's success started with their ability to provide well-designed computer devices. Then Apple began building an ecosystem, starting with the combination of iPod and iTunes. Apple continues to expand its ecosystem into cars, airplanes, movies, and TV. Google, Amazon, and Microsoft are now competing with Apple to build their own ecosystems in efforts to retain and grow their customer bases.

Through both acquisition and growth, Amazon has been systematically building an online retail ecosystem. This ecosystem began as an online bookstore and has expanded into a one-stop shopping experience. Amazon has built a supply chain and distribution system based on the integration of information systems, bar codes, automated conveyers, robotic technology, and shipping partners. At the end of the value chain is the customer and, for Amazon, the ideal customer has a Kindle. Kindle is the Trojan horse of the Amazon ecosystem. The Kindle business model involves offering the device itself at a low price, with hopes that the device will drive online sales. Sales revenue is generated when the Kindle is used and not necessarily when the device is purchased.[60]

To fulfill the value proposition promise, the innovation ecosystem must function holistically. The innovation ecosystem must be designed so that the risks are transparent and can be managed effectively rather than discovered after it is too late. When you expand your ecosystem, any subsystem in either the internal or external ecosystem can cause an innovation failure. By looking at the entire ecosystem, dependencies can be identified and managed. When innovation is part of an external ecosystem, there are two system risks that can affect an innovation, co-innovation risk and adoption chain risk.[61]

Co-Innovation Risk

In American football, the entire offensive line must function as a whole to prevent a defensive lineman from breaking through to tackle the quarterback. Like team sports, the process of innovation is enhanced when all collaborates work together to meet customer needs. Companies that are vertically integrated experience less co-innovation risk because they are less dependent on their suppliers. If you can produce all your parts for a product, then you can reduce your risk. The original IBM PC was successful partly because application software was more plentiful than that available for the Apple PC.

Co-innovation risk requires considering whether your partners delivered the co-innovations that are necessary for your innovation to be successful. For example, the Nokia 3G phone was not successful because Nokia was overly dependent on complementary digital products and services that were not in place when needed. Nokia failed to manage the relationship it had with co-innovations of key partners.

Amazon is an example of a company dependent on the products from their suppliers and for timely shipping from their shipping partners FedEx and UPS. If a new computer product is offered and the application software that was expected to be offered by a separate partner is not available, the computer product could fail.

Adoption Chain Risk

Innovations will fail if there is a gap in the customer value chain. For example, if a new innovative product is offered and there is no way to service that product, the new product will fail. Adoption chain risk considers whether your partners have adopted your innovation, so that a complete solution is available to customers.

When Monsanto developed genetically modified corn and soya bean seeds, they were taking a risk, hoping that the food manufacturers would buy the corn from the farmers and that the consumers would buy the food products from the retailers. If you have an innovative product or service that you intend to license to your partners, you are taking a risk, hoping that they will adopt your innovation. Monsanto's product was successful in that it was adopted across customers.

The Michelin run-flat tire was a technological innovation first developed by Michelin in the 1930s that allowed automobile drivers to operate safely for a limited distance and reduced speed after a drop in or loss of tire pressure.[62] The Michelin run-flat tire initially failed to take off, however, in part because the tire service centers did not adopt the innovation in a timely manner. By not ensuring that their service center partners had adopted the run-flat tire solution, customers had difficulty getting the tires serviced, resulting in poor customer acceptance.

Innovation Principles and Tenets

Leading innovative organizations develop a core ideology that comprises their purpose and a related set of guiding principles, while simultaneously stimulating innovation.[63] The *Webster's Dictionary* definition of a principle is "a comprehensive and fundamental law, doctrine, or assumption."[64]

Steve Jobs' Innovation Principles

In "The 7 Success Principles of Steve Jobs," Carmine Gallo described the innovation principles shown in Figure 2.9.[65]

1-Do What You Love. Think differently about your career.

2-Put a Dent in the Universe. Think differently about your vision.

3-Kick-Start Your Brain. Think differently about how you think.

4-Sell Dreams, Not Products. Think differently about your customers.

5-Say No to 1,000 Things. Think differently about design.

6-Create Insanely Great Experiences. Think differently about your brand experience.

7-Master the Message. Think differently about your story.

Figure 2.9 Illustration of Steve Jobs' Innovation Principles

Source: Adapted from Carmine Gallo, *The Innovation Secrets of Steve Jobs: Insanely Different: Principles for Breakthrough Success*, (New York: McGraw-Hill, 2011).

Vijay Govindarajan's Innovation Tenets

Vijay Govindarajan has provided a number of innovation tenets, encapsulating knowledge that has high utility. Govindarajan's seven innovation tenets are summarized in Figure 2.10.

1-Create a separate dedicated innovation team.

2-The innovation team must partner with the core (competencies) of the organization. The team cannot be isolated.

3-The innovation team should be held accountable for learning and not for short-term financial results.

4-Organizations (the core) are designed for the routine and efficiency to make tasks repeatable and predicable.

5-Innovation is about the non-routine

6-Innovation is not predictable.

7-Innovation is about how to convert non-consumers into consumers.

Figure 2.10 Illustration of Vijay Govindarajan's Innovation Tenets

Source: Adapted from Vijay Govindarajan, "Video Collection," accessed June 8, 2020, http://www.tuck.dartmouth.edu/people/vg/news/video

Applying Guiding Principles: Non-Profits

Water.org is a non-profit organization that focuses on providing clean water and sanitation to developing countries. A guiding principle for Water.org is to "get the right people on the bus," by being sure to screen, recruit, engage, and partner with local communities.[66] This is a high-opportunity endeavor since, according to Water.org, "[n]early one billion people lack access to safe water and 2.5 billion do not have improved sanitation. The health and economic impacts are staggering."[67]

Social activist Paul Polak is an advocate of a minimalist design approach to helping the poor in developing countries. The concept is based on designing extreme affordability into the products, services, and solutions for the huge markets wherein people are experiencing global poverty.[68] Polak created the zero-based design principle, which frames the poor as customers by focusing on developing innovative products and services designed explicitly for them.[69] Zero-based design is a guiding principle to solving big problems like poverty, clean water, and improving agriculture.

Applying Guiding Principles: For-Profits

Apple created the guiding principle "Think different" in the launch of the Macintosh in 1984, establishing them as a counterculture organization. "Don't be evil" is one of Google's guiding principles,[70] emphasizing their trustworthiness regarding personal data.[71] Google customers provide their personal data through Gmail and searches; Google uses this information for profit. Google applies another of their guiding principles, 70/20/10, an evidenced-based, multipurpose reference model attributed to Morgan McCall[72] to describe their resource allocation effort: 70% for core business tasks, 20% for projects related to the core business, and 10% for projects unrelated to the core business. Like Whole Foods, Disney, and Southwest Airlines, Amazon's dominant guiding principle is to focus on the customer experience. Amazon's guiding principles also include starting small and thinking big, "creativity must flow from everywhere," and "innovation can only come from the bottom. Those closest to the problem are in the best position to solve it."[73]

With P&G's Connect + Develop program, innovative solutions are sought both inside and outside the company. P&G's guiding principles include "Innovation is the cornerstone to our success," "We place great value on big, new consumer innovations," and "We challenge convention and reinvent the way we do business to better win in the marketplace."[74] P&G applies a set of innovation principles that are focused on global customer needs, where the consumer is the boss. Because consumers have the same core needs, the P&G product combination that best addresses these core needs will be the market leader. New ideas, big and small, need to transcend local markets and be scalable to global growth markets.[75]

Applying Guiding Principles: Shared Values

Michael Porter and Mark Kramer clearly identify the integrative and interactive nature of business and society: "The capitalist system is under siege. In recent years business increasingly has been viewed as a major cause of social, environmental, and economic problems. Companies are widely perceived to be prospering at the expense of the broader community."[76]

To address this interdependency, the triple bottom line was developed to advocate economic, environmental, and social responsibility.

> The triple bottom line (TBL) thus consists of three Ps: Profit, people, and planet. It aims to measure the financial, social, and environmental performance of the corporation over a period. Only a company that produces a TBL is taking account of the full cost involved in doing business.[77]

The TBL illustrates the need to be aware of how the business and social landscape is changing. "The purpose of the corporation must be redefined as creating shared value, not just profit per se," write Porter and Kramer. Speaking to the purpose of a venture as not just profit driven, but rather shared value, Porter and Kramer note, "This will drive the next wave of innovation and productivity growth in the global economy. It will also reshape capitalism and its relationship to society. Perhaps most important of all, learning how to create shared value is our best chance to legitimize business again."[78]

P&G products, for example, should improve the health and well-being of the lives of their consumers. With this in mind, "The P&G Children's Safe Drinking Water Program (CSDW)" distributes "P&G packets, a water purifying technology developed by P&G and the U.S. Centers for Disease Control and Prevention (CDC)."[79] P&G also developed a program known as the Tide of Hope, which sends mobile laundry facilities to disaster locations at no cost.[80] P&G serves as an example of an organization that uses innovation and entrepreneurship to approach multiple constituencies.

With the increased interested in sustainability throughout the world, the interest in stakeholder capitalism is growing. Stakeholder capitalism is the realization that firms should focus on more than their stockholders and participate more actively in social and environmental issues.

The triple bottom line (TBL) is based on environmental, social, and financial objectives, or environmental, social, and governance (ESG) without the governance. The purpose of the governance refers to public accountability and investment opportunities.[81]

Innovation Thresholds

Jim Collins first described innovation thresholds in his 2011 book, *Great by Choice*.[82] Innovation can provide a competition advantage, enabling an organization's sustainable growth success up to a certain threshold. An innovation threshold is a marker that each business sector needs to achieve to be competitive. To thrive, an organization cannot under-innovate, while over-innovation would be wasteful and ineffectual. Innovation thresholds range from low to high and are different for each business sector. Once an organization achieves the innovation threshold, additional innovation may not matter. After an organization exceeds the innovation threshold, other innovation and entrepreneurship competencies, such as creativity, culture, strategy, leadership, and technology, become increasingly important. Key innovation threshold concepts are shown in Figure 2.11.

Industry	Primary Innovation Dimension	Innovation Threshold
Semiconductors	New devices, products, and technologies	High
Biotechnology	New drug development, scientific discoveries, breakthroughs	High
Computers/ Software	New products, enhancements, and technologies	High
Medical Devices	New medical devices, application breakthroughs	Medium
Airlines	New service features, new business models and practices	Low
Insurance	New insurance products, new service features	Low

Figure 2.11 Illustration of Innovation Thresholds

Source: Adapted from Jim Collins and Morten T. Hansen, *Great by Choice*, (Harper Business, 2011), 75.

For example, airlines and insurance businesses have low innovation thresholds.[83] Because of this, organizations like Southwest Airlines and United Services Automobile Association (USAA) are free to build cultures that focus on providing an enhanced customer experience rather than on product innovation. Medical device manufacturers, on the other hand, have a medium threshold for innovation, while firms in the computer, biotechnology, and semiconductor segments have high thresholds.

Innovation Criteria

Three key criteria that can be used to evaluate an innovation are desirability, feasibility, and viability. This is depicted in Figure 2.12. An innovative design needs to be desirable, feasible, and aligned with a sustainable business model. It achieves desirability by fulfilling the unmet needs of consumers, and feasibility by providing a solution that is realistic and functionally possible. As important as these first two criteria are, they will be insufficient unless the innovative design is associated with a viable and sustainable business model.[84]

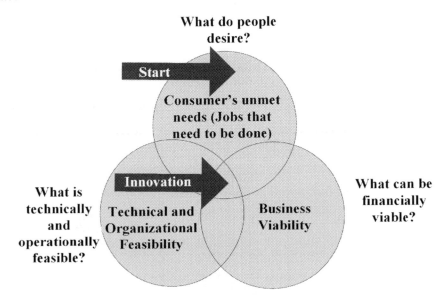

Figure 2.12 Illustration of Innovation Criteria

Source: Adapted from Tim Brown, *Change by Design*, (New York: Harper, 2009), 19.

Innovation Processes

Innovation processes are those disciplined steps that organizations follow to build what is new and hopefully unique, the imaginative content to meet the customer promise. The generic innovative process for building stand-alone solutions begins with defining the value proposition – defining *who* your customer is and defining *what* the requirements are for the solution.

Innovation Process Balance

When developing something new, the innovation process must be adapted to the circumstances; large-scale, complex, and high-risk innovations require more process, while small-scale, simple, and low-risk innovations require less. The innovative process must be carefully balanced to avoid either over- or under-engineering of the final innovative solution. Over-engineering results in wasted resources. Under-engineering risks failing to fulfill the customer promise and may result in costly defects. For example, the Intempo skyscraper in Benidorm, Spain was originally designed to be 20 stories high and include an elevator system to accommodate a building of that size. Although it was subsequently decided to extend the building to 47 stories, no thought was given to redesigning the elevator system.[85]

Defects that are introduced after the innovative solution is released to customers are expensive to fix and often result in a loss of credibility. The development of the Boeing Dreamliner required a highly disciplined process because under-engineering an aircraft would create unnecessary safety risks. Even though the Boeing Dreamliner engineers followed a disciplined process, the rollout revealed defects in the lithium-ion battery system.

Imaginative Content

Innovative processes are important, but they cannot replace imaginative content. The imaginative content that improves our lives and fulfills our dreams is highly valuable. In many ways, imaginative content is more important, even, than a disciplined process. What is (current state) need not override what might be, the imaginative content. What is new or what might be (future state) must not be sacrificed for what is.

Measure Learning Rather Than Financials

The evaluation criteria used during the process of developing something new and unique cannot be solely based on the traditional financial measures. Rather, the early results should be measured according to the extent of learning rather than in financial returns. The use of financial measures early in the process will kill new and unique ideas.

Model of the Innovation Process

In their book *Managing Innovation*, Tidd and Bessant have developed a valuable generic four-phase innovation process that encompasses the search, selection, implementation, and value capture of innovations.[86] Figure 2.13 captures the generic four-phase process.

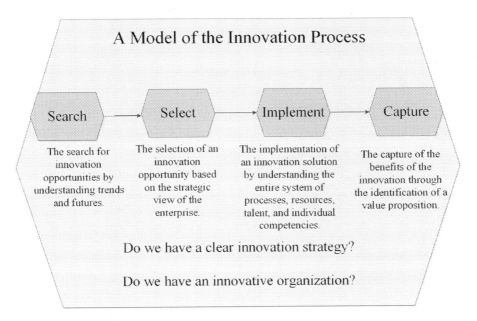

Figure 2.13 Illustration of a Generic Innovation Process

Source: Adapted from Joe Tidd, and John Bessant, J., *Managing Innovation: Integrating Technological, Market and Organizational Change*, 5th ed. (London: Wiley, 2013), 47.

Design Thinking

Design thinking is an empathetic innovation process, based on the work of Tom Kelley and Tim Brown, developed, and marketed by IDEO.[87] This is a specialized innovation process model that involves an empathetic relationship with the customer and continuous iterative prototyping. According to Tim Brown, design thinking "is a discipline that uses the designer's sensibility and methods to match people's needs with what is technologically feasible and what a viable business strategy can convert into customer value and market opportunity."[88] Design thinking applies concepts from both the humanities and science and is what innovators like Steve Jobs of Apple and Edwin Land of Polaroid were all about.[89]

Although many organizations have developed innovation processes, most tend to utilize an inspirational mental model followed by an implementable physical model. The mental creation in these cases always precedes the physical creation.[90] Design thinking is an iterative process that moves back and forth between ideation and creation to achieve consumer desirability, business viability, and technical feasibility. The iterative design thinking roadmap illustrated in Figure 2.14 provides for both the freedom to be creative and the discipline to achieve results.

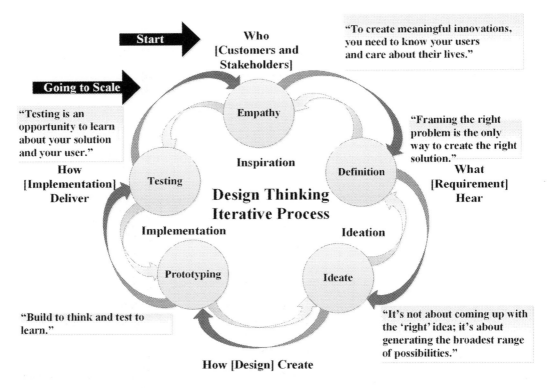

Figure 2.14 Illustration of the Design Thinking Process

Source: Adapted from "An Introduction to Design Thinking Process Guide," Institute of Design At Stanford.

The innovation process element or process steps for innovation are described in more detail in Chapter 17, "Applying Innovation Processes."

Innovation Diffusion and Adoption

Innovation adoption addresses how to successfully move innovations from *what might be* to *what is*. Everett Rogers first described innovation adoption in 2003 in *Diffusion of Innovations*. Diffusion theory explains how ideas and innovations are adopted by societies.[91] Using a bell-shaped curve, Rogers describes a technology adoption cycle composed of five separate stages for innovations to traverse.

Superimposed on Rogers' bell-shaped curve of diffusion theory in Figure 2.15 is Geoffrey A. Moore's *Crossing the Chasm,* which describes the difficult move from early adopters (visionaries) to the early majority (pragmatists) for revolutionary (discontinuous) innovations.[92]

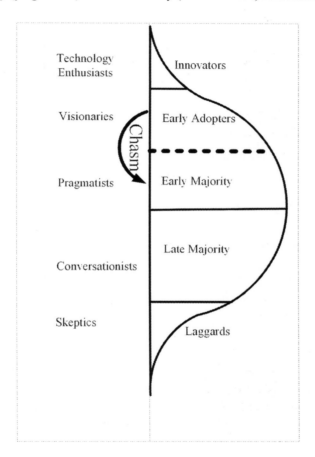

Figure 2.15 Innovation Adoption and Crossing the Chasm

Source: Adapted from Everett M. Rogers, *Diffusion of Innovations*, 5th ed., (New York: Free Press, 2003) and Geoffrey A. Moore, *Crossing the Chasm* (New York: Harper Business, 1991/1999).

3M has had many successful brands such as Scotch®, Post-it®, and Scotch-Brite®. 3M struggled initially with the Post-it® brand, but they were eventually able to hurdle the chasm. The adhesive was developed in 1968, by Dr. Spencer Silver, but no one could find a use for it. Later, Art Fry used the adhesive on bookmarks because they kept falling out of his books. The initial reaction to Post-it® was not favorable. No one used the product, and the product was not doing well. The product had hit the chasm.

Yet despite the initial dismal feedback from the marketing department and his peers, Fry and Silver believed in the potential of this unique product. Fry began by making the 3M corporate headquarters the marketing test site, supplying the entire company with the new reusable notes. Employees loved them and 3M launched in four cities under the then name "Press 'n Peel" with mixed results. Ultimately, 3M engaged in a massive marketing campaign and in what would become known as the Boise Blitz, over 90% who tried the product said they would buy it![93] Ultimately, Fry turned a failed product, the low tack adhesive, into a star product, the 3M Post-It® Note.

There are many examples of successful companies that have innovations that never transition across the chasm. Many Xerox PARC technology innovations did not cross; Apple's Lisa and Newton and Microsoft's Zune and Vista also failed to cross the chasm. The Apple Lisa was not affordable.[94] The Apple Newton was a product that was developed before the market was ready. The Microsoft Zune was not competitive and the Vista's user interface was not well-received.

Innovation and Organizational Change

Organizational change and the adoption of new ideas is one of the most perplexing challenges for leading innovators across the entire spectrum of innovation types. Innovation is facilitated when both the people and senior management support the change and when thought leaders are involved.

Facilitators of Innovation Adoption

If there is agreement that change is needed and there is a change champion, the process works. This is often the case when there is a serious operational set-back in an organization. For example, "In the spring and summer of 2000, P&G experienced one of the most demanding challenges in its history. After missing earnings commitments, the company's stock declined dramatically, resulting in a loss of nearly $50 billion in market capitalization."[95] This shockwave triggered a leadership and cultural shift at P&G that focused on the consumer-is-the-boss model. Instead of using focus groups and reading research reports, P&G sought to understand consumers directly through observation and empathy.

The year 2000 also inspired P&G to adopt Connect + Develop, an open innovation model, extending idea generation to anyone who was willing to provide productive ideas for the future. The Connect + Develop approach was a cultural shift for P&G to strategically focus on identifying external innovative solutions. Today, "Over 50% of P&G product initiatives involve significant external collaboration."[96]

In recent times, companies have become more open with their innovation process, leading to revolution described as "Open Innovation" by Chesbrough (2003). This "open innovation" model is a more dynamic model when compared to the traditional model as there is much more interaction between knowledge assets outside the company as well as inside. Henry Chesbrough (2003) in his book *Open Innovation: New Imperative for Creating and Profiting from Technology* defines open innovation as a concept in which companies must use ideas from inside as well as outside sources and find internal and external ways to reach the market to advance their technological capabilities.[97]

Barriers to Innovation Adoption

The barriers to innovation, adoption, and organizational change can be substantial, both internally and externally. In 1995, Coca-Cola introduced the New Coke, an incremental product innovation, in response to its declining market share due to competition from Pepsi-Cola. But "New Coke, a customer-driven product initiative that involved one of the most exhaustive market research projects in history with almost 200,000 consumer interviews at a cost of $4 million, resulted in one of the most embarrassing product failures of all time."[98] Consumers rejected the product, in part because head-to-head tastes tests failed to take into consideration that, while the New Coke product was preferred, consumers weren't seeing it as a replacement for traditional Coke. Coca-Cola consumers failed to see how this new product could be better than a product that was already considered the best.

Innovation Pacing

Innovation pacing (see Figure 2.16) encompasses the velocity or speed of a firm's innovation stream and the acceleration or increase in speed that is needed to compete. Pacing is influenced by your innovation capability and the ability of your customers to adopt those innovations. People have a slow pace adopting innovation because, as Stephen Covey said, "With people, if you want to save time, do not be efficient. Slow is fast and fast is slow."[99] People need time to adjust to what is new.

Figure 2.16 Illustration of Innovation Pacing

Elon Musk has an aspirational goal to reduce global warming by promoting the use of electric cars. He has a patent portfolio of inventions that have lowered the cost and improved the safety of battery packs. His solution is to offer his technology patents as open-source and expect nothing in return. He will not initiate patent lawsuits against those who use his technology. Musk believes that it is the pace of innovation that matters, and if he can out-invent his rivals, he can stay in a strong competitive position.[100]

Commodity product innovations are slow-paced because there is less opportunity to add value. For instance, innovations in food, gasoline, water, and salt have a slow pace. Innovations in technologies such as microprocessors are fast-paced because the opportunity to add value is extremely high. Moore's law has predicted that the number of transistors and integrated circuits will double every two years.[101] Intel continues to evolve by incrementally improving its price performance. Intel continues to evolve and adapt to the technology turmoil of the evolution of Windows operating systems but also Google's Android operating system.[102] The faster the pace, the more priority, processes, and resources will be required for the innovation.

Innovation Value

In the book *Blue Ocean Strategy*, W. Chan Kim and Renee Mauborgne use a red and blue ocean metaphor, wherein red oceans represent organizations (industries) that exist today. Red oceans have been the focus of much of the strategic thinking in the past, as evidenced by the early work of Michael Porter. Red ocean strategies utilize conventional warfare thinking, wherein organizational efforts are focused on how to achieve a competitive advantage over rivals. The red ocean mentality is a constraint because it overlooks the ability to adapt to change that is inherent in both individuals and many organizations.

Blue oceans represent organizations (industries), business models, or market segments that are not in existence today. Blue oceans are opportunities to create new markets and new business models for consumers. Opportunities that have been realized, such as the automobile, aviation, personal computing, discount retailing, smartphones, social networks, and home entertainment systems, were once blue oceans. Imagine what opportunities still exist – these are today's blue oceans.

Value is defined as the utility or relative worth that you receive in exchange for goods, services, or money.[103] "Value innovation is the cornerstone of blue ocean strategy."[104] Value without innovation is an improvement that may not be sufficient for organic growth. Innovation without value does not provide the utility that customers would be willing to purchase. Innovation needs to be aligned with value composed of utility, price, and cost.

"We call it value innovation," write Kim and Mauborgne, "because instead of focusing on beating the competition, you focus on making the completion irrelevant by creating a leap in value for buyers and your company, thereby opening up new and uncontested market space."[105] Instead of focusing on the traditional strategic trade-off of cost or differentiation, value innovation pursues cost and differentiation simultaneously.

The value innovation concept can be understood by examining Tesla's Blue Ocean Strategy and applying the four-action (ERRC) framework: eliminate, reduce, raise, and create.[106] As captured in Figure 2.17, Tesla sought to:

1. Eliminate reliance on fossil fuels, the need for marketing, and direct sales, thereby improving the environment and reducing the vehicle costs.
2. Reduce charge time, vehicle service costs (fewer parts to maintain and no oil changes) and vehicle energy costs because electricity is less expensive than gasoline.
3. Create a first mover advantage with a "green performance vehicle" that combined two customer segments, the concept of a "green" car and a fast sports car resulting in a new market segment.
4. Raise the customer experience with higher performance, longer driving ranges, several unique electronic vehicle models to mainstream consumers, and affordability with the newer models.

Disruptive Innovation

Disruptive innovation is based on Clayton Christensen's research for *The Innovator's Dilemma*.[107] Disruptive innovations are different from incremental, evolutionary, and revolutionary innovation degrees. A disruptive innovation is not a revolutionary innovation that makes other innovations, such as products and services, better. Rather, a disruptive innovation transforms any type of innovation that historically was expensive and complicated into an innovation that is affordable, simple, and available to broader markets. For instance, the personal computer opened computing to new consumers and new markets, even though personal computers were not as powerful, scalable, or reliable as mainframe computers.

Disruptive innovation occurs between entrants and incumbents. Start-ups, new entrants, can be successful launching disruptive innovations such as new market or new business innovations, but rarely will they succeed launching a sustaining innovation that targets the most valuable segments

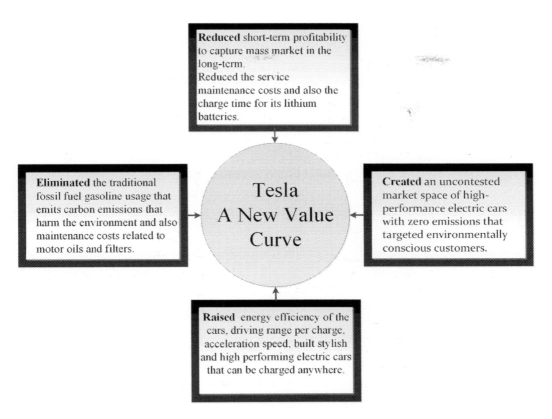

Figure 2.17 Illustration of the Value Innovation of Tesla

Source: Adapted from W. Chan Kim and Renee Mauborgne, *Blue Ocean Strategy*, (Boston, MA: Harvard Business Publishing, 2005), 29. http://analysiscasestudy.blogspot.com/search/label/Blue%20Ocean%20Strategy

of established markets.[108] As seen in Figure 2.18, entrant Netflix and incumbent Blockbuster provide a compelling example.

The entrant Netflix was founded in 1997, around two technologies: DVDs and an online website for ordering the DVDs. The company originally offered a digital subscription-service business model that used the US Postal Service to ship the DVD media. For about $20 per month, you would receive one DVD at a time. When you returned one DVD, you would receive another DVD based on your preference queue on the Netflix website.

The competition to the entrant Netflix was incumbent Blockbuster. At the time, the video-rental giant that had grown to 7,700 retail video stores. When renting with Blockbuster, you had to go to the store to pick up and return videos. If you were late returning the video, you had to pay fines, which was dissatisfying to the customers.[109]

In 2000, as Netflix was struggling for profits, co-founder Reed Hastings visited Blockbuster and offered a 49% stake to become Blockbuster's online service. This was during the period the dotcom bubble was bursting, between 1997 and 2000, and before the explosion of digital entertainment media. Blockbuster declined the offer from Reed Hastings, preferring to stay close to their current customers and the comfort of their retail store model.

Blockbuster was a late entrant into the online subscription service; by 2005, Netflix had 4.2 million subscribers. In 2007, Netflix initiated a new business service that streamed movies and

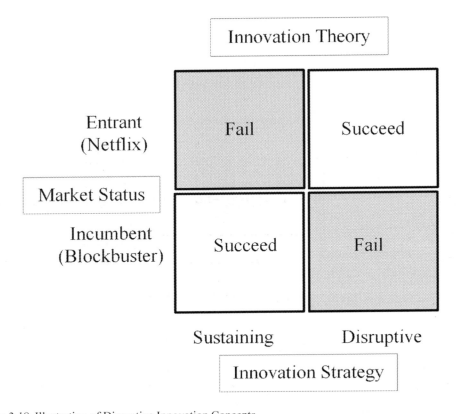

Figure 2.18 Illustration of Disruptive Innovation Concepts

Source: Adapted from Michael E. Raynor, "Disruption Theory as a Predictor of Innovation Success/Failure," *Strategy & Leadership* 39, no. 4 (2011): 27–30.

TV shows over the Internet to personal computers.[110] This service eliminated the customer dissatisfaction associated with the 20 minutes per hour of non-targeted advertising experienced by viewers of commercial TV. Netflix successfully disrupted Blockbuster; the former retail video giant filed for bankruptcy in 2010 and was later purchased by Dish Networks.[111]

An incumbent company like Blockbuster may know about an innovation that is being marketed by a new entrant, yet the incumbent could still fail because it invests in favor of the current customers rather than investing in innovations for new businesses and new markets. The agile entrant, like Netflix, can create a passing lane of disruption to move ahead of those stymied incumbents in the driving lane of sustaining improvements. Incumbents such as Blockbuster are not effective with disruptive innovations and new entrants tend to be less effective at sustaining innovations.

The broader topic known as innovation theory explains why managers can fail by applying the "best practice in business," though meeting and even exceeding the needs of their customers. Innovation theory is described in more detail in Chapter 10.

Summary

In this chapter, a common ground for what is meant by innovation, a term often misunderstood in both its use and scope, is provided. Working definitions of imagination and creativity are also given. The 12 elements of innovation (degrees, direction principles and tenets, criteria, diffusion, value, types, risk, thresholds, pacing, and finally, disruptive innovation) are discussed, which in turn inform the innovation and entrepreneurship competency framework outlined in the Introduction. Next, a closer examination into effective decision-making and its key role in the pursuit of innovation and entrepreneurship is undertaken.

Notes

1. Teresa Amabile, Regina Conti, Heather Coon, Jeffrey Lazenby, and Michael Herron, "Assessing the Work Environment for Creativity," *Academy of Management Journal* 39, no. 5 (1996), 1154–1184.
2. Keith R. Sawyer, *Explaining Creativity: The Science of Human Innovation* (New York: Oxford, 2012).
3. *Oxford Dictionaries Online*, s.v. "Innovation," accessed February 18, 2024, www.oxforddictionaries.com/us/definition/american_english/innovation?q=innovation.
4. *Oxford Dictionaries Online*, s.v. "Innovate," February 18, 2024, www.oxforddictionaries.com/us/definition/american_english/innovate.
5. *Oxford Dictionaries Online*, s.v. "Innovation," accessed February 18, 2024, www.oxforddictionaries.com/us/definition/american_english-thesaurus/innovation?q=innovation.
6. Merriam-Webster, "Innovation," accessed February 18, 2024, www.merriam-webster.com/dictionary/innovation.
7. Merriam-Webster, "Innovation," accessed February 18, 2024, www.merriam-webster.com/dictionary/innovation.
8. Joe Tidd and John Bessant, *Managing Innovation: Integrating Technological, Market and Organizational Change*, 5th ed. (New York: Wiley, 2013), 21–22.
9. Jeffrey Dance, "What Is Innovation? 30+ Definitions Lead to One Fresh Summary," *FreshConsulting*, accessed February 18, 2024, www.freshconsulting.com/what-is-innovation/.
10. Stephen Davies, *The Diffusion of Process Innovations* (Cambridge: Cambridge University Press, 1979).
11. Rod Coombs, Paolo Saviotti, and Vivien Walsh, *Economics and Technological Change* (Totowa, NJ: Rowman & Littlefield, 1987).
12. Bruce Nussbaum, "The Candidates on Innovation: What It Is and What They'll Do," *In Politics, Bloomberg Businessweek*, November 15, 2007, 5.
13. Mihaly Csikszentmihalyi, *Creativity: The Psychology of Discovery and Invention* (New York: Harper Perennial, 1997), 110.
14. Ken Robinson, *Finding Your Element* (New York: Viking, 2013), 23.
15. Karen Weintraub, "Brain a 'Creativity Machine,' If You Use It Right," *USA Today*, November 9, 2013, accessed August 14, 2020, www.usatoday.com/story/news/nation/2013/11/09/creativity-brain-science/3457735/.
16. Steven Johnson, "Where Good Ideas Come From," *YouTube Video*, posted by "RiverheadBooks," September 17, 2010, accessed February 18, 2024, www.youtube.com/watch?v=NugRZGDbPFU.
17. Jeff Dyer, Hal Gregersen, and Clayton Christensen, *The Innovator's DNA* (Boston: Harvard Business Review Press, 2009).
18. Valerie Liston, "Behind the Design: OXO's Iconic Good Grips Handles," January 31, 2017, accessed February 11, 2024, www.oxo.com/blog/behind-the-scenes/behind-design-oxos-iconic-good-grips-handles.
19. *Wikipedia*, s.v. "Outline of Academic Discipline," accessed February 18, 2024, https://en.wikipedia.org/wiki/Outline_of_academic_disciplines.
20. Tim Brown, *Change by Design* (New York: Harper Business, 2009), 162–164.
21. Clayton Christensen, "Christensen: We Are Living the Capitalist's Dilemma," *CNN*, January 21, 2014, accessed February 18, 2024, http://edition.cnn.com/2013/01/21/business/opinion-clayton-christensen/.
22. Dennis Berman, "Is a Peanut Butter Pop-Tart an Innovation?" *The Wall Street Journal*, December 3, 2013, accessed August 14, 2020, http://online.wsj.com/news/articles/SB10001424052702304854804579236601411310502.
23. Niraj Chokshi, "Electric Planes, Once a Fantasy, Start to Take to the Skies," November 3, 2023, revised November 4, 2023, accessed November 13, 2023, www.nytimes.com/2023/11/03/business/electric-planes-beta-technologies.html.
24. *Wikipedia*, s.v. "Johannes Gutenberg," last modified May 28, 2014, accessed February 18, 2024, http://en.wikipedia.org/wiki/Johannes_Gutenberg.
25. "Civil War Casualties," *HistoryNet.com*, accessed February 18, 2024, www.historynet.com/civil-war-casualties.
26. *Wikipedia*, s.v. "Joseph Lister," accessed February 18, 2024, http://en.wikipedia.org/wiki/Joseph_Lister,_1st_Baron_Lister.
27. "Wind Turbines with Integrated Electrolyzer Demonstrate Sustainable Hydrogen Production at Sea," August 23, 2021, accessed January 4, 2024, https://seawanderer.org/wind-turbines-with-integrated-electrolyzer-demonstrate-sustainable-hydrogen-production-at-sea.

28. Jena McGregor, "The World's Most Innovative Companies," with Michael Arndt, Robert Berner, Ian Rowley, Kenji Hall, Gail Edmondson, Steve Hamm, Moon Ihlwan, and Andy Reinhardt, *Business Week*, April 26, 2006, 64.

29. Flavio Martins, "Disney's 3 Keys to a Magical Customer Experience," April 2, 2012, accessed August 14, 2020, https://winthecustomer.com/disneys-magical-service-experiences/.

30. Gary Hamel, "The Why, What, and How of Management Innovation," *Harvard Business Review* 84, no. 2 (2006), 72–84.

31. *Wikipedia*, s.v. "Frederick Winslow Taylor," accessed February 18, 2024, http://en.wikipedia.org/wiki/Frederick_Winslow_Taylor.

32. "A Brief History of Lean," *Strategos*, accessed February 18, 2024, www.strategosinc.com/just_in_time.htm.

33. Peter F. Drucker, *Concept of the Corporation* (New Brunswick: Transaction Publishers, 1993).

34. Peter Drucker, "What Business Can Learn from Nonprofits," *Harvard Business Review*, July 1989, accessed February 18, 2024, http://hbr.org/1989/07/what-business-can-learn-from-nonprofits/ar/1.

35. Gary Hamel, "The Why, What, and How of Management Innovation," *Harvard Business Review* 84, no. 2 (2006), 72–84.

36. Gary Hamel, "The Why, What and How of Management Innovation," *Harvard Business Review* 84, no. 2 (2006), 72–84.

37. Paul Sloane, *The Leader's Guide to Lateral Thinking Skills* (London: Kogan Page Limited, 2006), 5.

38. Gary Hamel, "Management Must Be Reinvented," *YouTube Video*, posted by "HSM Americas Is Now WOBI," December 29, 2008, accessed February 18, 2024, www.youtube.com/watch?v=TVX8XhiR1UY.

39. Gary Hamel, *The Future of Management*, with Bill Breen (Boston: Harvard Business Press, 2007), 32.

40. Susan Schwab, "The US Growth Opportunity in Trading Knowledge-Intensive Products,' interview by McKinsey and Company, August 2013, accessed February 18, 2024, www.mckinsey.com/featured-insights/employment-and-growth/the-us-growth-opportunity-in-trading-knowledge-intensive-products.

41. Vijay Govindarajan, "The Other Side of Innovation: Solving the Execution Challenge," *YouTube Video*, posted by "VGgovindarajan," March 30, 2011, accessed February 18, 2024, www.youtube.com/watch?v=6pl1KTNA1G0.

42. Bill Chappell, "Tech Giants Launch Internet.org, A Global Plan to Widen Access," *The Two-Way* (blog), *NPR*, August 21, 2013, accessed February 18, 2024, www.npr.org/blogs/thetwo-way/2013/08/21/214117156/tech-giants-launch-internet-org-a-global-plan-to-widen-access.

43. Vindu Goel, "Facebook Leads an Effort to Lower Barriers to Internet Access," *The New York Times*, August 20, 2013, accessed February 18, 2024, www.nytimes.com/2013/08/21/technology/facebook-leads-an-effort-to-lower-barriers-to-internet-access.html?pagewanted=all.

44. "Is Connectivity a Human Right?" *Facebook*, accessed February 18, 2024, www.facebook.com/isconnectivityahumanright/isconnectivityahumanright.pdf.

45. Michelle Fay Cortez, "Abbott Labs Dissolving Heart Stent Helps Improve Recovery," *Business Week*, September 30, 2013, accessed February 11, 2024, www.bloomberg.com/news/articles/2013-09-30/innovation-abbott-labs-dissolving-heart-stent-helps-improve-recovery?embedded-checkout=true.

46. "Abbott Announces International Launch of the Absorb™ Bioresorbable Vascular Scaffold," *Abbott*, September 25, 2012, accessed February 18, 2024, www.prnewswire.com/news-releases/abbott-announces-international-launch-of-the-absorb-bioresorbable-vascular-scaffold-171140041.html.

47. Vijay Govindarajan and Chris Trimble, *Reverse Innovation: Create Far from Home, Win Everywhere* (Boston: Harvard Business Press, 2012).

48. Vijay Govindarajan, "Defining Reverse Innovation," video transcript, *BigThink*, February 18, 2024, http://bigthink.com/videos/defining-reverse-innovation.

49. Coimbatore K. Prahalad, *The Fortune at the Bottom of the Pyramid: Eradicating Poverty Through Profits*, Rev. ed. (Upper Saddle River, NJ: Pearson Education, 2010).

50. "The Dream of the Medical Tricorder," *The Economist*, December 1, 2012, accessed February 18, 2024, www.economist.com/news/technology-quarterly/21567208-medical-technology-hand-held-diagnostic-devices-seen-star-trek-are-inspiring.

51. Eurostat: Statistics Explained November 2019, update expected November 2020, accessed February 18, 2024, https://ec.europa.eu/eurostat/statistics-explained/index.php?title=Main_Page.

52. "Africa Has About One Doctor for Every 5,000 People, by Abairdqz," October 15, 2015, accessed February 18, 2024, https://qz.com/520230/africa-has-about-one-doctor-for-every-5000-people/#:~:text=In%202013%2C%20sub%2DSaharan%20Africa,to%204.3%20million%20by%202035.

53. Steven Hondrogiannis, "Head-Worn Device Uses Sonar to Rapidly Diagnose Stroke," *Gizmag*, March 31, 2011, accessed February 18, 2024, www.gizmag.com/submarine-technology-stroke-diagnosi s/18277/.

54. Max Little (director, Parkinson's Voice Initiative), interview by Ravi Parikh, *MedGaget*, August 20, 2012, accessed February 18, 2024, www.medgadget.com/2012/08/interview-with-max-little-ph-d-director-of-the-parkinsons-voice-initiative.html.

55. *Wikipedia*, s.v. "Tricorder," accessed February 18, 2024, http://en.wikipedia.org/wiki/Tricorder.

56. Jesse Sunenblick, "X Prize: Making the Tricorder a Reality," *Wired*, February 17, 2013, accessed February 18, 2024, www.wired.co.uk/magazine/archive/2013/02/features/tricorder/viewgallery/ 293759.

57. Sarah Buhr, "Scanadu to Shut Down Support for Its Scout Device Per FDA Regulation and Customers Are Mad," *TechCrunch*, 2016, accessed February 11, 2024, https://techcrunch.com/2016/12/13/ fda-orders-scanadu-to-shut-down-support-for-its-scout-device-and-customers-are-mad/.

58. "Scanadu," accessed February 11, 2024, https://dualdiagnosis.org/scanadu/.

59. Mariel Myers, "'Star Trek' Tricorder Becomes the Real McCoy," *CNet*, July 18, 2013, accessed February 11, 2024, www.cnet.com/science/star-trek-tricorder-becomes-the-real-mccoy/.

60. Martin Vendel, "The Amazon Kindle – A Successful Trojan Horse Strategy?" *BVD 2013* (blog), April 21, 2013, accessed February 18, 2024, http://bvd2013.wordpress.com/2013/04/21/the-amazon-kindle-a-successful-trojan-horse-strategy/.

61. Ron Adner, *The Wide Lens: A New Strategy for Innovation* (New York: Penguin, 2012).

62. "Run Flat Tire," *Michelin*, accessed February 11, 2024, https://en.wikipedia.org/wiki/Run-flat_tire# cite_note-1.

63. Bruce MacVarish, *Bruce MacVarish Notes* (blog), 2013, accessed February 11, 2024, https://macvarish. typepad.com/.

64. *Merriam-Webster*, s.v. "Principle," accessed February 18, 2024, www.merriam-webster.com/dictionary/ principle.

65. Carmine Gallo, "The 7 Success Principles of Steve Jobs," January 4, 2011, accessed February 18, 2024, www.forbes.com/sites/carminegallo/2011/01/04/the-7-success-principles-of-steve-jobs/.

66. "Solutions," *Water.org*, accessed February 18, 2024, http://water.org/solutions/.

67. "The Water Crisis," *Water.org*, accessed September 4, 2020, http://water.org/learn-about-the-water-crisis/ facts/.

68. Paul Polak, accessed February 18, 2024, www.paulpolak.com/design/.

69. Paul Polak, "The SunWater Project – Advanced Solar Technology for Poor Farmers," *Paul Polak* (blog), May 20, 2013, accessed February 18, 2024, www.paulpolak.com/the-sunwater-project-advanced-solar-technology-for-poor-farmers/.

70. *Wikipedia*, s.v. "Don't Be Evil," accessed February 11, 2024, http://en.wikipedia.org/wiki/Don't_ be_evil.

71. John Battelle, "The 70 Percent Solution," *CNN Money*, December 1, 2005, accessed February 11, 2024, https://money.cnn.com/2005/11/28/news/newsmakers/schmidt_biz20_1205/.

72. *Wikipedia*, s.v. "70/20/10 Model," accessed February 18, 2024, http://en.wikipedia.org/ wiki/70/20/10_Model.

73. Todd Hoff, "Amazon Architecture," *High Scalability* (blog), September 18, 2007, accessed February 18, 2024, http://highscalability.com/blog/2007/9/18/amazon-architecture.html.

74. "Innovation is the Cornerstone of Our Success," *P&G*, accessed February 11, 2024, https://us.pg.com/ policies-and-practices/purpose-values-and-principles/.

75. "Le Secret de Procter & Gamble," *Les Affaires* (blog), September 11, 2009, accessed February 11, 2024, www.lesaffaires.com/avant_garde.php/blogue/article/le-secret-de-procter-et-gamble/502571.

76. Michael E. Porter and Mark R. Kramer, "Creating Shared Value," *Harvard Business Review*, January 2011, accessed February 11, 2024, http://hbr.org/2011/01/the-big-idea-creating-shared-value/.

77. "Triple Bottom Line," *The Economist*, November 17, 2009, accessed February 18, 2024, www.economist.com/node/14301663.

78. Michael E. Porter and Mark R. Kramer, "Creating Shared Value," *Harvard Business Review*, January 2011, accessed February 18, 2024, http://hbr.org/2011/01/the-big-idea-creating-shared-value/.

79. "P&G Children's Safe Drinking Water Program," *P&G*, accessed September 7, 2020, https://csdw.org/ pg-purifier-of-water-packets.

80. "Tide Loads of Hope," *Tide*, accessed February 18, 2024, https://tide.com/en-us/our-commitment/ loads-of-hope.

81. "Five Ways That ESG Creates Value," November 14, 2019, accessed January 5, 2024, www.mckinsey.com/capabilities/strategy-and-corporate-finance/our-insights/five-ways-that-esg-creates-value.

82. Jim Collins and Morten T. Hansen, *Great by Choice* (New York: Harper Business, 2011), 75.

83. Jim Collins and Morten T. Hansen, *Great by Choice* (New York: Harper Business, 2011), 71–75.

84. Tim Brown, *Change by Design* (New York: Harper Business, 2009), 19.

85. Tyler Falk, "A 47-story Spanish Skyscraper Forgets the Elevator," *Smart Planet* (blog), August 8, 2013, accessed February 18, 2024, www.smartplanet.com/blog/bulletin/a-47-story-spanish-skyscraper-forgets-the-elevator/26115.

86. Joe Tidd and John Bessant, *Managing Innovation: Integrating Technological, Market and Organizational Change*, 5th ed. (New York: Wiley, 2013), 60.

87. Tim Brown, *Change by Design* (New York: Harper Business, 2009), 161–162.

88. Tim Brown, "Design Thinking," *Harvard Business Review* 86, no. 6 (2008), 86–92.

89. Walter Isaacson, *Steve Jobs* (New York: Simon and Schuster, 2011), xix.

90. Stephen Covey, *The Seven Habits of Highly Effective People* (New York: Simon and Schuster, 1989).

91. Everett M. Rogers, *Diffusion of Innovations*, 5th ed. (New York: Free Press, 2003).

92. Geoffrey A. Moore, *Crossing the Chasm* (New York: Harper Business, 1991/1999).

93. "History Timeline: Post-it® Notes," accessed February 18, 2024, www.post-it.com/3M/en_US/post-it/contact-us/about-us/.

94. "History of Computer Design: Apple Lisa," accessed February 18, 2024, www.landsnail.com/apple/local/design/lisa.html.

95. "A Company History, 1837–Today," *P&G*, accessed February 18, 2024, www.pg.com/translations/history_pdf/english_history.pdf.

96. "Business Engagement Partner Grows Relationship with P&G," July 31, 2018, accessed February 11, 2024, www.birmingham.ac.uk/news-archive/2018/business-engagement-partner-grows-relationship-with-pg.

97. Limali Panduwawala, Suvidha Venkatesh, Pedro Parraguez, and Xiajing Zhang, "Connect and Develop: P&G's Big Stake in Open Innovation," *University of Bath, MSC in Innovation and Technology Management*, November 27, 2009, 3, accessed February 11, 2024, www.bartleby.com/essay/Open-Innovation-PKXMCYSX73GEY.

98. Anthony Ulwick, *What Customers Want* (New York: McGraw-Hill, 2005), xiv.

99. Stephen R. Covey, *The 7 Habits of Highly Effective People: Restoring the Character Ethic* (New York: Free Press, 2004).

100. Ashlee Vance, "Why Elon Musk Just Opened Tesla's Patents to His Biggest Rivals," June 12, 2014, accessed February 18, 2024, www.bloomberg.com/news/articles/2014-06-12/why-elon-musk-just-opened-teslas-patents-to-his-biggest-rivals.

101. *Wikipedia*, s.v. "Moore's Law," accessed February 18, 2024, http://en.wikipedia.org/wiki/Moore's_law.

102. Gregg Keizer, "Intel Trumpets Android+Windows as 'More Choice'," *Computer World*, January 8, 2014, accessed February 18, 2024, www.computerworld.com/article/2701844/intel-trumpets-android-windows-as – more-choice-.html.

103. *Merriam-Webster*, s.v. "value," accessed February 18, 2024, www.merriam-webster.com/dictionary/value.

104. W. Chan Kim and Renee Mauborgne, *Blue Ocean Strategy* (Boston: Harvard Business, 2005), 12.

105. W. Chan Kim and Renee Mauborgne, *Blue Ocean Strategy* (Boston: Harvard Business, 2005), 12.

106. Four-Action Framework for Tesla, accessed February 18, 2024, https://mixcsy.wixsite.com/teslaensi313/blue-ocean-strategy.

107. Clayton Christensen, *The Innovator's Dilemma: When New Technologies Cause Great Firms to Fail* (Boston: Harvard Business School Press, 1997).

108. Michael E. Raynor, "Disruption Theory as a Predictor of Innovation Success/Failure," *Strategy & Leadership* 39, no. 4 (2011), 27–30.

109. "Netflix, Inc. History," *Funding Universe*, accessed February 18, 2024, www.fundinguniverse.com/company-histories/netflix-inc-history/.

110. Ken Atuletta, "Outside the Box," *The New Yorker*, February 3, 2014, 54.

111. *Wikipedia*, s.v. "Blockbuster," accessed February 18, 2024, http://en.wikipedia.org/wiki/Blockbuster_LLC.

3 Effective Decision-Making

In this chapter, the critical role that decision-making plays in the process of innovation and entrepreneurship is examined. Key questions are raised and addressed: What is effective decision-making? What does the decision-making framework and process look like? What role does implicit cognitive bias play in effective decision-making? In examining these questions and more, we explore how to improve decision-making effectiveness using a deliberate process. Several factors are outlined that provide guidance on the extent of the decision process, such as the decision-making frame, the category, the number of scenarios, the evaluation factors, and the choice dimensions.

Effective decision-making is an overarching lifelong competency that is required for building innovation capability to facilitate value creation in a global world of change, complexity, and competition.

Intuit

Intuit provides an interesting and illustrative example of the crucial role of decision-making in innovation and entrepreneurship. Inuit is a business and financial software company that provides a suite of financial, accounting, and tax preparation products and service for small businesses, accountants, and individuals. Through effective decision-making, the company has been able to successfully transform itself systematically using its strategic and execution capability that helped build a continuous competitive advantage.[1]

Intuit has been able to embed innovation within their strategic decision-making process by reinventing products, services, and their organization itself.[2] Intuit's first product was the personal-finance software product, Quicken, which led to a portfolio of products including Quick-Books, Mint, TurboTax, and Proconnect.

Intuit, as a start-up, was willing to take risks using both disruptive and nondisruptive creative pathways to provide new technology solutions and new business models. Intuit has succeeded in a combination of organic growth, active acquisitions, and divestures while simultaneously disrupting start-ups, such as Xerox, and formidable incumbents, such as Microsoft.

With the introduction of personal computers, Scott Cook, a former Procter & Gamble executive, realized that consumers wanted a better way to do paper-and-pencil based personal accounting. Scott Cook and Tom Proulz founded Intuit in 1983 and developed Quicken for the IBM PC and Apple II.[3]

The problem: accounting and tax preparation were a cumbersome process due to the complexity of the tax laws. The solution: Intuit was able to identify a job to be done and utilize the opportunity afforded by digital technologies by redefining how taxes are filed. Tax preparation services emerged as tax service businesses, certified public accounting firms, and national chains such as H&R Block or Jackson Hewitt. Even with the valuable expertise offered by these professionals, the process had several flaws and many customers had negative experiences.[4] As captured in the following quote, in the 1990s, the Intuit business products, QuickBooks and Turbo Tax, were introduced that displaced the need for accountants.

The customer needed to collect all documents comprehensively beforehand, and the fees were high. Many people procrastinated and then had to squeeze into scarce appointments before the

DOI: 10.4324/9781003034308-4

April 15 deadline, further adding to the stress. If you forgot or could not locate documentation for income, the tax calculations were inaccurate. Discovery of such income by the IRS led to audits with potential for penalties. And, if one did not remember or know about all their possible deductions – such as charitable contributions – and assemble the appropriate documentation beforehand, the customer would not get those deductions.[5]

In 1993, Intuit went public and used the proceeds to strategically acquire five firms, including tax preparation and payroll processing firms. In 1991, Microsoft became a competitor to Quicken by offering Microsoft Money. In 1994, Microsoft attempted to acquire Intuit, but it was disapproved by the United States Department of Justice.

Intuit launched new web-based products and solutions, putting more emphasis on QuickBooks and on TurboTax. In the 2000s they acquired ten firms, including Mint.com, a personal finance service. In the 2010s, they acquired 12 firms including Mobile Money Ventures, to position themselves for online and mobile banking; they sold seven firms.

In 2012, Microsoft withdrew their offering, Microsoft Money, from the market and no longer provided any of the personal accounting and bookkeeping/money management features of the legacy desktop program.[6] In 2016, Inuit sold the original Quicken (PC-based) personal software product offering to position themselves for cloud platforms. In the 2020, they acquired Credit Karma that offers free access to your credit scores, reports, and monitoring.[7]

Intuit has demonstrated an effective decision-making ability to combine an understanding of employee creativity, business trends, and a culture of innovation for discovering jobs that needed to be done. Intuit understood how to disrupt itself, reinventing its products and its business model before the competition.

What Is Effective Decision-Making?

Effective decision-making is the process of choosing a meaningfully significant course of action for various aspects of our lives. As illustrated in Figure 3.1, effective decision-making begins with the decision-maker. It is a process that can be learned and improved upon, forming an overarching meta-competency that is relevant in all organizations to multiply effectiveness, enhance the lives of all stakeholders, and facilitate adaptation and flexibility.[8] Stephen Covey, author of *The 7 Habits of Highly Effective People*, notes, "I am not a product of my circumstances, I'm a product of my decisions."

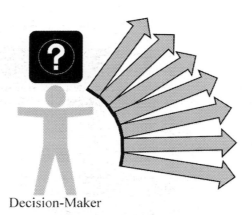

Decision-Maker

Figure 3.1 Illustration of the Decision-Maker

Steven Johnson writes, "Most decisions, big or small, are fundamentally predictions about the future. I choose vanilla ice cream over chocolate because I can predict, with an accuracy long-buffered by experience, that I will enjoy the vanilla more than the chocolate."[9] Johnson continues, "We make predictions about where all those different paths might lead us, given the variables at play; we reach a decision on a path by weighing the various outcomes against our overarching objectives."[10]

Why Is Decision-Making Important?

Roy "Wrong Way" Riegels, who played football for the University of California, Berkeley, is credited with the worst decision in the history of college football when he picked up a fumble in the 1929 Rose Bowl and ran toward his opponent's goal line, resulting in a safety. The opposing team Georgia Tech won 8–7.[11]

The effectiveness of our decision-making has a significant impact on our lives and on the lives of others. Decisions that matter the most in our individual lives and collectively in our organizations can dramatically result in sustainable progress. An effective decision-making process is essential to removing the many obstacles, such as implicit cognitive biases, which interfere with effective decision-making.

Decision-making is the most important cognitive process that is used in our daily lives. Decision-making is an essential, life-long meta-competency which enables us to make the right choices when confronted with new challenges experienced individually, in groups, and across organizations.

Effective decision-making is important because choices define our lives. Studies indicate that choices in large stakes domains, such as our behavior about exercise and nutrition, savings for retirement, choosing a mortgage, or investing in the stock market, are often sub-optimized.

In a recent McKinsey survey, 61 percent of executives said that at least half the time they spent making decisions, much of it surely spent in meetings, was ineffective. And just 37 percent of respondents said their organizations' decisions were both high-quality and timely.[12]

Teaching Effective Decision-Making

Making effective decisions is a learnable competency. Yet there are few if any courses devoted to the art and science of decision-making, even though the ability to make informed and creative decisions is a competency that applies to everyone. Decision-making is a part of our workplaces, our roles as parents or family members; our civic lives as voters, activists, or elected officials; and our day-to-day economic existence managing our monthly budget or planning for retirement.[13] Teaching effective decision-making involves multiple steps that are informed by several remarkable contrasts:

1. Effective decision-making is a meta-competency that is not typically taught in most educational systems. Surprisingly, many people are never trained in how to make effective decisions.
2. Decision-making is the *least* understood and *most* valuable high-order competency that we use in all aspects of our lives.

3. Decision-making is one of the most *frequent* cognitive tasks that we perform, yet we do not make the effort to learn how to do it effectively.
4. Decision-making has inherent invisible obstacles, such as implicit cognitive biases, which interfere with the clarity, completeness, and accuracy of our thoughts.

The Scientific Method

Effective decision-making starts with an understanding of the scientific method. The scientific method is a process that includes observations, questions, hypotheses, experimentation, conclusions, and results. "The process in the scientific method involves making conjectures (hypothetical explanations), deriving predictions from the hypotheses as logical consequences, and then carrying out experiments or empirical observations based on those predictions."[14] A hypothesis is a concept that can be tested to see if it might be true. Hypothesis-driven thinking involves formulating an early answer to a problem and then diving into the data to seek to improve and refine it.

The hypothesis-driven thinking process allows you to work through problems quickly and efficiently by holding your hypothesis loosely allowing you to keep an open mind.[15]

- Hold your hypotheses loosely by being willing to fundamentally reconsider your initial conclusions – and do so without defensiveness.
- Actively listen to understand, more than you talk.
- Leave your queries open-ended and avoid yes-or-no questions.
- Consider the counterintuitive to avoid falling into biased influence such as groupthink.
- Take time to process the problem, rather than making decisions unnecessarily quickly.

Decision-making is composed of both creative and critical thinking; both are essential competencies for building intellectual capability.[16] Creative thinking is a divergent process that elicits ideas that are novel, have value, and are useful. Critical thinking is a convergent process that assesses the worth or validity in something that exists. "Critical thinking entails an interpretation or analysis, even an evaluation or judgment about a claim that may or may not be valid, complete, or the best possible."[17] Critical thinking can be applied to understand how to separate facts from opinions and validate claims. The key to both creative and critical thinking is knowing how to formulate deep, different, and effective questions.

Joseph Rudyard Kipling was an English journalist, short-story writer, poet, and novelist who was awarded the Nobel Prize for Literature in 1907.[18] He created the Kipling method of open-ended questioning that is expanded here to include 12 decision-making elements. As illustrated in Figure 3.2, there are two elements for each question that provide focus and depth to the decision-making process.

- Who is involved in the decision: individual or group?
- What is the impact of the decision: tactical or strategic?
- Where does the decision take place: in-person or digital?
- When is the decision needed: short-term or long-term?
- Why is the decision important: aimless or purposeful?
- How is the decision to be made: reactive or proactive?

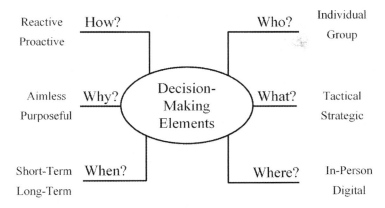

Figure 3.2 Illustration of the Decision-Making Elements

Source: Acknowledgement: John Coleman, "Critical Thinking Is About Asking Better Questions," *Harvard Business Review*, April 22, 2022, accessed April 26, 2022, https://hbr.org/2022/04/critical-thinking-is-about-asking-better-questions

What Is the Decision-Making Process?

Effective decision-making can be illustrated by applying a five-step process, as illustrated in Figure 3.3. Decision-making is a cognitive process of framing, categorization, identifying and choosing alternative scenarios, evaluating, and making a choice. The five-step decision-making process reveals the pathway to improve our ability to make decisions and to reflect on how we can improve our decisions.

Figure 3.3 Illustration of the Decision-Making Process

Source: Acknowledgement: Johnson, Steven. 2018. *Farsighted.* New York: Riverhead.

Effective Decision-Making Support Systems

Effective decision-making relies on accurately inputting, analyzing, and formulating alternatives often based on mutually attractive trade-offs. Questionable assumptions, information overload, misinformation, and haphazard pivoting, to name a few, are detrimental to effective decision-making. For example, an over emphasis of failing fast may lead to a quick decision for an investor, but may not be optimal to the entrepreneur as an effective decision. The ability to prevent dysfunction in decision-making can be addressed by creating a more robust decision-making model that enables informed choices. Several key questions must be addressed to optimize effective decision-making support systems:

1. How do we holistically combine the essentials of forward-thinking organizations into our decision-making?
2. How are guesswork, uncertainty, and inefficiency removed from decision-making?
3. How is a meaningfully significant mindset integrated into decision-making that empowers leadership of character?

4. How is a shared understanding of stakeholder capitalism, trends, and customers' changing needs cultivated?
5. How is a strategic growth mindset to win formulated for the future?
6. How do we align the efforts of our decision-making to be implicit cognitive bias-free?

According to author Ron Carucci, effective decision-making requires significant managerial attention, as summarized in Figure 3.4.[19]

Confusion over decision rights, accountability, roles and responsibilities.	"If your governance system is failing, people may grow confused about who is in charge of what — leading to a futile tug-of-war between departments or team members."
Competing and conflicting priorities.	"People who complain about overlapping or ever-changing priorities are often operating within an organization that is misaligned about what to focus on."
Lack of alignment of strategy and implement within organizations.	"If governing bodies are not managed correctly, they stick around long after their reasoning has ceased and generate activity and reports nobody cares about."
Unfocused communications, meetings, and discussions.	"Whereas effective meetings facilitate honest conversations that lead to smart choices, unfocused meetings often turn into long, irrelevant status updates with dishonest exchanges that paralyze effective decision making and risk making an already messy governance system worse."

Figure 3.4 Illustration of Effective Decision Making Support Systems

Source: Adapted from Ron Carucci, "How Systems Support (or Undermine) Good Decision Making," February 04, 2020, *Harvard Business Review*, acccessed February 5, 2020, https://hbr.org/2020/02/how-systems-support-or-undermine-good-decision-making

Defining a Decision-Making Framework

The decision-making framework for innovation is composed of three key components: character, creativity, and compassion, as illustrated in Figure 3.5.

1. Character is the foundation for effective decisions that are anchored to truthfulness, honesty, fairness, and excellence.
2. Creativity is the generation of ideas that have value that includes the willingness to transform from the obsolete to new value propositions when required. Creativity is essential because many decisions require the pursuit of unique alternatives.
3. Compassion is the capability to identify the emotions of others and how we would feel in the same circumstances.[20] Compassion is based on the ability to understand self-awareness and social awareness and resist implicit cognitive biases. Compassion is the ability to understand the consequences of the decision before the decision is made and afterward if corrective actions are needed. Compassion enables reflection, the process of thinking about thinking that underlies the significantly meaningful choices that we make.

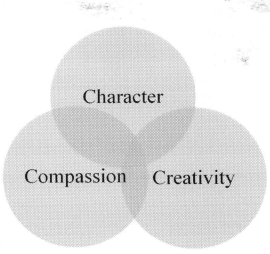

Figure 3.5 Illustration of the Decision Framework Components

Source: Adapted from Jennifer Riel and Roger L. Martin, *Creating Great Choices*, (Boston, Massachusetts: Harvard Business Review Press, 2017), 12.

Character is at the center of effective decision-making because it establishes trust. Trust is the underlying means for establishing relationships that provide a means for effective decisions. For example, a Pew Research Center report from 2019 found that many Americans see declining levels of trust making it more difficult to solve some of the country's problems. Seventy-five percent of Americans say that their fellow citizens' trust in the federal government has been decreasing. Sixty-four percent believe that peoples' trust in each other has also decreased.[21]

There are several examples of unethical behavior that have been identified in businesses and society worldwide. The US tobacco industry misled the public about the addictiveness of nicotine and the cancer-causing effects of tobacco, while DuPont polluted waterways with known toxins.[22,23] Wells Fargo inappropriately accessed customer accounts, and Volkswagen misreported emission controls.[24] Governments around the world have engaged in human rights violations and misinformation.

These three components of effective decision-making can be validated by imagining a decision-making process that reverses these. That is, decisions are made based on a lack of character (dishonesty), a lack of creativity (considering one option), or a lack of compassion (inability to understand the feelings of others).

A survey of more than 14,500 employees was conducted to better understand how Americans experience work by the Yale Center for Emotional Intelligence, in collaboration with the Faas Foundation. The sample represented the US economy in the distribution of industries represented and demographic diversity. The findings revealed that nearly one in four people felt pressured to do things they knew were wrong.[25]

What Does the Research Suggest?

A survey that was conducted by McKinsey & Company with more than 1,200 managers across a range of global companies "gave strong sings of" less-than-optimal decision-making processes, slow-paced decision-making deliberations, and decision-making outcomes of uneven quality.[26]

Fewer than half of the survey respondents say that decisions are timely, and 61 percent say that at least half the time spent making them is ineffective. The opportunity costs of this are staggering: About 530,000 days of managers' time potentially squandered each year for a typical Fortune 500 company, equivalent to some $250 million in wages annually.[27]

As summarized in Figure 3.6, respondents at winning organizations are twice as likely compared to all respondents to report their recent decisions have delivered returns of 20% or more (36/18).[28] The research suggests that the effectiveness of our decisions can be improved in most firms. "[Seventy-two] percent of senior-executive respondents to a McKinsey survey said they thought bad strategic decisions either were about as frequent as good ones or were the prevailing norm in their organization."[29]

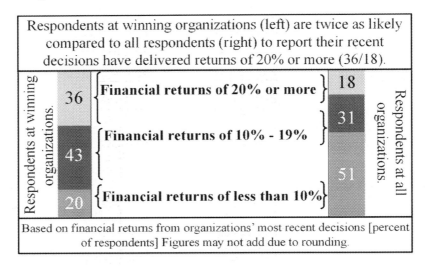

Figure 3.6 Illustration of the Value of Effective Decisions

Source: Acknowledgement: Iskandar Aminov, Aaron De Smet, Gregor Jost, and David Mendelsohn, "Decision making in the age of urgency," April 2019, McKinsey & Company, Retrieved from https://www.mckinsey.com/business-functions/organization/our-insights/decision-making-in-the-age-of-urgency

Making good business decisions is a critical part of every executive's job and is vital to every company's well-being. Based on a global survey from McKinsey & Company:[30]

1. Respondents at winning organizations are twice as likely (2 × 18 = 36) as others to say their recent decisions have delivered returns of 21% or more.
2. Respondents spend 37% of their time making decisions, and more than 50% of this time was thought to be spent ineffectively.
3. Only 20% of respondents say their organizations excel at decision-making.

Why Do Decisions Fail?

Have your ever watched a sport and disagreed with an umpire or judge's call? "Ample anecdotal and empirical evidence indicates that sports performance judgments are at least as prone to systematic errors (biases) as other social judgments."[31] According to Anderson and Pierce, there is cognitive bias in sports that has a balancing effect.[32] The leading teams tend to receive more fouls. Calling fouls against the leading team tends to keep games closer. The bigger the difference in fouls between the two teams playing, the more likely it was that the next call would come against the team with fewer fouls.

According to Prof. Paul C. Nutt at the Ohio State University, half of the decisions made in organizations fail, making failure far more prevalent than previously thought. He determined that the practices/processes followed to decide are the most important determinants of decision-making success.[33] The failures can be causally linked to the actions of decision-makers. Forces beyond the decision-maker's control, such as changes in customer tastes, budget cuts, and the like, can also prompt failure, but the practices/processes followed to decide are the most important determinants of success.

Decision-Making Errors

Professor Nutt identified three errors that lead to failed decisions:[34]

1. The first error is a **rush** by managers to identify a concern and select the first solution rather than taking time to look at other options.
2. The second error is the **misuse of resources** by spending time and money during decision-making on the wrong issue rather than gathering the intelligence and underlying data that is needed.
3. The third error is **applying failure-prone tactics** to make decisions, such as not involving those affected by the decision to participate in the decision-making process.

Journalist and book author Charles Duhigg writes,

> Destructive organizational habits can be found within hundreds of industries and at thousands of firms. And almost always, they are the products of thoughtlessness, of leaders who avoid thinking about the culture and so let it develop without guidance. There are no organizations without institutional habits. There are only places where they are deliberately designed, and places where they are created without forethought, so they often grow from rivalries or fears.[35]

Implicit Cognitive Bias

Decision-making and thinking errors can be caused by misperceptions due to implicit cognitive bias. That is, attitudes or judgments we hold about people or things, often unconsciously. For example, in a study using blindfolded violinists, six violins were compared: three high-quality modern violins with a Guarneri and two Stradivari instruments from the 18th century. There is a widespread belief that Giuseppe Guarneri violins rivals those by Antonio Stradivari as tonally superior. Yet the blindfolded violinists in the test could not reliably distinguish the violins of the old masters from the modern violins. The Guarneri and Stradivari violins do not, according to this blindfolded play-off, sound better than high-quality modern violin instruments.[36] This suggests that blind spots of accumulated bias play a role in effective decision-making.

Stephen Spielberg's *Jaws* was a popular movie about a disgruntled large great white shark that attacked swimmers in a small island community. Many people can easily recall John William's melodramatic musical theme from *Jaws*. The *Jaws* movie is an example of how our thinking can be affected into a form of bias, in this case shark bias. Biases are strongly held beliefs that are formed early in our lives and reformed by some significant emotional event. The *Jaws* movie created the impression that shark bites were high-risk for swimmers on the beaches of the oceans. It is counterintuitive to think that sharks are more at risk from people than people are at risk from sharks. Unlike the story in the movie, people are not on the shark's menu at all. Implicit cognitive biases are a constraint for all types of decision-making that involve people because they are deceptive and distort our thinking and the outcomes that we deserve.

Memory

About 60% of Americans believe that memory works like a video camera analogy where our experiences are recorded, stored, and later retrieved to viewing. Instead, our memory works more like a "mental paleontologist" that uncovers a fossil that represents a part of a species. Because the paleontologist does not have all the pieces, they must fill in the gaps.[37]

For example, in the late 1800s, Hermann Ebbinghaus conducted experiments on how memory works using nonsense syllables, such as lek, muf, vok, dal, sen, kep, nut, muf, ton, and gen, three random letters strung together.

> Hermann Ebbinghaus remembered thousands of three-letter strings and then tried to see how many he remembered the same day, the next week, the next year. He discovered something that many of us experience. Over time, he started to forget things. But since he was running an experiment, it allowed him to measure how much he was forgetting and how quickly. It led him to discover something that is today called the forgetting curve.[38]

The forgetting curve is the evidence that our recollections are fallible and that they interfere with decision-making that extends far beyond where we left our keys. The implications extend into high-stakes decision-making in our personal lives, in business settings, and in the court system where we ask people to make recollections or remember things under oath that can result in incorrect criminal convictions.[39]

The Lack of Evidence

The well-regarded statistician W. Edwards Deming says, "In God we trust, all others bring data." Rather than relying on intuition or experience, data and analytics can be used to create actionable insights for effective decision-making. To make progress in our complex and changing world we must create new data in new categories to discover new actionable insights.[40] We continue to experience staggering volumes of this new data that requires us to use technologies such as the combination of data, analytics, and artificial intelligence (AI).[41]

Deloitte conducted an online survey of 1,048 senior managers or higher executives of US-based companies with 501+ employees who interact with, create, or use analytics as part of their responsibilities that revealed significant opportunities for the utilization of data.[42] Figure 3.7 illustrates the salient aspects of a data-driven culture.

Leaders at all levels of an organization recognize the need to build a culture, the collective behaviors of an organization, to improve decision-making. Leaders who understand culture change can become data advocates, create new programs and educational initiatives, recognize early adopters and enlist them to help get others engaged, and build diverse cross-functional teams that combine people from many different disciplines.[43]

What Are the Factors That Influence Decision-Making?

Market Decision-Making

The efficient market theory is an economic model of how stocks and markets function. The theory is based on the notion that, ceteris paribus, stocks are always accurately priced and reflect all available information. Although you can search for undervalued securities, it is unlikely to find any, because efficient market theory predicts that you cannot beat the stock market. The theory is based on control, rationality, measurable risk, and efficiency. "The data clearly show that the efficient

Most executives do not believe their companies are insight-driven.	Sixty three percent (63%) of U.S. executives do not believe their companies are analytics-driven. They are aware of analytics but lack infrastructure, are still working in silos, or are expanding ad hoc analytics capabilities beyond silos.
Culture can be a catalyst or a culprit.	Among the thirty-seven percent (37%) of companies in the survey with the strongest analytics cultures, forty-eight percent (48%) significantly exceeded their business goals in the past 12 months, making them twice as likely to do so compared to the sixty-three percent (63%) that do not have as strong an analytics culture.
Aim high for analytics champions.	The CEO is the lead champion of analytics in twenty-nine percent (29%) of companies surveyed, and these companies are seventy-seven percent (77%) more likely to have significantly exceeded their business goals. They are also fifty-nine percent (59%) more likely to derive actionable insights from the analytics they are tracking.
Most executives are not comfortable accessing or using data.	Sixty-seven percent (67%) of those surveyed (who are senior managers or higher) say they are not comfortable accessing or using data from their tools and resources. The proportion is significant even at companies with strong data-driven cultures, where thirty-seven percent (37%) of respondents still express discomfort.

Figure 3.7 Illustration of Data-Driven Culture

Source: Adapted from Tom Davenport, Jim Guszcza, Tim Smith, and Ben Stiller, "Analytics and AI-driven enterprises thrive in the Age of With," accessed March 24, 2020, https://www2.deloitte.com/us/en/insights/topics/analytics/insight-driven-organization.html

market theory has fostered an economic system that, over the past two decades, has generated little innovation among most companies, weakened the middle class, widened inequality, and led to the relative decline of the United States."[44]

Efficient market theory has been questioned because it does not realistically include uncertainty. There are several examples of abrupt changes in the stock market that cannot be explained by this theory.[45] But efficient market theory is important because it has influenced the thinking of many managers in their quest for cost reduction and maximization of short-term financial results.

The markets do not always act in a rational manner. New value propositions that identify new opportunities exist in inefficient, unserved, underserved, and uncertain markets. Entrepreneurs are willing to tolerate the uncertainties of the dynamic changes in technologies and consumer needs that perpetually occur in the markets. Those who have been molded in their thinking by efficient market theory would be far less likely to be leading, inspirational forces for creative endeavors. Managers who operate under efficient market theory will focus on the "red ocean" of efficiency and cost reduction, sacrificing the "blue ocean" of creativity and innovation.

Markets work efficiently when all the gears are meshing, and things are normal in the global economy. Effective decision-making is essential throughout our lives but is severely impacted and pernicious during times of uncertainty and sentinel events. Markets are generally reliable to guide our choices except when black swan sentinel events occur, such as world wars, depressions, or recessions. During black swan sentinel events, rapid action is needed to manage the dynamic changes and complex coordination. The market mechanisms during black swan sentinel events do not work well to inform what decisions need to be made. Markets tend to be risk-adverse and focus on short-term profits. During the COVID-19 pandemic of 2020; for example, the following occurred:

1. Food shortages because farmers, to avoid supply gluts that drive down prices, dumped milk, broke eggs, and turned pork bellies to lard instead of bacon because sales to restaurants, hotels, and colleges declined.
2. Personal protective equipment and ventilators were not readily available because companies do not typically carry large inventories that would add cost burdens.

Behavioral Economics

The discipline of behavioral economics, led by social psychologists Daniel Kahneman and Amos Tversky, has revealed that our human brains distort decision-making processes.[46] Nobel laureate Daniel Kahneman, the author of *Thinking Fast and Slow*, provided insights into our decision-making processes when he described how implicit cognitive biases lead to sub-optimal decisions far removed from the rational choices assumed by classical economics.[47]

Decisions makers often base their decision-making processes on their past successes. For instance, those in decision-making positions can experience a phenomenon known as functional fixedness. Functional fixedness occurs when a decision-maker's experience with a particular function of an object impedes using the object in a novel way when searching for a solution to a problem.[48] Studies indicate that we make poor choices in large-stakes domains such as our health (exercise and nutrition), saving for retirement, choosing a mortgage, or investing in the stock market.

Normative Economics

Economic models taught in classical economics are normative theories that attempt to portray what ought to be through optimization, but they do not always predict behavior accurately. Normative economics is a perspective that reflects ideologically prescriptive judgments toward economic development, investment projects, statements, and scenarios.[49] Normative economics, however, cannot fully describe, explain, or predict choices of everyday people. The economic models are approximations based on people like the fictional character Mr. Spock, from the television series and later movie franchise *Star Trek*, completely rational and unbiased. Most people are not like Mr. Spock, however, because they have implicit biases and do not always optimize. These people may be unaware that they are not optimizing their decision-making at all. Economic models are based on normative theories that tell you the right way to think about some problem. In summary, normative economics attempts to optimize decisions.

Positive Economics

Positive economics is concerned with the description and explanation of economic phenomena that focuses on what is, facts, and cause-and-effect behavioral relationships.[50] Using behavioral economics, Kahneman describes how implicit cognitive biases lead to sub-optimal decisions far removed from the rational choices assumed by classical economics.

Behavioral economics is a blend of psychology and economics that explains our limitations and why people do not always think rationally. Behavioral economics uses descriptive theory to model real-life choices rather than normative theories based on economic optimization models. In summary, positive economics focuses on real-life choices to accurately portray human decision-making.

Heuristics

Heuristics are "rules of thumb" that we use to make decisions. We use heuristics to make decisions because we do not have the time or resources to acquire all the information that we need. Heuristics can result in implicit cognitive biases that can lead to decision-making errors.

Representativeness Heuristic

Representativeness is a concept that describes how our decision-making is influenced by the likelihood of uncertain events that we experience, and our thinking skills do not necessarily calculate the correct outcome. When we make judgments, we use subjective probabilities, guesses that can result in the wrong answers. Our decision-making is influenced by the likelihood of uncertain events that we experience, and our thinking skills do not necessarily calculate the correct outcome. We make a representative judgment that replaces a correct calculation of the odds.[51] For example, consider this hypothetical example: Linda is 31 years old, single, outspoken, and very bright. She majored in philosophy. As a student, she was deeply concerned with issues of discrimination and social justice and participated in anti-nuclear demonstrations.[52]

Which is more probable?[53]

1. Linda is a bank teller.
2. Linda is a bank teller and is an activist.

Even though the correct answer is (1), most people, 85% of those asked, chose option (2). This is because option (2) seems more "representative" of Linda based on the description of her even though it is mathematically less likely. As illustrated in Figure 3.8, this is because the probability of two events occurring together (in conjunction) is always less than or equal to the probability of either one occurring alone.

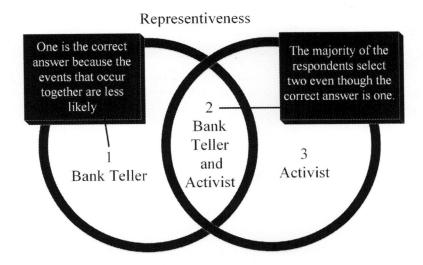

Figure 3.8 Illustration of Conjunctive Fallacy (Linda Problem)

Source: Adapted from Daniel Kahneman, *Thinking, Fast and Slow,* (New York: Farrar, Straus and Giroux, 2011), 156–158.

Prospect Theory

In addition to representative heuristics, understanding the notion of prospect theory is essential to managing implicit cognitive biases. Several implicit cognitive biases can be explained using prospect theory.

Prospect theory describes why people are more sensitive to losses, compared to gains of similar magnitude. Notice that the loss function (see Figure 3.9) on the left is steeper than the gain function on the right. People have tendencies to care less and less about increases in wealth. People tend to care increasingly about decreases in wealth.

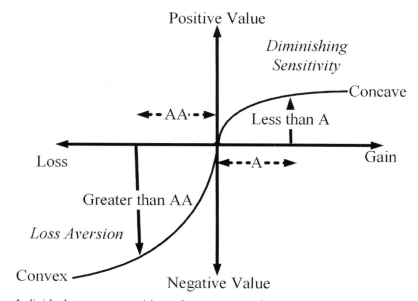

Individuals are more sensitive to losses compared to gains of similar magnitude.

Figure 3.9 Illustration of Prospect Theory

Source: Adapted from Nobel Laureate Daniel Kahneman and Amos Tversky https://econfix.wordpress.com/2013/03/27/behavioural-economics-propsect-theory/

Prospect Theory Example

Which of the following would you prefer?

1. *a. A certain win of $250*
    versus
    b. A 25% chance to win $1000 and a 75% chance to win nothing

2. *How about:*
    c. A certain loss of $750
    versus
    d. A 75% chance to lose $1000 and a 25% chance to lose nothing

Tversky and Kahneman's work shows that responses are different if choices are framed as a gain (1) or a loss (2). When faced with the first type of decision, a greater proportion of people will opt for the riskless alternative a), while for the second problem people are more likely to choose the riskier d). This happens because we dislike losses more than we like an equivalent gain: Giving something up is more painful than the pleasure we derive from receiving it.[54]

As depicted in Figure 3.9, prospect theory provides an explanation for decision-making associated with the concept of disruptive creation. Start-up new entrants are more likely to embrace new innovations because they have no endowments. In other words, entrants have less to lose. Established incumbents have endowments and a defined culture that supports the institutional memory shaping their success. This institutional memory can be an invisible decision-making force for those incumbents, often allowing them to be outmaneuvered by an agile start-up, for example.

Implicit and Explicit Cognitive Biases

There are two types of biases: implicit and explicit. Implicit biases are unconscious biases that affect the way we perceive, interpret, evaluate, or relate to other people. Explicit biases can be uncovered through observation, questioning, reflection, and introspection. The impact of cognitive decision-making biases is accentuated during high-stress circumstances, resulting in undesirable decisions that may be unbeknownst to the decision-makers themselves.

We all have hidden biases that influence how decisions and choices are made. These biases mean that, even in the face of rational evidence that supports proceeding in one direction, there is a likelihood that when given a choice an irrational choice occurs. "Biases are predispositions of a psychological, sociological, or even physiological nature that can influence our decision making. They often operate subconsciously and are outside the logical process on which decisions are purportedly based."[55]

Over optimism and risk aversion are examples of related cognitive biases that may affect effective decision-making. Learning organizations can enhance the decision-making process through a culture that explicitly seeks out the validity of claims that people initiate. The bias grid depicted in Figure 3.10 illustrates how different types of decisions are interwoven with the size, stakes, risks, and frequency of learning opportunities. Companies need to be aware that they are not always rationally factoring risk into decisions.[56]

1. In quadrant I, where there are large, high-stakes, and infrequent decisions, such as with mergers and acquisitions, there may be a tendency to take an overly optimistic view and accept unnecessary risk leading to an incorrect decision.
2. In quadrant II, where there are large, high-stakes, and frequent decisions, such as a new investment or the construction of a new plant using existing technology, there are ample learning opportunities, and the degree of risk aversion is likely to be reasonable.
3. In quadrant III, where there are small, low-stakes, and infrequent decisions, such as early research and development investments in mature businesses, optimism and loss aversion may counteract each other.
4. In quadrant IV, where there are small, low-stakes, and frequent decisions, such as small mergers and acquisitions and small product launches, excessive risk aversion is usually the dominant bias that may be unwarranted.

Deception Impact on Cognitive Biases

There are five cognitive biases summarized in Figure 3.11 that may result in deceptive decision-making. These cognitive biases when used in combination may have a significant impact on current decision processes and future innovation choices.

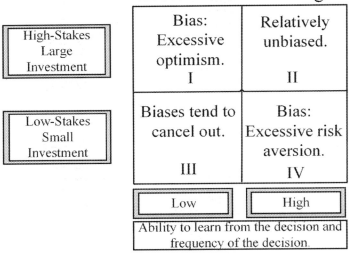

Factors that are most likely to affect decision-making

	Low	High
High-Stakes Large Investment	Bias: Excessive optimism. I	Relatively unbiased. II
Low-Stakes Small Investment	Biases tend to cancel out. III	Bias: Excessive risk aversion. IV

Ability to learn from the decision and frequency of the decision.

Figure 3.10 Illustration of Decision-Making Bias Grid

Source: Adapted from Dan P. Lovallo and Olivier Sibony, "Distortions and deceptions in strategic decisions," February 2006, accessed February 20, 2020, https://www.mckinsey.com/business-functions/strategy-and-corporate-finance/our-insights/distortions-and-deceptions-in-strategic-decisions

The Impact of Cognitive Biases on Decision-Making [Deceptions]

Decision-Making is Deceptive	Potential Results
The status quo bias is a defense for maintaining the current state that is caused by an inflexible mindset and behaviors.	Managers will keep doing what they did yesterday not what they should be doing in the future.
The short-termism bias is the tendency to focus on short-term results rather than making a deliberate rational and complete choice	Managers will focus on short-term incremental innovations and sacrifice future opportunities.
The sunk-cost fallacy or escalation of commitment is a preference to continue investing even though it is unwarranted by focusing our attention on historical costs that are not recoverable when deciding on future alternatives.	Managers should ignore sunk costs especially if there is a substantial innovation opportunity on the horizon.
The authority bias is the tendency to attribute greater accuracy to the opinion of a person who has the power in their authority. Sunflower management, related to authority bias, is the tendency for groups to align with the views of their leaders, through authority, whether expressed or assumed.	Individuals and managers will support the decisions of their leadership whether they are right or wrong. This phenomenon is accentuated in a culture with a directive and low autonomy leadership style.
Groupthink is the tendency to allow consensus to override the thoughtful and realistic appraisal of alternative courses of action.	Managers can choose the wrong alternative if contrary views are suppressed.

Figure 3.11 Illustration of Decision-Making Deception Grid

Source: Adapted from Dan P. Lovallo and Olivier Sibony, "Distortions and deceptions in strategic decisions," February 2006, accessed February 20, 2020, https://www.mckinsey.com/business-functions/strategy-and-corporate-finance/our-insights/distortions-and-deceptions-in-strategic-decisions

Distortion Impact on Cognitive Biases

There are five cognitive biases summarized in Figure 3.12 that may result in distorted decision-making. These cognitive biases singly or in combination may result in sub-optimal decisions being chosen.

The Impact of Cognitive Biases on Decision-Making [Distortions]	
Decision-Making is Distorted	Potential Result
Confirmation bias is the tendency to place more emphasis on information that is consistent with our beliefs, hypotheses, and experiences and to place less emphasis on information that contradicts them. Confirmation bias causes people to search for information in a way that confirms their preexisting beliefs or hypotheses.	Managers seek information that supports their antiquated beliefs without considering all of the facts.
The over-optimism bias is a phenomenon that describes the tendency to experience comparative unrealistic optimism.	Managers will underestimate the challenges of their innovation projects that have a large scope or long time frame.
The loss aversion bias is the tendency to feel losses more significantly than gains making us more risk-averse than rational behavior would suggest.	Managers will be unwilling to propose a new idea.
The overconfidence effect is the tendency for people to misjudge their own abilities that can result in forecasting unrealistic challenges.	Managers will understate risks for new investments, larger mergers, and acquisitions.
Stereotypes are representations of generalized categories of people that are used to make decisions. Stereotyping involves making a judgment about a person without having accurate information about the person.	Managers fail to hire the most qualified person or fail to promote the most competent person because of their race, religion, nationality, or sexual orientation.

Figure 3.12 Illustration of Decision-Making Distortion Grid

Source: Adapted from Dan P. Lovallo and Olivier Sibony, "Distortions and deceptions in strategic decisions," February 2006, accessed February 20, 2020, https://www.mckinsey.com/business-functions/strategyand-corporate-finance/our-insights/distortions-and-deceptions-in-strategic-decisions

Combinations of Cognitive Biases

Individual cognitive biases are inadvertently incorporated in our decisions but can occur in combinations that result in even more dysfunction. "Consider, for instance, a decision made by Blockbuster, the video-rental giant, in the spring of 2000. A promising start-up approached Blockbuster's management with an offer to sell itself for $50 million and join forces to create a 'click-and-mortar' video-rental model. Its name? Netflix."[57] The Blockbuster decision is an example of a common pattern that includes overconfidence, when an executive misjudges their own abilities; confirmation bias, when an executive seeks information that is consistent with their current views; and the sunk cost fallacy, where executives will continue to invest in the past even though better alternatives are present.

Managers can conduct a hypothetical bias buster exercise to evaluate their decisions in advance to achieve more objectivity.

This is an exercise in which, after a project team is briefed on a proposed plan, its members purposefully imagine that the plan has failed. The exercise prompts everyone to review the plan and anticipate potential threats and hurdles. The very structure of a pre-mortem makes it safe to identify problems. Under this approach, psychology is flipped, and blind support for ideas gives way to creative problem solving. In fact, we've seen team members compete to see who can raise the most worrisome issues, and those team members are admired for their foresight, not ostracized.[58]

The Decision-Making Process

Decision-making outcomes can be improved by understanding decision-making processes. Steven Johnson writes, "We have a tendency to emphasize the results of good decisions and not the process that led to the decision itself."[59] As depicted in Figure 3.13, the decision-making process can be described as a step-by-step process that includes framing, categorization, scenarios, evaluating, and choice. While the process needs to be adapted to the specific decision-making situations, overall, it provides insight into a complicated process.

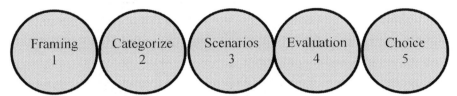

The process needs to be adapted to the decision-making circumstances.
Only the most complex, high-stakes, critical choices need the full comprehensive process.
Always ask yourself the question, what am I missing?

-Scope	-High-stakes	-Divergence	-Facts	-Customer focused
-Time	-Cross-cutting	-Brainstorming	-Expertise	-Implementation
-Effect	-Empowered	-Critique	-Context	Feasibility
			-Values	-Meaningful value

Figure 3.13 Illustration of the Decision-Making Process Steps
Source: Acknowledgement: Johnson, Steven. 2018. *Farsighted.* New York: Riverhead.

Framing

The first step of the decision-making process is framing. Framing is the process of defining the scope of the context associated with a question, problem, or event in a way that can influence how they are perceived and evaluated. There are three framing dimensions (scope, time, and consequence, illustrated in Figure 3.14) that should be considered at the outset prior to collecting data. The framing of a decision is based on determining the following:

1. What is the scope of the business innovation you are pursuing: low, medium, or high?
2. What is the time frame for the launch: right now, in the present, or in the future? If it is now, what time frame do you need to begin the decision-making process to collect facts needed to make the right decision?
3. What is the consequence of the decision? Will it have a positive or negative effect?

For high-stakes decision-making situations, all three of the frames should be considered to avoid missing a critical element needed. Last, ask, what is missing?

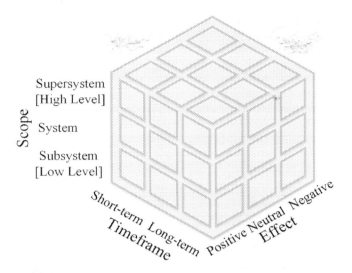

Supersystem
[High Level]

Scope

System

Subsystem
[Low Level]

Short-term Long-term
Timeframe

Positive Neutral Negative
Effect

Figure 3.14 Illustration of the Three Dimensions of Framing

Scope

Scope pertains to the breadth and depth of the decision. According to Ron Carucci, there are three categories of scope in decision-making:[60]

1. Corporate decisions include setting vision and direction for the company, appointing top leaders, defining company values and culture, and managing external reputation.
2. Strategic decisions include decisions about investments the company will make, which customers it will serve, capital expenditures, and setting corporate policies that all employees must comply with.
3. Operational decisions include budgeting, developing, and launching products, and managing talent.

Time

The short-term, medium-term, and long-term define the time framing of the issue. Time framing can be addressed by questions that are answerable with a yes-or-no regarding some course of action.

1. Should the company seek a new direction? Should individuals seek a new career [long-term]?
2. Should the company seek a new strategy? Should individuals seek new employment [medium-term]?
3. Should the company change its pricing? Should individuals go to work today [short-term]?

Effect

As captured in Figure 3.14, framing effects can result in dramatically different outcomes because an individual's response can be different depending on the levels of uncertainty involved and how the information is presented such as a loss or a gain.[61] In general, individuals tend to avoid risk when a positive frame is presented but seek risks when a negative frame is presented. This is the foundation of prospect theory discussed previously in this chapter.

Categories

The second step in the decision-making process is to determine the decision category (type) and who has responsibility for the decision. The three decision categories summarized in Figure 3.15 are high-stakes, cross-cutting, and empowered autonomous delegated decisions.

Decision Type	Examples	Who makes the decision	How to improve
High-stakes decisions: Infrequent, high risk, future shaping.	Mergers and acquisitions.	Top team, board.	Encourage productive debate: Assign roles to argue the case for and against a potential decision.
Cross-cutting decisions: Frequent, often high risk, collaborative.	Operations, planning, and pricing.	Business-unit heads; senior managers.	Focus on the process: The process should include objectives, measures, and targets.
Autonomous delegated decisions: Frequent, low risk, day-to-day.	Hiring, promotions, and marketing.	Individual, working teams.	Ensure commitment through empowerment: Each person should take responsibility.

Figure 3.15 Illustration of the Categories of the Decision Grid

Source: Acknowledgement: Aaron De Smet, Gregor Jost, and Leigh Weiss, "Three keys to faster, better decisions," May 2019, Mckinsey & Company, Retrieved from https://www.mckinsey.com/business-functions/organization/our-insights/three-keys-to-faster-better-decisions

The categorization provides for accountability regarding who makes the decision and how to improve the decision.[62] For instance, a high-stakes, infrequent, and risky decision would require substantial strategic thinking as compared to delegated decisions, which are the responsibility of individuals and managers.[63]

For example, discussing who should make which decision, Ron Carucci notes the need to assess at what level different types of decisions take place.

> Decision rights must be distributed thoughtfully to ensure everyone is clear on the boundaries of their departments and roles. There are a couple of major factors to consider when deciding where to allocate decision rights. Initially, you will need to determine what *level* different types of decisions should take place at. At the enterprise level, place decisions that will [affect] the company at large and need to be made centrally. At the department or business unit level, place decisions that must be discretely made for functions or geographies. At the local or individual level, place decisions that must be made with the uniqueness of employees and teams in mind.[64]

High-Stakes Decisions: Infrequent, High-Risk, and Future Shaping

High-stakes decisions are strategic, meaningful, and significant requiring comprehensive pre-work. Such decisions can change the entire direction of an organization and those that have a significant impact on the lives of individuals. High-stakes decisions are infrequent, unfamiliar, and high-risk.[65] Organizational high-stakes decisions are the responsibility of the top leadership team or the board of directors of an organization. Examples in business might include mergers and acquisitions, reengineering businesses (transformations), and new business opportunities. Individual high-stakes decisions impact how people live, such as marriage, children, healthcare, and job opportunities.

The high-stakes decision-makers need to be familiar with the implications of implicit cognitive biases that can cause decision-making errors. For high-stakes decision-making, McKinsey & Company has proposed four action steps, summarized in Figure 3.16.[66]

Appoint an executive sponsor.	"Each initiative should have a sponsor, who will work with a project lead to frame the important decisions for senior leaders to weigh in on—starting with a clear, one-sentence problem statement."
Break things down, and connect them up.	"Large, complex decisions often have multiple parts; you should explicitly break them down into bite-size chunks, with decision meetings at each stage. Big bets also frequently have interdependencies with other decisions. To avoid unintended consequences, step back to connect the dots."
Deploy a standard decision-making approach.	"The most important way to get big-bet decisions right is to have the right kind of interaction and discussion, including quality debate, competing scenarios, and devil's advocates. Critical requirements are to create a clear agenda that focuses on debating the solution (instead of endlessly elaborating the problem), to require robust prework, and to assemble the right people, with diverse perspectives."
Move faster without losing commitment.	"Fast-but-good decision making also requires bringing the available facts to the table and committing to the outcome of the decision. Executives have to get comfortable living with imperfect data and being clear about what 'good enough' looks like. Then, once a decision is made, they have to be willing to commit to it and take a gamble, even if they were opposed during the debate. Make sure, at the conclusion of every meeting, that it is clear who will communicate the decision and who owns the actions to begin carrying it out."

Figure 3.16 Illustration of the High-Stakes Decision Making

Source: Adapted from Aaron De Smet, Gerald Lackey, and Leigh M. Weiss, "Untangling your organization's decision making," June 2017, Mckinsey & Company, accessed April 26, 2020, https://www.mckinsey.com/business-functions/organization/our-insights/untangling-your-organizations-decision-making

A high-stakes decision can be improved by ensuring high-quality interaction and providing contrary evidence. A high-stakes decision involves three things:

1. Decision-makers explore assumptions and alternatives beyond the given information.
2. Decision-makers actively seek information that would disconfirm their initial hypotheses.
3. Decision-makers designate one or more members of the senior-executive committee to play devil's advocate and present counterarguments to the group.[67]

Cross-cutting Decisions: Frequent, Often High-Risk, Collaborative

Cross-cutting decisions are made by departments within and across organizations and groups with similar goals that are part of a collaborative network.[68] Cross-cutting decisions can be either strategic or tactical, they are frequent and high-risk decisions. Cross-cutting business decisions are the responsibility of business unit leaders and senior management. Examples of organizational cross-cutting decisions are business pricing, marketing, sales, and operational planning processes or new-product launches – that require participation from a wide range of stakeholders. The responsibility for group decision-making is for the formal and informal leaders that share a common purpose. Examples of group decision-making are churches, sports teams, volunteer organizations, and families (moving from one place to another).[69] According to best-selling author Ron Carucci, "Once you've identified which groups have the authority and resources to make which decisions, the next step is to link them to ensure effective coordination. None of these groups are making decisions in a vacuum, and many rely on each other to execute their choices."[70]

As summarized in Figure 3.17, cross-cutting decisions are often the culmination of many smaller decisions made over time and involve stakeholders in different parts of the organization. For effectiveness, the cross-cutting decisions focus on the how-to-processes, such as the running of decision-making meetings. The decision-making process includes how the decision is made, who is involved, when the decision is needed, and how the communications are managed.[71]

Map out the decision-making process, and then pressure-test it.	"Identify decisions that involve a cross-cutting group of leaders, and work with the stakeholders of each to agree on what the main steps in the process entail."
Run water through the pipes.	"Then work through a set of real-life scenarios to pressure-test the system in collaboration with the people who will be running the process."
Establish governance and decision-making bodies.	"Limit the number of decision-making bodies, and clarify for each its mandate, standing membership, roles (decision makers or critical 'informers'), decision-making protocols, key points of collaboration, and standing agenda."
Create shared objectives, metrics, and collaboration targets.	"These will help the persons involved feel responsible not just for their individual contributions in the process, but also for the process's overall effectiveness."

Figure 3.17 Illustration of the Cross-Cutting Decision-Making

Source: Adapted from Aaron De Smet, Gerald Lackey, and Leigh M. Weiss, "Untangling your organization's decision making," June 2017, Mckinsey & Company, accessed April 26, 2020, https://www.mckinsey.com/business-functions/organization-our-insights/untangling-your-organizations-decision-making

Autonomous Delegated Decisions: Frequent, Low-Risk, Day-to-day

Autonomous delegated decisions are frequent, familiar, and low-risk decisions and far narrower in scope than high-stakes decisions or cross-cutting ones. The decisions are tactical and involve day-to-day routine management. The authority to decide should be delegated to those who are closest to understanding the task relevant information needed and have the most relevant competencies to achieve the desired results. Those with the authority are expected to take responsibility for their role to deliver faster, better, and more efficiently the outcomes while also enhancing engagement and accountability.[72]

Autonomous business decisions are the responsibility of working teams and individuals who have received the authority delegated to them. Team decision-making is a shared responsibility. Examples are day-to-day management, in areas such as hiring, marketing, and purchasing. Autonomous individual decision-making is the sole responsibility of the individual. Examples include shopping, vacations, prescribing medicine, and recreational activities.

In most professions, autonomous delegated decision-making requires the use of explicit decision-making rules and best practices such as those for plumbers, electricians, welders, carpenters, physicians, lawyers, scientists, and airline pilots.[73] In business, an effective delegated decision depends on the leadership style, empowerment, mentoring, coaching, and the culture of the organization. "McKinsey survey respondents who report that employees at their company are empowered to make decisions and receive sufficient coaching from leaders were 3.2 times more likely than other respondents to also say their company's delegated decisions were both high quality and speedy."[74] Key elements of delegated decision-making are illustrated in Figure 3.18.

Delegate more decisions.	"Reassure them (and yourself) by creating transparency through good performance dashboards, scorecards, and key performance indicators (KPIs), and by linking metrics back to individual performance reviews."
Avoid overlap of decision rights.	"Doubling up decision responsibility across management levels or dimensions of the reporting matrix only leads to confusion and stalemates."
Establish a clear escalation path.	"Set thresholds for decisions that require approval (for example, spending above a certain amount)..."
Don't let people abdicate.	"One of the key challenges in delegating decisions is actually getting people to take ownership of the decisions."

Figure 3.18 Illustration of the Delegated Decision-Making

Source: Adapted from Aaron De Smet, Gerald Lackey, and Leigh M. Weiss, "Untangling your organization's decision making," June 2017, Mckinsey & Company, accessed April 26, 2020, https://www.mckinsey.com/business-functions/organization/our-insights/untangling-your-organizations-decision-making

Creating Scenarios

The third step in the decision-making process is the creation of alternative scenarios. How do you discover and identify the underlying nature of any decision? You begin by selecting alternative options and ordering them according to your priority. Once you have a list of alternatives for decision-making, you can eliminate those that are less relevant, repeating the process until you find the most useful outcome. The creation of scenarios is like the process of a detective solving a crime, the process that your physician uses to diagnose a medical problem, the differential diagnosis, or the process that a civil engineer uses to build a bridge.

Popular science author Steven Johnson observes:

1. "The most striking finding in Nutt's research was this: Only 15 percent of the case studies involved a stage where the decision-makers actively sought out a new option beyond the initial choices on the table at the onset. In a later study, Nutt found that only 29 percent of organizational decisions contemplated more than one alternative at all."[75]
2. "In one of his studies, Paul Nutt found that participants who considered only one alternative ultimately judged their decision a failure more than 50 percent of the time, while decisions that contemplated at least two alternatives were felt to be successes two-thirds of the time."[76]

Opportunity Costs and Trade-offs

In decision-making, the opportunity cost (alterative cost) is the loss of a potential gain from other alternatives when one alternative is chosen over the others. The goal of opportunity cost (alternative cost) is to ascertain the next valuable opportunity – for instance, a student who gives up going to see a movie to study for a test to get a better grade.[77]

In decision-making, a trade-off involves a choice where the selection of one thing increases and the other decreases in terms of quality, quantity, or attributes. The goal of a trade-off is to choose from two or more potential opportunities. For instance, a student decides to take a course in ethics rather than one in chemistry or differential equations.[78]

An opportunity cost represents the value of what could have been done with what was given up; a trade-off is about the choices sacrificed.

Divergence

As depicted in Figure 3.19, the broadest alternative scenarios can be created thorough divergence. Divergence is about expanding on the quantity, variety, and originality of alternatives through exploration.

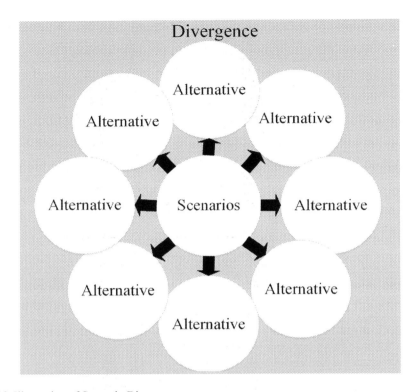

Figure 3.19 Illustration of Scenario Divergence

Scenario Creating Process

Creating scenarios is a process that can be achieved by updating the original brainstorming rules. The original brainstorming rules are:

1. The focus of group brainstorming is on idea quantity.
2. Criticism must be ruled out (evaluation of ideas should be withheld).
3. Freewheeling and big ideas are welcome.
4. Combination, refinement, and improvement are sought.

The original brainstorming rules have been extended to improve their effectiveness. As seen in Figure 3.20, the best practice for creating scenarios through brainstorming for innovation uses the following process: ideation (divergence), brainstorming, and role evaluation critiquing.[79]

Ideation Imagination

Each decision-maker writes down their best idea scenarios. Collect ideas from individuals first, then do group collaboration. The number of high-quality initial responses is superior for individuals over interacting groups.

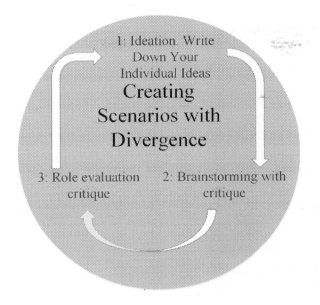

Figure 3.20 Illustration of Creating Scenarios

Brainstorming

Brainstorming for innovation extends the concept of the best practices for group interaction.[80] A group will brainstorm, discuss, and critique the idea scenarios and generate as many others as possible.

Group collaboration is effective only as a supplement to individual ideation. Using a group methodology is the combining of efforts of an equal number of individuals who previously worked alone.

Role Evaluation

Each decision-maker in the group will be assigned a role to evaluate the ideas: cautious, creative, constructive, intuitive, informative, and reflective. The role evaluation is needed to ensure that all aspects of each scenario are considered.

As suggested in Figure 3.21, there is a role for dissent and evaluation in creative idea generation. Everyone in the group should be assigned a different critique role – positive, negative, facts, creative, and empathy – for maximum effectiveness. Each person is given one of the following roles (Six Thinking Hats) and then asked to solve a problem of some type.

1. The blue hat role manages the process and defines the subject. What is the goal?
2. The white hat role focuses on the facts. What information is available?
3. The red hat role is focused on empathy and intuition.
4. The black hat role is focused on identifying reasons to be cautious and conservative.
5. The yellow hat role is focused on identifying benefits and the seeking of harmony.
6. The green hat role provides creativity, idea generation, and statements of provocation.

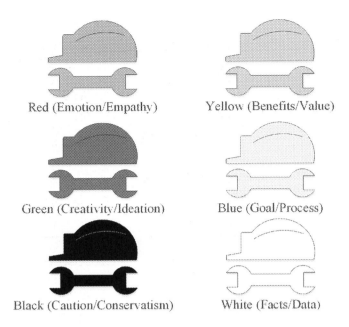

Figure 3.21 Illustration of the Six Thinking Hats

Source: Adapted from Edward de Bono, *Six Thinking Hats*, (New York: Little, Brown and Company, 1985).

Evaluation (Assessment)

The fourth step of the decision-making process, evaluation, uses critical thinking to validate the alternative scenarios by applying four elements. The four elements are evidence (facts and trends), expertise, context, and understanding the impact of values or strongly held beliefs on your decisions. As illustrated in Figure 3.22, the evaluation or assessment step is critical to ensure that all aspects of each scenario and choice are considered. Let's take a closer look at each of the four elements in the evaluation step.

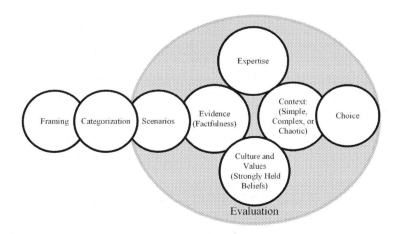

Figure 3.22 Illustration of the Decision-Making Evaluation Process

Source: Acknowledgement: Johnson, Steven. 2018. *Farsighted*. New York: Riverhead.

Evidence

The first element of the evaluation step is to discover the evidence. A fact is a statement that is consistent with reality or can be proven with evidence. The usual test for a statement of fact is verifiability, or whether it can be demonstrated to correspond to experience. For example, the story of *Silver Blaze*, by Sir Arthur Conan Doyle, gives us insight into using evidence and experience to inform decision-making. After the racehorse Silver Blaze was stolen, Sherlock Holmes notes that the dog did not bark. This fact in combination with others allowed him to determine more precisely who stole the racehorse. Verifiable facts, as described in Figure 3.23, are key to the role of evidence in evaluation.

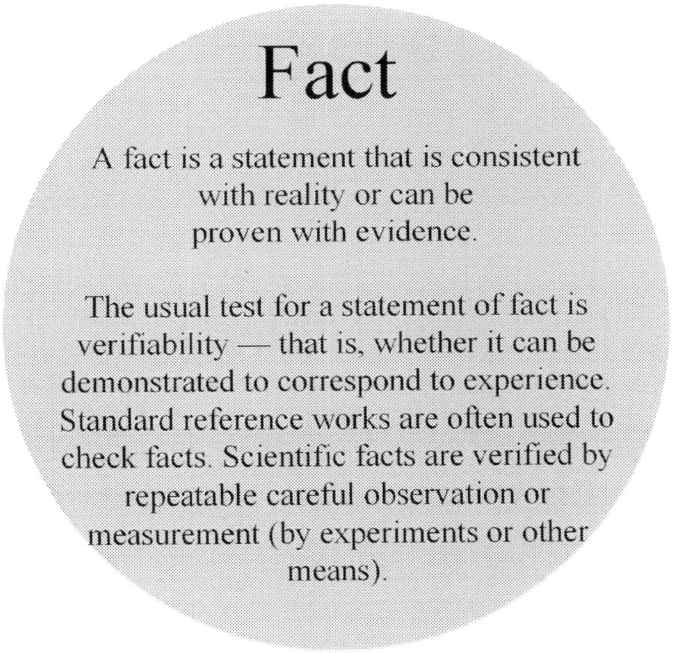

Fact

A fact is a statement that is consistent with reality or can be proven with evidence.

The usual test for a statement of fact is verifiability — that is, whether it can be demonstrated to correspond to experience. Standard reference works are often used to check facts. Scientific facts are verified by repeatable careful observation or measurement (by experiments or other means).

Figure 3.23 Illustration of Fact

Source: Acknowledgment: https://en.wikipedia.org/wiki/Fact

Steven Pinker, in his book *The Better Angels of Our Nature*, describes how the world is getting better, but our implicit cognitive biases are interfering with our perspective because we are drawn to dystopian headlines and overlook the positive trends.[81] Likewise, Hans Rosling was a Swedish physician, academic, and public speaker who studied global data. His research in the book *Factfulness* explains the extent to which we are ignorant about the world and why despite global inequalities, most of the world is better off than people think – and better off than it has ever been before.[82]

Expertise

The second element of evaluation is expertise. Expertise has a significant influence on decision-making, often evidencing itself via discipline, specific learning, and training. For instance, if you have heel pain and go to a surgeon, they will suggest an operation. If you go to a podiatrist with heel pain, they will want to give you orthotics. If you go to an internist, they will prescribe a muscle relaxant.

Although expertise is essential, it can inadvertently lead to blind spots, myopic vision, and lack of vision. As depicted in Figure 3.24, there is often a gap between what you know and what you think you know:

1. Expertise can cause a blind spot (implicit cognitive bias) that leads you to believe that you know more than you do. It is a misperception that we think we know more than we know as described in the circle of competence.
2. Overconfidence can lead you to believe that competence in one discipline can lead to competence in another very different discipline.
3. Deep knowledge, experience, and specialization caused by convergent thinking can leave leaders incurious, inflexible, and vulnerable – even in their own discipline. You have heard the statement, "Well, that's how we've always done it."

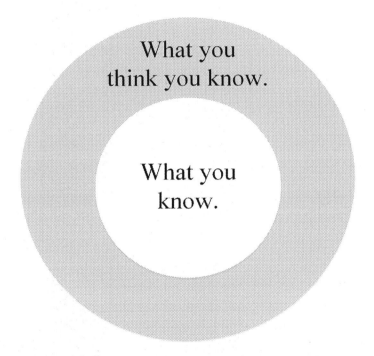

Figure 3.24 Illustration of the Circle of Competence

Context

The third element that influences the decision-making process is the context. As seen in Figure 3.25, context can be viewed in several ways from ordered to unordered, simple to complex, past to

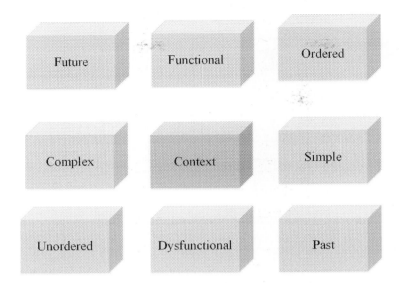

Figure 3.25 Illustration of the Context Framework

Source: Adapted from David J. Snowden, Mary E. Boone. A Leader's Framework for Decision Making Harvard Business Review, November 2007 Issue. Retrieved from https://hbr.org/2007/11/a-leaders-framework-for-decision-making

future, and functional to dysfunctional. The context framework is designed to provide you with insights into how to think about the context of a decision. For example, the decision-making that occurs in an emergency medicine department is quite different from what occurs at the meeting of the board of directors of a library.

Values

The fourth element of evaluation is understanding values. Values are strongly held beliefs that can influence your decision-making. Each person has different values that influence how they see the world. Decision-making is inherently filtered by one's values formed over time, filtered, and influenced by culture and media. At times, individual or group values can conflict with making decisions, making it even more of a challenge.

Values Filter

The values filter depicted in Figure 3.26 is the result of invisible, implicit, cognitive biases that we all have learned. The author Stephen Covey observes, "We don't see things as they are, we see them as we are." Just like an iceberg, our decision-making is only partially revealed above water. "Most impressions and thoughts arise in your conscious experience without you knowing how they got there."[83]

The implicit cognitive biases are caused in part by our values and strongly held beliefs that are formed over specific periods of time. Sociologist Morris Massey captures these concepts across generations in his writing and videos with this succinct notion: "What you are is where you were when."[84] You are a product of your decisions that are influenced by your value formation.[85]

Figure 3.26 Illustration of Values Filter

Generational Values

As can be clearly seen in Figure 3.27, values, our strongly held beliefs, are formed as we grow up. All our decisions are shaped by value formation. Each generation has different values that will affect their thinking and therefore the decisions that they make.

Birth Range	**Traditionalists (1900-45)**	**Baby Boomer (1946-64)**	**Gen X (1965-76)**	**Gen Y (1977-97)**	**Gen Z (After 1997)**
Context	Great Depression	Civil rights	Fall of the Berlin Wall	9/11 attacks	Mobility
	World War I & II	Anti-war movements	Space travel	Social networks	Climate change
	Suburbia	Personal computing	Emergence of the Internet	Questionable wars	Cyber insecurity
Behavior	Loyal to the workplace	Idealistic	Materialistic	Globalist	Truth seeking
	Financially insecure	Countercultural	Competitive	Self-orientated	Realistic
	Frugal	Collectivist	Individualistic	Questioning	Independent
Consumption	Conservation	Ideology	Status	Experience economy	Customization
	Saving	Movies and music	Brands and cars	Online retailing	Shared economy
	Caution	Mass media	Luxury articles	Travel and festivals	Ethical purchasing

Figure 3.27 Illustration of Generations

Source: Adapted from Tracy Francis and Fernanda Hoefel, "'True Gen': Generation Z and its implications for companies," McKinsey & Company, November 2018, accessed April 28, 2020 from https://www.mckinsey.com/industries/consumer packaged-goods/our-insights/true-gen-generation-z-and-its-implications-for-companies.

Adapted from "Five Generations Working Side by Side in 2020," accessed April 28, 2020 from https://www.technologyci tyinc.com/what-generation-am-i-in/

Pop Culture

Popular culture has a way of influencing an individual's beliefs toward certain topics and our underlying values. For example, the book and subsequent film *All the President's Men* was so inspiring that journalism schools across the US experienced higher enrollment numbers after its release. The film told the story of how Bob Woodward and Carl Bernstein, two reporters for the *Washington Post*, investigated the Watergate scandal that led to the resignation of President Richard Nixon. The film became part of popular culture, a set of the practices, beliefs, and objects that are dominant in society at a given point in time.

Impact of Media

Interestingly, during the dual significant events of the global COVID-19 pandemic and a contentious 2020 presidential election, the impact of all forms of media came under heightened scrutiny. It was commonly observed that in the past, journalists reported the facts and people formed opinions, while in 2020, journalists expressed opinions and people were left to ascertain if it was factual. The evolution of journalism is illustrative of the various roles that facts, expertise, context, and values play in decision-making. Journalism has undergone a transformation from oral content, to printed content, to digital content. Data journalism is the examination of data and statistics based on all types of content to provide actionable insights. Journalists and editors can use clicks as a metric to track how many people read each article, how long readers stay on a page, and how they found the story through real-time analytics. The knowledge of what gets read and what doesn't constitutes a major transformation from traditional print to digital journalism.[86]

Figure 3.28 shows relationship of availability bias or the tendency to think of examples of something as more representative than is the case. Media bias is the tendency of mass media news producers and journalists to report information selectively toward a point of view rather than

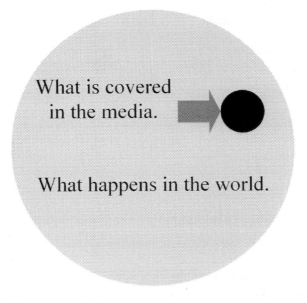

Figure 3.28 Illustration of Availability Bias

according to the standards of journalism. The standards of journalism are based on the practical acquisition and dissemination of information that adheres to a set of principles of accountability that include at least, impartiality, truthfulness, accuracy, objectivity, and fairness.[87]

Choice

Choice is the fifth element in the decision-making process. Choosing is the process of selecting and prioritizing decisions that are derived from high value creative alternatives. These alternatives should be original and breakthrough, highly feasible and useful, and meaningfully significant.

As illustrated in Figure 3.29, convergence is a narrowing of ideas and divergence is a broadening of ideas. When you are converging on your choice, recall the decision-making framework. This framework expects you to consider integrity, creativity, and reflection in your decision-making. Convergence is the process of narrowing the decision.

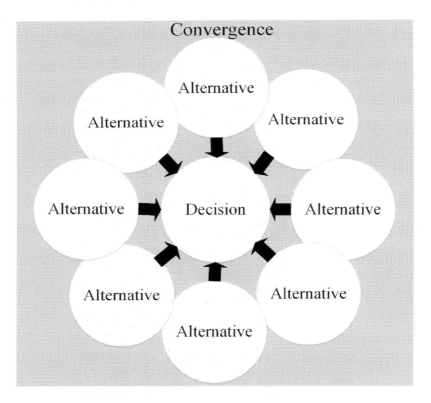

Figure 3.29 Illustration of Scenario Convergence

During the decision-making process, different perspectives are encouraged because there is no commitment without participation. In the end, when a decision is made, each participant is expected to commit to the decision. For example, "[i]n his April 2017 letter to Amazon shareholders, CEO Jeff Bezos reintroduced the concept of 'disagree and commit' with respect to decision making."[88]

Choice Dimensions

As depicted in Figure 3.30, there are three choice dimensions to consider when deciding: originality, feasibility, and meaningful significant value. Using established criteria provides a sense of discipline to eliminate what is not important and stick to what is important. The confidence in your choice of innovation will be increased if you consider these dimensions.

1. Your choice must target and fulfill the customer's need.
2. Your choice must be feasible to be successfully implemented within the time required.
3. Your choice must add meaningfully significant value. This means that the value proposition for the customer should provide affordability, accessibility, convenience, customization, selection, and simplicity that achieves economic, social, and environmental returns.

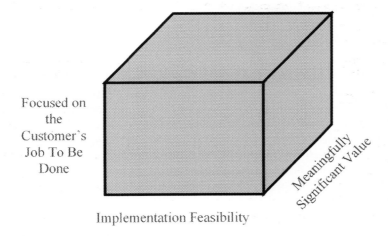

Figure 3.30 Illustration of the Three Dimensions of Choice

DECISION-MAKING ERRORS OF COMMISSION

In addition to the choice dimensions outlined in Figure 3.30, errors of commission and omission play a key role in choice. An error of commission is a wrong decision. It occurs when a person takes explicit action, directs something, orders something, or responds to some event, when they should not have done so. An example of an error of commission is when a friend is hired who lacks the relevant experience to be successful. Visible errors of commission are important because they are sources of learning for all of us.

The decision-making process to "get the right people on the bus" involves screening, selecting, and hiring people. This is a prevalent source of errors of commission. The knowledge, skills, and attitudes that a leader has learned are in direct proportion to what a person has developed and experienced over time from their successes and failures in life. Arguably, hiring should not be based on a candidate's innate ability or potential but rather on whether they have been exposed to a set of challenges that are similar to the challenges that they will be responsible for when they take their new role and whether they are open to continuous learning.[89] For example, from its founding in 1939, HP had a long period of success with Bill Hewlett and David Packard.[90] The subsequent hiring of executives Carly Fiorina, Mark Hurd, Patricia Dunn, and Léo Apotheker caused the company to start a trajectory of decline.[91]

Decision-Making Errors of Omission

An error of omission is a decision that is not made. It occurs when a person fails to take explicit action, leaves something out, or neglects something. An example of an error of omission is a viable investment opportunity that was passed by. Warren Buffet attests, "Errors of omission are the ones that are the big sins."[92] By unleashing our ability to think divergently, we can minimize the invisible errors of omission. Errors of omission are significant because they represent alternatives not considered and opportunities forever lost. Unfortunately, errors of omission, not doing something that should be done, are mostly invisible and so cannot be effective teaching moments.[93]

Errors of omission include failing to act on an opportunity, such as IBM's tardiness at offering cloud services, Xerox's failure to commercialize its discovery of many core computer technologies, RCA's failure to commercialize LCD technology, and Eastman Kodak's belated commercialization of its invention, the digital camera. All these companies made significant errors of omission at various points along their business journeys.

Decision-Making Matrix

Action or Inaction

If you create four quadrants and place actions and inactions on the Y-axis and closed-mindedness and open-mindedness on the X-axis, you can understand how to improve innovation decision-making. That is, in general, you are better off acting and risking an error of *commission* rather than inaction resulting in a decision that is not made through an error of *omission*.

You are better off developing your open mindedness through self-awareness rather than perpetuating your closed-mindedness that risks the introduction of thinking errors. What is covered in the media is only a small part of what happens in the world. The availability implicit cognitive bias is the making of decisions based on readily had information rather than harder to obtain information. These concepts are illustrated in Figure 3.31.

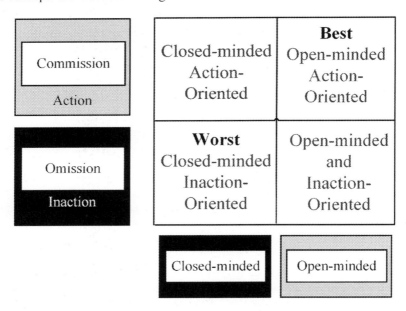

Figure 3.31 Illustration of Decision-Making Matrix of Action or Inaction

For example, in 1970, Xerox PARC (Palo Alto Research Center) was founded as a division of the Xerox Corporation. Xerox PARC was the inventor of many of the key components of the today's computing devices: laser printing, ethernet, the modern personal computer, graphical user interface (GUI), object-oriented programming, ubiquitous computing, amorphous silicon (a-Si) applications, and advancing very-large-scale-integration (VLSI) for semiconductors, and the mouse.[94] Xerox's inventions were not converted to innovations because of the Gordian knot of copier fixedness that resided in the Xerox executives in Norwalk, Connecticut.[95] But Xerox was unable to convert their many technological developments and significant inventions into successful commercial innovations. It took Steve Jobs and others to observe and make the connections to apply the graphical user interface concept to successful market solutions that were implemented in the Macintosh personal computer.

Understanding Reality Distortion

Reality Distortion

Steve Jobs was able to convince anyone of anything. "In the words of engineer Andy Hertzfeld, Jobs had a 'reality distortion field, a confounding mélange of a charismatic rhetorical style, an indomitable will, and an eagerness to bend any fact to fit the purpose at hand.'"[96] Reality distortion is created using a rhetorical style that distorts the facts to fit the outcome desired. Reality distortion can be categorized into whether there was an intent to harm and whether there is fabrication of the facts along the message chain from the sender to a receiver.

Historically, there are examples of organizations of all types that alter the facts to minimize the impact of their behavior, increase profits, or avoid losses. In a film series titled *Gaslit*, the Watergate scandal is used to describe gaslighting, a reality distortion technique, which focuses on Martha Mitchell, wife of the then Attorney General John Mitchell. Martha was the first person to publicly sound the alarm on Nixon's involvement in Watergate, causing both the presidency and her personal life to unravel.

Volkswagen intentionally programmed turbocharged direct injection (TDI) diesel engines to activate their emissions controls only during laboratory emissions testing, The firm Theranos promoted fraudulent blood-testing devices, Georgia-Pacific published fake science on asbestos, Brown and Williamson made false claims about tobacco that is described in the movie *The Insider*.

Dupont and 3M concealed evidence of the risks of forever chemicals that is described in the movie *Dark Waters*, based on the work of Rob Bilott, a Cincinnati attorney. The NFL minimized the impact of chronic traumatic encephalopathy (CET). Merck manipulated science regarding the drug Vioxx. Petrochemical companies downplayed the link between cancer and benzene and the extent of the climate change concerns.[97]

The fossil fuel industry has adopted the notion of the reality distortion field because it is incentivized to delay action on climate change to preserve their business models. "The research shows the oil and gas industry is now using social media as a key avenue for advertising, posting thousands of social issue, election, and political ads every year which are designed to prolong the use of oil and gas in the energy mix."[98] Similarly, climate activists have adopted elements of reality distortion in attempt to achieve scientizing climate policy. "Scientization of policy is a response to intractable political conflict that attempts to transform the political issues into scientific ones."[99]

Facts and Opinions

The basis of critical thinking is knowing how to use facts to validate a claim to ensure that it is accurate, complete, and transparent. A fact is something that has an actual existence in the real world and can be verified. Many people have difficulty separating facts from opinions. According to a survey by the Associated Press National Opinion Research Center (NORC) for Public Affairs, 29% of the respondents do not understand the difference between fact and opinion and 47% of the respondents believe it is difficult to know whether the information they encounter is correct.[100]

The Organisation for Economic Co-operation and Development (OECD) is an intergovernmental economic organization with 38 member countries, founded in 1961 to stimulate economic progress and world trade. PISA is the OECD's Programme for International Student Assessment that measures 15-year-olds' ability to use their reading, mathematics and science knowledge and skills to meet real-life challenges.[101] In the 2018 PISA assessment, students were asked to read a blog post that referenced a book review and then identify whether statements were facts or opinions offered by the author of the review.[102] The PISA findings revealed a gap in our students' ability to distinguish between facts and opinions. Survey findings revealed that "Only an estimated forty-seven percent of 15-year-old students were able to make this distinction."[103]

Contextual Deception

Contextual deception is the use of accurate information to frame an event, issue or individual, but maybe omitting needed information. With contextual deception, the communication process is incomplete, where some facts are left out and not conveyed at all.

> Contextual deception refers to the use of true but not necessarily related information to frame an event, issue or individual (e.g., a headline that does not match the corresponding article), or the misrepresentation of facts to support one's narrative (e.g., to deliberately delete information that is essential context to understanding the original meaning). While the facts used are true (unlike disinformation) and unfabricated (unlike misinformation), the way in which they are used is disingenuous and with the intent to manipulate people or cause harm.[104]

Disinformation

Disinformation is actively fabricated generally with intent to harm. In the message chain, a person may choose to intentionally pass on false information, disinformation, which is deliberately deceptive. "Disinformation refers to verifiably false or misleading information that is knowingly and intentionally created and shared for economic gain or to deliberately deceive, manipulate or inflict harm on a person, social group, organisation or country."[105]

Misinformation

Misinformation is not actively fabricated and there is no intent to harm. A person may convey misinformation that is false information, not deliberately conveyed, due to mistakes and incomplete critical thinking. "Misinformation refers to false or misleading information that is shared unknowingly and is not intended to deliberately deceive, manipulate or inflict harm on a person, social group, organisation or country."[106]

Cognitive Bias Distortion

Cognitive biases are **systematic patterns of deviation from rational judgment that further influence the message chain**. For instance, a bathroom scale is biased when it consistently underestimates our true weight by exactly four pounds.[107] People have implicit limitations in their rationality, accuracy of their memory, and cognitive biases, such as confirmation bias, which cause them to look for information in support of what they already believe. This can potentially result in ignoring significant information that could avoid a wrong decision. These cognitive biases may be unrealistic optimism, or biases like discrimination based on age, gender, or skin color. "When people consider errors in judgment and decision making, they most likely think of social biases like the stereotyping of minorities or of cognitive biases such as overconfidence and unfounded optimism. The useless variability that we call noise is a different type of error."[108]

Noise Distortion

Noise is unwanted variability (inconsistency) in judgments (measurements) that ought to be the same. An example of noise is a bathroom scale is noisy when it displays different readings if you repeatedly step on it. Variability across occasions occurs when decisions vary if the same case is presented more than once to the same individual, such as in the decision-making in recruitment and hiring. Variability across individuals occurs when different individuals, such as judges and physicians, in the same role, can make different decisions based on the same facts.[109]

The communication model, Figure 3.32, describes the message chain showing the flow of information from the sender to the receivers along with the obstacles that distort the communication. Like in the telephone game, there is a message chain that starts by whispering something, and before you know it, this message, transmitted from person to person, has become different.

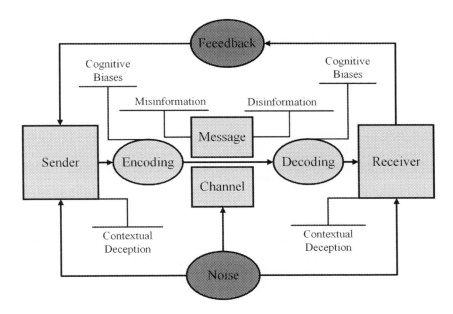

Figure 3.32 Illustration of Actual Communication Model

Source: Adapted from Daniel Kahneman, Andrew M. Rosenfield, Linnea Gandhi, and Tom Blase, "How to Overcome the High, Hidden Cost of Inconsistent Decision Making," October 2016, accessed September 8, 2021, https://hbr.org/2016/10/noise

Adapted from Daniel Kahneman, Oliver Sibony, and Cass R. Sunstein, Noise: A Flaw in Human Judgement, (New York: Little, Brown, Spark, 2021).

The message chain, Figure 3.33, illustrates how errors of judgment arise from the combination of context deception, disinformation, misinformation, cognitive bias, and noise.

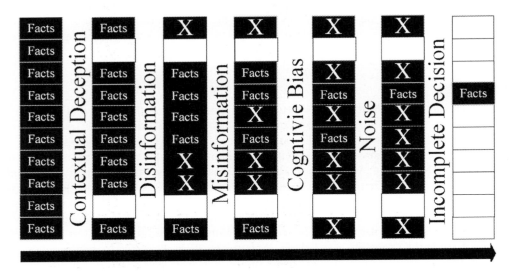

Figure 3.33 Illustration of How Incomplete Decisions Are Made

Source: Adapted from Daniel Kahneman, Andrew M. Rosenfield, Linnea Gandhi, and Tom Blase, "How to Overcome the High, Hidden Cost of Inconsistent Decision Making," October 2016, accessed September 8, 2021, https://hbr.org/2016/10/noise

Adapted from Daniel Kahneman, Olivier Sibony, and Cass R. Sunstein, *Noise: A Flaw in Human Judgement,* (New York: Little, Brown, Spark, 2021).

Risk and Reward

The quickening pace of change, the interconnectedness of globalization, population growth, limited resources, and increased technological complexity and impact all contribute to complex and challenging times. The competencies needed for effective decision-making to assess risk and reward are ever-evolving and require innovation and entrepreneurship competencies to create scalable solutions.

1. Organizations are needed that are fit for the future and all human beings that consider the need for diversity, equity, and inclusion.[110]
2. Organizations must seek to adopt the decision-making framework dimensions of character, for truth seeking, compassion, empathy, and creativity for idea generation.
3. The singular stockholder model of seeking profits needs to include an expansive model that includes stakeholders, advancing beyond economic factors to include the combination of governance, societal, and environmental progress measures.
4. There is a need to focus on our ability to apply the choice dimensions of innovation and entrepreneurship to provide feasible and meaningful value to customers.

Future effective decision-making requires a shift to a broader multidimensional risk and reward model that is illustrated in Figure 3.34.

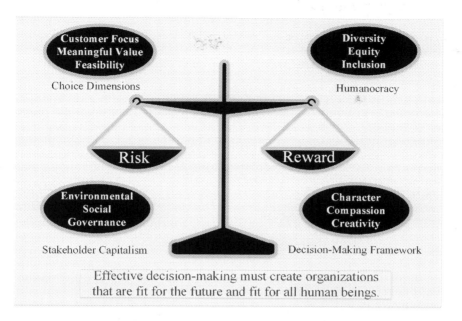

Figure 3.34 Illustration of Future Risk Reward Decision-Making

Source: Acknowledgement: Gary Hamel and Michele Zanini, *Humanocracy*, (Boston: Harvard Business Review Press, 2020).

Summary

In this chapter, how to improve decision-making effectiveness using a deliberate process is explored. There are several steps that provide guidance on the extent of the decision processes, including framing, categorization, scenarios, evaluation, and choice. Each step contains sub-dimensions that inform effective decision-making. For example, the evaluation step in decision-making is informed by four key elements: evidence, expertise, context, and culture/values.

Effective decision-making is an overarching lifelong competency that is required for building innovation capability to facilitate value creation in a global world of change, complexity, and competition. There are many examples of decision-making in start-ups and incumbent organizations that illustrate how some have lost their way while others have successfully found a path to the future.

Notes

1. Jay Kumar, "TurboTax by Intuit: Taxes Don't Have Be Taxing," February 1, 2018, accessed February 17, 2024, https://digital.hbs.edu/platform-digit/submission/turbotax-by-intuit-taxes-dont-have-be-taxing/.
2.. Reinaldo Fioravanti, "Intuit: Embracing the 'Innovator's Dilemma'," accessed February 9, 2020, accessed February 17, 2024, https://digital.hbs.edu/platform-digit/submission/intuit-embracing-the-innovators-dilemma/.
3. *Wikipedia*, s.v. "Intuit," accessed November 23, 2020, https://en.wikipedia.org/wiki/Intuit.
4. Jay Kumar, "TurboTax by Intuit: Taxes Don't Have Be Taxing," February 1, 2018, accessed February 19, 2024, https://digital.hbs.edu/platform-digit/submission/turbotax-by-intuit-taxes-dont-have-be-taxing/.
5. Jay Kumar, "TurboTax by Intuit: Taxes Don't Have Be Taxing," February 1, 2018, accessed February 11, 2024, https://digital.hbs.edu/platform-digit/submission/turbotax-by-intuit-taxes-dont-have-be-taxing/.
6. *Wikipedia*, s.v. "Microsoft Money," accessed February 11, 2024, https://en.wikipedia.org/wiki/Microsoft_Money.

7. *Wikipedia*, s.v. "Intuit," accessed November 23, 2020, https://en.wikipedia.org/wiki/Intuit.

8. *Oxford*, s.v. "Meta-competency," accessed February 11, 2024, www.oxfordreference.com/view/10.1093/oi/authority.20110803100152792.

9. Steven Johnson, *Farsighted* (New York: Riverhead, 2018), 26.

10. Steven Johnson, *Farsighted* (New York: Riverhead, 2018), 29.

11. *Wikipedia*, s.v. "Roy Riegels," accessed November 23, 2020, https://en.wikipedia.org/wiki/Roy_Riegels.

12. Aaron De Smet, Gregor Jost, and Leigh Weiss, "Want a Better Decision? Plan a Better Meeting," *McKinsey & Company*, May 2019, 1, accessed February 11, 2024, www.mckinsey.com/business-functions/organization/our-insights/want-a-better-decision-plan-a-better-meeting.

13. Steven Johnson, *Farsighted* (New York: Riverhead, 2018), 13.

14. *Wikipedia*, Scientific Method, accessed February 17, 2024, https://en.wikipedia.org/wiki/Scientific_method.

15. John Coleman, "Critical Thinking Is About Asking Better Questions," *Harvard Business Review*, April 22, 2022, accessed April 26, 2022, https://hbr.org/2022/04/critical-thinking-is-about-asking-better-questions.

16. Ahmad Kardoyo, Ahmad Nurkhin, Muhsin, and Hengky Pramusinto, "Problem-Based Learning Strategy: Its Impact on Students' Critical and Creative Thinking Skills," *European Journal of Educational Research* 9, no. 3 (2020), 1141–1150, https://doi.org/10.12973/eu-jer.9.3.1141.

17. Linda B. Nilson, *Teaching at Its Best a Research-Based Resource for College Instructors*, Jossey-Bass Higher and Adult Education Series, 4th ed. (US: Jossey Bass Ltd, 2016), 35.

18. *Wikipedia*, Rudyard Kipling, accessed February 17, 2024, https://en.wikipedia.org/wiki/Rudyard_Kipling.

19. Ron Carucci, "How Systems Support (or Undermine) Good Decision-Making," *Harvard Business Review*, February 4, 2020, accessed February 11, 2024, https://hbr.org/2020/02/how-systems-support-or-undermine-good-decision-making.

20. Ken Robinson and Lou Aronica, *Creative Schools: The Grassroots Revolution That's Transforming Education* (New York: Viking, 2015).

21. Lee Rainie and Andrew Perrin, "Key Findings about Americans' Declining Trust in Government and Each Other," July 22, 2019, accessed February 11, 2024, www.pewresearch.org/fact-tank/2019/07/22/key-findings-about-americans-declining-trust-in-government-and-each-other/.

22. K. Brownell and K. Warner, "The Perils of Ignoring History: Big Tobacco Play Dirty and Millions Died," *The Millbank Quarterly* 87, no. 1 (2009), 259–294, accessed February 11, 2024, www.ncbi.nlm.nih.gov/pmc/articles/PMC2879177/.

23. J. Kluger, "Companies Knew the Dangers of PFAS 'Forever Chemicals' – and Kept Them Secret," *Time*, 2023, accessed February 17, 2024, https://time.com/6284266/pfas-forever-chemicals-manufacturers-kept-secret/.

24. Zorana Ivcevic, Jochen I. Menges, and Anna Miller, "How Common Is Unethical Behavior in U.S. Organizations?" *Harvard Business Review*, March 20, 2020, accessed February 11, 2024, https://hbr.org/2020/03/how-common-is-unethical-behavior-in-u-s-organizations.

25. Zorana Ivcevic, Jochen I. Menges, and Anna Miller, "How Common Is Unethical Behavior in U.S. Organizations?" *Harvard Business Review*, March 20, 2020, accessed February 11, 2024, https://hbr.org/2020/03/how-common-is-unethical-behavior-in-u-s-organizations.

26. Aaron De Smet, Gregor Jost, and Leigh Weiss, "Three Keys to Faster, Better Decisions," *McKinsey & Company*, May 2019, accessed February 19, 2024, www.mckinsey.com/business-functions/organization/our-insights/three-keys-to-faster-better-decisions.

27. Aaron De Smet, Gregor Jost, and Leigh Weiss, "Three Keys to Faster, Better Decisions," *McKinsey & Company*, May 2019, 2, accessed February 17, 2024, www.mckinsey.com/business-functions/organization/our-insights/three-keys-to-faster-better-decisions.

28. Iskandar Aminov, Aaron De Smet, Gregor Jost, and David Mendelsohn, "Decision Making in the Age of Urgency," *McKinsey & Company*, April 2019, accessed February 19, 2024, www.mckinsey.com/business-functions/organization/our-insights/decision-making-in-the-age-of-urgency.

29. Aaron De Smet, Gerald Lackey, and Leigh M. Weiss, "Untangling Your Organization's Decision Making," *Mckinsey & Company*, June 2017, accessed February 19, 2024, www.mckinsey.com/business-functions/organization/our-insights/untangling-your-organizations-decision-making.

30. Iskandar Aminov, Aaron De Smet, Gregor Jost, and David Mendelsohn, "Decision Making in the Age of Urgency," *McKinsey & Company*, April 2019, accessed February 19, 2024, www.mckinsey.com/business-functions/organization/our-insights/decision-making-in-the-age-of-urgency.

31. H. Plessner and T. Haar, "Sports Performance Judgments from a Social Cognitive Perspective," *Psychology of Sport and Exercise* 7, no. 6 (2006), 555–575, accessed February 19, 2024, http://doi.org/10.1016/j.psychsport.2006.03.007.

32. K. J. Anderson and D. A. Pierce, "Officiating Bias: The Effect of Foul Differential on Foul Calls in NCAA Basketball," *Journal of Sports Sciences* 27, no. 7 (2009), 687–694.

33. Paul C. Nutt, *Why Decisions Fail: Avoiding the Blunders and Traps That Lead to Debacles* (San Francisco, CA: Berrett-Koehler, 2002).

34. Paul C. Nutt, *Half of Business Decisions Fail Because of Management's Blunders, New Study Finds* (Paul C. Nutt, *Why Decisions Fail: Avoiding the Blunders and Traps that Lead to Debacles* (San Francisco, CA: Berrett-Koehler, 2002)), accessed February 19, 2024, https://news.osu.edu/half-of-business-decisions-fail-because-of-managements-blunders-new-study-finds/.

35. Charles Duhigg, *The Power of Habit* (New York: Random House, 2014), 159–160.

36. Nicholas Wade, "In Classic vs. Modern Violins, Beauty Is in Ear of the Beholder," *New York Time*, January 2, 2012, accessed February 19, 2024, www.nytimes.com/2012/01/03/science/in-play-off-between-old-and-new-violins-stradivarius-lags.html.

37. Shankar Vedantam and Ayanna Thomas, "Did That Really Happen? How Our Memories Betray Us," *NPR*, December 16, 2019, accessed February 19, 2024, www.npr.org/2019/12/16/788422090/did-that-really-happen-how-our-memories-betray-us, www.npr.org/transcripts/788422090.

38. Shankar Vedantam and Ayanna Thomas, "Did That Really Happen? How Our Memories Betray Us," *NPR*, December 16, 2019, accessed February 19, 2024, www.npr.org/2019/12/16/788422090/did-that-really-happen-how-our-memories-betray-us, www.npr.org/transcripts/788422090.

39. Shankar Vedantam and Ayanna Thomas, "Did That Really Happen? How Our Memories Betray Us," *NPR*, December 16, 2019, accessed February 19, 2024, www.npr.org/2019/12/16/788422090/did-that-really-happen-how-our-memories-betray-us, www.npr.org/transcripts/788422090.

40. Karen Dillon, "Disruption 2020: An Interview with Clayton M. Christensen," *MIT Sloan Management Review*, accessed February 19, 2024, November 23, 2020, https://sloanreview.mit.edu/article/an-interview-with-clayton-m-christensen/.

41. Tom Davenport, Jim Guszcza, Tim Smith, and Ben Stiller, "Analytics and AI-driven Enterprises Thrive in the Age of With," accessed February 19, 2024, www2.deloitte.com/us/en/insights/topics/analytics/insight-driven-organization.html.

42. Tom Davenport, Jim Guszcza, Tim Smith, and Ben Stiller, "Analytics and AI-Driven Enterprises Thrive in the Age of With," accessed February 19, 2024, www2.deloitte.com/us/en/insights/topics/analytics/insight-driven-organization.html.

43. Thomas H. Davenport and Nitin Mittal, "How CEOs Can Lead a Data-Driven Culture," March 23, 2020, accessed February 19, 2024, https://hbr.org/2020/03/how-ceos-can-lead-a-data-driven-culture.

44. Bruce Nussbaum, *Creative Intelligence* (New York: Harper Business, 2013), 250.

45. Bruce Nussbaum, *Creative Intelligence* (New York: Harper Business, 2013), 227–229.

46. Thomas H. Davenport, "How to Make Better Decisions About Coronavirus," April 8, 2020, accessed February 19, 2024, https://sloanreview.mit.edu/article/how-to-make-better-decisions-about-coronavirus/.

47. Daniel Kahneman, *Thinking, Fast and Slow* (New York: Farrar, Straus and Giroux, 2011).

48. E. G. Chrysikou, K. Motyka, C. Nigro, S. Yang, and S. Thompson-Schill, "Functional Fixedness in Creative Thinking Tasks Depends on Stimulus Modality," *Psychology of Aesthetics, Creativity, and the Arts* 10, no. 4 (2016), 425–435. https://doi.org/10.1037/aca0000050.

49. *Investopedia*, s.v. "Normative Economics," accessed February 19, 2024, www.investopedia.com/terms/n/normativeeconomics.asp.

50. *Wikipedia*, s.v. "Positive Economics," accessed November 23, 2020, https://en.wikipedia.org/wiki/Positive_economics.

51. M. Lewis, *The Undoing Project* (New York: Norton, 2017), 183.

52. Daniel Kahneman, *Thinking, Fast and Slow* (New York: Farrar, Straus and Giroux, 2011), 158.

53. Daniel Kahneman, *Thinking, Fast and Slow* (New York: Farrar, Straus and Giroux, 2011), 156.

54. Alain Samson, "An Introduction to Behavioral Economics," accessed February 19, 2024, www.behavioraleconomics.com/resources/introduction-behavioral-economics/.

55. T. Baer, S. Heiligtag, and H. Samandari, "The Business Logic in Debiasing," *McKinsey & Company*, 2017, accessed February 19, 2024, www.mckinsey.com/business-functions/risk/our-insights/the-business-logic-in-debiasing?cid=other-eml-alt-mip-mck-oth-1705&hlkid=3821bc75543d474c8398b6ce4496a695&hctky=2468311&hdpid=04b7622e-702a-4405-9169-b64d6c6ffe98.

56. Dan P. Lovallo and Olivier Sibony, "Distortions and Deceptions in Strategic Decisions," February 2006, accessed February 19, 2024, www.mckinsey.com/business-functions/strategy-and-corporate-finance/our-insights/distortions-and-deceptions-in-strategic-decisions.

57. Philip Meissner, Olivier Sibony, and Torsten Wulf, "Are You Ready to Decide?" *McKinsey Quarterly*, April 2015, accessed February 19, 2024, www.mckinsey.com/business-functions/strategy-and-corporate-finance/our-insights/are-you-ready-to-decide.
58. Gary Klein, Tim Koller, and Dan Lovallo, "Bias Busters: Premortems: Being Smart at the Start," April 2019, accessed February 19, 2024, www.mckinsey.com/business-functions/strategy-and-corporate-finance/our-insights/bias-busters-premortems-being-smart-at-the-start.
59. Steven Johnson, *Farsighted* (New York: Riverhead, 2018), 18.
60. Ron Carucci, "How Systems Support (or Undermine) Good Decision-Making," *Harvard Business Review*, February 4, 2020, accessed February 19, 2024, https://hbr.org/2020/02/how-systems-support-or-undermine-good-decision-making.
61. Steven Johnson, *Farsighted* (New York: Riverhead, 2018), 21.
62. Aaron De Smet, Gregor Jost, and Leigh Weiss, "Three Keys to Faster, Better Decisions," *McKinsey & Company*, May 2019, accessed February 19, 2024, www.mckinsey.com/business-functions/organization/our-insights/three-keys-to-faster-better-decisions.
63. Dan P. Lovallo and Olivier Sibony, "Distortions and Deceptions in Strategic Decisions," *McKinsey & Company*, February 2006, accessed February 19, 2024, www.mckinsey.com/business-functions/strategy-and-corporate-finance/our-insights/distortions-and-deceptions-in-strategic-decisions.
64. Ron Carucci, "How Systems Support (or Undermine) Good Decision-Making," *Harvard Business Review*, February 4, 2020, accessed February 19, 2024, https://hbr.org/2020/02/how-systems-support-or-undermine-good-decision-making.
65. Aaron De Smet, Gregor Jost, and Leigh Weiss, "Three Keys to Faster, Better Decisions," *McKinsey & Company*, May 2019, accessed February 19, 2024, www.mckinsey.com/business-functions/organization/our-insights/three-keys-to-faster-better-decisions.
66. Aaron De Smet, Gerald Lackey, and Leigh M. Weiss, "Untangling Your Organization's Decision Making," *McKinsey & Company*, June 2017, accessed February 19, 2024, www.mckinsey.com/business-functions/organization/our-insights/untangling-your-organizations-decision-making.
67. Aaron De Smet, Gerald Lackey, and Leigh M. Weiss, "Untangling Your Organization's Decision Making," *McKinsey & Company*, June 2017, accessed February 19, 2024, www.mckinsey.com/business-functions/organization/our-insights/untangling-your-organizations-decision-making.
68. Aaron De Smet, Gregor Jost, and Leigh Weiss, "Three Keys to Faster, Better Decisions," *McKinsey & Company*, May 2019, accessed February 19, 2024, www.mckinsey.com/business-functions/organization/our-insights/three-keys-to-faster-better-decisions.
69. Aaron De Smet, Gerald Lackey, and Leigh M. Weiss, "Untangling Your Organization's Decision Making," *Mckinsey & Company*, June 2017, accessed February 19, 2024, www.mckinsey.com/business-functions/organization/our-insights/untangling-your-organizations-decision-making.
70. Ron Carucci, "How Systems Support (or Undermine) Good Decision-Making," *Harvard Business Review*, February 4, 2020, accessed February 19, 2024, https://hbr.org/2020/02/how-systems-support-or-undermine-good-decision-making.
71. Aaron De Smet, Gerald Lackey, and Leigh M. Weiss, "Untangling Your Organization's Decision Making," *Mckinsey & Company*, June 2017, accessed February 19, 2024, www.mckinsey.com/business-functions/organization/our-insights/untangling-your-organizations-decision-making.
72. Aaron De Smet, Gregor Jost, and Leigh Weiss, "Three Keys to Faster, Better Decisions," *McKinsey & Company*, May 2019, accessed February 19, 2024, www.mckinsey.com/business-functions/organization/our-insights/three-keys-to-faster-better-decisions.
73. Aaron De Smet, Gerald Lackey, and Leigh M. Weiss, "Untangling Your Organization's Decision Making," *Mckinsey & Company*, June 2017, accessed February 19, 2024, www.mckinsey.com/business-functions/organization/our-insights/untangling-your-organizations-decision-making.
74. Aaron De Smet, Gregor Jost, and Leigh Weiss, "Three Keys to Faster, Better Decisions," *McKinsey & Company*, May 2019, accessed February 19, 2024, www.mckinsey.com/business-functions/organization/our-insights/three-keys-to-faster-better-decisions.
75. Steven Johnson, *Farsighted* (New York: Riverhead, 2018), 67.
76. Steven Johnson, *Farsighted* (New York: Riverhead, 2018), 67.
77. *Wikipedia*, s.v. "Opportunity Cost," accessed January 20, 2021, https://en.wikipedia.org/wiki/Opportunity_cost.
78. *Wikipedia*, s.v. "Trade-off," accessed January 20, 2021, https://en.wikipedia.org/wiki/Trade-off.
79. O. Goldenberg and J. Wiley, "Quality, Conformity, and Conflict: Questioning the Assumptions of Osborn's Brainstorming Technique," *Journal of Problem Solving* 3, no. 2 (2011), 96–118.

80. O. Goldenberg and J. Wiley, "Quality, Conformity, and Conflict: Questioning the Assumptions of Osborn's Brainstorming Technique," *Journal of Problem Solving* 3, no. 2 (2011), 96–118.
81. Steven Pinker, *The Better Angels of Our Nature* (London: Lane, 2011).
82. Hans Rosling, Anna Rosling Rönnlund, Ola Rosling, Hans Freundl, Hans-Peter Remmler, and Albrecht Schreiber, *Factfulness* (Berlin: Ullstein, 2018).
83. Daniel Kahneman, *Thinking, Fast and Slow* (New York: Farrar, Straus and Giroux, 2011), 4.
84. *Wikipedia*, s.v. "Morris Massey," accessed November 23, 2020, https://en.wikipedia.org/wiki/Morris_Massey.
85. *Wikipedia*, s.v. "Morris Massey," accessed November 23, 2020, https://en.wikipedia.org/wiki/Morris_Massey.
86. Melissa De Witte, "What This Stanford Scholar Learned About Clickbait Will Surprise You," March 21, 2018, accessed February 19, 2024, https://news.stanford.edu/2018/03/21/this-stanford-scholar-learned-clickbait-will-surprise/.
87. *Wikipedia*, s.v. "Journalism Ethics and Standards," accessed November 23, 2020, https://en.wikipedia.org/wiki/Journalism_ethics_and_standards.
88. Aaron De Smet, Gregor Jost, and Leigh Weiss, "Three Keys to Faster, Better Decisions," *McKinsey & Company*, May 2019, accessed February 19, 2024, www.mckinsey.com/business-functions/organization/our-insights/three-keys-to-faster-better-decisions.
89. Morgan W. McCall Jr., *High Flyers: Developing the Next Generation of Leaders* (Boston: Harvard Business School Press, 1998).
90. David Packard, David Kirby, and Karen Lewis, *The HP Way: How Bill Hewlett and I Built Our Company* (New York: Collins Business Essentials, 2005).
91. David Goldman, "HP CEO Apotheker Fired, Replaced by Meg Whitman," *CNN Money*, September 22, 2011, accessed February 19, 2024, http://money.cnn.com/2011/09/22/technology/hp_ceo_fired/index.htm.
92. Warren Buffett, "Warren Buffett – My Biggest Mistake," *YouTube Video*, posted by "WarrenBuffettBlog's Channel," May 23, 2011, accessed February 19, 2024, www.youtube.com/watch?v=YJV-YZ1ZDL0.
93. Russell Ackoff, *System Thinking for Curious Managers* (Devon: Triarchy Press, 2012), 26.
94. Jeff Dyer, Paul Godfrey, Robert Jensen, and David Bryce, *Strategic Management: Concepts and Cases*, 2nd ed. (New York: John Wiley & Sons, Inc., 2018), 178.
95. *Wikipedia*, s.v. "Xerox PARC," accessed November 23, 2020, http://en.wikipedia.org/wiki/PARC_(company).
96. Kyle Jensen, Tom Byers, Laura Dunham, and Jon Fjeld, "Entrepreneurs and the Truth," July 2021, accessed August 12, 2021, https://hbr.org/2021/07/entrepreneurs-and-the-truth.
97. "The Disinformation Playbook, How Business Interests Deceive, Misinform, and Buy Influence at the Expense of Public Health and Safety," October 10, 2017, updated May 18, 2018, accessed June 12, 2022, www.ucsusa.org/resources/disinformation-playbook.
98. InfluenceMap, "Climate Change and Digital Advertising: The Oil and Gas industry's Digital Advertising Strategy," August 2021, accessed August 12, 2021, https://influencemap.org/report/Climate-Change-and-Digital-Advertising-a40c8116160668aa2d865da2f5abe91b.
99. Judith Curry, *Climate Uncertainty and Risk: Rethinking Our Response* (New York: Anthem Press, 2023).
100. USAFACTS, "State of the Facts Poll 2019," 10, accessed June 21, 2022, https://usafacts.org/, https://usafacts.org/state-of-the-facts, https://static.usafacts.org/public/resources/AP_NORC_Poll_2019.pdf.
101.. OECD PISA, accessed May 22, 2021, www.oecd.org/PISA/.
102. OECD PISA, accessed June 20, 2022, www.oecd.org/PISA/.
103. Gretchen Cheney, "Fact vs. Opinion: Digital Literacy Among Today's Students," May 22, 2021, accessed June 20, 2022, https://ncee.org/2021/05/fact-vs-opinion-digital-literacy-among-todays-students/.
104. Molly Lesher, Hanna Pawelec, and Arpitha Desai, "Disentangling Untruths Online: Creators, Spreaders and How to Stop Them," *Going Digital Toolkit Note, No. 23*, 2022, accessed February 19, 2024, https://goingdigital.oecd.org/data/notes/No23_ToolkitNote_UntruthsOnline.pdf.
105. Molly Lesher, Hanna Pawelec, and Arpitha Desai, "Disentangling Untruths Online: Creators, Spreaders and How to Stop Them," *Going Digital Toolkit Note, No. 23*, 2022, accessed February 19, 2024, https://goingdigital.oecd.org/data/notes/No23_ToolkitNote_UntruthsOnline.pdf.
106. Molly Lesher, Hanna Pawelec, and Arpitha Desai, "Disentangling Untruths Online: Creators, Spreaders and How to Stop Them," *Going Digital Toolkit Note, No. 23*, 2022, accessed February 19, 2024, https://goingdigital.oecd.org/data/notes/No23_ToolkitNote_UntruthsOnline.pdf.

107. Daniel Kahneman, Olivier Sibony, and Cass R. Sunstein, *Noise: A Flaw in Human Judgement* (New York: Little, Brown, Spark, 2021).
108. Daniel Kahneman, Andrew M. Rosenfield, Linnea Gandhi, and Tom Blaser, "Noise: How to Overcome the High, Hidden Cost of Inconsistent Decision Making," Harvard Business Review, October 2016, accessed September 8, 2021, https://hbr.org/2016/10/noise.
109. Daniel Kahneman, Olivier Sibony, and Cass R. Sunstein, *Noise: A Flaw in Human Judgement* (New York: Little, Brown, Spark, 2021).
110. Gary Hamel and Michele Zanini, Humanocracy (Boston: Harvard Business Review Press, 2020).

4 Innovative Behaviors

It is relatively well established that encouraging, promoting, and engaging in innovative behaviors benefit society across multiple dimensions (social, economic, political, education, technological, and more). Research suggests that the dynamics of human innovative behaviors are central in this benefit-driven assumption.[1] Yet the question remains, what behaviors are most directly related to innovation? In this chapter, we outline and discuss two key innovative behaviors, including discovery skills – which encompass questioning, observing, networking, experimenting, and associating – and delivery skills, such as analyzing, planning, detailed implementation, and disciplined execution. In addition, we also examine motivation within the context of innovative behaviors. Motivation, both extrinsic and intrinsic, is especially relevant with regard to inspiring people to engage in creative and innovative behaviors.

In this chapter, we look at why and how innovative behaviors are essential to improving the central role of innovation and entrepreneurship in economic advancement. These behaviors have variously been encouraged and/or discouraged over time, resulting in an uneven approach to the discovery that leads to innovation. We also discuss motivation within the context of innovative behaviors. As we shall see throughout this chapter, innovative behaviors and thinking (Chapter 5) are inextricably linked to each other in the overall framework of innovation and *entrepreneurship*.

Discovery Skills

Jeff Dyer, Hal Gregersen, and Clayton M. Christensen write in *The Innovator's DNA*, "A critical insight from our research is that one's ability to generate innovative ideas is not merely a function of the mind, but also a function of behaviours."[2] In their study of 5,000 executives and innovators from a large set of innovative companies like Intuit, eBay, Apple, Amazon, and Google, they noted a high proportion of discovery skills.[3] In fact, the leaders of highly innovative companies scored around the 88th percentile in discovery skills, while scoring around just the 56th percentile in delivery skills.[4]

Based on their research of the world's best innovators, five discovery skills, composed of four behavioral skills and one cognitive skill, distinguish innovators from typical executives.[5] As can be seen in Figure 4.1, the four behavioral skills are questioning, observing, networking, and experimenting. These skills facilitate the compilation of potential ideas. The lone cognitive skill identified, associating, allows for the combination of stock ideas and knowledge to create new, actionable insights.

Innovators and entrepreneurs are questioners. Innovators and entrepreneurs are willing to challenge why things are the way they are and ask how they might be changed. Questioning challenges the status quo, identifying new possibilities and searching for new opportunities. "Creativity starts with a penetrating research question, a startling vision for a new work of art, an urgent business

DOI: 10.4324/9781003034308-5

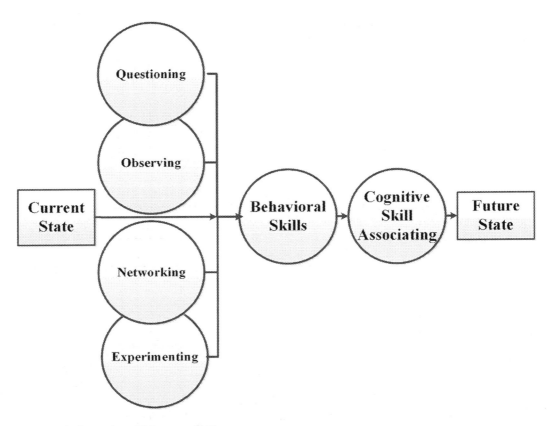

Figure 4.1 Illustration of Discovery Skills

Source: Adapted from Jeff Dyer, Hal Gregersen, and Clayton M. Christensen, *The Innovator's DNA,* (MA: Harvard Business Review Press, 2011), 27.

challenge, a predicament in your personal life. Mastering the discipline of asking means you're always looking for good problems, always seeking new inspiration."[6]

The five *whys* technique uses questions to understand the root cause of a problem. You start by asking why the problem occurred; for example, "Why are the employees not inspired or engaged?" Then for each reason given, ask why that reason happened until you get to the true root cause.

1. *Why?* – Our employees are not inspired or engaged. (First why)
2. *Why?* – Our teams are not inspired or engaged. (Second why)
3. *Why?* – Our managers of the teams are not inspired or engaged. (Third why)
4. *Why?* – Our executives are not inspired or engaged. (Fourth why)
5. *Why?* – Our president is not inspired or engaged. (Fifth why; a root cause)

Observing

Innovators and entrepreneurs are observers. They are willing to look around and see the world in different and new ways. As Yogi Berra, baseball legend and famed street philosopher opined, "You can observe a lot by watching." Observing the rapid growth of the Internet inspired many companies to start new business ventures.

When observing, "you are constantly and quietly aware. You don't just see what you expect to see. You see the new, the unusual, the surprising. You see what others take for granted, and what they incorrectly assume. You expose yourself to new experiences eagerly, without hesitation; you regularly seek out new stimuli, new situations, and new information."[7] In effect, observing allows you to see what is not there. Entrepreneurs are quite adept at seeing solutions to problems others do not. For example, Paul Polak, humanitarian and social entrepreneur, developed the ability to discover stealth knowledge.

When working with the farmers of Bangladesh, Polak realized that they needed a more effective way to irrigate their crops. Bangladesh is situated at the mouth of the Ganges River and surrounded by India. It is one of the poorest and most densely populated countries in the world.

The people of Bangladesh are part of C. K. Prahalad's "bottom of the pyramid"[8] because they have impoverished living standards and a low literacy rate. Paul Polak developed a leg-powered treadle pump that enabled the farmers to provide water more efficiently for their crops. Although this helped alleviate the water problem and crop yields, upon further observations and discussions he realized that an even more significant problem existed. What they also needed were jobs that would move them out of poverty. To improve the local economy, Polak required the treadle pumps to be built in Bangladesh rather than elsewhere, thereby providing jobs and income for the people.[9]

Networking

Innovators and entrepreneurs are networkers. Fundamentally, networking is building relationships and learning from others who are different from you, enabling you to uncover new insights and perspectives. Conventional wisdom suggests that you are not going to learn much from people just like you. Rather, seeking input, advice, and counsel from others, especially those individuals whose specialties relate to the pursuit of an innovative product, service, and/or new venture, can potentially provide considerable insight and benefit.

Indeed, networking has expanded with the use of social media, such as Twitter, LinkedIn, Facebook, Google+, and others. Over the years, researchers have suggested that there is a strong link between start-up success and social networks. Some have attributed this to "the organizational advantage" and creation of new intellectual capital that arises from robust social relationships within organizations.[10] Others believe the benefits that arise from social networks stem from the willingness and motivation of individuals to share knowledge.[11] All of these benefits are invaluable to a nascent innovation or venture.

Experimenting

Innovators and entrepreneurs are experimenters. They are willing to act and try new experiences, pilot new ideas, learn new skills, and work outside of their culture and in areas where others would be uncomfortable. Jeff Bezos, the founder and CEO of Amazon, experimented with selling books, building distribution centers, cloud computing, the Kindle electronic reader, subscription services, movies, and music. Thomas Edison and Leonardo da Vinci used experimenting to refine thinking and solve problems. Entrepreneur and innovator James Dyson combined observing and experimenting in his quest to solve the persistent problems when it came to using traditional vacuum cleaners.

Experimenting might include ideating across multiple problem/solutions sets, designing several concepts, and making either a design and/or working prototype of a new product or service from scratch. Making things can often be thought of as a "branch and prune" iterative process of trying new things. In his search for a marketable incandescent light bulb, Edison tried over 300 potential filaments, all of which ultimately failed, before he found the right one. Making and prototyping are described in more detail in Chapter 17, "Applying Innovation Processes."

Associating

Associating is a cognitive skill that involves combining unrelated ideas to create a new idea. The Power of And is based on associating. Associating is assembling what already exists to create something that did not exist. While associating is explored further as a creativity competency, essentially, it is connecting the dots. Innovation becomes a carefully orchestrated balancing and trade-off between the past, present, and future. As Steve Jobs said in his June 12, 2005, Stanford speech, "You can't connect the dots looking forward; you can only connect them looking backwards."[12] Fundamentally, knowledge by itself is insufficient unless we make connections between what we know and problems that need to be solved. In an interview for *Wired*, Jobs says it best:

> Creativity is just connecting things. When you ask creative people how they did something, they feel a little guilty because they didn't really do it, they just saw something. It seemed obvious to them after a while. That's because they were able to connect experiences they've had and synthesize new things.[13]

Associating is described in more detail in Chapter 8, "Creativity Insights."

Delivery Skills

As critical as discovery skills are, they are considerably different from delivery skills. As outlined in Figure 4.2, the four delivery skills often dominate conventional executives and, at times, can be counterproductive to innovation. Delivery skills include analyzing, planning, detail-oriented implementing, and disciplined executing. Interestingly, delivery skills are not new, beginning as far back as Socrates, Aristotle, and Plato. The Socratic method, for example, breaks problems down by seeking answers to a set of questions, systematically narrowing the line of inquiry.[14]

Clayton Christensen developed the concept of disruptive innovation in 1997, based on his research in *The Innovator's Dilemma*.[15] Disruptive innovation is a theory of organization failure that can be used to explain how change happens. Well-meaning instructors teach college students how to introduce change by creating novel, differentiated solutions (discovery skills) and, separately, how to meet the needs of their customers (delivery skills). Discovery skills are those that become dominant. Disruptive innovation occurs when start-ups incrementally add value to their offerings while the incumbents wait. This waiting decreases the window of opportunity for the incumbent. Disruptive innovation can be used for prediction because generally adaptable entrepreneurial start-ups see opportunity and act whereas incumbents see opportunity but are paralyzed to act.

The introduction of novel and unique change, effectively using discovery skills, and meeting the needs of customers using delivery skills are dramatically different and can be in conflict with one another. This phenomenon occurs when organizations choose to serve their customers rather than introduce novel change because leaders are not trained to reconcile the two opposing forces. "The key point here," write Dyer, Gregerson, and Christensen, "is that large companies typically fail at disruptive innovation because the top management team is dominated by individuals who have been selected for delivery skills, not discovery skills. As a result, most executives at large organizations don't know how to think different."[16]

Delivery skills could be considered conventional business skills. **Analyzing** breaks down an entity into its parts to increase understanding. Analysis is often considered the role of those employed in finance, accounting, systems analysis and programming, purchasing, and marketing. **Planning** is the process of determining a future course of action. In the field of project management, a common way of organizing an effort is to start from the top and break down the big pieces into smaller

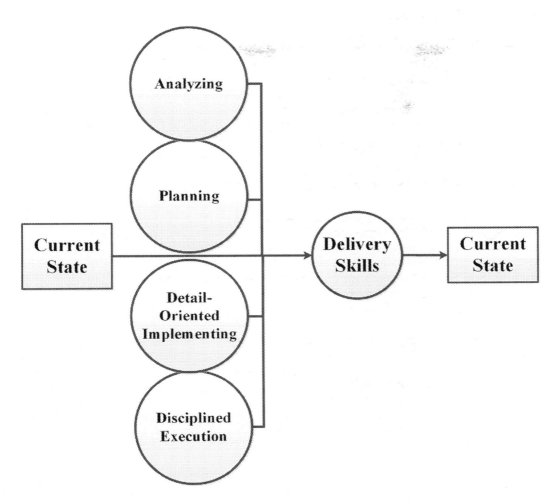

Figure 4.2 Illustration of Delivery Skills

Source: Adapted from Jeff Dyer, Hal Gregersen, and Clayton M. Christensen, *The Innovator's DNA,* (MA: Harvard Business Review Press, 2011), 32.

and smaller pieces. The creation of a project plan that is subdivided into smaller and smaller units is an example of this. Project management and operations management use **detail-oriented implementing** to transfer the plan into concrete results. **Disciplined execution** is the operationalization of the strategy. Disciplined execution relates to the need for both rough and more fine-grained implementation of ideas, as well as the need for balancing both deliberate and emergent strategies. Disciplined execution can often threaten innovation and entrepreneurship. It can be challenging to be precise and disciplined in execution of ideas without falling victim to dismissing new ideas because "this is the way we have always done it and that's the way it is going to be."

Motivation and Incentives

Leadership, motivation, and innovative behaviors are closely intertwined. A leader needs to create the conditions that will stimulate the intrinsic motivation of each follower. A leader should start with an understanding of the follower, their intrinsic needs, capabilities, and maturity. The leader will then select the leadership style to best match the follower, ideally providing the most autonomy possible for getting results and enabling the follower to grow and develop beyond where they are now.

Check Your Brains at the Door

Using incentives and efficiency, Henry Ford's increase in the wages of his employees and Frederick Taylor's increase in the productivity of manufacturing workers provided wealth and well-being for many. As organizations and institutions have morphed and changed over the years, the "check your brains at the door" model is less and less relevant in today's business environment. Interestingly, as long ago as the 1920s, studies done at the AT&T Western Electric plant discovered that the productivity of workers increased when interest was shown in them.[17] The so-called Hawthorne effect suggests that the work environment, including showing interest in the workers, positively affects productivity.

Although we still need incentives and efficiency, many economies have transitioned from an incentive-efficiency orientation toward a knowledge-oriented economy, requiring a more robust approach. While there may still be appropriate applications for an incentive-efficiency model in some organizations, generally speaking, the transition to a more innovation-based organization suggests that one size does not fit all.

Toyota Production System

In the early 1920s, innovator and entrepreneur Sakichi Toyoda invented a series of successful automated looms that provided a 20-fold increase in productivity compared to previous looms. Building on this initial success, Toyota Industries was established in 1929. In the 1930s, the company decided to branch out into automobiles. In 1939, the Toyota Motor Corporation was established, developing the Toyota Production System (TPS).[18] The principles underlying TPS and embodied in the Toyota Way were developed by Sakichi Toyoda, his son Kiichiro Toyoda, and the engineer Taiichi Ohno.[19]

TPS puts the customer at the forefront, viewing people as the most valuable resources. The Toyota philosophy had a shop-floor focus and fosters *kaizen*, or continuous improvement, setting the expectation that no defect shall be passed to the customer.

> Fifty years ago, most CEOs believed that "ordinary" employees were incapable of tackling complicated operational problems like quality and efficiency. To a modern executive, familiar with the benefits of kaizen, total quality management, and Six Sigma, such a belief seems like simple bigotry.[20]

The TPS (see Figure 4.3) was a departure from conventional thinking about people. Instead of asking workers to check their brains at the factory door, Toyota did the opposite. The TPS is sometimes known as the Thinking People System because employees are encouraged to aspire to develop perfect processes that prevent defects altogether. If defects occur, they are identified and remedied with a sense of urgency. The shop floor is the basis for the value-added activities that take place. Because the shop floor is constantly changing, managers and executives must be present to understand what events are occurring and to seek input from the workers who understand the business. As Gary Hamel observed,

> Amazingly, it took nearly 20 years for America's carmakers to decipher Toyota's advantage. Unlike its Western rivals, Toyota believed the first-line employees could be more than cogs in a soulless manufacturing machine. If given the right tools and training, they could be problem solvers, innovators, and change agents.[21]

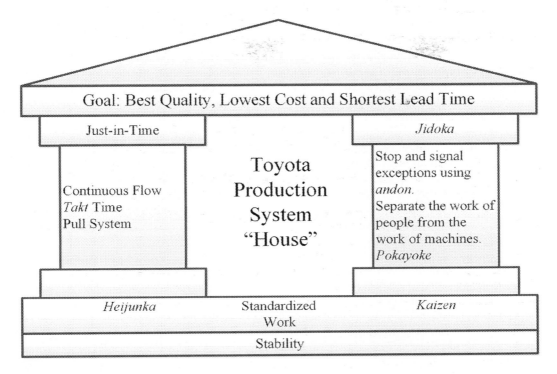

Figure 4.3 Illustration of the Toyota Production System

Source: Adapted from Jeffrey K. Liker, *The Toyota Way,* (New York: McGraw-Hill, 2004), 33.

Taiichi Ohno was the thought leader behind TPS, which was the predecessor to lean manufacturing in the United States. Ohno is credited with the development of "the seven wastes" and the application of "the five whys." The five whys questions-asking method mentioned earlier is used to explore cause-effect relationships in order to understand a particular problem.[22] Toyota business practices include an eight-step problem-solving process that is an expansion of the "plan, do, study/check, and act" model:[23]

1. Clarify the problem.
2. Break down the problem.
3. Set a target.
4. Determine the root cause.
5. Develop countermeasures.
6. See countermeasures through.
7. Confirm results and process.
8. Standardize successful processes.

The TPS is illustrated like the floor plan of a house. The house is used to describe the overall structure of the system. On the top floor are three goals: high quality, low cost, and short lead times. The middle of the house is composed of two pillars: just-in-time and *jidoka*. In the left column is just-in-time. Just-in-time is a pull system that delivers the right items in the right amounts at the right time. *Takt* time (units/time and continuous flow) is the rate of customer demand that allows for the balancing of over- and under-production. In the right column is *jidoka. Jidoka* is the ability to stop production if there is a defect. *Andon* is the signaling system used to request help, and *pokayoke* is the building of intelligence into the automation to both prevent and detect problems. On the bottom of the model is *heijunka*, the leveling of the production scheduling, standardized work, and *kaizen*, continuous improvement. At the lowest layer is the foundation of stability to achieve no variation. The strategy is to apply these concepts to achieving the three goals by focusing on the customer and the employees.[24]

As Toyota and other foreign automobile competitors invested in higher quality and more fuel-efficient technology for their vehicles, US automobile producers moved in the other direction, investing in larger, heavier, faster cars that required even more fuel. Ignoring the emerging environmental movement and the early development of hybrid vehicles, the US automobile industry continued to lobby against improved fuel-efficiency standards. Essentially, the US automobile industry failed to make connections and was slow to innovate, moving in a direction that was contrary to what many customers desired, to technological innovation, and to the emerging global trends concerning conservation of resources, energy independence, and climate change.

W. Edwards Deming was a leader in the quality movement, which focused on continuous improvement. Deming emphasized reducing rework and removing defects. He stressed the use of management practices that promote what are today known as the concepts of quality improvement. In the 1940s, Deming was unable to influence the US automobile industry to adopt his ideas on quality improvement. He was, however, able to influence the Japanese, who then developed the *kaizen* system of quality improvement. Before Deming, Japan was producing low-quality products. From the 1950s onward, Deming taught managers how to improve product design and to build systems and processes that prevented errors through the use of applied statistics. In Japan his ideas became the basis of the TPS of quality improvement.[25] TPS propelled Japan ahead of the United States to the forefront of quality products.[26]

Ironically, the inspiration for Toyota's success, TPS, was derived from US management thought, specifically as outlined by Deming. The success of the TPS has enabled Toyota to erode Ford and GM's market shares, eventually growing into the dominant passenger-automobile producer.[27]

The adoption of lean manufacturing techniques was based on the TPS principles of optimizing workflow and removing waste.[28] General Electric, for example, changed its business model to improve their ability to add value and remain competitive using lean manufacturing.

The TPS's emphasis on people makes it more than simply an efficiency model. Toyota replaced the old "check your brains at the door" model with a model that engaged the workers by asking them to participate in the problem-solving process. Those organizations still using the old model are currently being highlighted in studies revealing the lack of engagement among a large proportion of workers.

How Motivated Are People? Global Workforce Study

Employee engagement reflects the attitudes and behaviors of employees and their willingness to extend themselves to help their organizations succeed. Engagement is a determinant of the amount of discretionary effort that employees want to provide to their organization. Thirty-two thousand full-time workers participated in a Global Workforce Study prepared by Towers Watson. The nine-question survey results are organized into four categories: 35% of the participants were highly engaged; 22% were engaged, but lacking enablement and/or energy; 17% were detached, enabled, and/or energized, but lacking a sense of engagement; and 26% were disengaged. "When sustainable engagement starts to decline, companies become vulnerable not only to a measurable drop in productivity, but also to poorer customer service and greater rates of absenteeism and turnover."[29] When engagement is low, it becomes critical to engage the workforce through innovation and entrepreneurship. One approach uses creativity as a tool for inspiration. Next, we examine the roles of extrinsic and intrinsic motivation in more detail, with regard to simple and complex tasks.

Motivation: Simple and Complex Tasks

Figure 4.4 captures the complexity and interconnectedness of both the skills (past and future) and tasks (simple/routine and complex/creative) continua and the dynamics of extrinsic and intrinsic motivators. Daniel Pink explores how to inspire people to be more creative.[30] Pink concludes that

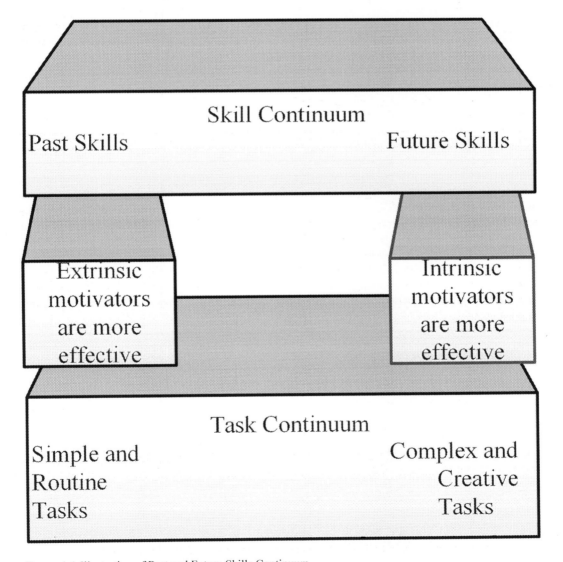

Figure 4.4 Illustration of Past and Future Skills Continuum

there is a mismatch between what behavioral science knows and what business does to inspire and motivate people. In the candle experiment developed by Karl Duncker, groups are given a box with some tacks, matches, and a candle; they have to figure out how to attach the candle to the wall without any additional elements. In experiment A, the tacks are in the box, and in experiment B, the tacks are outside the box. In experiment A, with the tacks inside the box, the group experiences cognitive bias, functional fixedness, because they cannot see how to use the tacks in a new way. The experiment B group, with the tacks outside the box, can find a solution more quickly.

Samuel Glucksberg used the candle experiment to incorporate incentives and discovered that they can undermine creative thought.[31] The results were counterintuitive. In experiment C, the incentivized group with tacks inside the box took even longer than experiment A, on average, to solve the problem. The incentive blocked their creativity. In experiment D, with tacks outside the box, the incentivized group did better than experiment B. Incentives (like the proverbial carrot and stick) work well for simple routine tasks of narrow focus (where you see the goal right there) but not for the complex cognitive tasks required for innovation because these extrinsic rewards cause people to narrow their focus and restrict possibilities.

Extrinsic motivators, also known as incentives, only work within a narrow band of tasks. Pink concludes that carrots and sticks do not work effectively for the creative and conceptual tasks of the future. He describes a future-oriented, inspirational approach that leads through valuing autonomy, mastery of excellence, and finding a meaningful purpose. For example, Microsoft's development of the now-obsolete Encarta online encyclopedia used an extrinsic model, while Wikipedia employs an intrinsic, "wisdom of the crowds" model. That is, Encarta was developed per the more extrinsic, pay-for-hire model, while Wikipedia relied on volunteers, or the more intrinsic, self-motivated model. The intrinsic reward for contributing to the building of knowledge produced far greater results than the extrinsic pay reward model. In the end, Wikipedia displaced Encarta. While Wikipedia inherently created an issue of corroboration or verification of information by promoting the volunteer model, the more intrinsic model produced and continues to produce information on a large scale. While caution needs to be exercised when using Wikipedia, since information can be contributed by anyone who wants to post material, it nonetheless provides a solid basic reference base. With over 1,500 site administrators and editors who monitor and make changes to content as appropriate, Wikipedia's success can be neither ignored nor dismissed. Caution, however, is the key word for its use and application, even as an example of intrinsically motivated innovation success.

The Power of Intrinsic Motivation

Progress Principle

Just as Mark Twain's *The Adventures of Tom Sawyer* reveals that painting a fence can be a source of motivation in and of itself, researcher Teresa Amabile notes that the secret to unleashing the creative potential of people is to enable them to experience a great inner work life. The single most powerful influence on that inner work life is progress in meaningful work. In their book, Amabile and Kramer outline two additional key forces that inform the impact of the power of small wins at work:[32]

- Progress in meaningful work (this is the single most important event)
- Catalysts (events that directly help project work)
- Nourishers (interpersonal events that uplift the people doing the work)

Multipliers and Diminishers

Multipliers are those leaders that make others feel valued by unleashing their intrinsic motivators. Multipliers are others-oriented and place people in the foreground by discovering ways to identify what is of high interest to those people. As Liz Wiseman writes in the book *Multipliers*,

> Multipliers have a rich view of the intelligence of people around them. Diminishers see the world of intelligence in black and white while Multipliers see it in Technicolor. Multipliers don't see a world where just a few people deserve to do the thinking; rather they see intelligence as continually developing.[33]

Diminishers are those leaders that put people in the background by making people feel devalued and disenfranchised.

> The Diminisher's view of intelligence is based on elitism and scarcity. Diminishers appear to believe that really intelligent people are a rare breed and I am one of the few really smart people. They then conclude, other people will never figure things out without me.[34]

Intrinsic Motivation Overshadows Extrinsic Motivation

The psychologist Frederick Herzberg (1968) conducted a study of 1,685 individuals to determine what factors cause job satisfaction and job dissatisfaction. The study resulted in Herzberg's motivation-hygiene theory, which uses motivators and hygiene factors as categories. The motivators are achievement, recognition, the work itself, responsibility, advancement, and growth. These are intrinsic motivators and can elicit positive job satisfaction. Hygiene factors are job security, salary, fringe benefits, and working conditions. The hygiene factors are extrinsic motivators. The key insight is that the hygiene factors do not motivate but are still needed to prevent job dissatisfaction.[35] Or put another way, money doesn't necessarily motivate, but its absence surely aggravates.

In Daniel Pink's *Drive: The Surprising Truth About What Motivates Us*, he highlights the importance of intrinsic motivation over both our biological drive and our need to seek rewards and avoid punishments (extrinsic motivation).[36] According to Pink, the three factors for effective motivation are autonomy, or self-direction; mastery, or the desire to get better and better at something that matters; and purpose or finding meaning.

In *A Whole New Mind: Why Right Brainers Will Rule the World*, Daniel Pink notes that we are transitioning from an economy and society earmarked by the Information Age into the Conceptual Age. He argues that creativity is required to be competitive. Pink describes the three dynamic economic and social forces – abundance (material and nonmaterial), Asia (globalization), and automation (technological progress) – that are nudging us into a new era that requires more conceptual thinking.[37] These megatrends, as he refers to them, are signaling to us that we need to expand our creative competencies or suffer the consequences:

- Abundance: material abundance that is deepening our nonmaterial yearnings
- Asia: globalization that is shipping white-collar work overseas
- Automation: powerful technologies that are eliminating certain types of work altogether

Pink outlines how we have progressed from the Agricultural Age (a society of farmers) to the Industrial Age (a society of factory workers) to the Information Age (a society of knowledge workers) to the Conceptual Age (a society of creators and empathizers). The Conceptual Age requires that we focus our efforts on enabling a new set of creative skills.

In the book *The Experience Economy*, authors Joseph Pine and James Gilmore describe a shift in consumer interest from basic products and services to one that includes more focus on the experience(s). This so-called experience economy represents a shift from passive consumption to active participation, where the memory of the experience itself becomes the product.[38]

Because of the affluence of the Western economies, Pink argues that once our basic needs are satisfied, we search for more meaningful customer experiences. New business service opportunities are being offered that go beyond our basic needs. For example, a family trip to Disney World can be a great experience because it fulfills an unmet need to engage and participate that goes beyond entertainment.[39] The Whole Foods customer experience goes beyond just shopping and the Southwest Airlines experience is beyond just a plane to travel in.

Empowerment

Empowerment (managed freedom) can multiply creativity whereas authoritarianism (managed control) can diminish creativity. As noted previously, a practical example of how this is implemented is in the value formation process used by 3M's William L. McKnight. He articulated a set of management principles and thereby established their innovative corporate culture. His basic rule of management was laid out in 1948:[40]

> As our business grows, it becomes increasingly necessary to delegate responsibility and to encourage men and women to exercise their initiative. This requires considerable tolerance. Those men and women, to whom we delegate authority and responsibility, if they are good people, are going to want to do their jobs in their own way.
>
> Mistakes will be made. But if a person is essentially right, the mistakes he or she makes are not as serious in the long run as the mistakes management will make if it undertakes to tell those in authority exactly how they must do their jobs.
>
> Management that is destructively critical when mistakes are made kills initiative. And it's essential that we have many people with initiative if we are to continue to grow.

The notion of empowerment is an effective way to encourage trust, build relationships, and encourage independent decision-making and alignment in an organization. Effective managers retain responsibility for decisions while simultaneously delegating authority to liberate and inspire their employees. Senior managers who take these actions not only free others but also free themselves for high-order tasks. As Clayton Christensen writes,

> Managers can't be there to watch over every decision as a company gets bigger. That's why the larger and more complex a company becomes, the more important it is for senior managers to ensure employees make, by themselves, prioritization decisions that are consistent with the strategic direction and the business model of the company.[41]

Drive for Progress: Continuous Improvement

The essence of a visionary company is to preserve its core ideology and stimulate progress. The core ideology does not change, but the goals, strategy, and operating practices will.[42] Inherent in successful individuals and organizations is a continual drive for progress.

This drive for progress is the fundamental underlying characteristic of quality improvement programs such as Six Sigma.[43] In the 1980s Motorola engineers needed a better way to measure defects in the manufacturing processes. In 1985, Motorola's Bill Smith developed a new approach known as Six Sigma to prevent manufacturing product defects by using statistical methods to reduce variability.[44] Under the leadership of Robert Galvin, son of company founder Paul V. Galvin, Motorola documented more than $16 billion in savings as a result of their continuous improvement efforts through Six Sigma.[45] Around 1995, Jack Welch, CEO of General Electric, adopted Motorola's Six Sigma process and integrated the program into GE's strategy.[46]

Summary

Innovative behaviors are essential to improving the central role of innovation and entrepreneurship in economic advancement. Key among these innovation skills and behaviors are discovery skills (including questioning, observing, networking, associating, and experimenting), and delivery skills (including analyzing, planning, detailed implementation, and disciplined execution). These behaviors have variously been encouraged and/or discouraged over time, resulting in an uneven approach to the discovery that leads to innovation. Motivation within the context of innovative behaviors was also examined. As we shall see in the next chapter, innovative behaviors and thinking are inextricably linked to each other in the overall framework of innovation and entrepreneurship.

Notes

1. Ying-Ting Lin, Xiao-Pu Han, and Bing-Hang Wang, "Dynamics of Human Innovative Behaviors," *Physica A: Statistical Mechanics and Its Applications* 394 (2014), 74–81.
2. Jeff Dyer, Hal Gregersen, and Clayton M. Christensen, *The Innovator's DNA* (Boston: Harvard Business Review Press, 2011), 3.
3. Jeff Dyer, Hal Gregersen, and Clayton M. Christensen, *The Innovator's DNA* (Boston: Harvard Business Review Press, 2011), 29.
4. Jeff Dyer, Hal Gregersen, and Clayton M. Christensen, *The Innovator's DNA* (Boston: Harvard Business Review Press, 2011), 176.
5. Jeff Dyer, Hal Gregersen, and Clayton M. Christensen, *The Innovator's DNA* (Boston: Harvard Business Review Press, 2011).
6. Keith Sawyer, *Zig Zag* (San Francisco: Jossey-Bass, 2013), 6.
7. Keith Sawyer, *Zig Zag* (San Francisco: Jossey-Bass, 2013), 6.
8. Coimbatore K. Prahalad, *The Fortune at the Bottom of the Pyramid: Eradicating Poverty Through Profits*, 5th ed. (Upper Saddle River, NJ: Pearson Education, 2010).
9. Bruce Nussbaum, *Creative Intelligence* (New York: Harper Business, 2013), 68–69.
10. Janine Nahapiet and Sumantra Ghoshal, "Social Capital, Intellectual Capital, and the Organizational Advantage," *Academy of Management Review* 23, no. 2 (1998), 242–266.
11. Ray Reagans and Bill McEvily, "Network Structure and Knowledge Transfer: The Effects of Cohesion and Range," *Administrative Science Quarterly* 48, no. 2 (2003), 240–267.
12. "Stay Hungry . . . Stay Foolish. Amazing Steve Jobs Speech at Stanford with English Subtitles," *YouTube Video*, posted by "Ramesh Ramanujan," October 6, 2011, accessed F, www.youtube.com/watch?v=JlptP2bpWD8.
13. Gary Wolf, "Steve Jobs: The Next Insanely Great Thing," *Wired*, February 1996, accessed February 19, 2024, www.wired.com/1996/02/jobs-2/.
14. *Wikipedia*, s.v. "Socrates," accessed December 10, 2020, http://en.wikipedia.org/wiki/Socrates.
15. Clayton M. Christensen, *The Innovator's Dilemma* (Boston: Harvard Business School Press, 1997).
16. Jeff Dyer, Hal Gregersen, and Clayton M. Christensen, *The Innovator's DNA* (Boston: Harvard Business Review Press, 2011), 37.
17. *Wikipedia*, s.v. "Hawthorne Effect," accessed December 10, 2020, http://en.wikipedia.org/wiki/Hawthorne_effect.

18. *Wikipedia*, s.v. "Toyota Industries," accessed December 10, 2020, http://en.wikipedia.org/wiki/Toyota_Industries#History.
19. *Wikipedia*, s.v. "Toyota Production System," accessed January 21, 2021, Toyota Production System – Wikipedia.
20. Gary Hamel, *The Future of Management* (Boston: Harvard Business School Press, 2007), 52.
21. Gary Hamel, *The Future of Management* (Boston: Harvard Business School Press, 2007), 29.
22. *Wikipedia*, s.v. "Five Whys," accessed December 10, 2020, http://en.wikipedia.org/wiki/5_Whys.
23. K. Holland, "Eight Steps to Practical Problem Solving," *Kaizen News*, 2013, accessed February 19, 2024, www.kaizen-news.com/eight-steps-practical-problem-solving/.
24. Jeffrey K. Liker, *The Toyota Way* (New York: McGraw-Hill, 2004).
25. *Wikipedia*, s.v. "Toyota Production System," accessed December 10, 2020, http://en.wikipedia.org/wiki/Toyota_production_system.
26. *Wikipedia*, s.v. "Edwards Deming," accessed December 10, 2020, http://en.wikipedia.org/wiki/W._Edwards_Deming.
27. *Wikipedia*, s.v. "Edwards Deming," accessed December 10, 2020, http://en.wikipedia.org/wiki/W._Edwards_Deming.
28. "Lean Manufacturing History," *Strategos Inc.*, accessed February 19, 2024, www.strategosinc.com/just_in_time.htm.
29. "2012 Global Workforce Study," *Willis Towers Watson*, accessed February 19, 2024, https://employeeengagement.com/wp-content/uploads/2012/11/2012-Towers-Watson-Global-Workforce-Study.pdf.
30. Daniel Pink, "Dan Pink: The Puzzle of Motivation," *YouTube Video*, posted by "Ted," August 25, 2009, accessed February 19, 2024, www.youtube.com/watch?v=rrkrvAUbU9Y.
31. Steven Zhang, "Solve This Problem, Receive $20," *The Cornell Sun*, via UWire College Press Release & Wire Service, September 14, 2010, accessed February 19, 2024, www.uwire.com/2010/09/14/column-solve-this-problem-receive-20/.
32. Teresa Amabile and Steven Kramer, *The Progress Principle* (Boston: Harvard Business Review Press, 2011).
33. Liz Wiseman, *Multipliers* (New York: Harper, 2010).
34. Liz Wiseman, *Multipliers* (New York: Harper, 2010).
35. Frederick Herzberg, "One More Time: How Do You Motivate Employees?" *Harvard Business Review* 46, no. 1 (1968), 53–62.
36. Daniel Pink, *Drive* (New York: Riverhead Books, 2009).
37. Daniel H. Pink, *A Whole New Mind* (New York: Riverhead Books, 2005).
38. B. Joseph Pine II and James H. Gilmore, *The Experience Economy* (Boston: Harvard Business School Press, 1999).
39. Tim Brown, *Change by Design* (New York: Harper, 2009), 112.
40. William L. McKnight, "Principles of 3M's Corporate Culture," *3M*, accessed February 19, 2024, https://en.wikipedia.org/wiki/William_L._McKnight#:~:text=Unsourced%20material%20may%20be%20challenged%20and%20removed.&text=this%20template%20message)-,William%20L.,the%20McKnight%20Foundation%20in%201953.
41. Clayton M. Christensen, James Allworth, and Karen Dillon, *How Will You Measure Your Life?* (New York: Harper, 2012), 126.
42. Jim Collins and Jerry I. Porras, *Built to Last* (New York: HarperCollins, 2002), 82.
43. Roger O. Crockett and Jena McGregor, "Six Sigma Still Pays Off at Motorola," *BusinessWeek*, December 3, 2006, accessed February 19, 2024, www.bloomberg.com/news/articles/2006-12-03/six-sigma-still-pays-off-at-motorola.
44. *Glossary*, s.v. "Bill Smith," accessed February 19, 2024, Bill Smith – Lean Manufacturing and Six Sigma Definitions (leansixsigmadefinition.com) and Lean Manufacturing and Six Sigma Definitions – Glossary terms, history, people and definitions about Lean and Six Sigma (leansixsigmadefinition.com).
45. "The History of Six Sigma," accessed February 19, 2024, www.isixsigma.com/new-to-six-sigma/history/history-six-sigma/.
46. *Wikipedia*, s.v. "Six Sigma," accessed December 10, 2020, http://en.wikipedia.org/wiki/Six_Sigma.

5 Innovative Thinking

Clayton Christensen and Andy Grove

One day at the Harvard Business School, the late Clayton Christensen received a surprise phone call and an opportunity of a lifetime from then Intel CEO, Andy Grove.[1]

Christensen picked up phone and listened.[2]

"Look, Clayton I'm a busy man and I don't have time to read drivel from academics but someone told me you had this theory . . . and I'm wondering if you could come out to present what you're learning to me and my staff and tell us how it applies to Intel."

Christensen, ecstatic from what he just heard, accepted the offer, and hopped on a plane out west to meet with the Intel team. Soon after arriving at Intel's offices to speak, he was greeted with a gruff response from Grove:

"Stuff has happened to us, but look we only have 10 minutes for you, so tell us what your theory means for Intel."

Christensen pushed back, saying,

"Andy I can't because I have no opinion about Intel, but my theory has an opinion . . . so I have to describe the theory."

Andy Grove sat back impatiently, and after 10 minutes of Christensen explaining his theory, he impatiently interrupted again, asking what it meant for Intel and Clayton pushed back again:

"Just give me five more minutes. I have to explain how this process of disruption worked its way through a totally different industry, just so you can envision what can happen to Intel."

When Clayton Christensen explained to Grove how the United States Steel integrated mills were disrupted by the Nucor mini-mills at the low-end of the market with rebar, Andy Grove understood the concept to where he could explain the theory himself. "Grove said, 'OK, I get it. What it means for Intel is . . . ,' and then Grove went on to articulate what would become the company's strategy for going to the bottom of the market to launch the Celeron processor."[3]

Christensen didn't teach the late Andy Grove "what to think" but rather "how to think." Teaching individuals how to think provides the ability to understand how to make effective decisions in different circumstances and contexts and enables individuals to recognize patterns so that they can more accurately make connections that are valuable for decision-making.[4]

Clayton Christensen was a thought leader who developed the theory of disruption. With a theory anyone can make predictions about what might happen even before you experience it.[5] The

DOI: 10.4324/9781003034308-6

Socratic-style Harvard Business School professor sought not to provide answers but instead to ask questions to help people learn how to think, not what to think.[6]

Businessman, educator, and author Michael Horn notes,

> As I read biographies of luminaries like Albert Einstein, I see echoes of Clay – people who were obsessed with discovering truth and causality in the world. Clay's view of how to form theory and how to revise it as one learned more about how the world works was consistent with the greatest scientists in history. It remains underappreciated by his detractors, just as was the case with some of Einstein's contemporaries.[7]

What Do We Mean by Thinking?

This chapter explores learning how to think more effectively. According to David Wallace, "'Learning how to think' really means learning how to exercise some control over how and what you think. It means being conscious and aware enough to choose what you pay attention to and to choose how you construct meaning from experience."[8]

"Learning how to think" means how you choose to view others through your belief template and the extent to which you are open or closed-minded about new experiences. A belief template is formed through and composed of the accumulation of experiences and strongly held beliefs and values that affect your thinking. Your belief template is like a map used to find out where to travel. If your map is wrong, you will travel in the wrong direction and reach a different location.

The notion of "learning how to think" is explored by understanding causation and correlation, thinking modes, convergence (including switch thinking) and divergence, critical thinking, multi-level systems thinking, and how to reflect on misperceptions and implicit biases to minimize thinking errors.

The thinking types and modes are visualized in Figure 5.1. Thinking types include causation and correlation, divergence and convergence, systems thinking, and critical thinking (deduction and induction). The four conceptual thinking modes include sleeping and default mode network (background) and fast and slow (foreground).

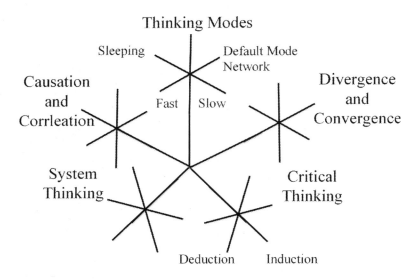

Figure 5.1 Illustration of the Thinking Competencies

Why Is Thinking Important?

Thinking is the antecedent to decision-making, a high-order meta-competency. Without effective thinking, effective decisions become problematic. As increasing levels of change and complexity are experienced, limits are reached on what can be achieved. Albert Einstein said, "The significant problems we face cannot be solved at the same level of thinking we were at when we created them."[9] Information and misinformation simultaneously tend to influence our consciousness from everyday news media, social media, and popular culture. These influences impact the ability to think effectively and make evidence-based decisions. Too often people limit their creativity, innovation, and new venture creation capabilities due to thinking skills that are poorly developed, shallow, and archaic.

The innovation and entrepreneurship mindset requires openness to ideas, yet people collectively tend to view things one way and not see other things at all. Each person needs to take responsibility to reduce the gravitational pull that draws their thinking in the wrong direction by enlarging their ability to see through the fog and "frosty windows" of our experiences.

Causation and Correlation

Daniel Bernoulli

Causation occurs when you identify the explicit reason that causes something to happen, such as flying a kite. What causes an airplane, bird, or kite to fly? A kite flies because of lift that enables flight. Lift is a result of air traveling over the kite's topside surface faster than the air on the underside resulting in reduced pressure on the topside in relation to the increased pressure on the bottom side. The phenomenon that describes the inverse relationship between the pressure and the speed of a fluid was discovered by the Dutch-Swiss mathematician Daniel Bernoulli in his book *Hydodynamica*, a study of fluid mechanics.

In contrast, a correlation occurs when two things move in the same direction but are not necessarily causal. For instance, wings and feathers of birds are correlated, but the feathers do not cause the lift, per se. Bernoulli's principle of hydrodynamics describes how lift in part is a consequence of the shape of the upper surface of the wing. That is, because as the air moves over the top of a wing, the wing can be designed (curved) so that it moves faster at the upper side, therefore causing lift by decreasing the pressure on the topside. Too often, correlation mistakenly is thought of as causal and care must be taken to be clear about what is actually the cause of a phenomenon.

As discussed earlier and illustrated in Figure 5.2, there is a fundamental difference between causation and correlation; correlation does not necessarily suggest that one variable causes the other. In general use, a theory is developed through a rational, at times abstract way of thinking about an occurrence. It is an educated but often an unsubstantiated guess as to causation. In science, the goal is to seek a well-substantiated explanation for why something occurs in nature, often via testable hypotheses derived from prior research, new evidence, logic, and empirical testing. By better understanding causation, it is possible to subsequently facilitate more accurate theoretical predictions. As Clayton Christensen writes, "We then use the theories to predict what problems and opportunities are likely to occur in the future for that company, and we use the theories to predict what actions the managers will need to take to address them."[10]

Dr. Ignaz Semmelweis

In 1846, at the General Hospital in Vienna, there were two maternity wards; one was staffed by all male doctors and medical students, while the other was staffed by female midwives.

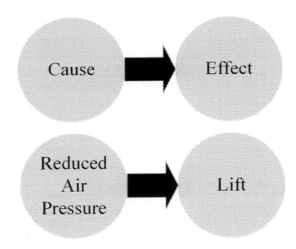

A causation between two variables
infers that one causes the other.

Figure 5.2 Illustration of Causation

Dr. Ignaz Semmelweis began collecting data on the number of deaths in the maternity wards to determine why so many women were dying from childbed fever or a postpartum bacterial infection of the reproductive tract that follows childbirth. Dr. Ignaz Semmelweis noticed that there was a disproportionate number of women in the clinic staffed by doctors and medical students that had the disease than women in the midwives' clinic. In the clinic staffed by doctors and medical students, the women died at a rate nearly five times higher than women in the midwives' clinic.[11]

A pathologist colleague of Dr. Ignaz Semmelweis pricked his finger while doing an autopsy on a woman who had died from childbed fever. When the pathologist died of the childbed fever, Dr. Semmelweis realized that this disease was something other people in the hospital could get sick from as well. Dr. Semmelweis discovered that the difference between the doctors' ward and the midwives' ward was that the doctors were doing autopsies and the midwives were not.

Dr. Ignaz Semmelweis hypothesized that there were infectious particles, little pieces of the corpse, that were getting on their hands from the cadavers that were being autopsied, and when babies were delivered, these particles would be transferred from the doctors and medical students to the women who would develop the disease and die. Semmelweis' hypothesized that if he could eliminate the infectious particles, it would reduce the death rate from childbed fever. He ordered his medical staff to start cleaning their hands and instruments with soap and a disinfectant chlorine solution before they delivered any babies. The death rate dropped immediately.

During the American Civil War doctors knew very little about germs and disease. There were a total number of 620,000 deaths, and the majority were caused by disease.[12] The ground-breaking research by Professor Joseph Lister in 1864, discovered that microorganisms cause diseases.[13] Moreover, we know that if medical instruments, operating theaters, surgeons' hands, and other surfaces are cleaned and/or sterilized, it will reduce the likelihood of transmitting germs and acquiring diseases during surgery and other procedures. With thorough handwashing, there will be a reduction in the transmission of microorganisms and the likelihood of diseases.

Dr. Benjamin Sandler

In 1921, at the age of 39, President Franklin Delano Roosevelt contracted the poliovirus, one of the thousands that were afflicted that year. Polio is a disease that affects the central nervous system and can result in paralysis. In 1949, Benjamin Sandler, MD, a nutritional expert at the Oteen Veterans' Hospital, observed that both polio and ice cream consumption increased during the summer. Summer was "polio season" and children were among the most susceptible to paralytic poliomyelitis (also known as infantile paralysis). He deduced that ice cream (because of the sugar) was causing polio. While the two phenomena were correlated, his fundamental error was he did not understand the difference between correlation and causation.[14] Figure 5.3 illustrates the risk of assuming correlation as causal.

By the early 1950s, 25,000 to 50,000 new cases of polio occurred each year. Rigorous scientific research revealed that poliomyelitis is caused by the poliovirus. The disease was finally brought under control when Jonas Edward Salk developed the first dead-virus polio vaccine that was approved in 1955. In 1961, Albert Bruce Sabin introduced an effective oral live-virus vaccine in the United States.[15]

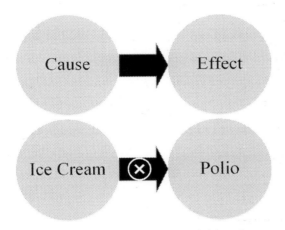

A correlation between two variables does not necessarily infer that one causes the other.

Figure 5.3 Illustration of Correlation

The Hummingbird Effect

Interestingly, it is possible to trace the causation chains historically. Author Steven Johnson has named these complex chains of influences the hummingbird effect, named after the famous butterfly effect. The butterfly effect is a concept from chaos theory – Edward Lorenz's famous metaphor for the idea that a change as imperceptible as the flap of a butterfly's wings can result in an effect as grand as a hurricane far away several weeks later.

Steven Johnson writes, "Innovations usually begin life with an attempt to solve a specific problem, but once they get into circulation, they end up triggering other changes that would have been extremely difficult to predict."[16] The hummingbird evolved in a novel way, allowing the bird to float midair in a strange leap of evolution. The *hummingbird effect* describes the cascading series of innovations leading from one to another. "The history of ideas and innovation unfolds in the same way, Johannes Gutenberg's printing press created a surge in demand for spectacles, as the new practice of reading made Europeans across the continent suddenly realize that they were farsighted; the market demand for spectacles encourages a growing number of people to produce and experiment with lenses, which led to the invention of the microscope, which shortly there-after enables us to perceive that our bodies were made up of microscopic cells."[17] As depicted in Figure 5.4, it is possible to trace the chains of influence by understanding how an innovation can trigger other innovations.

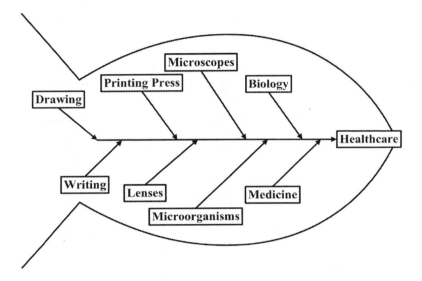

Figure 5.4 Illustration of the Chains of Influence

Source: Adapted from Steven Johnson, *How we got to now: Six innovations that made the modern world,* (New York: Riverhead Books, 2014), 3.

What Are the Thinking Modes?

As depicted in Figure 5.5, to better understand ideation, thinking processes can be organized into four conceptual thinking modes of your mind: background (default mode network and sleeping)

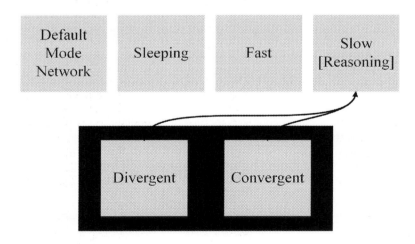

Figure 5.5 Illustration of Thinking Modes

and foreground (fast and slow). In background mode, the default is mind wandering, which occurs when you are daydreaming, driving, jogging, showering, walking, and reading.

Foreground mode is characterized by either fast or slow thinking, which is discussed in more detail later. Fast thinking is a rapid response to some event, like stopping your car to avoid a collision. Slow thinking is deliberate, explicit, and conscious. Slow thinking allows for switching between divergent broad thinking and convergent thinking, which is essential for critical thinking and encompasses the evaluation of the validity of various choices.

Default Mode Network

The default mode network is active when a person is not focused on the outside world and the mind is at wakeful rest, such as during daydreaming and mind wandering. The network activates by default when a person is not involved in an explicit task.

For example, when engaged in an activity such as driving a car, it is possible to invoke the default mode network and mind wandering and later realize you have traveled 20 miles down the highway. Or when running for exercise, the mind will automatically carry the body forward while another part of mind thinks deeply on another topic. One part of the mind is running, while another part is focused elsewhere.

When the default mode network is invoked, the mind is liberated to create ideas and associations. Generally speaking, this phenomenon occurs while listening to music, walking, and taking a shower. The default mode network creates a more relaxed state of being spawning divergent thinking.

Sleeping

When sleeping, the body is at rest, but interestingly the mind stays active. In fact, it is often difficult to "turn your brain off" at night to calm your mind when trying to go to sleep. The brain never stops working, running many of your body's functions like breathing, while simultaneously sorting through the day's information. Through the process of consolidation, it sorts, codifies, and locks learning into memory for later recall.

A circadian rhythm is basically a 24-hour internal clock that is running in the background of your brain and cycles between sleepiness and alertness at regular intervals. Basically, circadian rhythms bring together the physical and mental processes that affect our waking and sleeping lives. Moreover, it develops and changes over time. For example, the body clock changes at puberty, resulting in a shift in circadian rhythms by about two hours during the teenage years, meaning that teenagers feel sleepy a couple of hours later at night than adults. It is a challenging interface of the physiological and psychological aspects of thinking, in general and thinking modes, in particular affecting our overall thinking processes.

Dual Process Theory

Recognizing the importance of thinking processes, fast and slow thinking is a conceptual model that was developed by the Nobel Prize winner Daniel Kahneman. Kahneman conceived the dual-system theoretical framework that explains why our judgments and decisions often do not conform to the formal notions of rationality. Kahneman created the concept of two interacting systems: fast (system one) and slow (system two). These in combination describe our thinking processes.[18]

Fast Thinking (System One)

Fast thinking is intuitive, associative, metaphorical, automatic, impressionistic, experience-based, and relatively unconscious. It can't be switched off. System one is our subconscious system which operates automatically and quickly, with little or no effort and no sense of voluntary control. Judgments influenced by system one are rooted in impressions arising from mental content that is easily accessible to our cognitive process.[19]

System one provides an explanation of how cognitive bias and errors affect our thinking and decision-making. System one is prone to errors that can influence our decision-making.[20] Fast thinking is likely be a source of dysfunctional decisions, such as jumping wildly to conclusions. Similarly, it is subject to a fantastic suite of irrational biases and interference effects. Fast thinking is a rapid response to some event or stimulus such as applying your brakes to avoid a collision or recognizing a familiar face or identifying a song.

Slow Thinking (System Two)

Slow thinking is a conscious, rational system that is reflective, deliberate, explicit, controlled, analytical, rule-based, and high-effort. It represents our logical critical thinking steps. Slow thinking monitors our thinking processes and provides a check on mental operations and overt behavior – often unsuccessfully and allocates attention to the effortful mental activities that demand it, including complex computations.[21]

Slow thinking is better for decision-making as it tends to prevent interference from our bias templates. When things get difficult, slow thinking takes over rather unwillingly. As a result, it facilitates divergence, the broadening of your thinking and convergence, as well as the narrowing of your thinking that leads to choices. For example, reading and in some cases re-reading this textbook, you are using slow thinking.

Divergence and Convergence

As seen in Figure 5.6, divergent thinking is about expanding on ideas and generating new ideas, not necessarily about the right answer. Convergent thinking is assembling ideas from extant models and then narrowing the result. Both convergent and divergent thinking are interrelated and used together. "One of the most obvious differences between intelligence and creativity is that intelligence requires convergent thinking, coming up with the right answer, while creativity requires divergent thinking, coming up with many potential answers."[22]

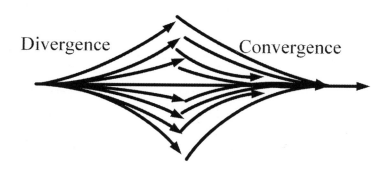

Figure 5.6 Illustration of Divergent and Convergent Thinking

Tectonic Plates

In general, ideas converge, diverge, and at times, conflict. A useful analogy is the formation and evolution of the earth's tectonic plates. The tectonic plates are gigantic pieces of rock in assorted sizes. Over 225 million years ago, the earth was composed of two major areas, a supercontinent of land known as Pangaea, which is a Greek word meaning "all lands," and an ocean known as Panthalassa, which is Greek for "all seas." Between then and now, the earth has been reorganized by huge forces exerted on tectonic plates. Various forces inside the earth, such as convection, cause the tectonic plates to move, resulting in a perpetual reorganization of the earth. Earthquakes and volcanoes reflect the dynamic turmoil of activity beneath the earth's surface.

In the world of geology, there are three types of tectonic plate boundaries. Divergent boundaries are those where the plates are being pulled apart. For instance, Iceland is now splitting and will eventually become two landmasses. Convergent boundaries are those where the plates are being forced to come together. For example, mountain ranges are created when an oceanic plate pushes under a land or continental plate. Finally, transform-fault boundaries are those where the plates are chafing or sliding horizontally against one another. For example, the San Andreas Fault zone in California continues to form and reform as the plates move against one another.[23] In organizations we have three analogous concepts surrounding innovative thinking: ideas that converge, ideas that diverge, and ideas that conflict.

According to IDEO's CEO Tim Brown,

> The innovation process is a series of divergent and then convergent activities – a very simple concept, but one with which leaders who are used to managing efficient processes in their businesses tend to struggle. By "divergence," I mean a willingness to explore things that seem far away from where you think your business is today. The discomfort that a lot of business leaders have with innovation is with divergence. They think that it's divergent forever and that they'll never be able to focus on something that makes business sense. I think that's where some business leaders, historically, have had a bit of a problem with their internal innovation units: The leaders have a sense that these units are endlessly divergent. If you understand that convergence follows divergence, and that it's really hard to converge without first diverging, maybe that's a bit comforting.[24]

Divergence

By contrast, divergence is characterized by thinking broadly and differently. Nobel Prize–winning physicist Richard Feynman often noted that thinking about a problem for a long time can make it harder to see the problem from a new perspective, thereby making it more difficult to arrive at fresh insights into the nature of the problem and discover optimal solutions. But if we step back and change our perspective slightly, we can see things in a different way, allowing new possibilities to emerge that we may not have seen before.[25]

Divergent thinking, a term created by Edward de Bono, a Maltese physician and writer, is concerned with broadening ideas, generating new ideas, and breaking out of old, outmoded ideas.[26] This type of thinking requires a fresh perspective to enable the generation of novel ideas. Divergent thinking may or may not result in creativity, however, in part since creativity is based on how ideas are associated or connected and what value the ideas provide.[27]

Divergent thinking can be viewed as a mini-paradigm shift, such as that which occurred with Copernicus's controversial idea that the sun was the center of our universe.[28] It is like digging a hole in a different place or changing to a different perceptual framework.[29] In essence, divergent thinking is concerned with restructuring patterns (actionable insights) and provoking new ones.

Olympic High Jump

For example, the Olympic high jump record for men is held by the American athlete Charles Austin, set in the 1996 Summer Olympic Games in Atlanta, Georgia. He earned a gold medal for the high jump for the height of 2.39 meters (7 feet, 10.9 inches). The women's Olympic high jump record is held by Yelena Slesarenko of Russia, who jumped 2.06 meters (6 feet, 9.1 inches) at the 2004 Games in Athens.[30] Both used a technique that has become known as the Fosbury flop (after its originator) because it provided better heights.

In the high jump, the jumper attempts to clear a horizontal bar placed at measured heights. The dominant jump model used to be the straddle – a technique for doing a high jump in which the jumper rotates his body belly-down around and over the horizontal bar. Having difficulty with the straddle, Dick Fosbury, at 16, created a new high-jump technique now known as the Fosbury flop. Instead of the traditional straddle, back-up and belly-down, the jumper leaps head-first, back-down and belly-up over the bar. This technique is now adopted by most high jumpers.[31] Dick Fosbury won an Olympic gold medal at the 1968 Olympics in Mexico with a height of 2.24 meters (7 feet, 4.19 inches). His unconventional approach, essentially the reverse of the previous technique, is an example of divergent thinking that changed the high jump forever.[32]

Natural Energy Saving

In another example of lateral divergent thinking, consider Microsoft's Christian Belady.

Frustration over escalating energy bills made Belady toss some computer servers into a tent in 2007, to tough out the Seattle winter. Belady, a data center expert at Microsoft, knew that servers are hardy machines. But the industry engineers who set air-conditioning standards had decreed that data centers operate best between 68 and 77 degrees Fahrenheit – a cautious edict that wasted hundreds of megawatts for unnecessary year-round cooling. Belady had grown up camping in national parks and figured that data centers could benefit from fresh air too. The servers hummed along in their tent for eight months without failure. He posted his results online, they went viral, and in 2009, the engineers changed their guidelines to a more flexible 64 to 81 degrees. This outside-the-building thinking has made Belady a pioneer in the greening of the data center.[33]

Suitcases

Prior to 1970, conventional thinking about luggage involved heavy suitcases with handles that had to be carried for long distances through airports. At best, putting the heavy suitcases on wheeled carts was the only solution to this backbreaking effort. In 1970, while traveling through the Aruba airport, Bernard Sadow, vice president of a US luggage company, observed a worker rolling machinery. He then realized that instead of carrying heavy luggage or putting the baggage on wheeled conveyances, he could add wheels to conventional luggage, thereby creating rolling luggage. His design was to add four wheels and pull the luggage on a towrope. His invention holds United States patent no. 3,653,474.[34] Although this was better than carrying the luggage, it was cumbersome because you tended to hit the back of your foot on the luggage. Around 1987, Bob Plath, a Northwest Airlines 747 pilot, improved on the Sadow design and changed how people travelled.[35] Plath created a new rectangular luggage design and flipped the horizontal luggage into a vertical position, attached two wheels, and added extendable handles. This Rollaboard® product design was more convenient that any luggage design previously developed. Pilots and flight attendants showcased the luggage, resulting in broad acceptance.[36]

Hoover Dam

In the late 1920s and early 1930s, the construction of dams to manage flooding, provide hydro-electric power, irrigation, and recreation was a fairly well-established process. One of the most ambitious dam projects in the United States took place during the Great Depression, between 1931 and 1936. The Hoover Dam was a megaproject constructed between Arizona and Nevada on the Colorado River.[37] The problem was that the concrete for the dam could not be delivered in a single pour because concrete contracts and generates considerable heat. On the other hand, waiting for the concrete to cool would result in missing the scheduled completion date. To solve the problem, the concrete was poured in squares 50 feet wide and 5 feet deep, including embedded pipes. The lateral idea was to embed pipes that carried cool water through the concrete during the curing process to dissipate the heat. The water was conveniently drawn from the Colorado River. The metal pipes remain in the dam.

Divergent thinking should precede convergent thinking. When engineering new solutions, divergent thinking is first used to identify ideas about the options. The preferred options are narrowed using convergent thinking. For example, convergent thinking was instrumental in the engineering and construction of the water systems in the United States. Los Angeles experienced a water shortage around 1900 that stalled the growth of the city. After identifying a set of alternatives using divergent thinking, William Mulholland led a public works project to build the Los Angeles aqueduct, supplying water from the Eastern Sierra Nevada Mountains into the city of Los Angeles.[38]

Convergence

Convergence is the narrowing of our thinking. The basic idea behind Western convergent thinking was designed about 2,300 years ago by the Greek gang of three: Socrates, Plato, and Aristotle. These three were the originators of convergent thinking style. Convergent thinking applies a set of prescribed steps, like those used when following a recipe to bake a cake.

Convergent thinking facilitates structure but can narrow creative thinking. We have strong tendencies to think in a convergent manner. Indeed, in certain circumstances, too much deviation from the convergent path can have less than optimal outcomes. The convergent thinking process is like that of the syllogism reflecting how one thinks in a step-by-step fashion:

- If all a are b,
- and if all b are c,
- then all a are c.

Convergent thinking is assembling ideas from the same model and then narrowing the result. For instance, in mathematics and physics, convergent thinking is valuable for how to compute the density of a compound or solve a mathematical equation.

Transportation

Convergent thinking was also instrumental in building transportation systems in the United States. The building process started with idea generation and divergent thinking to identify ideas. After the idea generation, convergent thinking was used to narrow and engineer the preferred solution selected for implementation. For example, the Panama Canal, built between 1904 and 1914, enabled more efficient shipping between the Atlantic and Pacific Oceans.[39] Robert Fulton developed the Clermont, the first commercial steamboat, which began traveling between New York City and Albany, New York, in 1807.[40]

The Erie Canal, which opened in 1825, was a transportation innovation of its day. The Erie Canal enabled commerce to be transferred between Albany, New York, and Lake Erie.[41] The first US transcontinental railroad was built from the East and from the West in two separate sections simultaneously. The railroad spanned the entire country and the two parts were joined on May 10, 1869, at Promontory Summit, Utah.[42] Telegraph lines were also built along the rail lines during the construction of the tracks. The US Interstate Highway system is a network of expressways and freeways which officially started in 1956, took 35 years to build for a total length of 46,876 miles, and cost over $425 billion.[43]

United States Space Program

The decision-making model starts with divergent thinking by looking outward and then shifting to convergent thinking by looking inward. The Space Program provides a kaleidoscope of colorful examples of the interplay of divergent and convergent thinking. After the 1957 Sputnik launch by the Russians, the United States formed the National Aeronautics and Space Administration (NASA) in 1958. President John F. Kennedy identified a set of novel ideas on how to compete with the Russians and then selected the idea to travel to the moon. The US Space Program has many examples of the synergism between divergent and convergent thinking as they built the rockets, spacesuits, and lunar modules to make the trip. In the Apollo 13 mission, a problem was experienced with the lithium hydroxide canisters that were used to remove carbon dioxide from the spacecraft. The NASA team first used divergent thinking to unleash their ideas and then used convergent thinking to implement a simple solution using duct tape.[44] These examples illustrate the powerful combination of first applying divergent thinking and then convergent thinking to achieve the most effective result.

Switch Thinking

Switch thinking is the ability to select the thinking mode that you need, based on the opportunity that you are pursuing. As illustrated in Figure 5.7, the concept is that you can manage your thinking modes by consciously being aware of what mode you are in at any one point in time and switching to a different one if needed.

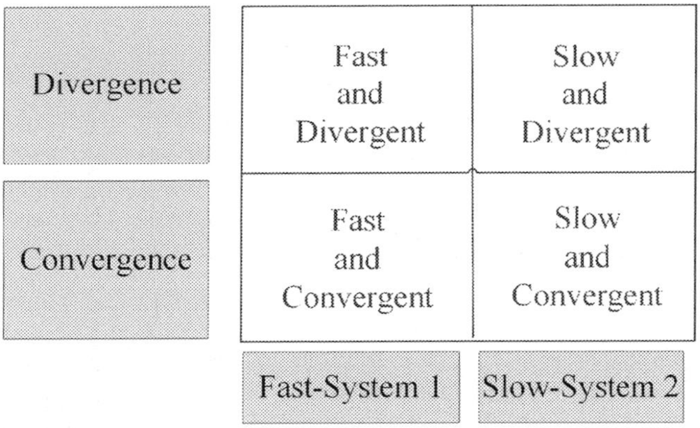

	Fast and Divergent	Slow and Divergent
Divergence	Fast and Divergent	Slow and Divergent
Convergence	Fast and Convergent	Slow and Convergent
	Fast-System 1	Slow-System 2

Figure 5.7 Illustration of Switch Thinking

Source: Adapted from Kahneman, D. (2011). *Thinking, fast and slow.* New York: Farrar, Straus and Giroux.

Effective thinkers are self-aware of their thinking modes and can learn to switch between the boxes. It is more effective if you switch your thinking to slow and divergent for creative tasks to facilitate imagination, planning, gathering evidence, and alternatives and switch your thinking to slow and convergent when you are ready for decision-making.

Critical Thinking

What is critical thinking? "Critical thinking entails an interpretation or analysis, even an evaluation or judgment about a claim that may or may not be valid, complete or the best possible."[45] Depicted in Figure 5.8, critical thinking is a set of cognitive tools that can improve thinking.

What is critical thinking?	Why is critical thinking important?	Why question a claim?
"Critical thinking entails an interpretation or analysis, even an evaluation or judgment about a claim that may or may not be valid, complete, or the best possible" (Nilson, 2016, p. 35). Both deduction and induction can facilitate critical thinking.	Critical thinking is a set of cognitive tools that can improve your thinking. It is an important part of decision making, problem solving, and being able to evaluate your judgements. An important behavior to facilitate critical thinking is self-awareness that fosters open-mindedness.	A claim is a declarative sentence that can be either true or false. To determine if a claim is true we need evidence to validate the truth. The conclusion may have been influenced by cognitive thinking errors. There are over a hundred implicit cognitive biases that can introduce thinking errors.

Figure 5.8 Illustration of Critical Thinking

Source: Adapted from Nilson, L. B. (2016). *Teaching at its best A research-based resource for college instructors* (4th ed.). US: Jossey Bass Ltd. Retrieved from http://www.vlebooks.com/vleweb/product/openreader?id=none&isbn=97804706123 30&uid=none

It is an important part of decision-making, problem solving and being able to evaluate claims. A claim is a declarative sentence that can be either true or false. To determine if a claim is true, evidence is needed to validate the information and avoid a conclusion that may have been influenced by cognitive thinking errors.

Reasoning

We might begin with formulating a *theory* about our topic of interest, which in turn is narrowed down into more specific testable *hypotheses*. Through the process of applying various research methods, measures, and analysis, it is possible to test the hypotheses with specific data – a *confirmation* (or not) of our original theories. The application of critical thinking includes the use of inductive and deductive reasoning.

Inductive reasoning is moving from specific observations often using data to broader generalizations and theories. In inductive reasoning, we begin with specific observations and measures, begin to detect patterns and regularities, formulate some tentative hypotheses that we can explore, apply rigorous empirical or qualitative research methods, and finally end up developing some general conclusions or theories.

Deductive reasoning starts with a general theory, statement, or hypothesis and then converges to narrow the conclusion based on evidence. The syllogism links premises with conclusions and if all premises are true and clear, the conclusion must also be true. For example, consider the syllogism.

1. Caffeine stimulates your brain.
2. A cup of coffee contains more caffeine than a cup of tea.
3. Therefore, a cup coffee is more stimulating to your brain than a cup of tea.

As seen in Figure 5.9, inductive and deductive reasoning seek to confirm a theory via testable hypothesis subjected to research methods and analysis but differ with regard to the initiation of the proposition leading to the testable hypothesis.

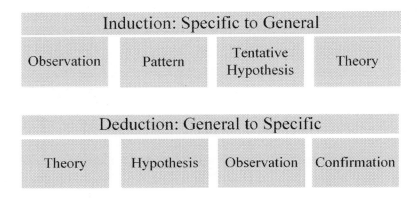

Figure 5.9 Illustration of Deduction and Induction

Source: Acknowledgement: https://socialresearchmethods.net/kb/dedind.php

Systems Thinking

Systems thinking is a way to understand how to solve complex and persistent problems in the near term and engage in ongoing learning and transformational change in the long term. A system is an organized set of interacting and interdependent subsystems that function together as a whole to achieve a purpose. If a subsystem changes, the overall system will change its behavior. There are seven foundational systems thinking concepts: mental models, aim, interaction, components, change, unexpected outcomes, and training. This systems thinking perspective is summarized in Figure 5.10.

The 12 boxes depicted in Figure 5.11 visualize systems thinking. A capability of systems thinking allows you to zoom in and out from incremental to revolutionary transformational change and simultaneously perform time travel by looking from the past to the future.

The System of Profound Knowledge

W. Edwards Deming developed the System of Profound Knowledge, a four-step process for diagnosing and improving any systems.[46] The System of Profound Knowledge was the foundation of the quality improvement movement that propelled Japan into the post–World War II automobile business that continues to this day. These four steps are illustrated in Figure 5.12.

1. Appreciation of a System. The system needs to be made visible by defining the system aim, leading (drivers) and lagging (outcome) metrics, boundaries, and stakeholders.

A System Thinking Perspective		
1	The mental models comprised of our values and beliefs influence our understanding of reality and underlie our decision-making.	Mental Models: Our mental models shape our systems perspective. The Copernican Revolution in astronomy was a paradigm shift from the view that the Sun revolves around the stationary "center of the universe"—the Earth—to the view that the Earth is one of several planets revolving around the Sun.
2	A system needs to be designed to fulfil its aim. A system achieves the results that it is designed to achieve.	Aim. When hurricane Katrina made landfall on the Gulf Coast it flooded New Orleans, it killed more than 1,800 people, and caused $100 billion in property damage. The storm's damage was greatly exacerbated by the failures of Congress, the administration, the Federal Emergency Management Agency (FEMA), and the Army Corps of Engineers because there were no agreed protocols for coordinating mutual support. Weather forecasters warned government officials about Katrina's approach, so they should have been ready for it. But they were not, and Katrina exposed major failures in America's disaster preparedness and response systems.
3	A system is a set of integrated and interacting component subsystems that function as a whole to achieve a desired goal.	Interaction: A human being is a system comprised of a set of interacting component subsystems. When your body moves, the respiratory system takes in the oxygen, the circulatory system to delivers the oxygen to the muscles, and the digestive system breaks the food down into nutrients like glucose.
4	In a system, the component subsystems are interdependent. All of the subsystems have a circular cause and effect relationship.	Components: SpaceX's Falcon rocket has multiple subsystem components that are in the shape of a spear structure. The system that enables it to fly into space will only work if all the components are fully functional and work in harmony. An airplane has an engine, fuselage (body), wing, flaps, aileron, elevator, rudder, and a person in the cockpit that all must be working together.
5	The way the systems components are organized and interact determines its behavior.	Change: If a component subsystem changes, the overall system will change its behavior. If the component subsystems are not balanced the system output will be lessened. All natural systems include component interconnected subsystems comprised of habitats, forests, waterways, oceans, air, trees, plants, and animals. An imbalance in any one imbalances the others.
6	A system may perform actions that are not expected.	Unexpected Outcomes: The law of unintended consequences. One of the opportunity costs of the FDA drug approval process is that people may die while waiting for the drug. Many people with advanced kidney disease could have been saved by the drug Interleukin-2 during the three years it took the FDA to approve it.
7	An understanding of system thinking can be learned.	Training: Education systems should encourage system thinking and the principles of quality improvement.

Figure 5.10 Illustration of the Seven System Concepts

Source: Adapted from Knowledgeworks, "Looking Beneath the Surface: The Education Changemaker's Guidebook to Systems Thinking," accessed July 24, 2020, https://knowledgeworks.org/resources/educationchangemakers-guidebook-systems-thinking/

Adapted from History, "Hurricane Katrina," accessed July 24, 2020, https://www.history.com/topics/natural-disasters-and-environment/hurricane-katrina

2. Knowledge about Variation. A system has variation that is either a common cause (a natural pattern that is part of the system) or special cause (a variation that is outside the historical experience of the system such as random errors made by employees).
3. Psychology. All human systems have elements that create positive and negative motivators. Intrinsic motivators are powerful and include achievement, recognition, responsibility, purpose, and personal growth. The less powerful extrinsic motivators are working conditions, policies, and rules, and compensation.
4. Theory of Knowledge. The theory of knowledge is an iterative approach of small steps to improve the system that focuses on planning (P), doing/experimenting (D), studying (S), and acting (A). The PDSA cycle aims to reduce non-productive special cause variation (errors people make) and remove negative motivational factors.

System Thinking

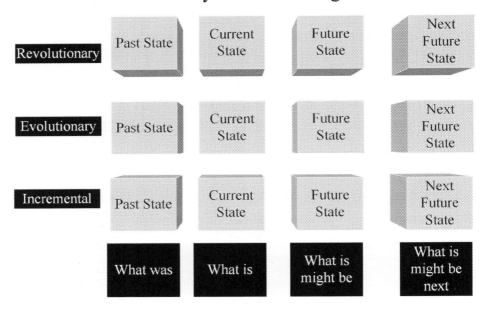

Figure 5.11 Illustration of the Twelve Boxes

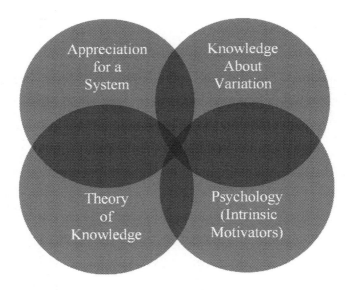

Figure 5.12 Illustration of the System of Profound Knowledge

Source: Adapted from Doug Hall, *Driving Eureka,* (La Vergne: Clerisy Press, 2018).

Integrating Disciplines

While specialization in many disciplines from art to science is highly valued, integrating disciplines promises to add value to the innovation and entrepreneurship process. "Modern work demands knowledge transfer: The ability to apply knowledge to new situations and different domains. Our most fundamental thought processes have changed to accommodate increasing complexity and the need to derive new patterns rather than rely only on familiar ones."[47] A generalist with a broad mindset can facilitate endless ways to access and connect knowledge to search for something better than before, the quest for integration.

The concept of integration as seen in Figure 5.13 is the notion that it is more effective to combine different disciplines for the highest level of innovation. Each of these different areas – science, technology, engineering, art, and design – provides insights that are more powerful as "and" rather than as "or." An interactive, interdisciplinary, and non-linear flow combines these five disciplines.[48]

1. Scientific exploration converts information into new knowledge.
2. Technology enables the acceleration of our knowledge transfer.
3. Engineering converts our knowledge into practical innovations that add value and affordability.
4. Art provides the means for creative expression, including using the natural world as the resource for engineering and design.
5. Design is the relationship between the human functional and form perspective.

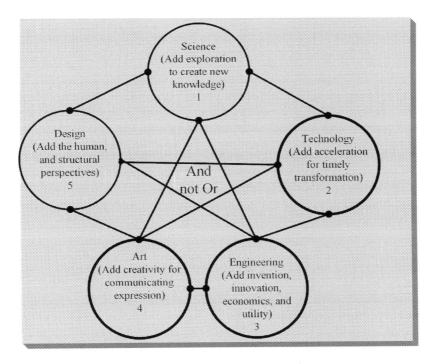

Figure 5.13 Illustration of Integration of Disciplines

Source: Adapted from Neri Oxman, *Abstract: The Art of Design, Netflix*, accessed July 24, 2020, https://www.netflix.com/title/80057883

Integrative Thinking: Analysis and Synthesis Contradictions

In the book *The Opposable Mind*, by Roger Martin, he proposes that effective leaders should be studied to understand their integrative thinking styles. Integrative thinkers practice salience, a broad view of all features to consider, multidimensional causality, visualization of the whole while working on the parts, and perform a search for creative resolution of the tensions.[49] Integrative thinking is "[t]he ability to face constructively the tension of opposing ideas and, instead of choosing one at the expense of the other, generate a creative resolution of the tension in the form of a new idea that contains elements of the opposing ideas but is superior to each."[50]

The common features of integrative thinkers are as follows:[51]

1. Integrative thinkers understand that the current models that exist are the best or only ones available but do not represent reality.
2. Integrative thinkers understand that conflicting models are to be valued not discarded.
3. Integrative thinkers understand that better models exist that are not yet available.
4. Integrative thinkers understand that better models can become a reality.
5. Integrative thinkers are willing to take responsibility for the new model.
6. Integrative thinkers understand and make the effort and time to create a better model.

Integrative thinking brings together both analysis and synthesis as well as contradictions. Analytical thinking breaks things down and focuses on both deductive and inductive reasoning to discover truths about the world.[52] Analytical thinking is formal, rational, convergent, and sterile. Simplification in problem solving is based on analytical thinking. Caution is urged, however, since simplification is useful but can result in reductionism.

Synthesis is the opportunity not only to combine the best ideas, but to do so in an empathetic and intuitive way.[53] Roger Martin, in *The Design of Business*, explains, "Integrative thinking is a metaskill of being able to face two (or more) opposing ideas or models and instead of choosing one versus the other, to generate a creative resolution of the tension in the form of a better model, which contains elements of each model but is superior to each (or all)."[54]

Synthesis is the integration, or bringing together, of things in a way that balances common trade-offs, such as cost, time, meeting customers' unmet needs, risk, and reliability, while also allowing the injection of something new and creative. These trade-offs are known as contradictions, and they distract from innovation.

Contradictions that result in compromise should be eliminated or at least reduced; otherwise, the consequences will be less than optimal.[55] A portable umbrella is an example of a system in balance. The portable umbrella must be broad, waterproof, and lightweight but also must be foldable so that it can be hidden away in a purse or briefcase.

Thinking Errors

Everyone makes thinking errors. Many of these errors can be attributed to a lack of training in critical thinking, lack of validation data, excessive amounts of episodic stress, and the inability to be self-aware of our implicit cognitive biases.

The Healthcare System

In 2007, Jerome Groopman, MD, published the book *How Doctors Think*, in which he argues that about 80% of medical mistakes are the result of flaws in physician thinking, predictable mental traps, or cognitive errors that bedevil all human beings; only 20% of medical mistakes are due to technical mishaps, specifically mixed-up test results or handwritten medical records and prescriptions.[56] Dr. Groopman writes of a 1995 report that stated that as many as 15% of all diagnoses are inaccurate.[57]

In *The Wall Street Journal*, Dr. Marty Makary reports that the healthcare system is wasteful and has an unacceptable rate of medical errors. It is estimated that from 20% to 30% of all medications, tests, and procedures are unnecessary, leading to considerable waste in the US healthcare system. Moreover, it is estimated that, in the United States, medical errors cause 98,000 deaths each year.

About 25% of all hospitalized patients will be harmed by medical errors. If medical mistakes were classified as a disease, they would be the 6th leading cause of death in America. US surgeons operate on the wrong body parts as often as 40 times a week. Medical mistakes cost tens of billions of dollars per year, and less than half of 65 surveyed US hospitals reported good teamwork.[58]

US airline crashes receive considerable exposure when they happen. Interestingly, the Virginia Injury Law Blog, citing an article in *The Wall Street Journal*, notes that medical mistakes result in patient deaths that would fill four jumbo jets each week.[59] Author and surgeon Marty Markay explains that the cause of the situation is that physicians and hospitals are not being held accountable for the outcomes. Hospital management is overly tolerant of physicians who are not qualified but are allowed to continue to treat patients. He argues that if patients and families had access to the outcomes of the physicians and hospitals, they would be better informed to select higher-performing healthcare systems and more likely to achieve better results. If physicians and nurses were more willing to take the initiative and report potential problems, healthcare errors could be more readily prevented.[60]

Not all the news is bad, however. In response to the need for a more responsive healthcare system, hospitals and healthcare providers have initiated a variety of innovative practices to improve patient care. For example, hospitals require healthcare providers throughout the system to follow strict patient identification and care protocols to ensure proper care and medication are provided. Patient admission and onboarding procedures include both digital and paper checks and safeguards. Lab work, examinations, and procedures are tied to unique identifiers to ensure the proper patient is receiving the appropriate care.

In addition, patients are taking greater responsibility for their healthcare by connecting with their own healthcare records through secure digital portals that connect the patient to their healthcare providers. Patients can view online doctor examination notes, lab results, and past, current, and future appointments and communicate with doctors, nurses, and other healthcare providers in real time and/or via email. On the wellness front, innovations in how patients pay for healthcare are being tested. For example, some employers provide cost sharing for employees who join and use fitness centers, reducing both time and cost in the healthcare system. With the advent of electronic portals, physicians and nurses who are part of a healthcare team can access and share real-time information, creating more accurate and timely diagnosis and treatment. Healthcare providers can share information that enables early detection and diagnosis, improves wellness, and reduces costly hospital and/or outpatient care. Future healthcare technology may even allow for virtual visits to doctors, reducing the cost of inpatient care. Innovation promises to redirect the course of healthcare in a number of positive ways. For example, advances have been and continue to be made in artificial intelligence, genetic editing engineering tools (clustered regularly interspaced short palindromic repeats [CRISPR]), genomics, stem cell research, surgical robotics, and personal early detection and diagnostic tools and techniques.

The Legal System

There are a number of examples of mistakes made in the legal system as the result of thinking dysfunctions. With new evidence, the decisions can be overturned, unfortunately often after considerable personal suffering. Movies such as *When They See Us* (1989 Central Park jogger case), *Just Mercy* (Walter McMillian), *Hurricane* (Ruben "Hurricane" Carter), and *Conviction* (Kenny Water) describe wrongful convictions.

Rubin "Hurricane" Carter

The legal system has itself fallen victim to imprecision in its practices that result in convicting people for crimes based on misperceptions. In 1966, in a tavern in Paterson, NJ, three white people were murdered by two black men. Although claiming not to be present in the tavern at the time, Rubin

"Hurricane" Carter, a middleweight boxer with a 27–12–1 record and 19 knockouts, and his friend John Artis were both convicted. Their conviction in 1967, largely based on the testimony of two thieves, was believed to be racially motivated. Bob Dylan, hearing about the conviction, wrote his song "Hurricane" to describe his passion for injustice and raise awareness about the conviction of Ruben "Hurricane" Carter.[61] To publicize the injustice, the movie *Hurricane* was produced starring Denzel Washington, who received an Academy Award nomination for playing Carter. After years of appeals, Carter's ordeal ended in 1985, when his conviction was set aside.[62] Recognizing the injustice that results in wrongful conviction, and with new technology available in the form of DNA testing, the Innocence Project innovated new approaches to addressing wrongful convictions.[63]

Kenny Waters

The Innocence Project, founded in 1992, by Barry Scheck and Peter Neufeld, is a national organization whose purpose is to identify and prevent injustice in the legal system.[64] According to the Innocence Project, eyewitness identification is frequently inaccurate: "Eyewitness misidentification is the single greatest cause of wrongful convictions nationwide, playing a role in nearly 75% of convictions overturned through DNA testing."[65] In May 1980, Katharina Brow was robbed and found stabbed to death in her Ayer, Massachusetts, home. In 1983, Kenny Waters was convicted of the crime, even though he was at work when it happened. Convinced of his innocence, to free her brother, Betty Anne Waters completed college and law school. Betty Anne Waters and the Innocence Project worked together and were able to use DNA evidence from the crime scene to prove Kenny's innocence. In 2001, after serving 18 years in prison, the DNA results proved that Kenny Waters was not the murderer, and he was exonerated. He died in a tragic accident later that same year.[66] The 2010 legal drama movie *Conviction,* starring Hilary Swank, describes the story. Innovations in technology (e.g., DNA testing) and approaches to solving crimes (e.g., evidence and witness protocols) hold promise for charting new directions in improvements in the legal system.

As these examples clearly illustrate, everyone makes thinking errors. While these errors can be attributed to a number of system failures, each provides a clarion call for better understanding of the variables contributing to the problems. As noted, better training in critical thinking, more accurate data validation, reduction in excessive amounts of episodic stress, and greater self-awareness of our implicit cognitive biases, to name a few, all play a role in moving forward.

Summary

In this chapter, the importance of *how* to think, rather than *what* to think, is examined within the context and process of innovation and entrepreneurship. Effective thinking is complementary to effective decision-making. We explored the notion of learning how to think by understanding causation and correlation, thinking modes, switch thinking, convergence and divergence, multi-level systems thinking, critical thinking, and how to reflect on your own misperceptions and implicit biases to minimize thinking errors. In today's fast-paced and globalized commerce and business environment, it is more important than ever before that start-ups and established ventures alike learn from past and current experiences, especially in relationship to keeping goods and services relevant in today's market.

Notes

1. Clayton M. Christensen, *How Will You Measure Your Life? (Harvard Business Review Classics)*, 1st ed. (Boston: Harvard Business Review Press, 2017).
2. "Christensen Taught Intel CEO How to Think and Why It's Important," accessed February 18, 2024, www.edgementoring.org/leadership-blog/clayten-christensen-taught-intel-ceo-what-to-think-not-how-to-think-and-why-thats-important.

3. Clayton M. Christensen, *How Will You Measure Your Life? (Harvard Business Review Classics)*, 1st ed. (Boston: Harvard Business Review Press, 2017).

4. "Christensen Taught Intel CEO How to Think and Why It's Important," accessed February 18, 2024, www.edgementoring.org/leadership-blog/clayten-christensen-taught-intel-ceo-what-to-think-not-how-to-think-and-why-thats-important.

5. Clayton M. Christensen, Michael E. Raynor, and Rory McDonald, "What Is Disruptive Innovation?" *Harvard Business Review*, accessed February 19, 2024, https://hbr.org/2015/12/what-is-disruptive-innovation.

6. *Wikipedia*, s.v. "Clayton Christensen," accessed April 13, 2021, https://en.wikipedia.org/wiki/Clayton_Christensen.

7. Michael Horn, "Clayton Christensen, The Gentle Giant of Innovation (1952–2020)," accessed February 18, 2024, www.forbes.com/sites/michaelhorn/2020/01/24/clayton-christensen-the-gentle-giant-of-innovation-19522020/#39b14f87a598.

8. David Foster Wallace, *This Is Water*, 1st ed. (New York: Little, Brown, 2009), 53–54.

9. *Quotes.net*, s.v. "Albert Einstein Quotes," accessed February 18, 2024, www.quotes.net/quote/9226.

10. Clayton M. Christensen, James Allworth, and Karen Dillon, *How Will You Measure Your Life*? (New York: Harper, 2012), 5.

11. Rebecca Davis, "The Doctor Who Championed Hand-Washing and Briefly Saved Lives," April 13, 2021, accessed February 18, 2024, www.npr.org/sections/health-shots/2015/01/12/375663920/the-doctor-who-championed-hand-washing-and-saved-women-s-lives.

12. *Wikipedia*, s.v. "American Civil War Casualties," accessed April 13, 2021, https://simple.wikipedia.org/wiki/American_Civil_War_casualties.

13. *Wikipedia*, s.v. "Joseph Lister," accessed April 13, 2021, https://en.wikipedia.org/wiki/Joseph_Lister.

14. Neil Z. Miller, "The Polio Vaccine: A Critical Assessment of Its Arcane History, Efficacy, and Long-Term Health-Related Consequences," accessed April 14, 2021, http://thinktwice.com/Polio.pdf.

15. "Jonas Salk and Albert Bruce Sabin," *Science History Institute*, January 8, 2017, accessed February 18, 2024, www.sciencehistory.org/historical-profile/jonas-salk-and-albert-bruce-sabin.

16. Steven Johnson, *How We Got to Now: Six Innovations That Made the Modern World* (New York: Riverhead Books, A Member of Penguin Group (USA), 2014), 3.

17. Steven Johnson, *How We Got to Now: Six Innovations That Made the Modern World* (New York: Riverhead Books, A Member of Penguin Group (USA), 2014), 4.

18. Daniel Kahneman, *Thinking, Fast and Slow* (New York: Farrar, Straus and Giroux, 2011).

19. Daniel Kahneman, *Thinking, Fast and Slow* (New York: Farrar, Straus and Giroux, 2011).

20. Daniel Kahneman, *Thinking, Fast and Slow* (New York: Farrar, Straus and Giroux, 2011).

21. Alain Samson, "An Introduction to Behavioral Economics," accessed February 18, 2024, www.behavioraleconomics.com/resources/introduction-behavioral-economics/.

22. R. Keith Sawyer, *Explaining Creativity: The Science of Human Innovation* (New York: Oxford, 2012), 46.

23. S. Schulz and R. Wallace, "The San Andreas Fault," *USGS*, 2016, last modified November 30, accessed February 19, 2024, https://pubs.usgs.gov/gip/earthq3/safaultgip.html#:~:text=Two%20of%20these%20moving%20plates,causing%20earthquakes%20along%20the%20fault.

24. Lenny T. Mendonca and Hayagreeva Rao, "Lessons from Innovation's Front Lines: An Interview with IDEO's CEO, Tim Brown, Whose Company Specializes in Innovation, Distills the Lessons of His Career," *McKinsey Quarterly*, November 2008, accessed February 19, 2024, https://codecamp.com.br/artigos_cientificos/lefr08.pdf.

25. *Wikipedia*, s.v. "Richard Feynman," accessed April 13, 2021, http://en.wikipedia.org/wiki/Richard_Feynman.

26. Edward de Bono, *Lateral Thinking* (New York: Harper, 1970).

27. Robert Weisberg, "Creativity and Knowledge – A Challenge to Theories," *Handbook of Creativity*, ed. Robert Sternberg (Cambridge: Cambridge University Press, 1999).

28. *Stanford Encyclopedia*, s.v. "Nicolaus Copernicus," accessed April 13, 2021, http://plato.stanford.edu/entries/copernicus/.

29. Edward de Bono, *Lateral Thinking* (New York: Harper, 1970).

30. *Wikipedia*, s.v. "High Jump," accessed April 13, 2021, http://en.wikipedia.org/wiki/High_jump.

31. *Wikipedia*, s.v. "Fosbury Flop," accessed April 13, 2021, http://en.wikipedia.org/wiki/Fosbury_Flop.

32. *Wikipedia*, s.v. "Dick Fosbury," accessed April 13, 2021, http://en.wikipedia.org/wiki/Dick_Fosbury.

33. David Ferris, "The Outdoor Fix," *Sierra*, November/December 2011, 25.

34. Joe Sharkey, "Reinventing the Suitcase by Adding the Wheel," *The New York Times*, October 4, 2010, accessed February 19, 2024, www.nytimes.com/2010/10/05/business/05road.html?_r=2&src=busln.

35. Marcia Wendorf, "Who Actually Invented the Wheeled Suitcase? Interesting Engineering, Inc," 2020, accessed February 19, 2024, https://interestingengineering.com/who-actually-invented-the-wheeled-suitcase.

36. Scott Applebee, "The History of Rolling Luggage," June 17, 2010, February 19, 2024, https://travel proluggageblog.com/2010/06/luggage/the-history-of-rolling-luggage/.
37. *Wikipedia*, s.v. "Hoover Dam," accessed April 13, 2021, http://en.wikipedia.org/wiki/Hoover_dam.
38. *Wikipedia*, s.v. "Los Angeles Aqueduct," accessed April 13, 2021, http://en.wikipedia.org/wiki/Los_Angeles_Aqueduct.
39. *Wikipedia*, s.v. "Panama Canal," accessed April 13, 2021, http://en.wikipedia.org/wiki/Panama_Canal.
40. *Wikipedia*, s.v. "Steamships," accessed April 13, 2021, http://en.wikipedia.org/wiki/Steam_ships.
41. *Wikipedia*, s.v. "Erie Canal," accessed April 13, 2021, http://en.wikipedia.org/wiki/Erie_canal.
42. *Wikipedia*, s.v. "Transcontinental Railroad," accessed April 13, 2021, http://en.wikipedia.org/wiki/Transcontinental_railroad.
43. *Wikipedia*, s.v. "Interstate Highway System," accessed April 13, 2021, http://en.wikipedia.org/wiki/Interstate_Highway_System.
44. Nancy Atkinson, "13 Things That Saved Apollo 13, Part 10: Duct Tape," February 19, 2024, accessed April 13, 2021, www.universetoday.com/63673/13-things-that-saved-apollo-13-part-10-duct-tape/.
45. Linda B. Nilson, *Teaching at Its Best a Research-Based Resource for College Instructors*, Jossey-Bass Higher and Adult Education Series, 4th ed. (San Francisco, CA: Jossey Bass Ltd, 2016).
46. Doug Hall, *Driving Eureka* (La Vergne: Clerisy Press, 2018), 74–78.
47. David Epstein, *Range: Why Generalists Triumph in a Specialized World* (London: Macmillan, 2019).
48. Neri Oxman, "Abstract: The Art of Design," *Netflix*, accessed February 19, 2024, www.netflix.com/title/80057883.
49. Roger Martin, *The Opposable Mind* (Boston: Harvard Business Review Press, 2007), 44–48.
50. Roger Martin, *The Opposable Mind* (Boston: Harvard Business Review Press, 2007), 15.
51. Roger Martin, *The Opposable Mind* (Boston: Harvard Business Review Press, 2007), 111–113.
52. Roger Martin, *The Design of Business* (Boston: Harvard Business Press, 2009), 5.
53. Roger Martin, *The Design of Business* (Boston: Harvard Business Press, 2009), 6.
54. Roger Martin, *The Design of Business* (Boston: Harvard Business Press, 2009), 165.
55. Howard Smith, "What Innovation Is," *European Office of Technology and Innovation* (CSC White Paper, 2005), 17.
56. Jerome Groopman, *How Doctors Think* (New York: Houghton Mifflin, 2007), 4–6, 24, 44, 56, 64, 75.
57. Jerome Groopman, *How Doctors Think* (New York: Houghton Mifflin, 2007), 24.
58. Marty Makary, "How to Stop Hospitals from Killing Us," *The Wall Street Journal*, September 21, 2012, accessed February 19, 2024, http://online.wsj.com/article/SB10000872396390444620104578008263334441352.html.
59. "Medical Errors Cause Enough Deaths Each Week to Fill Four Jumbo Jets," *Virginia Injury Law Blog*, January 8, 2013, accessed February 19, 2024, www.virginiainjurylawblog.com/medical_errors_cause_enough_de/.
60. Marty Makary, "How to Stop Hospitals from Killing Us," *The Wall Street Journal*, September 21, 2012, accessed February 19, 2024, http://online.wsj.com/article/SB10000872396390444620104578008263334441352.html.
61. City News, "Rubin 'Hurricane' Carter [05/06/1937–04/20/2014] Remembered by Family and Neighbors," *YouTube Video*, April 20, 2014, accessed February 19, 2024, www.youtube.com/watch?v=EIGxrQs9QTA.
62. "Rubin 'Hurricane' Carter, Boxer Who Inspired Bob Dylan, Dies at 76," *Billboard*, April 20, 2014, accessed February 19, 2024, www.billboard.com/articles/news/6062703/rubin-hurricane-carter-boxer-who-inspired-bob-dylan-dies-at-76.
63. "The Innocence Project," accessed February 19, 2024, www.innocenceproject.org/about.
64. "The Innocence Project," accessed February 19, 2024, www.innocenceproject.org/.
65. "Eyewitness Misidentification," February 19, 2024, www.innocenceproject.org/understand/Eyewitness-Misidentification.php.
66. "Kenny Waters," accessed February 19, 2024, https://innocenceproject.org/search/kenny+waters.

6 Problem Solving

Problem Finding and Solving

Innovators and entrepreneurs are problem solvers. As seen throughout this book in general, and Chapter 11, "Entrepreneurship," in particular, innovators and entrepreneurs seek to address some "pain or problem" point in practice and/or in the marketplace. Think of Levi Strauss in 1853, Maria Longworth (Rookwood Pottery) in 1880, King Gillette in 1901, Mary Kay Ash in 1973, Wally "Famous" Amos in 1975, Steve Jobs in 1976, Reed Hastings and Marc Randolf (Netflix) in 1997, Nick Woodman (GoPro) in 2002, Elon Musk in 2003, Sarah Blakely (Spanx) or Biran Chesky, Nathan Blecharczyk, and Joe Gebbia (Airbnb) in 2008, Reshma Saujani (Girls Who Code) in 2012, for example. From innovation in work clothes to ceramics, shaving, cosmetics, cookies, computers, streaming, videography, and electric cars, clothing, tourism, education, the list of individuals and teams seeking to solve a problem – for themselves, science, consumers, and more – is virtually endless.

Of course, problem solving is everyone's problem.[1] Problem solving is the ability to gather factual information, determine the root cause of the problem, create a set of alternative solutions, and then execute the best solution. Even though problem solving is a vital skill, it is unfortunately not taught as a skill or discipline very often.

Charles F. Kettering, an American inventor, engineer, and businessman and the holder of 186 patents, once observed that "a problem well defined, is a problem half solved." Of course, defining the problem is not easy. For example, in *How to Solve It*, George Pólya defines a four-step problem-solving process for use in mathematics. The four steps are understanding the problem, making a plan, carrying out the plan, and looking back. Pólya's insights led him to write "If you can't solve a problem, then there is an easier problem you can solve: find it" and "If you cannot solve the proposed problem, try to solve first some related problem. Could you imagine a more accessible related problem?"[2]

The importance of problem solving is highlighted in the research done by Mihaly Csikszentmihalyi, who performed a study to determine how creative works come into being. He discovered two distinct artistic approaches. There are those people who are known as problem solvers who formulate problems quickly and spend most of the time looking for a solution. Then there are those known as problem *finders* who spend most of their time understanding the problem and asking the right questions. At the end of the research study, the student problem finders were judged to be more creative. They were also, by and large, those who were the most successful six years later.[3]

In this chapter, we examine five problem-solving skills including analogy, visualization, ordering, simplification, and framing. See Figure 6.1. Each of these skills informs how we see, define, solve, and act on problems. Along the way, we will also see how various aspects of technology, nature, brain rules, mind mapping, prioritization, clarity of thinking, focus, and more contribute to the important tasks of identifying, defining, and solving problems and the critical role of doing so in innovation and entrepreneurship.

DOI: 10.4324/9781003034308-7

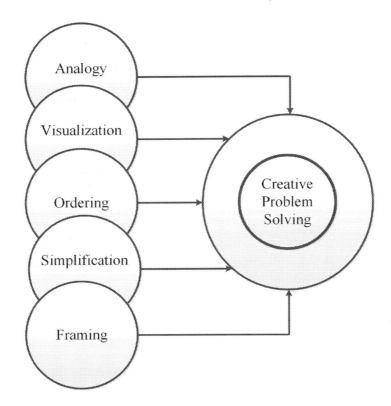

Figure 6.1 Illustration of Problem Solving Competencies

Analogy

Innovations can be derived from a variety of sources, including the discoveries of the past. Analogy is a problem-solving skill based on using existing solutions to solve new problems. For example, what an automobile technician learns the first time he or she encounters a problem can later be applied to other vehicles. It is not uncommon for the same car problem to occur in many vehicles, and thus analogy leverages the repairperson's learning surrounding identifying, defining, and solving the problem.

To use **analogy** means that when you find a new problem, you search for a past problem with a comparable solution. For example, medicines used for one population can be used for another. In 2011, the US Food and Drug Administration approved the use of Prevnar 13, a pneumococcal pneumonia vaccine, for people 50 and older. Previously, Prevnar 13 was only approved for use in children ages six weeks through five years.[4]

Colonial Williamsburg, Virginia, offers a historical experience of how we formerly made products, such as furniture, weapons, and clothing. Unlike in colonial times, today we use standard parts to assemble finished products. Standard reusable hardware components, such as microprocessors, memory, and LCDs, are found in PCs, laptops, smartphones, and tablets. Standard reusable software components are used extensively to improve the effectiveness of software development by providing common algorithms and functions, such as square roots, dates, or standard deviation computations.

Patterns are a useful form of analogy. In architecture and construction, there are many patterns such as doors, windows, electrical outlets, faucets, and tiles, which can be reused. Christopher Alexander even developed the concept of pattern language, which states that when building something, you need only look at classical patterns. "Each pattern describes a problem that occurs over and over again in our environment and then describes the core of the solution to that problem in such a way that you can use this solution a million times over without ever doing it the same way twice."[5]

Blocks, Tinkertoys, Erector Sets, and Legos are toys that let you use your imagination to assemble new objects from existing parts in unique ways. The parts can be different, such as wheels, caps, or couplings (like in Tinkertoys) or beams, nuts, and bolts (like in Erector Sets). The parts can be composed of uniform patterns of interlocking objects (such as Legos) that are much like using concrete blocks and bricks when constructing buildings. While uniform in dimension of each part, how they are combined is left to the imagination of the user, thus combining the best of both the standard pattern and the creativity of the user.

By using standard patterns, you can incrementally innovate by continuously improving operational processes through error reduction, error prevention, and the removal of unnecessary steps in procedures. This is the heart of most efforts in quality improvement.

Surgeons use standardized checklists before operating to minimize the chance of infection by ensuring that antibiotics are administered in advance. Other basic precautions include ensuring that the surgeon is operating on the correct place and that no surgical devices are left inside the patient. Once you have the checklist for one type of surgery, you can easily apply it to another. In this same way, airline pilots use standardized checklists before take-off to improve flight safety by reducing human error. You do not want to take up the landing gear when the plane is on the tarmac.

Analogy in Technology

One of the most compelling aspects of problem solving is that the solutions to problems often arise from making innovative connections between related and seemingly unrelated ideas, concepts, products, and processes. Both Apple and Microsoft have a history of reusing ideas that were proven by others. Microsoft's initial development of the Internet browser, gaming systems, and mobile devices, for example, stemmed from combining existing technologies in unique ways. Often, new product and/or process innovations can be traced back in time to an older existent concept or technology. Steve Jobs visited Xerox PARC in 1979, and observed some remarkable personal computer developments that influenced his early work on the Macintosh.[6]

What was new in the iPod? The original iPod looked very similar to Dieter Rams' 1958 T3 Transistor Radio. The colorful launch of the iPod and the five colors of the Kodak Vest Pocket Camera in 1928 are remarkably similar. Apple did not develop the first smartphone.[7] The touch screen technology existed in the Simon, a 1993 IBM Bell South smartphone cellular phone that likely influenced the Apple Newton and the iPhone.[8] Apple did not invent the digital compression technology, MP3, that reduces the number of digital bits and allows for speedy downloads and saved storage space in the iPod. Apple did not invent downloadable music. Instead, Apple connected existing technology and simple, effective design concepts to create a unique system. The success of the iPod and iTunes can be attributed to learning about and understanding past technological advancements, and having talented designers, like Jonathan Ive and his team, combine them in unique ways to create a marketable system of products.[9]

In the consumer appliance industry, Black & Decker applied reusable patterns to the design of standardized, scalable, universal electric motors for their appliance and tool products.[10] These generic motors allowed Black & Decker to build upon a unique core competency that provided a competitive advantage. They could manufacture a large number of appliance products that shared a relatively small number of universal motors, thereby reducing costs.

In the aerospace industry, the NASA human spaceflight shuttles were launched 135 times, proving their reusable design. The NASA space shuttle fleet operated for 30 years, from April 12, 1981, until July 21, 2011, carrying people into orbit using the Columbia, Challenger, Discovery, Atlantis, and Endeavour. The space shuttle enabled the crews to repair satellites, conduct research, and build the largest manmade structure in space, the International Space Station.[11]

Although the space shuttle was reusable, the rockets to propel the shuttle into space were not. For each launch of the space shuttle new rockets were used, increasing the cost of the space shuttle missions.[12] While the solid rocket boosters were recoverable, overall costs were underestimated and program funding not fully achieved. To reduce the cost of space travel, Elon Musk, CEO and CTO of the Space Exploration Technologies Corporation (SpaceX), developed a reusable rocket. Elon Musk is also the inventor and entrepreneur who co-founded the electronic payment system known as PayPal, the CEO and chief product architect of the Tesla electric car company, which includes SolarCity, a leader in providing solar power.

SpaceX has designed, tested, and implemented a reusable rocket that will dramatically reduce the cost of space travel. SpaceX is a private commercial rocket company that developed the Falcon 9.[13] The SpaceX Falcon 9 has a reusable launch system that is designed to bring the first and second stages of the rocket back to the launch pad.[14] Now that the space shuttle has been taken out of service, in 2020 US astronauts used the Space X Falcon 9 rocket to dock with the International Space Station.[15]

All these examples illustrate the power of the nexus of technology and analogy. Each provides not only a glimpse into the leveraged outcomes of making related and seemingly unrelated connections but also the enduring nature of the initial and subsequent connections. As compelling as technology and analogy is, however, it is nature that often provides the clues and solutions to everyday problems.

Analogy in Nature

Biomimicry is the use of insights discovered in nature for new opportunities and problem solving. A relatively new science, biomimetics or biomimicry (from the Greek *bios*, "life," and *mimesis*, "to imitate") is born out of the concept that nature has learned what works and what does not. As such, it poses a simple yet powerful question: What can nature teach us? Biomimicry is notable for its potential to solve problems from the very simple to the very complex. For example, George de Mestral was an engineer living in Commugny, Switzerland. In 1941, after returning from a hunting trip in the Swiss Alps, he noticed that his dog had burrs in its fur. He looked at the burrs under a microscope and observed that the burrs were attached to dog hairs with tiny hooks. These tiny hooks were the plant's way of grasping onto the fur of animals and the woven fibers of people's clothing to spread its seed. He paired the tiny hook with a tiny loop conceiving the fastener known as Velcro – innovation inspired by nature![16]

In the world of nature there are numerous activities, actions, and outcomes from which we can learn to solve problems. For example, when the Wright brothers were ideating and conceptualizing the potential for human flight, they observed how birds changed the shape of their wings to achieve turns, climbs, and descents. "From the first few days when humans watched birds fly, we have been in awe of their beauty and functionality," writes pilot Dan Pimentel. "With effortless ease, they take a few steps, flap their mighty wings, and launch skyward in a full STOL take-off that would make a Maule seem like a DC-10 cargo ship trying to plunder its way into the sky."[17]

Sometimes the observations and connections to the problem at hand are direct and obvious, but other times they are more oblique, informing innovation in an indirect light. While the Wright brothers are credited with inventing the first powered, fixed-wing airplane capable of human flight, their powerful use of analogy through observing nature is often overlooked.

The Wright brothers observed (an innovation behavior) how birds flew, and then performed hundreds of flying attempts to learn how to build the three-dimensional control system. Prior to the Industrial Revolution, craftsmen became adept at forming tools, furniture, and buildings by hand. Each part would be made from scratch, then assembled using what would now be viewed as a cumbersome and time-consuming process. Depending on the craftsman, each part might be slightly different from the previous one, requiring additional changes upon assembly of the final product. This same approach was used by the Wright brothers to build the first airplane.

Through this nature/analogy observation/innovation process, the Wright brothers' key innovation was the capability to navigate an airplane that used three controls simultaneously, known as the three-axis control design, based on the flying of birds. The three-axis control allows the pilot to control the pitch of the nose using the elevator, to use the rudder to move to the left and right, and to control the movement of the wings by using the ailerons to roll higher or lower. This remarkable invention is used today in modern aircraft, submarines, and spacecraft.[18]

The Wright brothers were artisan-craftsmen who built their airplanes by hand from spruce, a strong, lightweight wood. After a number of years of experiments and refinements, they created the Wright Flyer in 1905, launching the first practical airplane. It took them over 1,000 glider flights before they achieved a successful result.[19] Later, the trim tab, smaller surfaces attached to the trailing edge of a larger control surface was developed, enabling finer control over the operation of the airplane.[20]

German-based Arnold Glas also turned to biomimicry to address the growing problem of birds being injured or killed from flying into glass windows. Observation of the natural world enabled Arnold Glas to develop ORNILUX:

> The idea for ORNILUX glass came from understanding that birds have the ability to see light in the ultra-violet spectrum, and that some spiders incorporate UV reflective strands of silk in their webs to make them visible to birds. Alerting birds to the presence of a web preserves the spider's ability to capture prey without a bird crashing into it.[21]

As a result of their research into the natural world, Arnold Glas has successfully introduced a line of bird-friendly products while simultaneously raising awareness of the growing problem industry wide.

Visualization

Visualization is a problem-solving skill that enables us to powerfully combine our minds, vision, and physical actions. According to research, visualization is one of the strongest capabilities people have that can be used to expand our innovative potential. John Medina, in his book *Brain Rules*, describes Rule #10: vision trumps all other senses. Visualization, through pictures, diagrams, illustration, and more, is more powerful than text alone because to understand text your brain must decode the tiny alphabetic and numeric pictures before it understands the messages.

John Medina describes an experiment in which odorless and tasteless red dye was added to white wines in a wine-tasting: "When the wine tasters encountered the altered whites, every one of them employed the vocabulary of the reds. The visual inputs seemed to trump their other highly trained senses."[22]

Multimedia that uses a combination of pictures, animation, and videos can have a powerful impact on learning and understanding. These multi model effects are different depending on the characteristics of the learner. In a study published in the *Journal of Educational Psychology*, learners that have a high spatial ability were able to demonstrate more value from the multi models than those who scored low for special ability.[23]

With multimedia, there are a number of combinations that vary in their effectiveness. Using both verbal and visual models in teaching allows learners to make associations more effectively. In a separate study from that mentioned, learners who were presented with pictures and words to read generated 65% more solutions compared to those students who were presented with words alone.[24] Learners who were presented with an explanation using an animation while listening to a narrative resulted in 50% more solutions compared to those who viewed the animation and then listened to the narration.[25] Learners who viewed an animation and listened to a verbal narration were 50% more effective in generating useful solutions than those using the same animation with a display of the words. This study suggests that when presenting words, it is more effective to present the information in a narration verbally rather than visually.[26]

The field of psychology has long understood the power of visualization over physical reality. Athletes who have practiced visualizing the steps of their sports find that it is almost as valuable as the physical activity itself; research has shown that doing both – visualization and physical practice – is more effective than practicing either alone.[27] When it comes to innovation, visualization is useful for better understanding and communication of new solutions to problems.

There are a number of examples of the power of visualization as a key tool in innovation. With the advent and popularity of big data, visualization has become crucial for understanding large amounts of data. Big data are composed of a large quantity of unstructured and structured data that is taken from an assortment of sources. The data are analyzed and used to make predictions for improving business decisions. If a company can predict what consumers are planning to purchase, they can influence the consumer's decisions by offering them coupons or discounts. The visualization of the data allows for more effective interpretation of the results. In one of the most striking images of big data, instead of tables or graphs, intern Paul Butler uses the intensity of light on a map of the world to illustrate Facebook usage in the Americas, Europe, and Africa.[28]

Mind Mapping

Mind maps are two-dimensional, low-fidelity, visual models that enable the author and/or viewer to create associations between ideas, concepts, and themes. Mind mapping facilitates brain storming, business planning, and basically translating ideas into more concrete steps toward problem solving. As illustrated in Figure 6.2, to draw a mind map, you start with a central topic and then add more detail as the map radiates outward. Mind maps can be drawn by hand or facilitated by mind-mapping tools online or using freestanding software. Mind maps can improve learning by facilitating the building of associations.[29]

Options and Ordering

How is the nature of any problem discovered and identified? Basically, begin by selecting alternative options and ordering them according to some priority. Once a list of likely reasons for the problem is created, eliminate those that are less relevant until the best alternative remains.

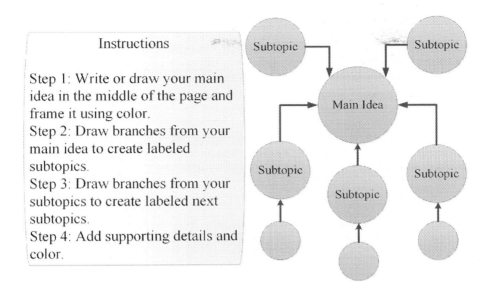

Instructions

Step 1: Write or draw your main idea in the middle of the page and frame it using color.
Step 2: Draw branches from your main idea to create labeled subtopics.
Step 3: Draw branches from your subtopics to create labeled next subtopics.
Step 4: Add supporting details and color.

Figure 6.2 Illustration of Mind Map

Like the work of a detective solving a crime, the process a physician uses to determine medical problem is known as differential diagnosis. Trisha Torrey explains:

> Using clues drawn from your descriptions of symptoms, your medical tests, his knowledge of medicine, and additional input, your doctor will make a list of all the possible diagnoses that could explain what is medically wrong with you. Then, one by one, using those same clues, he will begin to narrow down the list by finding clues that don't fit. That process of elimination is called "differential diagnosis." Ultimately, he will be left with one diagnosis, and that's the one he gives you.[30]

If you are concerned about the diagnosis, ask, "What else might it be?" and the process will restart.

Options and ordering are problem-solving skills that enable us to focus on alternatives and priorities, and thus sort through various options. Start with an outline of the list of alternatives and order the most important in sequence. Sutton's law, taught to medical students, suggests that you should first consider the obvious.[31] Another example is Pareto's 80/20 law, which states that 20% of the causes result in 80% of the effects.[32] Stephen Covey's third habit is to "put first things first."[33] Jim Collins writes, "Good is the enemy of the great. And that is one of the key reasons why we have so little that becomes great."[34] In his analogy, Collins argues that you are better off being a hedgehog (you know one big thing) than a fox (know many things) because the hedgehog understands the need to focus on what it takes to be great and what needs to be done to achieve that goal. The fox, who knows many good things of lesser importance, lacks the clear focus and instead is distracted and diffused.

Options and Ordering in Nature

Our natural ecosystems often follow an ordered sequence. Human development follows an ordered progression. In farming, there is an ordered development: plowing, seeding, fertilizing, continual watering, and finally harvesting. You cannot change the order.

Options and Ordering in Human Organizations

The book *The HP Way*, by David Packard, describes the early life and schooling of Packard and Bill Hewlett. The book then explains how they grew and nurtured the development of the HP organization and its culture:

> Any organization, any group of people who have worked together for some time, develops a philosophy, a set of values, a series of traditions and customs. These in total are unique to the organization. So it is with Hewlett-Packard. We have a set of values–deeply held beliefs that guide us in meeting our objectives, in working with one another, and in dealing with customers, shareholders and others.[35]

Simplification

In communication, it is more effective for understanding and learning to provide short, simple, and coherent verbal and visual information, rather than information that is lengthy, complex, and lacks focus.[36] In design, the adage "form follows function" describes the notion that functionality and structure should be related. This simple tenet is a useful design principle that improves the thinking process. If the functionality of a car requires that it have very high miles-per-gallon, the structure of the car must be designed to be aerodynamic.

Apple is brilliant at building ecosystems composed of products that are sequenced effectively for delivery, building on a growing and highly motivated customer base. Apple has consistently been ranked as one of the leading innovative companies.[37] This success has been achieved through Apple's providing excellent products with simple and natural design, not unlike the German Bauhaus school of design, which advocated high simplicity and functionality over decoration and adornments.

While Apple has revolutionized the personal computer industry and continues to evolve both as a company and in the larger context of the industry it helped create, it did not generate an extensive list of *computer* innovations, per se. Those innovations were the work of Xerox, Intel, IBM, and others. You can say, with fairness, that Apple is very skilled at simplicity by building products that fulfill the human experience, in part, because they had the dead-ends, traps, no-outlet streets, and other errors mostly debugged from their computers and devices before people used their products.

In product design, simplicity has high utility. Apple's iPod was designed for simplicity. The management of the music functionality was kept separate by building it into iTunes. The iPod has a simple user interface, and the unique combination of the iPod and iTunes allows users to listen to music and manage music collections while on the move.[38] "The iPod drew on the company's well-known skills in software, user-friendly product design, and imaginative marketing – all underexploited capabilities."[39] With iTunes, Apple became a world leader in online music, in part because the record companies were slow to respond to the potential of online music, failing to seize the market opportunity.[40]

Simplification in Money (M-Pesa)

M-Pesa (*M* is for "mobile," *pesa* is Swahili for "money") is a Kenyan mobile-phone money transfer service.[41] An electronic money transfer service is an efficient way to transact business because it is fast, affordable, and convenient. M-Pesa is a new digital form of banking that does not require traditional bank buildings.

In 2005, the M-Pesa pilot was conducted in Kenya as a joint venture between Vodafone and Safaricom, the country's largest mobile phone operator. The pilot allowed registered customers to transfer money and securely make payments to other registered customers, to deposit and withdraw money from their bank accounts, and to receive and repay microloans using their mobile phones. All three of these parts of the original service turned out to be too complicated for successful implementation, so the service was simplified to provide only the money transfer service without the banking account and microfinance services.

The simplified money transfer service uses text messages and a network of agents to deposit and withdraw money from an account that is stored on the customer's cell phone.[42] The M-Pesa customer deposits cash into their M-Pesa account by visiting one of the 40,000 Safaricom agents who credits the account. An M-Pesa customer withdraws the cash by visiting another Safaricom agent who debits the account. The customer is charged a small fee for these services. This simplification helped M-Pesa to become established. M-Pesa then adopted an incremental sequenced approach, adding retailers, ATMs (PesaPoint), international remittances (Western Union), and banking services such as microsaving, micro-insurance, and microfinance (M-Kesho).[43]

The M-Pesa money transfer system is now one of the most successful cash transfer systems in the world.[44] In the developing country of Kenya, the system is used by 17 million Kenyans, two-thirds of the adult population.[45] The M-Pesa mobile money transfer system is a social innovation because it brings poor communities a revolutionary financial service.[46] Moreover, it is an example of the exponential value of the network effect – the more customers, the more everyone benefits. This has been especially useful in a geographically dispersed country operating at the bottom of the economic pyramid.

Simplification in Manufacturing

Manufacturing has historically solved very simple problems. During US western expansion after the Civil War, for example, economical cattle fencing was created by simply twisting metal into barbed wire.[47] Elias Howe invented the zipper to fasten clothing, luggage, and camping gear.[48] George de Mestral developed the convenient fastener known as Velcro.[49]

Early glass was produced from sand, limestone, and other similar materials in batches known as flat glass or sheet glass.[50] In the 1950s, Sir Alastair Pilkington and Kenneth Bickerstaff invented a new process in which a ribbon of molten glass flows on top of molten tin.[51] This process produced windows that were flatter and more precise than ever before. In 1855, Henry Bessemer patented a low-cost method for mass-producing steel. In the Bessemer process, air is blown through molten iron to remove impurities.[52] Andrew Carnegie used the Bessemer process to build the US steel industry.[53]

The availability of economical steel to construct a new style of building in which the exterior surface was attached to a steel structure rather than having external brick walls, facilitated the growth of US cities.[54] The well-known triangular-shaped New York City Flatiron building was one of the first skyscrapers to use this type of steel fabrication.[55] Nucor Steel used electric, arc-furnace mini-mills to transform scrap metal into economical steel that competed effectively against steel created in integrated blast furnaces using the Bessemer process.[56]

Manufacturing progress involves how to organize the work through economies of scale, automated assembly lines, and other ways of organizing large numbers of self-managed people in order to produce high volumes of low-cost products. Recent advances in manufacturing have also been achieved through the increased use of robots for assembly, welding, and inspection of in-process and finished goods.

Baxter, a robot from Rethink Robotics, was an example of a new generation of robots that are intelligent and more economical.[57] In general, manufacturing robots reduce costs, but they can also result in the displacement of workers from one region of the world to another. As robotic innovation continues, however, new jobs arise as a result of shifting needs. For example, while the number of assembly line workers has decreased, the need for computer programmers, system analysts, and repair and maintenance personnel, to name just a few positions, has increased.

Framing

Framing is your perspective, point of view, or mindset regarding a problem or opportunity. "Framing in the social sciences refers to a set of concepts and theoretical perspectives on how individuals, groups, and societies organize, perceive, and communicate about reality."[58] As a competency, framing allows you to understand your perspectives about reality in order to improve your ability to think clearly by removing your misperceptions. Framing is the ability to change your perspective based on understanding your personal radar.

Imagine that you are in Mexico City. It is dark and rainy and you are trying to find your hotel. Then you get lost. It turns out that you have the wrong map. Your frame of Mexico City is completely wrong because your map is wrong. We all have established ways of thinking about the world based on the belief maps we have formed through our lives and careers. Our belief maps are the frames through which we see the world. We dynamically create our frames and then use them to interpret our reality. What if our belief maps are wrong? Do we have the self-awareness to check our maps for biases?

As Bruce Nussbaum so elegantly puts it in *Creative Intelligence: Harnessing the Power to Create, Connect, and Inspire*, "Framing is a focal lens that can guide us through the vagaries of a volatile world. Understanding your frame of reference – your way of seeing the world as it compares with other people's – is a key strategy no matter your aspirations or industry."[59]

Framing Effects

Framing effects occur when individuals differentially react to a particular choice, depending on whether it is presented as a loss or a gain. In general, individuals tend to avoid risk when a positive frame is presented but seek risks when a negative frame is presented. In most decision-making situations, only one of the two frames is generally considered, despite the fact that they can result in different choices.

Researchers Amos Tversky and Daniel Kahneman pioneered this line of inquiry when they conducted a study demonstrating how framing can affect outcomes.[60] The study was based on a hypothetical disease that could potentially affect 600 people.[61] The study had a positively framed scenario and a negatively framed scenario, both of which were mathematically identical. Both of the two scenarios had two options: In the positive framing scenario, vaccine A would save 200 people and vaccine B had a one-third probability of saving all 600 people and a two-thirds probability of killing 600 people. The majority (72%) of participants were risk averse and preferred vaccine A rather than vaccine B (28%).

As outlined in Figure 6.3, in the negative framing scenario, vaccine C would kill 400 people and vaccine D had a one-third probability of saving 600 people and a two-thirds probability of killing 600 people. The majority (78%) of the participants were risk takers and preferred vaccine D rather than vaccine C (22%).

Positive-Framed

- Response A (vaccine) would save 200 people.
- Response B (vaccine) had a one-third probability of saving everyone, but a two-thirds probability of saving no one.
- Results
  - 72% of participants preferred (vaccine) A.
  - 28% of participants preferred Response (vaccine) B.

Negative-Framed

- Response C (vaccine) would kill 400 people.
- Response D (vaccine) had a one-third probability of killing no one but a two-thirds probability of killing everyone.
- Results
  - 22% of participants choose response (vaccine) C.
  - 78% of participants preferred Response (vaccine) D.

Figure 6.3 Illustration of Framing Effects

Source: Adapted from Amos Tversky and Daniel Kahneman, "The Framing of Decisions and the Psychology of Choice," *Science*, New Series, 211(4481), (January 30, 1981): 453–458.

Framing Techniques

Framing techniques improve your overall focus regarding the scope of the problem or opportunity that you have identified. Focused thinking is a kind of pinpointing or zooming in on a particular question. By applying focused thinking, you can create the innovation of the right size, not too small and not too big.

Framing requires zooming in to observe details, as well as zooming out to look from a broader perspective. This is visually explained in the classic 1968 film, *Power of Ten*, commissioned by IBM and created by Charles and Ray Eames, renowned industrial designers. This video starts with a picnic scene in a park in Chicago and zooms out to space and then in again into the structure of atoms, depicting the exponential perspective of the magnitude of the powers of ten. By doing so, it makes you more aware of the need to frame or reframe how you think about the world.[62]

According to Rodolfo Llinás, a neuroscientist at the NYU School of Medicine, what we observe is largely a projection of us. "By Llinás' estimate, only 20 percent of our perceptions are based on information coming from the outside world; the other 80 percent, our mind fills in."[63] Educator, businessman, and author of the best seller *The Seven Habits of Highly Effective People*, Stephen Covey summarized this thought when he said, "We see the world, not as it is, but as we are – or, as we are conditioned to see it."[64] The way we interpret the world is more accurate if our beliefs or lenses are clear and precise. Most individuals can easily recognize what needs to change in the world, but most do not recognize that they must change and/or consider alternative frames. By understanding the role and impact of framing, we have a better foundation for developing clarity of thinking.

Clarity of Thinking

Clarity of thinking is needed to better achieve problem identification and ultimately innovative solutions. Framing plays an integral role in these relationships and is the foundation for clarity of thinking. To think openly is to have the self-awareness to see biases and know the filters through which the problem is seen. As noted earlier, "A problem well stated is half solved" is often attributed to Charles F. Kettering, who was head of research at General Motors from 1920 to 1947. Clarity of thinking requires observation of people and context, adapting to changes and trends when necessary. Clarity of thinking is facilitated through empathy to understand and acknowledge the differences of others. Moreover, the ability to *reframe* comes from an ability to self-correct thinking and not remain riveted to potentially obsolete thinking. In other words, how we think about or frame or reframe the problem is essential to the innovation and entrepreneurship process.

Figure 6.4 describes a comparison of old frames and new frames. Often it is as simple as how the problem is defined and the context or frame in which it is viewed that determines how we think about the problem, solution, and addressable markets.

Area	Old Frame	New Frame
Banking	Traditional banks	Mobile money (Alipay, Apple Pay, Google Pay, Kenya's M-PESA, and Venmo, and WeChat Pay)
Education	Traditional classroom	Blended learning (Academic Earth, Kahn Academy, and Coursera)
Energy	Energy from fossil fuel	Alternative energy (Vestas, NextEra Energy, Inc., and Siemens)
Financing start-ups	Traditional venture capitalists	Collaborative social media (Kickstarter)
Healthcare	Diseases and fee-for-service	Prevention, wellness and outcomes (Kaiser, Geisinger, CVS Health Corp, and UnitedHealth Group Inc.)
Medical Devices	Expensive medical devices	Personal medical devices (Blood Glucose Monitoring Devices)
Microfinance	Large amounts loaned to few individuals	Small amounts loaned to many individuals (Grameen Bank)
Packaging	Single-Use Packaging	Recyclable zero-waste packaging (Amcor, Ecover, Evian, L'Oréal, Mars, PepsiCo, The Coca-Cola Company, Unilever, Walmart, and Werner & Mertz)
Product Design	Engineering-Oriented	Consumer-oriented (Apple, Nike, Oxo, Unilever, Amazon, Alphabet/Google, Samsung, Tesla, Microsoft, Salesforce, and Dyson)
Retailing	Purchase at retail stores	Purchase online (Amazon, Alibaba, eBay, and Tencent)
Surgery	Expensive surgery	Bottom of the pyramid (BOP) inexpensive eye surgery (Aravind)
Technology	Mainframe computing	Personal mobile devices (Laptops, Tablets, and Smartphones)
Transportation	Gasoline and diesel vehicles	Electric vehicles (Tesla, Renault-Nissan, BMW, and Geely Holding Group)

Figure 6.4 Illustration of Framing Examples

Summary

In this chapter, five problem-solving skills – analogy, visualization, ordering, simplification, and framing – are outlined and discussed. Each informs how we see, define, solve, and act on problems and contributes to the important task of identifying, defining, and solving problems and the critical role of being able to do so in innovation and entrepreneurship. Each also informs and provides a foundation for how we go about the important task of knowledge building, which is explored in the next chapter.

Notes

1. Howard Smith, "What Innovation Is," *European Office of Technology and Innovation* (CSC White Paper, 2005), 29.
2. George Pólya, *How to Solve It: A New Aspect of Mathematical Method* (Princeton, NJ: Princeton University Press, 1948).
3. Keith Sawyer, *Zig Zag* (San Francisco: Jossey-Bass, 2013), 24–25.
4. "Licensure of 13-Valent Pneumococcal Conjugate Vaccine for Adults Aged 50 Years and Older," *Centers for Disease Control and Prevention*, accessed February 20, 2024, www.cdc.gov/mmwr/preview/mmwrhtml/mm6121a3.htm#:~:text=On%20December%2030%2C%202011%2C%20FDA,aged%2050%20years%20and%20older.
5. Christopher Alexander, Sara Ishikawa, Murray Silverstein, Max Jacobson, Ingrid Fiksdahl-King, and Shlomo Angel, *A Pattern Language* (New York: Oxford University Press, 1977).
6. "Making the Macintosh," accessed February 19, 2024, www-sul.stanford.edu/mac/parc.html.
7. The Week Staff, "Apple: The Singular Legacy of Steve Jobs," *The Week*, September 9, 2011.
8. Bruce Nussbaum, *Creative Intelligence* (New York: Harper Business, 2013), 64–65.
9. Bono, "The 2013 TIME 100," *Time Magazine*, April 18, 2013, accessed February 19, 2024, http://time100.time.com/2013/04/18/time-100/slide/jonathan-ive/.
10. Timothy W. Simpson, Zahed Siddique, and Roger Jianxin Jiao, *Product Platform and Product Family Design: Methods and Applications* (New York: Springer, 2006), 9.
11. "Space Shuttle," *NASA*, accessed February 19, 2024, www.nasa.gov/mission_pages/shuttle/main/index.html.
12. Robin Fearon, "Reusable Rockets: Expanding Space Exploration Possibilities with Retrievable Spacecraft," *Discovery*, accessed February 19, 2024, www.discovery.com/technology/Reusable-Rockets.
13. *Wikipedia*, s.v. "Elon Musk," accessed January 31, 2021, http://en.wikipedia.org/wiki/Elon_Musk.
14. *Wikipedia*, s.v. "SpaceX Reusable Rocket Launching System," accessed January 31, 2021, http://en.wikipedia.org/wiki/SpaceX_reusable_rocket_launching_system.
15. Catherine Thorbecke, "History-Making NASA-SpaceX Astronauts Returning from International Space Station," July 31, 2020, accessed February 19, 2024, https://abcnews.go.com/Technology/history-making-nasa-spacex-astronauts-returning-international-space/story?id=72092598.
16. "George de Mestral Velcro®," *Consumer Devices, Lemelson-MIT*, accessed February 19, 2024, https://lemelson.mit.edu/resources/george-de-mestral.
17. Dan Pimentel, "The Magic of Flight: Your Airplane Is a Close Relative to the Seagull," November 20, 2012, accessed January 31, 2021, www.av8rdan.com/2007/12/magic-of-flight-from-first-few-days.html.
18. *Wikipedia*, s.v. "Wright Brothers," accessed January 31, 2021, http://en.wikipedia.org/wiki/Wright_brothers.
19. *Wikipedia*, s.v. "Wright Brothers," accessed January 31, 2021, http://en.wikipedia.org/wiki/Wright_brothers.
20. *Wikipedia*, s.v. "Trim Tab," accessed January 31, 2021, http://en.wikipedia.org/wiki/Trim_tab.
21. Arnold Glas, "Ornilux Bird Protection Glass, Development and Testing," accessed January 31, 2021, www.ornilux.com/development.html.
22. John Medina, *Brain Rules* (Seattle, WA: Pear Press, 2008), 223–224.
23. Richard E. Mayer and Valerie K. Sims, "For Whom Is a Picture Worth a Thousand Words? Extensions of a Dual-coding Theory of Multimedia Learning," *Journal of Educational Psychology* 86, no. 3 (1994), 389–401, https://doi.org/10.1037/0022-0663.86.3.389.
24. Richard E. Mayer, "Systematic Thinking Fostered by Illustrations in Scientific Text," *Journal of Educational Psychology* 81, no. 2 (1989), 240–246, https://doi.org/10.1037/0022-0663.81.2.240.
25. Richard E. Mayer and Richard B. Anderson, "Animations Need Narrations," *Journal of Educational Psychology* 83, no. 4 (1991), 484–490.
26. Richard E. Mayer and Rosana Moreno, "Animation as an Aid to Multimedia Learning," *Educational Psychology Review* 14, no. 1 (2002), 87–99.
27. Philip Cohen, "Mental Gymnastics Increase Bicep Strength," *NewScientist*, accessed February 19, 2024, www.newscientist.com/article/dn1591-mental-gymnastics-increase-bicep-strength.html#.U6dY6fldVfA.
28. Sameer Khan, "20 Inspiring Big Data Visualization Examples," *Web Analytics and Multi-Channel Blog*, November 21, 2001, accessed February 19, 2024, www.keywebmetrics.com/2013/07/big-data-visualizations.

29. John W. Budd, "Mind Maps as Classroom Exercises," *The Journal of Economic Education* 35, no. 1 (2004), 35–46.
30. Trisha Torrey, "Differential Diagnosis: What Else Might Your Illness Be?" September 30, 2011, accessed February 19, 2024, http://patients.about.com/od/yourdiagnosis/a/diffdiagnosis.htm.
31. *Wikipedia*, s.v. "Sutton's Law," accessed September 19, 2012, http://en.wikipedia.org/wiki/Sutton's_law.
32. *Wikipedia*, s.v. "Pareto Principle," accessed January 31, 2021, http://en.wikipedia.org/wiki/Pareto_principle.
33. Stephen Covey, *The 7 Habits of Highly Effective People: Powerful Lessons in Personal Change* (New York: Simon and Schuster, 1989).
34. Jim Collins, *Good to Great: Why Some Companies Make the Leap . . . and Others Don't* (New York: HarperCollins, 2001), 1.
35. David Packard, *The HP Way* (New York: HarperCollins, 1995, 2005), 82.
36. Richard E. Mayer, William Bove, Alexandra Bryman, Rebecca Mars, and Lene Tapangco, "When Less Is More: Meaningful Learning from Visual and Verbal Summaries of Science Textbook Lessons," *Journal of Educational Psychology* 88, no. 1 (1996), 64–73, https://doi.org/10.1037/002-0663.88.1.64.
37. Mikael Markander, "Apple Named World's Most Innovative Company," July 2020, accessed February 19, 2024, www.macworld.co.uk/news/apple/apple-worlds-most-innovative-company-3793438/.
38. Dan Saffer, "The Cult of Innovation," *BusinessWeek*, March 5, 2007.
39. Chris Zook, "Googling Growth," *The Wall Street Journal*, April 9, 2007, A12.
40. Gary Hamel and Bill Breen, *The Future of Management* (Boston: Harvard Business Press, 2013), 44–45.
41. *Wikipedia*, s.v. "M-Pesa," accessed January 31, 2021, http://en.wikipedia.org/wiki/M-Pesa.
42. *Wikipedia*, s.v. "M-Pesa," accessed January 31, 2021, http://en.wikipedia.org/wiki/M-Pesa.
43. Ron Adner, *The Wide Lens* (New York: Portfolio/Penguin, 2012), 196–201.
44. Oumy Khairy Ndiaye, "Is the Success of M-Pesa 'Empowering' Kenyan Rural Women?" March 31, 2014, accessed February 19, 2024, www.opendemocracy.net/5050/oumy-khairy-ndiaye/is-success-of-mpesa-%E2%80%98empowering%E2%80%99-kenyan-rural-women.
45. "Why Does Kenya Lead the World in Mobile Money?" *The Economist*, May 2013, accessed February 19, 2024, www.economist.com/blogs/economist-explains/2013/05/economist-explains-18.
46. Wolfgang Fengler, Michael Joseph, and Philana Mugyenyi, "Mobile Money: A Game Changer for Financial Inclusion," *What Matters | Social Innovation* (Boston: McKinsey & Company, 2012).
47. *Wikipedia*, s.v. "Barbed Wire," accessed January 31, 2021, http://en.wikipedia.org/wiki/Barbed_wire.
48. *Wikipedia*, s.v. "Zipper," accessed January 31, 2021, http://en.wikipedia.org/wiki/Zipper.
49. *Wikipedia*, s.v. "Velcro," accessed January 31, 2021, http://en.wikipedia.org/wiki/Velcro.
50. *Wikipedia*, s.v. "Flat Glass," accessed January 31, 2021, http://en.wikipedia.org/wiki/Flat_glass.
51. *Wikipedia*, s.v. "Float Glass," accessed January 31, 2021, http://en.wikipedia.org/wiki/Float_glass.
52. *Wikipedia*, s.v. "Bessemer Process," accessed January 31, 2021, http://en.wikipedia.org/wiki/Bessemer_process.
53. *Wikipedia*, s.v. "Andrew Carnegie," accessed January 31, 2021, http://en.wikipedia.org/wiki/Andrew_Carnegie.
54. *Wikipedia*, s.v. "Steel Building," accessed January 31, 2021, http://en.wikipedia.org/wiki/Steel_Buildings.
55. *Wikipedia*, s.v. "Flatiron Building," accessed January 31, 2021, http://en.wikipedia.org/wiki/Flatiron_Building.
56. *Wikipedia*, s.v. "Nucor," accessed January 31, 2021, http://en.wikipedia.org/wiki/Nucor.
57. Erico Guizzo, Evan Ackerman, and IEEE Spectrum, "How Rethink Robotics Built Its New Baxter Robot Worker," *IEEE Spectrum*, October 2012, accessed February 19, 2024, http://spectrum.ieee.org/robotics/industrial-robots/rethink-robotics-baxter-robot-factory-worker.
58. *Wikipedia*, s.v. "Framing," accessed January 31, 2021, http://en.wikipedia.org/wiki/Framing_(social_sciences).
59. Bruce Nussbaum, *Creative Intelligence* (New York: Harper Business, 2013), 34.
60. Amos Tversky and Daniel Kahneman, "The Framing of Decisions and the Psychology of Choice," *Science* 211, no. 4481 (January 30, 1981), 453–458, accessed February 19, 2024, http://psych.hanover.edu/classes/cognition/papers/tversky81.pdf.
61. *Wikipedia*, s.v. "Framing," accessed January 31, 2021, http://en.wikipedia.org/wiki/Framing_(social_sciences).
62. Ray and Charles Eames, *Powers of Ten*, accessed February 19, 2024, www.eamesoffice.com/the-work/powers-of-ten/.
63. Keith Sawyer, *Zig Zag* (New York: Jossey-Bass, 2013), 75.
64. Stephen Covey, *The 7 Habits of Highly Effective People: Powerful Lessons in Personal Change* (New York: Simon and Schuster, 1989), accessed February 19, 2024, http://sourcesofinsight.com/stephen-covey-quotes/.

7   Knowledge Building

While it is largely accepted that knowledge building is critical to the process of innovation and entrepreneurship, *how* to build knowledge remains challenging. Research suggests that Western economies successfully created an optimal workforce for 20th-century national industries. For the 21st century, globally competitive industries, however, the growing need for innovation and entrepreneurship requires knowledge workers in addition to factory workers. Around the world, companies cite talent as their top constraint to growth:

> In the United States, for example, 85 percent of the new jobs created in the past decade required complex knowledge skills: Analyzing information, problem solving, rendering judgment, and thinking creatively. And with good reason: By a number of estimates, intellectual property, brand value, process know-how, and other manifestations of brain power generated more than 70 percent of all U.S. market value created over the past three decades.[1]

Knowledge Workers Underutilized

Innovation is highly dependent on knowledge building and on the creation of new knowledge. Making connections with existing knowledge to create something that adds unique value is essential. This knowledge can be created by scientists, researchers, educators, entrepreneurs, physicians, architects, accountants, financiers, engineers, or anyone with the knowledge building competency and the ability to use it. Collectively, these people are known as knowledge workers, a description attributed to Peter Drucker, an expert on managerial and future thinking. Knowledge workers have come to perform a dominant role in the global economy, augmenting the once dominant agriculture and manufacturing workers. The question is how to best improve the overall effectiveness of these knowledge workers?

Applying Social Technology

The McKinsey Global Institute (MGI) suggests that social technologies may improve the overall effectiveness of these knowledge workers. Essentially, social technologies facilitate social interactions among people at work and at home. Computers, mobile phones, smartphones, and a host of programs, sites, and applications, such as Facebook, Twitter, LinkedIn, WhatsApp, and WeChat, have brought social technologies to the forefront of knowledge building. MGI research notes that while a high percentage (72%) of firms use social technologies, firms need to continue to create value and develop not only outreach to consumers, but across and within the firms themselves.

> McKinsey Global Institute (MGI) finds that twice as much potential value lies in using social tools to enhance communications, knowledge sharing, and collaboration within and across

DOI: 10.4324/9781003034308-8

enterprises. MGI's estimates suggest that by fully implementing social technologies, companies have an opportunity to raise the productivity of interaction workers – high-skill knowledge workers, including managers and professionals – by 20 to 25 percent.[2]

As the proportion of knowledge workers and their labor costs continues to increase, a shift toward more effective ways of idea generation, thinking, problem solving, creativity, and innovation is critical. Better results could be achieved through the following systematic approach:

• Learn how to innovate by developing the innovation competencies.
• Systematically broaden our imaginations and increase idea generation to enhance our creative skills.
• Increase content sharing among the knowledge workers through collaboration tools.
• Simultaneously increase value-added knowledge-generating processes and decrease non-valued-added processes and tasks.
• Extend the reach of knowledge workers.

Knowledge Building

Central to this process is the critical innovation and entrepreneurship competency of knowledge building. Knowledge building refers to the process of creating new cognitive outcomes as a result of common goals, group discussions, and syntheses of ideas. Developed by Carl Bereiter and Marlene Scardamalia, knowledge-building theory outlines what a community of learners needs to accomplish in order to create knowledge. Knowledge building is essential in order to educate people for what Bereiter and Scardamalia describe as the *knowledge age* society, in which knowledge and innovation are pervasive.[3] They go on to note that in business, knowledge building connotes knowledge creation, while in education it tends to focus more on learning. As such, knowledge building fuels the cultural capital of society, resulting in innovation and entrepreneurship.

In the pursuit of a better understanding of knowledge building, in this chapter we explore critical aspects associated with developing effective learning systems, learning organizations, knowledge types, creation and integration of knowledge, the role of the empathic customer experience, including the voices of the customer, the job to be done, the open innovator, the dreamer, and the product, and five systematic inventive thinking patterns.

Education Today: Disruption

The higher education model is now undergoing change.[4] The overall cost of educational institutions is increasing, leading to an increase in the cost of tuition. This coincides with a decrease in funding for public education, causing increased borrowing by students. Furthermore, education systems are becoming more and more responsible for the instruction of students throughout their careers, as organizations attempt to adapt to global change and complexity. With free and low-cost online education now possible through technology, the education system's current business model is at risk. Moreover, the COVID-19 pandemic of 2020 accelerated the need for and deployment of advanced online systems. It has been argued that because of the COVID-19 pandemic, education in general, and higher education in particular, updated online technologies in months that would have taken years. Based on global trends and empirical research, there is an ongoing need to improve our education systems to balance the supply and demand for creative capability.

Clayton Christensen, a well-regarded thought leader, predicts that disruptive forces will revolutionize our education systems.[5] Christensen explored and developed the concept of disruptive innovation in his seminal 1997 book, *The Innovator's Dilemma*.[6] The theory of disruptive innovation can be used to explain how change happens in both business and education. Essentially, disruptive innovation occurs when innovative start-ups incrementally add value to their solutions while the incumbents wait. This hesitancy in the incumbents to act often allows the start-up to pass them by. Disruptive innovation predicts that start-ups, including education entrepreneurs, act on opportunities, while the incumbents, such as school systems, see the opportunity, but frequently are paralyzed by stagnant and outmoded thinking.

The Cycle of Learning

The cycle of learning proceeds as follows: First, the instructor must understand a student's learning needs, establish learning goals for that student, and engage the student to meet those needs by presenting accurate and current content in ways that help the student to meet those goals. Next, the student practices the skills and applies the knowledge learned. Finally, the instructor provides explicit corrective and value-added feedback.

The cycle of learning creativity can be improved using enriched models that enhance the learning experience.[7] First, general creativity skill-development courses are needed; second, creativity training needs to be embedded in all subjects, including language arts, chemistry, geometry, mathematics, and more; and finally, integrated courses that combine disciplines should be offered to enable the building of new associations or connections that may never occur otherwise.[8]

Developing Effective Learning Systems

Effective knowledge building starts with learning. Some people are visual learners, others learn best through reading and listening, and some learn kinesthetically through, for example, building something. When the appropriate learning style is combined with a subject one finds meaningful, an inner passion to collect information and build knowledge ignites.

Innovation is propelled by many sources, such as unexpected occurrences, process needs, changes in industry and/or market structures, demographics, even changes in perception or mood or meaning. Perhaps the most powerful source of innovation is brought about by development, discovery, and advancement of new knowledge.[9] By immersing ourselves in a wide variety of knowledge, we are able to more effectively increase our potential to be creative and innovative. Ideally, we develop both deep knowledge of a subject and a broad knowledge of many subjects. Keith Sawyer writes, "In a creative life, you're constantly learning, practicing, mastering, becoming an expert. You seek out knowledge not only in formal classrooms but also from mentors, experts, books, magazines, film, Web sites, nature, music, art, philosophy, science."[10]

A paradigm shift occurs when one realizes that existing knowledge is wrong and/or outdated and must be replaced by new knowledge. Prior to Galileo, for example, the dominant paradigm was that the earth was the center of the universe. Prior to the 1860s, many fatalities occurred because we did not know about the intricacies of germ theory. Even in the sports arena, paradigmatic shifts occur because of shifting knowledge. For example, conventional knowledge in Babe Ruth's time said that placing your best batter in the number three spot in the line-up would give you the most competitive advantage. Recent analysis into batting orders, however, indicates that the best batter should hit in the second position because it allows the best batters to have about 18 extra appearances per year.[11]

The Archer

In archery, the potential energy exists within the arm of the archer and the bent shaft of the bow. The string enables the potential energy to be transformed to kinetic energy as the arrow is released and glides through the air to the target. Similarly, our knowledge needs to be transformed into kinetic energy to spark innovation.[12] In order to provide value to customers, knowledge in the context of innovation needs to be organized, captured, and shared. Knowledge is the potential energy that is used to generate the kinetic energy to power an organization. The greater the accumulation of knowledge, the more potential is available to transform into new patterns and connect more knowledge.

Innovators are skilled at being able to associate knowledge from multiple sources in new and imaginative ways. For example, a rich understanding of customer needs is a main source for innovation. As we will see later in this chapter, knowledge about customer needs, product and service gaps, opportunities, obstacles, and trends is required to precisely define the course of action required for a strategic direction. The five sources of innovation are the voice of the customer, the voice of the job to be done, the voice of the open innovator, the voice of the dreamer, and the voice of the product.

Using new knowledge, making connections with existing knowledge, and combining knowledge in unique and creative ways can lead to innovations that continuously redefine both an industry and the customers' experience within that industry. For example, even though Apple did not have practical industrial experience in the mobile phone business in 2007, at the launch of the iPhone, Apple was able to grow new knowledge very quickly.

The success of the iPhone was due to Apple's creative use of new and emerging technologies (such as the touchscreen), the ability to leverage commodity and unique proprietary knowledge, and the use of standardized components from third-party vendors. The iPhone has been very profitable because of the embedded unique proprietary knowledge that was integrated into the mobile device. This knowledge includes the iPod music player, the web browser that enables you to perform searches and access online accounts, and the built-in applications that access the weather, stock prices, and YouTube videos. The creative use of technology and embedded knowledge enabled Apple to highly differentiate the product, while the standardized components enabled manufacturing efficiencies.[13] In the first quarter of 2011, Nokia sold nearly six times as many phones as Apple, but Apple still made more money as a result of this knowledge-oriented differentiation. This was because the average wholesale selling price for the Apple iPhone was $638 versus Nokia's $87.[14]

Combining knowledge in novel ways creates new knowledge. Facilitating the creation of new knowledge in an organization can be achieved by managing two tracks. On one track you have the standard processes for efficiency and order. On the other track, you liberate people to think about how to address the endless new problems that evolve in the white water of change.

Learning Models

Product, Process, Experimental

Learning how to learn is essential to successfully engage in the knowledge-building competency. There are a number of models that explain how people learn, including both learning as a product and learning as a process. Learning as a process includes learning theories such as behaviorist, cognitivist, humanist, and social and situational.[15] For example, David Kolb describes experiential learning as occurring through primary experience.[16] Rather than direct instruction, Maria Montessori advocates a discovery model where students learn independence and responsibility.[17]

Problem-Based Learning

In contrast to the traditional model of education, which is based on time-sequenced lectures and textbook chapters, problem-based learning gives students real problems to solve. Together the students discuss the problem and develop theories or hypotheses, with the teacher serving as a facilitator and coach. The students conduct independent research to better understand the nature of the problem. Finally, the students work together as a team to discuss their findings and refine their ideas.[18]

Learning Organizations

Today's problems cannot be solved with yesterday's knowledge. Rapid change requires rapid learning, and organizations must be designed to accomplish this. Successful organizations are learning organizations. According to Peter Senge, "'Learning organizations' [are] organizations where people continually expand their capacity to create the results they truly desire, where new and expansive patterns of thinking are nurtured, where collective aspiration is set free, and where people are continually learning to see the whole together."[19]

Double-Loop Learning

There are two types of learning: Single-loop learning improves your conventional thinking about how an organization solves problems, through training, for example. Double-loop learning challenges the existent culture by questioning the way things are done and can achieve a paradigm shift in the mental model.[20]

T-Shaped People

Learning organizations need to build the competencies to develop what has been termed "T-shaped people." (See Figure 7.1.)

Figure 7.1 Illustration of T-Shaped Person

T-shaped people have two kinds of characteristics, hence the use of the letter "T" to describe them. The vertical stroke of the "T" is a depth of their competency that allows them to contribute to the creative process. That can be from any number of different fields: An industrial designer, an architect, a social scientist, a business specialist or a mechanical engineer. The horizontal stroke of the "T" represents the broad competency set and the disposition for collaboration across disciplines. It is composed of two things: empathy and enthusiasm for other disciplines. Empathy is important because it allows people to imagine the problem from another perspective – to stand in somebody else's shoes. Second, learning organizations tend to get very enthusiastic about other disciplines, to the point that they may actually start to practice them. T-shaped people have both depth and breadth in their skills.[21]

T-shaped people are the antidote for over-specialization and compartmentalization. Specialization narrows your thinking – the only thing you learn is more and more about your specialty.

The more vertical and horizontal competencies you have, the more likely you will be able to combine the building blocks of knowledge in new and unique ways. A guiding principle of innovation requires that the customer to be placed at the center of the process.[22] This means the innovator must understand the unmet needs of the customer, as well as understanding what technology can be used to meet those needs, all while possessing a knowledge of both viable business models and the prevailing business trends.

Think, Learn, and Create

Catalytic leadership needs to provide the support for thinking, learning, and creating. Leaders should provide resources (money, time, and services) in order to promote creativity-induced organizational change. Leading organizations that are known for their creativity and innovation, like 3M, W. L. Gore, and Google, provide time and resources for their employees to work on projects that interest them. The purpose of this is to liberate divergent thinking, thereby utilizing the workforce more effectively. 3M, for example, is a historically recognized innovator that established the best practice of encouraging their employees to allocate 15% of their time to think, learn, and create. This best practice was adopted by W. L. Gore (at 10% allocation) and Google (at 20% allocation).[23]

Ten Thousand Hours

Anders Ericsson investigated the amount of effort required to gain expertise in a discipline. Ericsson's conclusion, known as the 10,000-hour rule, was popularized by Malcolm Gladwell in *Outliers*. It is important to recognize that the 10,000-hour rule approximates the effort required to develop knowledge expertise rather than a precise rule.[24]

Regardless of your genetics, you can improve your creative potential by building up your expertise through deliberate practice. It takes about 10,000 hours of practice over a period of ten years, at four hours per day for five days a week, to develop expertise in a particular discipline, whether it is a sport, a musical instrument, or a science. By building up your expertise (competencies), you will be able to improve your innovation capability.[25]

Your expertise will need to be extended to keep pace with change. You can extend vertically (depth of expertise) or horizontally (breadth of expertise). Using the competency framework, you can extend your expertise yourself to build on your existing strengths or add completely new competencies. Extending your competencies will allow you to create new associations.

Knowledge Types

As can be viewed in Figure 7.2, knowledge can be organized into four different types: articulate, implicit, tacit, and embedded.

Articulate
Articulate knowledge is that which we can explain to others. Articulate (explicit) knowledge is a type of knowledge that can be transferred to and from people. This is especially relevant for discovering the customer's unmet needs.

Implicit
Implicit knowledge is that knowledge which can be articulated by those who possess it but has not yet been articulated. Implicit knowledge can be extracted through a process of individual interviews and surveys.

Tacit
Tacit knowledge is difficult for people to convey to one another either in written or verbal form. There are many different skills that require tacit knowledge such as how ride a bicycle, ice skate, and play a musical instrument. Those people possessing tacit knowledge cannot articulate that knowledge to others. Tacit knowledge is not known explicitly, even by expert practitioners. Tacit knowledge is like the part of an iceberg that is under water. We know it is there but we do not see it. Michael Polanyi broadened the term knowledge by proposing the phrase about tacit knowledge: "We can know more than we can tell."

Embedded
Embedded knowledge is that which is contained in a tangible object, such as a hammer, a smartphone, a microprocessor, or a computer operating system. Embedded knowledge is part of a physical object, like the shape of the airfoil on an airplane wing that achieves lift. Products such as the Apple iPhone are loaded with embedded knowledge that is used as a product differentiator.

Figure 7.2 Illustration of Knowledge Types

Source: Acknowledgement Michael Polanyi, *The Tacit Dimension*, (Garden City, NY: Doubleday & Co., Inc., 1967). Acknowledgement https://en.wikipedia.org/wiki/Tacit_knowledge

Understanding the difference between articulate, implicit, and tacit knowledge can enhance the ability to seek out what is not known. Increasing knowledge increases the ability to assemble, connect, and create new knowledge. Then, by embedding existing and new knowledge content into all innovation types, you can achieve a unique competitive advantage and provide more utility and value to others.

Creation of New Knowledge

Conventional thinking about knowledge focuses on *what is* rather than *what might be*. A starting place for creating new knowledge is to ask the following questions: What might be? What should we be thinking? What is missing?

The Theory of Capabilities (Resources, Processes, and Priorities)

Understanding the knowledge types, the five voices, and technology advancements facilitates the use of the theory of capabilities to create new knowledge more effectively for innovation. The theory of capabilities describes the three building blocks that an organization uses to add capability: resources, processes, and priorities. This is summarized in Figure 7.3.

What Are Resources?

Resources are the assets of an organization. These include people, systems, equipment, information, finances, technology, designs, brands, and relationships. The most important resource in the knowledge-based economy is the intellect and ideation of people. Not only do you need to have enough people resources, but, even more importantly, you need to have the *right* people resources, the top talent. A key theme of Jim Collins' *Good to Great* is to make sure you get the right people on the bus and in the right seats and get the wrong people off the bus.[26]

There are three components to people resources: competency, quantity, and top talent. The 12 innovation and entrepreneurship competencies describe the skills and knowledge required for future innovation. To determine the quantity of people resources, you can employ **Packard's law**.

> Packard's Law: No company can grow revenues consistently faster than its ability to get enough of the right people to implement that growth and still become a great company. If your growth rate in revenues consistently outpaces your growth rate in people, you simply will not – indeed cannot – build a great company.[27]

Ultimately, it is the top talent that provides organizations with new top talent needed for future growth.

Resource considerations for the future need to go beyond the purely economic considerations to address both social and environmental factors. Sustaining our natural resources is increasingly important in order to protect the future of the planet for the next generation. Creative skills are central to innovation, entrepreneurship, and promoting resource reuse.

What Are Processes?

Processes encompass how people communicate, collaborate, and make decisions to achieve results. "Processes define how an organization transforms the sorts of inputs (resources) into things of greater value."[28] This transformative process determines how effectively an organization

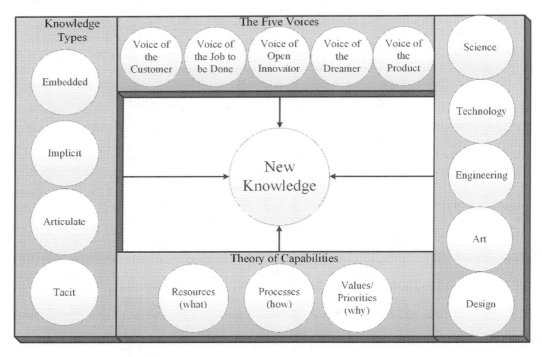

Figure 7.3 Illustration of Knowledge Types, Voices, and Capabilities

provides value to its customer. Processes need to be designed through consideration of the overall function desired. "Organizations create value as employees transform inputs or resources – people, equipment, technology, product designs, brands, information, energy, and cash – into products and services of greater worth."[29] Chapter 17, "Applying Innovation Processes," describes the characteristics of innovative processes.

What Are Priorities?

Values define the framework for decision-making to ensure that the key resources are aligned with the overall venture strategy. The organizational culture shapes the values, and the values drive the priorities, so that each person by themselves can operate with autonomy and accountability. As Clayton Christensen and Michael E. Raynor explain in *The Innovator's Solution*, "Value and processes come to constitute the organization's culture."[30]

The values and priorities address how decisions are made and the degree of autonomy permitted in the decision-making process. Decision-making is based on the values that are established by leadership and conveyed explicitly (by example) and implicitly (through the culture). "An organization's values," write Christensen and Raynor, "are the standards by which employees make prioritization decisions – those by which they judge whether an order is attractive or unattractive, whether a customer is more important or less important, whether an idea for a new product is attractive or marginal, and so on."[31]

The extent of autonomy that people are allowed is a very important element of high-functioning organizations. Leadership and the organizational culture provide the framework in which people are able to perform autonomously. "Culture enables employees to act autonomously and causes them to act consistently."[32] Chapter 9, "Culture Building," describes how culture can shape and guide human behavior. The larger and more complex a company is, the more importance needs to be placed on the extent of autonomy that is required. Generally, the degree of autonomy increases the larger and more complex the organization.

Knowledge Integration

Idea Generation and the Discovery of Customer Needs

There are two traditional ways to generate ideas and discover customers' unmet needs: individual-oriented and group-oriented. These are summarized in Figure 7.4.

Individual-Oriented Information Acquisition

Individual-oriented questionnaires, interviews, and observations are more effective for uncovering customer needs and generating ideas than group-oriented brainstorming and focus groups.[33] Individual idea generation favors revolutionary ideas that are often discouraged by group dynamics.

For example, Edward Jenner noticed that milkmaids did not generally get the smallpox disease. He hypothesized that the contact the milkmaids received with cowpox blisters protected them from smallpox, a similar virus.[34] "On 14 May 1796, Jenner tested his hypothesis by inoculating James Phipps, a young boy of 8 years (the son of Jenner's gardener), with material from the cowpox lesions that were present on the hand and arms of Sarah Nelmes, a milkmaid who had caught cowpox from a cow called Blossom."[35] Jenner inoculated James again in July of 1796, this time with smallpox lesions, and no disease developed.[36] This risky but successful inoculation led to Jenner's being recognized as the Founding Father of Immunology.[37] Today, while the field of immunology has led

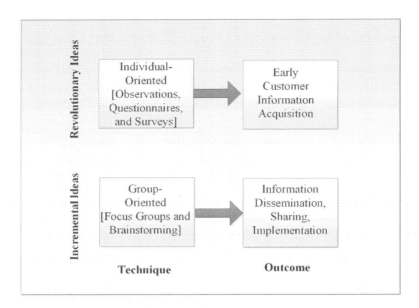

Figure 7.4 Illustration of Techniques for Customer Information Acquisition

Source: Adapted from: Gary R. Schirr, "Flawed Tools: The Efficacy of Group Research Methods to Generate Customer Ideas," *Journal of Product Innovation Management*, 29(3), (2012): 473–488.

© Copyright

to the virtual elimination of many life-threatening diseases, the war on disease continues with three countries, Afghanistan, Nigeria, and Pakistan, still fighting polio.[38] In this case, individual idea generation facilitated information acquisition resulting in an innovative outcome. It also highlights the need for ongoing investigation at both the individual and group orientation levels.

Group-Oriented Information Acquisition

As noted, individual-oriented methods to start gathering information for innovation efforts, such as the use of individual questionnaires, interviews, and observations, are more effective for initial idea generation. Group-oriented methods, by contrast, are more effective for improving ideas, information dissemination, and implementation.

Groups of people are often used to acquire information, generate and evaluate ideas, and determine what customers need and want in new product development. Group-oriented methods for acquiring customer information are not always the most effective approaches. For example, brainstorming is the conventional approach to idea generation. The participants follow the quantity over quality model; no criticism is permitted. The rationale for why focus and brainstorming groups kill or eliminate good ideas is the group effect. As we saw in Chapter 5, "Innovation and Thinking," groupthink occurs when individuals in a group situation may not be completely honest and may hold back their best ideas. This lack of transparency can be caused by a number of factors: group conformity, low levels of trust, low motivation to produce (if the group members feel their ideas are not being considered), idea blockage by other group members, or group members only performing at the level of the least productive member.[39]

In a study of brainstorming, though, one group of students was instructed to follow the conventional unstructured model of quantity over quality without criticism and the other group was instructed to follow a structured model of quality over quantity with criticism. The structured and constrained group had better results.[40] In the process of soliciting ideas, having an organized framework is both beneficial and impactful.

In summary, for maximum value, one might first employ individual-oriented efforts to acquire information and ideas, and then follow with group-oriented efforts for effective downstream information dissemination, sharing and organizational learning, and implementation.[41]

Empathic Innovation Sources

Innovation sources can be broad or narrow and do not reside in any one place. As illustrated in Figure 7.5, there are five sources (also called voices) for defining the path of innovation. The five voices are distinct yet complementary, each has value, and each has limitations. Because all five voices ultimately focus on people, all five voices need to be empathic. The five sources/voices of innovation are as follows:

- Voice of the customer
- Voice of the job to be done
- Voice of open innovation

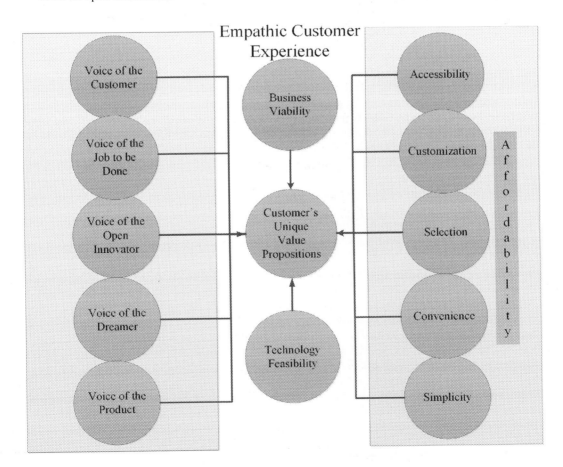

Figure 7.5 Illustration of the Five Voices

Source: © Copyright.

- Voice of the dreamer
- Voice of the product

When thinking about innovation, you will be limited if you only consider one source. For instance, a business must always understand who the customer is to whom it offers a unique value proposition (the voice of the customer), and a business must also understand what job, product, or service (innovation type) that customer has hired them to perform (the voice of the job to be done).[42] Customer-focused thinking should be integrated within the leadership, strategy, and culture. It is equally important to know who your customer is and know who your customer *is not*.

For example, around 2000, Procter & Gamble (P&G) underwent a crisis and the company needed a change. A. G. Lafley, P&G's CEO at the time, championed an integrated approach to managerial innovation by focusing synergistically on basic fundamentals. Lafley focused on the consumers and put them first. Because he knew that customer needs are learned best through direct observation (rather than just through research reports or focus groups), Lafley introduced observation methods to more fully understand the behavioral economics of the P&G customers. Lafley set an example for all of the P&G employees by spending time observing and listening to people inside their homes. He recognized in P&G a stagnant culture that needed change and encouraged idea generation and collaboration not only from the inside, but from the outside as well, stimulating open innovation through Connect + Develop.[43]

Voice of the Customer

It is not uncommon for products to fail to meet the wants and needs of customers because of unrealistic expectations, low value, and high prices. IBM's attempt to enter the home computer market, with the introduction of the IBM PCjr, failed due to a number of flawed features.[44] The Ford Edsel product line lost $350 million, or the equivalent of $2.76 billion in 2013 dollars, and its name became synonymous with a failed course of action.[45]

The voice of the customer is the conventional approach to new solutions and begins with defining a customer's unmet needs. Customers have unmet needs that are broad, such as the need for work/occupation, education, transportation, housing, entertainment, food, water, and health. Customers have unmet needs that are deep, such as unmet needs for a nutritious diet, exercise, and the prevention of acute (heart attacks and strokes) and chronic diseases (diabetes).[46]

Innovations can also be born out of quality improvement that aims to remove inefficiencies and errors from systems. The Toyota Production Systems (TPS) is sometimes known as the Thinking People System because employees are encouraged to aspire to develop perfect processes that prevent defects altogether. (For more details, see the "Toyota Production System" section in Chapter 4, "Innovative Behaviors," such as *jidoka* and *pokayoke*.) If defects occur, they are identified and remedied with a sense of urgency by shop floor employees. The shop-floor assembly-line employees are encouraged to take responsibility to act on problems at the time they occur and at their lowest cost point.[47] As we will see in more detail in Chapter 9, "Culture Building," Toyota uses its TPS competency very effectively to leverage worker skill and productivity in the workplace and satisfied customers that drive sales.

The voice of the customer has limitations. Incumbent organizations are often aware of innovations in their markets, but choose to stay close to their existing customers and attempt to evolve existing products rather than pursue new potentially innovative products focused on unserved or underserved market opportunities. The consequences of staying too close to customers are that the incumbents risk missing an innovation successfully implemented by a new or more innovative entrant. Intel avoided this common pitfall when it invested in a new low-end Celeron microprocessor yet continued to invest in their high-end microprocessors that were needed by their customers. In contrast, US Steel did not invest in a new electric manufacturing process to make steel and ignored a new entrant, Nucor Steel, which systematically took away a large proportion of US Steel's business by offering a lower-cost product.

There are limitations to the voice of the customer innovation source because customers have difficulty imagining products and services that do not yet exist. That is, they may not have the imagination or be well-informed about what scientific and technological advances have occurred. Subsequently, they may not understand what is realistic to pursue and lack the expertise to imagine what is possible. In addition, customers may not be able to describe their unmet needs, especially if the description of that unmet need involves tacit knowledge that the customer cannot articulate.

Conventional research that involves surveying competitors will not necessarily involve the creation of a differentiated product or a high degree of innovation.[48] Market research has limitations because of cost, time, accuracy, and availability of volunteers.[49] Market research is also constrained by the extent of the experience and expertise of those researched – the identical limitations of voice of the customers and voice of the lead user.

Voice of the Job to Be Done

The voice of the job to be done (JTBD) starts with the task a customer needs performed (see Figure 7.6). Tony Ulwick describes two important fundamentals of innovation: "First, it must know precisely who it is in the business of creating value for. In other words, it must know its customer: The person who is using its product to get a job done. Second, it must know what job that person hired the product to perform."[50] Traditionally, thermostats were sold through heating, ventilation, and air conditioning contractors. Energy-conscious consumers are often searching for value and improved ways to save energy and lower their energy costs. The start-up Nest provided a new way to get the job done when it realized that it could offer a smart thermostat directly to energy conscious consumers that they could install themselves, bypassing the contractor channel. The Nest thermostat product has been very successful because of its ability to self-learn how to adjust residential temperatures and its integration with smartphones.[51] The market in this example is first defined by the job to be done and second by the product offering.

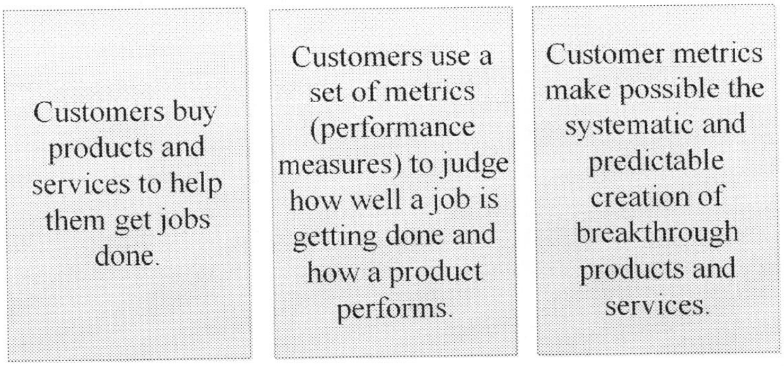

Customers buy products and services to help them get jobs done.	Customers use a set of metrics (performance measures) to judge how well a job is getting done and how a product performs.	Customer metrics make possible the systematic and predictable creation of breakthrough products and services.

Figure 7.6 Illustration of Job to Be Done

Source: Adapted from Anthony Ulwick, *What Customers Want,* (New York: McGraw-Hill, 2005), 17–18. © Copyright.

The voice of the JTBD does not focus on products and services but begins with the assumption that the job to be done is the cause behind the purchase of a product or service. By focusing on what job needs to be done, customers identify various solutions at various times. For example, if you need your home or apartment to be furnished, IKEA is a shopping experience that is organized around the JTBD.[52]

The Campbell Soup Company product, V8 juice, is an example of the JTBD combined with creative brand building and advertising. "For years, the advertising campaign for V8, a juice that promises the nutrients of eight different vegetables, had used the refrain, 'Wow, I could've had a V8!' It was sold as an alternative to refreshing drinks like apple juice, soft drinks and Gatorade and so on."[53] Campbell Soup Company later realized that V8 juice could be hired or linked to take on the job of providing the required daily vegetables more conveniently than having to prepare all of the vegetables. New V8 advertisements asked, "How many vegetables have you had today? Yeah, that's what I thought." In a year, Campbell Soup Company was able to quadruple the V8 juice revenue.

Clayton Christensen describes how a fast-food restaurant attempted to increase their milkshake sales by improving the features. The researcher started by asking the customers questions about how to improve their milkshakes. The question was: do you want chocolatier, cheaper, or chunkier milkshakes? After implementing the suggestions, there was no improvement in sales. The researchers then took a different approach. After direct observation and interviewing of the customers as they left the store, they discovered that the features were not the issue – it was the JTBD. Nearly half of the customers bought milkshakes in the morning for something to do during their long and uninteresting drives to work. Milkshakes worked better than bananas, bagels, and doughnuts.[54] The job to be done, the restaurant realized, was passing the time while stuck on a long commute. The market was first the JTBD, and second, the milkshake product.

The job of transportation is to get from one place to another. Consider the many alternatives: cars, bikes, trucks, trains, airplanes, taxis, and buses. What metrics do you compare in order to choose? Key elements considered might include customization (packages of options), affordability, simplicity, and convenience. When deciding on a car purchase or lease, total price, length of completeness of warranty, miles per gallon, resale value, reliability, and cost to maintain are filtered into the decision. From the oil crisis in 1973 and embargo of 1979, to the 2021 Colonial Pipeline Cybersecurity attack,[55] all resulting in fossil fuel availability disruption, customers are increasingly purchasing cars based on measuring the cost of gasoline against the miles per gallon metric. Manufacturers of cars study the metrics customers need and want to determine what to build next.

Building on the issues raised by the cost of fuel combined with efforts to be more sensitive to environmental impact, both companies and customers are responding to the overall challenge. Alternative modes of transportation, from electric to alternative fuel sources to shared commuting options, all speak to the future JTBD. For example, the 2013 minority-owned start-up, Orion Electronics, The Future of Urban Travel™, is focused on introducing its forward-thinking Smart E-Bike. Its goal is to redefine the micro-mobility market estimated at over $300 billion in the US and $900 billion globally. Building on its ORION Go® app, introducing its Smart E-Bike, seeks to not only focus on the JTBD by product, but also advancing the JTBD focused on the equity of clean, efficient, urban micro-transportation. Moreover, ORION Electronics Company, Inc., envisions an aggressive JTBD focused on an overall more innovative and sustainable future or what they call the Internet of Us™.[56]

Voice of the Open Innovator

As can be seen in Figure 7.7, open innovation is the realization that ideas for innovation can come from anywhere. "A recent trend in the evolution of innovation theory recognizes that not all good ideas come from inside the firm; neither need all good ideas emerging within the particular firm be commercialized by that same firm."[57] Henry Chesbrough is considered to be the father of the concept of open innovation.[58] He separates the concept of open innovation into two parts: outside-in open innovation opens up an organization to external sources of ideas, and inside-out open innovation opens up an organization to the notion that there are a wide range of internal sources in an organization that could be used externally.[59]

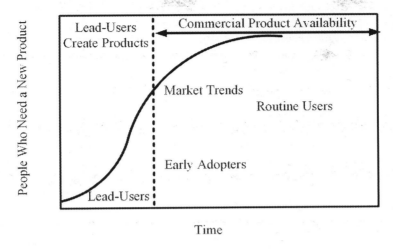

Figure 7.7 Illustration of Open Innovation or Lead-User Model

Source: Adapted from Eric von Hippel, Stefan Thomke, and Mary Sonnack, "Creating Breakthroughs at 3M," *Harvard Business Review*, 77(5), (1999), 47–57.

The closed model of innovation is based on using an organization's R&D infrastructure to generate organic growth for all innovation degrees and types. P&G realized that the closed model of innovation was limiting their potential and that external connections could add value to their innovation efforts. They concluded that there were 200 scientists or engineers outside of P&G for every P&G researcher, or about 1.5 million people that potentially could be accessed. P&G developed the Connect + Develop program to extend the reach of P&G's innovators to enable more external connections.[60]

Gary Hamel, Michele Zanini, and Polly LaBarre are co-founders of the Management Innovation eXchange (MIX). The MIX is an online, open innovation community to share ideas on how to innovate in ways that are beyond the ordinary.[61] The open innovator voice needs to meet the innovation criteria: business viability, technology feasibility, and consumer desirability.

OpenIDEO is a global, virtual, collaborative network of creative people who address social issues and environmental challenges.[62] To respond to the challenge, the process starts with asking ourselves "a big question."[63] For example, to address global poverty, what steps might be taken to provide an environment to promote innovation and entrepreneurship? "IDEO, a consultancy, has coined the slogan 'Fail often in order to succeed sooner.'"[64] OpenIDEO addresses social and environmental challenges. OpenIDEO's principles are optimism, continuous improvement, inclusiveness, community-centeredness, and collaboration.[65]

The lead-user model is an open innovation model based on the work of Eric von Hippel. Hippel challenges the belief that innovation comes solely from manufacturers of products. Rather, he argues, there are multiple sources of innovation, including end-users.[66] Hippel writes,

I define "lead users" of a novel or enhanced product, process or service as those who display two characteristics with respect to it: Lead users face needs that will be general in a market place – but face them months or years before the bulk of that marketplace encounters them, and – Lead users are positioned to benefit significantly by obtaining a solution to those needs.[67]

Hippel is an advocate of open innovation.[68]

> When I say that innovation is being democratized, I mean that users of products and services –
> both firms and individual consumers – are increasingly able to innovate for themselves.
> User-centered innovation processes offer great advantages over the manufacturer-centric inno-
> vation development systems that have been the mainstay of commerce for hundreds of years.[69]

Hippel writes,

> Our key finding was that approximately 80% of the innovations judged by users to offer them a
> significant increment in functional utility were in fact invented, prototyped and first field-tested
> by users of the instrument rather than by an instrument manufacturer.[70]

In his view the end-users (lead users) are a significant source of new innovation. He is one of the
most highly-cited social scientists writing on free and open-source software (FOSS).[71]

Sir Timothy John "Tim" Berners-Lee is considered to be a lead user and open innovator who
is credited with the invention of the World Wide Web.[72] This example demonstrates how you can
combine two voices: the job to be done and the open innovator. Berners-Lee wanted a way to get
the job done of sharing documentation that was inhibiting him from doing his work.

> Berners-Lee imagined combining the Internet with linked hypertext documents, to provide
> access to an open-ended body of interactive information. In March 1989, Berners-Lee pro-
> posed a global hypertext project, one that would permit researchers all over the world to share
> work-in-progress, transmitted instantaneously, without the delays associated with traditional
> scholarly publication or cumbersome mail groups. With collaborators at CERN, Berners-Lee
> wrote the "hypertext transfer protocol" (HTTP) for transmitting documents over the Internet.
> HTTP standardizes communication between web servers, where documents are stored, and the
> client programs, or browsers, used to view them. He also originated a system of identifying
> documents, originally known as the universal resource indicator, now known as the universal
> resource locator (URL).[73]

Rob McEwen, the CEO of Goldcorp, was struggling to find new gold deposits in Canada. Without
the discovery of new gold deposits, Goldcorp would likely have to close its 50-year-old mine and
go out of business. McEwen heard about the success of Linus Torvalds. While working over the
Internet, Torvalds and a group of volunteers developed a successful open-source commercial operating system. Linus shared all of the source code with his group of volunteers.

McEwen thought why not use the same approach as Linus Torvalds and solicit volunteer
"miners" over the Internet. Even though most of the information about a company in the gold
mining business is proprietary, he decided to use an open approach and share that information.
He created a contest with $575,000 in prize money and made available all of the geological in-
formation from about 55,000 acres of company property. He challenged the contestants to find
the gold; they did.

The Internet respondents provided new ways of locating gold deposits. The company grew from
a $100,000 company to a $9 billion company. McEwen devised a new creative approach using
lateral thinking. Instead of relying on his proprietary geological data and his staff of internal geolo-
gists, he enlisted voluntary contestants and made his data available to the public, thereby creating
a modern way to discover gold.[74]

Through the efforts of volunteers, the phenomenon known as "open source" has provided another source of innovation. The intrinsic motivation of unpaid individuals has driven the development of innovative technology-based solutions. These solutions include not only Wikipedia, which upstaged Microsoft's Encarta, but also software technologies that form the infrastructure for the delivery mechanism of information to web end-users. The open-source Linux operating system competes with the Windows operating system, the Firefox open-source browser competes with Microsoft's Edge, and the Apache open-source web server software competes against Microsoft's Internet Information Services web server.

Voice of the Dreamer

The dreamer provides the customer with something they did not necessarily request or even envision. These innovations often spring from the experiences, knowledge, and expertise of inventors, such as those of Thomas Edison, and R&D innovators, like Spence Silver's low tack glue and Arthur Fry's Post-it Note at 3M.

The voice of the dreamer generally envisions something without being sure someone will buy it. The voice of the dreamer is dramatically portrayed in the 1989 fantasy-drama movie *Field of Dreams*. The story is based on Ray Kinsella's troubled relationship with his deceased father and how he was encouraged to "ease his pain." Ray Kinsella, played by Kevin Costner, is walking through his cornfield in the twilight when he hears a quiet voice say three times, "If you build it, he will come." Ray, a devoted baseball fan, experiences a vision of a baseball diamond in his field. He later ploughs under his corn and builds a baseball field. Terrence Mann, played by James Earl Jones, convinced him that people would come to see a baseball game and they did. At the end, Ray invites his father to "play catch" in their field of dreams.[75]

"Just as good detectives are trained to hear the dog that did not bark – so too are good scientists trained to look, and listen for what's not there."[76] Alexander Fleming was performing research on the *Staphylococci* bacteria. He stored his cultures in the laboratory for safe-keeping while he went on vacation with his family. Upon his return he observed that one of the cultures was contaminated by a fungus and the bacteria in the vicinity of the fungus had been destroyed. By accident, he had discovered the antibiotic penicillin.[77]

The structure of DNA was discovered by two scientists, James D. Watson and Francis Crick. The discovery of DNA revealed the secrets of modern biological sciences and medicine. The innovation of flight was advanced by understanding the simple physics principle, discovered by Bernoulli, that increasing the speed of a fluid decreases its pressure. The voice of the dreamer is only limited by our divergent thinking. The ability to dream meaningful ideas is a function of associating individual experiences, deep knowledge, and expertise.[78]

The voice of the dreamer is based on finding products, services, and solutions that consumers may not even realize would make their day-to-day tasks better than before. Steve Jobs was a dreamer: "He saw himself as a designer of things that people didn't even know they wanted until he created them."[79] Jobs knew that big new ideas can only be nourished where there are markets that have high potential. He also knew that these high-potential markets do not exist today and, therefore, cannot be analyzed. When Jobs launched the Macintosh, he was asked what studies Apple had conducted to ensure there was a market for the computer. Steve Jobs replied, "Did Alexander Graham Bell do any market research before he invented the telephone?"[80] When Steve Jobs launched the iPad, he was asked how much research was done to guide Apple. Jobs responded, "None. It isn't the consumers' job to know what they want. It's hard for [consumers] to tell you what they want when they've never seen anything remotely like it."[81]

Steve Jobs' death was caused by respiratory arrest brought on by pancreatic cancer, a disease that can occur undetected until it is too late.[82] More specifically, he had a pancreatic neuroendocrine tumor.

A pancreatic neuroendocrine tumor, also called islet cell carcinoma, is a rare form of cancer that is most likely to be passed on through genetics, as there are few known risk factors that lead to this type of illness. Neuroendocrine tumors, which grow at a relatively slow rate, can be surgically removed. These tumors can release hormones prior to removal, which can cause recurrence or spreading of the cancer.[83]

Pancreatic cancer is one of the most pernicious forms of cancer because it is not easily detected. At the time of Jobs' death, there was no effective test to detect the presence of pancreatic cancer. Since then, Jack Andraka, inspired by the death of a family friend who had pancreatic cancer, is credited with developing a promising test for detecting the disease. At the age of 15, he developed a unique and inexpensive method to detect the presence of the cancer by measuring an increase of a protein. His talent was his ability to creatively put it all together.[84]

Voice of the Product

Many innovations can start with existing products by applying systematic inventive thinking based on the patterns derived from studying large numbers of patents.[85] You can create a new product by subtracting a component from an existing product. For example, an exercise bike is the result of removing one of the wheels from a bicycle. You can create a new product by creating, dissolving, or modifying the dependent relationships that exist between attributes of a product and/or attributes of its immediate environment. You can create a dependent relationship between the eyeglass lenses that change color when exposed to ultraviolet light on sunny days. As the ultraviolet light levels increase, the lenses increase in darkness. The dual-purpose lenses eliminate the need for a separate pair of glasses.[86]

The limitation to the voice of the product is that it is based on products that already exist. This approach can easily lead to incrementalism. **Incrementalism** is the tendency to build new variations of products rather than new scientific or technological breakthroughs of high degrees of innovation that are more likely from a dreamer.

Genrich Altshuller was a Russian scientist and engineer who studied existing patents searching for patterns. He discovered that 40 engineering analogies and abstractions could be used to explain the majority of inventions. He developed the theory of inventive problem solving (TRIZ), a deliberate, structured approach to classifying and solving engineering problems.[87]

Subir Chowdhury writes in *Design for Six Sigma*,

Systematic Innovation may seem an oxymoron, like jumbo shrimp, but with TRIZ, individuals can generate amazingly creative solutions without threatening the stability of the company – all in a step-by-step process that takes some of the fear and guesswork out of innovation. The reason DFSS-TRIZ works so effectively is the simple fact that over 90 percent of the underlying generic problems product and process designers face today at a given company have already been solved at another company or even in a completely different industry – perhaps even for entirely unrelated situations – using a fundamentally different technology or approach.[88]

Systematic Inventive Thinking

Systematic inventive thinking focuses on problem-framing by using patterns to organize ideas based on existing products. Systematic inventive thinking can provide a higher level of effectiveness for idea generation than conventional brainstorming because it allows for more focus on the problem itself. Rather than start with the customer's unmet needs, systematic inventive thinking starts with identifying existing products and the characteristics of those products.

Systematic inventive thinking is a disciplined approach that derives new product ideas from existing products using five generic innovation patterns.[89] The patterns provide a way to generate a set of manageable ideas within a defined frame of reference for ease of problem solving, in contrast to brainstorming, which has the potential to generate an overload of ideas.

Five Systematic Inventive Thinking Patterns

As outlined in Figure 7.8, the five innovation patterns are subtraction, multiplication, division, task unification, and attribute dependency change.[90] The subtraction pattern is based on removing features from existing products. Most airlines have international flights, long flights, and short flights; Southwest Airlines chose to offer short, direct flights only. An automated teller machine is an innovation in which the bank employee was removed. By removing frames from glasses, you have contact lenses, and by removing water from soup, you have a powered soup mix.[91]

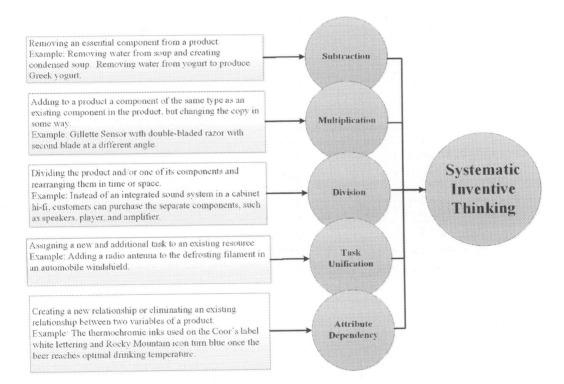

Figure 7.8 Illustration of Systematic Inventive Thinking

Source: Adapted from Drew Boyd and Jacob Goldenberg, *Inside the Box*, (New York: Simon and Schuster, 2013); and Yoni Stern, Idit Biton, and Ze'ev Ma'or, "Systematically Creating Coincidental Product Evolution Case Studies of the Application of the Systematic Inventive Thinking®(SIT) Method in the Chemical Industry." *Journal of Business Chemistry*, 3(1) (2006): 13–21.

The Knowledge Cycle

Building on the concept of systematic inventive thinking requires clear and concise communication. The knowledge cycle is a description of the pathways that illustrate how value is embedded into products and services. The pathway can start with clear communication based on articulate knowledge or unclear communication containing tacit and implicit knowledge. Because of the imprecise nature of communications, the knowledge cycle recognizes that five different voices are potentially needed to uncover the future unmet needs and opportunities.

The knowledge cycle path includes the actionable insights that are discovered by the innovator that allows them to integrate the attitudes, skills, and knowledge into a solution resulting in embedded knowledge in any innovation type. (See Figure 7.3 for summary of how knowledge types, the five voices, theory of capabilities, and discipline specific areas, such as art, science, technology, and others, inform new knowledge.)

For instance, the embedded knowledge for a smartphone is encoded using several integrated technologies, many types of hardware components, the operating system, the apps, and artificial intelligence. In 2011, Nokia sold nearly six times as many phones as Apple, but the Apple's phone's wholesale selling price was seven times that of the Nokia's phone. As illustrated in Figure 7.9, this difference can be attributed in part to the embedded knowledge in the Apple phone.[92]

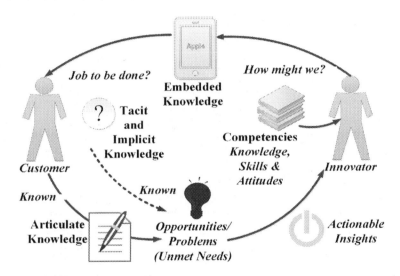

Figure 7.9 Illustration of the Knowledge Cycle
Source: © Copyright.

Summary

In this chapter, we explored the key innovation and entrepreneurship competency of knowledge building. We outlined a number of critical skills and elements of knowledge building, including developing effective learning systems; learning models, such as problem-based learning and learning organizations; knowledge types; creation and integration of new knowledge; the role of the empathic innovation sources, including the voices of the customer, the job to be done, the open innovator, the dreamer, and the product; and five systematic inventive thinking patterns. Finally, the knowledge cycle provides a description of the pathways that illustrate how value is embedded into products and services. Armed with this foundation, in the next chapter we visit the realm of creativity and the role it plays in propelling innovation and entrepreneurship.

Notes

1. Peter Bisson, Elizabeth Stephenson, and S. Patrick Viguerie, "The Productivity Imperative: To Sustain Wealth Creation, Developed Nations Must Find Ways to Boost Productivity; Product and Process Innovation Will be Key," *McKinsey & Company*, June 2010, accessed February 20, 2024, www.mckinsey.com/featured-insights/employment-and-growth/the-productivity-imperative#.

2. Michael Chui, James Manyika, Jacques Bughin, Richard Dobbs, Charles Roxburgh, Hugo Sarrazin, Geoffrey Sands, and Magdalena Westergren, "The Social Economy: Unlocking Value and Productivity Through Social Technologies," *McKinsey Global Institute*, July 2012, accessed February 20, 2024, www.mckinsey.com/industries/technology-media-and-telecommunications/our-insights/the-social-economy.

3. M. Scardamalia and C. Bereiter, "Knowledge Building," *Encyclopedia of Education*, ed. James W. Gutherie, 2nd ed., vol. 4 (New York: Macmillan Reference, 2003), 1370–1373.

4. "The Digital Degree," *The Economist*, June 28, 2014, 20–22.

5. "The Digital Degree," *The Economist*, June 28, 2014, 20–22.

6. Clayton M. Christensen, *The Innovator's Dilemma: When New Technologies Cause Great Firms to Fail* (Boston: Harvard Business School Press, 1997).

7. Thomas Skiba, Mei Tan, Robert J. Sternberg, and Elena L. Grigorenko, "Roads Not Taken, New Roads to Take: Looking for Creativity in the Classroom," in *Nurturing Creativity in the Classroom*, eds. Ronald A. Beghetto and James C. Kaufman (Cambridge: Cambridge University Press, 2010), 252–269.

8. R. Keith Sawyer, "Learning for Creativity," in *Nurturing Creativity in the Classroom*, eds. Ronald A. Beghetto and James C. Kaufman (Cambridge: Cambridge University Press, 2010), 172–190.

9. Peter Drucker, *Innovation and Entrepreneurship: Practice and Principles* (New York: Harper & Row, 1985).

10. Keith Sawyer, *Zig Zag: The Surprising Path to Greater Creativity* (San Francisco: Jossey-Bass, 2013), 6.

11. Joe Sheehan, "The Case For . . . Batting Your Stud Second," *CNN*, June 10, 2013, accessed May 19, 2021, https://vault.si.com/vault/2013/06/10/the-case-for-batting-your-stud-second.

12. *Wikipedia*, s.v. "Potential Energy," accessed May 12, 2021, http://en.wikipedia.org/wiki/Potential_energy.

13. Gary Hamel, *What Matters Now* (New York: Jossey-Bass, 2012), 139.

14. Johnny Evans, "Apple Now Bigger than Nokia in Mobile Biz," *Computerworld*, April 21, 2011, accessed February 20, 2024, www.computerworld.com/article/2471190/apple-now-bigger-than-nokia-in-mobile-biz.html.

15. "What Is Learning? A Definition and Discussion," accessed February 20, 2024, http://infed.org/mobi/learning-theory-models-product-and-process/.

16. Mark K. Smith, "David A. Kolb on Experiential Learning," accessed February 20, 2024, http://infed.org/mobi/david-a-kolb-on-experiential-learning/.

17. Mark K. Smith, "Maria Montessori and Education," *infed.org: Education, Community-Building, and Change*, 1997, updated January 7, 2013, accessed May 19, 2021, https://infed.org/mobi/maria-montessori-and-education/.

18. *Wikipedia*, s.v. "Problem-based Learning," accessed May 12, 2021, http://en.wikipedia.org/wiki/Problem-based_learning.

19. Peter Senge, *The Fifth Discipline: The Art and Practice of the Learning Organization* (New York: Doubleday, 1990), 3.

20. "Chris Argyris: Theories of Action, Double-loop Learning and Organizational Learning," accessed February 20, 2024, http://infed.org/mobi/chris-argyris-theories-of-action-double-loop-learning-and-organizational-learning/.

21. Morten T. Hansen, "IDEO CEO Tim Brown: T-Shaped Stars: The Backbone of IDEO's Collaborative Culture," January 21, 2010, accessed February 20, 2024, https://chiefexecutive.net/ideo-ceo-tim-brown-t-shaped-stars-the-backbone-of-ideoaes-collaborative-culture__trashed/orhttp://chiefexecutive.net/ideo-ceo-tim-brown-t-shaped-stars-the-backbone-of-ideoae%E2%84%A2s-collaborative-culture.

22. Alan G. Lafley and Ram Charan, *Game-Changer* (New York: Crown Business, 2008), 10.

23. Keith Sawyer, *Zig Zag* (New York: Jossey-Bass, 2013), 149.

24. David Bradley, "Why Gladwell's 10,000-hour Rule Is Wrong," *BBC*, November 12, 2012, accessed February 20, 2024, www.bbc.com/future/story/20121114-gladwells-10000-hour-rule-myth/1.

25. Keith Sawyer, *Zig Zag* (New York: Jossey-Bass, 2013), 50–51.

26. Jim Collins, *Good to Great: Why Some Companies Make the Leap . . . and Others Don't* (New York: HarperCollins, 2001).

27. Jim Collins, *How the Mighty Fall . . . and Why Some Companies Never Give In* (New York: Harper Collins, 2009).
28. Clayton Christensen and Michael E. Raynor, *The Innovator's Solution* (Boston: Harvard Business School Press, 2003).
29. Clayton Christensen and Michael E. Raynor, *The Innovator's Solution* (Boston: Harvard Business School Press, 2003).
30. Clayton Christensen and Michael E. Raynor, *The Innovator's Solution* (Boston: Harvard Business School Press, 2003).
31. Clayton Christensen and Michael E. Raynor, *The Innovator's Solution* (Boston: Harvard Business School Press, 2003), 185.
32. Clayton Christensen and Michael E. Raynor, *The Innovator's Solution* (Boston: Harvard Business School Press, 2003), 189.
33. Gary R. Schirr, "Flawed Tools: The Efficacy of Group Research Methods to Generate Customer Ideas," *Journal of Product Innovation Management* 29, no. 3 (2012), 473–488.
34. *Wikipedia*, s.v. "Edward Jenner," accessed May 12, 2021, http://en.wikipedia.org/wiki/Edward_Jenner.
35. *Wikipedia*, s.v. "Edward Jenner," accessed May 12, 2021, http://en.wikipedia.org/wiki/Edward_Jenner.
36. Stefan Riedel, "Edward Jenner and the History of Smallpox and Vaccination," accessed May 12, 2021, www.ncbi.nlm.nih.gov/pmc/articles/PMC1200696/.
37. Gareth Williams, "Dr. Jenner's House, the Birthplace of Vaccination," *Perspectives* 378, 307–308, www.lancet.com, accessed May 19, 2021, www.thelancet.com/pdfs/journals/lancet/PIIS0140-6736(11)61154-9.pdf.
38. Donald G. McNeil Jr., "Pakistan Battles Polio, and Its People's Mistrust," *The New York Times*, July 21, 2013, accessed May 12, 2021, www.nytimes.com/2013/07/22/health/pakistan-fights-for-ground-in-war-on-polio.html?nl=todaysheadlines&emc=edit_th_20130722&_r=0.
39. Gary R. Schirr, "Flawed Tools: The Efficacy of Group Research Methods to Generate Customer Ideas," *Journal of Product Innovation Management* 29, no. 3 (2012), 473–488.
40. Keith Sawyer, *Zig Zag* (New York: Jossey-Bass, 2013), 176.
41. Gary R. Schirr, "Flawed Tools: The Efficacy of Group Research Methods to Generate Customer Ideas," *Journal of Product Innovation Management* 29, no. 3 (2012), 473–488.
42. Tony Ulwick, "Innovation Starts by Targeting the Right Customer," accessed May 12, 2021, http://strategyn.com/2012/12/18/who-is-your-customer/.
43. "Connect + Develop," accessed May 12, 2021, www.pgconnectdevelop.com/.
44. *Wikipedia*, s.v. "IBM PCjr," accessed May 12, 2021, http://en.wikipedia.org/wiki/IBM_PCjr.
45. *Wikipedia*, s.v. "Edsel," accessed May 12, 2021, http://en.wikipedia.org/wiki/Edsel.
46. Tony Ulwick, "Secrets to Uncovering Unmet Customer Needs," accessed May 12, 2021, http://strategyn.com/2012/11/27/secrets-to-uncovering-unmet-customer-needs/.
47. Gary Hamel, *The Future of Management* (Boston: Harvard Business School Press, 2007), 29.
48. Yoni Stern, Idit Biton, and Ze'ev Ma'or, "Systematically Creating Coincidental Product Evolution Case Studies of the Application of the Systematic Inventive Thinking®(SIT) Method in the Chemical Industry," *Journal of Business Chemistry* 3, no. 1 (2006), 13–21.
49. Mary Jane and Demand Media, "The Disadvantages of Market Research on New Product Development," *The Houston Chronicle*, accessed May 12, 2021, http://smallbusiness.chron.com/disadvantages-market-research-new-product-development-23441.html.
50. Tony Ulwick, "Innovation Starts by Targeting the Right Customer," accessed May 12, 2021, http://strategyn.com/2012/12/18/who-is-your-customer/.
51. Tony Ulwick, "Innovation Starts by Targeting the Right Customer," accessed May 12, 2021, http://strategyn.com/2012/12/18/who-is-your-customer/.
52. Clayton M. Christensen, James Allworth, and Karen Dillon, *How Will You Measure Your Life?* (New York: Harper, 2012), 100–102.
53. Clayton M. Christensen, James Allworth, and Karen Dillon, *How Will You Measure Your Life?* (New York: Harper, 2012), 109.
54. Clayton M. Christensen, James Allworth, and Karen Dillon, *How Will You Measure Your Life?* (New York: Harper, 2012), 103–107.
55. Clifford Krauss, "Hackers and Climate Change Threaten U.S. Energy Independence," *The New York Times*, May 18, 2021, accessed May 19, 2021, www.nytimes.com/2021/05/18/business/energy-environment/colonial-pipeline-security-weather.html.

56. Dustan Tomlinson, "The Future of Urban Travel™: ORION Electronics Company, Inc.," *Ohio News Time*, March 31, 2021, accessed May 19, 2021, https://ohionewstime.com/the-future-of-urban-travel-orion-electronics-company-inc-ohio/112967/.

57. Johan Grönlund, David Ronnberg Sjödin, and Johan Frishammar, "Open Innovation and the Stage-Gate Process: A Revised Model for New Product Development," *California Management Review* 52, no. 3 (2010), 106–131.

58. Henry Chesbrough, *Open Innovation: The New Imperative for Creating and Profiting from Technology* (Boston: Harvard Business School Press, March 2003).

59. Oana-Maria Pop, "Open Innovation Past and Present: An Exclusive Interview with Henry Chesbrough," *Innovation Management*, July 25, 2013, accessed May 12, 2021, www.innovationmanagement.se/2013/07/17/open-innovation-past-and-present-an-exclusive-interview-with-henry-chesbrough/.

60. Larry Huston and Nabil Sakkab, "P&G's New Innovation Model," *Harvard Business Review*, March 20, 2006, accessed May 12, 2021, http://hbswk.hbs.edu/archive/5258.html.

61. "Gary Hamel," accessed May 19, 2021, www.mixprize.org/.

62. "OpenIDEO," accessed May 12, 2021, www.openideo.com/.

63. "Introduction to OpenIDEO/OpenIDEO.com," *YouTube Video*, posted by "IDEO," August 2, 2010, accessed May 12, 2021, www.youtube.com/watch?v=eUApgJBZU8M&feature=youtube.

64. "Fail Often, Fail Well," *Schumpeter* (blog), *The Economist*, April 14, 2011, accessed May 12, 2021, www.economist.com/node/18557776.

65. "OpenIDEO," accessed May 19, 2021, www.openideo.com/approach.

66. Eric von Hippel, *The Sources of Innovation* (Cambridge: Oxford University Press, 1988).

67. Eric von Hippel, "Lead Users: A Source of Novel Product Concepts," *Management Science* 32, no. 7 (1986), 791–805.

68. *Wikipedia*, s.v. "Eric von Hippel," accessed May 12, 2021, http://en.wikipedia.org/wiki/Eric_von_Hippel.

69. Eric von Hippel, *The Democratization of Innovation* (Cambridge, MA: MIT Press, 2005).

70. Eric A. von Hippel, "The Dominant Role of Users in the Scientific Instrument Innovation Process," *Research Policy* 5, no. 3 (1976), 212–239, accessed May 19, 2021, https://evhippel.files.wordpress.com/2013/08/1976-vh-instruments-paper.pdf.

71. *Wikipedia*, s.v. "Free and Open Software, FOSS," accessed May 12, 2021, http://en.wikipedia.org/wiki/Free_and_open_source_software.

72. Eric von Hippel, *The Democratization of Innovation* (Cambridge, MA: MIT Press, 2005).

73. Sir Tim Berners-Lee, "Academy of Achievement," accessed May 12, 2021, https://achievement.org/achiever/sir-timothy-berners-lee/.

74. Don Tapscott and D. Williams Anthony, *Wikinomics: How Mass Collaboration Changes Everything* (New York: Penguin Group, 2006), 7–9, 17.

75. *Wikipedia*, s.v. "Field of Dreams," accessed May 12, 2021, http://en.wikipedia.org/wiki/Field_of_dreams.

76. Bruce Nussbaum, *Creative Intelligence* (New York: Harper Business, 2013), 71.

77. *Wikipedia*, s.v. "Alexander Fleming," accessed May 12, 2021, http://en.wikipedia.org/wiki/Alexander_Fleming.

78. Bruce Nussbaum, *Creative Intelligence* (New York: Harper Business, 2013), 29–30, 33.

79. Bruce Nussbaum, *Creative Intelligence* (New York: Harper Business, 2013), 189.

80. Philip Elmer-DeWitt, "Fortune Names Steve Jobs the 'Greatest Entrepreneur'," *Fortune*, March 26, 2012, accessed May 19, 2021, https://fortune.com/2012/03/26/fortune-names-steve-jobs-the-greatest-entrepreneur/.

81. Philip Elmer-DeWitt, "Fortune Names Steve Jobs the 'Greatest Entrepreneur'," *Fortune*, March 26, 2012, accessed May 19, 2021, https://fortune.com/2012/03/26/fortune-names-steve-jobs-the-greatest-entrepreneur/.

82. Amanda Chan and Ramona Emerson, "Steve Jobs' Cause of Death Was Respiratory Arrest, Report Says," *The Huffington Post*, December 10, 2011, accessed May 12, 2021, www.huffingtonpost.com/2011/10/10/steve-jobs-cause-of-death_n_1004020.html.

83. AppleInsider Staff, "Steve Jobs' Cause of Death Officially Listed as Respiratory Arrest," *AppleInsider*, October 10, 2011, accessed May 12, 2021, http://appleinsider.com/articles/11/10/10/steve_jobs_cause_of_death_officially_listed_as_respiratory_arrest.html.

84. *Wikipedia*, s.v. "Jack Andraka," accessed May 12, 2021, http://en.wikipedia.org/wiki/Jack_Andraka.

85. Jacob Goldenberg, Roni Horowitz, Amnon Levav, and David Mazursky, "Finding Your Innovation Sweet Spot," *Harvard Business Review* 81, no. 3 (2003), 120–129.

86. Jacob Goldenberg, Roni Horowitz, Amnon Levav, and David Mazursky, "Finding Your Innovation Sweet Spot," *Harvard Business Review* 81, no. 3 (2003), 120–129.
87. Howard Smith, "What Innovation Is," *European Office of Technology and Innovation* (CSC White Paper, 2005), 19.
88. Subir Chowdhury, *Design For Six Sigma: The Revolutionary Process for Achieving Extraordinary Results* (Chicago: Dearborn, 2002), 114.
89. Jacob Goldenberg, Roni Horowitz, Amnon Levav, and David Mazursky, "Finding Your Innovation Sweet Spot," *Harvard Business Review* 81, no. 3 (2003), 120–129.
90. Drew Boyd and Jacob Goldenberg, *Inside the Box* (New York: Simon and Schuster, 2013).
91. Drew Boyd, "A Structured, Facilitated Team Approach to Innovation," *Organization Development Journal* 25, no. 3 (2007).
92. Johnny Evans, "Apple Now Bigger than Nokia in Mobile Biz," *Computerworld*, April 21, 2011, accessed May 12, 2021, www.computerworld.com/article/2471190/apple-now-bigger-than-nokia-in-mobile-biz.html.

8 Creativity Insights

The Beatles

Creativity is a time- and learning-dependent process composed of pathways that continually search for ideas that provide value. The creative pathways are determined by our attitudes, skills, and knowledge built up over time. The Beatles were creative music entrepreneurs who created their own pathways.

The Beatles are the best-selling music artists having achieved estimated sales of $600 million worldwide.[1] The Beatles received seven Grammy Awards, four Brit Awards, an Academy Award (for Best Original Song Score for the 1970 film *Let It Be*), and fifteen Ivor Novello Awards.[2] The Beatles' success stemmed in part via a creative process that integrated the song (lyrics and melodies), instrumentation, performances, production, and media in vibrant creative musical experiences.

During their early performances in Hamburg, the Beatles developed a creative style based on their playing and composing experience. The Beatles played for months in Hamburg's Reeperbahn district and Liverpool's Cavern night-club before being managed by Brian Epstein. Epstein approached many record companies to get a record contract, but he received continual rejection because of their *mediocre performances*. George Martin was introduced to the Beatles and noticed the potential talent and their distinctive harmonies. Their early albums were made up of simple compositions and cover songs from groups in America, but they became increasingly more creative using a combination of learnable competencies. What were the competencies that facilitated their creative processes? "Each creative output of The Beatles reflected its own combination of competition, team participation, and team dynamics."[3] The following are five creative competencies that the Beatles learned and applied: serious playing, associations, choosing, making, and pivoting. These are discussed in more detail later in this chapter and can be seen in Figure 8.2.

Serious Playing

The Beatles engaged in serious playing in a struggle of competition to achieve creative outcomes. "The propensity of competition to deliver creativity and innovation is one of the basic tenets of free market economics. The logic is that economic agents are forced to innovate to compete. The resulting innovation either creates value that contributes to human welfare and/or results in better resource utilization."[4]

The Beatles (John Lennon, Paul McCartney, George Harrison, and Ringo Starr) came to the US in February 1964. "By the time the Beatles had their first burst of success in 1964, in fact, they had performed live an estimated twelve hundred times."[5] The Hamburg practical experience was what separated them from other bands because most bands today do not perform twelve hundred times in their entire careers.

DOI: 10.4324/9781003034308-9

The Beatles were a team that had a dyadic mixture of cooperative teamwork and competitive rivalry.[6] The rivalry between the Beatles was *a contributor to their creative expression.* The "creative rivalry" came from both inside and outside the group. All four Beatles, especially Paul McCartney and John Lennon, worked together cooperatively. "There appears to be no 'holding back' in the Beatles and they were aware that sharing their ideas was one way of seeing the ideas developed and brought to fruition."[7] Yet, from the outset, John Lennon and Paul McCartney competed regarding their song writing capability.

Achievement, recognition, advancement, responsibility, the work itself, and learning are the elements of intrinsic motivation that are essential for creative thought.[8] The Beatles were intrinsically motivated by their love of music and extrinsically motivated from their financial incentives.[9] "External rewards such as getting on the A side, getting high in charts, fame, and surpassing their heroes were clear incentives for them, although some of them may have been more influenced by any particular reward than others. The structure of the reward system may play a large part in the cooperation–competition dichotomy."[10]

Associations

The Beatles relied on associations that enabled their creative minds working in combination to achieve a multiplicative effect. Their versatility was achieved by the combination of the composition of their own music and their ability to perform using multiple instruments. Paul McCartney and John Lennon working together added to their creative expression starting with their first album, *Please Me*, and continued with *Let It Be*.

It is the combination of all the musical elements that creates the emotional experience. As noted, there are five music elements including the following: **song** (lyrics, melody, harmony, rhythm, tempo, texture, and dynamics); **instrumentation** (the number of unique instrument combinations and their timbre); **performance** (natural talent of the musician, learned musical competencies, and choreography); **production** (the number and types of tracks and the use of technology); and **media** (film soundtracks and music videos).

Choosing

Externally, the Beatles were willing to learn from their competition, from other performers, by constantly looking at what others were doing and choosing to improve in different ways. As a result, the Beatles' music slowly became more sophisticated.[11] The competition raised the quality, not only of the Beatles output, but also the output of the groups with which they competed, such as their competition with the Beach Boys.[12]

Making

Da Vinci was one of the greatest known polymaths in history. We attribute the term Renaissance man to his developed expertise in painting, architecture, mathematics, and astronomy. His creativity was sourced not only through his immense curiosity, but also through the rigor that he applied in order to learn the details of these wide-ranging fields.[13]

The Beatles developed a combination of broad (horizontal) and deep (vertical) specialization like a T-shape when making their music. Their expertise in composing and instrumentation was driven by their intrinsic motivation and curiosity.

Pivoting

The Beatles were willing to take risks and be comfortable with uncertainty. The creative expression of the Beatles was the result of their adaptability and the synergistic integration of multiple musical components. The Beatles used experimentation, a creativity competency, to drive their musical expression. When they composed the song "Yesterday," they began departing from a standard rock 'n' roll model and started experimenting by using a string quartet and single acoustic guitar. Thereafter, the process of experimentation characterized their creative force to pivot in new directions.[14]

The Beatles were experimenters who were eager to incorporate different genres and try new ideas. The genres included skiffle, Merseybeat, folk rock, psychedelic rock, rock, pop rock, and blues.[15] The Beatles influenced and were influenced by many other musical groups such as Bob Dylan, the Beach Boys, Billy Joel, and Smokey Robinson.

The creative process of the Beatles successfully combined these five competencies that led to what could be called an "innovation pathway" or process that enabled them to move beyond set practices. By so doing, these competencies fostered the expansion of their musical talents to yield an outcome that was more than the sum of the individual parts.

Understanding Creativity

Creativity is the ability to generate new ideas that have value. Creativity can be thought of as the ability to transcend traditional ideas, rules, patterns, and/or relationships to devise new ideas, interpretations, and/or methods.[16] *Merriam-Webster* provides synonyms for creativity that include cleverness, imagination, ingeniousness, ingenuity, innovativeness, inventiveness, and originality.[17] Fundamentally, creativity, the generation of ideas that have value, is the prerequisite to innovation.

In the pursuit of innovation and entrepreneurship, the concept of creativity can be thought of as a dichotomy that distinguishes between "Big C" and "little c" creativity.[18] "Big C" creativity is legendary creativity with famous contributors, such as Einstein, Shakespeare, Newton, Leonardo, Michelangelo, Pasteur, Gutenberg, Darwin, Edison, Angelou, and Faraday.

Creativity, though, is not a Dionysian inspiration of the chosen few. Rather, everyday creativity, or "little c" creativity, is especially relevant because it can be applied and taught to students and studied using empirical research with large populations. Because of its applicability to education systems, "little c" creativity is particularly valuable in the pursuit of innovation and entrepreneurship. Although it might be dormant, creativity can be awakened and learned by individuals from all walks of life.

For example, Apple is known for its creative product and design innovations. Apple founder Steve Jobs created Apple University to provide employees with a sense of place, history, and change. Jobs wanted to give workers insights into more than just the organization as it was, but as it could be, including how they added value across the board, to each other, and to the customer in products and services. Jobs sought to add value by making complex technology easy to use for customers. To do this, Apple University teaches employees the art of innovation, Picasso-style:

> Apple has religiously embodied the notion that function and beauty come from elegant simplicity, and teachers in its internal training program sometimes point to a collection of Picasso lithographs that artfully illustrate the drive to boil down an idea to its most essential components.[19]

That is, by taking key design lessons from Picasso's style, revealing the essential elements behind the complex, employees can learn to create redefined products that are elegant, understandable, and user-friendly.

The Need for Creativity

Josh Linkner, founder and chairman of ePrize, succinctly notes the value and need for creativity in business and life.

> As economics and world markets continue to change, businesses are constantly being pulled into cost cutting, automation, and risk management. Although these are important elements of business success, we can't lose sight of the driving force of prosperity, the reason that any company exists in the first place, the source of both business and human fulfillment: *creativity*.[20]

Indeed, creativity can be seen in all aspects of living, working, leading, and more. Too often, however, creativity is only thought of as the domain of the arts such as dance, music, painting, or the theater. In reality it exists in all walks of life. As noted actor and writer, John Cleese observed, "Creativity can be seen in every area of life – in science, or in business, or in sport. Whenever you can find a way of doing things that is better than what has been done before, you are being creative."[21]

The Research Studies

In a 2010 American Management Association (AMA) study, creativity and innovation (along with critical thinking and problem solving, effective communication, and collaboration and team building) were identified as critical skills needed for business success today and in the future.[22] In 2010, International Business Machine conducted a study that was the largest known sample of one-on-one interviews of executives.[23] The study focused on determining what leadership skills are needed for the future. Creativity was identified as the number one leadership competency, followed by integrity and global thinking.[24] The IBM survey of "more than 1,500 Chief Executive Officers from 60 countries and 33 industries worldwide" found that "chief executives believe that – more than rigor, management discipline, integrity or even vision – successfully navigating an increasing [*sic*] complex world will require creativity."[25]

The OECD Global Creative Problem-Solving Study

The Organisation for Economic Co-operation and Development's (OECD) Programme for International Student Assessment (PISA) conducts a global evaluation of creative problem solving. The OECD PISA 2012 computer-administered assessment of creative problem solving included 85,000 15-year-old students in 44 countries and economies. From the 2012 study, the United Kingdom was ranked 11th, Germany was ranked 17th, and the United States was ranked 18th. The US score was 508, compared to the mean of 500. The top scores were from Singapore, Korea, and Japan at 562, 561, and 552, respectively.[26] Given the rapidly changing nature of work, education, society, technology, the environment, and more around the world, the need for creative problem solving is critical, especially in the context of innovation and entrepreneurship.

Intelligence and Creativity

Since the 1930s, there has been a worldwide increase in intelligence scores.[27] If there were a relationship between creativity and intelligence, creativity would be increasing as well. Kyung-Hee Kim, a professor of educational psychology at the College of William and Mary, conducted a meta-analysis study of the relationship between creativity and intelligence that synthesized results from studies between 1965 and 2005, concluding that the relationship between creativity and intelligence is negligible.[28] Research also suggests that the creativity capability of students in general is in decline.[29] Let us examine this in more detail.

Creativity Scores Declining

If creativity is viewed as a competency in terms of supply and demand, the evidence suggests that creativity competency demand is increasing and the creativity competency supply is decreasing.[30] Dr. Kim conducted a study to understand the relationship between creativity and intelligence over time.[31] She found that intelligence scores are increasing and US creativity scores are decreasing.[32] Kim found that US creativity scores steadily rose until 1990 and have since declined.[33] Kim's research sample included 272,599 Torrance Tests of Creative Thinking (TTCT) scores of an age-range of subjects (kindergarteners through adults) from 1966 to 2008.[34] The Torrance Tests of Creative Thinking (TTCT) is the most widely used test to ascertain a person's capacity to think of novel ideas and is the most reliable and valid measure of creativity available.[35]

If our creativity skills are diminishing, we are underutilizing the creative talents of the workforce.[36] Furthermore, there is little evidence to suggest that current education practices around the world focus on developing a creativity competency in students and future workers.

> According to Kim's research, all aspects of creativity have declined, but the biggest decline is in the measure called Creative Elaboration, which assesses the ability to take a particular idea and expand on it in an interesting and novel way. Between 1984 and 2008, the average Creative Elaboration score on the TTCT, for every age group from kindergarten through 12th grade, fell by more than 1 standard deviation. Stated differently, this means that more than 85% of children in 2008 scored lower on this measure than did the average child in 1984.[37]

Creativity and Ideation

Keith Sawyer, psychologist, jazz pianist, and former video game designer, is one of the world's leading experts on creativity. He notes, "The best way to come up with creative ideas is to come up with a lot of ideas."[38] Creative ideas are like buying lottery tickets: the more tickets you buy, the more likely you will succeed. A large proportion of the time you will fail.

Dean Keith Simonton is a distinguished professor of psychology at the University of California, Davis, and the author of *Genius, Creativity, and Leadership*. His research reveals a relationship between total lifetime quantity of works produced and creativity. Those who produce the highest quantity of works, such as published papers, are those who are the most creative, even though most of the papers published are never cited. For instance, Albert Einstein wrote 240 papers, of which only a few were viewed as having significant value.[39]

Innovation failures can themselves be valuable. In fact, they are often rationalized because you are learning something. "Thomas Edison, the American inventor, is synonymous with trial-and-error innovating. He would build a prototype, test it, and watch it go wrong, tweak the design and build another."[40] This model is in common use, but is there a better way to improve the brute force mentality to effectively innovate and be entrepreneurial?

While trial-and-error certainly has its place, these innovation and entrepreneurship iterations need to be focused on learning and the achievement of results. "It is easy to get carried away in the hunt for ideas: If you chase everything shiny and fast, you risk forgetting what you're seeking in the first place."[41]

The Innovation Power Number Law

To illustrate the complexities of creativity in practice, a tree serves as an interesting metaphor for innovation and entrepreneurship ideation. In the spring, the redbud tree produces bright and colorful reddish pink flowers. After the blossoms begin to disappear, many brown seedpods begin to emerge until they cover the entire tree interspersed between the deep-green, heart-shaped leaves.

Most of these seedpods never produce a new plant, and the ones that do take many years to grow because the walls of the seedpods are so hard. If the sunshine, temperature, moisture, carbon dioxide, and soil conditions are exactly right for the seed, a tree will grow. If the tree starts to grow, and it gets cut down, we will never know how beautiful it would have become. If the tree grows and we nurture it, it can become a most beautiful tree.

Thomas Edison used an iterative process of trial and error that revealed his remarkable solutions. He applied what could be called the "innovation power number law": it takes many ideas to generate a small number of high value results. By learning and understanding the creativity competencies, however, we can improve on this mining and extraction process.

Misleading Past Patterns

The patterns of our past decision-making shape our future decision-making and can result in the wrong choice. When we experience new situations, our mind will attempt to apply rules based on prior events to match the current context. There is a brain region called the dorsolateral prefrontal cortex (DLPFC) – think of it as the brain's "pattern seeker" – that searches for the extant patterns that can be applied to the new context to circumvent the chore of new learning.[42]

The decision-making process will first unfold in a way that reflects the need to overcome the imperatives of the patterns of experience, and the thinker will attempt to explore alternatives suggested in these patterns. The decision-maker may reach an impasse, "a state of mind that is accompanied by a subjective feeling of not knowing what to do and the cessation of overt problem-solving behaviour."[43]

In an experiment, subjects were given four types of matchstick arithmetic problems, each with a different rule set. "Once they got used to a rule, they were given a problem with another set of rules. So, to solve each new category of problem, they had to get out of the rut of the old way of thinking."[44] The matchsticks are used to form an incorrect equation consisting of roman numerals (I, II, etc.) and arithmetic operators (for example + and −). The participants would apply creativity to correct the equations by moving only one matchstick.[45]

- The problem: VI = VII + I and the solution VII = VI + I
- The problem: I = II + II and the solution I = III − II.
- The problem: III = III + III and the solution III = III = III
- The problem: XI = III + III and the solution VI = III + III.

The experiment revealed that people will apply their learned patterns to make sense of the present. "However, there is no guarantee that any particular extrapolation will succeed, and the complexity and the variability of the environment ensure that individuals will encounter problems and situations in which past experience is misleading."[46]

Your Creativity Machine

Creativity is a powerful competency. It can aid in uncovering truths and correcting misperceptions about others, our environment, and ourselves. Creativity is a multidimensional and interesting phenomenon involving the heart (passion), mind (thinking), and brain (physicality). One way to look at the creativity process is to think of the mind as the software and the brain as the hardware. The mind can be activated through training and practice, and the brain sustained and improved through exercise, diet, and sleep. Creativity does not reside in one place, but rather is the outcome of multiple functions (e.g., heart, mind, and brain) all working together.

As reporter Karen Weintraub notes from her interviews with Shelley Carson, Harvard lecturer and author of *Your Creative Brain*, and Bruce Adolphe, composer-in-residence at the Brain and Creativity Institute, creativity does not live in one spot. Creative potential is not solely on the right side or the left side of your brain or creativity machine. Rather, your creativity machine is a system with a cooperating set of subsystems that integrate your mind and brain.[47] As in all systems, optimum use requires that all parts operate in harmony.

Activating Your Creativity

Gordon MacKenzie was an artist at Hallmark cards who was concerned that the level of bureaucracy at Hallmark constrained creativity. How are new ideas generated and problems solved in a culture that encourages outdated behaviors and imagination? MacKenzie wondered if under-achievement occurred due to a lack or loss of imagination.

MacKenzie visited schools and did demonstrations about the craft of steel sculpture. As he proceeded from the first grade to the sixth, he would ask, "How many artists are in the room? Would you please raise your hands?"[48] The pattern remained the same. There were many hands raised in the lower grades and fewer in the upper grades; the number of hands raised was in inverse proportion to the grade level.

MacKenzie uses a Hairball as a metaphor for how corporations grow and constrain creativity. He writes, "Intricate patterns of effective behaviour have grown around the lessons of success, and failure, creating a Gordian knot of Corporate Normalcy (i.e., conformity with the 'accepted model, pattern or standard' of the corporate mind set)."[49] When culture constrains, people can get sent away, people go away voluntarily, or people can orbit the Hairball by learning how to discover ways to benefit from the corporate resources but not get stymied by the bureaucracy.

"Creativity can be cultivated through curiosity, training and specific exercises designed to foster the imagination," notes composer and musician Bruce Adolphe. "Our schools, however, often stifle creativity instead of promoting it," he says. Creativity can be inhibited through rote memorization and overemphasis on testing.[50] In contrast, creativity can be taught, learned, and practiced. British author, speaker, and international advisor on education in the arts, Sir Ken Robinson, believes that education systems drain creative skills from students. Further revealing the deepening divide and need to close the creativity education gap, Sir Robinson notes, "My contention is that creativity now is as important in education as literacy, and we should treat it with the same status."[51] According to Sir Robinson, we have educated ourselves out of our imaginations.[52] "We are educating ourselves out of creativity."[53] His stark conclusion is that we are underutilizing our imagination and our creative talent.[54]

Creativity is a linchpin concept. According to Bruce Nussbaum, author of *Creative Intelligence: Harnessing the Power to Create, Connect, and Inspire*, "Creativity drives capitalism."[55] In essence, creative insights are the source that leads to innovation of all types and degrees that have the potential to generate the highest economic value. Business efficiencies that are built from science, technology, engineering, and mathematics are important, but they will not necessarily result in the economic growth to sustain jobs and a viable standard of living in a hyper-competitive economy.

Our future creative economy requires a set of innovation competencies. Within these innovation competencies, there is an emphasis on the importance of creativity, especially as a driver of innovation and entrepreneurship. While start-ups are a large source of new jobs, large and less agile organizations must also work to build subcultures that promote creativity simultaneously with operational efficiencies that focus on speeding up tasks, removing waste, and preventing defects. (See also Toyota Production System innovation behaviors, such as *pokayoke* in Chapters 4, "Innovative Behaviors," and 7, "Knowledge Building.") Schools need to provide enriched curriculums based less on learning how to take tests and more on learning how to be a problem finder and definer, and then how to apply the innovation and entrepreneurship competencies.

Creativity Research

Research has discovered several insights about creative thought, including the role of nature versus nurture, brain dynamism, sleep, and whole-, right-, and left-brain considerations.

Nature or Nurture

We can learn to be creative; research studies involving creativity have found that nurture is more important than nature in this regard. A collection of studies suggests that two-thirds, or 67%, of our creativity skills come through learning, while only 25–40% of what we do innovatively has been shown to be determined by genetics.[56]

Moreover, a research study of 117 pairs of identical and fraternal twins aged 15 to 22 was conducted to determine the effect of genetics on creativity. The conclusion is that only about 30% of the performance of identical twins on a set of ten creativity tests could be attributed to genetics.[57]

Brain Dynamism

In the past, brain researchers thought that the brain was fixed and did not grow and develop new neurons. This outmoded thinking has since been reversed. Recent research has demonstrated that neurogenesis, the birth of neurons, does indeed continue into adult life.[58] Understanding that the brain is dynamic, and not static as previously thought, provides interesting opportunities for the role of creativity in innovation and entrepreneurship.

An example of the dynamic nature of the brain is the discovery of a significant inverse relationship between vision and hearing. This phenomenon, which could benefit those with hearing loss, has been observed in specific individuals, such as musicians and entertainers Ray Charles and Stevie Wonder, who lacked eyesight but had exceptional powers of hearing. If you simulate a loss of vision, the brain may compensate and augment another sense, hearing. Research done by Dr. Hey-Kyoung Lee, associate professor of neuroscience at Johns Hopkins University, and biologist Patrick Kanold at the University of Maryland, College Park, demonstrated this relationship.[59]

> The findings, which are published in the journal *Neuron*, show that adult mice who spend one week in complete darkness display a significant increase in their ability to respond to sounds. Compared to a control group that spent the same period in a naturally lit environment, these mice developed more complex nerve circuitry in the primary auditory cortex, the brain area that processes sounds.[60]

"The brain's many regions are connected by some 100,000 miles of fibers called white matter, enough to circle the Earth four times."[61] Each time something new is learned, a physical change occurs in the brain by forming a new connection between neurons. The human brain has a huge number of specialized connections with other cells known as synapses. For each of the 100 billion neurons, there are an average 10,000 synaptic connections to other neurons.[62]

This connection or phenomenon is like what has been called a runner's high. Researchers have shown that there is a relationship between exercise and the brain. "Running does elicit a flood of endorphins in the brain. The endorphins are associated with mood changes, and the more endorphins a runner's body pumps out, the greater the effect."[63]

A practical way to improve your creative thinking is through physical exercise and diet. If you maintain a healthy lifestyle your brain will function at a higher level. There is even a body of research that indicates that exercise improves creativity. Marily Oppezzo and Daniel Schwartz conducted four studies that demonstrated an increase in creative ideation from walking.

> The effect is not simply due to the increased perceptual stimulation of moving through an environment," they write, "but rather it is due to walking. Whether one is outdoors or on a treadmill, walking improves the generation of novel yet appropriate ideas, and the effect even extends to when people sit down to do their creative work shortly after.[64]

Exercise provides more blood flow to the brain, which has the effect of boosting intellectual performance. Nutrition ensures that all of your body's systems have the resources to function optimally.

In his book *Brain Rules*, molecular biologist John Medina describes how the brain works and how you can improve cognition.[65] The first brain rule is that exercise boosts brain power.

- The human brain evolved under conditions of almost constant motion. From this, one might predict that the optimal environment for processing information would include motion. That is exactly what one finds. Indeed, the best business meeting would have everyone walking at about 1.8 miles per hour.
- Researchers studied two elderly populations that had led different lifestyles, one sedentary and one active. Cognitive scores were profoundly influenced. Exercise positively affected executive function, spatial tasks, reaction times and quantitative skills.
- So researchers asked, if the sedentary populations become active, will their cognitive scores go up? Yes, it turns out, if the exercise is aerobic. Within four months of aerobic exercise, executive functions and memory scores improve.

Exercise improves cognition for two reasons:

- Exercise increases oxygen flow into the brain which reduces brain-bound free radicals. One of the most interesting findings of the past few decades is that an increase in oxygen is always accompanied by an uptick in mental sharpness.
- Exercise acts directly on the molecular machinery of the brain itself. It increases neurons' creation, survival, and resistance to damage and stress.[66]

Ultimately, each individual needs to take responsibility for their own health. Unique solutions that use social networks and gaming encourage individuals to change their behaviors by focusing on shared goals. Employees form teams with their colleagues, work together to collaborate on their goals, and they earn points providing reinforcement. The team with the most points wins the challenge.

A study by Damon Centola of MIT revealed that social gaming networks that are used for wellness programs have been shown to be effective in improving the health of the participants. "The results show that individual adoption was much more likely when participants received social reinforcement from multiple neighbors in the social network."[67]

Furthermore, a study reported by Keas, a firm that provides a number of employee-wellness programs, found that "[p]eople who reported weight loss shed an average of 5.5 pounds, and the proportion of people eating vegetables and fruits doubled from 37 to 73 percent. Half the employee participants said they were more physically active."[68]

What about creativity impacting your health? John Mirowsky and Catherine E. Ross found that employees that can be creative in their work enjoy better health. These health benefits are equal to or exceed the effects associated with education and income.[69]

Sleep Sustains Your Creativity

Most people do not realize that your human brain is running 24 hours a day, even while you sleep. You cannot turn your brain off. Studies of rats and baboons have revealed that during sleep the brain goes through a cleaning cycle like a dishwasher. During sleep, the brain cells shrink, increasing the space between the cells. The flow of the cerebrospinal fluid between the cells increases, washing away cellular waste, such as beta-amyloid. The presence of beta-amyloid, a plaque-like substance, is associated with dementia. Since sleep disorders are associated with dementia, it is plausible to conclude that inadequate sleep is related to brain damage.[70]

Your brain works especially hard during sleep, processing your ideas and solving your problems with no explicit effort on your part. Many "busy" people feel that they can get more done by shortening their sleep hours when it is more likely that they will get less done. Sleep improves your performance, memory, and learning.[71]

An incubation period, slack time, where a person leaves an idea for a while and returns to it later is crucial to creativity. "Dr. Ellenbogen's research at Harvard indicates that if an incubation period includes sleep, people are 33 percent more likely to infer connections among distantly related ideas, and yet, as he puts it, these performance enhancements exist 'completely beneath the radar screen.'"[72]

Whole Brain (Right or Left)

It is generally believed that creativity is a whole-brain activity rather than being dominated by either the left or right hemisphere of the brain. In a study to determine the effect of unilateral muscle contractions on the right hemisphere, the Remotes Associates Test was given to 40 people.[73] In the Remote Associates Test, subjects are given three words and asked to provide a fourth. Fifteen of the people were asked to squeeze a rubber ball with their left hand, fifteen people were asked to squeeze a ball with their right hand, and ten people did not squeeze a ball at all. The highest test scores were from the left-hand squeezer group (that activates the right side of the brain) and the lowest scores were from the right-hand squeezer group (that activates the left side of the brain).[74] The study has implications regarding the validity of the whole brain theory.

The Continuing Importance of Creativity

How important is creativity? In April 2013, Penn Schoen Berland conducted an online survey about creativity in the workplace, schools, and government among 2,040 US adult consumers for the Motion Picture Association of America, Microsoft, and *Time* magazine.[75] The results were quite interesting and clearly point to the continuing importance of creativity in general and creativity in the workforce in particular. In fact, when asked the value of six characteristics in others, creativity came out on top at 94%, followed by intelligence (93%), compassion (92%), humor (89%), ambition (88%), and beauty (57%). Moreover, 91% indicated creativity's importance in their personal lives, and 83% in their professional lives. For example, when it comes to creativity and the economy, slightly greater than seven in ten respondents say the current economic situation makes creativity more important. While slightly over eight in ten think the United States should be considered a global leader in creativity, among those who say the United States is not the current world leader in creativity, 31% say schools are not building creativity in students, 30%

think government is not doing enough to support creativity, 17% indicate businesses don't value creativity enough, and 8% say workers do not have the tools needed to be creative. Moreover, 55% reported that technology is making people more creative, and 62% say creativity is more important to success in the workplace than they anticipated it would be when they were in school.[76]

The role of technology, schools, and government notwithstanding, the question remains, what is it about creativity that we need to know in order to foster its use in innovation and entrepreneurship? In the next sections, we examine creativity archetypes (fine arts, drama and film, sports and ballet, design and architecture, and science, engineering, and technology) commonly seen in our lives and workplace and introduce the five creativity competencies (playing, associations, choosing, making, and pivoting).

Creativity Types

There are many creativity types beyond products and services. The creativity types include writing, music, and art; photography, painting, drama, and film; sports and dance; design and architecture; and science, engineering, and technology. The creativity types are shown in Figure 8.1.

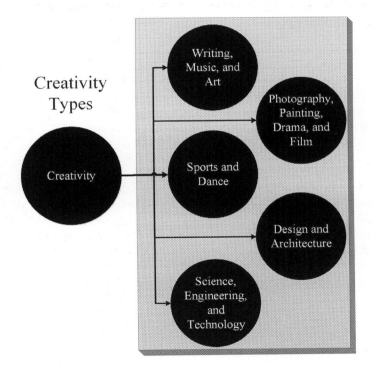

Figure 8.1 Illustration of Creativity Types

Fine Arts

On the surface, certain disciplines appear to be more amenable to creativity than others. For example, fine arts, such as writing, music, art, photography, painting, drama, and film, all lend themselves to the creative side of individuals and practices. Michelangelo's creative genius is apparent in his many sculptures and paintings. The creative voices and personas of stage actors, such as Sir Laurence

Olivier, stand as exemplars of creativity on stage and screen. Yet, upon closer examination, while each of these arts certainly relies on elements of creativity, each also has a structure and a discipline. For example, photography has evolved from primarily a chemical-based, silver-halide-driven process to the world of digital imagery. It epitomizes what Nicholas Negroponte identified in his 1995 book, *Being Digital*, as the transformation from an *atom*-based world to a *bit*-based world.[77] As such, it has transformed the entire value chain of inputs, throughputs, and outputs in virtually every industry. We are no longer bound by physicality, but unbounded by the virtual realm. The new nexus of creativity and discipline evolves from changes throughout the value chain.

Sports and Dance

Sports and dance have had an intriguing intersection over the years. In fact, football players from amateur to professional have often looked to ballet to improve their skills and game. Lynn Swann, Pittsburgh Steeler and Hall-of-Famer, credits his ballet training with substantially improving his athletic skills. He notes that ballet and football have a lot in common, not the least of which is the need for flexibility, strength, precision, and control.[78]

Classical ballet has been compared to high-intensity training and sports but with an artistic flair. Once again, we see the conundrum of the relationship between creativity and structure. From the sports side of the house, there would appear to be little room for creativity. Rules, guidelines, best practices, and more seem to restrict any creative license in the practice of the sport. Yet, over the years, we have seen this seeming conundrum result in advances in sport as we know it today. In American football in 1913, the forward pass was a novelty; today it is standard operating procedure at all levels of football. The forward pass was not against the rules; it just had not been done before.[79] Innovation in sports and dance share a common thread, creativity born of the careful balance of trying something new within the established norms of practice.

Design and Architecture

Nowhere can the nexus of creativity and practice, the new and the established, be seen more clearly than in design and architecture. Design cries out for creative elements, bold vision, and daring steps. Architecture, on the other hand, while not opposed to creativity, relies on the structural integrity of the object or program being built. While the term *architecture* conjures up images of skyscrapers and bridges, its meaning is much broader, from landscape architecture to computer language architecture to skyscrapers and everything in between. Creativity in design and architecture, as we see in all the creative types, relies on both vision and knowledge. Fueled by imagination and vision, tempered by science and practice, design and architecture push the envelope, moving the needle toward new innovations in product, process, and more.

Science, Engineering, and Technology

While the fine arts that were outlined at the beginning of this section obviously lend themselves to creativity, one might think that science, engineering, and technology would not be open to creativity. Appearances can be deceptive. In reality, creativity plays a key role in these fields. Once again, we find ourselves at the intersection of knowing and imagining. As French scientist Louis Pasteur once noted, "Chance favors the prepared mind."[80] That is, sudden flashes of brilliance or insight do not just happen. Rather, they emerge from a base of knowledge, connections, discovery, experimentation, and more. Gestalt psychology's central theme is that the mind organizes patterns and objects so that many parts can often seem whole or more than the whole. What seems like an "aha" or "eureka" moment is really the culmination of many simultaneous connections or patterns coming into focus. Such is the role of creativity in science, engineering, and technology. Creativity, in part, is developing a receptiveness or openness to change or advancement of thought beyond current practices.

Creativity Competencies

Creativity is a process that includes the following interactive competencies: serious playing, associations, choosing, making, and pivoting. Creativity is a dynamic, interactive process that can be improved through deliberate practice and adds to an overall personal competency bank account. The creativity competencies are illustrated in Figure 8.2.

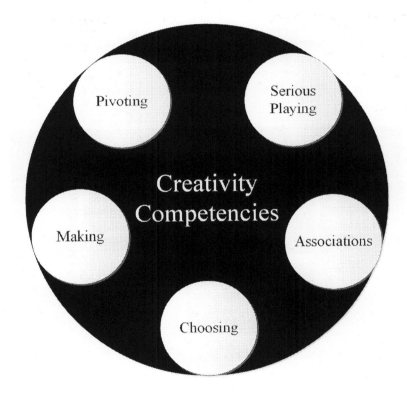

Figure 8.2 Illustration of Creativity Competencies

Serious Playing

Look back in time. Do you remember playing with a Slinky or a Rubik's Cube? Perhaps your imagination was triggered by playing with Lego building toys, whole toy systems created by Playmobile, or perhaps classic wooden blocks. "Playing is not just kid stuff; it's a complex behaviour that is driving the creation of life-altering technologies and companies," Bruce Nussbaum argues in *Creative Intelligence*. "By adopting a more playful mind-set we're more willing to take risks, explore possibilities, and learn to navigate uncertainty."[81]

Robert McKim founded Stanford's interdisciplinary product-design program, which combines engineering, art, science, and psychology.[82] McKim developed a multiple-circle visual exercise, designed to improve your ability to generate ideas.[83] The instructions are to draw as many pictures inside the circles as you can in one minute.

"The creative life is filled with play – the kind of unstructured activity that children engage in for the sheer joy of it," Keith Sawyer writes in *Zig Zag*. "You free your mind for imagination and fantasy, letting your unconscious lead you into unchartered territory. You envision how things might be; you create alternate worlds in your mind. 'The debt we owe to the play of imagination,' Carl Jung wrote, 'is incalculable.'"[84]

What memories do you have of playing as a child? What was it like to be able to have the freedom to play and try new things? What was it like to try a new toy, or the box the toy came out of? Sometimes the cardboard box was more fun than the toy! Remember your trips out on Halloween when you pretended to be some character like Snow White, Darth Vader, or Harry Potter? What would it be like to relive those experiences?

An effective way of improving your creativity is by relaxing and building an incubation period into your life. This can be done by getting enough sleep to refresh your brain, by exercising, and by letting your mind wander.[85] When you feel like your mind is wandering, it is probably working on your problems for you.[86] Serious playing is summarized in Figure 8.3.

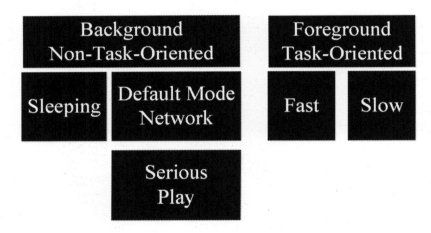

Figure 8.3 Illustration of the Serious Play Thinking Mode

A team of scientists worked for ten years to discover the molecular structure of a protein-cutting enzyme that plays a key role in the spread of AIDS. A game known as Foldit was crowdsourced to allow players to understand and unravel the problem using virtual molecular structures. A team of players known as the Foldit Contenders was able to figure it out in ten days.[87]

Combinatorial play, the Power of And, is a way to generate ideas and creativity insights.

- Einstein said, "Imagination is more important than knowledge."[88] To trigger your imagination, start with changing your perspective by choosing to learn something new that allows you to break away from what you are doing. This could be watching a movie, performing a sport, listening to music, playing a musical instrument, reading a book, meeting new people, or taking a vacation.

- Doing something that is fun and low-risk will let your mind wander and provide you with a clarity of thinking. For instance, Einstein attributed his scientific insight and intuition mainly to music. When he was confronted with a difficult challenge, he would turn to music.[89] Einstein said, "If I were not a physicist, I would probably be a musician. I often think in music. I live my daydreams in music. I see my life in terms of music. . . . I cannot tell if I would have done any creative work of importance in music, but I do know that I get most joy in life out of my violin."[90]
- Allow your mind to combine ideas, generating more ideas that you were not expecting. Einstein said, "Combinatory play seems to be the essential feature in productive thought."[91] Your mind will associate disparate ideas and stumble upon solutions that were otherwise hidden. "Celebrated creators – artists, writers, scientists, inventors – have always known the power of the synthesizing mind and have advocated for embracing the building blocks of combinatorial creativity."[92]

Arthur Koestler named this concept "bisociation" to describe the blending of elements drawn from two previously unrelated matrices of thought into a new matrix of meaning by way of a process involving comparison, abstraction and categorization, analogies, and metaphors.[93] "Einstein famously attributed some of his greatest physics breakthroughs to his violin breaks, which he believed connected different parts of his brain in new ways."[94]

Associations

In an inductive, grounded-theory study of innovative entrepreneurs, the findings suggest that the number one cognitive skill of innovation is associating.[95] That is, it is the associations (connections) that are important. Xerox PARC is credited with many technology innovations:

> Founded in 1970 as a division of Xerox Corporation, PARC has been responsible for such well known and important developments as laser printing, Ethernet, the modern personal computer, graphical user interface (GUI), object-oriented programming, ubiquitous computing, amorphous silicon (a-Si) applications, and advancing very-large-scale-integration (VLSI) for semiconductors.[96]

But Xerox was unable to convert their many technological developments and significant inventions into successful commercial innovations. It took Steve Jobs to observe and make the connections to apply the graphical user interface concept to successful market solutions that were implemented in the Macintosh personal computer.[97] The concept of idea association is shown in Figure 8.4.

"You're not born with a great ability to connect dots," writes Nussbaum. "You learn it. Some of us learn it in school, some at jobs, and others in life. It's not a difficult competence, but it is a deliberate one."[98] A practical example of associations is citation analysis. Citation analysis is a method to evaluate the impact of research through explicit linkages between related journal articles. A citation index uses these explicit linkages to derive a measurement that assesses the importance of a publication or journal article. There is a variety of services that provide citation metrics, including Thomson Reuters Web of Science, established by Eugene Garfield in the 1960s; Scopus, introduced by Elsevier in 2004; and Google Scholar, introduced in 2004.[99]

Sawyer writes,

> Creative minds are always bouncing ideas together, looking for unexpected combinations. Successful creativity never comes from a single idea. It always comes from any ideas in combination,

whether we recognize them or not. The creative life doesn't box its concepts into separate compartments; it fuses and re-fuses them.[100]

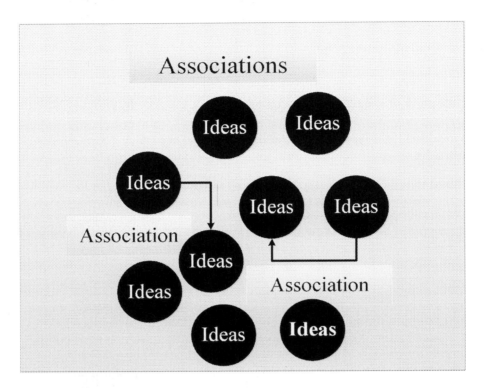

Figure 8.4 Illustration of Idea Associations

The big idea for Google came from creating a new association: "Google cofounder Larry Page created an odd combination by connecting two seemingly unrelated ideas – academic citations with Web search – to launch Google."[101] Larry Page and Sergey Brin wanted to change the world by organizing all of the information on the web in a way that would make it more useful. So they built the world's greatest search engine based on a simple association. "As a PhD student at Stanford, Page knew that academic journals and publishing companies rank scholars by the cumulative number of citations each scholar gets each year."[102] Larry Page and Sergey Brin decided to download the entire web and then look for patterns in the linkages. They discovered from the large dataset that they could use web page linkages to determine the viability of a targeted web page. They noticed that behind each targeted web page, there were web pages that are linked to it, known as backlinks. The more backlinks the more popular the target web page. The insight was that the backlinks could be used for rankings.

Page realized that Google could rank websites in the same way that academic citations rank scholars; Websites with the most links (that were most frequently selected) had more citations. This association allowed Page and cofounder Sergey Brin to launch a search engine yielding far superior search results.[103]

Medici Effect

In Florence Italy, around the 14th century, the Medici banking family funded a large number of artistic endeavors, phenomenally advancing the arts. During this period of history, there was a coalescence of ideas that had a multiplying effect known as the Medici effect.[104] Michelangelo Buonarroti's many achievements included the painting of the ceiling of the Sistine Chapel and sculpting both *David* and *Pieta*.[105]

The Medici effect was a synergistic result of a confluence of ideas, cultures, and disciplines brought together through association. The research discussed in *The Innovator's DNA* shows that "[e]very high-profile innovator excelled at associating (scoring at the 70th percentile or higher in the innovators' DNA assessment), with process inventors showing slightly less associational skill than other inventors (yet still more than non-innovators)."[106]

Something Old, Something New, Something Borrowed

You do not have to create something entirely new. What is right in front of you, such as your experiences, expertise, and observations, is often an excellent starting point. According to Andrew Hargadon, innovation is more about making connections with existing elements that are already in place rather than making new elements.[107] Innovation is not only about discovering the new biological advancements by getting the right people in the right labs and letting them work through experiments. Innovation is bringing ideas forward in different contexts. Innovation is taking pieces that are already out there and finding new ways to put them together. Innovation is synthesizing, organizing, and recombining known actionable insights and elements by moving these insights and elements from where they are known to where they are unknown.[108] Viagra was used originally as an intervention for angina, but the pharmaceutical failed in clinical trials. Pfizer then had to figure out why the patients refused to return the samples. It turned out that the "side effects" could be marketed for a completely different purpose.[109]

Choosing

Choosing is the process of prioritizing the creative ideas that have value to progress forward.

> A creative life is lived in balance, held steady by the constant tension between uncritical, wide-open idea generation (brainstorming, done right) and critical examination and editing. Choosing is essential, because not all ideas and combinations are ideal for any purpose. The key is to use the right criteria to critique them, so you can cull the best and discard any that would prove inferior, awkward, or a waste of your time.[110]

Using the right criteria requires a sense of discipline to eliminate what is not important and stick to what is important. The criteria for choosing should include the job to be done by the consumer, the vitality of the business model, and the realistic use of technology. These three criteria become competing constraints in the quest for innovations. Creativity choices that are both highly feasible and useful as well as original and breakthrough can have the biggest impact. A model of how to make effective choices is shown in Figure 8.5.

In *Great by Choice*, Jim Collins and Morten T. Hansen study a set of companies that demonstrate extraordinary performance, known as the 10Xers. The 10Xers have shareholder returns at least ten times greater than the comparison companies. The study compares the 10Xers, Amgen, Biomet, Intel, Microsoft, Progressive Insurance, Southwest Airlines, and Stryker, to Genentech,

Kirschner, AMD, Apple, Safeco, PSA, and United States Surgical. Based on their research, Collins and Hansen identify four distinguishing characteristics of great leaders: fanatic discipline, empirical creativity, productive paranoia, and ambition.[111]

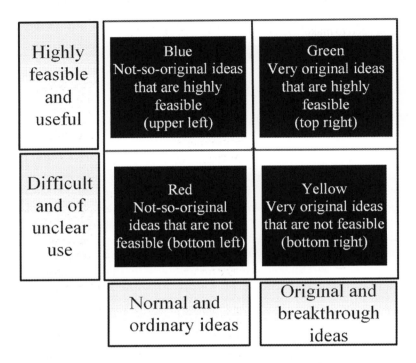

Figure 8.5 Illustration of the Creativity Quadrants for Choosing

Source: Adapted from Keith R. Sawyer, *Zig zag: The surprising path to greater creativity*, (San Francisco, California: John Wiley & Sons, 2013), 181.

Copyright ©.

Fanatic Discipline: The 20 Mile March

In *Great by Choice,* the 10Xers were guided by the 20 Mile March concept. The 20 Mile March requires meeting stepwise performance metrics that enable you to make disciplined choices. The concept is derived from Roald Amudsen's 1,400-mile hike to the South Pole, which he and his men completed by travelling 20 miles per day, and never more.

> The 20 Mile March is more than a philosophy. It's about having concrete, clear, intelligent, and rigorously pursued performance mechanisms that keep you on track. The 20 Mile March creates two types of self-imposed discomfort: (1) The discomfort of unwavering commitment to high performance in difficult conditions, and (2) the discomfort of holding back in good conditions.[112]

Making

The making competency is a successor to experimenting, one of the innovative behavior competencies. Experimenting can be viewed as the building of low-resolution prototypes through sketches, paper and masking tape models, or storyboards. The experimenting competency precedes making something. The combination of experimenting and making enables individuals and organizations to evolve and develop into the future.

Experimenting is achieved using an iterative process of refining and improving the working model to ensure that it is fit for use and fulfills the triple criteria: customer desirability, business viability, and technology feasibility. "In the creative life," Keith Sawyer explains, "it's not enough to just 'have' ideas. You need to make good ideas a reality. You continually externalize your thoughts – and not just the polished, finished ones. Making – a draft, drawing, a prototype, a plan – helps you fuse your ideas, choose among them, and build on what you like."[113] Experimenting allows you to fine-tune your low-resolution ideas. The interactions of making are shown in Figure 8.6.

Figure 8.6 Illustration of the Making Process

In making, you transition from low-resolution to high-resolution prototypes. Outsourcing and offshoring the making of products has been a trend to keep costs low. An assortment of changes is underway that could reduce this momentum and increase re-shoring. Three-dimensional printing and robotics have increased opportunities for cost-effective product manufacturing and mass customization. Crowdfunding has provided an alternative for start-ups to locate financial resources. The cloud has enabled start-ups to scale through the use of e-business infrastructure services provided by PayPal, Amazon, and Etsy. Social media, such as Facebook, LinkedIn, and Twitter, allow businesses to reach out to other entrepreneurs as well as customers for support and resources. Eco-entrepreneurs are interested in local markets and products to revitalize their neighborhoods and minimize the use of resources through recycling and reducing transportation costs.

Empirical Creativity: Firing Bullets, Not Cannonballs

Experimenting is an innovative behavior that can be viewed as early learning about an innovation. Making uses the results of experimenting but increases the fidelity of the prototype.

Making incorporates the knowledge gained from applying empirical creativity. Collins and Hansen write,

> When faced with uncertainty, 10Xers do not look primarily to other people, conventional wisdom, authority figures, or peers for direction; they look primarily to empirical evidence. 10Xers rely upon direct observation, practical experimentation, and direct engagement with tangible evidence. They make their bold, creative moves from a sound empirical base.[114]

Empirical creativity is the firing of metaphorical bullets instead of uncalibrated cannon balls. Leaders have a choice to make when building something new. Should they use metaphorically light, focused bullets first, or get distracted using a heavy cannonball first to explore new ideas? According to Collins and Hansen, you are better off collecting empirical data to test your creativity assumptions using precisely focused bullets. The disciplined approach would be to use bullets first because they are low-risk, low-cost, easy to produce, and easy to shoot. If what you learn from firing bullets is viable, then you shoot the cannonball. In Chapter 17, "Applying Innovation Processes," there is a description of making in more detail.

Pivoting

Pivoting, when used in relation to entrepreneurship, generally refers to a change in strategy or direction brought about by the ongoing search for the solution to a problem that adds value for potential customers. Sometimes the pivot is the result of early customer feedback. Pivoting occurs when individuals and organizations sense there is a need for change, and the time is right to take the risk and change direction. Evel Knievel was an American icon who took great risks with his own life as he completed ramp-to-ramp motorcycle jumps over increasingly more difficult objects and geographic challenges. Knievel was a successful entertainer in many ways, with one notable exception: his jumps resulted in his having 433 broken bones over his career, placing him in the *Guinness Book of World Records*.[115] When you pivot, the expectation is to land successfully. The key, of course, is to make the pivot without breaking too many bones. The key element of the creativity pivot is shown in Figure 8.7.

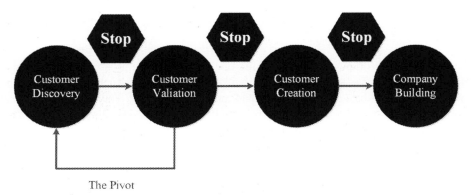

The Pivot

Figure 8.7 Illustration of the Creativity Pivot

Source: Adapted from Steve Blank, *The Four Steps to the Epiphany: Successful Strategies for Products that Win*, (3rd ed.), (Menlo Park: K&S Ranch Publishing LLC, 2013).

A pivot is a specific type of change to test a new hypothesis about creating a new strategy. Eric Ries in *The Lean Startup: How Today's Entrepreneurs Use Continuous Innovation to Create*

Radically Successful Businesses describes ten types of pivots, as can be seen in Figure 8.8.[116] You can use an engine of growth pivot, like that used by Facebook as it transitioned from a start-up to a broad social media product. You can use a zoom-out pivot by selling your business to a larger platform, such as when Google purchased YouTube or when eBay purchased Elon Musk's PayPal.

---

1. Zoom-in Pivot

A zoom-in pivot is a change from a single feature in a product that becomes the whole product.

2. Zoom-out Pivot

A zoom-out pivot is a change where a whole product becomes a single feature of a larger product.

3. Customer Segment Pivot

A customer segment pivot is a change from the original customer to a different customer.

4. Customer Need Pivot

A customer need pivot is a change from a former customer problem to a new customer problem.

5. Platform Pivot

A platform pivot refers to a change from an application to a platform or from a platform to an application.

6. Business Architecture Pivot

A business architecture pivot is when a startup switches architectures. A business architecture is a complex system model (high margin, low volume) or a volume operations model (low margin, high volume).

7. Value Capture Pivot

A value capture pivot is a change to how a company creates value.

8. Engine of Growth Pivot

An engine of growth pivot is a change in pacing to achieve faster or more profitable growth.

9. Channel Pivot

A channel pivot is a change to the way a company delivers its solution to customers.

10. Technology Pivot

A technology pivot is a change to a completely different technology to achieve the same solution.

Figure 8.8 Illustration of Pivot Types

Source: Adapted from Eric Ries, *The Lean Startup: How Today's Entrepreneurs Use Continuous Innovation to Create Radically Successful Businesses*, (New York: Crown Business, 2011).

Productive Paranoia: Leading Above the Death Line

Entrepreneurs need to embrace the possibility that there are dangers on the horizon, whether they pivot or not. Without making a pivot, you could fail. Inaction is behind the theory of disruptive innovation.[117] Whether you pivot or persevere, you are making a risk decision. Pivoting is a competence because the entrepreneur must always be aware that the world is turbulent and business conditions change. As Collins and Hansen write,

> 10Xers differ from their less successful comparison in how they maintain hyper vigilance in good times as well as bad. Even in calm, clear, positive conditions, 10Xers constantly consider the possibility that events could turn against them at any moment. Indeed, they believe that conditions will – absolutely, with 100 percent certainty – turn against them without warning, at some unpredictable point in time, at some highly inconvenient moment. And they'd better be prepared.[118]

Classical Model of Creativity

In 1924, Graham Wallas wrote *The Art of Thought*, describing a four-step creativity process.[119] His creative process steps are preparation, incubation, illumination, and verification.

- In the preparation stage, the problem is investigated in all directions. You begin by asking questions and making observations. You gather ideas, data, and information to build up your knowledge resources. You frame the problem to define a boundary around the problem.
- In the incubation stage the problem is at rest where no direct effort is expended. "The best ideas come while you're taking a long hot shower, going for a walk, or on vacation. Here, self-mastery comes from knowing when to let go, and knowing that you need to let go."[120]
- In the illumination stage there is an actionable insight that appears like that of the winning alignment of a slot machine.
- Finally, in the verification stage there is a conscious effort to create an explicit implementation. This could be a working model or a prototype.[121]

The middle two unconscious steps are sandwiched between two conscious steps, but it is important to understand that these are not progressive, linear steps. Wallas writes, "In the daily stream of thought these four different states constantly overlap each other as we explored different problems."[122]

Daniel Goleman, author of *Emotional Intelligence*, writing for *Psychology Today*, describes three examples:[123]

> George Lucas, for example, says that when he has to write a script or review one, he goes to a cottage behind his house, and just writes. Does he ever just let go into a reverie and see what comes to him? "No," he says, "I have to keep working all the time." That's how one creative genius works (but I suspect he has uniquely fluent creative circuitry).
>
> The second creative genius I talked to about this was the composer Phil Glass, one of the world's most renowned contemporary composers. I asked him, "When do you get your creative ideas?" His answer surprised me. He said, "I know exactly when they're going to come: Between 11 a.m. and 3 p.m. That's when I work on my new compositions."
>
> More usual though, might be a third creative expert I talked to: Adrienne Weiss, a woman who does product branding. She had an assignment to help rebrand the global ice cream shop chain Baskin-Robbins, including coming up with a fresh logo. She asked herself, "Well, what do we have? Baskin-Robbins is famous for its 31 flavors. How are we going to make that into something new and distinctive?" After getting nowhere just by thinking about this, one night

as she was sleeping, she woke up from a dream in which she saw the name "Baskin-Robbins." Highlighted in the loop of the "B" in Baskin was a "3," and in the stem of the "R" was a "1." That's "31," the number of their flavors. If you look at the new logo of Baskin-Robbins, you'll see that 31 pop out of the B and the R. And it came to her in a dream.[124]

Creativity Methods

Creativity Tests

Mednick developed the remote associates test in 1962, to assess creative potential.[125] Subjects are given three words and asked to provide a fourth word that is related. For example:

- If you are given the words *cream*, *skate*, and *water*, the correct response would be *ice*.
- If you are given the words *flower*, *friend*, and *scout*, the correct response would be *girl*.
- If you are given the words *stick*, *maker*, and *point*, the correct response would be *match*.[126]
- If you are given the words *rat*, *blue*, and *cottage*, the correct response would be *cheese*.
- If you are given the words *railroad*, *girl*, and *class*, the correct response would be *working*.
- If you are given the words *surprise*, *line*, and *birthday*, the correct response would be *party*.[127]

Guilford developed the alternative uses test. The alternative uses test stretches your creativity by giving you two minutes to think of as many uses as possible for an everyday object, like a paper clip, chair, coffee mug, or brick.[128]

Creativity Reversals

As we have seen throughout this chapter, creativity is a skill that can be taught and learned. "The fact is, creativity is a human aptitude, like intelligence, musical ability, or eye-hand coordination," Gary Hamel writes. "Like any other aptitude, it can be strengthened through instruction and practice."[129] Creativity tools can be useful in stimulating new ways of thinking.

Consider the reversal, an example of a creative thinking technique that looks at a problem in reverse or backward. In the book and movie *Pay It Forward*, instead of paying people back for something they have done for you, you pay the "debt" forward to someone else, often a complete stranger. Someone does a kindness for you, and then you do something positive for three other people. Those three people do something positive for three different people. Then those nine do something positive for three different people each, and then those 27 do something positive for three more people each, and so forth.[130]

In another example from the fine arts, in the movie *Night at The Museum*, instead of a Museum of Natural History full of dead animals and people, an ancient curse causes the animals and exhibits on display to come to life.[131] Traditionally, creative concepts have been introduced in movies and then licensed to toy manufacturers for toy making. Hasbro, however, reversed the model, by starting with toy making and then working with movie studios to create films based on the toys.[132] Figure 8.9 identifies reversal examples.

Social Network Analysis

Social network analysis studies relationships between people that can be useful in discovering associations and developing new innovations. Social network analysis, when combined with large datasets, is growing in popularity because it has the potential to make interpretations about what might lead to certain behaviors or outcomes. For instance, the US government is using electronic records of various types (such as phone records) to predict security threats.[133]

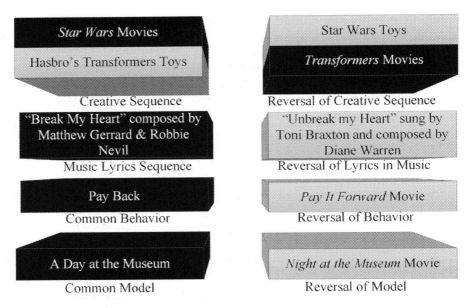

Figure 8.9 Illustration of the Reversal Examples

There are many different types of social networks, including social, professional, multimedia, and educational.[134] Facebook is a repository of social data that has the potential to provide information about all types of personal relationships, as well as connections to online searches, purchasing patterns, and more. These relationships can be depicted in social graphs that map the associations between people.[135] Facebook provides an application-programming interface (API) to develop these associations.[136] LinkedIn is a professional network that is used to share information about positions, skills, and job qualifications. YouTube is a multimedia network that provides videos of all types. Edutopia is an educational network, sponsored by the George Lucas Educational Foundation, for improving K–12 education.[137] All of these examples amplify the pace and power of social network connectivity and its potential in the realm of creativity and, ultimately, in the outcomes of innovation and entrepreneurship.

Creativity Scenarios

Creativity is the ability to generate ideas that have value. Where do good ideas come from?[138] Creative potential can be improved by increasing building blocks of knowledge, learning and practicing the competencies, and combining ideas in unique ways.

Creativity starts with building a personal competency bank account. If you build up your competencies in advance, they will be waiting for you to use them when a need arises. By being proactive, you can build up competencies that can be energized when they are needed to enhance your innovative potential. According to Keith Sawyer, "Exceptional creators see the world differently because they understand it more deeply."[139] The structure of the innovation competency framework is designed to enable you to improve your overall capabilities by focusing on understanding the underlying concepts of all the competencies.

When you are confronted with something new, you can access the specific competencies that you need from your competency bank account to enable you to build the scenarios that you need to create and pivot to business creations. Starting with an idea or a problem, you can use your imagination to create a set of competency scenarios that will likely begin with asking the right question and proceed by accessing a dynamic set of competencies.

Creativity is not approached along a singular linear path.[140] Creativity is like a moving ball zigzagging in different directions. Creativity follows zigzag pathways that are based on your accessing the relevant competencies. The zigzag pathways are shown in Figure 8.10.

Figure 8.10 Illustration of Creativity Scenarios

Source: Adapted from Sawyer, R. K. (2013). Zig zag: The surprising path to greater creativity. San Francisco, California: John Wiley & Sons.

The innovation competency framework provides the foundation for your bank account. You can create a set of scenarios that match the problem you have and then access the competencies from the innovation competency framework.

Creativity is achieved through devising a set of scenarios that draw on competencies, such as questioning, observation, networking, experimentation, thinking, problem solving, and association, resulting in actionable insights, or creations.[141] Your scenario path may be different for each creative insight that you find. You then pivot into innovation because creativity is a predecessor to innovation. You are always looking for new scenario paths. You might encounter a blockage and get stuck on a problem. These blockages are like bookmarks that are set in your mind to allow you to return to later, and hopefully discover a solution.[142]

New scenarios for new situations can be created. For any particular problem, why not be creative? Beginning with asking questions, observing, gathering knowledge, visualizing, stimulating your thinking through playing, associating, experimenting by making a prototype, observing, gathering more knowledge, refining the prototype, and then pivoting into a new product. For each new problem, a different set of scenarios is created.

Dispelling Creativity Myths

Leaders need to take responsibility for unlocking the creative talents of all people, overcoming the mythology, and the barriers to creativity. If we can get all people to contribute their own ideas that have value, everyone will benefit. Nilofer Merchant describes three creativity myths that highlight the core issues.[143]

Myth #1: Not everyone can be creative.

Many think creativity requires deep expertise or that you have to hire the "right" people. This filters out all the people whose fresh perspectives – which only they own – are needed and limits the scope of results. Break the barriers of roles, credentials, and qualifications by asking everyone, "What would you like to change for the better?"

Myth #2: Process kills creativity.

Many think that existing processes limit creativity. This is only true if the process is broken. A good process can serve as guardrails to clarify goals (timeline, resources available, and desired outcomes) yet leave the "how" open. The capacity to direct one's own work enables teams to share responsibility, self-organize, generate ideas, and collaborate.

Myth #3: Pay drives creativity.

Many have long thought that we need to financially reward creativity to get more of it. Money, while necessary, motivates neither the best people nor the best in people. More than a motivational carrot, finding and fulfilling a purpose is a fundamental human need. Think back to that analyst. Being able to draw on her passion for food and change the cafeteria was reward enough.

Summary

In this chapter, we explored what is involved in activating and sustaining creativity, reviewed the creativity research, examined creativity skills (playing, associations, choosing, making, and pivoting), and outlined working models of creativity and creativity tools. Two creativity models, developed by Bruce Nussbaum and Keith Sawyer, respectively, focus on creativity intelligence, creativity steps, and competencies. In exploring how you boost your ability to be creative, *Creative Intelligence* by Nussbaum describes five creative intelligence competencies: knowledge mining, framing, playing, making, and pivoting.[144] In *Zig Zag*, Sawyer outlines a creativity process composed of the eight steps: ask, learn, look, play, think, fuse, choose, and make. His actionable insight is that you can use the steps in a dynamic zigzag without an explicit ordering. Sawyer stresses the importance of practicing creativity.[145]

Next up, we look at the critical dimensions of building an innovative culture. As we shall see, whether a relatively new start-up or an established organization, fermenting and fostering an innovative culture is challenging, yet key, in building a competitive strategy.

Notes

1. . *Wikipedia*, s.v. "List of Best-Selling Music Artists," accessed June 10, 2021, https://en.wikipedia.org/wiki/List_of_best-selling_music_artists.
2. *Wikipedia*, s.v. "The Beatles," accessed June 10, 2021, https://en.wikipedia.org/wiki/The_Beatles.

3. Greg Clydesdale, "Creativity and Competition: The Beatles," *Creativity Research Journal* 18, no. 2 (2006), 129–139, 136.
4. Greg Clydesdale, "Creativity and Competition: The Beatles," *Creativity Research Journal* 18, no. 2 (2006), 129–139, 129.
5. Malcom Gladwell, *Outliers: The Story of Success* (New York: Little, Brown and Co., 2008), 47–50, 50.
6. Greg Clydesdale, "Creativity and Competition: The Beatles," *Creativity Research Journal* 18, no. 2 (2006), 129–139, 133.
7. Greg Clydesdale, "Creativity and Competition: The Beatles," *Creativity Research Journal* 18, no. 2 (2006), 129–139, 134.
8. Teresa M. Amabile, "How to Kill Creativity," *Harvard Business Review* 76 (1998), 77–87, 77.
9. Greg Clydesdale, "Creativity and Competition: The Beatles," *Creativity Research Journal* 18, no. 2 (2006), 129–139, 138.
10. Greg Clydesdale, "Creativity and Competition: The Beatles," *Creativity Research Journal* 18, no. 2 (2006), 129–139, 138.
11. Greg Clydesdale, "Creativity and Competition: The Beatles," *Creativity Research Journal* 18, no. 2 (2006), 129–139, 132.
12. Greg Clydesdale, "Creativity and Competition: The Beatles," *Creativity Research Journal* 18, no. 2 (2006), 129–139, 133.
13. Natalie W. Nixon, *The Creativity Leap*, 1st ed. (Oakland, CA: Berrett-Koehler Publishers, Inc, 2020), 28–29.
14. Greg Clydesdale, "Creativity and Competition: The Beatles," *Creativity Research Journal* 18, no. 2 (2006), 129–139, 132.
15. *Wikipedia*, s.v. "The Beatles, Genres," accessed June 10, 2021, https://en.wikipedia.org/wiki/The_Beatles.
16. *Dictionary.com*, s.v. "Creativity," accessed June 10, 2021, http://dictionary.reference.com/browse/creativity.
17. *Merriam-Webster Online*, s.v. "Creativity," accessed June 10, 2021, www.merriam-webster.com/dictionary/creativity.
18. Ronald A. Beghetto and James C. Kaufman, eds., *Nurturing Creativity in the Classroom* (Oxford: Cambridge University Press, 2010), 191–205.
19. Brian X. Chen, "Simplifying the Bull: How Picasso Helps to Teach Apple's Style: Inside Apple's Internal Training Program," *The New York Times*, August 10, 2014, accessed June 10, 2021, www.nytimes.com/2014/08/11/technology/-inside-apples-internal-training-program-.html?_r=0.
20. Josh Linkner, *Disciplined Dreaming: A Proven System to Drive Breakthrough Creativity* (San Francisco, CA: Jossey-Bass, A Wiley Imprint, 2011), 2.
21. John Cleese, *Creativity: A Short and Cheerful Guide* (New York: Crown, an Imprint of Random House, a Division of Penguin Random House LLC, 2020), 3–4.
22. "AMA 2010 Critical Skills Survey," *American Management Association*, accessed July 7, 2014, www.amanet.org/articles/ama-critical-skills-survey-workers-need-higher-level-skills-to-succeed-in-the-21st-century/.
23. Austin Carr, "The Most Important Leadership Quality for CEOs? Creativity," *Fast Company*, May 18, 2010, accessed June 10, 2021, www.fastcompany.com/1648943/creativity-the-most-important-leadership-quality-for-ceos-study.
24. "IBM 2010 Global CEO Study: Creativity Selected as Most Crucial Factor for Future Success," *IBM*, accessed June 12, 2021, www.ibm.com/news/ca/en/2010/05/20/v384864m81427w34.html.
25. "IBM 2010 Global CEO Study: Creativity Selected as Most Crucial Factor for Future Success," *IBM*, accessed June 12, 2021, www.ibm.com/news/ca/en/2010/05/20/v384864m81427w34.html.
26. "Problem Solving: Proficiency Levels (2012)," *National Center for Education Statistics, PISA*, accessed June 10, 2021, http://nces.ed.gov/surveys/pisa/pisa2012/pisa2012highlights_11.asp.
27. *Wikipedia*, s.v. "Flynn Effect," accessed June 10, 2021, http://en.wikipedia.org/wiki/Flynn_effect.
28. Kyung Hee Kim, "The Creativity Crisis in America!" *The Creativity Post*, July 10, 2012, accessed June 12, 2021, www.creativitypost.com/article/yes_there_is_a_creativity_crisis.
29. Peter Gray, "As Children's Freedom Has Declined, So Has Their Creativity," *Psychology Today*, September 17, 2012, accessed June 10, 2021, www.psychologytoday.com/blog/freedom-learn/201209/children-s-freedom-has-declined-so-has-their-creativity.
30. Erin Zagursky, "Professor Discusses America's Creativity Crisis in *Newsweek*," *William & Mary News & Media*, July 14, 2010, accessed February 22, 2024, www.wm.edu/news/stories/2010/professor-discusses-americas-creativity-crisis-in-newsweek-123.php.

31. Po Bronson and Ashley Merryman, "The Creativity Crisis," *Newsweek*, July 10, 2010, accessed February 22, 2024, www.newsweek.com/creativity-crisis-74665.
32. Kyung Hee Kim, "The Creativity Crisis in America!" *The Creativity Post*, July 10, 2012, accessed February 22, 2024, www.creativitypost.com/article/yes_there_is_a_creativity_crisis.
33. Erin Zagursky, "Smart? Yes. Creative? Not So Much," February 3, 2011, accessed June 10, 2021, www.wm.edu/research/ideation/professions/smart-yes.-creative-not-so-much.5890.php.
34. Kyung Hee Kim, "The Creativity Crisis: The Decrease in Creative Thinking Scores on the Torrance Tests of Creative Thinking," *Creativity Research Journal* 23, no. 4 (2011), 285–295.
35. "Torrance Tests of Creative Thinking," accessed June 10, 2021, www.ststesting.com/ngifted.html.
36. Peter Gray, "As Children's Freedom Has Declined, So Has Their Creativity," *Psychology Today*, September 17, 2012, accessed June 10, 2021, www.psychologytoday.com/blog/freedom-learn/201209/children-s-freedom-has-declined-so-has-their-creativity.
37. Peter Gray, "As Children's Freedom Has Declined, So Has Their Creativity," *Psychology Today*, September 17, 2012, accessed June 10, 2021, www.psychologytoday.com/blog/freedom-learn/201209/children-s-freedom-has-declined-so-has-their-creativity.
38. Keith Sawyer, *Zig Zag* (New York: Jossey-Bass, 2013), 132.
39. Keith Sawyer, *Zig Zag* (New York: Jossey-Bass, 2013), 130–132.
40. Charlie Burton, "The Seventh Disruption: How James Dyson Reinvented the Personal Heater," *Wired*, October 11, 2011, accessed June 10, 2021, www.wired.co.uk/magazine/archive/2011/11/features/the-seventh-disruption-james-dyson?page=all.
41. Bruce Nussbaum, *Creative Intelligence: Harnessing the Power to Create, Connect, and Inspire* (New York: Harper Business, 2013), 61.
42. Srini Pillay, "Can You Rewire Your Brain to Get Out of a Rut? (Yes You Can . . .)," March 9, 2018, updated March 14, 2018, accessed June 10, 2021, www.health.harvard.edu/blog/rewire-brain-get-out-of-rut-2018030913253.
43. Günther Knoblich, Stellan Ohlsson, Hilde Haider, and Detlef Rhenius, "Constraint Relaxation and Chunk Decomposition in Insight Problem Solving," *Journal of Experimental Psychology: Learning, Memory, and Cognition* 25, no. 6 (1999), 1534.
44. Srini Pillay, "Can You Rewire Your Brain to Get Out of a Rut? (Yes You Can . . .)," March 9, 2018, updated March 14, 2018, accessed June 10, 2021, www.health.harvard.edu/blog/rewire-brain-get-out-of-rut-2018030913253.
45. Srini Pillay, "Can You Rewire Your Brain to Get Out of a Rut? (Yes You Can . . .)," March 9, 2018, updated March 14, 2018, accessed June 10, 2021, www.health.harvard.edu/blog/rewire-brain-get-out-of-rut-2018030913253.
46. Günther Knoblich, Stellan Ohlsson, Hilde Haider, and Detlef Rhenius, "Constraint Relaxation and Chunk Decomposition in Insight Problem Solving," *Journal of Experimental Psychology: Learning, Memory, and Cognition* 25, no. 6 (1999), 1553.
47. Karen Weintraub, "Brain a 'Creativity Machine,' If You Use It Right," *USA Today*, November 9, 2013, accessed June 10, 2021, www.usatoday.com/story/news/nation/2013/11/09/creativity-brain-science/3457735/.
48. Gordon MacKenzie, *Orbiting the Giant Hairball* (New York: Viking, 1996), 18–20, 19.
49. Gordon MacKenzie, *Orbiting the Giant Hairball* (New York: Viking, 1996), 30–33, 30.
50. Karen Weintraub, "Brain a 'Creativity Machine,' If You Use It Right," *USA Today*, November 9, 2013, accessed June 10, 2021, www.usatoday.com/story/news/nation/2013/11/09/creativity-brain-science/3457735/.
51. "Sir Ken Robinson: Do Schools Kill Creativity?" *YouTube Video*, posted by "TED," January 6, 2007, accessed June 10, 2021, www.youtube.com/watch?v=iG9CE55wbtY.
52. "Sir Ken Robinson: Do Schools Kill Creativity?" *YouTube Video*, posted by "TED," January 6, 2007, accessed June 10, 2021, www.youtube.com/watch?v=iG9CE55wbtY.
53. "Sir Ken Robinson: Do Schools Kill Creativity?" *YouTube Video*, posted by "TED," January 6, 2007, accessed June 10, 2021, www.youtube.com/watch?v=iG9CE55wbtY.
54. Sir Ken Robinson, *Out of Our Minds* (Mankato, MN: Capstone, 2011).
55. Bruce Nussbaum, *Creative Intelligence: Harnessing the Power to Create, Connect, and Inspire* (New York: HarperCollins, 2013), 239–240.
56. Jeff Dyer, Hal Gregersen, and Clayton M. Christensen, *The Innovator's DNA* (Boston: Harvard Business Review Press, 2011), 22.

57. Marvin Reznikoff, George Domino, Carolyn Bridges, and Merton Honeyman, "Creative Abilities in Identical and Fraternal Twins," *Behavior Genetics* 3, no. 4 (1973), 365–377.
58. Ananya Mandal, "Neurogenesis – What Is Neurogenesis?" accessed June 10, 2021, www.news-medical.net/health/Neurogenesis-What-is-Neurogenesis.aspx.
59. Latarsha Gatlin, "Simulated Blindness Can Help Revive Hearing, Researchers Find," February 5, 2014, accessed June 12, 2021, https://releases.jhu.edu/2014/02/05/simulated-blindness-can-help-revive-hearing-loss-researchers-find/.
60. John Ericson, "Hard of Hearing May Benefit from Time in the Dark: Temporary Blindness Boosts Brain's Auditory Cortex," *Medical Daily*, February 5, 2014, accessed June 10, 2021, www.medicaldaily.com/hard-hearing-may-benefit-time-dark-temporary-blindness-boosts-brains-auditory-cortex-268676.
61. Carl Zimmer, "Secrets of the Brain," *National Geographic*, February 2014, 34.
62. Carl Zimmer, "Secrets of the Brain," *National Geographic*, February 2014, 39.
63. Gina Kolata, "Yes, Running Can Make You High," *The New York Times*, March 27, 2008, accessed June 10, 2021, www.nytimes.com/2008/03/27/health/nutrition/27best.html?_r=0.
64. Marily Oppezzo and Daniel Schwartz, "Give Your Ideas Some Legs: The Positive Effect of Walking on Creative Thinking," *Journal of Experimental Psychology: Learning, Memory, and Cognition* 40, no. 4 (2014), 1142–1152, https://doi.org/10.1037/a0036577.
65. John Medina, *Brain Rules: 12 Principles for Surviving and Thriving at Work, Home, and School* (Seattle, WA: Pear Press, 2008).
66. John Medina, *Brain Rules*, Videos: Exercise, accessed June 12, 2021, https://brainrules.net/brain-rules-video/.
67. Damon Centola, "The Spread of Behavior in an Online Social Network Experiment," *Science* 329, no. 5996 (2010), 1194–1197.
68. Bruce Nussbaum, *Creative Intelligence: Harnessing the Power to Create, Connect, and Inspire* (New York: Harper Business, 2013), 130.
69. John Mirowsky and Catherine E. Ross, "Creative Work and Health," *Journal of Health and Social Behavior* 48, no. 4 (2007), 385–403.
70. "Brains Sweep Themselves Clean of Toxins During Sleep," blog post by Jon Hamilton, *Shots: Health News from NPR*, October 17, 2013, accessed June 10, 2021, www.npr.org/blogs/health/2013/10/18/236211811/brains-sweep-themselves-clean-of-toxins-during-sleep.
71. Leslie Berlin, "We'll Fill This Space, But First a Nap," *The New York Times*, September 27, 2008, accessed June 10, 2021, www.nytimes.com/2008/09/28/technology/28proto.html?_r=0.
72. Leslie Berlin, "We'll Fill This Space, But First a Nap," *The New York Times*, September 27, 2008, accessed June 10, 2021, www.nytimes.com/2008/09/28/technology/28proto.html?_r=0.
73. Abraham Goldstein, Ketty Revivo, Michal Kreitler, and Nili Metuki, "Unilateral Muscle Contractions Enhance Creative Thinking," *Psychonomic Bulletin & Review* 17, no. 6 (2010), 895–899.
74. Keith Sawyer, "Raise Your Left Hand for Greater Creativity!" *Psychology Today*, March 13, 2013, accessed June 10, 2021, www.psychologytoday.com/blog/zig-zag/201303/raise-your-left-hand-greater-creativity.
75. Jeffrey Kluger, "Assessing the Creative Spark," *Time Magazine*, May 9, 2013, accessed June 10, 2021, http://business.time.com/2013/05/09/assessing-the-creative-spark/?iid=obinsite.
76. Elizabeth Dias, "Creativity Conference," *Time Magazine*, April 26, 2013, accessed June 10, 2021, http://business.time.com/2013/04/26/the-time-creativity-poll/slide/introduction/.
77. Nicholas Negroponte, *Being Digital* (New York: Alfred A. Knopf, 1996).
78. Judy Fisk, "Can Ballet Lessons Improve Your Football Skills?" *Demand Media, AZCentral, A Gannett Company*, accessed June 10, 2021, http://healthyliving.azcentral.com/can-ballet-lessons-improve-football-skills-2944.html.
79. Harry Cross, "Inventing the Forward Pass," *The New York Times*, November 1, 1913, accessed June 10, 2021, www.nytimes.com/packages/html/sports/year_in_sports/11.01.html.
80. Louis Pasteur, accessed June 10, 2021, www.goodreads.com/quotes/9178-chance-favors-the-prepared-mind.
81. Bruce Nussbaum, *Creative Intelligence: Harnessing the Power to Create, Connect, and Inspire* (New York: Harper Business, 2013), 35.
82. Robert H. McKim, *Experiences in Visual Thinking* (Boston, MA: PWS Engineering, 1980).
83. Alex Soojung-Kim Pang, "Mighty Mouse," *Stanford Magazine*, March/April 2002, accessed June 10, 2021, http://alumni.stanford.edu/get/page/magazine/article/?article_id=37694.

84. Keith Sawyer, *Zig Zag: The Surprising Path to Greater Creativity* (New York: Jossey-Bass, 2013), 6.
85. Keith Sawyer, *Zig Zag: The Surprising Path to Greater Creativity* (New York: Jossey-Bass, 2013), 112.
86. Leslie Berlin, "We'll Fill This Space, But First a Nap," *The New York Times*, September 27, 2008, accessed June 10, 2021, www.nytimes.com/2008/09/28/technology/28proto.html?_r=0.
87. Alan Boyle, "Gamers Solve Molecular Puzzle That Baffled Scientists," *NBC News*, September 18, 2011, accessed June 10, 2021, www.nbcnews.com/science/gamers-solve-molecular-puzzle-baffled-scientists-6C10402813.
88. George Sylvester Viereck, "Imagination Is More Important Than Knowledge" *Quote Investigator*, accessed June 12, 2021, https://quoteinvestigator.com/2013/01/01/einstein-imagination/.
89. Robert and Michele Root-Bernstein, "Einstein on Creative Thinking: Music and the Intuitive Art of Scientific Imagination," 2010, accessed June 10, 2021, www.psychologytoday.com/us/blog/imagine/201003/einstein-creative-thinking-music-and-the-intuitive-art-scientific-imagination.
90. Einstein, Albert, Libquotes, accessed February 14, 2021, https://libquotes.com/albert-einstein/quote/lbx4e3o.
91. Maria Popova, "How Einstein Thought: Why 'Combinatory Play' Is the Secret of Genius," August 14, 2013, accessed June 10, 2021, www.brainpickings.org/2013/08/14/how-einstein-thought-combinatorial-creativity/.
92. Maria Popova, "Combinatorial Creativity and the Myth of Originality," June 6, 2012, accessed February 14, 2021, www.smithsonianmag.com/innovation/combinatorial-creativity-and-the-myth-of-originality-114843098/.
93. *Wikipedia*, s.v. "The Act of Creation," accessed June 12, 2021, https://en.wikipedia.org/wiki/The_Act_of_Creation.
94. Maria Popova, "Networked Knowledge and Combinatorial Creativity," August 1, 2012, accessed June 10, 2021, www.brainpickings.org/2011/08/01/networked-knowledge-combinatorial-creativity/.
95. Jeffrey H. Dyer, Hal B. Gregersen, and Clayton Christensen, "Entrepreneur Behaviors, Opportunity Recognition, and the Origins of Innovative Ventures," *Strategic Entrepreneurship Journal* 2, no. 4 (2008), 317–338.
96. *Wikipedia*, s.v. "Xerox Parc," accessed June 10, 2021, http://en.wikipedia.org/wiki/PARC_(company).
97. Carmine Gallo, "To Unlock Creativity, Learn from Steve Jobs," October 2010, accessed June 12, 2021, www.carminegallo.com/to-unlock-creativity-learn-from-steve-jobs/.
98. Bruce Nussbaum, *Creative Intelligence: Harnessing the Power to Create, Connect, and Inspire* (New York: Harper Business, 2013), 62.
99. Anne-Wil Harzing, "Citation Analysis Across Disciplines: The Impact of Different Data Sources and Citation Metrics," accessed June 10, 2021, www.harzing.com/data_metrics_comparison.htm.
100. Keith Sawyer, *Zig Zag: The Surprising Path to Greater Creativity* (New York: Jossey-Bass, 2013), 7.
101. Jeff Dyer, Hal Gregersen, and Clayton M. Christensen, *The Innovator's DNA* (Boston: Harvard Business Review Press, 2011), 52.
102. Jeff Dyer, Hal Gregersen, and Clayton M. Christensen, *The Innovator's DNA* (Boston: Harvard Business Review Press, 2011), 52.
103. Jeff Dyer, Hal Gregersen, and Clayton M. Christensen, *The Innovator's DNA* (Boston: Harvard Business Review Press, 2011), 52.
104. Frans Johansson, *Medici Effect: What Elephants and Epidemics Can Teach Us About Innovation* (Boston: Harvard Business School Press, 2006).
105. *Wikipedia*, s.v. "The Agony and the Ecstasy," accessed June 10, 2021, http://en.wikipedia.org/wiki/The_Agony_and_the_Ecstasy_(novel).
106. Jeff Dyer, Hal Gregersen, and Clayton M. Christensen, *The Innovator's DNA* (Boston: Harvard Business Review Press, 2011).
107. "Andrew Hargadon Innovation Is About Connection," *YouTube Video*, posted by "Bright Sight Group," April 15, 2009, accessed June 10, 2021, www.youtube.com/watch?v=RWwTjxx4WxE.
108. Andrew Hargadon, *How Breakthroughs Happen: The Surprising Truth About How Companies Innovate* (Boston, MA: Harvard Business Press, 2003).
109. "Andrew Hargadon – Innovation and Invention," *YouTube Video*, posted by "Bright Sight Group," January 14, 2009, accessed June 10, 2021, www.youtube.com/watch?v=iD6iRxaZQrE.
110. Keith Sawyer, *Zig Zag: The Surprising Path to Greater Creativity* (New York: Jossey-Bass, 2013), 7.
111. Jim Collins and Morten T. Hansen, *Great By Choice* (New York: Harper, 2011).
112. Jim Collins and Morten T. Hansen, *Great By Choice* (New York: Harper, 2011), 45.
113. Keith Sawyer, *Zig Zag: The Surprising Path to Greater Creativity* (New York: Jossey-Bass, 2013), 7.

114. Jim Collins and Morten T. Hansen, *Great By Choice* (New York: Harper, 2011), 36–37.
115. *Wikipedia*, s.v. "Evel Knievel," accessed June 10, 2021, http://en.wikipedia.org/wiki/Evel_Knievel.
116. Eric Ries, *The Lean Startup: How Today's Entrepreneurs Use Continuous Innovation to Create Radically Successful Businesses* (New York: Crown Business, 2011).
117. "Eric Ries: 10 Classic Strategies for a Fast, User-Focused Company Reboot," June 4, 2012, accessed February 22, 2024, www.fastcodesign.com/1669814/eric-ries-10-classic-strategies-for-a-fast-user-focused-company-reboot.
118. Jim Collins and Morten T. Hansen, *Great By Choice* (New York: Harper, 2011), 29.
119. Graham Wallas, *The Art of Thought* (London: Jonathan Cape, 1926).
120. Dan Goleman, "New Insights on the Creative Brain," *Psychology Today*, August 10, 2011, accessed February 22, 2024, www.psychologytoday.com/blog/the-brain-and-emotional-intelligence/201108/new-insights-the-creative-brain.
121. Maria Popova, "The Art of Thought: A Pioneering 1926 Model of the Four Stages of Creativity," accessed June 12, 2021, www.brainpickings.org/2013/08/28/the-art-of-thought-graham-wallas-stages/.
122. Graham Wallas, *The Art of Thought* (London: Jonathan Cape, 1926).
123. Dan Goleman, "New Insights on the Creative Brain," *The Brain and Emotional Intelligence* (blog), *Psychology Today*, August 10, 2011, accessed June 10, 2021, www.psychologytoday.com/blog/the-brain-and-emotional-intelligence/201108/new-insights-the-creative-brain.
124. Dan Goleman, "New Insights on the Creative Brain," *The Brain and Emotional Intelligence* (blog), *Psychology Today*, August 10, 2011, accessed June 10, 2021, www.psychologytoday.com/blog/the-brain-and-emotional-intelligence/201108/new-insights-the-creative-brain.
125. Sarnoff A. Mednick, "The Associative Basis of the Creative Process," *Psychological Review* 69, no. 3 (1962), 220–232, https://doi.org/10.1037/h0048850.
126. "Remote Associates Test," accessed June 10, 2021, www.remote-associates-test.com/.
127. Sarnoff A. Mednick, "The Remote Associates Test," *The Journal of Creative Behavior* 2 (1968), 213–214.
128. J. P. Guilford, *The Nature of Human Intelligence* (New York: McGraw-Hill, 1967).
129. Gary Hamel, *The Future of Management* (Boston: Harvard Business Review Press, 2007), 52.
130. *Wikipedia*, s.v. "Pay It Forward," accessed June 10, 2021, http://en.wikipedia.org/wiki/Pay_it_forward.
131. *Wikipedia*, s.v. "Night at the Museum," accessed June 10, 2021, http://en.wikipedia.org/wiki/Night_at_the_museum.
132. Ron Adner, *The Wide Lens* (New York: Portfolio/Penguin, 2012), 206.
133. Jacob Davidson, "Spy Gains," *Time Magazine*, July 8–15, 2013, accessed June 12, 2021, http://content.time.com/time/subscriber/article/0,33009,2146443,00.html.
134. Mary White, "What Types of Social Networks Exist?" accessed June 10, 2021, http://socialnetworking.lovetoknow.com/What_Types_of_Social_Networks_Exist.
135. *Wikipedia*, s.v. "Social Graphs," accessed June 10, 2021, http://en.wikipedia.org/wiki/Social_graph.
136. *Wikipedia*, s.v. "Facebook Platform," accessed June 10, 2021, http://en.wikipedia.org/wiki/Facebook_Platform#Open_Graph_protocol.
137. "Edutopia," accessed June 10, 2021, www.edutopia.org/.
138. "Where Good Ideas Come from by Steven Johnson," *YouTube Video*, posted by "Riverhead Books," September 17, 2010, accessed June 10, 2021, www.youtube.com/watch?v=NugRZGDbPFU.
139. Keith Sawyer, *Zig Zag: The Surprising Path to Greater Creativity* (New York: Jossey-Bass, 2013), 50.
140. Keith Sawyer, *Zig Zag: The Surprising Path to Greater Creativity* (New York: Jossey-Bass, 2013), 222–223.
141. Jeff Dyer, Hal Gregersen, and Clayton Christensen, *The Innovator's DNA* (Boston: Harvard Business Review Press, 2011).
142. Keith Sawyer, *Zig Zag: The Surprising Path to Greater Creativity* (New York: Jossey-Bass, 2013), 77.
143. Nilofer Merchant, "Your Employees Have All the Creativity You Need. Let Them Prove It," November 01, 2019, accessed June 10, 2021, https://hbr.org/2019/11/your-employees-have-all-the-creativity-you-need-let-them-prove-it.
144. Bruce Nussbaum, *Creative Intelligence: Harnessing the Power to Create, Connect, and Inspire* (New York: Harper Business, 2013), 33–220.
145. Keith Sawyer, *Zig Zag: The Surprising Path to Greater Creativity* (New York: Jossey-Bass, 2013).

9 Culture Building

The Importance of Culture

When it comes to a culture of innovation, an organization's culture is the foundation of its organizational health. Culture has been defined as "the tacit social order of an organization: It shapes attitudes and behaviours in wide-ranging . . . ways."[1] Strong performance cultures are built on clear aspirational goals that are linked to specific, observable behaviors that everyone follows – from leaders to the front line. Culture can have a significant impact on creativity, innovation, and ventures because top-quartile cultures enjoy three times the returns to shareholders as bottom-quartile rivals.[2]

Accenture, a multinational management consulting company, conducted a study titled "Corporate Innovation Is Within Reach: Nurturing and Enabling an Entrepreneurial Culture," which involved 1,000 individuals composed of 600 corporate employees, 200 corporate business decision-makers, and 200 self-employed individuals.[3] The study revealed that individuals are willing to contribute ideas, but there is, generally, a lack of managerial support for these ideas. Other insights from the study include:

- Thirty-six percent say they are too busy doing their job to pursue new ideas.
- Twenty-seven percent have avoided pursuing an idea within their company because they think there may be negative consequences.
- Forty-nine percent believe that management support for new ideas is important, yet only twenty percent report that their organization does this well.
- Forty-two percent believe that tolerance for failure is important to support innovation, but only twelve percent believe their company does a good job of providing this.[4]

Innovation, however, is a key factor in entrepreneurship and economic growth in general, and in job growth, in particular. Given its critical multidimensional role, it is important to ask what can be done to increase the prevalence and potential of innovation and entrepreneurship. While the importance of behaviors such as thinking, problem solving, knowledge, and creativity in innovation and entrepreneurship have been discussed, our attention now turns to the challenge of building a culture of innovation and entrepreneurship.

The significance of the influence of culture on innovation was demonstrated in a study by researchers Gerard J. Tellis, Jaideep C. Prabhu, and Rajesh K. Chandy that included 759 companies based in 17 major markets. The results revealed that corporate culture was a more important driver of radical innovation than labor, capital, government, or national culture.[5] When it comes to innovation, corporate culture matters.

DOI: 10.4324/9781003034308-10

The Roles of Culture and Innovation

If culture is a key factor that influences innovation, how is an innovative culture built? Jay Rao, Professor of Technology and Innovation, and Joseph Weintraub, Professor of Management, both at Babson College, describe six building blocks of culture to enable organizations to multiply their innovative potential: resources, processes, values, behavior, climate, and success.[6]

The theory of capabilities described earlier in Chapter 7, "Knowledge Building," encompasses the first three building blocks of culture in the context of adding capability: resources, processes, and values/priorities. The resources are the assets, tangible and intangible, of an organization and include its people, systems, equipment, information, finances, technology, designs, brands, time, and relationships. One of the most important resources in the future economy is the ideation potential and intellect of people. Processes encompass how people communicate, collaborate, and make decisions to achieve results. Processes also include those mechanisms through which the inputs are transformed to the outputs or innovations. This transformation process determines how entrepreneurs create value – effective organizations provide continued value to their customers. Values and priorities define the cultural framework for decision-making to ensure that resources are aligned with the strategy. An organization's values shape its culture, and together the values and culture drive the priorities, so that each person can manage him or herself and operate with autonomy while being held accountable.

The second group of three building blocks includes behavior, climate, and success. Behaviors describe how people act in an organization to foster innovation. Actions speak louder than words, and the higher the level of the innovation competence, the more effectively people can imagine, create, and innovate. Rao and Weintraub describe climate as "the tenor of workplace life. An innovative climate cultivates engagement and enthusiasm, challenges people to take risks within a safe environment, fosters learning and encourages independent thinking."[7]

Organizational success has been traditionally defined based on financial measures such as revenue, cost, and profits. Michael E. Porter and Mark R. Kramer view the optimization of short-term financial performance as an outdated notion. They have introduced the concept of shared value, suggesting organizations take a long-term view and redefine success to include improving economic and social conditions in their communities. For example, organizational success should include reduced resource consumption, such as energy and water use, as well as improving employee wellness and skills.[8] "More generally, success reinforces the enterprise's values, behaviours and processes, which in turn drive many subsequent actions and decisions: Who will be rewarded, which people will be hired and which projects will get the green light."[9]

The six building blocks of culture – resources, processes, values, behavior, climate, and success – are summarized in Figure 9.1.[10] These building blocks are synergistic. The upper left blocks are more measurable, while the lower right blocks are less measurable.

Rao and Weintraub developed a survey to evaluate the six building blocks of culture. The survey organizes each of these blocks into three factors, and each of the factors into three survey questions, for a total of 54 questions.[11]

> The final average of the six building blocks represents the company's overall score, which we call the "Innovation Quotient." The Innovation Quotient can be a useful benchmark for comparing the overall level of innovation between companies, divisions, and teams based in different regions. However, executives we have worked with tell us that the most important value of the Innovation Quotient assessment is its ability to rank the factors and elements that support innovation. This gives them an easy-to-understand scorecard that allows them to zero in on the strengths and weaknesses of their organization's innovation culture.[12]

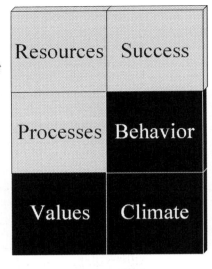

The *upper left* blocks are more easily measured.

The *lower right* blocks are less easily measured.

Figure 9.1 Illustration of the Six Building Blocks of Culture

Source: Adapted from Jay Rao and Joseph Weintraub, "How Innovative Is Your Company's Culture," *MIT Sloan Management Review*, (Spring), 2013.

© Copyright.

The Force

Culture is a set of group-specific behaviors in a team or organizational setting that guide behavior and decision-making. A culture based on trust and commitment needs to be based on a set of guiding core values, a purpose, and a drive for progress. Organizational culture is shared learning that is a result of people working together to solve problems and achieve their goals.[13] One way to learn about a culture is by observing the collective behaviors of the respected leaders. The people inside an organization are the ones who can best describe the culture in which they are immersed. According to a study done by KPMG, cultural issues cannot be avoided. They reported that one of the top challenges was "company culture or entrenched attitudes" and that politics, turf wars, and culture were some of the top obstacles cited by innovators.[14]

The powerful impact of a culture has been described by the following phrase, attributed to Peter Drucker: "Culture eats strategy for breakfast."[15] Effective cultures, such as that at Southwest Airlines, understand that treating the employees well encourages them to treat the customers well in turn. Treating employees well also liberates them to think and learn beyond where they are now – times of rapid change require rapid learning.

To borrow an analogy from popular culture, organizational culture is like the concept of the Force used by Jedi Knights for noble acts in the *Star Wars* movie series. In the original *Star Wars* movie, Han Solo speaks to Luke Skywalker, saying, "May the Force be with you," before the attack on the Imperial Death Star. In the movie, the Force is a metaphysical power that the characters relied on in order to perform positive and negative acts. The Jedi use the Force for peaceful, humble, and selfless acts, but the Force also has a dark side that feeds on the negative emotions of anger, jealousy, and hate.[16] Likewise, culture can be a defining concept in an organization, a motivating and empowering *force* that can be either positive or negative.

Whirlpool developed its own force by building innovation into their culture. "In 1999, Dave Whitwam, then chairman of Whirlpool challenged his colleagues to make innovation a deeply embedded core competence."[17] Whirlpool decided to take a holistic approach to their vision known as Innovation from Everyone Everywhere.[18] They built a learning organization that focused on culture and values, leadership and organization, and people and skills that leads to innovation improving life at home while addressing a sustainable future. "It is this commitment that uniquely positions us to both aid the energy transition and deliver compelling innovation with meaningful societal impact."[19]

The focus of Whirlpool was to build a culture that involved all of the people and facilitated the elimination of the cultural barriers to innovation, such as the fear of failure, not-invented here, and risk aversion.[20] At Whirlpool, innovative thinking is considered the responsibility of every employee and has become a core component of the company's worldwide culture to strengthen their competitive position, "by focusing on driving consumer preference by embedding innovation as a core competency – which everyone at Whirlpool would be part of."[21]

While culture is foundational, it requires strategy and leadership to transform companies into innovation machines. "The Whirlpool journey is not for every company. But for those companies looking to build a deep and lasting innovation capability . . . there is no better place to look than Whirlpool."[22]

The Guiding Hand of Culture

Culture is highly effective in guiding the decision-making process by providing the framework that guides the invisible hand of self-management, unleashing people to think. In a corporation of knowledge workers, less oversight is required, increasing the importance of delegation. Instead of directing people on how to do their jobs, leaders should be mentoring and coaching. A culture can create the conditions that liberate people to make autonomous decisions within a framework.

Culture can also provide a framework to keep a company focused on its core mission to customers and employees, and not focused only on financial returns. For example, in 1982, Johnson & Johnson, makers of the over-the-counter pain and fever reducer Tylenol, was faced with a critical decision when they learned that someone had laced Extra Strength Tylenol capsules with lethal doses of potassium cyanide, resulting in multiple deaths across a dispersed geographic area in Chicago.

Even though the deaths occurred only in the Chicago area, Johnson & Johnson removed all Tylenol capsules from the entire US market. Following the Tylenol incident, the US Food and Drug Administration reported 270 separate product-tampering incidents. Although the case has never been solved, drug manufacturers designed new tamper-proof packaging to minimize future incidents.[23] Johnson & Johnson confronted the brutal facts by adhering to what they call "Our Credo." The credo, published in 1943, established the core ideology of the company, which places customers and employees ahead of stockholder returns.[24]

A culture can have a powerful impact on the behavior of innovators. A steady stream of innovation depends on an underlying innovative culture that can either diminish or multiply innovation. Some cultures are designed to encourage self-management and foster innovation, while others are based on control and efficiency. Firms such as 3M, Intuit, Alphabet, Amazon, Microsoft, and Apple have been able to continuously and simultaneously balance current operational efficiency and the development of creative insights that lead to future innovations.

As important as having a strong, positive culture is, it does not guarantee success; a company can lose sight of their culture. Hewlett-Packard, for example, has turned its focus toward financial rewards and operational efficiency, eroding their founders' innovative culture known as the HP Way.[25]

The two-dimensional model shown in Figure 9.2 illustrates the potential impact of culture. The X-axis is the coaching continuum, and the Y-axis is the individual capability continuum. Generally, individuals who are highly capable prefer autonomy, and individuals that have low capability need mentoring and coaching. The upper-left and lower-right quadrants are mismatches that decrease organizational effectiveness. The lower left should represent only individuals who are new in their roles. The guiding force of culture should facilitate the transition of everyone from the lower-left quadrant of dependence to the upper-right quadrant of independence.

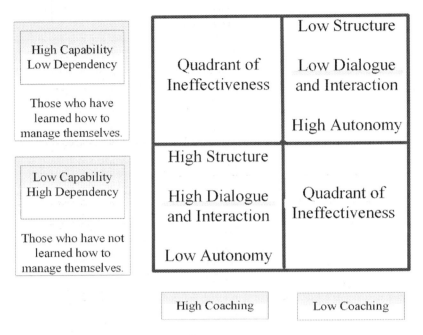

Figure 9.2 Illustration of the Guiding Force
Source: © Copyright.

Core Ideology

In *Built to Last,* authors Jim Collins and Jerry I. Porras study successful companies to better understand what distinguishes one company from another.[26] They find that exceptional organizations (and people) have a dynamic balance, a duality that includes an unchanging core ideology and a built-in, dynamic adaptability to pursue progress. The duality includes preserving the core ideology (guiding principles and purpose) while leading (drive for progress) the organization into the future.

In an example that illustrates Collins and Porras's findings, Apple's Tim Cook describes Apple's business ideology around product, process, and people:

> We believe that we're on the face of the earth to make great products and that's not changing. We're constantly focusing on innovating. We believe in the simple, not the complex. We believe that we need to own and control the primary technologies behind the products we make and participate only in markets where we can make a significant contribution. We believe in saying no to thousands of projects so that we can really focus on the few that are truly important and meaningful to us. We believe in deep collaboration and cross-pollination of our groups, which allow us to innovate in a way that others cannot. And frankly, we don't settle for anything less than excellence in every group in the company, and we have the self-honesty to admit when we're wrong and the courage to change. And I think regardless of who is in what job, those values are so embedded in this company that Apple will do extremely well.[27]

Core Ideology: Guiding Principles (Core Values)

The culture framework shown in Figure 9.3 describes a set of guiding principles; core values that are never to be sacrificed for profits or short-term expediency; purpose, or a reason for being; and a drive for progress.[28]

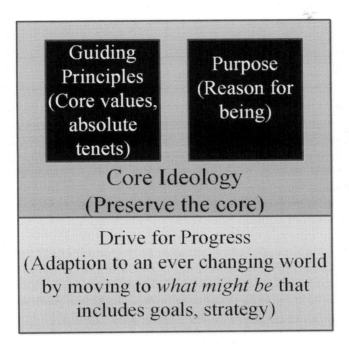

Figure 9.3 Illustration of a Culture Framework

Source: Adapted from Jim Collins and Jeffy I. Porras, *Built To Last: Successful Habits of Visionary Companies*, (New York: HarperCollins, 1994, 1997, 2002), 47.

Some examples of core values from company founders are as follows:

- William McKnight's 3M core values were to solve problems, respect individual initiative, personal growth, and tolerance for honest mistakes.
- Robert J. Johnson's core values for Johnson & Johnson were based on a hierarchy with customers first followed by employees, society at large, and shareholders last.
- Sam Walton's core values were putting the customer ahead of everything.
- David Packard and Bill Hewlett's core values were respect and concern for the individual and affordable quality for customers.
- Paul V. Galvin's core values for Motorola were continuous improvements, and honesty, integrity, and ethics in all aspects of business.
- George W. Merck's core values included honesty, integrity, corporate social responsibility, and science-based innovation.[29]

Core values inform individual and organizational thought and action. For example, Marc Benioff, founder, chairman, and CEO of the computing company salesforce.com, pioneered the philanthropic concept *Share the Model*. "Benioff pioneered the 1/1/1 Integrated Philanthropic model, by which companies contribute 1 percent of profits, 1 percent of equity, and 1 percent of employee hours back to the communities it serves."[30] Salesforce.com has given over $708 million in total, 59K nonprofits and schools using technology given for free or discounted, and completed over 8.9 million volunteer hours.[31] The salesforce.com model is based on their cultural values:

> The Sales-force.com Foundation is based on a simple idea: Leverage Salesforce.com's people, technology, and resources to improve communities throughout the world. We call our integrated philanthropic approach the 1/1/1 model. It's easy to get started and the benefits grow exponentially as your company grows.[32]

Core Ideology: Purpose

Simon Sinek uses the Golden Circle in *Start With Why* to describe the importance of purpose. The Golden Circle is based on the concept of the Golden Ratio, a mathematical formula that describes symmetry and order in nature.[33] The Golden Circle offers symmetry and order in human behavior. Inspiration starts inside the concentric circles, with a *why*, a purpose, rather than with a *what* or a *how* as shown in Figure 9.4.

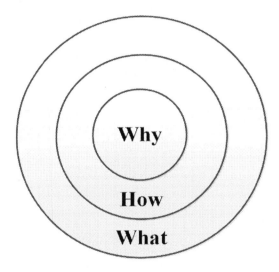

Figure 9.4 Illustration of the Golden Circle

Source: Adapted from Simon Sinek, *Start With Why: How Great Leaders Inspire Everyone to Take Action*, (New York: Penguin, 2009), 37.

© Copyright.

Purpose describes the reason, beyond making money, an organization exists.[34] Some examples of purpose from the founders of leading organizations are as follows:

- William McKnight's purpose was innovation, more explicitly, "Thou shalt not kill a new product idea."[35]
- Robert J. Johnson's purpose was to alleviate pain and disease.
- Sam Walton's purpose was to make the lives of customers better through a broad selection of products at affordable prices.

- David Packard and Bill Hewlett's purpose was to contribute to the communities in which they operated.
- Paul V. Galvin's purpose was to service the community by providing affordable quality products and services.
- George W. Merck's purpose was preserving and improving human life.[36] "Medicine is for the patient; not for the profits. The profits follow."[37] Onchocerciasis, river blindness, is an infectious disease that is caused by parasitic worms. If the disease is left untreated, it will cause blindness.[38] Merck developed the drug Mectizan to treat the disease and later decided to give the drug to anyone who needed it at no cost.[39]

The purpose of an organization is what provides its meaning. Viktor E. Frankl, in his compelling chronicle, *Man's Search for Meaning*, describes his horrifying experiences in Auschwitz during World War II.[40] Despite the extreme despair and suffering he witnessed and experienced, Frankl passionately articulates that the meaning of life is found in every moment of life. He writes that we must each take responsibility for finding meaning in our lives. We have the freedom to choose. One can even find meaning during suffering and despair. "In the death camps of Nazi Germany, Frankl saw men who walked through the huts comforting others, giving away their last piece of bread."[41] Those that survived found meaning in their suffering by helping others.

Similarly, in *Good to Great: Why Some Companies Make the Leap . . . and Others Don't*, Collins tells the story of Admiral Jim Stockdale who spent eight years in the "Hanoi Hilton," a Vietnam prisoner of war camp, from 1965 to 1973. Stockdale survived the brutal treatment because he was able to retain the faith that he would prevail even when confronted with the most brutal facts. Sadly, those who were unrealistic and expected to be released "early" were not as fortunate as Stockdale.[42] Both Frankl and Collins captured and conveyed how essential culture and a core ideology are in instilling purpose and focus in our lives and pursuits.

CVS Health (formerly known as CVS Caremark) demonstrated its purpose to support a healthy lifestyle with a commitment to end the sale of cigarettes and other tobacco products in 2014. "Ending the sale of cigarettes and tobacco products at CVS/pharmacy is the right thing for us to do for our customers and our company to help people on their path to better health," Larry J. Merlo, president and CEO of CVS Health, said in a statement. "Put simply, the sale of tobacco products is inconsistent with our purpose."[43]

The Drive for Progress

All organizations need to adapt to change for survival and vitality. Most organizations, however, do not fully understand how to develop and engage their company cultures for self-management, creative thinking, and adaptation to change, because the cultures are built to run an operational engine. Organizations say they want more innovation but have not created and sustained the cultures that provide the autonomy to inspire their people to ideate.

Some organizations considered to have innovative cultures are Google, Apple, 3M, Corning, W. L. Gore, Whirlpool Corporation, Steelcase, and Whole Foods. Apple's culture is different even from other identified innovative companies. Apple spends relatively little on R&D, does not have a formal stage gate funnel process, makes a small set of vertically integrated products, and, historically, has been led by a strong-willed leader and his "worshippers."[44] The stage gate funnel is a formal prescriptive process for building an object. The object to be built is separated into discrete substeps, where a deliverable (part of the object) is produced, followed by a gate that checks conformance to a predefined specification. A deliverable must pass the gate to get to the next step in the process.[45] In contrast, the drive for progress for an innovative culture would be based on using an iterative and adaptable process that matches the object to be built.

The drive for progress is not set in stone by following an overly rigorous and costly process, but rather is molded by the values and purpose to be accomplished. If you focus on the wrong criteria for the gate, you could be excluding the best ideas. The value of early learning may be more useful than financial returns.

Creating a Cultural Duality

F. Scott Fitzgerald writes, "The test of a first-rate intelligence is the ability to hold two opposed ideas in mind at the same time and still retain the ability to function."[46] Fitzgerald's concept of duality is both a theme of and a challenge to innovation. A cultural duality exists wherein discipline and creativity function together like two roads side by side. Effective innovation cultures value both entrepreneurship and accountability, freedom within a framework.

The creative culture at Apple lives this duality every day.

> Every week, design teams at Apple have two meetings: A right-brain creative meeting and a left-brain production one. At the creative meeting people are to brainstorm, to forget about constraints, to think freely, and to go crazy. At the production meeting the designers and engineers are required to nail everything down, to work out how this crazy idea might work. This process and organization continue throughout the development of any application. The balance shifts as the application progresses. Options are kept for creative thought even at a late stage.[47]

All the concepts developed in Collins' *Good to Great* were derived by making empirical deductions directly from the data.[48] Collins writes, "When you blend a culture of discipline with an ethic of entrepreneurship, you get a magical alchemy resulting in superior performance."[49] This is precisely the issue with respect to process. Innovation and process represent differing yet complementary perspectives. Innovation is associated with entrepreneurship; process is associated with discipline.

As important as core ideology is, it must exist in relationship with creativity and discipline. In *Great by Choice*, Collins and Hansen write,

> The combination of creativity and discipline, translated into the ability to scale innovation with great consistency, better explains some of the greatest success stories – from Intel to Southwest Airlines, from Amgen's early years to Apple's resurgence under Steve Jobs – than the mythology of big-hit, single-step breakthroughs.[50]

The duality of creativity and discipline is illustrated in Figure 9.5.

In *Good to Great*, Collins describes a freedom-in-a-framework model: hire entrepreneurial and creative people and then hold them accountable by building a culture of discipline.[51] Collins identifies four distinguishing characteristics of great leaders based on his research into extraordinarily successful companies: fanatic discipline, empirical creativity, productive paranoia, and humble ambition.[52]

Separate Spaces and Processes

The Magic Circle

Core ideology and creativity may resonate on a theoretical plane, but how can they be translated into the so-called real world? Imagine that there are two concentric circles. The area of these two

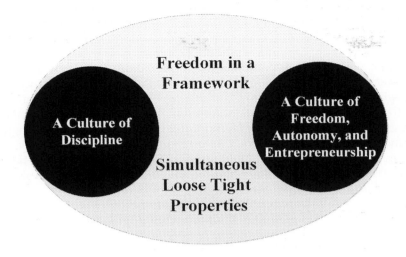

Figure 9.5 Illustration of Cultural Dyad

Source: Adapted from: Hofstede, Kluckhohn-Strodbeck, Schein, Drucker, Collins, Peters and Waterman.
© Copyright.

concentric circles represents employees in an organization. You start with the outermost circle that represents the real world where people perform their work. The area of the outermost circle includes those individuals who have the knowledge to perform their work and may have ideas on how to improve the way that work is done. This space is the frenzy of disciplined operational activities that occur in factories, retail stores, business offices, schools, hospitals, and airlines. In the outermost circle, a whirlwind of day-to-day activity sustains the short-term and defines what individuals do to meet the needs of the organization and their leadership. This circle is important because it is the foundation of the organization – the discipline element – but it is not conducive to creative thought.

Imagine that you want to create something new. Imagine a circle that is inside the outer circle as shown in Figure 9.6. The inner circle becomes the freedom (play) element that defines the magic

Figure 9.6 Illustration of the Magic Circle

circle.[53] Magic circles are places separate from the whirlwind of traditional activity, where talented individuals who have trusting relationships can share ideas, visualize product concepts, and learn from each other. This magic circle is a special place away from the whirlwind that liberates individuals to unlock their creative potential. The magic circle draws on the knowledge of the outer circle but is different because it exists in the eye of the whirlwind.

Vijay Govindarajan, a Tuck School of Business professor, describes the need to maintain a separation of the performance engine, the outer circle, from the dedicated innovation team, the inner magic circle.[54] The magic circle builds on trust and teamwork and provides for learning and experimentation. Lockheed's skunk works, IBM's original PC division in Boca Raton, Florida, and Apple's design studio are examples of magic circles.[55] The magic circles provide freedom within a framework. The extent of the freedom within the framework is provided by the cultural factors that are shared among the team members.

The Power of Culture

Edison's Research Laboratory

Thomas Edison created a space for invention and innovation known as the corporate research laboratory at Menlo Park. He realized that building a separate dedicated team and a protected learning and experimentation process are critical to making innovation happen.[56] Edison intuitively understood and appreciated the need for structure and discipline to drive progress, along with the equally important aspects of creativity and imagination to fuel innovation and entrepreneurship.

Al Capp's Li'l Abner and "Skunk Works"

In today's business parlance, a "skunk works" project is essentially a small experimental laboratory or department of an organization, often independent, charged with research and development of a radical innovation. "The term 'Skunk Works' came from Al Capp's satirical, hillbilly comic strip Li'l Abner, which was immensely popular in the 1940s and '50s."[57] In an interesting and long-running parody, cartoonist Al Capp published *Li'l Abner*, a comic strip about a fictional Appalachian family. The main character in the story was Li'l Abner Yokum, from Dogpatch, Kentucky. In the story, the Skunk Works was a dilapidated factory containing a still that emitted toxic smelly fumes because of the worn shoes and dead skunks used for the ingredients.[58] The term "skunk works" was later applied to the secret aerospace World War II project, known as the Lockheed Martin Advanced Development Programs (ADP) that was used during the development of early jet aircraft. The ADP was located near a smelly plastics factory, thereby acquiring the name Skunk Works.[59]

Li'l Abner and Lockheed share a common thread: product, process, and people working on a project in an unconventional manner, separate from the whirlwind of an organization. AT&T Bell Laboratories was an effective Skunk Works that developed the transistor.[60] Xerox PARC was a skunk works project that developed a number of the key components of modern computing.[61] Steve Jobs used a skunk works project for the development of the Macintosh computer.[62]

The locations where major innovations are conceived are often kept separate from the mainstream culture. Skunk works live on, for instance, Alphabet's Google founded X Development LLC (formerly Google X) in January of 2020 as an American semi-secret research and development facility and organization. The X headquarters are separated by about a mile and a half from Alphabet's corporate headquarters, the Googleplex, in Mountain View, California. X focuses on artificial intelligence, computational neuroscience, healthcare, and biotechnology.[63]

IBM

Behind skunk works is the notion that to make change, we must sometimes distance the new concepts from established practices. The original IBM PC from the 1980s was not developed at the IBM headquarters in Armonk, New York; instead, it was developed in Boca Raton, Florida, because the PC business model was substantially different from the mainframe business model. IBM was able to prevent disruption by creating a separate and independent organization.

> Christensen concluded that the only way a big company could avoid being disrupted was to set up a small spinoff company, somewhere far away from headquarters, that would function as a start-up, make the new low-end product, and be independent enough to ignore what counted as sensible for the mother ship.[64]

Later as IBM grew, they realized that, just like in a forest, there is a difference between the growth of large mature oaks trees and growing an acorn seed into a sapling. An acorn seed needs sunshine, water, and soil nutrients to create the new growth. Without these elements, the seed will not grow into a sapling or will be stunted to less than its potential. Even then the ratio of seeds to saplings is very low. Around the year 2000, IBM realized they had to make a change. IBM launched the new Emerging Business Opportunities (EBO) management process "for identifying, staffing, funding, and tracking new business initiatives across IBM."[65] IBM built an entirely new management process, one that dovetailed with the old and helped offset the short-term bias of IBM's management culture. They kept the old tracks and laid down some new tracks and had the trains running in parallel.[66]

Blue Zones

An outlier is a statistical concept that describes a set of one or more observations that are separate and significantly different from other observations.[67] In explaining factors that lead to high levels of success, Malcolm Gladwell, in his book, *Outliers*, describes the Roseto effect. The Roseto effect refers to the good heart health of the residents of a small town, Roseto, Pennsylvania, which Gladwell attributes to the stable social structure the Italians brought with them when they immigrated to the United States. He calls the residents of Roseto, Pennsylvania, "outliers," to describe their unique, although temporary, characteristics.[68] The homogeneous Italian American Roseto effect disappeared after the community was Americanized.[69] The Roseto effect is an example of how a healthy, unique, homogenous culture can exist within a larger, different culture. If an outlier can exist in a community, why not apply it to an organization in the form of a magic circle?

A similar concept to Gladwell's outliers is the Blue Zone, a term used by Dan Buettner to describe geographical areas where people have long lifespans. In Buettner's book, *The Blue Zones: 9 Lessons for Living Longer From the People Who've Lived the Longest*, he identifies five areas – Sardinia, Italy; Okinawa, Japan; Loma Linda, California; Nicoya Peninsula, Costa Rica; and Icaria, Greece – where the residents have high life spans. Buettner credits the Power 9™ lessons with the longer lifespans: exercise, finding your purpose, slowing down, limiting eating, eating more vegetables and less meat, drinking red wine, joining a social network, spiritualism, and family life.[70]

Similarly, in business, culturally innovative outliers, like 3M, Google, W. L. Gore, Apple, Whole Foods, and Whirlpool, have been created by their leadership to exhibit multiplicative, innovative characteristics. It is a strikingly simple concept, yet companies struggle to give way to new ideas while entrenched in the success of current practices. For example, while not the inventor of the combi steamer oven, the German company, Rational, pioneered its development, production, and distribution. Invented in the 1960s by Burger Eisenwerke (now part of Electro-lux), the combi steamer oven combines the functionality of a convection oven with a steam cooker. Its smaller footprint saves space in crowded restaurant and professional kitchens while simultaneously reducing electricity and water usage.

Despite its advantages, though, it was slow to catch on. Undaunted, Rational, then a privately held company and already an industry leader in convection ovens, put its resources behind the development, refinement, and sales of the new, innovative combi steamer oven. Led by its visionary founder Siegfried Meister in 1973, the company made the bold move to abandon its convection oven line and focus almost exclusively on the combi steamer oven. Subsequently, Rational has grown from 18 to over 2,000 employees and has become a publicly traded company with subsidiaries worldwide, and nearly €205 million net income, earnings before interest and taxes (EBIT).[71]

3M: Power of Culture

3M has developed a unique culture that allows people to devote a portion of their time at work to thinking, learning, and creating. These cultural behaviors are fragile, and as an organization grows, they need to be protected from the bureaucratic forces that could crush them. A GE executive hired by 3M injected a popular methodology known as Lean, which promoted efficiency and waste removal. 3M's culture of creativity began to deteriorate as a result of this move toward a culture of efficiency. Fortunately, the former GE executive left 3M, and a new leader reversed the downward spiral.[72]

Microsoft: Power of Culture

As noted, culture building is important because it can have a powerful influence on whether innovation is multiplied or diminished. Consider the continued success of Apple's innovation, led by Steve Jobs, in contrast to the plateau of Microsoft under Steve Ballmer. Both companies have had many successful and unsuccessful products.

Despite setbacks with some of its releases, such as Vista, Microsoft has been successful with its Windows operating system. Microsoft also introduced a number of products that never caught on, from the Zune music player to the Windows mobile operating system. Microsoft introduced the Encarta encyclopedia only to remove it from the market after the success of Jimmy Wales and Wikipedia.

Microsoft had an opportunity to capture market share in the mobile device market with the development of a secret new tablet product under the code name Courier. Courier had innovative new features, such as an icon-rich user interface and multitouch, stylus-friendly, dual screens. Unfortunately, although the head of the entertainment and devices division was optimistic about securing additional funding for the project, in April 2010, Microsoft CEO Steve Ballmer denied the request and cancelled the project on the basis that it was "unnecessary." Ballmer instead wanted to incorporate the innovative new features in Courier into the next version of Windows.[73]

Culture Theories

Culture includes teams, organizations, tribes, communities, states, and nations. The theoretic basis for understanding culture has been conceived by a number of experts, some of whom are discussed in the following.

Geert Hofstede

Geert Hofstede proposed an influential five-dimensional model that can be used to quantify differences in cultures. The model includes a power distance index (the acceptance of an uneven distribution of power), individuality and collectivism, masculinity and femininity (the relative value placed on stereotypically male or female personality characteristics and actions), an uncertainty avoidance index, and long-term orientation.[74]

Comparing countries on the individualism and collectivism dimension highlights several differences. Those "individuals who grow up in societies that promote community versus individualism and hierarchy over merit – such as Japan, China, Korea, and many Arab nations – are less likely to creatively challenge the status quo and turn over innovations (or win Nobel Prizes)."[75] For example, the United States is high on the individualism dimension and China is low. The United States has been awarded 383 Nobel Prizes and China only 6.[76]

As assessed by Hofstede's five cultural dimensions, China and the United States are quite different. The United States is high on individualism and low on collectivism, whereas China is the reverse. The United States tends toward a short-term orientation, focusing on immediate results and the present, whereas China tends toward long-term orientation that focuses on perseverance and the future.[77] The United States is more consultative, whereas China is more autocratic.[78]

A competitive, complex, and changing world is placing increased emphasis on both creativity and innovation. Creativity and innovation are the outcomes of a culture of collaboration. The dynamic, collaborative office-of-the-future designed by Steelcase provides a way to use space for motivating employees by facilitating teamwork, collaboration, and innovation.[79] The Steelcase innovation quotient highlights the connection between physical environments and innovation. The innovation quotient is derived from a 21-question survey.[80] The first question is "Has your space been designed to help employees better understand the organization's strategy, brand and culture?"[81]

Steelcase conducted a study in 11 countries between 2006 and 2011 to investigate the connection between space and culture. The 11 countries studied were China, France, Germany, Great Britain, India, Italy, Morocco, the Netherlands, Spain, Russia, and the United States.[82] Steelcase used Hofstede's model and combined it with the concept of proxemics, developed by anthropologist Edward T. Hall Jr., to create a six-dimensional model. Proxemics deals specifically with how space can affect behavior.

The result was Hofstede's five cultural dimensions, combined with Hall's high and low context. "In High context cultures (HCC), an understanding of unspoken rules of engagement is required, therefore indirect implicit communication is essential. In Low context cultures (LCC) a direct and explicit approach is key to cooperation between independent individuals."[83] Each of the countries studied was at a different place on each of the six dimensions. By understanding these cultural differences, more effective teams can be built based on trust and empathy.

The United States is low in context, which means that communication occurs primarily through language and explicit rules. In contrast, China is high in context, which means that communication occurs primarily through gestures, posture, status, connotation, and even seating arrangements.

It is important to note that no culture is completely high-context or low-context, since all societies contain at least some parts that are both high and low. For example, while the United States is a low-context culture, family gatherings (which are common in the American culture) tend to be high-context.[84]

Edgar Schein

Former MIT Sloan School of Management professor Edgar Schein writes, "Culture is an abstraction, yet the forces that are created in social and organizational situations that derive from culture are powerful. If we don't understand the operation of these forces we become victims of them."[85] Schein conceived a three-level pyramidal model of organizational culture, composed of artifacts (the visible elements of a culture), espoused values (guiding principles), and shared basic assumptions.[86]

- Artifacts are tangible, overt, or verbally identifiable elements in any organization. Organizational artifacts are the visible elements in a culture such as the office layout, furniture, and dress code. For example, "The Palo Alto office of IDEO famously has an airplane wing jutting out from one wall, a surprising and puzzling artifact if one doesn't understand IDEO's culture of playful experimentation and free expression."[87]
- Espoused values are the stated guiding principles, values, and rules of behavior that are used to represent the organization. The espoused values may be expressed as employee growth and development, customer orientation, shareholder orientation, and community social responsibility. Herb Kelleher, Southwest Airlines, was known for responding to a variety of proposals from his colleagues with the phrase "low-cost airline" that reaffirmed the espoused value of affordability.[88]
- Shared basic assumptions are hidden, tacit, embedded, automatic behavioral forces of the culture. For example, "Zappos call center employees share a strong belief that providing outstanding service will result in loyal customers, so much so that employees send potential customers to other retailers if Zappos doesn't have the item in stock."[89]

In Search of Excellence (Tom Peters and Robert Waterman)

In 1982, Tom Peters and Robert Waterman published *In Search of Excellence*, in which they proposed eight common themes that were responsible for the success of the selected corporations.[90] The corporations were selected based on their excellence according to established criteria created by the authors. One theme they found is simultaneous loose-tight properties; another is autonomy and entrepreneurship. These two themes are central to understanding the duality needed for innovation.

- Active decision-making – "getting on with it"
- Close to the customer – learning from the people served by the business
- Autonomy and entrepreneurship – fostering innovation and nurturing "champions"
- Productivity through people – treating rank and file employees as a source of quality
- Hands-on, value-driven – management philosophy that guides everyday practice – management showing its commitment
- Stick to the knitting – stay with the business that you know
- Simple form, lean staff – some of the best companies have minimal HQ staff
- Simultaneous loose-tight properties – autonomy in shop-floor activities plus centralized values

Workplace Culture Types

Culture is the collective behavior of an organization that represents the tacit social order shaping decision-making. Culture influences attitudes and behaviors by defining what is encouraged, discouraged, accepted, or rejected within a group. Culture is expressed through the core values and purpose that guide autonomous decision-making to drive progress. If culture is aligned with core values and purpose, it becomes the kinetic energy that sustains the drive for progress.

Workplace culture in organizations can be understood as the way workers view and describe their work environments. Because it is people and leader driven, each workplace is substantially different. Overall, workplace cultures can be categorized into eight types: caring, purpose, learning, enjoyment, results, authority, safety, and order. These are summarized in Figure 9.7. It is important to note that there is no one best way to organize or perfect culture.

1	Caring	Disney	"Caring focuses on relationships and mutual trust. Work environments are warm, collaborative, and welcoming places where people help and support one another. Employees are united by loyalty; leaders emphasize sincerity, teamwork, and positive relationships."
2	Purpose	Whole Foods	"Purpose is exemplified by idealism and altruism. Work environments are tolerant, compassionate places where people try to do good for the long-term future of the world. Employees are united by a focus on sustainability and global communities; leaders emphasize shared ideals and contributing to a greater cause."
3	Learning	Tesla	"Learning is characterized by exploration, expansiveness, and creativity. Work environments are inventive and open-minded places where people spark new ideas and explore alternatives. Employees are united by curiosity; leaders emphasize innovation, knowledge, and adventure."
4	Enjoyment	Zappos	"Enjoyment is expressed through fun and excitement. Work environments are lighthearted places where people tend to do what makes them happy. Employees are united by playfulness and stimulation; leaders emphasize spontaneity and a sense of humor."
5	Results	GlaxoSmithKline	"Results is characterized by achievement and winning. Work environments are outcome oriented and merit-based places where people aspire to achieve top performance."
6	Authority	Huawei	"Authority is defined by strength, decisiveness, and boldness. Work environments are competitive places where people strive to gain personal advantage. Employees are united by strong control; leaders emphasize confidence and dominance."
7	Safety	Lloyd's of London	"Safety is defined by planning, caution, and preparedness. Work environments are predictable places where people are risk-conscious and think things through carefully. Employees are united by a desire to feel protected and anticipate change; leaders emphasize being realistic and planning ahead."
8	Order	Securities and Exchange Commission	"Order is focused on respect, structure, and shared norms. Work environments are methodical places where people tend to play by the rules and want to fit in. Employees are united by cooperation; leaders emphasize shared procedures and time-honored customs."

Figure 9.7 Illustration of Workplace Culture Types and Dimensions

Source: Adapted from Boris Groysberg, Jeremiah Lee, Jesse Price, and J. Yo-Jud Cheng, "The Leader's Guide to Corporate Culture," HBR, accessed August 3, 2020, https://hbr.org/2018/01/the-culture-factor?referral=00060 and https://hbr.org/video/5686668254001/the-8-types-of-company-culture

People Interactions

An organization's orientation toward people interactions and coordination spans a spectrum from highly independent to highly interdependent.[91] Cultures that are more independent place greater value on autonomy, individual action, and competition. Those that are more interdependent place greater emphasis on integration, managing relationships, and coordinating group effort. People in the interdependent cultures tend to collaborate and to see success through the group mindset.[92]

Response to Change

Moreover, an organization's orientation toward agility spans a spectrum from stability to flexibility. Cultures that are stable focus on prioritizing consistency, predictability, and maintenance of the status quo. The stable cultures follow rules, use control structures such as seniority-based staffing, reinforce hierarchy, and strive for efficiency. Cultures that are flexible are adaptable, dexterous, and receptive to change. The flexible cultures tend to prioritize innovation, openness, diversity, and a longer-term orientation.[93]

In Figure 9.8, the X-axis, independent to interdependent, and Y-axis, stability to flexibility, illustrate the workplace culture types and dimensions.

These eight culture types and company examples provide perspective of how firms have evolved around these archetypes. Again, no one type is necessarily better or worse than any other, but each culture is specific to the company, industry, and customer needs. The best culture is that which works best to achieve the vision, mission, objectives, and strategy within a specific organization.

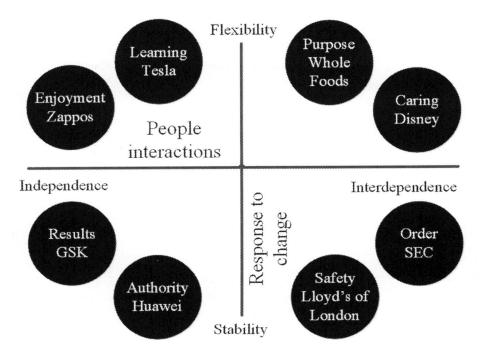

Figure 9.8 Illustration of Workplace Culture Types and Dimensions

Source: Adapted from Boris Groysberg, Jeremiah Lee, Jesse Price, and J. Yo-Jud Cheng, "The Leader's Guide to Corporate Culture," HBR, accessed March 13, 2018, https://hbr.org/2018/01/the-culture-factor?referral=00060 and https://hbr.org/video/5686668254001/the-8-types-of-company-culture

Stable and Interdependent-Order

The US Securities and Exchange Commission (SEC) is considered to have an order-centric culture with a three-part mission:[94]

1. The SEC protects investors by ensuring that they have access to certain basic facts about an investment prior to buying it.
2. The SEC maintains fair, orderly, and efficient markets to protect the public.
3. The SEC facilitates capital formation that includes capital goods, such as equipment, tools, transportation assets, and electricity.

"Rule making is a key function of the commission. And when we are setting the rules for the securities markets, there are many rules we, the SEC, must follow." – Jay Clayton, Chairman.[95]

Stable and Independent Results

GlaxoSmithKline is a science-led global healthcare company that is considered to have a results-oriented culture that uses scientific innovation to deliver the next generation of transformational medicines and vaccines for patients.[96]

1. GlaxoSmithKline focuses on science related to the immune system and the use of human genetics and advanced technologies, and is driven by the multiplier effect of Science × Technology × Culture.
2. GlaxoSmithKline plans to disrupt the discovery, development, and manufacturing of vaccines.
3. GlaxoSmithKline develops products in five categories: oral health, pain relief, respiratory, nutrition and gastrointestinal, and skin health.

"I've tried to keep us focused on a very clear strategy of modernizing ourselves." – Sir Andrew Witty, former CEO GSK.[97]

Flexible and Independent Learning

Tesla is considered to have a learning culture that challenges conventional wisdom as it disrupts combustion-engine vehicles, and builds batteries, and solar panels.[98]

1. Tesla's design model is like that of a software product with dynamic regular improvements and few and simple modular parts. Tesla builds cars by developing software on unique hardware.
2. Tesla has a simple online buying process for customers and builds products with minimal vehicle maintenance requirements.
3. Tesla has a core competency in battery technology that minimizes the total vehicle cost.
4. Tesla's purpose is aligned with the going green megatrend to reduce the impact of climate change.

"I'm interested in things that change the world or that affect the future and wondrous new technology where you see it and you're like 'Wow, how did that even happen?' – Elon Musk, cofounder, and CEO"[99]

Flexible and Interdependent Caring

The Walt Disney Company is a multinational mass media conglomerate that includes Walt Disney Pictures, Walt Disney Animation Studios, Pixar, Marvel Studios, Lucasfilm, 20th Century Studios, Searchlight Pictures, and Blue-Sky Studios.[100] Disney launched a new streaming service in November of 2019, now in competition with Netflix and Amazon.

1. Disney has a culture that provides a high-value customer experience.
2. Disney has developed a brand that engages the loyalty of families.
3. Disney has developed a unique value proposition that is difficult to copy.

"It is incredibly important to be open and accessible and treat people fairly and look them in the eye and tell them what is on your mind." – Bob Iger, CEO.[101]

GM and Toyota Decision-Making

While culture is unique to each organization or company, it must also evolve to fit that organization's vision, mission, goals, and strategy. The challenge is how to adapt to change and evolve for the organization to survive and thrive.

GM is an example of a stable and interdependent culture. Older more established bureaucratic cultures, such as that of General Motors, worked well initially but eventually can create challenges. For instance, in an older more bureaucratic culture, workers would have to be told to fix obvious problems rather than taking the initiative to fix problems expeditiously as they occur. For example, in 2014, it was revealed that GM had installed faulty ignition switches in over a million cars during a period of over ten years. The faulty switch was implicated in the deaths of 13 people. By 2005, the company had received multiple reports of the symptoms of the faulty switch stalling vehicles and preventing airbags from deploying. "With so much at stake, why didn't GM act sooner? The answer, according to many people familiar with the automaker, is a corporate culture reluctant to pass along bad news."[102]

Toyota is an example of a stable and independent culture. Toyota, with their results-oriented, team-based culture, encourages employees to solve problems in real-time through their implementation of a more effective experience, known as the Toyota Production System. Every line worker is trained as a knowledge worker and has the power and support to "stop the line" if they see a defect or problem. Implementing this culture was a bold move that has raised quality and reduced costly errors at the source, putting Toyota in the "driver's seat" of the automotive industry.

As noted earlier, there is no one best way to organize or the perfect organizational culture. These examples rather illustrate the unique aspects and challenges that occur, especially over time, with regard to managing innovation in various organizations and cultures. The key question to ask is "Are we building and optimizing the culture that best fits with the leadership, vision, mission, objectives, and policies of our organization?"

Summary

In this chapter, the role of how organizational culture influences innovation in multiple ways was explored. The six building blocks of an innovative culture, the guiding force of culture, its relationship to a firm's core ideology, the role of culture as a driving force for progress, and the role of culture to empower innovation as a force for change were described. The eight different culture types (caring, purpose, learning, enjoyment, results, authority, safety, and order) all convey the need to develop a culture that is specific to each company's unique leadership, vision, mission, objectives, strategies, and policies. There is no one best way to organize or perfect culture, yet each company or organization must seek to build and optimize the culture that best fits with its leadership and vision. We now turn our attention to the theoretical foundations of innovation. As noted psychologist Kurt Lewin once offered, "There is nothing more practical than a good theory."[103]

Notes

1. B. Broysberg, L. Jeremiah, J. Price, and J. Yo-Jud Cheng, "The Leader's Guide to Corporate Culture," *Harvard Business Review*, January–February 2018.
2. Aaron De Smet, Chris Gagnon, Elizabeth Mygatt, and Richard Steele, "The Nine Traits of Future-Ready Companies," February 23, 2024, accessed June 30, 2021, www.mckinsey.com/business-functions/organization/our-insights/the-nine-traits-of-future-ready-companies.
3. "Corporate Innovation Is Within Reach: Nurturing and Enabling an Entrepreneurial Culture," *Accenture*, December 16, 2013, accessed June 30, 2021, www.fintech-ecosystem.com/assets/study-corp-innovat-n-entrepreneur-l-culture-accenture-fall-2015.pdf.

4. Elaine Pofeldt, "What to Do When Your Boss Won't Support Your Great Ideas," *Forbes*, December 31, 2013, accessed February 23, 2024, www.forbes.com/sites/elainepofeldt/2013/12/31/what-to-do-when-your-boss-wont-support-your-great-ideas/?goback=.gde_35222_member_5825651092066680833#.
5. Gerard J. Tellis, Jaideep C. Prabhu, and Rajesh K. Chandy, "Radical Innovation Across Nations: The Preeminence of Corporate Culture," *Journal of Marketing* 73, no. 1 (2009), 3–23.
6. Jay Rao and Joseph Weintraub, "How Innovative Is Your Company's Culture?" *MITSloan Management Review* 54, no. 3 (2013), 29–37.
7. Jay Rao and Joseph Weintraub, "The Building Blocks of Innovation Survey," *MITSloan Management Review*, accessed February 23, 2024, http://sloanreview.mit.edu/files/2013/03/1d3719138f2.pdf.
8. Michael E. Porter and Mark R. Kramer, "Creating Shared Value," *Harvard Business Review* 89, no. 1–2 (2011), 62–77.
9. Jay Rao and Joseph Weintraub, "The Building Blocks of Innovation Survey," *MITSloan Management Review*, Spring 2013, accessed February 23, 2024; June 30, 2021, http://sloanreview.mit.edu/files/2013/03/1d3719138f2.pdf.
10. Jay Rao and Joseph Weintraub, "How Innovative Is Your Company's Culture?" *MITSloan Management Review* 54, no. 3 (2013), 29–37.
11. Jay Rao and Joseph Weintraub, "The Building Blocks of Innovation Survey," *MITSloan Management Review*, Spring 2013, accessed February 23, 2024, http://sloanreview.mit.edu/files/2013/03/1d3719138f2.pdf.
12. Jay Rao and Joseph Weintraub, "The Building Blocks of Innovation Survey," *MITSloan Management Review*, Spring 2013, accessed February 23, 2024, http://sloanreview.mit.edu/files/2013/03/1d3719138f2.pdf.
13. Clayton M. Christensen, James Allworth, and Karen Dillon, *How Will You Measure Your Life?* (New York: Harper, 2012), 159–161.
14. KPMG, "Benchmarking Innovation Impact 2020," accessed February 23, 2024, https://info.kpmg.us/content/dam/info/en/innovation-enterprise-solutions/pdf/2019/benchmarking-innovation-impact-2020.pdf, 4.
15. George Bradt, "How TriZetto's CEO Changed Its Culture By Changing Its Attitude," *Forbes*, accessed February 23, 2024, www.forbes.com/sites/georgebradt/2012/08/29/how-trizettos-ceo-changed-its-culture-by-changing-its-attitude/.
16. *Wikipedia*, s.v. "Force," accessed June 30, 2021, http://en.wikipedia.org/wiki/Force_(Star_Wars).
17. Gary Hamel, *The Future of Management* (Boston: Harvard Business Review Press, 2007), 29.
18. Pierre Loewe and Jennifer Dominiquini, "Overcoming the Barriers to Effective Innovation," *Strategy & Leadership* 34, no. 1 (2006), 24–31.
19. Whirlpool Corporation, "To Our Stakeholders, A Message from Marc Bitzer, Chairman and CEO," *2020 Sustainability Report*, accessed February 23, 2024, www.whirlpoolcorp.com/2020SustainabilityReport/approach/ceo-message.php.
20. Pierre Loewe and Jennifer Dominiquini, "Overcoming the Barriers to Effective Innovation," *Strategy & Leadership* 34, no. 1 (2006), 24–31.
21. Noreña, Moisés, "Whirlpool's Innovation Journey: An On-Going Quest for a Rock-Solid and Inescapable Innovation Capability," *Management Innvoation eXchange*, January 23, 2013, accessed February 23, 2024, www.managementexchange.com/story/whirlpools-innovation-journey.
22. Whirlpool's Commitment to Innovation, accessed February 23, 2024, https://strategos.com/whirlpools-commitment-innovation/.
23. Dan Fletcher, "A Brief History of the Tylenol Poisonings," *Time*, February 9, 2009, accessed June 30, 2021, http://content.time.com/time/nation/article/0,8599,1878063,00.html.
24. Jim Collins and Jerry I. Porras, *Built to Last: Successful Habits of Visionary Companies* (New York: HarperCollins, 2002), 58–61.
25. Bill Taylor, "How Hewlett-Packard Lost the HP Way," September 23, 2011, accessed February 23, 2024, https://hbr.org/2011/09/how-hewlett-packard-lost-the-h.
26. Jim Collins and Jerry I. Porras, *Built to Last: Successful Habits of Visionary Companies* (New York: HarperCollins, 2002).
27. Jonny Evans, "Tim Cook Has Now Led Apple for Nine Years," August 24, 2020, accessed June 27, 2021, www.computerworld.com/article/3572550/tim-cook-has-now-led-apple-for-nine-years.html.
28. Jim Collins and Jerry I. Porras, *Built to Last: Successful Habits of Visionary Companies* (New York: HarperCollins, 2002), 73.

29. Jim Collins and Jerry I. Porras, *Built to Last: Successful Habits of Visionary Companies* (New York: HarperCollins, 2002), 68–71.
30. *Wikipedia*, s.v. "Marc Benioff," accessed August 3, 2020, http://en.wikipedia.org/wiki/Marc_Benioff.
31. Salesforce.com, "Our Impact: 25 Years of Giving Back," accessed July 31, 2024, https://www.sales force.com/company/philanthropy/.
32. Salesforce Foundation, "1% Model," accessed June 30, 2021, www.salesforce.org/pledge-1/.
33. Simon Sinek, *Start with Why: How Great Leaders Inspire Everyone to Take Action* (New York: Penguin, 2009).
34. Jim Collins and Jerry I. Porras, *Built to Last: Successful Habits of Visionary Companies* (New York: HarperCollins, 2002), 76.
35. Jim Collins and Jerry I. Porras, *Built to Last: Successful Habits of Visionary Companies* (New York: HarperCollins, 2002), 88.
36. Jim Collins and Jerry I. Porras, *Built to Last: Successful Habits of Visionary Companies* (New York: HarperCollins, 2002), 68–71.
37. Jim Collins and Jerry I. Porras, *Built to Last: Successful Habits of Visionary Companies* (New York: HarperCollins, 2002), 16.
38. *Wikipedia*, s.v. "Onchocerciasis," accessed June 30, 2021, http://en.wikipedia.org/wiki/Onchocerciasis.
39. Jim Collins and Jerry I. Porras, *Built to Last: Successful Habits of Visionary Companies* (New York: HarperCollins, 2002), 47.
40. Viktor Frankl, *Man's Search for Meaning* (New York: Pocket Books, 1984).
41. Alex Pattakos, *Prisoners of Our Thoughts* (San Francisco: Berrett-Koehler, 2010), 25.
42. Jim Collins, *Good to Great: Why Some Companies Make the Leap . . . and Others Don't* (New York: HarperCollins, 2002), 83–87.
43. Elizabeth Landau, "CVS Stores to Stop Selling Tobacco," *CNN*, February 5, 2014, accessed February 23, 2024, www.cnn.com/2014/02/05/health/cvs-cigarettes/index.html.
44. Bruce Nussbaum, *Creative Intelligence: Harnessing the Power to Create, Connect, and Inspire* (New York: Harper Business, 2013), 12.
45. Robert G. Cooper, "Stage-Gate Systems: A New Tool for Managing New Products," *Business Horizons* 33, no. 3 (1990), 44–54.
46. F. Scott Fitzgerald, *The Crack-Up* (New York: New Directions Publishing, 1945).
47. "Apple's Design Process," *Lessons from Business Legends*, accessed February 23, 2024, www. 1000ventures.com/business_guide/cs_innovation-npd-design_apple.html.
48. Jim Collins, *Good to Great: Why Some Companies Make the Leap . . . and Others Don't* (New York: HarperCollins, 2001).
49. Jim Collins, "A Culture of Discipline," accessed February 23, 2024, www.jimcollins.com/concepts/a-culture-of-discipline.html.
50. Jim Collins and Morten T. Hansen, *Great by Choice* (New York: Harper Business, 2011), 97–98.
51. Jim Collins and Morten T. Hansen, *Great by Choice* (New York: Harper Business, 2011).
52. Jim Collins and Morten T. Hansen, *Great by Choice* (New York: Harper Business, 2011).
53. Johan Huizinga, *Homo Ludens: A Study of the Play-Element in Culture* (Boston: Beacon Press, 1955).
54. Vijay Govindarajan, "Executing on Innovation," *YouTube Video*, posted by "Harvard Business Review," September 28, 2010, accessed June 30, 2021, www.youtube.com/watch?v=bQpNhZ1SndQ.
55. Bruce Nussbaum, *Creative Intelligence: Harnessing the Power to Create, Connect, and Inspire* (New York: Harper Business, 2013), 126.
56. "The Thomas Edison Center at Menlo Park," accessed June 30, 2021, www.menloparkmuseum.org/.
57. *Wikipedia*, s.v. "Lockheed Martin's Advanced Development Programs (ADP)," accessed June 30, 2021, http://en.wikipedia.org/wiki/Lockheed_Martin_Advanced_Development_Programs.
58. *Wikipedia*, s.v. "Li'l Abner," accessed March 8, 2013, http://en.wikipedia.org/wiki/Li'l_Abner.
59. *Wikipedia*, s.v. "Skunk Works," accessed June 30, 2021, http://en.wikipedia.org/wiki/Skunk_Works.
60. *Wikipedia*, s.v. "Bell Labs," accessed June 30, 2021, http://en.wikipedia.org/wiki/Bell_Labs.
61. Malcolm Gladwell, "Creation Myth," *The New Yorker*, May 16, 2011, accessed June 30, 2021, www.newyorker.com/reporting/2011/05/16/110516fa_fact_gladwell.
62. *Wikipedia*, s.v. "Skunkworks Project," accessed February 23, 2024, http://en.wikipedia.org/wiki/Skunkworks_project.
63. *Wikipedia*, s.v. "X Development," accessed August 3, 2020, https://en.wikipedia.org/wiki/X_ (company).
64. Larissa MacFarquhar, "When Giants Fail," *The New Yorker*, May 14, 2012, 87.

65. Gary Hamel, *The Future of Management* (Boston: Harvard Business School Press, 2007), 219–220.
66. Gary Hamel, *The Future of Management* (Boston: Harvard Business School Press, 2007), 218–219.
67. *Wikipedia*, s.v. "Outlier," accessed June 30, 2021, http://en.wikipedia.org/wiki/Outlier.
68. Malcolm Gladwell, *Outliers: The Story of Success* (New York: Little, Brown and Company, 2008).
69. B. Egolf, J. Lasker, S. Wolf, and L. Potvin, "The Roseto Effect: A 50-Year Comparison of Mortality Rates," *American Journal of Public Health* 82, no. 8 (1992), 1089–1092.
70. Dan Buettner, *The Blue Zones, Second Edition: 9 Lessons for Living Longer from the People Who've Lived the Longest* (Washington, DC: National Geographic Society, 2012).
71. *Wikipedia*, s.v. "Rational AG, 2010 Annual Report," accessed June 27, 2021, http://en.wikipedia.org/wiki/Rational_AG.
72. Brian Hindo, "At 3M, A Struggle between Efficiency and Creativity," *BusinessWeek*, June 10, 2007, accessed June 30, 2021, www.effectuation.org/wp-content/uploads/2016/06/3m-struggle-between-efficiency-and-creativity.pdf.
73. *Wikipedia*, s.v. "Microsoft Courier," accessed June 30, 2021, http://en.wikipedia.org/wiki/Microsoft_Courier.
74. Geert Hofstede and Gert Jan Hofstede, *Cultures and Organizations: Software of the Mind*, 2nd ed. (New York: McGraw-Hill, 2005).
75. Jeff Dyer, Hal Gregersen, and Clayton M. Christensen, *The Innovator's DNA* (Boston: Harvard Business Review Press, 2011), 22.
76. "Nobel Prize Winners by Country," accessed February 23, 2024, www.worldatlas.com/articles/top-30-countries-with-nobel-prize-winners.html.
77. "What Is Hofstede's Cultural Dimensions Theory," *Peak Frameworks*, accessed February 23, 2024, www.peakframeworks.com/post/hofstede-cultural-dimensions#:~:text=China%2C%20with%20a%20high%20LTO,social%20obligations%2C%20and%20quick%20results.
78. Christina Larson, "Office Cultures: A Global Guide," *Bloomberg Business Week*, June 13, 2013, accessed June 30, 2021, www.bloomberg.com/news/articles/2013-06-13/office-cultures-a-global-guide.
79. "How Place Fosters Innovation," *Steelcase*, accessed February 23, 2024, www.steelcase.com/asia-en/research/articles/topics/design/place-fosters-innovation/.
80. "Amplify Your Innovation Quotient: The New I.Q.," *360°, 360.steelcase.com*, Issue 66, p. 30.
81. "Amplify Your Innovation Quotient: The New I.Q.," *360°, 360.steelcase.com*, Issue 66, p. 30.
82. "Culture Code," *360°, 360.steelcase.com*, Issue 65, p. 24.
83. "Culture Code," *360°, 360.steelcase.com*, Issue 65, p. 24.
84. "High-Context Culture: Definition, Examples," accessed February 23, 2024, http://education-portal.com/academy/lesson/high-context-culture-definition-examples-quiz.html#lesson.
85. Edgar Schein, *Organizational Culture and Leadership*, 3rd ed. (San Francisco, CA: Jossey-Bass, A Wiley Imprint, 2004).
86. *Wikipedia*, s.v. "Edgar Schein," accessed March 4, 2021, Edgar Schein – Wikipedia.
87. David Burkus, "How to Tell If Your Company Has a Creative Culture," December 2, 2014, accessed February 23, 2024, https://hbr.org/2014/12/how-to-tell-if-your-company-has-a-creative-culture.
88. David Burkus, "How to Tell If Your Company Has a Creative Culture," December 2, 2014, accessed February 23, 2024, https://hbr.org/2014/12/how-to-tell-if-your-company-has-a-creative-culture.
89. David Burkus, "How to Tell If Your Company Has a Creative Culture," December 2, 2014, accessed February 23, 2024, https://hbr.org/2014/12/how-to-tell-if-your-company-has-a-creative-culture.
90. Thomas J. Peters and Robert H. Waterman, *In Search of Excellence: Lessons from America's Best-Run Companies* (New York: Harper & Row, 1982).
91. Boris Groysberg, Jeremiah Lee, Jesse Price, and J. Yo-Jud Cheng, "The Leader's Guide to Corporate Culture," January–February 2018, accessed February 23, 2024, https://hbr.org/2018/01/the-culture-factor.
92. Boris Groysberg, Jeremiah Lee, Jesse Price, and J. Yo-Jud Cheng, "The Leader's Guide to Corporate Culture," January–February 2018, accessed February 23, 2024, https://hbr.org/2018/01/the-culture-factor.
93. Boris Groysberg, Jeremiah Lee, Jesse Price, and J. Yo-Jud Cheng, "The Leader's Guide to Corporate Culture," January–February 2018, accessed February 23, 2024, https://hbr.org/2018/01/the-culture-factor.
94. U.S. Securities and Exchange Commission, "The Role of the SEC," accessed June 30, 2021, www.investor.gov/introduction-investing/investing-basics/role-sec.
95. Boris Groysberg, Jeremiah Lee, Jesse Price, and J. Yo-Jud Cheng, "The Leader's Guide to Corporate Culture," January–February 2018, accessed February 23, 2024, https://hbr.org/2018/01/the-culture-factor.
96. GlaxoSmithKline, "Research and Development," accessed February 23, 2024, www.gsk.com/en-gb/research-and-development/.

97. Boris Groysberg, Jeremiah Lee, Jesse Price, and J. Yo-Jud Cheng, "The Leader's Guide to Corporate Culture," January–February 2018, accessed February 23, 2024, https://hbr.org/2018/01/the-culture-factor.

98. Lou Shipley, "How Tesla Sets Itself Apart," February 28, 2020, accessed February 23, 2024, https://hbr.org/2020/02/how-tesla-sets-itself-apart.

99. Boris Groysberg, Jeremiah Lee, Jesse Price, and J. Yo-Jud Cheng, "The Leader's Guide to Corporate Culture," January–February 2018, accessed February 23, 2024, https://hbr.org/2018/01/the-culture-factor.

100. *Wikipedia*, s.v. "The Walt Disney Company," accessed June 30, 2021, https://en.wikipedia.org/wiki/The_Walt_Disney_Company.

101. Boris Groysberg, Jeremiah Lee, Jesse Price, and J. Yo-Jud Cheng, "The Leader's Guide to Corporate Culture," January–February 2018, accessed February 23, 2024, https://hbr.org/2018/01/the-culture-factor.

102. Michael A. Fletcher and Steven Mufson, "Why Did GM Take So Long to Respond to Deadly Defect? Corporate Culture May Hold Answer," *The Washington Post*, March 30, 2014, accessed February 23, 2024, www.washingtonpost.com/business/economy/why-did-gm-take-so-long-to-respond-to-deadly-defect-corporate-culture-may-hold-answer/2014/03/30/5c366f6c-b691-11e3-b84e-897d3d12b816_story.html.

103. Kendra Cherry, "Quotes from Psychologist Kurt Lewin," April 21, 2020, accessed February 23, 2024, www.verywellmind.com/kurt-lewin-quotes-2795692.

10 Innovation Theory

Experience without theory is blind, but theory without experience is mere intellectual play.
— Immanuel Kant

In this chapter, we focus on why innovation theory and practice are important, especially about how it leads to developing innovation capabilities. To paraphrase the noted German philosopher Immanuel Kant, "theory without practice is meaningless, but practice without theory is blind." Interestingly, innovation and music have quite a bit in common when it comes to how each discipline is organized from theory to form to function.

For example, music is a universal language of creativity that inspires our human experiences while intersecting very different and diverse cultures. Our imaginations create insights that spark vibrant musical sounds. The language of music includes a set of symbols that are combined into melodies and harmonies that are illustrated on music scores. Music theory is the understanding of how to make and describe the language of music. That is, music theory is an organized way for creating music that allows musicians to communicate their ideas to one another in a musical composition. The music elements of melody, harmony, and rhythm are the building blocks that allow us to read, play, study, and write music. In a similar way, the innovation elements, degrees, and types previously outlined in Chapter 2, "Elements," form a matrix that marks the inception of the innovation theory pathways that provide a way for a common understanding that enables the field of innovation to advance as discipline.

Innovation theory is important especially with a focus on applying innovation theory in general to inform the innovation and entrepreneurship competency framework and the building of core capabilities. Specifically, we examine the evolution of a micro and macro theory of innovation, economic growth, and how innovation is managed. The interactions between the elements, degrees and types are used to explicitly define the innovation discipline. For example, later in this chapter, Figure 10.3 outlines ten key innovation types that cover a broad spectrum of innovation capabilities. The degrees and types form a matrix that marks the inception of the innovation theory pathways to provide a way to understand how to achieve meaningfully significant progress.

The Innovation Discipline

Why Is Innovation Theory Important?

Innovation theory provides for the understanding of the language of innovation. Innovation theory is an organized way for facilitating how ideas are communicated to one another. While a theory describes a specific realm or knowledge and attempts to explain how it works, applied disciplines

DOI: 10.4324/9781003034308-11

can be described as realms of study and practice that are understood in their application and used in practice.[1] The innovation elements are the building blocks that allows us to focus on our imaginations, creativity, and innovation competencies to establish the innovation discipline in theory and practice.

To build innovation capability, decision-making should be based on an understanding of discipline of innovation to achieve a sustainable competitive advantage that adds value and strives to lower costs. Too often, however, when talking about innovation, it is the equivalent of the Tower of Babel where each person often speaks their own language when describing innovation. For innovation to progress to a discipline, clear terminology, innovation training for everyone, and measurements of our progress are needed. That is, innovation needs to be grounded in theory and tested in practice.

Innovation and entrepreneurship are two of the most important and popular concepts in business and economics today. Yet the two terms have become so ubiquitous they are in danger of becoming almost meaningless, and an underlying, generally agreed-upon theory of innovation remains a challenge.

Micro-Theory of Innovation

Genrich Alshuller was a Soviet engineer, inventor, and writer who created the theory of inventive problem solving, known by its Russian acronym TRIZ, or TIPS in English. Alshuller's theory is grounded in research into 40,000 patent abstracts to determine how innovation had taken place. Based on the notion that you can use an existing solution and adapt it to the current problem; his research revealed a set of 40 principles of invention that could be applied in multiple situations or contradictions.[2]

For example, principle #1, segmentation, focuses on disaggregation. If a small furniture store seeks to increase inventory, you could design the furniture in component parts, build the product's parts, package the flattened product to save space, and sell the flattened product for assembly by the customer. When addressing a problem, a contradiction that needs to be resolved is often experienced. An example of a contradiction is the improvement in a furniture product may result in an increase in weight which can be a disadvantage to the product. A solution would be to use a lighter material, principle #40, composite materials.[3]

Building on TIPS, Greg Yezersky worked toward capturing a more general theory of innovation (GTI), centered on reactive innovation (considered defensive; value proposition is known), proactive innovation (offensive; value proposition is unknown), and on-demand innovation capability.[4] Yezersky is quick to note, however, that his GTI is not a "quick fix" for a company's ongoing quest for innovation and growth. Rather, he argues it is "a potent theory that is capable of controlling the process of innovation, which would effectively work for any specific application."[5]

Macro-Theory of Innovation

While Yezersky focused more on the micro-analytic level of innovation that was based on methodologies and tools to develop his general theory of innovation, others have taken a macro level approach. Researchers at Aalborg University in Sweden and the IKE-group have examined the need for a general theory of innovation from the perspective of national systems of innovation. Their learning-centered approach suggests that "[t]he important elements of the process of innovation tend to become transnational and global rather than national" and that these elements "will be most important in science-based areas where the communication is easier to formalize and codify."[6] The Aalborg IKE-group research promises to inform ongoing policy needs in the area of innovation and entrepreneurship.

The discipline of economics provides insights into the understanding of the relationship between innovation and subsequent economic growth. While multiple factors, such as human intellectual capital, new knowledge, and population growth can influence economic growth, the next section provides an overview of the role of the field of economics in the development of an applied theory of innovation.

Economic Growth – Schumpeter

The Austrian-born American economist Joseph Schumpeter is largely credited with one of the earliest attempts to outline a theory of innovation, stressing the core and pivotal role of continuous innovation in economic "disequilibrium" and "creative destruction." As noted by researchers Magnus Henrekson and Tino Sanandaji, "This Schumpeterian definition of the entrepreneur as an innovator and as a driver of growth dominates in theoretical entrepreneurship research and in entrepreneurship policy."[7] While certainly foundational toward a general theory of entrepreneurship, Schumpeter's theory only partly addresses the need for a general theory of innovation.

Exogenous Economic Growth Model

In 1987, Robert M. Solow received the Nobel Prize for his economic growth model. Solow built an economic model to study the question of why some economies grow faster than others. He proposed a model wherein long-term economic growth is a function of the supply of labor (L) and education (e), capital (K) accumulation (the supply of savings to invest in technology), and ideas (A) that result in increases in productivity through innovation and technological progress (Solow, 1956).[8] The addition of more capital and labor inputs and ideas and new technology causes economic growth. The most important factor that he discovered was ideas (A) that stimulate technological progress are the leading factor for economic growth.[9] "The Solow Growth Model is an exogenous model of economic growth that analyzes changes in the level of output in an economy over time as a result of changes in the population growth rate, the savings rate, and the rate of technological progress."[10]

Endogenous Economic Growth Model

Robert Solow introduced the notion that ideas and technological innovation are the primary drivers of economic growth but had not modeled how economic decisions and market conditions determine the creation of new technologies. Solow concluded that technological change was a key driver of economic growth and that technological change was based on an exogenous growth model, not something determined in the model, but an outside factor.[11]

In 2018, Paul Romer received the Nobel Prize for his work on innovation and economic growth. He proposed the notion of endogenous growth theory that was both conceptual and practical, that is, growth is based on internal and not external forces. He explained how ideas are different from other goods and require specific conditions to thrive in a market.[12] The investment of human intellectual capital, innovation, and knowledge is a contributor to economic growth. Specifically, "[t]he endogenous growth theory primarily holds that the long run growth rate of an economy depends on policy measures. For example, subsidies for research and development or education increase the growth rate in some endogenous growth models by increasing the incentive for innovation."[13]

The role of ideas and technological progress is part of the exogenous and endogenous growth models. The difference is that in the exogenous growth model the determining factors are outside the economic system, whereas in the endogenous model, the activities within the economic system, such as explicit and deliberate polices, can achieve economic growth.

Collectively considered, these micro- and macro-approaches to the development of innovation theory hold considerable promise for unifying the general field. Currently, there is no universally accepted general theory of innovation. Still, the immediate question is this: how does theory relate to our current needs in innovation and entrepreneurship? In addition, based on the various studies, the success rate for innovations is relatively low and needs to improve; what can be done to improve the innovation success rate and prevent failures?

While theories and models are often used interchangeably, they are quite different. Theories generally rely on models to illustrate key aspects, while models do not necessarily require a theoretical foundation. Applied theories, as noted earlier, reveal the larger representation of a set of activities. We posit, in part, that the continued clarification of an applied theory of innovation includes identifying and codifying a comprehensive innovation and entrepreneurship process model. The innovation and entrepreneurship competency framework provides a comprehensive overview of behaviors, thinking, problem solving, knowledge, creativity, culture, theory, entrepreneurship, strategy, leadership, ecosystems, and technology.

What Is the Discipline of Innovation?

This raises the question of what is the discipline of innovation? As noted throughout this text, innovation is the process of making changes in something established, especially by introducing new methods, ideas, or products.[14] In essence, innovation is a humanistic process to add meaningfully significant value and achieve sustainable outcomes that can improve the world in many ways. Ultimately, the discipline of innovation accomplishes this via putting people first.

To achieve a discipline of innovation requires training for everyone that provides an understanding of the elements of innovation to include degrees and types of innovation. There are degrees of innovation from low-value, incremental to evolutionary, to high-value revolutionary and disruptive innovations. There are types of innovation that span products, services and experiences, solutions, systems, processes, business models, managerial, platforms, brand, and science and technology that when combined are synergistic.

How Is Innovation Managed?

The eminent Austrian-born American management consultant, educator, and author, Peter Drucker, is often regarded as the father of modern business management. He notes, "Most of what we call management consists of making it difficult for people to get their work done."[15] In many respects, the way we manage today was an important innovation in the 1920s by those who were born in the middle of the 1800s. Even though the world is now dramatically different, the way we manage today is often rooted in the past. Our aspirational goal should be to integrate imagination, creativity, and innovation into how we lead future organizations. While the way we manage has changed in many ways, from the advent of the computer to artificial intelligence, the Internet of things, the industrial Internet of things, the emergence of the gig economy to the democratization of funding via crowd source funding and beyond, there is always a need for both new and established ventures to continuously innovate or run the risk of becoming obsolete. Figure 10.1 illustrates the intersection of imagination, creativity, and innovation. It is here that companies must explore what is, what is next, and what is next after next.

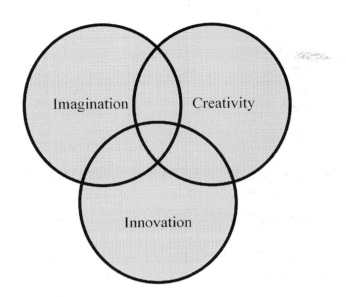

Figure 10.1 Illustration of the Intersection of Imagination, Creativity, and Innovation

Why Is Innovation Theory and Practice Important?

Innovation theory and practice is important for several reasons. As noted, innovation theory is important for building innovation capability. There continues to be a need for a common language and understanding for the discipline of innovation to have structural integrity. Moreover, innovation theory and practice are important essentially because they are drivers for better standards of living, creating a sustainable advantage, economic growth, and job opportunities. Companies are impacted by both a lack of innovation capability as well as attending to building innovation capability. For example, the Procter & Gamble Company did well with incremental innovations, such as adding enzymes to Tide®, stannous fluoride to Crest®, and select-a-size to Bounty® paper towels. Despite talent and resources, however, their innovation efforts have slowed. An example of a product launch was Swiffer® in 1999, that originated from a separate firm, Kao in Japan. Swiffer® product variants continue to be offered as well as the replacement refills and pads. In theory, innovation consists of the realm of a set of variables describing a system, which leads to an outcome. In practice, the question becomes one of building continuous innovation capability.

Innovation Research

Building Innovation Capability

The international strategy consulting firm Strategyn sponsored independent research to study the success rates of traditional innovation methods as compared to its Outcome-Driven Innovation™ (ODI) process. This study included 12 sources, such as the *Harvard Business Review*, the consulting firm Frost & Sullivan, the professional services firm PricewaterhouseCoopers, the Product Development Management Association (PDMA), the Corporate Strategy Board, and others. The study found that the average innovation success rate was 17%, as compared to Strategyn's ODI 86% success rate.[16]

In an innovation study by Accenture in 2018, despite increased spending on innovation, overall participants reported a 27% decline on the return on innovation-related spending over the past five years.[17] The implication is that if a company pursues innovation haphazardly, much of the investment ends up being non-strategic, poorly linked to the business, and undermanaged.

Accenture's survey of C-level executives suggests a way to build innovation capability is to focus on three key elements:[18]

1. Creating a willingness to be change oriented, overcome the status quo, and transition to the future.
2. Creating a willingness to change the outcome to focus on innovation results.
3. Creating a willingness to invest more aggressively in truly disruptive innovation initiatives.

All of this suggests the need for an innovation and entrepreneurship competency framework that provides both a comprehensive overview as well as detailed outline of how the complexities and intricacies of innovation unfold in theory and practice.

Innovation Success Rates

In a survey that was conducted by the National Science Foundation titled the "2008 Business R&D and Innovation Survey (BRDIS)," it was reported that "overall about 9% of the estimated 1.5 million for-profit companies were active product innovators in 2006–08."[19]

In 2000, P&G was achieving a 15% success rate for innovations, based on meeting revenue and profit targets. P&G undertook several steps to systematize innovation, such as developing the Connect + Develop program to increase innovative ideas from external sources and intersect with other disciplines. Realizing they needed to do more, P&G started an initiative for a new-growth factory based on Christensen's disruptive innovation theory: develop new solutions that are accessible, simple, affordable, and convenient for customers in new markets. The success rate has since improved from 15% to 50%.[20]

The Pace of Change

"We live in interesting, shape-shifting times. Our world is turning faster than ever, and the pace of change is accelerating on a global scale with more complexity and more interconnections than ever before. And one thing is for sure: It will only go faster in the future."[21] We are experiencing exponential change, hyper-competition, and commoditization of knowledge. Organizations need to reimagine their leadership and managerial models by innovating faster than their peers to adapt to change, build cultures for everyone to innovate, and create new knowledge.[22] To innovate faster everyone needs to reinvent leadership and management by setting high aspirational goals to improve the well-being of the workforce, challenging the prevailing dogma, and operating on the edge of the herd.

Simultaneously organizations need to demonstrate a meaningfully significant purpose built upon true north core values focused on integrity. Because the pace of change has increased, without high-order value innovations, the successful companies of the present may not be successful in the future.

Standard and Poor's 500 Index

The makeup of the S&P testifies to the number of firms that have failed to adapt because of competitive forces. Numerous factors can influence a company's innovation advantage, such as its research and development, organizational culture, intellectual property, modern workforce competencies, decision-making capabilities, and the strength of the higher education systems.

The Standard and Poor's 500 index is continually changing as companies are added and subtracted based on their fulfilling the required criteria, as well as subsequent mergers and acquisitions. These changes reflect the perpetual turbulence of the "creative destruction," suggested by Joseph Schumpeter and the difficulty of managing organizations effectively.[23]

An indication of the dynamic volatility that is occurring is the length of time that an S&P company remains in the index. In 2007, at the 50th anniversary of the S&P 500, only 86 original companies remained, which brings to question as to why only a small proportion of original firms were still listed.[24] The average tenure of S&P 500 companies in 1965 was 33 years, and in 1990 it was 20 years. Innosight forecasts the tenure of companies in the index to shrink to 14 years by 2026. According to Innosight's forecast, about 50% of the S&P 500 will be replaced over the next 10 years if the trend continues.[25]

Innovation Theory and Practice

Given the pace of change and indication of dynamic volatility revealed in the S&P 500, how do we use innovation theory to inform practice? Research suggests that there are three key aspects related to how we continue to innovate into the future. The first is **improving the way we innovate innovation**. The second is **creating organizations that are adaptable to change**. The third speaks directly to organizations **building innovation capabilities**.

Innovate Innovation

How do we move to the future? The most effective way to improve our ability to innovate is to improve the way we *innovate innovation:*[26]

1. How do you build organizations that are fit for the future?
2. How do you build organizations that are fit for people? Are people reluctant to generate ideas, or do they feel that it is their responsibility?
3. How do you ensure that the people are continuously inspired to engage in fulfilling the purpose of their organizations and be a part of high-performing teams?
4. How do we ensure that the people are healthy and engaged in wellness programs that promote their well-being, their intellect and creativity, and, therefore, their individual competencies?

Adaptable Organizations

To manage innovation requires that we build organizations that are adaptable to change as fast as change itself and that provide the leadership to inspire the employees to want to come to work every day and give their creative gifts. Each person must feel that innovation is part of everyone's job.[27]

1. Is your organization adaptable to change?
2. Has your organization made innovation everyone's job?
3. Are the employees excited to come to work and inspired to give their creativity?

Building Capability

Many organizations are focused on incremental improvements in their execution capability through the implementation of small changes, the removal of waste, and the elimination of defects in their products and processes. In contrast, few organizations have dramatically improved their overall ability to manage innovation and systemically renew their overall organizations.[28]

1. Have the employees been trained to be innovators?
2. If you have an idea, how would you get approval for the funds and free time to pursue the opportunity?
3. Is the organization's innovation performance being measured?
4. The discipline of innovation and entrepreneurship can be understood and learned using a competency-based approach. The 12 elements of innovation outlined in Chapter 2 provide clarity for increasing the awareness and understanding of innovation and entrepreneurship. The 12 competencies provide a framework for defining what needs to be learned to improve innovation capability and promise that we can revitalize our human resource talent's knowledge, skills, and attitudes, as well as our economy and our overall well-being. With the innovation and entrepreneurship competency framework as a foundation, we can outline a learning architecture for adaptability.

Innovation Foundation

Like music theory, the innovation theory can be used to explicitly define the discipline of innovation using the degrees and type elements that were described in Chapter 2.

Innovation: Degrees and Types

Innovation Degrees

As Gary Hamel notes, the only way to create value is to innovate.[29] Innovations have increasing degrees of scale from incremental, evolutionary, revolutionary, to disruptive. For example, revolutionary degrees encompass several paths such as non-disruptive creations and disruptive creations (superior or inferior displacement). The innovation degrees are the foundation for understanding the innovation paths. These innovation degrees are outlined in Figure 10.2.

Innovation Types

Similarly, music has genres such as classical, blues, folk, hip-hop, country, pop, jazz, and rock. Innovations have genres or types that include products, services/experiences, solutions, systems, processes, business models, platform, brand, and science and technology. Figure 10.3 outlines ten key innovation types that cover a broad spectrum of innovation capabilities.

Singular innovation types in innovation processes have been used to drive innovation in many businesses. For instance, Ford's assembly line, the Toyota Production System, and the Pilkington Glass Process have had a significant impact. When the Hoover Dam was constructed from 1931 to 1936, the engineers determined that it would take 125 years for the concrete to cool using a continuous pour process. Because concrete heats and contracts, the engineers changed the process to insert one-inch steel pipes in the fifty-foot-square and five-foot-high forms. To prevent cracking and crumbling, they used the cool Colorado River water to cure the concrete.[30]

The most effective innovators pursue multiple innovation types simultaneously. For example, Apple has created a vast ecosystem of products, services/experiences, business models, platforms, technology, and brands to support its mission.

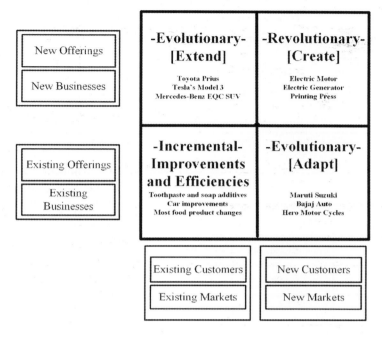

Figure 10.2 Illustration of Innovation Degrees

Source: Adapted from: Tim Brown, *Change by Design*, (New York: Harper, 2009), 161.

Products	Apple (iPod, iPhone, iPad design at premium prices), Alphabet/Google (Advertising models).
Customer Experience	Ikea (assemble furniture yourself); FedEx, Disney (recreation), Southwest Airlines (affordable enjoyable experience). Solutions: Dell (selling custom built PC direct to buyers), Zipcar (alternative to car buying), IBM (moved away from mainframes to solutions), and Uber (mobile app driven transportation service).
Solutions	McKinsey & Company, Accenture, Boston Consulting Group, Bain and Company, and PWC.
Systems	Supply chain systems like Target, Wal-Mart (high quantity and low margins); Ikea (assemble furniture yourself and save). Cost is strategic and price is a tactic.
Processes	Toyota production system, Pilkington Glass, Ford assembly line, Nucor (steel using electric arc mini mills), and IDEO's design thinking.
Business Models	Amazon (Prime subscription service); Apple (iTunes digital music service), Netflix's subscription model, Xerox (pay per copy); ARM Holdings (licensing of their designs); and HP (print cartridges) use the razor-and-blades business model.
Managerial	Peter Drucker's management concepts; companies such as Intuit, Netflix, Google, 3M, Steelcase, and Whirlpool.
Platform	Platform innovations are based on architecture and design concepts of extensible modularity. Some platform examples are Amazon's cloud services, Netflix's video streaming, Uber's platform that allows drivers and passengers to engage for a ride-sharing service; Airbus and Boeing airliners; GE and Rolls Royce jet engines; microprocessors from Intel and Samsung, ARM Holdings (microprocessor designs); Lego blocks; Tesla automobiles; SpaceX reusable rockets; and Google (Android), Microsoft (Windows 7 and 10) and Apple (iOS) operating systems.
Brands	P&G (brand management, premium branded products), Trademarks (Intel inside); Disney magic; ecosystem branding of Meta (Facebook), Apple, Alphabet, Amazon, and Microsoft.
Science and Technology	Copernicus's heliocentric model, Mendeleev's periodic table, Franklin's lightning as electrical, Mendel's laws of inheritance, Bohr's model of the atom, Watson and Crick's discovery of the structure of DNA, William Shockley, John Bardeen and Walter Brattain's invention of the first transistor, Charles Darwin and Alfred Wallace's theory of evolution by natural selection, and Louis Pasteur's germ theory.

Figure 10.3 Illustration of Innovation Types

Innovation Matrix

The breadth and depth of the discipline of innovation can be understood using an innovation matrix (see Figure 10.4) that combines innovation degrees and types. If one combines degrees and types into a matrix, then one can expand his or her understanding of opportunities that can be simultaneously pursued.

The Innovation Matrix				
Innovation Types	Innovation Degrees			
	Incremental	Evolutionary	Revolutionary	Disruptive
Products	Product additives	Smartphones	Xerox, heart-lung machine	Transistor radio
Services	Automated checkout	IKEA, Whole Foods	Disney, Sesame Street	Netflix
Solutions	Airplane Wi-Fi	Heliocopter	Airplane	Wikipedia
Systems	Windows and Apple OS	Artificial intelligence	The Internet	Bell System
Processes	Design thinking	Lean and Six Sigma	Ford assembly line	Electric arc furnaces
Business Models	Subscription model	One-stop shopping	Microfinance	Discount retailers
Managerial	Participative leadership styles	Statistical process control	Decentralization	Scientific management
Platforms	Jet engine efficiency	Airbnb and Uber	Intel x86 Microprocesors	Alibaba and Amazon
Brands	Branded ecosystems	Coca-Cola	Trademarks	Starbucks Customer Experience
Science and Technology	Antibacterial paint	Refrigeration	Vaccines	CRISPR, GMO seeds

Figure 10.4 Illustration of the Innovation Matrix

Paths to Innovations

Effective forward-thinking organizations must *provide a clear path on how anyone* can be free to implement their high-order actionable insights. Innovative organizations must balance the discipline provided by an architectural framework and the autonomy that is provided by inspired people.

As can be seen in Figure 10.5, there are several paths to innovation that have very different impacts: incremental, often to achieve an efficiency, evolutionary sustaining (extended and adapted), inferior disruptive creation, superior disruptive creation, and revolutionary nondisruptive creation. The innovation paths are like a baseball game; you can hit a single, double, triple, or home run. A home run or "swing for the fences" occurs when a significant impact on improving the livelihoods of everyone results.

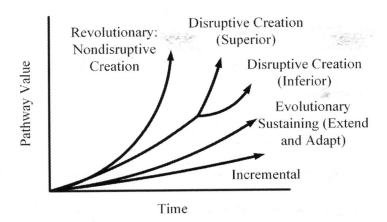

Figure 10.5 Illustration of Innovation Pathways

Incremental Innovations

Incremental innovation is solving an existing problem in a better way through marginal improvements. Incremental innovations can be **feature additions** that are implemented in existing offerings, products, and services, or they can be **efficiency innovations** that enable firms to do more with less resources.

Incremental Feature Additions

A company focuses on incremental innovations to provide a continuing revenue stream for existing customers to maintain their base. For example, because of the complexity of many software systems such as Microsoft's Windows, Apple's operating systems, and the software that powers Tesla's electric cars, incremental improvements are essential to sustain existing products.

While Gillette's initial development of twin blade for the men's wet shaving market may have been disruptive, subsequently adding additional blades to a razor becomes more incremental or evolutionary. Examples of incremental innovation might include better fuel economy in vehicles, additives in toothpaste and detergents, and colorful athletic shoes. Incremental innovations that improve on existing product attributes rarely provide any meaningful competitive advantage. While incremental innovation certainly has its place, an over-reliance on incremental innovations can easily detract from investing in potentially more powerful innovations.

One example of the power of incremental innovation, however, can be seen in improving our global efforts toward sustainability. Sustainability is a global system problem that can be improved through incremental improvements though the management of our renewable and non-renewable resources, the reduction of greenhouse gases emission, improvements in the circular value chains through the reuse of plastics, and the elimination of air, water, and soils contamination. This is achieved by each person taking responsibility for changing their behavior that can result in accumulative value. (See Chapter 19 for a discussion on innovation and sustainability.)

Balancing Efficiency and Innovation

Incremental efficiency innovations are those that enable companies to do more with less resources. A carpenter knows to measure twice and cut once. Just as a carpenter learns how to use specific tools for certain tasks, thinking and problem-solving tools can be learned and used to improve efficiency. By reducing the variation in cutting wood, the amount of waste can be reduced and over time eliminated. Many quality improvement programs focus on incremental innovations to reduce waste, such as the assembly of a product in less time, reducing product defects, and underutilizing the talents of employees.

Quality improvement efforts are management programs to deliver products and services that meet customer requirements by eliminating waste and inefficiency. Quality improvement efforts focus on five principles:[31]

1. Specify *value from customer's perspective.*
2. Identify the *value stream* for each product or service.
3. Make value *flow* without interruptions from beginning to end.
4. Let the customer *pull* value from our process.
5. Pursue *perfection* – continuous improvement.

Once the customer's requirements are understood, anything below or above those customer requirements should be eliminated. For instance, customers expect a certain response time from information systems, and the less variation in the times the better. The longer times would be considered waste in lost human productivity.

Six Sigma and Lean are fast-based, data-driven, statistical quality improvement methods. Six Sigma was developed by Motorola in 1986 and focuses on reducing process variation and enhancing process control in manufacturing. Lean is a quality improvement method that focuses on removing waste (non-value-added processes and procedures) and promotes work standardization and flow.

Lean Six Sigma is the integration of the two quality improvement methods that can create a single language, mindset, and purpose across all functions and levels of an organization, provide education and professional growth opportunity for employees, and build a strong foundation for the incorporation of other powerful business and process models.[32]

The analytics used in Lean Six Sigma were originally based on an American statistician, W. Edwards Deming, who influenced Japanese businesses to adopt his concepts in the 1950s. By the 1970s, Japanese automobiles and electronics surpassed US products in quality and reputation.[33] Lean Six Sigma is especially useful to prevent defects where safety is required such as in airplane manufacture, nuclear power plants, and hospital medical systems.

Organizations that focus on quality improvement can reduce costs and increase profits but are at risk for long-term innovation opportunities. For some organizations, improving overall efficiency using quality improvement effort even has the potential to eliminate jobs.

The 3M Company, formerly known as the Minnesota Mining and Manufacturing Company, is a US-based multinational company that created Post-it Notes. Based in Saint Paul, Minnesota, they are an incremental innovation machine that sells some 55,000 products, ranging from adhesives to electronic materials.[34] 3M has thousands of scientists and researchers around the world that enable them to generate a steady stream of unique products for customers.

3M invests about 5.8% of their sales back into the science that enables them to continue their innovation stream that results in 3,000 patents each year.[35]

One critical balance at 3M is between present AND future concerns. Quarterly results are important but should not be the sole focus; staying relevant is also important but cannot come at the cost of current performance. 3M has several mechanisms to sustain this "and thinking." Employing the Thirty Percent Rule, 30% of each division's revenues must come from products introduced in the last four years. This is tracked rigorously, and employee bonuses are based on successful achievement of this goal.[36]

Under Jack Welch, General Electric adopted Six Sigma from Motorola in 1995. Six Sigma became part of the corporate culture after the company invested more than $1 billion in training thousands of employees and the system was adopted by every GE business unit. The imbalanced use of Lean Six Sigma can influence a singular minded culture by discouraging opportunity discovery and innovation potential.[37]

In 2001, 3M experienced a period of low profitability that prompted a change in senior leadership. 3M brought in Jim McNerney as the CEO, formerly a vice president of General Electric (GE) under Jack Welch. When 3M adopted Six Sigma, they decided to use a hybrid model and implement it within the subcultures where there was a best fit to avoid a clash with the 3M entrepreneurial mindset that was the cultural model of 3M's product innovation.[38]

Figure 10.6 illustrates the generic facets of incremental and efficiency innovations. In the following section, we explore the facets of evolutionary extended and adapted sustaining innovation depicted in Figure 10.7.

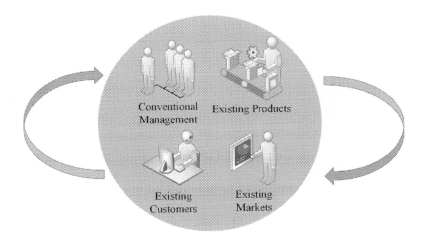

Figure 10.6 Illustration of Incremental and Efficiency Innovations

Evolutionary Sustaining Innovations

Evolutionary sustaining innovations are the next higher pathway above incremental innovations. These innovations provide more opportunity to serve a job that customers need to have done, especially for those who are undershot, those who are not satisfied with their existing solutions, or the underserved, where there are few providers.[39]

Evolutionary sustaining innovations involve larger sets of improvements, often in combination, that provide actual and/or perceived value to the customer.[40] Some examples include the use of multi-core microprocessors that enable simultaneous faster processing, airplanes that use fuel-saving technologies that allow them to fly farther on less fuel, analog to digital telecommunications, and innovations that transformed black-and-white television to color. Ironically, the transition to color television receiver capability was prolonged because initially networks were not broadcasting in color and subsequently, there was not a rush to purchase a color television. Networks were reluctant to spend the time and resources to broadcast in color because no one had

Evolutionary extended sustaining innovations are created when new offerings and new business models are provided to existing customers in existing markets. For example, hybrid and electric vehicles.

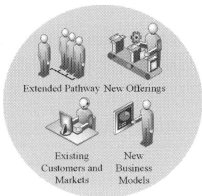

Evolutionary adapted sustaining innovation are created when existing offerings and existing business models are adapted for new customers and new markets. For example, affordable vehicles in developing countries.

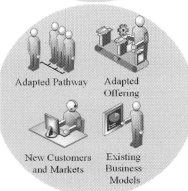

Figure 10.7 Illustration of Evolutionary Innovation

Source: Adapted from Tim Brown, *Change by Design*, (New York: Harper, 2009), 161.

color television. This conundrum was finally solved when RCA (a manufacturer of color televisions) acquired NBC.[41]

"Sustaining innovation, which most understand, is the process of making good products better. This is important for any economy, but once a market is mature, it generates little net growth in terms of new factories, new jobs, new technology investments, and so forth."[42]

Evolutionary sustaining innovation can occur through extensions and adaptation:

1. Evolutionary sustaining *extended* innovations are created when new offerings and new business models are provided to existing customers in existing markets, such as hybrid or electric vehicles.
2. Evolutionary sustaining *adapted* innovations are created when existing offerings and existing business models are provided to new customers and new markets, such as offering very affordable vehicles in developing countries.

Innovation Theory: Postulation to Practice

What if you could investigate a crystal ball and predict the future? What if you could predict the next innovation? Clayton Christensen was a leading thinker who developed the theory of disruption to predict innovations. With a theory, it is possible to make predictions about what might happen even before you experience it.[43] Christensen's disruptive innovation theory can be used to explain how expensive, complicated products and services are transformed into simple, convenient, and more affordable ones for lower tiers of a market.[44]

The theory of disruptive innovation does just that. It is based on research described in Clayton Christensen's book *The Innovator's Dilemma*.[45] Imagine that David is the start-up and Goliath is the incumbent. Disruptive innovation theory can be used to make predictions about why existing companies and incumbents are successfully launching incremental and evolutionary sustaining degrees of innovation but not disruptive innovations. Start-ups, or new entrants, are successful at launching disruptive innovations, such as new market or new business innovations, but rarely will they succeed at launching an evolutionary sustaining innovation that targets the most valuable segments of established markets.[46]

Innovation theory describes how organizations become so riveted on taming the operational whirlwind of execution that they become stuck in quicksand when it comes to the future. By fulfilling the needs of and pursuing incremental improvements for their existing customers, incumbents are unable to break from the gravity pull of their existing mindsets, forsaking potentially huge opportunities right in their sights. These organizations fail to pull the innovation trigger on the next big idea.

If existing organizations can overcome their blind spots and be proactive, they can be disruptive and avoid being disrupted. Organizations are in a race for survival to protect their aspirational success. If organizations understand how to best apply innovation theory, it will enable them to lead in the race and avoid getting passed. Start-ups are always looking for opportunities to pass the incumbents in the race for survival. Disruptive innovations have the potential to provide start-ups a competitive advantage and overcome the incumbents. As can be seen in Figure 10.8, innovation pathways include both continuous and disruption innovation. Figure 10.9 illustrates the process over time.

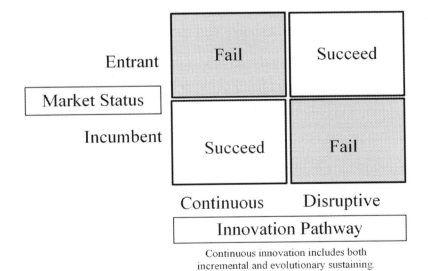

Continuous innovation includes both incremental and evolutionary sustaining

Figure 10.8 Illustration of Disruptive Innovation Theory

Source: Adapted from Michael E. Raynor, "Disruption Theory as a Predictor of Innovation Success/Failure," *Strategy & Leadership* 39, no. 4 (2011): 27–30.

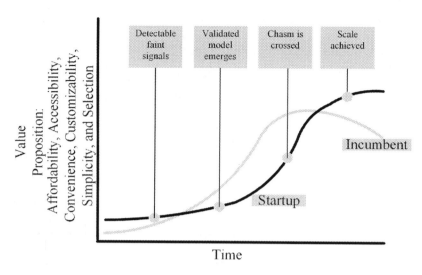

Figure 10.9 Illustration of Disruptive Innovation

Source: Adapted from Bradley, C., & O'Toole, C. (2016). An incumbent's guide to digital disruption. Retrieved from http://www.mckinsey.com/business-functions/strategy-and-corporate-finance/our-insights/an-incumbents-guide-to-digital-disruption

Disruptive Creations

Disruptive creations are the next pathway above evolutionary sustaining innovations. A disruptive creation occurs when a product or service displaces something that already exists either with an inferior or superior offering.

Disruption is the foundation of the concept known as the *innovator's dilemma*. The innovator's, dilemma is a failure model that focuses on the inaction of well-managed organizations and the action-orientation of entrepreneurial start-ups. Many incumbent organizations have a gravitational pull that guides them to stick too closely to the existing customers that drive their revenue stream. The result of this pull often leads to ignoring viable opportunities for those willing to take the risk.

Blockbuster, Sears & Roebuck, Digital Equipment Corp., and Eastman Kodak are examples of once dominant companies that have been displaced through disruptive creations. The disruptive creation can occur in two ways: an inferior solution displaces what exists in the market or a superior solution that displaces what exists in a market.[47]

Inferior Disruptive Creation Low-End Disruptive Innovation

The inferior disruptive creation (low-end) occurs when a new product or service is launched in the most price-sensitive segment of the market, and then moves upmarket as the experience curve improves.[48]

Inferior disruptive creation occurs when a low-end innovation displaces an existing offering in underserved or overshot markets and then systematically moves up market. Inferior disruptor creations transform markets by providing simple, convenient, affordable, and accessible products and services rather than over-complicated and expensive products and services. These inferior disruptive creations may not perform as well and often have less capability than the original product or service but are positioned for new customers (non-consumers) who are less demanding and tolerate a lower level of features.[49]

Disruptive creation (low-end) facilitates the reshaping of markets and creates new businesses by addressing customers that are overshot or overserved. Because companies at times can innovate faster than customers can adapt and/or adopt, the new features potentially provide an opportunity for an entrant to introduce a product or service that is disruptive. With disruptive creation (low-end), companies with lower-cost business models start at the bottom of the market and then frequently move up-market.

US Steel relied on a substantial investment in blast furnaces and integrated steelworks. US Steel was aware of a new electric mini-mill technology but failed to adopt it.[50] The new entrant, Nucor Steel, entered the market producing an affordable and less elegant product known as rebar. Rebar is steel reinforcing rods that are hidden in poured concrete. For the rebar, Nucor choose a new solution: electric. Today most steel is produced using more efficient electric mini-mills rather than the large, infrastructure-heavy, inefficient old steel mills.

Led by Nucor, the innovations of the electric mini-mills allowed manufacturers to reduce their prices without significantly and adversely affecting their profit margins. New entrants achieve early results and begin the process of transitioning up-market, taking customers away from the incumbents.

Inferior Disruptive Creative (Low-End Disruptive) Examples

There are several examples of disruptive creation (low-end):

1. Netflix displaced Blockbuster by using the US post office for distribution of videos. Netflix subsequently upgraded to media streaming services
2. Canon displaced Xerox by using a combination of product and process innovation to create a line of desktop printers that were more affordable and convenient than the existing model of centralized copying centers.
3. Target and Wal-Mart displaced Sears through the implementation of discount retailing by innovating their supply chains to save costs and unleash aggressive price competitiveness and inventory turns.
4. Nucor Steel's mini-mills' electric arc furnaces displacing US Steel's use of the Bessemer process in the manufacture of rebar for concrete reinforcement.[51]
5. Vanguard's affordable indexed mutual fund stock investments displaced full-service brokers.
6. Southwest Airlines was successful based on customer service, regional affordable flights, quick turnarounds, and a single airplane model within existing markets.
7. Toyota used design and manufacturing innovation to produce the Corona, a low-cost, low-maintenance, and economical car to disrupt some Ford and General Motors product lines.
8. Skype offered affordable and often free phone service that moved upmarket that was disruptive to Verizon, AT&T, Sprint, and T-Mobile.[52] MCI Long Distance used advances in analog and later digital technology to implement low-cost long distance to disrupt AT&T.
9. Dell's Direct-to-Customer Business Model used a customer-centric ordering and distribution chain to disrupt IBM retail store distribution.
10. Honda offered small motorcycles and used the profits from a large volume of small motorcycle sales to build larger motorcycles that were offered in Harley Davidson's markets.[53]
11. Southern New Hampshire University is one of the world's most innovative and largest universities with over 130,000 students enrolled.[54] SNHU takes students from Pennsylvania's community colleges from the Pennsylvania's State System of Higher Education that is now losing enrollments.[55]

Superior Disruptive Creative (High-End Disruptive)

Whereas the inferior disruptive creation targets the price-sensitive markets and moves up-market, the superior disruptive creation targets price-insensitive markets and moves downward into mainstream markets. The superior disruptive creation (high-end) occurs when a new product or service is launched in the most price-insensitive segment of the market, and then moves down market as the experience curve improves.[56]

Superior disruptive creation occurs when a high-end innovation displaces an existing offering. The superior disruptive creation, or high-end disruption, occurs when a new product or service outperforms an existing product or service in a market that improves the customer experience.[57]

The cellphone originally targeted the high-end price-insensitive market; as the cost experience decreased, it became available to the mass market. Tesla offered high-end electric vehicles, such as the Model S and Model X, and then moved down market with the Model 3 and Model Y.[58]

The personal computer is an example of a superior disruptive creation. Personal computers were originally premium-priced, targeting a narrow market. As the customer experience improved in affordability and performance, they took business away from mainframe companies like Control Data Corporation (CDC) and minicomputer companies like Digital Equipment Corporation (DEC). The business model at DEC forced them to make bigger and more profitable minicomputers rather than inexpensive, low-margin personal computers. According to Clayton Christensen, "of all the companies that made mainframe computers, IBM was the only one to become a leading maker of minicomputers; and of all the companies that made minicomputers, IBM was the only one that became a leading maker of personal computers."[59]

Superior Disruptive Creative (High-End Disruptive) Examples

1. IBM's PC and Apple PC innovations disrupted Digital Equipment Corporation's minicomputer opening personal computing for everyday people, computer cathode ray tubes (CRT) were displaced by liquid crystal displays (LCD).
2. Digital MP3 technology disrupted CD and album sales and provided opportunities for music stream. Apple's iPod device was superior to the Sony Walkman transistor radio.[60]
3. Amazon's online retailing model provides an online customer experience, broader product selections, and affordability over the conventional retail model.
4. Starbucks's introduction of coffee products and beverage experiences, while widely misunderstood as an incremental innovation, was revolutionary and became disruptive as they were accepted broadly over many local coffee shops.
5. Humphry Davy invented the first electric bulb that produced light; it was not practical because it did not last long. Thomas Edison developed a longer-lasting bulb that made it practical. Light bulbs with tungsten filaments replaced CFL bulbs and LED bulbs displaced CFL bulbs.
6. Many generations of storage technology have been displaced – floppy disks, zip drives, flash drives, hard drives, and solid-state devices.
7. Digital photography displaced photographic film.
8. Diesel and gasoline engines were more efficient than steam engines; jet planes flew faster and higher than propeller planes; steamboats that did not require wind were more practical than sailing ships.
9. The Bell Telephone network and telephone devices provided significant improvement over Western Union and the then disruptive telegraph.

10. Geisinger Health System is a regional healthcare provider to central, south-central, and north-eastern Pennsylvania and southern New Jersey that provides better health outcomes and affordability than their competition.
11. Alphabet's AdWords and AdSense advertising model continues to displace print advertising.

Figure 10.10 captures the generic processes illustrating inferior and superior disruptive creation

The superior disruptive creation [high-end] occurs when a new product or service is launched in the most price-insensitive segment of the market, and then moves down market as the experience curve improves

The inferior disruptive creation [low-end] occurs when a new product or service is launched in the most price-sensitive segment of the market, and then moves upmarket as the experience curve improves

Figure 10.10 Illustration of Disruptive Creation

Source: Adapted from W. Chan Kim and Renee Mauborgne, *Blue Ocean Shift*, (New York, NY: Hachette, 2017), 30–32.

Nondisruptive Creation

Nondisruptive creations are the next pathway after disruptive creations. Nondisruptive creations focus on new demand in uncontested space. Instead of the red ocean of intense close competition, the concept is to add unique value and low-cost in vast open waters of blue oceans.

Blue ocean shifts target markets where consumers are not consuming products or are consuming the product in inconvenient or outmoded settings. A nondisruptive creation aims to make the competition irrelevant by focusing on non-consumption through breakthrough solutions, redefining an industry's existing problem and solving it, and identifying and solving a brand-new problem or seizing a brand-new opportunity.[61]

Paul Polak is a solid example of this often-seismic shift as he has been successfully combining reverse and new market disruptive innovation. Polak is a psychiatrist, social entrepreneur, and author of *Out of Poverty* and *The Business Solution to Poverty*, who works in developing countries to alleviate poverty. Instead of taking the conventional approach to alleviating poverty through charitable assistance, Polak combines reverse innovation (designing explicitly for the unmet needs of consumers in developing countries) and disruptive innovation (providing a customer-centric solution that is simple, convenient, and accessible to a larger population).

For example, Polak and his colleagues designed a unique, simple water pump for irrigation, and then provided employment opportunities by enabling local people to build and sell the water pumps. "It was brilliantly simple, it could be manufactured by local workshops, and a local driller could dig a 40-foot well and install it for $25. Studies showed that farmers made $100 in one season on that investment."[62] The combination of the pump and local employment opportunities enabled the community to become self-sufficient and less dependent on outside assistance.

Nondisruptive Creation Examples

Market creating nondisruptive creative innovations have dramatically improved our life spans and well-being. Figure 10.11 captures the relationship between the previously discussed disruptive creative innovations and the following nondisruptive creative innovations.

Nondisruptive Creation	Disruptive Creation	
A nondisruptive creation (revolutionary) focuses on nonconsumption and identifies and solves a brand-new problem or seizes a brand-new opportunity. Nondisruptive creations focus on new demand in uncontested markets. Examples: Sesame Street edutainment, vaccines, pharmaceuticals, and online dating.	The superior disruptive creation offers a solution to an existing business problem by displacing its predecessor in the most price-insensitive market segments. Examples: ICEs over steam engines, jet planes over propeller planes, steamboats over sailing ships, LCDs over CRTs, LEDs over CFL, the telephone over the telegraph, digital media over DVDs and CDs.	The inferior disruptive creation offers a solution to an existing industry problem by displacing its predecessor in the most price-sensitive market segments. Examples: Netflix displaces Blockbuster, Nucor steel over US Steel Bessemer process, Amazon over conventional retailing and department stores, and index mutual funds over managed mutual funds.

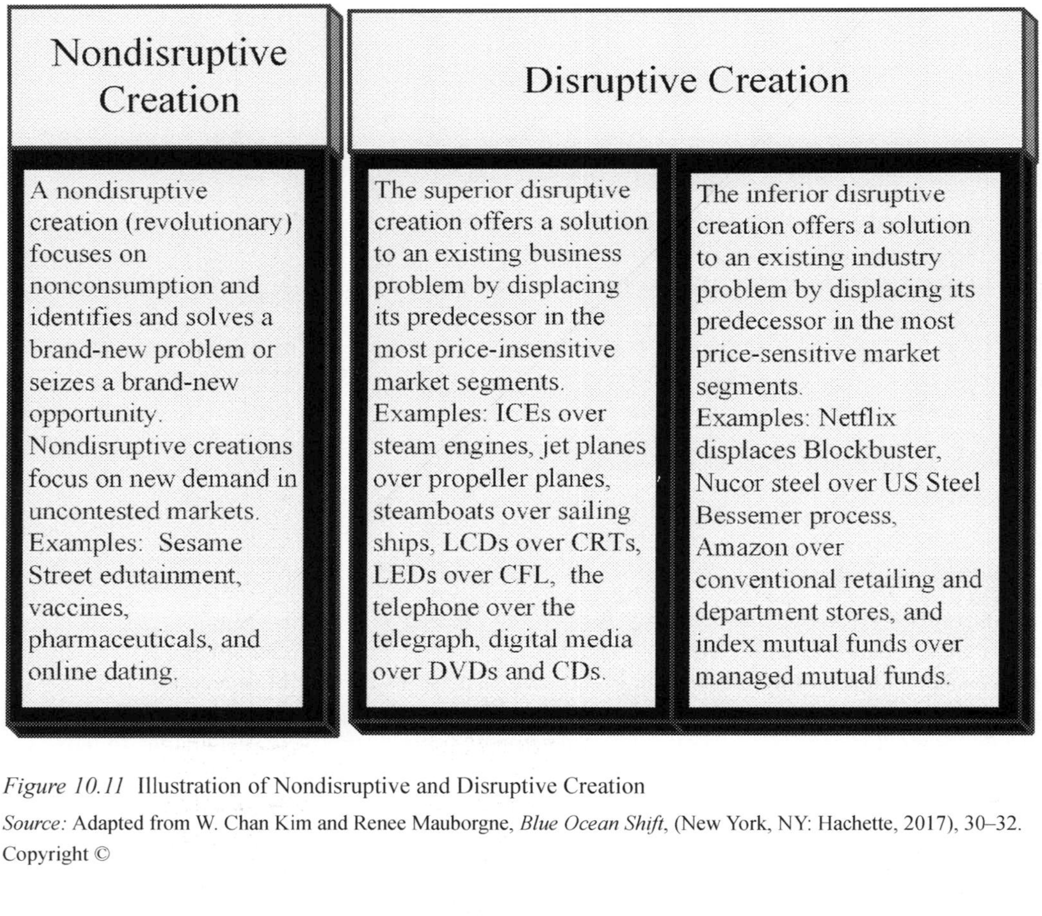

Figure 10.11 Illustration of Nondisruptive and Disruptive Creation

Source: Adapted from W. Chan Kim and Renee Mauborgne, *Blue Ocean Shift*, (New York, NY: Hachette, 2017), 30–32.
Copyright ©

1. Charles Darwin and Alfred Wallace's theory of evolution by natural selection
2. Copernicus's heliocentric model, Mendeleev' periodic table, and Bohr's model discovery of the atom.
3. Bernoulli's principle (an increase in the speed of a fluid occurs simultaneously with a decrease in static pressure, giving lift) and the Wright brothers' discovery of flight.
4. Marconi's radio, Gutenberg's printing press, and Edison's motion picture camera and phonograph.
5. Louis Pasteur's germ theory and vaccines of all types that eliminated smallpox and polio and significantly reduced mumps, measles, rubella, and whooping cough. Sanitation and clean water have diminished infectious diseases like cholera. Pharmaceuticals of all types and biomedical devices.
6. The experiments on pea plants conducted by Gregor Mendel, father of modern genetics, led to the understanding of inheritance.[63] Watson and Crick's discovery of the structure of DNA, and related discoveries in genomics and CRISPR.
7. Norman E. Borlaug, an American agronomist, was awarded the Nobel Peace Prize in 1970 for his application of genetics that led to increases in agriculture production, termed the Green Revolution.[64]
8. Nikola Tesla's alternating current electricity distribution system, Faraday's electric motor and generator, and Edison's alkaline storage battery and research lab for experimentation.
9. William Shockley, John Bardeen, and Walter Brattain's invention of the first transistor that led to Intel's development of microprocessors.
10. Grameen Bank and microfinance
11. Sesame Street's edutainment model.

Innovation Pathways

The innovation pathways have very different impacts. The overall impact increases when moving from the left to the right because of the increased job opportunities and competitive separation advantage. As noted earlier, innovation pathways are key in securing competitive advantage. This is illustrated in Figure 10.12.

The innovation pathways can be combined into variations. The slow decline of the Ringling Brothers Circus opened an opportunity for a new entertainment concept. Cirque du Soleil combined nondestructive and destructive creation by redefining and solving an existing business problem. Cirque du Soleil created new demand and broke away from the competition by reconstructing the market boundaries.

Cirque du Soleil built on the strengths of alternative businesses and *created* theater themes, acrobatics, Broadway shows, traditional circus, and the opera to offer a totally new high-value, premium-priced entertainment model.[65] They *raised* a unique venue, they *eliminated* the star performers, animal shows, and aisles concession, and they *reduced* the fun, humor, thrills, and danger.[66]

As introduced in Chapter 2, "Elements," combinatorial innovations join two or more other innovations of any degree except incremental. Overall, combinatorial innovation offers a lens for understanding how innovation can occur leveraging creativity, resourcefulness, and existing knowledge, making it a relevant and insightful concept for innovation theory. Integrated products of all types join innovations of varying degrees, such as the Apple iPhone, Tesla EVs, and the Microsoft product line with the addition of generative artificial intelligence. This topic is also discussed in Chapters 8, 15, 19, and 20.

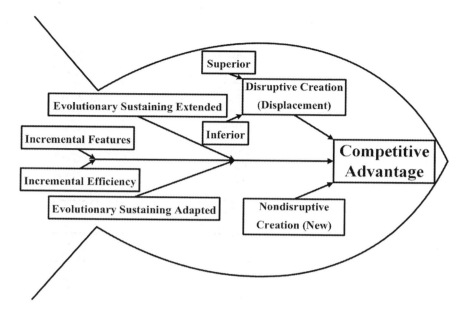

Figure 10.12 Illustration of Seven Innovation Pathways

Source: Adapted from W. Chan Kim and Renée Mauborgne, "Nondisruptive Creation: Rethinking Innovation and Growth," MIT Magazine, Spring 2019, February 21, 2019, accessed January 6, 2020, https://sloanreview.mit.edu/article/nondisruptive-creation-rethinking-innovation-and-growth/ Adapted from Tim Brown, *Change by Design*, (New York: Harper, 2009), 19.

The Capitalist Dilemma

Clayton Christensen conceived a new concept known as the capitalist dilemma. The capitalist dilemma states that an imbalance toward efficiency can result in loss of job opportunities for the entire economy.[67] "At the heart of this paradox is a doctrine of finance employing measures of profitability that guide capitalists away from investments that can create growth."[68] Business leaders have been trained to optimize their business operations by reducing costs and improving efficiencies while sacrificing future, long-term opportunities. The implications of their executive training are to focus on improving their financial measures and optimizing efficiency. Unfortunately, this mentality lowers the prospect of long-term employment. Job creation increases as you move up along the innovation pathways. The essence of the capitalist dilemma is illustrated in Figure 10.13.

Leadership Essentials for Innovation

Leadership is the most important capability that is needed for building innovation capability within an organization because it directly influences the essential human factors. Leadership is essential for applying innovation theory and building innovation capability. A survey was conducted to determine the practices of effective innovators. The survey largely represented the innovation, R&D, or strategy group inside large organizations to determine the essential aspects of successful innovators.[69] As can be seen in Figure 10.14, six key aspects from having a culture of innovation to transformation innovation are identified. Each is in relation to effective leadership for what it takes for an organization to be innovative.

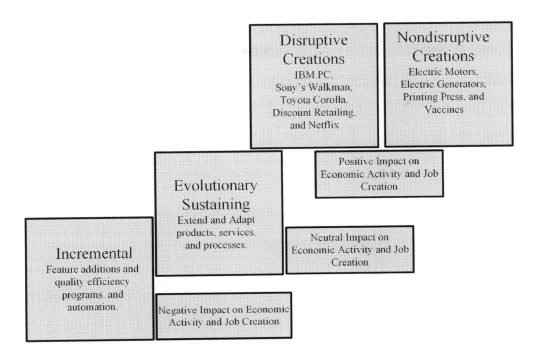

Figure 10.13 Illustration of the Capitalist Dilemma

Source: Adapted from Clayton Christensen, "A Capitalist's Dilemma, Whoever Wins on Tuesday," *The New York Times*, November 3, 2012, accessed December 27, 2020, http://www.nytimes.com/2012/11/04/business/a-capitalists-dilem ma-whoever-becomes-president.html?pagewanted=all& _r=O

Summary

In this chapter, we described the importance of innovation theory in general, disruptive innovation theory, and the value and role of the innovation and entrepreneurship competency framework in the further refinement of innovation theory and practice. Innovation theory, the innovation elements and competencies, and the innovation pathways are the foundation for the discipline of innovation. For example, as can be seen in Figure 10.5, there are several pathways that can be used to predict the likelihood of meaningful significant transformational change from incremental to evolutionary to revolutionary.

Macro and micro theories of innovation are explored and discussed, along with parallels to macro- and microeconomics. The value of innovation theory is seen in the compilation of innovation degrees and types, yielding a more robust innovation matrix. For example, incremental, evolutionary, revolutionary, and disruptive innovation degrees, along with the role of new entrants, low-end and new market disruptive innovation are reviewed. Multiple innovation types – from science and technology to products and services and everything in between; the capitalist dilemma; efficient market theory; balancing efficiency and innovation; and measuring innovation – are discussed. For example, disruptive innovation theory is based on new entrants being more likely to be successful with a disruptive solution, and the incumbents are more likely to focus on sustaining solutions and fulfilling the needs of their current customer base. Also discussed is the importance of leadership essentials for applying innovation theory and building innovation capability. The innovation competencies described in these chapters increase individual and organizational innovation through the enhancement of attitudes, skills, and knowledge. Next up, we look at the foundational role of entrepreneurship as a key competency in the innovation and entrepreneurship competency framework.

Transformational innovation	The organizations spend less time and energy on incremental innovation and small process improvements, and devote proportionately more effort to the creation and transformation of entirely new businesses.
Collaboration	The organizations focus on the collaboration with key partners on strategy, corporate venture capital, and corporate development.
Staffing	The organizations and their innovation teams are staffed in accordance with the point of the process of the implementation, systematically increasing as the value unfolds.
Meaningful incentives	The organizations need to offer several kinds of incentives to those who are engaged in innovation activities: recognition and awards; dedicated time to further develop projects; employee bonuses; seed funding; and even a financial stake in the new offerings they create.
Monitoring the impact	The organizations need to provide a scorecard that includes broad measures that include at least economic, social, and governance measures of viability to ensure that what is being delivered is effective.
A culture of innovation	A culture of innovation is needed to ensure that the shared goals are being implemented harmoniously and aligned with the long-term strategy of the organization.

Figure 10.14 Illustration of Effective Innovation Leadership

Source: Adapted from Scott Kirsner, "What Companies That Are Good at Innovation Get Right," November 29, 2019, accessed January 25, 2020, https://hbr.org/2019/11/what-companies-that-are-good-at-innovation-get-right

Notes

1. Richard A. Swanson and Thomas J. Chermack, *Theory Building in Applied Disciplines* (San Francisco, CA: Berrett-Koehler Publishers, Inc, 2013).
2. *Wikipedia*, s.v. "TRIZ," accessed February 24, 2024, https://en.wikipedia.org/wiki/TRIZ.
3. "40 TRIZ Principles," *Triz40*, accessed February 24, 2024, www.triz40.com/aff_Principles_TRIZ.php.
4. Greg Yezersky, "General Theory of Innovation," in *Trends in Computer Aided Innovation* (Boston: Springer, 2007), 45–55.
5. Greg Yezersky, "General Theory of Innovation," in *Trends in Computer Aided Innovation* (Boston: Springer, 2007), 45–55.
6. Bengt-Åke Lundvall, ed., *National Systems of Innovation: Toward a Theory of Innovation and Interactive Learning* (New York: Anthem Press, 2010), 4, accessed February 23, 2024, https://anthempress.com/national-systems-of-innovation-pb.
7. Magnus Henrekson and Tino Sanandaji, "Small Business Activity Does Not Measure Entrepreneurship," *IFN Working Paper No. 959*, 2013, 2, Research Institute of Industrial Economics, accessed February 23, 2024, www.ifn.se/wfiles/wp/wp959.pdf.
8. Robert M. Solow, "A Contribution to the Theory of Economic Growth," *The Quarterly Journal of Economics* 70, no. 1 (1956), 65–94, https://doi.org/10.2307/1884513.
9. Robert M. Solow, "Why Do Some Economies Grow Much Faster Than Others?" *Robert M. Solow | UBS Nobel Perspectives*, 2016, accessed February 23, 2024, www.ubs.com/microsites/nobel-perspectives/en/laureates/robert-solow.html.

10. *Corporate Finance Institute*, s.v. "Solow Growth Model," accessed February 23, 2024, https://corporate-financeinstitute.com/resources/knowledge/economics/solow-growth-model/.
11. *Corporate Finance Institute*, s.v. "Solow Growth Model," accessed February 23, 2024, https://corporate-financeinstitute.com/resources/knowledge/economics/solow-growth-model/.
12. Kate Vitasek, "Nobel Laureate Paul Romer: The Path to Economic Growth and Innovation," November 19, 2018, accessed May 25, 2020, www.forbes.com/sites/katevitasek/2018/11/19/paul-romer-the-path-to-economic-growth-and-innovation/#19e51a95139d.
13. *Wikipedia*, s.v. "Endogenous Growth Theory," accessed May 25, 2020, https://en.wikipedia.org/wiki/Endogenous_growth_theory.
14. *Oxford Dictionaries Online*, s.v. "Innovate," accessed February 23, 2024, www.oed.com/search/dictionary/?scope=Entries&q=innovate.
15. *Brainyquote.com*, s.v. "Peter Drucker," accessed February 23, 2024, www.brainyquote.com/search_results?x=0&y=0&q=peter+drucker.
16. Anthony Ulwick, "Outcome-Driven Innovation® (ODI): Jobs-to-be-Done Theory in Practice," *Stratgyn Whitepaper*, 2017, accessed February 22, 2024, https://strategyn.com/.
17. Omar Abbosh, Paul Nunes, Vedrana Savic, and Michael Moore, "How to Unlock the Value of Your Innovation Investments," *Accenture*, 2018, accessed February 24, 2024, https://newsroom.accenture.com/news/2018/high-growth-companies-buck-trend-of-declining-returns-on-innovation-accenture-report-finds.
18. Omar Abbosh, Paul Nunes, Vedrana Savic, and Michael Moore, "Discover Where Value's Hiding," *Accenture*, 2018, accessed February 22 2024, https://urmh.edu.mx/download/b9fb1_discover-where-value-s-hiding-accenture.
19. "Business R&D and Innovation Survey," *National Science Foundation*, originally accessed August 14, 2014, accessed via archive February 22 2024, https://wayback.archive-it.org/5902/20181003215119/www.nsf.gov/statistics/infbrief/nsf11300/.
20. Bruce Brown and Scott D. Anthony, "How P&G Tripled Its Innovation Success Rate Inside the Company's New-growth Factory," *Harvard Business Review*, June 2011.
21. Statista TrendCompass 2020 Report, accessed February 23, 2024, www.statista.com/study/69166/statista-trendcompass/.
22. Gary Hamel, *Reinventing Management for the 21st Century*, Gary Hamel: Reinventing the Technology of Human Accomplishment, May 21, 2011, accessed February 24, 2024, www.youtube.com/watch?v=aodjgkv65MM.
23. "S&P 500's 50-Year Club," *Bloomberg Business Week*, March 5, 2007, accessed February 23, 2024, www.bloomberg.com/news/articles/2007-03-05/s-and-p-500s-50-year-clubbusinessweek-business-news-stock-market-and-financial-advice.
24. "S&P 500's 50-Year Club," *Bloomberg Business Week*, March 5, 2007, accessed February 23, 2024, www.bloomberg.com/news/articles/2007-03-05/s-and-p-500s-50-year-clubbusinessweek-business-news-stock-market-and-financial-advice.
25. Scott D. Anthony, S. Patrick Viguerie, Evan I. Schwartz, and John Van Landeghem, "2018 Corporate Longevity Forecast: Creative Destruction is Accelerating," *Innosight*, 2018.
26. Gary Hamel, *Reinventing Management for the 21st Century*, Gary Hamel: Reinventing the Technology of Human Accomplishment, May 21, 2011, accessed February 24, 2024, www.youtube.com/watch?v=aodjgkv65MM.
27. "Gary Hamel at Dell: What Are the Biggest Challenges for Organizations Today?" *YouTube Video*, posted by "mlabvideo," March 9, 2011, accessed February 23, 2024, www.youtube.com/watch?v=-Sq0-vtWHLM.
28. "Gary Hamel at Dell: How Are Leaders Innovating Today?" *YouTube Video*, posted by "mlabvideo," April 26, 2011, accessed February 23, 2024, www.youtube.com/watch?v=xO_sgdc_jTs.
29. "Gary Hamel at Dell: How Are Leaders Innovating Today?" *YouTube Video*, posted by "mlabvideo," April 26, 2011, accessed February 23, 2024, www.youtube.com/watch?v=xO_sgdc_jTs.
30. *Wikipedia*, s.v. "Hoover Dam," accessed February 25, 2018, https://en.wikipedia.org/wiki/Hoover_Dam.
31. "Lean Thinking and Practice," accessed February 23, 2024, www.lean.org/whatslean/principles.cfm.
32. "What Is Six Sigma?" accessed February 23, 2024, https://asq.org/quality-resources/six-sigma.
33. Oliver Staley, "Whatever Happened to Six Sigma?" September 3, 2019, accessed February 23, 2024, https://qz.com/work/1635960/whatever-happened-to-six-sigma/.
34. Statista, "3M's Spending on Research and Development from 2010 to 2019 (in Million U.S. Dollars)," accessed February 23, 2024, www.statista.com/statistics/733585/3m-spending-on-research-and-development/.
35. 3M, "3M Research & Development," accessed February 23, 2024, www.3m.com/3M/en_US/company-us/about-3m/research-development/.

36. Vijay Govindarajan and Srikanth Srinivas, "The Innovation Mindset in Action: 3M Corporation," August 6, 2013, accessed February 23, 2024, https://hbr.org/2013/08/the-innovation-mindset-in-acti-3.
37. Mary J. Benner and Michael Tushman, "Process Management and Technological Innovation: A Longitudinal Study of the Photography and Paint Industries," *Administrative Science Quarterly* 47 (2002), 676+.
38. Kevin Hurren, "The Challenge of Change: 3M, Six Sigma, and Corporate Culture," July 13, 2015, accessed February 23, 2024, www.nbs.net/articles/the-challenge-of-change-3m-six-sigma-and-corporate-culture.
39. Clayton Christensen, Scott D. Anthony, and Erik Roth, *Seeing What's Next* (Boston: Harvard Business School Press, 2004).
40. Clayton Christensen, Scott D. Anthony, and Erik Roth, *Seeing What's Next* (Boston: Harvard Business School Press, 2004).
41. Clayton Christensen, Scott D. Anthony, and Erik Roth, *Seeing What's Next* (Boston: Harvard Business School Press, 2004).
42. Karen Dillon, "Disruption 2020: An Interview with Clayton M. Christensen," *MIT Sloan Management Review*, February 4, 2020, accessed February 23, 2024, https://sloanreview.mit.edu/article/an-interview-with-clayton-m-christensen/.
43. Clayton M. Christensen, Michael E. Raynor, and Rory McDonald, "What Is Disruptive Innovation?" *Harvard Business Review*, accessed February 23, 2024, https://hbr.org/2015/12/what-is-disruptive-innovation.
44. Clayton Christensen, *The Innovator's Dilemma* (New York: HarperCollins, 2003).
45. Clayton Christensen, *The Innovator's Dilemma* (New York: HarperCollins, 2003).
46. Michael E. Raynor, "Disruption Theory as a Predictor of Innovation Success/Failure," *Strategy & Leadership* 39, no. 4 (2011), 27–30.
47. W. Chan Kim and Renee Mauborgne, *Blue Ocean Shift* (New York: Hachette, 2017), 30–32.
48. Jeff Dyer, Paul Godfrey, Robert Jensen, and David Bryce, *Strategic Management: Concepts and Cases*, 2nd ed. (New York: John Wiley & Sons, Inc, 2018), 182.
49. Clayton Christensen, Jerome Grossman, and Jason Hwang, *The Innovator's Prescription* (New York: McGraw-Hill, 2009).
50. John Hagedoorn, "Innovation and Entrepreneurship: Schumpeter Revisited," *Industrial and Corporate Change* 5, no. 3 (1996), 883–896.
51. Clayton M. Christensen, Michael E. Raynor, and Rory McDonald, "What Is Disruptive Innovation?" *Harvard Business Review* 93, no. 12 (2015), 44–53, accessed February 23, 2024, https://hbr.org/2015/12/what-is-disruptive-innovation.
52. Jeff Dyer, Paul Godfrey, Robert Jensen, and David Bryce, *Strategic Management: Concepts and Cases*, 2nd ed. (New York: John Wiley & Sons, Inc, 2018), 183.
53. Jeff Dyer, Paul Godfrey, Robert Jensen, and David Bryce, *Strategic Management: Concepts and Cases*, 2nd ed. (New York: John Wiley & Sons, Inc, 2018), 183.
54. Susan Adams, "Meet the English Professor Creating the Billion-Dollar College of the Future," March 28, 2019, accessed February 23, 2024, www.forbes.com/sites/susanadams/2019/03/28/meet-the-english-professor-creating-the-billion-dollar-college-of-the-future/.
55. Michael Horn, "Why Disruption Is Stealing Pennsylvania's Students," January 30, 2020, accessed February 23, 2024, www.forbes.com/sites/michaelhorn/2020/01/30/why-disruption-is-stealing-pennsylvanias-students/#77497e71e777.
56. Jeff Dyer, Paul Godfrey, Robert Jensen, and David Bryce, *Strategic Management: Concepts and Cases*, 2nd ed. (New York: John Wiley & Sons, Inc, 2018), 184.
57. Jeff Dyer, Paul Godfrey, Robert Jensen, and David Bryce, *Strategic Management: Concepts and Cases*, 2nd ed. (New York: John Wiley & Sons, Inc, 2018), 184.
58. Jeff Dyer, Paul Godfrey, Robert Jensen, and David Bryce, *Strategic Management: Concepts and Cases*, 2nd ed. (New York: John Wiley & Sons, Inc, 2018), 184.
59. Clayton Christensen, Jerome Grossman, and Jason Hwang, *The Innovator's Prescription* (New York: McGraw-Hill, 2009), 8.
60. Leslie Kwoh, "You Call That Innovation?" *The Wall Street Journal*, May 23, 2012, accessed February 23, 2024, http://online.wsj.com/article/SB10001424052702304791704577418250902309914.html.
61. W. Chan Kim and Renee Mauborgne, *Blue Ocean Shift* (New York: Hachette, 2017), 36.
62. Donald G. McNeil, Jr., "An Entrepreneur Creating Chances at a Better Life," *The New York Times*, September 27, 2011, accessed February 23, 2024, www.nytimes.com/2011/09/27/health/27conversation.html?pagewanted=all&_r=2&.
63. *Wikipedia*, s.v. "Gregor Mendel," accessed February 23, 2024, https://en.wikipedia.org/wiki/Gregor_Mendel.

64. *Wikipedia*, s.v. "Normal Borlaugh," accessed December 25, 2019, https://en.wikipedia.org/wiki/Norman_ Borlaug.
65. W. Chan Kim and Renee Mauborgne, *Blue Ocean Shift* (New York: Hachette, 2017), 39–40.
66. W. Chan Kim and Renee Mauborgne, *Blue Ocean Shift* (New York: Hachette, 2017), 220–222.
67. Nadya Zhexembayeva, "Stop Calling It 'Innovation'," February 19, 2020, accessed February 23, 2024, https://hbr.org/2020/02/stop-calling-it-innovation.
68. Clayton Christensen, "Christensen: We Are Living the Capitalist's Dilemma," *CNN*, February 23, 2024, accessed March 28, 2014, http://edition.cnn.com/2013/01/21/business/opinion-clayton-christensen/.
69. Scott Kirsner, "What Companies That Are Good at Innovation Get Right," November 29, 2019, accessed February 23, 2024, https://hbr.org/2019/11/what-companies-that-are-good-at-innovation-get-right.

11 Entrepreneurship

Entrepreneurship in Practice

Innovation and entrepreneurship have played and continue to play a critical role in the advancement of agriculture. Entrepreneurs Mike Zelkind and Tisha Livingston left their corporate careers to pursue a big vision: making farming and food better, utilizing completely indoor practices, renewable energy, no pesticides, and reduced time to market. The new venture was called 80 Acres Farms, "inspired by the amount of food we can grow, not the amount of land we use to grow it."[1,2] To produce more in a smaller space, they innovated and developed a vertical farming strategic direction and functional business model that incorporates the environmental, social, and governance stakeholder model.[3] As a result, 80 Acres Farms was nominated as one of the ten most innovative North American companies.[4]

> This vertical farming company runs farms that produce 300 times more food than traditional, Old McDonald-style operations with the same land equivalent. By turning to automation, 80 Acres increased yields while reducing labor costs, making it the first profitable indoor farming company. It also boasts a 30,000-square-foot facility that grows more than a ton of tomatoes weekly without sunlight – another first. In 2019, 80 Acres contributed no pesticides, wasted just 3% of its produce compared to the agriculture industry average of 40%, and used 97% less water than traditional farming. During the pandemic, it opened its largest facility yet in Ohio and fed thousands of New Yorkers from its tomato farm at the Guggenheim, expanding its commitment to growing organic food locally while reducing its environmental impact.[5]

Vertical farming is the practice of growing crops in vertically stacked layers that incorporate a controlled agriculture environment.[6] Vertical farming systems use buildings, shipping containers, tunnels, and abandoned mine shafts for year-round produce and employment. Everything is grown indoors – often using robots and artificial intelligence. Vertical farming has several advantages over conventional farming including increased crop yield, smaller land requirements, protection from weather variations and seasonality, and locally grown produce that is fresher and has lower shipping costs.[7]

This market is growing and provides for organic job growth. The global market for hydroponics in vertical farming is projected to have a compounded annual growth rate (CAGR) of 19.7% between 2020 and 2027.[8] The global indoor farming technology market size is expected to reach approximately $12.03 billion by 2024. The increase in value would be over $6 billion from 2019, when the market size was around $5.92 billion.[9]

The sustainability plan for 80 Acres Farms includes renewable energy and the reduction of their greenhouse gas emission that is dramatically less in comparison to that of a traditional farm.[10] Most of the operations are located near a source of hydroelectric power that is used for renewable energy.[11] The use of indoor farming protects the crops from weather variability of all types. 80 Acres Farms uses

DOI: 10.4324/9781003034308-12

different LED light spectrums and fixture types to grow each plant crop.[12] For instance, a vine crop like tomatoes will be grown under a different fixture and light spectrum than leafy greens or herbs.[13]

Through the practice of Innovation and Entrepreneurship, 80 Acres Farms continues to successfully pursue its mission to eliminate food waste and cut back on water usage.[14] Using hydroponically grown crops, the plant's roots hang out in nutrient-rich water – no soil is needed.[15] There is no need for pesticides.[16] If the water supply contained fluoride, it would have to be removed.[17] Sensors are used to measure the nutrients that plants are soaking up that results in a 97% reduction in water consumption. With this approach, 80 Acres Farms does not add to agricultural runoff – a significant source of pollution of rivers and streams.[18] The company continuously tests the water that is recycled through its irrigation system relying on sensors to identify the changes needed for the nutrient mix.[19]

Entrepreneurship

As illustrated in the 80 Acres Farms example, Entrepreneurship is the engine that drives the economy, and creativity and innovation are its fuel. Driven by a passion to improve food and farm production, 80 Acres Farms is doing what entrepreneurs do best, redefining markets by addressing market inefficiencies in creative and innovative ways. This is an excellent example of marrying mission with practice and provides a window into the entrepreneurship process of ideation, conceptualization, formulation, and implementation. It captures the focus of new ventures creation creating a product/service, addressing customer needs, and assessing the competition. Further, it illustrates the role of the entrepreneur providing creativity, innovation, leadership, and communication. It considers the internal and external environmental forces that include uncertainty, ambiguity, and other outside forces. It demonstrates the execution and engagement of seizing underserved market opportunities, identifying key resources, defining competencies, and building an integrated team. Most importantly, it captures the clear foundation of creating and crafting a compelling value proposition upon which the process of entrepreneurship must be built. These concepts are captured in Figure 11.1.

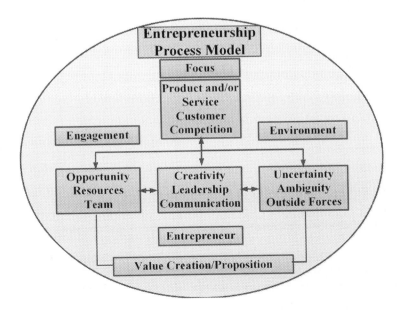

Figure 11.1 Illustration of Entrepreneurship Process Model

What is entrepreneurship? Entrepreneurship is the creation of venture and value for multiple constituencies, including but not limited to customers, employees, communities, and countries. It is the discipline of venture creation that propels and transforms ideas into action, an enterprise that provides value. In its broadest terms, entrepreneurship is an economic phenomenon, a scholarly domain, and a teaching subject.[20] It is a multifaceted, complex, social, and economic phenomenon.[21] "Entrepreneurship is a mindset that can empower ordinary people to accomplish the extraordinary."[22]

Because entrepreneurship is perceived, often incorrectly, to be so many things, it is important to underscore that it is the practice of new venture creation that provides the way to address unserved and/or underserved market opportunities and market inefficiencies that arise from the turbulence that occurs during creative destruction. New opportunities are a blend of unmet customer needs, a viable business model, and various types of technology, incorporating various innovations and business trends to achieve wealth and social value.

Where is entrepreneurship? Entrepreneurship is everywhere. It is about venture creation – individual, corporate, and social. It is the attempt to create value through the recognition of a business opportunity, the management of the risk appropriate to the opportunity, and the management of the resources (people, money, and materials) that bring the venture to fruition. Entrepreneurship is a way of thinking, reasoning, and acting that is opportunity-obsessed, holistic in approach, and leadership-balanced.[23]

Who pursues entrepreneurship? Entrepreneurs are individuals, acting alone or with others, who manage the risks and take actions to create the venture and value for the multiple constituents. Entrepreneurship is driven by imagination, creativity, and innovation, but it is also informed by knowledge that spans specific domain-knowledge and interdisciplinary business practices.

Entrepreneurship is about creating new ventures and expanding value. New ventures can be either accelerated-/scalable-growth aspirant ventures or small-business/steady-state-growth aspirant ventures. Entrepreneurs are the individuals, acting alone or with others, who manage the risks and resources and engage in the process of entrepreneurship.

Present and future economic development requires business leaders, inventors, innovators, designers, marketers, financial planners, and more to have acquired – either on their own or through academics – competencies in domain specific areas. Inventors and innovators are not synonyms for entrepreneurs. Innovation and invention have domain-specific knowledge as well but are more universally applied in other disciplines and do not rely on the common denominator of business as entrepreneurship or venture creation does.

In this chapter we explore the challenge of entrepreneurship (the conundrum/paradox of understanding entrepreneurship: viewing firms in their present success while understanding them at their genesis and nascence), the four critical entrepreneurship continuums (growth, funding, strategy, and planning), entrepreneurship types (individual, corporate, social, and global entrepreneurs), the lean start-ups process, and five entrepreneurship competencies every entrepreneur needs to sell his or her venture.

Entrepreneurship Starting Questions

As will be seen in more detail in the planning continuum later in this chapter, the answers to five deceptively simple questions can often provide the starting point for the new venture creation process:

1. What is the pain/problem you are addressing?
2. What is your primary product and/or service? (Solution)
3. What is the purpose of your business? (Be precise and concise)

4. What type of business do you have? (For example, platform, app, product, or service)
5. Who are your target customers? (Is the market of sufficient size, quality, and durability to sustain your venture? Are buyers and users one in the same?)

With these five questions as a guide, it is possible to explore more fully the process of entrepreneurship and how it differs across multiple continuums of growth aspirant venture type, funding, strategy, and planning.

The Entrepreneurship Conundrum

The "Conundrum of Understanding Entrepreneurship" is essentially the tendency of viewing firms in their present success while needing to understand them at their genesis and nascence. It is a challenging paradox. Before we delve too deep into the world of entrepreneurship, more than any other discipline, understanding entrepreneurship is vexed by the complexity of knowing successful ventures in their success today, but needing to understand them at the beginning of their journeys. This paradox creates the challenge of entrepreneurship shown in Figure 11.2.

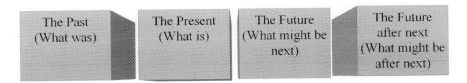

Figure 11.2 Illustration of the Four Time Periods

Source: Adapted from Vijay Govindarajan and Chris Trimble, "The CEO's Role in Business Model Reinvention," *Harvard Business Review*, 89(1–2), (2011): 109.

For example, in 1837, two young would-be entrepreneurs named James Gamble and William Procter started a small business in Cincinnati, Ohio, on the banks of the Ohio River. Procter, a candlemaker from England, and Gamble, an apprentice soap maker from Ireland, met by chance. In fact, Gamble's family was headed on past the Ohio River Valley, but James became ill and, by the time he recovered, the family decided to settle in Cincinnati. By coincidence, Procter and Gamble each married daughters of a prominent local candlemaker and businessman named Alexander Norris. Norris urged his new sons-in-law to form their own new venture, and on October 31, 1837, with funding from friends and family and total assets of $7,000, they signed the partnership agreement that formed the Procter & Gamble Company. Fast forward to today, Procter & Gamble is known as a multibillion-dollar global provider of consumer goods.[24]

Snapshots and Movies

In the book *How Will You Measure Your Life?* Clayton Christensen provides insights into why success is so hard to sustain.[25] Most companies are evaluated based on a snapshot in time. Later, a snapshot is taken with the same group of people and things are different. The snapshot does not tell how the company got to where it is now, nor does it tell where it is going. A movie, on the other hand, might explain more effectively how a company got to where it is and how it can proceed to the next step.

This is the conundrum, or paradox if you will, of entrepreneurship and strategy; we tend to see company success (e.g., now famous brands and wealth creation) as an outcome, not the rigorous and often lengthy process that comprises the real path to success. The time continuum from nascent entrepreneurial or venture start-up activity to the present provides a challenging and changing picture to the learner, depending on where in the process it is first viewed. For example, today's student only knows Procter & Gamble as an 80-plus-billion-dollar global purveyor of consumer goods. Of course, in 1837, it was a small business venture destined to become what is known today as a scalable high-growth potential venture.

Entrepreneurship Continuums

In addition to the entrepreneurship conundrum/paradox evidenced by the time continuum in Figure 11.2, there are four additional continuums captured in Figure 11.3 that are focused on the nexus of innovation, strategy, and entrepreneurship: growth aspirations, funding, strategy, and planning.

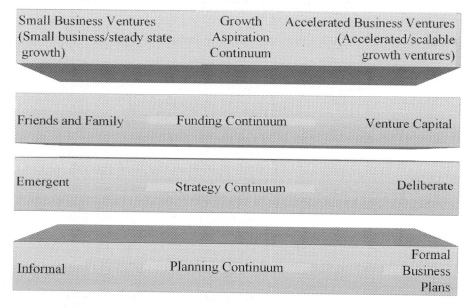

Figure 11.3 Illustration of the Four Continuums

Source: Adapted from Henry Mintzberg & John A. Waters, "Of strategies, deliberate and emergent," *Strategic Management Journal*, 6(3), (1985): 257–273.

Growth Aspiration Continuum

The growth aspiration continuum spans small-business/steady-state-growth aspirant entrepreneurs that seek local market success to accelerated-/scalable-growth aspirant entrepreneurs that seek to change market conditions. Both play a vital role in economic growth and stability. Too often, however, accelerated-growth potential ventures are overemphasized. This is due to the high growth potential and scalability that portends jobs and return of investment for equity investors. High-growth aspirant ventures capture 80% of the headlines, they comprise less than 2% of start-ups, while small-business-growth ventures comprise 80% plus of start-ups.

Accelerated-/Scalable-Growth Aspirant Entrepreneurs

Accelerated-/scalable-growth aspirant ventures are those that have high aspirations to pursue new ideas, identify new markets, and redefine industry standards. Accelerated-/scalable-growth aspirant ventures typically provide a new and unique innovation and may redefine markets or businesses. Accelerated-/scalable-growth ventures are uniquely suited to compete where there is no competition by creating temporary monopolies.

While both small-business/steady-state-growth and accelerated-/scalable-growth ventures seek to create new value propositions, the most distinguishing difference is the scalable nature of accelerated growth aspirant ventures. An excellent case in point is the now globally recognized brand, Starbucks.

Howard Schultz, the founder of Starbucks as it is known today, created a new value proposition after he visited Italy by copying the experience he observed while frequenting the espresso bars there. He was able to successfully import the coffee experience with a premium product and service that made customers feel comfortable and willing to come back again and again. Initially, however, Starbucks was a single store in the historic Pike Place Market in Seattle, Washington. In 1971, Starbucks was founded primarily as a retailer of the world's finest whole-bean coffees. Co-founders Jerry Baldwin, Zev Siegel, and Gordon Bowker only wanted to sell whole-bean coffee. Selling brewed coffee was not on their radar and would only come later. Starbucks would begin to scale with the purchase of Schultz's then-nascent chain in 1987. Shultz, a former employee, left to start his own European-style coffeehouse, Il Giornale, only to return a few years later to build and grow the Starbucks brand, resulting in its initial public offering (IPO) in 1992.[26]

Small-Business/Steady-State-Growth Aspirant Entrepreneurs

Start-up micro, small, and medium-sized enterprises (MSMEs) are usually the result of entrepreneurs who build new ventures to sustain their lifestyles. While both accelerated/scalable potential ventures and MSMEs are opportunity driven, MSMEs are sometimes called "income substitution" ventures since they often substitute for the income the founders would have received had they gone to work for an already established company. Small-business/steady-state-growth aspirant ventures are typically independently owned and operated, not dominant in their fields, and not seeking to redefine industry standards on a scalable level. MSMEs often will compete in intense competitive situations, offering similar products and services in existing markets. MSMEs include businesses such as restaurants, stylists, plumbers, landscapers, franchises, and remodeling, with a focus on local or regional value propositions. Some ventures that start out as small-business/steady-state-growth aspirant ventures morph into accelerated-/scalable-growth aspirant ventures and vice versa. Small business ventures that seek "local scalability," on the other hand, generally launch with capital from friends, family, and founders and, as such, rarely seek outside equity capital.

Funding Continuum

The funding continuum starts with personal funds (cash and credit cards) and continues to friends and family and founders and then to angel and venture capital and everything in between. The primary function of providing goods and services is to deliver value of sufficient scope consistently and clearly such that your customer is willing to exchange value for it. Indeed, confirmation of great business ideas only comes with this exchange of value; that is, the willingness of a customer to pay or barter for what is being offered. Initially, however, it takes start-up capital to get the venture off the ground. Over 80% of all ventures are small-business/steady-state-growth aspirants, less than 20% are accelerated-/scalable-growth aspirants. Correspondingly, angel and venture capital investors are generally only interested in the accelerated-/scalable-growth ventures, while funding from friends, family, and founders fuels the small-business/steady-state-growth ventures.

Start-Up Paths

In general, only ventures with the potential to scale and provide significant return in a relatively short period of time are attractive to equity investors such as private placement, angel, or venture capitalists. Micro, small, and medium enterprises generally are only attractive to friends, family, and founders.

Focusing on high-growth-potential or scalable start-ups, there are several possible funding paths For example, a start-up may attempt to accelerate its growth in order to scale, possibly with a goal of an initial public offering (IPO) (detailed here in Chapter 11). Or as the venture scales, it may seek to be acquired or merge with another firm (see mergers and acquisitions [M&A] discussed in Chapter 15 in relation to horizontal integration). Alternatively, a start-up may pivot and change its initial trajectory as a result of feedback on a minimally viable product (MVP) and change its strategy (see the pivot discussed in Chapter 8). If a start-up venture is successful, it may displace an incumbent and accelerate its expansion overtaking the incumbent (see the theory of disruption discussed in Chapter 10). A start-up may seek to exit by discontinuing operations because it cannot cross the chasm between the early adopters of an offering and the strategic moves of competitors. While not an exhaustive list, it illustrates the impact the start-up path has on seeking financial resources, especially for high-growth potential start-ups along the funding continuum.

Start-Up Funding Across the Continuum

Given the relative importance placed on new venture funding, it is desirable to take a deeper look at start-up funding across the continuum. Start-up financing varies depending on type of venture (MSME vs. accelerated-/scalable-growth potential), as well as the different stages of the firm's maturity. Initially, both MSMEs and accelerated-/scalable-growth ventures are funded by the founders themselves or by friends and family and often through crowdfunding. While MSMEs are rarely, if ever, attractive to outside equity investors, accelerated-/scalable-growth potential ventures may be attractive.

For example, angel investors and venture capitalists provide funds to emerging firms with one objective in mind: to get a return on their investment. They manage the risks by providing the financing to a range of start-ups in their portfolio with the expectation that an exceedingly small number of the start-ups will ultimately attain profitability and the expected return on investment.

Unless funded by internal sources, angel investors, or private placement, venture capital is essential when it comes to scaling high growth potential ventures.

> Venture capital (VC) is a form of private equity financing that is provided by venture capital firms or funds to start-ups, early-stage, and emerging companies that have been deemed to have high growth potential or which have demonstrated high growth (in terms of number of employees, annual revenue, scale of operations, etc.).[27]

For example, in 1987, Howard Schultz recognized the scalable potential of specialty coffees and convinced a group of investors to join him in refocusing, rebranding, and recasting Starbucks outside its founding city of Seattle to rapidly expand the fledgling chain.

The potentially scalable start-up may grow and pursue an initial public offering, exit by being acquired or through a merger, pivot to a new strategy, displace an incumbent, or may fail. Figure 11.4 illustrates these funding stages and types of funding on a two-dimensional chart.

Interestingly, results from a longitudinal research study on nascent entrepreneurial ventures (the Panel Study of Entrepreneurial Dynamics) suggest that simple forms of financing are preferred over more complex forms. The most common sources of start-up capital include the founder's own money (90%), followed by credit cards (30.6%), spouse (25.1%), friends and family (13.8%), bank loan (12.1%), and friends and family of team members (9.4%). The sample of over 800 nascent entrepreneurs reported that only 3.2% were even seeking venture capital for their start-up.[28]

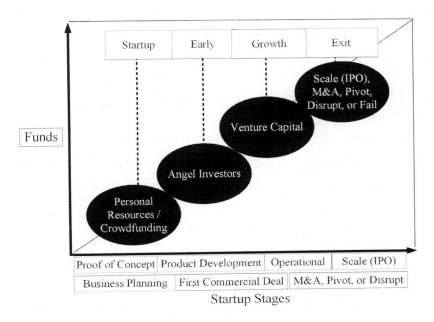

Figure 11.4 Illustration of the Generalized Start-up Financing Stages

Source: Adapted from "Venture capital," accessed January 11, 2021, https://en.wikipedia.org/wiki/Venture_capital and https://www.mbaknol.com/business-finance/stages-of-venture-capital-financing

Debt and Equity

The source notwithstanding, there are basically only two types of funding for new start-ups: debt and equity. Debt is capital that must be repaid at specified interest over a stated period. Equity is capital that is provided in exchange for a percentage of ownership of the venture. There is one variation on the dual capital theme, convertible debt. That is, debt can be obtained, which, upon the satisfaction of certain conditions, converts to equity at a specified time and amount. For example, a loan might be obtained at 5% interest over seven years. If the venture reaches certain specified milestones or "triggers," the debt converts from repayment with interest to a specified portion of ownership.

Crowdsourcing

Crowdsourcing is "the practice of obtaining needed services, ideas, or content by soliciting contributions from a large group of people and especially from the online community rather than from traditional employees or suppliers."[29] Crowdsourcing applies the wisdom of the crowd to solve problems. Top crowdsourcing websites include crowdSPRING, 99Designs, DesignCrowd, Elance, oDesk, and Innocentive.[30] For example, crowdSPRING is a crowdsourcing website that enables creative individuals to find customers and allows customers to find creative talent.[31]

Crowdfunding

Crowdfunding is crowdsourcing relatively small amounts of money from large numbers of people using social networking. With crowdfunding, small amounts of money can be pooled and used to implement big ideas. Crowdfunding is a way for individuals to fund start-ups wherein the participants vote with their dollars. In the past, entrepreneurs have been constrained by the ability to acquire funds for the start-up and growth phases of their ideas. Entrepreneurs traditionally had to seek out friends and families, venture capitalists, and financial institutions for resources.

Benefitting from a renewed presence thanks to the reach and scope of the Internet, crowdfunding is the time-tested process of seeking start-up capital via raising small amounts of funds from many people. Crowdfunding is a variation of the "friends, family, and founders" end of the continuum. As seen later in this chapter, the advent of the Internet has greatly broadened the reach and scope of seeking small amounts of debt or equity from many people and thus moved it more toward the middle of the funding continuum. With crowdfunding now a global phenomenon, *Forbes* reported that London is now the world capital of crowdfunding, displacing New York and San Francisco as the most active. Using data compiled from the Crowdfunding Centre, it is estimated that over 250,000 crowdfunding campaigns were launched internationally in 2014, with an average of nearly $18,000 raised and a little over 30% reaching their full funding target.[32] It is estimated that crowdfunding platforms have raised more than $34 billion worldwide through 2021.[33] Moreover, in 2024, crowdfunding volume in the US and Canada is estimated to bey nearly $74 billion, and the global crowdfunding market is estimated to be over $3.5 trillion by 2030.[34]

While online fundraising is relatively new, crowdfunding as a concept is not. For example, for the Statue of Liberty, $250,000 was funded through crowdfunding by the working people of France. Because there were not enough funds for the pedestal for the Statue of Liberty, Joseph Pulitzer, publisher of the *New York World*, wrote an article to appeal to the working people of America to donate funds. Approximately 125,000 people responded to his appeal with contributions totaling $100,000 for the construction of the stone pedestal that was placed in New York Harbor.[35] The average crowdfunding contribution was 83 cents. Regardless of the size of the contribution, Pulitzer published the names of each person in his newspaper.[36]

Crowdfunding has reframed the nascent ventures fundraising process by enabling interested individuals to invest directly into new ventures, bypassing the more conventional ways of funding entrepreneurs. In general, crowdfunding can be broken down into three types: rewards, debt, and equity. Essentially, the Statue of Liberty example illustrates the rewards crowdfunding, similar to what is seen on Kickstarter or Indiegogo. In exchange for a small amount of funds, the funder receives rewards, such as recognition, early order access, or other perks/swag. Top crowdfunding websites include Kickstarter, Indiegogo, Crowd Supply, Crowdfunder, Patreon, GoFundMe, and SeedInvest Technology, to name a few.[37] For example,

> Kickstarter is full of projects, big and small, that are brought to life through the direct support of people like you. Since our launch in 2009, more than 4.2 million people have pledged over $638 million, funding more than 42,000 creative projects. Thousands of creative projects are raising funds on Kickstarter right now.[38]

In addition to these rewards crowdsourcing platforms, by 2019, the number of FINRA-registered (Financial Industry Regulatory Authority) regulation crowdfunding (Reg CF) portals that engage in equity or debt funding has reached over 50. For example, the top four funding portals ranked by the number of Form C filings (both ITD and 2019 YTD) are StartEngine, WeFunder, SeedInvest, and Republic.[39] Other equity and debt crowdsourcing portals include NextSeed, Microventures, Wunderfund, and Netcapital. By 2024, the number of funding portals regulated by FINRA was approaching 100.[40]

Fintech: A Blend of Finance and Technology

Fintech, shorthand for financial technology, refers to the use of technology to reconfigure, improve, and automate the delivery and use of financial services across multiple users and platforms. In short, it is "new tech that seeks to improve and automate the delivery and use of financial services."[41]

Essentially, Fintech encompasses a wide range of innovations, from mobile banking payment apps, crowdfunding platforms, investment apps, robo-advisors, cryptocurrencies, and more. It is a rapidly evolving field with the potential to transform the way both personal as well as start-up finances are managed that include potential benefits as well as notable challenges for innovators and entrepreneurs. While a comprehensive review of the evolving field of fintech is beyond the scope of this chapter, several examples of fintech application and key benefits, challenges, and takeaways can be identified.

Examples of Fintech Applications

Interestingly, as consumers become more familiar with the evolution of fintech, there is growing adoption by consumers to connect their fintech accounts to other digital services. For example, Plaid is a financial services company based in San Francisco, California. The company builds a data transfer network that powers fintech and digital finance products. Plaid's product, a technology platform, enables applications to connect with users' bank accounts.[42,43]

Again, while far from comprehensive, here are a few examples of how fintech is playing and continues to play a role in innovation and entrepreneurship:

- Mobile banking: Apps like Venmo, Cash App, and Zelle are peer-to-peer mobile payment apps that allow users to send and receive money easily and instantly.
- Payment processing: Companies such as Stripe and PayPal facilitate online payments for businesses and individuals.
- Crowdfunding: Unregulated platforms like Kickstarter and GoFundMe, as well as regulated platforms like the Wunderfund or StartEngine Capital LLC, enable individuals to raise funds for projects or businesses.
- Robo-advisors: Algorithmic tools like Wealthfront and Betterment provide automated investment advice and management.
- Blockchain: This distributed ledger technology has the potential to revolutionize areas like payments, lending, and asset management.

Fintech Benefits, Challenges, and Takeaways

When it comes to advantages of fintech, a number have emerged as leading benefits. Among these are convenience, lower costs, greater choices, financial inclusion, and transparency. Arguably, fintech makes financial tasks easier and quicker to complete, although keeping track of multiple apps can be challenging in and of itself. Also, automated processes and increased competition can potentially lead to lower fees and charges while simultaneously providing consumers access to a wider range of financial products and services than ever before. As a result, fintech can help bring financial services to those who were unbanked, unaware of or excluded from the benefits of having and connecting financial tools. Interestingly, fintech innovations can enable greater transparency in financial transactions, thus making it attractive for innovators and entrepreneurs.

While fintech is promising, it is not without its challenges. Chief among these are security concerns, regulatory issues, potential for job displacement, and access. Data breaches and other security issues are a major concern in the digital world. Adding to the security concerns is that the rapid evolution of fintech can outpace regulatory agencies. For example, as noted earlier, when it comes to regulated crowdsource funding, there are challenges. "To protect investors and ensure the market's integrity, FINRA Financial Industry Regulatory Authority is a government-authorized not-for-profit organization that oversees U.S. broker-dealers."[44] Added to the security and regulatory challenges is the possibility that fintech could lead to job displacement in certain sectors. Finally, while continuing to improve, not everyone has access to technology as it advances. Combined with the consumer learning curve, while fintech holds much promise for innovation and entrepreneurship, it is not a panacea and requires consumers to keep up-to-date.

Strategy Continuum

Building on the work of management scholar Henry Mintzberg, strategy can be viewed from a purely emergent perspective (facilitates learning but precludes structure) to a purely deliberate perspective (facilitates structure but precludes learning) and everything in between.[45] Decision-making within new ventures is often more emergent than deliberate due to newly uncovered information and results achieved along the way, which require modifying the original assumptions of the business.[46]

For example, the networking technology for text messaging, or short messaging service (SMS), was created by the Anglo-Dutch information technology firm known as CMG. The original purpose of SMS was to communicate to customers about service problems with the network. It was never intended for use in personal communications between friends and family or by the young generations, who today find it so popular.[47] Some of the customers found out how to use the service and serendipitously began using it from customer to customer (but only through the same carrier). The "free" service was not so much deliberately planned as it was emergent. Later, the technology model was revised to incorporate a business model that charged customers for the use of the service.[48] In 2010, this service was reported to have earned $114.6 billion globally.[49] For more on innovation and entrepreneurship strategy, see Chapter 12.

Planning Continuum

While the debate continues around the value of writing a business plan, and research is mixed as to its direct value to the financial performance of firms, having a plan from which to vary is more valuable than not. What is often overlooked is the fact that planning exists on a continuum that spans from strictly informal/unwritten/in your head to formal/written and everything in between. This is analogous to music that can be played on a continuum from a pick-up garage band to a formal classical orchestra.

Both informal and formal planning provides benefits that add value to the venture.

1. Planning provides a point of reference as well as a point of departure. It is hard to know where you are going (or when you have arrived) if you do not have an idea of what that looks like.
2. Planning allows for flexibility while simultaneously providing structure.
3. Planning facilitates change; while little can be guaranteed in the start-up process, change, both internal and external to the firm, will certainly occur.

4. Planning provides value not only in the completed plan, but in the planning process itself. Simply the fact that a plan must be updated is value added to the new venture.

Planning for a new venture is fundamentally different from that of more established businesses. An established business can extrapolate its plans from past experiences, blending that with their future. In contrast, at the start of a new venture, less is known and more is assumed. As a result, it is important to carefully articulate the planning assumptions on which a nascent venture business plan is built. The well-worn phrase "failing to plan is planning to fail" is still a very viable thought. Planning, whether informal or formal, is crucial to the sustained success of a new venture. As noted earlier, the answers to the five deceptively simple questions about the new venture start-up process can reveal a great deal about its viability.

Ideation, Conceptualization, Formulation, Implementation

The genesis of entrepreneurship begins with an idea. It is the first of four steps that lead to new venture creation. Once the idea takes shape, it moves toward conceptualization, the second step. Conceptualization gives an idea shape, substance, and form and helps transform the idea from its rudimentary beginning to a more developed stage. Conceptualization enables the third step, formulation. Formulation considers the details of what it takes to get the conceptualized idea off the ground and the new venture up and running. Typically, formulation encompasses the business planning process, from informal to formal written plans. Formulation thus empowers the fourth step, implementation. Implementation is ongoing, never ceasing until the venture ceases to exist. These four steps form the genesis of the entrepreneurship process model.

Entrepreneurship Process Model

The challenge of understanding entrepreneurship is that ventures are only seen in their success, but entrepreneurship is about understanding ventures at the beginning. Considering the multidimensional entrepreneurship process model, that venture understanding generally begins with the entrepreneur. One of the best examples of the quintessential entrepreneur is King C. Gillette. He embodies what can be called the entrepreneur's three-dimensional vision: drive, determination, and dedication. His start-up journey parallels the timeless challenges facing entrepreneurs then and now. As we will see in the full entrepreneurship process model, Gillette epitomizes the three essential tasks of the entrepreneur, both as a start-up begins and as a venture matures – creativity, leadership, and communication.

Building on the work of the late Jeffry Timmons, a robust model of the new venture creation process that is formed on the **foundation of value creation** is developed. As seen in Figure 11.1, four key aspects of the entrepreneurship process model are identified: the **entrepreneur** (creativity, leadership, and communication), the **environment** (uncertainty, ambiguity, outside forces), the **engagement** (opportunity, resource, team), and the **focus** (product/service, customer, competition). All of this unfolds on the foundation of creating value for multiple constituents – customers, employees, suppliers, vendors, communities, and even countries.

As noted previously, entrepreneurship is about creating venture and value. New ventures can be either small-business/steady-state-growth aspirant ventures or accelerated-/scalable-growth aspirant ventures. Entrepreneurs are the individuals, acting alone or with others, who manage the risk and resources to form new stand-alone ventures, corporate ventures, or socially driven ventures, both small-business or accelerated-growth ventures. It is these entrepreneurs who are engaged in the process of entrepreneurship.

Present and future economic development requires business leaders, inventors, innovators, designers, marketers, financial planners, and more to have acquired – either on their own or through academics – competencies in domain specific areas. Inventors and innovators are not synonyms for entrepreneurs. Innovation and invention have domain-specific knowledge as well, but are more broadly applied in other disciplines and do not rely on the common denominator of business as entrepreneurship or venture creation does.

This entrepreneurship process model integrates how a start-up can begin with an innovative idea that develops into a small business or high-growth company and includes strong leadership from the founder or co-founders. It illustrates the role of complementary talents and team work (internal and/or external to the venture); skill and ingenuity in finding, managing, and controlling resources; and the financial backing (self, friends, and family, to venture capital and everything in between) to "chase" the opportunity. Let's begin by examining the role of the entrepreneur.

The Entrepreneur

Central to the entrepreneurship process is the entrepreneur. That the entrepreneur must simultaneously wear multiple hats is legendary in the lore of new start-ups. With so many distractions, creativity, leadership, and communication are the entrepreneur's most vital weapons.

Creativity

As seen in Chapter 8, "Creativity Insights," it all begins with an idea. At the turn of the 20th century, the dominant method for men to obtain a close shave was the straight edge, strop, whetstone, mug, brush, and soap. Gillette envisioned a reusable steel-blade-and-holder shaving system that did not need stropping or honing and that would provide a clean, safe shave at a fraction of the cost of going to a barber while also avoiding the usual labor- and time-intensive system. The entrepreneur sees a problem, clarifies it, and seeks a solution. It is the entrepreneur's creativity and innovation that provides the spark that ignites change. One of the greatest sources of creativity is seeking solutions to everyday problems. It might be driven by new knowledge, technology, or even changes in mood and meaning.

Leadership

As we will see in Chapter 13, "Catalytic Leadership," if there is one thing that sets entrepreneurs apart, it is their leadership in translating ideas into action and making things happen. King Gillette initially was ahead of his time. His solution, while innovative, was not immediately embraced. The engineers at MIT said it couldn't be done. Undaunted, he continued to pursue his vision for nearly six years, until another MIT-educated machinist, William Nickerson, partnered with him to introduce the Gillette Safety Razor in 1903. It would have been easy to give up, but leadership is about overcoming obstacles and working with others to see and understand what needs to be done and how to do it. The entrepreneur lives the classic definition of leadership: facilitating individual and collective efforts to accomplish shared objectives.

Communication

As good as a creative solution to a problem might be, it is only as good as the entrepreneur's ability to effectively communicate that idea. This is one of the most perplexing challenges for most entrepreneurs. Great innovators are not always the best communicators. The key is recognizing that there is limited time available to clearly, concisely, and effectively present how the problem, solution, and market opportunity all come together. It is tempting to talk tech, become immersed in the detail, and/or lose sight of key objectives. When communicating, keep it clear, clean, precise, and concise. Moreover, it is important to know your audience. For example, while the core message remains crisp and customer-centric, investors are going to want to know more about the returns on their investments.

As important as these three tasks are to the launch of a new venture, they are equally essential to the ongoing growth and success of the business over the long term. Gillette, for example, was one of the first entrepreneurs to recognize the need to continuously innovate products and services, provide ongoing leadership, and leverage the power of advertising by crafting a simple, compelling message for the consumer – a clean, close, safe shave without stropping or honing, at a fraction of the price of a barbershop shave. Of course, that message has been refined over the years as the product has evolved. Entrepreneurs challenge traditional definitions of value and embrace market inefficiencies (seeking to make them more efficient).

Identifying, capturing, and taming ideas are never easy. The entrepreneur must be relentless in the pursuit of his or her idea. The entrepreneur must recognize his or her own strengths and weaknesses and determine the roles to which he or she is best suited.

The Environment

Blaise Pascal, a 17th-century French mathematician, physicist, inventor, and writer, once noted, "Il n'est pas certain que tout soit incertain," or "It is not certain that everything is uncertain."[50]

A changing business, economic, legal, political, social, and technological landscape suggests that there is a critical need to continually assess the environments in which we conduct business. Uncertainty, ambiguity, and outside forces inevitably impinge on and/or distract from how business in done.

Uncertainty

Life and business are full of uncertainty. Simply stated, incomplete information, doubt, or lack of access to information can compromise the degree of certainty about future actions and outcomes. For researchers and practitioners, the planning/performance equation has always been of great interest. While the debate continues around the direct efficacy of the planning and performance relationship, in general, both steady-state/small-business-growth and accelerated-/scalable-growth aspirant ventures can benefit from more sophisticated planning.[51] Research has also shown that as uncertainty increases, formal planning tends to decrease.[52] One possible explanation is simply human nature. Why engage in detailed plans when the outcome is uncertain? Of course, every entrepreneur must strive to balance the benefits of planning without succumbing to either environmental uncertainty or analysis paralysis.

Ambiguity and Outside Forces

There is always going to be ambiguity and mixed signals in doing business. For example, what markets are best to enter or avoid? Can you stay ahead of the direct competition while not losing ground to indirect competition? What is the volatility of interest rates or lines of credit? Will government regulations impact the business? There are key players/stakeholders and a host of outside forces, many of which are outside your control, with which you must deal on a daily basis. For example, players/stakeholders can include communities, customers, creditors, employees, labor unions, governments, special interest groups, suppliers, trade associations, and others. When combined with economic, political/legal, societal, and technological forces, environmental uncertainty can lead to an overwhelming sense of distraction and loss of focus and direction.

The difficult part is to stay the course and engage in sufficient planning to develop clear objectives, core competencies, and market objectives. Monitor key aspects of the environment that are important with regard to how and where you do business. For example, increasing costs of transportation may suggest that alternative delivery options need to be explored. Develop meaningful metrics to assess both your progress toward objectives and goals as well as the potential impact of changes in the environment. For example, define objectives in quantifiable terms (increase sales 10%) over a specified period of time (annually), and collect data at regular intervals (quarterly sales revenue). Using these key variables and metrics, develop contingency plans, but stay focused. Knowing the options ahead of time can be critical in terms of time, money, and peace of mind.

The Engagement

The popular definition of opportunity refers to a favorable set of circumstances or a chance for advancement, as in the opportunity to buy a computer on sale or an opportunity to go to college. While useful in most situations, when it comes to business and entrepreneurship in particular, this definition misses the mark at best and can even be downright misleading.

Opportunity

The word "opportunity" is used to cover everything from *action* opportunities (e.g., the opportunity to expand geographic markets or add product/service lines) to *expense* opportunities (e.g., the opportunity to lease a larger retail space or buy a discounted computer system) and everything in between. In reality, the opportunity of interest in innovation and entrepreneurship is *market* opportunity. "What is the unserved and/or underserved *market opportunity* that having this larger retail space will allow you to better serve?"[53] Moreover, the market opportunity needs to be of sufficient size, quality, and durability to sustain the business venture in which you are engaged. The opportunity is not to start the venture but rather to identify a problem or pain point, devise a solution, and discern the dimensions of the unserved and/or underserved market potential. This can be tricky. For example, advancing technology can lead to goods and/or services that address problems for which previously there might not have been a viable market. If you were born before 1942, do you really need a smartphone? If you were born after 1992, could you possibly live without one?

Resources

Identifying a market opportunity is one thing, assembling the necessary resources is quite another. For example, building on memories of "snurfing" in high school, by 1977, Jake Burton Carpenter envisioned a more sophisticated way to "surf on snow" and introduced the first Burton Snow Board. But like other entrepreneurs, he was ahead of his time, and his early attempt failed because he improperly calculated the potential market for this new entry in sports equipment. By 1980, however, he had brought together the resources to simultaneously innovate the board itself, put the wheels in motion to "create" the emerging sport of snowboarding (now an Olympic sport), and launch the manufacturing, distribution, and sale of products targeted at an emerging market. The entrepreneur constantly balances scarce resources for optimal impact to define and develop the product/service offering, build brand awareness and acceptance, and gain a market entry point.

Today, Burton Snow Board products are in over 4,300 stores worldwide with a 40–70% market share, depending on the category.

Team

Entrepreneurs by their very nature are not timid, especially when it comes to their ideas. Yet they are always quick to note that the secret to their success is surrounding themselves with people who are better, brighter, and smarter than they are. Building a cohesive and focused team is both an art and a science. While we are familiar with team sports and the reliance on each member of the team performing as a unit to achieve excellence, it is often overlooked that even in individual sports there is a reliance on a team that may go unseen yet is equally important to success. Entrepreneurship is both an individual and a team sport, and identifying core team members in the short, intermediate, and long term is essential. Team is critical to execution, and while investors would like every new venture to be an "A" idea and an "A" team, they are often drawn to an "A" team with a "B" idea over a "B" team with an "A" idea.

Focus

Keep in mind that the entire entrepreneurship process model is underscored by what must be a rock-solid foundation: the creation of value for the customer. This value proposition must be sufficiently compelling to induce a value exchange between your goods and/or service and the customer's need, want, desire, pain, or problem. Entrepreneurs who solve problems, no matter what the size, create a solid value proposition.

Naturally, it is difficult yet critical not to be distracted along the way. The key is focus, focus, focus. Even a casual perusal of successful new ventures reveals a clear and persistent focus on three core elements: the product and/or service offered, the customer, and the competition. An excellent example of a new venture start-up that lived, breathed, and executed this focus principle is the Boston Beer Company. Founded in 1983 by native Cincinnatian Mr. James Koch, the Boston Beer Company personifies the entrepreneurship conundrum presented earlier in this chapter.

When Koch first conceived his new venture idea in 1983, entering the brewing industry was not very attractive. In fact, breweries were closing, not opening, growth was stagnant, and there was excess brewing capacity throughout the industry. Initial thoughts toward building a brewery were quickly abandoned, as potential investors were naturally reluctant to participate. Given this relative lack of overall industry attractiveness, what did Koch know that would set him apart? The short answer: focus on product/service, customers, and competitors.

Product and/or Service

Samuel Adams Lager would become the cornerstone of what would eventually become an entire product line of beer that would be targeted to just 2% of the beer drinking market. Pursuing a focused differentiation strategy demanded that the product attributes not only meet but exceed the customer's expectations. Since the premium product attributes (especially taste) were paramount, considerable time was spent perfecting the heart and soul of the company – the product. While the Boston Beer example focuses on product development, the same processes apply to service offerings. Service offerings can actually be thought of as "products" of service companies. For example, the product that a personal tax preparation service company offers is timely, accurate, quality tax analysis and preparation for individual taxpayers. In addition, product and service offerings frequently occur in combination. Starbucks is an excellent example of a product (a selection of premium coffee and tea beverages) and service (a premium coffee and tea beverage experience).

Customer

For Jim Koch crafting the Boston Beer Company, the customer segment was small but of sufficient size quality and durability to support a new entrant. By conceding 98% of the brew-drinking market to the dominant domestic breweries, Boston Beer was able to successfully focus on the 2% of beer drinkers that sought a premium or super premium product – an emerging segment addressed at that time only by the imported or specialty beer producers.

Competitors

In the early years, Koch correctly assessed that the major domestic players would be unable and/or unwilling to respond to a new entrant in the premium beer segment. They were committed to the larger, non-premium segment and had conceded the premium/specialty segment to the imported beers. While he knew the imported beer makers would respond, focusing on product attributes the customer sought, he would gain valuable time and space on his eventual emerging competitors. Through the early 1990s, microbrewing and craft brewing were still highly fragmented, giving Boston Beer first-mover advantage. In 2021, trends shaping the craft beer industry continue to change, creating a much different competitive landscape. Shaped in part by the innovation sparked by Boston Beer in the 1980s, today's craft brewers face new challenges requiring continuous creativity and innovation.

By the late 2000s, the business landscape had changed dramatically, which brings the entire entrepreneurship process model back into focus. It is a dynamic and interactive process that balances all four core elements of the entrepreneurship process underscored by creating value for the customer: There must be a clear focus (product and/or services, customers, and competition) and constant scanning of a changing landscape/environment (uncertainty, ambiguity, and external forces) guided by the entrepreneur (creativity, leadership, and communication) and relentlessly engaged/executed (opportunity, resources, and team).

Value Propositions

A value proposition is a promise made to a customer to provide value that meets or exceeds the customer's expectation. The value proposition defines how a product, process, or service fulfills a customer's unmet needs in a way that does a job for them. A value proposition meets the customer's needs in a simple, convenient, timely, and affordable manner. A high-potential value proposition is one that addresses an unserved and/or underserved market opportunity.

Entrepreneurship and Entrepreneur Types

Building on the core elements of the entrepreneurship process model, entrepreneurship transforms ideas into action, or, more precisely, creates an enterprise that provides value. The strategic intent of the enterprise can encompass social, economic, and/or environmental objectives, individually or in various combinations. Entrepreneurship is everywhere. Individual entrepreneurship accounts for 95% of firms, which are the small- and medium-sized enterprises. Corporate entrepreneurship encompasses large firms, which often need to compete through *intrapreneurship* (i.e., innovation, venturing, and strategic renewal). Social entrepreneurship includes, typically, but not exclusively, not-for-profit ventures that seek to meet an unmet, unserved, and/or underserved social objective.

As noted, the enterprise can be any type or size, from small-business/steady-state-growth aspirant to accelerated-/scalable-growth aspirant ventures. Entrepreneurship is a broad concept that encompasses multiple new venture pursuits by a variety of entrepreneurs: individual and serial entrepreneurs, small business entrepreneurs, corporate entrepreneurs, family-owned business entrepreneurs, and social entrepreneurs. The three core entrepreneurship types are shown in Figure 11.5.

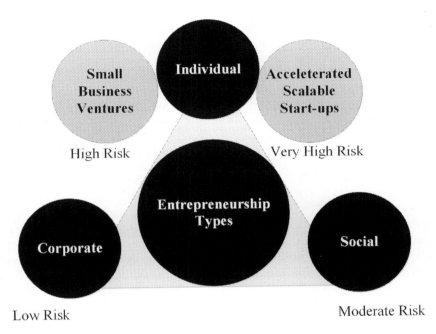

Figure 11.5 Illustration of Entrepreneurship Types

Source: Adapted from Steve Blank https://steveblank.com/2010/06/10/you%E2%80%99re-not-a-real-entrepreneur/

Individual Entrepreneurs

Entrepreneurship is practiced by individual entrepreneurs who transform ideas into value propositions. Often, individual entrepreneurs repeat this value proposition process over and over, becoming serial entrepreneurs who can repeatedly create and build successful and sustainable ventures. These are the individuals, alone or with others, pulling together teams that have become synonymous with entrepreneurship throughout time. The list of notable entrepreneurs, including King Gillette, James Gamble and William Procter, Mariah Longworth, Mary Kay Ash, Andrew Carnegie, James Koch, Howard Schultz, Bill Gates, Steve Jobs, Mohammad Yunus, Jeff Bezos, Fred Smith, and Oprah Winfrey, barely scratches the surface of the incredible pantheon of entrepreneurs whose names are identified with ventures that create value to solve a need and address underserved and/or unserved markets.

While there are many whose names are known, there are tens of thousands whose names are not as well known, yet whose pursuits in both small-business/steady-state-growth aspirant to accelerated-/scalable-growth aspirant ventures have transformed the business landscape. For example, John D. Goeken, nicknamed Jack the Giant Killer, was instrumental in breaking up the huge AT&T monopoly when he installed microwave technology that was used for long-distance communications between Chicago and Saint Louis.[54] Donald "Buddy" LaRosa founded a single pizzeria in 1954 in Cincinnati, Ohio, that today has "locally scaled" into the dominant pizza chain in the city with over 60 locations, industry-leading sales, and market-share dominance. In fact, LaRosa not only innovated a food product, pizza, at a time when most people in the United States were not familiar with it, but he would continually innovate new processes, such as home delivery and "one number" ordering for the entire chain.[55]

Corporate Entrepreneurs

Corporate entrepreneurship can be successful but needs to be managed differently from other aspects of the business, since it requires an emphasis on experimentation and learning over short-term profits. For example, to overcome internal stagnation, Procter & Gamble has successfully introduced a form of open innovation by soliciting ideas from outside the corporation.

Research in corporate entrepreneurship has identified five specific dimensions that are important determinants of an environment conducive to entrepreneurial behavior: (1) top management support, (2) work discretion/autonomy, (3) rewards/reinforcement, (4) time availability, and (5) organizational boundaries.[56]

Corporate New Venture Boundaries

Corporate entrepreneurs' efforts can be achieved within existing organizations, such as Amazon, Google, 3M, IBM, and Whirlpool, but require boundaries. Corporate entrepreneurship can be part of the corporate culture yet may require a separate organization that is linked to the core organization through the application of simultaneous loose-tight properties. Corporate leadership will need to create an organizational boundary that separates the corporate discipline (tight) that is needed for the operational performance engine and the innovation improvisation (loose) that is needed for creative insights. Some historical examples include Xerox Palo Alto Research Center (computer technology),[57] Bell Labs (transistors),[58] Lockheed Martin's Advanced Development Programs (ADP) (aircraft designs),[59] and the US Department of Defense ARPANET (Internet)[60]

Corporate New Venture Conditions

A survey of 50 equity analysts to gain a better understanding of the value at stake for corporate entrepreneurs (incumbents) that launch new venture start-ups has revealed the following findings.[61]

- Corporate entrepreneurs must demonstrate that their new business ventures are validated from outside the parent company. These start-ups must be able to secure funding independently from investors in the market as proof of a start-up's value.
- Value creation must be assessed using tangible metrics such as top-line revenue.
- Corporations must make a commitment to the growth venture that has the necessary capital and opportunity. The new venture should be a dedicated unit to protect it from short-term earnings pressures on the parent company.

The corporate entrepreneurs that want to create new ventures that generate significant value must create conditions that enable rapid growth. There are two ingredients that are essential:[62]

- The original idea must be disruptive and counterintuitive. A breakthrough idea may not appear to be a breakthrough at all. This means that corporate entrepreneurs should focus on the pathways that have the most impact, such as disruptive and nondisruptive creations rather than incremental innovations.
- The new venture must maximize its learning speed, informed by data-driven insights from structured tests with real customers. This means that corporate entrepreneurs should adopt processes that focus on testing hypotheses, gathering early and frequent customer feedback, and showing "minimum viable products" to prospects. "A minimum viable product (MVP) is a version of a product with just enough features to be usable by early customers who can then provide feedback for future product development."[63]

Social Entrepreneurs

Social entrepreneurships seek out value propositions that provide a social return on investment. Social entrepreneurs focus on a broad set of core ideologies that include reducing poverty, providing local jobs and independence, developing local economies, using local agriculture for food products, and sustaining resources through recycled, reusable, and biodegradable packaging. To have the largest impact, social entrepreneurships focus on the architecture of participation to achieve collaborative synergism using social technologies such as crowdfunding and crowdsourcing. The Safepoint Trust founder, Mark Koska, is an example of a social entrepreneur who designed the K1 Auto-Disposable syringe that cannot be reused, thereby reducing the likelihood of spreading infections such as AIDS.[64]

In 1974, Mohammad Yunus, an economist at Chittagong University in India, was travelling through Jobra, Bangladesh.[65] This was during a time of great famine in which people were dying. He encountered a woman earning two cents a day making beautiful stools. Yunus agreed to lend the woman 25 cents with which to purchase bamboo from a dealer, under the condition that she sell the bamboo stools back to Yunus, at the price he established, when the furniture was finished.[66]

Yunus felt that the furniture-maker's poverty was unnecessary and that this woman was receiving a fair business proposition. He decided to loan money to people like her, not as a charity but as a business loan, so the borrowers would be independent and could offer their products at a market price. Instead of loaning large amounts of money to a small number of people who had collateral, he loaned small amounts of money to large numbers of people who did not have any collateral. Yunus observed that the borrowers were dependable, reliable, and tenacious, with the potential for a high repayment rate.[67] He created the concept of microfinance and was awarded the 2006 Nobel Peace Prize for his pursuit of social entrepreneurship.

The Foods Resource Bank (FRB) is a US non-profit organization composed of a network of churches and rural farmer groups that provides resources to support farmers in developing countries. Their reason for being is to increase awareness of the fight against hunger as well as to improve agriculture and sustainability. There are ample opportunities to fulfill their purpose, as it is estimated that over 70% of the population of developing countries are rural farmers, compared to just over 1% in the United States.[68,69]

Social entrepreneurs often provide resources to local farmers in developing countries in order to improve food production and not just focus on the food itself. "In the past seven years, agricultural projects in 19 states raised $7 million. That amount has been matched by $3 million from the public-private partnership initiative of the U.S. Agency for International Development."[70] "The churches help finance the growing of crops or cattle dedicated to particular rural development projects, most of them in Africa."[71] The crops and cattle are sold, and the profits are than used to fund an assortment of projects that can have a big impact. For example, the people of Archbold, Ohio, provided $3,000 in funds to design and build the Mercy of God cement dam in Africa. "Before the water projects, local residents, mainly the women and children, would trudge as far as 10 miles to collect water for their crops, their cattle and themselves."[72]

For-Profits versus Non-Profits

Individual and corporate entrepreneurs generally form for-profit organizations, whereas social entrepreneurs tend to form non-profit ventures. There are notable exceptions, such as Tom's Shoes which is a for-profit venture with a strong social mission fulfilled by Tom's Shoes donating a pair of shoes for every pair sold. There are several noteworthy differences between for-profit and non-profit organizations as shown in Figure 11.6.

Description	For Profit	Nonprofit
Categories	Corporation (described in column below), Limited Liability Companies (LLC), Partnerships, Sole Proprietorship...	Public: Public colleges and universities, hospitals, etc. Private: Foundations, social services and charities, private schools, and universities described in the column below.
Success Criteria	Profit for Stockholders / Stakeholders.	Mission and / or client value and impact.
Owns	Stockholders	No one person or group of people can own a nonprofit organization.
Governance Body	Optional paid governing board.	The Governance provided by the Board of Directors. Minimum 3-person uncompensated volunteers. The bylaws state how to operate. Organized into committees.
Board Responsibilities	Governing body, strategic direction (shared), fiduciary, and ambassadors.	Governing body, strategic direction (shared), ensures necessary resources, fiduciary, risk management, culture, and ambassadors.
Top Management	Reports to Board of Directors	Reports to Board of Directors
Target Market	Customer / Consumer	Client / Society Beneficiary
Startup and/or Operating Funds	Venture capital, stock and bond offering, sales revenue and cash flow, bank loans / lines of credit, and grants	Donations, investments, fee for service, bank loans / lines of credit, and grants.
Use of Earnings	Grow business and / or increase dividend	Only for IRS approved exempt purposes.
Taxation	Taxable	Generally tax exempt, subject to unrelated business income (UBIT), payroll, and state taxes.
Personnel	Paid employees	Combination of paid staff and / or volunteers.
Political Activity	Lobbying, campaign contributions and candidate endorsement permitted as decided in the US Supreme Court case Citizens United v. Federal Election Commission.	IRS restriction on percent of revenue, Johnson amendment prohibits all 501(c)(3) non-profit organizations from endorsing or opposing political candidates.

Figure 11.6 Illustration of Comparison of For Profit and Non-Profit Organizations

Source: Adapted from Connie Hinitz, "Essentials of Nonprofit Organizations," OneSource Center for Nonprofit Excellence.

- While both are mission driven, a for-profit corporation focuses on profits for stockholders. A non-profit focus is on the stakeholders.
- A for-profit corporation is owned by stockholders. There is no one person who owns a non-profit.
- A for-profit start-up relies on venture capital, stocks, and bond offerings. A non-profit relies on donations and fees for services.

- A for-profit corporation is taxable and is permitted to lobby politicians. A non-profit is non-taxable and is not permitted to lobby politicians.

A mission-driven stakeholder strategy used by most non-profit social entrepreneurs creates some key differences when compared to a mission driven stockholder strategy. For example, the metrics for a non-profit might emphasize the number of people served, percent of administrative funds, and explicit outcomes, such as a clean environment, improved education or healthcare, and creating job opportunities.

Social Activism

Conventional approaches to social change often include violence, and the response to the violence is more violence. The Freedom Riders were different.[73] In May 1961, the Freedom Riders, civil rights activists made up of six white and seven black activists, rode two public interstate buses into the southern United States to challenge segregation. Their purpose was to test the Supreme Court's ruling in *Boynton v. Virginia* (1960).[74] Bruce Boynton was an African American student who was arrested for trespassing because he refused to move from the "white section" to the "colored section" of a lunchroom in a bus terminal in Richmond, Virginia. The Supreme Court ruled,

> We are not holding that every time a bus stops at a wholly independent roadside restaurant the act applies . . . [but] where circumstances show that the terminal and restaurant operate as an integral part of the bus carrier's transportation service . . . an interstate passenger need not inquire into documents of title or contractual agreements in order to determine whether he has a right to be served without discrimination.[75]

The Freedom Riders were harassed and eventually thrown in the Mississippi State Penitentiary to discourage their efforts. The Freedom Riders felt that they could not let violence overcome nonviolence. The principles of nonviolence were advocated earlier by Dr. Martin Luther King in *Stride Toward Freedom: The Montgomery Story*.[76] The activism of the Freedom Riders was later supported by the efforts of both Dr. Martin Luther King and the office of the President of the United States.

Change.org is a for-profit, social-activist, web-based organization wherein individuals petition for a change.

> John Lauer has been fighting fires for 6 years, all without health care. After he started his petition, more than 126,000 people joined him to ask Obama for health care for wild-land firefighters. And he won! On July 10, President Obama announced that he would direct federal agencies to ensure that wildland firefighters like John qualify for health care coverage.[77]

Global Entrepreneurship

Global entrepreneurship is the expansion of ventures beyond a national border throughout the global economy. New models, such as reverse innovation, benefit from the large number of potential consumers at the bottom of the pyramid. Older models, such as an overreliance on outsourcing, are being questioned as the cost structures change, the emphasis on protecting core competencies and intellectual property increases, and customer-driven innovation increases.

The McKinsey Global Institute has projected a geographic shift in global corporate power by 2025. The number of Fortune Global 500 companies from emerging economies has increased from a presence of 5% in 2000 to 17% in 2010 and is projected to grow to more than 45% by 2025. The rationale is that today 75% of the 8,000 companies with annual revenue of $1 billion or more are based in developed economies. By 2025, an additional 7,000 companies could reach $1 billion, and 70% (or 4,900 companies) will be based in emerging economies.[78]

New Global Entrepreneurship Models Are Arriving

General Electric is an example of global corporate entrepreneurship with its successful use of reverse innovation by building affordable devices for sale in developing countries and then later selling them in developed countries. The developing markets represent underserved and unserved market opportunities as consumers increase their standard of living and wealth.

Old Global Entrepreneurship Models Are Evolving

The viability of global entrepreneurship is based on a dynamic set of multiple factors, such as the proximity to the customers (to learn their dreams, ideas, and unmet needs), differentials in national wage rates, currency exchange rate fluctuations, and the availability of resources in the supply chain. Other factors include the cost of technology, such as additive manufacturing, three-dimensional printing, and robotics; the technology skills of the workforce; the stability of the governments of other nations; sourcing; and the cost of transportation for bulky and heavy merchandise.

For example, global businesses and entrepreneurs have been outsourcing their manufacturing because of lower labor costs outside of the United States. But the dynamics are changing; there is some indication that companies are in the process of reshoring some of their manufacturing businesses.[79] "Stories of foreign investment in the U.S. have been matched in the past few years with the 're-shoring' of overseas work back to the U.S.," writes Ben W. Heineman in an 2013 article for the *Atlantic*. "Iconic American companies like Apple, Google, Caterpillar, Ford, Emerson, GE, and Intel are adding plants and jobs in the U.S. or North America."[80]

Dell outsourced so much of their technology skills and knowledge that they lost control over their supply chain. There is some indication that, globally, the value of outsourcing has reached its limit. The growth rate of manufacturing wages in China is exceeding that of the United States, resulting in the narrowing of the comparative difference in wages.[81] This is expected to benefit the United States and has the potential to reduce offshoring and increase the reshoring of manufacturing jobs.[82] There are other factors that benefit the United States, such as labor productivity, faster delivery because of the proximity of consumers to factories, no long-distance shipping costs, and new sources of less expensive energy.[83]

Start-Ups

Start-ups are vital to economic growth and employment opportunities. There are many types of start-ups that have very different perspectives regarding the outcomes that they are expected to achieve and their growth potential. All types of entrepreneurships have the potential for the creation of new businesses and new markets, whether they are using existing value propositions or realizing innovation using new value propositions.

Start-Ups: Red, Blue, Simple, and Complex Offerings

Entrepreneurs search for a gap or inefficiency in an underserved and/or unserved market and attempt to assemble the resources needed to create a venture with a core value proposition to address that market gap. The new venture may exist in a unique space, a first mover, for example, or quickly accelerate past an incumbent that is inattentive to changes in the market. If the start-up offers a unique or complex product, it has a temporary advantage because the product may be hard to duplicate. On the other hand, when offering a simple product that can be easily duplicated, current or other new entrants can overcome the start-up through duplication or acquisition. Obtaining a patent on an innovation gives the start-up a temporary monopoly that allows for a limited reprieve from the red ocean of competition. In the red ocean of fierce competition, underserved and unserved market opportunities abound, but only if recognized and acted upon.

The US healthcare industry is amid dramatic changes that will result in multiple market opportunities for entrepreneurs, start-ups, and investors. For example, the 2013 Affordable Care Act requires businesses to provide health insurance for their uninsured workers, affecting their employee costs. Payments to providers that have high rates for hospital-acquired infections will mean lower reimbursements, providing an incentive for hospitals and entrepreneurs to act. Five major preventable hospital acquired infections in the United States are estimated to cost at least $10 billion annually.[84]

To address this market inefficiency, IntelligentM's smart bracelet uses RFID tags on handwashing and sanitizing stations to track whether healthcare workers wash their hands. The device uses an accelerometer to detect the amount of time that a healthcare worker spends washing. The smart bracelet buzzes once if it's done correctly and three times if it's not.[85]

The conventional food and beverage industry also provides an example of how and where entrepreneurs identify market inefficiencies and act to provide new and/or unique products and/or services to underserved markets. Entrepreneur Hamdi Ulukaya took an existing but little known Greek yogurt product in 2007 and created a temporary monopoly as he grew Chobani into a company that sold over $1 billion of yogurt in less than six years. By removing whey, the liquid portion of the curdled milk, he was able to develop a recipe that increased the protein in the yogurt, thereby making it attractive to many health-conscious consumers.

Several large yogurt producers – such as Fage S.A., a Greek dairy company; Groupe Danone, a French food-products multinational corporation; General Mills; and the French dairy cooperative Sodiaal, the producer of Yoplait – responded late with similar products. It is a pattern that even well-managed organizations are often slow to respond to opportunities that seem obvious and actionable.[86]

Some start-ups are built to flip, that is, seek to exit sooner than later by selling or merging the venture as the result of successful growth. Innovative start-ups identify the gap in the market (often defined as a pain or problem point), devise a viable solution, and identify a market of sufficient size and quality to allow the venture to scale. Ultimately, the results of sustained market growth become attractive to a larger organization. The larger company may have become paralyzed in its innovative thinking, may be falling behind, or its analysis might suggest that it is more cost-effective to acquire the necessary resources to produce innovative products than to build the means of production from a less-than-favorable position. For example, baby food has been traditionally sold in jars for spoon-feeding. Plum Organics innovated packaging for baby food that utilized pouches with spouts. Consumers responded enthusiastically, enabling Plum Organics to acquire a fifth of the American baby food market. Recognizing the value proposition, market potential, and balance of resources needed to compete, the Campbell Company acquired Plum Organics.[87]

Some start-ups have a temporary monopoly that allows them to build momentum in the market, but then reposition the product from a specialty to more of a commodity. For example, the single-serving coffee producer Keurig has been able to grow their coffee business with the protection of a patent on the unique aspects of the coffee pod. After successful scaling of the product offering, Keurig now will be challenged to transition from the blue to the red ocean with a commodity product.[88]

Innovating Entrepreneurism

As noted earlier, the role of planning, even in lean start-ups, is especially critical when the process of both deliberate and emergent strategy is considered.

Lean Start-Up Model: Steven Blank

Steve Blank's book *The Four Steps to the Epiphany* launched the lean start-up approach to new ventures that focuses on learning and discovery.[89] A main theme of the book is that start-ups are not small versions of large companies. Blank writes,

> Instead of executing business plans, operating in stealth mode, and releasing fully functional prototypes, young ventures are testing hypotheses, gathering early and frequent customer feedback, and showing "minimum viable products" to prospects. This new process recognizes that searching for a business model (which is the primary task facing a start-up) is entirely different than executing against that model (which established firms do).[90]

The lean start-up is how most innovators build start-ups and innovate inside incumbent companies. Steven Blank's lean start-up consists of three parts:[91]

1. Business Model Canvas – to frame hypotheses
2. Customer Development – to test those hypotheses in front of customers
3. Agile Engineering – to build minimum viable products to maximize learning

In essence, Blank advocates for a lean, fail-fast model, as the entrepreneur seeks to create a temporary organization in search of a scalable, repeatable, profitable business model. Large companies, on the other hand, due to their size and evolved corporate culture, find disruptive innovation difficult. The four steps to epiphany lean start-up model are summarized in Figure 11.7.

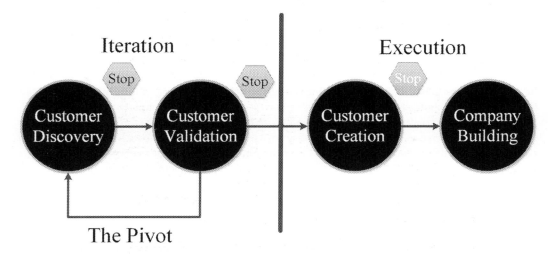

Figure 11.7 Illustration of the Four Steps to the Epiphany

Source: Adapted from Steve Blank, *The Four Steps to the Epiphany: Succesful Strategies for Products that Win.* 3rd ed. (Menlo Park: K&S Ranch Publishing LLC., 2013).

Lean Start-up Model: Eric Ries

Eric Ries extended the lean start-up model that was based on three cascading chains of innovations, each dependent on the previous:

1. Edward Deming's System of Profound Knowledge[92]
2. Taiichi Ohno's Toyota Production System (TPS) model, which focused on removing waste in manufacturing known as lean manufacturing[93]
3. Steven Blank's customer development methodology based on *The Four Steps to Epiphany*[94]

The core component of lean start-up methodology is the build-measure-learn feedback loop to address the extreme uncertainty that is experienced by entrepreneurs. This is achieved by developing a minimum viable product (MVP) to validate the concept and begin the process of learning as quickly as possible.[95] Ries conceived the notion of a pivot, a change of strategy without a change in vision while preserving what has been learned.[96] Pivots are inflection points that suggest a deviation from a prescribed course of action that are not always prospectively planned for. Changes may be needed due to business conditions, resource needs, the internal and/or external environment changes, or the product market fit. Ries acknowledges how the critical role of uncertainty can lead to one or more pivot points that fundamentally change the course of action being pursued by the entrepreneur. Parallelism can be achieved with the split test by using different versions of the MVP at the same time.[97] The lean start-up model is shown in Figure 11.8.

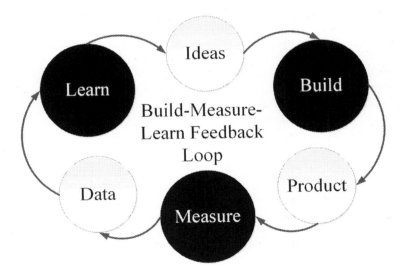

Figure 11.8 Illustration of the Lean Start-Up Process

Source: Adapted from Eric Ries, *The Lean Startup: How Today's Entrepreneurs Use Continuous Innovation to Create Radically Successful Businesses,* (New York: Crown Business, 2011), 75.

Essentially, the lean start-up model proposes an iterative process to determine the customer requirements for a solution to get to the market as quickly as possible to solicit feedback, adjust, and repeat. This lean start-up process is akin to making continuous adjustments in products or services based on market reaction. The challenge of any entrepreneurial process is balancing the amount of discipline (ceremony) that is needed. Technology-based products, such as those from Apple and

Samsung, move aggressively toward what customers expect and the limits of what technology can make possible, even beyond that of which they may be aware. Entrepreneurs must be adept at creating, leading, and communicating the balancing process surrounding the start-up process.

The process of lean start-ups and the role of the pivot can be seen in the collaboration between American Airlines and AT&T on ideating, conceptualizing, formulating, and implementing new applications that address the growing sophistication of technology to change how the world travels. American Airlines partnered with AT&T to host the first air travel hack-a-thon to encourage new technology-driven applications to address the changing airline travel market. From the more than 60 developers who were invited to compete at the South by Southwest (SXSW) event in Austin, Texas, 15 emerged to vie for the top three spots and a $10,000 first-place grand prize. The grand prize winner was a new venture called AirPing. AirPing gives flyers real-time updates for flight changes, as well as estimated travel time to the airport. More than just information for the traveler, however, the app also keeps the airline up-to-date on the location of its passengers to help the airline better plan the flight manifest in real time.[98] Garnering feedback at competitions is an excellent way to discern the next pivot point.

American Airlines took it to the next level and made the process more than just an on-the-ground competition, moving the hack-a-thon onto an actual flight to further conceptualize new technology-driven ideas. The process of garnering feedback and pivoting came to life in 2014, with a cross-country hack-a-thon hosted by American Airlines on Flight 59 from New York to San Francisco. From 22 teams of developers who submitted ideas, four were chosen to give actual in-flight demonstrations to a select group of passengers to garner real-time feedback on their applications. For the flight feedback event, American Airlines partnered with the Wearable World Labs incubator in San Francisco, which provided a 90-day development opportunity for the winner to use the feedback, refine the product/service, and sell their idea to American Airlines.[99] While the on-the-ground competition provided one way to garner feedback (in this case from potential funders), the in-the-air competition provided a direct consumer feedback mechanism to gather product and/or service feedback. Considering, refining, and possibly incorporating this feedback becomes part of the entrepreneurial journey and potential pivot points.

Wearable World, Inc., pioneering wearable technology innovation, is itself a good example of the lean start-up. Recognizing the evolving and intersecting aspects of technology and its impact on how people interact with technology and daily activities, Wearable World seeks constant feedback on how to proceed next. For the four finalists on Flight 59, the chance to solicit feedback in the actual travel environment creates a win-win for the nascent entrepreneurs as well as the airline and its partners.

Entrepreneurship Competencies

While entrepreneurship and innovation are inexorably intertwined (e.g., entrepreneurship is a competency in the innovation frame), entrepreneurship encompasses five essential competencies that small business and accelerated growth entrepreneurs must develop and demonstrate as shown in Figure 11.9. These distinct competencies enable communication of the venture and value both internally and externally. It all begins with knowing who you are and why you are in business.

Resilience

Resilience is a key entrepreneur competence that is needed to purse a new venture. Louis Silvie "Louie" Zamperini was an American World War II prisoner of war survivor, inspirational speaker, and Olympic distance runner. He is an example of courage and resilience. In 2010, Laura Hillenbrand wrote a best-selling book about his experiences, which was adapted into the film *Unbroken*

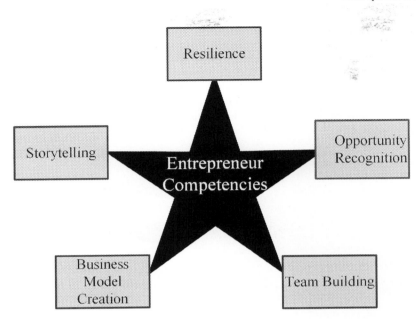

Figure 11.9 Illustration of Entrepreneur Competencies

in 2014. As illustrated in Figure 11.10, resilience is a term that encompasses the passion an entrepreneur must have in pursuing innovation and entrepreneurship:[100]

- The willingness to face reality and understand your talents
- The willingness to discover a meaningful purpose in life
- The willingness to continuously strive for improvement

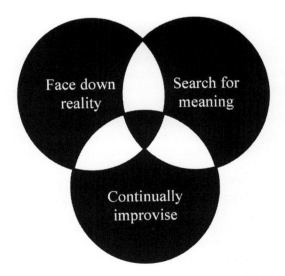

Figure 11.10 Illustration of the Resilience

Source: Adapted from Diane L. Coutu, "How Resilience Works". *Harvard Business Review*, 80(5), (2002), 46–55.

Opportunity Recognition

Opportunity recognition is a process for discovering jobs that need to be done. The job to be done (JTBD) starts with understanding the progress that a customer wants to achieve that is defined in the context of the circumstances. Ask the question, what job is the customer trying to get done? The JTBD is a prerequisite to predictable success in innovation because the job becomes the focal point around which the entire innovation process is executed.[101] Figure 11.11 identifies JTBD questions for opportunity recognition.

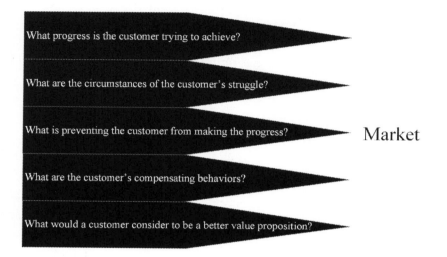

What progress is the customer trying to achieve?

What are the circumstances of the customer's struggle?

What is preventing the customer from making the progress? — Market

What are the customer's compensating behaviors?

What would a customer consider to be a better value proposition?

Figure 11.11 Illustration of the Jobs-To-Be-Done

Source: Adapted from Clayton Christensen, Taddy Hall, Karen Dillon, David S. Duncan, *Competing Against Luck*, (New York: HarperCollins, 2016), 32–33.

You must know:[102]

1. The customer who is using the solution to get a job done
2. All dimensions of the job that include the functional and social
3. The whole job, not part of the job, that the customer hired the solution to perform

As noted earlier, the word "opportunity" is used to cover everything from *action* opportunities to *expense* opportunities and everything in between. Since the opportunity of interest is *market* opportunity or more specifically underserved or unserved market opportunity, the product/market fit is key.

Product/Market Fit

The new opportunity must achieve product/market fit that can be ascertained by the creation of a minimum viable product. The product/market fit is the degree to which a product satisfies strong market demand. "One metric for product/market fit is if at least 40% percent of surveyed customers indicate that they would be 'very disappointed' if they no longer have access to a particular product or service."[103] A way to determine the product/market fits is to create a minimum viable product that addresses and solves a problem or need that exists. A minimum viable product (MVP) is a version of a product with just enough features to be usable by early customers who can then provide feedback for the next iteration of the innovation. This decision would be to continue, pivot, or discontinue development.[104]

Team Building

As noted, Entrepreneurship is both an individual and a team "sport," and identifying core team members in the short, intermediate, and long term is essential. Patrick Lencioni created a pyramid that is organized into five layers starting at the bottom and proceeding to the top. The five layers of the pyramid are as follows: (1) absence of trust, (2) fear of conflict, (3) lack of commitment, (4) avoidance of accountability, and (4) inattention to results. The underlying layers of the pyramid must be achieved before ascending to the upper layers. Patrick Lencioni created a five-layer model that is described in his book titled the *Five Dysfunctions of Teams* shown in Figure 11.12.[105]

Figure 11.12 Illustration of the Five Dysfunctions of Teams

Source: Adapted from Patrick Lencioni, *The Five Dysfunctions of a Team*, (San Francisco, CA: Jossey-Bass, 2002).

Business Model Creation

The strategy and business model are quite different concepts. A strategy is about the *future*, how you create new markets, products, and services through competitive separation from your rivals. A business model is about the *present*, how value is created for customers and how organizations conduct continuous improvement.

Essentially, the business model is a value exchange model built on the innovation value proposition. The customer must be willing to exchange value (usually money) with your business for your innovation. The business model canvas is a way to create a comprehensive business model.

Business Model Canvas

A business model includes all the elements that are needed to realize a firm's strategy. Alex Osterwalder conceived the concept of the business model canvas (BMC). There are nine building blocks that enable the design of the optimal business model, ultimate possibilities, and numerable alternatives. The nine building blocks provide a way to combine the essential components of a business together. It is not a single building block but rather an integrated combination. Alex Osterwalder notes, "Great products are becoming a commodity. It's the combination between great products and a great business model that is going to keep you ahead of the competition in the coming decade."[106]

The business model canvas is a tool that can be used to develop and refine a business model. The nine blocks are described and summarized here and in Figure 11.13.[107]

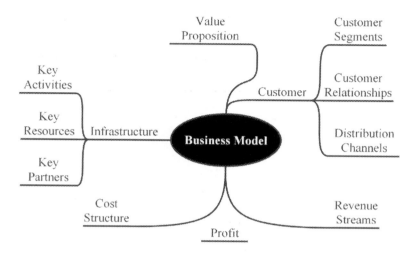

Figure 11.13 Illustration of the Business Model Canvas Mind Map

Source: Adapted from Alexander Osterwalder, Yves Pigneur, and Tim Clark. Business Model Generation: A Handbook for Visionaries, Game Changers, and Challengers. (Hoboken, NJ: Wiley, 2010). Adapted from Alexander Osterwalder: The Business Model Canvas, accessed July 22, 2021, https://www.youtube.com/watch?v=2FumwkBMhLo

1. The value proposition of what is offered to the market
2. The segment(s) of clients that are addressed by the value proposition
3. The communication and distribution channels to reach clients and offer them the value proposition
4. The relationships established with clients
5. The key resources needed to make the business model possible
6. The key activities necessary to implement the business model
7. The key partners and their motivations to participate in the business model
8. The revenue streams generated by the business model (constituting the revenue model)
9. The cost structure resulting from the business model

Business Models

Business models can be placed in types: asset builders, service providers, technology creators and network orchestrators. Libert, Beck, and Wind with Deloitte examined 40 years of financial data for S&P 500 companies and proposed four business models (2014). The four models are shown in Figure 11.14.[108]

Business Model Types		
Type	Description	Examples
Asset Builders	The asset builders develop, manufacture, and lease physical assets to market, sell, and distribute physical things.	Boeing, Ford, Wal-Mart, and FedEx.
Service Providers	The service providers employ talent who provide services to customers or produce chargeable billable hours.	Deloitte, United Healthcare, Accenture, and JP Morgan.
Technology Creators	The technology creators develop and provide software, analytics, pharmaceuticals, and biotechnology.	Microsoft, IBM, Oracle, and Amgen.
Network Orchestrators	The network orchestrators create a network of customers and partners in which all of the participants interact and share in the value creation. The network orchestrators may sell products or services, build relationships, share advice, give reviews, collaborate, and co-create.	eBay, Linkedin, Facebook, and Visa, Uber, Tripadvisor, and Alibaba.

Figure 11.14 Illustration of Four Business Models

Source: Adapted from Libert, B., Beck, M., & Wind, Y. (2016). Why are we still classifying companies by industry? Harvard Business Review, Retrieved from https://hbr.org/2016/08/why-are-we-still classifying-companies-by-industry?referral=00563& cm_mmc=email-_-newsletter-_-daily_alert-_-alert_date&utm_source=newsletter_daily_alert&utm_medium=email&utm_campaign=alert_date

Storytelling: The Pitch

How do you communicate your passion? Know who you are, what brought you to this point, and why you are pursuing this venture. Also, when it comes to telling and selling your venture idea, know your audience and something about them ahead of time if possible. Do not outline your life's journey here; less is more. When appropriate, include a personal anecdote that brought you where you are today, but, in general, keep it simple and focus their attention on clearly defining the pain/problem/underserved market opportunity nexus.

The pitch is the term used by founders and funders to make the case for why, what, and how the pain/problem, solution, and addressable market come together. The elevator pitch is a condensed version, often one to two minutes in length, of the longer pitch. Generally speaking, if more than ten slides are needed to explain a business, you probably do not have a clear business proposal.

Define the Problem

Clearly define the pain/problem/opportunity nexus. This is the venture trifecta – keep it clear, simple, and direct. Try to avoid engaging in what could be called "MBA hyperbole," such as "the market is enormous," "the opportunity is limitless," or "sales are limitless." Clearly articulate the underserved and/or unserved market opportunity, the entry point for your goods/services, and the growth potential. For example, the pain: heavy travel bags; the problem: traveler discomfort with heavy bags; the underserved market opportunity, total addressable market, and initial addressable market: thousands of weary travelers toting heavy luggage.

Innovate the Solution

This is the heart and soul of the venture. It is how the venture in general, and the goods and/or services in particular, address the unserved and/or underserved market experiencing the "pain" outlined earlier. It may be desirable to save some of the details for later, but basically this is the moment to put the spotlight on the value proposition and get others to agree that this makes sense. For example, the initial solution to the heavy luggage problem noted earlier might be a lightweight luggage dolly that the traveler can put the bag on and take on the plane. Later solutions might include incorporating the wheels right on the luggage itself.

Devise a Salient Business Model

The overarching question is "Will this make money?" This needs to be tied to the business plan assumptions and financials, but overall you need to outline the plan to sell your goods and/or services and explain who the customer/buyer will be. Remember, buyers and users may be different, but be clear that you have a sales plan. (See the following for more, under "Marketing and Sales.")

Apply Technology/Inside the Black Box

This is often described as the "secret sauce," or magic behind your product or service. Avoid going too "techno" here unless of course your audience is scientific or technology based. The general rule of thumb for most audiences is it is not necessary to open up the black box, only ensure that it works or what it will take to make it work. For example, let's say you develop a sophisticated health-monitoring application for a smartphone connected to wearable technology that allows the user to update his or her online personal profile in real time while working out. If you are pitching this idea to a group of investors, focus on the market gap, scalability, and product features, not pages of code and/or telemetry processes that enable it to work. Eventually, investors will want to do due diligence to confirm the technology, but save the tech talk until then. Often a picture or diagram is worth a thousand words, as described in the visualization competency.

Marketing and Sales

As noted under the business model, the buyers and users may be different, so it is key to have a clearly articulated sales plan. Essentially, the business/sales model is a value exchange model built on your product or service value proposition. The customer must be willing to exchange value (usually money) with your business for your goods and/or services. For example, if developing a premium product or service, what is the appropriate pricing model? Too high and it might not be attractive or competitive, but too low might convey that it is not high-end.

Assess the Competition

Never say you don't have any competition – there is always competition. Products and services competing for your customer's earned and disposable income are everywhere. Often, a one-page pictorial or a simple verbal comparison outlining how you compete on value, offerings, and features is more powerful than just listing who your competitors are. For example, when Ely Calloway was developing his now well-established metal drivers in the golf equipment industry, wood drivers were his direct competition. Later, metal drivers would compete from other companies, and, of course, there is always indirect competition for leisure sports equipment. This is discussed in Chapter 12, "Innovation Strategy."

Build and Cultivate a Team

The key question: Do you have the right team? If not, what are you doing to get it? Many potential funders, once interested, look past the idea and prefer to invest in the person and/or team. As noted earlier, at the scalable end of the venture spectrum, angel and venture capital investors often like to say they would rather invest in an "A" team with a "B" idea than an "A" idea with a "B" team. This is discussed in more detail in Chapter 13, "Catalytic Leadership."

Develop Key Projections, Metrics, and Milestones

This should be tied to the business plan timeline and should clearly outline the sources and uses of funds, and how progress is measured. As has been attributed to management sage Peter Drucker and others, "What gets measured gets done." This applies not only to financial measures, which are often critical for assessing the financial health of the venture and providing time-sensitive updates to investors, but also to sales- and employee-growth objectives. Objectives should be quantifiable, measurable, and attainable. As a rule of thumb, for new start-ups without financial history, on the financial planning front, tie the planning assumptions (projected sales, markets, and timing) together to provide three key financial projections or pro forma statements: cash flow analysis, income statement, and break-even analysis.[109]

Note Current Status and Timeline

Progress reporting requires the team to communicate a results-oriented approach to the current status, as well as accomplishments to date, and future plans. No matter how good your ideas, plans, and/or intentions, failure to communicate the value proposition and progress toward your goals and objectives puts your venture in jeopardy. As noted throughout this text, good communication is essential to moving innovation and entrepreneurship to the forefront of multiple constituents, including investors, customers, suppliers, and buyers, among others.

Provide a Clear Summary and Call to Action

While it all begins with knowing who you are and why you are in business, a clear, concise, precise summary tied to a specific call to action puts everything in perspective. The section to include addresses key questions, such as "What are the next steps?" "What is needed from the audience?" "What key team members are needed?" and "What is needed to succeed in the short-term, intermediate term, and long-term?"

Guy Kawasaki, author of the *Art of the Start*, succinctly articulates the top ten slides, as seen in Figure 11.15.

Summary

In this chapter we discussed the main conundrum of understanding entrepreneurship – seeing firms in the present success, but needing to understand them at their genesis and nascency. Also discussed is how the four critical entrepreneurship continuums (growth, funding, strategy, and planning) inform each other and line up in terms of the growth aspirations of the venture. For example, angel and venture capital sources of funding, at one end of the continuum, match up with

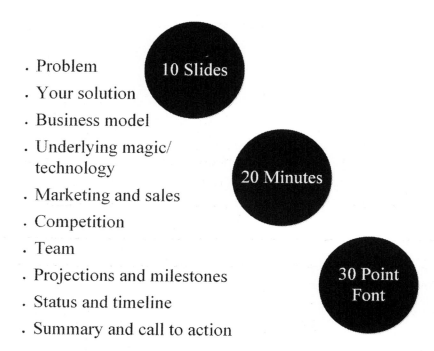

- Problem
- Your solution
- Business model
- Underlying magic/ technology
- Marketing and sales
- Competition
- Team
- Projections and milestones
- Status and timeline
- Summary and call to action

10 Slides

20 Minutes

30 Point Font

Figure 11.15 Illustration of Story Telling Pitch Presentation Structure
Source: Acknowledgement: Guy Kawaski.

accelerate/scalable growth aspirant ventures, while at the other end, friends, family, and founder sources match up with small-business-growth aspirant ventures. A fully developed entrepreneurship process model ties multiple critical elements together. The chapter includes a discussion about individual, corporate, and social entrepreneurs; global entrepreneurship; lean start-ups; social activism; and the five entrepreneurship competencies every entrepreneur needs to create his or her venture. Next up, we outline the key elements of innovation strategy in the innovation and entrepreneurship competency framework.

Notes

1. "80 Acres Farms.com," accessed July 8, 2021, www.80acresfarms.com/our-story/.
2. Eric Schwartzberg, "Dilapidated Hamilton Building Transforms into an Industry-Changing Grow Facility," July 20, 2019, accessed July 14, 2021, www.journal-news.com/news/dilapidated-hamilton-building-transforms-into-industry-changing-grow-facility/SK6EX3v4sUzidii80f2NhN/.
3. "80 Acres Farms Fully Automated Indoor Farm of The Future," accessed July 14, 2021, https://rural-livingtoday.com/gardens/80-acres-farms-automated-farm/.
4. "The 10 Most Innovative North American Companies," March 9, 2021, accessed July 14, 2021, www.fastcompany.com/90600362/north-america-most-innovative-companies-2021.
5. "The 10 Most Innovative North American Companies," March 9, 2021, accessed July 14, 2021, www.fastcompany.com/90600362/north-america-most-innovative-companies-2021.
6. *Wikipedia*, s.v. "Vertical Framing," accessed July 14, 2021, https://en.wikipedia.org/wiki/Vertical_farming.
7. *Wikipedia*, s.v. "Vertical Framing," accessed July 14, 2021, https://en.wikipedia.org/wiki/Vertical_farming.
8. M. Shahbandeh, "Global Vertical Farming Annual Growth Rate 2020–2027, by Technology," October 23, 2020, accessed July 14, 2021, www.statista.com/statistics/1181856/global-vertical-farming-annual-growth-rate-by-application/.

9. M. Shahbandeh, "Global Indoor Farming Technology Market Size 2019–2024," October 22, 2020, accessed July 14, 2021, www.statista.com/statistics/1087999/global-indoor-farming-technology-market-value/.

10. "80 Acres Farms Fully Automated Indoor Farm of the Future," accessed July 14, 2021, https://rurallivingtoday.com/gardens/80-acres-farms-automated-farm/.

11. Eric Schwartzberg, "Dilapidated Hamilton Building Transforms into an Industry-Changing Grow Facility," July 20, 2019, accessed July 14, 2021, www.journal-news.com/news/dilapidated-hamilton-building-transforms-into-industry-changing-grow-facility/SK6EX3v4sUzidii80f2NhN/.

12. Eric Schwartzberg, "Dilapidated Hamilton Building Transforms into an Industry-Changing Grow Facility," July 20, 2019, accessed July 14, 2021, www.journal-news.com/news/dilapidated-hamilton-building-transforms-into-industry-changing-grow-facility/SK6EX3v4sUzidii80f2NhN/.

13. GIE Media Horticulture Group, "Top-Shelf Growing with LEDs," May 30, 2018, accessed July 14, 2021, www.greenhousemag.com/article/top-shelf-growing-with-philips-lighting-leds-80-acres-farms/.

14. "80 Acres Farms Fully Automated Indoor Farm of the Future," accessed July 14, 2021, https://rurallivingtoday.com/gardens/80-acres-farms-automated-farm/.

15. "80 Acres Farm," accessed July 14, 2021, www.80acresfarms.com/faq/.

16. Eric Schwartzberg, "Dilapidated Hamilton Building Transforms into an Industry-Changing Grow Facility," July 20, 2019, accessed July 14, 2021, www.journal-news.com/news/dilapidated-hamilton-building-transforms-into-industry-changing-grow-facility/SK6EX3v4sUzidii80f2NhN/.

17. Eric Schwartzberg, "Dilapidated Hamilton Building Transforms into an Industry-Changing Grow Facility," July 20, 2019, accessed July 14, 2021, www.journal-news.com/news/dilapidated-hamilton-building-transforms-into-industry-changing-grow-facility/SK6EX3v4sUzidii80f2NhN/.

18. "80 Acres Farm," accessed July 14, 2021, www.80acresfarms.com/faq/.

19. Eric Schwartzberg, "Dilapidated Hamilton Building Transforms into an Industry-Changing Grow Facility," July 20, 2019, accessed July 14, 2021, www.journal-news.com/news/dilapidated-hamilton-building-transforms-into-industry-changing-grow-facility/SK6EX3v4sUzidii80f2NhN/.

20. Scott Shane and Sankaran Venkataraman, "The Promise of Entrepreneurship as a Field of Research," *Academy of Management Review* 25, no. 1 (2000), 217–226.

21. David B. Audretsch, "The Dynamic Role of Small Firms: Evidence from the U.S.," *Small Business Economics* 18 (2002), 13–40.

22. Gary Schoeniger and Clifto Taulbert, *Who Owns the Ice House? Eight Lessons from an Unlikely Entrepreneur* (Mentor, OH: ELI Press, 2010).

23. Rob Adams and Stephen Spinelli, *New Venture Creation: Entrepreneurship for the 21st Century* (New York: McGraw Hill-Irwin, 2008).

24. "P&G History: A Legacy of Forward Thinking," *Company History, the Procter & Gamble Company, P&G*, accessed July 14, 2021, https://us.pg.com/pg-history/.

25. "Clayton Christensen at University of Louisville College of Business," *YouTube Video*, posted by "Cindy McDonald," February 7, 2012, accessed July 14, 2021, www.youtube.com/watch?v=OvWwotY4APc.

26. "History of Starbucks," accessed July 14, 2021, www.starbucks.com/about-us/company-information; *Wikipedia*, s.v. "Starbucks," accessed July 14, 2021, http://en.wikipedia.org/wiki/Starbucks.

27. *Wikipedia*, s.v. "Venture Capital," accessed July 14, 2021, https://en.wikipedia.org/wiki/Venture_capital.

28. Charles H. Matthews, Mark T. Schenkel, Matthew W. Ford, and Sherrie E. Human, "Financing Complexity and Sophistication in Nascent Ventures," *Journal of Small Business Strategy* 23 (2013), 15–29.

29. *Merriam-Webster*, s.v. "Crowdsourcing," accessed July 14, 2021, www.merriam-webster.com/dictionary/crowdsourcing.

30. "Top 6 Crowdsourcing Websites," accessed July 14, 2021, www.ichitect.com/best-crowdsourcing/.

31. "crowdSPRING," accessed July 14, 2021, www.crowdspring.com/.

32. Jason Hesse, "London Is Now the World's Crowdfunding Capital," *Forbes*, August 15, 2014, accessed July 14, 2021, www.forbes.com/sites/jasonhesse/2014/08/15/forget-nyc-or-san-francisco-london-is-the-worlds-crowdfunding-capital/.

33. Mary Kearl, "Best Crowdfunding Platforms: Raise the Money You Need Fast," *Invetopedia*, 2021, accessed July 10, 2021, www.investopedia.com/best-crowdfunding-platforms-5079933.

34. "Statista: Crowdfunding – Statistics & Facts," 2024, accessed February 2, 2024, www.statista.com/topics/1283/crowdfunding/#topicOverview.

35. "Statue of Liberty," *National Park Service*, accessed July 14, 2021, www.nps.gov/stli/historyculture/joseph-pulitzer.htm.

36. Slava Rubin, "How to Raise $1 Million in 30 Days," *Crowdfund Insider*, August 30, 2013, accessed July 14, 2021, www.crowdfundinsider.com/2013/08/21737-slava-rubin-how-to-raise-1-million-in-30-days-video/.

37. Aman Jain, "These Are the Top 10 Crowdfunding Platforms," *Entrepreneur*, March 11, 2021, accessed July 10, 2021, www.entrepreneur.com/article/366972.
38. "Kickstarter," accessed July 18, 2021, www.kickstarter.com/help/stats?ref=about_subnav.
39. Crowdwise, "Top Equity Crowdfunding Sites 2019 – Deal Flow and Capital Raised," August, 26, 2019, accessed February 2, 2024, https://crowdwise.org/all/top-2019-reg-cf-funding-portals-and-websites/.
40. "FINRA: Funding Portals We Regulate," December 2023, accessed February 2, 2024, www.finra.org/about/firms-we-regulate/funding-portals-we-regulate.
41. Julia Kagan, "Financial Technology (Fintech): Its Uses and Impact on Our Lives," *Investopedia*, December 20, 2023, accessed February 2, 2024, www.investopedia.com/terms/f/fintech.asp.
42. Ginger Baker, "Leading Fintechs Join the Plaid Network," November 4, 2021, accessed February 2, 2024, https://plaid.com/blog/leading-fintechs-join-the-plaid-network/.
43. "Why Plaid?" accessed February 2, 2024, https://plaid.com/products/auth/?utm_source=Google&utm_medium=paid&utm_campaign=DEPT_SEM_Google_Brand_ACQ_Performance_NAMER_US-CA_Core_CPA-ROAS_BAU_Exact&utm_term=Core_KW-Exact_plaid-banking&utm_content=plaid%20banking&gad_source=1&gclid=CjwKCAiAq4KuBhA6EiwArMAw1IrCPGb42aqSkSKwwPvxYjhuMRn4B3Yo8z0aItFx_8fGKeyhBF-ATRoC4skQAvD_BwE.
44. "About FINRA," December 2023, accessed February 2, 2024, www.finra.org/about.
45. Karl Moore, "Porter or Mintzberg: Whose View of Strategy Is the Most Relevant Today?" *Forbes*, March 28, 2011, accessed July 14, 2021, www.forbes.com/sites/karlmoore/2011/03/28/porter-or-mintzberg-whose-view-of-strategy-is-the-most-relevant-today/?sh=7c935a5a58ba.
46. Rita Gunther McGrath and Ian C. MacMillan, "Discovery-Driven Planning," *Harvard Business Review*, July 1995, accessed July 14, 2021, http://hbr.org/1995/07/discovery-driven-planning/ar/1.
47. Richard Wray, "First with the Message-Interview: Cor Stutterheim, Executive Chairman, CMG," *The Guardian*, March 15, 2002, accessed July 14, 2021, www.theguardian.com/business/2002/mar/16/5.
48. Keith Sawyer, *Zig Zag* (New York: Jossey-Bass, 2013), 101–102.
49. *Wikipedia*, s.v. "Short Message Service," accessed July 14, 2021, http://en.wikipedia.org/wiki/Short_Message_Service.
50. Blaise Pascal, *Pascal's Pensees*, accessed February 20, 2024, www.goodreads.com/author/quotes/10994.Blaise_Pascal.
51. For example, see C. Chet Miller and Laura B. Cardinal, "Strategic Planning and Firm Performance: A Synthesis of More than Two Decades of Research," *Academy of Management Journal* 37, no. 6 (1994), 1649–1665; Benson Honig, "Entrepreneurship Education: Toward a Model of Contingency-Based Business Planning," *Academy of Management Learning & Education* 3, no. 3 (2004), 258–273.
52. Charles H. Matthews and Susanne G. Scott, "Uncertainty and Planning in Small and Entrepreneurial Firms: An Empirical Assessment," *Journal of Small Business Management* 33, no. 4 (1995), 34–52.
53. Charles H. Matthews, "See an Opportunity, and Be Ready for It," *The Cincinnati Enquirer*, May 26, 2013.
54. T. Rees Shapir, "John Goeken," *The Washington Post*, September 18, 2010, accessed July 17, 2021, www.washingtonpost.com/wp-dyn/content/article/2010/09/17/AR2010091706452.html.
55. *Wikipedia*, s.v. "LaRosa's Pizzeria," accessed July 14, 2021, https://en.wikipedia.org/wiki/LaRosa's_Pizzeria.
56. Donald F. Kuratko, Jeffrey S. Hornsby, and Jeffrey G. Covin, "Diagnosing a Firm's Internal Environment for Corporate Entrepreneurship," *Business Horizons* 57 (2014), 37–47.
57. *Wikipedia*, s.v. "PARC," accessed July 14, 2021, https://en.wikipedia.org/wiki/PARC_(company).
58. *Wikipedia*, s.v. "Bell Labs," accessed July 14, 2021, https://en.wikipedia.org/wiki/Bell_Labs.
59. *Wikipedia*, s.v. "Skunk Works," accessed July 14, 2021, https://en.wikipedia.org/wiki/Skunk_Works.
60. *Wikipedia*, s.v. "ARPANET," accessed July 14, 2021, https://en.wikipedia.org/wiki/ARPANET.
61. Philipp Hillenbrand, Dieter Kiewell, Ivan Ostojic, and Gisa Springer, "Scale or Fail: How Incumbents Can Industrialize New-Business Building," March 13, 2021, accessed July 14, 2021, www.mckinsey.com/business-functions/mckinsey-digital/our-insights/scale-or-fail-how-incumbents-can-industrialize-new-business-building.
62. Philipp Hillenbrand, Dieter Kiewell, Ivan Ostojic, and Gisa Springer, "Scale or Fail: How Incumbents Can Industrialize New-Business Building," March 13, 2021, accessed July 14, 2021, www.mckinsey.com/business-functions/mckinsey-digital/our-insights/scale-or-fail-how-incumbents-can-industrialize-new-business-building.
63. *Wikipedia*, s.v. "Minimum Viable Product," accessed July 14, 2021, https://en.wikipedia.org/wiki/Minimum_viable_product.

64. Healthcare Heroes: The Passion Project, "Mark Koska the Disposable Syringe That Has Saved Over Nine Million Lives," accessed July 18, 2021, https://healthcare-heroes.com/heroes/marc-koska.

65. Muhammad Yunus and Alan Jolis, *Banker to the Poor: Micro-Lending and the Battle Against World Poverty* (New York: PublicAffairs, 2003), accessed July 17, 2021, www.economist.com/media/globalexecutive/banker_to_the_poor_yunus_e.pdf.

66. "Muhammad Yunus, Banker to the World's Poorest Citizens, Makes His Case," *Knowledge @ Wharton*, May 9, 2005, accessed July 14, 2021, http://knowledge.wharton.upenn.edu/article.cfm?articleid=1147.

67. Kathleen Kingsbury, "Microfinance: Lending a Hand," *Time*, April 5, 2007, accessed July 17, 2021, http://content.time.com/time/subscriber/article/0,33009,1607256,00.html.

68. Gustavo Anriquez and Livor Stloukal, "Rual Population Change in Developing Countries: Lessons for Policymaking," *European View, Sage Journals* 7, no. 2 (December 2008), 309–317, accessed July 17, 2021, https://journals.sagepub.com/doi/10.1007/s12290-008-0045-7.

69. Lepley, Sara, "9 Mind-Blowing Facts about the US Farming Industry," *Market Insider*, May 30, 2019, accessed July 17, 2021, https://markets.businessinsider.com/news/stocks/farming-industry-facts-us-2019-5.

70. Roger Thurow, "A Dam Connects Machakos, Kenya, to Archbold, Ohio," *The Wall Street Journal*, April 23, 2007, accessed July 14, 2021, http://online.wsj.com/article/SB117729086351978575.html?mod=hps_us_pageone.

71. Roger Thurow, "A Dam Connects Machakos, Kenya, to Archbold, Ohio," *The Wall Street Journal*, April 23, 2007, accessed July 14, 2021, http://online.wsj.com/article/SB117729086351978575.html?mod=hps_us_pageone.

72. Roger Thurow, "A Dam Connects Machakos, Kenya, to Archbold, Ohio," *The Wall Street Journal*, April 23, 2007, accessed July 14, 2021, http://online.wsj.com/article/SB117729086351978575.html?mod=hps_us_pageone.

73. *Wikipedia*, s.v. "Freedom Riders," accessed July 14, 2021, http://en.wikipedia.org/wiki/Freedom_Riders.

74. "The Freedom Rides," accessed July 14, 2021, www.core-online.org/History/freedom%20rides.htm.

75. "The Road to Civil Rights," accessed July 14, 2021, www.fhwa.dot.gov/highwayhistory/road/s25.cfm.

76. Martin Luther King, *Stride Toward Freedom: The Montgomery Story* (New York: Harper & Brothers, 1958).

77. John Lauer, "Give Health Care to Firefighters Who Battle Wildfires," *Change.org*, July 2012, accessed July 14, 2021, www.change.org/petitions/give-health-care-to-firefighters-who-battle-wildfires.

78. Richard Dobbs, Jaana Remes, Sven Smit, James Manyika, Jonathan Woetzel, and Yaw Agyenim-Boateng, "Urban World: The Shifting Global Business Landscape," *McKinsey Global Institute*, October 1, 2013, accessed July 17, 2021, www.mckinsey.com/featured-insights/urbanization/urban-world-the-shifting-global-business-landscape.

79. Steve Denning, "Why Apple and GE Are Bringing Back Manufacturing," *Forbes*, December 7, 2012, accessed July 17, 2021, www.forbes.com/sites/stevedenning/2012/12/07/why-apple-and-ge-are-bringing-manufacturing-back/?sh=75e2439f6c4b.

80. Ben W. Heineman, "Why We Can All Stop Worrying about Offshoring and Outsourcing," *The Atlantic*, March 26, 2013, accessed July 14, 2021, www.theatlantic.com/business/archive/2013/03/why-we-can-all-stop-worrying-about-offshoring-and-outsourcing/274388/.

81. Sam Ro, "America's Manufacturers Should Get Ready to Eat China's Lunch," accessed July 17, 2021, www.businessinsider.in/americas-manufacturers-should-get-ready-to-eat-chinas-lunch/articleshow/29290695.cms.

82. Jackie Northam, "As Overseas Costs Rise, More U.S. Companies Are 'Reshoring'," *NPR*, accessed July 14, 2021, www.npr.org/blogs/parallels/2014/01/22/265080779/as-overseas-costs-rise-more-u-s-companies-are-reshoring.

83. Rana Foroohar, "How 'Made in the USA' is Making a Comeback," *Time Magazine*, April 11, 2013, accessed July 14, 2021, http://business.time.com/2013/04/11/how-made-in-the-usa-is-making-a-comeback/#ixzz2R7gFFU71.

84. Susan Scutti, "5 Major Hospital-Acquired Infections That Cost the U.S. $10B Each Year," *Medical Daily*, September 13, 2013, accessed July 14, 2021, www.medicaldaily.com/5-major-hospital-acquired-infections-cost-us-10b-each-year-256727.

85. Christopher Matthews, "The Obamacare Start-Up Boom-Health Ventures Rush to Cash in on the Law," *Time Magazine*, August 12, 2013, accessed July 14, 2021, http://content.time.com/time/subscriber/article/0,33009,2148639,00.html.

86. "Cultural Revolution," *The Economist*, August 31, 2013, accessed July 14, 2021, www.economist.com/news/business/21584353-greek-yogurt-phenomenon-america-left-big-food-firms-feeling-sour-they-are-trying-get.
87. "Cultural Revolution," *The Economist*, August 31, 2013, accessed July 14, 2021, www.economist.com/news/business/21584353-greek-yogurt-phenomenon-america-left-big-food-firms-feeling-sour-they-are-trying-get.
88. "Cultural Revolution," *The Economist*, August 31, 2013, accessed February 20, 2024, www.economist.com/news/business/21584353-greek-yogurt-phenomenon-america-left-big-food-firms-feeling-sour-they-are-trying-get.
89. Steve Blank, *The Four Steps to the Epiphany: Successful Strategies for Products that Win*, 3rd ed. (Menlo Park: K&S Ranch Publishing LLC., 2013).
90. Steve Blank, "Why the Lean Start-up Changes Everything," *Harvard Business Review* 91, no. 5 (2013), 63–72.
91. Steve Blank, "The Mission Model Canvas – An Adapted Business Model Canvas for Mission-Driven Organizations," February 23, 2016, accessed July 18, 2021, https://steveblank.com/category/business-model-versus-business-plan/.
92. *Wikipedia*, s.v. "W. Edwards Deming," accessed July 14, 2021, https://en.wikipedia.org/wiki/W._Edwards_Deming.
93. *Wikipedia*, s.v. "Lean Manufacturing," accessed July 14, 2021, https://en.wikipedia.org/wiki/Lean_manufacturing.
94. Steve Blank, *The Four Steps to the Epiphany: Successful Strategies for Products that Win*, 3rd ed. (Menlo Park: K&S Ranch Publishing LLC., 2013).
95. Eric Ries, "The Lean Startup," accessed July 14, 2021, http://theleanstartup.com/principles.
96. Eric Ries, *The Lean Startup: How Today's Entrepreneurs Use Continuous Innovation to Create Radically Successful Businesses* (New York: Crown Business, 2011), 149.
97. Eric Ries, *The Lean Startup: How Today's Entrepreneurs Use Continuous Innovation to Create Radically Successful Businesses* (New York: Crown Business, 2011), 136.
98. Nathan Chandra, "AT&T and American Airlines | The SXSW Party & Hackathon Recap," *TechZulu*, March 13, 2013, accessed July 18, 2021, http://techzulu.com/att-and-american-airlines-the-sxsw-party-hackathon-recap/.
99. Scott McCartney, "This Cross-Country Flight Is the Future of Flying," *The Wall Street Journal*, July 17, 2014, D1.
100. Diane L. Coutu, "How Resilience Works," *Harvard Business Review*, May 2002, accessed July 14, 2021, http://hbr.org/2002/05/how-resilience-works/ar/1.
101. Tony Ulwick, "Innovation Starts by Targeting the Right Customer," accessed July 14, 2021, http://strategyn.com/2012/12/18/who-is-your-customer/.
102. Tony Ulwick, "Jobs-To-Be-Done Examples and Rules," accessed July 14, 2021, https://strategyn.com/jobs-to-be-done/jobs-to-be-done-examples/.
103. *Wikipedia*, s.v. "Product/Market Fit," accessed January 15, 2021, https://en.wikipedia.org/wiki/Product/market_fit.
104. *Wikipedia*, s.v. "Minimum Viable Product," accessed July 14, 2021, https://en.wikipedia.org/wiki/Minimum_viable_product.
105. Patrick Lencioni, *The Five Dysfunctions of a Team* (Hoboken: Wiley, 2012).
106. Alexander Osterwalder, "The Business Model Canvas," July 14, 2021, https://ecorner.stanford.edu/in-brief/the-business-model-canvas/.
107. Alexander Osterwalder, Yves Pigneur, and Tim Clark, *Business Model Generation: A Handbook for Visionaries, Game Changers, and Challengers* (Hoboken, NJ: Wiley, 2010).
108. Barry Libert, Yoram Wind, and Megan Beck, "What Airbnb, Uber, and Alibaba Have in Common," *Harvard Business Review*, accessed July 14, 2021, https://hbr.org/2014/11/what-airbnb-uber-and-alibaba-have-in-common.
109. While full detailed financial planning tools are beyond the scope of this text, there are a number of excellent online resources that can provide help with this aspect of planning your venture. One excellent such resource is provided by the U.S. Small Business Administration and can be found at www.sba.gov/content/financial-projections. Also, while writing the business plan is also beyond the scope of this book, the U.S. SBA also provides an excellent overview of the business planning process at www.sba.gov/writing-business-plan.

12 Innovation Strategy

Strategy Importance

Vital to the economic revitalization of national economies and global competitiveness, both inno-vation and entrepreneurship rely on creating a strategic direction. A strategic direction is informed and guided by the choices that are made by management. Yet, despite this intuitive and empirical sense of the importance of strategy to inform innovation and entrepreneurship, and ultimately competitiveness, strategy often remains elusive, even in companies where innovation is consid-ered important and valuable. The global management consulting company Accenture conducted a survey of 519 executives in the United States, the United Kingdom, and France titled "Why 'Low Risk' Innovation Is Costly."[1] Accenture's study indicates that innovation expectations are not being met in many companies. The study revealed a significant strategic gap, with 67% of responding organizations indicating they were strongly dependent on innovation for their long-term strategy, but only 18% rating innovation as their top strategic priority.[2]

Louis V. Gerstner started his career at McKinsey & Company before moving on to American Express, RJR Nabsico, and IBM. While at IBM from 1993 to 2002, he is credited with a significant turnaround of the company. Gerstner's prior experience gave him an insider's view of the central problem: lack of a clearly defined process for providing meaning and depth to the strategic plan-ning and its key role in decision-making. On the importance of strategic decisions, Gerstner writes,

> The fact remains that in the large majority of companies corporate planning tends to be an aca-demic, ill-defined activity with little or no bottom-line impact. Observations of many compa-nies wrestling with the strategic-planning concept strongly suggest that this lack of real payoff is almost always the result of one fundamental weakness, namely, the failure to bring strategic planning down to current decisions.[3]

Given the relative importance of strategy in the health and viability of organizations, and its central role in the pursuit of innovation and entrepreneurship, in this chapter we begin with a core question: what is strategy? From there, we examine strategy with a particular focus on its applica-tion in the innovation space, beginning with a set of five core strategy decisions and cascading choices, followed by an overview of the importance of strategic thinking, a review of the impor-tance of assessing and measuring strategy (e.g., the balanced scorecard), the challenge of strategy execution, the importance of strategic agility, and the moments of truth model.

What Is Strategy?

In its broadest terms, business strategy is adding value to a company, its employees, customers, investors, stakeholders, and the community through decisions designed to integrate actions that

DOI: 10.4324/9781003034308-13

exploit a firm's competencies (core and distinctive), in order to secure a competitive advantage in the marketplace. Strategy is making future-thinking decisions about how to create what could be termed "competitive separation." As seen in the following and throughout this chapter, as important as operational effectiveness is, strategy is not directed only at operational effectiveness as driven by efficiency. Rather, strategy is focusing on something that is envisioned for the future that adds value to employees and customers – and that your competitors will not, cannot, and/or are not willing to do – that creates the separation.

Strategic value can include product innovations (e.g., the iPhone or Samsung smartphones) that are generally hard to copy; process innovations, often driven by the development of unique intellectual property (IP; e.g., Ford's first assembly line or Gillette's patentable IP surrounding the design, manufacturing, and production of multiple blade men's and women's wet shaving systems); the application of the network effect where the value of the solution increases as more people are added (such as eBay, Facebook, and LinkedIn); or unique customer experiences (such as those provided by Southwest Airlines, Disney, Starbucks, United Services Automobile Association, and IKEA). Moreover, strategic value can be created even in what might appear to be a mature, saturated market. For example, Gillette dominated the men's and women's wet shaving market through multiple blade innovation combined with a dual differentiation and cost strategy. As successful as Gillette was, innovation in product and process by new entrants such as Dollar Shave Club and Harry's illustrated that there is no such thing as an unattractive mature market.

Strategy Elements

While not exhaustive, the six key elements of innovation strategy are shown in Figure 12.1. It provides a clear framework for how vision, mission, core values, shared values, objectives, and goals interact in the formulation and execution of business strategy.

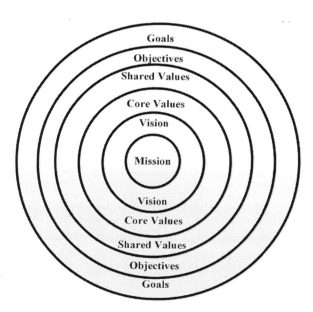

Figure 12.1 Illustration of the Six Key Elements of Strategy

To start, the firm's leadership must provide a clear vision for a firm's existence and convey the importance of the mission – the reasons for being – the why of their work. People whose energies are channeled toward a purpose tend to respond positively in the workplace. Employees who say they are "living their purpose" at work are four times more likely to report higher engagement levels.[4] Second, it is not sufficient for management to provide just the "here and now mission-driven goals," but leaders and managers must express a vision for the future, what the organization wants to become. The vision is the aspirational statement of the future direction of the organization to fulfill the mission (operational). Third, the core values and strongly held beliefs of what the organization stands for, such as excellence, fairness, integrity, diversity, inclusion, and more, must be shared throughout the organization. Fourth, the shared (stakeholder) values that include environmental, social, and governance issues should be a part of the entire organization. Fifth, the firm's leadership and management must provide not only the short and intermediate term objectives, but the longer-term aspirational goals that describe what the organization aims to achieve. Clearly articulated goals and objectives that can be quantified, measured, and attained keep firms on mission but at the same time provide a path toward aspirational goals. Finally, the circular dimensionality of the Figure 12.1 suggests the ever-important role of the evaluation, review, and feedback loop that is essential in any strategic framework.

The Strategy Challenge

Strategic thinking is all about the present in relation to the future and the future next that can be viewed through the window of time as illustrated in Figure 12.2. That is, strategic thinking, just as we observed earlier in the context of innovation and entrepreneurship, can be viewed as four time periods: the past state or institutional memory, the present or current operational whirlwind, and, most importantly, creating the future and the future after next, simultaneously.

Why do established corporations struggle to find the next big thing before new competitors do? The problem is pervasive; the examples are countless. The simple explanation is that many companies become too focused on executing today's business model and forget that business models are perishable. Success today does not guarantee success tomorrow.[5]

Execution	Strategy	
Execution Managing the Present	Next Strategy	Strategy After Next
Competing for the present, applying knowledge to strengthen the core business efficiencies.	Selectively choosing new aspirational goals and forgetting and abandoning the past.	Selectively choosing the next aspirational goals while performing discovery and testing of assumptions.
What is	What might be	

Figure 12.2 Illustration of the Three Strategy Boxes

Source: Adapted from Vijay Govindarajan and Chris Trimble, "The CEO's Role in Business Model Reinvention," *Harvard Business Review*, 89(1–2), (2011): 111.

As seen later in this chapter, in addition to the strategy challenge over time, there are two broad strategy models – blue ocean and red ocean. Generally speaking, organizations of all types are more likely to achieve more effective innovation results through the pursuit of a market-creating strategy (blue oceans). Market-competing conventional strategies (red oceans) that focus on beating rivals in existing markets often produce short term results, but don't always stretch an organization to reach new heights.

Michael Porter's Innovation in Strategic Thinking

Author and Harvard Business School professor Michael E. Porter provides compelling insight into the world of competitive strategy in his ground-breaking 1985 book, *Competitive Strategy: Techniques for Analyzing Industries and Competitors*. Porter outlines three generic strategies: low cost, differentiation, and focus (which relies on pursuing a low cost and/or differentiation strategy in a market niche).[6]

Essentially, a low-cost position entails having the lowest cost of producing your goods and/or services when compared with competitors. Note that this focuses on cost, not price. Cost is the sum of expenditures it takes to produce goods and/or services. Price is what you ask or charge your customer. Cost is the exchange of value for production; price is the exchange of value with the buyer. From an applied perspective, cost is strategic; price is tactical. Due to a lack of knowledge of your competitor's costs and changing costs of supply a low-cost position is very difficult to achieve. It is also worth noting achieving a low-cost position does not necessarily require the lowest price. While a full treatment of the art and science of pricing is beyond the scope of this text, pricing must always follow the product or service position in the market. That is, a luxury or premium good priced too low, or a commodity product priced too high, sends the wrong signal to the buyer about its market position and ultimately affects its desirability.

Pursuing a differentiation strategy entails distinguishing your product and/or service from your competition by creating actual or perceived unique attributes that are sought by the buyer. While quality is used most often to differentiate a product or service, products and services can be differentiated on several attributes. Pursuing a differentiation strategy can be challenging since it is not always possible to know what attributes are or will be embraced by the customer. Differentiation also generally entails additional cost to the good and/or service, adding to the cost of production and, ultimately, to the price of the good and/or service.

Pursuing a focus strategy entails targeting goods and/or services in a market niche. Within this niche, you will want to pursue either a low cost or differentiation strategy. The Boston Beer Company is an example of a successful focus differentiation strategy. Founder Jim Koch recognized in 1986 that the premium beer product he envisioned, Sam Adams Lager, would appeal to less than 2% of the beer-drinking population. Looked at another way, 98% of the beer-drinking population was satisfied with the products provided by the major breweries at that time: Coors, Miller, and Anheuser Busch. Koch innovated a premium product, using excess capacity in the industry to contain costs, and introduced Sam Adams Lager to compete with the imported beers that catered to the focus premium segment. Koch knew that the larger breweries would not be interested in the small segment (at least not at the outset); he realized that the segment was of enough size, quality, and durability to support his innovative product offering.

While it is tempting to try to pursue a low-cost leadership and a differentiation strategy simultaneously, it is extremely difficult. In practice, only a handful of companies have been able to successfully pursue both low cost and differentiation. For example, the Gillette Company, by continuously pushing down the cost of production of its multiblade wet shaving systems through process innovation while simultaneously reinventing and differentiating its core products (e.g., Sensor, Sensor Excel, Mach3, Fusion, complete with innovative technologies on the front and back of the blade cartridge, and beyond), was able to garner the lowest industry cost structure while creating a demonstrably superior product. Even though Gillette (now owned by Procter & Gamble) has the lowest industry cost structure and could charge less, its superior technology and product differentiation allows Gillette to price its product as a premium good.

As compelling as Porter's seminal work was, he addressed the issue of "What is strategy?" again in 1996. Writing in the *Harvard Business Review*, Porter notes that while operational effectiveness and strategy are both essential ingredients of competitiveness, they are not the same. "Strategy is the creation of a unique and valuable position, involving a different set of activities. If there were only one ideal position, there would be no need for strategy."[7] Porter emphasizes that strategy is adding value for customers and differentiation from the competition. He distinguishes this from developing strategic positions, which essentially emerge from three distinct but overlapping sources: serving the few needs of many customers (variety-based positioning), serving the broad needs of few customers (needs-based positioning), and serving the broad needs of many customers in a narrow market (access-based positioning). While Porter contributed to innovative strategic thinking with his five forces model, shown in Figure 12.3, it is important to note its application in innovation and Entrepreneurship must be carefully considered.

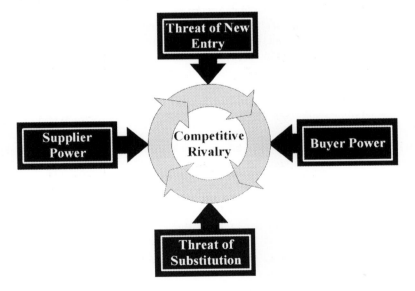

Figure 12.3 Illustration of the Five Forces Model

Source: Adapted from Michael E. Porter, "How Competitive Forces Shape Strategy." *Harvard Business Review* 57, no. 2 (March-April 1979): 137–145, accessed August 12, 2020, https://hbr.org/1979/03/how-competitive-forces-shape-strategy

The five forces model provides a holistic perspective for understanding the rules of competition between companies and between nations. It describes a process for evaluating new competitors, the threat of substitutes, the bargaining power of buyers, the bargaining power of suppliers, and the rivalry among the existing competitors. The five forces model informs whether firms will yield positive results in the red ocean.[8] Moreover, as a starting point for industry analysis, the five forces model empowers managers and entrepreneurs with information that reflects the industry environment and the venture's situation in that environment. Armed with this information, managers and entrepreneurs are more keenly aware of how they can effect change and chart the evolution of innovation and entrepreneurship as a change agent in an industry.

While fairly clear in a red ocean environment, when it comes to blue ocean pursuits, it should be carefully noted that often a five forces analysis will suggest a start-up is not advisable. It should not be taken to be solely definitive and should always be considered with other analyses. For example, a five forces analysis in the early 1980s of the circus entertainment industry would suggest that opening a new circus would not be advisable – circus attendance was declining not expanding; circuses were closing not opening; competition was consolidated into the hands of a few; while buyer and supplier power were limited, threats of substitute entertainment options were very high. Taken alone, this analysis would argue against a start-up. Of course, entrepreneur street performers Guy Laliberté and Gilles Ste-Croix were not dissuaded by this analysis but rather saw an underserved market opportunity. In 1984, they redefined the circus entertainment industry founding the Montreal-based Cirque du Soleil, growing from humble beginnings to global dominance opening innovative performances around the world by 2021.[9]

Playing to Win

In Playing to Win, A. G. Lafley, former Procter & Gamble chairman, CEO, and president, and Roger L. Martin, former dean of the Rotman School of Management at the University of Toronto, note, "Strategy is an integrated set of choices that uniquely positions the firm in its industry so as to create sustainable advantage and superior value relative to the competition."[10] Strategic innovation is a set of thinking and decision-making processes on how to improve organizational effectiveness, competitiveness, and competencies. When evaluating strategic innovation, consider the following questions:

- What is your winning aspiration? The purpose of the enterprise, its motivating aspiration. The company must seek to win in an explicit place and in an explicit way.
- Where will you play? A playing field where to best achieve that aspiration. The questions to be asked focus on where the company will compete – in which markets, with which customers and consumers, in which channels, in which product categories, and at which vertical stage(s) of the industry in question.
- How will you win? To determine how to win, an organization must decide what will enable it to create unique value and sustainably deliver that value to customers in a way that is distinct from the firm's competitors.
- What capabilities must be in place? The set and configuration of capabilities required for winning in the chosen way. Capabilities are the map of activities and competencies that critically underpin specific where-to-play and how-to-win choices.
- What management systems are required? The systems and measures that enable the capabilities and support the choices. These are the systems that foster, support, and measure the strategy.

The Five Strategy Decisions

As noted, Lafley and Martin emphasize that the outcome of strategy is to win. "Winning is at the heart of any strategy. In our terms, a strategy is a coordinated and integrated set of five choices: A winning aspiration, where to play, how to win, core capabilities, and management systems."[11] It is driven by the answers to five questions depicted in Figure 12.4.

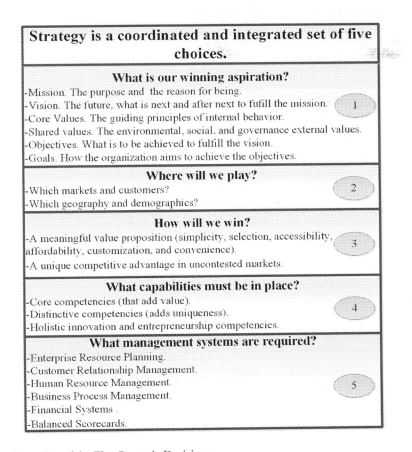

Figure 12.4 Illustration of the Five Strategic Decisions

Source: Adapted from A. G. Lafley, Roger L. Martin, *Playing To Win: How Strategy Really Works*, (Boston, MA: Harvard Business Review Press, 2013).

Strategy: An Integrated Set of Cascading Choices

The five strategic choices must be cascaded top-down throughout the organization. The winning aspiration encompasses the mission, vision, objectives, guiding principles (core values), and shared values. For example, Google's mission is "to organize the world's information and make it universally accessible and useful."[12] Where you play addresses the markets, customers, geography, and demographics. How we win identifies the value proposition. What capabilities must be in place is focused on future innovation and entrepreneurship competencies. Management systems are the foundation for implantation and tracking of results.

As noted earlier, Lafley and Martin describe strategy as the answer to five questions, using a hierarchical and cascading model. The cascades are shown as a set of five linked boxes conveying forward action. These linked boxes are organized in a hierarchy showing their relationships at multiple levels. The lattice shows the intersection points of the questions and the interaction of the levels.[13] Figure 12.5 shows the lattice of the integrated set of cascading choices and shows the relationship between the corporate decision-makers, the division and departments, and the individuals and groups.

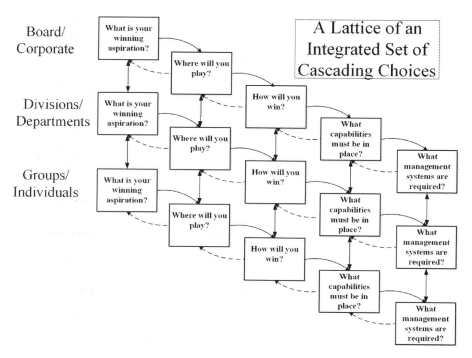

Figure 12.5 Illustration of the Strategic Lattice

Source: Adapted from A. G. Lafley, Roger L. Martin, *Playing To Win: How Strategy Really Works*, (Boston, MA: Harvard Business Review Press, 2013), 3–16.

Strategic Thinking: No Commitment Without Involvement

Strategic decision-making needs to take a holistic perspective that includes all people in the organization because there is no commitment without involvement. Google allows its workers time to experiment and make things to achieve involvement, thereby recognizing the valuable ideas of its employees. Google then chooses what to keep, incubate, and develop further.

Similarly at Apple, Michael Lopp, senior engineering manager, discussed Apple's design process at a South by Southwest (SXSW) conference. Teams meet to describe their dream products and outline what they want from any new application, ultimately, through paired design meetings, one in which there are no constraints, the other a production meeting in which designers and engineers "are required to nail everything down." Lopp notes that while it is a lot of work and time, ultimately, dream products are crafted into deliverables.[14]

Strategic Thinking: Time

Strategic thinking can be viewed as a set of four boxes focused on time shown in Figure 12.6. Strategic thinking's focus is on the future but there needs to be a balance of the past, present, future, and future after next. The longer the time frame the more agility that will be necessary to adapt to changes in trends.

More formally, innovation strategy is what you want to achieve, and the capabilities needed to achieve it: the organizational processes, how an organization allocates its precious resources, how an organization determines its priorities, and how an organization responds to and balances the opportunities and threats along the way.[15]

Figure 12.6 Illustration of the Strategic Challenge

Source: Adapted from Vijay Govindarajan and Chris Trimble, "The CEO's Role in Business Model Reinvention," *Harvard Business Review*, 89(1–2), (2011): 109.

Strategic Thinking: Agility

When conditions change, an organization needs to be agile and adapt to changed circumstances. As Yogi Berra quipped, "The future ain't what it used to be." Strategy includes aspects of managing the present, selectively abandoning the past, and creating the future after next.[16] Strategic thinking must consider how an organization can be adaptable enough to respond to and anticipate rapid change. "Building organizations that are deeply adaptable, that are innovative at their core, and that are engaging, exciting places to work – building healthy organization – requires some deep rethinking about how we put our organizations together."[17]

Strategic thinking has a duality that contrasts deliberate and emergent paths and the need to adapt to changed circumstances.[18] The viability of a company's innovation strategy depends on its ability to evolve, not on its static view of today's business. For instance, at Google, "Brin and Page understand that in a discontinuous world, what matters most is not a company's competitive advantage at a single point in time, but its evolutionary advantage over time. Hence their desire to build a company that is capable of evolving as fast as the Web itself."[19]

Effective strategic thinking explores the relationship between the intended deliberate strategies and the realized emergent strategies shown in Figure 12.7. Deliberate strategies are created using a due diligence process of careful analysis of future markets, customers, competitors, resources, processes, and values. "Planning suggests clear and articulated intentions, backed up by formal controls to ensure their pursuit, in an environment that is acquiescent."[20]

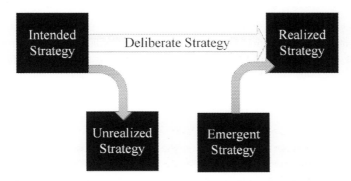

Figure 12.7 Illustration of Deliberate and Emergent Strategy

Source: Adapted from Henry Mintzberg and John A. Waters, "Of Strategies, Deliberate and Emergent," *Strategic Management Journal*, 6(3), (1985): 257–273.

Emergent strategies, by contrast, are those that are realized despite, or in the absence of, intention. Innovation is often driven by three continuously changing conditions: people's capabilities (talent and competencies), trends, and scientific and technological advancement.

In this context, entrepreneurs may discover that the deliberate strategy originally articulated is not viable and needs to be updated. This can result in what is commonly referred to as a pivot or shift in a venture's business strategy to address a change in the industry or customer preference often expressed when feedback is received from a minimally viable product (MVP). Eric Reis notes that a pivot is a change in strategy without a change in vision. "That change is called a pivot: a structured course correction designed to test a new fundamental hypothesis about the product, strategy, and engine of growth."[21] In reality, it is often more complicated, as a number of start-up ventures' pivots represent both a change in vision and in strategy. For example, Twitter began as a podcasting platform before becoming a social media giant.[22] When it comes to innovation and entrepreneurship, deliberate and emergent strategy clearly play notable roles.

The Time Periods

The Past

Strategic thinking should consider what has been learned from past experiences and related historical data to extract what is practical and what is not practical. Institutional memory is vital for learning from successes and failures, but it can also be debilitating and distracting if strategic thinking becomes locked to the past, creating a "No Outlet" street.

The Present

Managing the present is about how to deliver results now. Most organizations' efforts are focused on the present. Managing the present is the skill of execution, not necessarily strategy. Execution deals with competition for the present and can feel like a perpetual whirlwind to sustain the current operations, satisfy the current customer base, and improve upon the processes, resources, and decision-making of the execution model.[23] For effective execution, it is necessary to establish goals that are aligned with the strategy.[24] Start with focusing on your strategic goals – the strategic goals need to be focused and have a finish line.

Lagging Measures

Lagging measures are outcomes that measure your history. The goal might be to increase profits, increase market share, increase employee satisfaction, improve sustainability, or improve the customer experience. However, these are lagging measures, which deal with the past. For instance, if you were watching your weight, your weight would be a lagging (outcome) measure. The outcomes can only be measured in retrospect.

Leading Measures

Leading measures are predictive and focus on the future. Learning to predict or estimate that something will happen is based on leading measures. Predictive theories and processes are useful because they can help understand causation, how you got to where you are, and how to best estimate where you are going. Execution needs to be linked to causation to best estimate what will happen and what things can be done to increase your ability to achieve success, strategic goals, and ultimately what becomes the lagging measures.

The strategic job to be done is to devise leading measures that can influence the lagging measures. For instance, if you were watching your weight, leading measures would be calorie reduction and increased exercise. The leading measures are predictive ways that can influence weight loss, the lagging measure.

Scorecard

A scorecard can be used to display lagging measures (outcomes) and leading measures so that total performance can be monitored.[25] By having a scorecard, you can create a model of accountability that ensures the leading measures are moving the lagging measures. Where each individual or team commits to the measures and is held accountable, you can determine with certainty that you are executing your strategy effectively.[26] The steps for building a scorecard are shown in Figure 12.8.

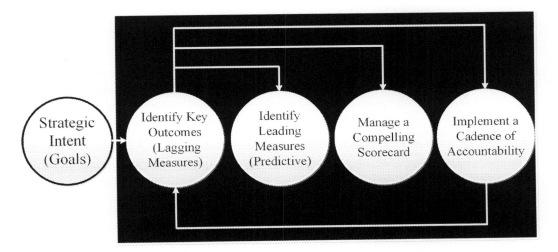

Figure 12.8 Illustration of Disciplined Strategic Management System

Source: Adapted from: Chris McChesney, Sean Covey, and Jim Huling, *The Four Disciplines of Execution: Achieving Your Wildly Important Goals*, (New York: Free Press, 2013).

American Airlines Outcome Measurements

Airlines use measurements to determine their level of efficiency and effectiveness. For instance, American Airlines uses the following measures: an available seat mile (ASM) is a measure of capacity that is calculated by multiplying seats (empty or filled) in a plane times the miles flown. A 100-seat plane flying 200 miles would create 20,000 ASMs. The revenue passenger mile (RPM) is a measure of production that is calculated by multiplying the number of paying passengers times each mile flown. That is, 100 passengers flying 100 miles would generate 10,000 RPMs. The load factor is a comparison of production to capacity. It is calculated by dividing RPMs by ASMs, such as 10,000 RPMs/20,000 ASMs for 50%. The revenue per passenger mile is the yield that is calculated by dividing the passenger revenue by the total RPMs. Building on the previous example, $10 billion in passenger revenue divided by 100 billion RPMs would result in a yield of 10 cents per mile. The revenue per available seat mile (R/ASM) is the load factor times the yield. For example, 50% times 10 cents would result in a 5 cent R/ASM. The cost per available seat mile (C/ASM) is the operating expenses divided by the total ASM. For example, $20 billion in operating expenses divided by 100 billion ASM, or 20 cent C/ASM.[27]

Strategic measures are derived from the strategic goals of an organization. Only by using measures will you know if you are achieving your goals. This example describes how an airline uses measures to manage its operations to evaluate its effectiveness against their goals.

Scandinavian Airlines Wrong Measures

Jan Carlzon, in his book *Moments of Truth*, describes how the Scandinavian Airlines System (SAS) determined that they were using the wrong measures for their cargo operation. SAS's customer promise was both timely and accurate cargo delivery. SAS was interested in determining how well they were serving their customers on these two promises, so they sent 100 packages throughout Europe in an experiment to gather empirical data. From the experiment they learned that the average delivery time was four days. They realized that they failed in their promise to the cargo customers. SAS ascertained that the reason for their performance was that the air cargo operation measured how well they were able to fill the available capacity or volume in each plane, and not by the timely and accurate cargo delivery.[28]

Carlzon writes,

> We had caught ourselves in one of the most basic mistakes a service-oriented business can make: Promising one thing and measuring another. In this case, we were promising prompt and precise cargo delivery, yet we were measuring volume and whether the paper work and packages got separate en route.[29]

SAS was measuring the wrong thing – volume was important to the company, but timeliness of delivery was ultimately more important to the customer. From a cargo customer perspective, the measurement of cargo volume was not relevant because cargo customers were more interested in the timeliness of the delivery to the designated target locations, not the volume of cargo of the airline. In response, SAS's cargo employees developed new measures of customer service that included the timeliness of delivery. By having customer-focused measures and a scorecard, SAS could make timely and corrective action. The SAS example points out the need for a scorecard to add value to the concept of strategic innovation, which is discussed in the next section.[30]

A Balanced Scorecard

Drs. Robert Kaplan and David Norton developed the concept of a balanced scorecard that performance management systems could use for tracking performance against strategic goals.[31] The balanced score is organized into four perspectives: financial, customer, internal business process, and learning and growth.[32] Organizations that are innovation-oriented should consider adding innovation and entrepreneurship competency objectives, targets, measures, and initiatives pertaining to learning and growth, and should consider adding innovation as a fifth enhanced perspective. An example of a balance scorecard is shown in Figure 12.9.

The Future

Strategy is all about the future and beyond. How do you create what might be? You build a bridge from the future strategy to the future strategy after next. The bridge allows for transitioning to the strategy after next and selectively forgetting the past.[33]

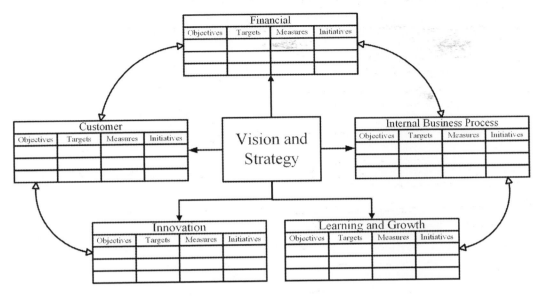

Figure 12.9 Illustration of a Balanced Scorecard for Innovation

Source: Adapted from Robert S. Kaplan and David P. Norton, "Linking the Balanced Scorecard to Strategy," *California Management Review*, 39(1), (1996): 53–79.

The Blue Strategy

The blue strategy is a market-creating strategy that is based on creating pathways from incremental, evolutionary, inferior, and superior disruptive creation and ultimately nondisruptive creation.

The blue strategy is about the pathways in which a venture seeks to pursue a strategic intent and achieve its big dreams. James Collins and Jerry Porras refer to this as identifying and pursuing a "Big Hairy Audacious Goal," or BHAG, such as putting a man on the moon in 1969.[34] Strategy is capturing the future trends, making the competition irrelevant, selecting the top talent, developing the innovation competencies of the people (their knowledge, attitudes, and skills), and the creation of a team-based culture.

The blue strategy is a metaphor to encapsulate how to think about strategy composed of the blue winds, the blue ocean, the blue sky, and the blue zones. The blue strategy metaphor is shown in Figure 12.10.

The Blue Winds

The blue winds are a metaphor for the drivers of innovation: people's capabilities (talent and competencies), trends, and science and technological advancement that are continuously changing. There are constant dynamic shifts that are occurring with respect to societal, economic, and technological upheavals. These dynamic shifts are a mix of competitive forces – the dynamics of hyper-global change and the increasing complexity of our experiences.

The Blue Sky

The blue sky is a metaphor for the 21st-century competencies that are described in the innovation and entrepreneurship competency framework that are required for building innovative

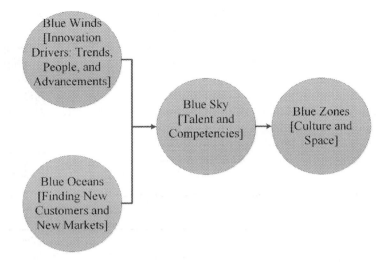

Figure 12.10 Illustration of Blue Strategy

organizations. It is a clarion call to reverse the declines in creative skills and foster more divergent thinking and creative capacity.

The Blue Zones

The blue zones are new ways of creating organizational cultures and spaces to enable innovation. As described in Chapter 9, "Innovation Culture," organizations like Google, 3M, and Intuit are creating these blue zones to attract the top talent needed for the future. Top talent will seek out blue zone organizations to fulfill their aspirational goals by avoiding zones of mediocrity that pervade many businesses and institutions.

The Blue Ocean

The blue ocean strategy is a way of strategic thinking that encourages you to use the innovation competencies to think about the future and the future after next. Instead of competing in the red ocean of relentless struggles of hyper-competition, why not create a new blue ocean where you can navigate in less crowded waters?

In the search for uncontested markets, IBM has adopted a strategy based on the Watson supercomputer. The Watson supercomputer includes ultrafast computing, data storage, and natural language question-answering technology. The Watson is expected to be used in both healthcare and finance, industries that rely on expensive human advisors. If the Watson can be used to increase the effectiveness of expensive physicians and financial advisors, it represents an innovative opportunity to pioneer new markets and increase IBM's organic growth.[35]

Rivals can become partners and create blue oceans. In 2014, a partnership between Apple, with their customer design expertise, and IBM, with their enterprise-wide business expertise, was announced. This strategic partnership has the potential to enhance Watson's strengths.[36] For example, "IBM, the health insurer WellPoint and Memorial Sloan-Kettering Cancer Center announced two Watson-based applications – one to help diagnose and treat lung cancer and one to help manage health insurance decisions and claims."[37] To implement this new strategy, IBM has formed a new division known as the IBM Watson Group. The strategy includes the cloud to build an open Watson ecosystem of independent Watson application developers. Furthermore, to realize the strategy in 2013, IBM purchased Softlayer, a cloud-computing company, for an estimated $2 billion.[38]

The innovation and entrepreneurship competencies allow companies to use a blue ocean strategy rather than a red ocean strategy. As W. Chan Kim and Renee Mauborgne explain in their 2005 book, *Blue Ocean Strategy*,

> In the red oceans, industry boundaries are defined and accepted, and the competitive rules of the game are known. Here, companies try to outperform their rivals to grab a greater share of existing demand. As the marketplace gets crowded, prospects for profits and growth are reduced. Products become commodities, and cutthroat competition turns the red ocean bloody. Blue oceans, in contrast, are defined by untapped market space, demand creation and the opportunity for highly profitable growth.[39]

You can choose to compete in the red ocean of intense competition, or compete in the blue ocean and make the competition irrelevant. Monsanto, for example, used patented biotechnology to develop corn and soya bean seeds that were resistant to the herbicide Roundup. They sold the seeds and the herbicides to farmers – a double value-added product set allowing them to stand apart from their competitors.

Patents are effective ways to implement the blue ocean strategy. As we will see in more detail in Chapter 16, "The Importance of Intellectual Property," patent laws are used to reward those who have made considerable research investments in the development of the innovation. For example, the cost to develop a new pharmaceutical can be $100,000 million.[40]

Innovations that provide a competitive advantage will be patented and kept secret to give the provider a substantial temporary advantage. For example, Pfizer's Lipitor has been a top-selling and highly profitable pharmaceutical for lowering cholesterol and thereby preventing the buildup of plaque inside of blood vessels, reducing the risk of heart disease. The patent expired in November 2011, thereby moving the pharmaceutical from the blue to the red ocean.[41] In the red ocean, the competition is in the generic market, resulting in large revenue decreases for Pfizer.[42]

Value Innovation

Value innovation is created when an organization's actions favorably affect both its cost structure (striving to achieve the lowest industry costs) while simultaneously differentiating its offering in a way that is valued by its customers (real or perceived). While attractive, it is very difficult to achieve both a cost (sum total of what it takes to produce a good or service) and a differentiation advantage (a real or perceived desired product attribute) simultaneously. Strategically, value innovation must address both the why and the how questions clearly and precisely. For example, on the cost side, it must describe continuous reduction in the sum total it takes to produce a good or service, with a focus on key customer needs to more effectively provide accessibility, affordability, customization, convenience, simplicity, and selection, which directly address the job that a customer needs to have done (removing the customer's pain). As shown in Figure 12.11, value innovation is focused on both cost and differentiation value simultaneously. Cost savings are generated by eliminating and reducing the elements that the business sector competes on. Buyer value is lifted by creating and raising the elements the business sector has inadequately or never offered.[43]

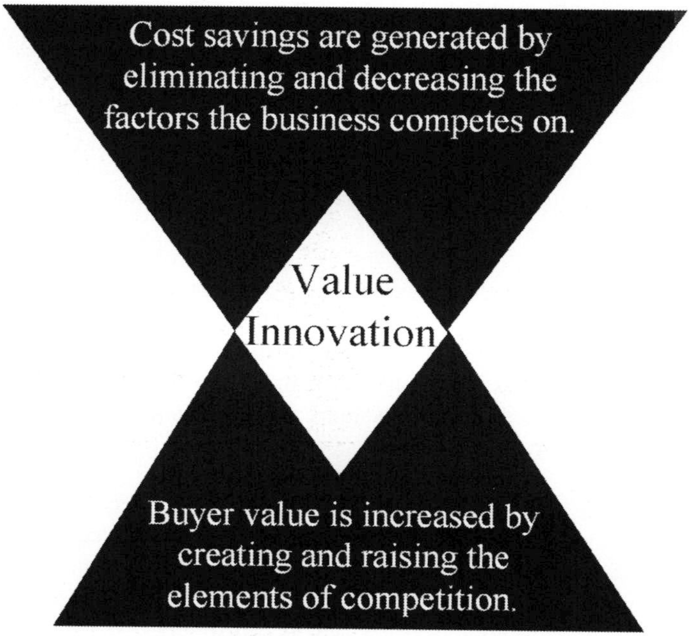

Value Innovation

Cost savings are generated by eliminating and decreasing the factors the business competes on.

Buyer value is increased by creating and raising the elements of competition.

Figure 12.11 Illustration of Value Innovation

Source: Adapted from W. Chan Kim and Renee Mauborgne, *Blue Ocean Strategy*, (Boston, MA: Harvard Business Publishing, 2005), 16.

Four Actions Framework

In *Blue Ocean Strategy*, Kim and Mauborgne describe a four-action framework that introduces four questions to build a strategic model.[44]

1. Which of the factors that an industry takes for granted should be eliminated?
2. Which factors should be reduced well below the industry's standard?
3. Which factors should be raised well above the industry's standard?
4. Which factors should be created that the industry has never offered?

Amazon has been effective by implementation of a strategy that can be explained using the four-action framework shown in Figure 12.12

Three Tiers of Non-Customers

If you can transform latent non-customers into customers, you can unleash new blue ocean opportunities. Kim and Mauborgne propose that there are three tiers of non-customers who differ in their relative distance from the market. The first tier is non-customers closest to your market and those who sit on the edge. The second tier is non-customers who have declined your offerings. The third tier is non-customers who have never considered your offerings.[45] From the blue ocean perspective, the three tiers shown in Figure 12.13 represent market opportunities.

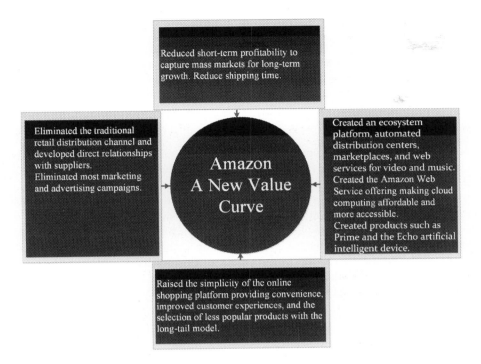

Figure 12.12 Illustration of the ERRC Grid

Source: Adapted from W. Chan Kim and Renee Mauborgne, *Blue Ocean Strategy*, (Boston, MA: Harvard Business Publishing, 2005), 29. http://insights.wired.com/profiles/blogs/amazon-innovates-with-its-business-model-not-drones?xg_source=activity#axzz2rmMQDwPb

© Copyright

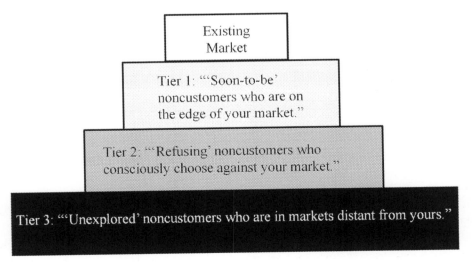

Figure 12.13 Illustration of the Enhanced Three Tiers of Noncustomers

Source: Adapted from W. Chan Kim and Renee Mauborgne, *Blue Ocean Strategy*, (Boston, MA: Harvard Business Publishing, 2005), 104.

Strategic Marketing

Strategic marketing can be used for increasing the awareness of new emerging innovations through either conventional or digital marketing. Marketing strategies are used to increase brand awareness among consumers and generate revenue streams. The transition from conventional marketing to digital marketing could be viewed as a disruptive innovation.[46]

Conventional Marketing

The conventional mass marketing paradigm uses a single, uniform, push-based strategy that attempts to reach all consumers. Historical examples of conventional mass marketing are the Michelin Guide that provided drivers with information on auto maintenance, accommodations, and other travel tips and Ben Franklin's *Poor Richard's Almanack* to promote his printing business.[47]

In the mass marketing push model, the customer is the passive receiver of mass media, such as television. Today this conventional outbound marketing is achieved when a company sends messages out to an audience through the general media using TV advertising, newsletters, and emailing. The use of broadcast TV and newspapers can provide advertisers with a targeted audience. For example, an audience would be differentially targeted if an ad is placed during a sports game broadcast versus in the sports section of a newspaper that is likely to be read by sports fans.[48]

Digital Marketing

Digital marketing includes the use of innovations that provide advantages: better customer experience, streamlined operations, and new lines of businesses.[49] Digital marketing uses the World Wide Web, online platforms, and digital technologies to promote products and services to reach customers more effectively by targeting market segments.[50]

> The digital marketing approach and its channels are critical for overcoming the declining effectiveness of traditional approaches to campaign management, such as interruptive, push mass-blast campaigning. Marketers need to use engagement techniques that continue to develop from digital marketing for a complete, multichannel campaign management strategy.[51]

The Dollar Shave Club launched an online digital marketing promotional campaign for their new subscription service using a YouTube video costing $4,500. In the first 48 hours they had over 12,000 people signing up for the service. The video won "Best Out-of-Nowhere Video Campaign" at the 2012 AdAge Viral Video Awards. By November 2015, the video had more than 21 million views.[52]

Security and Privacy Implications

Google and Facebook make most of their revenue from advertisements that are based on the information they collect about client interests. Digital marketers capture client information and demographics that are used to build profiles to determine the most productive prospective targets. The collecting of this personal digital information has privacy implications. The more information that is collected about the consumer in the profile, the more precise the digital marketing targeting and segmentation.

Digital Technologies: Tracking Pixels and Cookies

Tracking pixels are essentially tiny snippets of code that allow digital marketers to gather information about visitors to a website or to determine if an email was read or forwarded. The identifying information that can be accessed includes the Internet Protocol address, the time the request was made, the type of web browser, the activities on the website during the session, and the existence of cookies previously sent by the host server.[53]

A web cookie is a small piece of data stored on the user's computer by the web browser while browsing a website. The purpose of a cookie is to remember stateful information that can include a record of the user's browsing activity, clicking buttons, logging in, web page visits, information that the user previously entered in form fields, and items added in the shopping cart.[54]

Digital Marketing Components

There are six components of digital marketing that include content marketing, search engine optimization, search engine marketing, social media marketing, email marketing, and interactive websites shown in Figure 12.14.[55]

Figure 12.14 Illustration of the Digital Marketing

Source: Adapted from multiple sources based on wikipedia.org

Taking a closer look at each of the key components of digital marketing, it is possible to grasp a better understanding of the value of the various elements in relation to innovation and entrepreneurship.

1. Content marketing involves the use of content, blogs, articles, social updates, videos, and landing pages that improve brand recall and engagement. The content is created to attract (pull) customers. This inbound marketing is achieved by creating, providing, and distributing valuable content.[56]

2. Search engine optimization is the process of improving the quantity and quality of website traffic to a website from search engines. The purpose of search engine optimization (SEO) is to achieve a high website rank on the search engine results page.
    SEO techniques may be used to improve the visibility of business websites and brand-related content based on search queries. Search engines use indices that are built by crawlers that automatically operate in the background. Google, Microsoft, and Yahoo use crawlers to find the web pages for indexing algorithms that are used when a search is performed.[57]

3. Search engine marketing involves the pay per clicks (PPC) model. PPC focuses on the use of prominent advertising space, visible positions atop search results pages, and websites. Pay-per-click advertisers bid on keyword phrases relevant to their target market and pay when ads are clicked. Pay-per-click advertising is associated with search engines such as Google Ads, Amazon Advertising, and Microsoft Advertising.[58]

4. Social media marketing is the use of social media platforms and websites to promote a product or service. The use of social media in marketing provides a communications channel for current and prospective clients to find information about the organization using the social media. Social media platforms like Facebook, Instagram, Twitter, and YouTube are used for interacting with clients to increase the revenue streams, brand awareness, and increase community engagement.[59]
    The Facebook platform has at least 2.8 billion active users; they have been the subject of user privacy (as with the Cambridge Analytica data scandal), political manipulation (as with the 2016 US elections), fake news content, copyright infringement, and facilitating the spread of inappropriate speech.[60]

5. Email marketing is the sending of email messages to current or previous customers with the purpose of enhancing a relationship between a for-profit or non-profit organization for enhancing customer loyalty, increasing brand awareness, acquiring new customers, retaining existing customers, asking for donations, and purchasing products and services.[61]
    Marketing emails that you receive include images that are not embedded in the email message, but instead the images are hosted on a marketing server. When you open the email, a request is sent to download the image from the marketing server. When the request is sent to download the image, information about your device and your approximate location is provided back to the sender of the email. The marketer uses this information to determine the effectiveness of the marketing content.

6. Interactive websites are platforms hosted by for-profit and non-profit organizations that are used to communicate interactively with their clients by providing content in the form of web pages. Websites are built by organizations of all types to provide news, education, commerce, entertainment, or social networking. Websites rely on two meaningfully significant innovations: the World Wide Web and the Internet.
    Websites that are publicly accessible are known collectively as the World Wide Web. The World Wide Web was created by the British CERN physicist Tim Berners-Lee to provide a technology that enabled the interlinking of hypertext documents to provide the free interchange of information. Hypertext is an innovation that is credited to Ted Nelson. Hypertext is the use of documents that are interconnected by hyperlinks that are activated by a mouse click, by keypress set, or by touching the screen.[62]

The Internet is a global network of interconnected computer systems that provide the underlying infrastructure for the World Wide Web. The Internet has a local and global reach consisting of private, public, academic, business, and government subnetworks. The ARPANET that was established by the Advanced Research Projects Agency (ARPA) of the United States Department of Defense is considered to be the creator of the Internet.[63]

The Moments of Truth Model

The digitalization of the media, the explosion of consumer choices, and the advancement of social media have resulted in an increased role for shoppers and retailers.[64] The buying experience has changed to an increasingly efficient market. This customer-centered model actively engages shoppers to seek what they need rather than providing the shoppers with what sellers have.

The buying experience change is described in the moments of truth model, shown in Figure 12.15, which is based on the notion that every purchasing decision is done through a process.[65] While the buying process is composed of many moments of truth where a customer compares and decides among the alternatives, there are four core moments of truth.

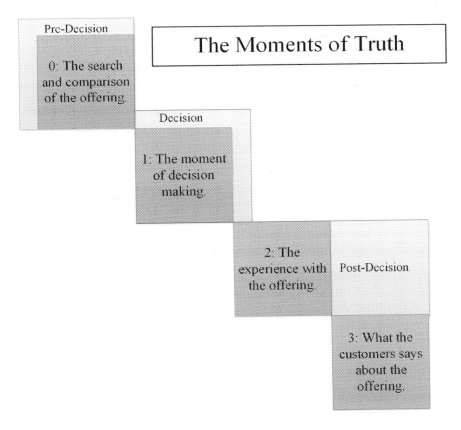

Figure 12.15 Illustration of the Moments of Truth Model

Source: Adapted from: Jan Carlzon, *Moments of Truth: New Strategies for Today's Customer-Driven Economy,* (New Your: Harper, 1987); and Jim Lecinski, "The Zero Moment of Truth," accessed March 19, 2021, https://www.scribd.com/document/59940378/Winning-the-Zero-Moment-of-Truth

Zero Moment of Truth

The zero moment of truth is the prework to understand more about the product or service before the purchase that will define what path the customer wants to take.

> Shoppers today want to explore and think about how products can improve their lives. They do reconnaissance to gain the insights they need, and they're driven to bond with others and enrich relationships as they learn. They are motivated by a desire to take charge of their own identities and the well-being of their families and homes.[66]

Shoppers use smartphones to search for a product's pricing, available coupons, and competitive offerings. Shoppers can actively search for online ratings and provide their own online ratings. This information is used by services, such as Angie's List and Consumer Reports, which provide empirical data about products and services for consumers. If you are looking for skis, you can view a video of someone describing the ski experience. Dimensional Research, in a recent study, found that "an overwhelming 90 percent of respondents who recalled reading online reviews claimed that positive online reviews influenced buying decisions, while 86 percent said buying decisions were influenced by negative online reviews."[67]

The first, second, and third moment of truth concepts were introduced by Procter & Gamble in 2005. Google introduced the zero moment of truth in 2011, which describes the predecessor to the first moment of truth to describe what consumer jobs need to be done and what they are searching to accomplish.[68] For example, if you are buying a used car, you can use Carfax to access a car's maintenance and repair history, and you can access information from Edmonds, Kelly's Blue Book, and National Automobile Dealers Association (NADA) all online. You can request bids if you want to sell your car using Craigslist, eBay, or MaxTradeIn (consumer to business (C2B)) where the dealers bid for your car.[69] Innovators in retail used car buying, purchasing and trade-ins such as Carvana, CarMax, Vroom, and WeBuyAnyCar.com continue to proliferate as customer preferences evolve.

First Moment of Truth

The first moment is dependent on the zero moment. "We face the first moment of truth at the store shelf, when she decides whether to buy a P&G or a competitor's brand."[70] The first moment of truth is when the customer observes what is on the shelf and decides what to purchase. For digital retailing, this would be the point when they click "Add to Cart" and proceed through the steps to purchase the product.

Second Moment of Truth

The second moment is dependent on the first moment. "If we win at the first moment of truth, we get a chance to win at the second, which occurs at home when she and her family use our product and decide whether we've kept our brand promise."[71] The second moment of truth is the customer experience with the product or service in the home or business. If the purchase was a book, for example, the second moment would be your experiences with the book and what value you feel you have received.

Third Moment of Truth

The third moment is dependent on the second. Endless surveys attempt to capture our experiences with products and services. Using an example of a book purchase, the third moment would be what the purchaser writes about the book.[72] The third moment is what the customer will communicate to others about the product or service and the extent to which customers can express themselves and provide their perspective about the products and services.

Summary

In this chapter, we examined the importance of strategy in the health and viability of organizations and its central role in the pursuit of innovation and entrepreneurship. Starting with a core question, "What is strategy?" we examined strategy with a particular focus on its application in the innovation space, beginning with a set of five core decisions and cascading choices, followed by an overview of the importance of strategic thinking, a review of the importance of assessing and measuring strategy (e.g., the balanced scorecard), the challenge of strategy execution, importance of strategic agility, and the impact of moments of truth. Taken together, we see the strategic foundation of innovation and entrepreneurship in creating technology-driven change and gain and to maintain competitive advantage. Up next, we examine the critical role of leadership in the ongoing quest for innovation for entrepreneurship.

Notes

1. Wouter Koetzier and Adi Alon, "Accenture Study: Innovation Efforts Falling Short Despite Increased Investment," 2013, accessed July 28, 2021, https://newsroom.accenture.com/subjects/supply-chain-management/accenture-study-innovation-efforts-falling-short-despite-increased-investment.htm.
2. Wouter Koetzier and Adi Alon, "Accenture Study: Innovation Efforts Falling Short Despite Increased Investment," 2013, accessed July 28, 2021, https://newsroom.accenture.com/subjects/supply-chain-management/accenture-study-innovation-efforts-falling-short-despite-increased-investment.
3. Louis V. Gerstner, Jr., "Can Strategic Planning Pay Off?" *McKinsey Quarterly*, December 1973, accessed July 28, 2021, www.mckinsey.com/business-functions/strategy-and-corporate-finance/our-insights/can-strategic-planning-pay-off.
4. Aaron De Smet, Chris Gagnon, Elizabeth Mygatt, and Richard Steele, "The Nine Traits of Future-Ready Companies," February 9, 2021, accessed February 23, 2024, www.mckinsey.com/business-functions/organization/our-insights/the-nine-traits-of-future-ready-companies.
5. Vijay Govindarajan and Chris Trimble, "The CEO's Role in Business Model Reinvention," *Harvard Business Review* 89, no. 1–2 (2011), 109.
6. Michael E. Porter, *Competitive Strategy: Techniques for Analyzing Industries and Competitors* (New York: The Free Press, 1985).
7. Michael E. Porter, "What Is Strategy?" *Harvard Business Review* 74, no. 6 (1996), 68.
8. Michael Porter, "The Five Competitive Forces That Shape Strategy," *Video*, January 2008, accessed February 23, 2024, http://hbr.org/2008/01/the-five-competitive-forces-that-shape-strategy/.
9. "Cirque du Soleil Entertainment Group Announces Additional Reopening Plans," *Cirque du Soliel Press Release*, accessed February 24, 2024, www.cirquedusoleil.com/press/news/2021/cirque-du-soleil-etertainment-group-announces-additional-reopening-plans.
10. Alan G. Lafley and Roger L. Martin, *Playing to Win* (Boston: Harvard Business Review Press, 2013), 5.
11. Alan G. Lafley and Roger L. Martin, *Playing to Win* (Boston: Harvard Business Review Press, 2013), 3.
12. "About Google," *Google Inc.*, accessed July 28, 2021, https://about.google/.
13. Alan G. Lafley and Roger L. Martin, *Playing to Win* (Boston: Harvard Business Review Press, 2013), 16–30.
14. Michael Lopp, "Apple's Design Process," accessed February 24, 2024, https://konigi.com/blog/apples-design-process/.
15. Clayton M. Christensen, James Allworth, and Karen Dillon, *How Will You Measure Your Life?* (New York: Harper, 2012), 22.
16. "Vijay Govindarajan, – Ten Rules for Strategic Innovators," *London Business Forum, YouTube Video*, May 10, 2010, accessed Steve Moilanen, "Pivots (Sometimes) Require a Change in Vision," *Too*, 2019, www.youtube.com/watch?v=DHdHw8HbgWk.
17. Gary Hamel, "Forward," *Beyond Performance*, eds. Scott Keller and Colin Price (New York: Wiley, 2011), ix–x.
18. Henry Mintzberg and John A. Waters, "Of Strategies, Deliberate and Emergent," *Strategic Management Journal* 6, no. 3 (1985), 257–273.
19. Gary Hamel, *The Future of Management* (Boston: Harvard Business Press, 2007), 103.
20. Henry Mintzberg and James A. Waters. "Of Strategies, Deliberate and Emergent," *Strategic Management Journal (Pre-1986)* 6, no. 3 (1985), 257–273, 259.
21. Eric Ries, *The Lean Startup: How Today's Entrepreneurs Use Continuous Innovation to Create Radically Successful Businesses* (New York: Crown Business, 2011), 149.

22. *Wikipedia*, "Twitter," accessed February 24, 2024, https://en.wikipedia.org/wiki/Twitter#:~:text=Twitter%20was%20created%20in%20March,25%20offices%20around%20the%20world.
23. Vijay Govindarajan and Chris Trimble, "The CEO's Role in Business Model Reinvention," *Harvard Business Review* 89, no. 1–2 (2011), 109–110.
24. Stephen R. Covey, "Work-Life Balance: A Different Cut," *Forbes*, March 21, 2007, accessed February 23, 2024, www.forbes.com/2007/03/19/covey-work-life-lead-careers-worklife07-cz_sc_0319covey.html.
25. Dan Schawbel, "The 4 Disciplines of Business Execution," *Forbes*, April 23, 2012, accessed February 23, 2024, www.forbes.com/sites/danschawbel/2012/04/23/the-4-disciplines-of-business-execution/.
26. Chris McChesney, Sean Covey, and Jim Huling, *The Four Disciplines of Execution: Achieving Your Wildly Important Goals* (New York: Free Press, 2013).
27. "Basic Measurements in the Airline Business," *American Airlines*, accessed July 28, 201, www.scribd.com/doc/208655410/Basic-Measurements-in-the-Airline-Business.
28. Jan Carlzon, *Moments of Truth* (New York: Harper, 1989), 107–112.
29. Jan Carlzon, *Moments of Truth* (New York: Harper, 1989), 108.
30. Jan Carlzon, *Moments of Truth* (New York: Harper, 1989), 110.
31. Robert S. Kaplan and David P. Norton, "Linking the Balanced Scorecard to Strategy," *California Management Review* 39, no. 1 (1996), 53–79.
32. Robert S. Kaplan and David P. Norton, "Using the Balanced Scorecard as a Strategic Management System," *Harvard Business Review*, July 2007, accessed February 23, 2024, http://hbr.org/2007/07/using-the-balanced-scorecard-as-a-strategic-management-system/ar/1.
33. Vijay Govindarajan and Chris Trimble, "The CEO's Role in Business Model Reinvention," *Harvard Business Review* 89, no. 1–2 (2011), 109.
34. James C. Collins and Jerry I. Porras, "Building Your Company's Vision," *Harvard Business Review* 74, no. 5 (1996), 65–77.
35. "A Cure for the Big Blues," *The Economist*, January 11, 2014, accessed February 23, 2024, www.economist.com/news/business/21593489-technology-giant-asks-watson-get-it-growing-again-cure-big-blues?zid=291&ah=906e69ad01d2ee51960100b7fa502595.
36. "Apple's Partnership with IBM Is About the Victory of Design Over Data," *Forbes*, accessed February 23, 2024, www.forbes.com/sites/anthonykosner/2014/07/16/apples-partnership-with-ibm-is-about-the-victory-of-design-over-data/.
37. Jim Fitzgerald, "Watson Supercomputer Offers Medical Expertise," *USA Today*, February 8, 2013, accessed February 23, 2024, www.usatoday.com/story/tech/2013/02/08/watson-supercomputer-ibm/1902807/.
38. "A Cure for the Big Blues," *The Economist*, January 11, 2014, accessed February 23, 2024, www.economist.com/news/business/21593489-technology-giant-asks-watson-get-it-growing-again-cure-big-blues?zid=291&ah=906e69ad01d2ee51960100b7fa502595.
39. W. Chan Kim and Renee Mauborgne, *Blue Ocean Strategy* (Boston: Harvard Business Review Press, 2005), 4.
40. *Wikipedia*, s.v. "Drug Development," accessed July 27, 2021, http://en.wikipedia.org/wiki/Drug_development.
41. Trefis Team, "Pfizer Q1 Earnings Slump on Lipitor Patent Expiry," *Forbes*, May, 2, 2012, accessed February 23, 2024, www.forbes.com/sites/greatspeculations/2012/05/02/pfizer-q1-earnings-slump-on-lipitor-patent-expiry/?sh=2b7eec9d1a2f.
42. *Wikipedia*, s.v. "Atorvastatin," accessed July 27, 2021, http://en.wikipedia.org/wiki/Atorvastatin.
43. W. Chan Kim and Renee Mauborgne, *Blue Ocean Strategy* (Boston: Harvard Business Publishing, 2005), 16.
44. W. Chan Kim and Renee Mauborgne, *Blue Ocean Strategy* (Boston: Harvard Business Publishing, 2005), 29.
45. W. Chan Kim and Renee Mauborgne, *Blue Ocean Strategy* (Boston: Harvard Business Publishing, 2005), 103–104.
46. Ginna Hall, "How Digital Is Changing Retail Across EMEA," May 8, 2019, accessed February 23, 2024, www.marketingweek.com/digital-changing-retail-emea/.
47. *Wikipedia*, s.v. "Content Marketing," accessed July 27, 2021, https://en.wikipedia.org/wiki/Content_marketing.
48. *Wikipedia*, s.v. "Social Media Marketing," accessed July 27, 2021, https://en.wikipedia.org/wiki/Social_media_marketing.
49. Jean-Michel Sahut, Dana Léo-Paul, and Michel Laroche, "Digital Innovations, Impacts on Marketing, Value Chain and Business Models: An Introduction," *Canadian Journal of Administrative Sciences/Revue Canadienne des Sciences de l'Administration* 37, no. 1 (2020), 61–67, accessed March 20, 2021, https://doi.org/10.1002/CJAS.1558, 1.

50. *Wikipedia*, s.v. "Digital Marketing," accessed July 27, 2021, https://en.wikipedia.org/wiki/Digital_marketing.

51. Adam Sarner, "Digital Marketing: The Critical Trek for Multichannel Campaign Management," April 11, 2021, accessed February 23, 2024, https://zednercomunicaciones.wordpress.com/2011/04/20/digital-marketing-the-critical-trek-for-multichannel-campaign-management/and original source from www.gartner.com/DisplayDocument?ref=clientFriendlyUrl&id=1560514 (Login required).

52. *Wikipedia*, s.v. "Content Marketing," accessed July 27, 2021, https://en.wikipedia.org/wiki/Content_marketing.

53. *Wikipedia*, s.v. "Web Beacon," accessed July 27, 2021, https://en.wikipedia.org/wiki/Web_beacon.

54. *Wikipedia*, s.v. "HTTP Cookie," accessed July 27, 2021, https://en.wikipedia.org/wiki/HTTP_cookie.

55. *Wikipedia*, s.v. "Digital Marketing," accessed July 27, 2021, https://en.wikipedia.org/wiki/Digital_marketing.

56. *Wikipedia*, s.v. "Content Marketing," accessed March 19, 2021, https://en.wikipedia.org/wiki/Content_marketing.

57. *Wikipedia*, s.v. "Search Engine Optimization," accessed July 27, 2021, https://en.wikipedia.org/wiki/Search_engine_optimization.

58. *Wikipedia*, s.v. "Pay-Per-Click," accessed July 27, 2021, https://en.wikipedia.org/wiki/Pay-per-click.

59. *Wikipedia*, s.v. "Social Media Marketing," accessed July 27, 2021, https://en.wikipedia.org/wiki/Social_media_marketing.

60. *Wikipedia*, s.v. "Facebook," accessed July 279, 2021, https://en.wikipedia.org/wiki/Facebook.

61. *Wikipedia*, s.v. "Email Marketing," accessed July 27, 2021, https://en.wikipedia.org/wiki/Email_marketing.

62. *Wikipedia*, s.v. "Hypertext," accessed July 27, 2021, https://en.wikipedia.org/wiki/Hypertext.

63. *Wikipedia*, s.v. "Internet," accessed July 27, 2021, https://en.wikipedia.org/wiki/Internet.

64. Rad Ewing, "P & G Innovation Marketing Presentation," *University of Cincinnati*, February 14, 2013.

65. Jan Carlzon, *Moments of Truth: New Strategies for Today's Customer-Driven Economy* (New York: Harper, 1987).

66. Jim Lecinski, "The Zero Moment of Truth," accessed February 23, 2024, www.scribd.com/doc/193128210/The-Zero-Moment-of-Truth.

67. Amy Gesenhues, "Survey: 90% of Customers Say Buying Decisions Are Influenced by Online Reviews," *Marketing Land*, April 9, 2013, accessed February 23, 2024, https://martech.org/survey-customers-more-frustrated-by-how-long-it-takes-to-resolve-a-customer-service-issue-than-the-resolution/.

68. Chad Anderson, "Google's Zero Moment of Truth," February 25, 2016, accessed February 23, 2024, https://emfluence.com/blog/googles-zero-moment-of-truth.

69. *Wikipedia*, s.v. "Consumer to Business," accessed July 27, 2021, https://en.wikipedia.org/wiki/Consumer-to-business.

70. Alan G. Lafley and Ram Charan, *The Game Changer* (New York: Crown Business, 2008), 34.

71. Alan G. Lafley and Ram Charan, *The Game Changer* (New York: Crown Business, 2008), 34.

72. Pete Blackshaw, "The 'Three Moments of Truth' Web Site Checklist," *Clickz*, July 24, 2007, accessed February 23, 2024, www.clickz.com/clickz/column/1696512/the-three-moments-truth-web-site-checklist.

13 Leadership

Leadership and Innovation: Sputnik and Beyond

On October 4, 1957, the Union of Soviet Socialist Republics (USSR) deployed Sputnik, the first artificial satellite that was placed in Earth's orbit.[1] This event signaled what would become known as the "dawn of the space age" and created in the United States a sense of urgency surrounding science, technology, and space that resulted in the establishment of the National Aeronautics and Space Administration (NASA) in 1958. On April 12, 1961, the Soviet Union won the race to put a man into space when Yuri Alekseyevich Gagarin successfully completed an orbit of Earth.[2]

On May 25, 1961, John F. Kennedy delivered a speech to a joint session of Congress that proposed landing a man on the moon before 1970.[3] President Kennedy provided the vision and the impetus to launch the United States on a remarkable journey and develop the scientific breakthroughs that came along the way.[4] With these words, "First, I believe that this nation should commit itself to achieving the goal, before this decade is out, of landing a man on the moon and returning him safely to the earth," he began what would be known as the "Space Race."[5]

In 1969, NASA leaders used imagination, innovation, and sheer determination to create the Apollo space program. Apollo 11 enabled the US space program to conceive, create, innovate, and build the technology to produce the products and processes required to land a man on Earth's moon. Short on fuel, with only 15 seconds left, astronaut Neil Armstrong became the first person to manually land the Eagle lunar module spacecraft on the surface of the moon. With Command Module Pilot Michael Collins in moon orbit, Apollo 11 enabled Commander Neil Armstrong and Lunar Module Pilot Edwin "Buzz" Aldrin Jr. to step on the surface of the Earth's moon, establishing the lunar base Tranquility.[6]

Armstrong was a uniquely private and humble man who had the will and passion necessary for landing on Earth's moon.[7] While it could be said that there was no one like him, the character and competence with which he approached his life demonstrate the foundation for catalytic leadership. Indeed, astronauts of the world, including Armstrong, achieved significant success through catalytic leadership of innovation, often putting their own lives at risk.

Dare Mighty Things

While it is encouraging that Neil Armstrong and others are not alone in exhibiting the leadership required in the relentless pursuit of innovations that are taking us to space and beyond, the fundamental question remains: are individuals and organizations today willing and capable of the bold innovations of the past? Innovations are needed to meet the challenges of today in government, education, manufacturing, finance, supercomputers, biotechnology, transportation, insurance, healthcare, the environment, and more. It is a daunting challenge, but one for which we can prepare.

DOI: 10.4324/9781003034308-14

Engraved on the wall at the NASA Jet Propulsion Lab in Pasadena, California, in bold capital letters, are the following words: "DARE MIGHTY THINGS." This is a most appropriate sentiment for innovators and entrepreneurs. The words are taken from a longer speech titled "The Strenuous Life," delivered by Theodore Roosevelt in 1899, before the Hamilton Club in Chicago, Illinois. "Far better is it to dare mighty things, to win glorious triumphs, even though checkered by failure . . . than to rank with those poor spirits who neither enjoy nor suffer much, because they live in a gray twilight that knows not victory nor defeat."[8] Roosevelt's speech calls to mind a similar sentiment expressed 2,000 years earlier by the Roman philosopher, author, and politician, Lucius Annaeus Seneca, "It is not because things are difficult that we do not dare; it is because we do not dare that they are difficult."[9] Meeting the challenge requires effective leadership, even in the face of failure.

When it comes to innovation and entrepreneurship, the task of leadership is continuously challenging and at times fraught with peril. On January 27, 1967, astronauts were performing a launch pad test for Apollo 1 when a spark from a live wire ignited the 100% oxygen in the command module of the Apollo/Saturn space vehicle. In the flash fire, Gus Grissom, Ed White, and Roger Chaffee all were killed.[10] While we may be encouraged by "daring mighty things," daring can come at a price.

A young Greek courtier to King Dionysius of Syracuse also demonstrates the serious nature of leadership:

> Damocles was a courtier in Greece in the fourth century BC. The story has it that he used to flatter the king by saying what a marvelous life he had. When the king offered to swap places with him for a day, Damocles agreed, only to find himself sitting beneath a huge sword that was hanging by a single hair from a horse's tail. He couldn't move without putting his life in danger. The episode taught Damocles a sharp lesson about the gravity of a leader's responsibilities.[11]

Indeed, there are many examples in history of leaders who performed courageous acts and wound up under the precarious specter of imminent danger: Abraham Lincoln, Nelson Mandela, Mahatma Gandhi, Winston Churchill, and Mother Teresa, to name just a few.[12]

The challenges and results that were achieved by the Sputnik space program and the subsequent lunar landing are examples of high-order innovations that are possible only if we are collectively willing to take on the responsibility of leadership and to develop the competencies necessary for dramatic breakthroughs.

Catalytic Leadership

Leadership is equally about creating a climate where the truth is heard, and the brutal facts are confronted. Catalytic leadership is a choice that individuals make to challenge existing practices and theories, having the courage and wisdom to challenge what exists. Challenging what exists is necessary because organizational cultures will perpetuate the past even though change is needed. Catalytic leaders are those that create an atmosphere where ideas flow freely both upward and downward, like gentle breezes; they must recognize that the leader's personality and position can be a hindrance to getting the best information.

Catalytic leadership requires the two-step learning process. The first step of effective leadership is to learn the competencies: attitudes, skills, and knowledge. The second step is to apply the competencies by practicing the leadership behaviors. Just like learning to play the piano, one must first learn about music concepts and the instrument and second, must practice the instrument.

In this chapter, we take the Innovation and Competency Framework to the next level and examine the importance of catalytic leadership. Catalytic leadership development can be viewed as a set of five concentric rings: character and competence capability of everyone, the contributing team members, the competent manager, the effective leader, and the catalytic leader. Emotional intelligence, servant leadership, and the window and the mirror are also discussed. Goleman's six leadership styles and the effects of each on the corporate climate are explored: pacesetter, authoritative, affiliative, coercive, coaching, and democratic are explored. The role of "mavericks" in the workplace, transforming management, the two-step leadership learning process, and resilient leadership are also outlined and discussed.

Leadership Importance

Gallup conducted a survey in more than 130 countries to discover how people rated the leadership of Germany, China, the United States, and Russia.[13] Germany was rated at 39%, the highest of the four countries; China ranked at 34%, the United States ranked at 31%, and Russia ranked at 30%. These ratings have important implications on the effectiveness of the leadership of these countries and how they may influence the future.

The Conference Board and McKinsey & Company conducted a survey and associated focus groups on the state of human capital. Over 500 executives were asked to rank their top three human-capital priorities. Leadership development and succession management was identified by almost two-thirds of the respondents as their number one concern, followed by talent acquisition and retention and strategic workforce planning.[14] McKinsey & Company reports that "U.S. companies alone spend almost $14 billion annually on leadership development. Colleges and universities offer hundreds of degree courses on leadership, and the cost of customized leadership-development offerings from a top business school can reach $150,000 a person."[15]

There is a leadership gap in the willingness of executives to support their innovation-empowered people, but some evidence that the gap may be closing. In a study done by Accenture in 2013, 49% of respondents say management support is very important for trying something new and the generation of entrepreneurial ideas, yet only 20% report that their organization does this very well. Forty-two percent of the respondents consider tolerance of failure from management as being very important in fostering an entrepreneurial attitude, yet only 12% of the respondents report that their organization does this very well.[16]

In 2021, Accenture published research on building a culture that drives sustained growth. For this study, innovation was defined as a "new way of doing things that adds value." Using a multi-method research design, including surveys, interviews, case studies, and economic and statistical analyses, they surveyed 1,000 C-suite executives at 1,000 companies. The report suggests, "Building and maintaining an innovation culture is crucial but often elusive." The Accenture report notes that companies that fostered a strong innovation culture benefitted via higher growth and enhanced financial performance.[17]

Those organizations with the leadership and cultures that foster high engagement are more profitable than those that do not have high engagement.[18] Engagement includes the willingness of an employee to exceed expectations, to take responsibility for doing their jobs effectively, to take the initiative and embrace empowerment, and to achieve a sense of purpose.[19]

Willis Towers Watson, a global advisory firm, focuses on three components of sustainable engagement in its research: engaged, enabled, and energized. Results of their survey regarding the level of sustained employee engagement of full-time workers suggest that nearly two-thirds (60%) of the participants in the study were not highly engaged:[20]

- Forty percent of employees were highly engaged.
- Nineteen percent were unsupported.
- Seventeen percent were detached.
- Twenty-four percent were disengaged.

Leadership is key when it comes to creating an engaged, enabled, and energized team. Of course, leadership is important on multiple fronts and continues to garner considerable attention from researchers and practitioners alike. For example, a three-year study of over 3,000 middle-level managers completed by Daniel Goleman and his research team highlights the role of leadership on a company's climate and the bottom-line. The research suggests that leadership style accounts for up to 30% of the venture's profitability.[21]

The Leadership Elements

While a full treatment of the complexities of leadership topics is beyond the scope of this chapter, it is possible to identify and outline six core elements of leadership depicted in Figure 13.1. These six elements bridge the theoretical and practical aspects of leadership that are key in the process of innovation and entrepreneurship. While not meant to be exhaustive, each element provides a fundamental representation of leadership for innovative start-ups and beyond.

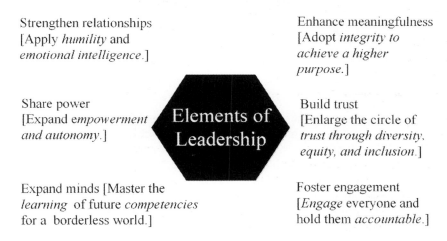

Strengthen relationships [Apply *humility* and *emotional intelligence.*]

Enhance meaningfulness [Adopt *integrity to achieve a higher purpose.*]

Share power [Expand e*mpowerment and autonomy.*]

Build trust [Enlarge the circle of *trust through diversity, equity, and inclusion.*]

Expand minds [Master the *learning* of future *competencies* for a borderless world.]

Foster engagement [*Engage* everyone and hold them *accountable.*]

Figure 13.1 Illustration of the Elements of Leadership

Source: Adapted from "Management Innovation Xchange Moonshots," accessed August 15, 2020, http://www.managementexchange.com/moonshots

Finding Your Voice

In addition to the elements of leadership outlined earlier, leadership is facilitated by finding your voice. Stephen Covey captures this thought brilliantly in his book *The 8th Habit: From Effectiveness to Greatness*. Essentially, to be an effective leader, one must be an effective person. This requires that each person takes responsibility for unlocking their talents, building on their strengths, and relying on character, always pointing to truth north. True north is a metaphor for the pursuit of complete integrity as demonstrated through character. For Covey, the nexus of passion, talent, need, and conscience is voice.[22] Once you have found your voice, it is possible to inspire others to find their voice. That is, we must amplify our voices and help others to find their voice. Combining the six elements outlined with Covey's concept of voice provides a powerful path to understand and practice leadership. The three voices are summarized in Figure 13.2.

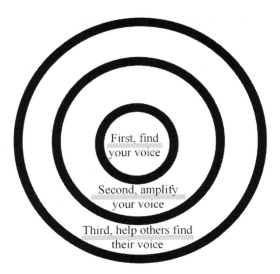

Figure 13.2 Illustration of the Three Voices

Source: Adapted from Stephen R. Covey, *The 8th Habit: From Effectiveness To Greatness*, (New York: Free Press, 2005).

Leadership and Management

Leadership and management are inexorably linked, but they are not the same thing. Despite key differences, leadership and management are often viewed interchangeably, largely due to overlap especially in practice. Management, however, has a tactical implementation orientation that focuses on order and stability: analyzing, planning, organizing, controlling, rules, and risk avoidance.

In contrast, leadership has a strategic future orientation that focuses on vision: enhanced meaningfulness, trust, engagement, the growth mindset, empowerment, and building on the strengths of people and relationships. While both leaders and managers may motivate and inspire in their own ways, managers administer, while leaders innovate.[23] Some of the key differences between the two are identified in Figure 13.3.

The Five Rings of Catalytic Leadership

Catalytic leaders are those willing to act to create the future, what might be. Catalytic leaders build organizations that are creation machines, where the big ideas flow from everyone.

Catalytic leaders remove barriers and organizational inertia that interfere with innovation progress. Catalytic leaders develop and impart creative skills throughout their organizations. Catalytic leadership development can be viewed as a set of five concentric rings that are shown in Figure 13.4.

The five concentric rings represent the character and competence of capable individuals, the contributing team members, the competent manager, the effective leader, and the catalytic leader. To reach the catalytic leadership level, the leader must develop the skills to advance as they progress from the innermost ring to the outermost ring.

The innermost ring is a blend of character and competence. Both are needed. Character, in this context, is the ability to draw out the truth. Once the emerging leader has mastered the self-management anchored in these skills, they can progress outward in the rings.

Yes, leadership is about vision. But leadership is equally about creating a climate where the truth is heard and the brutal facts confronted. There is a huge difference between the opportunity to

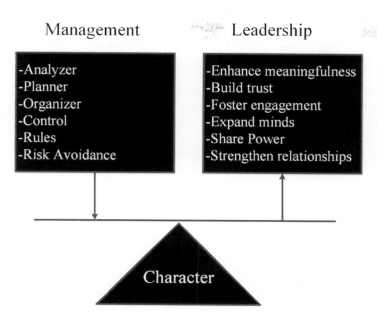

Figure 13.3 Illustration of Leadership and Management

Source: Adapted from Warren G. Bennis, *On Becoming a Leader*, (New York: Basic Books, 2009).

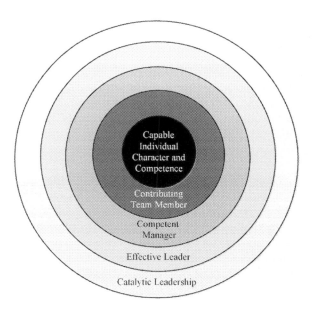

Figure 13.4 Illustration of the Five Rings

Source: Adapted from Jim Collins, *Good to Great: Why Some Companies Make the Leap... and Others Don't*, (New York: Harper Collins, 2001).

"have your say" and the opportunity to be *heard*. The good-to-great leaders understood this distinction, creating a culture wherein people had a tremendous opportunity to be heard and ultimately, for the truth to be heard.[24]

If someone is placed in a ring without the prerequisite skills, there will be a mismatch, resulting in the probability of failure. Those "leaders" who are low in willfulness, low in humility, and high in self-absorption will rarely make it to the outer rings because they focus on their needs instead of the organization's needs.

If an organization does not have a way of identifying the quality of the managerial talent, such as 360 reviews and statistically validated surveys, the mismatched manager can operate endlessly in a marginal state. If this occurs, the organization will incur a hidden intangible tax on the effectiveness of its people, as unqualified leaders diminish their resource talent.

Leadership is not about personality.[25] When looking into five personality dimensions, there were no significant differences between those who scored low and those who scored high on the factor result of leadership.[26] In contrast, one might think that introverts have no place in any of the rings. Not so, says Adam Grant.

According to a team of researchers led by the Wharton management professor Adam Grant, introverted leaders typically deliver better outcomes than extroverts, because they're more likely to let proactive employees run with their ideas. Extroverted leaders, who like to be at the center of attention, may feel threatened by employees who take too much initiative (but do outperform introverts when managing less proactive workers who rely on their leader for inspiration).[27]

Capable Individual: Character and Competence

100% of the Time

Leaders are more effective if they demonstrate authentic integrity 100% of the time to build the foundation for trusting relationships. In *How Will You Measure Your Life?* Christensen, Allworth, and Dillon describe the difference between 100% people and 98% people: "Many of us have convinced ourselves that we are able to break our own personal rules, 'just this once.' In our minds, we can justify these small choices. None of those things, when they first happen, feels like a life-changing decision."[28]

The tobacco industry senior management deceived the American public when they lied about the addictiveness of cigarettes and nicotine.[29] The movie *The Insider* describes the true story of whistleblower Jeffrey Weigand, a 100% person who, at great risk to his family, exposed the tobacco industry's lies when he revealed that cigarettes were a nicotine-delivery instrument.[30] The facts indicate that the tobacco companies designed cigarettes to make them more additive, that the nicotine in tobacco is addictive, and that tobacco causes cancer.[31]

The movie *Chariots of Fire* describes the story of Eric Liddell, a 100% person who refused to run on Sunday in the 1924 Olympics because of his religious beliefs, even though he was likely to win. Clayton Christensen would have recognized Eric Liddell as someone who adhered to his personal rules 100% of the time. Christensen had an identical experience when he refused to play basketball on a Sunday in the finals of the British equivalent of the NCAA tournament.[32]

98% of the Time

There are plenty of examples of false steps made by people in visible positions. Christensen would have called Lance Armstrong a person who adhered to his personal rules 98% of the time. Lance

Armstrong could justify his breaking the rules, just this once, because he would do anything to win in sports, rationalizing that the end justifies the means. After years of very convincing lying, in January 2013, Armstrong admitted to Oprah Winfrey that he used banned drugs in order to win in all seven of his Tour de France victories.

Best Buy's Brian Dunn made the list as one of the worst CEOs of 2012. Effective leaders need to set high standards of behavior and demonstrate those behaviors. Dunn demonstrated both a lack of professional conduct and a lack of competence.[33] He resigned in April 2012. Dish Network Corporation, the second largest satellite network, was founded by Charlie Ergen and is considered by the 24/7 Wall Street website to be the worst company to work for in America.[34] Ergen has a reputation for creating a poisonous work environment and being unnecessarily harsh not only on his employees, but also his partners. The future will decide whether this level of people-competence is sustainable.

Contributing Team Members

The lone wolf is the traditional model for the hiring and promoting of leaders that relies on individualism, intelligence, and scientific or technical skills. This model is based on the ability of the perceived competence of new employees to adapt and learn rapidly in times of change. In the poem, "The Law of the Jungle," Rudyard Kipling writes, "For the strength of the Pack is the Wolf,/ and the strength of the Wolf is the Pack."[35] Creativity is more dynamic in a team setting rather than as a solo performance. In a leadership position, selecting employees based on individualism is very risky and can easily result in failure. A leadership position requires the ability to choose the right person who can effectively function within a team.

The relatively unknown Larry Gelwix, coach of the successful Highland Rugby Team, is an advocate of character-oriented sports. Gelwix says, "If you lose your integrity, you've lost everything."[36] John Wooden, former English teacher and coach of the UCLA basketball team, is another example of a catalytic leader who focused on character development. Wooden says, "Be more concerned with your character than your reputation, because your character is what you really are, while your reputation is merely what others think you are."[37]

In *Coach Wooden's Pyramid of Success*, Wooden writes, "The star of the team is the team. 'We' supersedes 'me.'"[38] Innovation and entrepreneurship are often attributed to individuals, such as Michelangelo, Steve Jobs, and Mark Zuckerberg. These innovation and entrepreneurship leaders, however, are also often the first to acknowledge that the process of innovation and entrepreneurship is a collaborative activity that needs to be built into the cultural fabric of a team and, ultimately, an organization. Innovation and entrepreneurship, while leadership-driven, are ultimately based on our ability to apply collective intelligence, the coalescing of ideas from multiple sources, and then connecting and refining those thoughts, discoveries, and connections to unfold something new and unique.

In *The Five Dysfunctions of a Team*, author Patrick Lencioni describes a five-layer pyramidal model of pitfalls that prevent effective team functioning. The five dysfunctions are absence of trust, fear of conflict, lack of commitment, avoidance of accountability, and inattention to results. The reason character is important is that it is the prerequisite for trustworthiness; trustworthiness is the prerequisite to team functioning. Individuals may not be comfortable sharing their ideas with others they are uncomfortable with. Likewise, individuals may not be comfortable confronting others about the value of their ideas if they are uncomfortable with each other. "Trust lies at the heart of a functioning, cohesive team. Without it, teamwork is all but impossible."[39]

Teams that function at a high level are composed of individuals that trust each other to build on the strengths of each member. That is, teams that are trustworthy, supportive, transparent, and diverse. "Choose people who trust each other enough to suspend judgment for a time. Trust is hugely important; people need to be willing to fall on their faces, make asses out of themselves, and learn from it."[40]

Functional and Dysfunctional Conflict

When working with a team, all of the different types of thinking can be in conflict. If conflict results in better decision-making, it is productive. It is the responsibility of leadership to manage the balance between productive and non-productive conflict. By learning more about how to apply the types of thinking, we can expand our effective thinking skills.

Leader-Member Exchange

Building on theory and practice, research suggests there are multiple domains within the concept of leadership: the leader, the follower, the relationship, the team, the organization, and more. In the world of innovation and entrepreneurship, given its central focus on a relationship-based approach to leadership, the leader-member exchange (LMX) theory is especially appealing and applicable. Researchers George B. Graen and Mary Uhl-Bien outline four stages in the development of LMX: (1) discovery of vertical dyads between leaders and members (VDL); (2) the shift from VDL to relationship exchange between leaders and members and a focus on outcome (LMX); (3) building on the LMX research, evolving to more of a "leadership making" focus on leadership as a partnership among team members including the leader; and (4) finally, viewing LMX not as a series of independent dyads or relationships, but rather a system of interdependent or network of relationships.[41] Innovation and entrepreneurship rely on the key relationships that exist between the members of the team. From the entrepreneur to the organizational team leader, the relationships developed are essential for the cross-fertilization of ideas, concepts, formulation, and implementation.

Competent Manager: Tame the Whirlwind

Leadership and management are not the same thing. The competent manager is the one who can tame the whirlwind. The competent manager focuses on improving the execution of the present by "organiz[ing] people and resources toward the effective and efficient pursuit of predetermined objectives."[42] Author and former University of Cincinnati president and professor emeritus Dr. Warren Bennis succinctly describes the difference between managers and leaders.[43]

- The manager administers; the leader innovates.
- The manager is a copy; the leader is an original.
- The manager maintains; the leader develops.
- The manager focuses on systems and structure; the leader focuses on people.
- The manager relies on control; the leader inspires trust.
- The manager has a short-range view; the leader has a long-range perspective.
- The manager asks how and when; the leader asks what and why.
- The manager has his or her eye always on the bottom line; the leader's eye is on the horizon.
- The manager imitates; the leader originates.
- The manager accepts the status quo; the leader challenges it.
- The manager is the classic good soldier; the leader is his or her own person.
- The manager does things right; the leader does the right thing.

While not an exhaustive list, it more than adequately illustrates working elements of both management and leadership, exposing key differences.

Effective Leaders: Getting the Right Leaders on the Bus (School of Experience)

Studies by Zenger and Folkman identified ten leadership shortcomings. Every one of the failed leaders that they identified had at least one of these shortcomings. The leadership shortcomings are: a lack of energy and enthusiasm, acceptance of their own mediocre performance, lack of clear vision and direction, poor judgment, failure to collaborate, violating behavior performance standards, resistance to new ideas, not learning from mistakes, lack of interpersonal skills, and failure to support and develop others.[44] How does one select leaders that do not have these shortcomings?

The inability to function effectively in any new position can be explained using the school of experience theory. Morgan McCall conceived the school of experience theory, which argues that one can predict whether or not a person can effectively solve a problem they have in the present based on whether they had learned to solve a similar problem in the past.[45] The school of experience theory can be used to predict whether someone will be successful when performing a future job assignment. For example, if someone is admitted to a college partly on non-academic grounds, and the person hasn't previously been an accomplished academic, he or she might struggle with academic coursework, leading to poor outcomes and less learning for that person. In a similar manner, if an individual is hired for a leadership position and has not been through the school of experience, it is likely that the person will struggle and that struggle will lead to poor outcomes for not only the leader, but also for those people that the person leads.

John Wooden's life as a devoted player, teacher, coach, and poet is an example of the school of experience.[46] Over a period of 40 seasons of playing and coaching, his high school and college teams won 80% of their games. Wooden was a star player on the 1927 Martinsville Indiana High School state championship basketball team. From 1930 to 1932, he was an All-American basketball player at Purdue and an Academic All-American. He was a high school basketball coach at Dayton High School in Kentucky, and from 1934 to 1943 he coached basketball at Central High School in South Bend, Indiana. In 1948, after military service during World War II, he became the coach of the UCLA Bruins. His school of experience is represented by the "The Pyramid of Success," a description of the accumulation of characteristics he regarded as having determined his school of experience.[47]

Catalytic leaders need to resist the urge to push, control, and clamp down when the going gets tough. If a catalytic leader has to overmanage an experienced individual, the organization has made a mistake, and that individual needs to "get off the bus." Conversely, if a "leader" is over-managing an individual that has the character and commensurate competence for their role, the "leader" needs to "get off the bus."[48]

Effective Leadership: "When in Rome, Do as the Romans Do"

St. Ambrose, bishop of Milan, famously said, "When I am at Rome, I fast on a Saturday; when I am at Milan, I do not. Follow the custom of the church where you are."[49] Researchers have studied the intersection of leadership and culture and have come to the same conclusion.

Introduced earlier in this book, Hofstede's five cultural dimensions are a power distance index (the acceptance of an uneven distribution of power), individuality and collectivism, masculinity and femininity (the relative value placed on stereotypically male or female personality characteristics and actions), an uncertainty avoidance index, and long-term orientation.[50] Robert J. House of the Wharton School of Business at the University of Pennsylvania expanded on the five cultural dimensions and conceived the "Global Leadership and Organizational Behavior Effectiveness" (GLOBE) Research Program.

In 2004, "Culture, Leadership, and Organizations: The GLOBE Study of 62 Societies" was published.[51] The study is based on results from about 17,300 middle managers from 951 organizations in the food processing, financial services, and telecommunications services industries. In 2007, "Culture and Leadership across the World: The GLOBE Book of In-Depth Studies of 25 Societies" was published. It complements the results from the first volume regarding leader behavior in those 25 cultures.[52]

The GLOBE studies provide a comprehensive description of how cultures are similar or different from one another. The GLOBE study used nine cultural dimensions: power distance, uncertainty avoidance, humane orientation, collectivism I (institutional), collectivism II (in-group), assertiveness, gender egalitarianism, future orientation, and performance orientation. The results were placed in clusters.

The findings were organized by leadership styles: charismatic/value-based style, team-oriented style, participative style, humane style, self-protective style, and autonomous style. The findings of the research highlight the contextual nature of leadership styles. Specifically, the effectiveness of leadership is associated with the cultural norms, values, and beliefs of those being led.

Researchers Badrinarayan Pawar and Kenneth Eastman suggest four contextual variables that are influential in the process of transformational leadership: organization, structure, culture, and strategy. They argue that these contextual variables affect individual and organizational receptivity to leadership in general and transformational leadership in particular.[53] By extension, it is reasonable to say that context and leadership styles are interrelated and dynamic.

Leadership Competencies

Catalytic Leadership

Catalytic leadership is a choice that individuals make to challenge existing practices and theories.[54] Having the courage and wisdom to challenge what exists is necessary because organizational cultures will perpetuate the past even though change is needed. Catalytic leaders are those that choose to transform *what is* into *what might be* through *how we might*.

Authentic Leadership

Bill George writes,

> In researching my book, *True North*, we interviewed 125 authentic leaders and learned that the essence of leadership comes not from having pre-defined characteristics but from knowing yourself – your strengths and weaknesses – by understanding your unique life story and the challenges you've experienced.[55]

In *Primal Leadership*, Daniel Goleman, Richard Boyatzis, and Annie McKee describe a set of leadership competencies that focus on emotional intelligence.[56]

Emotional Intelligence

Catalytic leaders are those who confront the brutal facts to overcome the obstacles that impede innovation. They are those individuals who are willing to facilitate the counterculture of an organization by constantly searching for new ideas and discarding outmoded beliefs. People in conventional organizations expect leaders to say, "Here's where we are headed."[57] But this is wrong, because this kind of leadership may be overlooking those talented people who know something that could be useful in formulating that decision. "Great decisions begin with really great people and a simple statement: I don't know."[58] Catalytic leaders have the competency building blocks of emotional intelligence.[59] There are 12 competencies within four categories illustrated in Figure 13.5.

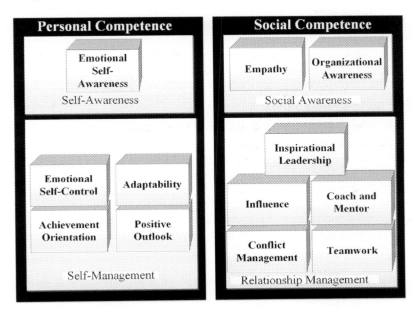

Figure 13.5 Illustration of Leadership Competencies

Source: Adapted from Daniel Goleman, et. al., *Building Blocks of Emotional Intelligence*, (Florence, MA: Key Step Media, 2017) Daniel Goleman, Richard Boyatzis and Annie McKee, *Primal Leadership*, (Boston: Harvard Business School Press, 2004), 253–256.

Key takeaways from reviewing emotional and social intelligence leadership competencies include the following:

- Self-awareness is the emotional self-awareness to recognize one's own feelings and how they affect one's effectiveness.
- Self-management is the ability to manage oneself, to develop emotional self-control, and to develop an achievement orientation.
- Social awareness is the ability to discern others' emotions, concerns, and needs through empathy and organizational awareness.
- Relationship management is the ability to apply authentic interpersonal skills for inspirational leadership, coaching and mentoring, team building, ethical influencing, and managing conflict.

Servant Leadership

Catalytic leadership makes it easier for individuals and organizations to adapt and renew themselves, to grow and develop beyond where they are now. Catalytic leaders understand that they have not achieved anything until they have helped others achieve something meaningful. Catalytic leaders apply servant leadership.

> Servant leadership is based on the premise that to bring out the best in their followers, leaders rely on one-on-one communication to understand the abilities, needs, desires, goals, and potential of those individuals. With knowledge of each follower's unique characteristics and interests, leaders then assist followers in achieving their potential.[60]

Servant leadership enables the expansion of human capabilities to provide a path to learn and grow beyond where each person is now, explore the limits of their talents, and create new knowledge. Catalytic leaders are those that can create a human framework where there is less need for oversight, which has the potential to reduce latitude and inspiration if overused.

The Broken Window: Bad to Great

> In 1982, criminologist George L. Kelling and political scientist James Q. Wilson described what they called the "broken windows" theory: They observed that in neighborhoods where one broken window was left unrepaired, the remaining windows would soon be broken, too. Allowing even a bit of bad to persist suggests that no one is watching, no one cares, and no one will stop others from doing far worse things.[61]

The broken windows theory is instructive in the application of catalytic leadership.
McKinsey suggests that the prerequisite to catalytic leadership is first to eliminate destructive behaviors.

> The researchers discovered that negative interactions with bosses and co-workers had five times more impact on employees' moods than positive interactions. This "bad is stronger than good" effect holds in nearly every other setting studied, from romantic relationships to group effectiveness.[62]

Catalytic leaders need to bring about change by focusing on what competency gaps need to be filled in their organizations.

The Window and Mirror: Good to Great

Jim Collins used the window and mirror analogy to describe catalytic leadership.[63] By acknowledging that leaders are willing to take responsibility for their lack of knowledge and missteps (by looking in an imaginary mirror when there is a problem) while, at the same time, giving sincere credit to others for meaningful results (by looking out the imaginary window to reward the results of others), they set performance expectations for bi-directional accountability. It happens all too often in the whirlwind of organizations that if leadership has not developed bi-directional accountability where each employee takes responsibility, the leadership blames the employees and the employees blame the leadership when things go wrong.

The Little Bighorn

Unlike the flamboyant General George Custer, whose leadership hubris ultimately led to his demise at the battle of Little Bighorn,[64] catalytic leaders possess the willfulness and humility to drive strategic intent into the future by overcoming the inertia of outmoded beliefs.[65]

Catalytic leaders understand and apply this notion by being willful enough to achieve a larger aim beyond them and humble enough to acknowledge others for their contributions. Although completely different individuals, John Wooden, Neil Armstrong, Thomas Edison, Abraham Lincoln, Nelson Mandela, Mohandas Karamchand Gandhi, and Franklin D. Roosevelt all demonstrate the characteristics of catalytic leaders.

Edgar Schein believes that the leader of the future must give and receive help. Globalization, technology, the changing nature of work, and increasing complexity have created a situation in which leaders will be unable to lead effectively without relying on their teams. This will require a new sense of humility on behalf of the leader. Leaders must admit that they need help to overcome their vulnerabilities.[66]

Gentle Breezes

Catalytic leaders are those that create an atmosphere where ideas flow freely both upward and downward, like gentle breezes; they have to recognize that the leader's personality and position can be a hindrance to getting the best information.

Catalytic leaders are the facilitators for others, not themselves. Self-absorbed leadership that focuses too much on the needs and preferences of the leader over the needs of others in the organization vacuums away the spirit to innovate. Catalytic leaders are those who know how to connect people and who know that important achievements are accomplished through others. The ability to increase people connections also facilitates the ability to create innovative associations.

In hierarchical organizations there is an implicit expectation that management improvements need to start at the top, and that needed change will come from above. This is wrong because a one-way downdraft results in no dialogue. If people feel that they cannot speak up and engage the senior leadership, then they cannot be part of the solution. Effective organizations need a two-way dialogue and are built on the capability to confront the brutal facts combined with the tenacity to prevail.[67]

Mavericks (Insubordination or Entrepreneurship)

According to Tim Brown of IDEO, "A culture that believes that it is better to ask forgiveness afterward rather than permission before, that rewards people for success but gives them permission to fail, has removed one of the main obstacles to the formation of new ideas."[68]

As we discussed in Chapter 3, Richard Drew became an inventor for 3M in 1923. When Drew noticed that car painters were having difficulty with the tape they were using to separate the colors on two-tone cars, he began working on a new tape. Despite what seemed to a ludicrous idea, mounting obstacles, setbacks, material shortages, and more, he persisted.[69] Drew invented what would become one of the most practical items to be found in any home or office: transparent adhesive tape. Scotch cellophane tapes went on to become one of the most famous and widely used products in 3M history. In 2021, 3M sells enough Scotch brand tape to encircle the Earth 165 times. 3M's Drew was posthumously inducted into National Inventors Hall of Fame on May 4, 2007.[70]

Chuck House, an engineer at HP, while working on oscilloscope technology, developed a new prototype of a display monitor. He was asked to stop working on the display monitor. Instead, he demonstrated the display monitor to some HP customers in order to determine the strengths and weaknesses of his new prototype. Based on the feedback from the customers, he proceeded with his work, even though David Packard told him to discontinue the project. House was able to get the monitor into production and it sold more than 17,000 units.[71]

How do you know how much autonomy to give to individuals? How are leaders to distinguish between individuals like Richard Drew and Chuck House? Are they insubordinate or are they entrepreneurial? According to David Packard, the difference lies in the intent of the individual. David Packard writes, "Several years later, at a gathering of HP engineers, I presented Chuck with a medal for 'extraordinary contempt and defiance beyond the normal call of engineering duty.'"[72]

Management Innovation

Foundations of Management

In general, the foundation of managerial thinking is built upon the insights of Frederick Taylor, Henry Ford, Peter Drucker, and Edwards Deming. In 1939, upon reading Drucker's *The End of Economic Man*, Winston Churchill declared Drucker "one of those writers to whom almost anything can be forgiven because he not only has a mind of his own, but has the gift of starting other minds along a stimulating line of thought."[73]

Transforming Management

Is it time to transform our thinking about management and leadership? Peter Drucker is often credited with saying, "The best way to predict the future is to create it."[74] Gary Hamel is an advocate of managerial innovation. He believes that organizations can achieve a competitive advantage if they develop leadership skills in employees at all levels. He is one of the founders of the open-innovation platform known as the Management Innovation eXchange.[75]

> The Management Innovation eXchange (MIX) is an open innovation project aimed at reinventing management for the 21st century. The premise: While "modern" management is one of humankind's most important inventions, it is now a mature technology that must be reinvented for a new age.[76]

Leadership Styles

The most successful leaders have strengths in the emotional intelligence competencies: Self-awareness, self-management, social awareness, and relationship management. According to Daniel Goleman, there are six basic leadership styles. "Each derives from different emotional intelligence competencies, works best in particular situations, and affects the organizational climate in different ways."[77]

1. The coercive style of leadership demands immediate compliance and may be necessary in some situations. It is the least effective in most situations due to its negative impact, as it restricts bi-directional communication, lessens motivation and flexibility.
2. The authoritative style of leadership provides positive direction and enables employees to choose their own means of achieving it. It is less effective when the leader is working with a team of experts who are more experienced.
3. The affiliative style is effective for building positive team harmony, empathy, communications, and relationships but less effective if specific direction is needed.
4. The democratic style of leadership builds consensus by engaging people in decisions, builds organizational flexibility and responsibility, but is less effective when direction is needed.
5. The pacesetting style of leadership sets high performance expectations for those employees who are self-motivated and highly competent but can have a negative impact on the climate if it is resented by employees who feel overwhelmed.

6. The coaching style of leadership focuses more on personal development than results This style is effective for those people who are receptive to changing their behavior and not for those who are resistant to changing their ways.

The leadership situation determines the most effective style to be applied. The leader who can switch among the authoritative, affiliative, democratic, and coaching styles will likely achieve the best outcome. Figure 13.6 illustrates all six leadership styles.

Figure 13.6 Illustration of Leadership Styles

Source: Adapted from Daniel Goleman, "Leadership that Gets Results." Harvard Business Review 78, no. 2 (2000): 78–90.

Leadership Attitudes, Skills, Knowledge, and Behaviors

There are two steps to effective leadership. Step 1 of effective leadership is to learn the attitudes, skills, and knowledge competencies. Yet this is not enough. Step 2 is required, applying the competencies by practicing the behaviors. Just like in most sports, it is especially relevant for new leaders to have a coach so that they can receive the feedback from their performance. The two-step process is identified in Figure 13.7.

Resilient Leadership

As previously noted, Louis Silvie "Louie" Zamperini was an American World War II prisoner of war survivor, inspirational speaker, and Olympic distance runner. He is an example of resilience that encompasses courage. In 2010, Laura Hillenbrand wrote a best-selling book about his experiences, which was adapted into the film *Unbroken* in 2014. All of the competencies require resilience and practice that is driven by your passion.

Step-1: Learning the Competencies	Attitudes	Leadership attitudes are the wanting to do. A positive attitude about learning leadership is based on the growth mindset. Attitudes include agility, compassion, curiosity, fairness, humility, inclusivity, open-mindedness, and resilience anchored to character.
	Skills	Leadership skills are the how to do. The capabilities to perform a task or activity that can be measured include communication, collaboration, creativity, critical thinking, emotional intelligence, problem solving and styles.
	Knowledge	Leadership knowledge is the what to do. The understanding of facts and concepts that includes system thinking, domain expertise, understanding culture, planning, organizing, and staffing.
Step-2: Behavior-Applying the Competencies	Behaviors	Leadership behaviors are actions that are based on the competency times practice that results in achievement and mastery. The behaviors include coaching and mentoring, effective decision-making, engaging, facilitating, gratitude, networking, reflection, risk tolerance, strategic thinking, team building, vision and future orientation.

Figure 13.7 Illustration of Leadership Attitudes, Skills, Knowledge, and Behaviors

Source: Adapted from Warren G. Bennis and Burt Nanus, *Leaders: The strategies for taking charge (1st ed.)*, (New York: Harper Business Essentials, 1985) Daniel Goleman, *Emotional intelligence*, (New York: Bantam Books, 1997).
Carol S. Dweck, *Mindset: The new psychology of success (1st ed.)*, (New York: Random House, 2006).

According to Diane L. Coutu, there are three essential components of resilience:[78]

1. Facing reality to understand your talents
2. Finding a meaningful purpose in your life
3. Striving for continuous improvement

The resilience leadership attitudes for effective leadership are described in Figure 13.8.

Summary

In this chapter, we examined the critical importance of leadership in the process of innovation and entrepreneurship. Catalytic leaders are mastery-driven, not ego-driven. When mastery-driven leaders improve themselves, they can more effectively develop others. Catalytic leadership development can be viewed as a set of five concentric rings: the five concentric rings are the character and competence capability of the individuals, the contributing team members, the competent manager, the effective leader, and the catalytic leader. We examined emotional intelligence, servant leadership, and the window and the mirror. While teams and the relationships between and among the team and leaders are critical, we also examined the role of "mavericks" in the workplace. We explored transforming management, leadership styles, the two-step leadership learning process, and resilient leadership.

Next up, we look at the ongoing role of innovation ecosystems and the importance of the inter-dependencies operating through the ecosystem.

1. Design from the heart ... and the head.	"In crisis, the hardest things can be the softest things. Resilient leaders are genuinely, sincerely empathetic, walking compassionately in the shoes of employees, customers, and their broader ecosystems. Yet resilient leaders must simultaneously take a hard, rational line to protect financial performance from the invariable softness that accompanies such disruptions."
2. Put the mission first.	"Resilient leaders are skilled at triage, able to stabilize their organizations to meet the crisis at hand while finding opportunities amid difficult constraints."
3. Aim for speed over elegance.	"Resilient leaders take decisive action—with courage—based on imperfect information, knowing that expediency is essential."
4. Own the narrative.	"Resilient leaders seize the narrative at the outset, being transparent about current realities—including what they don't know—while also painting a compelling picture of the future that inspires others to persevere."
5. Embrace the long view.	"Resilient leaders stay focused on the horizon, anticipating the new business models that are likely to emerge and sparking the innovations that will define tomorrow."

Figure 13.8 Illustration of Leadership Resilience

Source: Adapted from Punit Renjen, "The heart of resilient leadership: Responding to COVID-19," Deloitte Insights, March 16, 2020, accessed March 31, 2020, https://www2.deloitte.com/global/en/insights/economy/covid-19/heart-of-resilient-leadership-responding-to-covid-19.html

Notes

1. *Wikipedia*, s.v. "Sputnik 1," accessed August 11, 2021, https://en.wikipedia.org/wiki/Sputnik_1.
2. *Wikipedia*, s.v. "Yuri Gagarin," accessed August 11, 2021, http://en.wikipedia.org/wiki/Yuri_Gagarin.
3. John F. Kennedy, "Excerpt from the 'Special Message to the Congress on Urgent National Needs'," *President John F. Kennedy, Delivered in Person Before a Joint Session of Congress*, May 25, 1961, accessed August 14, 2021, www.nasa.gov/vision/space/features/jfk_speech_text.html.
4. *Wikipedia*, s.v. "John F. Kennedy," accessed August 11, 2021, http://en.wikipedia.org/wiki/John_Kennedy.
5. John F. Kennedy, "Special Message to the Congress on Urgent National Needs," May 25, 1961, accessed February 24, 2024, www.nasa.gov/vision/space/features/jfk_speech_text.html.
6. *Wikipedia*, s.v. "Apollo 11," accessed August 11, 2021, http://en.wikipedia.org/wiki/Apollo_11.
7. Jeffrey Kluger, "Remembering Neil Armstrong, a Man of Profound Skill and Preternatural Calm," *Time Magazine*, August 25, 2012, accessed February 24, 2024, http://science.time.com/2012/08/25/remembering-neil-armstrong-a-man-of-profound-skill-and-preternatural-calm/?xid=newsletter-daily.
8. Doreen Rappaport and C. F. Payne, *To Dare Mighty Things: The Life of Theodore Roosevelt* (New York: DisneyHyperion, 2013).
9. *Stanford Encyclopedia of Philosophy*, s.v. "Seneca," October 17, 2007, revised November 21, 2011, accessed February 24, 2024, http://plato.stanford.edu/entries/seneca/.
10. "Apollo 1," accessed February 24, 2024, www.history.nasa.gov/Apollo204/.
11. *Wikipedia*, s.v. "Damocles," accessed August 11, 2021, http://en.wikipedia.org/wiki/Damocles.
12. "Courageous People," accessed February 24, 2024, www.biographyonline.net/people/famous/courageous.html.
13. "Rating World Leaders: The U.S. vs. Germany, China, and Russia," *Gallup*, accessed February 24, 2024, www.gallup.com/analytics/247040/rating-world-leaders-2019.aspx.

14. "The State of Human Capital 2012 – Why the Human Capital Function Still Has Far to Go," *McKinsey and Company*, January 1, 2012, accessed February 24, 2024, www.mckinsey.com/business-functions/organization/our-insights/the-state-of-human-capital-2012-report.
15. Pierre Gurdjian, Thomas Halbeisen, and Kevin Lane, "Why Leadership Programs Fail," *McKinsey and Company*, January 1, 2014, accessed August 14, 2021, www.mckinsey.com/featured-insights/leadership/why-leadership-development-programs-fail.
16. "Corporate Innovation Is Within Reach: Nurturing and Enabling an Entrepreneurial Culture, A 2013 Study of U.S. Companies and Their Entrepreneurial Cultures," *Accenture*, 2013.
17. S. Vora, T. Kuczmarski, S. Bhattacharya, Y. Seedat, and J. Sherman, "Innovation Unleashed," *Accenture*, 2021, accessed February 24, 2024, www.accenture.com/content/dam/accenture/final/a-com-migration/r3-3/pdf/pdf-169/accenture-innovation-unleashed-final.pdf.
18. Eric Mosley and Derek Irvine, *Winning with a Culture of Recognition: Recognition Strategies at the World's Most Admired Companied* (Southborough, MA: Globoforce Limited, 2010).
19. Eric Mosley and Derek Irvine, *Making Work Human: How Human-Centered Companies Are Changing the Future of Work and the World* (New York: McGraw Hill, 2020).
20. "Global Trends in Employee Attraction, Retention, and Engagement," *Willis Towers Watson*, October 2014, accessed February 24, 2024, www.willistowerswatson.com/en-US/Insights/2014/10/global-trends-in-employee-attraction-retention-and-engagement.
21. Daniel Goleman, "Leadership That Gets Results," *Harvard Business Review* 78, no. 2 (2000), 78–90.
22. Stephen Covey, *The 8th Habit: From Effectiveness to Greatness* (New York: Free Press, 2004).
23. Warren Bennis, *On Becoming a Leader* (Reading, MA: Addison-Wesley Pub. Co., 1989).
24. Jim Collins, *Good to Great* (New York: Harper Business, 2001), 74.
25. Jeffery D. Houghton, T. W. Bonham, Christopher P. Neck, and Kusum Singh, "The Relationship Between Self-Leadership and Personality: A Comparison of Hierarchical Factor Structures," *Journal of Managerial Psychology* 19, no. 4 (2004), 427–441, accessed February 24, 2024, www.researchgate.net/publication/235308381_The_relationship_between_self-leadership_and_personality_A_comparison_of_hierarchical_factor_structures.
26. Ole Boe and Torill Holth, "The Relationship between Developmental Leadership, the Results of Leadership and Personality Factors," *Procedia Economics and Finance* 26 (2015), 849–858, accessed February 24, 2024, www.researchgate.net/publication/283954693_The_Relationship_between_Developmental_Leadership_the_Results_of_Leadership_and_Personality_Factors.
27. Susan Cain, "Hire Introverts," *The Atlantic*, June 19, 2012, accessed February 24, 2024, www.theatlantic.com/magazine/archive/2012/07/hire-introverts/309041/.
28. Clayton M. Christensen, James Allworth, and Karen Dillon, *How Will You Measure Your Life?* (New York: Harper, 2012), 189.
29. Associated Press, "Tobacco Companies Are Told to Correct Lies about Smoking," *The New York Times*, November 28, 2012, accessed February 24, 2024, www.nytimes.com/2012/11/28/business/tobacco-companies-are-told-to-correct-lies-about-smoking.html?_r=0.
30. "60 Minutes' Most Famous Whistleblower," *60 Minutes Overtime*, February 4, 2016, accessed September 5, 2021, www.cbsnews.com/news/60-minutes-most-famous-whistleblower/.
31. "Judge Orders Tobacco Companies to Say They Lied," *USA Today*, November 27, 2012, accessed February 24, 2024, www.usatoday.com/story/news/nation/2012/11/27/judge-smoking-cigarettes-tobacco-lied/1730305/.
32. Clayton M. Christensen, James Allworth, and Karen Dillon, *How Will You Measure Your Life?* (New York: Harper, 2012), 189–190.
33. Sidney Finkelstein, "The Five Worst CEOs of 2012," *The Washington Post*, December 18, 2012, accessed February 24, 2024, www.washingtonpost.com/national/on-leadership/the-five-worst-ceos-of-2012/2012/12/18/0f353f14-4940-11e2-ad54-580638ede391_story.html.
34. Caleb Hannan, "Dish Network, the Meanest Company in America," *Bloomberg Businessweek*, January 2, 2013, accessed February 24, 2024, www.bloomberg.com/news/articles/2013-01-02/dish-network-the-meanest-company-in-america.
35. Rudyard Kipling, *The Jungle Book* (Garden City, NY: Doubleday, Page, 1894).
36. Larry Gelwix, "Forever Strong," accessed February 24, 2024, https://quotefancy.com/quote/1615921/Larry-Gelwix-If-you-lose-your-integrity-you-ve-lost-everything#:~:text=Larry%20Gelwix%20Quote%3A%20%E2%80%9CIf%20you,you've%20lost%20everything.%E2%80%9D.
37. John Wooden, "John Wooden Quote," accessed February 24, 2024, www.goodreads.com/author/quotes/23041.John_Wooden.

38. John Wooden and Jay Carty, *Coach Wooden's Pyramid of Success: Building Blocks for a Better Life* (New York: Regal, 2009).
39. Patrick Lencioni, *The Five Dysfunctions of a Team: A Leadership Fable* (New York: Jossey-Bass, 2002), 195.
40. Bruce Nussbaum, *Creative Intelligence* (New York: Harper Business, 2013), 127.
41. George B. Graen and Mary Uhl-Bien, "Relationship-Based Approach to Leadership: Development of Leader-Member Exchange (LMX) Theory of Leadership Over 25 Years: Applying a Multi-Level Multi-Domain Perspective," *Leadership Quarterly* 6, no. 2 (1995), 219–247.
42. Jim Collins, *Good to Great: Why Some Companies Make the Leap . . . and Others Don't* (New York: Harper Collins, 2001), 20.
43. Warren Bennis, *On Becoming a Leader* (Reading, MA: Addison-Wesley, 1989).
44. Jack Zenger and Joseph Folkman, "Ten Fatal Flaws That Derail Leaders," *Harvard Business Review* 87, no. 6 (2009), 18.
45. Morgan W. McCall, Michael M. Lombardo, and Ann M. Morrison, *Lessons of Experience: How Successful Executives Develop on the Job* (Lexington, MA: Lexington Books, 1988).
46. "Pursuing the Best in Yourself – The Difference Between Winning and Succeeding – John Wooden," *YouTube Video*, posted by "Sales Drive," May 7, 2013, accessed August 11, 2021, www.youtube.com/watch?v=KlKlBOi8KS4; "UCLA Coach John Wooden (1910–2010)," *YouTube Video*, posted by "805Bruin," October 14, 2009, accessed February 24, 2024, www.youtube.com/watch?v=cZ358_YrFAM&list=PL702CFFF128FC9525.
47. John Wooden and Jay Carty, *Coach Wooden's Pyramid of Success* (New York: Regal, 2005), 151–155.
48. Jim Collins, *Good to Great* (New York: Harper, 2001).
49. Saint Augustine, "Oxford Reference," accessed February 24, 2024, www.oxfordreference.com/display/10.1093/acref/9780191826719.001.0001/q-oro-ed4-00000253#:~:text=St%20Ambrose%20c.&text=Ubi%20Petrus%2C%20ibi%20ergo%20ecclesia,there%20must%20be%20the%20Church.&text=When%20I%20go%20to%20Rome,to%20give%20or%20receive%20scandal.
50. Geert Hofstede and Gert Jan Hofstede, *Cultures and Organizations: Software of the Mind*, 2nd ed. (New York: McGraw-Hill, 2005).
51. Robert J. House, Paul J. Hanges, Mansour Javidan, Peter W. Dorfman, and Vipin Gupta, eds., *Culture, Leadership, and Organizations: The GLOBE Study of 62 Societies* (Thousand Oaks, CA: Sage, 2004).
52. Jagdeep S. Chhokar, Felix C. Brodbeck, and Robert J. House, eds., *Culture and Leadership Across the World: The GLOBE Book of In-Depth Studies of 25 Societies* (Mahwah, NJ: Lawrence Erlbaum, 2007).
53. Badrinarayan Pawar and Kenneth Eastman, "The Nature and Implications of Contextual Influences on Transformational Leadership: A Conceptual Examination," *Academy of Management Review* 22, no. 1 (1997), 80–109.
54. "Stanley McChrystal: Leadership Is a Choice," *YouTube Video*, posted by "Stanford School of Business," February 17, 2007, accessed February 24, 2024, www.youtube.com/watch?v=p7DzQWjXKFI.
55. Bill George, "Leadership Skills," *Leadership Excellence* 28, no. 6 (2011), 13.
56. Daniel Goleman, Richard Boyatzis, and Annie McKee, *Primal Leadership* (Boston: Harvard Business School Press, 2004), 253–256.
57. Jim Collins, Verne Harnish, and the Editors of *Fortune*, "Foreword: The Greatest Business Decisions of all Time," *Fortune*, October 2012, 15.
58. Jim Collins, Verne Harnish, and the Editors of *Fortune*, "Foreword: The Greatest Business Decisions of all Time," *Fortune*, October 2012, 15.
59. Daniel Goleman, *Emotional Intelligence* (New York: Bantam Books, 2005).
60. Robert Liden, Sandy Wayne, Hao Zhao, and David Henderson, "Servant Leadership: Development of a Multidimensional Measure and Multi-Level Assessment," *The Leadership Quarterly* 19, no. 2 (2008), 162.
61. Huggy Rao and Robert I. Sutton, "Bad to Great: The Path to Scaling Up Excellence," *McKinsey*, February 2014, accessed February 24, 2024, www.mckinsey.com/business-functions/organization/our-insights/bad-to-great-the-path-to-scaling-up-excellence.
62. Huggy Rao and Robert I. Sutton, "Bad to Great: The Path to Scaling Up Excellence," *McKinsey*, February 2014, accessed February 24, 2024, www.mckinsey.com/business-functions/organization/our-insights/bad-to-great-the-path-to-scaling-up-excellence.
63. Jim Collins, *Good to Great* (New York: Harper, 2001).

64. "Battle of the Little Big Horn," *Britannica*, accessed February 24, 2024, www.britannica.com/event/Battle-of-the-Little-Bighorn.
65. Jim Collins, *Good to Great* (New York: Harper, 2001).
66. "MIT's Ed Schein on Why Managers Need to Ask for Help interview by McGill's Karl Moore," *You-Tube Video*, posted by "Karl Moore," January 12, 2010, accessed February 24, 2024, www.youtube.com/watch?v=hasdKAhXhZg.
67. Jim Collins, *Good to Great* (New York: Harper Business, 2001).
68. Tim Brown, *Change by Design* (New York: Harper Business, 2009).
69. "Scotch Transparent Tape: National Historic Chemical Landmark," *Commemorative Booklet, Produced by the National Historic Chemical Landmarks Program of the American Chemical Society*, 2007, accessed February 24, 2024, www.acs.org/content/acs/en/education/whatischemistry/landmarks/scotchtape.html.
70. "3M's Richard Drew Inducted into National Inventors Hall of Fame," *Adhesives and Sealants Industry*, August 1, 2007, accessed February 24, 2024, www.adhesivesmag.com/articles/86815–3m-s-richard-drew-inducted-into-national-inventors-hall-of-fame.
71. David Packard, *The HP Way* (New York: HarperCollins, 1995), 107–108.
72. David Packard, *The HP Way* (New York: HarperCollins, 1995), 108.
73. "Peter Drucker's Life and Legacy," *Drucker Institute*, June 13, 2006, accessed February 24, 2024, www.drucker.institute/news-post/peter-druckers-life-and-legacy/.
74. Peter Drucker, accessed February 24, 2024, www.brainyquote.com/quotes/peter_drucker_131600.
75. Gary Hamel, "Leaders Everywhere: A Conversation with Gary Hamel," *McKinsey*, accessed February 24, 2024, www.mckinsey.com/business-functions/organization/our-insights/leaders-everywhere-a-conversation-with-gary-hamel.
76. "Management Innovation Xchange," *Management Innovation Xchange*, accessed February 24, 2024, www.managementexchange.com/faq.
77. Daniel Goleman, "Leadership That Gets Results," *Harvard Business Review* 78, no. 2 (2000), 1–13.
78. Diane L. Coutu, "How Resilience Works," *Harvard Business Review*, May 2002, accessed February 24, 2024, http://hbr.org/2002/05/how-resilience-works/ar/1.

14   Ecosystem Interdependencies

Ecosystems

Honeybees provide an interesting representation of a natural ecosystem and can inform our thinking on nature and the scope of ecosystems. The overarching honeybee ecosystem is a highly organized society of honeybees, beekeepers, and all types of flowers. The micro honey ecosystem functions like a manufacturing plant, wherein each honeybee has a specialized role. The hardworking honeybees will make many separate trips to the flower to collect pollen. The honeybees locate flowers of all types, extract the pollen, attach the pollen to the stiff hairs on their legs in a part of their body called pollen baskets, and then fly back to the hive. At the hive, the bees will mix the pollen with nectar and add an enzyme to the special solution before it is placed into the honeycomb. The honeybees fan the honeycomb to remove the excess moisture until it is ready. The honeybees have special glands that produce the wax that is used for holding the inventory.

Each of the bees performs a specific assignment to achieve their goal of sustaining their ecosystem. The beekeeper entrepreneurs remove the honey used for sustaining the bee community and sell it to their customers. The hive comprises the internal ecosystem and the beekeeper, flowers, and community make up the external ecosystem. To produce the most honey for sale, all parts of the ecosystem must function optimally. If there are too few flowers available for the honeybees, there will be a system imbalance, resulting in a decrease of honey and a shortage for the customers. Recently, impact from the external ecosystem has been linked to a decline in the honeybee population. If this continues, it will impact pollination and, subsequently, agriculture and the growing of fruits and nuts. This natural ecosystem is shown in Figure 14.1.

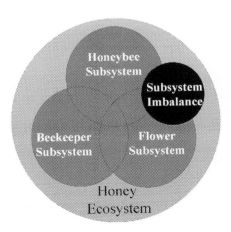

Figure 14.1 Illustration of a Natural Ecosystem

DOI: 10.4324/9781003034308-15

Interconnectedness, Wasps, and Bees

The nexus of nature and business reveals the power of the interconnectedness of ecosystems. Biomimetics, or biomimicry, is at the heart of this nexus. Biomimetics is observing, studying, and applying systems, subsystems, elements, models, and more from nature to address challenging and complex problems in science, economics, business, design, and other disciplines. It holds great promise as applied in the world of innovation and entrepreneurship.

The secrets of the interconnectedness of the natural world continue to be revealed by scientists such as researcher Duccio Cavalieri.[1] Cavalieri and his team are studying the science of genomics to understand yeast variation and its interaction with the immune system. Cavalieri is using a systems approach to study the interaction between yeasts and cellular functionality to understand the differences between both the harmful and beneficial effects of microorganisms.[2]

Even seemingly unrelated occurrences and processes can illustrate the interconnectedness of nature and society. For example, what do wasps and wine have in common? More than one might think.

Scientists say that wine drinkers can thank wasps and hornets for the complex aroma and taste of their favorite vino, NPR reports. The insects help by biting grapes on the vine and leaving behind yeast from their guts that spurs fermentation. This is partly why winemakers have planted flowers near their vines since Roman times – to attract various insects.[3]

This chapter examines the world of systems and ecosystems and how nature informs our approach to systems thinking, and an innovation and entrepreneurship ecosystem. We review a set of innovation concepts that build on Ron Adner's work in *The Wide Lens: A New Strategy for Innovation*, that include adoption chain risk, co-innovation risk, the value blueprint, the leadership prism, and the costs and benefits of innovation.[4] We then discuss how co-innovation dependencies affect the first mover advantage, the ecosystem continuum, integrative thinking, innovation and entrepreneurship ecosystems, and sustainability.

System Interconnectedness

In broad terms, the process of effective innovation and entrepreneurship can be viewed as a system of interacting parts that need to synergistically operate as one whole. Yet despite the value of this synergy, companies are not viewed as highly effective in their innovation efforts. In a survey conducted by Strategos of 550 large companies about their innovation practices, the majority of respondents considered innovation to be critical, yet less than 20% of the respondents considered their companies to be effective in their innovation efforts. The survey identified not one, but six obstacles to innovation:[5]

1. Short-term focus.
2. Lack of time, resources, or staff.
3. Leadership expects payoff sooner than is realistic.
4. Management incentives are not structured to reward innovation.
5. Lack of a systematic innovation process.
6. Belief that innovation is inherently risky.

While it is constructive to view innovation and entrepreneurship as a system of interacting parts, clearly there remains an inherent set of obstacles to its full realization. To address these obstacles, we turn to the concept of an ecosystem in general, and an innovation and entrepreneurship ecosystem in particular, to explore how innovation and entrepreneurship interact with and become part of a dynamic and evolving environment, simultaneously giving, and drawing energy that stimulates change and economic advancement.

Systems and Ecosystems

A system is an organized set of interacting and interdependent subsystems that function together as a whole to achieve a purpose. If a subsystem changes, the overall system will change its behavior. For example, imagine you are baking a cake in your kitchen. Although baking a cake represents a simple system, if you incorrectly apply the ingredient/process mix – say add too many eggs, add too little sugar, or bake it for too short or too long a time – the fundamental outcome is affected. Being out of balance, the cake may or may not be appealing to the consumer.

In general, an ecosystem is a purposeful collaborating network of dynamic interacting systems and subsystems that have an ever-changing set of dependencies within a given context. For discussion purposes, we can think of external or overarching macro-ecosystems (e.g., natural environments such as air, land, or natural resources or community efforts around start-up ecosystems to support development of new businesses and jobs), and internal/organizational micro-ecosystems. For example, an internal ecosystem is about balancing the parts or subsystems of an organization and its value chain of inputs, throughputs, and outputs. In an organization there are sometimes conflicts between the drive for competitive efficiency and the drive for innovative competitive separation. The organizations of the past are not necessarily designed for both. To survive and thrive, however, the organizations of the future must be designed for both. Future external and internal ecosystems will need to integrate efficiency and innovation.

Naturally occurring ecosystems provide excellent examples of this powerful dynamic interaction to blend efficiency and innovation, which takes place every day. For example, natural environment ecosystems are undergoing constant evolution and change due to both naturally occurring and commercially generated impacts on the environment. As one part of the ecosystem changes, the ecosystem overall will respond.

In 1993, James F. Moore observed that there is a parallel between natural ecosystems and business ecosystems. He writes, "In a business ecosystem, companies coevolve capabilities around a new innovation: They work cooperatively and competitively to support new products, satisfy customer needs, and eventually incorporate the next round of innovations."[6] Moore observed that there are four stages of an evolutionary business ecosystem. "Every business ecosystem develops in four distinct stages: Birth, expansion, leadership, and self-renewal – or, if not self-renewal, death."[7] In business, for example, the Boeing Dreamliner was designed and built as a complete system using modern composite materials that are lighter than metal. Although based on the success of earlier versions of Boeing aircraft platform design, the renewed plane was designed holistically, including the embedded computer hardware and software.

Business ecosystems and natural ecosystems interact with each other in remarkable ways, some positive, some less so. Many businesses and communities strive to be responsible stewards of the natural ecosystem. Companies routinely engage in eco-friendly materials and product recycling efforts, responsible handling of hazardous materials, development of alternative and/or green sources of energy such as wind and/or solar, and volunteer and philanthropic efforts to care for and renew the natural ecosystem. For example, many companies engaged in the building of new or repurposing of older buildings seeking Leadership in Energy and Environmental Design (LEED) certification to promote environmental sustainability. The LEED rating system, created in 1998 and overseen by the US Green Building Council, has grown to all states in the United States and over 135 countries, encompassing more than 54,000 projects and 10.1 billion square feet of construction.[8]

Often, however, businesses' impact on the natural world is undesirable and the social costs not accounted for. For example, the Reid Gardner Generating Station near Las Vegas has not optimized its waste disposal over the years.

Since 1965, the coal-fired Reid Gardner Generating Station, about fifty miles northeast of Las Vegas, has dumped its combustion waste into uncovered "ponds" beside the Moapa Band of

Paiutes Reservation. Tribal members believe that the coal ash – which contains mercury, arsenic, selenium, and other toxins and blows into their village in dust storms – has caused asthma attacks, cancer, heart disease, and many premature deaths among the 200 residents there.[9]

Coal ash is like volcanic ash that the Romans used to build the structures such as the Colosseum and aqueducts. Coal ash has properties that can strengthen concrete. "Between 1966 and 2017, coal-mining companies and utilities dumped more than 4 billion tons of coal ash across the United States."[10] Because of the devastating impact of the pollution, the Reid Gardner station has been closed and the plant demolished.[11] The Moapa Southern Paiute Solar Project is a 250-megawatt photovoltaic power plant. This power plant is the first utility-scale solar project located on North American tribal lands in the United States.[12]

Innovation Ecosystem

Ecosystems can be externally or internally focused. Systems and subsystems within both the external and internal ecosystems are interdependent. For example, Amazon announced the introduction of Fire, its first entry into the burgeoning smartphone market. Amazon exists and interacts in multiple external ecosystems, including generic external systems such as retail and online shopping, and industry systems such as electronics, books, and more. It also operates within multiple internal ecosystems, including research and development, operations, and others. The product, Fire, represented the latest systems thinking in terms of features and capabilities, including an innovative three-dimensional feature called Dynamic Perspective, which is enabled by technology recently made available and applied in a unique, innovative way. Indeed, Amazon's entry into the smartphone "ecosystem" is designed to attract customers to a digital ecosystem that itself includes tens of thousands of apps, books, games, movies, and more. By looking at the entire ecosystem, dependencies, interactions, and synergies that can affect innovation and entrepreneurship can be examined and assessed to optimize a positive effect and eliminate negative aspects.

An organization may have an internal ecosystem where they develop innovative solutions of all types and degrees independent of other firms. Inevitably, however, the organization is also part of external ecosystems that create relationships and rely on the interconnectedness of multiple players. These ecosystem partners all need to be coordinated to support the customer promise.

Ecosystem Importance

We live in an interdependent world, bound together by the global exchange of goods, services, capital, people, data, and ideas. These flows have facilitated the construction of global value chains, contributing to a more prosperous world. Despite the turbulence of our times, these connections have demonstrated remarkable resilience, underscoring the deep interconnectivity of our world. While no region is entirely self-sufficient, the challenge lies in leveraging the advantages of this interconnectivity while mitigating the risks and drawbacks of dependency, especially when products are concentrated in their places of origin.[13]

The single largest economic transformation in the history of the planet is now underway. "For ten thousand years, everything – the whole economy – was organized across traditional industry lines, and now it's breaking up. It's getting reorganized across customer needs."[14]

The borders between traditional economic sectors are evolving: construction, real estate, information technology, automotive manufacturing, energy financial services, and healthcare.[15] Businesses are organizing into new, more dynamic configurations centered not on the things that have always been done but on people's needs. Networks of ecosystems across different sectors are driving the transformation.[16] Ecosystems companies include Apple, Alphabet, Amazon, Meta, and Microsoft.[17] It is projected that the $4 trillion integrated ecosystem economy is estimated to be expanding to drive $70 to $100 trillion of revenue.[18]

The Triple Challenge: Independence to Interdependence

The triple challenge is to discover ideas that excite and provide value to customers, deliver on those customer expectations, and implement those ideas better than the competition. Firms are learning that to achieve the triple challenge, they need to shift their thinking from independence to interdependence.

Economies are experiencing a trend toward more complexity and interaction. This shift requires that leadership look at innovation as a set of internal and external ecosystems. Organizations that partner and work together to achieve common goals can provide more economic and social value than those working singly.

Although these partnerships and close collaborations have the potential to achieve more value, they also create ecosystem dependencies.[19] For example, there were high expectations set for the product benefits and resulting projected revenue of Pfizer's inhalable insulin drug, Exubera. Inhalable insulin was thought to be better than both syringes and insulin pumps because its use would reduce pain and improve the quality of life of diabetics. Because Pfizer had considerable experience in drug development, manufacturing, marketing, and sales, it appeared that Pfizer did everything right and addressed all the issues that would lead to success.

Before Exubera could be administered to a patient, the FDA required a lung-function test using a device called a spirometer, which was available in general practitioners' offices to test for asthma. This test was not typically done in the offices of endocrinologists. Because the initial rollout of the inhalable insulin was targeted to experienced, specialized endocrinologists, the patient would have to be referred to a general practitioner, lab, or nurse practitioner, and then return to the endocrinologist, requiring up to three visits. The dependency was accentuated because access to endocrinologists is limited by the supply of these specialists, thereby increasing appointment waiting times and the delay of treatment.[20]

Pfizer inadvertently created a dependency on the general practitioner performing the lung-function test, resulting in an inconvenient extra step for patient treatment. Exubera was withdrawn from the market in the third quarter of 2007 because of a lack of acceptance and is considered to be a major pharmaceutical failure.

What can we learn from this failure? As the Value Blueprint outline in Figure 14.2 shows, there are two key takeaways. First, recognition of the key co-dependencies in the value chain is critical. Second, in examining these relationships, the blueprint addresses where potential bottlenecks are likely to appear as well as cause problems in the delivery of the customer value proposition. In the next section, we examine the bottleneck problem and examples of these interrelationships.

The Search for Bottlenecks

Dr. Eliyahu Goldratt, an Israeli physicist, wrote *The Goal*, a story that describes how the fictional character Alex Rogo improved the effectiveness of a factory by applying the theory of constraints. The theory of constraints is based on how to find effective balance in a system by optimizing performance, understanding variability, and eliminating the bottlenecks and constraints.[21]

Goldratt's story describes the transformation of an inefficient manufacturing plant that is losing money and is about to be closed. Alex, the plant manager, goes on a Boy Scout trip with his son. As the boys are marching on a hike, Alex notices that there is one boy, Herbie, who is slowing down

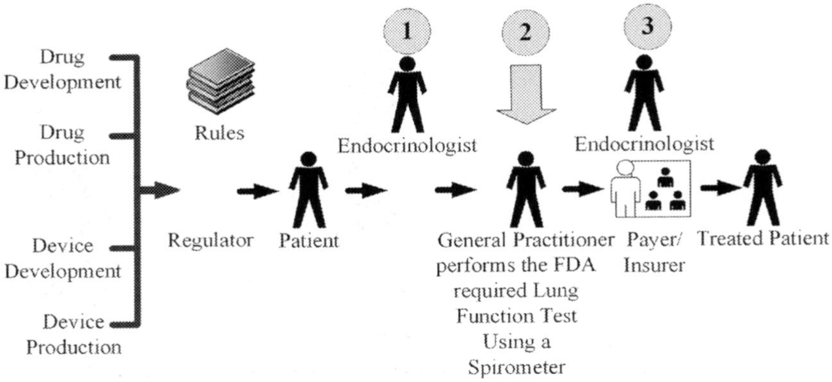

Figure 14.2 Illustration of Value Blueprint Inhalable Insulin Ecosystem

Source: Adapted from Ron Adner, *The Wide Lens: A New Strategy For Innovation*, (New York: Portfolio / Penguin, 2012), 110.

the hike. Herbie is the bottleneck. The solution is to find the "Herbies" in the plant by looking at two issues. To start, they find two bottlenecks: in heat treatment and with a machine tool named the NCX010. The dependent events (a series of events that must take place before another begins) and statistical fluctuations (the length of events and outcomes) are not completely deterministic. A deterministic system is one where there is no randomness and that will produce the same output from a given starting condition or initial state.[22] By focusing on these two issues, Alex, with the help of Jonah, a trained physicist consultant, can improve the overall system flow and identify bottlenecks throughout the plant.

A bottleneck can be removed by adding more capacity. You can find capacity by making sure the machines are never idle, increasing the cycle time on the machine, adding another duplicate machine, outsourcing work to a vendor, inspecting the quality of the parts before the bottleneck (making sure the inputs into the bottleneck are quality parts), and only working on parts that are needed for priority work, as compared to those you are adding to inventory.[23] Once you add more capacity to the bottlenecks, the throughput will increase. As you add more capacity to the initial bottlenecks, though, you will find different bottlenecks.

Apple

One of the keys to managing the ecosystem interrelationships is to build the multiple ecosystem dynamics into the corporate culture from the beginning. Apple and its relentless pursuit of innovative products is an excellent example of systems thinking that has evolved based on both external and internal ecosystem thinking. As we have noted, ecosystems thinking is a holistic approach that focuses on the relationships of the parts within a whole entity in a way that expands the total perspective.

Apple has created an ecosystem that is conceptually shown in Figure 14.3. There is more to Apple products than their aesthetics. Their appearance suggests that they are connected as one "family" of products. Commercial services allow music and other entertainment to be purchased with ease in an ever evolving "cloud" that represents designers' dreams of connectivity. "Each app allows consumers to 'personalize' their access to Apple and interaction with other users."[24] Apple represents a company ecosystem, tied to multiple external ecosystems, as well as multiple synergistic internal ecosystems, such as its innovative product ecosystem that has grown from the Macintosh to the iPod, iPhone, iMac, Apple Watch, iCloud, Mac Pro, Mac Studio, Vision Pro headset, and beyond.

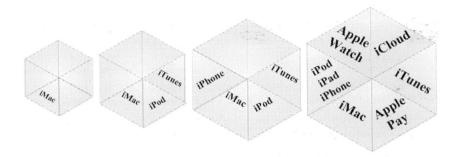

Figure 14.3 Illustration of Apple's Ecosystem

Planes, Trains, and Automobiles

Throughout history there have been interesting and informative examples of the formation, development, and dynamics of innovation ecosystems – some forming and performing in quite unpredictable ways. All illustrate the intricacies, interrelationships, and interdependencies of innovation ecosystems. Three such examples include the development and deployment of the P-51 Mustang during WWII, innovating lubricating advances for locomotives, and the role of modern global positioning systems (GPS) for truckers in Finland.

The P-51 Fighter Plane

In contrast to Apple, during World War II the fighter planes had to be built very quickly. While an overarching external ecosystem involving governments, politics, global conflict, and industry existed, many of the planes were not built from a systems perspective. The engines, airframes, and weapon systems were designed and built separately. It was more by coincidence than system design that one plane, the P-51, was destined to become more effective over the others.[25]

The ultimate success of a complex system is often an integration of technology and people. During World War II, it would be the highly motivated Tuskegee Airmen who would become famous for flying those agile P-51s that escorted bombers over Europe. For those now celebrated Tuskegee Airmen, it was their talent, execution, and the serendipitous P-51 plane acting in concert that enabled them to overcome two wars – the Axis powers on the warfront and discrimination on the home front.[26]

The Real McCoy

Inventor and entrepreneur Elijah McCoy's impact on today's modern economic ecosystem cannot be overestimated and illustrates how multiple ecosystem paths intersect in ways that are not always fully seen at the time. Born in 1844 in Canada, his parents were fugitive slaves who escaped from Kentucky in the US north to Canada via the aptly named "underground railroad," formed by abolitionists seeking to address the evils of slavery. His innovation and entrepreneurship journey would take him from Kentucky, to Canada, to Scotland, and back to Ypsilanti, Michigan, returning in the 1860s, as a highly trained, certified mechanical engineer.

Determined to overcome the prejudice of the day, he attacked the problem of lubricating machinery in general and locomotive engines in particular. His first patent, in 1872, for an automatic lubricator for oiling steam engines, would be the first of nearly 60 patents he would file over his lifetime. Products produced by the Elijah Manufacturing Company were high quality and highly sought after, resulting in imitation products, leading to the legacy of buyers seeking out "the real McCoy." While the origins of the iconic phrase may be attributed to multiple sources, there is no question, Elijah was indeed the real McCoy.[27]

Driving Direction(s)

The role of modern global positioning systems (GPS) has evolved over time, encompassing ecosystems in space, land, sea, and air. Its global impact can be seen everywhere on smartphones that speak directly to the interconnectedness of ecosystems on multiple planes. Nowhere can this be seen more clearly than in Finland where it is estimated that 40% of transport companies consist of one person and one truck providing delivery of essential goods around the clock. Modern technology enables companies to aggregate and update voluminous transport industry data, but often it was not available or actionable.

The problem was compounded by the fact that some legacy systems did not talk to other systems and timely and useful data were not always available while on the road. Attacking the problem head on, Janne Lausvaara, founder of ESRI start-up partner Tietorahti Oy, created a map-based mobile app that empowers drivers to customize information to their needs. Collecting data from multiple ecosystem partners was challenging but aptly illustrates the power of ecosystem interdependencies and connections to solve an overwhelming problem with a significant impact.[28]

Black Swans: Innovation Risk

A black swan is a metaphor for a significant unexpected event. The name "black swan" is based on the notion that black swans are rare. Black swan theory is a useful way to view risk where the event is a surprise to the observer, has a major effect, and is rationalized by hindsight. The black swan theory is not an attempt to predict a black swan or surprise event, but to build robustness against negative events that occur and be able to exploit positive ones.[29] In the discipline of innovation, how do you prepare for the possibility of black swan events? There are two ecosystem risks that can affect an innovation: co-innovation risk and adoption chain risk.[30]

Co-Innovation Risk

Have your partners delivered the co-innovations that are necessary for your innovation to be successful? Smartphone retailers, such as Apple App Store, Google Play, BlackBerry World, Windows Phone Store, and Amazon Appstore, depend on outside developers to provide apps for their devices. Apple is dependent on semiconductor manufacturers, shipping firms to deliver their products to customers in a secure and timely manner, wireless service providers for their smartphones, and musicians for all their music. Apple, so far, has been able to successfully manage the co-innovation of its partners.

Nokia's 3G Mobile Phone: The Burning Platform

Nokia had a history of building successful mobile phones. Their strategy at the time was to use 3G to encourage their existing customers to switch to new phones and related service. Nokia framed the 3G as a mobile lifestyle experience that went far beyond a better cell phone handset. Their 3G vision depended on the delivery of related technologies from the partners that they undermanaged. Nokia's mistake was their blindness to the fact that their success depended on a variety of complementary digital products and services to enable their 3G vision. Their focus solely on their core competency, the handset device business, and not on the entire ecosystem caused them to create a burning platform.[31]

Nokia's co-innovation risk is shown in Figure 14.4. The Nokia 3G phone was not successful because Nokia was dependent on complementary and essential digital products and services that were not in place when needed. Nokia failed to manage the co-innovations of their partners.

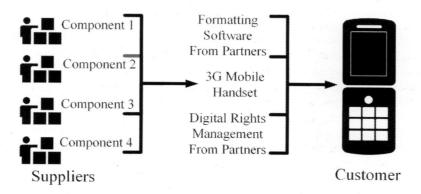

Figure 14.4 Illustration of Nokia's Co-Innovation Risk

Source: Adapted from Ron Adner, *The Wide Lens: A New Strategy For Innovation*, (New York: Portfolio / Penguin, 2012), 46.

On February 11, 2011, Nokia CEO Stephen Elop distributed his "Burning Platform" memorandum, which included the following:

> The battle of devices has now become a war of ecosystems, where ecosystems include not only the hardware and software of the device, but developers, applications, ecommerce, advertising, search, social applications, location-based services, unified communications and many other things. Our competitors aren't taking our market share with devices; they are taking our market share with an entire ecosystem. This means we're going to have to decide how we either build, catalyze or join an ecosystem.[32]

Elop's solution was to form an alliance with Microsoft and transition to the Windows phone operating system.

Adoption Chain Risk

Have your partners adapted your innovation so that a complete solution is available to customers? The Michelin run-flat tire product failed because the tire service centers did not adopt the entire run-flat tire solution in a timely manner.

Michelin Man

The bias automobile tire was manufactured using multiple overlapping rubber plies, in which the tread (crown) and sidewalls are interdependent. This design results in a tire that is less flexible and more sensitive to overheating. Michelin introduced the radial tire, designed so that the tread (crown) and sidewall were independent, resulting in better flexibility and performance.[33] In the

1990s, with the success of the Michelin radial tire product, the company grew into the largest tire company in the world.[34]

In 1998, Michelin introduced the run-flat tire, designed to operate even if the tire was punctured. The run-flat tire was safer than the bias and radial tires because it prevented the effects of blowouts, flats, and underinflated tires. This would also create space in the vehicle since the spare tire would no longer be needed. The run-flat design required that the wheel and tire be combined into an assembly, instead of using independent parts provided by separate suppliers. The assembly design of the entire wheel added a layer of complexity to the product and necessitated that Michelin become a system integrator.

Michelin formed a partnership with Goodyear, licensed the run-flat technology with tire manufacturers, and signed-up automobile manufacturers, such as Mercedes, Cadillac, Renault, Audi, Rolls-Royce, and Honda. Michelin met the triple challenge, except for one thing: the service network. Because of the tire design, the service centers needed new equipment and technician certification training to perform service and repairs. Customer complaints about the lack of adequate service and repair facilities resulted in Michelin discontinuing the product in 2007.[35]

Michelin did not fully understand or consider the impact that the run-flat tire design would have on the tire ecosystem. The traditional path to rolling-out tire innovations was through the tire replacement market, rather than through the new vehicle market. Innovations in the new vehicle market are often provided as *options* on new vehicles rather than as required components. But in this case, the assembly design for the run-flat tires became a required component in a new vehicle.

The run-flat tire was introduced through new vehicle sales, resulting in a small number of run-flat tires on the road. The lack of sufficient run-flat tire volumes prevented tire service centers from investing in the equipment and training to service the new design. The lack of run-flat customer service caused consumers to complain, resulting in a failure in the value proposition, the promise to the customer.

The run-flat tire service centers were a dependency within the innovation ecosystem. Because this dependency was not fulfilled, it became a critical resource that affected the value proposition and caused Michelin to fail.[36] The market share for run-flat tires remains low, within the US it is below 1%. The run-flat tires are double the cost of other comparable tires. Their value is limited because they cannot run flat if the sidewall is damaged, a common cause of a flat, and their speed and range are limited.[37]

The tire-pressure monitoring-system technology was designed to reduce blowouts and improve vehicle safety by preventing vehicular accidents and thereby injuries and deaths. A tire-pressure-monitoring system (TPMS) is independent of the tire design. Because one could achieve a safety advantage with any tire design and TPMS, the relative interest in run-flat tires decreased, further accentuating the demise of run-flat tires. Today, TPMSs are now required in all new passenger vehicles.[38] Michelin's value blueprint and adoption chain risk is shown in Figure 14.5.

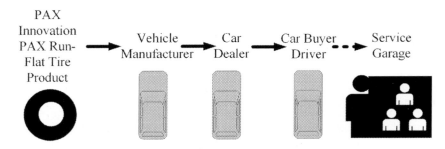

Figure 14.5 Illustration of Michelin's Adoption Chain Risk

Source: Adapted from Ron Adner, *The Wide Lens: A New Strategy For Innovation*, (New York: Portfolio / Penguin, 2012), 28.

Figure 14.6 is a cause-and-effect illustration that summarizes both the co-innovation and adoption chain risks.

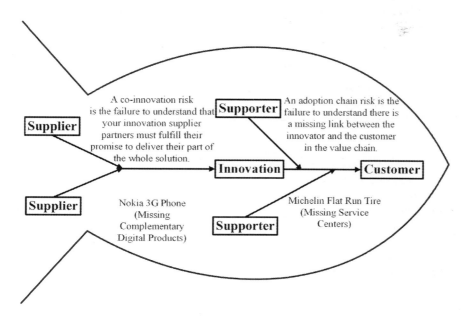

Figure 14.6 Illustration of Innovation Risks

Source: Ron Adner and Rahul Kapoor, "Value Creation in Innovation Ecosystems," *Strategic Management Journal*, 31:3, (2010): 309.

Monsanto

Monsanto was the world's largest seed and weed company due to their pairing of engineered seeds and herbicides to produce herbicide-resistant soybeans, corn, and other gene-modified products.[39]

> A genetically modified organism (GMO) is any organism whose genetic material has been altered using genetic engineering techniques. The exact definition of a genetically modified organism and what constitutes genetic engineering varies, with the most common being an organism altered in a way that "does not occur naturally by mating and/or natural recombination."[40]

GMOs are a sensitive issue to some consumers because there are differing perspectives on their impact on health.

Monsanto's production of genetically modified products is an example of adoption chain risk.[41] The adoption chain for genetically modified organisms includes governments, regulatory boards, farmers, food manufacturers, restaurants, and consumers of products that use GMO ingredients.

In the United States, there are three agencies that have responsibilities for biotechnology.

> The U.S. Government agencies responsible for oversight of the products of agricultural modern biotechnology are the USDA's Animal and Plant Health Inspection Service (USDA-APHIS), the U.S. Environmental Protection Agency (EPA), and the Department of Health and Human Services' Food and Drug Administration (FDA).

Within USDA, the Animal and Plant Health Inspection Service (APHIS) is responsible for protecting agriculture from pests and diseases. Under the Plant Protection Act, USDA-APHIS has regulatory oversight over products of modern biotechnology that could pose such a risk.

The EPA through a registration process regulates the sale, distribution, and use of pesticides to protect health, and the environment, regardless of how the pesticide was made or its mode of action. This includes regulation of those pesticides that are produced by an organism through techniques of modern biotechnology.

The FDA is responsible for ensuring the safety and proper labeling of all plant-derived food and feed, including those developed through genetic engineering. All food and feed, whether imported or domestic and whether derived from crops modified by conventional breeding techniques or by genetic engineering techniques, must meet the same rigorous safety standards.[42]

Outside of the United States, other countries' regulatory boards must approve Monsanto's seed and weed products in their respective countries. Adoption chain risk occurs because it is plausible that regulators may not sanction Monsanto's GMO products, food manufacturers and restaurants may stop using them, and/or consumers may stop purchasing them.

Monsanto uses licensing as an element of their strategy, and this licensing of innovations can also be an adoption chain risk. For example, Monsanto broadly licensed germplasm and its trait innovations so farmers and partners could collectively reach the fullest potential. After acquiring Monsanto, Bayer continued a focus on product stewardship.[43]

Even though Bayer was aware of a controversy that alleged Roundup caused cancer, in 2018 Bayer acquired Monsanto, the manufacturer of Roundup, for $63 billion. Bayer based their decision on a lack of scientific evidence establishing Roundup's risks. The first court trial, two months after the takeover, resulted in $289 million in damages in favor of the plaintiff. It was concluded that Monsanto's glyphosate-based weed killers, including the flagship Roundup brand, were the cause of a former school groundskeeper's cancer. Bayer, like Monsanto before it, insisted the popular herbicide was safe.[44]

Acquisitions can add value for an organization, but they can introduce substantial innovation risk. In 2020, with mounting lawsuits increasing to 18,400, Bayer agreed to make a payment of as much as $10.9 billion to resolve about three-quarters of the existing Roundup lawsuits and address potential future ones in an attempt to bring its herbicide woes to a close.[45]

Cost and Benefits of Innovation

Cost-benefit analysis is always instructive when it comes to assessing the strengths, weaknesses, costs, and ultimate trade-offs of pursuing a course of action. It is especially illuminating when it comes to costs and trade-offs that are not immediately apparent when considering the benefits. For example, adopting new technology that enables secure credit card access might be beneficial to increasing sales, but there will be costs associated with equipment, training, upgrades, and more.

Traditionally, cost-benefit analysis looks at internal aspects of the value chain in relation to the trade-offs. In Ron Adner's book, *The Wide Lens: A New Strategy for Innovation*, he extends the scope and contrasts the innovator and customer perspectives on costs and benefits.[46] He notes that the innovator's perspective on benefits is different from the customer's perspective. Innovators view benefits in absolute terms, based on what the solution provides. Customers, on the other hand, tend to view benefits in relative terms compared to what alternatives are available to them.

The innovator's perspective on the ultimate price to the consumer is quite different from the customer's perspective. The innovator views the price they charge as a tactic based on their development, production, and delivery costs, as well as desired profit. The customer views their *cost* as the price charged by the retailer plus all the other costs for them to use the solution, such as training and upgrades. For example, if you switch from the iPhone N to the iPhone N+1, your total purchase price will include not only the price of the device, but also a new case (the size of the device is smaller or larger), cell phone wireless communication plan, and more resource capability.

The customer will purchase the solution if the relative real or perceived benefits of the solution exceed the total solution price. For those organizations that did not upgrade from Office 20NN to Office 20NN+1, for example, the relative solution benefits were less than the total solution cost that they would have incurred to transition.[47]

Figure 14.7 shows the benefits and costs from the innovator and customer perspective.

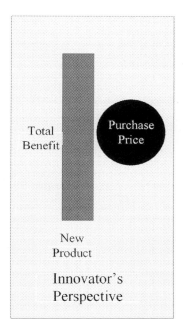 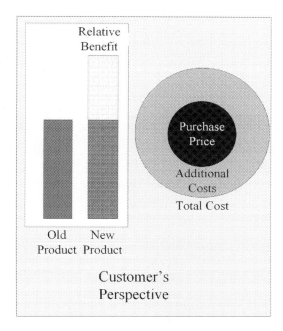

Figure 14.7 Illustration of Benefits and Cost from the Innovator and Customer Perspective

Source: Adapted from Ron Adner, *The Wide Lens: A New Strategy For Innovation*, (New York: Portfolio / Penguin, 2012), 57.

The Value Blueprint

In general terms, the value proposition for a good and/or service is the promise to deliver on the real and/or perceived benefits to the customer. Adner encompasses this in the value blueprint, a visual representation of how the ecosystem interacts to fulfill the value proposition. Each part of a multipart ecosystem is organized into a map of successor and predecessor relationships that depicts the dependencies. A dependency that is not resolved becomes a bottleneck preventing progress.

Each part of the ecosystem has a responsible actor (person or organization) who is accountable for delivering their part of the promise to the customer. It is the job of the actor to complete their part of the ecosystem. The actors will not participate unless they feel that they are receiving a reward for their efforts. It is only when all the parts of the ecosystem are functioning together that the promise to the customer can be delivered.

As we saw earlier in this book, compared to other developed nations, the US healthcare industry has a challenging history of patient safety, costs, errors, and undesirable outcomes. For example, healthcare in general has been a follower in adopting information technology, especially electronic health record solutions that have the potential to improve efficiency and eliminate errors.

The value blueprint in Figure 14.8 outlines the process. While electronic health record (EHR) systems have been initially slow to progress in their implementation, they are gaining momentum. To implement an EHR system, all the steps of the ecosystem need to work together to achieve the value proposition. The opportunity cost is significant for physicians as they transition to an EHR system because of the steep learning curve, the amount of effort required entering the patient information, and the reluctance to sacrifice patient eye contact. Physicians became the bottleneck when many were reluctant to adopt EHR systems. In-person patient contact can be sacrificed if the physician spends an inordinate amount of their patient contact time looking at the EHR system user interface on the computer device rather than at the patient. Physicians would prefer learning about the latest medical advancements rather than being data entry clerks.[48]

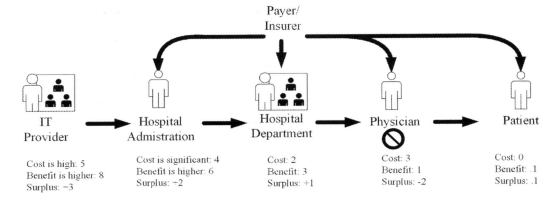

Figure 14.8 Illustration of Electronic Health Records Value Blueprint

Source: Adapted from Ron Adner, *The Wide Lens: A New Strategy For Innovation,* (New York: Portfolio / Penguin, 2012), 123–132.

The Leadership Prism

Leadership competencies are essential to the identification, transformation, and implementation of innovation and entrepreneurship. The leadership prism is a visual representation that provides clarification on who is the leader and who are the followers in an ecosystem. Adner uses the leadership prism to describe the electronic health records ecosystem.[49]

The five actors – IT provider, hospital administration, hospital department, physician, and patient – were not able to lead the drive toward electronic health administration. A set of new actors emerged who looked at patients as groups rather than as individuals. The new actors were the Veterans Health Administration; large healthcare systems, such as Geisinger, Intermountain, and Kaiser Permanente; and the US government. Federal laws provided funding to hospitals and physicians to incentivize EHR adoption.[50]

The leadership prism shown in Figure 14.9 is a visualization that identifies key actors in the Electronic Healthcare Records ecosystem. The general purpose of the leadership prism is to clarify who is the leader and who are the followers.[51] What became clear in the healthcare example was that large aggregators were the only ones who could provide the leadership and resources required to break through the bottleneck.

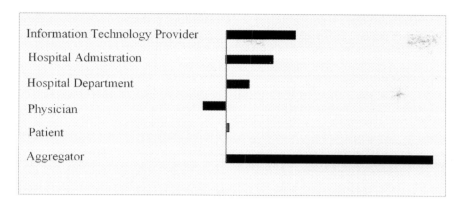

Figure 14.9 Illustration of Electronic Health Records Leadership Prism
Source: Adapted from Ron Adner, *The Wide Lens: A New Strategy For Innovation*, (New York: Portfolio / Penguin, 2012), 129.

Co-Innovation Dependencies Affect First Mover Advantage

When you are competing in an ecosystem, it is important to understand if your partners can help or hinder your success. Being first to market can provide an advantage, but it depends on the characteristics of the innovative solution within the ecosystem. There are two variables to consider: the execution difficulty and the extent of co-innovation dependency. Execution difficulty is the amount of effort required for a firm to build and market the innovative solution. Co-innovation dependency is the extent to which your rollout depends on whether other innovative solutions are needed at the time your innovation is available.[52]

When there is a low execution challenge and low co-innovation challenge, early movers have a distinct advantage, and the value proposition can be fulfilled. Akio Morita and his team at Sony created a set of new market disruptive innovations between 1950 and 1982, including the Sony battery-powered transistor radio and the Sony Walkman stereo cassette player.[53] The first mover advantage that is easy to duplicate may be only temporary, though, because it opens up opportunities for the competition.

When there is a high execution challenge and a low co-innovation challenge, early movers have a considerable advantage. This is because difficulty in implementing an innovative solution becomes a barrier for the competition. The more difficult the execution for the innovative solution, the more likely the competition can be minimized. For example, there is the potential for less competition and high rewards for complex operating system software, such as Microsoft Windows and Apple's Mac OS, because they are so hard to duplicate.

The pioneer start-up has minimal advantage when you have low execution and a high set of co-innovation challenges. The ecosystem dynamics result in the value proposition being unfulfilled, because the first firm to overcome its execution challenge needs to wait for others. Being first does not matter if the co-innovations are not in place at the right time. For example, SaeHan's MPMan, the world's first portable digital audio player was available in 1998. Being first is not useful if you are too early. It stalled because of the lack of availability of MP3 digital audio and the slow speed of the Internet for downloading music.[54] Nokia in 3G was too early and failed.[55] Sony in e-books was too early and succumbed to the same fate.[56] Apple launched a proprietary solution with the combination of the iPod and iTunes in 2001, when all the co-innovations needed were in place for an extremely successful product launch.

When co-innovation and execution challenges are both high at the time of entry, the advantage of the first mover will depend on which challenge is resolved first. If you can solve the co-innovation challenge, the solution shifts to high execution and low co-innovation, a desirable place. If you solve the execution challenge, the solution shifts to low execution and high co-innovation, an undesirable place to be because of the timing.

The relationship between the execution challenge and the co-innovation dependency is shown in Figure 14.10.

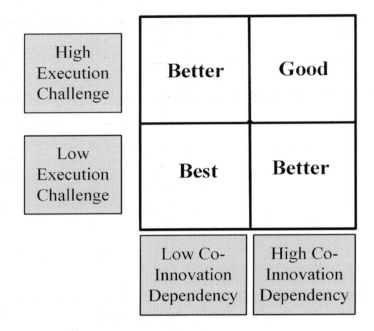

Figure 14.10 Illustration of the First Mover Matrix

Source: Adapted from Ron Adner, *The Wide Lens: A New Strategy For Innovation*, (New York: Portfolio / Penguin, 2012), 149.

The Ecosystem Continuum

As noted throughout this book, innovation and entrepreneurship are informed by and unfold along multiple continuums that exist in the innovation and entrepreneurship competency framework. External and internal ecosystems can be viewed along just such a continuum. A central challenge of innovation and entrepreneurship is to envision what currently does not exist or what is next.

Figure 14.11 illustrates the four major aspects of the ecosystem continuum from *what was* (interestingly often the result of earlier innovation and entrepreneurship) to *what is next* (itself driven by the constant discovery of innovative ideas).

Integrative Thinking: Ecosystems and Strategy

The combining of ecosystem and strategic thinking enables the thought leader to build a better model for the future. Martin suggested that when you are confronted with opposing models, you

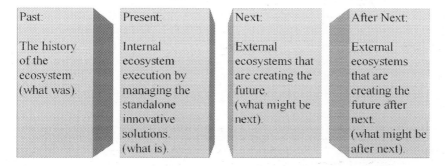

Figure 14.11 Illustration of the Integrative Ecosystem Evolution

Source: Adapted from Ron Adner, *The Wide Lens: What Successful Innovators See That Others Miss*, (New York: Portfolio / Penguin, 2012); and Vijay Govindarajan, "Video Collection," accessed February 2, 2015, http://www.tuck.dartmouth.edu/people/vg/news/video

can integrate your thinking by choosing the exemplary aspects of each model to create a new model rather than being forced to choose one model over another.[57]

An ecosystem can be viewed from a time-sequenced integrative perspective. Martin's concept of integrative thinking can be used to combine strategic thinking in parallel form with ecosystem thinking through the window of time. Integrative thinking can be used to superimpose ecosystem and strategic thinking together into four time periods: the past ecosystem, the present ecosystem, the future ecosystem, and the creation of the bridge to the future after next ecosystem. This interactive perspective seeks to optimize integrative thinking through applying past learning to improve and build current and future ecosystems, both internal and external.

- Applying learnings from your former ecosystems
- Improving your current internal ecosystems composed of standalone innovation solutions
- Building of external ecosystems through partnerships (suppliers and supporters)
- Building a bridge from the next external ecosystem to the external ecosystem after next

Innovation and Entrepreneurship Ecosystems

While the focus has been on the internal and external ecosystems specifically surrounding the nexus of nature, innovation, and industry, it is also interesting to note that over the past 20 years, there has been an increase in start-up ecosystems in cities and countries around the world. These start-up ecosystems are designed to foster innovation and entrepreneurship through identifying start-up resources (e.g., funding, universities, counseling) and support mechanisms (incubators, mentors, training), while often providing incubation facilities to promote local and regional economic development. For example, East London Tech City was formed via local and national government agencies to encourage the creation of a cluster of tech start-ups on par with California's Silicon Valley. From Los Angeles to New York; Melbourne, Australia; Toronto, Canada; Santiago, Chile; Paris, France; Berlin, Germany; Moscow, Russia; Singapore; and more, countries and cities are recognizing the value of having vibrant start-up ecosystems.

An Innovation and Entrepreneurship Ecosystem

An ecosystem for promoting innovation and entrepreneurship can be designed to provide services, resources, and coordination of key areas that include incubators; accelerators; university research and innovation programs; local and outside funders; regional support; venture development; entrepreneurship support groups; local, state, regional, and national government resources; and more. Within each of these overarching areas, multiple participants cooperate and network to provide a wide array of resources, services, and funding, which come together to form a fully functioning ecosystem.

The progress and interconnectedness of a model entrepreneurship ecosystem in the Greater Cincinnati and Northern Kentucky region is summarized in Figure 14.12.

Figure 14.12 Illustration of the Entrepreneur Ecosystems

Source: Acknowledgement Cintrifuse https://www.cintrifuse.com/wp-content/uploads/2014/07/GreaterCincinnatiEntrepreneurialEcosystem.pdf

Leading the formation and development of the Greater Cincinnati and Northern Kentucky Entrepreneurship Ecosystem is Cintrifuse. The mission of Cincinnati-based Cintrifuse is to lead and accelerate the development of a disruptive, tech-based innovation ecosystem to stimulate the economy and engage the community. Cintrifuse's efforts are designed to create jobs, attract talent and investment, and facilitate innovation in a wide range of start-ups and businesses. Its vision is to provide leadership as the principal start-up hub in the Midwest and among the top innovation hubs in the nation.[58] Cintrifuse provides resources for high-growth, technology-based start-ups with tools and services such as office space, specialized workshops, curated venture building services, and an active network of members. Cintrifuse uses a three-part model:

1. Build a community of winning entrepreneurs. Cintrifuse collaborates with entrepreneurs to start up new ventures and to connect them with global industry-investors.
2. Expand a venture fund and a national coalition of investors. The Cintrifuse Syndicate Fund invests in early-scale venture capital firms focusing on information technology, human capital, digital health, media, and marketing. Cintrifuse offers a venture fund to access innovative technologies, generate strong financial returns, and create investment pools for entrepreneurs. The Cintrifuse Syndicate Fund provides exposure to a network of over six hundred venture capital fund managers and thousands of start-ups, driving access to the best emerging technologies.[59]
3. Grow partnerships with Fortune 500 corporations. Cintrifuse assists the largest corporations in the region to discover the innovations and innovators.

Cintrifuse's mission is unique in the Greater Cincinnati Northern Kentucky Entrepreneurship Ecosystem in that it operates like an accelerator fostering start-up processes but does not invest directly. Rather, it has created and operates more as a "fund of funds." It is worth noting the distinction between an incubator and an accelerator and the role of each in an entrepreneurship and innovation ecosystem, as each has evolved over time often with overlapping missions. In general, an incubator is an organization that helps new and start-up companies to develop by providing services such as training and office space.[60] An accelerator, on the other hand, is an organization that provides the functions of an incubator but limits the amount of time of direct engagement.[61] For example, the functions of an accelerator might include:

1. The application process is open to anyone, but highly competitive. Start-ups are accepted and supported in cohort classes.
2. A seed investment in the start-ups is usually made in exchange for equity.
3. The focus is on small teams, not on individual founders. A single person is insufficient to manage all the work associated with a start-up.
4. The start-ups must "graduate" by a given deadline, typically after three months. During this time, they receive intensive mentoring and training.
5. Accelerators end their programs with a "Demo Day" where the start-ups present to investors.

For example, the Brandery is a nationally ranked accelerator, founded in Cincinnati, Ohio, in 2010, that offers a program focused on turning ideas into successful, brand-driven start-ups.[62] The Brandery is an example of the synergy that an innovation and entrepreneurship ecosystem can add to the economic and social vibrancy of a region. The start-ups are paired with world-class creative agencies with expertise in branding, marketing, and design and have access to some of the biggest companies in the world, including Procter & Gamble and Kroger.[63] The Brandery claims to have created over 3,000 jobs that benefit the region. The Brandery targets investment in five companies per program and provides the following terms:[64]

1. $20,000 cash investment in exchange for 6–7% common stock equity
2. $80,000 of guaranteed follow-on capital from the Brandery (uncapped convertible note)
3. Access to staff interns (development, design, marketing, social media, journalism, business development, sales and more)

4. $1M+ in deals and benefits from vendors like SoftLayer, Rackspace, Amazon, PayPal, Zendesk, and Microsoft
5. Support from the Brandery team and network of alumni and mentors

The program culminates in "Demo Day," where the start-ups can showcase their ventures to an audience of potential investors, future employees, and others. Thirty-seven percent of the Brandery alumni have raised more than $1M in follow-on financing or have been acquired and 61% of the Brandery alumni have raised more than $250K in follow-on financing or have been acquired.[65]

McKinsey & Company, through its Center for Government (Global), identified two key bottlenecks for cities in the formation and success of start-up ecosystems: keeping pace with the rapid change in the start-up environment and managing multiple stakeholders, sometimes with competing interests.

> The ability to keep pace with the start-up environment. The start-up world is volatile; investors and founders, and their needs and activities, change rapidly. Policy makers cannot pick winners in such an environment. Instead, they should focus on enabling structures that can address more fundamental requirements.
>   The ability to succeed in a multi stakeholder environment. When starting initiatives to spur innovation, there are many competing interests: Stakeholders from the private sector, such as venture capitalists, corporations, and start-ups; diverse levels of governments; and universities and research institutes. Bringing together and managing those stakeholders and interests are essential to successful implementation.[66]

Because start-up failure can be high in an entrepreneurship ecosystem, start-ups can improve their likelihood of success by using clearly defined metrics and red flags. The distinct phases of ecosystem development require quite different managerial focal points and explicitly need to adopt suitable metrics as needed. If the ecosystem is performing weakly on one or more metrics or experiencing red flags, the underlying drivers should be identified to prevent future dysfunction.

> In the *launch* phase, the focus should be on developing a strong value proposition for all ecosystem participants (the orchestrator, partners, and customers) and on finding the right initial design. After the ecosystem is established, it enters the *scale* phase, in which the key focus is to increase the number and intensity of interactions in the ecosystem and to decrease the unit cost of each interaction. An ecosystem that has successfully scaled enters the *maturity* phase, in which growth slows and focus turns to bolstering customer and partner loyalty, and on erecting barriers to entry by competitors. Once a defensible position is attained, the ecosystem enters the *evolution* phase, in which the focus shifts to expanding the offering and innovating continuously.[67]

While Silicon Valley in California and Boston's Route 128 in Massachusetts are often considered the genesis of start-up ecosystems, a 2012 report by Telefonica clearly suggests that start-up ecosystems around the world are growing. The Telefonica report collected data from over 50,000 start-ups around the world to identify eight components in its Global Start-Up Ecosystem Index: start-up output, funding, company performance, mindset (focus on the founder's vision, resilience, risk, work ethic, overcome obstacles), trendsetter (how quickly the start-up ecosystem adopts new technologies, etc.), support, talent, and differentiation (using Silicon Valley as the benchmark).[68] Telefonica's deep dive into the top start-up ecosystems suggests that innovators and entrepreneurs are not operating in isolation, that they can reach out to multiple agents to seek assistance, and that they are part of a robust resurgence in what is next, a global start-up revolution.

Ecosystems: Sustainability

As will be seen in more detail in Chapter 19, "Sustainability," the concept of sustainability provides an interesting lens through which innovation and entrepreneurship in general, and natural ecosystems can be viewed. In an economic, managerial, and environmental view, sustainability is the oversight for managing our present resource needs without compromising the ability of future generations to meet their needs while preserving a wider global environment, social systems, and economic structures. Sustainability ensures a viable community or ecosystem in the long view.

We are experiencing a shift in the earth's social, economic, and environment ecosystems. Global growth requires more resources such as energy, water, and space that must be carefully balanced. Creativity, innovation, and entrepreneurship play a key role in addressing today's challenges for a better future. Figure 14.13 presents a framework for understanding and improving the interdependencies of a sustainability ecosystem.

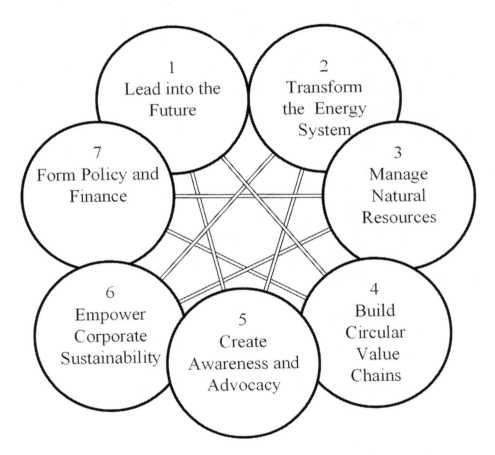

Figure 14.13 Illustration of the Innovation and Entrepreneurship Sustainability Framework

Source: Adapted from Alejandro Sandoval, Bill Lacivita, and, Ignacio Marcos. October 2019. "Transform the whole business, not just parts," McKinsey & Company, accessed January 6, 2020, https://www.mckinsey.com/business-functions/operations/our-insights/transform-the-whole-business-not-just-parts

Summary

In this chapter, we saw how the world of systems and ecosystems, in both nature and business, informs our approach to systems thinking and an innovation and entrepreneurship ecosystem. We also look specifically at adoption chain risk and co-innovation risk. Building on Ron Adner's work in *The Wide Lens: A New Strategy for Innovation*, the costs and benefits of innovation are outlined and his value blueprint, leadership prism, and innovator execution challenge matrix in the context of an innovation and entrepreneurship ecosystem are examined. The ecosystem continuum and a model of a regional innovation and entrepreneurship ecosystem is outlined with its promise, as a systematic approach, to promote and support innovation and entrepreneurship and economic development. Next, we tackle the world of technology accelerators and ecosystems as key components in the rapidly advancing world of innovation and entrepreneurship.

Notes

1. Duccio Cavalieri, "Evolution of Transcriptional Regulatory Networks in Yeast Populations," *Wiley Interdisciplinary Reviews: Systems Biology and Medicine* 2, no. 3 (May–June 2010), 324–335, https://doi.org/10.1002/wsbm.68. PMID: 20836032.
2. Duccio Cavalieri, "Evolution of Transcriptional Regulatory Networks in Yeast Populations," *Wiley Interdisciplinary Reviews: Systems Biology and Medicine* 2, no. 3 (May–June 2010), 324–335, https://doi.org/10.1002/wsbm.68. PMID: 20836032.
3. Rob Quinn and Newser Staff, "Wasps: The Wine Lover's Best Friend?" *Newser*, August 4, 2012, accessed January 15, 2024, www.newser.com/story/151318/wasps-the-wine-lovers-best-friend.html.
4. Ron Adner, *The Wide Lens: A New Strategy for Innovation* (New York: Portfolio/Penguin, 2012).
5. Pierre Loewe and Jennifer Dominiquini, "Overcoming the Barriers to Effective Innovation," *Strategy & Leadership* 34, no. 1 (2006), 24–31.
6. James F. Moore, "Predators and Prey: A New Ecology of Competition," *Harvard Business Review* 71, no. 3 (1993), 76.
7. James F. Moore, "Predators and Prey: A New Ecology of Competition," *Harvard Business Review* 71, no. 3 (1993), 76.
8. "U.S. Green Building Council (USGBC)," accessed August 20, 2021, www.usgbc.org/.
9. Steve Hawk and Ami Vitale, "The Cost of Coal," *Sierra Club Magazine*, November/December 2012, accessed January 15, 2024, http://vault.sierraclub.org/sierra/costofcoal/nevada/default.aspx.
10. Austyn Gaffney, "From the Ashes," March–April 2021, accessed January 15, 2024, https://digital.sierramagazine.org/publication/?m=43145&i=693875&p=26, 28.
11. *Wikipedia*, s.v. "Reid Gardner Generating Station," accessed January 15, 2024, https://en.wikipedia.org/wiki/Reid_Gardner_Generating_Station.
12. *Wikipedia*, s.v. "Moapa Southern Paiute Solar Project," accessed January 15, 2024, https://en.wikipedia.org/wiki/Moapa_Southern_Paiute_Solar_Project.
13. Jeongmin Seong, Olivia White, Jonathan Woetzel, Sven Smit, Tiago Devesa, Michael Birshan, and Hamid Samandari, "Global Flows: The Ties That Bind in an Interconnected World," November 15, 2022, accessed January 18, 2024, www.mckinsey.com/capabilities/strategy-and-corporate-finance/our-insights/global-flows-the-ties-that-bind-in-an-interconnected-world.
14. Venkat Atluri and Miklós Dietz, "Author Talks: Prepare Your Business for the Cross-Sector Ecosystem Economy," January 26, 2023, accessed January 16, 2024, www.mckinsey.com/featured-insights/mckinsey-on-books/author-talks-prepare-your-business-for-the-cross-sector-ecosystem-economy.
15. Venkat Atluri and Miklós Dietz, *The Ecosystem Economy: How to Lead in the New Age of Sectors Without Borders* (Hoboken, NJ: Wiley, 2023), 1.
16. Venkat Atluri and Miklós Dietz, *The Ecosystem Economy: How to Lead in the New Age of Sectors Without Borders* (Hoboken, NJ: Wiley, 2023), 2.
17. Venkat Atluri and Miklós Dietz, *The Ecosystem Economy: How to Lead in the New Age of Sectors Without Borders* (Hoboken, NJ: Wiley, 2023), 7.
18. Venkat Atluri and Miklós Dietz, *The Ecosystem Economy: How to Lead in the New Age of Sectors Without Borders* ((Hoboken, NJ: Wiley, 2023), 8.
19. Ron Adner, *The Wide Lens: A New Strategy for Innovation* (New York: Portfolio/Penguin, 2012), 16.

20. Ron Adner, *The Wide Lens: A New Strategy for Innovation* (New York: Portfolio/Penguin, 2012), 108–112.
21. Eliyahu M. Goldratt, *The Goal* (Great Barrington, MA: North River Press, 1984).
22. *Wikipedia*, s.v. "Deterministic System," accessed January 15, 2024, https://en.wikipedia.org/wiki/Deterministic_system.
23. Eliyahu M. Goldratt, *The Goal* (Great Barrington, MA: North River Press, 1984).
24. Bruce Nussbaum, *Creative Intelligence: Harnessing the Power to Create, Connect, and Inspire* (New York: Harper Business, 2013), 189.
25. *Wikipedia*, s.v. "North American P-51 Mustang," accessed January 18, 2024, https://en.wikipedia.org/wiki/North_American_P-51_Mustang.
26. *Wikipedia*, s.v. "Tuskegee Airmen," accessed January 15, 2024, https://en.wikipedia.org/wiki/Tuskegee_Airmen.
27. Lois Haber, *Black Pioneers of Science and Invention* (San Diego, CA: An Odyssey Book, Harcourt Brace & Company, 1970).
28. ESRI, "In Finland, A Geospatial App Gives Transport Drivers the Information They Need," *ArcNews, ESRI* 43, no. 1 (Winter 2021), 12–13.
29. *Wikipedia*, s.v. "Black Swan Theory," accessed January 15, 2024, http://en.wikipedia.org/wiki/Black_swan_theory.
30. Ron Adner, *The Wide Lens: A New Strategy for Innovation* (New York: Portfolio/Penguin, 2012).
31. Ron Adner, *The Wide Lens: A New Strategy for Innovation* (New York: Portfolio/Penguin, 2012), 38–52.
32. "Full Text: Nokia CEO Stephen Elop's 'Burning Platform' Memo," *The Wall Street Journal*, February 11, 2011, accessed January 15, 2024, http://blogs.wsj.com/tech-europe/2011/02/09/full-text-nokia-ceo-stephen-elops-burning-platform-memo/.
33. "Bias and Radial Technology," *Michelin*, accessed September 17, 2021, www.michelinearthmover.com/eng_ca/Welcome/Tires/Why-choose-MICHELIN/The-technology-of-MICHELIN-R-radial-tires.
34. Ron Adner, *The Wide Lens* (New York: Portfolio/Penguin, 2012), 16.
35. Ron Adner, *The Wide Lens* (New York: Portfolio/Penguin, 2012), 16–31.
36. Ron Adner, *The Wide Lens* (New York: Portfolio/Penguin, 2012), 16–31.
37. *Wikipedia*, s.v. "Run-Flat Tire," accessed January 15, 2024, https://en.wikipedia.org/wiki/Run-flat_tire.
38. Ron Adner, *The Wide Lens* (New York: Portfolio/Penguin, 2012), 30.
39. Jack Kaskey, "Monsanto Will Let Bio-Crop Patents Expire," *Bloomberg Businessweek*, January 21, 2010, accessed January 15, 2024, www.bloomberg.com/news/articles/2010-01-21/monsanto-will-let-bio-crop-patents-expire.
40. *Wikipedia*, s.v. "Genetically Modified Organism," accessed January 15, 2024, http://en.wikipedia.org/wiki/Genetically_modified_organism.
41. Planes, Alex, "Why Is Monsanto the Most Hated Company in the World?" *The Motley Fool*, June 8, 2013, updated October 11, 2018, accessed September 17, 2021, www.fool.com/investing/general/2013/06/08/why-is-monsanto-the-most-hated-company-in-the-worl.aspx.
42. "How the Federal Government Regulates Biotech Plants," accessed September 17, 2021, www.usda.gov/topics/biotechnology/how-federal-government-regulates-biotech-plants.
43. "Farmer and Partner Resouces: Providing the Tools to Grow Together," *Bayer*, accessed September 17, 2021, www.cropscience.bayer.com/who-we-are/farmer-partner-resources.
44. Andrew Marc Noel, "How Monsanto's Roundup Herbicide Went from Bayer Asset to Burden," June 24, 2020, accessed August 20, 2021, www.bloomberg.com/news/articles/2020-06-24/how-monsanto-s-roundup-herbicide-went-from-bayer-asset-to-burden?sref=3u20Kc68.
45. Andrew Marc Noel, "How Monsanto's Roundup Herbicide Went From Bayer Asset to Burden," June 24, 2020, accessed Augsust 20, 2021, www.bloomberg.com/news/articles/2020-06-24/how-monsanto-s-roundup-herbicide-went-from-bayer-asset-to-burden?sref=3u20Kc68.
46. Ron Adner, *The Wide Lens* (New York: Portfolio/Penguin, 2012).
47. Ron Adner, *The Wide Lens* (New York: Portfolio/Penguin, 2012), 56–58.
48. Ron Adner, *The Wide Lens* (New York: Portfolio/Penguin, 2012), 127–127.
49. Ron Adner, *The Wide Lens* (New York: Portfolio/Penguin, 2012), 131.
50. Ron Adner, *The Wide Lens* (New York: Portfolio/Penguin, 2012), 131.
51. Ron Adner, *The Wide Lens* (New York: Portfolio/Penguin, 2012), 118.
52. Ron Adner, *The Wide Lens* (New York: Portfolio/Penguin, 2012), 141–155.
53. Clayton Christensen and Michael E. Raynor, *The Innovator's Solution* (Boston: Harvard Business School Press, 2003), 79.

54. "MPMan- The World's First MP3 Player in Your Pocket," accessed January 15, 2024, https://historictech. com/mpman-and-the-birth-of-the-personalized-playlist/.
55. *Wikipedia*, s.v. "Nokia," accessed January 15, 2024, https://en.wikipedia.org/wiki/Nokia.
56. *Wikipedia*, s.v. "E-book," accessed January 15, 2024, https://en.wikipedia.org/wiki/Ebook.
57. Roger L. Martin, *The Opposable Mind: How Successful Leaders Win Through Integrative Thinking* (Boston: Harvard Business School Press, 2007).
58. Cintrifuse, accessed January 15, 2024, www.cintrifuse.com/about/.
59. Cintrifuse, accessed January 15, 2024, www.cintrifuse.com/how-it-works/syndicate-fund/.
60. Business Incubator, accessed January 15, 2024, https://en.wikipedia.org/wiki/Business_incubator.
61. Startup Accelerator, accessed January 15, 2024, https://en.wikipedia.org/wiki/Startup_accelerator.
62. The Brandery, accessed January 16, 2024, www.brandery.org/.
63. The Brandery, accessed January 16, 2024, www.brandery.org/.
64. The Brandery, accessed January 16, 2024, www.brandery.org/apply.
65. The Brandery, accessed January 16, 2024, www.brandery.org/statistics.
66. Julian Krichherr, Gundbert Scherf, and Katrin Suder, "Creating Growth Clusters: What Role for Local Government?" *McKinsey & Company, McKinsey Center for Government (Global)*, July 2014, accessed January 15, 2024, www.mckinsey.com/industries/public-and-social-sector/our-insights/creating-growth-clusters-what-role-for-local-government.
67. Ulrich Pidun, Martin Reeves, and Edzard Wesselink, "How Healthy Is Your Business Ecosystem?" March 9, 2021, accessed January 15, 2024, https://sloanreview.mit.edu/article/how-healthy-is-your-business-ecosystem/.
68. Bjoern Lasse Herrmann, Max Marmer, Ertan Dogrultan, and Danny Holtschke, "Start-Up Ecosystem Report 2012 Part 1," *Telifonica Digital and Startup Genome*, accessed January 15, 2024, https://media. rbcdn.ru/media/reports/StartupEcosystemReportPart1v1.2.pdf.

15 Technology Accelerators

Nobel Prizes

When research discovers new knowledge, the opportunities for innovation are significantly expanded. Research is the transformation of intellectual capital into knowledge and innovation is the transformation of knowledge into new value. Prizes are often offered to accelerate, as well as provide encouragement and recognition to pursue innovation and entrepreneurship. The awarding of a Nobel Prize is the preeminent example of recognition that marks new pathways for advancement in science and technology.

Alfred Bernhard Nobel was a Swedish chemist, engineer, inventor, businessperson, and philanthropist. Nobel discovered that when nitroglycerine was added to an absorbent inert substance like diatomaceous earth it became safer and more convenient to handle. The mixture was patented as "dynamite" and led to his financial success. Nobel held 355 different patents, dynamite being the most famous. The synthetic element nobelium was named after him. In his last will and testament, he bequeathed most of his estate to establish five Nobel Prizes to be awarded annually without distinction of nationality. The Nobel Prizes are significant awards because they represent innovations of all types.[1]

The first prizes in Chemistry, Literature, Peace, Physics, and Physiology or Medicine were awarded in 1901. Although not one of the original Nobel Prizes, a sixth prize, the Nobel Memorial Prize in Economic Sciences, officially the Sveriges Riksbank Prize in Economic Sciences in Memory of Alfred Nobel, was established in 1968 by a donation from Sweden's central bank, Sveriges Riksbank, to the Nobel Foundation. The sixth award is administered by the Nobel Foundation and is regarded as the Nobel award in Economics.[2]

There is a variation in the countries that received the most Nobel Prizes. The rank order of Nobel Prize recipients is the United States, the United Kingdom, Germany, France, Sweden, Russia/Soviet Union, Switzerland, Japan, Canada, and Austria, respectively.[3] A majority share of Nobel Prizes in the science categories have gone to US institutions. Out of the Nobel laureates that were exclusively affiliated with US institutions, 30% of the Nobel laureates were born abroad.[4]

There have been over 992 Nobel laureates awarded; because the awards for physics, chemistry, and medicine are typically awarded once the achievement has been widely accepted, some candidates do not receive the award because posthumous awards are prohibited. For instance, Daniel Kahneman received the Nobel award, but not his colleague, Amos Tversky, who died at 59. This can result in their achievements not being recognized.[5]

Marie Curie was the first female to receive the Nobel Prize in 1903, and again in 1911, the only one to receive it twice. Marie Curie shared the 1903 Nobel Prize in Physics with her husband, Pierre Curie, and the physicist Henri Becquerel. They developed the theory of radioactivity using techniques she invented for isolating radioactive isotopes. She won the 1911 Nobel Prize in Chemistry for the discovery of two elements, polonium, and radium.[6]

DOI: 10.4324/9781003034308-16

In 2020, the Nobel Prize in Chemistry went to Emmanuelle Charpentier and Jennifer Doudna, for the DNA-editing method known as CRISPR-Cas9 that provides the ability to re-write genes.[7] This discovery can be used to customize genes in microbes, plants, animals, and (potentially when it is ethically appropriate) humans. The CRISPR gene-editing technology is meaningfully significant because of the potential for innovations in medicine and agriculture. It has the capability to engineer plants to address food production, climate change, pests, and diseases.[8]

Technology Accelerators

As the Nobel Prize awards illustrates, one of the critical dimensions of innovation and entre-preneurship is the role of leadership to integrate technology within the venture and/or organiza-tion to accelerate development. Yet despite its importance, leadership and technology are often misaligned. MIT Sloan Management Review and Capgemini Consulting conducted a survey of executives and managers that indicated most CEOs are not providing leadership in the use of digital technology to empower significant improvements for their organizations. The respondents included 1,559 people from 106 countries, representing small and large organizations across the business spectrum.[9]

The survey indicates that most companies lack experience in emerging digital technologies. The results suggest that organizations fall into four digital maturity levels, from the lowest level, Begin-ner companies (65% of respondents), to Conservative (14%), to Fashionista (6%), and finally, to the highest, Digirati (15%).

The results also suggest that there is a high need for digital transformation, but low will to act. Seventy-eight percent of respondents report that digital transformation is critical to their or-ganization's future, while 39% indicate the major obstacle is that there is no urgency or "burning platform." Only 38% of the respondents believe that a digital transformation is a priority or "per-manent fixture" of the leadership.

Despite the lower cost of technology and the abundance of digital and analytics transforma-tions underway across the business landscape, few companies are achieving the results they ex-pect. According to a McKinsey survey, only 14% of the respondents say their efforts have made and sustained performance improvements, and just 3% report complete success at sustaining their change.[10]

McKinsey reports that those who achieve the greatest levels of success in pursuing digital trans-formations follow five practices listed in the following list and illustrated in Figure 15.1.

1. Ruthlessly focus on a clear set of objectives.
2. Be bold when setting the scope.
3. Create an adaptive design.
4. Adopt agile execution approaches and mind-sets.
5. Make leadership and accountability clear.

The Future of Science and Technology

Technology trends are important because each can be used to increase the likelihood of creative disruption. Fifteen of the major trends, summarized in Figure 15.2, have the potential to improve environmental, social, and governance challenges. These trends are expected to have a broad im-pact on innovation and entrepreneurship, on how people live and work, and on industries and economies.[11]

Figure 15.1 Illustration of the Five Best Practices

Source: Adapted from Jonathan Deakin, Laura LaBerge, and Barbara O'Beirne, "Five moves to make during a digital transformation," April 24, 2019, McKinsey and Company, accessed September 15, 2020, https://www.mckinsey.com/business-functions/digital-mckinsey/our-insights/five-moves-to-make-during-a-digital-transformation

1. Applied artificial intelligence	2. Industrializing machine learning	3. Generative artificial intelligence
4. Next-generation software development	5. Trust architectures and digital identity	6. Web3
7. Advanced connectivity	8. Immersive-reality technologies	9. Cloud and edge computing
10. Quantum technologies	11. Future of mobility	12. Future of bioengineering
13. Future of space technologies	14. Electrification and renewables	15. Climate tech beyond electrification and renewables

Figure 15.2 The Future of Science and Technology

Source: Adapted from Michael Chui, Mena Issler, Roger Roberts, and Lareina Yee, "Technology Trends Outlook 2023," July 20, 2023, accessed November 20, 2023, https://www.mckinsey.com/capabilities/mckinsey-digital/our-insights/the-top-trends-in-tech#new-and-notable

Applied Artificial Intelligence

Artificial intelligence is the simulation of any cognitive tasks by training algorithms to make predictive insights from data. Artificial intelligence includes machine learning, natural language processing, computer vision, robotics, expert systems, and neural networks.

Artificial intelligence can perform functions typically requiring human intelligence, such as reasoning, automating tasks, improving decision, learning from experience, and problem-solving.[12] The applications of artificial intelligence include natural language processing (NLP), image recognition, computer vision, predictive analytics, generation of original content, self-driving vehicles, medical diagnosis (expert systems), search engines, smartphones (NLP), targeting online advertisements, and renewables and energy storage.[13]

In 1950, Alan Turing introduced the "imitation game," a test to determine if a machine's intelligent behavior was indistinguishable from that of a person.[14] This was the initial step toward applied artificial intelligence, the use of machine learning (ML), computer vision, and natural-language processing (NLP), speech or image recognition, to solve real-world problems and to derive insights to automate processes, add or augment capabilities, and make better decisions. Artificial intelligence systems can learn patterns from existing data and generate text, images, music, and code.

The importance of artificial intelligence includes the potential to provide a competitive advantage to those who adopt it effectively. It has the capability to reduce the cost of intellectual capability to think effectively and generate the information needed to make decisions about creativity and innovation. The potential economic value at stake from applied AI is estimated to be $17 trillion to $26 trillion, and the share of companies pursuing that value has been increasing.[15]

An artificially intelligent model depends on both (1) large amounts of high-quality text datasets, on which the system is trained and (2) specialized artificially intelligent chips. The specialized chips are used to detect relationships within and among the datasets. The model can be improved by increasing the quantity of data in the datasets and by increasing the functionality and speed of the specialized chips. Quality text-based well-written evidence-based information is valued. The data is extracted from the Internet, with or without permission, using sources such as Wikipedia, textbooks, and software code. An example of a source for code would be the software repository, GitHub. It is a platform and cloud-based service for developers to store and manage their code.[16]

There are concerns that artificial intelligence could surpass human abilities and become a threat to human survival in contrast to the value AI can provide for our society. While there are concerns, there is also optimism that progress should be made subject to our trust in those who can provide it responsibly.[17] There are risk factors associated with the advent of artificial intelligence such as a practical concern about the possibility of the replacement of human workers by computers and "bad actors" who would try to use artificial intelligence for "bad things."[18] Geoffrey Hinton, the godfather of artificial intelligence, is an advocate for responsible artificial intelligence and has expressed the warning that artificial brains are better than ours, may start to think for themselves, and even seek to take over or eliminate human civilization.[19]

Industrializing Machine Learning (ML)

Industrializing machine learning (ML), commonly referred to as ML operations, describes the engineering processes of using software and hardware solutions to accelerate the development and deployment of machine learning. Organizations that industrialize ML successfully can reduce the production time frame for ML applications (from proof of concept to product) by about eight to ten times and reduce development resources by up to 40%.[20]

Generative Artificial Intelligence

Generative artificial intelligence systems use mathematical algorithmic models to generate new content.[21] The content is derived from training an artificially intelligent system using large sets of existing broad data (prose, code, images).[22] Generative artificial intelligence can be used to create new content, including audio, code, images, text, simulations, and videos.[23] Artificial intelligence can provide "outputs from generative AI models [that] can be indistinguishable from human-generated content."[24]

Generative artificial intelligence is based on large language models. Large language models use massive amounts of data and complex algorithms that understand natural language patterns to generate human-like text. Large language models are constructed from data that is taken from the Internet, which means it can include personal information and business proprietary information. Large language models are not explicitly using reasoning, rather they are making predictions.

The creation of a large language model like ChatGPT involves a two-step process:[25]

1. Pre-training. The model is trained on a massive dataset containing parts of the Internet. Web-crawling software is used to build *large* language models by scanning books, articles, websites, and more. The large language model learns to predict the next word in a sentence by considering the previous words, learns to associate words, understand context, learn language patterns, and even generate coherent text.
2. Fine-tuning. After pre-training, the model is fine-tuned on a narrower dataset that is generated with the assistance of human reviewers. These reviewers follow guidelines to review and rate possible model outputs for various example inputs.

Next-Generation Software Development

The concept of next-generation software development includes the latest trends that facilitate the development of software applications and improve processes and software quality throughout the software development life cycle. Next-generation software development includes low-code/no-code platforms, code that is generated by artificial intelligence, and automated code reviews and testing. New online digital products are expected to drive the demand for more effective software development practices.[26]

Trust Architectures and Digital Identity

Digital-trust technologies refer to the infrastructure and systems that enable organizations to manage technology and data risks, accelerate innovation, and protect assets. The technologies include zero-trust architectures (ZTAs), digital-identity systems, and privacy engineering. The technologies help build trust by building explainability, transparency, security, and bias minimization principles into the design of artificially intelligent systems.[27]

Web3

Web1 started in the in the 1990s and early 2000s with the use of "open protocols" on the Internet for exchanging information that can be used by anyone, rather than just one entity or organization. Web2 developed in the mid-2000s, when start-up Internet companies – like Facebook, Twitter (now X), and Wikipedia – empowered users to create their own content. The Web3 Internet incorporates blockchain technology, smart contracts, and digital assets and tokens that are communally controlled by its users.[28]

Web3 goes beyond the typical understanding of cryptocurrency investments – it more significantly refers to a future model for the internet that decentralizes authority and redistributes it to users, potentially giving them increased control over how their personal data are monetized and stronger ownership of digital assets.[29]

Advanced Connectivity

Advanced connectivity is the technology that includes wireless low-power networks, short-range wireless technologies, 5G/6G cellular, Wi-Fi 6 and 7, and low-Earth-orbit satellites that support a host of digital solutions that can drive growth and productivity across industries today and tomorrow. Advanced-connectivity technologies will enhance user experiences for consumers worldwide and increase productivity in industries such as mobility, healthcare, and manufacturing.[30]

Immersive-Reality Technologies

Immersive-reality technologies merge the physical world with a digital or simulated reality to create distinct experiences. They use spatial computing to interpret physical space; simulate the addition of data, objects, and people to real-world settings; and enable interactions in virtual worlds with various levels of immersion provided by augmented reality (AR), virtual reality (VR), and mixed reality (MR).[31] "Immersive-reality technologies use sensing technologies and spatial computing to help users 'see the world differently' through mixed or augmented reality or 'see a different world' through virtual reality."[32]

Cloud and Edge Computing

In both cloud and edge computing workloads are distributed across locations, such as hyperscale remote data centers, regional centers, and local nodes, to improve latency, data-transfer costs, adherence to data regulations, autonomy over data, and security. "Cloud computing is the use of comprehensive digital capabilities delivered via the internet for organizations to operate, innovate, and serve customers. It eliminates the need for organizations to host digital applications on their own servers."[33]

Edge computing is a distributed computing model that involves processing data closer to the source of the data generation, the edge of the network. Edge computing provides flexibility for organizations to process data closer to their origins faster (ultra-low latency) and achieve data sovereignty and enhanced data privacy.[34]

Quantum Technologies

Quantum computing (QC) is a fundamentally different computing approach that is based on the laws of quantum mechanics. QC holds enormous potential because it allows certain computations to be performed far more quickly and efficiently than traditional computing.[35]

Quantum technologies take advantage of the unique properties of quantum mechanics to perform specific types of complex calculations exponentially more efficiently than classical computers, secure communication networks, and provide a new generation of sensors capable of massive improvements in sensitivity over their classical counterparts.[36]

For example, quantum computing can improve the computer-aided drug-design (CADD) process enabling an increase in the accuracy of molecular simulations and the reduction in the costs of pharmaceutical development.

Future of Mobility

The future of mobility is expected to improve the efficiency and sustainability of land and air transportation of people and goods using autonomous, connected, electric, and shared solutions. The mobility technologies include a shift toward autonomous driving, connectivity, the electrification of vehicles, and shared mobility (ACES) technologies. ACES is an acronym for four key technological trends: autonomous driving, connectivity, electrification, and smart mobility. These technologies are expected to facilitate new companies, and new business and revenue models that have the potential to alter the way consumers interact with vehicles.[37]

Future of Bioengineering

Bioengineering is the application of engineering principles to biological systems. Future advances in bioengineering include miniaturization, material innovations, personalized medicine, and additive manufacturing, which enable new design options for biomedical devices and products. Bioengineering includes bioprinting and tissue engineering that can create artificial organs and tissues for transplantation or testing, artificial intelligence can improve the diagnosis, treatment, and research, and gene therapy can modify or replace defective genes to treat or prevent diseases.[38]

CRISPR (clustered regularly interspaced short palindromic repeats) is a system that enables the modification of a cell's DNA in a way that is comparable to editing a document. With CRISPR you can switch off the disease-causing mutated version of genes, delete fragments of DNA to treat conditions, and insert new genes to produce therapeutically relevant proteins.[39] Jennifer Doudna, co-discoverer of CRISPR-Cas9, notes, "It's taking a protein that can be targeted to a particular position in the genetic information in a cell and trigger a change."[40]

Future of Space Technologies

Economies of scale have enabled the future of space technology to achieve lower component costs that have been propelled by reductions in the size, weight, power, and cost of satellites and launch vehicles.

These reductions have led to changes in system architectures, such as the shift from individual, large geosynchronous-equatorial-orbit (GEO) satellites to smaller, distributed low-Earth-orbit (LEO) satellites, as well as the increasing interest in space technologies from traditional nonspace companies.[41]

Electrification and Renewables

Electrification and renewables are expected to facilitate net-zero commitments. They include solar-, wind-, and hydro-powered renewables and other renewables; nuclear energy; hydrogen;

sustainable fuels; band electric-vehicle charging.[42] McKinsey describes the power supply and demand trends:[43]

1. Power consumption is expected to triple by 2050 as electrification and living standards grow.
2. Renewables are expected to become the new baseload, accounting for 50% of the power mix by 2030 and 85% by 2050.
3. Flexible assets like gas plants, batteries, and hydrogen electrolyzers are key for grid stability and decarbonization.
4. Technologies like carbon capture, utilization, and storage (CCUS) and nuclear will likely see additional growth if renewables build-out is constrained.

Climate Technology

Climate technology beyond electrification and renewables is aimed at solutions for addressing climate change, reducing greenhouse gas emissions, and promoting sustainability.[44]

> Climate technologies include carbon capture, utilization, and storage (CCUS); carbon removals; natural climate solutions; circular technologies; alternative proteins and agriculture; water and biodiversity solutions and adaptation; and technologies to track net-zero progress.[45]

Electrification, renewables, and climate technology are described in Chapter 19, "Sustainability."

The Importance of Technology

IBM conducted a survey of 3,000 global CEOs to answer the central, overarching question of this new era: what will it take to be essential – to customers, employees, community, and investors? There was near uniform emphasis to focus on the sharpest edge of the business, differentiation to deliver the most distinctive value, and eliminating diversions and indulgences while rooting out "tradition for tradition's sake."[46]

The finding identified two groups: the outperformers and underperformers. The outperformers were those who reported (1) high revenue growth compared to their peers over the three years prior to the study year and (2) performance on par with or exceeding peers during the study period itself. About one in five respondents met the two-pronged standard of outperformance.[47] The differences between outperformers and underperformers became apparent in each of the five key areas of outperformer focus: leadership, technology, employees, open innovation, and cybersecurity.[48]

1. Leadership comes first. Purposeful engagement and creating flatter, faster, and more flexible structures are key.
2. Technology is more than a tool. While the Internet of things, cloud computing, and artificial intelligence (AI) are essential tech tools, outperformers focus on the "forward-looking risks and opportunities of emerging technologies."[49]
3. Employees – the hybrid workplace cannot be taken for granted. Stakeholders fit into the hybrid workforce that blends in-person employees with virtual colleagues that affects organizational culture and needs new management approaches with upgraded capabilities. Moreover, outperformers place a higher focus on employee well-being, even at the expense of near-term profit.
4. Partner to win with open innovation. Partnerships to facilitate open innovation to achieve higher performance to fulfill strategic goals and unlock fresh opportunities.

5. Cybersecurity provides a foundation. Digital security and trust are of strategic importance as the currency of business ecosystems.

The IBM survey findings discovered the importance of technology as the core of a business. When asked to identify which other members of the C-suite will play the most crucial role in the future for their organizations, it revealed the increased importance of the technology role. The findings revealed 57% chief financial officers (CFOs), 56% chief operating officer (COOs), and 39% chief information officers (CIOs), and chief technology officers (CTOs).[50]

The Technology Accelerator Pathways

Of course, technology in all its forms continues to move forward, despite the absence of organizational leadership to embrace and integrate it in mission-critical aspects of their organizations. Given this gap, technology accelerators have become more prominent in the pursuit of new venture creation, as well as organizational renewal and advancement.

In general, technology accelerators empower the utilization of human, social, and digital technology to transform and facilitate the strategic direction of a firm. Technology accelerators provide a foundation for the strategic direction of individual firms and thus impact the course of industries. Because technology in general is an enabler of innovation, firms need to continuously seek new ways to expand their competencies to innovate new product and/or service offerings to reach underserved and unserved market opportunities. For example, the Internet is a technology that enables multiple adaptations and alignments of the value chain across the firm. Wholesale sellers and retail buyers have expanded capabilities to facilitate inventory stocking/order entry processes.

There are three broad technology-accelerator pathways of interest to innovation and entrepreneurship: technology convergence, innovation integration, and technology ecosystems as shown in Figure 15.3.

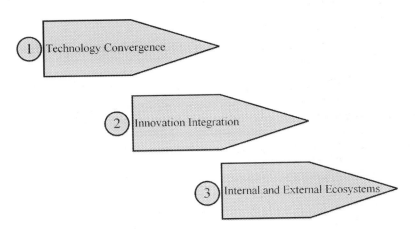

Figure 15.3 Illustration of Three Broad Technology Accelerator Movements

1. Technology convergence occurs when products and services are integrated in one solution to address a market need and/or gap in the market. For example, technology convergence is evident in an electronic device, such as a smartphone, which integrates voice, text, talk, web browsing, maps, gaming technologies, apps, and integration into ecosystem platforms.

2. Innovation integration is achieved by growing an innovation capability horizontally and/or vertically. Horizontal integration takes place by merging and/or acquiring similar companies or divisions of similar companies. Vertical integration creates growth through partnerships, mergers, and acquisitions that enable a company to better manage and control the innovation process throughout the entire value chain, from inputs to throughputs to outputs.

3. Technology ecosystems include internal/organizational and external perspectives. Internal technology ecosystems are built by businesses that synergistically integrate key success factors that drive innovation and entrepreneurship. These key success factors can be core and distinctive competencies (such as supply chain management), as well as core products and/or services (such as devices, operating systems, movies, music, games, books, apps, and storage). External technology ecosystems consist of key support agencies that provide (directly or indirectly) advice, space, mentoring, education, training, funding, or some combination of these. In this chapter, we will focus on the role of the internal or organizational technology ecosystem accelerator. These concepts build on Chapter 14, "Ecosystems Interdependencies."

It is the combination of the pathways that provide the key insight that underscores the Power of And.

Technology Convergence

Technology convergence is achieved through the combination of different yet complementary technologies applied in the building of a single integrated product to serve an underserved and/or unserved market need. Smartphones and tablets are examples of how technology convergence can include both software and hardware. For example, Samsung's Galaxy smartphones and watches, Google's Pixel smartphones, Nintendo's Wii, and Apple's iPhone, iPad, and Apple Watch all illustrate achieving technology convergence via synergistic technologies.

Technology convergence also involves the combining of product components, services, and applications into a single device, such as a smartphone or tablet. Most consumers focus on the latest mobile electronic devices because they are useful for performing everyday personal and business communication tasks, like phone calls, email, text messaging, accessing information (including directions, stock market quotes, coupons, products, and the weather forecast), and entertainment (such as gaming and social media).

Technology convergence, illustrated in Figure 15.4, however, also serves as a key entry point into integration and technology ecosystem platforms. For example, Amazon's Echo smart speaker and Google's Home smart speaker, enabled by artificial intelligence, extend the integration into their respective platforms. Artificial-intelligence-enabled devices can better manage the market base and offer a set of complementary and integrated products and services. For example, the Amazon Echo is fully integrated with the Amazon retail network, creating, and managing a goods-and-services offering via the Internet.

The smartphone continues to be one of the best examples of technology convergence generating multiple players coming and going developing a robust market. The estimated global smartphone 2020 market share in rank order was Samsung, Apple, Huawei, Xiaomi, Oppo, Vivo, Realme, Lenovo, LG, and Tecno, while LG announced that they were shutting down their smartphone business in 2021.[51]

Innovation Integration

Innovation integration involves the application of horizontal and vertical integration strategies. Horizontal integration occurs when a company seeks growth through creating and/or acquiring

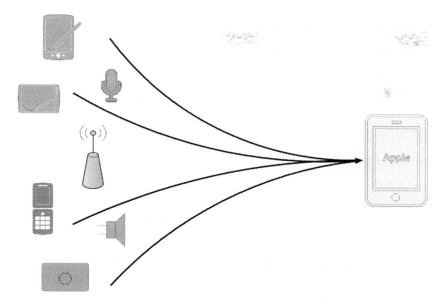

Figure 15.4 Illustration of Technology Convergence

the same and/or similar lines of business, usually via mergers and acquisitions. For example, if a bakery specializing in wedding cakes wants to expand to specialty cakes for all occasions, it might seek to acquire other smaller bakeries that have a great reputation for cakes. Over the years, Disney provides multiple examples of how it skillfully used mergers and acquisitions to build key technologies to achieve core and distinctive competencies to maintain a competitive edge, as illustrated in Figure 15.5.

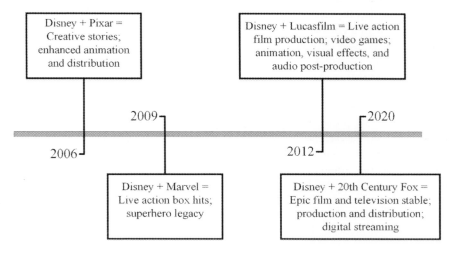

Figure 15.5 Illustration of Disney's Horizontal Integration

Source: Adapted from Wikipedia s.v. "List of acquisitions by Disney" accessed November 17, 2021, https://en.wikipedia.org/wiki/List_of_acquisitions_by_Disney

Vertical integration occurs when a company seeks to own all the components of the value chain from raw materials to finished good. Vertical integration can be forward or backward in the value chain. Building on the previous example, if the cake bakery wants to own all the components of production, it might expand its business backward toward raw materials and acquire a flour plant or a sugar processor. While it could be argued that some of the Disney examples cited earlier could be viewed as vertical integration as means of production, overall, the pursuit was more horizontal in scope.

Innovation integration enables firms to minimize the deleterious impact of both co-innovation and adoption chain risk. Backward vertical integration occurs when a company acquires the means of managing and controlling the inputs used in the production of its products. One example of backward innovation integration is Apple's design and delivery of their chips.[52] In addition, Apple has contracts with Samsung for the building of their chips and related hardware components.[53] Forward vertical integration occurs when a company grows by building and controlling distribution centers and retailers where its products are sold. For example, Apple used forward vertical integration when it designed and implemented the Apple stores. Both forward and backward integration are illustrated in Figure 15.6.

The vertical integration model allows for simplicity, lower costs, and higher levels of design integration over the resulting products. The degree of effective vertical integration depends, in part, on the extent to which an organization controls its supply chain, including its distribution centers and retailers where the products and services are offered.

Samsung

Samsung effectively uses vertical integration to expand its reach into the manufacture, supply, and distribution of digital components. Samsung has a competitive hardware advantage over Apple because Samsung's products are based on a tightly integrated set of hardware components that it manufactures. Samsung controls and manufactures the building blocks of its electronic products.

Samsung's ability to manage its hardware components also enables it to achieve a time-to-market advantage. Samsung has the capacity to increase the production of the components quickly, which provides Samsung with a competitive advantage over other manufacturers.[54] Apple manufactures and sells a few models, whereas Samsung can manufacture a larger number of models. Apple relies on many suppliers for its product components, including Samsung, requiring more coordination between all the companies in the value chain.[55]

Google (Alphabet)

The advantages of vertical integration of an operating system can be understood by comparing the Android operating systems with Apple iOS.[56] Google acquired the Android start-up in 2005 from the founder Andy Rubin. Android is an open-source operating system that can be customized for different devices that are offered by carriers and manufacturers. The open-source model can result in fragmentation, complexity, and extra effort in product rollouts if it is not managed with a balance of discipline and entrepreneurism. Because of the number of companies using it for their products (e.g., Samsung, Sony, Ericsson, Google, Motorola, and Amazon), Android needs to support over 600 screen sizes. Google provides periodic new software versions, resulting in various versions of Android being used at the same time by different customers. If you multiply the customizations by the devices by the screen sizes by the older operating system versions, you have a prolific number of contemporaneous variations of Android.

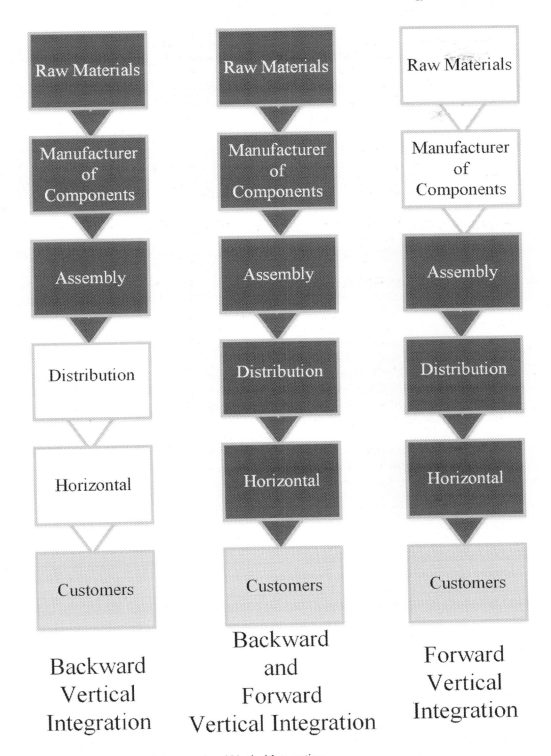

Figure 15.6 Illustration of Horizontal and Vertical Integration

Apple

Apple's strategy is to use vertical integration, a form of combinatorial innovation, with its computers systems, a term that describes the physical components (hardware) and the programs (software). Vertical integration is a business strategy in which a company controls multiple stages of its production process and supply chain that allow for streamlining operations, reducing costs, and improving efficiency by eliminating the need to rely on external contractors or suppliers.

Apples' computer architecture is the deliberate interconnection of hardware components that provide the functional, performance and cost goals of its systems. Apple's proprietary operating systems, such as iOS, iPadOS, watchOS, tvOS, macOS, and visionOS are designed to work exclusively with Apple computer architecture. This integration has enabled Apple to set the pace for mobile computing and has been a key factor in the company's value proposition. Apple demonstrated the ability to adapt its product line by transitioning its computer architecture four times over its history.[57]

1. Apple used the Motorola 68K chip in the Macintosh, Lisa, and PowerBook 190 computers from 1984 to 1995.
2. Apple transitioned away from the traditional CPU architectures toward Reduced Instruction Set Computing (RISC) from 1994 to 2005 to the PowerPC. An alliance formed between Apple, IBM, and Motorola was formed to tackle Microsoft-Intel domination – therefore creating the Power PC chip used in the Power Macintosh 6100.
3. Apple changed the computer architecture to use the Intel x86 chip from 2006 to 2020 that included the Intel iMacs and the MacBook Pros.
4. Apple initiated the move to Apple Silicon in 2020 with the introduction of system on a chip (SOC) that used the ARM-based design. Apple Silicon (M1-MN) is fast and more energy-efficient than Intel chips. Arm Limited, a UK-based technology company, licenses their intellectual property for architectural designs.

Apple has a potential software advantage over Samsung because Apple's products are tightly integrated with its operating system in all its devices. Apple's vertical software integration has a competitive advantage over Samsung because of its reliance on Google for the Android operating system.[58]

Intel

When it comes to understanding the importance of skillfully using convergence, integration, and ecosystem interdependencies, there is perhaps no better example than Intel. Founded in 1968, by the legendary team of Robert Noyce, co-founder of the integrated circuit, and Gordon Moore, namesake of Moore' Law, the premise was simple: make semi-conductor memory more practical and affordable. Shortening "integrated electronics" to Intel, the race for silicon innovation was on.[59]

Intel has made several strategic decisions over time that have impacted its competitive position in quite different ways.

1. In 1985, the Intel CEO Andy Grove decided to move out of the memory chip business "disrupting itself" to focus on higher value chips.[60]
2. In 2007, the Intel CEO Paul Otellini decided to not manufacture mobile chips because he felt it could not be done profitability; this resulted in the loss of that market.[61]
3. In 2008, Intel attempted to re-enter the market but was not able to produce a competitive low-power- chip.[62]

In 2021, Intel pivoted its strategy in three ways to regain its competitive advantage that was seized by competitors like Taiwan Semiconductor and Samsung.[63]

1. Intel decided to pursue a major expansion in manufacturing capacity to build chip plants in the US. Intel is expected to build extra capacity so it could become a major manufacturer of chips for other companies that build on their manufacturing expertise.[64] This is identical to the business model of competitors Taiwan Semiconductor Manufacturing Company and Samsung that provide chips for the major chip designing companies like Apple and Nvidia.[65]
2. Intel relies on the vertical integration model to control their design and manufacturing. Intel plans to outsource the manufacturing of some of its upcoming products to rivals like TSMC.[66]
3. Intel plans to collaborate with IBM on research into new chip designs and ways of packaging components: "IBM has several research groups working on novel approaches to microprocessor design and manufacturing."[67]

Technology Ecosystems: Integrated Ecosystem Economy

The borders between traditional sectors of our economy are fading away: construction, real estate, information technology, automotive manufacturing, energy financial services, and healthcare.[68] Today, technology is all about ecosystems.[69]

Now businesses are organizing into new, more dynamic configurations, which are focused not on the things that have always been done, but on people's needs. Networks of ecosystems across different sectors are driving the transformation.[70] The companies that comprise the integrated ecosystem economy include Alibaba, Apple, Alphabet, Amazon, Meta, and Microsoft.[71] It is projected that the integrated ecosystem economy is already here and expanding to what could potentially amount to $80 trillion in revenue.[72]

An integrated ecosystem is a large, integrated suite of additional brands, products, and services that enable these companies to manage, retain, and attract new customers and achieve reliable revenue streams.[73] "But what turned Apple into the most valuable company on the planet was that Jobs did more than just create cool new devices. Rather, he presided over the creation of new market ecosystems, with those devices at their heart."[74]

Technology convergence provides the means for the development and deployment of mobile electronic devices that have become one of the key entry points into the world of technology ecosystems. These integrated devices are the digital door for buyers and consumers as they compare, contrast, and choose between the various incremental updates and features that the next device offers. These mobile digital doors open a vast array of offerings through vertically and horizontally integrated technology ecosystems to retain and attract customers.

Internal technology ecosystems provide an integration of an entire system of evolving products, services, and solutions and external technology ecosystems consist of key support agencies that provide (directly or indirectly) advice.

Since 1975, we have continued to experience the growth of large technological ecosystem companies.

It is a war between vast ecosystems made up of hardware, software and online services, not just individual pieces of hardware and software. Purchase an iPhone, for example, and you're buying into the entire Apple ecosystem, including operating systems, apps, add-ons, music, movies, books and more. The big money isn't in your single purchase, but in encouraging you to purchase only products and services that interact with each other – and your wallet.[75]

The integrated ecosystems companies are examples of start-ups that have become technology giants, in part because of their development of technology ecosystems. By controlling the design and/or production of electronic devices and the core operating systems of the device used for the entry point into their ecosystems, these companies can better manage their customer base.

Figure 15.7 illustrates the relationship in firms between the lower and higher innovation degrees on the Y-axis and the lower and higher levels of ecosystem innovation on the X-axis.

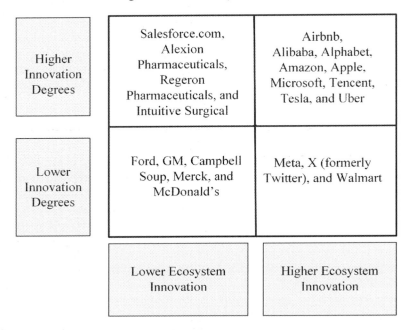

Higher Innovation Degrees	Salesforce.com, Alexion Pharmaceuticals, Regeron Pharmaceuticals, and Intuitive Surgical	Airbnb, Alibaba, Alphabet, Amazon, Apple, Microsoft, Tencent, Tesla, and Uber
Lower Innovation Degrees	Ford, GM, Campbell Soup, Merck, and McDonald's	Meta, X (formerly Twitter), and Walmart
	Lower Ecosystem Innovation	**Higher Ecosystem Innovation**

Figure 15.7 Illustration of a Set of Organizational Technology Ecosystems

The three broad technology-accelerator movements discussed here when combined have resulted in significant growth in the overall critical technology accelerator ecosystems. Figure 15.8 summarizes and illustrates key aspects of the three technology accelerator pathways.

Strategic Intent, Technology Accelerators, and Action

The power of an internal or organizational technology accelerator is its ability to transform and facilitate the strategic intent of an organization. In "Strategic Intent," Gary Hamel and C. K. Prahalad write, "Strategic intent is the essence of winning."[76] Winning is accomplished by customer-driven organizations that are composed of thought leaders capable of balancing present and future customer needs. As important as digital technology accelerators are, they are strictly secondary in relation to the strategic intent.

Digital technology can accelerate innovation, but the real drivers are the wills of the people, their teamwork, inspiration, competency, persistence, and talent. For instance, only one of 3M's seven pillars of innovation is technology. The 3M seven pillars are:

- Commitment to innovation
- Nurturing an innovation culture
- Application of a broad technology base

- Networking and communication
- Management of individual expectation and rewards for outstanding work
- Measurements to determine the amount of revenue from products introduced in the last four years
- Association of research with the customer[77]

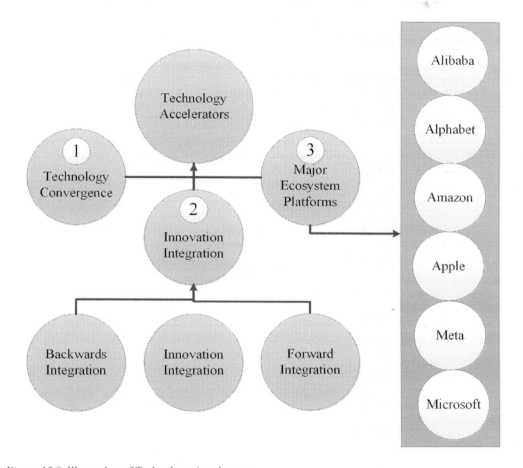

Figure 15.8 Illustration of Technology Accelerators

Source: Adapted from Violet Chung, Miklós Dietz, Istvan Rab, and Zac Townsend, "Ecosystem 2.0: Climbing to the next level," September 11, 2020, McKinsey Quarterly, accessed September 15, 2020 https://www.mckinsey.com/business-functions/mckinsey-digital/our-insights/ecosystem-2-point-0-climbing-to-the-next-level

Innovation and entrepreneurship can be facilitated by technology, but the spirit of the innovators and entrepreneurs – their determination and willingness to answer a call to action – make innovation and entrepreneurship happen.

Winning: The Willingness to Act

Innovation and entrepreneurship success can be attributable to a willingness to act. For example, Chester Carlson invented the mimeograph, a process of electrophotography that used dry ink for copying instead of a wet process.[78] In 1959, Xerox introduced the first plain-paper copier using the electrophotography process, the Xerox 914.[79] The original Xerox 914 business model was to sell the expensive copying machines below cost and to profit by selling the supplies. This business model did not work because the alternative solutions were less expensive than the xerography supplies. Xerox changed its business model to leasing the Xerox 914 and charging a copy fee.[80] The solution to the problem was to change the business model and offer copies per page rather than have the customer purchase the copier.

Losing: The Unwillingness to Act

Innovation failures can often be attributable to an unwillingness to act. Xerox was able to conceptualize many technological ideas and transform them into innovations but often did not follow through. Although Xerox PARC developed many technology innovations, they were not able to effectively commercialize them.

> PARC was founded in 1970 and incorporated as a wholly owned subsidiary of Xerox in 2002. It is best known for inventing laser printing, Ethernet, the modern personal computer graphical user interface (GUI) paradigm, ubiquitous computing, and advancing very-large-scale-integration (VLSI).[81]

One of the most profound inventions in modern software, object-oriented technology, was invented by Xerox in conjunction with the Smalltalk programming language. Xerox developed the graphical user interface concept (windows) that influenced the software that was commercialized by both Apple and Microsoft.[82]

That is not to say that successful companies do not have technological failures – they do. Both Apple and Microsoft had many setbacks, but, by comparison, none of them were as significant as Xerox's unwillingness to act. Apple was unsuccessful in the development of the Lisa prior to the Macintosh, the Apple III, and the Apple Newton, a predecessor of the PDA.[83] Microsoft has a list of unsuccessful attempts at innovation progress, such as Zune, Bob, Windows ME, Windows CE, Vista, the tablet PC, and the smartwatch.[84] Failure is part of the innovation and entrepreneurship process.

An Unlikely Place for Technology

There are many market inefficiencies that reveal unserved and/or underserved market opportunities awaiting our creative thinking. For instance, the challenge in agriculture is to increase crop yields while simultaneously reducing costs to feed an ever-growing population. There are two problems with traditional farming. Tilling increases the likelihood of erosion and the loss of precious topsoil. Worldwide each year, one hectare (area equal to 10,000 square meters) of farmland loses an average of 30 metric tons of topsoil.[85]

With precision agriculture, farmers can use technology known as real-time kinematics (RTK), where the accuracy of seed and fertilizer placement can be pinpointed within a few centimeters, in contrast to global positions systems at three meters. Broadcasting fertilizer results in waste because it is spread over areas that do not have any seeds. Using RTK, the farmer can cut grooves in the soil to sow the seeds and precisely apply a band of fertilizer exactly where it is needed. Farmers need a picture of soil variability because composition of soil is not uniform. Mapping technology can be used to determine the water-holding capacity, yield potential, soil acidity, and some types of nutrients. By knowing the explicit characteristics of the soil, the farmer will know how much and where to apply water and fertilizer. This is an innovation opportunity because precision agriculture has not yet been widely adopted in developed or developing countries.[86]

Four Core Technology Competencies

There are four technologies that were once scarce but are now plentiful and affordable. When these four are integrated, they provide the potential for high added value: semiconductors, sensors, wireless connectivity, and databases.[87] Figure 15.9 illustrates the important role the IoT has when combined with the capability to apply the four core technology competencies.

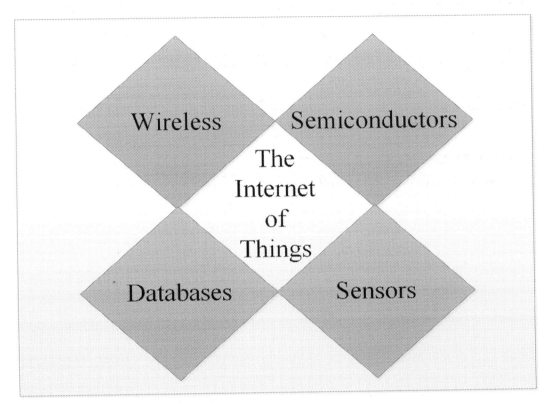

Figure 15.9 Illustration of The Four Technology Competencies and the Internet of Things

Semiconductors

Semiconductors are used in every aspect of our lives; they are an integral part of electronic devices, including all types of computers, and they are responsible for the functionality of the devices.[88]

1. A semiconductor is a material that has electrical conductivity between a conductor and an insulator. It can conduct electricity when certain conditions are met, and it can be an insulator when other conditions are met.
2. A transistor is a device that can switch a current on and off. The transistor was invented by William Shockley, John Bardeen, and Walter Brattain at Bell Labs in Murray Hill, New Jersey, in 1947 for which they were awarded the Nobel Prize in Physics in 1956. The invention was a three-electrode circuit element utilizing semiconductive materials.[89] There are around 15 billion transistors on an iPhone.[90]

3. An integrated circuit refers to a complete circuit that is integrated onto a single semiconductor such as silicon. A microchip or chip is a specific type of integrated circuit is used to control a small device or system.[91] The terms "microchip" and "semiconductor" are often used interchangeably, but they are not the same.

The semiconductor industry, also known as the chip industry, is a critical sector of the global economy and is a key driver for advancing technology and enabling innovation. Semiconductors are critical innovation building blocks of modern electronic devices and have a fundamental role in advancing. They provide the underlying ability for us to empower artificial intelligence (AI), machine learning (ML), cloud computing, and the Internet of things (IoT).[92]

Semiconductors drive the systems and products used for our employment, transportation and travel, medical equipment, renewable energy, automotive electronics, appliances, dishwashers, refrigerators, microwaves, industrial machinery, and wireless communications. Semiconductors used in devices like thermocyclers, spectrophotometers, and mass spectrometers facilitate our innovation capability and make new scientific discoveries possible.[93]

Industry Characteristics

The semiconductor industry is one of the world's most advanced manufacturing and research and development sectors.[94] The global semiconductor industry is an organized network of interdependent value chains of exceptional length and complexity located in the United States, Japan, the Netherlands, and Taiwan; our modern economy cannot function without them.[95]

The semiconductor business is characterized by intense global competition that requires continuous innovation, rapid technological advancements, and major investments in research and development. The semiconductor industry must protect its intellectual property, manage the trust in the supply chain, optimize manufacturing processes, design next generation chip layouts, and facilitate the discovery of new materials.

The semiconductor industry is an *oligopoly* that is dominated by a small number of large companies that can influence supply, pricing, and innovation. These major firms include Intel, Samsung, TSMC (Taiwan Semiconductor Manufacturing Company), Nvidia, AMD, Micron technologies, and Qualcomm.

1. The experience curve for the semiconductor business shows the inverse relationship between the cost of production and the cumulative production quantity of a product; the more a company produces and markets a product, the more it gains in efficiency and lowers its unit costs.
2. High barriers to entry, because of the sizable capital investment required, make it difficult for new firms to participate.
3. Ecosystem cooperation based on trust is essential for partnerships and alliances because of the interdependence of separate competing firms that share the same manufacturers.

The factors that determine the investment decision for new semiconductor facilities are industrial policy and programs, economic, and strategic factors.[96]

1. The industrial policy programs in the US are expected to increase the capability of the semiconductor industry and decrease the dependence on foreign producers. For instance, the US government funding is supporting the building of large facilities by Taiwan Semiconductor Manufacturing Company, Samsung, Intel, and Micron Technology.

2. The economic factors that determine where to build large facilities are the cost of electricity, land and capital, the availability of workers, and the proximity of suppliers.
3. The strategic factors that influence decision-making are human capital and talent, market factors and trends, and technological innovation that leads to more powerful capability and energy efficiency, and intellectual property portfolio protection.

Strategic Importance

Global semiconductor strategy is based on how a firm chooses to create new intellectual property, recruit top talent, vertically integrate, and manage the trust needed in its supply chain. Both firms and nations are sensitive to the vital importance of the implications of semiconductor strategy.

Semiconductors are an increasingly critical element of corporate strategies – and of the global economy. All our electronic devices are full of semiconductors that are responsible for computing, sensing, communicating, and managing data. For instance, a car can have over a thousand chips that are composed of semiconductor components.[97] According to McKinsey, the global semiconductor industry is expected to grow to be a one-trillion-dollar industry by 2030, assuming average price increases of about 2% a year and a return to balanced supply and demand after current volatility.[98]

Integrated circuits have strategic importance because there are international defense and competitiveness implications especially when the manufacturing of strategic resources resides outside a country. In the United States, the CHIPS and Science Act of 2022 includes nearly $250 billion in semiconductor and scientific research and development (R&D). The legislation seeks to strengthen the United States role in chipmaking.[99] Because integrated circuits that contain semiconductor components are used in defense systems such as the F-35 jet fighter for its command, control, and communication (C3) systems, this use has implications as to where the semiconductors components are manufactured.[100]

Global Competition

Semiconductor companies invest heavily in research and development focusing on chip design, process technology, performance, energy efficiency, and cost-effectiveness. The global semiconductor industry is composed of the design, manufacture, and distributions of semiconductors. It functions are an organized network of interdependent value chains of exceptional length and complexity located in the United States, Europe, China, South Korea, Japan, and Taiwan; our modern economy cannot function without them.[101]

Semiconductor Firms

The semiconductor business includes the design, manufacture, and sales of semiconductor products in intensely competitive international markets.[102] Semiconductor firms are critical in driving technological innovation and economic growth because they provide the building blocks of all modern electronic devices, from smartphones and computers to automobiles and appliances. The four semiconductor product categories are as follows:[103]

1. Transistors are semiconductor devices that can act as amplifiers or switches.
2. Memory provides temporary storage.
3. Microprocessors are the central processing units.

4. Integrated circuits are complete circuits that are integrated onto a single semiconductor such as silicon.
5. System on a chip is an integrated circuit that manages the entire system's capability (SoC).

The semiconductor business can be categorized into design, fabrication, foundries, manufacturing equipment firms, architecture design firms, and packaging, assembly, and testing. Understanding the semiconductor business is essential for innovation.[104]

Design

The process starts with semiconductor design companies, which create complex circuit designs and architectures for various applications. These designs are typically implemented using computer-aided design (CAD) tools and advanced software. Apple, Nvidia, and Advanced Micro Devices design their semiconductors but do not fabricate their semiconductors. Rather, they outsource their manufacturing to foundry firms like Taiwan Semiconductor Manufacturing Company Limited (TSMC), the world's biggest contract chip maker, or to South Korea's Samsung Electronics Co. Ltd.[105]

Fabrication

Fabricators, also known as semiconductor manufacturers or fabs, are companies that produce semiconductor wafers through the process of semiconductor fabrication. Fabricators typically design and manufacture their own semiconductor chips.[106] The semiconductor fabrication firms design and manufacture integrated circuits (ICs): Intel, Samsung, SK Hynix, and Micron Technologies.

Foundries

The semiconductor companies specialize only in manufacturing and are called foundries. They provide fabrication services for other semiconductor design companies that do not have their own manufacturing facilities. TSMC (Taiwan Semiconductor Manufacturing Company) provides manufacturing services for various semiconductor companies, including leading technology firms like Apple, Nvidia, AMD, and Qualcomm. GlobalFoundries is another major player in the foundry business. It was initially spun off from AMD's manufacturing division and now operates as an independent company. Samsung, the South Korean electronics giant, has a semiconductor foundry division known as Samsung Foundry. United Microelectronics Corporation (UMC) is a foundry based in Taiwan that offers semiconductor manufacturing services to a diverse range of customers.

Manufacturing Equipment Firms

The firms that develop, produce, and market semiconductor manufacturing equipment, specifically machines to produce chips through lithography are Applied Materials Inc, ASML Holding N.V., KLA Corporation, LAM Research Corp, and Tokyo Electron. A new type of lithography, more precise, using smaller-wavelength light in the ultraviolet spectrum is necessary to get the precision, but it was also extraordinarily complex to produce. These machines are the most complex machines humans have ever made and they require one of the most powerful lasers that has ever been deployed in a commercial device that is 40 or 50 times hotter than the surface of the sun.[107]

Gordon Moore, co-founder of Intel Corporation, observed as the director of research and development at Fairchild Semiconductor that the number of transistors on a semiconductor chip was doubling approximately every two years while the cost per transistor was decreasing.

Whether or not Moore's law will continue will depend on further innovations in lithography tools, especially extreme-ultraviolet (EUV) lithography technology. EUV uses short-wavelength light sources to scale feature sizes below 10 nanometers (nm).[108] The transistor density timelines are as follows.

1. Seven nanometers – 2018
2. Five nanometers – 2020
3. Three nanometers – 2022
4. Two nanometers ~ 2024

Sensors

A sensor is an electronic device or transducer that changes from one form of signal to another and detects and measures changes in physical properties or environmental conditions. The sensors convert the inputs into outputs in the form of electrical signals that are sent to control systems, electronic devices, and data acquisition systems. Sensors are used in many everyday applications to collect data measure vibration, viscosity, optics, and detect temperature and pressure.[109]

Operational technology (OT) in manufacturing includes the integration of many machines, devices, and control mechanisms operating together. Information technology (IT) is the computer systems, cloud-based storage systems, and network architecture that is used for processing and storing of information. Online (IT/OT) sensors and valves – for flow, density, and turbidity – can be used to manage the collection of data inside an automation system and choose a set point for monitoring. "Overlaying real-time advanced analytics on data from online sensing can help to stabilize operations and increase capacity in water-treatment facilities."[110] For example, water can be reclaimed after treatment to remove metals, reagents, or suspended solids to provide fresh water to be reused to reduce operating expenses especially in low water stressed areas.

Sensors are used in complex systems in manufacturing and machinery, airplanes and aerospace, cars, medicine, robotics, and in autonomous vehicle technology components that include driver assistance systems, automotive radars, Advanced Driver-Assistance Systems (ADAS) ultrasonic wave components, and Laser Imaging, Detection, and Ranging (LiDAR) system sensors, among many others.[111]

Wireless Technologies

A computer network is composed of both wired and wireless connectivity that is integrated using digital interconnection to computer systems and devices of all types. Ethernet is a set of computer networking technologies that are widely used in homes and businesses. Ethernet is standardized and is one of the key technologies that is used for the Internet. Ethernet uses coaxial cable as a shared medium, twisted pair, and fiber optic links. The Internet Protocol is commonly carried over Ethernet, and so it is considered one of the key technologies that make up the Internet.[112]

Wireless technologies like low-power wide-area networks (LPWAN), Wi-Fi 6, low-to mid-band 5G, and short-range connections like radio-frequency identification (RFID) are expected to provide a quantum leap in the speed and scope of digital connections that have the potential to stimulate innovation.[113]

Database Technologies

A database is an organized collection of data that is stored and accessed from many types of computer systems. A database management system is used to define how the data is organized, provide access to the different views of the data, and manage the updates and backups. A database provides significant value because it provides a single place for all types of data, the enforcement of data integrity, and the prevention of invalid data and duplications.[114] The data can be organized in different models. For instance, in a relational database system, the views of the data are organized into row and column tables. Structured query language (SQL) is a standard language that is used to administer, define, update, and retrieve the data.[115]

The Internet

The Internet is a revolutionary innovation that has become an integral part of our daily lives, providing us with a wealth of information, entertainment, and communication options. It has had a significant impact on the economy, creating jobs and contributing to innovation by improving processes and products; the Internet has become indispensable in the modern world of information and communication. It began as a tool of the US government, which arose because of a need for interoperability of digital communication.[116] For example, the United Parcel Service relies on the Internet to meet their customers' needs. UPS's core competency is getting letters and packages from point A to point B in a timely and cost-effective manner.[117] The Internet has grown to become the backbone of many businesses that provide integrated ecosystems applications, such as Salesforce.com and cloud services offered by Microsoft, Apple, and Amazon.

The Internet of Things (IoT)

The Internet of things (IoT) provides the infrastructure to enable the communication of sensors, networks, and data that allows information to be sent to and received from digital devices of all types. The industrial Internet of things (IIoT) is a related term that is used to describe the integration of connected smart sensors, actuators, and other devices with industrial applications, including manufacturing and energy management. The IoT digital devices span cars, trucks, trains, airplanes, ships, manufacturing control systems, robots, appliances, security systems, smartphones, smart speakers, electric grids, city traffic and congestion monitoring, air and water monitoring, smart home security systems, intelligent HVAC systems, vertical farming, autonomous farming equipment, wearable health monitors, smart manufacturing control systems, wireless inventory trackers, biometric cybersecurity scanners, satellites, supply chain tracking of logistics and shipping containers, data analytics, and artificially intelligent systems.[118]

1. IoT sensors can be used any connected car to provide automatic crash response, roadside assistance, and the ability to locate the vehicle, unlock it, and even start its ignition – all from a smartphone. Both Tesla and OnStar, a subsidiary of GM, provide these capabilities.
2. IoT sensors can be used to monitor temperature, soil moisture, nutrients, and humidity levels in crops. This data can be used to optimize irrigation and fertilization schedules, reduce water usage, and increase crop yields.
3. IoT sensors can be used to monitor air and water quality providing data that can be used to pinpoint pollution locations, track pollution trends, and develop targeted interventions to reduce pollution.

Cloud Computing

The term cloud computing is a metaphor for a set of scalable services composed of low-cost computer systems and storage device resources that provide on-demand availability. Cloud computing eliminates the need for customers to have the physical hardware and infrastructure themselves enabling them to use these resources on-demand and pay only for what they use. The increase in demand for cloud computing has led to the development of hyperscale data centers that can support hundreds of thousands of servers and consume tens or hundreds of megawatts of power. The major providers are Amazon Web Services (AWS), Microsoft Azure, Google Cloud, Oracles Cloud, and IBM Cloud.[119]

Network Effect

Arthur Rock was an early investor in Intel and Apple Computer. His criterion for identifying opportunities was to "look for business concepts that will change the way people live or work."[120] The early Bell telephone is an example of technology that changed the way people communicated through the network effect. As each new home and business was added to the network, the telephone achieved an exponential increase in utility. Pierre Omidyar's eBay used the network effect as a successful strategy. eBay provided a web software platform where buyers and sellers are brought together in an online auction.[121] The more buyers and sellers, the more value for everyone.

Meta uses the network effect as the foundation of their strategy and then complements it with low cost, differentiation, and the customer experience. It is not one, but all combined that has changed the way people live and work. Meta's consumer-managed personal profile allows ads to be targeted to specific potential buyers.[122]

The Meta business model is based on providing targeted display ads that use the personal profile. The ads are targeted based on the personal profile of demographics provided by the consumer, including birthdays, emails, employment histories, and hometowns. "The whole premise of the site is that everything is more valuable when you have context about what your friends are doing," says Meta co-founder and chief executive officer Mark Zuckerberg, who started accepting ads on Meta (Facebook) as a Harvard sophomore in 2004 to cover the costs of the server.[123] "An advertiser can produce the best creative ad in the world, but knowing your friends really love drinking Coke is the best endorsement for Coke you can possibly get.[124]

The Value of Technology Accelerator Pathways

The technology accelerator pathways: technology convergence, innovation integration, and technology ecosystems add broad value to the global economy. The technology accelerator pathways can promote creativity, increase knowledge expertise, liberate routine thinking, support resource sustainability, enable predictions to create new knowledge, provide execution efficiency, make predictions to create new knowledge, and empower mass customization. The value provided by the technology accelerators is shown in Figure 15.10.

Creativity and Technology

The skillful and synergistic combination of creativity and technology can accelerate the likelihood that your strategic thinking and execution will be successful.[125] Technology has opened opportunities for the expression of creative thinking. Technology has provided access to information, improved ways of learning, and provided tools to create new forms of art, music, and fiction.

Graphic design software like Adobe Photoshop and Illustrator allows designers to create visuals. Social media platforms provide a way for everyone to share their creative ideas and connect with other creatives. Video games provide a platform for people to create and explore new worlds, characters, and stories. YouTube is a platform that provides a way for people to share their creative

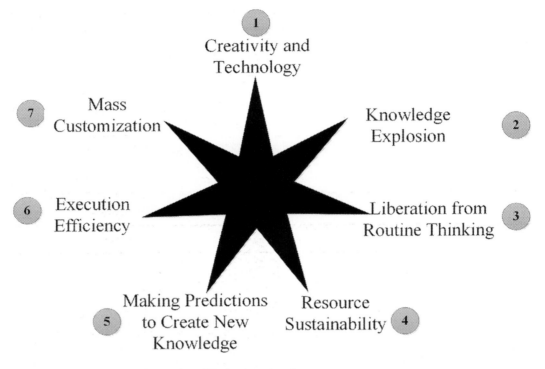

Figure 15.10 Illustration of the Value of Technology Accelerators

ideas with the world and get feedback. Generative artificial intelligence tools like Copilot, Gemini can create lyrics for a song. Artificial intelligence tools like Mupert, Jukebox, and Loudly can produce audio sounds.

Knowledge Explosion

Advances in information technology have created a virtual explosion in available knowledge on multiple levels. The Internet is the digital pipeline for businesses, enabling them to be versatile, and more valuable than ever before. However, while the digital pipeline has created an excess of information, this information needs to be filtered for quality and distributed to people in a specific, task-relevant, and timely manner. Enter technology accelerators.

Technology accelerator pathways provide a platform that can be used to bring together consumers and sellers, giving them access to information about products, prices, and availability. The technology accelerators facilitate the optimal operation of Adam Smith's invisible hand. Smith provided the foundations of classical free market economic theory.[126] In 1988, Joe Ricketts had the actionable insight to allow investors to use a touch-tone phone instead of a stockbroker for investment transactions. He later founded TD Ameritrade and grew the company into the largest online discount broker (measured in transactions per day).[127]

In response to the need for a more responsive healthcare system, hospitals and healthcare providers have initiated a variety of innovative practices to improve patient care. For example, hospitals require healthcare providers throughout the system to follow strict patient identification and care protocols to ensure proper care and medication are provided. Patient admission and onboarding procedures include both digital and paper checks and safeguards. Lab work, examinations, and procedures are tied to unique identifiers to ensure the proper patient is receiving the appropriate care.

In addition, patients are taking greater responsibility for their healthcare by connecting with their own healthcare records through secure digital portals that connect the patient to their healthcare providers. Patients can view online doctor examination notes, lab results, and past, current, and future appointments and communicate with doctors, nurses, and other healthcare providers in real time and/or via email.

Liberation from Routine Thinking

An increasingly important strategy in the new global economy is to innovate. This requires that people spend more time on high-order thinking, such as innovation, and less time on routine tasks. The digitalization of these routine tasks is the outcome of viable enterprise technology architecture, such as Amazon's integrated technology infrastructure. The transformation of paper-based systems into reengineered workflows is an iterative and incremental process that will proceed endlessly as new technology provides features that make new things possible.

Resource Sustainability

The sustainability challenges faced moving forward are noteworthy. The challenges include innovative stakeholder leadership; the management of renewable and non-renewable resources; addressing climate change; issues of reusability in local, regional, national, and global value chains; environmental stewardship; compelling sustainability education; and an increasing need for breakthrough innovation. To overcome these challenges, a combination of public-sector funding and private business innovation based on technology is essential.

The growth of hyperscale data centers that can support hundreds of thousands of servers and consume tens or hundreds of megawatts of power, has resulted in the increased focus on reducing energy consumption and increasing efficiency. To manage their electrical consumption, data centers have implemented various strategies.

1. Renewable energy sources, such as solar, wind, and hydroelectric power.
2. Energy-efficient hardware, such as servers with low-power processors and solid-state drives.
3. Virtualization allows for the consolidation of multiple physical servers into a single server, thereby reducing the number of servers required and the energy consumed.
4. Power management software to monitor and control the power usage of servers and other equipment.
5. Within a large data center, there are two competing electrical power consumption systems – one generating heat and the other providing cooling: free cooling, which uses outside air to cool the data center instead of air conditioning, and hot aisle/cold aisle containment, which separates hot and cold air streams to improve cooling efficiency.

The location of the data centers is a factor in resource sustainability. In the northwestern United States, for example, the area around the Columbia River boasts affordable land, abundant water, inexpensive electricity, and fiber-optic connectivity.[128] Meta (Facebook) has implemented data centers in Sweden, less than 70 miles from the Arctic Circle. Instead of using air conditioning, this frigid location allows the data center to use cool air from the outside to combat the warm air that is generated by the servers. Finally, the data center uses affordable, renewable, and clean energy that is supplied mainly by hydroelectric dams.[129]

Future-minded resource consuming organizations need to be leaders in the support of sustainability. An example of a renewable-energy-efficient data center that uses renewable hydroelectric power and free cool air can be seen in Figure 15.11, illustrating a snapshot of an innovative data center. Sustainability is addressed in more detail in Chapter 19.

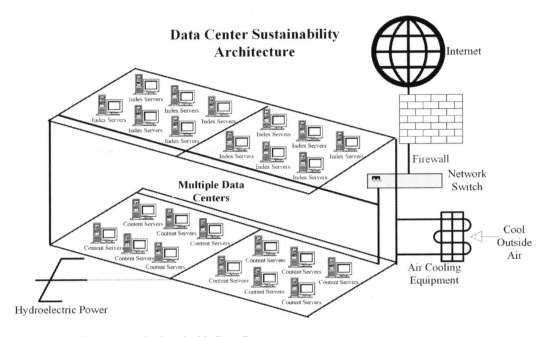

Figure 15.11 Illustration of a Sustainable Data Center

Making Predictions to Create New Knowledge

While it is not possible to predict the future, data-driven decision-making can provide a compelling picture of potential outcomes. From a commercial perspective, making predictions can provide a competitive advantage. From politics to retail to sports and everything in between, using data effectively and efficiently is a big business.

The Bridal Registry

Using technology, data can be economically analyzed on a large scale to understand and predict consumer behavior. Retailers purchase demographic information about their customers, collect purchasing history through loyalty and credit cards, collect survey results, collect what coupons their customers prefer to use, and contact customer service representatives to build aggregate customer profiles that can be used to build their businesses by attracting and retaining customers.

A statistical analyst at Target mined purchasing data from women who were signed up for Target's bridal registry.[130] From the data that they accumulated, Target used statistics to uncover patterns in purchasing products such as unscented lotions and vitamin supplements. They determined that there was a bundle of about 25 products that could be used to predict a pregnancy and the delivery date. Using this information, they distributed coupons to these women based on their predictions.[131] This new information allowed them to seek new baby business before information about the births showed in the public records.

Moneyball: Billy Beane's Dream

The book *Moneyball* describes the Oakland Athletics baseball team's 2002 season attempts to develop a competitive team by using evidence over conjecture to offset their financial limitations due to their relatively small market.[132]

There are resource-abundant baseball teams, and there are resource-constrained baseball teams, often determined by the market size of the team's home city. How do the resource-constrained teams from small markets (like the Cincinnati Reds or Milwaukee Brewers) that cannot pay large market salaries like the Yankees or Dodgers compete? What impact do baseball salaries have on success? Salaries do matter, but not in all cases. Consider the Oakland Athletics, where success starts with the players, many of whom have more latent talent than people think.

In the early 2000s, Billy Beane, general manager of the Oakland Athletics, did not have the resources that the big teams had. To compete, Beane broke from conventional baseball thinking and got creative.[133] He used data and analytics to make predictions about performance from under-valued players. He used overlooked statistics that were better indicators than the more commonly used batting averages and runs batted in. He found that offense information was more important than defense. That is, on-base percentages (a measure of how often a batter reaches base for any reason except for fielding error, fielder's choice, or dropped/uncaught third strike)[134] and slugging percentages (a measure of total bases divided by at bats) were more valid in determining the most effective players.[135]

Beane understood the market inefficiencies of baseball. As reported by Albert Chen in *Sports Illustrated,*

> There are no high first-round draft picks in the line-up. There are no sticker-shock free agents. There are, in fact, only five players making more than $5 million; the AL East champion Red Sox, by contrast, have 12 on their roster. There's never been a Billy Beane team that has better exemplified the Moneyball ethos than the 2013 Oakland A's, a 96-win club that waltzed away with the AL West and did so with the 27th-highest payroll.[136]

Stuck in Time

Founded in 1880 by entrepreneur George Eastman, the Eastman Kodak Company was an exceptional pioneer in photography and the leading producer of photographic cameras, film, and film processing. Yet despite its industry leadership, built on state-of-the-art technology, Kodak was slow to respond to competitive threats built on new technologies. Fujifilm of Japan successfully employed process technology to lower production costs, which allowed them to sell competitive products at lower prices, eroding Kodak's profit margins. The demand for digital cameras increased and reduced the market for film cameras and film. Even though Eastman Kodak's Steve Sasson invented the digital camera, the company remained stuck in the photographic film business.[137]

Kodak relied on its soon-to-be-outdated, chemical-based photographic competencies far too long, overinvesting in *what is* and not *what might be*. Kodak was focused on the low-end camera market, dependent on the chemical-based photographic processing competencies, and missed the initial instant photographic market (conceding that to another photographic entrepreneur, Dr. Edwin Land, founder of the Polaroid Company), and even though it held the initial key to the coming wave of digital photography, it was unable to unlock the future. Soon the very market that Kodak created (making memories through photography) was transformed by new technologies that produced new products, such as smartphones, with ever improving embedded cameras. Kodak sold significant digital imaging patents to raise cash, yet because they fell so far behind, they filed for bankruptcy protection in January 2012.[138]

Execution Efficiency

A challenge of organizations of all types, sizes, and missions is how to manage the duality of improving internal efficiency while simultaneously deciding on what new non-disruptive creations to implement. Technology can be used to economically streamline the distribution of information to decision-makers, enabling efficient markets. For example, Amazon's business model is dependent on technology accelerators to provide a virtually limitless inventory by applying the long tail strategy. The long tail strategy enables online retailers to sell small volumes of a broad selection of unpopular and hard-to-find merchandise, such as red-striped shoelaces, to customers. In contrast, conventional retailers sell large volumes of a narrow selection of more popular merchandise, such as Crest toothpaste, to customers. Technology properly configured and strategically applied can enable both broad and narrow selection strategies in support of a profitable business model.

Mass Customization

Technology can enable mass customizations that are ultimately markets for a single person. Markets are not made up of people always wanting the same thing; rather, there is an underlying challenge to meet their demands for variety and increasing customization. There has always been a market for personalized custom-made goods-and similarly custom configured services, for example, personal shoppers, personal travel agents, and personal physicians.

Mass customization through personalization enables customer lock-in. Mass customization represents a powerful driver as we move from conditions where products are in short supply to one of mass production so the demand for differentiation increases. The illustration Figure 15.12, by Joe Pine, describes the progression of economic value in four stages starting with the extraction of commodities, such as minerals and food, to the making of goods, such as cars, to the delivery of services, and finally to the staging of distinct experiences.

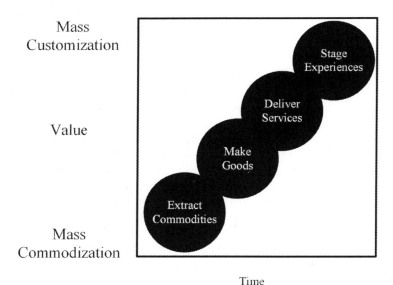

Figure 15.12 Illustration of the Progression of Economic Value

Source: Adapted from Joseph B. Pine and James H. Gilmore, "Welcome to the Experience Economy," Harvard Business Review, Vol. 76, July–August 1998 Issue, accessed September 15, 2020, https://hbr.org/1998/07/welcome-to-the-experience-economy

Strategy and Implementation of Technology Accelerators for Competitive Advantage

Businesses' top goals are unreachable without new *ideas and technological innovation* to achieve a competitive advantage. It is the combination of a strategic decision-making combined with the implementation of accelerated technology transformations that can provide the most long-term value. For example, in McKinsey's annual IT strategy survey, the results point to the value of technology innovation. The data suggest that more than three-quarters of technology initiatives have yielded some or significant cost reductions and improvements to employee experience. Two-thirds of the respondents indicated that technology initiatives increased revenue from existing streams, and more than half cite the creation of new revenue streams such as a new product line or new business.[139]

The Role of Ideas and Technological Progress

Robert Solow

Robert Solow, an American economist, received the Nobel Memorial Prize in Economic Sciences in 1987 for his work on the theory of economic growth. In his model, long-term economic growth is based on factors outside the economic system, such as savings, population growth, and technological progress.[140] The model assumes that technological progress is exogenous, independent of economic forces.

Robert Solow introduced the notion that *ideas and technological innovation* are the primary driver of economic growth; he discovered that the key to sustained growth is a country's ability to create, absorb and use new technology innovation.[141] Solow concluded that technological change was a key driver of economic growth, and that technological change was based on an exogenous growth model, not something determined in the model, but was an outside factor.[142] In summary, he demonstrated that technological innovation generates a significant portion of economic growth.

Paul Romer

Paul Romer, an American economist, was awarded the Nobel Memorial Prize in Economic Sciences in 2018. He developed the theory of endogenous technological change, where the search for new ideas by profit-maximizing entrepreneurs and researchers drives economic growth. The theory focuses on how technological change is the result of efforts by researchers and entrepreneurs who respond to economic incentives; the investments in human capital, innovation, and knowledge are crucial contributors to steer economic growth.[143]

Endogenous growth theory thus holds that economic growth is primarily the result of internal and not external forces, which is the idea that the investment in human capital, innovation, and knowledge are crucial contributors to economic growth. He proposed the notion of endogenous growth theory and how ideas are different from other goods and require specific conditions to thrive in a market.[144] The investment of human intellectual capital, innovation, and knowledge are the contributors to economic growth. Specifically,

> The endogenous growth theory primarily holds that the long run growth rate of an economy depends on policy measures. For example, subsidies for research and development or education increase the growth rate in some endogenous growth models by increasing the incentive for innovation.[145]

The role of *ideas and technological innovation* is part of the exogenous and endogenous growth models. The difference is that in the exogenous growth model the determining factors are outside the economic system, whereas in the endogenous model, the activities within the economic system, such as explicit and deliberate polices, can achieve economic growth. Both provide different frameworks for understanding economic growth.

Strategic leadership is needed to drive *ideas and technological innovation*. The broad means of building innovation capability for the future are critical. A changing world requires transformations that compel a shift in mindset, culture, competencies, talent, and leadership to be ready for the future. *Leadership is not about maintaining the status quo*; rather, it is the creation of a bridge between the past, through the present, and into the future. Four key aspects of strategy that lead to innovation and entrepreneurship are described as follows.

1. Strategy: Technology-accelerated business model
2. Strategy: Organizational transformation for technology acceleration
3. Strategy: The two-sided network ecosystem
4. Strategy: The importance of combinations

Strategy: Technology-Accelerated Business Model

In the past, entrepreneurs had to divert their precious resources away from building their core products and services and toward creating expensive technology infrastructures before they were able to grow their businesses. They had to build websites, implement servers, purchase expensive manufacturing machines, and potentially hire skilled technical staff.

The concept and process of technology accelerators have helped to produce a cadre of ventures that have created goods and services that can be used to fast-track start-ups. Entrepreneurs with viable value propositions and business models can launch a new business using existing e-business platforms, such as eBay, Amazon, or Etsy.

In addition to value proposition delivery systems such as eBay, entrepreneurship can turn to virtual technology to help raise start-up and operating capital, as well as for cash management systems. Entrepreneurs can use crowd funding such as Kickstarter for financial resources, use PayPal for customer payments, purchase advertisements from Google, and integrate their businesses into social media platforms, such as LinkedIn, Facebook, Twitter, and Tumblr.

Entrepreneurs can use the cloud for their server and database needs, create diagrams of the design models with Google Sketchup, and build new products with both three-dimensional printing and affordable programmable robotics. Business services are available through Shapeway and Ponoko to take the diagram of the design model and build an agile prototype. Entrepreneurs can use YouTube to market and promote their new creations. With the Internet and the World Wide Web, entrepreneurs, limited only by their imaginations, can immediately become international businesses.[146]

A competitive advantage with technology can be achieved in four completely different ways as viewed on separate continuums:

1. Technology convergence of devices can provide a pathway into ecosystems such as those of Google, Microsoft, Amazon, and Apple. This is especially valuable for those with proprietary solutions.
2. Innovation integration enables firms to minimize the deleterious impact of both co-innovation and adoption chain risk.
3. Ecosystem knowledge accumulation enables firms to multiply their ability to associate more and more ideas.
4. Finally, product complexity and added value provide a shield against competitive copying.

Figure 15.13 illustrates the four-technology continuums that provide competitive advantage.

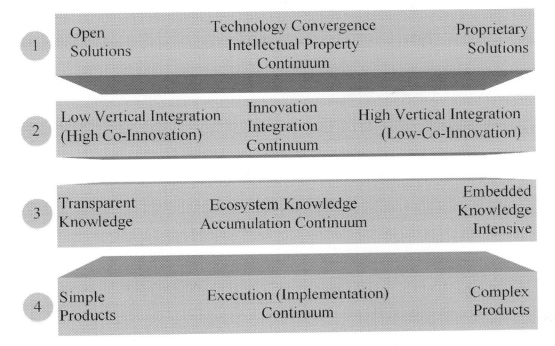

Figure 15.13 Illustration of the Technology Competitive Advantage Continuums

Strategy: Organizational Transformations for Technology Acceleration

Organizations can accelerate technology by building innovation capability through several types of transformations. The firm must take responsibility for the ownership of all impacts and consequences of their technology, intended or not.[147] Firms can use transformations to:

1. Operate for the long-term-benefit of business and society as viewed by the environmental, societal, and governance model (ESG).
2. Create positive outcomes for all stakeholders through human capital development, fostering the growth mindset, building creative cultures, enhancing innovation competencies, recruiting top talent, and growing leadership expertise.
3. Accelerate the adoption of technology to streamline assets, extend digital capabilities, provide economies of scale, lower costs, and simplify unnecessary complexity.[148]

The following describes practical examples of organizational transformations that can build long-term human capital and innovation capability.[149]

1. Transformative horizontal mergers can build innovation capability when organizations with similar business lines of products or services are combined to expand their markets, such as Microsoft's acquisition of LinkedIn, Apple's acquisition of Beats, Amazon's acquisition of the robotics firm Kiva Systems, and the merger of Daimler-Benz and Chrysler.
2. Transformative vertical mergers can build innovation capability when organizations in the same industry adapt by extending their value chain, such as the merger of the Internet provider America Online (AOL) with media conglomerate Time Warner.

3. Transformative market-extension mergers can build innovation capability when two firms produce or sell the same type of product or service but to different markets with the purpose to extend their market such as RBC (Royal Bank of Canada) Centura acquiring Eagle Bancshares, Inc.

4. Transformative product extension or congeneric mergers can build innovation capability when organizations whose products or services are associated or co-consumed together create a meta product such as Broadcom, a Bluetooth system firm, and Mobilink Telecom, a supplier of chips. The two firms do not produce the same product or service.

5. Transformative conglomerates are created when companies in different businesses pursue the broadening of their services and products such as the merger of the Walt Disney Company and the American Broadcasting Company. Alphabet is a conglomerate holding company create a collection of separate firms. Conglomerates can be restructured if they have become ineffective, such as General Electric dividing into separate companies focused on aviation, healthcare, and energy.[150]

Selected examples are shown in Figure 15.14.

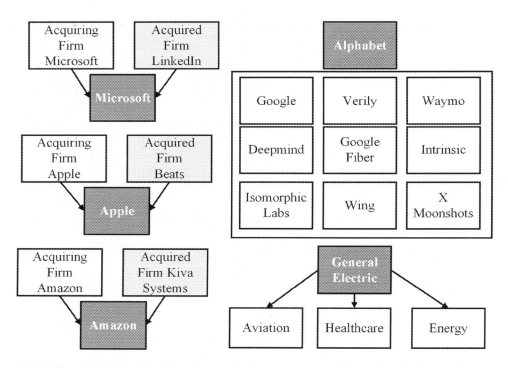

Figure 15.14 Illustration of Organizational Transformations to Accelerate Technology Implementation

Strategy: The Two-Sided Network Ecosystem

A two-sided network *strategy* utilizing technology accelerators provides a competitive advantage. A two-sided network (two-sided market) is a platform with two distinct user groups that provide each other with network benefits. The underlying phenomenon of the network effect occurs when an increased numbers of participants improve the value of a good or service exponentially.[151]

For example, an electric vehicle is a two-sided platform, the two sides are an installed base of car buyers and a large network of geographically dispersed multi-stall rapid-charging stations.[152]

There are many examples of two-sided networks, including credit cards (composed of cardholders and merchants), mobile apps (end-users and developers), publications (advertisers and consumers), video-game consoles (gamers and game developers), recruitment sites (job seekers and recruiters), and search engines (advertisers and users).[153]

The Tesla ecosystem strategy is based on providing all the components needed for the consumer's job to be done. The two main components are the design and manufacturing of electric vehicles at scale and a charging station network. The investment to build a massive charging network makes sense only if there is a large enough user base and demand for these chargers. Tesla has achieved a first mover advantage because they built out a proprietary charging network for their cars across the country.[154] A two-sided network is illustrated in Figure 15.15.

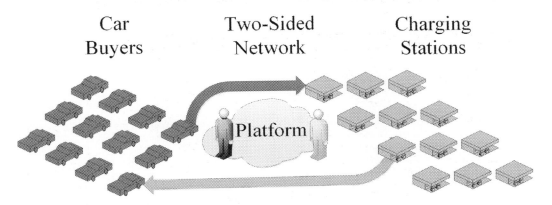

Figure 15.15 Illustration of the Two-Sided Network

Source: Adapted from Hemant Bhargava, Jonas Boehm, and Geoffrey G. Parker, "How Tesla's Charging Stations Left Other Manufacturers in the Dust," January 27, 2021, accessed February 10, 2021, https://hbr.org/2021/01/how-teslas-charging-stations-left-other-manufacturers-in-the-dust

Tesla has created a proprietary two-side network strategy that enabled the platform owner to coordinate the two sides of the market, that is, the installed base of cars and the network of charging stations. Because Tesla owns the charging network, it can choose the price charged to the customer (whether to charge or make charging free and monetize only the car), the number of stations, roll-out timing, and location. Because Tesla was an early adopter, the two-sided network gives them a significant first mover competitive advantage.[155]

Strategy: The Importance of Combinations

According to the McKinsey Global Institute, US productivity growth has slowed in the last 15 years to 1.4% annual growth (as compared to long-term rates of 2.2% since 1948). They also found striking variations in productivity among leading and lagging firms within each sector – a gap that is only widening.[156]

The most productive companies follow a strategy that combines these four elements:

1. The firms capture value from digitization.
2. The firms invest in intangibles (such as R&D or workforce capabilities).
3. The firms build a future-ready workforce.
4. The firms take a systems approach.

McKinsey projects that if more firms followed these four elements and brought the US closer to 2.2% growth, it could be worth $10 trillion in cumulative GDP by 2030.

Summary

In this chapter, the role and value of technology accelerators in the process of innovation and entrepreneurship were reviewed. Specifically, three aspects of technology acceleration: technology convergence, innovation integration, and internal and external ecosystems were discussed. We described four core technology competencies: semiconductors, sensors, wireless, and databases.

How the technology accelerators add value was outlined and how start-ups can use existing platforms to their advantage is described. Finally, several examples of businesses and industries that were either leaders or followers in the ongoing transformation of industries due to the relentless advances in technology were discussed. Next, in Chapter 16 the importance and value of protecting intellectual property in the pursuit of innovation and technology are explored.

Notes

1. *Wikipedia*, s.v. "Alfred Nobel," accessed October 9, 2020, https://en.wikipedia.org/wiki/Alfred_Nobel.
2. *Wikipedia*, s.v. "Nobel Memorial Prize in Economic Sciences," accessed October 9, 2020, https://en.wikipedia.org/wiki/Nobel_Memorial_Prize_in_Economic_Sciences.
3. *Wikipedia*, s.v. "List of Nobel Laureates by Country," accessed October 9, 2020, https://en.wikipedia.org/wiki/List_of_Nobel_laureates_by_country.
4. Katharina Buchholz, "Immigrants' Big Share of Nobel Prizes in the Sciences," October 8, 2020, accessed February 22, 2024, www.statista.com/chart/19646/science-nobel-prizes-by-country-and-immigrant-share/.
5. *Wikipedia*, s.v. "Nobel Prize," accessed June 22, 2024, https://en.wikipedia.org/wiki/Nobel_Prize.
6. *Wikipedia*, s.v. "Marie Curie," https://en.wikipedia.org/wiki/Marie_Curie.
7. Emma Reynolds and Katie Hunt, "Nobel Prize in Chemistry Awarded to Scientists Who Discovered CRISPR Gene Editing Tool for 'Rewriting the Code of Life'," October 7, 2020, accessed March 15, 2021, www.cnn.com/2020/10/07/health/nobel-prize-2020-winner-chemistry-scn-intl/index.html.
8. Nell Greenfieldboyce and Mark Katkov, "2 Scientists Awarded Nobel Prize in Chemistry for Genome Editing Research," October 7, 2020, accessed February 22, 2024, www.npr.org/2020/10/07/921043046/2-female-scientists-awarded-nobel-prize-in-chemistry-for-genome-editing-research.
9. Michael Fitzgerald, Nina Kruschwitz, Didier Bonnet, and Michael Welch, "Embracing Digital Technology," *Sloan Review*, October 8, 2013, accessed October 4, 2021, http://sloanreview.mit.edu/projects/embracing-digital-technology/.
10. Jonathan Deakin, Laura LaBerge, and Barbara O'Beirne, "Five Moves to Make During a Digital Transformation," *McKinsey and Company*, April 24, 2019, accessed October 4, 2021, www.mckinsey.com/business-functions/digital-mckinsey/our-insights/five-moves-to-make-during-a-digital-transformation.
11. Michael Chui, Mena Issler, Roger Roberts, and Lareina Yee, "McKinsey Technology Trends Outlook 2023," July 20, 2023, accessed November 19, 2023, www.mckinsey.com/capabilities/mckinsey-digital/our-insights/the-top-trends-in-tech#new-and-notable.
12. Michael Chui, Mena Issler, Roger Roberts, and Lareina Yee, "Technology Trends Outlook 2023," July 2023, accessed July 29, 2023, www.mckinsey.com/capabilities/mckinsey-digital/our-insights/the-top-trends-in-tech#/.
13. *Wikipedia*, s.v. "Artificial Intelligence," accessed November 21, 2023, https://en.wikipedia.org/wiki/Artificial_intelligence#Applications.
14. *Wikipedia*, s.v. "Turing Test," accessed November 21, 2023, https://en.wikipedia.org/wiki/Turing_test.
15. Michael Chui, Mena Issler, Roger Roberts, and Lareina Yee, "McKinsey Technology Trends Outlook 2023," July 20, 2023, accessed November 19, 2023, www.mckinsey.com/capabilities/mckinsey-digital/our-insights/the-top-trends-in-tech#new-and-notable.
16. Economist, "AI Is Setting Off a Great Scramble for Data," August 19, 2023, accessed August 19, 2023, www.economist.com/business/2023/08/13/ai-is-setting-off-a-great-scramble-for-data.

17. Kevin Roose, "The Chaos at OpenAI, Explained," November 21, 2023, accessed February 17, 2024, www.nytimes.com/2023/11/21/briefing/open-ai-sam-altman-microsoft.html.
18. Zoe Kleinman and Chris Vallance, "AI 'Godfather' Geoffrey Hinton Warns of Dangers as He Quits Google," May 2, 2023, accessed November 20, 2023, www.bbc.com/news/world-us-canada-65452940.
19. Joshua Rothman, "Why the Godfather of A.I. Fears What He's Built," November 13, 2023, accessed November 20, 2023, www.newyorker.com/magazine/2023/11/20/geoffrey-hinton-profile-ai.
20. Michael Chui, Mena Issler, Roger Roberts, and Lareina Yee, "McKinsey Technology Trends Outlook 2023," July 20, 2023, accessed November 19, 2023, www.mckinsey.com/capabilities/mckinsey-digital/our-insights/the-top-trends-in-tech#new-and-notable.
21. Michael Chui, Mena Issler, Roger Roberts, and Lareina Yee, "McKinsey Technology Trends Outlook 2023," July 20, 2023, accessed November 19, 2023, www.mckinsey.com/capabilities/mckinsey-digital/our-insights/the-top-trends-in-tech#new-and-notable.
22. Richelle Deveau, Sonia Joseph Griffin, and Steve Reis, "AI-Powered Marketing and Sales Reach New Heights with Generative AI," May 11, 2023, accessed July 6, 2023, www.mckinsey.com/capabilities/growth-marketing-and-sales/our-insights/ai-powered-marketing-and-sales-reach-new-heights-with-generative-ai.
23. "What Is Generative AI?" January 19, 2023, accessed January 24, 2023, www.mckinsey.com/featured-insights/mckinsey-explainers/what-is-generative-aiLinks to an external site.
24. "What Is Generative AI?" January 19, 2023, accessed January 24, 2023, www.mckinsey.com/featured-insights/mckinsey-explainers/what-is-generative-aiLinks to an external site.
25. GPTBot, accessed August 26, 2023, https://platform.openai.com/docs/gptbot?tpcc=NL_Marketing.
26. Michael Chui, Mena Issler, Roger Roberts, and Lareina Yee, "McKinsey Technology Trends Outlook 2023," July 20, 2023, accessed November 19, 2023, www.mckinsey.com/capabilities/mckinsey-digital/our-insights/the-top-trends-in-tech#new-and-notable.
27. Michael Chui, Mena Issler, Roger Roberts, and Lareina Yee, "McKinsey Technology Trends Outlook 2023," July 20, 2023, accessed November 19, 2023, www.mckinsey.com/capabilities/mckinsey-digital/our-insights/the-top-trends-in-tech#new-and-notable.
28. "What Is Web3?," October 10, 2023, accessed November 19, 2023, www.mckinsey.com/featured-insights/mckinsey-explainers/what-is-web3.
29. Michael Chui, Mena Issler, Roger Roberts, and Lareina Yee, "McKinsey Technology Trends Outlook 2023," July 20, 2023, accessed November 19, 2023, www.mckinsey.com/capabilities/mckinsey-digital/our-insights/the-top-trends-in-tech#new-and-notable.
30. Michael Chui, Mena Issler, Roger Roberts, and Lareina Yee, "McKinsey Technology Trends Outlook 2023," July 20, 2023, accessed November 19, 2023, www.mckinsey.com/capabilities/mckinsey-digital/our-insights/the-top-trends-in-tech#new-and-notable.
31. Michael Chui, Mena Issler, Roger Roberts, and Lareina Yee, "McKinsey Technology Trends Outlook 2023," July 20, 2023, accessed November 19, 2023, www.mckinsey.com/capabilities/mckinsey-digital/our-insights/the-top-trends-in-tech#new-and-notable.
32. Michael Chui, Mena Issler, Roger Roberts, and Lareina Yee, "McKinsey Technology Trends Outlook 2023," July 20, 2023, accessed November 19, 2023, www.mckinsey.com/capabilities/mckinsey-digital/our-insights/the-top-trends-in-tech#new-and-notable.
33. "What Is Cloud Computing?" August 17, 2022, accessed November 24, 2023, www.mckinsey.com/featured-insights/mckinsey-explainers/what-is-cloud-computing.
34. Michael Chui, Mena Issler, Roger Roberts, and Lareina Yee, "McKinsey Technology Trends Outlook 2023," July 20, 2023, accessed November 19, 2023, www.mckinsey.com/capabilities/mckinsey-digital/our-insights/the-top-trends-in-tech#new-and-notable.
35. Anna Heid and Ivan Ostovic, "Open Interactive Popup Recalculating the Future of Drug Development with Quantum Computing," October 23, 2020, accessed October 4, 2021, www.mckinsey.com/industries/pharmaceuticals-and-medical-products/our-insights/recalculating-the-future-of-drug-development-with-quantum-computing.
36. Michael Chui, Mena Issler, Roger Roberts, and Lareina Yee, "McKinsey Technology Trends Outlook 2023," July 20, 2023, accessed November 19, 2023, www.mckinsey.com/capabilities/mckinsey-digital/our-insights/the-top-trends-in-tech#new-and-notable.
37. Michael Chui, Mena Issler, Roger Roberts, and Lareina Yee, "McKinsey Technology Trends Outlook 2023," July 20, 2023, accessed November 19, 2023, www.mckinsey.com/capabilities/mckinsey-digital/our-insights/the-top-trends-in-tech#new-and-notable.
38. Michael Chui, Mena Issler, Roger Roberts, and Lareina Yee, "McKinsey Technology Trends Outlook 2023," July 20, 2023, accessed November 19, 2023, www.mckinsey.com/capabilities/mckinsey-digital/our-insights/the-top-trends-in-tech#new-and-notable.

39. Nessan Bermingham, Katrine Bosley, Samarth Kulkarni, Tom Ruby, and Navjot Singh, "Realizing the Potential of CRISPR," January 24, 2017, accessed October 4, 2021, www.mckinsey.com/industries/pharmaceuticals-and-medical-products/our-insights/realizing-the-potential-of-crispr.
40. Jennifer Doudna and Michael Chui, "Programming LIfe: An Interview with Jennifer Doudna," June 4, 2020, accessed October 4, 2021, www.mckinsey.com/industries/pharmaceuticals-and-medical-products/our-insights/programming-life-an-interview-with-jennifer-doudna.
41. Michael Chui, Mena Issler, Roger Roberts, and Lareina Yee, "McKinsey Technology Trends Outlook 2023," July 20, 2023, accessed November 19, 2023, www.mckinsey.com/capabilities/mckinsey-digital/our-insights/the-top-trends-in-tech#new-and-notable.
42. Michael Chui, Mena Issler, Roger Roberts, and Lareina Yee, "McKinsey Technology Trends Outlook 2023," July 20, 2023, accessed November 19, 2023, www.mckinsey.com/capabilities/mckinsey-digital/our-insights/the-top-trends-in-tech#new-and-notable.
43. "Global Energy Perspective 2022," April 26, 2022, accessed November 19, 2023, www.mckinsey.com/industries/oil-and-gas/our-insights/global-energy-perspective-2022.
44. "McKinsey Platform for Climate Technologies," accessed November 19, 2023, www.mckinsey.com/capabilities/sustainability/how-we-help-clients/mckinsey-platform-for-climate-technologies.
45. Michael Chui, Mena Issler, Roger Roberts, and Lareina Yee, "McKinsey Technology Trends Outlook 2023," July 20, 2023, accessed November 19, 2023, www.mckinsey.com/capabilities/mckinsey-digital/our-insights/the-top-trends-in-tech#new-and-notable.
46. "2021 CEO Study: Find Your Essential," accessed October 4, 2021, www.ibm.com/thought-leadership/institute-business-value/c-suite-study/2021-ceo.
47. "2021 CEO Study: Find Your Essential," accessed October 4, 2021, www.ibm.com/thought-leadership/institute-business-value/c-suite-study/2021-ceo.
48. "2021 CEO Study: Find Your Essential," accessed October 4, 2021, www.ibm.com/thought-leadership/institute-business-value/c-suite-study/2021-ceo.
49. "2021 CEO Study: Find Your Essential," accessed October 4, 2021, www.ibm.com/thought-leadership/institute-business-value/c-suite-study/2021-ceo.
50. "2021 CEO Study: Find Your Essential," accessed October 4, 2021, www.ibm.com/thought-leadership/institute-business-value/c-suite-study/2021-ceo.
51. Felix Richter, "LG Drops Out of the Smartphone Race," April 6, 2021, accessed October 4, 2021, www.statista.com/chart/24569/global-smartphone-market-share/.
52. Victor Hristov, "Apple A7 Chip Specs and Details Surface," October 30, 2013, accessed October 4, 2021, www.phonearena.com/news/Apple-A7-chip-specs-and-details-surface_id48860.
53. *Wikipedia*, s.v. "Apple A7," accessed October 4, 2021, http://en.wikipedia.org/wiki/Apple_A7.
54. Michal Lev-Ram, "Samsung's Road to Global Domination," *Fortune*, January 22, 2013, accessed October 4, 2021, https://fortune.com/2013/01/22/samsungs-road-to-global-domination/.
55. Ian Sherr, Eva Dou, and Lorraine Luk, "Apple Tests iPhone Screens as Large as Six Inches," *The Wall Street Journal*, September 5, 2013, accessed October 4, 2021, http://online.wsj.com/news/articles/SB10001424127887324577304579057262388733816.
56. Brad Stone, "Google's Sundar Pichai Is the Most Powerful Man in Mobile," *Bloomberg Businessweek*, June 24, 2014, accessed October 4, 2021, www.bloomberg.com/news/articles/2014-06-24/googles-sundar-pichai-king-of-android-master-of-mobile-profile.
57. Josephine Nuamah, "The Evolution of the Apple Processor," Sepetember 22, 2022, accessed November 18, 2023, www.megamac.com/blog/the-evolution-of-the-apple-processor.
58. Brad Reed, "The Biggest Threat to Samsung's Gadget Empire," December 16, 2013, accessed October 4, 2021, http://bgr.com/2013/12/16/samsung-future-gadget-innovation/.
59. "Intel. Silicon Valley Historical Association," 2008, accessed September 24, 2021, www.siliconvalley-historical.org/intel-history.
60. "Intel: 50 Years of Leadership," accessed October 4, 2021, www.chiphistory.org/intel-ceo-history.
61. Agam Shah, "How Intel Knocked Itself Out of the Smartphone Chip Market," *PC World*, May 4, 2016, accessed October 4, 2021, www.pcworld.com/article/3065894/how-intel-knocked-itself-out-of-the-smartphone-chip-market.html.
62. Will Knight, "Intel Chases a More Power-Efficient Future," September 14, 2011, accessed October 4, 2021, www.technologyreview.com/2011/09/14/191309/intel-chases-a-more-power-efficient-future/.
63. Aaron Pressman, "Intel's CEO Reveals New Strategy: Go Big or Go Home," March 23, 2021, accessed October 4, 2021, https://fortune.com/2021/03/23/intel-ceo-gelsinger-strategy-new-chip-plants-big-spending/.

64. Will Knight, "Intel Wants to Revive US Chipmaking – But It Has to Catch Up First," March 24, 2021, accessed October 4, 2021, www.wired.com/story/intel-wants-revive-us-chipmaking-catch-up-first/.

65. Aaron Pressman, "Intel's CEO Reveals New Strategy: Go Big or Go Home," March 23, 2021, accessed October 4, 2021, https://fortune.com/2021/03/23/intel-ceo-gelsinger-strategy-new-chip-plants-big-spending/.

66. Aaron Pressman, "Intel's CEO Reveals New Strategy: Go Big or Go Home," March 23, 2021, accessed October 4, 2021, https://fortune.com/2021/03/23/intel-ceo-gelsinger-strategy-new-chip-plants-big-spending/.

67. Will Knight, "Intel Wants to Revive US Chipmaking – But It Has to Catch Up First," September 14, 2011, accessed October 4, 2021, www.wired.com/story/intel-wants-revive-us-chipmaking-catch-up-first/.

68. Venkat Atluri and Miklós Dietz, *The Ecosystem Economy: How to Lead in the New Age of Sectors Without Borders* (Hoboken, NJ: Wiley, 2023), 1.

69. Tiernan Ray, "Apple: It's All About the Ecosystem, Raymond James Tells CNBC," *Barron's*, July 1, 2013, accessed October 4, 2021, http://blogs.barrons.com/techtraderdaily/2013/07/01/apple-its-all-about-the-ecosystem-raymond-james-tells-cnbc/.

70. Venkat Atluri and Miklós Dietz, *The Ecosystem Economy: How to Lead in the New Age of Sectors Without Borders* (Hoboken, NJ: Wiley, 2023), 2.

71. Venkat Atluri and Miklós Dietz, *The Ecosystem Economy: How to Lead in the New Age of Sectors Without Borders* (Hoboken, NJ: Wiley, 2023), 7.

72. Venkat Atluri and Miklós Dietz, *The Ecosystem Economy: How to Lead in the New Age of Sectors Without Borders* (Hoboken, NJ: Wiley, 2023), 8.

73. Byron Acohido, "Brand Champ: Microsoft-Nokia Bests Google-Motorola," *USA Today*, September 4, 2013, accessed October 4, 2021, www.usatoday.com/story/tech/2013/09/04/brand-champ-microsoft-nokia-bests-google-motorola/2768929/.

74. James Surowiecki, "How Steve Jobs Changed," *The New Yorker*, October 17, 2011, accessed October 4, 2021, www.newyorker.com/talk/financial/2011/10/17/111017ta_talk_surowiecki.

75. Michael deAgonia, Preston Gralla, and J. R. Raphael, "Battle of the Media Ecosystems: Amazon, Apple, Google and Microsoft," *Computer World*, August 2, 2013, accessed October 4, 2021, www.computer-world.com/s/article/9240650/Battle_of_the_media_ecosystems_Amazon_Apple_Google_and_Micros oft?taxonomyId=229&pageNumber=2.

76. Gary Hamel and C. K. Prahalad, "Strategic Intent," *Harvard Business Review* 67, no. 3 (1989), 63–76.

77. Michael Arndt, "3M's Seven Pillars of Innovation," *Bloomberg Businessweek*, May 9, 2006.

78. *Wikipedia*, s.v. "Mimeograph," accessed October 4, 2021, http://en.wikipedia.org/wiki/Mimeograph.

79. *Wikipedia*, s.v. "Xerox," accessed October 4, 2021, http://en.wikipedia.org/wiki/Xerox.

80. "The Business Model," accessed October 4, 2021, www.quickmba.com/entre/business-model/.

81. *Wikipedia*, s.v. "PARC (Company)," accessed October 4, 2021, http://en.wikipedia.org/wiki/Xerox_PARC.

82. Malcolm Gladwell, "Creation Myth, Xerox PARC, Apple, and the Truth About Innovation," *The New Yorker*, May 16, 2011, accessed October 4, 2021, www.newyorker.com/reporting/2011/05/16/110516fa_fact_gladwell?currentPage=all.

83. Rod Chester, "Overpriced and Undersold: Apple's Ten Biggest Flops," July 14, 2013, accessed October 28, 2021, https://amp.news.com.au/technology/overpriced-and-undersold-apple8217s-ten-biggest-flops/news-story/876fb81400f5060785348b0f40dcb137.

84. Rod Chester, "Windows Drawn on Microsoft's 10 Biggest Failures," July 18, 2013, accessed October 28, 2021, www.adelaidenow.com.au/technology/news/windows-drawn-on-microsoft8217s-10-biggest-failures/news-story/42f021b06eb32c2713b1bcfaea4cc336.

85. Ariel Bleicher, "Farming by the Numbers," *IEEE Spectrum*, May 30, 2013, accessed October 4, 2021, http://spectrum.ieee.org/computing/it/farming-by-the-numbers/?utm_source=computerwise&utm_medium=email&utm_campaign=061213.

86. Ariel Bleicher, "Farming by the Numbers," *IEEE Spectrum*, May 30, 2013, accessed October 4, 2021, http://spectrum.ieee.org/computing/it/farming-by-the-numbers/?utm_source=computerwise&utm_medium=email&utm_campaign=061213.

87. Adam Richardson, "The Four Technologies You Need to Be Working With," *Harvard Business Review*, September 12, 2011, accessed October 28, 2021, https://hbr.org/2011/09/the-four-technologies-you-need.

88. *Wikipedia*, s.v. "Computer Architecture," accessed October 4, 2021, https://en.wikipedia.org/wiki/Computer_architecture.

89. "Who Invented the Transistor?" accessed November 24, 2023, www.physlink.com/Education/AskExperts/ae414.cfm.

90. Ezra Klein, "Transcript: Ezra Klein Interviews Chris Miller," April 4, 2023, accessed, November 24, 2023, www.nytimes.com/2023/04/04/podcasts/transcript-ezra-klein-interviews-chris-miller.html.

91. "Microchip vs Semiconductor: Meaning and Differences," accessed November 24, 2023, https://thecontentauthority.com/blog/microchip-vs-semiconductor.

92. Angeet Kaur Bouns, "Intel (INTC) vs. Taiwan Semiconductor Manufacturing (TSM) – Determining the Profitability of Chip Stocks," November, 10, 2023, accessed November 18, 2023, www.entrepreneur.com/finance/intel-intc-vs-taiwan-semiconductor-manufacturing-tsm/465204#.

93. "Insights on Semiconductors," accessed November 16, 2023, www.mckinsey.com/industries/semiconductors/our-insights.

94. "Semiconductors Power the Modern World," accessed November 21, 2023, www.semiconductors.org/.

95. David Leonhardt, "The Semiconductor Struggle," July 14, 2023, accessed July 14, 2023, www.nytimes.com/2023/07/14/briefing/semiconductors.html.

96. Don Clark and Ana Swanson, "U.S. Pours Money Into Chips, But Even Soaring Spending Has Limits," January 1, 2023, accessed August 6, 2023, www.nytimes.com/2023/01/01/technology/us-chip-making-china-invest.html.

97. Ezra Klein, "Transcript: Ezra Klein Interviews Chris Miller," April 4, 2023, accessed, November 24, 2023, www.nytimes.com/2023/04/04/podcasts/transcript-ezra-klein-interviews-chris-miller.html.

98. Ondrej Burkacky, Julia Dragon, and Nikolaus Lehmann, "The Semiconductor Decade: A Trillion-Dollar Industry," April 1, 2022, accessed July 22, 2023, www.mckinsey.com/industries/semiconductors/our-insights/the-semiconductor-decade-a-trillion-dollar-industry.

99. Jim Probasco, "What Is the CHIPS and Science Act of 2022?" April 10, 2023, accessed July 27, 2023, www.investopedia.com/chips-and-science-act-6500333.

100. Paul Brandus, "Intel's Build-in-America Emphasis Is About More Than Profits-It's Also About National Security," January 28, 2021, accessed August 9, 2021, www.msn.com/en-us/news/world/intel-s-build-in-america-emphasis-is-about-more-than-profits-it-s-also-about-national-security/ar-BB1daCSv.

101. David Leonhardt, "The Semiconductor Struggle," July 14, 2023, accessed July 14, 2023, www.nytimes.com/2023/07/14/briefing/semiconductors.html.

102. "McKinsey on Semiconductors," acccessed November 16, 2023, www.mckinsey.com/industries/semiconductors/our-insights/mckinsey-on-semiconductors.

103. *Investopedia*, s.v. "Semiconductor," accessed October 4, 2021, www.investopedia.com/terms/s/semiconductor.asp.

104. "What Is a Semiconductor?" May 15, 2023, accessed November 16, 2023, www.mckinsey.com/featured-insights/mckinsey-explainers/what-is-a-semiconductor.

105. Paul Brandus, "Intel's Build-in-America Emphasis Is about More than Profits-It's also about National Security," January 28, 2021, accessed August 9, 2021, www.msn.com/en-us/news/world/intel-s-build-in-america-emphasis-is-about-more-than-profits-it-s-also-about-national-security/ar-BB1daCSv.

106. Thomas L. Friedman, "Is There a War Coming Between China and the U.S.?" April 27, 2021, accessed August 9, 2021, www.nytimes.com/2021/04/27/opinion/china-us-2034.html.

107. Ezra Klein, "Transcript: Ezra Klein Interviews Chris Miller," April 4, 2023, accessed July 14, 2023, www.nytimes.com/2023/04/04/podcasts/transcript-ezra-klein-interviews-chris-miller.html.

108. Harald Bauer, Jan Veira, and Florian Weig, "Moore's Law: Repeal or Renewal?" December 1, 2013, accessed July 21, 2023, www.mckinsey.com/industries/semiconductors/our-insights/moores-law-repeal-or-renewal.

109. *Wikipedia*, s.v. "Sensor," accessed October 4, 2021, https://en.wikipedia.org/wiki/Sensor.

110. Jay Agarwal, Lapo Mori, Fritz Nauck, Johnathan Oswalt, Dickon Pinner, Robert Samek, and Pasley Weeks, "Optimizing Water Treatment with Online Sensing and Advanced Analytics," October 29, 2020, accessed October 4, 2021, www.mckinsey.com/industries/metals-and-mining/our-insights/optimizing-water-treatment-with-online-sensing-and-advanced-analytics.

111. *Wikipedia*, s.v. "Lidar," accessed October 4, 2021, https://en.wikipedia.org/wiki/Lidar.

112. *Wikipedia*, s.v. "Ethernet," accessed October 4, 2021, https://en.wikipedia.org/wiki/Ethernet.

113. Lutz Goedde, Joshua Katz, Alexandre Ménard, and Julien Revellat, "Agriculture's Connected Future: How Technology Can Yield New Growth," October 9, 2020, accessed October 4, 2021, www.mckinsey.com/industries/agriculture/our-insights/agricultures-connected-future-how-technology-can-yield-new-growth.

114. *Wikipedia*, s.v. "Database," accessed October 4, 2021, https://en.wikipedia.org/wiki/Database.

115. *Wikipedia*, s.v. "SQL," accessed October 4, 2021, https://en.wikipedia.org/wiki/SQL.

116. *Wikipedia*, s.v. "Internet," accessed October 4, 2021, http://en.wikipedia.org/wiki/Internet.

117. "UPS Deploys Purpose-Built Navigation for UPS Service Personnel," accessed October 28, 2021, www.globenewswire.com/news-release/2018/12/04/1661762/30428/en/UPS-Deploys-Purpose-Built-Navigation-For-UPS-Service-Personnel.html.

118. *Wikipedia*, s.v. "Internet of Things," accessed October 4, 2021, https://en.wikipedia.org/wiki/Internet_of_things.

119. *Wikipedia*, s.v. "Cloud Computing," accessed November 25, 2023, https://en.wikipedia.org/wiki/Cloud_computing.

120. *Wikipedia*, s.v. "Arthur Rock," accessed October 4, 2021, http://en.wikipedia.org/wiki/Arthur_Rock.

121. David Silverstein, Philip Samuel, and Neil DeCarlo, *The Innovator's Toolkit: 50+ Techniques for Predictable and Sustainable Organic Growth*, 2nd ed. (Boston: Harvard Business School Publishing, 2009), 111.

122. Brad Stone, "How Facebook Sells Your Friends," *Bloomberg Businessweek*, September 24, 2010, accessed November 25, 2023, www.bloomberg.com/news/articles/2010-09-22/facebook-sells-your-friends.

123. Brad Stone, "How Facebook Sells Your Friends," *Bloomberg Businessweek*, September 24, 2010, accessed November 25, 2023, www.bloomberg.com/news/articles/2010-09-22/facebook-sells-your-friends.

124. Brad Stone, "How Facebook Sells Your Friends," *Bloomberg Businessweek*, September 24, 2010, accessed November 25, 2023, www.bloomberg.com/news/articles/2010-09-22/facebook-sells-your-friends.

125. Walter Isaacson, *Steve Jobs* (New York: Simon and Schuster, 2011), 21.

126. *Wikipedia*, s.v. "Adam Smith," accessed October 4, 2021, https://en.wikipedia.org/wiki/Adam_Smith.

127. *Wikipedia*, s.v. "Joe Ricketts," accessed October 4, 2021, http://en.wikipedia.org/wiki/Joe_Ricketts.

128. Jennifer Reingold, "The New Billionaire Political Activist," *Fortune*, October 8, 2012, 103; Randy H. Katz, "Tech Titans Building Boom," *Spectrum, IEEE* 46, no. 2 (2009), 40–54.

129. Ashlee Vance, "Inside the Arctic Circle, Where Your Facebook Data Lives," *Bloomberg Businessweek*, October 4, 2013, accessed October 28, 2021, www.fbcoverup.com/docs/library/2013-10-04-Inside-the-Artic-Circle-Where-YourFacebookDataLives-by-Ashlee-Vance-Business-Week-Oct-4-2013.pdf.

130. Charles Duhiff, "How Companies Learn Your Secrets," *The New York Times*, February 16, 2012, accessed October 4, 2021, www.nytimes.com/2012/02/19/magazine/shopping-habits.html?pagewanted=all.

131. Kashmir Hill, "How Target Figured Out a Teen Girl Was Pregnant before Her Father Did," *Forbes*, February 16, 2012, accessed October 4, 2021, www.forbes.com/sites/kashmirhill/2012/02/16/how-target-figured-out-a-teen-girl-was-pregnant-before-her-father-did/.

132. M. Lewis, *Moneyball*, 1st ed. (New York: Norton, 2004).

133. Adam Sternbergh, "Billy Beane of 'Moneyball' Has Given Up on His Own Hollywood Ending," *The New York Times*, September 21, 2011, accessed October 4, 2021, www.nytimes.com/2011/09/25/magazine/for-billy-beane-winning-isnt-everything.html?pagewanted=all&_r=0.

134. *Wikipedia*, s.v. "On-Base Percentage," accessed October 4, 2021, http://en.wikipedia.org/wiki/On-base_percentage.

135. Tyler Bleszinski, "Still Playing Moneyball," October 25, 2012, accessed October 4, 2021, www.athletic-snation.com/2012/10/25/3553788/still-playing-moneyball-an-exclusive-interview-with-billy-beane.

136. Albert Chen, "American League: Right on the Moneyball," *Sports Illustrated*, October 7, 2013, accessed October 28, 2021, https://xqubits.com/3zplp/sports-illustrated-wiki#.

137. *Wikipedia*, s.v. "Steven Sasson," accessed October 4, 2021, http://en.wikipedia.org/wiki/Steven_Sasson.

138. Michael J. De La Merced, "Eastman Kodak Files for Bankruptcy," *The New York Times*, January 19, 2012, accessed October 4, 2021, http://dealbook.nytimes.com/2012/01/19/eastman-kodak-files-for-bankruptcy/.

139. Anusha Dhasarathy, Ross Frazier, Naufal Khan, and Kristen Steagall, "Seven Lessons on How Technology Transformations Can Deliver Value," *McKinsey Digital*, March 11, 2021, accessed November 20, 2021, www.mckinsey.com/business-functions/mckinsey-digital/our-insights/seven-lessons-on-how-technology-transformations-can-deliver-value.

140. Peter Dizikes archive, "The Productive Career of Robert Solow," December 27, 2019, accessed November 26, 2023, www.technologyreview.com/2019/12/27/131259/the-productive-career-of-robert-solow/.

141. Nobel Perspectives, "Robert M. Solow," accessed November 26, 2023, www.ubs.com/microsites/nobel-perspectives/en/laureates/robert-solow.html.

142. *Corporate Finance Institute*, s.v. "Solow Growth Model," accessed November 26, 2023, https://corporate-financeinstitute.com/resources/knowledge/economics/solow-growth-model/.

143. *Wikipedia*, s.v. "Paul Romer," accessed November 26, 2023, https://en.wikipedia.org/wiki/Paul_Romer.

144. Kate Vitasek, "Nobel Laureate Paul Romer: The Path to Economic Growth and Innovation," November 19, 2018, accessed November 26, 2023, www.forbes.com/sites/katevitasek/2018/11/19/paul-romer-the-path-to-economic-growth-and-innovation/#19e51a95139d.

145. *Wikipedia*, s.v. "Endogenous Growth Theory," accessed May 25, 2020, https://en.wikipedia.org/wiki/Endogenous_growth_theory.
146. Bruce Nussbaum, *Creative Intelligence* (New York: Harper Business, 2013), 166–169.
147. Polman Paul and Andrew Winston, *Net Positive* (La Vergne: Harvard Business Review Press, 2021), 30.
148. Paul Daume, Tobias Lundberg, Patrick McCurdy, Jeff Rudnicki, and Liz Wol, "How One Approach to M&A Is More Likely to Create Value Than All Others," October 13, 2021, accessed November 21, 2021, www.mckinsey.com/business-functions/strategy-and-corporate-finance/our-insights/how-one-approach-to-m-and-a-is-more-likely-to-create-value-than-all-others.
149. Marshall Hargrave, "Merger," March 22, 2021, accessed November 16, 2021, www.investopedia.com/terms/m/merger.asp.
150. Rick Clough and Ryan Beene, "How GE's Larry Culp Found a Way Out of the Mess Jack Welch Made," November 11, 2021, accessed November 19, 2021, www.bloomberg.com/news/articles/2021-11-11/how-ge-ceo-larry-culp-decided-to-split-conglomerate-into-three-companies.
151. *Investopedia*, s.v. "Network Effect," accessed November 23, 2021, www.investopedia.com/terms/n/network-effect.asp.
152. Hemant Bhargava, Jonas Boehm, and Geoffrey G. Parker, "How Tesla's Charging Stations Left Other Manufacturers in the Dust," January 27, 2021, accessed February 10, 2021, https://hbr.org/2021/01/how-teslas-charging-stations-left-other-manufacturers-in-the-dust.
153. *Wikipedia*, s.v. "Two-Sided Markets," accessed February 10, 2021, Two-sided market – Wikipedia.
154. Nathan Furr and Jeff Dyer, "Lessons from Tesla's Approach to Innovation," February 12, 2020, accessed November 16, 2021, https://hbr.org/2020/02/lessons-from-teslas-approach-to-innovation.
155. Hemant Bhargava, Jonas Boehm, and Geoffrey G. Parker, "How Tesla's Charging Stations Left Other Manufacturers in the Dust," January 27, 2021, accessed February 10, 2021, https://hbr.org/2021/01/how-teslas-charging-stations-left-other-manufacturers-in-the-dust.
156. Charles Atkins, Asutosh Padhi, and Olivia White, "What the Most Productive Companies Do Differently," February 16, 2023, accessed February 13, 2024, https://hbr.org/2023/02/what-the-most-productive-companies-do-differently.

16 The Importance of Intellectual Property

[T]o promote the progress of science and useful arts, by securing for limited times to authors and inventors the exclusive right to their respective writings and discoveries.
– The US Constitution, Article I, Section 8, Clause 8

Intellectual Property

Intellectual property plays an important role in the process of innovation and entrepreneurship. With considerable foresight, in 1787, the framers of the United States Constitution included protection for those whose pursuits and work directly promoted progress in the sciences and useful arts, thereby contributing to the growth of the new nation. The intellectual property clause enumerates two of the powers of the US Congress: giving authors the sole right to their writing for a set period (the basis for US copyright law) and likewise assuring inventors the rights to their discoveries for a set period (the basis of US patent law).

To begin the chapter, it is important to note that the authors are not attorneys, and this material is not intended as legal advice. As always, it is recommended that in all legal matters pertaining to your business, it is best to seek the advice and counsel of a licensed attorney.

With that in mind, there are several interesting and important aspects about intellectual property that should be considered in the context of innovation and entrepreneurship. In this chapter, we examine the ongoing key role of intellectual property protection including the four major types: trade secrets, copyrights, trademarks and branding, and patents. Armed with these basics, we explore the role of intellectual property in practice as a key component in innovation and entrepreneurship. Nowhere is this seen more clearly than in the music industry over time.

Intellectual Property in Music

The music business has transitioned from vinyl to CD to digital distribution that includes digital download and music streaming. During the period between 2001 and 2010, there was a 60% decline in annual global music revenue resulting in a drop of $14 billion. In the same period digital music revenue increased to $4 billion but was not sufficient to offset the revenue gap; the music business revenue bottomed out in 2014.

The music business began to see an uptick in recordings and sales with the increased adoption of music streaming services. By 2020, streaming services accounted for 62% of worldwide music revenues.[1] The International Federation for Information Processing (IFPI) Global Music Report states that the total global recorded music revenues for 2020, were $21.6 billion.[2] "Growth was driven by streaming, especially by paid subscription streaming revenues, which increased by 18.5%. There were 443 million users of paid subscription accounts at the end of 2020."[3] The global music revenue would follow a U-shape from the period from 2001 to 2020.

DOI: 10.4324/9781003034308-17

Traditionally, in the music business, composers (who provide the lyrics and melody), record labels (who provide the audio recording), and recording artists protect their intellectual property using copyrights that acknowledge their ownership.

When someone buys a song from iTunes, Google Play or any other digital store, money from that sale is paid out to creators via both copyrights – composition and sound recording – with the rates depending on label size, distributor size and specific negotiations between the two as well as any other middle parties involved.[4]

For example, in the music industry, the copyright belongs to artists and whatever label is behind them. Copyrighted music is offered through licenses that generate royalties if a song is played on streaming services, AM/FM radio, satellite radio, and/or Internet radio. In addition, there are licenses for reproduction rights (i.e., for sales of physical CDs or digital music files), and synchronization rights (i.e., for music used in film, television, commercials, and other media).[5]

Fair use is a doctrine of law that permits limited use of copyrighted material without having to first acquire permission from the copyright holder. The fair use right is a general exception to copyright law that applies to music.[6] Fair use is very subjective and is decided on a case-by-case basis. For instance, if music is incorporated into training materials the fair use doctrine might be applicable but would likely be narrow.[7]

When creating music, the composer may include samples from other music.[8] Sampling is the reuse of a portion (or sample) of a sound recording in another recording. Sampling may introduce several elements of music. The elements that can be sampled are the melody (tune), the lyrics that convey the message in "verse" and "chorus" structures, the harmony, and the rhythm.[9] "Sampling without permission can infringe copyright or may be fair use. The process of acquiring permission for a sample is known as clearance, a potentially complex and costly process; samples from well-known sources are now often prohibitively expensive."[10]

In 1969, the soul group, the Winstons, released a single where both the A-side and the B-side received notoriety. The A-side single by the composer Richard Lewis Spencer, won a Grammy Award for Best R&B song titled "Color Him Father."[11] On the B-side song, "Amen, Brother," there is a drum break that lasts about seven seconds known as the "Amen break."[12] The break of drums in "Amen, Brother" is at the 01:26 mark; it is a sample that has been used extensively in popular music.[13] Figure 16.1 illustrates the use of sampling from the song "Amen, Brother."

The "Amen break" has been used in thousands of recordings by rock bands and in television show themes.[14] Even though you may never have heard of the song "Amen, Brother," it is likely you have listened to a specific part of the track because the "Amen break" is the most sampled piece of music of all time.[15] The copyright owner of the "Amen break," Richard Lewis Spencer, never received royalties for its use.[16]

The following are songs that have been sampled most often by other artists.[17]

1. "Amen, Brother"
2. "Think (About It)," Lyn Collins
3. "Change the Beat" (Female Version)
4. "Funky Drummer," James Brown
5. "La Di Da Di," Doug E. Fresh and Slick Rich

The single "Funky Drummer" was recorded on November 20, 1969, in Cincinnati, Ohio, and released by King records in 1970.[18] The recording contains one of the most frequently sampled and

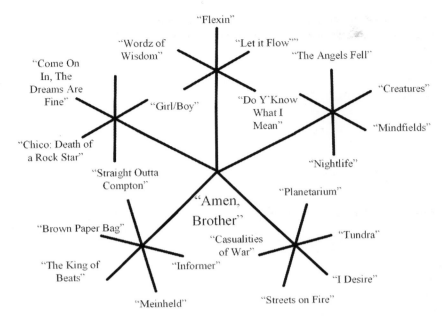

Figure 16.1 Illustration of the Sampling in Music

Source: Acknowledgment: https://www.samples.fr/secret-de-sample-the-amen-break/

one of the most influential pieces of music.[19] The sample break was improvised by the drummer Clyde Stubblefield for which he was not credited.

Stubblefield was featured in the 2009 PBS documentary *Copyright Criminals*, which addressed the creative and legal aspects of sampling in the music business. "'People use my drum patterns on a lot of these songs,' he said, 'They never gave me credit, never paid me. It didn't bug me or disturb me, but I think it's disrespectful not to pay people for what they use.'"[20] Stubblefield received an honorary Doctor of Fine Arts from the University of Wisconsin–Madison that was conferred posthumously in 2017. The sample has been used for decades by hip-hop groups and rappers, such as Public Enemy, Run-DMC, N.W.A, Raekwon, LL Cool J, Beastie Boys, and Prince.[21]

While the music business provides an interesting glimpse into the multifaceted world of intellectual property in a popular and ever-changing industry, the role of intellectual property impacts a global economy. While the global economy continued to underperform in 2011, worldwide intellectual property protection filing was robust. Patent applications worldwide passed the two-million mark in 2011, growing nearly 8% over 2010. Similarly, trademark application worldwide increased by 13.3% over 2010. In 2011, for the first time, more patent applications were filed at the patent office of China than at any other country patent office in the world, joining the patent offices of Germany, Japan, and the United States as the world leaders.[22]

Intellectual Property Types

According to the World Intellectual Property Organization (WIPO), intellectual property refers to creations of the mind: inventions, literary and artistic works, and symbols, names, and images used in commerce.[23] From a legal perspective, intellectual property (IP) refers to legal property rights involving creations of the mind, both artistic and commercial.[24] In a manner of speaking, intellectual property protection is about building fences around ideas. Consequently, there are four types of intellectual property protection, shown in the following list and in Figure 16.2, that are essential for understanding how to protect ownership rights in innovation and entrepreneurship:

1. Trade secrets
2. Copyrights
3. Trademarks and branding
4. Patents

Figure 16.2 Illustration of Intellectual Property Types

Trade Secrets

The Uniform Trade Secrets Act (UTSA) defines a trade secret as information, including a formula, pattern, compilation, program, device, method, technique, or process, that (1) derives independent economic value from not being generally known or readily available by legal means and (2) is the subject of efforts that are reasonable under the circumstances to maintain its secrecy.[25]

For example, the formula for Coca-Cola is a trade secret. While copyright, trademark, and patent protection have been sought for other aspects of the production, bottling, sale, and distribution of Coca-Cola products, the original recipe formulated by inventor and entrepreneur Dr. John Pemberton is still protected to this day as a trade secret.

Trade or business secrets, unlike published patents and copyrights, are available for the world to see and they derive their value from not being disclosed publicly. Rather, a trade secret is information that derives value from being unknown. While non-disclosure adds a measure of protection, continuous effort is required to maintain a trade secret.

Unlike patents and copyrights, trade secret protection can last forever. Once disclosed, however, protection is lost forever. Trade secrets are protected under federal and state laws. Most states have a version of the UTSA, with the exceptions of North Carolina and New York. Moreover, at the federal level, the Economic Espionage Act of 1996 makes it a federal crime to steal a trade secret or to possess information that is known to be stolen.

Examples of items that are often protected via trade secrets include computer software and databases; customer lists and information; drawings, designs, and plans; formulas; internal cost and pricing information; internal company systems, operations, and marketing strategies; research pertaining to product formulations; request for proposals (RFPs) and bids; specialized training materials; and supplier and distributor information.

Protection of intellectual property via trade secrets provides perpetual protection that can extend broadly to business know-how, is timely and automatic (no filing necessary), and requires no proof of novelty. It does, however, require constant vigilance since once disclosed the secret is lost forever. When relying on trade secrets, it is always advisable to secure employee confidentiality and non-compete agreements and customer/vendor non-disclosure agreements where appropriate. In addition, it is advisable to review consultant work-for-hire agreements to ensure that you own what you pay for and that it is protected. This will have implications for copyrights as well.

Copyrights

According to the US Copyright Office, a unit of the Library of Congress, a copyright protects original works of authorship fixed in a tangible medium of expression. It covers both published and unpublished work, as well as the way an idea is expressed. It does not, however, protect the idea itself.[26] That is, a copyright is a form of protection for the way a story is told but not the idea, per se. A copyright is given automatically when someone puts a pen to paper or from the time the work is created in fixed form. "However, registration with the Copyright Office is a pre-requisite to infringement lawsuits and important benefits accrue when a work is registered within three months of initial publication."[27] That is, while a work is copyrighted or protected from the time pen is put to paper, legal action, or a lawsuit to protect the work is predicated on having an officially registered copyright.

Registration with the US Copyright Office provides two distinct advantages: (1) a solid foundation for maintaining the copyright and (2) a stronger foundation for legal recourse should the copyright be violated. It is essential that copyright holders conduct periodic checks for copyright infringement. The Internet can provide a means for identifying potential infringement. Vigorous vigilance and proper notice of the copyright itself, as well as pursuit of any subsequent infringement, are essential elements of maintaining a copyright. Copyright notice alerts potential infringers and prevents them from claiming "innocent infringement." Proper notice of the copyright includes the use of the circled "c" (©) or "copyright" – for example, "©20NN. All Rights Reserved. Company/Individual Name."

What is copyrightable? While not an exhaustive list, copyrights apply to architectural works; art, sculpture, and photographs; building designs and blueprints; computer software; dramatic works, including any accompanying music; literary works; motion pictures, video, video games, and audiovisual works; musical works, including the score and lyrics; pantomimes and choreographic works; and sound recordings. There are categories of material that are not eligible for federal copyright protection, such as works that have not been fixed in a tangible medium or form of expression (e.g., improvisational speeches that have not been recorded). In addition, ideas, concepts, and works that consist of common property and contain no original authorship (e.g., lists or tables taken from public documents or common sources) would not be eligible.

As noted earlier, works made for hire should be fully considered when it comes to copyright protection. In general, in the case of a work made for hire, the employer, and not the employee, is considered the "author." While the work of an independent contractor is not considered a work for hire, a work prepared by an employee within the scope of his or her employment or work specifically ordered or commissioned by the employer is. For example, part of collective work, supplementary work, instructional materials, or a compilation of materials could be considered work for hire. Of course, it is always advisable to consult with a licensed attorney since there are cases where artists, advertising agencies, and contract programmers could be exceptions.

Copyrights in Music

The music industry introduced earlier in the chapter provides an interesting insight into copyrights. The public performance of a song requires a license whether the music is played in a retail store, at a conference, or in a restaurant by a live band, by a CD, or by a DJ. The public performance licenses are issued by country; for instance, in the US, the performing rights organizations (PROs) are ASCAP, BMI, SESAC, and GMR.[28] In the music business, there is a difference between a composition of a song and a sound recording, and each may have a separate copyright.

COMPOSITION

There is a copyright for the composition of a song that consists of a melody and any accompanying lyrics that is normally owned by the songwriter or the songwriter's music publishing company.[29] These publishing rights for a copyright are described using sheet music that has the music notation and lyrics.

For example, Bob Dylan has sold his entire song writing catalog – more than 600 songs – to Universal Music Publishing Group for $300,000.[30] "The owner of publishing rights typically controls whether or not songs are cleared for inclusion in TV, film, and ads."[31] "Songwriting rights – that is, ownership of a song's melody and lyrics – are figured and paid out separately from recording rights."[32]

SOUND RECORDING

There is a separate copyright for a sound recording, which is generally owned by the record label that released the recording.[33] For instance, Taylor Swift's $300 million catalogue was acquired by a private investment group that covered recorded rights but not the composition rights.[34]

Independent Musicians

Independent musicians can create a recording on their own, or pay for studio time and session fees, but it is the musician who copyrights the composition and owns that sound recording.[35] Copyright protection lasts for the life of the author plus an additional 70 years. Once the copyright term ends, the music enters the public domain, and anyone is free to use it.[36]

It is worth noting that as soon as you start using a trademark with your goods or services, the USPTO considers that the point of ownership. That is, rights in your trademark are established by using it, "but those rights are limited, and they only apply to the geographic area in which you're providing your goods or services."[37] By contrast, while it is not necessarily required to register a trademark, a USPTO registration provides broader rights and protections than an unregistered one. Trademarks and branding are explored in more detail next.

Trademarks and Branding

What is a trademark? According to the US Patent and Trademark Office (USPTO), a trademark is any word, name, symbol, or device (i.e., pictures, colors, sounds) used to identify the source of one's product and distinguish it from the products of others.[38] Functions of trademarks/service marks include: identification of source(s), a "guarantee" of the constancy or consistency of the quality, and a repository of goodwill and foundation for advertising of goods and/or services. For example, the Nike swoosh is a trademark. While it is not required to file for a trademark, it is preferred for optimizing notice and protection.

For companies such as Apple, Amazon, Microsoft, and others, a trademark represents a significant amount of their intangible assets. For example, Coca-Cola is considered one of the most recognizable brands and one of the most valuable trademarks in the world, worth between $55 billion and $80 billion. Interbrand, a brand consulting company, ranks the top 100 most valuable brands based on criteria that include financial performance and the role the brand plays in influencing consumer choices. In addition to the top three listed earlier, which make up 62.3% of the total value of the top ten brands, Google, Samsung, Coca-Cola, Toyota, Mercedes-Benz, McDonalds, and Disney round out the top ten.[39] All ten of these firms were started by entrepreneurs who would be viewed as innovative and grew the ventures to the success we see today. As noted in earlier chapters, the paradox of innovation and entrepreneurship education is that we see these ventures in their success but need to understand them at the beginning of the journey.

Given the value and importance of trademarks, it is important to consider their search, registration, and level of protection. In general, trademarks can be viewed on a continuum from weak to strong: generic, descriptive, suggestive, and arbitrary or fanciful.

Trademarks distinguish your products and services from those of your competitors and protect your investment in brand loyalty and goodwill. While any word, symbol, slogan, logo, or design may qualify for trademark protection, it is important to conduct a thorough search and selection process to ensure the best possible outcome. Selecting and searching your trademarks can include using the Internet, a public database like the USPTO, and/or professional search companies.

After a thorough search, a trademark can be obtained by using the mark in trade and commerce (although it may be limited to a geographic area of use). There are both federal and state registration processes, but a federal registration is the most common. The circled "R" (®) means the mark is federally registered, while "TM" indicates that the mark is unregistered, in process, or registered at the state level. The more you use your mark to identify your goods and/or services, the stronger it will become.

It goes almost without saying, but it is best to choose as strong a mark as possible. Arbitrary or fanciful marks are among the strongest and receive the most protection. Arbitrary is when a common word is used in an unfamiliar way (e.g., Apple® or Shell®). Fanciful/inherently distinctive occurs when words are invented solely for its use as the trademark (e.g., Kodak® or Xerox®). Suggestive marks are the most common and receive some level of protection since they rely on imagination, thought, or perception to link it to the good and/or service (e.g., Blu-ray® or Play-Station®). Descriptive marks may put you in a gray zone and could go either way (e.g., Small Business Institute® or Computer Land®).

One way to protect a descriptive mark is by establishing "secondary meaning." For example, the words "small" "business" and "institute" in and by themselves would be considered generic (generic words cannot be protected) and could not be trademarked. Taken collectively, however, "Small Business Institute®" represents a non-profit educational association devoted to the advancement of experiential small business and entrepreneurship education, and thus, by establishing secondary meaning, the term can be trademarked. In addition, demonstrating exclusive and continuous use for five years contributes to the protection of a descriptive mark.

Of equal importance to the process of searching, registering, and strengthening a trademark is maintaining a trademark. Marking your products and marketing materials (e.g., using ® for federally registered marks), establishing policies and guidelines for use, and policing your marks are all important. For example, "Escalator" was originally a registered trademark of the Otis Elevator Company but has become generic. "Popsicle" is a registered trademark of the Unilever Company, which it vigorously defends to this day.

Branding in Action

In this ever-changing society, the most powerful and enduring brands are built from the heart. They are real and sustainable.

– Howard Schultz, chairman and CEO, Starbucks

One of the most perplexing aspects of innovation and venture creation is building brand aware-ness, acceptance, and loyalty. Apple, Coca-Cola, Disney, Facebook, Ford, Microsoft, McDonald's, Nike, and Toyota are all examples of what have become iconic brands among the most recogniz-able (and valuable) in the world – *presently*. As noted earlier in this text, however, they illustrate the conundrum of understanding innovation and entrepreneurship; that is, we come to know ven-tures in their success, but as innovators and entrepreneurs just at the beginning of the journey, we need to understand these ventures in their infancy.

For example, Howard Schultz has shown on numerous occasions that he has considerable in-sight when it comes to innovation, entrepreneurship, and building a brand. Beginning its entre-preneurial journey in 1971, Starbucks has risen from a single store in Seattle, Washington, to a global phenomenon. Today, we know Starbucks as the dominant global purveyor of the finest coffee (and now tea also) beverages in the world. The journey to that global position is quite instructive. For Starbucks, the brand was not just the coffee beverage but rather the coffee beverage experience. It was about educating consumers who sought a higher-end beverage product and service experi-ence. This required a relentless pursuit of a focused differentiation strategy. It recognized that not everyone was going to be a Starbucks customer, but for those who would become its customers, building brand awareness, acceptance, and loyalty were paramount.

With that in mind, the question becomes, what is involved in building an enduring brand? The strategy for building a brand, especially via trademarks and/or catch phrases, is nicely captured in the simple rubric of knowing your ABCs.

A IS FOR AUTHENTIC

From the previous example, Schultz most definitely gets an "A" for his insights into building a brand. "Authentic brands don't emerge from marketing cubicles or advertising agencies. They emanate from everything the company does."[40] When it comes to brand awareness and acceptance, consumers are very sensitive to the value proposition, how the company has positioned itself, and how it interacts with the customer. A company can destroy its brand image quickly if it is not re-sponsive to consumer needs. The formula for branding success is to focus on developing primary product and/or services offerings; to develop, build, and maintain core and distinctive competen-cies; and to deliver value that exceeds your customers' expectations.

Nike's mantra of "authentic athletic apparel" illustrates why Phil Knight's dream of a better run-ning shoe is the global brand we know today. Knight and his former track coach and future busi-ness partner, Bill Bowerman, initially only sought to develop a better running shoe. Together they formed Blue Ribbon Sports and began selling Tiger running shoes, produced by Onitsuka in Japan, from the trunk of Knight's car. Signing their first employee, Jeff Johnson, Blue Ribbon Sports began a transition to making and designing its own athletic footwear. This included an innovative waffle outer-sole design, and rebranding the start-up as Nike, complete with the now ubiquitous Nike swoosh logo designed by a Portland State graphic design student, Carolyn Davidson.[41] Both Schultz and Knight built authentic brands from the ground up, innovating products and processes, creating industries that today have multiple competitors, each striving for new innovations in the delivery of their goods and services.

B IS FOR BOLD

Building brands can often require bold moves. Ted Turner's early days of building the cable news industry is a perfect example of the relationship between brand and bold. Indeed, the beginning of the cable television industry we know today involved several bold moves. Perhaps the boldest was even believing that broadcast television as it was known in the late 1960s could be transformed in both scope and delivery. Beginning in 1970, Turner purchased the struggling, number-four television station, UHF Channel 17 WJRJ, in a four-station Atlanta market. He immediately renamed it WTCG (for Turner Communications Group) and set out on a programming path built on old movies, a heavy dose of sports, and rebroadcasts of syndicated sitcoms and dramas, ultimately building the "superstation" vision that would become TBS. Along the way, Turner optioned on all the NBC shows the local Atlanta affiliate (the top-rated station at the time) didn't pick up that year. Soon, Turner Communication billboards all over Atlanta proclaimed WTCG the new NBC affiliate in Atlanta. If success can be measured by the number of letters one receives from NBC lawyers, the campaign was a huge success! Of course, the billboards came down, but the road to what would become nearly universally known brands in the cable television industry, TBS, CNN, Turner Broadcasting, and more, had already been paved.[42]

C IS FOR CREATIVE

When it comes to innovation and entrepreneurship, as we have seen in earlier chapters, creativity is a key factor. Considered one of the most creative start-ups of the 20th century, Walt Disney Productions took a very interesting route to building the Disney brand we know today. Walt Disney began his entrepreneurial journey driving a Red Cross ambulance in France in 1919. On his return home to Kansas, he failed at his first venture attempt, sold his meager possessions, connected with his brother selling vacuums in California, convinced him to be his partner in a motion picture production company, and successfully negotiated a solid contract that looked like the start of something. The success was short-lived. While Disney was in New York on business, the studio executive who hired the fledgling venture fired them because they had wasted the studio's money. Disney was determined not to let this setback deter him and, not wanting to break up the team, began to write the scenario for the first feature production of his newly rebranded company, Walt Disney Productions, Ltd. Disney, on the train back to California. He decided that his new cartoon hero would be a mouse because mice are little, cute, and always up to mischief. The first Mickey Mouse cartoon reel was produced in a cramped space over the Disney garage. Of course, finding a new studio was a considerable challenge until, undaunted, he found an equally bold independent producer willing to take a chance on Disney's dream.[43] Today, the Disney brand is among the most valuable in the world. Walt Disney has received the most individual Academy Award (Oscar) wins with 22 and nominations with 59.[44]

Building a brand creates expectations on both the part of the venture and the customer. It becomes a rallying point for how your company is viewed internally by the founders, funders, and employees, and externally by customers and other key stakeholders. The ABCs of building a brand (authenticity, boldness, and creativity) enable innovators and entrepreneurs to deliver in a way that is enduring. If you believe in your business, so will your backers, employees, and customers. The common theme in building a brand is designing and executing the reason to believe in your products or services. This includes aligning your goals, the organization you build, and the customer experience with your core products and services and speaking to building brand awareness, acceptance, and, ultimately, loyalty.

Branding in Music

Again, the music industry provides some interesting insights into the roles of branding in innovation and entrepreneurship. For example, "Rock and Roll" as both an innovative musical genre and a commercial brand name was created in the 1950s but was similar to "Rhythm and Blues," which had been around since the 1940s, in a 12-bar blues form that was faster and infused with livelier rhythms and more pronounced beats.[45] The intent behind expanding "Rhythm and Blues" by calling it "Rock and Roll" was to reach a wider audience.

Innovation in the music industry can be seen in two classic recordings, "Good Rockin' Tonight" and "Rock Around the Clock," both of which featured a 12-bar blues form, boogie-woogie bass line, and backbeats. Each became precursors of music innovation that would spark a new music genre and ultimately a new music brand – Rockabilly and Rock and Roll.

In 1947, Wynonie Harris's "Good Rockin' Tonight" had characteristics of music marketed as "Rhythm and Blues," 12-bar blues form, the up-tempo boogie-woogie bass line, the honking saxophone, the backbeat, and heavy emphasis on beats two and four of every measure. The instrumentation was the saxophone, drums, bass, piano, and at the very outset, a jazzy muted cornet.

By 1954, Bill Haley and His Comets recorded "Rock Around the Clock" again using the boogie-woogie bass line, the straightforward 12-bar blues form, and the drums with an emphasis on the backbeat (beats two and four of every bar). The instrumentation, however, included a saxophone, heavy drums, bass, and electric guitar, recalling the urban blues bands of the 1950s. Ultimately, the differences rebranded "Rhythm and Blues," as "Rock and Roll" emerged directed at different audiences, designed to capture changing popular musical interests and tastes. From baroque to classical to jazz, big band to swing, rhythm and blues to rockabilly to rock and roll, heavy metal to rap, and beyond, the music industry is an evolving branding exemplar.

Patents

What is a patent? According to the US Patent and Trademark Office, a patent is

> a property right granted by the Government of the United States of America to an inventor "to exclude others from making, using, offering for sale, or selling the invention throughout the United States or importing the invention into the United States" for a limited time in exchange for public disclosure of the invention when the patent is granted.[46]

In brief, a patent is a contract between the government and the inventor. As seen in the US Constitution Article I, Section 8, Clause 8, quoted at the beginning of this chapter, the government receives the disclosure of the invention for the general promotion of the sciences, while the inventor receives the right to exclude others from making, using, selling, and importing the invention for a specified period (14 years for a design patent and 20 years for a utility patent). While there are multiple types of patents, the three most common are utility, design, and plant patents, and of these, utility patents are the most prevalent. In addition, although not a patent, statutory invention registration is a process by which an inventor or applicant effectively blocks others from getting a patent on the same invention, even after the patent application is abandoned.[47]

In a manner of speaking, patents are temporary monopolies granted to individuals and firms by governments. Each country has its own patent laws, and, as such, the laws are territorial. Worldwide, the top countries by patents granted in 2019 were China, United States, Japan, the European Patent Office, the Republic of Korea, the Russian Federation, India, Canada, Germany, Australia, France, and Brazil.[48] As an indication of the scale involved, in the United States, approximately 7,544,797 patents were granted as of 2020, with 3,890,902 of US origin and 3,653,895 of foreign origin.[49]

It is often said that anything under the sun that is made by man can be patented. According to US patent laws, though, to obtain a patent, the concept must generally be "any new and useful process, machine, manufacture, or composition of matter, or any new and useful improvement thereof."[50] While a patent can be sought for almost any kind of invention, certain things are not patentable, such as laws of nature (e.g., $E = mc^2$), physical phenomena, mental processes, or abstract ideas. Patents are somewhat counterintuitive in that they do not give you the right to make something. What they do provide can be summed up in one word: exclusivity. A patent excludes others from making, using, or selling your invention. Unlike a copyright, which only protects actual copying, patents can protect against commercial use of an idea and its functional equivalent. A patent gives the holder the right to preclude functionally equivalent works, thereby protecting intellectual property.

Once it is determined that an idea or concept is patentable, three additional requirements must be met. Patents must be useful, new (novelty), and not obvious to one skilled in the discipline. First, the useful/utility condition, while usually the easiest of the three requirements to establish, is not to be overlooked. Always ask the obvious question, "What and to whom is this idea useful and why?" Clarity of thought concerning usefulness helps establish the fundamental basis for the patent.

Second, when it comes to new/novelty, an invention cannot be patented if (1) it was described in a publication more than one year prior to the filing date or (2) it was used publicly or offered for sale to the public more than one year prior to the filing date. In general, an inventor who does not file for patent protection on an invention within this one-year grace period will lose all right to obtain patent protection on the invention. Most other countries do not grant a grace period. It is almost always preferable to file a patent application before any public disclosure of the invention.

Finally, the idea must be non-obvious to someone skilled in the technical area in which the invention is derived. The invention must be a non-obvious improvement over prior art. The determination is made by deciding whether the invention seeking patent would have been obvious to a person having ordinary skill in the art. This notion refers to a fictional person considered to have the normal skills and knowledge in a particular technical field (an art) without being a genius.[51]

Patents are valuable for several reasons. They allow the inventor to monopolize a given area of commerce for a limited time. Moreover, patents provide an aura of credibility in the marketplace, while simultaneously signaling a "scare" factor to potential competition. A patent can also be an asset used in licensing, trading, or even rewarding employees.

The penalties for patent infringement can be significant. In 2021, Intel lost a patent-infringement trial over technology related to chip-making because they infringed on two patents owned by VLSI Technology. They were told to pay $1.5 billion for infringement of one patent and $675 million for infringement of the second.[52]

Three types of patents exist: utility, design, and plant. Each is briefly discussed in the following sections, along with a brief discussion of statutory invention registration.

Utility Patent

A utility patent protects the way an article is used and works. Utility patents are the most common kinds of patents and, in general, protect new and useful processes, machines, manufacturing, or compositions of matter, or any new and useful improvement. In other words, it protects what is useful about an invention.

For example, entertainer Michael Jackson was a co-patent holder (#5,255,452, October 26, 1993) of an anti-gravity illusion that is described as

[a] system for allowing a shoe wearer to lean forwardly beyond his center of gravity by virtue of wearing a specially designed pair of shoes which will engage with a hitch member movably projectable through a stage surface. The shoes have a specially designed heel slot which can be

detachably engaged with the hitch member by simply sliding the shoe wearer's foot forward, thereby engaging with the hitch member.[53]

Other types of utility patents (lasting 20 years from filing date) include apparatus, processes, articles of manufacture, and compositions of matter.

Design Patents

"Whoever invents any new, original, and ornamental design for an article of manufacture may obtain a patent" (35 U.S.C. § 171).[54] Generally speaking, a design patent, lasting 14 years from the date of issue, protects the way an article looks, including non-functional, ornamental inventions, such as the shape or style of a good.

Design patents have no requirement for utility and generally protect the appearance of a functional article. It covers only the non-functional aspects of a product design (e.g., the design of an automobile body unrelated to functionality such as ornamental tail fins or the unique appearance of a Chevrolet Corvette).

In relation to trademarks, design patents protect the ornamental design of an article, while trademarks protect the public identity of the product. Using the automotive example, the auto manufacturer would apply for a design patent for the overall design or look of the car, such as the General Motors design patents for the Chevrolet Corvette, but would also apply for a trademark for the term describing the car, such as GM owning the trademark registration for the name "Corvette."

Plant Patents

"Whoever invents or discovers and asexually reproduces any distinct and new variety of plant, including cultivated spores, mutants, hybrids, and newly found seedlings, other than a tuber propagated plant or a plant found in an uncultivated state" (35 U.S.C. § 161).[55] No bacteria or similar single-cell organisms need apply!

This protection is limited to "a living plant organism which expresses a set of characteristics determined by its single, genetic makeup or genotype, which can be duplicated through asexual reproduction, but which cannot otherwise be 'made' or 'manufactured.'" Moreover,

> Spores, mutants, hybrids, and transformed plants are comprehended; spores or mutants may be spontaneous or induced. Hybrids may be natural, from a planned breeding program, or somatic in source. While natural plant mutants might have naturally occurred, they must have been discovered in a cultivated area. Algae and macro fungi are regarded as plants, but bacteria are not.[56]

William Radler, a Wisconsin rose breeder, worked for more than 15 years crossbreeding rose varieties to produce a beautiful, hardy, adaptable, disease-resistant rose known as the "Knock Out" rose.[57] The rose is available in red, pink, yellow, and multicolored varieties. The Conard-Pyle Company holds the patent for the "Knock Out" rose. It is illegal to propagate this rose because it is protected with a plant patent and trademark.[58]

Statutory Invention Registration

A statutory invention registration has the defensive attributes of a patent, but is not a patent, and therefore does not have the enforceable attributes of a patent. In the case where an individual has invented an item solely for personal use and not for commercial production or sale and desires to prevent someone else from later obtaining a patent on his or her invention, the inventor can register a statutory invention and have it published by the patent office. Once published, it cannot be claimed by another person, and the inventor does not have to immediately go through the effort and expense of obtaining a patent. The Patent and Trademark Office (PTO) publishes a statutory invention registration "containing the specifications and drawings of a regularly filed application for a patent without examination, providing the patentee meets all the requirements for printing, waives the right to receive a patent on the invention within a certain period of time prescribed by the PTO, and pays all application, publication and other processing fees" (37 U.S.C. § 157).[59]

What About Business Method Patents?

Business method patents are a class of patents which disclose and claim new methods of doing business in e-business, software systems, manufacturing, insurance, banking, and tax compliance.[60] Up until about 2000, the USPTO took the position that "methods of doing business" are not patentable.[61] Business method patents are relatively new; historically, "methods of doing business" were not patentable because they did not fall into any of the four categories of invention: Process, machine, manufacture, or composition of matter. Indeed, while "innovation and investment may be bolstered, . . . corporations may find themselves in a minefield of intangible business methods patents."[62] The rapid development of information technology has created new opportunities for innovation in the business methods and has led to an increase interest in patents sought in business methods.[63]

Intellectual Property in Practice

In 1938, Roy J. Plunkett, a DuPont chemist, was conducting experiments to develop a better refrigerant. During experiments, he combined tetrafluoroethylene, or TFE, with hydrochloric acid and obtained a solid, white material that he was not expecting. The result was the discovery of polytetrafluoroethylene (PTFE), commonly known as Teflon, patented in 1941.[64] Teflon is now an important material used for coating kitchen utensils.

In 1966, stretched polytetrafluoroethylene (ePTFE) was invented by John Cooper. He kept the ePTFE as a trade secret rather than filing a patent. In 1969 Wilbert Gore, Rowena Taylor, and Robert W. Gore independently co-invented the material. They introduced this new material under the trademark Gore-Tex. Gore-Tex was waterproof, porous, breathable fabric made from a form of the material polytetrafluoroethylene (PTFE) known as stretched or expanded polytetrafluoroethylene (ePTFE). They also filed for patent protection and received three patents. Later, in a patent infringement case in the 1970s, *Gore v. Garlock*, the court held that John Cooper relinquished his right to the invention.[65]

Natural rubber latex is taken from a tapped and wounded Pará rubber tree (*Hevea brasiliensis*). The tree responds to the wound by producing even more natural rubber.[66] In 1839, Charles Goodyear discovered that if you removed sulfur from the natural rubber latex and heated the rubber, it would remain elastic.[67] This process became known as vulcanization and was patented in 1844, following five years of work. The vulcanization of rubber is important because it is used in automobile tires, enabling the growth of the transportation industry.[68]

Wilson Greatbatch, an American engineer, invented the first practical, implantable cardiac pacemaker entirely by accident.[69] When building an oscillator to record heartbeats, he mistakenly used the wrong-sized resistor. The device then began producing electrical impulses that reminded him of heartbeats. Greatbatch designed and patented the device that was later manufactured by Medtronic. About a half-million cardiac pacemakers are implanted each year, saving millions of lives.[70]

The little blue pill, Viagra (sildenafil), was originally studied by Pfizer for use in treating high blood pressure and severe chest pain. During the studies, it was discovered that the drug could be used as an intervention for erectile dysfunction (ED).[71] Pharmaceutical companies, because of a cultural shift and growing acceptance of communications about sex, now market Viagra directly to the public. The drug Viagra has little to do with a medical indication and is more for recreation.[72] In 2017, the patent on Viagra expired and is now available as a generic medication.[73]

All the products described thus far, Gore-Tex, vulcanized rubber, pacemakers, and sildenafil citrate, are excellent examples of the role of intellectual property protection in innovation and entrepreneurship. From initial protection to product development to commercialization, intellectual property is an essential ingredient in the process of creating and adding value for companies, employees, and customers. Of course, it is more than just protecting a product and/or process. It is also a key factor in the building of brand awareness, acceptance, and loyalty that speaks directly to building core competencies as well as competitiveness.

Summary

Given the important role of protecting and promoting intellectual property, it is essential that innovators and entrepreneurs have a basic understanding of what is involved in IP protection and how it plays a role in product and/or service development and venture growth. In this chapter, we saw the ongoing importance of intellectual property protection regarding innovation and entrepreneurship. While not meant to be exhaustive, we reviewed the four major types of intellectual property protections – trade secrets, copyrights, trademarks/branding, and patents. Armed with these basics, we explored the role of intellectual property in practice as a key component in innovation and entrepreneurship. In the next chapter, we turn our attention to the art and science of making things, using the innovation and entrepreneurship competency framework processes.

Notes

1. Felix Richter, "Streaming Drives Global Music Industry Resurgence," March 24, 2021, accessed November 9, 2021, www.statista.com/chart/4713/global-recorded-music-industry-revenues/.
2. "IFPI Issues Global Music Report 2021," March 23, 2021, accessed November 9, 2021, www.ifpi.org/ifpi-issues-annual-global-music-report-2021/.
3. "IFPI Issues Global Music Report 2021," March 23, 2021, accessed November 9, 2021, www.ifpi.org/ifpi-issues-annual-global-music-report-2021/.
4. Amy X. Wang, "How Musicians Make Money – Or Don't at All – in 2018, What Do 'Royalties' in Music Actually Comprise?" August 8, 2018, accessed November 9, 2021, www.rollingstone.com/pro/features/how-musicians-make-money-or-dont-at-all-in-2018–706745/.
5. Amy X. Wang, "How Musicians Make Money – Or Don't at All – in 2018, What Do 'Royalties' in Music Actually Comprise?" August 8, 2018, accessed November 9, 2021, www.rollingstone.com/pro/features/how-musicians-make-money-or-dont-at-all-in-2018-706745/.
6. *Wikipedia*, s.v. "Fair Use," accessed November 9, 2021, https://en.wikipedia.org/wiki/Fair_use.
7. Joy Butler, "Music Licensing: What Is Considered Fair Use?" June 6, 2017, accessed November 9, 2021, www.copyright.com/blog/music-licensing-fair-use/.
8. Martin Armstrong, "The Most Sampled Tracks of All Time," February 4, 2020, accessed November 9, 2021, www.statista.com/chart/20709/most-sampled-tracks/.
9. *Wikipedia*, s.v. "Sampling (Music)," accessed November 9, 2021, https://en.wikipedia.org/wiki/Sampling_(music).
10. *Wikipedia*, s.v. "Sampling (Music)," accessed November 9, 2021, https://en.wikipedia.org/wiki/Sampling_(music).
11. *Wikipedia*, s.v. "Color Him Father," accessed November 9, 2021, https://en.wikipedia.org/wiki/Color_Him_Father.

12. "The Most Sampled Loop in Music History," accessed November 9, 2021, www.youtube.com/watch?v=v89CjsSOJ_c.
13. *Wikipedia*, s.v. "Amen Break," accessed November 9, 2021, https://en.wikipedia.org/wiki/Amen_break.
14. *Wikipedia*, s.v. "Sampling," accessed November 9, 2021, https://en.wikipedia.org/wiki/Sampling_(music)#Legal_and_ethical_issues.
15. Martin Armstrong, "The Most Sampled Tracks of All Time," February 4, 2020, accessed November 9, 2021, www.statista.com/chart/20709/most-sampled-tracks/.
16. *Wikipedia*, s.v. "Richard Lewis Spencer," accessed November 9, 2021, https://en.wikipedia.org/wiki/Richard_Lewis_Spencer.
17. Martin Armstrong, "The Most Sampled Tracks of All Time," February 4, 2020, accessed November 9, 2021, www.statista.com/chart/20709/most-sampled-tracks/.
18. *Wikipedia*, s.v. "Funky Drummer," accessed November 9, 2021, https://en.wikipedia.org/wiki/Funky_Drummer.
19. Jason Gordon, "James Brown: Most Sampled Man in the Biz," December 26, 2006, accessed November 9, 2021, www.rollingstone.com/music/music-news/james-brown-most-sampled-man-in-the-biz-115798/.
20. Ben Sisario, "Living Legend Tries to Make a Living," March 29, 2011, accessed November 9, 2021, www.nytimes.com/2011/03/30/arts/music/clyde-stubblefield-a-drummer-aims-for-royalties.html.
21. *Wikipedia*, s.v. "Clyde Stubblefield," accessed November 9, 2021, https://en.wikipedia.org/wiki/Clyde_Stubblefield.
22. "2012 World Intellectual Property Indicators," *World Intellectual Property Office (WIPO)*, accessed November 9, 2021, www.wipo.int/export/sites/www/freepublications/en/intproperty/941/wipo_pub_941_2012.pdf.
23. "What Is Intellectual Property?" *World Intellectual Property Office (WIPO), WIPO Publication No. 450(E)*, accessed November 10, 2021, www.wipo.int/about-ip/en/.
24. "What Is Intellectual Property?" *World Intellectual Property Organization (WIPO), WIPO Publication No. 450(E)*, accessed November 10, 2021, https://tind.wipo.int/record/28588?ln=en.
25. "Uniform Trade Secrets Act with 1985 Amendments," *Uniformlaws.org*, accessed October 28, 2021, www.uniformlaws.org/HigherLogic/System/DownloadDocumentFile.ashx?DocumentFileKey=e19b2528-e0b1-0054-23c4-8069701a4b62.
26. "United States Copyright Office," accessed October 28, 2021, www.copyright.gov/.
27. "The Authors Guild," *Authorsguild.org*, accessed November 9, 2021, www.authorsguild.org/services/legal-services/improving-your-book-contract/.
28. Joy Butler, "Music Licensing: The Difference Between Public Performance and Synchronization Licenses," May 16, 2017, accessed November 9, 2021, www.copyright.com/blog/music-licensing-public-performance-license-synchronization/.
29. Joy Butler, "Music Licensing: The Difference Between Public Performance and Synchronization Licenses," May 16, 2017, accessed November 9, 2021, www.copyright.com/blog/music-licensing-public-performance-license-synchronization/.
30. Anastasia Tsioulcas, "Bob Dylan Sells Songwriting Catalog in 9-Figure Deal," December 7, 2020, accessed November 9, 2021, www.npr.org/2020/12/07/943818966/bob-dylan-sells-songwriting-catalog-in-nine-figure-deal.
31. Simon Vozick-Levinson, "What Bob Dylan Selling His Music Catalog Does and Doesn't Mean," December 7, 2020, accessed November 9, 2021, www.rollingstone.com/pro/news/bob-dylan-catalog-sale-takeaways-1099117/.
32. Anastasia Tsioulcas, "Bob Dylan Sells Songwriting Catalog in 9-Figure Deal," December 7, 2020, accessed November 9, 2021, www.npr.org/2020/12/07/943818966/bob-dylan-sells-songwriting-catalog-in-nine-figure-deal.
33. Joy Butler, "Music Licensing: The Difference Between Public Performance and Synchronization Licenses," May 16, 2017, accessed November 9, 2021, www.copyright.com/blog/music-licensing-public-performance-license-synchronization/.
34. Simon Vozick-Levinson, "What Bob Dylan Selling His Music Catalog Does and Doesn't Mean," December 7, 2020, accessed November 9, 2021, www.rollingstone.com/pro/news/bob-dylan-catalog-sale-takeaways-1099117/.
35. Greg Majewski, "Music Copyright Guide for Indie Musicians," March 22, 2021, accessed November 9, 2021, https://diymusician.cdbaby.com/music-rights/copyright-for-musicians/.
36. K. Fleisher Alexander, "Confused by Music Copyright? Here Are 5 Things You Definitely Need to Know," March 11, 2018, accessed November 9, 2021, www.digitalmusicnews.com/2018/03/11/music-copyright-basics/.

37. "Owning a Trademark vs. Having a Registered Trademark," *USPTO*, accessed November 9, 2021, www.uspto.gov/trademarks/basics/what-trademark.
38. "What Is a Trademark?" *USPTO*, accessed November 10, 2021, www.uspto.gov/trademarks/basics/what-trademark.
39. "Best Global Brands 2021," *Interbrand Online*, accessed November 10, 2021, https://interbrand.com/best-global-brands/.
40. Howard Schultz and Dori Jones Yang, *Pour Your Hearts Into It: How Starbucks Built a Company One Cup at a Time* (New York: Hyperion, 1999), 353.
41. Jack Meyer, "History of Nike: Timeline & Facts," *The Street, Bloomberg News*, August 14, 2019, accessed November 10, 2021, www.thestreet.com/lifestyle/history-of-nike-15057083.
42. Arthur A. Thompson and A. J. Lonnie Strickland, III, "Turner Broadcasting Systems in 1992," in *Strategic Management: Concepts & Cases*, 7th ed. (Boston: Irwin, 1993).
43. Neal N. Gabler, *Walt Disney: The Triumph of the American Imagination* (New York: Knopf, 2006).
44. *Wikipedia*, s.v. "Walt Disney," accessed November 9, 2021, https://en.wikipedia.org/wiki/Walt_Disney.
45. Lorenzo Candelaria and Daniel Kingman, *American Music: A Panorama*, 5th ed. (Stamford, CT: Cengage Learning, 2015).
46. "Patents," *United State Patent and Trademark Office (USPTO)*, accessed 28 October 2021, www.uspto.gov/patents/basics/general-information-patents.
47. "Statutory Invention Registration," *35 ISC 157 (pre-AIA)*, U.S. Patent and Trademark Office, accessed November 9, 2021, www.uspto.gov/web/offices/pac/mpep/mpep-9015-appx-l.html#d0e304339.
48. "Rankings of the 20 National Patent Offices with the Most Patent Grants in 2019," 2019, accessed November 10, 2021, www.statista.com/statistics/257152/ranking-of-the-20-countries-with-the-most-patent-grants/ Statista.
49. "Patents by Country, State, and Year – All Patent Types," *USPTO*, accessed November 9, 2021, www.uspto.gov/web/offices/ac/ido/oeip/taf/cst_all.htm. Also, "Calendar Year Patent Statistics (January 1 to December 31 Years 2016–2020)," accessed 10 November 2021, www.uspto.gov/web/offices/ac/ido/oeip/taf/reports_stco.htm.
50. "35 USC 101: Inventions Patentable," accessed November 9, 2021, https://uscode.house.gov/view.xhtml?req=(title:35%20section:101%20edition:prelim)%20OR%20(granuleid:USC-prelim-title35-section101)&f=treesort&edition=prelim&num=0&jumpTo=true.
51. *Wikipedia*, s.v. "Person Having Ordinary Skill in the Art," accessed November 9, 2021, https://en.wikipedia.org/wiki/Person_having_ordinary_skill_in_the_art.
52. Susan Decker and Matthew Bultman, "Intel Ordered to Pay $2.2 Billion after Losing Patent Lawsuit," April 2, 2021, accessed November 9, 2021, https://fortune.com/2021/03/02/intel-patent-infringement-lawsuit-payordered-to-pay-2-2-billion/.
53. "Method and Means for Creating Anti-Gravity Illusion," accessed November 9, 2021, https://patents.google.com/patent/US5255452A/en.
54. United States Code – PATENTS, 2006 Edition, Supplement 5, Title 35.
55. United States Code – PATENTS, 2006 Edition, Supplement 5, Title 35.
56. "Plant Patents," *United States Patent and Trademark Office*, accessed October 28, 2021, www.uspto.gov/patents/basics/types-patent-applications/general-information-about-35-usc-161.
57. M. H. Dyer, "Can You Plant Knock Out Roses from Seeds?" accessed November 9, 2021, https://homeguides.sfgate.com/can-plant-knock-out-roses-seeds-62199.html.
58. "Grower Caught Illegally Propagating Knock Out Roses," October 2, 2011, accessed November 9, 2021, www.greenhousemag.com/article/grower-caught-illegally-propagating-knock-out-roses/.
59. United States Code – PATENTS, 2006 Edition, Supplement 5, Title 35.
60. *Wikipedia*, s.v. "Business Method Patent," accessed November 9, 2021, https://en.wikipedia.org/wiki/Business_method_patent.
61. *Wikipedia*, s.v. "Business Method Patent," accessed November 9, 2021, https://en.wikipedia.org/wiki/Business_method_patent.
62. "35 U.S. Code § 101 – Inventions Patentable," April 2, 2021, accessed November 9, 2021, www.law.cornell.edu/uscode/text/35/101.
63. Advisory Council on Intellectual Property, "Report on a Review of the Patenting of Business Systems," September 2003, accessed November 10, 2021, www.ipaustralia.gov.au/sites/default/files/final_report_review_of_patenting_of_business_systems.pdf.

64. Roy J. Plunkett, "Science History Institute," accessed October 28, 2021, www.sciencehistory.org/historical-profile/roy-j-plunkett.
65. *Wikipedia*, s.v. "Gore-Tex," accessed November 9, 2021, http://en.wikipedia.org/wiki/Gore-Tex.
66. *Wikipedia*, s.v. "Natural Rubber," accessed October 28, 2021, http://en.wikipedia.org/wiki/Natural_rubber.
67. "Charles Goodyear and the Vulcanization of Rubber," accessed October 28, 2021, https://connecticuthistory.org/charles-goodyear-and-the-vulcanization-of-rubber/.
68. *Wikipedia*, s.v. "Charles Goodyear," accessed November 9, 2021, http://en.wikipedia.org/wiki/Charles_Goodyear.
69. Barnby Feder, "Wilson Greatbatch, Inventor of Implantable Pacemaker, Dies at 92," *The New York Times*, September 28, 2011, accessed October 28, 2021, www.nytimes.com/2011/09/28/business/wilson-greatbatch-pacemaker-inventor-dies-at-92.html?pagewanted=all&_r=0.
70. *Wikipedia*, s.v. "Wilson Greatbatch," accessed October 28, 2021, http://en.wikipedia.org/wiki/Wilson_Greatbatch.
71. *Wikipedia*, s.v. "Sildenafil," accessed November 9, 2021, https://en.wikipedia.org/wiki/Sildenafil.
72. Jerome Groopman, *How Doctors Think* (New York: Houghton Mifflin, 2007).
73. *Wikipedia*, s.v. "Sildenafil," accessed November 9, 2021, https://en.wikipedia.org/wiki/Sildenafil.

17 Applying Innovation Processes

Apply Innovation Processes

As seen in Chapter 2, "Elements of Innovation," defining innovation can be a challenging task. From an applied perspective, however, innovation can be viewed as the process of *transforming* an idea into reality and capturing value from it. That is, applying a creative concept (e.g., something fresh, new, original, and/or improved) to an existing person, place, process, or thing. This could include products, customer experiences, solutions, systems, processes, business models, management, platforms, brands, science, technology, and more. In addition to something new, it provides value to all stakeholders while simultaneously generating revenue and profits.

In this chapter we explore the design thinking, an innovation process, that starts with building emphatic relationships through watching, listening, observing, and engaging customers. While the innovation and entrepreneurship journey begins with an idea, to move forward it must be transformed into something that is implementable. The act of making things is a driver of imagination, creativity, innovation, and new venture creation. Capturing value is building the infrastructure for the new venture to commercialize the innovation initiative to derive the benefits.

Because innovation is a process, it is possible to apply these concepts in practice and see how the process can be applied effectively. One of the interesting aspects of innovation and entrepreneurship is that both are iterative. That is, we don't just wake up one morning or walk into a meeting room and say, "Let's innovate" or "Let's start a company." But, as French microbiologist Louis Pasteur once famously observed, "Chance favors the prepared mind." Preparation occurs over time. It is not possible to successfully climb Mount Everest just by deciding one day to go do it. It takes time, knowledge, understanding, physical conditioning, and practice to improve the chances of success.

For example, discontinuous innovation in processes and revolutionary innovations can result in dramatic progress. At the turn of the 20th century, with the automobile industry still in its infancy, an automobile, or "horseless carriage," was custom-built by hand, one at a time. Henry Ford knew this process; more importantly, he knew that it could be improved. His innovation was to change the basic production model from a customized craft process that provided a handmade product for a few customers to a mass-produced, affordable product for many customers. Ford didn't invent the automobile; he invented the modern manufacturing process to produce the automobile. In so doing, he encapsulated the innovation and entrepreneurship competency framework: innovative behaviors, thinking, problem solving, knowledge, creativity, culture building, innovation theory, entrepreneurship, strategy, leadership, ecosystems, and technology acceleration.

Innovation processes can provide a unique competitive advantage for organizations if they are able to unleash ideas that have value and transform those ideas into results. For example, the social networking pioneer, Facebook, organizes all-night events known as hackathons that provide employees a way to ideate, initiate, and create prototypes.[1]

DOI: 10.4324/9781003034308-18

This novel approach and process enables Facebook to unleash its innovation strengths. Tim Campos, the former CIO of Facebook, said,

> Hackathons are very much engrained in our culture – we have one every few weeks. There's no purpose to them; they're a complete license to fail. You spend your time doing something that is or isn't related to the company. The point is to be as creative and innovative as possible. It's bragging rights for employees, too.[2]

Applying innovation processes provides an avenue to explore, achieve, and fail, and explore, achieve, and fail some more.

In this chapter, we focus on applying the concepts, competencies, and tools of the innovation and entrepreneurship competency framework. We begin by reviewing divergent, convergent, and emergent thinking and discuss a generalized innovation process. The process of managing innovation and the use of design-thinking in innovation and entrepreneurship are reviewed and outlined.

Finally, six perspectives (empathic, cognitive, perceptual, conceptual, physical, and emotional) and four communication dimensions (line, plane, solid, space-time) are discussed, along with the 11 design principles of Apple's former SVP of design, Jonathan Ive. An overview of project management and the triple constraint round out the chapter.

Making Things Using Processes

Turning ideas into action through making things can lead to greater creativity and is essential to the creative process.[3] Even though Michael Faraday did not have a formal education in science or mathematics, he was one of the most influential scientists in history for inventing the electric motor and the first electric generator. How did he do this? His innovations were based on experimenting, prototyping, and making things.[4]

From July of 1508 to October of 1512, Michelangelo Buonarroti painted the ceiling of the Sistine Chapel. While his finished work is an inspiration to behold, initial drawings demonstrate trial and error and provide us with insights into the importance of translating ideas into action. Before he transferred his images onto the ceiling's damp plaster, Michelangelo used an iterative process of continuous refinement by preparing sketches. This contrasts with the use of a monolithic, sequential process. The intermediate drawings he prepared were temporary creations awaiting more revisions and expansion.[5]

In the past, it was thought that creativity starts with an initial mental idea, and once it is completely thought through, that idea is transformed into something real. New research, however, suggests that creativity starts with an initial mental idea, but the idea is expanded and enhanced through an iterative process of making sketches, drawings, and objects that later result in a more powerful idea. As Keith Sawyer writes in *Zig Zag*, "Successful creators engage in an ongoing dialogue with their work. They put what's in their head on paper long before it's fully formed, and they watch and listen to what they've recorded, zigging and zagging until the right idea emerges."[6]

While the innovation and entrepreneurship journey begins with an idea, to move forward it must be transformed into something tangible or concrete. That is, the simple act of making something can be a driver of imagination, creativity, innovation, and new venture creation. It is an interesting exercise to go back in time and recall what you did when you were young. Did you make things with wooden blocks, Tinkertoys, or an Erector set? What did you draw with your crayons and pencils? What did you make with those large cardboard appliance boxes? Did you ever fold a sheet of paper into an airplane and then fly it across a room? Did you ever build a sandcastle on the beach? Did you ever create multidimensional designs using the multicolored beads of Bindeez? Perhaps you recall drawing with the Etch A Sketch? In the late 1950s, André Cassagnes invented the visual eye-hand-coordination toy, the Etch A Sketch, that allowed you to draw and erase end-lessly. The product was acquired by the Ohio Art Company and became a best-selling toy.[7] All of these activities share a common bond of melding ideas and action together with an outcome based on that creative synergy.

If you did any of these ideation translation activities, you experienced a form of **rapid proto-typing**. Rapid prototyping is taking your ideas and making something simple and concrete. As we see with Michelangelo's painting of the Sistine Chapel, the act of making something allows you to improve your creativity and thinking. Writing about the revival of interest in making things, Bruce Nussbaum notes, "The revival of a 'maker culture,' combining open-source philosophy new chan-nels for distribution made possible by social philosophy, and a shift to DIY, Made-in-the-Hood consumerism, has helped Making become a critical component of innovation once again."[8]

Innovation Processes

The generic innovative and entrepreneurship process to build new standalone solutions follows multiple steps. You start by identifying and defining a problem or "pain" in the market. The problem or "pain" can be a gap, something missing or in need of totally new thinking to solve the problem. In ideating and conceptualizing a solution, you simultaneously define the value proposition, defining *who* the customer is for whom you are building a new solution and defining *what* the requirements are for the new solution. Once you have considered the problem, the solution, and market feasibility, the value proposition drives the ultimate value exchange between the seller and the buyer.

The five voices of the empathetic customer experience described in Chapter 7, "Knowledge Building," provide insights into different approaches that can be used to generate ideas on what types of solutions will be the most useful. The five voices include the following:

- Voice of the customer
- Voice of the job to be done
- Voice of open innovation
- Voice of the dreamer
- Voice of the product

Each informs the unique value proposition that helps define the relationship between the business and the customer.

After the *what*, the process proceeds to the *how*. Limited prototypes (often low-fidelity paper models) of the solution are developed to better understand the concept and to solicit feedback from customers. Iterations of the limited prototype are often necessary to refine the solution and grow it into a high-fidelity, computer-aided prototype that more closely approximates the complete solution.

Once you have identified a viable solution that addresses the problem or pain point, implemen-tation may include a pilot or prototype. This pilot or prototype can be made available to a limited audience so that further feedback can be elicited before the solution is rolled out to a larger market. Feedback can be used to evaluate a more refined and/or complete solution and so on as the market potential and/or size increases.

Organizations may incorporate "stage-gates" into the innovation process as checkpoints for decision-making. The purpose of these stage-gates is to decide if resources should be allowed to continue or if the effort on the solution should be stopped. For innovation solutions, the criteria should include both learning and financial measures. If financial measures alone are used, the solu-tion may be stopped prematurely.

For standalone innovations that have no dependencies, the pilot/prototype iterative approach has been a prevalent and viable method. The introduction of an innovative solution of any type and degree into an internal organizational ecosystem that has dependencies, though, requires extra precautions to mitigate both co-innovation and adoption chain risks. In an internal organizational ecosystem, it might be necessary to create a set of staging scenarios where you start with a subset of the value proposition and incrementally build it over time. For example, in the M-Pesa mobile wallet platform piloted by Vodaphone, the rollout had many unresolved, interwoven, and complex dependencies that resulted in initial failure. A simpler value proposition was conceived to gain the learning and experience to perform a staged incremental expansion using multiple, properly sequenced, limited sub-pilots.

Apple's design process provides insights into this iterative innovation dynamic and an interesting view into the way they innovate:[9]

- Apple matches ideas from the top with ideas from the bottom, thereby empowering everyone to participate. It is not enough to rely on ideas only from top management. All people should be involved in the innovation process. CEO Tim Cook says,

  Everybody in our company is responsible to be innovative, whether they're doing operational work, or product work or customer service work. So, in terms of the pressure, all of us put a great deal of pressure on ourselves. And yes, part of my job is to be a cheerleader, and getting people to stop for a moment and think about everything that's been done.[10]

- Apple uses paired design meetings during their development process. Each week there are two separate meetings: in the first meeting, the participants remove the constraints on their thinking and apply creativity, and in the second meeting, the participants do the antithesis and figure out how to perform the implementation and transition to production. This duality builds on the strengths of their creative talent and implementation talent.[11]
- Apple develops perfect mock-ups to reduce ambiguity (experimenting and making competencies).
- Apple uses a divergent to convergent decision-making process to choose (a creative competency) from many ideas. The selection is narrowed from ten ideas to three ideas to one idea that emerges into a product. This is illustrated in Figure 17.1.

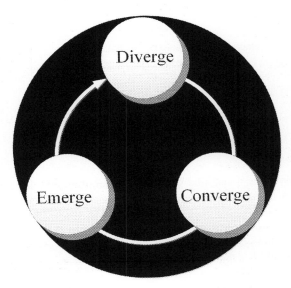

Figure 17.1 Illustration of Diverge, Converge, and Emerge Process

Generalized Innovation Process

Joe Tidd and John Bessant provided in their book, *Managing Innovation*, a generic, four-phase innovation process that encompasses the search, selection, implementation, and value capture of innovations. This is shown in Figure 17.2 and described as follows.[12]

- Searching involves scanning of the internal and external ecosystem for generating *actionable insights* about what is possible.
- Selecting is the decision-making process to transform the actionable insights into the most relevant *strategic initiatives* about what is going to be implemented and why.
- Implementing is the process of transforming the strategic initiatives into value-added *results*. Implementation is an iterative process as new learnings influence the outcome.
- Capturing value is building the infrastructure for the *new venture* to commercialize the innovation initiative to derive the benefits. Capturing value requires built-in mechanisms to learn how to improve the innovation and may require protection to prevent duplication.

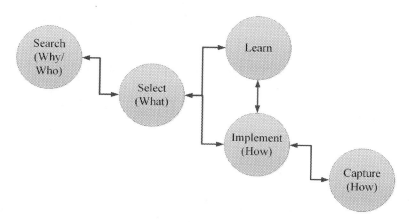

Figure 17.2 Illustration of a Generic Innovation Learning Process

Source: Adapted from Joe Tidd, and John Bessant, J., *Managing Innovation: Integrating Technological, Market and Organizational Change*, 5th ed. (London: Wiley, 2013), 47.

Copyright ©

IDEO's Design Thinking

IDEO is the global innovation consulting firm that created design thinking for use with their customers. IDEO's design thinking is an empathetic iterative process that uses high-functioning, diverse teams to compound and accumulate ideas that build agile prototypes that become prerequisites to innovations. According to IDEO's CEO and president, Tim Brown, "Put simply, [design thinking] is a discipline that uses the designer's sensibility and methods to match people's needs with what is technologically feasible and what a viable business strategy can convert into customer value and market opportunity."[13] Design thinking is the application of a proven concept that combines (the Power of And) the humanities and sciences. For example, the works of Albert Einstein,

Thomas Edison, Steve Jobs, and Edwin Land of Polaroid all illustrate the power of synergistically leveraging the humanities and sciences.[14]

Connect with People

Design thinking is based on the generic innovation process, and starts with building emphatic relationships through watching, listening, observing, and engaging customers. IDEO anthropologists observe people as they experience products and services to understand and learn how to meet the needs of customers more effectively. "Psychologist Jane Fulton Suri, who leads IDEO's human factors projects, has been called a 'bird watcher with attitude,' except the birds she specializes in are humans. Nearly all IDEO projects now include an element of 'bird watching.'"[15]

IDEO's Five Steps of Design Thinking

Design thinking uses a multi-step, iterative process (empathize, define, ideate, prototype, and test) that is based on meeting consumer desirability, business viability, and technical feasibility criteria.[16]

The team selects a problem/opportunity that motivates a search for a solution through research and direct observation.[17] The process uses ideation to generate, develop, and test ideas that may lead to solutions. Teams visualize and brainstorm potential solutions. The team will produce a prototype. The team makes sketches and (if appropriate) they test, modify, and test again, in an iterative process that is at the heart of design thinking.[18]

What: Discovery with Empathy

Empathy is the ability to look at things from someone else's point of view.

> Empathy is the centerpiece of a human-centered design process. The Empathize mode is the work you do to understand people, within the context of your design challenge. It is your effort to understand the way they do things and why, their physical and emotional needs, how they think about the world, and what is meaningful to them.[19]

When you empathize, you question, observe, and network with the customer; you watch and listen and engage them to participate in the solution.

What: Scope Definition

The scope definition is a statement of the frame (a problem-solving competency) and customer requirements.

> The Define mode of the design process is all about bringing clarity and focus to the design space. It is your chance, and responsibility, as a design thinker to define the challenge you are taking on, based on what you have learned about your user and about the context.[20]

It is important to focus on the customer and identify a manageable set of unmet needs that focus on some job that need to be done. An important outcome of scope definition is to transition from actionable insights into *what might be.*

How: Generate and Ideate

Ideation is the application of divergent thinking to create a design solution. You can use an assortment of techniques, such as mind mapping, brainstorming, and sketching to ideate.

> Ideate is the mode of the design process in which you concentrate on idea generation. Mentally, it represents a process of "going wide" in terms of concepts and outcomes. Ideation provides both the fuel and the source material for building prototypes and getting innovative solutions into the hands of your users.[21]

How: Experimentation and Prototyping

An important step in design thinking is the building of agile prototypes, working models that are used to experiment and ultimately learn about the customers' needs and the extent of the value added. By engaging the customers interactively when building a prototype, the learning process can be accelerated. The prototype does not have to be perfect; the purpose of the prototype is to increase understanding and learning. The risks and costs are low. You can fail early and often with minimal consequences.

> The Prototype mode is the iterative generation of artifacts intended to answer questions that get you closer to your final solution. In the early stages of a project that question may be broad – such as "do my users enjoy cooking in a competitive manner?" In these early stages, you should create low-resolution prototypes that are quick and cheap to make (think minutes and cents) but can elicit useful feedback from users and colleagues.[22]

Using modern software tools, it is increasingly economical to prototype user interfaces, build models of objects, and conduct low-cost simulations that ask "what if" questions before committing to an initial design. Experimenting with visual prototypes in the early stages of a design allows improvements to be made quickly. Customers can interact and simultaneously remove errors at the lowest cost point in a design innovation. Beginning in the early 1930s, Walt Disney originated the use of storyboards when creating a movie. A storyboard is a linear ordering of images and words that are used in a time-sequence.[23]

In 1978, *The Flight of the Gossamer Condor* won the Academy Award for the best documentary short subject. The film tells the story of how Paul MacCready and his team built a set of prototypes over a period of a year that proved that human-powered flight was a reality. The iterations of the prototypes allowed the team to learn how to refine the prototypes to win the prize.[24]

In the mid-1970s, MacCready was inspired by his theoretical knowledge of the soaring patterns of birds to conquer a very practical challenge. In 1959, the British industrialist Henry Kremer had offered a prize of £50,000 for the first substantial flight of a human-powered airplane. In 1977, MacCready's Gossamer Condor made the first sustained, controlled flight by a heavier-than-aircraft powered solely by its pilot's muscles. For this feat, he received the $95,000 Henry Kremer Prize.

Two years later, MacCready's AeroVironment team, with DuPont sponsorship, created the Gossamer Albatross, another 70-pound craft with a 96-foot wingspan. This time, they hoped to meet the Kremer prize committee's challenge for the first human-powered flight across the English Channel. That flight, made by "pilot-engine" and bicycle racer Bryan Allen, took almost three hours, and covered more than 20 miles. It won the new Kremer prize of $213,000, which was, at the time, the largest cash prize in aviation history.[25]

Both low-fidelity and high-fidelity prototypes can be used for innovation projects. Low-fidelity prototypes are made from whatever is handy, such as paper, clay, masking tape, or string. High-fidelity prototypes make use of more sophisticated processes, such as SketchUp, Adobe Illustrator, or Microsoft Visio, to produce 2D diagrams. 3D printing can be used to develop physical models that can streamline the process from idea to product.

How: Evolution and Testing

Testing is an iterative process of evolution that ensures that the solution meets both product specification and the customer's requirements. As seen in Figure 17.3, first introduced in Chapter 2, "The Elements of Innovation," testing also draws out the discovery and learning that is necessary to focus on the most practical solution.

> The Test mode is when you solicit feedback about the prototypes you have created, from your users and have another opportunity to gain empathy for the people you are designing for. Testing is another opportunity to understand your user, but unlike your initial empathy mode, you have now likely done more framing of the problem and created prototypes to test.[26]

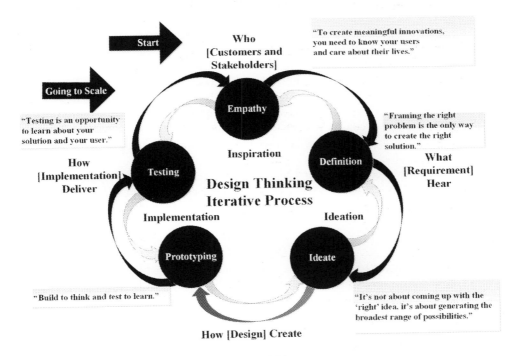

Figure 17.3 Illustration of the Five Steps of Design Thinking

Source: Adapted from "An Introduction to Design Thinking PROCESS GUIDE," Institute of Design At Stanford.

Applying the Design Thinking Process: The Acela Express

At the dawn of the 21st century, Amtrak initiated a project to study opportunities to improve transportation on the Acela Express route. The Acela Express is a high-speed Amtrak route on the East Coast from Washington, DC, to New York and Boston. IDEO was asked to focus on the design of the seats.[27] Instead of focusing just on the seats, a convergent thinking concept, IDEO focused on the broader customer experience and applied divergent thinking to differentiate rail travel from cars and airlines. "IDEO identified ten steps in the passenger's journey, from learning about Amtrak and planning a trip through to arriving at the destination and continuing on."[28] The resulting actionable insight was that passengers did not take their seats until step 8 and that most of the travel experience did not involve the train at all. "Every one of the prior steps was an opportunity to create a positive interaction, opportunities that would have been overlooked if they had focused only on the design of the seats."[29] It is the entire customer journey, not a single step in the process, which is important; otherwise, opportunities for improving the experience would be overlooked.

Design Thinking and Montessori Concepts

The educational philosophy and process of Montessori education, first conceived by Maria Montessori at the turn of the 20th century, provides an interesting parallel to the concepts of design thinking. The core concepts of Montessori education are based on a model of human development and include purposeful activities such as abstraction, creativity, and exploration. Design thinking can be viewed as an adaptation of the Montessori concepts that are applied to innovation. If the Montessori education concepts are applied within a business environment, we will have the following:[30]

- Formation of diverse heterogeneous teams.
- Individuals choose activities from within a prescribed range of options.
- Focused blocks of work time with both freedom and constraints.
- Individuals learn concepts from working with physical materials, rather than by direct instruction.
- Building working models (prototypes) and applying constructivism. "Constructivism is a theory to explain how knowledge is constructed in the human being when information comes into contact with existing knowledge that had been developed by experiences."[31]

The characteristics of design thinking and Montessori concepts are remarkably similar. Both promote critical thinking with a purpose, while overcoming the constraints of over-rigidity inhibiting creative thinking and action.

Process Match

When developing something new, often the innovation process must be adapted to the circumstances. There are four variables to consider: risk, complexity level, scale, and formality. Innovations of high risk, complexity, and scale are best matched with a formal process.

Innovations of low risk, complexity, and scale are best matched with an informal process. The innovation process must be carefully balanced to avoid either over- or under-engineering of the final solution. Over-engineering results in wasted resources. Under-engineering risks failing to fulfill the customer promise and may result in costly defects and rework. The process and solution match are illustrated in Figure 17.4.

Design Concepts

The fundamentals of innovation design concepts include perspectives, dimensions, and principles. Perspective is a powerful force in the promotion of innovation and entrepreneurship. Alan Kay, considered the father of the personal computer, is often credited with the saying, "Perspective is worth 80 IQ points."[32]

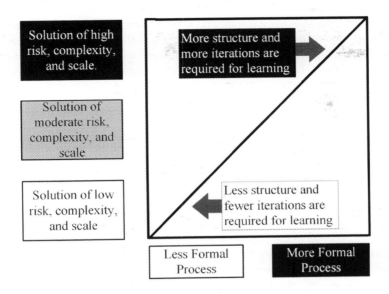

Figure 17.4 Illustration of Process and Solution Match

The Six Perspectives

In the 1989 Academy Award–winning movie *Dead Poets Society*, there is a powerful scene in which the main character, teacher John Keating, portrayed by actor Robin Williams, exhorts his poetry students to stand on top of their desks. More than just a random activity, he challenges them to look around and take in the view, or in other words, change their perspective. Interestingly, in the movie, his purposeful activity is interrupted by the headmaster, who puts a stop to what he perceives as foolish, irresponsible behavior. This raises this question: how can we best balance the relationship between imagination and more established practices of learning leading to ideation and activity? The short answer is perspective. The six perspectives – empathetic, cognitive, perceptual, conceptual, physical, and emotional – are illustrated in Figure 17.5.

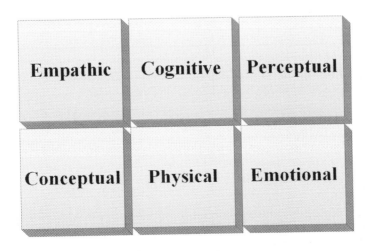

Figure 17.5 Illustration of the Six Perspectives

A way to broaden your imagination is by enabling yourself to think from different perspectives. Start by imagining a problem from multiple perspectives. For example, consider the perspective of an accountant, artist, journalist, policeman, judge, engineer, lawyer, or physician. How would each look at the same problem? Think about an approach or solution to the problem. For example, an engineer might approach a problem from a linear perspective, while an artist might see the problem in terms of an emergent perspective.

In addition, we can outline six generic perspectives that take us from our unique perspective to more fully considering the perspectives of others. These six generic perspectives are empathic, cognitive, perceptual, conceptual, physical, and emotional. For example, empathize by imagining yourself as a hospital patient struggling to breathe or cope with pain. Or cognitively, think back about your best teachers and how they were able to challenge you and expand your intellect and why they were so effective. Perceptually, think about an incident when you were completely wrong about someone or something based on a misperception and how that misperception manifested itself. Conceptually, think about a new concept that you imagined before anyone else that either you acted on or failed to act on. Physically, imagine yourself with a disability or age-related physical impairment, perhaps in a wheelchair physically dependent on others for your basic needs. Emotionally, reconnect with the experiences of births, schooling, work, marriage, deaths, and other life-altering experiences. All six of these generic perspectives speak to us on different levels about how we live, work, learn, and change over time. Perspective fuels our imagination, sparks our creativity, empowers our thinking, and provides a foundation for innovation and entrepreneurship.

The Four Dimensions of Communication

Applying the innovation and entrepreneurship concepts requires strong communication. There are four general dimensions to communication. Your ability to design, structure, and restructure ideas can be enhanced by learning to apply all four dimensions of communications. Moreover, all four have individual utility and/or can be used together.

The four dimensions are useful during experimentation, especially while prototyping. The purpose of a prototype is to use limited resources to learn something about your idea. A prototype can use any of the four dimensions to build, branch, and prune. A prototype can be low-fidelity, using basic resources, such as scrap paper and crayons, or it can be high-fidelity if you choose to use computer software or 3D printing.

First Dimension

The first dimension of communication is about the language of communication. It is represented by a line and includes words, numbers, poetry, singing, and the connotations (tone) of the voice. As Yogi Berra advises, "When you come to a fork in the road. . . . Take it." Or as Robert Frost more poetically states:

> Two roads diverged in a yellow wood,
> And sorry I could not travel both
> And be one traveler, long I stood
> And looked down one as far as I could
> To where it bent in the undergrowth;
>
> Then took the other, as just as fair,
> And having perhaps the better claim,

Because it was grassy and wanted wear;
Though as for that the passing there
Had worn them really about the same,

And both that morning equally lay
In leaves no step had trodden black.
Oh, I kept the first for another day!
Yet knowing how way leads on to way,
I doubted if I should ever come back.

I shall be telling this with a sigh
Somewhere ages and ages hence:
Two roads diverged in a wood, and I –
I took the one less traveled by,
And that has made all the difference.
– Robert Frost,
"The Road Not Taken"

Second Dimension

The second dimension of communication is focused on translating or transforming an idea into a concept, usually by drafting a representation on paper. It is represented by a physical plane, such as a square, rectangle, or triangle, and includes deliverables such as sketching, blueprints, painting, typography, diagrams, and icons. For example, a wireframe is a hierarchical way of designing a web page. Mind maps are visual two-dimensional models that focus on a central idea and then branch outward into leaves. This can be done by placing Post-it Notes on a wall and rearranging them by topics. Painting can be done alla prima, or wet-on-wet, without a sketch, or more formally with a detailed plan. The sketchbooks kept by Charles Darwin on his sea voyages, Thomas Edison as he pursued his experiments, and Leonardo da Vinci as he imagined painting and sculpting are all examples of using the second dimension.

Third Dimension

The third dimension of communication is related to the physical aspects of how we communicate. It includes a solid, such as a cube, and/or physical and sculptural forms. This might include building a small working model of an object such as an airplane, a medical device, a house, or a car. The Wright brothers successfully used working models of airplanes to experiment with their aerodynamic designs.

Fourth Dimension

The fourth dimension of communication is the space-time continuum. When asked what time it was, Yogi Berra said, "You mean now?" This dimension includes media such as sound, movies, animation, comic books, and storyboards. Walt Disney is given credit for early use of storyboards for preparing cartoons. "A storyboard is a series of sketches that maps out a story and allows film-makers to visualize the sequence of the plot. Story sketches are created to depict the key storytelling moments of a film."[33] The storyboard captures the space-time dimensions in a "freeze frame" format, giving seemingly unrelated concepts a coherent presence.

Storyboards are prepared by stringing together a set of pictures in a time sequence. When working with customers, it is useful to prepare a storyboard of the customer journey that describes the idea from a time perspective, showing visualizations, and narratives. Storyboarding gives dimensionality to a story and allows it to be captured in other media. For example, cinematography is the production of motion pictures. This includes the use of focus, lighting, composition (or arrangement), and appropriate camera movement to tell stories. The four dimensions are illustrated in Figure 17.6.

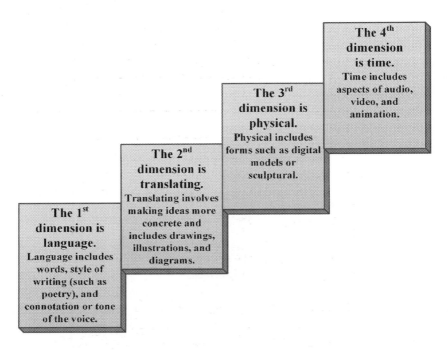

Figure 17.6 Illustration of the Four Dimensions of Communication

Collectively, these four dimensions provide a window into the ongoing process of innovation and entrepreneurship. Each defines and expands on current thinking while simultaneously providing a point of reference and departure for forward thinking. When considered with the six perspectives in various combinations, the potential is virtually limitless. Next, we consider the 11 innovation principles articulated by Sir Jonathan Ive, the senior vice president of design at Apple.

Jonathan Ive's Design Principles

Humble Sir Jonathan Ive was the senior vice president of design at Apple and the principal designer for their products. He is listed as an inventor of hundreds of patents. In 2012, he was knighted by Princess Anne in Buckingham Palace.[34] Ive has been instrumental in the design of the iMac, iPod, and iPhone. Bono writes,

> To watch him with his workmates in the holy of holies, Apple's design lab, or in a night out is to observe a very rare esprit de corps. They love their boss, and he loves them. What the

competitors don't seem to understand is you cannot get people this smart to work this hard just for money. Jony is Obi-Wan. His team are Jedi whose nobility depends on the pursuit of greatness over profit, believing the latter will always follow the former, stubbornly passing up near-term good opportunities to pursue great ones in the distance.[35]

Ive has identified innovation design principles that are illustrated in Figure 17.7.[36]

```
1-Have a Thirst for Knowledge and
Understanding
2-Keep the Focus
3-Obsess About the Details
4-Look to be Wrong
5-Iterate and Reduce
6-Be Better, Not Different
7-Work and Win as a Team
8-Embrace Technology
9-Stick to What You're Good At
10-Keep the Faith
11-Work Hard
```

Figure 17.7 Illustration of Jonathan Ive's Innovation Principles

Source: Adapted from John Webb, "10 success principles of apple's innovation master Jonathan Ive," June 13, 2012, accessed September 17, 2020, from https://in2marketing.wordpress.com/2012/06/13/10-success-principles-of-apples-innovation-master-jonathan-ive/

Each of these innovation principles speaks to the deliberate and emergent process of innovation and entrepreneurship. The first two principles, thirst for knowledge/understanding and focus, speak directly to the need for constant curiosity, but with focus, to avoid getting too far off task. Obsessing over the details, the third principle, speaks to the need to articulate a connection and direction for solving a problem. It is rare to get it right from the beginning, so the fourth principle, looking to be wrong, keeps us honest. It is not possible to be right 100% of the time. Inevitably, we will have to iterate and reduce to gain traction, the fifth principle. Naturally, there is a tendency to see creativity as just being different. The reality is that we need to be better, not just different, as in the sixth principle. The seventh principle, working and winning as a team, speaks directly to the need to leverage the strengths of those around us. The eighth principle, embracing technology, almost goes without saying, but not all technology is created equal. While we need to embrace technology selectively, embrace it we must. It is often challenging to stick to what we know best, the ninth principle, when new technologies are constantly pressuring us to adopt new tools and new rules. Yet despite the sometimes-chaotic approach that technology adaptation can bring, we are also challenged to keep the faith, the tenth principle. In the end, we must be our own best counsel, in concert with the team that results in hard work that leverages the first ten principles.

Project Management

In general, innovation projects need to have oversight that increases with the size, complexity, and risk factors. Project management is the process that applies attitudes, skills, knowledge, talent, resources, and tools to an innovation project to satisfy stakeholder needs and expectations. Project management is a discipline that has international standards, such as *Guidance on Project Management,* an international standard developed by the International Organization for Standardization.[37] A generic project management innovation project can have up to 12 project steps, shown in Figure 17.8.

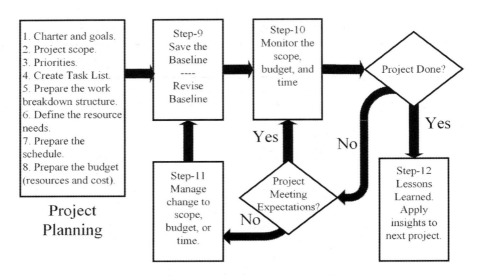

Figure 17.8 Illustration of the Twelve Steps of Project Management

There are 12 steps to the generalized project management process.

1. A project charter would be prepared that provides an overview of the goals of what is to be achieved. The project charter is a key document for formally recognizing the existence of a project.
2. A scope document would be prepared that defines what is or is not to be done. The scope or customer performance specification refers to all the work involved in creating the products of the project and the processes used to create them.
3. The priorities and phasing are defined based on high level estimates. Each project would be organized into sub-projects that can be packaged into phases that are time-boxed into approximately 30–60 days total duration.
4. A task list is created that represents the basic building blocks of any project. Tasks identify the work to be done to accomplish the goals of the project. Tasks describe work in terms of sequence, estimated effort, and resource requirements.
5. A work breakdown structure is prepared that shows how the work tasks are organized. A work breakdown structure (WBS) is a results-oriented grouping of the work involved in a project that defines the total scope of the project. A WBS is often depicted as a task-oriented family tree of activities, like an organizational chart. It is a foundation document for managing the project.

6. The resource needs would be defined that include the talent, expertise, and competencies.
7. The schedules are prepared using task estimates on what needs to be done, by whom, and when.
8. The budget is prepared that includes the total cost of personnel, hardware, and software.
9. The project baseline is the combination of the scope, budget, and schedule that would have the commitment of all stakeholders and defines a set of realistic expectations.
10. A project is monitored by tracking actual progress on the scope, budget, and schedule. The actual work would be done in an iterative manner based on the priorities and project phasing.
11. The change is managed by comparing the actual performance against the scope, budget, and schedule. If the project is on target, no additional action is required. If there is a change to the project, the variance can be accommodated by adjusting the triple constraint. This can be achieved by reducing the scope, adding resources to the budget, or adding time. Managing a scope change involves the adaptation of the scope (specification), budget, or schedule. If there is a scope change (new or changed requirements), the change needs to be managed by assessing the impact on the current project (and existing projects), and if accepted by the customer, the schedule and budget would be modified. Changes must be agreed to and approved.
12. A lesson learned would be conducted to evaluate what went right and wrong and the causes of variances. This information should be used to improve the next project.

All projects have three principal constraints: scope (i.e., customer or performance specifications), budget, and schedule. The triple constraints and the priorities are different for each project. Figure 17.9 illustrates the triple constraint. Keeping these three constraints in balance helps maintain the confidence and commitment of all stakeholders. Changing one constraint affects the others and can result in trade-offs.

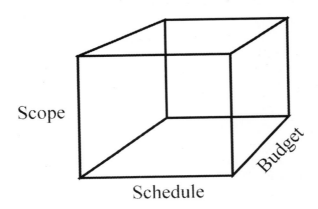

Figure 17.9 Illustration of the Triple Constraint

The scope (customer or performance specification) is the desired job to be done or outcome of the innovation project. When the scope is changed there is almost always a concomitant change in the budget and/or schedule.

The critical path is determined by identifying the longest stretch of dependent activities and measuring the time required to complete them from start to finish.[38] The three elements of the triple constraint determine the critical path. The one constraint that has the highest priority (most important) identifies the driver.

- If the scope *cannot* be changed, this is a driver. Examples of performance drivers are nuclear power plants, the practice of medicine, and all powered aircrafts.
- If the budget *cannot* be changed, this is a driver. Examples are residential construction, public schools, and most non-profit organizations.
- If the schedule *cannot* be changed, this is a driver. Some examples are commercial construction, buildings and roads, a concert, holidays, the year 3000, agriculture (crops), and tax deadlines.

The triple constraint priorities vary by level of management.

- Upper-level management places emphasis on long-term performance results.
- Middle management tends to focus on the budgets and costs.
- Individual employees will most likely focus on performance results. For example, engineers may focus on the quality of their results and may not worry about the cost.

There are several solutions to rebalance a project: add cost to solve a problem, add time to solve a problem, or subtract from performance to solve a problem.

- If the innovation project is *not* performance driven, reduce scope.
- If the innovation project is *not* cost driven, add resources (dollars). You can also create a parallel or overlapping set of tasks, but this adds risk to the project.
- If the innovation project is not time driven, adjust/negotiate the start time and/or end time.

Project management is an essential competence that will be needed for most innovation projects.

Summary

In this chapter, the process of applying the concepts, competencies, and tools of the innovation and entrepreneurship competency framework is outlined. The premise of the values of making things and the role of divergent, convergent, and emergent thinking form the starting point of this discussion.

The design thinking multi-step process and the process solution match are outlined. Innovations of low risk, complexity, and scale are best matched with an informal process. The innovation process must be carefully balanced to avoid either over- or under-engineering of the final solution.

Finally, six perspectives (empathic, cognitive, perceptual, conceptual, physical, and emotional) and four communication dimensions (line, plane, solid, space-time) are outlined and discussed, along with Apple's former SVP of design Jonathan Ive's 11 design principles. Project management and the triple constraint round out this discussion.

Next up, the increasingly import role of identifying and implementing an innovation education architecture.

Notes

1. Hackathon, accessed November 16, 2021, www.facebook.com/hackathon.
2. Kristin Burnham, "Facebook's CIO Shares IT Innovation Successes and Failures," *CIO*, June 2, 2011, accessed November 16, 2021, www.cio.com/article/2407573/facebook-s-cio-shares-it-innovation-successes-and-failures.html.
3. Keith Sawyer, *Zig Zag: The Surprising Path to Greater Creativity* (New York: Jossey-Bass, 2013), 213.

4. Michele and Robert Root-Bernstein, "Imagine That!" *Psychology Today*, August 21, 2008, accessed February 22, 2024, www.psychologytoday.com/blog/imagine/200808/thinkering.

5. Irving Stone, *The Agony and the Ecstasy* (New York: Doubleday, 1961).

6. Keith Sawyer, *Zig Zag: The Surprising Path to Greater Creativity* (New York: Jossey-Bass, 2013), 199–200.

7. *Wikipedia*, s.v. "Etch a Sketch," accessed November 16, 2021, http://en.wikipedia.org/wiki/Etch_A_Sketch.

8. Bruce Nussbaum, *Creative Intelligence: Harnessing the Power to Create, Connect, and Inspire* (New York: Harper Business, 2013), 36.

9. Vadim Kotelnikov, "Apple's Design Process," accessed November 16, 2021, www.innovarsity.com/coach/bp_product_design_apple.html.

10. Josh Tryangiel, "Tim Cook's Freshman Year: The Apple CEO Speaks," *Businessweek*, December 6, 2012, accessed November 16, 2021, www.bloomberg.com/news/articles/2012-12-06/tim-cooks-freshman-year-the-apple-ceo-speaks.

11. Helen Walters, "Apple's Design Process," *Bloomberg Business Week*, March 8, 2008, accessed December 1, 2021, www.eng.auburn.edu/~troppel/Apple-design-process.htm.

12. Joe Tidd and John Bessant, *Managing Innovation: Integrating Technological, Market and Organizational Change*, 5th ed. (New York: John Wiley, 2013), 60.

13. Tim Brown, "Design Thinking," *Harvard Business Review* 86, no. 6 (June 2008), 86.

14. Tim Brown, "Design Thinking," *Harvard Business Review* 86, no. 6 (June 2008), 86; Walter Isaacson, *Steve Jobs* (New York: Simon and Schuster, 2011), 19.

15. Howard Smith, "What Innovation Is," *European Office of Technology and Innovation* (CSC White Paper, 2005), 10.

16. Hasso Plattner Institute of Design at Stanford, "An Introduction to Design Thinking Process Guide," accessed June 22, 2024, https://web.stanford.edu/~mshanks/MichaelShanks/files/509554.pdf.

17. John Leger, "Technology Innovation Awards," *The Wall Street Journal*, October 17, 2011, accessed December 01, 2021, www.wsj.com/articles/SB10001424052970203914304576626971938467958.

18. Hasso Plattner Institute of Design at Stanford, "An Introduction to Design Thinking Process Guide," accessed June 22, 2024, https://web.stanford.edu/~mshanks/MichaelShanks/files/509554.pdf.

19. Hasso Plattner Institute of Design at Stanford, "An Introduction to Design Thinking Process Guide," accessed June 22, 2024, https://web.stanford.edu/~mshanks/MichaelShanks/files/509554.pdf.

20. Hasso Plattner Institute of Design at Stanford, "An Introduction to Design Thinking Process Guide," accessed June 22, 2024, https://web.stanford.edu/~mshanks/MichaelShanks/files/509554.pdf.

21. Hasso Plattner Institute of Design at Stanford, "An Introduction to Design Thinking Process Guide," accessed June 22, 2024, https://web.stanford.edu/~mshanks/MichaelShanks/files/509554.pdf.

22. Hasso Plattner Institute of Design at Stanford, "An Introduction to Design Thinking Process Guide," accessed June 22, 2024, https://web.stanford.edu/~mshanks/MichaelShanks/files/509554.pdf.

23. *Wikipedia*, s.v. "Storyboard," accessed November 16, 2021, http://en.wikipedia.org/wiki/Storyboard.

24. Paul MacCready, accessed January 26, 2021, Paul MacCready | Lemelson (mit.edu). *Wikipedia*, s.v. "Paul MacCready," accessed December 6, 2020, Paul MacCready – Wikipedia, Ben Shedd, "The Flight Of The Gossamer Condor," August 20, 2020, accessed December 6, 2020, https://gossamercondor.com/remembering-paul-maccready/.

25. Paul MacCready, accessed January 26, 2021, Paul MacCready | Lemelson (mit.edu). *Wikipedia*, s.v. "Paul MacCready," accessed December 6, 2020, Paul MacCready – Wikipedia, Ben Shedd, "The Flight of the Gossamer Condor," August 20, 2020, accessed December 6, 2020, https://gossamercondor.com/remembering-paul-maccready/.

26. Hasso Plattner Institute of Design at Stanford, "An Introduction to Design Thinking Process Guide," accessed June 22, 2024, https://web.stanford.edu/~mshanks/MichaelShanks/files/509554.pdf.

27. "Amtrak® Acela Express® Accommodates All," December 11, 2000, The Center for Universal Design, accessed November 16, 2021, www.ncsu.edu/ncsu/design/cud/projserv_ps/projects/case_studies/acela.htm.

28. Ritesh Bhavnani, "IDEO: Service Design (A)," Originally published 2006, revised April 7, 2017, accessed November 29, 2021, www.thecasecentre.org/products/view?id=70718.

29. Tim Brown, *Change by Design* (New York: Harper, 2009), 94.

30. *Wikipedia*, s.v. "Montessori Education," accessed November 16, 2021, https://en.wikipedia.org/wiki/Montessori_education.

31. *Wikipedia*, s.v. "Constructivism (Philosophy of Education)," accessed November 16, 2021, https://en.wikipedia.org/wiki/Constructivism_(philosophy_of_education).

32. *Wikipedia*, s.v. "Alan Kay," accessed November 16, 2021, https://en.wikiquote.org/wiki/Alan_Kay.

33. "Storyboards," the Walt Disney Family Museum, accessed November 11, 2021, www.waltdisney.org/blog/open-studio-storyboards.

34. "Apple Design Chief Jonathan Ive Is Knighted," *BBC*, May 23, 2012, accessed November 16, 2021, www.bbc.com/news/uk-18171093.

35. Bono, "Jonathan Ive," *Time*, April 29–May 6, 2013.

36. John Webb, "10 Success Principles of Apple's Innovation Master Jonathan Ive," April 30, 2012, accessed December 01, 2021, www.disruptorleague.com/blog/2012/04/30/10-success-principles-of-apples-innovation-master-jonathan-ive/.

37. *Wikipedia*, s.v. "Project Management," accessed November 16, 2021, https://en.wikipedia.org/wiki/Project_management.

38. *Wikipedia*, s.v. "Critical Path Method," accessed November 16, 2021, https://en.wikipedia.org/wiki/Critical_path_method.

18 Education Architecture for Innovation

Human Capital, Education, and the University of Bologna

An education system is an organized program for learning that performs a critical role in research, knowledge creation, and knowledge transfer.[1] Our standard of living is a direct result of our ability to learn new knowledge and translate that new knowledge into results. Because about two-thirds of our innovation skills come through learning, rather than from genetics, anything that promotes learning has the potential to accelerate innovation.[2] As John F. Kennedy observed, "Our progress as a nation can be not swifter than our progress in education." The education system facilitates the process of learning competencies and training that impact our well-being.[3]

In general, human capital is "the economic value of worker's experience and skills." Human capital is an intangible asset that includes explicit competencies: attitudes, skills, knowledge, and values. By providing education and training, human capital can be improved to achieve economic growth, productivity, and profitability.[4] By extension, the human capital theory of education is the concept that when the education system teaches students competencies it is providing value and offering employment opportunities. That is, "Once you enter the labor market, the theory says, you will be rewarded with a better job, brighter career prospects, and higher wages."[5] The human capital theory, however, is fulfilled only if the education system provides forward thinking competitive value and affordability.

Today's education systems have not kept up with our need for the combination of personal growth, societal change, economic prosperity, environmental challenges, and cultural shifts that we are experiencing. Too often they morph into monoliths, designed a century ago to solve a quite different set of problems than the ones faced today.[6] Many of the education systems still in use were built based on the first industrial revolution model. In general, education systems are organized in stages of increasing specificity: early childhood education or kindergarten, primary education, or elementary school sometimes up to middle school, secondary or high school, and tertiary, higher education, or vocational schools.[7] For example, a university is a tertiary institution for higher learning that is organized into academic disciplines of increasing levels of specialization for both education and research.

The University of Bologna, founded in 1088, is considered by many to be the oldest university in the world.[8] The University of Bologna created the concept of academic freedom, which guaranteed the right of the academics to pursue their interests in education unhindered.[9] It is interesting to note, and no coincidence, that a picture of a classroom at the University of Bologna from hundreds of years ago would resemble any classroom today. The University of Bologna "design" of the past has been adopted by colleges and universities around the world.

While the University of Bologna model worked well in its day and some of its vestiges are still valuable, the world has changed and, consequently, innovative approaches are needed. This

DOI: 10.4324/9781003034308-19

chapter examines the overall understanding of the attitudes, skills, knowledge, and experiences that are needed to increase imagination, creativity, innovation, and new venture creation capability, especially about education innovation. Innovation and entrepreneurship are important for individual personal growth, local and regional industry growth, national economic growth, and worldwide economic prosperity. Innovation and entrepreneurship need to be included in the fundamental training and strategic thinking of every organization.

Throughout this book, the value of innovation and entrepreneurship at the individual, organizational, local, regional, national, and international levels have been emphasized. Innovation and entrepreneurship are important for individual personal growth, local and regional industry growth, national economic growth, and worldwide economic prosperity. This book is designed for people who want to improve their ability to generate ideas, develop creative insights, and become more capable of innovation by applying the innovation and entrepreneurship competency framework. The innovation and entrepreneurship competency framework developed and outlined in this book serves to improve the overall understanding of the knowledge, skills, attitudes, and experiences that are needed to increase imagination, creativity, innovation, and new venture creation capability. People are the innovators and innovation drives competitiveness. The well-being of the global economy is related to everyone's capability and capacity for innovation and competitiveness.

In addition, the state of innovation and competitiveness is explored by examining comparative measurements of global innovation and competitiveness and ways to increase innovation capacity and competitiveness and discussing the value of a learning architecture for applying the innovation and entrepreneurship competency framework.

Education Systems

Universities add buildings, sports facilities, administrators, and incorporate new electives in the curriculums without considering or altering the overall education foundation. There is a significant difference between offering new electives vs. including the forward-thinking concepts in every required educational program and class. The problem, however, goes deeper than superficial changes. This conundrum is captured in an old saying: you can always change the saddle, but it is the same old horse. According to a 2023 survey, Americans' confidence in higher education has fallen to 36%, lower than in two prior readings in 2015 (57%) and 2018 (48%).[10]

Sir Ken Robinson writes,

> If you design a system to do something specific, don't be surprised if it does it. If you run an education system based on standardization and conformity that suppresses individual, imagination, and creativity, don't be surprised if that's what it does.[11]

The tribal wisdom of the Dakota Indians, passed on from generation to generation, states that when you find out that you are riding a dead horse, the best strategy is to dismount.

How do you design an education system for innovation? Innovation is a human-centered process that can provide meaningful value to improve the education system. Innovation is important because it is a driver for better standards of living, creating a sustainable advantage, economic growth, and job opportunities. Innovation is a vital discipline that needs to be understood, organized, and deliberately managed and led.

In the book, *Creative Schools*, Sir Ken Robinson writes, "As I see it, the aims of the education system are to enable students to understand the world around them and the talents within them so they can become fulfilled individuals and active, compassionate citizens."[12] Social, economic, environmental, and cultural changes are continually appearing on the horizon. As a result, he notes, education must embrace not only mechanistic processes but organic as well.

According to Robinson, an adaptable education architecture is essential to achieving these future aims. Sir Ken Robinson suggested that to engage and succeed, education systems need to develop on three fronts.

1. Education systems should foster diversity by offering a broad curriculum and encourage individualization (personalization) of the learning process.
2. Education systems should promote curiosity through creative teaching, which depends on high quality teacher training and development.
3. Education systems should focus on awakening creativity through alternative didactic processes that put less emphasis on standardized testing, thereby giving the responsibility for defining the course of education to individual schools and teachers.[13]

Architectural Organizing Framework

Education architecture is a high-level design representation for an education system. It is dyadic because it must be able to function effectively both internally and externally.

1. The internal education ecosystem focuses on creating an architectural structure that is dynamic, adaptable, and flexible for breaking out of the status quo, dismantling silos, and injecting new concepts into the organizational culture.
2. The external education ecosystem focuses on building entrepreneur and innovation capability for students to be citizens in their communities that achieve personal, social, cultural, and economic goals in the workforce.

The question becomes this: what can be done to improve the teaching and application of innovation at colleges and universities to achieve the most cost-effective impact and include all stakeholders? The starting point is to develop a strategic innovation learning architectural framework is to build innovation capability that focuses on the future unmet needs of all. Ideally, everyone should be taught the fundamentals of innovation to achieve the most impact.

A new learning architecture would add value to building innovation capability. Traditional campus structures and systems often discourage transformational change, limit collaboration, and constrain creative thinking through physical and cultural silos. The architectural organizing framework model is illustrated in Figure 18.1 that focuses on inputs, progression, output, outcomes, and impact.

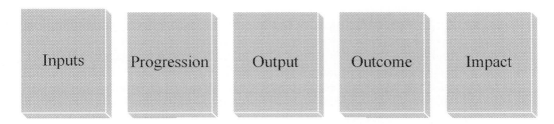

Figure 18.1 Illustration of the Organizing Framework

Source: Adapted from OECD (2023), Education at a Glance 2023: OECD Indicators, OECD Publishing, Paris, https://doi.org/10.1787/e13bef63-en, January 2024, accessed January 12, 2024, https://www.oecd-ilibrary.org/docserver/e13bef63-en.pdf, 11

Trends Shaping Education

According to Patricia Morton, writing in the *Journal of Professional Nursing,*

> As a nation we are facing unprecedented challenges – social, economic, and environmental. These challenges, coupled with the extraordinary speed of technology development couched in an era of globalization, provide enormous opportunities for higher education to meet the needs of future generations of learners. Children launching their educational journey in 2018 will be young adults in 2030. The educational system must prepare them for jobs that have not yet been created, for technologies that we can't begin to imagine, and for solving problems that we are unable to anticipate.[14]

Moreover, we are experiencing population life spans shifts, and economic affluence, leading to greater consumption that is impacting our ability to sustain our environment.[15]

> The unprecedented digital transformation of the global economy and society is likely to increase the complexity of the modern world, as well as the speed of change, largely because of increased connectivity and more educated individuals worldwide. These two elements – complexity and speed of change – mean that connecting education to the trends shaping the world we live in has never been so urgent.[16]

> The challenge remains: how is the education system keeping pace with the trends of the changing world? Those forward thinkers who understand the shifting trends can create powerful and strategic opportunities. Effective leadership needs to take responsibility to understand these shifts. The current attitudes, skills, knowledge, and values of the worldwide workforce will not likely be enough for the future.[17]

McKinsey's Manyika, Pinkus, and Tuin directly address this problem when they write:

> While inequality between countries has decreased, inequality within countries has increased, most acutely in the United States. Economic mobility has slowed, and the middle class that has been much celebrated as critical to the American economy has been especially squeezed, declining over the past half-century from 61 percent of American households to 52 percent. A primary source of this inequality is a fundamental change in the US economy from one driven by manufacturing to one driven by services and consumption, which has reduced the income available to workers, and this inexorable shift is unlikely to reverse itself.[18]

The Organisation for Economic Co-operation and Development (OECD) is an international group of 36-member countries to advocate for policies to increase prosperity, equality, opportunity, and well-being for all.[19] The OECD identified five emerging trends shaping education: a shifting in the global balance of power, a reliance on competencies of the citizens for civics, the need for security in a turbulent world, an increasing life span, and the influence of modern cultures on education, work, and life. These are described in more detail in Figure 18.2.

The OECD noted that addressing ongoing trends is challenging. "In a complex and quickly changing world, this might require rethinking the relationships between formal and informal learning and reimagining education content and delivery."[20] In 2022, the OECD explored five megatrends shaping the future of education: economic growth, home and work life, knowledge and power, identity and belonging, and the changing nature of our lives. In a broader sense, these trends suggest education is a way to prepare for the unexpected.[21]

Education Trends	
1	Economic Growth: Economic growth is influencing education in various ways. "Education can foster adaptability in a changing global economy and encourage reflection on the type of future we want to build."
2	Living and Working: The changing nature of life and work is having a profound influence on education. "Education can continue to help us grow personally and professionally."
3	Knowledge and Power: The dynamics of knowledge and power are impacting education. "Education equips people with knowledge and helps reinforce the values and skills needed to make it meaningful in their own contexts."
4	Identity and Belonging: Issues of identity and belonging are becoming increasingly relevant to education. "Education can help support the needs of diverse learners and their communities while cultivating global competences."
5	Our Changing Nature. Educational institutions are expected to face significant impacts due to climate change over the next decade. "Education can nurture healthy and sustainable relationships with ourselves and our surroundings."

Figure 18.2 Illustration of Education Trends

Source: Adapted from OECD "Trends Shaping Education 2022," accessed January 12, 2024, http://www.oecd.org/education/trends-shaping-education-22187049.htm

Innovation in Education Systems

Innovating education means solving real problems in new, simple, but not simplistic ways that promote meaningful and equitable learning. It is the combination of the need for personal growth, societal change, economic prosperity, and cultural shifts that are the basis for the need to focus on a new education architecture to drive innovation.

As previously noted, an education architecture is dyadic because to build innovation capability it should focus both (1) inward to create an adaptable thriving inspirational ecosystem within the education systems itself and (2) outward to empower students to apply their entrepreneur and innovation capabilities to improve our well-being through organizations and communities.

The need to integrate innovation, the force for adapting to change, into an education architecture is evidenced in a rapid pace of change and a lagging ability to keep pace. The challenges faced within education systems are to rearchitect the education systems to accommodate new perspectives and ideas while simultaneously providing innovation and entrepreneurship competencies for the students to learn.

Mass education is a powerful force multiplier investment that can help people live better by allowing them to make new discoveries and learn from their past mistakes.[22] Education outcomes can improve our standard of living and create meaningful jobs; the increased levels of education results in high earnings.[23] It is challenging, however, for an education system to innovate itself.

Five ways that innovation can be used to improve education itself might include:

1. Applying an evidence-based foundation
2. Empowering the talent of everyone
3. Building competence capability foresight

4. Strengthening the education workforce
5. Facilitating opportunities for self-expression

1.   Applying an Evidence-Based Foundation

Evidence-based data can be used to identify areas of improvement to inform decisions regarding future investments in education. The data can be used to guide policy and practice toward the creation of a more equitable and effective education system.

Empirical evidence can support an understanding of how to identify novel approaches to teaching and learning. When designing education policies, the evidence can be used to understand how to collaborate with all types of stakeholders, teachers, parents, and community members to develop innovative solutions that meet the needs of all students.[24]

Apply Science to Learning Gap

The teaching of reading is an example of how our education system maintains the status quo in which there is evidence for the need to change. Are we using the wrong model to teach reading? There is an ongoing debate between two teaching models: the balanced literacy and the science of reading. The National Assessment of Educational Progress (NAEP) is a test that is administered by the National Center for Education Statistics, the research arm of the Education Department. The NAEP is the largest continuing and nationally representative assessment of what US students know and can do in various subjects.[25] This national assessment includes the performance of about 600,000 students in reading and math. The results indicate that America's fourth and eighth graders are below expectation in their ability to read literature and academic texts.[26] The below-expectations reading test scores fuel this conversation: traditional educators prefer to focus on the balanced literacy theory, which is based on reading literature, as compared to the science of reading, which emphasizes phonics.[27]

In the balanced literacy theory, students learn to read a wide range of books like those written by Dr. Seuss and Maya Angelou without too much emphasis on technically complex texts or sounding out words. The traditional balanced literacy theory dominates the nation's colleges of education.[28] The science of reading approach is based on a body of research produced by linguists, psychologists, and cognitive scientists that emphasizes phonics, the sound of words. Even though research has demonstrated that systematic phonics is the most reliable way to learn how to read words, the science of reading approach has not made its way into many preservice programs.[29]

2.   Empowering the Talent of Everyone

The achievement gap refers to any disparity in educational achievement between distinct groups of students. The denying of education to individuals limits the breadth of what might be possible in our societies. Curriculums should be based on future competencies but also reflect the diverse cultural perspectives of their local communities. Schools should aim to integrate diversity, equity, and inclusion in education systems to achieve a more interconnected system that is crucial for creating a more equitable and just society.[30]

The High-Performing and Low-Performing Achievement Gap

The National Assessment of Educational Progress (NAEP) Grade 12 results in the United States has found that the achievement gap between high- and low-performing students has widened significantly in both math and reading.[31]

The Socioeconomic Opportunity Gap

Using the National Assessment of Educational Progress (NAEP), the Trends in International Mathematics and Science Survey (TIMSS), and the Program for International Student Assessment (PISA), a study has revealed that the opportunity gap – that is, the relationship between socioeconomic status and achievement – has persisted for the last 50 years.

> Contrary to recent perceptions, we find the opportunity gap – that is, the relationship between socioeconomic status and achievement – has not grown over the past 50 years. But neither has it closed. Instead, the gap between the haves and have-nots has persisted.[32]

The Racial College Completion Rate Gap

The US has a persistent academic achievement disparity across income levels and between white students and students of Black and Hispanic heritage that was first identified in 1966. According to McKinsey, "The achievement gap costs the United States hundreds of billions of dollars – and also exacts a long-term cost in social cohesion."[33] The question of how to design an education system for innovation is critical in addressing this gap.

The completion rates for four-year colleges demonstrate clear racial disparities. Asian (71%) and white students (63%) graduate in high numbers and with increasing rates of completion. The Hispanic graduation rate (50%) is increasing, but the completion rates for Black people (38%) and Native American (35%) students continue to fall.[34] According to Bound, Lovenheim, and Turner, as much as a quarter of the decline in college completion rates can be attributed to declines in college spending.[35]

The Rich and Poor College Gap

Based on funds that are spent on full-time equivalent students, there are wide variations in college spending, even among similar colleges. This is important because research studies are making strong links between college spending and student outcomes.[36] "Much like America's household income inequality, American colleges and universities are deeply unequal when it comes to their finances."[37]

Community colleges and regional public universities, defined as those that admit 80–100% of applicants, spend a little less than $15,000 on academic basics for each full-time-equivalent student; in comparison, highly selective institutions, defined as those that admit less than 40% of applicants, spend just over $52,000 per student.[38]

> Because Black, Hispanic, Native, Pell recipient, and low-income students disproportionately attend broad access colleges, and broad access colleges spend the least per FTE across all classifications outlined above, persistent spending gaps disproportionately affect low-income students and students of color.[39]

THE DIVERSITY, EQUITY, AND INCLUSION GAP

According to Bourke and Dillon,

> Our view is that the goal is to create workplaces that leverage diversity of thinking. Why? Because research shows that diversity of thinking is a well-spring of creativity, enhancing innovation by about 20 percent. It also enables groups to spot risks, reducing these by up to 30 percent. And it smooths the implementation of decision by creating buy-in and trust.[40]

Better outcomes can be achieved by building cultures that support diversity, equity, and inclusion.[41]

1. Diversity is defined as the acceptance of a group of people having a wide range of characteristics, seen and unseen, which they were born with or have acquired. Diversity is all the ways that people differ and includes characteristics, such as gender identity, race or ethnicity, military or veteran status, sexual orientation, talent and ability, experience, skill set, and perspective.[42]
2. Equity is justice according to natural law or right.[43] Equity is the fair treatment for all people through the prevention, detection, and elimination of implicit cognitive biases. There are several interventions that can promote equity that start with emotional intelligence: self-awareness, self-management, social awareness, and social skills.
3. Inclusion is defined as the practice of making all members of an organization feel accepted and welcomed and giving everyone an equal opportunity to build relationships and connect with each other. Inclusion encourages contributions from each person to enable them to grow beyond where they are now. Inclusion is the creation of a climate where any individual or group is respected. Inclusion is achieved by advancing each person's skill set, promoting their careers, and ensuring that they are comfortable and confident at being their authentic selves.[44]

3. *Building Competence Capability Foresight*

Competencies are the interrelated attitudes, skills, and knowledge that are relevant, measurable, and transferable that can be applied throughout a learner's lifetime. Each learner in a competency-based system is given the opportunity to reach their fullest potential and master competencies through flexible pathways and personalized support.

The competency gap refers to the mismatch between the capabilities that students possess and the those that are required to succeed in the workforce. The competency gap refers to the difference between the current level of attitudes, skills, and knowledge of a person and the level of attitudes, skills, and knowledge required for a particular role, such as a student or an employee. There is a changing breadth of competencies that need to be included in education systems for the 21st-century economy.

By implementing targeted strategies, the education system can help bridge the competency gap and prepare students for success in the workforce. The education curriculum, the lessons and academic content taught in a school, needs to reflect (1) the breadth of needs of all citizens; (2) the attitudes (wanting to), skills (how to), and knowledge (what to) that are in demand in the workforce, such as citizenship, critical thinking, creative thinking, collaboration, communication, emotional intelligence; and the (3) specialized skills for science, technology, engineering, art and design, and mathematics. The strategies are:

1. Partnering and collaboration with the industry to understand their unmet needs
2. Revising the curriculum to incorporate the competencies that are in demand in the workforce[45]
3. Providing career counseling to guide students on what career paths are available for their talents

Comparative International Test Scores

The Organisation for Economic Co-operation and Development (OECD) advocates for policies to increase prosperity, equality, opportunity, and well-being for all.[46] The OECD Program for International Student Assessment (PISA) is a worldwide study of both member and non-member nations to evaluate educational systems. The PISA study is conducted every three years by measuring the skills and knowledge of 15-year-old students' scholastic performance in science, reading and mathematics (plus collaborative problem solving and financial literacy) from randomly selected schools.[47]

Based on global comparative scores from the OECD's worldwide PISA study of scholastic performance, many developed countries are lacking in foundational skills. The results are a harbinger of the future and a signal for those countries and economies to modernize their educational systems.[48] The future of the world is dependent on strong education systems that need to focus on strengthening the foundational competencies.[49]

PISA results are crucial because they are the best indicator available that has the potential to predict global intellectual capital in the future. OECD PISA 2022 evaluated nearly 700,000 15-year-old students in 81 OECD member countries and partner economies on mathematics, reading, and science. This was the first study to collect data on student performance, well-being, and equity before and after the COVID-19 pandemic. On average, the PISA 2022 assessment saw an unprecedented drop in performance across the OECD. Compared to 2018, mean performance fell by 10 score points in reading and by almost 15 score points in math. The 2022 Program for International Student Assessment (PISA) scores are listed in Figure 18.3.[50]

Eighteen countries and economies performed above the OECD average in mathematics, reading and science in 2022. Between 2018 and 2022, mean performance in mathematics across OECD countries fell by a record 15 points. Reading fell 10 points, twice the previous record, whereas science performance did not change significantly. On average, reading and science trajectories had been falling for a decade, though math had remained stable between 2003–2018. Colombia, Macao (China), Peru and Qatar improved in all three subjects on average since they began to take part in PISA.[51]

	Math (Average 472)				Reading (Average 476)				Science (Average 485)		
1	Singapore	575	6	1	Singapore	543	-7	1	Singapore	561	10
2	Macao (China)	552	-6	2	Ireland	516	-2	2	Japan	547	17
3	Chinese Taipei	547	16	3	Japan	516	12	3	Macao (China)	543	0
4	Hong Kong (China)	540	-11	4	Korea	515	1	4	Chinese Taipei	537	22
5	Japan	536	9	5	Chinese Taipei	515	13	5	Korea	528	9
6	Korea	527	1	6	Estonia	511	-12	6	Estonia	526	-4
7	Estonia	510	-13	7	Macao (China)	510	-15	7	Hong Kong (China)	520	4
8	Switzerland	508	-7	8	Canada	507	-13	8	Canada	515	-3
9	Canada	497	-15	9	United States	504	-1	9	Finland	511	-11
10	Netherlands	493	-27	10	New Zealand	501	-5	10	Australia	507	4
11	Ireland	492	-8	11	Hong Kong (China)	500	-25	11	New Zealand	504	-4
12	Belgium	489	-19	12	Australia	498	-5	12	Ireland	504	8
13	Denmark	489	-20	13	United Kingdom	494	-10	13	Switzerland	503	7
14	United Kingdom	489	-13	14	Finland	490	-30	14	Slovenia	500	-7
15	Poland	489	-27	15	Denmark	489	-12	15	United Kingdom	500	-5
16	Austria	487	-12	16	Poland	489	-23	16	United States	499	-3
17	Australia	487	-4	17	Czech Republic	489	-2	17	Poland	499	-12
18	Czech Republic	487	-12	18	Sweden	487	-19	18	Czech Republic	498	1
19	Slovenia	485	-24	19	Switzerland	483	-1	19	Latvia	494	7
20	Finland	484	-23	20	Italy	482	5	20	Denmark	494	1
21	Latvia	483	-13	21	Austria	480	-4	21	Sweden	494	-6
22	Sweden	482	-21	22	Germany	480	-18	22	Germany	492	-11
23	New Zealand	479	-15	23	Belgium	479	-14	23	Austria	491	1
24	Lithuania	475	-6	24	Portugal	477	-15	24	Belgium	491	-8
25	Germany	475	-25	25	Norway	477	-23	25	Netherlands	488	-15
26	France	474	-21	26	Latvia*	475	-4	26	France	487	-6
27	Spain	473	-	27	Spain	474	-	27	Hungary	486	5
28	Hungary	473	-8	28	France	474	-19	28	Spain	485	-
29	Portugal	472	-21	29	Hungary	473	-3	29	Lithuania	484	2
30	Italy	471	-15	30	Lithuania	472	-4	30	Portugal	484	-7
31	Viet Nam	469	-	31	Slovenia	469	-27	31	Norway	478	-12
32	Norway	468	-33	32	Viet Nam	462	-	32	Italy	477	9
33	Malta	466	-6	33	Netherlands	459	-26	33	Viet Nam	472	-
34	United States	465	-13	34	Slovak Republic	447	-11	34	Malta	466	9
Key: 1-Rank, 2-Country, 3-Mean score, and 4-Score difference (PISA 2018 to PISA 2022)											

Figure 18.3 Illustration of International Test Scores

Source: Acknowledgement: PISA 2022 Results (Volume I): The State of Learning and Equity in Education, accessed, December 6, 2023, https://www.oecd-ilibrary.org/sites/9149c2f5-en/index.html?itemId=/content/component/9149c2f5-en

The Competency Skill Gaps

The Organisation for Economic Co-operation and Development (OECD) has launched *The Future of Education and Skills 2030* project to help countries find answers to two far-reaching questions:[52]

1. What attitudes, skills, knowledge, and values will today's students need to thrive and shape their world?
2. How can education systems develop these attitudes, skills, knowledge, and values effectively?

There is an ever-widening skills gap between what schools are teaching and what the economy needs. Tony Wagner has recommended seven overlapping competencies (survival skills) for the future: critical thinking and problem solving, collaboration across networks and leading by influence, agility and adaptability, initiative and entrepreneurism, effective oral and written communication, accessing and analyzing information, and curiosity and imagination.[53]

In a survey done by McKinsey, 87% of the respondents say they are currently experiencing skill gaps now or expect them within a few years. Specifically, the findings suggest that 43% of the companies surveyed currently have skills gap and that 44% of the respondents say their organizations expect skill gaps within the next five years. The top skill areas that were identified in the survey are critical thinking and decision-making, leadership and management, advanced data analysis and math skills, project management, and adaptability and continuous learning.[54] The top skill areas are shown in Figure 18.4.

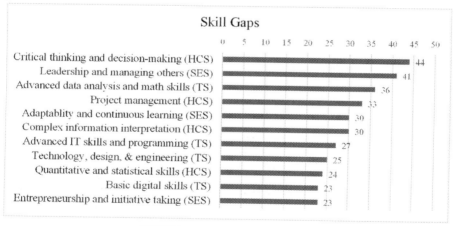

HCS [Higher Cognitive Skills]
TS [Technological Skills]
SES [Social and Emotional Skills]

Figure 18.4 Illustration of Skill Gaps

Source: Adapted from Sapana Agrawal, Aaron De Smet, Pawel Poplawski, and Angelika Reich, "Beyond hiring: How companies are reskilling to address talent gaps," McKinsey & Company, February 2020, accessed March 10, 2020, https://www.mckinsey.com/www.mckinsey.com/business-functions/organization/our-insights/beyond-hiring-how-companies-are-reskilling-to-address-talent-gaps

4. Strengthening the Education Workforce

Once an education architecture is in place, the strengthening of the education workforce begins with the adoption of a structured pedagogy framework that provides an effective way to design and implement courses to achieve meaningful outcomes. The structured pedagogy framework is an architectural concept that uses evidence to describe the elements for implementing an effective educational program.[55]

The structured pedagogy framework for a competency-based education is a stepwise process beginning with the performance objectives (what the learner will learn), the assessments, and then the instructional strategies. All three should be aligned with each other and linked to the course competency content.[56]

Competency-based education courses that focus on attitudes (wanting to), skills (how to), and knowledge (what to) would align the performance objectives, assessments, and instructional strategies. The competencies would be personalized for every student to receive a completely unique educational approach that's fully customized to his or her individual abilities and needs.

Next Generation of Teacher Training Gap

The strategies that support strengthening the education workforce are as follows:

1. Teachers should be trained to educate the whole person, including those competencies that support lifelong learning and that are in demand in the workforce.
2. Teachers should collaborate with families and the community members to engage in improvements in the educations system.
3. Teachers should be trained to encourage creativity and innovation mindsets by embedding active learning exercises, projects, and technology into their coursework.

The transformation of the education system to adopt innovation and entrepreneurship competencies can be accelerated with teacher training. The key to transforming education is the teaching experience that inspires students to learn. The role of teaching is the facilitation and support of student learning.[57] According to Sir Ken Robinson, great teachers perform three essential purposes.

1. Inspiration: They inspire their students with their own passion for their disciplines and to achieve at their highest levels within them.
2. Confidence: They help their students to acquire the skills and knowledge they need to become confident, independent learners who can continue to develop their understanding and expertise.
3. Creativity: They enable their students to experiment, inquire, ask questions, and develop the skills and disposition of original thinking.[58]

A critical measure of the education system is that students complete their degrees and graduate.

The six-year completion rates, the percentages of students who graduate from a four-year program within six years, are 55% for public and 64% percent for private non-profit universities. The six-year completion rates for public and private non-profit universities have hovered around 56% to 58% for the past ten years.[59]

If value is achieved through innovation, it should be expected that teachers complete innovation training. Innovation training is a prerequisite to building innovation capability. All teachers should understand innovation so that it can be integrated into the classroom experience. Creativity and innovation training need to be embedded in all subjects, including language arts, chemistry, geometry, mathematics, etc. The three ways of organizing creativity for education are shown in Figure 18.5.

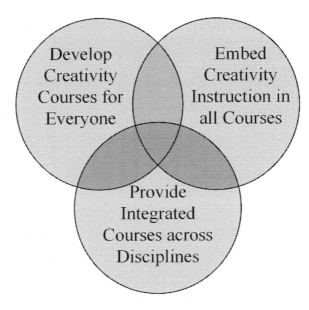

Figure 18.5 Illustration Organizing for Creativity Education

5.   *Facilitating Opportunities for Self-Expression*

Education systems that prioritize conformity over individuality can limit the opportunity for self-expression. A focus on these competency sets when combined (Power of And) can accelerate self-expression.

1. Behavioral competencies: questioning, observing, networking, and experimentation. Chapter 4.
2. Thinking competencies: causation versus correlation, divergent and convergent thinking, switch thinking, critical thinking, and systems and integrative thinking. Chapter 5.
3. Problem-solving competencies: visualization, ordering, analogy, simplification, and frame. Chapter 6.
4. Knowledge competencies: learning efficacy and knowledge creation. Chapter 7.
5. Creativity competencies: questioning, observing, networking, and experimenting. Chapter 8.

The use of evidence-based technology learning tools, such as gamification, virtual and augmented reality, and generative artificial, can be especially effective in stimulating ideation. Students should be given opportunities to apply their competencies in real-world settings through internships, apprenticeships, and other work-based learning programs.

The Montessori method is an example of an educational model that is based on the notion of self-expression. It emphasizes self-motivated learning, hands-on activities, and a nurturing environment that fosters the development of the whole child. "The Montessori method fosters rigorous, self-motivated growth for children and adolescents in all areas of their development – cognitive, emotional, social, and physical."[60]

Education Disruption

Today's education systems are posed for disruption because the systems were built like castles that are representations of institutions architected not for adaptability but rather to defend past decisions and hold onto their power. Rosabeth Moss Kanter notes:

The world is littered with literal and figurative castles. In Europe, they are museums to a medieval past. In America, castles take a more modern physical form as suburban corporate headquarter campuses, heavily guarded office towers, gated communities with hidden delivery entrances, or massive government buildings with intimidating security lines. These edifices are designed to protect executives and functionaries from unwelcome intrusions – or the need to change.[61]

Education systems need to evolve from the castle model to develop the flexibility and adaptability needed to face the challenges of a changed and changing world. Innovation and entrepreneurship competencies are valuable for identifying, addressing, and resolving significant problems across complex educational, as well as geographic, environmental, social, legal, political, economic, sociological, healthcare sectors and more.[62]

One way to achieve this evolution in education is through innovation in general, and disruptive innovation in particular. For example, Thomas Charmorro-Premuzic and Becky Frankiewicz, writing in *Harvard Business Review*, note that while there is no clear path to disrupting higher education, there are many issues or "pain points" that need to be addressed. They succinctly capture the challenge: "The reality in today's digital-first world is that we need to teach every generation how to learn, unlearn, and relearn – quickly – so they can transform the future of work, rather than be transformed by it."[63] Figure 18.6 illustrates multiple aspects of the potentional for disruption in higher education.

Why Disruption is Needed in Higher Education	
Employers need adaptable skills, not just knowledge.	The future of the education system will be based on adaptability and learnability, rather than earning college credentials that may not be matched with current employer needs.
Students want meaningful jobs and financial stability.	Students investment (time and money) in a college education that yields under-employment, with up to 40% of college graduates over qualified for their jobs.
Students are paying more and more to get less and less.	In the U.S. the cost of higher education has increased some 200% in the past 20 years (145% above the inflation rate) and student debt increased 600%, reaching an all-time-high of $ 1.4 trillion in America.
Students have unrealistic expectations about college.	To attract students universities build impressive facilities for students and market themselves by setting high expectations by promising to upgrade each student's talent for exceptional employment opportunities. These expectations are not realistic for all students and may explain the prevalence of low employee engagement outcomes.
Many elite universities prioritize research, often at the expense of teaching.	For some university cultures, teaching can become less important than publishing and getting research grants. The incentives in higher education include higher salaries, autonomy, tenure, and a lower teaching load, which can result in less importance placed on teaching.
Instead of boosting meritocracy, universities reinforce inequality, an untenable trend.	A student's socio-economic status is inversely related to the value that a university can provide. The enrollment choices that a university makes influences the opportunity gap because students from a lower social-economic group receive more added value than a student from a high-economic group.

Figure 18.6 Illustration of Disruption in Education

Source: Adapted from Tomas Chamorro-Premuzic, Becky Frankiewicz, "6 Reasons Why Higher Education Needs to Be Disrupted," November 19, 2019, Harvard Business Review, accessed January 13, 2024, https://hbr.org/2019/11/6-reasons-why-higher-education-needs-to-be-disrupted

This suggests three needs moving forward: (1) There is a need to address not just the future of work, but the future of education as well. (2) There needs to be a continuously evolving education architecture that takes innovation into consideration. (3) The principles and competencies of innovation and entrepreneurship can be applied to the education system itself.

Education Purpose

The purpose of the education system should extend far beyond learning skills for employment. Rather it is how to prepare young people for life beyond school; helping them to build capability intellectually, emotionally, and socially so that they can cope well with uncertainty and complexity.[64] "This purpose for education is valuable for all young people and involves helping them to discover the things that they would really love to be great at, and strengthening their will and skill to pursue them. This confidence, capability, and passion can be developed since real-world intelligence is something that people can be helped to build up."[65]

According to Sir Ken Robinson, there are four purposes for education: personal, social, economic, and cultural, as shown in Figure 18.7.[66] That is, education is personal – enabling everyone to engage their unique talents; social – enabling everyone to engage in active, compassionate citizenship; economic – enabling everyone to take responsibility for applying acquired competencies to achieve meaningful results; and cultural – enabling everyone to understand and appreciate their cultural groups, respect others, and demonstrate their values.

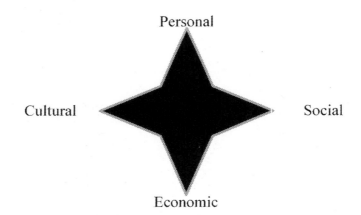

Figure 18.7 Illustration of the Four Purposes of Education

Source: Adapted from Robinson, K., & Aronica, L. (2015). Creative schools: The grassroots revolution that's transforming education. New York: Viking, p. 45–53.

Education Learning Framework

Education can provide learners with a sense of purpose, and the competencies they need, to find their voice in their own lives, amplify their voice, and help others find their voice by contributing to the lives of others. The OECD Learning Framework 2030 offers a vision and some guiding principles for the future of education systems.[67]

1. Need for innovative solutions in a rapidly changing world
2. Need for broader education goals: Individual and collective well-being
3. Learner agency: navigating through a complex and uncertain world

4. Need for a broad set of knowledge, skills, attitudes, and values in action
5. Competencies to transform our society and shape our future to address new sources of growth
6. Design principles for moving toward an eco-systemic change[68]

The OECD notes that curriculum change results from an ecosystem with multiple stakeholders: students, teachers, school leaders, parents, national and local policymakers, academic experts, unions, and social and business partners.[69] From these, five core stakeholder groups emerge: students, teachers, employers (unions), leaders (school and academic experts, policymakers), and community (parents, social and business partners).

Students have an opportunity to master the competencies essential to achieve the learning objectives before advancing to the next subject. This allows each individual student to take responsibility for their learning. *Teachers* can customize instruction and content to fulfill the unmet needs of each student. *Employers* have an opportunity to share their evolving needs with educational institutions. *Leaders* can transparently provide oversight and focus on supporting, evaluating, and reporting on students' essential mastery of specific learning objectives. *An actively engaged community* provides the cohesion to bring all the partners together. The five core stakeholders are shown in Figure 18.8, which summarizes the OECD Learning Framework.

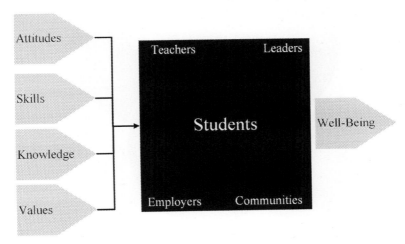

Figure 18.8 Illustration of The OECD Learning Framework 2030: Work-in-progress

Source: Adapted from OECD, "The Future of Education and Skills Education 2030," 2018, accessed January 13, 2024, http://www.oecd.org/education/2030-project/contact/E2030_Position_Paper_(05.04.2018).pdf

There is increasing interest in expanding the perspective of organizations beyond focusing on economics. Peter Tufano, Moores Professor of Finance and former dean at the University of Oxford's Said Business School, writing in the *Harvard Business Review*, captures this emphasis in stakeholder value when he notes the following.

The Business Roundtable statement and the Davos Manifesto are statements of intent for firms to acknowledge and advance the interests of multiple stakeholders, rather than simply accept the primacy of shareholders. To turn these good intentions into reality, schools should:

1. Teach students to understand the nature and implications of stakeholder capitalism.

2. Create courses that allow students to understand the needs and concerns of all stakeholders, rather than treating them as instrumental groups to be dealt with in the service of enhancing shareholder value.
3. Create new metrics to capture the degree to which firms are addressing the needs of their broader constituencies.
4. Research and design new feedback mechanisms (e.g., new forms of management accounting and stakeholder accounting, new measures of investment performance, new contractual structures to create incentives for advancing stakeholder interests, etc.).[70]

Formal Education Architecture

Any formal education architecture is based on the teaching-learning process that is made up of three main elements: curriculum, teaching, and assessments. These are standardized in many national education systems and are illustrated in Figure 18.9 and discussed in the following.[71]

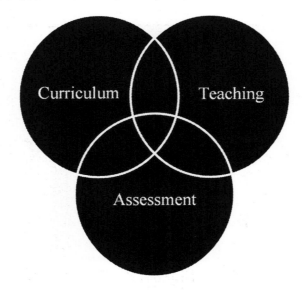

Figure 18.9 Illustration of the Elements of Formal Education

Source: Adapted from Ken Robinson and Lou Aronica, *Creative Schools: The Grassroots Revolution That's Transforming Education*, (New York: Viking, 2015), 11.

Curriculum

The first element in formal education is the curriculum. A curriculum is the content structure to achieve the performance objectives of a learner. Our interconnected worldwide community requires the building of a solid foundation: literacy, mathematics, science, and the arts. A major purpose of the education system is to prepare people for citizenship and employment opportunities in all types of organizations; some of these opportunities do not yet exist. In the education system, education, broad, and training, more specialized, are both offered in a curriculum that focuses on competencies.

The principles of a curriculum should include diversity, depth, and dynamisms.[72] Imagine an organization as a tree. At the top of the tree, you will find the outputs and at the bottom of the tree the inputs. At the bottom of the tree is the root system that represents the competencies. The roots are the entry point for the pathways to provide the resources that are transferred to the leaves. Sunlight is used by the leaves to produce the products of the tree, which are flowers, nuts, and fruits, which represent the desired behaviors. Therefore, learning of competencies becomes the root system for any organization.[73] The distinct competencies cannot become rigid because the dynamics of technological advancements may require new competencies to be integrated into the organizational learning.

Traditional Education Programs

In traditional education programs, the path to completion is based on accumulating education credits using semester-long courses. Students' progress is measured primarily by the accumulation of credit hours and the achievement of minimum grade-point averages.[74]

The structure of most curriculums today is based on the concept of discrete subjects that are organized in a hierarchy where the perceived value can be ascertained explicitly whether the subject is required, optional or not offered at all and by the amount of time and resources that are given to each subject.[75]

The building block for the curriculum is the course that is offered in classes. Each course can be viewed as a story in a narrative form that is told by the educator. The hierarchy has math, languages, and science at the top. At the middle would be social studies, geography, and history. At the bottom would be physical education and the arts, which would include music, art, theater, and ballet.[76]

In traditional education programs, students learn competencies: attitudes, skills, knowledge, and values. The fundamental building block competencies are literacy, mathematics, and science such as biology, chemistry, botany, and physics. There are also distinct competencies that are specialized for growing and sustaining effective organizations. For instance, to build a jet engine, you need metallurgy and engineering competencies. To build a dam, you need civil engineering and strength of material competencies.

Competency-Based Education and Learning Programs

Competency-based education and learning programs are learner-centered programs designed for students to demonstrate a set of competencies: attitudes, skills, knowledge, and values. The students advance through a program based on demonstrated mastery of a competency set defined by their discipline.[77] According to the American Institutes for Research's Postsecondary Competency-Based Education Research, to be classified as a competency-based education and learning program, the program must contain at least one of the following characteristics:[78]

- Learning is measured in competencies and either quantified without reference to seat time or mapped to measures of seat time.
- Students advance from the course or complete the program based on mastering all required competencies.
- Courses or programs offer flexible pacing.

Competency-based education and learning focuses on mastering and applying measurable evidence-based competencies.[79] The adoption of competency-based education and learning in educational systems differs widely because programs have unique needs and goals. The foundation of competency-based education is the notion that students have (1) clear expectations described in performance objectives regarding what they are expected to learn, (2) their learning is measured by assessments that are aligned with the expectations, and (3) instructional strategies to enhance their learning.

Competency-based education and learning can be viewed on a continuum that is integrated into a time-bound traditional education program, a complete competency-based education and learning self-paced degree program, or an experimental competency-based education and learning program.[80]

Integrated into a Traditional Curriculum

In a competency-based curriculum, within the traditional model, the course may be time-bound, have well-defined competencies that are embedded in the course, have assessments that directly evaluate student mastery of the competencies, and attract more traditional students. The course can be online, classroom, or blended and offered by any university that requires synchronization with a group of students. The building of a competency-based curriculum would be useful as a bridge to a competency-based education and learning program. The learning of a musical instrument, such as the piano, in curriculums is competency-based and often self-paced. Learning how to play the piano requires the interaction of affective, psychomotor, and cognitive domains.[81]

Teaching

The second element in formal education is teaching. Teaching refers to strategies that are designed to facilitate the learning of attitudes, skills, and knowledge. Many education systems, however, are based on a labyrinth of theories and terminology from the past that may or may not match with current educational needs. There are several theories of how people learn, such as behaviorism, cognitivism, and constructivism, which are instructive in this process.

Behaviorism explains learning as a process of reacting to external stimuli. This means that behavior can be explained without considering the mental states of consciousness. Cognitivism explains learning as a process of acquiring and storing information. Changes in behavior reflect what is in people's minds. Constructivism explains learning as a process of constructing subjective reality based on previous knowledge and objective reality. In constructivism, behavior is the result of testing personal hypotheses and forms the basis for the Montessori method of education.

Basic Learning Models

Learning is the process of acquiring new knowledge and skills using passive and active strategies.

Passive Learning Strategy

The conceptual framework for traditional learning provides one curriculum model for everyone based on passive time-sequenced lectures, textbook reading, and test taking. In the traditional education model, teachers lecture and students listen, read textbooks, and may conduct research and write essays. There is an emphasis in most educational systems on learning science, technology, engineering, and mathematics. Students are rarely introduced to creativity, thinking, or problem solving as learnable skills. In traditional learning, a student's progress is based on their putting in a fixed amount of time (a semester of effort) while they learn a set of competencies. The students must fulfill the time requirement, or they will not receive credit for their course work.

In many teaching and learning models, the student focuses on what will be assessed. For college and graduate school admission, for example, students may take the SAT, ACT, and GRE. These tests measure reading, math, and writing competencies. The innovation competency model provides an opportunity for broadening the content and can be used in traditional time-based education, competency-based education without time constraints.

Active Learning Strategy

Learning can come alive through student-centered models, such as constructivism and problem-based learning. In constructivism, the teacher serves as a learning guide. The student's knowledge is constructed rather than transmitted. In problem-based learning, the teacher serves as a facilitator and coach. Students are given a real problem, which they discuss together to develop theories or hypotheses. The students conduct independent research to better understand the nature of the problem. Finally, the students work together as a team to discuss their findings and refine their ideas.

Active learning allows students to combine their talents, attitudes, skills, and knowledge with innovation. Active learning facilitates the application of the innovation elements and competencies. Active learning can be achieved using multiple visual instructional models that focus on the narrated content, videos, exercises, contemporary innovation stories, innovation research, challenge-based team learning, online discussion groups, team projects, individual research, and the personalization of assignments. The more the competencies are practiced, the more effective is the behavioral mastery.

Assessments

The third element in formal education is assessment. Assessments in education are to evaluate students' attitude, skills, and knowledge outcomes. These assessments measure student progress, identifying areas of strength and areas for improvement by informing instructional decisions and providing feedback for both students and teachers. Assessments are composed of a set of methods that serve different purposes throughout the educational experience. Common types of assessments in education are as follows:[82]

1. Formative assessments: These assessments occur during the learning process and are designed to provide ongoing feedback to students and teachers. They help identify student understanding, misconceptions, and areas that require further instruction. Examples include classroom discussions, quizzes, homework assignments, and in-class activities.
2. Summative assessments: These assessments are typically administered at the end of a learning unit, course, or academic year to evaluate a student's overall understanding and mastery of the material. Examples include final exams, standardized tests, projects, and research papers.
3. Diagnostic assessments: These assessments are conducted at the beginning of a learning cycle to gather information about students' prior knowledge, skills, and readiness for new content. They help identify individual student needs and inform instructional planning. Diagnostic assessments can include pre-tests, surveys, and interviews.
4. Performance assessments: These assessments require students to demonstrate their knowledge and skills by completing real-world tasks or projects. They often involve hands-on activities, presentations, portfolios, or simulations. Performance assessments focus on the application of knowledge rather than mere recall.

Structured Pedagogy Framework for Courses

There are two course design models: forward design and backward design. The traditional forward course design starts with what content the teacher will teach. Backward course design focuses on what the learner will learn rather than what the teacher will teach. The structured pedagogy framework for a competency-based education starts with the performance objectives (what the learner will learn), then assessments, and finally the instructional strategies. All three should be aligned with each other and linked to the course content.[83]

The design of a course would also include flexible scheduling, online delivery, project-based learning, and a higher level of mentoring and coaching. Because competency-based education allows students to learn the content at their own pace, it works well for online delivery.

Competency-based education or learning programs can provide a personalized learning experience for every student to receive a completely unique educational approach that's fully customized to his or her individual abilities and needs. Personalization can directly increase students' motivation and reduce their likelihood of dropping out.

Southern New Hampshire University's College for America, Capella University, and the University of Wisconsin System offer competency-based education and learning degree programs. They have received approval from accreditors and the federal government to offer an aggressive form of competency-based education called direct assessment, which is not based on the credit hour.[84]

Within the elements there is a three-step process needed to ensure alignment of course content.

1. Define the learning (performance) objectives to achieve the desired outcome. The goals and objectives are the starting point in course development by beginning with the end. This is achieved by creating clear measurable goals and objectives that define the competencies of what students will be able to do. Competencies are determined by what students and business want and need.[85]
2. Create assessments to ensure understanding. Assessments should be created to measure student progress. Formative assessments allow measuring progress during the learning: observations, journals, and discussion. Summative assessments define the outcome on the path to success: portfolios, essays, and projects.
3. Create instructional strategies to facilitate the student learning. The instructional strategies and experiences are based on what assignments are relevant to achieve the goals and objectives. This would include group assignments, debates, guest speakers, practical exercises, and field trips.

The structured pedagogical framework instructional design seeks to ensure that the learning or performance objectives, assessments, and instructional strategies are aligned. "The performance required in the objectives must match the performance required in the test item or task."[86] The performance objectives, the assessment and the instructional strategy must be congruent around the content as shown in Figure 18.10.

Step 1: Performance Objectives

A performance objective is a detailed description of what the learners will be able to do when they complete the instruction. A tri-lateral model for preparing performance objectives based on the behavior, the conditions and the criteria are shown in Figure 18.11.[87]

- Does the statement describe what the learner will be doing (behavior) when he is demonstrating that he has reached the objective?
- Does the statement describe the important conditions (givens and/or restrictions) under which the learner will be expected to demonstrate his competence?
- Does the statement indicate how the learner will be evaluated? Does it describe at least the low limit of acceptable performance?

Step 2: Assessments

Assessment is the process of making judgments about students' progress and attainment against expectations.[88] Student assessments are ways to support personal progress and

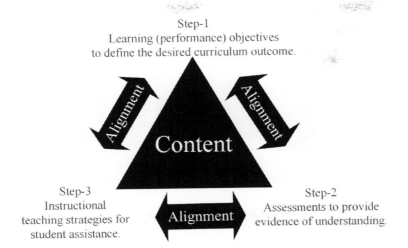

Figure 18.10 Illustration Structured Pedagogy Framework

Source: Adapted from Walter Dick, Lou Carey, and James O. Carey, *The systematic design of instruction.* (Upper Saddle River, N.J: Merrill/Pearson, 2009).

Adapted from Holly Gould, "A 3-Question Checklist for Better Course Design," June 21, 2022, accessed June 24, 2022, https://he.hbsp.harvard.edu/2022-06-21-the-faculty-lounge.html

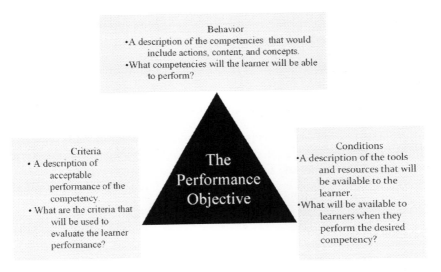

Figure 18.11 Illustration Parts of Performance Objective (Terminal Objective)

Source: Adapted from Walter Dick, Lou Carey, and James O. Carey, *The systematic design of instruction.* (Upper Saddle River, N.J: Merrill/Pearson, 2009), 115.

achievement. An assessment is an instrument that is composed of explicit tasks that directly measure the competencies described in one or more performance objectives. The assessment items are used to determine the adequacy of a learner's performance in meeting the performance objectives in the instructional unit.[89] The assessment types and purposes are described in Figure 18.12.

Diagnostic	Formative	Summative
A diagnostic assessment is used to identify the current competency level or a misconception about a topic.	A formative assessment is use to gather information to support progress and provide feedback during the instructional process to determine growth.	A summative assessment is used to determine the mastery of the overall performance objectives at the end of a program of work.
Diagnostic Examples	**Formative Examples**	**Summative Examples**
• Pre and post-tests • Self-assessment • Discussion board responses • Observations • Polling	• Student observations • Assignments and exercises • Reflection journals • Socratic discussions • Peer reviews	• High-stakes tests • Capstone projects • Portfolios • Essays • Rubrics

Figure 18.12 Illustration of Assessment Types and Purposes

Source: Adapted from The Institute for Arts Integration and STEAM, "Assessment Strategies for Arts Integration and STEAM," accessed March 19, 2020, https://educationcloset.com/assessment-strategies/

Adapted from Ken Robinson and Lou Aronica, *Creative Schools: The Grassroots Revolution That's Transforming Education*, (New York: Viking, 2015), 170.

Step 3: Instructional Strategies

Instructional strategies are ways to enhance the student's ability to learn the content.[90]

The instructional strategy categories are direct instruction, interactive instruction, indirect instruction, independent study, and experimental learning that are shown in Figure 18.13.

For instance, project-based learning (PBL) is an indirect method that is achieved by expecting the students to explore and generate solutions to real-world problems and challenges. All instructional strategies should accommodate accessibility for those in need.

Content Perspectives

We are currently preparing students for jobs that don't yet exist . . . using technologies that haven't been invented . . . in order to solve problems we don't even know are problems yet.

– Richard Riley, former secretary of education

This is a considerable challenge suggesting that education-focused organizations across the country should promote a broad approach to curriculum and learning.[91] We should extend our education system to include broad content described in the innovation and entrepreneurship competency framework.[92]

We live in a world that is demanding a 21st-century competency set, yet education systems in general have not kept pace with providing these vital competencies. Robinson and Aronica write, "First, all students have great natural abilities. Second, the key to developing them is to move beyond the narrow confines of academicism and conformity to systems that are personalized to the real abilities of everyday students."[93]

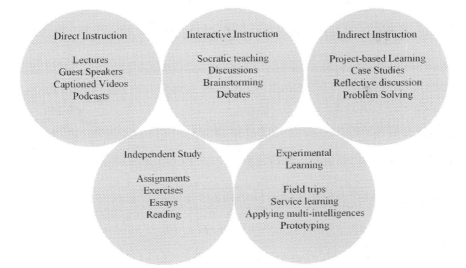

Figure 18.13 Illustration of Instructional Strategies

Source: Adapted from Giani Petri, "A Method For The Evaluation Of The Quality Of Games For Computing Education," Thesis, November 2018, accessed March 18, 2020, https://www.researchgate.net

Adapted from Saskatchewan Education, "Instructional Approaches A Framework for Professional Practice," accessed March 18, 2020, https://wikieducator.org/images/e/e2/Instructional-Approaches_Handbook.pdf

Broad and Narrow Education

The T-shaped person represents the combination of the vertical depth of horizontal breadth that is represented by the competency framework. The education of a democratic society needs to be both broad and deep to encourage critical thinking, effective problem solving, and creative thinking. "Counterintuitive thought, for sure, as we observe the steady disassembling of classic liberal arts programs and colleges, driven by the blend of chronic budget problems and the long-running strategies of educational entrepreneurs to gleefully monetize alternative pathways for students."[94]

A liberal arts education consists of the natural sciences, social sciences, arts, and humanities. A liberal arts degree program contrasts with those that are principally vocational, professional, or technical.[95] Today's complex problems require a foundation of an interdisciplinary liberal arts education that is combined with vocational, professional and technical education. "At its core, liberal education consists of two contradictory yet complementary streams: The pursuit of truth and the creation of virtuous citizens in the community."[96]

For example, nowhere is this need seen more clearly than in the field of engineering. Sorby, Fortenberry, and Bertoline, writing in *Issues in Science and Technology*, note the need to transform engineering education and build a framework that "includes identifying structural racism and inequalities and suggesting possible remedies while integrating cognitive, affective, and kinesthetic domains of learning to prepare students to have more expansive perspectives when approaching society's problems."[97]

The Framework for P–12 Engineering Learning is expected to add structure and coherence to the P–12 engineering community by serving as a foundation for the development of engineering programs in schools, informing state and national standards-setting efforts, and providing researchers with a common starting point to better investigate and understand P-12 engineering learning.[98] The Framework for P–12 Engineering Learning, shown in Figure 18.14, is a step to move forward by democratizing engineering learning across all grade levels, preschool through high school.[99]

Habits Of Mind	Engineering Practice	Engineering Knowledge
Optimism	Processes (Engineering Design)	Sciences
Resilience (Persistence)	Making (Material Processing)	Engineering Mathematics
Collaboration	Quantitative Analysis	Interdisciplinary (Engineering
Creativity	Professionalism	Technical Applications)
Ethical Choices (Conscientiousness)		
Systems Thinking		

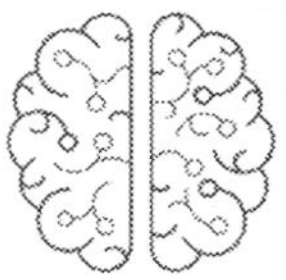

Figure 18.14 Illustration of the Framework for P-12 Engineering Learning

Source: Advancing Excellence in P-12 Engineering Education & American Society for Engineering Education, "Framework for P-12 Engineering Learning," 2020, accessed October 26, 2021, https://pl2framework.asee.org/wp-content/uploads/2020/11/Framework-for-P-l 2-Engineering-Learning-l.pdf

Next Generation Curriculum

In general, the US education system is incomplete in terms of innovation and entrepreneurship competencies. That is, it needs to consider more fully incorporating innovation and entrepreneurship competencies for the whole person. Fundamentally, there is an increased demand for creativity, critical thinking, and problem solving across education, life skills, and employment.

For example, Michael B. Horn and Bob Moesta, co-authors of *Choosing College: How to Make Better Learning Decisions Throughout Your Life*, note,

> Employers are staring at a chasm between the skills they require and what would-be employees bring to the workforce. According to the World Economic Forum, for example, just under 30 percent of companies believe they have the digital talent they require, and a *Wall Street Journal* survey showed that 89 percent of executives struggle to find candidates with the right mix of soft skills – things like teamwork, communication, and adaptability. Higher education has yet to step up and meet the gap. A stunning number of students learn little in college, and far too many – 40 percent – don't complete four-year programs in six years.[100]

The next generation curriculum should be viewed as an integrated set of interdisciplinary building blocks. Each education system should build an adaptable educational architecture that is based on a competency-based curriculum guided by a body of attitudes, skills, knowledge, and values to achieve future outcomes.

1. Integrated courses that combine disciplines should be offered to enable the building of new associations or connections that may never occur otherwise across colleges.

2. A competency-based curriculum needs to be designed to enable students to demonstrate that they have learned the attitudes, skills, knowledge, and values they are expected to learn as they progress through a course.
3. Social-emotional learning (SEL) is based on students learning emotional intelligence that includes responsible decision-making, empathy, self-efficacy, self-awareness, self-management, social awareness, and resilience.
4. Discipline-specific professional competencies that are essential for students to be competitive in the workplace include leadership skills, teamwork skills, communication skills, design skills, and interdisciplinary skills.[101]

In *Creative Schools,* Robinson and Aronica advocate for eight core competencies that inform how students succeed rather than just a "collection of separate subjects." These competencies are curiosity, creativity, criticism, communication, collaboration, compassion, composure, and citizenship.[102] That is, a liberal arts education can provide the competencies that are needed to educate the whole person. A compilation of 21st-century competencies, starting with personal character, are shown in Figure 18.15.

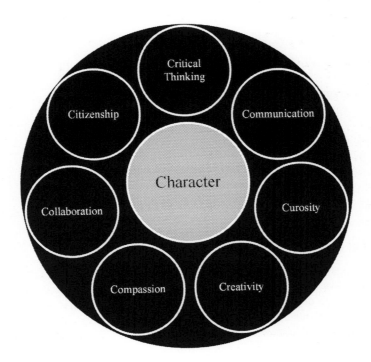

Figure 18.15 Illustration of the 21st-Century Competencies

Source: Adapted from Tony Wagner. 2014. *Global Achievement Gap: Why Even our Best Schools Don't Teach the New Survival Skills our Children Need-and what we can do about It.* New York: Basic Books.

Adapted from Ken Robinson and Lou Aronica, *Creative Schools: The Grassroots Revolution That's Transforming Education,* (New York: Viking, 2015).

The Innovation and Entrepreneurship Education Challenges

An educational architecture is a structure that fulfills a unique functional duality.

1. Empower innovation inward to dynamically adopt an entrepreneurship spirit with new cost-effective value-added continuous improvement concepts and
2. Empower innovation outward to provide students with impactful capability to learn how to apply entrepreneurial innovation competencies for their career journey.

Education is a powerful force that increases a person's chances of achieving their career opportunities, a better standard of living, and more effective citizenship.[103] Yet internally, according to Horn and Pulsipher, "Altogether, post-secondary institutions now spend more than \$670 billion per year – yet interestingly, four-year public and other private nonprofit colleges devote just one third of their total spending on course delivery and instruction."[104]

Colleges and universities have cultures that are built for knowledge transfer, prefer stability, and avoid risk, therefore making it difficult for them to innovate internally because colleges and universities are not designed for transforming the education experience.

> For educational institutions to remain viable, there is an urgent imperative for colleges and universities to recognize the need for change, to act deliberately and strategically to reduce costs and generate revenue, and to challenge the status quo in everything they do. No longer can an educational institution assume that society embraces the value of higher education and that its longevity is assured.[105]

Can colleges and universities adapt to change and respond with agility amidst their significant challenges?[106]

While the education architecture in general and higher education in particular face considerable issues moving forward, the higher education system has challenges.

1. Value and cost of innovation education
2. Innovation opportunities
3. Education rearchitected
4. Strategic opportunities
5. Going for the gold

Value and Cost of Innovation Education

According to a 2022 survey of responses from 6,008 US adults, three-quarters of currently enrolled college and prospective college students report that a college education is either more important than it was 20 years ago or equally as important. However, only about a quarter of currently enrolled or prospective students believe that all or most Americans have access to quality, affordable education after high school if they want it.[107] And in a survey from 2023 of currently enrolled bachelor's degree students nationally at US institutions, around three-quarters strongly agree or agree that the degree they are receiving is worth the cost.[108]

The value/benefits and cost/challenges related to innovation capability internally and externally are summarized in Figure 18.16.

Value/Benefits	Cost/Challenges
Economic Impact: Higher levels of education are associated with increased earning potential and reduced unemployment rates	Ensuring High-Quality Education: Affordability, outdated curricula, teacher training, and resources [Brown]
Global Competitiveness: The nations with well-developed education systems are more likely to be competitive in the global marketplace	Outcomes and Costs: Outcomes and spending are not always correlated. The US outspends the OECD average by roughly 50 percent, yet it falls behind the competency standards [Feldman]
Innovation and Technological Advancement: The nations with well-educated populations tend to be more innovative and technologically advanced	Educational Inequality: There are disparities in educational opportunities based on socioeconomic status, race, and geographic location that can impede human capital
Democratic Values and Civic Engagement: Education is positively associated with civic engagement, political participation, and a commitment to democratic values	Mismatch Between Education and Labor Market Needs: The skills vs needs mismatch can lead to unemployment or underemployment.
Lifelong Learning and Adaptability: Education promotes a positive attitude toward lifelong learning and adaptability to manage under changing circumstances	Overcoming the Status Quo: Rapid societal and technological changes pose challenges to education systems that must adapt to meet evolving needs [Morton]

Figure 18.16 Illustration of Value and Cost of Innovation Education

Source: Adapted from Anna Brown, "Most Americans say higher ed is heading in wrong direction, but partisans disagree on why," July 2018, Pew Research Center, accessed June 25, 2020, https://www.pewresearch.org/fact-tank/2018/07/26/most-americans-say-higher-ed-is-heading-in-wrong-direction-but-partisans-disagree-on-why/

Adapted from Sarah Feldman, "U.S. Outspends Other Developed Nations in the Classroom," Sep 10, 2018, March 21, 2023, https://www.statista.com/chart/15404/us-outspends-other-developed-nations-in-the-classroom/

Adapted from Patricia Gonce Morton, "Higher Education - is the Value Worth the Cost?" Journal of Professional Nursing 34, no. 5 (Sep, 2018): 327–328, doi:10.1016/j.profnurs.2018.08.001, accessed June 25, 2020, https://www.sciencedirect.com/science/article/abs/pii/S8755722318301285?via%

Innovation Opportunities

The innovation opportunities include measurement indicators, design, competency-based education, omni channels, digital learning, personalization, open education resources, and shareable components.

According to Anna Brown of the Pew Research Center,

> Among Americans who say the country's higher education system is going in the wrong direction, 84% cite high tuition costs as a major reason they think this is the case. About two-thirds (65%) say students not getting the skills they need in the workplace is a major reason, while roughly half cite colleges and universities being too concerned about protecting students from views, they might find offensive (54%) or professors bringing their political and social views into the classroom (50%).[109]

Measurement Indicators

The measurement of higher education outcomes should focus on the student competencies (attitudes, skills, knowledge, and values) that are associated with the purpose of education that contribute to economic, cultural, social, and personal growth.[110] Competency-based education is the core of the innovation and entrepreneurship framework.

The OECD's Indicators of Education Systems (INES) program is an authoritative source for accurate and relevant information on education around the world that provides a useful model for determining the value added.[111] The measurement themes are shown in Figure 18.17.

The output of educational institutions, and the impact of learning	How many students finish secondary [high school] and tertiary education [college]?
	How does educational attainment affect participation in the labor market?
	What are the social outcomes of education?
	What are the earnings premiums from education?
The financial and human resources invested in education	How much public and private investment in education is there?
	How much do tertiary students pay, and what public subsidies do they receive?
	On what resources and services is education funding spent?
Access to education, participation and progression	Who participates in education?
	How many students will enter tertiary education?
	Who studies abroad, and where?
	How have 15 to 29-year-olds transitioned from school to work?
The learning environment and organization of schools	How much time do students spend in the classroom?
	What is the student-teacher ratio, and how big are classes?
	How much are teachers paid?

Figure 18.17 Illustration of Performance Measurement Themes

Source: Adapted from OECD, "OECD Indicators of Education Systems," https://www.oecd.org/education/skills-beyond-school/49338320.pdf

For example, the Association for the Advancement of Sustainability in Higher Education (AASHE) provides the Sustainability Tracking, Assessment & Rating System (STARS), a self-evaluation framework used by hundreds of colleges and universities to measure, report, and improve their contributions to global sustainability.[112] The Sustainable Campus Index (SCI) identifies the top-performing colleges and universities overall by institution type in 17 sustainability impact areas. The performance measures are grouped into several categories: academics, engagement, operations, planning and administration, and innovation and leadership.[113]

Adaptable and Multi-Purpose Design

In a complex, changing, global community, course design needs to be adaptable for the future of education, or in terms of our time challenge, *what might be*. Education systems need to continuously improve based on a multidimensional, adaptable learning architecture.

An adaptable learning design for the future would be based on organizing competencies into modularized components that can be individually mastered. The adaptable learning architecture is explicitly designed to support modularized components that can be reused and updated as new knowledge is discovered. This allows and enables new knowledge and technology advancements to be easily integrated, to maximize learning effectiveness, while keeping the overall design the same.

Any course for a broad discipline, like innovation, should be designed for multiple purposes. When designing a course, it should be built for the future so that it can be offered for *omni-channels*. The instructional content should be designed to be offered in multiple ways: online, blended, and traditional classroom using four delivery methods.

The high-level learning architectures has four models that are shown in Figure 18.18.

1. Offline traditional classroom-based instruction
2. Offline self-study

3. Online competency-based education
4. Online traditional education

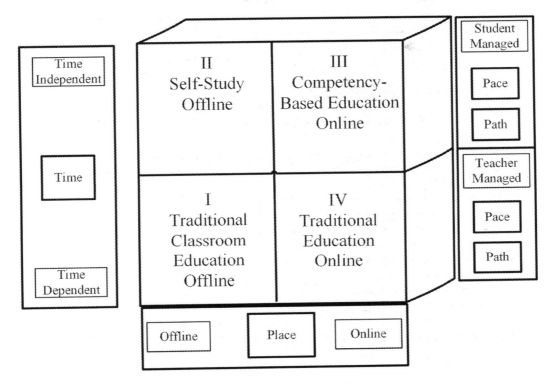

Figure 18.18 Illustration of a Learning Architecture by Time, Place, Pace, and Path

Any of the innovation and entrepreneurship competency categories can be inserted into one of the four quadrants of the learning architecture. This book is future-oriented and is designed to support multiple learning models.

Competency-Based Education Online

A widespread practice of educators is to create competency-based commoditized content from scratch without regard to reusability and sharing with others. The notion of reusable and shared competency-based commoditized content for selected courses in science, mathematics, and history can provide value and lower costs. Much of the competency-based commoditized content is the same across both national and global education systems.[114]

With digital educational technology platforms, it is now possible to incorporate reusable competency-based commoditized content into many courses that require little personalization or human interaction. Students can learn at their own pace and place.

The commoditized content can be offered using multimedia technology that augments the content with images, videos, and music. Using digital educational technology platforms, competency-based commoditized content can be scaled to education systems at a relatively low cost without sacrificing the value of the classroom experience.

The shared reusable competency-based commoditized content online model frees resources from courses that can be commoditized. This frees resources for research-based teaching and more effort can be devoted to the courses where personalized problem solving and mentorship are needed. The students would benefit because they could learn competency-based commoditized content with more affordability, from anyplace, and at any time.

Learning Omni Channels

The delivery channels should fulfill our core educational mission for the students.[115] There are three principal omni channels for the delivery of content. In the adaptable design, a course should be designed for all three. The instructor would seamlessly offer any of the three as students prefer.

Blended learning can be an effective formal education program because it has the potential to improve the value proposition available to students through accessibility, affordability, convenience, customization, selection, and simplicity. With blended learning, the student has some control over time, place, path, and/or pace.

Blended learning uses both synchronous and asynchronous models for learning. Blended learning is organized in several parts that are shown in Figure 18.19.

1. The student learns through online learning.
2. The student engages in practice in a classroom location.
3. The student can participate in challenge-based learning. Challenge-based learning is a student-centered methodology (pedagogy) in which students learn about a subject such as creativity and innovation. Challenge-based learning integrates knowing and doing by applying what students know to solve authentic problems and produce results that matter.

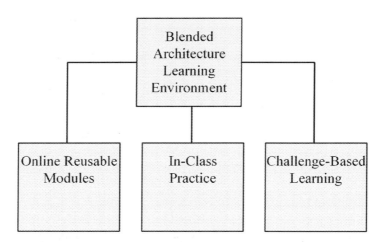

Figure 18.19 Illustration of Blended Learning Architecture

Source: Adapted from Hannafin, M. J., Hannafin, K. M., Land, S. M., & Oliver, K. (1997). Grounded practice and the design of constructivist learning environments. *Educational Technology Research and Development, 45(3),* 101–117.

Adapted from Michael B. Horn and Heather Staker, *Blended: Using disruptive innovation to improve schools.* (San Francisco, California: Jossey-Bass, 2015), 34–35.

Digital Learning Stages for Education Institutions

The progress toward digital learning in educational institutions can be understood by categorizing them into three stages: digital newcomers, emerging adopters, and advanced institutions shown in Figure 18.20. Examples of education institutions that are considered in the advanced institutions category are the University of Michigan, Imperial College London, Duke University, and Coursera.[116]

Digital Newcomers	Digital newcomers are institutions that lack the necessary prerequisites of online learning and remote teaching. These institutions have few courses available online and limited experience teaching online, and they have not funded exploring or expanding online content. Students and faculty have no or limited access to software (collaboration tools, video conferencing) and computer hardware. Digital newcomers have poor or no Internet connectivity.
Emerging Adopters	Emerging adopters are institutions that have successfully experimented with online learning, have basic communication and collaboration tools in place, and have some departments delivering programs online. Emerging adopters need to accelerate their digital transformation journey with institutional intent and a task force dedicated to building online strategy.
Advanced Institutions	Advanced institutions have robust technical infrastructure, a large catalog of digital content, and a faculty that is experienced in teaching online. Advanced institutions usually have dedicated centers of academic innovation driving their digital strategy, and use online courseware as digital textbooks, developed by their own instructors or by integrating courses produced by other institutions.

Figure 18.20 Illustration of the Digital Learning Stages for Educational Institutions

Source: Adapted from James DeVaney, Gideon Shimshon, Matthew Rascoff and Jeff Maggioncalda, "Higher Ed Needs a Long-Term Plan for Virtual Learning," May 05, 2020, accessed May 6, 2020, https://hbr.org/2020/05/higher-ed-needs-a-long-term-plan-for-virtual-learning

The education architecture for innovation and entrepreneurship for the future undoubtedly has and will continue to have a digital premise and presence. For example, building on the innovation and entrepreneurship competency model (see Figure 0.4), leadership plays a key role in discerning the best path forward for how digital competencies contribute to a strong education innovation and entrepreneurship architecture.

Personalized Learning

In contrast to these group-focused models, personalized learning offers a unique curriculum that adapts to each student. With software technology, each student has a customized curriculum like a personal playlist. The software allows the educator and student to monitor progress and access personal tutors where gaps in learning are identified.[117]

Personalized learning environment inspires each student to nurture his or her passions, make connections between different learning experiences and opportunities, and design their own learning projects and processes in collaboration with others.[118] A model of personalization is shown in Figure 18.21.

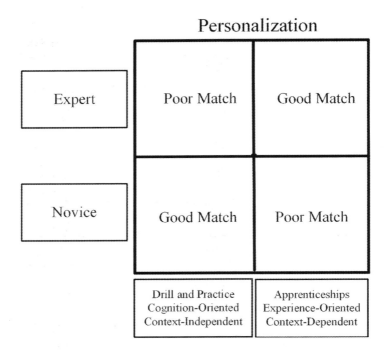

Figure 18.21 Illustration of the Personalization Grid

Source: Acknowledgement: John Pane, Elizabeth D. Steiner, Matthew D. Baird and Laura S. Hamilton. Continued Progress: Promising Evidence on Personalized Learning. Santa Monica, CA: RAND Corporation, 2015. http://www.rand.org/pubs/research_reports/RR1365.html

Personalization Continuum

Personalization in learning is an educational strategy that aims to customize learning for each student's interests and their extant level of attitudes and skills; each student gets a learning plan that's based on what they know and how they learn best. Understanding learners helps the teacher to better design instruction and materials; it can also offer learners a way to understand how they can increase their self-awareness of how they learn best.[119] Personalization can be viewed on a continuum as an extension of the current direct instruction model to a more radical learning model that is shown in Figure 18.22.

Open Educational Resources

According to the United Nations Educational, Scientific and Cultural Organization,

> Open Educational Resources (OER) are teaching, learning and research materials in any medium – digital or otherwise – that reside in the public domain or have been released under an open license that permits no-cost access, use, adaptation and redistribution by others with no or limited restrictions.[120]

The value proposition for Open Education Resources (OER) is to make education accessible by providing both free (no cost) resources for anyone to access and to legally modify to include retain, reuse, revise, remix, and redistribute.[121] The Creative Commons licenses would be used to

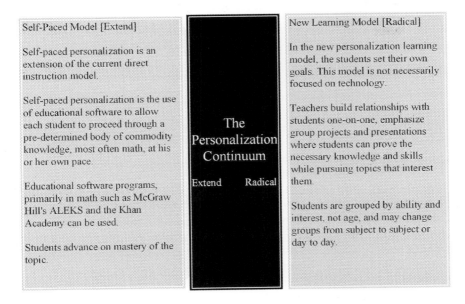

Figure 18.22 Illustration of the Personalization Continuum

Source: Adapted from Anya Kamenetz, Robbie Feinberg, and Kyla Calvert Mason, "The Future Of Learning? Well, It's Personal," NPR, November 16, 2018, accessed May 10, 2020, http://www.npr.org/2018/11/16/657895964/the-future-of-learning-well-it-s-personal

license content as OER, where licensing is required. This excludes those resources with restrictions that permit re-distribution but do not permit changing marked as CC-ND (no derivatives).[122]
Several of the strategic goals for OER are:[123]

1. Reducing barriers to education, including access, cost, language, and format
2. Enabling the free access to and reuse of expressions of human knowledge, in all their forms
3. Ensuring educators have the legal rights to retain, reuse, revise, remix, and redistribute educational resources as they determine – without having to ask permission
4. Increasing the efficiency and effectiveness of public funds spent on education
5. Transforming teaching, learning, and enabling effective, open pedagogy
6. Connecting communities of educators and learners around open content
7. Expanding the use of the Internet and digital technologies in education
8. Enhancing educational opportunities to foster development and more productive, free societies
9. Empowering educators to have more agency in the classroom

Just like most changes, resistance from publishers, policymakers, and teachers has been identified as a major barrier to adopting OER.[124]

Shareable Components

The curriculum, a form of learning architecture, can be viewed as a series of reusable building blocks. A narrow perspective would not provide the value that can be achieved by considering the overall curriculum architecture for innovation across the university.

Traditional higher education uses a "walled garden" model.

A walled garden is a garden enclosed by high walls for horticultural rather than security purposes, although originally all gardens may have been enclosed for protection from animal or human intruders. In temperate climates, the essential function of the walls surrounding a walled garden is to shelter the garden from wind and frost, though they may also serve a decorative purpose.[125]

In the education system, a walled garden is a closed ecosystem in which the learning process and the content is controlled by the ecosystem educators. It is atypical for an educator to share their course content with others. With the walled garden, it is near impossible to introduce innovation concepts because learning from others is essential. In contrast, a shared garden in education occurs where educators openly share their courses at least with other educators, even sharing their content, so that others can learn from them.

Effective learning requires the sharing of intellectual capital. Today, most *instructional content is commoditized.*[126] The instructional content for many education systems was developed like the way we manufactured products in colonial times. Just go to *Williamsburg, Virginia,* and you can see how we create instructional content where each product is painstakingly made from scratch. The concept of knowledge LEGOS is the sharing of knowledge. The building of a shared knowledge base of instructional content will enable costs to decrease over the long term through reuse. Some examples of solutions that have organized and provided free access to commoditized content are http://kahnacademy.org and http://wikipedia.org.

Modularity is a fundamental principle of design. Modularized components can be added, shared, and changed without changing the structure of the learning architecture. In construction, it would be like updating your kitchen cabinets without redesigning your entire house. Any course should be built using sharable components to facilitate an interdisciplinary shared knowledge base of instructional innovation content that can provide a cost-effective, convenient, and collaborative means for continuous learning. Instead of the development of unnecessary duplicate instructional content, content reuse will be promoted, costs will be reduced, and ideas will be shared.

There are often barriers, such as no or low incentives, which preclude acting upon and fostering a culture of innovation. Building a culture of innovation requires a shared knowledge base of instructional innovation content to increase understanding. The interdisciplinary innovation model is based on sharing ideas across organizations. Figure 18.23 shows the concept of the shared garden.

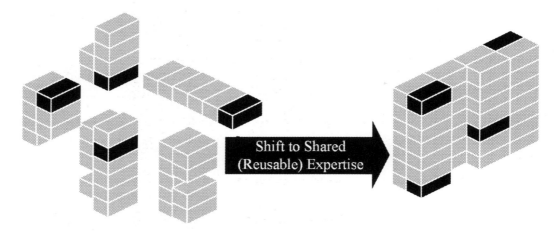

Figure 18.23 Illustration of Shift to Shared Expertise

Education Rearchitected

Architecture and Design

The curriculum for a broad discipline, like innovation, should be designed to be a total learn-ing experience. If a university is to achieve its goals, it needs a curriculum that is aligned with a future-oriented strategic plan.

Education architecture is the structure for the education system that is powered by a culture of innovation. A culture of innovation requires that everyone be involved in innovation, not just the elite. It isn't that employees aren't creative or innovative enough to build the culture, it's that they haven't been taught how to innovate, they haven't been given the inspiration to conduct low-cost experiments, there are no resources to innovate, and there isn't a documented innovation process.[127]

Our education systems were designed before the middle of the 19th century primarily to meet the needs of the Industrial Revolution. The Industrial Revolution, which ranged from 1760 to sometime between 1820 and 1840, focused on efficiency, standardization, and mass production.[128] After World War II, the US economy was one of the few that was functioning.

Because our economic system was working well, it appeared that it was an effective system. During the post–World War II era, W. Edwards Deming was a leader in advocating the use of statistical pro-cess control, operational definition and the process improvement model known as plan-do-study-act, known as the Walter Shewhart cycle. Deming's theory of profound knowledge is a managerial theory that takes data, raw facts, and converts the data into information and then into new knowledge.

After World War II, unable to influence US businesses to adopt his ideas, he visited Japan, where he was well received. Deming is credited by many with inspiring the Japanese post-war economic miracle of 1950 to 1960, when Japan ascended to the second-largest economy in the world through process improvement. Edwards Deming said, "I should estimate that in my experi-ence most troubles and most possibilities for improvement add up to the proportions something like [the following]."[129]

1. Ninety-four percent belongs to the system (responsibility of management).
2. Six percent includes special causes (outside the system, such as blaming a person for a mistake).

Once the system is working, whether it is effective or not, it continues to operate. A way to detect dysfunction is to measure the value provided by the entire system, not just the subsystem. It is the entire system that needs to improve, not just the subsystems independently.

It is more effective to improve the entire system from end to end rather than a part of the sys-tem. Then, the subsystems will complement the whole and reinforce each other. There are many examples of effective systems: baseball teams, orchestras, executive teams, and education cur-riculums.[130] In order to build an effective system, all the independent subsystems (colleges, depart-ments, divisions, etc.) need to achieve broad strategic goals. If two or more of the subsystems are working toward narrow tactical goals, the result will be less than peak performance and potentially dysfunction.[131] The systems concept is shown in Figure 18.24.

Future education systems need to focus on student-centered learning objectives that determine the assessment and learning strategies shown in Figure 18.25. In contrast to teacher-centered learning where the teacher talks, controls the classroom and learning strategies, and the students listen.

The Flow of Knowledge

To have an effective system, the flow of knowledge needs to move in many directions. A university is organized into colleges that are independent business units. The flow of knowledge is vertical

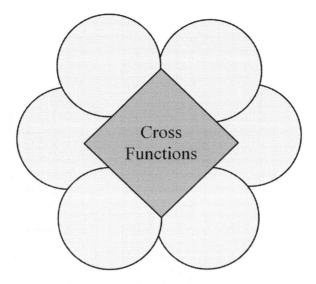

Figure 18.24 Illustration of Cross-Functions

Source: Adapted from Alejandro Sandoval, Bill Lacivita, and, Ignacio Marcos. October 2019. "Transform the whole business, not just parts," McKinsey & Company, accessed September 14, 2020, https://www.mckinsey.com/ business-functions/ operations/our-insights/transform-the-whole-business-not-just-parts

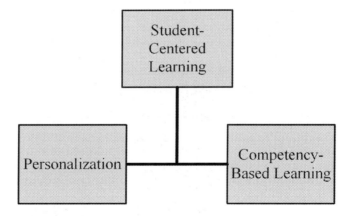

Figure 18.25 Illustration of Student-Centered Learning

rather than horizontal. Vertical knowledge is useful for efficiency and less so for effectiveness. Most colleges are focused on vertical flows, not horizontal. The vertical and horizontal flows are shown in Figure 18.26.

Extending the Reach

Described in the musical *Come From Away* and the book *The Day the World Came to Town: 9/11 in Gander, Newfoundland*, during the 9/11 terrorist attacks 6,700 passengers had to be rerouted to

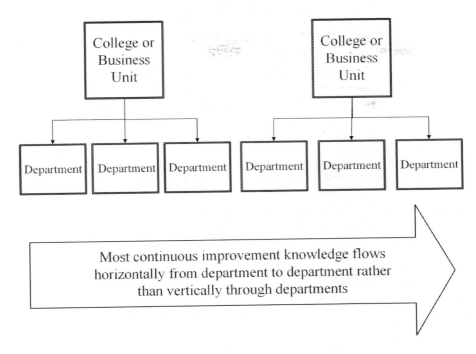

Figure 18.26 Illustration of Vertical and Horizonal Knowledge

Gander, Newfoundland, population 10,000, where they were welcomed and at least temporarily extended the reach of their community. During this period, the entire community worked together to receive all the new visitors.[132]

> Theresa Amabile's *The Progress Principle* and Daniel Pink's *Drive* both demonstrated that making progress towards a shared mission is the most motivating force a professional can feel. Communities deliver these benefits, creating a sense of shared accountability and a set of values while preserving individual autonomy.[133]

Many universities are building innovation centers to extend their reach into the community and build relationships with business partners. These innovation centers are intended to facilitate bringing the academic and business worlds more closely together. Partnerships between business, community and the university can be synergistic.

Scott DeRue, the dean of University of Michigan's Ross School of Business, is an advocate for improving the horizonal cross-cutting skills in colleges, such as collaboration and complex problem solving, that can be developed by partnerships between business and universities.[134] The shared content can be offered to the business community. The shared knowledge base of instructional content would provide a cost-effective, convenient, and collaborative means for continuous learning to extend *beyond the reach* of the university.

Strategic Opportunities for the Education System

The dyadic nature of an education architecture should function both inward and outward. The addition of practical innovation concepts into curricula should align with the strategic direction of the university across various academic units. Ideally, innovation and entrepreneurship concepts go beyond a focus on a single course.

Of course, university outcomes are broader than student outcomes. They are both direct and indirect. Direct measures of outcomes are comprehensive examinations, capstone course assessments, certification and licensure examination, and successful start-ups. Indirect outcomes can be surveys of graduating seniors, exit interviews, and employer surveys.[135] All parts of the education system should be managed using meaningfully significant outcome measures.

Progressive education for transformational change needs to continuously innovate teaching and learning. "In dynamic classrooms, students are engaged in active learning and utilize mobile devices to respond to follow-up questions in real time. Data gathered before and in class can feed predictive analytics systems that guide both interventions and student expectations."[136]

To address the needs for the future, a reimagined and redesigned education system would include the structure of the curriculum, the content of the instructional material, the instructional design mode of active learning, and the cultural experience of the learning environment.

As change, globalization, and cultural shifts continue, the question remains, can the education system progress to new opportunities? Knowledge Works, a non-profit organization dedicated to advancing personalized learning, identified five opportunity areas for building strategies that will lead the future of learning.[137] These are shown in Figure 18.27.

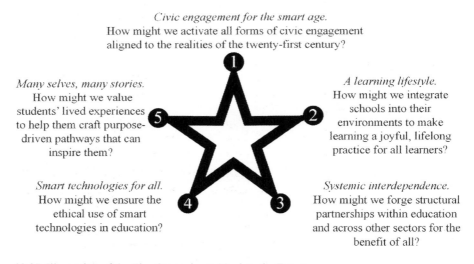

Figure 18.27 Illustration of the Five Strategies to Naviate the Future

Source: Acknowledgement Katherine Prince, Jason Swanson, Ben Moran and Andrea Saveri, "Navigating the Future of Learning: A Strategy Guide," accessed January 30, 2024, https://knowledgeworks.org/wp-content/uploads/2019/06/knowledgeworks-forecast-strategy-guide.pdf

Going for the Gold: Innovation and Entrepreneurship Maturity Model

A maturity model is a way to assess the overall effectiveness of an organization. The purpose of this education architectural model is to improve the awareness and understanding of the innovation and entrepreneurship elements on the Y-axis as well as the development of innovation and entrepreneurship capability on X-axis that are shown in Figure 18.28.

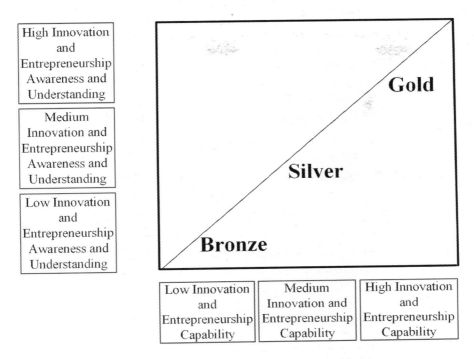

	High Innovation and Entrepreneurship Awareness and Understanding			
	Medium Innovation and Entrepreneurship Awareness and Understanding		**Gold**	
	Low Innovation and Entrepreneurship Awareness and Understanding	**Silver**		
		Bronze		
	Low Innovation and Entrepreneurship Capability	Medium Innovation and Entrepreneurship Capability	High Innovation and Entrepreneurship Capability	

Figure 18.28 Illustration of the Innovation and Entrepreneurship Maturity Model

It is suggested here that organizations develop measurements to assess their overall innovation and entrepreneurship capability as they strive to reach the aspirational gold level. Just like in the Olympics, innovation success is based on winning most of the events using an assortment of measures such as speed, accuracy, endurance, and agility.

To win an Olympic event requires the highest level of performance from each athlete. Innovation needs to be part of everyone's job, just like the rigorous training and practice that is expected of all Olympic athletes. The successful management of innovation initiatives is dependent on the talents and competencies of all the players, the building of forward-thinking organizations, and the total integration of all the organization's innovation initiatives in collaboration with all its partners.

A Future Model of Education

Considering the issues and challenges outlined in this chapter, the question becomes this: what would a future model of education look like? Educators need to consider new ways to design courses for the future. Writing for *Harvard Business Publishing* about creating a more impactful asynchronous course model, Dr. Rikke Duus, University College London, develops a very straightforward yet dynamic model that could inform a broader perspective on the impact of innovation, entrepreneurship, and education. Her 3Cs framework suggests a way to create more impactful course material that in turn amplifies educator skills needed to move forward. The focus on the model is the course content that is connected to the real world. The 3Cs model, shown in Figure 18.29, outlines the roles of the creator, curator, and connector – all focused on making those connections[138]

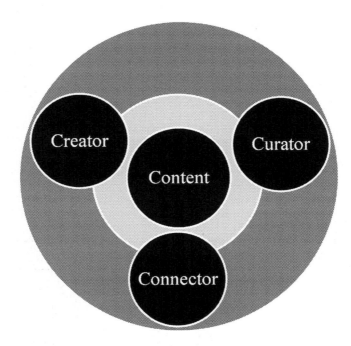

Figure 18.29 Illustration of a Future Model of Education

Source: Adapted from Rikke Duus, "Develop More Impactful Asynchronous Course Material," January 21, 2021, accessed January 12, 2024, https://hbsp.harvard.edu/inspiring-minds/develop-more-impactful-asynchronous-course-material

Creator

The creator designs and develops the framework and core content into organized modules. The creator shares the content with the students who take responsibility for learning at their own pace, place, and time.

Curator

The curator provides external material for the course to enhance understanding of practical real-world applications.

Connector

The connector provides the student an opportunity to combine the core content with the external material. The student would explore creative and critical thinking using practical assignments.

Summary

The education architecture especially with respect to innovation and entrepreneurship is experiencing unpreceded challenges – sustainability, global economic turbulence, an aging population, automation impacting jobs, pandemics, and mass migrations, to name a few. These and other challenges require an education architecture that is built on and fosters innovation and entrepreneurship competencies focused on creating the best possible environment to produce needed outcomes.

Education systems are the essential building blocks for providing life-long competencies essential for everyone. Effective education systems are different because they need to be architected to provide a functional duality both inward and outward.

Education systems need to focus inward to dynamically adopt an enterprising spirit to themselves, with new unique evidence-based education concepts. All education systems need continuous innovation and renewal to maintain their viability. The more effective the education system, the more likely it can address the complex challenges and the shifting cultures of today's world. Education systems need to (1) measure their outcomes to achieve the highest overall value to achieve personal social, economic, and cultural value; (2) provide the greatest diversity, equity, and inclusion for all stakeholders; (3) provide affordable education with the most effective overhead and cost; and (4) strengthen the education workforce to maintain discipline currency and in specific disciplines have practical experiences.

Education systems need to focus outward to ensure that students have the entrepreneurial and innovative capability for their career journey. The education system needs to (1) develop the next leaders for transformational change; (2) empower students with the future competencies to become the change agents; (3) inspire student to apply independent thinking to engage with employers, teachers, community groups, non-profits, and elected policymakers; and (4) foster the confidence in students to facilitate opportunities for self-expression.

Notes

1. Ken Robinson and Lou Aronica, *Creative Schools: The Grassroots Revolution That's Transforming Education* (New York: Viking, 2015), xx.
2. Jeff Dyer, Hal Gregersen, and Clayton M. Christensen, *The Innovator's DNA* (Boston: Harvard Business Review Press, 2011), 22.
3. Ken Robinson and Lou Aronica, *Creative Schools: The Grassroots Revolution That's Transforming Education* (New York: Viking, 2015), xx.
4. *Investopedia*, s.v. "Human Capital," accessed, November 6, 2021, www.investopedia.com/terms/h/humancapital.asp.
5. "Why Higher Education in America Is Ripe for Disruption," June 14, 2017, accessed February 19, 2024, https://latest.13d.com/why-higher-education-in-america-is-ripe-for-disruption-b5f2e49cea98.
6. Marc Tucker, *Leading High-Performance School Systems* (Alexandria: Association for Supervision & Curriculum Development, 2019), xi.
7. *Wikipedia*, s.v. "Education Stages," accessed March 13, 2020, https://en.wikipedia.org/wiki/Educational_stage.
8. *Wikipedia*, s.v. "University of Bologna," accessed May 20, 2022, https://en.wikipedia.org/wiki/University_of_Bologna.
9. *Wikipedia*, s.v. "University," accessed March 4, 2020, https://en.wikipedia.org/wiki/University.
10. Megan Brenan, "Americans' Confidence in Higher Education Down Sharply," July 11, 2023, accessed February 3, 2024, https://news.gallup.com/poll/508352/americans-confidence-higher-education-down-sharply.aspx.
11. Ken Robinson and Lou Aronica, *Creative Schools: The Grassroots Revolution That's Transforming Education* (New York: Viking, 2015), xxii.
12. Ken Robinson and Lou Aronica, *Creative Schools: The Grassroots Revolution That's Transforming Education* (New York: Viking, 2015), xxiv.
13. *Wikipedia*, s.v. "Ken Robinson," accessed January 29, 2024, Ken Robinson (educationalist) – Wikipedia.
14. Patricia Gonce Morton, "Higher Education – Is the Value Worth the Cost?" *Journal of Professional Nursing* 34, no. 5 (September–October 2018), 327–328, https://doi.org/10.1016/j.profnurs.2018.08.001. PMID: 30243688.
15. "Trends Shaping Education 2019," accessed February 19, 2024, www.oecd.org/education/trends-shaping-education-22187049.htm.
16. "Trends Shaping Education 2019," accessed February 19, 2024, www.oecd.org/education/trends-shaping-education-22187049.htm.

17. Joseph Tidd and John Bessant, *Managing Innovation: Integrating Technological, Market and Organizational Change*, 5th ed. (New York: John Wiley, 2013), 204–205.

18. James Manyika, Gary Pinkus, and Monique Tuin, "Rethinking the Future of American Capitalism," *McKinsey Global Institute*, November 2020, accessed February 19, 2024, www.mckinsey.com/featured-insights/long-term-capitalism/rethinking-the-future-of-american-capitalism, 4.

19. Organisation for Economic Co-operation and Development (OECD), accessed February 19, 2024, www.oecd.org/about/.

20. OECD, "Executive Summary," in *Trends in Shaping Education 2022* (Paris: OECD Publishing, 2022), accessed February 19, 2024, https://doi.org/10.1787/cf62066f-en.

21. OECD, "Executive Summary," in *Trends in Shaping Education 2022* (Paris: OECD Publishing, 2022), accessed February 19, 2024, https://doi.org/10.1787/cf62066f-en.

22. David Leonhardt, *Ours Was a Shining Future* (New York: Random House, 2023), 344.

23. David Leonhardt, *Ours Was a Shining Future* (New York: Random House, 2023), 345.

24. "How States and Districts Support Evidence Use in School Improvement," June 2020, accessed December 18, 2023, https://ies.ed.gov/ncee/pubs/2020004/pdf/2020004.pdf.

25. *Wikipedia*, s.v. "National Assessment of Educational Progress," accessed February 16, 2020, https://en.wikipedia.org/wiki/National_Assessment_of_Educational_Progress.

26. Erica L. Green and Dana Goldstein, "Reading Scores on National Exam Decline in Half the States," December 5, 2019, accessed February 16, 2020, www.nytimes.com/2019/10/30/us/reading-scores-national-exam.html.

27. Dana Goldstein, "An Old and Contested Solution to Boost Reading Scores: Phonics," February 15, 2020, accessed February 19, 2024, www.nytimes.com/2020/02/15/us/reading-phonics.html.

28. Madeline Will, "Will the Science of Reading Catch on in Teacher Prep?" December 3, 2010, accessed February 19, 2024, www.edweek.org/ew/articles/2019/12/04/most-ed-professors-favor-balanced-literacy.html.

29. Sarah Schwartz and Sarah D. Sparks, "How Do Kids Learn to Read? What the Science Says," October 2, 2019, accessed February 19, 2024, www.edweek.org/ew/issues/how-do-kids-learn-to-read.html.

30. Jill Anderson, "5 Ways Educators Can Start Innovating," August 20, 2021, accessed December 18, 2023, www.gse.harvard.edu/ideas/usable-knowledge/21/08/5-ways-educators-can-start-innovating.

31. National Center on Education and the Economy, "The Widening Achievement Gap in the U.S.," November 6, 2020, accessed February 19, 2024, https://ncee.org/2020/11/the-widening-achievement-gap-in-the-u-s/.

32. Eric A. Hanushek, Paul E. Peterson, Laura M. Talpey, and Ludger Woessmann, "The Achievement Gap Fails to Close," *Education Next* 19, no. 3 (2019), accessed February 19, 2024, www.educationnext.org/achievement-gap-fails-close-half-century-testing-shows-persistent-divide/.

33. Emma Dorn, Bryan Hancock, Jimmy Sarakatsannis, and Ellen Viruleg, "COVID-19 and Student Learning in the United States: The Hurt Could Last a Lifetime," *McKinsey & Company*, June 1, 2020, accessed February 19, 2024, www.mckinsey.com/industries/public-sector/our-insights/covid-19-and-student-learning-in-the-united-states-the-hurt-could-last-a-lifetime.

34. Emma Dorn, Andre Dua, and Jonathan Law, "Rising Costs and Stagnating Completion Rates: Who Is Bucking the Trend?" October 12, 2020, accessed November 18, 2020, www.mckinsey.com/industries/public-and-social-sector/our-insights/rising-costs-and-stagnating-completion-rates-who-is-bucking-the-trend.

35. John Bound, Michael Lovenheim, and Sarah Turner, "Why Have College Completion Rates Declined? An Analysis of Changing Student Preparation and Collegiate Resources," *American Economic Journal: Applied Economics* 2, no. 3 (December 2009), 129–157. See also: John Bound, Michael Lovenheim, and Sarah Turner, "Increasing Time to Baccalaureate Degree in the United States," *Education Finance and Policy* 7, no. 4 (September 27, 2012), 375–424, www.mitpressjournals.org/doi/10.1162/EDFP_a_00074; John Bound and Sarah Turner, "Cohort Crowding: How Resources Affect College Attainment," *Journal of Public Economics* 91, no. 5–6 (August 2006), 877–899.

36. Nick Hillman, "Why Rich Colleges Get Richer & Poor Colleges Get Poorer: The Case for Equity-Based Funding in Higher Education," November 20, 2020, accessed February 19, 2024, www.thirdway.org/report/why-rich-colleges-get-richer-poor-colleges-get-poorer-the-case-for-equity-based-funding-in-higher-education-and-Why-Rich-Colleges-Get-Richer-and-Poor-Colleges-Get-Poorer.pdf (imgix.net).

37. Nick Hillman, "Why Rich Colleges Get Richer & Poor Colleges Get Poorer: The Case for Equity-Based Funding in Higher Education," November 20, 2020, accessed November 20, 2020, www.thirdway.org/report/why-rich-colleges-get-richer-poor-colleges-get-poorer-the-case-for-equity-based-funding-in-higher-education and Why-Rich-Colleges-Get-Richer-and-Poor-Colleges-Get-Poorer.pdf (imgix.net).

38. Madeline St. Amour, "Report: Rich Colleges Keep Getting Richer," November 20, 2020, accessed February 19, 2024, www.insidehighered.com/news/2020/11/20/report-stark-inequity-higher-ed-funding.

39. Nick Hillman, "Why Rich Colleges Get Richer & Poor Colleges Get Poorer: The Case for Equity-Based Funding in Higher Education," November 20, 2020, accessed February 19, 2024, www.thirdway.org/report/why-rich-colleges-get-richer-poor-colleges-get-poorer-the-case-for-equity-based-funding-in-higher-education and Why-Rich-Colleges-Get-Richer-and-Poor-Colleges-Get-Poorer.pdf (imgix.net).

40. Juliet Bourke and Bernadette Dillon, "The Diversity and Inclusion Revolution: Eight Powerful Truths," *Deloitte Review*, no. 22 (January 2018), accessed January 29, 2024, www2.deloitte.com/content/dam/insights/us/articles/4209_Diversity-and-inclusion-revolution/DI_Diversity-and-inclusion-revolution.pdf.

41. Juliet Bourke and Bernadette Dillon, "The Diversity and Inclusion Revolution: Eight Powerful Truths," *Deloitte Review*, no. 22 (January 2018), accessed January 29, 2024, www2.deloitte.com/content/dam/insights/us/articles/4209_Diversity-and-inclusion-revolution/DI_Diversity-and-inclusion-revolution.pdf.

42. Mike Fucci and Terri Cooper, "The Inclusion Imperative for Boards: Redefining Board Responsibilities to Support Organizational Inclusion," *Deloitte University Press*, April 2, 2019, accessed January 29, 2024, www2.deloitte.com/us/en/insights/topics/value-of-diversity-and-inclusion/redefining-board-responsibilities-to-support-organizational-inclusion.html?nc=1.

43. *Merriam-Webster*, s.v. "Equity," accessed December 7, 2020, Equity | Definition of Equity by Merriam-Webster (merriam-webster.com).

44. Mike Fucci and Terri Cooper, "The Inclusion Imperative for Boards: Redefining Board Responsibilities to Support Organizational Inclusion," *Deloitte University Press*, April 2, 2019, accessed January 29, 2024, www2.deloitte.com/us/en/insights/topics/value-of-diversity-and-inclusion/redefining-board-responsibilities-to-support-organizational-inclusion.html?nc=1.

45. "4D Competencies Framework," January 2024, accessed January 29, 2024, https://curriculumredesign.org/framework/.

46. "Organisation for Economic Co-operation and Development (OECD)," accessed February 19, 2024, www.oecd.org/about/.

47. Anna Fleck, OECD PISA 2022, "The Top Performing Places for Education," December 6, 2023, accessed January 29, 2024, www.statista.com/chart/7104/pisa-top-rated-countries-regions-2016/.

48. "PISA 2018," *National Center for Education Statistics*, accessed February 19, 2024, https://nces.ed.gov/surveys/pisa/pisa2018/#/.

49. OECD, "The Future of Education and Skills," *Education 2030, The Future We Want*, accessed February 19, 2024, www.oecd.org/education/2030/E2030%20Position%20Paper%20(05.04.2018).pdf.

50. Organisation for Economic Co-operation and Development (OECD), Programme for International Student Assessment, accessed December 18, 2023, www.oecd.org/pisa/.

51. OECD, "PISA 2022 Results," accessed January 13, 2024, www.oecd.org/publication/pisa-2022-results/index.

52. OECD, "The Future of Education and Skills Education 2030," 2018, accessed February 19, 2024, www.oecd.org/education/2030-project/contact/E2030_Position_Paper_(05.04.2018).pdf.

53. Tony Wagner, *Global Achievement Gap: Why Even Our Best Schools Don'T Teach the New Survival Skills Our Children Need-and What We Can Do about It* (New York: Basic Books, 2014).

54. Sapana Agrawal, Aaron De Smet, Pawel Poplawski, and Angelika Reich, "Beyond Hiring: How Companies Are Reskilling to Address Talent Gaps," *McKinsey & Company*, February 2020, accessed February 19, 2024, www.mckinsey.com/business-functions/organization/our-insights/beyond-hiring-how-companies-are-reskilling-to-address-talent-gaps.

55. Bjorn Lomborg, "Best Things First," *Copen Consensus Center*, 2023, 69.

56. "Where to Start: Backward Design," accessed December 19, 2023, https://tll.mit.edu/teaching-resources/course-design/backward-design/.

57. Ken Robinson and Lou Aronica, *Creative Schools: The Grassroots Revolution That's Transforming Education* (New York: Viking, 2015), 100.

58. Ken Robinson and Lou Aronica, *Creative Schools: The Grassroots Revolution That's Transforming Education* (New York: Viking, 2015), 127.

59. Emma Dorn, Andre Dua, and Jonathan Law, "Rising Costs and Stagnating Completion Rates: Who Is Bucking the Trend?" October 12, 2020, accessed November 18, 2020, www.mckinsey.com/industries/public-and-social-sector/our-insights/rising-costs-and-stagnating-completion-rates-who-is-bucking-the-trend.

60. "What Is Montessori Education?" accessed December 18, 2023, https://amshq.org/About-Montessori/What-Is-Montessori.

61. Rosabeth Moss Kanter, *Think Outside the Building*, 1st ed. (New York: PublicAffairs, 2020), 1.

62. Rosabeth Moss Kanter, *Think Outside the Building*, 1st ed. (New York: PublicAffairs, 2020), 5.

63. Chamorro-Premuzic and Becky Freankiewicz, "6 Reasons Why Higher Education Needs to be Disrupted," *Harvard Business Review*, November 19, 2019, accessed May 20, 2022, https://hbr.org/2019/11/6-reasons-why-higher-education-needs-to-be-disrupted.

64. Ken Robinson and Lou Aronica, *Creative Schools: The Grassroots Revolution That's Transforming Education* (New York: Viking, 2015), 112.

65. Ken Robinson and Lou Aronica, *Creative Schools: The Grassroots Revolution That's Transforming Education* (New York: Viking, 2015), 112.

66. Ken Robinson and Lou Aronica, *Creative Schools: The Grassroots Revolution That's Transforming Education* (New York: Viking, 2015), 45–53.

67. OECD, "The Future of Education and Skills Education 2030," 2018, accessed May 20, 2022, www.oecd.org/education/2030-project/contact/E2030_Position_Paper_(05.04.2018).pdf.

68. OECD, "The Future of Education and Skills Education 2030," 2018, accessed, February 10, 2023, www.oecd.org/education/2030-project/contact/E2030_Position_Paper_(05.04.2018).pdf.

69. OECD, "The Future of Education and Skills Education 2030," 2018, accessed February 10, 2023, www.oecd.org/education/2030-project/contact/E2030_Position_Paper_(05.04.2018).pdf.

70. Peter Tufano, "A Bolder Vision for Business Schools," March 11, 2020, accessed February 19, 2024, https://hbr.org/2020/03/a-bolder-vision-for-business-schools.

71. Ken Robinson and Lou Aronica, *Creative Schools: The Grassroots Revolution That's Transforming Education* (New York: Viking, 2015), 11.

72. Ken Robinson and Lou Aronica, *Creative Schools: The Grassroots Revolution That's Transforming Education* (New York: Viking, 2015), 157.

73. C. K. Prahalad and Gary Hamel, "The Core Competence of the Corporation," *Harvard Business Review* 68, no. 3 (May–June 1990), 82.

74. "15 Best Competency Based Degree Programs [2020 Guide]," accessed February 19, 2024, www.mydegreeguide.com/competency-based-degrees/.

75. Ken Robinson and Lou Aronica, *Creative Schools: The Grassroots Revolution That's Transforming Education* (New York: Viking, 2015), 12.

76. Ken Robinson and Lou Aronica, *Creative Schools: The Grassroots Revolution That's Transforming Education* (New York: Viking, 2015), 134.

77. "National Survey of Postsecondary Competency-Based Education," accessed February 19, 2024, www.air.org/project/national-survey-postsecondary-competency-based-education.

78. "State of the Field Findings from the 2019 National Survey of Postsecondary Competency-Based Education," 2019, accessed February 19, 2024, www.air.org/sites/default/files/National-Survey-of-Postsecondary-CBE-Lumina-October-2019-rev.pdf.

79. Maria Henri, Michael D. Johnson, and Bimal Nepal, "A Review of Competency-Based Learning: Tools, Assessments, and Recommendations," *Journal of Engineering Education* 106, no. 4 (2017).

80. "What Competency-Based Education Looks Like," *American Council on Education (ACE)*, accessed February 19, 2024, www.acenet.edu/Documents/What-Competency-Based-Education-Looks-Like.pdf.

81. Barbara Sicherl Kafol, Olga Denac, Jerneja Žnidaršič, and Konstanca Zalar, *Analysis of Music Education Objectives in Learning Domains*, vol. 186, 2015, accessed February 19, 2024, https://doi.org/10.1016/j.sbspro.2015.04.069. www.sciencedirect.com/science/article/pii/S1877042815023290.

82. "Describe Assessments in Education," *ChatGPT*, accessed June 13, 2023.

83. "Where to Start: Backward Design," accessed December 19, 2023, https://tll.mit.edu/teaching-resources/course-design/backward-design/.

84. Paul Fain, "Slow and Steady for Competency-Based Education," January 28, 2019, accessed February 19, 2024, www.insidehighered.com/news/2019/01/28/slow-growth-competency-based-education-survey-finds-interest-and-optimism-about-it.

85. Holly Gould, "A 3-Question Checklist for Better Course Design," June 21, 2022, accessed January 9, 2024, https://he.hbsp.harvard.edu/2022-06-21-the-faculty-lounge.html or https://hbsp.harvard.edu/inspiring-minds/a-3-question-checklist-for-better-course-design.

86. Walter Dick, Lou Carey, and James O. Carey, *The Systematic Design of Instruction* (Upper Saddle River, NJ: Merrill/Pearson, 2009), 132.

87. Robert F. Mager, *Preparing Instructional Objectives* (Palo Alto, CA: Fearon Publishers, 1962), 52.

88. Ken Robinson and Lou Aronica, *Creative Schools: The Grassroots Revolution That's Transforming Education* (New York: Viking, 2015), 170.

89. Walter Dick, Lou Carey, and James O. Carey, *The Systematic Design of Instruction* (Upper Saddle River, NJ: Merrill/Pearson, 2009), 132.

90. Walter Dick, Lou Carey, and James O. Carey, *The Systematic Design of Instruction* (Upper Saddle River, NJ: Merrill/Pearson, 2009), 166.

91. "P21's Frameworks for 21st Century Learning," accessed February 19, 2024, http://static.battelleforkids. org/documents/p21/P21_Framework_Brief.pdf.

92. Battelle for Kids, accessed February 19, 2024, www.battelleforkids.org/.

93. Ken Robinson and Lou Aronica, *Creative Schools: The Grassroots Revolution That's Transforming Education* (New York: Viking, 2015), 82.

94. Matthew C. Moen, "Opportunity Knocks for Liberal Education," December 17, 2020, accessed February 19, 2024, www.insidehighered.com/views/2020/12/17/how-liberal-education-has-exceptional-opportunity-help-fix-what-most-ails-our.

95. *Wikipedia*, s.v. "Liberal Arts Education," accessed October 19, 2021, https://en.wikipedia.org/wiki/Liberal_arts_education.

96. Matthew C. Moen, "Opportunity Knocks for Liberal Education," December 17, 2020, accessed December 19, 2020, www.insidehighered.com/views/2020/12/17/how-liberal-education-has-exceptional-opportunity-help-fix-what-most-ails-our.

97. Sheryl Sorby, Norman L. Fortenberry, and Gary Bertoline. "Stuck in 1955, Engineering Education Needs a Revolution," *Issues in Science and Technology*, September 13, 2021, accessed March 16, 2023, https://issues.org/engineering-education-change-sorby-fortenberry-bertoline/#.YXL5LKmWVVc.link.

98. Sheryl Sorby, Norman L. Fortenberry, and Gary Bertoline. "Stuck in 1955, Engineering Education Needs a Revolution," *Issues in Science and Technology*, September 13, 2021, accessed March 16, 2023, https://issues.org/engineering-education-change-sorby-fortenberry-bertoline/#.YXL5LKmWVVc.link.

99. Advancing Excellence in P-12 Engineering Education & American Society for Engineering Education, "Framework for P-12 Engineering Learning," 2020, accessed March 16, 2023, https://p12framework.asee.org/wp-content/uploads/2020/11/Framework-for-P-12-Engineering-Learning-1.pdf.

100. Michael B. Horn and Bob Moesta, "Do Colleges Truly Understand What Students Want from Them?," *Harvard Business Review*, October 15, 2019, accessed October 31, 2021, https://hbr.org/2019/10/do-colleges-truly-understand-what-students-want-from-them.

101. Maria Henri, Michael D. Johnson, and Bimal Nepal, "A Review of Competency-Based Learning: Tools, Assessments, and Recommendations," *Journal of Engineering Education* 106, no. 4 (2017).

102. Ken Robinson and Lou Aronica, *Creative Schools: The Grassroots Revolution That's Transforming Education* (New York: Viking, 2015), 135–141.

103. World Population Review, accessed February 19, 2024, https://worldpopulationreview.com/country-rankings/education-rankings-by-country.

104. Michael B. Horn and Scott Pulsipher, "Higher Ed Spending Problem Demands Attention No Matter Court's Opinion," August 2, 2023, accessed August 2, 2023, https://michaelbhorn.substack.com/p/higher-ed-spending-problem-demands.

105. Patricia Gonce Morton, "Higher Education – Is the Value Worth the Cost?" *Journal of Professional Nursing* 34, no. 5 (September 2018), 327–328, https://doi.org/10.1016/j.profnurs.2018.08.001, accessed February 19, 2024, www.sciencedirect.com/science/article/pii/S8755722318301285?via%3Dihub.

106. André Dua, Jonathan Law, Ted Rounsaville, and Nadia Viswanath, "Reimagining Higher Education in the United States," October 26, 2020, accessed February 19, 2024, www.mckinsey.com/industries/public-and-social-sector/our-insights/reimagining-higher-education-in-the-united-states.

107. Stephanie Marken, "Americans Value College Education Despite Barriers," May 11, 2023, accessed February 3, 2024, https://news.gallup.com/poll/505727/americans-value-college-education-despite-barriers.aspx.

108. Stephanie Marken and Zach Hrynowski, "Current College Students Say Their Degree Is Worth the Cost," June 1, 2023, February 3, 2024, https://news.gallup.com/poll/506384/current-college-students-say-degree-worth-cost.aspx.

109. Anna Brown, "Most Americans Say Higher Ed Is Heading in Wrong Direction, But Partisans Disagree on Why," *Pew Research Center*, July 2018, accessed February 19, 2024, www.pewresearch.org/fact-tank/2018/07/26/most-americans-say-higher-ed-is-heading-in-wrong-direction-but-partisans-disagree-on-why/.

110. Max Roster, "Measuring Education: What Data Is Available?" February 23, 2018, accessed April 28, 2023, https://ourworldindata.org/measuring-education-what-data-is-available.

111. OECD, "OECD Indicators of Education Systems," accessed February 19, 2024, www.oecd.org/education/skills-beyond-school/education-indicators-in-focus.htm.

112. "Association for the Advancement of Sustainability in Higher Education," accessed February 19, 2024, AASHE, www.aashe.org/.

113. "Sustainable Campus Index (SCI)," 2019, accessed February 19, 2024, www.aashe.org/wp-content/uploads/2019/08/SCI-2019-Updated.pdf.

114. Vijay Govindarajan and Anup Srivastava, "What the Shift to Virtual Learning Could Mean for the Future of Higher Ed," March 31, 2020, accessed February 19, 2024, https://hbr.org/2020/03/what-the-shift-to-virtual-learning-could-mean-for-the-future-of-higher-ed.

115. André Dua, Jonathan Law, Ted Rounsaville, and Nadia Viswanath, "Reimagining Higher Education in the United States," February 19, 2024, accessed October 26, 2020, www.mckinsey.com/industries/public-and-social-sector/our-insights/reimagining-higher-education-in-the-united-states.
116. James DeVaney, Gideon Shimshon, Matthew Rascoff, and Jeff Maggioncalda, "Higher Ed Needs a Long-Term Plan for Virtual Learning," May 5, 2020, accessed February 19, 2024, https://hbr.org/2020/05/higher-ed-needs-a-long-term-plan-for-virtual-learning.
117. "Nurturing Nature," review of Kathryn Asbury and Robert Plomin, "G Is for Genes: The Impact of Genetics on Education and Achievement," *The Economist*, November 30, 2013, accessed February 19, 2024, www.economist.com/news/books-and-arts/21590881-genes-count-lot-schooling-whether-schools-can-adapt-knowledge-less.
118. OECD, "The Future of Education and Skills Education 2030," 2018, accessed February 19, 2024, www.oecd.org/education/2030-project/contact/E2030_Position_Paper_(05.04.2018).pdf.
119. Robin Kanaan, "Learner Profiles," October 26, 2023, accessed December 20, 2023, https://knowledgeworks.org/resources/learner-profiles-what-why-how/.
120. United Nations Educational, Scientific and Cultural Organization, "Open Educational Resources (OER)," accessed February 19, 2024, https://en.unesco.org/themes/building-knowledge-societies/oer.
121. Nicole Allen, Delia Browne, Mary Lou Forward, Cable Green, and Alek Tarkowski, "Foundations for OER Strategy Development," accessed February 19, 2024, www.oerstrategy.org/home/read-the-doc/index.html.
122. Creative Commons Attribution NoDerivs (CC-ND), accessed February 19, 2024, https://tldrlegal.com/license/creative-commons-attribution-noderivs-(cc-nd)
123. Nicole Allen, Delia Browne, Mary Lou Forward, Cable Green, and Alek Tarkowski, "Foundations for OER Strategy Development," accessed February 19, 2024, www.oerstrategy.org/home/read-the-doc/index.html.
124. Fengchun Miao, Sanjaya Mishra, and Rory McGreal, "Commonwealth of Learning," (Paris: United Nations Educational, Scientific and Cultural Organization, 2016), accessed February 19, 2024, www.academia.edu/25790186/Open_Educational_Resources_Policy_Costs_and_Transformation_PERSPECTIVES_ON_OPEN_AND_DISTANCE_LEARNING.
125. *Wikipedia*, s.v. "Walled Garden," accessed June 27, 2021, https://en.wikipedia.org/wiki/Walled_garden.
126. Scott DeRue, *The Future of MBA Education*, February 19, 2024, accessed February 24, 2018, https://hbr.org/ideacast/2018/02/the-future-of-mba-education.
127. Terri Williams, "How Innovation Engineering Can Transform Your Company," *Economist*, accessed February 19, 2024, https://execed.economist.com/blog/industry-trends/how-innovation-engineering-can-transform-your-company.
128. Ken Robinson and Lou Aronica, *Creative Schools: The Grassroots Revolution That's Transforming Education* (New York: Viking, 2015), xxiii.
129. William Edwards Deming, *Out of the Crisis*, 1st ed. (Cambridge, MA: MIT Press, 2000), https://mitpress.mit.edu/9780262541152/out-of-the-crisis/.
130. Terri Williams, "How Innovation Engineering Can Transform Your Company," *Economist*, accessed February 19, 2024, www.eureka1europe.com/innovation-resources.
131. Terri Williams, "How Innovation Engineering Can Transform Your Company," *Economist*, accessed February 19, 2024, www.eureka1europe.com/innovation-resources.
132. *Wikipedia*, s.v. "Come from Away," accessed July 10, 2021, https://en.wikipedia.org/wiki/Come_from_Away.
133. Jeffrey Bussgang and Jono Bacon, "When Community Becomes Your Competitive Advantage," January 21, 2020, accessed June 8, 2023, https://hbr.org/2020/01/when-community-becomes-your-competitive-advantage.
134. Scott DeRue, "The Future of MBA Education," February 14, 2018, accessed February 19, 2024, https://hbr.org/ideacast/2018/02/the-future-of-mba-education.
135. "Assessment in Academic Programs," accessed October 24, 2021, www.calu.edu/inside/faculty-staff/assessment/academic-programs/index.aspx.
136. Ryan Craig, "The Top 10 Higher Education Issues We All Agree On," January 20, 2017, accessed May 31, 2023, www.forbes.com/sites/ryancraig/2017/01/20/the-top-10-higher-education-issues-we-all-agree-on/#31dac28ffa87.
137. Katherine Prince, Jason Swanson, Ben Moran, and Andrea Saveri, "Navigating the Future of Learning: A Strategy Guide," accessed January 30, 2024, https://knowledgeworks.org/wp-content/uploads/2019/06/knowledgeworks-forecast-strategy-guide.pdf.
138. Rikke Duus, "Develop More Impactful Asynchronous Course Material," January 21, 2021, accessed June 8, 2023, https://hbsp.harvard.edu/inspiring-minds/develop-more-impactful-asynchronous-course-material.

19 Sustainability

The Wine Story

Some of the most famous wines in the world are produced in the Bordeaux region of France.[1] The Bordeaux wines are controlled by the French wine-governing body known as the National Institute of Origin and Quality (INAO), which authorizes what grape varieties can be used in the Bordeaux wines.[2] Vintners must adapt to the rise in average temperatures and summer draughts as change in weather patterns is impacting how quickly wine grapes ripen, how much acid they have, and how much sweetness is in the product.[3]

Wine grapes are particularly susceptible to weather. For example, hail, fierce winds, heavy rain in the flowering season or frost in spring can be especially problematic, as the devastating April frost that destroyed 40% of Bordeaux's 2017 harvest[4] illustrated.

Wine producers have dealt with weather issues for centuries and have developed innovative processes and management strategies. The French wine industry may be the "canary in a coal mine" indicator of what can be expected for the future of agriculture. Using an experimental 25-acre Bordeaux vineyard laboratory, French wine scientists are studying dozens of varieties of heat-tolerant grapes from southern and eastern Europe to explore the yield, fruit quality, and composition. Because some of the existing grapes in the region may not be able to survive the impact of climate change, the INAO approved the use of seven new grape varieties for certain categories of Bordeaux wines.[5]

As climate issues challenge vineyards across Europe, American hybrid varieties provide bountiful harvests without irrigation, without fertilizers and without pesticide treatment. These American hybrid varieties named Jacquez, red grape varieties that originate from America, have been banned by the French government since 1934. The preference for natural wines that are grown without pesticides and the threat of climate change has added momentum to the adoption of the forbidden American hybrids. "French authorities have tried to outlaw hardy American hybrids for 87 years. But climate change and the natural wine movement are giving renegade winemakers a lift."[6]

For wine makers, climate is a two-edged sword.

> Climate is both friend and foe to the winemaking industry. The geology, landscape, soil and, most importantly, the temperature determine what grape varieties can be grown as well as shaping the quality and yield of the harvest. When the climatic conditions are good, then you can expect a great vintage.[7]

The continuing challenge is innovation and entrepreneurship's role in addressing sustainability, production, and core issues surrounding the future of wine. It is a classic example of the nexus of environmental, economic, and social sustainability.

DOI: 10.4324/9781003034308-20

Sustainability

What is sustainability? Generically, sustainability is the ability of some thing or process to be maintained or continued at a certain rate or level. For example, sustaining a level of output of performance or continuous production of goods and services. More specifically, sustainability has come to be a key element addressing changes in how we live, learn, work, and lead on the planet earth, especially regarding use of natural resources and fossil fuels.

Overall, there are three key parts or types of sustainability: environmental, economic, and social. Environmental sustainability "focuses on the conservation of biodiversity without forgoing economic and social progress." Economic sustainability, in general, "refers to the organization's ability to manage its resources and responsibly generate profits in the long term." Finally, social sustainability seeks to strengthen the stability of society or social groups.[8]

The challenge is how to best address these three parts to balance priorities and bring about desired outcomes in the near, intermediate, and long terms. While all three are important, examining environmental sustainability provides a solid starting point as it has led to a deep dive into the environmental, greenhouse gas effects, carbon dioxide emissions, and more as it affects weather and climate change.

Defining Environmental Sustainability

Environmental sustainability is the oversight for managing present resource needs without compromising the ability of future generations to meet their needs while preserving our wider global environment, social systems, and economic structures. Sustainability is informed by the process of learning how to lead individual, organizational, and societal change from a multidisciplinary perspective.[9]

The environmental sustainability challenges are increasingly evident. The challenges include a lack of stakeholder leadership, the overuse of renewable and non-renewable resources, undermanaging climate change, a lack of reusability in our value chain, environmental contamination, providing a compelling sustainability education, and increasing breakthrough innovations. To address these challenges, a combination of public-sector funding and private investments in business technology driven innovations are needed.

Sustainability Importance

Sustainability is important because of the need for viable communities for everyone. Sustainability represents a meaningfully significant challenge that can be targeted using the capabilities of the discipline of innovation. It requires an understanding of the fundamentals of how our natural world is delicately balanced as a holistic system. To understand sustainability, it is essential to incorporate an evidence-based problem-solving system level model. As indicated in Chapter 1, human ecology or sustainability can be seen as a megatrend, especially as it transitions through what could be called a transition state opportunity zone. That is, an opportunity to transform the environment via the role of sustainability, innovation, and entrepreneurship to improve how we live, learn, work, and lead. This is captured in Figure 19.1, the sustainability megatrend paradigm shift.

The Global Sustainability Challenge

Presently, humanity confronts an array of unique and pressing global sustainability challenges. The world constitutes a complex system composed of interconnected subsystems encompassing people, animals, plants, rivers, oceans, lakes, and land, all of which display signs of imbalance. This disruption is manifesting in the natural world.

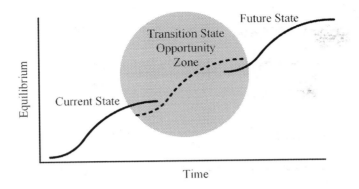

Figure 19.1 Illustration of Sustainability Megatrend Paradigm Shift

Source: Acknowledgment: Thomas Kuhn, *The Structure of Scientific Revolutions.* 2d, enl ed. Vol. 2, no. 2. Chicago: University of Chicago Press, 1970. Wikipedia, s.v. "Paradigm shift," accessed December 11, 2020, https://en.wikipedia.org/wiki/Paradigm_shift

Addressing the sustainability imbalance necessitates a comprehensive understanding of the system to elevate awareness, encourage behavioral change, and unveil the underlying processes in play. A clear illustration of this dynamic challenge is found in the impact of fossil fuels utilized during the industrial revolution. Fossil fuels are extracted from the earth and utilized for energy generation, resulting in the emission of greenhouse gases contributing to global warming. The challenges faced today and in the future require a dynamic interactive approach to better align sustainability system level strategic processes. Figure 19.2 depicts an integrated trilateral strategic framework that provides a way to achieve an integrated approach through research, remediation, and regulation.

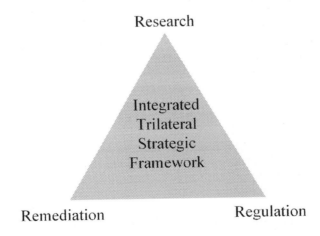

Figure 19.2 Illustration of the Integrated Trilateral Strategic Framework

Trilateral Strategic Framework

Research

Research driven by innovation is an important requirement to better understand prevailing sustainability predicaments and formulate novel solutions. Investigation into methods for preserving global sustainability, averting adverse consequences, and detecting contamination is paramount. A systematic exploration into the origins of the disrupted natural ecosystem and the formulation of robust, forward-thinking, practices, policies and solutions that do not jeopardize overall well-being is essential. This undertaking demands imaginative, innovative thinking to ensure favorable outcomes.

Regulation

Regulation can create oversight that fosters innovation and simultaneously protects our global community, preventing and detecting any harm such as contamination of air, water, and land. The precautionary principle is a broad epistemological, philosophical, and legal approach to innovation that emphasizes caution when introducing *innovations* that have potential for causing harm when extensive scientific knowledge on the matter is lacking.[10] The precautionary principle in environmental regulation states that an activity, such as the manufacture of a new chemical compound, which raises threats of harm to human health or the environment should have measures taken even if some cause-and-effect relationships are not fully established scientifically.[11] For example, the forever chemicals, PFAS chemical compounds, are now present in our groundwater and are considered to have harmful effects.[12] This PFAS water contamination is poorly reversible and difficult to remediate and could have high monetary and societal costs to clean up.[13]

Remediation

Environmental remediation is the removal of legacy contamination from soil and groundwater, the reversal of environmental damage in particular locations, and the return of the locations to a more natural state. Examples of environmental remediation include bioremediation, phytoremediation (the use of plants to absorb heavy metals or other contaminants from soil), soil vapor extraction (VPE), dredging, waste solidification/stabilization, and barrier systems. Environmental remediation projects can vary widely in scale and complexity, depending on the type and extent of contamination and the desired outcome. The choice of remediation method depends on site-specific factors, such as the nature of the contaminants, the hydrogeology of the area, and the local ecological context. Additionally, regulatory agencies play a significant role in determining the appropriate remediation approach and ensuring compliance with environmental regulation.

The Climate Problem

When it comes to sustainability in the context of innovation and entrepreneurship, one of the most compelling long-term issues is climate change. Climate change is inextricably linked to sustainability because it represents one of the most significant and urgent challenges to the well-being of people and the planet. Climate change is a crucial aspect of any discussion on sustainability on multiple fronts:

- Global impact: Climate change is a global phenomenon that affects the entire planet. It transcends national boundaries and impacts people, ecosystems, and economies worldwide. Sustainability, which seeks to ensure that current and future generations can meet their needs, inherently depends on addressing global challenges like climate change.
- Interconnectedness: Climate change is interconnected with various other sustainability issues. It affects biodiversity, water resources, food security, energy production, and more. Addressing climate change often involves addressing these interconnected challenges, making it a vital component of a holistic sustainability approach.
- Threat to ecosystems: Climate change poses a severe threat to ecosystems and the services they provide, such as pollination, clean water, and carbon sequestration. Sustainability aims to

protect and maintain these ecosystems for the long term, making climate change mitigation and adaptation essential for achieving sustainability goals.

- Economic implications: Climate change can have profound economic repercussions. Extreme weather events, sea-level rise, and shifts in temperature and precipitation patterns can disrupt agriculture, infrastructure, and industries. By addressing climate change, it is possible to build resilience, to prepare for threats and hazards, adapt to changing conditions, and withstand and recover rapidly from adverse conditions and disruptions and mitigate these economic risks to promote sustainable economic development.[14,15,16]

Managing Climate Change

Climate change refers to long-term shifts in temperatures and weather patterns. Such shifts can be natural due to changes in the sun's activity or large volcanic eruptions. But since the 1800s, human activities have also contributed to long-term climate change, primarily due to the burning of fossil fuels like coal, oil, and gas.

According to the IPCC Sixth Assessment Report (AR6) Working Group One (WGI) report,

Human activities, principally through emissions of greenhouse gases, have unequivocally caused global warming, with global surface temperature reaching 1.1°C above 1850–1900 in 2011–2020. Global greenhouse gas emissions have continued to increase, with unequal historical and ongoing contributions arising from unsustainable energy use, land use and land-use change, lifestyles and patterns of consumption and production across regions, between and within countries, and among individuals (high confidence).[17]

The aim is to manage climate change and decarbonization to provide solutions to hold warming below 1.5 degrees Celsius compared to preindustrial levels. The current global average temperature has already increased by around 1 degree Celsius of warming. Alternative energy sources, investor activism, and evolving climate legislation are changing the dynamics of energy markets.

A paradigm is currently underway, transforming the energy sector with the goal of achieving net-zero emissions. A transition strategy is required to guide the movement into the future while maintaining a manageable balance.

Net zero does not mean zero emissions. It means that any remaining, hard-to-avoid anthropogenic emissions need to be zeroed out by carbon dioxide removal – that is, taking some amount of carbon out of the atmosphere and putting it someplace else.[18]

Net zero, shown in Figure 19.3, is a balance of greenhouse-gas emissions and greenhouse gas removals so that the result is net zero.

Fossil fuels are the largest contributor to human-made greenhouse gas emissions followed by animal agriculture, the second largest contributor and the leading cause of deforestation, water and air pollution, and biodiversity loss.[19] Twenty-four percent of global greenhouse gas emissions come mostly from agriculture (cultivation of crops and livestock) and deforestation.[20] A transition to alternative protein sources could limit greenhouse gases. For instance, China's animal-agriculture sector if improved could result in a one-billion-metric-ton reduction of carbon dioxide emissions.[21] As shown in Figure 19.4, climate change is impacted by human activities, especially the burning of pernicious fossil fuels.

Climate change is a long-term shift in temperatures and weather patterns resulting in the increase in heat intensity, melting of snow and ice, and the rising of sea levels. The extra carbon dioxide is absorbed by oceans resulting in the buildup of carbonic acid changing the pH balance. Carbon dioxide dissolves into seawater and the water and carbon dioxide combine to form carbonic acid (H_2CO_3), a

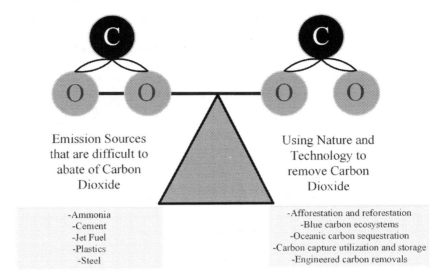

Figure 19.3 Illustration of Net-Zero

Source: Adapted from John Doerr, *Speed and Scale: An Action Plan for Solving our Climate Crisis Now*, (US, UK, & Canada: Penguin Business), 2021.

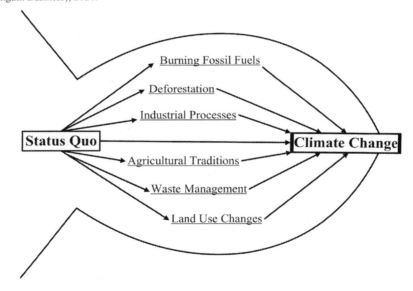

Figure 19.4 Illustration of the Human Causes of Climate Change

weak acid that breaks into hydrogen ions (H$^+$) and bicarbonate ions (HCO$_3$). The heat impact causes weather disruptions that impact agriculture resulting in increased risk to the global food system.[22]

Research suggests that human activity contributes to climate change and global warming based on several factors:

1. Direct physical understanding of how human and natural factors influence climate.
2. Indirect estimates of climate changes over the last 1,000 to 2,000 years are obtained from living things and their remains (like tree rings and corals), which provide a natural archive of climate

variations. These indicators show that the recent temperature rise is unusual in at least the last 1,000 years.

3. Computer model forecasts of how we expect climate to behave under certain human influences.[23]

The Intergovernmental Panel on Climate Change (IPCC) is the scientific group assembled by the United Nations to monitor and assess global science related to climate change. While the IPCC Assessment Reports "do not support the concept of imminent global catastrophe associated with global warming,"[24] the IPCC's 6th Assessment Report (AR6 WGIII) indicates that there is a need to reduce emissions and remove some of the carbon that's already in the atmosphere.[25] "To limit global warming to around 1.5C (2.7°F), the IPCC report insisted that global greenhouse gas emissions would have to peak 'before 2025 at the latest, and be reduced by 43 per cent by 2030.'"[26]

Tipping Point

In 49 BC, Julius Caesar led his army across the Rubicon River, violating Roman law. The metaphorical phrase "crossing the Rubicon" describes a pivotal moment where a choice is made that cannot be undone. The climate change tipping point in Figure 19.5 illustrates a critical moment in the ongoing environmental crisis when the consequences of global warming reach the time that leads to accelerated and potentially irreversible impacts.

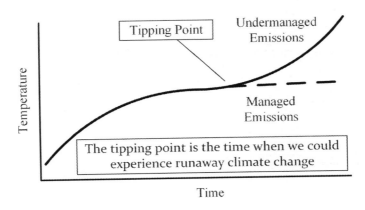

Figure 19.5 Illustration of the Tipping Point

Source: Adapted from Grove, A., S. (1996). *Only the paranoid survive: How to exploit the crisis points that challenge every company and career.* New York: Currency Doubleday.

The Innovation and Entrepreneurship Sustainability Framework

The Innovation and Entrepreneurship Sustainability Framework is a conceptual representation designed to provide direction for the future and increase the understanding, comprehension, and awareness of the importance of sustainability.[27] The sustainability framework is a holistic model for understanding and improving the overall sustainability ecosystem. Improving a part of a complex system does not necessarily improve the complete system. More effective outcomes can be achieved by focusing on improving the complete system, the parts, and the interdependencies between the parts.

To understand why, think about other team-based endeavors. Improving a single athlete's performance can help improve a basketball team's record, for instance, but improving all the players while also teaching the group to work better as a team leads to far stronger overall improvement. Or consider an orchestra. A top-flight oboist can't improve a group's musical performance nearly as much as a conductor who works with every section in the orchestra, emphasizing the ways their musical parts interact.[28]

In our global system, there are interdependencies between the economy and the environment resulting in unintended consequences. "Globally, humans have never been that good at recycling – only about 9% of all plastic ever produced has been made into something new."[29]

During 2020, there was a global oil price collapse that reduced the cost of new (virgin) plastic that is used to make fossil fuels. This decrease in the price of oil resulted in a decrease in the likelihood of plastic recycling and the aspirational goal to achieve "waste-free economy."

Transformative leadership and strategic direction are needed to address the global sustainability imbalance. The imbalance requires a collective global sustainability transformation that focuses on the following:

1. Lead into the future
2. Transform the energy system
3. Manage natural resources
4. Build circular value chains
5. Create awareness and advocacy
6. Empower corporate sustainability
7. Form policy and finance

The Innovation and Entrepreneurship Sustainability Framework is shown in Figure 19.6.

Lead into the Future

While leadership is more extensively covered in Chapter 13, "Catalytic Leadership," leadership encompasses a guiding vision built on character, courage, and compassion; these are the forces for good that empower us to solve the endless challenges we face.[30] As Warren Bennis stated, "Leadership is the wise use of power. Power is the capacity to translate intention into reality and sustain it."

Teddy Roosevelt: Creative Conservation Leadership

In 1903, Teddy Roosevelt traveled to Yosemite, California, to camp with the naturalist John Muir. They went on a wilderness trip throughout Yosemite Valley including Mariposa Grove, Sentinel Dome, and Glacier Point. "The president left convinced that Yosemite should be fully under control of the federal government."[31] The camping trip with President Theodore Roosevelt was significant in conservation history because Muir was able to persuade Roosevelt to return Yosemite Valley and the Mariposa Grove to federal protection as part of Yosemite National Park.[32]

This camping trip was instrumental in the expansion of the America's National Park System, including Yellowstone, Glacier, Yosemite, and Arches. When the National Park Service was created in 1916, Roosevelt led the creation of 23 national parks and monuments.[33] Teddy Roosevelt, a transformational leader, helped establish the 230 million acres of public lands of which 150 million acres were set aside as national forests. In 1905, he created the United States Forest Service to conserve forests to insure the sustainability of those resources. He created 51 federal bird reserves that would later become today's national wildlife refuges, managed by the United States Fish and Wildlife Service (USFWS).

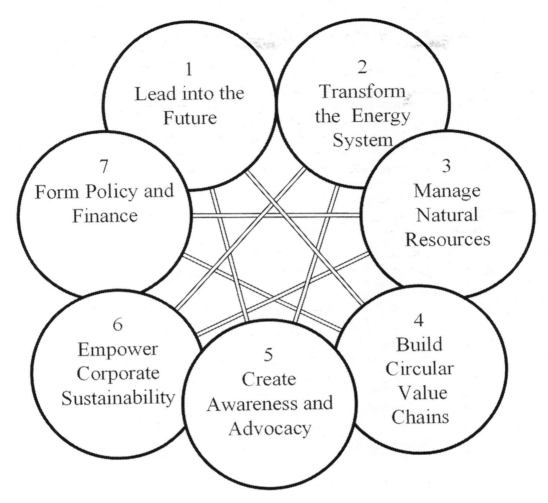

Figure 19.6 Illustration of the Innovation and Entrepreneurship Sustainability Framework

Source: Adapted from Alejandro Sandoval, Bill Lacivita, and, Ignacio Marcos. October 2019. "Transform the whole business, not just parts," McKinsey & Company, accessed January 6, 2020, https://www.mckinsey.com/business-functions/operations/our-insights/transform-the-whole-business-not-just-parts

There are many ways for an organization to innovate for sustainability. Most of the ways to promote innovation require open-mindedness about all aspects of a firm's business model that especially includes redefining people's roles, responsibilities, and incentives.[34] The aim is to facilitate research, innovation, and an entrepreneurship mindset. For example, about climate change,

Combating climate change has entered the mainstream, and corporate and venture capital investment in climate technologies is on the rise. In 2020, US investors doubled the money they put into exchange-traded funds focused on environmental, social, and governance (ESG) criteria – rising to $25 billion. Industry groups, such as the influential Business Roundtable in the US, are emphasizing the need to embrace sustainable practices and lead the way through investment and innovation.[35]

Stakeholder Capitalism

Is the purpose of a corporation solely to maximize shareholder profit? Stakeholder capitalism, the notion of "good governance," includes a wider variety of stakeholders – not only shareholders but also employees, customers, communities, and more. Stakeholders and the boards that govern them should be aligned. For individuals, diversity, equity, and inclusivity are the lens through which this alignment is viewed. If there is incongruity between the stakeholders and the board, it can raise questions about the organization's integrity and the sincerity of their commitment.[36]

Stakeholder capitalism is the capacity of the private sector to harness the innovative, creative power of individuals and teams to generate long-term value for shareholders, for all members of society and for the planet we share. The World Economic Forum's (WEF) International Business Council (IBC) has aligned with the United Nation's Sustainable Development Goals (SDGs) to serve the interests of all stakeholders and align their mainstream reporting on performance against environmental, social, and governance (ESG) indicators through a set of stakeholder capitalism metrics.[37] Figure 19.7 outlines the UN SDGs.

United Nations: The Sustainable Development Goals
1. No Poverty
2. Zero Hunger
3. Good Health and Well-being
4. Quality Education
5. Gender Equality
6. Clean Water and Sanitation
7. Affordable and Clean Energy
8. Decent Work and Economic Growth
9. Industry, Innovation, and Infrastructure
10. Reducing Inequality
11. Sustainable Cities and Communities
12. Responsible Consumption and Production
13. Climate Action
14. Life Below Water
15. Life on Land
16. Peace, Justice, and Strong Institutions
17. Partnerships for the Goals
Sustainable Development Goals, accessed November 5, 2023, https://sustainabledevelopment.un.org/sdgs

Figure 19.7 Illustration of Sustainable Development Goals

Source: Adapted from Sustainable Development Goals, accessed November 5, 2023, https://sustainabledevelopment.un.org/sdgs

What prevents corporations that have talents and resources from expanding their purpose to include environmental, social, and governance purposes? According to McKinsey, "Sustainability endeavors often make good business sense, promising to deliver revenue gains, cost savings, and other benefits that lift enterprise value."[38]

For example, McKinsey has identified five advanced technologies that are long-term, high-impact, and most important for making progress on sustainability and stopping climate change. By explicitly targeting these advanced technologies the most value can be achieved and has the potential to facilitate the support of government, businesses, and the community.[39]

1. Electrifying transportation, buildings, and industry
2. Launching the next green revolution in agriculture
3. Remaking the power grid to supply clean electricity
4. Delivering on the promise of hydrogen
5. Expanding carbon capture, use, and storage

Transform the Energy System

Relying on yesterday's thinking to solve the problems that we face today is problematic. Fresh solutions are needed for the challenges and opportunities that lie ahead. Transforming the energy system aligns with the principles of sustainability by reducing environmental impact, encourages innovation and entrepreneurship fostering the creation of new markets and technologies, and offers economic and societal benefits that can drive long-term sustainable development.

El Hierro Innovation

El Hierro is a tiny active volcanic island that is the most remote of Spain's Canary Islands with a population of 10,000.[40] Using conventional renewable energy technology, the island combined a mix of wind and hydropower to build the Gorona del Viento powerplant that can generate 48 gigawatt hours per year. El Hierro previously used barges to ship diesel fuel to power its electricity generators.

When there is high wind energy from five wind turbines, water is pumped up the mountain from the lower reservoir to the upper reservoir for storage. When there is little wind the water "battery" in the upper reservoir is streamed down a pipe in the mountain. Hydropower is used to drive the turbines to generate electricity. The water accumulates in the lower reservoir for storage and then is pumped back to the top reservoir when the renewable energy resumes.

As soon as sensors detect the wind force slowing, the hydro component of the system automatically starts to provide continuous electrical energy to the people of the island. The creativity in this sustainability solution is in the combination of the wind turbines and water that is managed between the upper and lower reservoirs. This unique solution provides for a sustainable energy future for this remote island. Moreover, the island plans to adopt electric vehicles as part of its long-term plan.[41]

Sustainability requires a focus on climate change mitigation to reduce the effects of global warming.

1. Electrify transportation (cars, vans, buses, trucks, planes (low-carbon fuel), and ships).
2. Decarbonize the grid (solar, wind, and storage) and implement the smart grid.
3. Reduce reliance on fossil fuels and end subsidies and loans to fossil fuel firms.

Renewable energy, like wind and solar power, is becoming increasingly affordable because of improving technology, growing economies of scale, and fierce competition. Electrification from renewable energy is expected to be a significant force to offset climate change because infrastructure projects are needed by automobile manufacturers to sell their vehicles. Major automobile manufacturers cannot sell their vehicles unless they have a viable charging structure, a modern electrical grid, and over time a renewable electrical and storage infrastructure. There is a major shift by the automobile manufactures. There are many auto manufacturers, including GM, Volkswagen, and Tesla, that have made strategic commitments to electronic vehicles (EVs) because they expect the demand for internal combustion engine vehicles (ICEs) to decrease.

Niagara Falls

Niagara Falls, a spectacular natural wonder which drains Lake Erie into Lake Ontario, was subject to entrepreneurs promoting a host of tourist attractions. New York Governor David B. Hill signed legislation creating the Niagara Reservation, New York's first state park, in 1885. New York State began to purchase land from developers under the charter of the Niagara Reservation State Park. In the same year, on the Canadian side the province of Ontario established the Queen Victoria Niagara Falls Park for protection. Nikola Tesla developed the alternating current system which allowed for the transmission of hydroelectric power generated along the Niagara River to be used for homes and businesses in the region. The Niagara Power Project is New York State's biggest electricity producer, providing up to 2.6 million kilowatts of clean electricity. "That clean energy is generated by two facilities, the Robert Moses Niagara Power Plant and the Lewiston Pump Generating Plant, with a combined 25 turbines spun by 748,000 gallons of water per second."[42]

There are several energy system sustainability innovations that have become part of our lives, some of which are taken for granted. Examples of innovations in this category are clean drinking water, solar panels, efficient wind turbines, smart grids for alternating current electrical distribution, and sensors for detecting contamination.[43]

Manage Natural Resources

Building on material previously covered in Chapter 14, "Ecosystems," sustainability benefits from a focus on resource management.

1. Achieve net-positive capital by revitalizing, regenerating, and restoring resources.
2. Adopt sustainable agriculture, stop overuse of fertilizers, and reduce food waste.
3. Implement practices to effectively manage our biodiversity populations.

Resource management focuses on the wise use of both renewable and non-renewable resources throughout the supply chain. Worldwide population growth cannot be sustained by current levels of resource consumption. For example, many food retailers, including Kroger and Whole Foods are advocates for food sustainability. The reduction of food waste by 15% could feed more than 25 million Americans every year.[44] Kroger has created a comprehensive set of long-term sustainability goals on greenhouse gases (GHG) emissions reductions, sustainable packaging for Our Brands products, responsible sourcing (including zero deforestation in Our Brands products), and extended zero waste.[45]

Leadership is essential to manage precious natural resources critical to living on the planet. Resource balance includes the management of the renewable resources consumed from natural ecosystems – water, air, forests, wildlife, and food (animals, plants, and fish) – and the avoidance of non-renewable resource depletion.

For example, mined minerals and metals, such as nickel, cobalt, copper, lithium, gold, and rare earths, are a critical part of clean energy for use in wind turbines, electric vehicles, battery technology, and electric grids. These nonrenewable resources are often extracted without regard to how to source sustainably mined products. To build sustainable products like electronic vehicles, sustainable mining processes are essential. The supplies of cobalt and lithium that are required for making the batteries that power electric cars and mobile phones are likely to be limited by 2050.[46] The scarce minerals, lithium, and cobalt can be recycled or substituted with another mineral.[47] A zero-carbon product requires a zero-carbon mineral supply chain.[48]

Natural renewable resource overuse is the consumption of a resource faster than it can be replenished. Renewable resources of all types, such as aquifers, forests, farmland soils, and fish species, in international waters have been undermanaged and depleted. Congestion on urban highways contributes to air pollution, overused antibiotics result in the increase of resistant diseases, and eliminating forests reduces carbon absorption. Deforestation results in habitat loss and causes a reduction in species and biodiversity.

Figure 19.8 illustrates the human driven sustainability resource management focus.

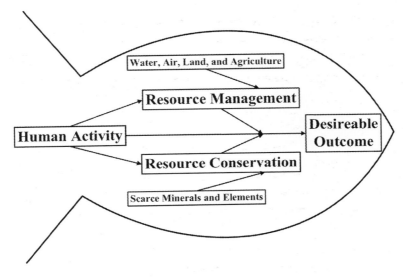

Figure 19.8 Illustration of Management of Natural Resources

Source: Adapted from Ron Adner and Rahul Kapoor, "Value Creation in Innovation Ecosystems," Strategic Management Journal, 31:3, (2010): 309.

As a nation becomes increasingly wealthy, the amount of food wasted by its people increases linearly. There is a direct relationship between consumer affluence and consumer food waste that emerges when consumers reach a threshold of approximately $6.70/day/capita level of expenditures for food. The United Nations Food and Agricultural Organization (FAO) has estimated that one-third of the world's food supply around the globe is wasted due to the rotting of harvested vegetables and families throwing out leftovers. The estimate of calories purchased minus calories consumed results in 527 calories per person per day wasted by people around the globe.[49]

Conserving Natural Systems

The world has a finite set of resources, and the conservation of our natural systems can be achieved by eliminating air, water, and soil contamination. An imbalance in our natural systems has been created, as evidenced by adverse health effects resulting from the presence of contaminants, which encompass various harmful and toxic elements.

Florida Keys National Marine Sanctuary

The Florida Keys National Marine Sanctuary has North America's only coral reef in the continental United States that ranges from south of Miami to the Dry Tortugas. "According to a 2011 government study, the sanctuary's habitats were in fair to poor condition, meaning that mangroves, coral gardens and seagrass weren't healthy enough for marine life to thrive."[50] The National Oceanic and Atmospheric Administration (NOAA) has prepared a blueprint to address the poor conditions and expand protection to the habitat to allow manatees, sea turtles, and fish to survive and thrive.[51]

In general, the aim is to preserve natural systems and prevent contamination of the natural environment. A natural system needs to be monitored for balance and possible rebalance across water, land, and air, as shown in Figure 19.9.

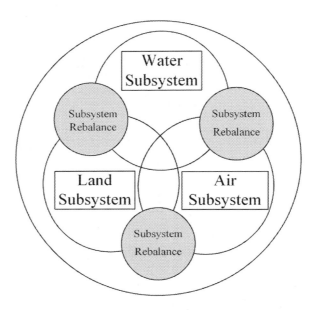

Figure 19.9 Illustration of the Global Ecosystem Balance

The Intergovernmental Science-Policy Platform on Biodiversity and Ecosystem Services (IP-BES) prepared a summary report that states, "Nature and its vital contributions to people, which together embody biodiversity and ecosystem functions and services, are deteriorating worldwide."[52] "The Report finds that around 1 million animal and plant species are now threatened with extinction, many within decades, more than ever before in human history."[53] Some of the causes of the decline in biodiversity are shown in Figure 19.10.

The Tragedy of the Commons

The tragedy of the commons is an illustrative example of what can happen when attention is not paid to managing natural resources. The tragedy of the commons occurs when individuals overconsume a resource at the expense of society. For example, in New England in the 17th century, immigrants formed villages in which they had privately owned homesteads and gardens, but they also set aside community-owned pastures, called commons, where all the villagers' livestock could

(1) Changes in land and sea use.

(2) Direct exploitation of organisms.

(3) Climate change.

(4) Pollution.

(5) Invasion of alien species.

Figure 19.10 Illustration of a Causes of Biodiversity Deterioration

Source: Adapted from Intergovernmental Science-Policy Platform on Biodiversity and Ecosystem Services (IPBES), "UN Report: Nature's Dangerous Decline 'Unprecedented'; Species Extinction Rates 'Accelerating,'" May 2019, http://www.un.org/sustainabledevelopment/blog/2019/05/nature-decline-unprecedented-report/

graze.[54] The settlers had an incentive to avoid overuse of their private lands, so they would remain productive in the future. This self-interested stewardship of private lands, however, did not extend to the commons. A vicious circle of design-manufacture-marketing-consumption can occur when the shared resources of a community are overused.[55]

Sustainability builds on conserving pure natural ecosystems: clean water, air, and land.

1. Preserve, protect, prevent, and detect harm to our natural capital.
2. Monitor and eliminate all types of contamination from the forests, air, land, oceans, and waterways.
3. Take responsibility for research, remediation, and regulation of our natural capital.

Figure 19.11 illustrates the tragedy of the commons in terms of a plant's carry capacity and the maximum population size the plant ecosystem can sustainably support.

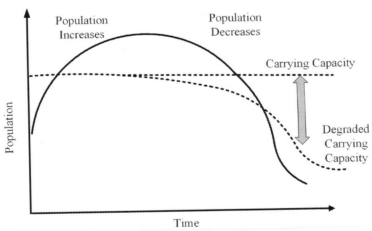

The carrying capacity in a plant refers to the maximum population size it can sustainably support within its ecosystem based on available resources and environmental conditions.

Figure 19.11 Illustration of Nature-Based Carrying Capacity

Source: Acknowledgement: Douglas Tallamy, *Nature's Best Hope*, (Portland, Oregon: Timber Press, 2019), 83.

For example, trees provide one of the simplest and most effective ways to capture carbon. *A tree stores carbon in wood, in the trunks, branches, and root system, as well as the leaves.* Wood is an organic material that is a natural composite of cellulose fibers.[56] A single hardwood tree might store a ton of carbon over a period of 40 years. Growing new trees, protecting existing forests and peatlands, and reforesting logged over, burned, or otherwise degraded lands are essential.[57] Figure 19.12 provides an illustration of achieving nature-based value.

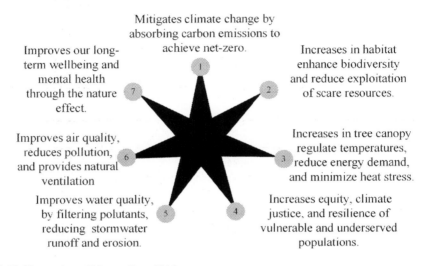

Figure 19.12 Illustration of Nature-Based Value

Source: McDonald RI, Biswas T, Sachar C, Housman I, Boucher TM, Balk D, et al. (2021) The tree cover and temperature disparity in US urbanized areas: Quantifying the association with income across 5,723 communities. PLoS ONE 16(4): e0249715. https://doi.org/10.1371/journal.pone.0249715

Build Circular Value Chains

Circular value chains and linear value chains represent two distinct approaches to resource management and economic production, each with its own set of advantages and disadvantages. Circular value chains are important for sustainability, innovation, and entrepreneurship because they tend to align economic growth with environmental and social responsibility. They offer opportunities for businesses to reduce their environmental impact, drive innovation, and create new markets while promoting a more sustainable and circular economy.

In general, circular value chains are seen as more sustainable and environmentally responsible compared to linear value chains. The transition from linear to circular models, however, can be challenging and costly for some industries. There are calls to end the waste generated by the linear value chain needs and increase the number of interconnected circular supply chains. The World Economic Forum, for example, has identified a new ecosystem for circular value chains that needs to focus on plastics, electronics, food, and fashion/textiles.[58]

Which approach is better depends, in part, on the specific goals and circumstances of a business or industry. Many organizations are increasingly recognizing the benefits of circular value chains and are taking steps to transition to align with sustainability goals and consumer demands. The choice between circular and linear value chains should be guided by a commitment to sustainability and long-term economic viability.

Building a Circular Economy

The concept of a circular economy is driven by the need to address pressing global challenges such as resource depletion, climate change, pollution, and waste management. By shifting from a linear to a circular economic model, societies and businesses can reduce their environmental footprint while still pursuing economic prosperity. The goal of a fully circular economy is to generate zero waste and keep products and materials in use while simultaneously preventing the contamination of natural systems.

> One model that holds great promise is the circular economy (CE) – instead of digging up materials, using them once, and then throwing them away, companies in a CE recapture the enormous volume of resources in their value chain in order to use them again and again.[59]

Honda

For example, Honda has a life cycle assessment (LCA) model for managing the impact of its products and operations on the environment in development, purchasing, manufacturing, and sales and service. This model focuses on designing end-of-life products that reduce the environmental impacts and increase the use of renewable (recycled and remanufactured) component parts to reduce waste. The LCA model establishes expectations for emission in its plants and with its partner suppliers. Honda designs its products so that they are easy to disassemble and process for recycling at the end of their useful life. The LCA model reduces the likelihood that harmful substances will be released into the environment.[60]

Linear and Circular Value Chains

A value chain is rooted in a business model that describes all the activities needed by a firm to deliver a valuable product, service, or experience. The value chain is composed of the functional activities that involve bringing an offering from conception to distribution and everything in between – in short, inputs, throughputs, and outputs.

The functions include procuring raw materials, manufacturing functions, and marketing and sales functions.[61] A value chain can be linear or circular. A linear value chain is a set of activities that a firm operating in a specific industry performs to deliver a valuable product, service, or experience that is based on "make, use, and dispose."[62] Historically, production systems are designed using a linear value chain.

In contrast, the circular economy is a systems concept that focuses on designing out waste and continuously reusing resources.[63] The primary driver of a circular economy is the development and implementation of circular value chains. For example, instead of disposing of potentially useful resources, a circular value chain seeks to design products and packaging so that they continue to function in the circular economy and not waste essential materials, such as plastics, clothing, cans, paper, wood, glass, and electric motors. The linear and circular value chain are shown in Figure 19.13.

Sustainability relies on a change from linear value chains to the circular value chains. Circular value chains focus on designing out waste and continuously reusing resources.[64]

1. Adopt circular sustainable value chains.
2. Design sustainable products for reuse.
3. Implement recyclable packaging.

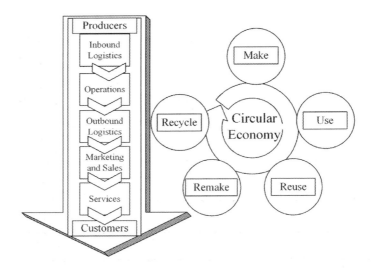

Figure 19.13 Illustration of the Value Chain and Circular Economy

Source: Adapted from Porter, M. E. (1985). Competitive advantage (5. print. ed.). New York: Free Press u.a.

Building a circular economy and viable circular value chains are crucial for sustainability, innovation, and entrepreneurship. Resource conservation, environmental sustainability, economic efficiency, innovation, market opportunities, job creation, resilience, ethical, social benefit, resource security, and long-term viability all provide compelling reasons for strong interest by business and society.

1. Consumers, especially millennials and Generation Z, seek reusable packaging options and rank sustainability as a key factor in their purchasing decisions.
2. Consumer companies, such as Walmart and Coca-Cola, are moving away from single-use plastics – toward materials that are recyclable, reusable, or compostable.[65]
3. Policymakers are starting to create regulations that support consumer-driven change, particularly in the European Union. "French President Emmanuel Macron signed a law in 2020 that established concrete goals, including recycling 100% of plastics by 2025 and the end of single-use plastic packaging by 2040."[66]

Create Awareness and Advocacy

We are viewing the global sustainability problem through an obsolete black-and-white cathode-ray vacuum tube television set.[67] The environmental, social, and governance challenges we face are significant and unprecedented. The solutions are to seek to understand the importance of awareness, advocacy, and consumer behavior.

Awareness

Awareness is the state of being *cognizant* or conscious of something. Sustainability awareness is recognition of the interconnectedness of the world and the impact of human actions on the environment. The aim of awareness is to acknowledge the problem and discover innovative solutions that can be accelerated through learning and education.

Education is one of the keys to raising awareness of climate change concerns.[68] Richard Feynman notes that, "Scientific knowledge is an enabling power to do either good or bad – but it does not carry instructions on how to use it."[69] The education system is a powerful force for transformational change that can increase sustainability awareness. In addition, education systems have the opportunity to provide the leadership to promote sustainability for all students beyond the traditional classroom into nature-based outside experiences. A more extensive treatment of education architecture can be found in Chapter 18.

In *Upheaval*, Jared Diamond provides an examination of how countries have coped with transformational crises as shown in Figure 19.14. He describes 12 factors that can influence how both whole nations and individual people can respond to big challenges.[70] It is a useful framework for examining awareness and advocacy and education for sustainability.

Awareness and Advocacy Factors to Consider for Sustainability Education
1. Acknowledging the problem (crisis)
2. Accepting responsibilty to take action
3. Isolating (frame) the problems that need solving
4. Getting resources from others (individuals and groups (countries))
5. Using others as role models of how to solve problems
6. Building ego-strength (self-awareness, confidence, and humility)
7. Self-appraising with honesty confronts the brutal facts.
8. Applying experiences of previous crisis (for example, ozone depletion)
9. Exercising patience
10. Exercising personal flexibility
11. Identifying core values (strongly held beliefs)
12. Focusing, freeing oneself from personal constraints, and liberating oneself from routine thinking (creativity)

Figure 19.14 Illustration of Awareness and Advocacy Factors to Consider for Sustainability Education

Source: Adapted from Diamond, J. M. (2019). Upheaval. [London], UK: Allen Lane, an imprint of Penguin Books.

Advocacy

Advocacy is the act of taking responsibility on behalf of a cause. Advocacy requires an understanding of the issues and knowledge of the subject matter. Advocates use evidence, facts, relationships, media, and messaging to educate stakeholders.

Sustainability advocacy is taking responsibility for promoting and encouraging everyone to make choices that improve the environment for future generations. The aim of advocacy is to increase the quantity and quality of sustainability responsibility among individuals, businesses, governments, and education systems, interwoven together like a fabric.

Historically, management of all types of organizations acting in their own self-interest can override what is best for a community. Sustainability requires advocacy networks for community awareness and advocacy powered by education. The education system is a major force that defines our progress forward.

1. Adopt universal primary and secondary sustainability education.
2. Promote advocacy networks among communities, business, and government partnerships.
3. Counter contextual deception, disinformation, misinformation, cognitive biases, and noise.

The concept of advocacy at the grassroots level focuses on collective community action. Advocacy networks that lift public awareness and organize solutions can be formed that drive broad transformational change. The message is, pay now to protect the environment or pay more later to correct the environment. There is a need to build momentum through education.

Consumer Behavior

One of the key aspects of creating awareness and advocacy is consumer behavior. Behavior refers to the way in which someone *conducts* themselves in response to different actions they experience. Habits are the things a person does *repeatedly* until such a time that it becomes automatic. Consumer habits are a crucial factor in explaining purchasing decisions. Consumers can be organized into three sustainability groups as follows:

1. Engaged and willing to accept trade-offs in price and performance
2. Engaged and aware but not willing to accept trade-offs in cost and performance
3. Indifferent to sustainability and its importance to our future

There is a dynamic shift that is occurring toward those willing to make trade-offs in process and performance as shown in Figure 19.15.

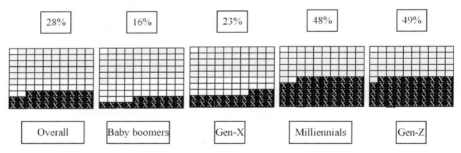

Figure 19.15 Illustration of Consumer Insights on Sustainability [Attitudes Toward Tradeoffs-Consumer Willingness to Pay Premiums for Sustainable Products]

Source: Adapted from Bill Aull, Prabh Gill, Dymfke Kuijpers, Nancy Lu, Eric Marohn, and Griffin McLaughlin, "The state of grocery in North America 2023," September 25, 2023, accessed October 23, 2023, https://www.mckinsey.com/industries/retail/our-insights/the-state-of-grocery-in-north-america-2023 and https://www.mckinsey.com/featured-insights/sustainable-inclusive-growth/chart-of-the-day/buying-into-sustainability

Empower Corporate Sustainability

Procter & Gamble's Tide Detergent

Procter & Gamble has focused on decarbonizing laundry from design, manufacturing, and distribution to consumer use by reducing greenhouse gas emissions, minimizing energy use in the wash cycle, and exploring carbon capture and utilization technology. P&G created a formula that uses enzymes designed for lower wash temperatures to help break down stains in colder water to save energy.[71] Enzymes are proteins that act as biological catalysts by accelerating chemical reactions.[72] P&G scientists used directed evolution to optimize enzymatic activity to make them work effectively at colder and colder temperatures for washing thereby saving energy.[73] Tide's cold-water washing initiative is a significant part of its efforts to minimize energy use in the wash cycle. Tide's research found that over two-thirds of all greenhouse gas emissions in the laundry lifecycle result from consumer use.[74]

Both local and global economies need the private and public sectors to work together to commit to creating well-targeted sustainability transformations. Forward thinking companies seeking to make the most of sustainability focus on innovation to manage the complex transitions that are needed by concentrating on adding value, growth, and opportunity. Kathleen McLaughlin and Andrew Steer write,

> We believe that businesses that embrace a high-efficiency, low-carbon model will have a better chance to survive and grow in the 21st century. Innovation is essential for any business, but especially in the face of the growing risks and uncertainty of climate change.[75]

Figure 19.16 identifies way to create sustainable value.

Creating Value through Sustainability		
	Strong environmental, social, and governance value proposition	Weak environmental, social, and governance value proposition
Growth	Organizations can attract clients by offering sustainable products and experiences.	Organizations will lose clients when they fail to fulfill essential needs due to insufficient sustainability measures.
Cost reduction	Organizations can offset rising operating expenses through lower energy consumption and the use of continuous improvement and waste reduction programs.	Organizations that are wasteful, do not recycle, and expend resources on poorly designed processes, equipment, and packaging.
Policy, regulatory, and legal interventions	Organizations can achieve greater impact in their strategic decision-making by adopting sustainability policies, committing to 100% renewables, and functionally deregulating bureaucracy.	Organizations that incur fines, penalties, enforcement actions, and nonproductive restrictions.
Employee productivity and purpose	Organizations with a purposeful sustainability mission can increase engagement and productivity, as well as retain and attract quality employees.	Organizations can inadvertently create dissatisfaction if they are not aligned with a purpose-driven culture.
Investment and asset optimization	Organizations can improve innovation returns by allocating capital to more promising and sustainable opportunities, such as renewables, waste reduction, and new markets.	Organizations can lose their competitive advantage by missing valid opportunities for long-term growth.

Figure 19.16 Illustration of How to Create Sustainable Value

Source: Adapted from Witold Henisz, Tim Koller, and Robin Nuttall, "Five ways that ESG creates value," McKinsey & Company, November 2019, accessed November 25, 2019, https://www.mckinsey.com/business-functions/strategy-and-corporate-finance/our-insights/five-ways-that-esg-creates-value

Environmental, Social, and Governance (ESG)

Business strategy and education in the past has focused on profit maximization in the interest of shareholders compared to an emphasis on all stakeholders. To maintain balance in the ecosystems, innovation is needed to address the most pressing problems. Business models need to change more rapidly to favor renewables to adapt our infrastructure to minimize the cost impact of the disruptive effects of climate change.

Strategic framing is needed to bring to the forefront long-term objectives that are the most important and have the highest impact.

> **Ample evidence shows** that when executives consistently make decisions and investments with long-term objectives in mind, their companies generate more shareholder value, create more jobs, and contribute more to economic growth than do peer companies that focus on the short term.[76]

For example, in a McKinsey Global Survey, the findings indicate that most of the executives and investment professionals believed that ESG programs create short- and long-term value and will do so even more five years from now.[77] The ESG model, shown in Figure 19.17, outlines ways ESG has the potential to create value.

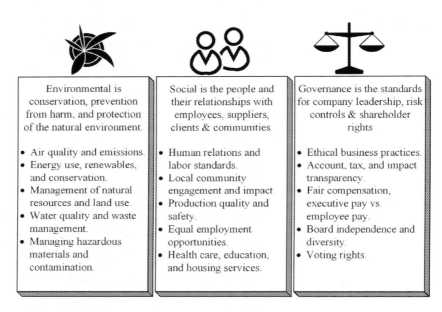

Environmental is conservation, prevention from harm, and protection of the natural environment.	Social is the people and their relationships with employees, suppliers, clients & communities.	Governance is the standards for company leadership, risk controls & shareholder rights
• Air quality and emissions. • Energy use, renewables, and conservation. • Management of natural resources and land use. • Water quality and waste management. • Managing hazardous materials and contamination.	• Human relations and labor standards. • Local community engagement and impact. • Production quality and safety. • Equal employment opportunities. • Health care, education, and housing services.	• Ethical business practices. • Account, tax, and impact transparency. • Fair compensation, executive pay vs. employee pay. • Board independence and diversity. • Voting rights.

Figure 19.17 Illustration of the Environmental, Social, and Governance Elements

Source: Adapted from https://investor.vanguard.com/investing/esg/

Adapted from Witold Henisz, Tim Koller, and Robin Nuttall, "Five ways that ESG creates value," McKinsey & Company, November 2019, accessed January 5, 2020, https://www.mckinsey.com/business-functions/strategy-and-corporate-finance/our-insights/five-ways-that-esg-creates-value

Form Policy and Finance

Sustainability Policy

When it comes to sustainability, climate change is one of the most widely discussed and controversial areas. For example, worldwide policies and legislation have been approved to mitigate environmental disruption and rebalance sustainability. The 1987 Montreal Protocol targeted depletion of the ozone layer that was caused by chlorofluorocarbons (CFCs), halons, and carbon tetrachloride. The 1997 Kyoto Protocol was an international treaty aimed at combatting climate change and remains a significant foundation for climate diplomacy. The Paris Agreement is an international treaty on climate change. The European Green Deal is a comprehensive plan to make the EU's economy sustainable. The Climate Change Act is a UK law that sets legally binding targets for reducing greenhouse gas emissions.

The United States government has implemented several legislative programs that deal with environment:

1. The Inflation Reduction Act is the largest and most ambitious climate legislation Congress has ever passed. It includes $369 billion in climate and clean energy investments.
2. The Clean Air Act gives the Environmental Protection Agency (EPA) the responsibility to address climate pollution while providing new tools and funding to protect communities.
3. The American Clean Energy and Security Act is aimed to establish a cap-and-trade system to reduce greenhouse gas emissions.
4. The Energy Policy Act provides tax incentives for renewable energy production, including wind, solar, geothermal, and biomass.
5. The Energy Independence and Security Act aims to increase energy efficiency across all sectors of the economy, including buildings, lighting, appliances, transportation, and industry.

Pillars of Sustainability

To achieve positive outcomes creating sustainability policy, three pillars can be identified. Figure 19.18 focuses on these three pillars dealing with the pursuit of environmental policy: mitigation, adaptation, and loss and damage.[78,79,80]

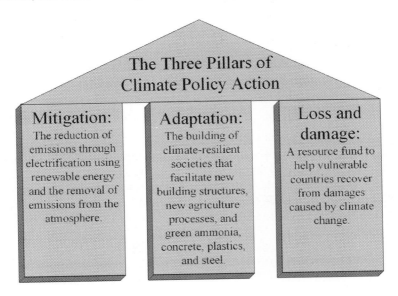

Figure 19.18 Illustration of the Three Pillars

Source: Vaclav Smil, *How the World Really Works, The Science Behind How We Got Here and Where We're Going,* (UK: Viking, Penguin Random House, 2022). "A new UN fund for "loss and damage" emerges from COP27," November 20, 2022, accessed October 30, 2023, https://www.economist.com/international/2022/11/20/a-new-un-fund-for-loss-and-damage-emerges-from-cop27

1. Mitigation: Measures to reduce the amount and rate of future climate change by reducing emissions of heat-trapping gases (primarily carbon dioxide) or removing greenhouse gases from the atmosphere.
2. Adaptation: The process of adjusting to an actual or expected environmental change and its effects in a way that seeks to moderate harm or exploit beneficial opportunities.
3. Loss and damage: A resource fund to help vulnerable countries recover from damages caused by climate change.

Net-Zero Policy

With respect to sustainable environmental policy, for example, net zero is the point in time where heat-trapping greenhouse gases are added to the atmosphere. Figure 19.19 provides an overview timeline of current policymaking, greenhouse emissions, and achieving net-zero.

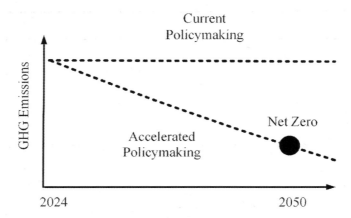

Figure 19.19 Illustration of the Impact of Policy on Net Zero

Source: Adapted from John Doerr, Speed and Scale, (UK: Penguin Random House 2021).

Cost-Effectiveness

Kathleen McLaughlin and Andrew Steer write,

> As climate impacts intensify, they are projected to become more costly. According to the recent *National Climate Assessment*, by the end of the century, warming at the current trajectory would cost the American economy hundreds of billions of dollars from crop damage, lost labor and the consequences of extreme weather. Similarly, the National Bureau of Economic Research found that climate change could cost the United States 10.5 percent in real income by 2100.[81]

According to research by the Global Commission on Adaptation, the investment of $1.8 trillion globally in five areas from 2020 to 2030 could generate $7.1 trillion in total net benefits. The five areas that they have proposed are "early warning systems, climate-resilient infrastructure, improved dryland agriculture, mangrove protection, and investments in making water resources more resilient."[82]

The Global Commission on Adaptation stated that their proposal only represents a portion of the total investment needed and total benefits available. The Global Commission on Adaptation believes that adaptation actions bring multiple benefits, which are called the triple dividend.

The first dividend is avoided losses, that is, the ability of the investment to reduce future losses. The second is positive economic benefits through reducing risk, increasing productivity, and driving innovation through the need for adaptation; the third is social and environmental benefits.[83]

Carbon Pricing/Markets

Carbon markets are trading systems in which carbon credits are sold and bought. There are two types of carbon markets: regulated (public) and voluntary (private).

A regulated (public) carbon market is a trading system regulated by government organizations where carbon credits are bought and sold to compensate for greenhouse gas emissions. Regulated carbon markets, also known as emissions trading systems or cap-and-trade programs, are regulatory mechanisms designed to reduce greenhouse gas emissions by putting a price on carbon.

Regulated markets work by setting a limit (cap) on the total amount of emissions that can be released within a given period and then allowing companies and organizations to buy and sell permits or credits that represent the right to emit a specific quantity of carbon. In a cap-and-trade public program, government organizations cap emissions at a certain overall level and assign limits to countries or companies, covered under the rules. An entity that doesn't need to use all the carbon credits it has been issued can sell them to someone that expects to exceed its limits. "The trading of carbon credits can help companies – and the world – meet ambitious goals for reducing greenhouse-gas emissions."[84]

Voluntary (private) carbon markets are specialized financial trading systems markets where carbon credits can be bought and sold to offset greenhouse gas emissions. Voluntary carbon credits are not regulated by governments or international organizations. In the voluntary (private) market, carbon offsets can be obtained through activities such as nature-based solutions, such as reforestation and regenerative agriculture, and engineered solutions, such as direct air capture and combusting methane emitted from landfills to generate electricity.[85] A person or organization can fund climate change (avoid, remove, or reduce) instead of taking actions themselves to lower their own carbon emissions.

Carbon credits are created from projects that remove GHGs from the atmosphere or that avoid the generation of GHG emissions. The criteria for a carbon credit project would require at least additionality. This means the project would not have occurred without the expected revenue from selling the carbon credit. For a project to be additional, the revenues from selling the carbon credits must play a decisive role in the project developer's decision to implement the project.[86]

Carbon markets are important to sustainability, innovation, and entrepreneurship for a few reasons, including economic incentives, cost-effective emissions reduction, promotion of clean technologies, job creation, investor confidence, and others. Figure 19.20 illustrates the value of regulated and voluntary carbon markets.

Sustainability Innovation and Entrepreneurship Strategy

The strategic conceptual framework presented here is a representation designed to provide direction for the future and increase the understanding, comprehension, and awareness of the importance of sustainability.[87] Strategic thinking facilitates the ability to understand the complete system, the parts, and the interdependencies between the parts.

The sustainability strategy framework focuses on the choices that are needed to implement the highest impact transformational changes needed to improve sustainability. To achieve credibility and minimize resistance, we need to adopt a collaborative direction where there are no explicit political positions about candidates or parties. The framework focuses on the choices that are needed to implement the highest impact transformational changes needed to improve sustainability.

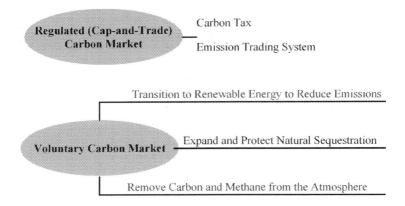

Figure 19.20 Illustration of The Carbon Markets

Source: Acknowledgement: "The Ultimate Guide to Understanding Carbon Credits," accessed July 4, 2022, https://carbon-credits.com/the-ultimate-guide-to-understanding-carbon-credits/

Acknowledgement: Gabrielle Walker and Bruno Giussani, "Carbon Credits Should Be One of Our Best Tools to Fight Climate Change If We Use Them Right," July 20, 2022, accessed July 20, 2022, https://time.com/6197651/carbon-credits-fight-climate-change/

Strategic Decision-Making

Strategy is about making decisions regarding what to do now to shape the future by adding value.[88] Strategy is about the "fundamentals of how an organization works: The sources of value creation, the drivers of the cost to deliver it, and the basis of competition."[89] In the book *Playing to Win*, Lafley and Martin write, "In our terms, strategy is a coordinated and integrated set of five choices: a winning aspiration, where to play, how to win, core capabilities, and management systems."[90]

Strategies can be deliberate and follow a defined pathway of direction or strategies can be emergent (transformative) and change pathways. Pivoting refers to a change in strategy or direction brought about by the ongoing search for the solution to a problem that adds value for potential customers. Strategies that are broad and shallow are less effective than those that are narrow and deep. Too many times we have seen companies trying to focus on too many things and, as a result, getting little success with any of them. It is like having too many planes in the air but not enough runways to land them all. The planes are the ideas, and the runways are the commercial abilities of a company to make those ideas happen.

A strategic pathway is one of several directions, based on customer wants and needs, to take to ensure alignment with the customer expectations. The search for a customer fit is to ensure alignment between the solutions and what the client expects. This might be customized or off-the-shelf solutions for a client.

The Strategy Framework Model

Business Model Defined

A business plan/model describes how to manage the core business to achieve peak profitability in the present. It describes how an organization operates to deliver products, services, and solutions in a customer segment so that value is provided to all the stakeholders. An organizational transformation can refer to the strengthening and optimization of the value chain. The value chain refers to the process of how an organization adds value by transforming inputs into outputs, such as products, services, and solutions, to customers.

A business model is a conceptual tool that contains a set of elements and their relationships and allows expressing the business logic of a specific firm. It is a description of the value a company offers to one or several segments of customers and of the architecture of the firm and its network of partners for creating, marketing, and delivering this value and relationship capital, to generate profitable and sustainable revenue streams.[91]

The value chain encompasses those activities that improve upon nine elements: value proposition (the customer promise), marketing and market segments, distribution channels, client relationships, key resources, key activities, key partners, revenue streams, and cost structure. An organizational transformation can refer to strengthening of key partners that would include the board of directors.

Strategy Defined

Strategy is an integrated set of choices about what is done in the present to create the objectives that fulfill the mission and future vision of the organization. Vijay Govindarajan and Chris Trimble proposed that while a CEO manages the present business model, he or she must also selectively forget the past to create the future strategy.[92] The business model of all companies will be affected by the transition to a sustainable net-zero economy; sustainability must be part of the strategic planning process of all organizations.[93]

The strategy framework integrates the present, the future next, and the future after next that is shown in Figure 19.21.

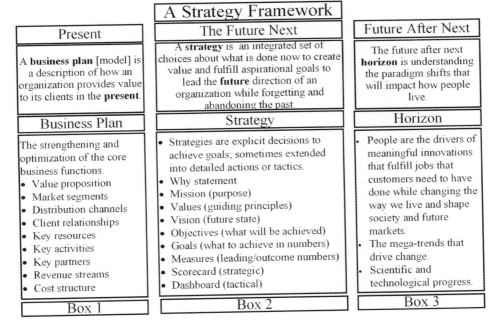

Figure 19.21 Illustration of a Strategy Framework

Source: Adapted from Vijay Govindarajan and Chris Trimble, "The CEO'S Role in Business Model Reinvention," Harvard Business Review, 89(1–2), (2011): 111.

Adapted from A. G. Lafley, Roger L. Martin, Playing To Win: How Strategy Really Works, (Boston, MA: Harvard Business Review Press, 2013), 3–16.

Adapted from Alexander Osterwalder, Yves Pigneur, and Tim Clark. Business Model Generation: A Handbook for Visionaries, Game Changers, and Challengers, (Hoboken, NJ: Wiley, 2010).

The Strategy Process

The way to have the highest impact is to focus on a direction that contributes to broad collaboration with businesses, legislators, everyday people, and the community. Ideally, the goal is to create a direction that can join stakeholders together on issues. The creation of a strategic direction must involve all internal stakeholders (staff, volunteers [if non-profit], and board) and external stakeholders (clients, customers, consumers).

The process enables stakeholders to determine what will be the most effective direction (pathway) to make sustainability progress.

1. Definition: Conduct discussions to understand the mission and values.
2. Discovery: Determine what is now, the current state.
3. Dream: Determine the most impactful (what might be) future state direction.
4. Design: Determine the objectives by identifying the gaps between the current and future state.
5. Deliver: Commit to the objectives by preparing the goals, measures, and scorecard. Implement the direction that has the outcomes with the most impact and broadest support.

A strategic planning process can be formulated using the process shown in Figure 19.22

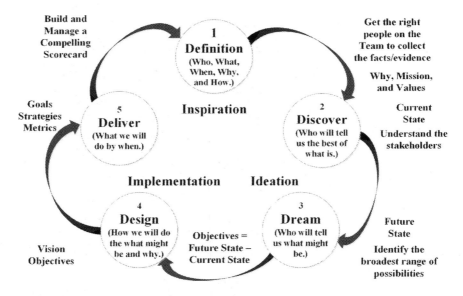

Figure 19.22 Illustration of the Strategic Planning Process

Source: Adapted from "An Introduction to Design Thinking PROCESS GUIDE," Institute of Design At Stanford Adapted from the Appreciative Inquiry Conceptual Process for Strategic Planning, Joe Kane.

Innovation

Sustainability, innovation, and entrepreneurship requires a focus on creating impactful innovations. As noted in Chapter 10, "Innovation Theory," Figure 10.5, there are several paths to innovation that have quite different impacts: incremental (often to achieve an efficiency), evolutionary sustaining (extended and adapted), inferior disruptive creation, superior disruptive creation, and revolutionary nondisruptive creation. In terms of sustainability and innovation, those pathways are critical.

1. Incremental changes (decrease cost of electricity, energy efficiencies, and sustainable fuel)
2. Evolutionary methods (next generation, artificially intelligent smart grids, green steel, and desalination)
3. Disruptive (renewable energy, energy storage, sustainable agriculture)
4. Revolutionary materials (carbon removal, fusion, green hydrogen, and carbon-neutral fuels)

There are several sustainability innovations that have become part of our lives, some of which are taken for granted. Examples of innovations in this category are clean drinking water, solar panels, efficient wind turbines, smart grids for alternating current electrical distribution, and sensors for detecting contamination.[94]

To break free from the tendency of clinging to the past, one must avoid repeating the same actions while anticipating different outcomes. As Einstein said, "We can't solve problems by using the same kind of thinking we used when we created them."[95] Innovations of all types are needed.

Expanding on the foundation in Chapter 10, the innovation pathways, shown in Figure 19.23, illustrate the choices that leadership can make that are most impactful in sustainability. In general, the outcome pathway value increases over time.

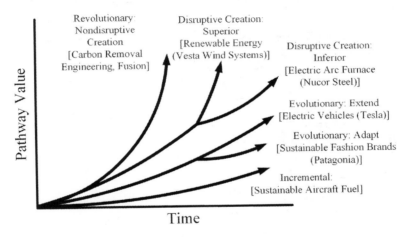

Figure 19.23 Illustration of Innovation Pathways

Source: Adapted from Mckinsey & Company, "What is net zero?" November 28, 2022, https://www.mckinsey.com/featured-insights/mckinsey-explainers/what-is-net-zero

Incremental Innovation

Incremental innovation is improving upon an existing solution by adding features to the solution or making the solution more efficient. Feature improvements to existing offerings would include the use of natural materials rather than plastics in products or the manufacture of safer batteries. Efficiency innovations to existing offerings would include longer charges in batteries and energy star products and services that provide more utility (outputs) with less energy resource inputs.

Incremental innovation can include regenerative agriculture practices, carbon accounting measures in scorecards and dashboards, and the adoption of carbon footprint labeling on products. The substitution of conventional aircraft fuel with sustainable aviation fuel can reduce emissions. Sustainable aviation fuel (SAF) is a biofuel, biomass-derived fuel from plants or waste used to power aircraft. Sustainable aviation fuel (SAF) is a viable way to reduce the carbon footprint impact of aviation. This is because depending on which type of biomass is used, the biofuel could lower CO_2 emissions by 20–98% compared to conventional jet fuel.[96]

Evolutionary Innovation

Evolutionary innovations can occur through extensions and adaptation.

Extend

Evolutionary extended innovations are created when new offerings and new business models are provided to existing customers in existing markets. Evolutionary extended innovations include electric vehicles, cars, trucks, electric scooters, and e-bikes. Electronic vehicles of all types provide value because of their long-term savings on maintenance and repairs and lower operational costs. Electric planes extend existing offerings that result in new offerings that solve the unmet needs of current customers or markets.[97]

Solar power plants could use mirrors to concentrate sunlight, which heats up hundreds or thousands of tons of salt until it melts.

> This molten salt then is used to drive an electric generator, much as coal or nuclear power is used to heat steam and drive a generator in traditional plants. These heated materials can also be stored to produce electricity when it is cloudy, or even at night.[98]

Adapt

Evolutionary adapted innovations are created when existing offerings and existing business models are provided to new customers and new markets such as the retrofitting of residences and commercial buildings to use less energy through insulation, heating, ventilation, and air conditioning upgrades.

Disruptive Creation

A disruptive creation involves a new venture that targets overlooked customers with a novel but modest offering and gradually moving upmarket to challenge the industry leaders. Disruptive creations provide an inferior or superior solution by displacement.

Inferior Disruptive

The inferior disruptive creations occur when a new product or service is launched in the most price-sensitive segment of the market and then moves upmarket as the experience curve improves.[99] There has and continues to be a transition from relatively low-cost animal power, mills powered by streams of water and wind to a mix of solutions, such as wood, coal, oil, gas, geothermal, and hydropower, that are increasingly moving upmarket. That transition path continues to renewables that have increasingly more value including wind, solar, and biomass as energy sources in various combinations.

Superior Disruptive

The superior disruptive creation occurs when a new product or service is launched in the most price-insensitive segment of the market, and then moves down market as the experience curve improves.[100] For example, the transition to increasingly superior lighting solutions that provide value in the progression from candles, gaslights, incandescent bulbs, florescent, to light-emitting diodes for illumination (LEDs). The waste generated by the linear value chain is displaced by a fully circular value chain. For example, a new ecosystem for circular value chains focused on plastics, electronics, food, and fashion/textiles.[101]

Revolutionary Nondisruptive Creation

Revolutionary nondisruptive creations focus on meaningful transformations and new demand in uncontested space. The target markets for revolutionary nondisruptive creations occur where consumers are not consuming products or are consuming the product in inconvenient or outmoded settings.

A revolutionary nondisruptive creation aims to make the competition irrelevant by focusing on non-consumption through breakthrough solutions, redefining an industry's existing problem and solving it, and identifying and solving a brand-new problem or seizing a brand-new opportunity.[102] Hydrogen cells and nuclear fusion are examples of nondisruptive creations because they provide, if proven implementable, clean energy with cost savings and minimal side effects. Figure 19.24 illustrates the impact of creative adaptation on value and cost.

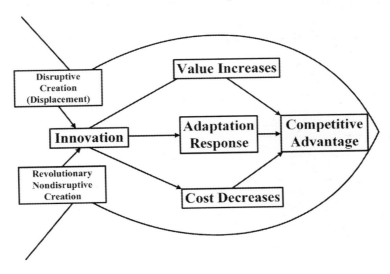

Figure 19.24 Illustration of the Power of Innovations

Source: Adapted from W. Chan Kim and Renée Mauborgne, "Nondisruptive Creation: Rethinking Innovation and Growth," MIT Magazine, Spring 2019, February 21, 2019, accessed January 6, 2020, https://sloanreview.mit.edu/article/nondisruptive-creation-rethinking-innovation-and-growth/

The Innovation Types

Creative adaptation is the ability to generate transformative ideas that have value to explore new sustainability pathway solutions. Creativity is the generation of ideas that have value. Creativity and innovation to sustainability is needed. Tackling climate change will take more than eliminating fossil fuels. Creativity comes from expanding your imagination by learning, exercising, and stimulating your mind with the elements of attitudes, skills, knowledge, sights, sounds, emotions, and experiences. Your mind will make associations among the elements and assemble your thoughts into new insights.

One of the keys is to break out of the tendency to cling to the past. Doing the same things repeatedly and expecting different results is self-defeating. As Einstein said, "We can't solve problems by using the same kind of thinking we used when we created them."[103] Innovations of all types are needed. Figure 19.25 outlines a set of sustainability innovation types with examples.

Innovation Type	Description	Examples
Products	Create new offerings by discovering unmet customer needs and identify underserved customer segments.	Interface, Inc. (sustainable manufacturing), Tide Laundry Detergent (cold water), ENERGY STAR® Certified Products, and Fair Trade Certified Coffee.
Customer Experience	Redesign customer interactions across all aspects of a service offering.	Amazon Logistics, Netflix Personalization Algorithms, IKEA Group (assemble furniture yourself).
Solutions	Create new consulting solutions to lead business progress.	Colorifix Ltd, Xylem Inc. (water solutions), Vestas Wind Systems A/S, H2 Green Steel, Solidia Technologies (green cement systems).
Systems	Create integrated and customized offerings that solve end-to-end customer problems.	Tesla, Schneider Electric, Siemens, Johnson Controls, First Solar, and the Honda Life Cycle Assessment (LCA).
Processes	Redesign core operating processes to improve efficiency and effectiveness.	IDEO (Design Thinking), Toyota Production System (TPS), Nucor Steel's Electric Arc Furnace (EAF) Steelmaking, and Loop and TerraCycle (zero waste).
Business Models	Rethink business models including distribution channels, value propositions, and shorter supply-chains.	Whole Foods Market, Eileen Fisher, Target, Wal-Mart, and The Body Shop International Limited.
Managerial	Build purposeful cultures that attract talent. Enhance engagement, function, or organizational form.	Nike, National Geographic Partners, Walt Disney, Intuit, Alphabet, 3M, Steelcase, and Whirlpool.
Platform	Use sharable building block modules to create derivative offerings.	Airbnb and Zipcar (shared economy), Airbus, Boeing, GE, Rolls Royce, ARM, Intel, and Samsung.
Brands	Reuse a brand for a new concept.	Patagonia (Circular Economy Model), Unilever, Danone, Adidas, Puma, Allbirds, Reformation, Birchbox, and Thinx.
Science and Technology	Create new innovations that build new markets or underserved markets.	Novo Nordisk, Carbon Engineering, Bloom Energy, Ecotricity, Ecovative Design, GE Grid Solutions, Enphase Energy, and Skanska (LEED).

Figure 19.25 Illustration of Innovation Types

Source: Adapted from Mohanbir Sawhney, Robert C. Wolcott, and Inigo Arroniz, "The 12 Different ways for Companies to Innovate," Spring 2006, MIT Sloan Management Review accessed https://sloanreview.mit.edu/article/the-different-ways-for-companies-to-innovate/

Artificial Intelligence

In terms of potential for disruption innovation, artificial intelligence (AI) has and will continue to have a broad range of impacts. AI technology can provide meaningful sustainability solutions. Figure 19.26 shows examples of how artificially intelligent innovations can support climate engineering.

Artificial Intelligence for Climate Engineering	
1	Artificial intelligence can be integrated with sensors, the internet of things, and machine learning to implement a smart grid that monitors electrical use to take preemptive action to improve efficiency and reduce costs.
2	Artificial intelligence can distill and coalesce data into actionable insights. For example, data analytics company Kayrros uses satellite images and machine learning to help spot methane leaks.
3	Artificial intelligence can optimize complicated systems. For example, Fero Labs, based in the U.S. and Germany, uses machine learning to improve energy efficiency at cement, steel and chemical companies. And WeaveGrid is helping electric grid operators better integrate electric-vehicle charging.
4	Artificial intelligence can be used to accelerate scientific discovery. For example, the startup Aionics helps speed up the experiments needed to find a new battery material.
5	Artificial intelligence can be used to provide climate simulations quicker. For example, researchers are using artificial intelligence to reduce the time needed to process large, complex climate models.
6	Artificial intelligence can be used to improve predictions. For example, the start-up Kettle uses neural networks to improve forecasts of wildfire risk.

Figure 19.26 Illustration of the Artificial Intelligence Climate Applications

Source: Adapted from Akshat Rathi, "Artificial Intelligence Could Dramatically Speed Up Climate Action," July 27, 2021, accessed July 27, 2021, https://www.bloomberg.com/news/articles/2021-07-27/can-ai-help-tackle-climate-change

Adapted from David González Fernández and Diego Hernandez Diaz, "Staying connected: The investment challenge for electric grids," July 28, 2021, accessed August 6, 2021, https://www.mckinsey.com/business-functions/operations/our insights/staying-connected-the-investment-challenge-for-electric-grids

The Power of Combinatorial Innovations

An analogy can be drawn between Bach's "St. Matthew Passion" and the power of combinatorial innovations needed to address the future of sustainability. "St. Matthew Passion" is a masterpiece of baroque choral music that combines multiple orchestras, choirs, a soloist, and instruments, including strings, woodwinds, brass, and keyboards, like the harpsichord and organ. It is the power of combinations that provides the rich harmonic textures and emotional depth in the music. Similarly, today's complex sustainability challenges require the same level of combinations of innovation. Figure 19.27 illustrates the power of combinatorial innovations in the realm of emissions.

Summary

This chapter presents a seven-part innovation and entrepreneurship sustainability framework model that describes the action steps that are needed for adaptation, mitigation, and resilience. Each part provides a compelling picture of the role innovation and entrepreneurship play in the future of sustainability.

The seven interconnected system parts include leading into the future, transforming the energy system, managing natural resources, building circular value chains, creating awareness and advocacy, empowering corporate sustainability, and forming policy and finance.

The focus is on *how best to build capability* to understand how to apply the combination of innovation, entrepreneurship, and strategy to accelerate and educate for sustainability. The action steps are shown in Figure 19.28.

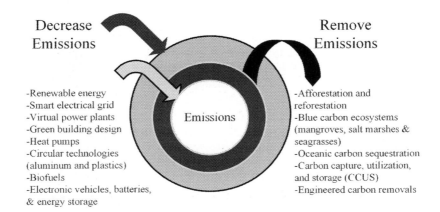

Figure 19.27 Illustration of the Power of Combinatorial Innovations

Source: Adapted from IEA (2023), Net Zero Roadmap: A Global Pathway to Keep the 1.5 °C Goal in Reach, IEA, Paris https://www.iea.org/reports/net-zero-roadmap-a-global-pathway-to-keep-the-15-0c-goal-in-reach, 24, License: CC BY 4.0

Adapted from Ali Shayegan-Rad, Ali Zangeneh, "7 - VPP's participation in demand response aggregation market," Editor(s): Ali Zangeneh, Moein Moeini-Aghtaie, Scheduling and Operation of Virtual Power Plants,

Elsevier, 2022, Pages 163–178, ISBN 9780323852678, https://doi.org/10.1016/B978-0-32-385267-8.00012-3. (https://www.sciencedirect.com/science/article/pii/B9780323852678000123)

Adapted from National Oceanic and Atmospheric Administration, https://oceanservice.noaa.gov/facts/bluecarbon.html

Adapted from Bernd Heid, Martin Linder, Sebastian Mayer, Anna Orthofer, and Mark Patel, "Preview: What would it take to scale critical climate technologies?" December 1, 2023, accessed December 3, 2023, https://www.mckinsey.com/capabilities/sustainability/our-insights/what-would-it-take-to-scale-critical-climate-technologies

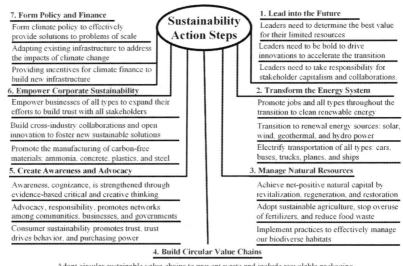

Figure 19.28 The Sustainability Framework Impact Areas

Source: Adapted from John Doerr, *Speed and Scale: An Action Plan for Solving our Climate Crisis Now*, Penguin Business, 2021.

Notes

1. *Wikipedia*, s.v. "Bordeaux Wine," accessed February 19, 2024, https://en.wikipedia.org/wiki/Bordeaux_wine.

2. "The National Institute of Origin and Quality – Institut National de l'origine et de la qualité (INAO)," accessed September 1, 2021, www.inao.gouv.fr/.

3. Jillian Kramer, "English Sparkling Wines Challenge the Supremacy of Champagne, France – Thanks to Climate Change," January 27, 2020, accessed February 19, 2024, www.smithsonianmag.com/science-nature/english-sparkling-wines-challenge-supremacy-champagne-francethanks-climate-change-180974057/.

4. Anson, Jane, "Bordeaux Counts Cost of Frost for 2017 Vintage," *Decanter*, February 1, 2018, accessed July 4, 2023, www.decanter.com/wine-news/opinion/news-blogs-anson/bordeaux-wine-frost-2017-vintage-383633/.

5. Eleanor Beardsley, "Climate Change Is Disrupting Centuries-Old Methods of Winemaking in France," *NPR*, November 5, 2019, accessed February 19, 2024, www.npr.org/sections/thesalt/2019/11/05/773097167/climate-change-is-disrupting-centuries-old-methods-of-winemaking-in-france.

6. Norimitsu Onishi, "For France, American Vines Still Mean Sour Grapes," August 29, 2021, accessed September 1, 2021, www.nytimes.com/2021/08/29/world/europe/france-wine-usa.html.

7. Sean McAllister, "How Is Climate Change Affecting Wine?" *Zurich, News & Media, Magazine*, February 7, 2023, accessed July 4, 2023, www.zurich.com/en/media/magazine/2021/how-does-climate-change-affect-wine.

8. "What Is Sustainability? Definition, Types and Examples," 2022, Satander Universities, June 4, 2022, accessed July 14, 2023, www.becas-santander.com/en/blog/what-is-sustainability.html.

9. "What Is Sustainability? Definition, Types and Examples," 2022, Satander Universities, June 4, 2022, accessed July 14, 2023, www.becas-santander.com/en/blog/what-is-sustainability.html.

10. *Wikipedia*, s.v. "Precautionary Principle," accessed June 21, 2022, https://en.wikipedia.org/wiki/Precautionary_principle.

11. A. Wallace Hayes, "The Precautionary Principle," *Arhiv za Higijenu Rada i Toksikologiju* 56, no. 2 (June 2005), 161–166. PMID: 15968832, accessed October 16, 2021, https://pubmed.ncbi.nlm.nih.gov/15968832/.

12. Center for Disease Control, "Per- and Polyfluoroalkyl Substances (PFAS)," accessed October 16, 2021, www.cdc.gov/niosh/topics/pfas/default.html.

13. Ian T. Cousins, Robin Vestergren, Zhanyun Wang, Martin Scheringer, and Michael S. McLachlan, "The Precautionary Principle and Chemicals Management: The Example of Perfluoroalkyl Acids in Groundwater," *Environment International* 94 (2016), 331–340. https://doi.org/10.1016/j.envint.2016.04.044, accessed February 19, 2024, www.sciencedirect.com/science/article/pii/S0160412016301775.

14. "Fifth National Climate Assessment," accessed November 14, 2023, https://nca2023.globalchange.gov/ and www.globalchange.gov/our-work/fifth-national-climate-assessment.

15. "Our Changing Planet-The U.S. Global Change Research Program for Fiscal Year 2023," accessed November 14, 2023, https://downloads.globalchange.gov/ocp/ocp2023/Our-Changing-Planet_FY2023.pdf.

16. "U.S. Global Change Research Program 2022–2031 Strategic Plan," accessed November 14, 2023, https://downloads.globalchange.gov/strategic-plan/2022/USGCRP_2022-2031_Decadal_Strategic_Plan.pdf.

17. Intergovernmental Panel on Climate Change, "Climate Change 2023, Synthesis Report, Summary for Policymakers," accessed July 11, 2023, www.ipcc.ch/report/ar6/syr/downloads/report/IPCC_AR6_SYR_SPM.pdf, 4.

18. Holly Jean Buck, "Carry the Zero," June 14, 2022, accessed June 26, 2022, www.sierraclub.org/sierra/2022-2-summer/feature/carry-the-zero-carbon-dioxide-removal.

19. "Animal Agriculture's Impact on Climate Change," accessed January 29, 2021, https://climatenexus.org/climate-issues/food/animal-agricultures-impact-on-climate-change/.

20. "Global Greenhouse Gas Emissions Data," accessed February 19, 2024, www.epa.gov/ghgemissions/global-greenhouse-gas-emissions-data.

21. Charlie Campbell, "How China Could Change the World by Taking Meat Off the Menu," January 22, 2021, accessed January 29, 2021, https://time.com/5930095/china-plant-based-meat/.

22. Judith A. Curry, *Climate Uncertainty and Risk: Rethinking Our Response* (London: Anthem Press Wimbledon Publishing Company, 2023).

23. "Global Climate Change Indicators," accessed November 3, 2023, www.climate.gov/news-features/understanding-climate/climate-change-global-temperature#:~:text=According%20to%20NOAA's%202021%20Annual,0.18%20%C2%B0C)%20per%20decade.

24. Judith A. Curry, *Climate Uncertainty and Risk: Rethinking Our Response* (London: Anthem Press Wimbledon Publishing Company, 2023), 3.
25. "The Latest IPCC Report: What Is It and Why Does It Matter?" April 2022, accessed May 31, 2022, www.nature.org/en-us/what-we-do/our-insights/perspectives/ipcc-report-climate-change/.
26. "UN Climate Report: We're on Fast Track to Disaster, Warns Guterres," April 4, 2022, accessed September 15, 2023, www.globalissues.org/news/2022/04/04/30515.
27. David Gray, "What Makes Successful Frameworks Rise Above the Rest," November 3, 2023, accessed July 7, 2023, https://sloanreview.mit.edu/article/what-makes-successful-frameworks-rise-above-the-rest/.
28. Alejandro Sandoval, Bill Lacivita, and Ignacio Marcos, "Transform the Whole Business, Not Just Parts," *McKinsey & Company*, October 2019, accessed July 7, 2023, www.mckinsey.com/capabilities/operations/our-insights/transform-the-whole-business-not-just-the-parts.
29. Emily Chasan, "The Oil Crash Created a Recycled Plastic Trap," May 6, 2020, accessed September 1, 2021, www.bloomberg.com/news/articles/2020-05-06/oil-crash-means-single-use-plastic-is-back-as-recycling-struggles.
30. Warren Bennis, *On Becoming a Leader* (Reading, MA: Addison-Wesley, 1989).
31. Anna Maria Gillis, "Read a Biographical Essay, John Muir: Nature's Witness," March 17, 2011, accessed September 1, 2021, www.pbs.org/wnet/americanmasters/john-muir-in-the-new-world-read-a-biographical-essay-john-muir-natures-witness/1806/.
32. Anna Maria Gillis, "Read a Biographical Essay, John Muir: Nature's Witness," March 17, 2011, accessed September 1, 2021, www.pbs.org/wnet/americanmasters/john-muir-in-the-new-world-read-a-biographical-essay-john-muir-natures-witness/1806/.
33. Theodore Roosevelt and Conservation, *National Park Service*, accessed February 19, 2024, www.nps.gov/thro/learn/historyculture/theodore-roosevelt-and-conservation.htm.
34. Mohanbir Sawhney, Robert C. Wolcott, and Inigo Arroniz, "The 12 Different Ways for Companies to Innovate," *MIT Sloan Management Review*, Spring 2006, accessed February 19, 2024, https://sloanreview.mit.edu/article/the-different-ways-for-companies-to-innovate/.
35. Kanika Chandaria, Marco Duso, Michel Frédeau, Jesper Nielsen, Dennis Pamlin, and Cornelius Pieper, "The Next Generation of Climate Innovation," March 22, 2021, accessed August 26, 2021, www.bcg.com/publications/2021/next-generation-climate-innovation.
36. Simran Jeet Singh, "Boards Need Real Diversity, Not Tokenism," August 31, 2021, accessed September 1, 2021, https://hbr.org/2021/08/boards-need-real-diversity-not-tokenism.
37. World Economic Forum, "Measuring Stakeholder Capitalism Towards Common Metrics and Consistent Reporting of Sustainable Value Creation," September 22, 2020, accessed February 19, 2024, www.weforum.org/reports/measuring-stakeholder-capitalism-towards-common-metrics-and-consistent-reporting-of-sustainable-value-creation.
38. Anna Granskog, Eric Hannon, Solveigh Hieronimus, Marie Klaeyle, and Angela Winkle, "How Companies Capture the Value of Sustainability: Survey Findings," April 28, 2021, accessed November 3, 2023, www.mckinsey.com/business-functions/sustainability/our-insights/how-companies-capture-the-value-of-sustainability-survey-findings.
39. Tom Hellstern, Kimberly Henderson, Sean Kane, and Matt Rogers, "Innovating to Net Zero: An Executive's Guide to Climate Technology," October 28, 2021, accessed November 1, 2021, www.mckinsey.com/business-functions/sustainability/our-insights/innovating-to-net-zero-an-executives-guide-to-climate-technology.
40. *Wikipedia*, s.v. "El Hierro," accessed January 12, 2020, https://en.wikipedia.org/wiki/El_Hierro.
41. Lauren Frayer, "Tiny Spanish Island Nears Its Goal: 100 Percent Renewable Energy," *NPR*, September 28, 2014, NPR, accessed September 15, 2023, www.npr.org/sections/parallels/2014/09/17/349223674/tiny-spanish-island-nears-its-goal-100-percent-renewable-energy.
42. Niagara Power Project, accessed September 1, 2021, www.nypa.gov/power/generation/niagara-power-project.
43. Stephen, Johnson, *How We Got to Now: Six Innovations That Made the Modern World* (New York: Riverhead, 2014).
44. "Food Waste," accessed April 19, 2021, www.hsph.harvard.edu/nutritionsource/sustainability/food-waste/.
45. "Kroger's 2020 Environmental, Social & Governance (ESG) Report," accessed January 26, 2021, http://sustainability.kroger.com/index.html.
46. Cecilia Jamasmie, "Electric Car Dreams May Be Dashed by 2050 on Lack of Cobalt, Lithium Supplies," March 16, 2018, accessed August 26, 2021, www.mining.com/electric-cars-dreams-may-shattered-2050-lack-cobalt-lithium-supplies/.
47. Kelly Rippy, "These 3 Energy Storage Technologies Can Help Solve the Challenge of Moving to 100% Renewable Electricity," August 26, 2021, accessed August 26, 2021, https://theconversation.

com/these-3-energy-storage-technologies-can-help-solve-the-challenge-of-moving-to-100-renewable-electricity-161564.

48. Emily Chasan, "Mining Rare Earths for a Renewable Future," July 29, 2020, accessed February 19, 2024, www.bloomberg.com/news/articles/2020-07-29/mining-rare-earths-for-a-renewable-future-green-insight.

49. Monika van den Bos Verma, Linda de Vreede⊃a, Thom Achterbosch, and Martine M. Rutten "Consumers Discard a Lot More Food Than Widely Believed: Estimates of Global Food Waste Using an Energy Gap Approach and Affluence Elasticity of Food Waste," *PLoS ONE* 15, no. 2 (February 19, 2024), e0228369, https://doi.org/10.1371/journal.pone.0228369.

50. Florida Keys National Marine Sanctuary 2011 Condition Report, accessed July 7, 2023, https://sanctuaries.noaa.gov/science/condition/fknms/.

51. Florida Keys National Marine Sanctuary Restoration Blueprint, accessed July 7, 2023, https://floridakeys.noaa.gov/blueprint/.

52. IPBES (2019): Summary for policymakers of the global assessment report on biodiversity and ecosystem services of the Intergovernmental Science-Policy Platform on Biodiversity and Ecosystem Services. S. Díaz, J. Settele, E. S. Brondízio, H. T. Ngo, M. Guèze, J. Agard, A. Arneth, P. Balvanera, K. A. Brauman, S. H. M. Butchart, K. M. A. Chan, L. A. Garibaldi, K. Ichii, J. Liu, S. M. Subramanian, G. F. Midgley, P. Miloslavich, Z. Molnár, D. Obura, A. Pfaff, S. Polasky, A. Purvis, J. Razzaque, B. Reyers, R. Roy Chowdhury, Y. J. Shin, I. J. Visseren-Hamakers, K. J. Willis, and C. N. Zayas, eds., *IPBES Secretariat*, Bonn, Germany, 56, accessed February 19, 2024, https://doi.org/10.5281/zenodo.3553579.

53. "Intergovernmental Science-Policy Platform on Biodiversity and Ecosystem Services (IPBES) Global Assessment Report," 2019, accessed March 19, 2024, www.un.org/sustainabledevelopment/blog/2019/05/nature-decline-unprecedented-report/.

54. McFadden Daniel, "The Tragedy of the Commons," September 10, 2001, accessed February 19, 2024, www.forbes.com/asap/2001/0910/061.html.

55. Tim Brown and Barry Kātz, *Change by Design: How Design Thinking Transforms Organizations and Inspires Innovation* (New York: Harper Business, 2009), 201.

56. United States Department of Agriculture, "Forest Carbon FAQs," accessed May 28, 2022, www.fs.usda.gov/sites/default/files/Forest-Carbon-FAQs.pdf.

57. Paul Rauber, "Suck It Up," June 14, 2022, accessed June 26, 2022, www.sierraclub.org/sierra/2022-2-summer/feature/suck-it-up-carbon-dioxide-removal.

58. "The Circular Transformation of Industries: Unlocking New Value in a Resource-Constrained World," *White Paper, World Economic Forum, in Collaboration with Bain & Company*, University of Cambridge, and INSEAD, accessed October 5, 2023, www3.weforum.org/docs/WEF_Circular_Transformation_of_Industries_2022.pdf.

59. Karolin Frankenberger, Fabian Takacs, and Richard Stechow, "A Step Toward Making Your Company More Sustainable," *Harvard Business Review*, January 11, 2021, accessed October 5, 2023, https://hbr.org/2021/01/a-step-toward-making-your-company-more-sustainable.

60. Honda, "2019 North American Environmental Report," accessed November 3, 2023, https://global.honda/en/sustainability/cq_img/report/pdf/2023/Honda-SR-2023-en-004.pdf.

61. *Investopedia*, s.v. "Value Chain," accessed March 27, 2021, www.investopedia.com/terms/v/valuechain.asp.

62. *Wikipedia*, s.v. "Value Chain," accessed November 3, 2023, https://en.wikipedia.org/wiki/Value_chain.

63. Shardul Agrawala Peter Börkey, "Business Models for the Circular Economy," *OECD*, October 2018, accessed February 19, 2024, https://dokumen.pub/business-models-for-the-circular-economy-opportunities-and-challenges-for-policy-9264311416-9789264311411.html.

64. Shardul Agrawala Peter Börkey, "Business Models for the Circular Economy," *OECD*, October 2018, accessed November 3, 2023, www.oecd.org/environment/waste/policy-highlights-business-models-for-the-circular-economy.pdf.

65. Elizabeth Elkin, "Green Packaging Isn't Good Enough Anymore," May 8, 2021, accessed October 5, 2023, www.bloomberg.com/news/articles/2021-05-08/the-no-packaging-movement-is-gaining-momentum-on-climate-worries.

66. Elizabeth Elkin, "Green Packaging Isn't Good Enough Anymore," May 8, 2021, accessed October 5, 2023, www.bloomberg.com/news/articles/2021-05-08/the-no-packaging-movement-is-gaining-momentum-on-climate-worries.

67. *Wikipedia*, s.v. "Cathode-Ray Tube," accessed December 16, 2019, https://en.wikipedia.org/wiki/Cathode-ray_tube.

68. "OECD Skills Outlook 2023," accessed December 19, 2023, www.oecd.org/education/oecd-skills-outlook-e11c1c2d-en.htm.

69. Richard Feynman, accessed February 19, 2024, http://en.wikiquote.org/wiki/Richard_Feynman.

70. Jared M. Diamond, *Upheaval* (London: Allen Lane, an imprint of Penguin Books, 2019).
71. "P&G Pro Line Coldwater Laundry Detergent," accessed November 1, 2023, https://pgpro.com/en-us/brands/tide-professional/coldwater-laundry-detergent.
72. "Enzymes, Directed Evolution, and the Science of Clean Laundry," accessed November 12, 2023, www.statnews.com/sponsor/2018/02/22/clean-laundry-enzyme-science/.
73. "Tide Detergent Ingredients A-Z," accessed November 12, 2023, https://tide.com/en-us/our-commitment/ingredients-and-safety/tide-detergent-ingredients-a-to-z.
74. "Tide Reinvents Clean on Journey to Decarbonize Laundry with Efforts to Turn Consumers to Cold, Explore Carbon Capture and Reduce Virgin Plastic," March 18, 2021, accessed November 1, 2023, https://news.pg.com/news-releases/news-details/2021/Tide-Reinvents-Clean-on-Journey-to-Decarbonize-Laundry-with-Efforts-to-Turn-Consumers-to-Cold-Explore-Carbon-Capture-and-Reduce-Virgin-Plastic/default.aspx.
75. Kathleen McLaughlin and Andrew Steer, "Why Walmart and Other Companies Are Sticking With the Paris Climate Deal," *New York Times*, November 2019, accessed February 19, 2024, www.nytimes.com/2019/11/06/opinion/climate-change-walmart-paris.html.
76. Ariel Babcock, Sarah Keohane Williamson, and Tim Koller, "How Executives Can Help Sustain Value Creation for the Long Term," July 22, 2021, accessed February 19, 2024, www.mckinsey.com/business-functions/strategy-and-corporate-finance/our-insights/how-executives-can-help-sustain-value-creation-for-the-long-term.
77. Kevin Sneader and Shubham Singhal, "The Next Normal Arrives: Trends that Will Define 2021 – And Beyond," January 4, 2021, accessed January 9, 2021, www.mckinsey.com/featured-insights/leadership/the-next-normal-arrives-trends-that-will-define-2021-and-beyond, 12.
78. "Fifth National Climate Assessment," accessed November 14, 2023, https://nca2023.globalchange.gov/ and www.globalchange.gov/our-work/fifth-national-climate-assessment.
79. "Our Changing Planet-The U.S. Global Change Research Program for Fiscal Year 2023," accessed November 14, 2023, https://downloads.globalchange.gov/ocp/ocp2023/Our-Changing-Planet_FY2023.pdf.
80. "U.S. Global Change Research Program 2022–2031 Strategic Plan," accessed November 14, 2023, https://downloads.globalchange.gov/strategic-plan/2022/USGCRP_2022-2031_Decadal_Strategic_Plan.pdf.
81. Kathleen McLaughlin and Andrew Steer, "Why Walmart and Other Companies Are Sticking with the Paris Climate Deal," *New York Times*, November 2019, accessed February 19, 2024, www.nytimes.com/2019/11/06/opinion/climate-change-walmart-paris.html.
82. "Global Commission on Adaptation," September 13, 2019, accessed March 19, 2024, https://gca.org/global-commission-on-adaptation/report *and* https://gca.org/about-us/the-global-commission-on-adaptation/.
83. "Global Commission on Adaptation," September 13, 2019, accessed March 19, 2024, https://gca.org/global-commission-on-adaptation/report *and* https://gca.org/about-us/the-global-commission-on-adaptation/.
84. Christoper Blaufelder, Cindy Levey, Peter Mannion, and Dickon Pinner, "A Blueprint for Scaling Voluntary Carbon Markets to Meet the Climate Challenge," *McKinsey Sustainability*, January 29, 2021, accessed October 19, 2023, www.mckinsey.com/capabilities/sustainability/our-insights/a-blueprint-for-scaling-voluntary-carbon-markets-to-meet-the-climate-challenge.
85. Varsha Ramesh Walsh and Michael W. Toffel, "What Every Leader Needs to Know About Carbon Credits," December 15, 2023, https://hbr.org/2023/12/what-every-leader-needs-to-know-about-carbon-credits.
86. Varsha Ramesh Walsh and Michael W. Toffel, "What Every Leader Needs to Know About Carbon Credits," December 15, 2023, https://hbr.org/2023/12/what-every-leader-needs-to-know-about-carbon-credits.
87. David Gray, "What Makes Successful Frameworks Rise Above the Rest," April 29, 2021, accessed November 03, 2023, https://sloanreview.mit.edu/article/what-makes-successful-frameworks-rise-above-the-rest/.
88. Stephen Bungay, "5 Myths About Strategy," *Harvard Business Review*, April 9, 2019, accessed April, 2024, https://hbr.org/2019/04/5-myths-about-strategy.
89. Stephen Bungay, "5 Myths About Strategy," *Harvard Business Review*, April 9, 2019, accessed June 26, 2021, https://hbr.org/2019/04/5-myths-about-strategy.
90. Alan G. Lafley and Roger L. Martin, *Playing to Win* (Boston: Harvard Business Review Press, 2013), 5.
91. Alexander Osterwalder, Yves Pigneur, and Y. Christopjer, "Clarifying Business Models: Origins, Present and Future of the Concept," *Communications of the Assoc. of Information Systems* 15, no.

May (July 2005), accessed May 18, 2021, www.researchgate.net/publication/37426694_Clarifying_Business_Models_Origins_Present_and_Future_of_the_Concept.

92. Vijay Govindarajan and Chris Trimble, "The CEO's Role in Business Model Reinvention," January–February 2011, accessed September 7, 2021, https://hbr.org/2011/01/the-ceos-role-in-business-model-reinvention.

93. Aaron De Smet, Wenting Gao, Kimberly Henderson, and Thomas Hundertmark, "Organizing for Sustainability Success: Where, and How, Leaders Can Start," August 10, 2021, accessed November 1, 2021, www.mckinsey.com/business-functions/sustainability/our-insights/organizing-for-sustainability-success-where-and-how-leaders-can-start.

94. Johnson Stephen, *How We Got to Now: Six Innovations That Made the Modern World* (New York: Riverhead, 2014).

95. BrainyQuotes, accessed September 1, 2021, www.brainyquote.com/quotes/albert_einstein_385842.

96. *Wikipedia*, s.v. "Aviation Biofuel," accessed August 26, 2021, https://en.wikipedia.org/wiki/Aviation_biofuel#Sustainable_fuels.

97. Niraj Chokshi, "Electric Planes, Once a Fantasy, Start to Take to the Skies," November 3, 2023, revised November 4, 2023, accessed November 13, 2023, www.nytimes.com/2023/11/03/business/electric-planes-beta-technologies.html.

98. Kelly Rippy, "These 3 Energy Storage Technologies Can Help Solve the Challenge of Moving to 100% Renewable Electricity," August 26, 2021, accessed November 3, 2023, https://theconversation.com/these-3-energy-storage-technologies-can-help-solve-the-challenge-of-moving-to-100-renewable-electricity-161564.

99. Jeff Dyer, Paul Godfrey, Robert Jensen, and David Bryce, *Strategic Management: Concepts and Cases*, 2nd ed. (New York: John Wiley & Sons, Inc, 2018), 182.

100. Jeff Dyer, Paul Godfrey, Robert Jensen, and David Bryce, *Strategic Management: Concepts and Cases*, 2nd ed. (New York: John Wiley & Sons, Inc, 2018), 184.

101. "The Circular Economy Challenge," https://initiatives.weforum.org/the-circular-transformation-of-industries/home.

102. W. Chan Kim and Renee Mauborgne, *Blue Ocean Shift* (New York: Hachette, 2017), 36.

103. BrainyQuotes, accessed September 1, 2021, www.brainyquote.com/quotes/albert_einstein_385842.

20 Innovation Architecture

The Orchestra

The Full Score

In the world of orchestral music, a score is a manuscript in written form for a musical composition. The printed form of a musical score is known as sheet music. The score is made up of a set of staffs, a set of five horizontal lines and four spaces on which notes (tones) are placed. A full orchestral score is used by the conductor that shows all the parts of a large work, with each part on separate staffs in vertical alignment.[1] The full score is the music architecture that contains each of the four sections of the orchestra ordered from the highest to the lowest sounding: woodwinds, brass, percussion, and strings. Each musician plays their part from their music score as the conductor of the orchestra leads the musicians using the full score with a baton to signal instructions to the performers.

The conductor's full score is unique, important, and practical because it enables the composers and performers to have the freedom to create and innovate within an organized discipline. When conducting a symphony, the full score is the architecture that enables the conductor to understand what each performer should be playing with their instruments. The full score provides the framework to enable the musician to play with a sense of autonomy of self-expression. The orchestra cannot play effectively without a conductor using a full score.

Innovation architecture is like a full score that can enable an organization to increase their innovation capability more effectively. Imagine that organizations apply the orchestra full score concept to the discipline of innovation to facilitate the freedom of creativity within the discipline of a structure framework.

Like the full score for an orchestra, innovation architecture is the way a new venture or an organization can be led to perform at the highest level. Innovation architecture is the structure to transform a venture or organization from the present to the future and the future next. Each person is given the freedom to perform in an architectural framework as they are guided along a pathway to the desired destination.

Innovation in a discipline like music, architecture, or engineering needs an architectural framework to allow managers to make a set of five integrated choices: people, partnerships, purpose, performance, and processes. Just like a suspension bridge, an organization needs an architectural framework to provide meaningful value and simultaneously adapt to the turbulence of our world. Bridge building is just like organizational innovation building. Organizations that are forward thinking cannot *effectively* pursue any degree or type of innovation without a future-centric architectural framework.

DOI: 10.4324/9781003034308-21

Introduction

In developing an innovation architecture framework, it can be organized into five sections: people, partnerships, purpose, performance, and process. An innovation architectural framework is a blueprint for how innovation can be systematized, organized, and accelerated. For example, building a bridge can be a metaphor for an entrepreneur or an organization building a new venture or innovating. Creating innovation architecture is akin to constructing a bridge between the aspirations of entrepreneurs and organizations and their desired destinations. It serves as a pivotal blueprint for the systematic, organized, and accelerated pursuit of innovation. In essence, it provides the scaffolding and guidance necessary to transform ambitious visions into tangible realities.

People. "High tech versus high touch" is a key struggle in today's fast-paced world. The people component emphasizes the significance of the human element in innovation. Entrepreneurs and organizations are driven by individuals with diverse skills, knowledge, and perspectives. Innovation architecture ensures that these talents are harnessed efficiently, fostering a culture of creativity and collaboration. By nurturing an environment where individuals are empowered to generate novel ideas and solutions, this framework catalyzes the innovation process.

Partnerships. Partnerships represent a foundational cornerstone. Collaboration with external entities, whether other businesses, research institutions, or communities, injects fresh insights and resources into the innovation ecosystem. An effective innovation architecture strategically identifies and nurtures these partnerships, thereby expanding the collective knowledge and capabilities available to entrepreneurs and organizations.

Purpose. The purpose is about defining the "why" behind innovation. Clarity in purpose not only aligns efforts, but also inspires and motivates teams. It provides a guiding star, ensuring that innovation efforts remain directed toward meaningful goals.

Performance. Performance measurement is crucial to ensure the efficacy of innovation initiatives. The architecture allows for the establishment of key performance indicators, enabling the continuous assessment of progress and the ability to adjust strategies as needed. A data-driven approach helps entrepreneurs and organizations stay on course.

Process. Lastly, the process component provides the roadmap for bringing ideas to fruition. It delineates the stages, from idea generation to market implementation, ensuring that innovation is not a haphazard venture but a well-structured and efficient process.

The creation of an innovation architecture adds value for innovators, entrepreneurs, and organizations. It offers a systematic approach to navigate the complex journey of innovation, leveraging human potential, fostering strategic partnerships, defining purpose, measuring performance, and following a well-defined process. By embracing such a framework, future generations gain the ability to transform concepts into impactful innovations, bridging the gap between vision and reality. It is the blueprint for building the bridges that connect dreams with achievements, fueling progress and growth.

Architectural Concepts

The discipline of architecture provides an interesting analogy when it comes to innovation and entrepreneurship. It is the art and science of designing and building structures. An architectural blueprint is created using a deliberate decision-making process to describe how the components are selected to achieve the most useful holistic function. Each of the components are designed to interact collaboratively with one another to achieve the highest level of effectiveness.

The innovation architectural framework, like the conductor's full musical score, provides a way for all components of an organization to be integrated holistically as a system rather than haphazardly. An innovation architectural framework balances the autonomy and discipline that allows everyone to build innovation capability by contributing to the five integrated choices: people, partnerships, purpose, performance, and process.

Innovation Importance

McKinsey analyzed about 650 of the largest public companies that achieved profitable growth relative to their industry between 2016 and 2021 while also excelling in innovation. The McKinsey research has identified a group of companies known as innovation growers that out-innovate and outgrow their peers. "In the face of constant disruptions, leading companies become 'innovative growers,' excelling at growth and innovation – and outperforming their peers in the process."[2]

While some of these companies outgrew their peers, and others were more innovative than competitors, 53 "innovative growers" managed to do both. The research is based on mastery of the evidenced based eight essentials of innovation that correlate with strong financial performance. "Most of our innovative growers achieved total shareholder returns (TSR) above their industry median between 2012 and 2022."[3] This research suggests that companies that are deliberate about innovation and adopt an innovation architecture's structured model can add measurable value to corporations.

McKinsey's evidence-based research has identified essentials that enhance understanding of innovation architecture. This research describes a set of cross-cutting human practices and processes to build capability. The first four (aspire, choose, discover, and evolve) are strategic and creative in nature and help set and prioritize the terms and conditions under which innovation is more likely to thrive. The next four essentials (accelerate, scale, extend, and mobilize) deal with how to deliver and organize innovation repeatedly over time and with enough value to contribute meaningfully to overall performance.[4]

Growth or Extinction

Innovation is widely regarded as being important, yet a full understanding of how to utilize the discipline of innovation is not universally understood. In a study done by McKinsey & Company, it was revealed that 84% of executives believed that innovation was critical to their business's growth, but only 6% were satisfied with their company's current innovation performance.[5]

KPMG (Klynveld Peat Marwick Goerdeler) conducted two studies, the first with 215 respondents and the second with about 25 "role model" companies. Nearly 60% of respondents indicated that they were at the earliest stages of their innovation efforts.[6] The "role model" companies were at the more advanced end of the innovation maturity spectrum. "Among the role model set, there is less focus on incremental and adjacent innovation, and more (37 percent, compared to 25 percent) on transformational work."[7]

In general, when an organization stops producing new ideas and ceases to innovate it will eventually become extinct. Striving for innovation provides the promise for human ingenuity to be the transformational force to provide broad value for all stakeholders. Many organizations are built to repeat specific past outcomes, but lack the innovation architecture for transforming themselves forward into the future. In this chapter we focus on how to ensure that an innovation architecture can provide the vitality to never let organizations become extinct.

The Bridge Metaphor

Blending the architecture and bridge metaphors provides an illuminating insight into creating an innovation architecture. For example, a bridge is built based on a blueprint of the architecture that describes the entire structure and how it is to be constructed. Forward-thinking innovators know that it would be unwise for an organization to pursue any innovation pathway without first having an innovation architecture.

The purpose of a bridge is to move people to their next destination. A bridge that does not have a sustainable architectural framework will fail if it encounters turbulence from winds and floods. For example, the city of Sweetwater, Florida, built a walkway that was opened on March 10, 2018, over a busy thoroughfare spanning the campus of Florida International University. It collapsed five days later March 15, 2018.[8]

In one of the most famous bridge collapses, the first Tacoma Narrows Bridge in the state of Washington was opened on July 1, 1940. This suspension bridge spanned the Tacoma Narrows strait of Puget Sound. On November 7, 1940, the bridge collapsed due to a wind-induced physical phenomenon known was aerostatic flutter.[9] Aerostatic flutter is an instability due to the interaction between aerodynamic, inertial, and elastic forces.[10] The bridge's swaying and gyrations in the wind eventually caused the structure to collapse.

Just like a bridge, an organization needs an architectural framework to provide the strategic flexibility to sustain the dynamic forces of complexity, change, and competition. An architectural framework provides an integrated pathway to the future by facilitating the building of scalable, meaningful, and significant innovation capability to move people to their next destination while simultaneously improving their lives.

Bridge building is like people and organization building. Just like a suspension bridge, an organization needs an architectural framework to provide meaningful value and simultaneously adapt to the turbulence of our world. An architectural framework provides a richer understanding of the major components that are needed to achieve a meaningful holistic humanistic design to provide high-order value creation known as innovation.

Architectural Framework

An architectural framework to build innovation capability is an effective way to achieve meaningful progress and build a discipline of innovation. According to a study by Accenture,

> The effective innovators had developed comprehensive approaches to pursuing innovation. They had integrated their capabilities together in a single architecture. In contrast, more than half of the executives in our study said that innovation was "an ad-hoc creative process" – in other words, moments of inspiration produced by isolated teams located a safe distance from the core business.[11]

Like a full orchestral score in music, an innovation architecture framework can be organized into sections: people, partnerships, purpose, performance, and process as shown in Figure 20.1.

An innovation architectural framework is a blueprint for how innovation can be systematized, organized, and accelerated. For example, bridge-building is just like organizational innovation building. Organizations that are forward thinking cannot effectively pursue any degree or type of innovation without a future-centric architectural framework. For example, consider a bridge.

1. The architecture of a bridge has three sections: foundation, substructure, and superstructure. Just like a suspension bridge, an organization needs an architectural framework to provide meaningful value and simultaneously adapt to the turbulence of our world.
2. A bridge has two basic characteristics: degree and type. A bridge has degrees that can be viewed in scale from a small step-stone bridge to a medium-sized covered-bridge and to a large cantilever bridge. There are types of bridges, such as suspension, truss, cable-stayed, arch, and bowstring.

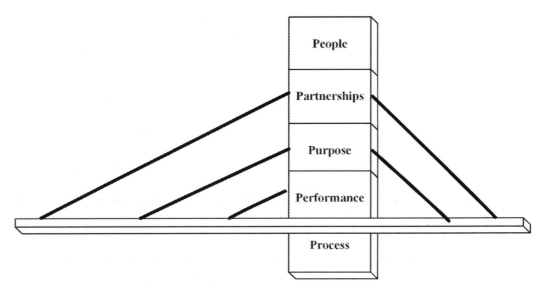

Figure 20.1 Illustration of the Architectural Framework for Building Innovation Capability

Source: Acknowledgements: Omar Abbosh, Vedrana Savic, Paul Nunes, & Michael Moore, How to unlock the value of your innovation investments, Accenture, https://www.accenture.com/gb-en/insights/consulting/innovation-investment-value

Omar Abbosh, Vedrana Savic, & Michael Moore, What Sets the Most Effective Innovators Apart, Harvard Business Review, March 8, 2019.

When building a step-stone bridge, there is little need for an architectural blueprint. For instance, a small bridge could be built incrementally without a blueprint because there is little risk even if it breaks. A small bridge built incrementally, like many innovations, provides some value but nowhere near the impact of a large bridge. In contrast, when building a large cantilever bridge, no one would build the bridge without an architectural blueprint. If a large bridge is built incrementally without a blueprint, it would break under demanding conditions.

People

Millau Viaduct

Continuing the bridge metaphor, there are many types of bridges that connect people and communities together and simultaneously beautify their environment. Travelers use the Millau Viaduct to connect Paris and Spain; it is one of the world's most significant engineering achievements.[12] The cable-stayed bridge has a length of 8,070 feet that rises above and spans the gorge valley of the Tarn near Millau in Southern France. This bridge is the tallest in the world with a structural height of 1,104 feet from where the piers emerge from the supporting surface to the top of a bridge tower.

The Millau Viaduct rises higher than the clouds, its form providing not only functionality but also inspiration. This innovation in bridge architecture was based on the unique talents of the team who managed the construction project led by Michel Virlogeux, a bridge structural engineer and the British architect Norman Foster.

Innovation is all about people who conceive and implement inspirational creations. Michel Virlogeux has received several awards for this achievements, such as the IABSE Prize in Venice, the Award of Excellence of the Engineering News Record, the Gold Medal of the Institution of Structural Engineer, the Gold Medal of the Institution of Civil Engineers, the Gustave Magnel Medal, and the Fritz Leonhardt Prize.[13] Norman Foster was been recognized with the Knight Bachelor, granted the title Sir, the Order of Merit (OM), and the Baron Foster of Thames Bank, of Reddish; elected an Associate of the Royal Academy (ARA), a Royal Academician, and Honorary Fellow of the Royal Academy of Engineering; and received a Stirling Prize.[14]

People-Centered Innovation

The top companies understand that talent is their scarcest and most precious form of capital and pursue its development with the rigor of any other business strategy. They promote diversity, equity, and inclusion while energizing the work environments matching the top talent to critical roles to stay ahead of the competition.[15]

There are two aspects of people-centered innovation. The first is that everyone learns the fundamentals of innovation to achieve the most impact. "An innovation is the *conversion* of a novel concept (an invention) into a product, process, or business model that generates revenue and profits."[16] Organizations need to provide an opportunity for each person to develop the competencies, risk tolerance, and resilience that are the foundation for building innovation capability.[17]

The second is to empower people by providing a framework and the freedom to pursue innovation. Each person is expected to take responsibility for significantly meaningful value creation and simultaneously be held accountable.

> The good-to-great companies built a consistent system with clear constraints, but they also gave people freedom and responsibility within the framework of that system. They hired self-discipline people who didn't need to be managed, and then managed the system, not the people.[18]

Learning Organizations

Top innovative organizations focus on continual learning, a growth mindset, curiosity, and deep enthusiasm for experimentation. As circumstances change, a learning orientation enables employees to adapt quickly, reinvent themselves successfully, and repeat the process of renewal.[19]

Today's problems cannot be solved with yesterday's knowledge. Rapid change requires rapid learning, and organizations must be designed to accomplish this. Successful organizations are learning organizations. According to Peter Senge,

> "Learning organizations" [are] organizations where people continually expand their capacity to create the results, they truly desire, where new and expansive patterns of thinking are nurtured, where collective aspiration is set free, and where people are continually learning to see the whole together.[20]

The spirit of building innovation capability resides in the people: the leadership and teams that bridge the gap between the old and new. A culture of innovation has a blend of authority, autonomy, agility, and an action-orientation to effectively instill a willingness to integrate unique ideas into the status quo. A meta-analysis on empowered leadership revealed:

> Our analysis yielded a few main results: First, empowering leaders are much more effective at influencing employee creativity and citizenship behaviour (i.e., behaviour that is not formally recognized or rewarded like helping coworkers or attending work functions that aren't mandatory) than routine task performance.[21]

Consider J. K. Rowling, who was inspirational because of her relentless resilience, pursuit of continuous learning, and adaptability to change. Clayton Christensen says,

> It's not any one set of skills – rather, it's the ability to acquire them. The pace of change – of technology, of our economy – continues to increase. In any environment, it's not necessarily the strongest or smartest that are best able to survive. It's who is best suited to the changing conditions. In today's world, which means always being willing to learn.[22]

Overcoming and Closing Gaps

There are multiple gaps that can affect innovation capability and the competitiveness of businesses and countries throughout the world. According to Hamel and Tennant,

> If your company is really serious about building an innovation engine, then it needs to upgrade everyone's innovation skills, agree on what counts as innovation, establish comprehensive metrics, hold leaders accountable for innovation, and retool its management processes so they foster innovation everywhere, all the time. These can't be isolated initiatives; they must work in harmony.[23]

Three of the most notable gaps in pursing innovation and entrepreneurship are effective decision-making, competencies for the 21st century, and the business/university gap.

The Effective Decision-Making Gap

Future innovation capability ultimately relies on effective decision-making, a meta-competency. As discussed extensively in Chapter 3, "Effective Decision-Making," a meta-competency is an overarching competency that is relevant in a broad range of organizations to multiply innovation and facilitate adaptation and flexibility. Effective decision-making is an essential high-order meta-competency that is needed to apply all competencies.

Over time, our lives are shaped by thousands of decisions. The viability of significant choices, both in individual and organizational contexts can substantially impact the standard of living. The art of making effective decisions is a meta-competency that is not typically taught in traditional education systems. The inclusion of effective decision-making skills and 21st-century competencies throughout all levels of education programs to facilitate the enhancement of decision-making and expertise is ultimately boosting innovation capability.

The 21st-Century Competency Gap

The four super forces of the Fourth Industrial Revolution – technology, society, culture, and the economy – are driving the need for 21st-century competencies that will require the reskilling of more than one billion people by 2030.[24] The World Economic Forum has launched a Reskilling Revolution, a multi-stakeholder initiative aiming to provide better education, new skills, and better work to a billion people around the world by 2030.[25]

According to McKinsey & Company, "Social, emotional, and technological skills are becoming more crucial as intelligent machines take over more physical, repetitive, and basic cognitive tasks."[26] They report that the top missing soft skills are problem solving, critical thinking, innovation and creativity, ability to deal with complexity and ambiguity, and communication. This creates a road map for educators to follow in preparing the next generation of decision-makers.

The Center for Curriculum Redesign has outlined a framework of key 21st-century competencies, which includes character, critical thinking, communication, creativity, curiosity, compassion, and collaboration. Individually and collectively, each offers an opportunity to stimulate creativity and overcome narrow thinking. Figure 20.2 identifies many of the essential 21st-century competencies to facilitate innovation and entrepreneurship.[27] These competencies stem from the four basic purposes of education: personal, social, economic, cultural.[28]

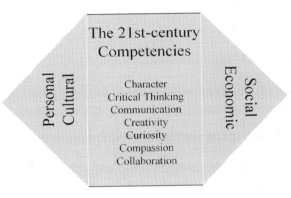

Figure 20.2 Illustration of the 21st-Century Competency

Source: Adapted from Ken Robinson and Lou Aronica. *Creative Schools: The Grassroots Revolution that's Tranforming Education,* (New York: Viking, 2015), 135.

The Business and University Gap

As noted previously, there is a divide between what businesses need and what educational systems provide. Studies continue to highlight the importance of the innovation competencies that are in demand by businesses but not necessarily met by universities. Examples of the top future competencies include communication, problem solving, critical thinking, creativity, emotional intelligence, and collaboration. Social emotional learning that focuses on deep self-knowledge, emotional regulation, and empathy and perspective taking are increasingly relevant.[29]

Scott DeRue, the dean of University of Michigan's Ross School of Business, is an advocate for improving horizonal cross-cutting skills in colleges because many of the core subjects taught have become commodities. Collaboration and complex problem solving can be developed by partnerships between business and universities.[30] Businesses are asking for future competencies and universities are behind in helping students to learn the future interdisciplinary and collaborative competencies that are necessary to provide modern firms a competitive advantage through innovation.

Scott DeRue describes the importance of cross-cutting skills that include interdisciplinary competencies, such as science, technology, art, engineering, and design.[31]

And so, what we're hearing from companies whether they're in technology, whether in professional services, consulting, finance otherwise is they expect, they assume that the core fundamentals, the knowledge of different business functions, finance, marketing, et cetera, they assume that's a given.

What they're really looking for is they want what I often call these horizontal skills, these cross-cutting skills. They want folks who can lead and build teams. They want folks that can enable units to collaborate. They want folks who can really thrive in the context of highly ambiguous, highly complex situations and not get overwhelmed by that, but simplify it, make sense of it and lead to action. They want folks who can deal with the change that's happening in their different industries and sectors and really thrive in that adaptive leadership world."

Partnerships

The Øresund Bridge

A bridge is a connector metaphor that provides a pathway to a destination. By connecting people to share their knowledge and unique and value-added actionable insights, organizations can build a culture and network of innovation. Partnership networks between countries have been proven to add significant value. In the Baltic region, to cross the Øresund strait connecting Malmö, Sweden, and Copenhagen, Denmark you travel over the Øresund Bridge, which runs nearly 8 kilometers (5 miles) to Peberholm, an artificial island, where you enter the Drogden tunnel under the strait for another 4 kilometers (2.5 miles), which allows the ships to travel above. The tunnel has two railway tubes, two road tubes, and one emergency tube.

The Øresund Bridge is a classical cable-stayed bridge structure that has four road lanes and two railway tracks. The bridge project was a collaborative project across the borders of two countries to create a new economic region. In the partnership, the bridge was not built over the narrowest distance between Elsinore, Denmark, and Helsingborg; rather, a longer structure was chosen to provide high value by connecting the overall Øresund Region.

The Medici Effect

In Florence Italy, around the 14th century, a banking family known as the Medicis funded many artistic endeavors, phenomenally advancing the arts. During this period of history, there was a coalescing of ideas that had a multiplying effect known as the "Medici effect."[32] Creative thinking is stimulated through associations. Associations are the ability to make connections by combining concepts across domains of knowledge.[33] Sculpting both *David* and *Pieta* and painting *The Last Judgment* and the ceiling of the Sistine Chapel are examples of Michelangelo Buonarroti's many achievements using associations.[34]

The Medici effect was a synergistic result of a confluence of ideas, cultures, and disciplines brought together through networking. By connecting people to share their knowledge and unique and value-added actionable insights, organizations can build a culture and network of innovation. Research of the world's best innovators has identified networking as one of the essential discovery skills that distinguishes innovators from typical executives.[35]

William Shakespeare's timeless story in the play *Romeo and Juliet* formed the basis for the musical *West Side Story*, which combined dance, music, and a new setting in New York involving two street gangs, the Sharks and the Jets. *West Side Story* is an example of using associations to create a new work of art.

Partnership Networks

Effective organizations develop rich networks of external partners – and manage them as extensions of themselves. The key focus is to create mutually interdependent relationships and flexible boundaries, then expand the value you share by letting each partner focus on the one unique thing that defines their strengths.[36] Research of the world's best innovators has identified networking as one of the essential discovery skills that distinguishes innovators from typical executives. Partnership networks between business firms and universities have been advocated for the future of education. Figure 20.3 depicts this tapestry of interdependent relationships and boundaries.

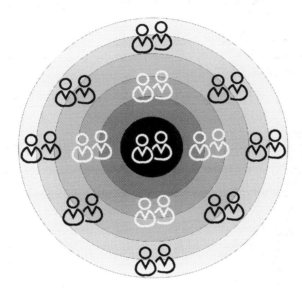

Figure 20.3 Illustration of Partnerships Networks

Scott DeRue, the dean of University of Michigan's Ross School of Business, is an advocate for improving the horizonal cross-cutting skills, interdisciplinary competencies, in colleges such as collaboration and complex problem solving, which can be developed by partnerships between business and universities.[37] DeRue is an advocate of partnership between the world of business and academics, noting, "But I think the future of management education and business education is actually *bringing those two worlds* together."[38] Therefore, a program that focuses on bringing more closely together these two worlds can drive innovation capability. The integration of academics, research, and business partners to achieve shared knowledge, teamwork, and meaningful outcomes can drive innovation.

Business and academic partnerships are built on the principles that elicit trust, the foundation for *bi-directional relationships*. Partnerships are needed to understand the future needs of business so that they can be incorporated into the education systems. This cooperation provides a way for universities to provide talent that is aligned with business needs.

For high-value innovation solutions, pilot projects are needed that are embedded deeply into business and academics. While informed by the past, new models of collaboration need to integrate businesses, students, researchers, and open-minded faculty not bound by the past. By creating a tightly integrated *bi-directional relationship* between business and academics, both can learn from others through an all teach all learn model. Partnership can provide a way to connect people in universities and businesses who have unique and value-added ideas for practical solutions.

Community Partnerships

According to Bussgang and Bacon, writing in *Harvard Business Review,* consumers are looking for more meaningful interactions with the company and fellow buyers of the product or service. In a survey nearly 80% of start-up founders reported that building a community of users was important to their business, with 28% describing it as their competitive moat and critical to their success. "The top five brands in 2019 – Apple, Google, Microsoft, Amazon, and Facebook – have all invested significantly in digital and in-person community engagement across their various product portfolios."[39] Examples of start-ups that have made contributions to the community are shown in Figure 20.4.

There are seven key elements of community partnerships, according to Bussgang and Bacon that are identified in Figure 20.5.[40]

Purpose

The Golden Gate Bridge

Bridges are important for connecting people, but they can influence our lives, hopes, and dreams. The Golden Gate Bridge connects San Francisco with Marin County, crossing the strait known as the

Codeacademy	Codeacademy has more than 50 million people who have taken interactive educational content courses. Codeacademy's success has been its ability to link learners who contribute to the catalog and collaborate to improve their skills.
Fitbit	Fitbit has a brought together a community of more than 25 million members who share and refine their exercise regimes.
Harley Davidson	Harley Davidson has created more than 1,400 local chapters around the world for enthusiasts to get together in person and discuss their bikes.
HITRECORD	HITRECORD has brought more than 750,000 artists, writers, and filmmakers together to collaborate on productions, many of which have shown at Sundance.
Kahn Academy	The Kahn Academy has built a community network that provides free access to commoditized content.
LinkedIn	LinkedIn has created a network of professionals that facilitates the sharing of expertise.
Salesforce	Salesforce created a community of nearly 2 million members who support each other, organize events, produce content, and have become an integral part of its global operations.
Wikipedia	Wikipedia through a community of volunteer editors using open collaboration and the wisdom of the crowds created the largest popular general reference work on the World Wide Web.

Figure 20.4 Illustration of Extending the Reach

Source: Adapted from Jeffrey Bussgang and Jono Bacon, "When Community Becomes Your Competitive Advantage," January 21, 2020, https://hbr.org/2020/01/when-community-becomes-your-competitive-advantage

1. A shared purpose and values.	"As former Instagram executive Bailey Richardson puts it, the community must be able to answer the question 'Why are we coming together?'"
2. Simple, easily accessible value consumption.	"Prospective and existing members can easily see what they're getting: support, events, documentation, the ability to download and use technology, etc. This value is not hidden or buried, it is clearly organized and available."
3. Simple, easily navigable value creation.	"Members can easily create new value for others in the group to consume. This contribution process is (a) crisply defined, (b) simple and intuitive, and (c) provides almost-immediate gratification."
4. Clearly defined incentives and rewards.	"Quality contributions (e.g. content, support, technology, etc.) and community-centric behavior (e.g. mentoring, leadership, and growth) are acknowledged and applauded to build a sense of belonging, unity, and satisfaction."
5. Carefully crafted accountability.	"There is a clearly defined, objective peer review and workflow — for example, reviewing content, code, and events. This doesn't just produce better, more diverse results, it also increases collaboration and skills development."
6. Healthy, diverse participation driven by good leadership.	"When you are intentional about diversity and good conduct and have leaders who embody and empower these important principles, you reduce toxicity and increase value."
7. Open, objective, governance and evolution.	"There is clear, objective governance, and community members can play an active role in reshaping its structure and operational dynamics together, giving them 'skin in the game' and, thus, a sense of ownership and responsibility."

Figure 20.5 Illustration of Community Partnerships

Source: Adapted from Jeffrey Bussgang and Jono Bacon, "When Community Becomes Your Competitive Advantage," January 21, 2020, https://hbr.org/2020/01/when-community-becomes-your-competitive-advantage

Golden Gate. The bridge has a purpose beyond its function because it is valued for the scenic beauty of the Pacific Ocean. Likewise, organizations are not driven solely by their function and profits; they need an inspirational overarching purpose that is driven by their values and guiding principles.

Core Ideology

True competitive advantage through innovation is based on the establishment of guiding principles and purpose. The guiding principles and purpose are the anchor to withstand the turbulence of change. The guiding principles and purpose enable the stability for building trust that is the basis of relationships.

Innovations are transformational and need an anchor to separate the stable operations from the agility that can facilitate breakthrough progress. The stable-operations structure is a whirlwind of distractions that is spinning in the same place in contrast to the agility needed to drive progress by moving forward and upward. These dyadic structures are separated but linked to build on the strengths of each.

In *Built to Last*, authors Jim Collins and Jerry I. Porras studied successful companies to better understand what distinguishes one company from another.[41] They found that exceptional organizations (and people) have a dynamic balance, a duality that includes an unchanging core ideology and a built-in, dynamic adaptability to pursue progress. The duality includes preserving the core ideology (guiding principles and purpose) while leading (drive for progress) the organization into the future.

Exceptional organizations have a core ideology composed of a purpose and guiding principles coupled with a dynamic drive for progress that is illustrated in Figure 20.6. This dyadic model can be achieved by empowering everyone to improve based on a blend of discipline (core ideology) and autonomy (drive for progress) that the architectural framework provides.[42]

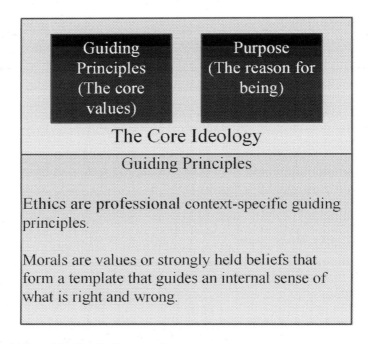

Figure 20.6 Illustration of the Dyadic Framework

Source: Adapted from Jim Collins and Jerry I. Porras, *Built To Last: Succesful Habits of Visionary Companies*, (New York: HaiverCollins, 1994, 1997, 2002), 47.

Adapted from Eric Pliner, "A Framework for Leaders Facing Difficult Decisions," October 13, 2020, https://hbr.org/2020/10/a-framework-for-leaders-facing-difficult-decisions

The Purpose of an Organization

The purpose of an organization provides its meaning. While it sounds simple, the process of finding a purpose can be challenging. Viktor E. Frankl, in his compelling chronicle *Man's Search for Meaning*, describes his horrifying experiences in Auschwitz during World War II.[43] Despite the extreme despair and suffering he witnessed and experienced, Frankl passionately articulates that the meaning of life is found in every moment of life. He writes that we must each take responsibility first to find our voice and then second help others to find their voice. We have the freedom to choose. One can even find meaning during suffering and despair. "In the death camps of Nazi Germany, Frankl saw men who walked through the huts comforting others, giving away their last piece of bread."[44] Those that survived found meaning in their suffering by helping others to find their voice. While extreme, Frankl's experience underscores the critical importance of searching for and identifying purpose in our lives and, by extension, the purpose for our actions, a start-up, or an organization.

Ridley Scott was the director of an Apple advertisement that aired during the Super Bowl in 1984, to launch the Macintosh computer. The ad was based on the George Orwell novel *1984*, which describes a dystopian world led by Big Brother, who promoted conformity. In the ad a female athlete, who represents the Macintosh counterculture, is in a movie theater with an audience of gray-faced men. As she races toward the movie screen carrying a sledgehammer, she thrusts the sledgehammer at the movie screen and destroys the image of Big Brother, who represents the traditional culture of the then-dominant IBM.[45] In the ad, Apple established its purpose to challenge the status quo by inspiring its followers to start with why (a cause or belief), not what or how.[46]

Similarly, with respect to environmental impact, Tesla's purpose is "to accelerate the world's transition to sustainable energy."[47] Tesla's purpose is encompassing to its mission, including providing Tesla patents to their competition. In a counterintuitive move,

> Tesla Motors was created to accelerate the advent of sustainable transport. If we clear a path to the creation of compelling electric vehicles, but then lay intellectual property landmines behind us to inhibit others, we are acting in a manner contrary to that goal. Tesla will not initiate patent lawsuits against anyone who, in good faith, wants to use our technology.[48]

The Guiding Principles of Organizations

The physicist Enrico Fermi was an advocate of the first principles. He won a Nobel Prize in Physics in 1938 and is considered the "father of the nuclear age."[49] Tesla's Elon Musk, like Fermi, applies the first principles that are based on pursing the fundamental assumptions of a system. The concept of the first principles was articulated by the ancient Greek philosopher Aristotle, more than 2,000 years ago. He believed we learn more by understanding a subject's fundamental principles, those "things better known and clearer to us"[50] or, more simply, known by nature. First principles focus on the fundamental truths for what is best for an organization and building on that knowledge.

Elon Musk said,

> You know, the sort of first principles reasoning. Generally, I think there are – what I mean by that is, boil things down to their fundamental truths and reason up from there, as opposed to reasoning by analogy. Through most of our life, we get through life by reasoning by analogy, which essentially means copying what other people do with slight variations. And you have to do that. Otherwise, mentally, you wouldn't be able to get through the day. But when you want to do something new, you have to apply the physics approach. Physics is really figuring out how to discover new things that are counterintuitive, like quantum mechanics. It's really counterintuitive.[51]

True Competitive Advantage

Purpose provides a basis for creating a competitive advantage. While competitive advantage has traditionally focused on generic principles, such as cost or differentiation, either broadly or within a niche (customer value), a more robust competitive advantage equation is based on innovation and entrepreneurship that also considers both the customer value advantage and the environmental (sustainability), social (equality), and governance (leadership), or ESG, advantage. A model of competitive advantage that more fully considers both the customer and society is shown in Figure 20.7.

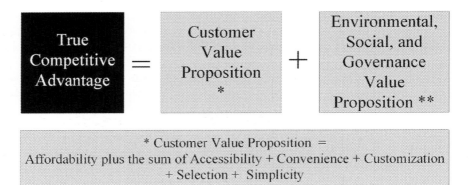

True Competitive Advantage = Customer Value Proposition * + Environmental, Social, and Governance Value Proposition **

* Customer Value Proposition = Affordability plus the sum of Accessibility + Convenience + Customization + Selection + Simplicity

** Environmental, Social, and Governance Value Proposition = The sum of Environmental Factors (e.g., clean energy, conservation of land, air, and water, and climate justice), Social Factors (fair labor practices, human rights, and product safety), and Governance Factors (e.g., net-zero leadership, business ethics, and stakeholder capitalism).

Figure 20.7 Illustration of the True Competitive Advantage Innovation Equation

Performance

Gateshead Millennium Bridge

The Gateshead Millennium Bridge that spans the River Tyne in England is a dyadic structure known as the "blinking eye bridge."[52] Its function is derived from its form that is composed of two parabolic arcs that are shaped like the letter "V": one arc is for people crossing, and the second arc functions as a counterbalance for support. The "V" structure has a stable form that allows people to cross when tilted one way and an agile form that rotates on huge joints to tilt the other way allowing the river boats to travel beneath. The Gateshead Millenium Bridge illustrates the performance value of a dyadic structure that has both stability and agility.

For example, Scandinavian Airlines Systems (SAS) promised its customers both *timely and accurate cargo delivery*. SAS was interested in determining how well they were serving their customers on these two promises, so they sent 100 packages throughout Europe in an experiment to gather empirical data. From the experiment, they learned that the average delivery time was four days. They realized that they failed in their promise to the cargo customers.

SAS ascertained that the reason for their performance was that the air cargo operation measured how well they were able to fill the available capacity or volume in each plane, and not by the timely and accurate cargo delivery.[53]

We had caught ourselves in one of the most basic mistakes a service-oriented business can make: Promising one thing and measuring another. In this case, we were promising prompt and precise cargo delivery, yet we were measuring volume and whether the paperwork and packages got separated en route.[54]

SAS was measuring the wrong thing, volume (important to the company), instead of timeliness of delivery (important to the customer).

The Innovation Scorecard

Nearly everyone agrees that innovation is important, but there is no agreed upon valid way to measure it. There is a broad array of economic statistics such as the GDP and CPI, but there are no standardized measures of innovation. Governments and businesses globally are looking for new sources of economic growth and new ways to identify opportunities to solve difficult social problems. It seems that everyone is searching for novel solutions to improve lives and well-being by reducing poverty, preventing disease, improving educational opportunities, and dealing with climate change.

A balanced scorecard is a strategic performance management tool that is used to track measurements that evaluate the outcomes of an organization to ensure that the strategic direction is aligned. A balanced scorecard includes leading (causes) and lagging (outcome) measures that can be used to build a culture of innovation. Individuals, organizations, and nations all need accurate leading measures that can inform us about what causes innovation and the lagging or outcome measures that provide the results that we want to achieve.[55]

Employee performance measures would include learning and growth, engagement, training, working conditions, pay, safety, and organizational culture. Customer performance measures would include service, convenience, customization, simplicity, safety, selection, accessibility, and affordability. Financial performance measures would include revenue from new products and profits. Business process improvements would include reduction in waste, circular value chains, and productivity. The general balanced scorecard for innovation, shown in Figure 20.8, would include key performance indicators (KPIs) that drive meaningfully significant innovations.[56]

Building the Innovation Scorecard

There are five steps to build a scorecard, which are listed and illustrated in Figure 20.9.

1. The creation of viable performance measurements begins with the identification of the strategic goals of all stakeholders: customers, employees, stockholders, investors, partners, and the community.[57]
2. The innovation scorecard's outcome measures provide a way to define the innovation outcomes and align the incentives for improving capability. The outcome measures provide a way for an organization to achieve meaningfully significant value to ensure that the organization is competitive from the stakeholder's perspective.
3. The building of innovation capability requires an understanding of the leading measures that drive the desired innovation outcomes for each organization. What are the starting dominos that kick off the innovations?
4. A transparent integrated scorecard is needed to demonstrate progress to achieve.[58]
5. Everyone must take responsibility for their part and then expect to be held accountable for the results.

Direct and Indirect Measures of Innovation

When it comes to assessing innovation capability, an ideal model would measure collective innovation capability through a set of leading measures and a set of outcome measures demonstrating innovation progress. While direct measures of what drives innovation remain elusive, the search for key indicators that lead to innovation continues. More studies are needed.

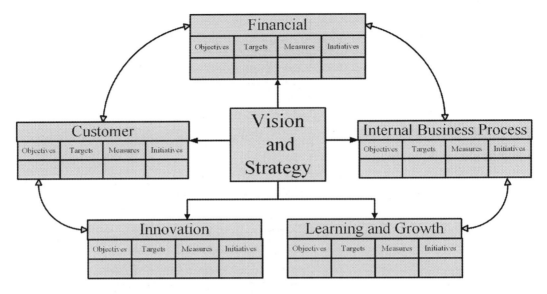

Figure 20.8 Illustration of a Balanced Scorecard for Innovation

Source: Adapted from Robert S. Kaplan and David P. Norton, "Linking the Balanced Scorecard to Strategy," *California Management Review*, 39(1), (1996): 53–79.

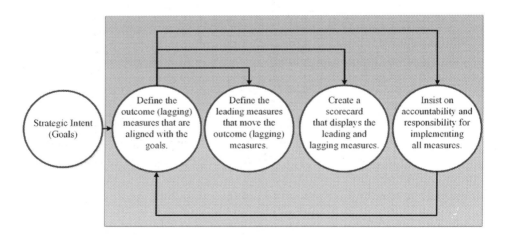

Figure 20.9 Illustration of How to Measure Innovation

Source: Adapted from Sean Covey, Jim Huling, and Chris McChesney. The 4 Disciplines of Execution. London: Simon & Schuster, Limited, 2012.

In the absence of direct measures, however, nine indirect measures can serve as proxies to provide a better understanding of how to create and innovate. Examples of indirect leading measures are innovation capability, business research and investment, university research and investment, government research and investment, company culture, and organization culture. Examples of indirect lagging measures are new product revenue, the innovation premium, and patents. The indirect measures of innovation are shown in Figure 20.10.

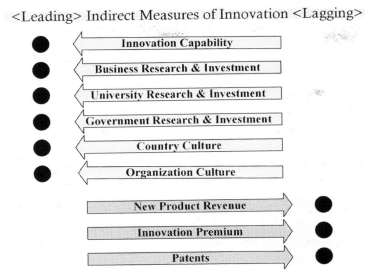

Figure 20.10 Illustration of Indirect Measures of Innovation

Innovation Indices

As noted throughout this book, innovation and entrepreneurship are critical in multiple aspects of living, working, leading, and more. Innovations have powerful impacts for business and society. For example, there are several innovation indices that rank countries. The Global Innovation Index (GII), discussed in Chapter 1, measures the most innovative economies in the world, ranking the innovation performance of around 132 economies while highlighting innovation strengths and weaknesses.[59]

Innovation Capability

The most important leading measure to drive innovation is the innovation capability of the people. Journalist Roger Ebert writes, "We are put on this planet only once, and to limit ourselves to the familiar is a crime against our minds."[60] The aspirational goal is for everyone to develop continuous innovation capability anytime and anywhere.

The learning of evidence-based innovation competencies is expected to improve innovation capability, provide a competitive advantage, and add value to all organizations. The building of innovation capability requires intellectual bravery to streamline the bureaucracy and construct a way to create an innovation flywheel. Timothy Clark writes:[61]

> Intellectual bravery is a willingness to disagree, dissent, or challenge the status quo in a setting of social risk in which you could be embarrassed, marginalized, or punished in some way. When intellectual bravery disappears, organizations develop patterns of willful blindness. Bureaucracy buries boldness. Efficiency crushes creativity. From there, the status quo calcifies, and stagnation sets in.
>
> The responsibility for creating a culture of intellectual bravery lies in leadership. As a leader, you set the tone, create the vibe, and define the prevailing norms. Whether or not your company has a culture of intellectual bravery depends on your ability to establish a pattern of rewarded rather than punished vulnerability.

Intellectual bravery requires leadership that is willing to be bold and take risks. During the Civil War General George McClellan was ideally suited to lead but refused to act in force against the confederacy. Abraham Lincoln eventually replaced McClellan with Ulysses S. Grant who was deliberate in his decision-making. Likewise, Elon Musk is a leader who is willing to take risks to bring his bold vision into reality. Tesla's Elon Musk has a clear core ideology of a purpose to accelerate sustainable energy and the application of first principles to pursue the fundamental truths.

Business Research and Investment

In a study by Akcali and Sismanoglu, the findings indicate that there is a positive correlation between research and development, innovation, and economic growth.[62] In addition, writing in the *Harvard Business Review*, Gina O'Connor notes, "Overall, our study supports what I have found across years of research at numerous companies: That investing in innovation pays off, but not if it is limited to R&D."[63]

There is more to innovation, however, than research and development expenditures. Booz Allen Hamilton Holding Corporation conducted a study of 1,000 companies and concluded that aggregate research and development expenditures are not necessarily a determinant of innovation; you cannot necessarily spend your way to successful innovation.

It is not strictly money; rather, it is the combination of resources, processes, and priorities that are used for innovation purposes. The theory of capabilities described in Chapter 7, "Knowledge Building," provides actionable insights into the three building blocks that an organization uses to add capability: resources, processes, and priorities. Key among these are the resources that include people and their leadership.

The top ten research and development spenders are not necessarily the top innovators. Interestingly, there does not appear to be a direct correlation between company rankings on innovation and R&D expenditures.[64] Moreover, Jaruzelski, Chwalik, and Goehle, writing in *strategy+business*, write:[65]

Our analysis reveals that both the high-leverage innovators and the larger universe of companies that report relative high performance have six key characteristics. The first five are widely understood, though executed to varying degrees. The sixth is something that only the best innovators accomplish.

1. They closely align innovation strategy with business strategy.
2. They create company-wide cultural support for innovation.
3. Their top leadership is highly involved with the innovation program.
4. They base innovation on direct insights from end-users.
5. They rigorously control project selection early in the innovation process.
6. They excel at each of these first five characteristics and have been able to integrate them to create unique customer experiences that can transform their market.

Examples of start-ups that have become global innovators are listed in Figure 20.11.

University Research and Investment

Universities that conduct research are critical in generating innovation-based economic growth and driving US global innovation leadership.[66] The United States is continuing to fall behind other developed nations in funding for university research according to The Information Technology & Innovation Foundation.[67] That's despite the US being home to world-leading research universities

1	Amazon.com, Inc.	United States	Consumer Discretionary	Retailing
2	Alphabet Inc.	United States	Information Technology	Software and Services
3	Volkswagen Aktiengesellschaft	Germany	Consumer Discretionary	Automobiles and Components
4	Samsung Electronics Co., Ltd.	South Korea	Information Technology	Technology Hardware and Equipment
5	Intel Corporation	United States	Information Technology	Semiconductors and Semiconductor Equipment
6	Microsoft Corporation	United States	Information Technology	Software and Services
7	Apple Inc.	United States	Information Technology	Technology Hardware and Equipment
8	Roche Holding AG	Switzerland	Healthcare	Pharmaceuticals, Biotechnology and Life Sciences
9	Johnson & Johnson	United States	Healthcare	Pharmaceuticals, Biotechnology and Life Sciences
10	Merck & Co., Inc.	United States	Healthcare	Pharmaceuticals, Biotechnology and Life Sciences

Figure 20.11 Illustration of Top R&D Global Expenditures Rankings

Source: Adapted from "The Global Innovation 1000 study," Strategy &, 2018, accessed October 18, 2020, https://www.strategyand.pwc.com/gx/en/insights/innovation1000.html

Adapted from Barry Jaruzelski, Robert Chwalik, and Brad Goehle, "What the Top Innovators Get Right," Tech & Innovation, October 30, 2018, Winter 2018, Issue 93, accessed October 18, 2020, https://www.strategy-business.com/feature/What-the-Top-Innovators-Get-Right

that have played an important role in driving American technological supremacy since the Second World War.

Historically, colleges and universities have made significant innovation contributions. Even though colleges and universities provide for knowledge creation and transfer, the challenge for colleges and universities is to develop agility and speed to facilitate their capability to drive innovation to meet the needs of the next generation.

Colleges and universities are key to building cultures that drive innovation and catalyze economic development. Farnam Jahanian, then president of Carnegie Mellon University, identified four ways that colleges and universities can improve their ability to drive innovation.[68]

1. Fostering entrepreneurship
2. Encouraging collaboration with the private sector
3. Promoting diversity, equity, and inclusion
4. Exploring the nexus of technology and society[69]

Government Research and Investment

The Capitalism Model

Capitalism has provided significant gains in economic growth and prosperity to many nations. During the Great Depression of the 1930s, the focus was on the John Maynard Keynes economic model that advocated the use of fiscal and monetary policies to stimulate growth and job creation. In the 1970s, the Milton Friedman model made influential contributions to monetary macroeconomics and promoted the notion that "the social responsibility of business is to increase its profits."[70] In the 2020s, there is an interest in stakeholder capitalism due to discontent about rising inequality, heightened competition from economies with different models, and possible threats from climate change.[71] Building on the work of Keynes and Friedman, governments have several ways to stimulate innovation and create economic growth: supply-side and demand-side macroeconomics.

Supply-Side Macroeconomics

Supply-side macroeconomics is implemented through lowering taxes and decreasing regulations. The concept is that lower taxes and fewer regulations enable businesses to invest more in research and development of new products and services. For example, many Apple products created new consumer demand by producing new unique goods and services.[72] While individually and organizationally driven, the technological innovations of Apple, Amazon, Google, Microsoft, and many others have also benefitted from the support of federal, state, and local government policies.

Demand-Side Macroeconomics

Demand-side macroeconomics involves government spending to increase economic activity that can create jobs. The government manages the supply of money by altering interest rates or selling or buying government-issued bonds. For example, interest rates can influence business and residence construction that influence economic activity.[73]

"In Silicon Valley, for example, the government has acted as a strategic investor through a decentralized network of public institutions: The Defense Advanced Research Projects Agency, NASA, the Small Business Innovation Research program (SBIR), and the National Science Foundation."[74] The US Defense Advanced Research Projects Agency (DARPA) is a research and development agency of the United States Department of Defense that contributed to the creation of the global positioning system (GPS) and the Internet.[75]

The US National Aeronautics and Space Administration (NASA) created the space program and has provided aeronautics and space research.[76] NASA has been instrumental in producing more than 2,000 spinoffs since 1976.[77] "A NASA spinoff is a technology, originally developed to meet NASA mission needs, that has been transferred to the public and now provides benefits for the Nation and world as a commercial product or service."[78] The American National Institute of Health funds studies that lead to new pharmaceuticals. The National Science Foundation provided a grant that produced the Google search algorithm.[79]

According to McKinsey, "Federal spending on education, infrastructure, and scientific research fell from approximately 2.5 percent of GDP in 1980 to less than 1.5 percent of GDP today."[80] The reduction in resources to these institutions lessens the ability for government investments to stimulate innovative breakthroughs.

Thomson Reuters, in reviewing an article by Wendy Schacht who writes about the Bayh-Dole Act, notes,

> The United States has had a long tradition of R&D tax credits, annually renewed by Congress and with broad-based political support. Acts such as Bayh-Dole (1980) and subsequent policies have created more robust innovation collaboration between government and the private sector, ultimately resulting in the emergence of tech startups, venture capital and private equity and an increase in mergers and acquisitions.[81]

Country Culture

Research by Pamela Cox and Raihan Khan at SUNY Oswego suggests that innovative societies are characterized by the following cultural values: individualism, relationships, pragmatism/

long-term orientation, and improvisation. Their study results suggest "that cultural dimensions do influence decisions that affect the innovation capabilities of a country."[82] Examining the relationship between Hofstede's cultural dimensions and the Global Innovation Index (GII), they suggest the following:

1. Individualistic societies will be more innovative than collectivist societies.
2. Feminine societies (low masculinity) will be more innovative than masculine societies.
3. Pragmatic societies will be more innovative than normative societies. That is, a longer-term perspective focuses on the values of perseverance and effort, whereas the shorter-term focuses on the values of the past and the present.
4. Indulgent societies will be more innovative than normative societies. This suggests that improvisation-oriented societies (the extent to which people can be adaptable, flexible, and spontaneous) will be more innovative than societies that follow rules and norms.[83]

Cox and Khan's research suggests that countries with cultures that are adversely predisposed to innovation may not be able to grow economically and compete effectively with more innovative societies.

Culture has a powerful effect on human behavior within countries.

This is one reason that individuals who grow up in societies that promote community versus individualism and hierarchy over merit – such as Japan, China, Korea, and many Arab nations – are less likely to creatively challenge the status quo and turn out innovations (or win Nobel prizes).[84]

Nobel Prizes may be influenced by a country's culture, but more research is warranted to unravel the complexities. For example, the top five Nobel Prize laureates' countries were the United States (385), United Kingdom (133), Germany (108), France (70), and Sweden (32). Japan had 28 winners, India 12, China 8, and Korea 2.[85] When comparing the number of prizes relative to country population, the top five were Saint Lucia (2), Luxembourg (2), Switzerland (28), Sweden (30), and Iceland (1), respectively. The United Kingdom was ranked 9th and the United States 15th in Nobel Prizes per capita.[86]

Organization Culture

As suggested in Chapter 9, "Culture Building," an organization that has a monolithic, top-down decision-making structure is at risk of diminishing its human talent. This can be ameliorated with a dual organizational culture that offers discipline and freedom to break away from the whirlwind.

An organizational environment where innovation can flourish may be characterized by the following:[87]

1. Challenging the status quo (individualism)
2. Sharing of information and the promotion of collaboration (relationships)
3. Encouragement of achievement and long-term thinking (pragmatism)
4. Creating new technology to improve life (improvisation)

Organizations that support the ideas of their employees in a tangible way are in a strong position to support innovation. For example, Google employees can spend 20% of their time working on inspirational projects, which is how Gmail and AdSense, two of the company's most successful products, were developed. Google provides resources, including infrastructure, money, time, and people, for innovation. 3M allows employees to spend 15% of their time on projects that go beyond their core responsibilities. 3M provides seed money of between $30,000 and $75,000, called Genesis Grants, to employees for developing ideas.[88]

New Product Revenue

Revenue is a lagging or outcome measure of innovation in an organization. While forms of inorganic growth, such as acquisitions, can provide a boost to the bottom line, in general, viable new product revenue is often the result of organic growth. Steady-state growth from internal frameworks can provide a long-term focus on revenue, not just the immediate bottom line. To grow, organizations need to increase idea-generation and new product lines. "The top line is the bottom line." The top line is total revenue, and the bottom line is profit. New products are necessary because, in the product lifecycle, revenue grows, tapers, and then declines, resulting in a need to add new products to their portfolios for growth.[89]

Innovation Premium

Innovation premium is a lagging measure that is the added value that a company derives from having a reputation as an innovate leader in its industry. The authors of *The Innovator's DNA*, along with HOLT, a division of Credit Suisse, developed a methodology for measuring innovation known as the innovation premium.[90]

> The Innovation Premium is a measure of how much investors have bid up the stock price of a company above the value of its existing business based on expectations of future innovative results (new products, services, and markets). Members of the list must have $10 billion in market capitalization, spend at least 2.5% of revenue on R&D and have seven years of public data.[91]

The implication is that a company is better positioned to innovate and fuel future growth.

Patents

Granted patents, rather than filed patents, can be used as an outcome (lagging) proxy measure for innovations. Examples of patent grants by country are listed in Figure 20.12. "Patent activity has always been an indicator of innovation. However, innovation comprises much more than mere patent filing volume." Patent studies do not necessarily support the notion that patents are leading measures of innovation, as explained in "Patents and the Regress of Useful Arts."[92]
What is the relationship between patents and innovation?

> When you look at most of the products that have changed our lives over the past decades – from Facebook to Twitter, Amazon to eBay – they are almost invariably start-ups offering surprising new products or services. Their success had nothing to do with the number of patents or the amount spent on R&D, and so it was impossible to measure these companies using the same metrics of more established organizations.[93]

Process

Rialto Bridge

During the Renaissance, in Venice, Italy, the Rialto Bridge was built as a single stone arch that spanned the Grand Canal. The Rialto Bridge was a 15th-century experimental structure designed to

Patent Grants		
1	China	432,147
2	U.S.	307,759
3	Japan	194,525
4	European Patent Office	127,603
5	South Korea	119,012
6	Russian Federation	35,774
7	Canada	23,499
8	Australia	17,065
9	Germany	16,367
10	India	13,908

Figure 20.12 Illustration of Granted Patents

Source: Adapted from Wikipedia, s.v. "Patent Grants," accessed April 11, 2020, https://en.wikipedia.org/wiki/World_Intellectual_Property_Indicators

connect the two sides of Venice. To build the bridge they used a process that started with imagination, followed by design, model building, and then the implementation of the stone construction. Bridge building uses a problem-solving process that depends on the job to be done that includes considerations for the distance, height, terrain, and resources.

Similarly, innovation is a process where mental creation precedes physical creation. According to Scott Kirsner, "One key enabler of innovation, referenced by more than half of our survey respondents, was the 'ability to test, learn, and iterate.' How well does your company run quick-and-dirty experiments, gather the results, and then try again?"[94] Building on this, three key concepts inform process: design thinking, lean start-up models, and the human-centered process.

Design Thinking Process

Tim Brown, David Kelly, and Tom Kelly of IDEO are proponents of the iterative empathic human-centered design thinking process that has demonstrated practical applicability.[95] The design thinking process uses three steps: inspiration, ideation, and implementation. The first step, inspiration, the team must select a problem/opportunity to serve a set of customers/consumers that is based on a job that needs to be done. Jobs-to-be-done focuses on the meaningfully significant measurable jobs and outcomes of people that are unmet or underserved.[96] The second step, ideation, involves the process of generating, developing, and testing ideas that may lead to solutions. In the third step, implementation, the team produces a minimally viable product (MVP) or prototype. The team makes sketches and models (if appropriate) that they test, modify, and test again, in an iterative process that is at the heart of design thinking.

Given that the process of innovation involves considerable trade-offs, (e.g., status quo, risk, costs, employee buy-in and others), Jeanne Liedtka, Darden School of Business, suggests that design thinking addresses the behaviors that hamper innovation. Moreover, she notes,

Design thinking provided a structured process that helps innovators break free of counterproductive tendencies that thwart innovation. Like TQM, it is a social technology that blends practical tools with insights into human nature.[97]

Entrepreneurship

Lean Start-up Process

Steve Blank and Eric Ries are proponents of the lean start-up model that focuses on building minimum viable products that can be validated with direct customer experiences rather than formal business plans.[98] Steve Blank advocates for a lean, fail-fast model, which is perpetually testing low-cost solutions as the entrepreneur seeks to create a temporary organization in search of a scalable, repeatable, profitable business model. The actionable insight is that scalable start-ups are not mini versions of large organizations. New ventures should focus on a search for a business model that describes how the organization will operate, not executing the business model.[99] A new venture is started by sketching out critical hypotheses. The iterative process is used to build a minimum viable product that can be used with customers to validate the hypotheses.[100]

Venture Capital Funding Process

Venture capital firms or funds provide equity financing to start-ups, early-stage and emerging companies that have demonstrated high growth or have been deemed to have high growth potential. The venture capital funding typically has six stages that correspond to a company's progress.[101]

1. Seed funding is the earliest round of financing that is used to prove a new idea, often provided by angel investors. Seed funding can be provided through crowdsourcing.
2. Start-ups need funding for expenses associated with marketing and product development.
3. The first round is for growth that is typically provided by venture capitalists using terms like Series A round, Series B, Series C rounds and so on.
4. The second round is the working capital for early-stage companies that are selling products, but not yet turning a profit.
5. The third round is for expansion or mezzanine financing; these funds are targeted for a newly profitable company.
6. In the fourth round, the venture capitalist may exit through secondary sale or an initial public offering (IPO) or an acquisition.

Both design thinking and the lean start-up movement capture the customer's job-to-be-done by shifting the innovation process from a high-ceremony model to a low-ceremony, agile, iterative, and experimental process.[102] Innovation is a human-centered process for adding value and lowering costs. An innovation process adaptable to scale and complexity can improve innovation capability. Both design thinking and the lean start-up movement test solutions by simultaneously applying processes that are adaptable, iterative, and experimental.

The Human-Centered Process

Innovation is a human-centered process for transforming actionable insights into value-added results that can provide a sustainable strategic advantage for any organization. Organizations need to provide an opportunity for each person to develop the competencies, risk tolerance, and resilience that are the foundation for building innovation capability.[103] An integrated model of a human-centered innovation process is shown in Figure 20.13.

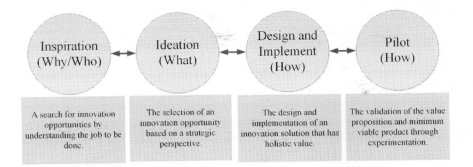

Figure 20.13 Illustration of Generic Innovation Process

Source: Adapted from Tim Brown, *Change by Design*, (New York: Harper, 2009), 19

Adapted from Steve Blank, Why the lean start-up changes everything. *Harvard Business Review, 91*(5), 63–74 Adapted from Joe Tidd, and John Bessant, J., *Managing Innovation: Integrating Technological, Market and Organizational Change,* 5th ed. (London: Wiley, 2013), 47.

Culture: Creativity and Structure

A culture of duality in innovation is the balance between structure and the enterprising spirit of creativity within an organization. "When you blend a culture of discipline with an ethic of entrepreneurship, you get a magical alchemy resulting in superior performance."[104] The balance is crucial for fostering an environment that encourages innovation while maintaining a level of discipline and order necessary for effective implementation and execution.[105]

Creativity Summary

During the development of the Macintosh, Steve Jobs and his team flew a pirate flag over their own Macintosh building at Apple as a symbol to convey their counterculture attitude. The team decided that best way for the Mac team to mark its territory would be to fly its own pirate flag above the building.[106] The pirate flag on the Apple building was the symbol that describes alchemy. The core is to understand how to apply the multiple theories that contribute to explaining and applying creativity.

1. Cognitive psychology is a field that examines the thinking processes that engage in creative thinking, such as divergent thinking, convergent thinking, critical thinking, combinatorial innovations (associations, the Power of And), and analogical reasoning. An example of an analogy: a book is to read as music is to listen. These concepts were explored in Chapters 4, 5, and 8.
2. Personality psychology is a field that explores individual characteristics that are associated with creativity, such as openness to experience, tolerance for ambiguity, intrinsic versus extrinsic motivation, and risk-taking. Examples are fixedness and the status quo bias that result in closed-mindedness. These concepts were explored in detail in Chapter 3.
3. Cultural psychology provides insights into those factors that affect creativity, such as the physical, social, organizational, and cultural context. For example, organizational culture can amplify creativity or diminish creativity. Learning organizations can enhance the creative decision-making process through a culture that explicitly promotes self-expression and seeks out the validity of claims that people initiate.[107] These concepts were explored in Chapters 7 and 9.
4. Neuroscience is a field that uses neuroimaging techniques, such as EEG (electroencephalogram), fMRI (Functional magnetic resonance imaging), and TMS (transcranial magnetic stimulation),

to examine the brain regions and networks that participate in creative thinking. For example, creativity resides in multiple brain regions rather than being right-brained (left-handed) or left-brained (right-handed). These concepts were explored in Chapter 8.

Structure Summary

A **structure** is a framework for creative people to understand expectations and to be held accountability for the organization's objectives, key focus areas, core capabilities, and commitments to stakeholders.[108] The structure is built to enable leaders to inspire and empower their teams, providing resources, autonomy, and a safe space for innovation.[109]

The ISO 56000 Standard for Innovation Management provides a framework for managing innovation within an organization.[110] The Innovation Management ISO 56000 standard supports the concept of innovation architecture by providing internationally agreed-upon guidelines that describe the best practices for managing the innovation process. The ISO standards represent the collective competencies, attitudes, skills, and knowledge of experts that understand the long-term strategic needs of organizations. The standards facilitate innovation progress, reduce costs, increase effectiveness, improve service and safety, and enhance the likelihood of a successful outcome.[111] The ISO standard is shown in Figure 20.14.

ISO 56000:2020	Innovation management — Fundamentals and vocabulary
ISO/AWI 56001	Innovation management — Innovation management system — Requirements
ISO 56002:2019	Innovation management — Innovation management system — Guidance
ISO 56003:2019	Innovation management — Tools and methods for innovation partnership — Guidance
ISO/TR 56004:20	Innovation Management Assessment — Guidance
ISO 56005:2020	Innovation management — Tools and methods for intellectual property management — Guidance
ISO 56006:2021	Innovation management — Tools and methods for strategic intelligence management — Guidance
ISO/DIS 56007	Innovation management — Tools and methods for idea management — Guidance
ISO/CD 56008	Innovation management — tools and methods for innovation operation measurements — Guidance
ISO/DTS 56010	Innovation management - Illustrative examples of ISO 56000

Figure 20.14 International Standards Organization – Innovation Management

Source: Acknowledgment: ISO 56000, accessed January 28, 2024, https://en.wikipedia.org/wiki/IS0_56000

To achieve meaningfully significant performance, an organization's innovation architecture should ideally provide a dyadic structure of both creative agility (flexibility) and operational stability (discipline). For example, in discussing enterprise agility, McKinsey senior partner, Shail Thaker, notes,

> But also, if you think of agile as an outcome of a particular setup where you're putting the Lego bricks right around which bits are dynamic and which bits need to be stable for me to be able to deliver speed and be nimble and all that good stuff, start-ups have a ton of dynamic, not a whole lot of stable. Incumbents: Huge amounts of stable, not a lot of dynamic.[112]

Leadership is essential for the construction of an organizational dyadic structure (yin and yang) and provides a way to separate the creative agility and operational stability. Both are needed to drive performance and progress. Creative agility and operational stability are separated but linked to achieve the sharing of the embedded expertise of the competencies. The enterprising spirit of creative agility is measured by ideation, learning, and experimentation. Operational stability is measured by outcomes, such as employee satisfaction, customer satisfaction, revenue, costs, and profit.

Innovation Architecture Framework

It is time to apply an architectural framework to build a foundation for the discipline of innovation that encompasses the five integrated choices: people, partnerships, purpose, performance, and process as shown in Figure 20.15.

Innovation Architecture Framework	
The innovation architecture framework for the foundation for building innovation capability.	
Outcome	What is the desired outcome?
People	Everyone should master the fundamentals of innovation and 21st-century competencies to achieve the most impact. Build a results-oriented culture of innovation that includes a flat organization comprised of open-minded, diverse, and cross-functional teams.
Partnerships	Build an internal partnership network within the organization linked externally to a partnership network between Universities and businesses, and between cities, regions, and countries to foster open innovation.
Purpose	Pursue a meaningfully significant purpose for all stakeholders. Adopt the innovation equation based on the combination of the value proposition and social advantage.
Performance	Create a scorecard of measures to track innovation progress. The scorecard would incorporate leading innovation and outcome measures based on people, partnerships, purpose, performance, and process.
Process	Adopt an adaptable, agile, and experimental innovation process that spans imagination to implementation. The process should define what jobs customers need to have done that are validated with evidence.

Figure 20.15 Illustration of Innovation Architecture Framework

The discipline of innovation can be practiced using an architectural framework to enable anyone to be part of the movement to achieve meaningful progress. Effective forward-thinking organizations must *provide a clear path on how anyone* can be free to implement their high-order actionable insights. Organizations must balance the discipline provided by an architectural framework and the autonomy that is provided by inspired people.

Conclusion

Innovation is a humanistic discipline that requires each person to have the competencies, behaviors, and confidence for their career journey. Universities are catalysts for helping students to learn the future interdisciplinary and collaborative competencies that are necessary to provide modern firms with a way to build their innovation capability. Therefore, an innovation architectural blueprint that focuses on people, partnerships, principles, performance, and process can provide the guardrails to add value for all stakeholders: students, business partners, educators, and administrators.

If your company is really serious about building an innovation engine, then it needs to upgrade everyone's innovation skills, agree on what counts as innovation, establish comprehensive metrics, hold leaders accountable for innovation, and retool its management processes so they foster innovation everywhere, all the time. These can't be isolated initiatives; they must work in harmony.[113]

Starting early in the learning process, educators are expected to provide opportunities for students to develop imagination, creativity, innovation, and entrepreneurship skills to ensure our future competitiveness.[114] The education systems of the future will need to teach the competencies that enable people to create and connect very different domains of knowledge. An innovation architectural framework can facilitate the movement.

Notes

1. *Britannica*, s.v. "Score," accessed January 21, 2024, www.britannica.com/art/score-music.
2. Matt Banholzer, Rebecca Doherty, Alex Morris, and Scott Schwaitzberg, "Are You an Innovative Grower?" November 1, 2023, accessed January 23, 2024, www.mckinsey.com/quarterly/the-five-fifty/five-fifty-are-you-an-innovative-grower.
3. Matt Banholzer, Rebecca Doherty, Alex Morris, and Scott Schwaitzberg, "Innovative Growers: A View from the Top," November 1, 2023, accessed November 16, 2023, www.mckinsey.com/capabilities/strategy-and-corporate-finance/our-insights/innovative-growers-a-view-from-the-top.
4. Marc de Jong, Nathan Marston, and Erik Roth, "The Eight Essentials of Innovation," April 1, 2015, accessed November 16, 2023, www.mckinsey.com/capabilities/strategy-and-corporate-finance/our-insights/the-eight-essentials-of-innovation [Includes Video].
5. Gina O'Connor, "Real Innovation Requires More than an R&D Budget," December 19, 2019, accessed February 20, 2024, https://hbr.org/2019/12/real-innovation-requires-more-than-an-rd-budget and cite "Strategic Growth & Innovation," accessed February 8, 2024, www.mckinsey.com/capabilities/strategy-and-corporate-finance/how-we-help-clients/Strategic-Growth-and-Innovation.
6. KPMG, "Benchmarking Innovation Impact 2020," accessed February 20, 2024, https://info.kpmg.us/content/dam/info/en/innovation-enterprise-solutions/pdf/2019/benchmarking-innovation-impact-2020.pdf.
7. KPMG, "Benchmarking Innovation Impact 2020," accessed February 20, 2024, https://info.kpmg.us/content/dam/info/en/innovation-enterprise-solutions/pdf/2019/benchmarking-innovation-impact-2020.pdf.
8. Marwa Eltagouri, "The Deadliest Bridge Collapses in U.S. History," March 16, 2018, accessed February 20, 2024, www.washingtonpost.com/news/retropolis/wp/2018/03/16/looking-back-at-five-of-the-deadliest-bridge-collapses-in-u-s-history/?utm_term=.b6665e9d517c.
9. *Wikipedia*, s.v. "Tacoma Narrows Bridge," accessed February 25, 2018, https://en.wikipedia.org/wiki/Tacoma_Narrows_Bridge_(1940)

10. *Wikipedia*, s.v. "Aeroelasticity," accessed March 6, 2021, https://en.wikipedia.org/wiki/Aeroelasticity#Flutter.
11. Omar Abbosh, Vedrana Savic, and Michael Moore, "What Sets the Most Effective Innovators Apart," March 8, 2019, accessed February 20, 2024, https://hbr.org/2019/03/what-sets-the-most-effective-innovators-apart.
12. *Wikipedia*, s.v. "Millau Viaduct," accessed March 6, 2021, https://en.wikipedia.org/wiki/Millau_Viaduct.
13. *Wikipedia*, s.v. "Michel_Virlogeux," accessed March 6, 2021, https://en.wikipedia.org/wiki/Michel_Virlogeux.
14. *Wikipedia*, s.v. "Norman Robert Foster, Baron Foster of Thames Bank," accessed March 6, 2021, https://en.wikipedia.org/wiki/Norman_Foster,_Baron_Foster_of_Thames_Bank.
15. Aaron De Smet, Chris Gagnon, Elizabeth Mygatt, and Richard Steele, "The Nine Traits of Future-Ready Companies," February 9, 2021, accessed February 9, 2021, www.mckinsey.com/business-functions/organization/our-insights/the-nine-traits-of-future-ready-companies.
16. Jeff Dyer, Paul Godfrey, Robert Jensen, and David Bryce, *Strategic Management: Concepts and Cases*, 2nd ed. (New York: John Wiley & Sons, Inc, 2018).
17. Diane L. Coutu, "How Resilience Works," *Harvard Business Review*, May 2002, accessed November 13, 2023, http://hbr.org/2002/05/how-resilience-works/ar/1.
18. Jim Collins, *Good to Great: Why Some Companies Make the Leap . . . and Others Don't* (New York: HarperBusiness, 2001), 125.
19. Aaron De Smet, Chris Gagnon, Elizabeth Mygatt, and Richard Steele, "The Nine Traits of Future-Ready Companies," February 9, 2021, accessed February 9, 2021, www.mckinsey.com/business-functions/organization/our-insights/the-nine-traits-of-future-ready-companies.
20. Peter M. Senge, *The Fifth Discipline* (London: Century Business, 1992).
21. Allan Lee, Sara Willis, and Amy Wei Tian, "When Empowering Employees Works, and When It Doesn't," March 2, 2018, accessed February 20, 2024, https://hbr.org/2018/03/when-empowering-employees-works-and-when-it-doesnt. Meta analysis: Allan Lee, Sara Willis, and Amy Wei Tian, "Empowering Leadership: A Meta-Analytic Examination of Incremental Contribution, Mediation, and Moderation," *Journal of Organizational Behavior* 39, no. 3 (2018), 306–325, accessed February 20, 2024, https://doi.org/10.1002/job.2220.
22. Dan Schawbel, "How Will You Measure Your Life?" June 5, 2012, accessed February 24, 2024, www.forbes.com/sites/danschawbel/2012/06/05/how-will-you-measure-your-life/#2552e5614d09.
23. Gary Hamel and Nancy Tennant, "The 5 Requirements of a Truly Innovative Company," April 27, 2015, accessed November 13, 2023, https://hbr.org/2015/04/the-5-requirements-of-a-truly-innovative-company.
24. Saadia Zahidi, "We Need a Global Reskilling Revolution – Here's Why," January 22, 2020, accessed February 20, 2024, www.weforum.org/agenda/2020/01/reskilling-revolution-jobs-future-skills/.
25. World Economic Forum, "The Reskilling Revolution: Better Skills, Better Jobs, Better Education for a Billion People by 2030," January 22, 2020, accessed February 20, 2024, www.weforum.org/press/2020/01/the-reskilling-revolution-better-skills-better-jobs-better-education-for-a-billion-people-by-2030.
26. "Soft Skills for a Hard World," *McKinsey & Company*, accessed February 20, 2024, www.mckinsey.com/featured-insights/future-of-work/five-fifty-soft-skills-for-a-hard-world.
27. Center for Curriculum Redesign, "Competencies/Subcompetencies Framework," July 2019, accessed November 13, 2023, https://curriculumredesign.org/framework/.
28. Ken Robinson and Lou Aronica, *Creative Schools: The Grassroots Revolution That's Transforming Education* (New York: Viking, 2015).
29. C. Aguilar and C. Bridges, "A Guide to the Core SEL Competencies [+ Activities and Strategies]," *Panorama Education*, 2024, accessed February 20, 2024, www.panoramaed.com/blog/guide-to-core-sel-competencies.
30. Scott DeRue, *The Future of MBA Education*, February 14, 2018, accessed February 20, 2024, https://hbr.org/ideacast/2018/02/the-future-of-mba-education.
31. Scott DeRue, *The Future of MBA Education*, February 14, 2018, accessed February 20, 2024, https://hbr.org/ideacast/2018/02/the-future-of-mba-education.
32. Frans Johansson, *Medici Effect: What Elephants and Epidemics Can Teach Us about Innovation* (Boston: Harvard Business School Press, 2006).
33. Jeff Dyer, Hal Gregersen, and Clayton M. Christensen, *The Innovator's DNA* (Boston: Harvard Business Review Press, 2011), 41–64.
34. *Wikipedia*, s.v. "The Agony and the Ecstasy," accessed August 6, 2011, http://en.wikipedia.org/wiki/The_Agony_and_the_Ecstasy_(novel).
35. Jeff Dyer, Hal Gregersen, and Clayton M. Christensen, *The Innovator's DNA* (Boston: Harvard Business Review Press, 2011), 24.

36. Aaron De Smet, Chris Gagnon, Elizabeth Mygatt, and Richard Steele, "The Nine Traits of Future-Ready Companies," February 9, 2021, accessed February 9, 2021, www.mckinsey.com/business-functions/organization/our-insights/the-nine-traits-of-future-ready-companies.

37. Scott DeRue, *The Future of MBA Education*, February 14, 2018, accessed February 20, 2024, https://hbr.org/ideacast/2018/02/the-future-of-mba-education.

38. Scott DeRue, *The Future of MBA Education*, February 14, 2018, accessed February 20, 2024, https://hbr.org/ideacast/2018/02/the-future-of-mba-education.

39. Jeffrey Bussgang and Jono Bacon, "When Community Becomes Your Competitive Advantage," January 21, 2020, accessed December 6, 2023, https://hbr.org/2020/01/when-community-becomes-your-competitive-advantage.

40. Jeffrey Bussgang and Jono Bacon, "When Community Becomes Your Competitive Advantage," January 21, 2020, accessed January 21, 2024, https://hbr.org/2020/01/when-community-becomes-your-competitive-advantage.

41. Jim Collins and Jerry I. Porras, *Built to Last: Successful Habits of Visionary Companies* (New York: HarperCollins, 2002).

42. Jim Collins and Jerry I. Porras, *Built to Last: Successful Habits of Visionary Companies* (New York: Harper Business Essentials, 1994).

43. Viktor Frankl, *Man's Search for Meaning* (New York: Pocketbooks, 1984).

44. Alex Pattakos, *Prisoners of Our Thoughts* (San Francisco: Berrett-Koehler, 2010), 25.

45. *Wikipedia*, s.v. "Riley Scott," accessed March 27, 2018, https://en.wikipedia.org/wiki/Ridley_Scott.

46. Simon Sinek, *Start With Why: How Great Leaders Inspire Everyone to Take Action* (New York: Penguin, 2009).

47. "About Tesla," accessed January 21, 2024, www.tesla.com/about.

48. Elon Musk, 2014, "All Our Patent Are Belong to You," June 12, 2014, accessed January 21, 2024, www.tesla.com/blog/all-our-patent-are-belong-you.

49. "Enrico Fermi, Father of the Nuclear Age," January 4, 2018, accessed January 21, 2024, www.economist.com/news/books-and-arts/21733971-new-biography-italian-physicist-considered-last-man-know-everything-enrico.

50. Terence Irwin, *Aristotle's First Principles*. Clarendon Aristotle Series. New ed. (Oxford: Clarendon Press, 1988), https://doi.org/10.1093/0198242905.001.0001, http://lib.myilibrary.com?ID=205200.

51. Elon Musk, "The Mind Behind Tesla," *SpaceX, and Solar City*, February 2013, accessed January 21, 2024, www.ted.com/talks/elon_musk_the_mind_behind_tesla_spacex_solarcity.

52. *Wikipedia*, s.v. "Gateshead Millennium Bridge," accessed January 21, 2024, https://en.wikipedia.org/wiki/Gateshead_Millennium_Bridge.

53. Jan Carlzon, *Moments of Truth* (New York: Harper, 1989), 107–112.

54. Jan Carlzon, *Moments of Truth* (New York: Harper, 1989), 108.

55. Robert S. Kaplan and David P. Norton, "Using the Balanced Scorecard as a Strategic Management System," *Harvard Business Review* 85, no. 7, 8 (2007), 150–161.

56. Graham Kenny, "Create KPIs That Reflect Your Strategic Priorities," *Harvard Business Review*, February 4, 2020, accessed February 20, 2024, https://hbr.org/2020/02/create-kpis-that-reflect-your-strategic-priorities.

57. Graham Kenny, "Create KPIs That Reflect Your Strategic Priorities," *Harvard Business Review*, February 4, 2020, accessed January 21, 2024, https://hbr.org/2020/02/create-kpis-that-reflect-your-strategic-priorities.

58. Robert S. Kaplan and David P. Norton. 2007. "Using the Balanced Scorecard as a Strategic Management System," *Harvard Business Review* 85, no. 7, 8 (July/August 2007), 150–161.

59. Global Innovation Index, accessed February 9, 2024, www.wipo.int/global_innovation_index/en/.

60. Jon Terbush, "Roger Ebert's Most Memorable Quotes on Life, Death and the Movies," *The Week*, April 4, 2013, accessed January 21, 2024, http://theweek.com/article/index/242364/roger-eberts-most-memorable-quotes-on-life-death-and-the-movies.

61. Timothy R. Clark, "To Foster Innovation, Cultivate a Culture of Intellectual Bravery," October 13, 2020, accessed January 21, 2024, https://hbr.org/2020/10/to-foster-innovation-cultivate-a-culture-of-intellectual-bravery.

62. Burcay Yasar Akcali and Elcin Sismanoglu, "Innovation and the Effect of Research and Development (R&D) Expenditure on Growth in some Developing and Developed Countries," *Procedia – Social and Behavioral Sciences* 195 (2015), https://doi.org/10.1016/j.sbspro.2015.06.474, accessed February 20, 2024, www.sciencedirect.com/science/article/pii/S1877042815039531.

63. Gina O'Connor, "Real Innovation Requires More Than an R&D Budget," December 19, 2019, accessed January 21, 2024, https://hbr.org/2019/12/real-innovation-requires-more-than-an-rd-budget.
64. "The World's Most Innovative Companies," accessed February 2, 2024, www.forbes.com/innovative-companies/list/.
65. Barry Jaruzelski, Robert Chwalik, and Brad Goehle, "What the Top Innovators Get Right," *Tech & Innovation*, October 30, 2018, Winter 2018, Issue 93, accessed February, 2024, www.strategy-business.com/feature/What-the-Top-Innovators-Get-Right.
66. Robert D. Atkinson Caleb Foote, "U.S. Funding for University Research Continues to Slide," October 21, 2019, accessed February 2, 2024, https://itif.org/publications/2019/10/21/us-funding-university-research-continues-slide.
67. Robert D. Atkinson Caleb Foote, "U.S. Funding for University Research Continues to Slide," October 21, 2019, accessed February 2, 2024, https://itif.org/publications/2019/10/21/us-funding-university-research-continues-slide.
68. Farnam Jahanian, "4 Ways Universities Are Driving Innovation," January 17, 2018, accessed February 2, 2024, www.weforum.org/agenda/2018/01/4-ways-universities-are-driving-innovation.
69. Farnam Jahanian, "4 Ways Universities Are Driving Innovation," January 17, 2018, accessed February 2, 2024, www.weforum.org/agenda/2018/01/4-ways-universities-are-driving-innovation.
70. Milton Friedman "A Friedman Doctrine – The Social Responsibility of Business Is to Increase Its Profits," September 13, 1970, accessed February 2, 2024, www.nytimes.com/1970/09/13/archives/a-friedman-doctrine-the-social-responsibility-of-business-is-to.html.
71. James Manyika, Gary Pinkus, and Monique Tuin, "Rethinking the Future of American Capitalism," *McKinsey Global Institute*, November 2020, accessed February 2, 2024, www.mckinsey.com/featured-insights/long-term-capitalism/rethinking-the-future-of-american-capitalism.
72. *Wikipedia*, s.v. "Supply-Side Economics," accessed February 2, 2024, https://en.wikipedia.org/wiki/Supply-side_economics.
73. *Wikipedia*, s.v. "Demand-Side Economics," accessed February 2, 2024, https://en.wikipedia.org/wiki/Demand-side_economics.
74. Mariana Mazzucato, "What Is Government's Role in Sparking Innovation?," April 7, 2015, accessed February 2, 2024, www.weforum.org/agenda/2015/04/what-is-governments-role-in-sparking-innovation/.
75. *Wikipedia*, s.v. "DARPA," accessed February 2, 2024, https://en.wikipedia.org/wiki/DARPA.
76. *Wikipedia*, s.v. "NASA," accessed February 2, 2024, https://en.wikipedia.org/wiki/NASA.
77. "NASA Spinoff," accessed February 2, 2024, https://spinoff.nasa.gov/.
78. "NASA Spinoff," accessed February 2, 2024, https://spinoff.nasa.gov/.
79. "The Entrepreneurial State," *The Economist*, August 31, 2013, accessed February 2, 2024, www.economist.com/business/2013/08/31/the-entrepreneurial-state.
80. James Manyika, Gary Pinkus, and Monique Tuin, "Rethinking the Future of American Capitalism," *McKinsey Global Institute*, November 2020, accessed February 2, 2024, www.mckinsey.com/featured-insights/long-term-capitalism/rethinking-the-future-of-american-capitalism.
81. "Thomson Reuters 2013 Top 100 Global Innovators: Honoring the World Leaders in Innovation," *Findings and Methodology*, October 2013, accessed February 2, 2024, www.fichier-pdf.fr/2013/12/24/thomson-reuters-2013-top-100-global-innovators/; Wendy Schacht, "The Bayh-Dole Act: Selected Issues in Patent Policy and the Commercialization of Technology," December 3, 2012, U.S. Congressional Research Service.
82. Rihan Khan and Pamela Cox, "Country Culture and National Innovation," *Archives of Business Research* 5, no. 2 (March 3, 2017), accessed February 2, 2024, https://doi.org/10.14738/abr.52.2768.
83. Rihan Khan and Pamela Cox, "Country Culture and National Innovation," *Archives of Business Research* 5, no. 2 (March 3, 2017), accessed February 2, 2024, https://doi.org/10.14738/abr.52.2768.
84. Jeff Dyer, Hal Gregersen, and Clayton M. Christensen, *The Innovator's DNA* (Boston: Harvard Business Review Press, 2011), 22.
85. *Wikipedia*, s.v. "Nobel Laureates," accessed April 11, 2020, http://en.wikipedia.org/wiki/List_of_Nobel_laureates_by_country.
86. *Wikipedia*, s.v. "Nobel Laureates Per Capita," accessed April 11, 2020, http://en.wikipedia.org/wiki/List_of_countries_by_Nobel_laureates_per_capita.
87. P. Cox and R. H. Khan, "Country Culture and National Innovation," *Archives of Business Research* 5, no. 2 (2017), 85–101, accessed February 2, 2024, https://doi.org/10.14738/abr.52.2768.
88. Accenture, "Corporate Innovation Is Within Reach: Nurturing and Enabling an Entrepreneurial Culture," accessed February 20, 2024, https://newsroom.accenture.com/news/2013/us-employees-eager-to-be-corporate-entrepreneurs-but-lack-support-and-rewards-from-employers-accenture-research-finds.

89. John Kotter, "Why New Innovation and Revenue Growth Strategies Fail," *Forbes*, January 12, 2012, accessedFebruary2,2024,www.forbes.com/sites/johnkotter/2012/01/12/why-new-innovation-and-revenue-growth-strategies-fail/.

90. Jeff Dyer, Hal Gregersen, and Clayton M. Christensen, *The Innovator's DNA* (Boston: Harvard Business Review Press, 2011), 159–160.

91. Jeff Dyer and Hal Gregersen, "The World's Most Innovative Companies," *Forbes*, August 2013, accessed February 19, 2024, www.forbes.com/innovative-companies/.

92. Andrew W. Torrance and Bill Tomlinson, "Patents and the Regress of Useful Arts," *The Columbia Science & Technology Law Review* 10 (2009), 130, accessed February 2, 2024, https://papers.ssrn.com/sol3/papers.cfm?abstract_id=1411328.

93. Bruce Nussbaum, *Creative Intelligence* (New York: Harper Business, 2013), 12.

94. Scott Kirsner, "The Biggest Obstacles to Innovation in Large Companies," July 30, 2018, accessed February 2, 2024, https://hbr.org/2018/07/the-biggest-obstacles-to-innovation-in-large-companies.

95. Tim Brown, "Design Thinking," *Harvard Business Review* 86, no. 6 (2008), 84–92.

96. *Wikipedia*, s.v. "Outcome Driven Innovation," accessed March 6, 2021, https://en.wikipedia.org/wiki/Outcome-Driven_Innovation.

97. J. Liedtka, "Why Design Thinking Works," *Harvard Business Review*, September–October 2018, 2–9.

98. Steve Blank, "Why the Lean Start-Up Changes Everything," *Harvard Business Review* 91, no. 5 (2013), 63–74.

99. Steve Blank, "Why the Lean Start-Up Changes Everything," *Harvard Business Review* 91, no. 5 (2013), 63–74.

100. "Why the Lean Start-Up Changes Everything," January 16, 2018, accessed February 2, 2024, https://hbr.org/video/5712986167001/why-the-lean-startup-changes-everything.

101. *Wikipedia*, s.v. "Venture Capital," accessed November 1, 2020, https://en.wikipedia.org/wiki/Venture_capital.

102. Clayton M. Christensen, Taddy Hall, Karen Dillon, and David S. Duncan, *Competing Against Luck* (New York: HarperCollins, 2016), 27–29.

103. Diane L. Coutu, "How Resilience Works," *Harvard Business Review* 80, no. 5 (2002), 46–55.

104. Jim Collins, "A Culture of Discipline," accessed January 28, 2024, www.jimcollins.com/concepts/a-culture-of-discipline.html.

105. Gary P. Pisano, "The Hard Truth About Innovative Cultures," January–February 2019, accessed February 7, 2024, https://hbr.org/2019/01/the-hard-truth-about-innovative-cultures.

106. Computer History Museum, accessed February 7, 2024, https://computerhistory.org/exhibits/hello-the-mac-at-40/.

107. Waguih Ishak, "Creating an Innovation Culture," September 28, 2017, accessed February 7, 2024, www.mckinsey.com/capabilities/strategy-and-corporate-finance/our-insights/creating-an-innovation-culture.

108. Waguih Ishak, "Creating an Innovation Culture," September 28, 2017, accessed February 7, 2024, www.mckinsey.com/capabilities/strategy-and-corporate-finance/our-insights/creating-an-innovation-culture.

109. Nick Jain, "What Is a Culture of Innovation? Definition, Process and Best Practices," July 14, 2023, accessed February 7, 2024, https://ideascale.com/blog/what-is-a-culture-of-innovation/.

110. Diana Porumboiu, "The ISO 56000 Series for Innovation Management Explained," July 26, 2023, accessed February 7, 2024, www.viima.com/blog/iso-56000-innovation-management.

111. ISO 56000:2020 Innovation Management Fundamentals and Vocabulary, accessed February 7, 2024, www.iso.org/standard/69315.html.

112. Sherina Ebrahim, Shail Thaker, and Diane Brady, "The Journey to Agile: How Companies Can Become Faster, More Productive, and More Responsive," October 5, 2020, accessed January 21, 2024, www.mckinsey.com/business-functions/organization/our-insights/the-journey-to-agile-how-companies-can-become-faster-more-productive-and-more-responsive.

113. Gary Hamel and Nancy Tennant, "The 5 Requirements of a Truly Innovative Company," April 27, 2015, accessed February 2, 2024, https://hbr.org/2015/04/the-5-requirements-of-a-truly-innovative-company.

114. Tom Peters, "Educate for a Creative Society," accessed February 2, 2024, www.youtube.com/watch?v=h_w4AfflmeM.

Index

Note: Page numbers in *italic* indicate a figure and page numbers in **bold** indicate a table on the corresponding page.

618   *Index*

Printed in the United States
by Baker & Taylor Publisher Services